AUSTRALIAN DICTIONARY
OF BIOGRAPHY

General Editor
DIANE LANGMORE

AUSTRALIAN DICTIONARY OF BIOGRAPHY

VOLUME 17 : 1981-1990

A - K

General Editor
DI LANGMORE

Deputy General Editor
DARRYL BENNET

MELBOURNE
UNIVERSITY
PRESS

MELBOURNE UNIVERSITY PUBLISHING
(an imprint of Melbourne University Publishing)
187 Grattan Street, Carlton, Victoria 3053, Australia
mup-custom@unimelb.edu.au
www.mup.com.au

First published 2007

Text © Australian National University 2007
Design and typography © Melbourne University Publishing 2007

Typeset by Syarikat Seng Teik Sdn. Bhd., Malaysia
Printed in Australia by Ligare

National Library of Australia Cataloguing-in-Publication entry

Australian dictionary of biography. Volume 17 A-K.

Bibliography.
ISBN 9780522853827 (hbk.).

1. Biography. 2. Australia—Biography—Dictionaries.
I. Langmore, Dianne. II. Bennet, Darryl.

920.094

PREFACE

Six hundred and seventy individuals with surnames from Abdullah to Kyle are included in Volume 17 of the *Australian Dictionary of Biography*. The first entry in the volume is George Henry Abdullah, an Aboriginal community leader. The last is Sir Wallace Kyle, air chief marshal and governor. Between them is a host of men and women from all walks of life who died in the years from 1981 to 1990. It is the first of two volumes for this period. Work has begun on the second volume (L-Z), which will complete the decade.

Volume 17 illustrates such vast topics in Australian history as immigration, accelerating industrialisation, urbanisation and suburbanisation, and war (World War II, Korea, Malaya and Vietnam). While other themes are also illuminated—material progress, increasing cultural maturity, conservative and progressive politics, conflict and harmony, loss of isolation—the emphasis of the biographies is on the individuals. The entries throw light on the complexity of the human situation, and on the greatness and the littleness of moral response and actual behaviour that this can evoke.

The longest-lived subjects of Volume 17 are two centenarians: Leslie Claude Hunkin, a public servant born in 1884, and Harry Jacobs, a musician born in 1888 who, immaculately dressed in bow-tie and tails, led an orchestra that played light classics before film screenings at the Palais Theatre, Melbourne. The briefest life is that of Barry Goldsmith (1946-84), a swimmer and an early AIDS victim. While a minority of the subjects in the volume were born in the late nineteenth century, most of those included lived their lives in step with the twentieth century, being born in its early decades, experiencing the Depression, often serving in World War II, and leading lives that reached fulfilment in the prosperous postwar decades.

The two volumes of the 1788-1850 section of the *ADB*, the four of the 1851-1890 section and the six of the 1891-1939 section were published between 1966 and 1990. Volumes 13-16, covering the 1940-1980 section, were published in 1993-2002. Douglas Pike was editor for Volumes 1 to 5, Bede Nairn for Volume 6, Nairn and Geoffrey Serle for Volumes 7 to 10, Serle for Volume 11, and John Ritchie for Volumes 12 to 15 and, with Diane Langmore, Volume 16. The chronological division was designed to simplify production. In Volumes 1-12 the placing of each individual's name was determined by when he/she did his/her most important work (*floruit*). In contrast, the 1940-1980 and the 1981-1990 sections include only individuals who died in this period. The 'date of death' principle will be maintained in future volumes. An Index to Volumes 1-12 was published in 1991 and a *Supplement* of 'missing persons' in 2004.

In 2006 the *ADB Online* was launched. It is a free, illustrated and searchable electronic database containing the articles on all 11 244 individuals included in the *ADB*. Entries from Volume 17 will be added to it in 2008.

The choice of subjects for inclusion in this volume required prolonged consultation. After quotas were estimated, working parties in each State together with the Armed Services and Commonwealth working parties prepared provisional lists that were widely circulated and carefully amended. Many individuals were obviously significant and worthy of inclusion as leaders in politics, business, the armed services, the church, the professions, the arts and the labour movement. Some have been included as representatives of ethnic and social minorities, and of a wide range of occupations; others have found a place as innovators, notorieties or eccentrics. As in previous volumes a number have had to be omitted through pressure of space or lack of material. Thousands of these names, and information about them, have been gathered in the biographical register at the ADB's headquarters at the Australian National University.

Most authors were nominated by working parties. The burden of writing has been shared almost equally by the staff of universities and by a variety of other specialists.

The *ADB* is a collaborative project based on consultation and co-operation. The Research School of Social Sciences at the ANU has borne the cost of the headquarters staff, of much research and of occasional special contingencies, while other Australian universities have supported the project in numerous ways. The *ADB*'s editorial board, comprising distinguished historians and other academics, determines policy. The board and the staff keep in touch with historians at many universities, and with working parties, librarians, archivists and other local experts, as well as with research assistants in each Australian capital city and correspondents abroad. With such widespread support, the *ADB* is truly a national project.

ACKNOWLEDGMENTS

The Australian Dictionary of Biography is a program fully supported by the Research School of Social Sciences at the Australian National University. Special thanks are due to the vice-chancellor, Professor Ian Chubb, to Professor Frank Jackson and Professor Rod Rhodes, retired and current directors of the RSSS, and to Professor Jill Roe and Professor Tom Griffiths, as successive chairs of the editorial board. Those who helped in planning the shape of the work have been acknowledged in earlier volumes.

Within Australia the ADB is indebted to many librarians and archivists, schools, colleges, universities, institutes, historical and genealogical societies, and numerous other organisations; to the National Library of Australia, the Australian War Memorial, the Commonwealth Scientific and Industrial Research Organisation, the Australian Institute of Aboriginal and Torres Strait Islander Studies and the National Archives of Australia; to the archives and public records offices in the various States and Territories, and to registrars of probates and of the Supreme and Family courts, whose co-operation has solved many problems; to various town and shire clerks; to the Australian Department of Defence and State education departments.

Other national institutions that have assisted our research include the Australian Broadcasting Corporation, the Royal Australasian College of Surgeons, the Australian Medical Association, the Australian Red Cross, the Australian Psychological Society, the Royal Australian and New Zealand College of Psychiatrists, the Australasian section of the International College of Dentists, the Royal Life Saving Society, the Australian College of Theology, the Australian College of Education, the Royal Australian Institute of Architects, the Australian Institute of International Affairs, the Institute of Public Administration Australia, the Australian Institute of Librarians, the Australian Academy of Technological Sciences and Engineering, the Australian Society of Veterinary Scientists, the Society of Automotive Engineers Australasia, the Australian Speleological Federation, the Australian Music Examinations Board, the National Trust of Australia, the Fellowship of Australian Composers, the Australian Writers' Guild, the Australian Film Institute, Chartered Secretaries Australia, CPA Australia, the Reserve Bank of Australia, the Commonwealth Bank of Australia, Westpac, the Keep Australia Beautiful Council and the Sport Australia Hall of Fame.

The ADB is also indebted to the Royal Humane Society of New South Wales, the Air Ambulance Service of New South Wales, the Sydney Water Corporation, the Sydney Opera House, the Clarinet Society of Sydney, the Children's Hospital, Westmead, the Sir Moses Montefiore Jewish Home, Hunters Hill, the Coogee Surf Lifesaving Club, all in Sydney, and to the Dubbo Museum and Historical Centre, New South Wales; to the Royal Commonwealth Society (Victoria), the Royal Society of Victoria, the Royal Melbourne Zoological Gardens, the Presbyterian Church of Victoria, the United Grand Lodge of Victoria, and the Rotary Club of Aspendale, all in Melbourne, and History House, Glenelg, Victoria; to the Queensland Clarinet and Saxophone Society, Brisbane, and the Australian Stockman's Hall of Fame, Longreach, Queensland; and to the Berndt Museum of Anthropology, Perth.

Warm thanks for the free gift of their time and talents are due to contributors, to members of the editorial board and to the working parties. For particular advice the ADB owes much to Matthew Ciolek, Bob Douglas, Bill Gammage, Ian Hancock, Ken Inglis, Elisabeth Lebensaft, John Molony, Hank Nelson and F. B. Smith.

ACKNOWLEDGMENTS

Essential assistance with birth, death and marriage certificates has been provided by the co-operation of registrars in New South Wales, Queensland, South Australia, Tasmania, Victoria, Western Australia, the Northern Territory and the Australian Capital Territory; by the General Register offices in London, Dublin and Belfast; by the registrar-general in Papua New Guinea; by the mayor of Vence, France; by the consul-general for Poland in Sydney; by the Apostolic Nuncio, and the embassies of Germany, Italy, the Netherlands, Norway, Spain, Sweden and Switzerland, and the high commissions of India and Singapore, Canberra; by the Ministry of Foreign Affairs and Trade, Barbados, the Royal Danish Embassy, Singapore, and the Australian embassies in Paris, Berlin and Tel Aviv.

For other assistance overseas, thanks are due to Judith Farrington and Pamela Ayshford, London, Betty Iggo, Edinburgh, and Roger Joslyn, New York; to the universities of Birmingham, Cambridge, Leeds, Liverpool, London, Manchester and Oxford, England; to the universities of Aberdeen, Edinburgh and Glasgow, Scotland; to the University of Wales, Aberystwyth; to Trinity College, Dublin; to Pontificus Universitas Urbaniana, Rome; to the University of Vienna; to Friedrich-Alexander Universität, Erlangen, Germany; to Vilnius University, Lithuania; to Columbia University, New York, and the state universities of Kansas, Nevada, New York, Ohio, Pennsylvania and Washington, USA; to McGill University and the University of British Columbia, Canada; to Sardar Patel University, India; and to Massey University, New Zealand.

Gratitude is also due to Trinity College of Music, the Royal College of Surgeons of England, the Royal Geographical Society, the Royal Anthropological Institute of Great Britain and Ireland, the British Psychological Society, the British Interplanetary Society, the Royal Institute of British Architects, the Royal Society for the Encouragement of the Arts, Manufactures and Commerce, and the Ministry of Defence, all in London; to the Bethlehem Royal Hospital, Kent, England; to the Smithsonian Institution, Washington, DC, the American College of Physicians, the American Academy of Pediatrics, the National Speleological Society, the Robert Frost Foundation, Lawrence, Massachusetts, and the National Personnel Records Center, St Louis, Missouri, USA; to the Yad Vashem Archives and the JDC Archives, Jerusalem, and to the New Zealand Defence Force, Wellington; to the staffs of the *Oxford Dictionary of National Biography*, *Österreichisches Biographisches Lexikon*, Vienna, the *Dictionary of Canadian Biography*, Toronto, the *Dictionary of New Zealand Biography*, Wellington, and the *Northern Territory Dictionary of Biography*; and to other individuals and institutions who have co-operated with the ADB.

The ADB deeply regrets the deaths of such notable contributors as Patsy Adam-Smith, N. W. Archbold, Allan Ashbolt, H. D. Attwood, D. W. A. Baker, Peter Balmford, Geoffrey Barnes, John Behr, A. L. Bennett, J. H. W. Birrell, Andrew Bisset, John B. Blanden, Keith Macrae Bowden, F. Maxwell Bradshaw, Cecil J. Broome, Rodger S. Brown, Ken Buckley, K. J. Cable, A. E. Cahill, Frank Callaway, Margaret Carnegie, L. T. Carron, Alex C. Castles, C. B. Christesen, Nina Christesen, Beryl Cigler, Eric G. Clancy, Axel Clark, Joan Clarke, K. W. Cleland, James H. Coleman, Gordon D. Combe, Margaret H. Connah, W. F. Connell, Frank Cranston, W. R. Crocker, C. J. Cummins, Greg Curnow, W. J. Cuthill, Alison M. Dolling, Austin Dowling, Ian Downs, Sophie C. Ducker, Mary Durack, Robin Eaden, V. A. Edgeloe, David F. Elder, Ann Elias, Ronald Elmslie, R. Else-Mitchell, Susan E. Emilsen, Frank Engel, Lloyd Evans, Kevin Fahy, Frank Farrell, Marcus de Laune Faunce, H. A. Finlay, Philippa L. Fletcher, Alan Fraser, Eric L. French, Bryan Gandevia, R. O. Giles, Aline Gillespie, Lyall Gillespie, Douglas Gordon, Noel Goss, Donald Grant, David Griffin, C. M. Gurner, J. P. Haldane-Stevenson, Rupert Hamer, Ralph Harry, A. Heatley, Ursula Hoff, Vic Honour, K. A. R. Horn, J. C. Horner, Patricia Horner, W. M. Horton, Keith Issacs, Barbara James, Alex Jelinek,

ACKNOWLEDGMENTS

A. G. Kenwood, Joan Kerr, John D. Kerr, Hugh King, Allan Knight, J. L. Knight, Don Lancaster, Robert Langdon, T. F. C. Lawrence, Stuart Lee, D. C. Lewis, A. L. Lougheed, Alan H. Loxton, Davis McCaughey, Andrew D. McCredie, Annie J. McElligott, Ian MacFarling, Eileen Macintyre, A. M. Mackerras, N. D. McLachlan, C. C. Manhood, Leslie R. Marchant, Max Marginson, N. D. Martin, Robert Mather, H. E. Maude, T. B. Millar, R. J. Moir, Charles E. Moorhouse, Richard Morris, I. D. Muecke, Bede Nairn, Kevin Newman, Patrick O'Farrell, Warren Osmond, C. A. S. Page, Geoffrey W. Page, R. S. Parker, Joy E. Parnaby, C. G. Pearce, Noel Pelly, H. H. Penny, Julian Phillips, Yvonne A. Phillips, John Playford, R. B. Potts, S. A. Prentice, Anthony Proust, Benjamin Rank, Ira D. Raymond, John Ritchie, W. Ritchie, Rutherford Robertson, Stephen Salsbury, Margaret Scott, Clement Semmler, Margaret Sharpe, Rodney P. Shearman, D. Shineberg, Caroline Simpson, M. R. Sims, D. C. S. Sissons, I. H. Smith, Sasha Soldatow, G. D. Solomon, R. V. Southcott, R. L. Southern, J. G. Starke, Frank Strahan, Kay Sweeney, Leonard B. Swinden, Robert I. Taylor, Colin Thiele, Joyce Thomson, Joy Thwaite, M. Borgia Tipping, Prudence Torney-Parlicki, W. A. Townsley, B. H. Travers, Ursula Trower, J. W. Turner, E. Cole Turnley, Alison M. Turtle, Constance E. Vickers, Gavin Walkley, R. L. Wallace, Jack Watson, Phillipa Weeks, L. W. Weickhardt, Neville Whiffen, Jean P. Whyte, J. Atherton Young, Howard Zelling, H. J. Zwillenberg.

Grateful acknowledgment is due to the director and staff of Melbourne University Press, to Professor Jill Roe, who retired from chairmanship of the editorial board in 2006, and to two long-serving members of the ADB staff, Martha Campbell and Joyce Gibberd, who retired while the volume was being produced. Martha Campbell worked for the ADB from 1967 to 2002, has written 169 articles for its volumes and, as New South Wales research editor, prepared for publication some thousands more. Joyce Gibberd served the ADB as South Australian research assistant for thirty years.

The ADB expresses its deep appreciation of generous contributions of the late Mrs Caroline Simpson and the Myer Foundation, Melbourne, which helped in the production of this volume.

xi

WORKING PARTIES

Armed Services
Peter Burness, Chris Clark, John Coates, Peter Dennis, Alec Hill, David Horner
(chair), John McCarthy, Perditta McCarthy, Philip Mulcare, Anthony Staunton, Alan
Stephens, David Stevens, A. J. Sweeting.

Commonwealth
Nicholas Brown (chair), David Carment, Patricia Clarke, John Farquharson, Bill
Gammage, Robert Hyslop (retired), John Nethercote, Graeme Powell, Libby Robin,
John Thompson, Jill Waterhouse.

Indigenous
Aileen Blackburn, Nicholas Brown, Dawn Casey, Ann Curthoys, Stephen Kinnane,
Frances Peters-Little (chair), Kaye Price, Peter Read, Tim Rowse.

New South Wales
John Carmody, Chris Cunneen, Ross Curnow, Nancy Cushing, Barrie Dyster, Stephen
Garton, Bridget Griffen-Foley, Murray Goot, Warwick Hirst, Beverley Kingston
(chair), John Kennedy McLaughlin, Glenn Mitchell, Andrew Moore, Jill Roe, Regina
Sutton, Alan Ventress.

Queensland
Pat Buckridge (chair), Manfred Cross, Kay Ferres, Richard Fotheringham, M. French,
Jennifer Harrison, Lorna McDonald, Belinda McKay, S. J. Routh, Joanne Scott.

South Australia
Margaret Allen, Roger André, Carol Fort, Joyce Gibberd, R. M. Gibbs, David Hilliard,
P. A. Howell (chair), Helen Jones, Judith Raftery, Jenny Tilby Stock, Patricia Stretton.

Tasmania
Peter Chapman, Shirley Eldershaw, Margaret Glover-Scott, Elizabeth McLeod, Stefan
Petrow, Anne Rand, Michael Roe (chair), John Taylor.

Victoria
John Arnold, Geoff Browne, Mimi Colligan, B. J. Costar, Jim Davidson, David Dunstan,
Charles Fahey, F. J. Kendall, John Lack (chair), Peter Love, Janet McCalman, David
Merrett, Robert Murray, J. R. Poynter, Carolyn Rasmussen, John Rickard, Judith
Smart.

Western Australia
Wendy Birman, David Black, G. C. Bolton (chair), Michal Bosworth, Dorothy
Erickson, Charles Fox, Sue Graham-Taylor, Jenny Gregory, Lenore Layman, John
McIlwraith, Jenny Mills, C. Mulcahy, Jan Ryan, Tom Stannage.

THE ADB'S SECOND GENERAL EDITOR

Bede Nairn (1917-2006) was born on 6 August 1917 at Turill, near Mudgee, New South Wales, youngest of six children of Robert John (Jack) Nairn, labourer, and his wife Rose Ann, née Hopkins. He was baptised Noel Bede but was known by his second Christian name—reputedly his parents' intention to name him Lloyd George had been foiled by the officiating priest. In 1923 the Nairns moved to Sydney where Jack worked as a council watchman and cleaner and the family lived in Bathurst Street. 'We were still poor, damned poor', Bede later said, but 'one step up from real poverty'; Rose probably financed the piano she purchased and Bede's music lessons by taking in boarders. Educated at St John's Poor School, in Kent Street, and by the Christian Brothers at St Mary's Cathedral School, after completing the Intermediate certificate (1934) he took a job with the New South Wales Electoral Office. His poor eyesight meant that he wore glasses for the rest of his life and was rejected for service in World War II. While studying for matriculation part time he worked as a clerk at the Sydney Technical College; later he was an evening student at the University of Sydney (BA Hons 1945; MA 1955). He married Jean Hayward on Australia Day 1943 at St Mary's Cathedral.

In 1948 Nairn taught at the Sydney Technical College, Ultimo, then from 1949 lectured in history at the newly founded New South Wales University of Technology (later University of New South Wales). He became senior lecturer and head of the school of history at UNSW in 1956 and in 1961 associate professor of history. In 1957, on a Rockefeller grant, he went with the family to Balliol College, Oxford, England, where he researched British trade unions. From 1959 to 1976 he was a trustee (councillor) of the Public (State) Library of New South Wales and in 1971-82 represented it on the New South Wales Archives Authority.

An influential figure in the Australian Society for the Study of Labour History from its foundation in 1961, Nairn was a member of its executive and of the editorial board of *Labour History*. In Gerry Walsh's words, 'he wrote history according to the evidence and not according to an ideology: his canons were integrity and common sense'. In 1963 his article 'Writing Australian History' in the journal *Manna* was both an insightful review of Volume 1 of Manning Clark's *History of Australia* and a refutation of attacks by critics such as Malcolm Ellis; it was praised in *The Times* of London as 'one of the first great essays in historical criticism in Australia'. With G. J. Abbott, Nairn co-edited *Economic Growth of Australia 1788-1921* (1969). His groundbreaking *Civilising Capitalism: The Labor Movement in NSW 1870-1900* (1973) stressed, as John Merritt has written, 'the pragmatic reform agendas of men and women seeking independence and security within a capitalist society'. He followed this in 1986 with *The Big Fella*, a biography of Jack Lang and an account of the Labor Party in New South Wales to 1949.

In 1962 Nairn had become chairman of the New South Wales working party of the *Australian Dictionary of Biography*. In 1965 he moved to Canberra to join the *ADB* staff at the Australian National University. When Douglas Pike fell ill in 1973 Nairn became *ADB* general editor for volume 6. In a significantly harmonious partnership, he and Geoffrey Serle were joint general editors for Volumes 7 to 10.

Warm and approachable as leader of the ADB team in Canberra, Nairn had a firm commitment to continuing the high standards set by Pike. A fine administrator, sensitive to human frailties and fiercely devoted to the project, Nairn consolidated the dictionary's achievements. He was a skilful editor, as adept at cutting a superfluous phrase as in summarising a wordy paragraph. His own writing was clear and graceful (with occasionally a Beethovian deliberate discord). He retired as general editor in 1984. Among the most notable of the eighty *ADB* entries he wrote himself are those on Sir John Robertson, Jack Lang, Jack Beasley and Chris Watson, politicians, Frank Dickson, trade unionist, Archie Jackson and Victor Trumper, cricketers, and Jimmie and 'Darby' Munro, jockeys.

Nairn had joined the Royal Australian Historical Society in 1964, and was elected a fellow in 1987. In the society's *Journal* he chose to publish major articles such as 'The Political Mastery of Sir Henry Parkes' (March 1967). His last publication in the *JRAHS* was 'The Governor, the Bushranger and the Premier' (December 2000). Throughout his career he supported young scholars, and was much in demand as a sympathetic examiner, and a generous adviser on manuscripts. He had a world-wide circle of friends and correspondents. In 1988 he was appointed AO for service to education as an historian and a biographer. The History Council of New South Wales presented a citation to him in 2000 in recognition of his contribution to Australian biography and history.

A tall, gentle man, with a neat moustache and a good head of hair, Nairn spoke softly but held his opinions firmly. His Catholic faith was a lifelong commitment. Politics were also an abiding interest—he had joined the Australian Labor Party at the age of 16 and though he ceased his membership when he moved to Canberra, he remained strongly committed to the party and scornful of the failings of 'the conservatives' who opposed it. He was a devoted and loving family man. Nairn combined a keen interest in philosophy and religion with a passion for sport and music. He had an enduring love for Beethoven's piano works. A good cricketer in his youth, he played regularly before moving to Canberra, and occasionally after. He was a combative New South Wales patriot in sport (and in other matters as well) and both a practical and theoretical devotee of horse-racing, which he saw as a metaphor for life. Nairn died in Canberra on 21 April 2006 and after a Requiem Mass was buried in Gungahlin Lawn Cemetery. His wife, their three sons and three daughters, seventeen grandchildren and eight great-grandchildren survived him; he was also close to his niece who lived in Canberra.

Rugby League had been an abiding enthusiasm. South Sydney was his team and his last entry for the *ADB* was an article on the 'Little Master' Clive Churchill; it appears in this volume. For Bede Nairn, as for his colleagues and friends Pike, Serle and Ritchie, it can be said: for his memorial, turn these pages.

Chris Cunneen

THE ADB'S FOURTH GENERAL EDITOR

John Ritchie (1941-2006), son of John and Evelyn Ritchie, was born on 4 April 1941 in East Melbourne and educated at Northcote High School and Trinity College, University of Melbourne (BA Hons). He was a middle distance runner of some distinction, once competing against the great athlete Herb Elliott. After graduating with honours in history, he obtained a Dip.Ed. and then in 1964 became a teaching fellow at Monash University. When he had completed a Ph.D. at the Australian National University, Manning Clark appointed him to a lectureship in history in 1969. On 20 December that year he married Joan McDermott.

Ritchie became a legendary teacher, first in British history. Then for many years he taught first-year students a survey course in Australian history that for scores of them became the foundation of their later knowledge, even through to doctoral level. From the 1970s he was a key member of the team of teachers of Australian history that flourished at the ANU around Manning Clark and included Don Baker, Bob Gollan, Barbara Penny, Eric Fry, Ian Hancock, John Merritt and John Molony. They were inspiring times and the ANU's history department became a leader in the field.

Ritchie, attired in his old university gown, gave meticulously prepared lectures to an ever growing number of students. His lectures were a model of presentation. Structure and the development of an argument emerged through a flowing narrative, which became a form of high entertainment in itself. In that way he attracted a multitude of students to the discipline of history. His tutorials were tightly controlled exercises designed to encourage the first steps in the systematic use of primary sources. The students' essays, rigorously marked both as to content and structure, were employed by Ritchie not merely to develop their knowledge of the subject but also to ensure that they carried into later life a conviction that to write English with clarity, correct spelling, proper punctuation and a sense of direction was a hallmark of an educated person. Later-year teachers only had to look at the bibliography in an essay to recognise Ritchie's share in the making of the student. He ensured that students went to their sources and made a proper record of their use.

Convinced that a sense of place was fundamental to the study of history, Ritchie took great pains to organise for his students field trips to Sydney, the 'Macquarie towns' and Victoria's north-east. He also played a major role in offering weekend residential study sessions for teachers and pupils from local schools and the outlying country areas. The university, as well as his department, benefited from a subsequent growth in enrolments.

During the twenty years Ritchie gave to teaching he did not neglect his obligation to research and write. He first turned to the material of his Ph.D., from which two notable publications were drawn: *Punishment and Profit* (1970) and *The Evidence to the Bigge Reports* (1971). A popular history, *Australia as Once We Were*, followed in 1975. Enriched by several years of thought and research, some of it on sabbatical leave in the British Isles, his masterly work, *Lachlan Macquarie: A Biography*, appeared in 1986. He wrote the introduction to *A Charge of Mutiny* (1988). During those years Ritchie successfully edited the journal *Labour History* and helped thereby to establish it on a national footing as a scholarly publication. He made a wide contribution to the life of the university from 1971 to 1975 as deputy warden of Burton Hall and became acting warden in 1976. He undertook the responsible duties of acting dean of the Faculty of Arts in 1986 and 1987 and remained mindful that his proper function was to serve the faculty rather than control it.

In the 1980s Ritchie taught a stimulating fourth-year honours course in the theory and practice of biography. This activity ceased when, in 1988, he was appointed a professorial fellow (professor 1992) in the Research School of Social Sciences and general editor of the *Australian Dictionary of Biography*, in succession to Geoffrey Serle. His experience as an author and editor had equipped him admirably for this task, but nothing could have prepared him for the rigours of a position that had contributed to the ill health of the three previous editors. Ritchie threw himself totally into the seemingly endless grind of seeing thousands of short biographies through the process of their development from draft manuscripts to polished entries in the *ADB*. By 2000 he had seen Serle's Volume 11 through the press and edited Volumes 12 to 15. He co-edited Volume 16 with Di Langmore.

After some years at the ADB Ritchie had decided to cease working on weekends, and in whatever spare time he could muster he researched and wrote *The Wentworths, Father and Son* (1997). The volume dealt thoroughly with the father, Darcy Wentworth, but was able to take the son, William Charles, only through his formative years and then touch lightly on the vast contribution to colonial Australia made by that lion of our early history. Volume 2 of this monumental work had not progressed far when, in 2001, Ritchie was forced to lay down his pen after a stroke. No man had come to know W. C. Wentworth as Ritchie had done and Wentworth stood fair to be highly honoured by his biographer.

Ritchie was a fellow of the Australian Academy of Humanities, the Academy of Social Sciences in Australia and the Royal Historical Society, and an honorary fellow of the Royal Australian Historical Society. Retiring in 2002, he was appointed AO that year and emeritus professor, ANU, in 2003. He died on 10 May 2006 at his home in Aranda, Canberra, and, after a Requiem Mass, was cremated.

Throughout his life John Ritchie was not one to play for popularity among his peers and even less towards those above him. Thus he stuck by his convictions and uttered them without fear. A man with a generally conservative outlook, he never cherished the past for its own sake or rejected its values when the prevailing wind blew against them. In his devotion to work and to what he saw as his duty, he spared neither himself nor others. A lover of good food and fine wine, of the opera and ballet, of literature (above all Dickens), and a creator rather than a teller of jokes, Ritchie was loyal to his God, to his friends, to his country and to his football club, Carlton. Before all else Ritchie preserved his private life in the sanctuary of his home. There, with his beloved wife and son, Joan and Christopher, John Ritchie, editor, historian and genuine Australian, lived out the roles he truly held dear on earth: those of husband and father.

John Molony

AUTHORS

ABDULLAH, Yasmin Jill:
Abdullah.
ANDERSON, Hugh:
Hill, E.
ANDERSON, Patricia:
Gall.
ARCHBOLD, N. W.*:
Hills.
ARGENT, A.:
Ferguson; Jenkins.
ARNOLD, John:
Campbell, J. M.; Cheshire; Cugley.
ARROW, Michelle:
Howell, E.
ATCHISON, John:
Knight, J. F.

BAKER, Joe:
Barnes, J.
BALLARD, Chris:
Champion.
BANKS, Joan M.:
Jarrett, T.
BARBER, Stella M.:
Coles, A., K., E. & N.
BATEMAN, Sam:
Burrell.
BECKETT, Jeremy:
Hogbin.
BEGGS, Hugh S.:
Bakewell.
BELL, Michael:
Hibberd.
BENNET, Darryl:
Davidson, C.; Hyland.
BENNETT, Scott:
Bourke, W.; Crisp, L.; Everett.
BERKMAN, D. A.:
Evans, H. J.
BERZINS, Baiba:
Jones, P.
BEST, Ysola:
Brady.
BILLETT, Bill:
Cliff.
BINNS, Georgina:
Buck.
BIRMAN, Wendy:
Baker, C.; Beeck.
BISHOP, Geoffrey C.:
Haselgrove.
BLACK, David:
Graham, H.; Howell, L.

* deceased

BLACK, Paul D.:
Gilbert.
BLACKMAN, Danny:
Cluff.
BLAIR, Dale:
Cameron, L.
BLEVIN, W. R.:
Giovanelli.
BLOOD, D. C.:
Fethers.
BOADLE, Donald:
Bury.
BOLAND, T. P.:
Campbell, J. S.
BOLTON, G. C.:
Baker, H.; Birman; Blythe, L.
BOMFORD, Janette:
Doig.
BONGIORNO, Frank:
Brack.
BOOTH, Douglas:
Chalmers; Curlewis.
BOUGHEN, Robert K.:
Grimes.
BOURKE, Helen:
Cook, P.
BOWDEN, Tim:
Davis.
BOWMAN, Linda:
Cleary.
BOYCE, Peter:
Gairdner.
BRAGA, Stuart:
Brown, H.; Else.
BRANAGAN, D. F.:
King, H.
BRENNAN, Richard:
Kennedy, B.
BRIGNELL, Lyn:
Brindle.
BROMFIELD, David:
Blumann.
BROOK, David N.:
Eastick.
BROOKS, G. H.:
Hobbs.
BROOME, Richard:
Bennett, E.
BROWN, D. J.:
Albert.
BROWN, Elaine:
Cairns.
BROWN, Nicholas:
Dunk.
BROWN, Robert:
Benn.

BROWNE, Elspeth:
Cuthbert Browne.
BROWNE, Geoff:
Herring, E.; Keon.
BROWNRIGG, Jeff:
Davidson, J.
BUCKNALL, John:
Bin Bin.
BUCKRIDGE, Patrick:
Gilliland.
BUNBURY, Bill:
Brearley.
BURNESS, Peter:
Hutchison.
BURNSWOODS, Jan:
Booth.
BUTCHER, Barry W.:
Cummins.
BUXTON, Jeremy:
Johnston, F.

CAHILL, Peter:
Chin.
CAMPBELL, Peter:
Glass; Kennedy, I.
CAPELL, K.:
Healy, George.
CAREY, Jane:
Blackwood, M.; Clark, E.
CARMENT, David:
Fong Lim.
CARMODY, John:
Dintenfass; Dowd.
CARNELL, Ian:
Deegan.
CARR, Andy:
Farrell.
CARR-BOYD, Ann:
Goodman.
CARROLL, V. J.:
Henderson, R.
CASHMAN, R. I.:
Bosisto; Carruthers; Fingleton.
CATHIE, Ian:
Barber.
CHAPMAN, Barbara:
Darbyshire.
CHAPMAN, R. J. K.*:
Binns.
CHOO, Christine:
Brennan, G.
CLARK, Chris:
Anderson, C. G.; Kyle.
CLARKE, Patricia:
Commins.
CLEMENTS, Gail:
Czulak.
CLEREHAN, Neil:
James.
CLOSE, Cecily:
Derham, D.

* deceased

CLUNE, David:
Kane.
COATES, John:
Jordan, D.
COHEN, Kay:
Barton; Holt, J.
COLEMAN, Peter:
Hulme; Krygier.
COLLIGAN, Mimi:
Crawford, D.; Jacobs, H.
COLLINS, Diane:
Dyer.
CONNORS, Tom:
Chaffey.
CONSANDINE, Marion:
Boyer.
COOKE, Glenn R.:
Barker, C.
COOKE, Marie:
Burbidge.
COOPER, Alastair:
Gatacre.
COPPEL, Charles A.:
Dimmick.
CORNISH, Selwyn:
Burton.
COSSART, Yvonne:
Black, R.
COSTAR, B. J.:
Feltham; Field, F.
COSTIGAN, Michael:
Jackson, D. G.
COTTLE, Drew:
Alexander, H.
CRICHTON, Pam:
Chauvel; Hamilton, L.
CROCKETT, Cheryl:
Herring, M.
CROMPTON, Robert W.:
Huxley, L.
CRONIN, Stephen:
Grainer.
CROOK, Karen:
Cameron, K.
CROSS, Manfred:
Hiley; Hooper.
CROSS, Roger:
Dawbarn.
CROWLEY, James:
Casey, D.
CUNNEEN, Chris:
Bolton; Evatt.
CURNOW, Ross:
Goodsell.
CURRY, Robert:
Anderson, G.
CURTIS, Campbell:
Bourke, M.

DALLY, John:
Hudson, W.
DALY, John A.:
Hele; Knoke.

DAVIDSON, Dianne:
  Kastner.
DAVIDSON, Jim:
  Hancock.
DAVIDSON, P. A.:
  Beyer.
DAVIDSON, Ron:
  Kirwan Ward.
DAVIES, Chris Lawe:
  Bingham.
DAWSON, Daryl:
  Aickin.
DEMACK, Alan:
  Bennett, A.
DENGATE, John:
  Affley.
DENNIS, Peter:
  Gillon.
DI FRANCESCO, Michael:
  Bourke, J.
DIBBLE, Brian:
  Hart-Smith.
DINGLE, Tony:
  Croxford.
DOCKER, Rose:
  Kinghorn.
DONOVAN, Peter:
  Connellan.
DORAN, Stuart:
  Blakeney.
DRUMMOND, Doug:
  Hartigan, T.
DUGGAN, Kevin:
  Chamberlain, R.
DUNSTAN, David:
  Antcliff; Bolte; Evans, B.; Howard, F.
DUNSTAN, Keith:
  Irving.
DUTTON, Kenneth R.:
  Auchmuty.

EAGLE, Mary:
  Drysdale.
EDDY, J.:
  Casey, J.; Johnston, H.
EDGAR, P. L.:
  Axford.
EDGAR, Suzanne:
  Fitzhardinge.
EDMONDS, Angus A.:
  Busch.
EDMONDS, Leigh:
  Hamilton, K.; Kleinig.
EDQUIST, Harriet:
  Harvie.
EDWARDS, Deborah:
  Dadswell.
EDWARDS, John:
  Crebbin.
EDWARDS, Peter:
  Henderson, W.
EDWARDS, Vivian E.:
  Edwards, C.

EDWARDS, W. H.:
  Duguid.
ELDER, David F.*:
  Eyre.

FAHEY, Charles:
  Ansett; Chadwick; Gawith; Heffernan.
FAIRWEATHER, D. F.:
  Jacka.
FALK, Barbara:
  Austin, A.
FALLON, Patricia:
  Jordan, E.
FARQUHARSON, John:
  Fitchett; Hicks; Knight, J. W.
FARRELL, Frank*:
  Crowley, D.
FIELD, Michael:
  Fagan.
FINLAY, H. A.*:
  Crisp, M.
FINLAY, Ric:
  Badcock.
FINNANE, Mark:
  Cilento, R.
FISHER, E. M.:
  Elphick.
FITZGERALD, Criena:
  Anderson, C. W.; Anstey.
FLETCHER, B. H.:
  Black, H.
FOGARTY, Mike:
  Collins, P.
FORT, Carol:
  Hunkin.
FRENCH, M.:
  Anderson, J.; Featherstone; Joyce.
FUNNELL, Ray:
  Hewitt.
FYFE, Christopher:
  Fyfe.

GAMMAGE, Bill:
  Black, J.; Joynt.
GARDEN, Donald S.:
  Jennings, D.
GARE, Deborah:
  Edis.
GARGETT, Kathryn:
  Drew.
GARTON, Stephen:
  Bailey; Clifford.
GASCOIGNE, S. C. B.:
  Allen, C.
GIBBERD, Joyce:
  Hart, I.
GIBSON-WILDE, Dorothy M.:
  Halberstater.
GILLBANK, Linden:
  Carr.
GILLESPIE, James:
  Grieve.

* deceased

xix

HUMPHRIES, Michael E.:
Heymanson.
HUNT, D. W.:
Aikens.
HUNT, Jane E.:
Helmrich.
HUNT, Rod:
Hursey.
HUNTER, Cecily:
Hailes.
HURST, Doug:
Bennett, W.; Hudson, R.
HUTCHISON, D. E.:
Currie.

INGAMELLS, Michael:
Kemsley.

JAMIESON, Suzanne:
Clancy.
JENNER, J. D.:
Begg.
JENNINGS, Rosemary:
Hook.
JOHNSON, K. A.:
Cobley.
JOHNSON, R. W.:
Everist.
JOHNSTON, Allan:
Harper.
JOHNSTON, Mark:
Bell; Bugg.
JOHNSTON, W. Ross:
Greenwood, G.
JOLLY, Bridget:
Irwin.
JONES, Barry O.:
Galbally.
JONES, Helen:
Gell.
JONES, Peter D.:
Collins, J.
JORDENS, J. T. F.:
Basham.
JOYCE, E. B.:
Gill, E. D.

KEATING, Michael:
Higgins.
KENDALL, F. J.:
Green, K.; Jungwirth.
KENNEDY, K. H.:
Hilton.
KENT, Jacqueline:
Campbell, R.; Cook, K.
KENWOOD, A. G.*:
Clark, C.
KERR, Anthea:
Gentle.
KERR, John D.*:
King, N.

KEYS, David:
Bush.
KEYS SMITH, Gordon:
Galbraith.
KINGSLAND, Richard:
Hartnell.
KINNANE, Garry:
Colahan.
KIRKPATRICK, Rod:
Darwen; Groom, W.
KLEINERT, Sylvia:
Cooper, R.
KNOTT, John:
Delandro.
KOTAI-EWERS, Trisha:
Beilby.
KRATZMANN, Gregory:
Kratzmann.
KYNASTON, Bruce:
Cooper, A.

LACK, John:
Banks; Cuming; Fidge; Good(e).
LAFFIN, Josephine:
Beovich.
LAKE, P. S.:
Butcher.
LANCASTER, Don*:
Cooper, G. A.
LANE, Richard:
Foster, D.; Jacklin.
LANE, Terence:
Hughan.
LANGMORE, Diane:
Casey, E.; Chatterton.
LAVERTY, John:
Groom, T.
LAWN, Meredith:
Hill, M.
LAWSON, Valerie:
Clinch.
LAX, Mark:
Boyle.
LEASK, Margaret:
Haag.
LEE, David:
Ballard.
LEE, Stuart*:
FitzGerald, R.
LEMON, Andrew:
Badger; Davies, A. T.
LEVINE, David:
Berkelouw.
LEWIS, D. C.*:
Fairfax-Ross.
LISTON, Carol:
Geeves.
LLOYD, Brian:
Daley, F.
LLOYD, Neil:
Forde.

* deceased

* deceased

LOVE, Peter:
Bridges; Kennelly.
LOW, John:
Dark, E. P.
LOWE, David:
Beale.
LOWE, Doug:
Foster, A.
LYNCH, Peter:
Healy, Gertrude.

MACCALLUM, Monica:
Dyason.
MCCALMAN, Janet:
Arnold; Campbell, K.
MCCARTHY, Dayton:
Bishop.
MCCARTHY, John:
Bennett, D.; Hardman.
MCCONVILLE, Chris:
Grant.
MCCONVILLE, Kieran:
Diplock.
MCDONALD, Lorna:
Golding.
MCDOUGALL, Russell:
Herbert.
MCFADYEN, R. E.:
Dodd.
MCFARLANE, Brian:
Hardy, M.
MCGINNESS, Mark:
Crosby; Fitzgerald, P.; Hart, B.
MCHUGH, Siobhán:
Jeromin.
MCILWRAITH, John:
Agnew; Holmes à Court.
MACINTYRE, Pam:
Christie.
MACINTYRE, Stuart:
Brown, J.; Gibson, R.
MCKAY, Judith M.:
Hutton, B.
MCKNIGHT, David:
Bialoguski.
MCLAUGHLIN, John Kennedy:
Evatt; Hutley.
MCNEILL, Barry:
Blythe, S.
MCPHERSON, Ailsa:
Archdale; Fitton.
MAHONEY, Mary D.:
Cilento, P.
MANDEL, Daniel:
Atyeo.
MANSFIELD, Joan:
Grove.
MARCHANT, Sylvia:
Dobson, R.
MARGINSON, Ray:
Kaye.
MARKUS, Andrew:
Fink.

MARTIN-CHEW, Louise:
Johnstone.
MATTHEWS, Emma:
Corder.
MAY, Dawn:
Atkinson.
MAY, T. W.:
Beaton.
MILLER, J. D. B.:
Bull; Crawford, J.
MILLS, Jenny:
Grey-Smith.
MITCHELL, Alex:
Godfrey.
MOORE, Andrew:
Doyle; Ellis; Irvine.
MOORE, Keith:
Campbell, A.
MORAN, Brendan:
Coombe.
MORANT, Andrew:
Baker, H.
MOREMON, John:
Allen, L.
MORRIS, John:
Craig, C.
MORRIS, Richard*:
Elliott.
MULCAHY, Clement:
Baron-Hay.
MUNRO, Craig:
Hall.
MURPHY, Lynne:
Gibson, G.
MURRAY, Pamela:
Kelly, M.
MURRAY, Robert:
Avery; Brockhoff; Holt, R.
MURRAY, W. J.:
Curran.

NAIRN, Bede*:
Churchill.
NASH, David:
Bill.
NELSON, H. N.:
Gunther; Hampshire; Karava.
NEWTON, Dennis:
Ifould.
NEWTON, Peter J. F.:
Capell.
NIALL, Brenda:
Boyd, G.; Boyd, J.
NICHOLSON, Sally-Anne:
Huppatz.
NICKLIN, Lenore:
Komon.
NOBBS, Alanna M.:
Hawthorne.
NOLAN, Sybil:
Dexter.

* deceased

NORTH, Marilla:
Cusack.
NOSSAL, G. J. V.:
Burnet.

O'BRIEN, Angela:
Diamond.
O'BRIEN, Anne:
Daly, J.
O'BRIEN, Michael:
Jackson, D. R.
O'BRIEN, Tom:
Bostock.
O'CONNOR, Desmond:
Giordano.
O'NEIL, Bernard:
Glaessner.
OLIVER, Bobbie:
Chamberlain, F.
OPPENHEIMER, Melanie:
Barnes, K.; Bate.
OSMOND, Gary:
Herford.

PAGE, Vilma:
Craven-Sands.
PAINTER, Alison:
Jacobs, R.
PARKER, Dorothy:
Hodgkin.
PARKER, Pauline F.:
Gainfort.
PARKIN, Russell:
Berry.
PARNABY, Owen:
Johnson.
PARRY, Suzanne:
Gault.
PATON, Simon:
Diplock.
PATRICK, Alison:
Fitzpatrick.
PATTERSON, G. W.:
Evans, H. J.
PAYNE, Pauline:
Both.
PAYNE, Trish:
Burgess.
PAYTEN, Marianne:
Burrow.
PEERS, Juliet:
Duldig.
PELLY, Noël*:
Kellaway.
PEMBERTON, P. A.:
Holt, Z.
PENDAL, Phillip:
Hawke.
PERKINS, John:
Adler.

* deceased

PERRY, Peter W.:
Colquhoun.
PHILLIPS, Harry C. J.:
Dolan; Jamieson.
PHILLIPS, Murray G.:
Herford.
PLEVIN, John E.:
Haldane.
POULOS, Judy:
Andrews, W.
POWELL, Alan:
Boye-Jones.
POWELL, Graeme:
de Berg.
POWELL, Stephen M.:
Clayton.
POYNTER, J. R.:
Fitts.
PRATTEN, Garth:
Anderson, A.
PRIESTLEY, Susan:
Brazill; Cooper, J.
PRYOR, Arthur:
Butler.

QUINN, Catriona:
Best.

RADBOURNE, Jennifer:
Felgate.
RADCLIFFE, John C.:
Donald.
RADFORD, Ron:
Cant.
RADI, Heather:
Cashman; Kelly, E.
RADIC, Thérèse:
Heinze.
RAE, Ian D.:
Blackwood, R.; Boas; Kelsall.
RAE, Ruth:
Bonnin.
RAFTERY, Judith:
Hampton.
RAITER, Laura:
Einihovici.
RALPH, Gilbert M.:
Clark, G.
RAND, A.:
Brain; Cuthbert.
RASMUSSEN, Carolyn:
Croxford; Greenwood, J.
REFSHAUGE, Richard:
Blackburn.
REID, Brian:
Fenton.
REID, Richard E.:
Corkhill.
REILLY, Dianne:
Craig, S.
RENNER, J. T. E.:
Hebart.

REYNOLDS, Peter:
  Freeland; Herman.
RICH, Joe:
  Hartnett.
RICHARDS, Duncan:
  Iwanoff.
RICHARDS, Jonathan:
  Barraclough; Huxley, V.; Kennedy, M.
RICKARD, John:
  Hoban.
RIDLEY, Ronald T.:
  Culican.
ROBERTSON, Enid:
  Ashby.
ROBERTSON, Peter:
  Bok.
ROBIN, Libby:
  Frith.
ROBINSON, Suzanne:
  Glanville-Hicks.
ROE, Jill:
  Barnard; Collisson; Helmrich; Ingamells.
ROE, Michael:
  Dallas.
ROGERS, David N.:
  Gibson, W.
ROSE, Deborah Bird:
  Danayarri (Danaiyarri).
ROSENZWEIG, Paul A.:
  Driver; England.
ROUTH, S. J.:
  Corbould; Edwards, C.; Kruger.
ROWSE, Tim:
  Barwick; Boney; Cook, C.
RUSHWORTH, G. D.:
  Kentwell.
RUSSELL, R. Lynette:
  Doherty.
RUTLAND, Suzanne D.:
  Freedman; Freilich.
RUTLEDGE, Martha:
  Barbour; Cowper; Crowley, B.; Fair; Green, I.
RYAN, Alan:
  Cameron, C.
RYAN, Peter:
  Ball.

SAUNDERS, Malcolm:
  Adams, N.; Forde.
SCHILD, Maurice:
  Albrecht.
SCOTT, Joanne:
  Camm.
SCOTT, Stan:
  Chisholm.
SCULLY, P. J.:
  Adams, J.
SEARS, J. S.:
  Armstrong, J.
SENYARD, J. E.:
  Kernot.

SEXTON, Christopher:
  Helpmann.
SHELTON, J. J.:
  Chinn.
SHERLOCK, Peter:
  Buxton; Gaden.
SHERSON, Susan:
  Gainfort.
SIERAKOWSKI, K. (Charles):
  Andrzejaczek.
SIMPSON, Caroline*:
  Blaxland.
SIMS, M. R.*:
  Begg.
SINNAMON, Ian:
  Cummings.
SITSKY, Larry:
  Evans, H. L.
SMART, Judith:
  Couchman; Gill, E. E.
SMITH, Bernard:
  Counihan.
SOUTER, Gavin:
  Browne; Hastings.
SPARGO, Sheila:
  Dickson.
SPATE, Andy:
  Jennings, J.
SPAULL, Andrew:
  Connolly; Cranley.
SPEARRITT, Gordon D.:
  Brandon.
SPEARRITT, Peter:
  Campbell, J. K.; Finey; Korman.
SPURLING, Kathryn:
  Bland; Croll.
STACY, Bill:
  Hurren.
STAFFORD, G. A.:
  Buick.
STARCEVICH, Judith:
  Goble.
STAUNTON, Anthony:
  Cawthorne.
STEPHENS, Alan:
  Dale.
STEVENS, David:
  Humphries; Knight, A.
STOCK, Jenny Tilby:
  Finger.
STODDART, Brian:
  Ferrier.
STRANGIO, Paul:
  Di Salvo.
STRAWHAN, Peter:
  Cooper, G. C.
STRETTON, Hugh:
  Duncan.
STUBBS, Brett J.:
  Foyster.

* deceased

SUDRABS, Zaiga:
Krips.
SUNTER, Anne Beggs:
Bartrop.
SWIFT, Robert S.:
Armstrong, R.
SWINDEN, Greg:
Knight, A.

TAMPKE, Jürgen:
Hammerman.
TANNER, Howard:
Guertner.
TATE, Audrey:
Byrne; Jarrett, P.
TAYLOR, Robert I.*:
Carne.
TAYLOR, Tracy:
Clark, A.
TEALE, Ruth:
Knox, D.
TEBBUTT, John:
Barcs.
THOMAS, Daniel:
Horton.
THOMSON, D. S.:
Daley, E.
TIFFIN, Chris:
Hadgraft.
TOBIAS, Phillip V.:
Dart.
TONKINSON, Robert:
Berndt.
TORNEY-PARLICKI, Prudence*:
Hughes.
TRELOAR, Michael:
Dunstan.
TRIBE, Kenneth W.:
Berg.
TRINCA, Mathew:
del Piano.
TROY, P. N.:
Harrison, P.
TULLY, Bill:
Hartigan, W.
TYLER, Peter J.:
Anderson, K. McC.
TYQUIN, Michael B.:
Ford.
TYRELL, Sarah:
Guthrie.

UREN, Nick:
Downes.

VAN DER POORTEN, Alf:
Chandler.
VAN STRATEN, F.:
Hayes.

* deceased

VELTRI, Damian:
Bandt; Kilpatrick.
VENTRESS, Alan:
Alam.
VICK, Lesley:
Cook, W. G.
VON OPPELN, C. A.:
Crowther.

WALKER, J. D.:
Johnston, E.
WALLACE-CRABBE, Chris:
Buckley.
WALSH, G. P.:
Bayliss; Cooke; Freeman, G.; Hardy, W.; Kelly, J. H.; Knight, J. L.
WALSH, Greg:
Anderson, K. S.
WALTER, James:
Davies, A. F.
WANNA, John:
Field, A.
WARD, Peter:
Ballantyne.
WARNE, Ellen:
Daly, M.
WARREN, Alan:
Bowring.
WATERHOUSE, Jill:
Holt, B.
WATERHOUSE, Richard:
Cook, W. H.; Kenna.
WATERS, Ian B.:
Knox, J.
WATSON, Pamela Lakin:
Duncan-Kemp.
WESTLAKE, Donald:
Amadio.
WHIMPRESS, Bernard:
Farmer; Favell.
WHITAKER, Anne-Maree:
Goldsmith.
WHITE, M. W. D.:
Douglas.
WHITE, Margaret H.:
Derham, F.
WHITE, Richard:
Halliwell.
WHITELAW, J.:
Dyke.
WILLIAMS, Paul D.:
Katter; Keeffe.
WILLIAMS, Robyn:
Daley, M.
WILLIAMS, Ross:
Cochrane.
WILLSON, Robert:
Dougan.
WILSON, David:
Campbell, S.; Harrison, A.
WILSON, Rose:
Dobson, A.; Hayward.

AUTHORS

WILTSHIRE, Kenneth:
  Fraser.
WINTER, Christine:
  Bergmann.
WOOD, Ronald:
  English.
WOODARD, Garry:
  Bourchier.
WOODHOUSE, Fay:
  Knox, A.

WORBY, Gus:
  Cherry.
WYNDHAM, Marivic:
  Dark, E.

YOUNG, John:
  Korman.
YU, John:
  Dods.

A NOTE ON SOME PROCEDURES

Differences of opinion exist among our authors, readers and the editorial board as to whether certain information should normally be included—such as cause of death, burial or cremation details, and value of estate. In this volume our practices have been as follows:

Cause of death: usually included, except in the case of those aged over 70.

Burial/cremation: included when details available.

Value of estate: included where possible for categories such as businessmen, and if the amount is unusually high or low.

Some other procedures require explanation:

Measurements: we have used imperial system measurements when historically appropriate, followed by the metric equivalent in brackets.

Money: we have retained £ (for pounds) for references prior to 14 February 1966 (when the conversion rate was A£1 = A$2).

Religion: stated whenever information is available, but there is often no good evidence of actual practice; e.g., the information is confined to marriage and funeral rites.

[q.v.]: the particular volume is given for those included in Volumes 1-16 and the *Supplement*, but not for those in this volume. Note that the cross-reference [q.v.] now accompanies the names of all who have separate articles in the *ADB*. In Volumes 1-6 it was not shown for royal visitors, governors, lieutenant-governors and those Colonial Office officials who were included.

Small capitals: used for relations and others when they are of substantial importance, though not included in their own right; these people are also q.v.'d.

Floruit and 'date of death': for the period 1788 to 1939, the placing of subjects in Volumes 1 to 12 was determined by when they flourished; in contrast, Volumes 13 to 16 (for the period 1940 to 1980) and this volume (for the period 1981–1990) only include people who died in those years.

* An asterisk against an author's name indicates deceased.

CORRIGENDA

Every effort is made to check every detail in every article, but a work of the *ADB*'s size and complexity is bound to contain some errors.

Corrigenda have been published with each volume. A consolidated list, including corrections made after the publication of volume 12 (1990), forms part of the *Index* (1991). A list of corrigenda compiled since 2002 accompanies Volume 17.

Only corrections are shown; additional information is not included; nor is any reinterpretation attempted. The exception to this procedure occurs when new details about parents, births, marriages and deaths become available.

Documented corrections are welcomed. Additional information, with sources, is also invited, and will be placed in the appropriate files for future use. In both cases, readers should write to:

> The General Editor
> Australian Dictionary of Biography
> Research School of Social Sciences
> Coombs Building, No 9
> Australian National University
> CANBERRA ACT 0200
> Australia
> Email: adb@anu.edu.au

REFERENCES

The following and other standard works of reference have been widely used, though not usually acknowledged in individual biographies:

Biographical registers for various Australian parliaments: (A. W. Martin & P. Wardle and H. Radi, P. Spearritt & E. Hinton and C. N. Connolly—New South Wales; D. Black & G. Bolton—Western Australia; K. Thomson & G. Serle and G. Browne—Victoria; D. B. Waterson and D. B. Waterson & J. Arnold—Queensland; H. Coxon, J. Playford & R. Reid—South Australia; S. & B. Bennett—Tasmania; and J. Rydon—Commonwealth)

Oxford Dictionary of National Biography (2004)

C. A. Hughes and B. D. Graham, *A Handbook of Australian Government and Politics 1890-1964* (1968) and *1965-1974* (1977) and *1975-1984* (1986) and *1985-1999* (2002); *Voting for the Australian House of Representatives 1901-1964*, with corrigenda (1974) and *1965-1984* (1995), *Queensland Legislative Assembly 1890-1964* (1974), *New South Wales ...* (1975), *Victoria ...* (1975), and *South Australian, Western Australian and Tasmanian Lower Houses ...* (1976), D. Black, *An Index to Parliamentary Candidates in Western Australian Elections 1890-2006* (2006)

J. Statton (ed), *Biographical Index of South Australians 1836-1885*, 1-4 (Adel, 1986)

P. Serle, *Dictionary of Australian Biography*, 1-2 (Syd, 1949); D. Carment et al (eds), *Northern Territory Dictionary of Biography*, 1 (1990), 2 (1992), 3 (1996); D. Horton (ed), *The Encyclopaedia of Aboriginal Australia*, 1-2 (Canb, 1994); J. Arnold and D. Morris (eds), *Monash Biographical Dictionary of 20th Century Australia* (1994); A. Millar (ed), *The Biographical Dictionary of the Australian Senate*, 1 (2000), 2 (2004)

P. Parsons (ed), *Companion to Theatre in Australia* (1995); W. Bebbington (ed), *The Oxford Companion to Australian Music* (1997); S. Sadie (ed), *The New Grove Dictionary of Music and Musicians*, 1-29 (2001)

W. Moore, *The Story of Australian Art*, 1-2 (1980); A. McCulloch, *Encyclopedia of Australian Art*, revised S. McCulloch, 1-2 (2004)

E. M. Miller, *Australian Literature from its Beginnings to 1935* (Melb, 1940), extended to 1950 by F. T. Macartney (Syd, 1956); H. M. Green, *A History of Australian Literature Pure and Applied*, revised D. Green, 1-2 (1984-85); W. H. Wilde, J. Hooton & B. Andrews, *The Oxford Companion to Australian Literature* (1994)

Who's Who (London) and *Who's Who in Australia*

Jobson's Year Book of Public Companies

ABBREVIATIONS USED IN BIBLIOGRAPHIES

A'asia/n	Australasia/n	JCU	James Cook University, Qld
ABC	Australian Broadcasting Commission/Corporation	jnl	journal
ACT	Australian Capital Territory	LA	Legislative Assembly
ADB	Australian Dictionary of Biography	LC	Legislative Council
		lib	library
ADFA	Australian Defence Force Academy		
		mag	magazine
ALP	Australian Labor Party	mfm	microfilm
ANU	Australian National University	*MJA*	*Medical Journal of Australia*
ANZAAS	Australian and New Zealand Association for the Advancement of Science	ms/s	manuscript/s
		NAA	National Archives of Australia
AOT	Archives Office of Tasmania	nd	date of publication unknown
assn	association	NFSA	National Film and Sound Archive
Aust/n	Australia/n		
AWM	Australian War Memorial	NGA	National Gallery of Australia
		NLA	National Library of Australia
Basser Lib	Adolph Basser Library, Australian Academy of Science	no	number
		NSW	New South Wales
bd	board	NT	Northern Territory
BHP	Broken Hill Proprietary Co. Ltd	NTA	Northern Territory Archives Service
bib	bibliography		
biog	biography, biographical	NY	New York
		NZ	New Zealand
c	circa		
C of E	Church of England	*ODNB*	*Oxford Dictionary of National Biography*
CAE	College of Advanced Education		
co	company	p/p	page/s
comp	compiler	*PD*	*Parliamentary Debates*
corp/s	corporation/s	*PIM*	*Pacific Islands Monthly*
Crt	Court	PNG	Papua New Guinea
CSIRO	Commonwealth Scientific and Industrial Research Organisation	*PP*	*Parliamentary Papers*
		PRO	Public Record Office
ctte	committee	procs	proceedings
Cwlth	Commonwealth	pt/s	part/s
dept	department	Qld	Queensland
		QSA	Queensland State Archives
ed/s	editor/s	qtrly	quarterly
edn	edition		
Eng	England	RMIT	Royal Melbourne Institute of Technology (Univ)
geog	geographical		
govt	government	SA	South Australia/n
		sel	select
HA	House of Assembly	SLNSW	State Library of New South Wales
hist	history/historical		
HR	House of Representatives	SLQ	State Library of Queensland
		SLSA	State Library of South Australia
Inc	Incorporated	SLT	State Library of Tasmania
inst	institute	SLV	State Library of Victoria
instn	institution	SLWA	State Library of Western Australia
intro	introduction, introduced by	*SMH*	*Sydney Morning Herald*

ABBREVIATIONS USED IN BIBLIOGRAPHIES

soc	society	univ	university
SRNSW	State Records NSW	UNSW	University of New South Wales
SRSA	State Records of South Australia	UPNG	University of Papua New Guinea
SRWA	State Records Office of Western Australia	USA	United States of America
		UWA	University of Western Australia
supp	supplement		
Tas	Tasmania/n	*V&P*	*Votes and Proceedings*
trans	transactions	Vic	Victoria/n
ts	typescript/transcript	vol/s	volume/s
UK	United Kingdom		
UNE	University of New England	WA	Western Australia/n

A

ABDULLAH, GEORGE CYRIL (1919-1984), community leader, was born on 9 August 1919 at Guildford, Western Australia, youngest of five children of Joseph Benedict Abdul, a labourer from Calcutta, India, and his Aboriginal wife Mary Salina, née Griffin. Educated at the Benedictine Mission, New Norcia, George was a farm labourer at Goomalling for six years before beginning full-time service in the Militia on 15 April 1942. Employed as a driver with the Bulk Issue Petrol and Oil Depot at Salter Point, Perth, he transferred to the Australian Imperial Force on 11 August but remained at the BIPOD. He was discharged on medical grounds on 28 October 1943. On 6 December 1944 at Holy Trinity Catholic Church, New Norcia, he married Gladys Martha Kelly, from Moore River Native Settlement; they were together for only a short period of time.

From 1946 Abdullah worked as a labourer, truck driver, and linesman with the South Australian Railways. He participated in a number of Perth organisations and committees promoting Aboriginal rights. Granted citizenship on 23 January 1947, he was an early member of the Coolbaroo League, a welfare group that administered the Allawah Grove settlement and held social functions for Aborigines at Northbridge and Eden Hill. In 1952 he called a public meeting to discuss citizenship rights for Aboriginal people, as a result of which the short-lived Original Australians Welfare and Progress Association was formed. Also in 1952 he helped to establish the Western Australia Native Welfare Council (from 1963 the Aboriginal Advancement Council of Western Australia). Divorced in 1956, he married with Churches of Christ forms Vera Alwyn Moore on 15 June that year at her parents' North Perth residence.

Abdullah travelled to Sydney, Adelaide and Perth in the early 1950s to address meetings of diverse groups about the plight of Aboriginal people, and on Sundays regularly spoke from a soapbox at the Perth Esplanade. For some years he ensured that a float representing Aboriginal interests was entered in the Trades and Labour Day procession. He was a member of the local United Nations committee on human rights. In 1958 he established the Western Australian Youth Club, which catered for both Aboriginal and non-Aboriginal children and adolescents. He organised an all-Aboriginal conference in Western Australia in September 1962. For several months in 1966 he managed the Aboriginal Advancement Council's centre at Beaufort Street, Perth.

In 1970 Abdullah was involved in setting up the Aboriginal Rights Council (later Aboriginal Rights League); he was a founding executive member of the National Tribal Council (1970) and of the Aboriginal Publications Foundation (1972-81). He established the Aboriginal Development and Cultural Council at Geraldton and was employed in the early 1970s as a liaison officer with the Commonwealth Office of Aboriginal Affairs in Canberra. He was active in the National Aboriginal Consultative Committee (from 1977 the National Aboriginal Conference) and stood unsuccessfully for the Senate as an Independent at the Federal election in December 1975.

A charismatic leader, Abdullah fought for forty years for equal rights for Aboriginal people, saying 'don't be ashamed. Be proud of being an Aboriginal'. He died of coronary artery disease on 6 August 1984 at Nedlands and was buried with Catholic rites in Guildford cemetery. His wife and their daughter and three sons survived him.

R. Gilbert, *Living Black* (1977); *West Australian*, 4 Sept 1962, p 12, 17 Sept 1962, p 8, 7 Dec 1975, p 8, 9 Aug 1984, p 13; *Newsletter for the Aboriginal People of WA*, Oct 1972, p 35; B883, items WX2518 and WX33318 (NAA); personal knowledge.

YASMIN JILL ABDULLAH

ADAMS, JOHN IRWIN ('BAY') (1922-1990), air force officer, was born on 6 December 1922 at Mordialloc, Melbourne, fourth of five children of Victorian-born parents Albert Warnock Adams, engineer, and his wife Ruby Constance, née Jenkins, a nurse. His elder siblings and their friends would go 'to the bay' to swim and John would call out 'bay too, bay too'; the nickname 'Bay' stuck. He began his flying career by jumping off the 60 ft (18 m) cliffs at Beaumaris with a home-made parachute and converting his bicycle into a glider. His father soon put a stop to his attempts to become airborne. Educated to Intermediate certificate level at Malvern Church of England Grammar School, he was a member (1938) of the first XVIII and the athletics team. After leaving school, he worked as a clerk for a South Yarra real-estate agent, Williams & Co.

On 7 November 1941 Adams enlisted in the Royal Australian Air Force. He trained in South Australia and in Canada, where he qualified as a pilot and was made an instructor. Rising to flight sergeant in June 1943, he proceeded to Britain in April 1944 and was commissioned in July. Next month he joined

No.3 Squadron, Royal Air Force. Flying Hawker Tempests, he shot down two V-1 flying bombs, shared in the destruction of a third and was engaged in much dangerous activity against German ground targets. Late in April 1945 he and Pierre Clostermann were the only survivors of an attack by eight Tempests on the German airfield at Schwerin. According to Clostermann, Adams 'was quite imperturbable and feared neither God nor the Devil'. On 30 April he shot down one German aircraft and three days later shared two further victories with Clostermann. Serving with the occupation forces after the war in Europe ended, he was promoted to flight lieutenant in July. He returned to Australia in February 1946 and transferred to the Permanent Air Force.

Early in 1948 Adams joined the British Commonwealth Occupation Force in Japan as a flight commander in No.77 Squadron. Initially based at Iwakuni, he was involved in a mid-air collision on 17 March 1949, resulting in a parachute descent from his Mustang into the freezing waters of the Sea of Japan. At Holy Trinity Church of England, Iwakuni, on 13 August that year he married Bonnie Jean Brien, a teacher at the base's school. In December he obtained the highest individual score at the Far East Air Forces gunnery competition at Yokota. For this achievement he was awarded the Air Force Cross (1951).

From July 1950 No.77 Squadron was engaged in escort, ground-attack, close-support and armed-reconnaissance missions over Korea; by September Adams, flying Mustangs, had completed fifty sorties. He was awarded the American Air Medal (1950) and, for his courage, leadership and devotion to duty, the Distinguished Flying Cross (1951). In October 1950 he returned to Australia.

Sent to Malta in July 1952 as commanding officer of No.76 Squadron, Adams again displayed exceptional weapons skills. In 1955 he attended the RAAF Staff College, Point Cook, Victoria. He held further flying posts in 1958-61 as commanding officer of No.22 and No.75 squadrons. Stationed in the United States of America in 1961-64, he completed the course at the Armed Forces Staff College, Norfolk, Virginia, before serving as an intelligence officer at the Australian Embassy, Washington. In November 1966 he was promoted to group captain and given command of RAAF Base, Townsville, Queensland. From October 1968 he commanded the RAAF Contingent Vung Tau, Republic of Vietnam (South Vietnam). Returning home a year later, he was appointed CBE (1970).

In November 1971 Adams rose to air commodore and became director, joint operations and plans, Canberra. He was again posted overseas as air commander of the Australia-New Zealand-United Kingdom Force in Singapore (1974) and commander of the Integrated Air Defence System at Penang, Malaysia (1975-77). His final appointments were as chief of air force operations, Canberra (1978), and air officer commanding Operational Command, Glenbrook, New South Wales (1978-79). On 7 November 1979 he retired, having served in every rank from aircraftman to air vice-marshal (promoted 31 January 1975).

Six ft 2 ins (188 cm) tall, with azure blue eyes, Adams was a gregarious, larger-than-life character. He earned the respect of all who knew him and was revered by his pilots. Air Chief Marshal Sir Neville McNamara summed him up: 'Bay was a natural fighter pilot, completely at home in the world of fighter squadrons and ... active operations'. Survived by his wife, their daughter and one of their two sons, Adams died of a cerebrovascular accident on 7 September 1990 at Broadbeach Waters, Queensland, and was buried with full military honours in Southport lawn cemetery.

P. Clostermann, *The Big Show* (1953); A. Stephens, *Going Solo* (1995); D. Newton, *Clash of Eagles* (1996); T. Hall, *Typhoon Warfare* (2000); *Australian*, 19 July 1968, p 2, 10 Sept 1990, p 5; *RAAF News*, Feb 1975, p 3, Oct 1990, p 7; *Sun* (Sydney), 23 Aug 1978, p 25; *Canberra Times*, 9 Sept 1990, p 2; Adams, John Irwin, series A12372 (NAA); private information.   P. J. SCULLY

ADAMS, NOEL DARWIN (1906-1989), journalist, was born on 7 March 1906 at Waratah, Tasmania, third child of Oliver Linley Adams, a Tasmanian-born surveyor, and his wife Leonora, née Battanta, who came from Victoria. Educated at the Church Grammar School, Launceston, and the University of Tasmania (BA, 1929), where he majored in English and history, Adams first worked for the Hobart *Mercury* and then for the Melbourne *Argus*. Early in the 1930s he followed his parents to Argentina and spent two years on the staff of the Buenos Aires *Standard*. He returned to Australia via Europe in 1933 and joined the Adelaide *Advertiser* as a 'special writer', soon becoming a leader-writer in the editorial section. On 3 May that year at St Paul's Church of England, Adelaide, he married Joan Patricia Irvine.

On 27 September 1941 Adams enlisted in the Australian Imperial Force. He was posted to the 58th Anti-Aircraft Searchlight Company in February 1942 and promoted to lance sergeant. Discharged on 26 October, he was accredited as a war correspondent for the *Advertiser*. He witnessed the Huon Peninsula campaign in New Guinea in December 1943-January 1944 and the landings at Tarakan and Labuan Islands, Borneo, in May 1945. Between assignments in South-East Asia, he wrote stories which often had a military theme, and also covered local issues.

Late in 1944 Adams toured areas along the Murray River in South Australia and in south-west New South Wales investigating the impact of the long drought. A colleague, Stewart Cockburn, believed that the resulting dozen articles heightened public and governmental awareness in South Australia of the dangers of soil erosion to the fruit and grain industries, and led to greater use of contour ploughing and other land-management techniques. The *Advertiser* released Adams for a few months in 1946 to be press relations officer to the governor-general, the Duke of Gloucester [q.v.14]. Representing the Australian metropolitan morning newspapers, he accompanied Princess (Queen) Elizabeth and the Duke of Edinburgh on their royal tours of 1952 and 1953-54.

As the *Advertiser*'s foreign editor during the 1950s and 1960s, and former president of the local branch of the Australian Institute of International Affairs, Adams established himself as an authority on international relations. He read widely and often travelled overseas. Although he maintained his interest in South America, he paid particular attention to South-East Asia, and among highlights of his career were interviews with prime ministers Lee Kuan Yew, of Singapore, and Tunku Abdul Rahman, of Malaysia. One year he substituted for his friend Douglas Pike [q.v.16] and taught Asian history at the Workers' Educational Association of South Australia. Foreign governments invited him to visit their countries. In 1962 the West German government suggested that he write a series of articles on the Berlin Wall; in 1965, awarded a scholarship by the Department of State, United States of America, he focused on that country's Black civil rights movement. He regularly wrote one of the *Advertiser*'s two weekday editorials, but was occasionally upset by interference from the newspaper's conservative management headed by Sir Lloyd Dumas [q.v.14]. For example, during the Suez crisis of 1956 he was called back to the office in the early hours of the morning to rewrite a piece in which he was critical of the British government's actions—an incident he never forgot.

Adams became a well-known figure on radio and television. For some years he was a commentator on the Australian Broadcasting Commission's radio program 'Notes on the News', and early in the 1960s he was the host of 'Meet the Press', on Adelaide's ADS-7. After retiring in March 1971 he continued to write articles and book reviews for the *Advertiser*, made documentaries for television, and travelled. For most of their married life he and his wife lived in rented premises in North Adelaide; only when their son and daughter had grown up did they buy a house, at Wattle Park. Tall and slim, with a dark complexion, Adams was attractive to women and seemed younger than his years. He contracted Parkinson's disease, and in 1985 the Adamses moved to the Helping Hand Centre, North Adelaide. Survived by his wife and their son, he died there on 31 March 1989 and was cremated. In 1991 Cockburn described Adams, renowned for his elegant style, as 'one of the most gifted writers in the history of the *Advertiser*'.

Advertiser PI, Jan-Feb 1971, p 2, Mar 1989; *Advertiser* (Adelaide), 6 Mar 1971, p 8, 1 Apr 1989, p 13; B883, item SX14700 (NAA); private information.
MALCOLM SAUNDERS

ADLER, LAWRENCE JAMES (1931-1988), businessman, was born on 2 November 1931 in Budapest, Hungary, and named Ladislaus (Laszlo), only son of Bela Adler, button manufacturer, and his wife Antonia, née Vorosvary. Laszlo attended technical high school in Budapest. Previously prosperous, the family suffered privation during World War II; Bela had died in a camp at Mühlhausen, Germany, by 1945. With the communists in control in Hungary, Laszlo tried to leave; he was successful on his second attempt, escaping in 1949 via Austria, where, after a brief stay in a displaced persons' camp, he accepted a free passage to Australia in return for two years' indentured labour. He arrived in Melbourne in March 1950.

Known as 'Larry' in Australia, he started the two years' allocated employment in Adelaide with the South Australian Railways. In 1950 he moved to Sydney, where he worked as a petrol-pump attendant, storeman, motorcar-parts procurer, sales manager and taxi owner-driver. He operated an electrical goods store, then a record shop in the mid-1950s. Concurrently, he ran an investment business, the Prosperity & Security Corporation Ltd. He dabbled in real estate before forming a used-car dealership, Eagle Motors Pty Ltd (named after the English translation of the German *Adler*). He was naturalised in 1952. On 11 March 1956 Adler married Ethel Kaminer, a secretary, at the Great Synagogue, Sydney. He officially adopted the name Larry by deed poll in 1957 and changed it to Lawrence James in 1965.

In 1960 Adler had established the Fire & All Risks Insurance Co. Ltd, known as FAI. He was chairman and managing director. The company's initial paid-up capital was £7500 (soon increased to £25 000 to give the impression of solid backing for the company), its prime asset being a small building in King Street. Initially the company conducted fire, marine and accident insurance, but in 1965 it bought the Car Owners' Mutual Insurance Co. Ltd. FAI was an innovator, offering generous no-claim bonuses and an honour plan for minor repairs. Progress was not always smooth: the company suffered reverses due to heavy exposure in Darwin property and car insurance when Cyclone Tracy caused devastation in 1974.

Diversification within the insurance field began in the mid-1960s, with the company acquiring the Falkirk & Stirlingshire Assurance Co. Ltd in 1966 (which gave it the ability to offer life insurance); buying Automotive & General Industries Ltd of Melbourne in 1967 for 'asset stripping'; and purchasing Australian & International Insurances Ltd and Omnibus & General Insurance Brokers Pty Ltd in 1968. Australian & International Insurances Ltd acquired Fire & All Risks in 1971, achieving public company status for the whole group, and changed its name to FAI Insurances Ltd in 1973.

From 1969 Adler expanded his activities beyond insurance through Cumberland Holdings Ltd (previously Cumberland Credit Corporation Ltd), which began to operate nursing homes, followed by private hospitals. Not all his activities were successful. The 1981 purchase of Horwood, Bagshaw [q.v.3] Ltd, an Adelaide agricultural and mining equipment manufacturer, was a disaster, as was the 1982 acquisition of Offshore Oil NL. In the 1980s Adler made a fortune for FAI and himself as a corporate raider, acquiring shareholdings in underperforming companies likely to attract takeovers. In 1987 the strategic holdings he acquired in Pioneer Concrete Services Ltd and Ampol Ltd netted a profit of $194 million. The stock market crash of 1987 halved FAI's market valuation of $1.6 billion but Adler rode out this crisis too, in spite of not obeying the risk-averse investment pattern of most insurance companies.

Adler was frequently involved in civil law suits, as both plaintiff and defendant, against the insurance commissioners and various businesses. A member of the board of the Insurance Council of Australia from 1985 until his death, he was appointed AO in 1988. Though never a regular synagogue-attender, he remained proud of his Jewish identity. For relaxation he owned a yacht and tried some sports: 'I work golf. I work tennis. But I play business'. But his leisure time was mainly spent with his family and watching television at his Vaucluse home. A diabetic, he suffered his first heart attack in 1979. He died of diabetes and myocardial infarction on 13 December 1988 at Camperdown and was buried in the Northern Suburbs Jewish cemetery, North Ryde. His wife and their son and two daughters survived him. On his death FAI's share value dropped fifty cents (one-sixth of their value) overnight.

R. Ostrow, *The New Boy Network* (1987); P. Denton, *From Cabbie to Chairman* (1991); *Bulletin*, 24 Feb 1981, p 94; *SMH*, 2 Mar 1985, p 5, 10 Aug 1985, p 45, 14 Dec 1988, p 20; *Austn Financial Review*, 29 July 1985, p 11, 14 Dec 1988, p 6; *Age* (Melbourne), 14 Dec 1988, p 25; private information.

JOHN PERKINS

AFFLEY, DECLAN JAMES (1939-1985), musician, was born on 8 September 1939 in Cardiff, Wales, son of James Affley, labourer and amateur musician, and his wife Winifred Anne, née Samuel. Declan's Catholic working-class parents were both descended from Irish families. He began learning the clarinet when he was 8 years old and later enrolled in the Royal Welsh College of Music. He attended several Catholic schools and maintained that they 'caused no permanent damage'.

Having joined the British merchant navy at the age of 16, Affley arrived in Sydney in 1960. The folk-music movement was just beginning and he sang in what he referred to as 'low dives' such as the Royal George pub. By this time, he had abandoned the clarinet in favour of the guitar, banjo and tin whistle. In 1967 he started playing the fiddle and in 1970 the Irish (uillean) pipes. Devoted to his craft, Affley is best remembered for his singing and guitar (his 'harp') accompaniments. His voice was deep, resonant and powerful.

On 11 December 1967 at the office of the government statist, Melbourne, he married Colleen Zeita Burke, a stenographer and poet. Working as a boat-builder, Affley lived (1967-69) in Melbourne and performed at the Dan O'Connell Hotel and at Frank Traynor's [q.v.] folk and jazz club. In 1969 he founded a bush band, 'The Wild Colonial Boys', which combined traditional Australian and Irish music. Back in Sydney from 1970, he played at the Troubadour coffee lounge, Edgecliff. His last band was 'Lazy Harry's'. Affley was a regular performer at the Boîtes: concerts featuring Turkish, Greek, Irish and Australian music. He busked on the streets and was occasionally subjected to censorship by council officials for singing left-wing political material, but such suppression encouraged rather than deterred him. Some of the political songs he sang were broadcast on radio by the Australian Broadcasting Commission and performed on concert tours. In 1970 the National Folk Foundation of New Zealand invited him to attend its festival. He was a member of the committee of the New South Wales Folk Federation in the early 1970s.

Affley participated as a singer in an award-winning ABC television documentary, 'The Restless Years' (1966), which presented Australian history through songs, stories and poetry. In 1972 he accompanied Peter O'Shaughnessy and Marian Henderson to

Ireland to perform a dramatised stage version at the Dublin Theatre Festival. He contributed to films including Tony Richardson's *Ned Kelly* (1970), Peter Weir's *The Last Wave* (1977) and Richard Lowenstein's *Strikebound* (1984).

Supporting the advancement of the Australian Indigenous people, Affley taught music at the Eora Centre in Redfern (1984-85). He regarded himself as a socialist 'with a fair degree of anarchy'. Outspoken and informed, especially on Australian and Irish working-class politics, he supported the New South Wales Builders' Labourers' Green Bans, Irish hunger strikers and the Gurindji's struggle for land rights at Wave Hill, Northern Territory. He enjoyed discussing cricket and Rugby League over a convivial ale. Articulate but unpretentious and egalitarian, he shared his skills and knowledge. Affley died of a dissecting aneurysm of the aorta on 27 June 1985 at Newtown and was cremated. His wife and their daughter and son survived him. The Declan Affley songwriting award is made annually at the Australian National Folk Festival.

G. B. Davey and G. Seal (eds), *Oxford Companion to Australian Folklore* (1993); NSW Folk Federation, *Newsletter*, Aug 1970, p 11, Feb 1972, p 13, May 1972, p 8, June 1972, p 3, Dec 1972, p 1, no 23, nd, p 6, no 24, nd, p 3, Dec 1980, p 20; *Cornstalk Gazette*, Aug 1985, p 3, July 1986, p 17; C686, correspondence file: Declan Affley (NAA); private information.

JOHN DENGATE

AGNEW, SIR ROBERT DAVID GARRICK (1930-1987), sportsman and businessman, was born on 21 September 1930 at Nedlands, Perth, son of Western Australian-born parents Robert Gordon Carlisle Agnew, municipal engineer, and his wife Dorothy Jean, née Wilson. Garrick attended Perth Modern School and in 1949 entered the University of Western Australia to study engineering. A champion freestyle swimmer, he won the annual long-distance 'swim through Perth' race in the Swan River that year, and the 440-yards and the 880-yards finals at the Australian championships in 1950. He competed in the London Olympic Games (1948), and won the gold medal for the 440-yards freestyle at the 1950 British Empire Games in Auckland, New Zealand. In 1950 he secured a sporting scholarship in the United States of America at Ohio State University, Columbus (BS, 1952); majoring in psychology, he graduated summa cum laude. At the Helsinki Olympic Games (1952) he competed in the 1500-metres event. He undertook postgraduate studies at Harvard University's Graduate School of Business Administration (MBA, 1954), this time on an academic scholarship, and returned to Perth.

A restless individual, with an original turn of mind, as a young man Agnew considered using tank-landing craft to ferry iron ore to bulk carriers offshore. Instead he acquired an old 'tramp steamer' and began exporting minerals and live cattle. He formed Garrick Agnew Pty Ltd and went into business as an ore broker. On 4 April 1959 at the Perth Society of the New Church, Adelaide Terrace, he married Fay Ma-belle Ferguson, a stenographer. In 1966 he established an evaporative salt and gypsum mine at Shark Bay, near Carnarvon; the enterprise ran at a loss for some years but eventually flourished. He was known as a 'great gambler' who, with little capital of his own, was able to persuade affluent partners to back his ventures. Having a financial interest (through his company, Mt Enid Iron Co. Pty Ltd) in the original consortium holding the prospecting rights to the reserves covering the Robe River iron ore deposits, Agnew acquired a 5 per cent stake in Robe River Ltd when it became a public company in 1970 and began mining. He benefited from considerable royalties before selling his interest in 1977.

In 1970 the Agnew group of companies had merged with Clough Holdings Pty Ltd to form Agnew Clough Ltd, with Agnew as chairman. Four years later the company embarked on a project to mine and process vanadium, and in 1980 announced plans to build a silicon metal smelter at Wundowie, near Perth. That year Agnew helped to found the Australian Bank Ltd, the first new trading bank in the country for fifty years, and was appointed its founding chairman. Also chairman of several Australian Bank subsidiaries, including Australian Liquid Assets Management Ltd and Australis Securities Ltd, he was a director of Qantas Airways Ltd (1981-87) and the Australian Industry Development Corporation (1974-80). Determined, far-sighted and self-effacing, Agnew was 'a down-to-earth man with straightforward ideas' and a style that was a mixture of 'doggedness and flair'. He amassed a fortune estimated by the *Australian* as $100 million. He was appointed CBE in 1978 and knighted in 1983.

A 'big healthy man, with a brown face, big forehead and curly hair', Sir Garrick swam regularly throughout his life to keep fit. He was an outstanding big game fisherman, taking his cruiser every year from Fremantle to North Queensland in pursuit of marlin. In 1983 at Rottnest Trench he set a Western Australian record when he caught a 319-kg Pacific Blue Marlin. He was a member of the Weld, Royal Freshwater Bay Yacht and Perth Game Fishing clubs. His wife died in 1981 and his younger daughter in 1983. On 29 November 1986 at St Columba's Presbyterian Church, Mosman Park, he married Elizabeth Margaret, née Ahern, a divorcee and an interpreter. He died of coronary artery disease on 3 August

1987 at the University of Western Australia swimming pool complex, Crawley, after a training session, and was cremated with Anglican rites. His wife and the two sons and elder daughter of his first marriage survived him.

Austn Financial Review, 6 May 1971, p 10, 5 Aug 1987, p 4; *People with Pix*, 29 Sept 1977, p 5; *West Australian*, 4 Aug 1987, p 16; *Australian*, 13 Feb 1981, p 19, 5 Aug 1987, p 2; private information.

JOHN MCILWRAITH

AH LING, GEORGE; *see* LAU

AICKIN, SIR KEITH ARTHUR (1916-1982), judge, was born on 1 February 1916 at East Malvern, Melbourne, younger son of James Lee Aickin, a schoolmaster from Ireland, and his Victorian-born wife Edith Clarabel, née Knight. Keith attended Melbourne Church of England Grammar School, where his father was senior mathematics master (1909-37). He proceeded to the University of Melbourne (LL B, 1937; LL M, 1939) and graduated with first-class honours, the E. J. B. Nunn scholarship and the Supreme Court judges' prize. On 1 May 1939 he was admitted to practise as a barrister and solicitor. That year he became associate to Justice (Sir) Owen Dixon [q.v.14] of the High Court of Australia.

At the request of Dixon, who chaired the Central Wool Committee and the Shipping Control Board, Aickin was attached (1941-42) to those two bodies. When Dixon was appointed Australian minister in Washington in 1942, he insisted that Aickin accompany him as third secretary of the Australian legation. In 1944 Aickin went on to London, where he became legal adviser to the European office of the United Nations Relief and Rehabilitation Administration. He was called to the Bar at the Middle Temple in 1948. This initiative allowed him, many years later, to appear in the House of Lords as a member of the English Bar to argue a copyright case for an Australian company.

In 1948 Aickin was appointed to the legal department of the United Nations in New York. Returning to Australia in 1949, he signed the Victorian Bar roll on 4 February and read with A. D. G. (Sir Alistair) Adam. Aickin's practice expanded rapidly. Within two years he was appearing without a leader in the High Court. He also lectured (1951-56) in company law at the University of Melbourne. On 10 December 1957 he took silk. At St John's Church of England, Toorak, on 17 April 1952 he had married Elizabeth May Gullett.

Aickin's skills, pre-eminently those of an appellate advocate, extended over the wide areas of company and commercial law; taxation; constitutional law; and intellectual property, including patent law. He was an effective cross-examiner, particularly in matters involving scientific or technical evidence. His calm and deliberate manner often belied a certain steeliness. Once in a criminal appeal, on a pro bono brief, Aickin was asked by an impatient judge why he was wasting the court's time when his client had obviously been guilty. Aickin replied, 'That is not the point of the exercise your Honour. The point of the exercise is whether he had a fair trial'.

It was rare for Aickin to appear in a criminal court. In the more complex civil matters he excelled. He was able to argue difficult cases with a subtlety disguised by an apparent simplicity. His presentation of a case was the result of the painstaking dissection of an argument in order to strip away its inessential elements and expose its strengths. The argument would then be lucidly delivered with a logical precision that was compelling.

Aickin was a formal, quietly spoken man. He was reserved, but capable of real warmth with those he knew well. He was modest, yet aware of his ability so that his arguments and opinions were confidently expressed. His proficiency gained him a nationwide reputation in the areas in which he practised and his advice was widely sought. In 1969 he declined appointment to the High Court when Sir Alan Taylor [q.v.16] died. His abilities had by this time been recognised beyond his practice as a barrister. Honorary secretary (1951-59) of the Australian Institute of International Affairs, he also became a director of Mayne Nickless Ltd (1958-76), P & O Australia Ltd (1969-76), Comalco Ltd (1970-76) and the Broken Hill Proprietary Co. Ltd (1971-76). He was a member of the interim council (1966) and council (1966-74) of La Trobe University.

On 20 September 1976, following the retirement of Sir Edward McTiernan [q.v.], Aickin finally accepted appointment to the High Court. Two months later he was appointed KBE. He did not attain the same stature as a judge as he had enjoyed as a member of the Bar. This was partly because his time on the bench was so short, but his judgments tended to contain lengthy passages from previous judgments and did not display the same penetrating analysis as his arguments and advice as counsel.

Sir Keith died on 18 June 1982 in South Melbourne, as a result of injuries suffered in a motorcar accident two weeks earlier. Survived by his wife, and their daughter and son, he was cremated. His estate was sworn for probate at $587 754.

G. Fricke, *Judges of the High Court* (1986); T. Blackshield et al (eds), *The Oxford Companion to the High Court of Australia* (2001); *BHP Jnl*, Autumn

1972, p 26; *Austn Law Jnl*, vol 56, no 8, 1982, p 438, vol 56, no 9, 1982, p 482; *Austn Tax Review*, vol 11, no 3, 1982, p 133; *Univ of Qld Law Jnl*, vol 12, no 2, 1982, p 3.
                                          DARYL DAWSON

AIKENS, THOMAS (1900-1985), politician, was born on 28 April 1900 at Hughenden station, Queensland, second of three children of John Aikens, an itinerant labourer, and his wife Emily, née Wilkinson, both born in Queensland. After Tom's father deserted the family in 1904, his mother moved with the children to Charters Towers, where she took in washing. In 1910 she went west to work in hotels, returning to visit each Christmas. Tom lodged with a friend and attended local state primary and high schools. He started work in 1915, first with the post office, and then as a roustabout in the Julia Creek area. In January 1916 he joined Queensland Railways at Cloncurry as a locomotive cleaner. He progressed to fireman and, in 1925, to engine driver. On 16 February 1921 at St Andrew's Church of England, Cloncurry, he married Margaret Ann Myers, a barmaid.

A large man, 6 ft (183 cm) tall and weighing approximately 16 stone (102 kg), Aikens was a keen Rugby League footballer, a gifted bass singer and a drinker. He was an avid reader with a remarkable memory, eagerly consuming Voltaire, Daniel Defoe, Charles Dickens, Robert Ingersoll and Eugene Debs. Less enthusiastic about his paid employment, he earned the nickname 'Energy' or 'Enjo'. He held various sub-branch positions in the Australian Railways Union from 1918 and was secretary of the local branch of the Australian Labor Party. In 1924 he was elected to the Cloncurry Shire Council and three years later became deputy-chairman. Transferred by the railways to Townsville in 1930 because of his 'political activism', he joined the newly formed Hermit Park ALP branch. He stood unsuccessfully at the 1933 Townsville municipal elections, but won a seat in 1936. At the 1939 election Labor won control of the council and Aikens was elected deputy-mayor.

Despite his electoral popularity, in October 1940 Aikens was expelled from the ALP, ostensibly for his drinking, which had reached epic proportions, but really because the Queensland party's dominant Australian Workers' Union faction opposed his brand of socialism. He was saved from political oblivion when the State branch's central executive expelled the entire Hermit Park membership in September 1942, because of its connection with a local 'aid to Russia' committee. The ousted branch formed itself into a new party, the 'Hermit Park ALP', and welcomed back Aikens. In 1943 it won seven of the ten aldermanic positions (with Aikens topping the poll),

and in loose coalition with the Communist Party of Australia ran the Townsville City Council for three years. The council instituted an extensive program of municipal ownership of facilities—an electrical appliance store, a wood depot, a fruit and vegetable mart, an iceworks and a child-care centre—which was more a response to the exigencies of wartime than to ideology. These circumstances, coupled with Aikens's ability to articulate northern resentment of remote government, saw him elected to the Legislative Assembly as Hermit Park Labour member for Mundingburra on 15 April 1944. He resigned as deputy-mayor and gave up drinking for good.

In 1949 the party became the North Queensland Labour Party, and in 1960 Mundingburra was renamed Townsville South. By then the party name (from which 'Labour' was dropped in 1974) was merely a medium for Aikens's political career. He was re-elected continuously until 1974, winning an absolute majority in eight successive elections from 1953 to 1972. Moving progressively to the Right, 'Tory Tom' was the 'perfect provincial populist', reflecting the views and prejudices of his electorate. He travelled around his electorate on his bicycle and worked hard advising and representing his constituents. As an Independent he did not exert much influence on government—although this did not prevent him from claiming responsibility for several legislative amendments.

Speaking often in parliament, usually without notes but with scattered literary references, he was fluent and loud, frequently humorous, but sometimes ponderous and verbose. He could be vicious and vindictive: he regularly denounced the ALP, and sharply criticised the medical and legal professions and, increasingly, the 'bludgers, parasites and time-servers' of the universities. Railing against the evil of pornography, he called for the castration of rapists and provided graphic descriptions of their crimes. In 1974 he was a member of the select committee on punishment of crimes of violence in Queensland.

By 1977 his views attracted fewer voters. Narrowly defeated by the ALP candidate in the election on 12 November, Aikens retired from politics. As president and later patron of the Townsville Choral and Orchestral Society, he continued to enjoy singing. He died on 30 November 1985 at Townsville and, although religion had played little part in his life, was cremated with Catholic rites. His wife and their daughter survived him.

C. A. Hughes, *Images and Issues* (1969); I. Moles, *A Majority of One* (1979); D. J. Murphy et al (eds), *Labor in Power* (1980); *PD* (Qld), 8 Aug 1944, p 74, 3 Oct 1944, p 666, 2 Mar 1945, p 2000, 5 Sept 1963, p 232, 8 Sept 1971, p 431, 26 Aug 1976, p 71, 15 Sept

1977, p 676, 4 Dec 1985, p 3199; *North Aust Research Bulletin*, Sept 1977, p 58; *Australian*, 12-13 Nov 1977, 'Weekend Mag', p 2; *Townsville Bulletin*, 3 Dec 1985, p 6.   D. W. HUNT

ALAM, ANTHONY ALEXANDER (ALEC) (1896-1983), politician, merchant and builder, was born on 23 January 1896 at Plattsburg, New South Wales, eldest child of Syrian (Lebanese)-born parents Joseph Alam, dealer, and his wife Mary, née Hashem. Alec was educated at De La Salle College, Armidale. He lived at various country centres in New South Wales and worked in the family business J. J. Alam, merchants, of The Rock, Dubbo and Dunedoo. Alam married Theresa (Therese) Anthony on 26 April 1924 at St Columba's Catholic Church, Charters Towers, Queensland. They moved to Sydney in the 1930s and lived at Drummoyne, then Mosman. Alec was managing director of the Australian Fur Export Co. and later a contract builder, and director of Mala (Alam spelt backwards) Homes Pty Ltd, Alam Homes Pty Ltd and Zebra Motels Pty Ltd.

Active in the Australian Labor Party, Alam was president of the Gwydir, Dubbo and Wammerawa branches. He represented Labor in the NSW Legislative Council for almost forty-two years in 1925-58 and 1963-73, and was the third-longest-serving member of the council, after Frank Spicer and John Mildred Creed [q.v.3]. In 1941 Alam, then president of the Phillip electorate council, had unsuccessfully contested the Macquarie ward at the Sydney Municipal Council elections. In October 1948 he was defeated in a preselection ballot conducted by the State ALP executive for the Phillip ward.

Alam's time in State parliament was contentious and he was frequently the subject of censure, more often than not from his own party. He was criticised for absences from the Legislative Council due to travel overseas, for using parliamentary privilege to impugn a policeman and for opposing reform of the council. Some Labor Party members could not reconcile his support for the party with his personal wealth: his attendance at a State ALP conference as a delegate of the Shop Assistants' Union seemed incongruous in view of his substantial business assets and investments. Alam could not see why 'just because a man is Labor, he should not be a better businessman than a Liberal. I am'.

In 1957 Alam was not selected for the ALP ticket for the Legislative Council elections. His success in a council by-election in 1963, when he was formally nominated by Premier R. J. Heffron, caused divisions in the party. Because of Alam's age (67) and that of others, the wisdom of a twelve-year term for council members was questioned. Despite his ambivalent relationship with the ALP hierarchy, late in 1971 Alam said that he would give away some of his parliamentary pension to the ALP, because he wanted to put it to good work: in his view all the great social legislation, including that affecting widows' pensions, workers' compensation, the status of women, and maternity wings in hospitals, had emanated from the ALP.

Therese Alam was a driving force behind fund-raising efforts during World War II in the Lebanon League of Australia, of which she was president. The community raised £352 000 for Commonwealth War Loans as well as funds to purchase ambulances and medical equipment for the Australian armed forces. On one occasion in 1943, the Lebanon Ladies War Comforts League of Australia had raised £6000 mainly through a then popular 'ugly man' competition at the Sydney Town Hall. After the war Therese Alam continued her fund-raising activities for projects in Australia and the Middle East.

Both the Alams helped migrants to settle in Australia. Alam was awarded many honours by foreign governments and the Lebanese community in Australia. He was appointed to the National Order of the Cedar (Lebanon), the Order of Nichan Iftikhar (France), the Légion d'honneur (France) and the Royal Order of the Phoenix (Greece). Therese Alam was awarded the Order of Merit (1st class) of the Lebanon. Alam died on 9 August 1983 at Darlinghurst. Survived by his wife, he was buried in the Catholic section of Rookwood cemetery. They had no children.

PD (LC, NSW), 20 Jan 1926, p 4186, 4 Aug 1937, p 22; *SMH*, 12 June 1923, p 9, 14 Oct 1926, p 9, 6 Aug 1937, p 11, 24 Aug 1956, p 5, 6 Nov 1963, p 5, 8 Nov 1963, p 2, 13 Nov 1963, p 16, 18 Nov 1963, p 2, 20 Nov 1963, p 1, 31 Oct 1969, p 4, 12 Nov 1971, p 10; Austn-Lebanese Hist Soc, *Newsletter*, Nov 2000, p 3.
ALAN VENTRESS

ALBERT, ADRIEN (1907-1989), medical chemist, was born on 19 November 1907 in Sydney, only son of Jacques Albert [q.v.7 M. F. Albert], a music publisher from Switzerland, and his third wife Mary Eliza Blanche, née Allan, who was born in Victoria. His parents separated and his father died when he was a small child. Adrien attended primary schools at Randwick and Coogee, and, on a scholarship, Scots College. After passing botany (1926), chemistry (1926) and materia medica (1927) at the University of Sydney, he was registered as a pharmacist on 12 February 1929. However, the business aspects of pharmacy did not appeal to him and he soon returned to the University of Sydney (B.Sc., 1933), where he graduated with first-class honours and the university medal in pharmaceutical science. He worked briefly at the university and then for a fabric-dyeing firm to accumulate funds for postgraduate study in London. Arriving there in 1934, he undertook research with W. H. Linnell at the College of the Pharmaceutical Society, University of London. Despite recurrent illness, he received his Ph.D. in 1937 for synthetic work on acridine antiseptics, a pointer to his future focus on heterocyclic and medicinal chemistry.

Back at the University of Sydney in 1938, Albert enjoyed reasonable research facilities as a lecturer in organic chemistry. During World War II he collaborated with J. C. Earl [q.v.14] in the industrial-scale preparation of the antiseptic proflavine, required urgently in the Pacific war zone. He also developed practical syntheses for the antimalarial drug mepacrine (Atebrin), then in equally desperate demand, and for a new and improved antiseptic, aminacrine (Monacrine), that replaced proflavine later in the war.

The National Health and Medical Research Council began to fund Albert's research in 1944 and he quickly built up a 'chemotherapy team' to study the relationship between the structure and activity of synthetic antimicrobial agents. For this and earlier work, subsequently reviewed in his book *The Acridines* (1951), the University of London awarded him a D.Sc. (1948). He was a research fellow (1947-48) at the Wellcome Research Institution, London, before being appointed foundation professor of medical chemistry at the John Curtin [q.v.13] School of Medical Research, Australian National University, in 1949. As no building was yet available in Canberra, he inaugurated his department in hired laboratories in London, where fundamental work on pteridines and the like (mainly as anti-cancer agents) was soon under way. The department moved to Canberra in 1956.

Meanwhile, Albert had been developing a novel concept, known as selective toxicity, to explain the ability of chemical substances to affect certain cells without harming others, applying the principle not only to human and veterinary medicine, but to pesticides and herbicides. He first enunciated this in a series of public lectures at University College, London, in 1948, followed by the small first edition of *Selective Toxicity* (1951); the concept, probably Albert's greatest contribution to the progress of medicinal chemistry, was gradually extended over the next thirty-five years, culminating in the massive seventh edition (1985) and a companion book, *Xenobiosis* (1987).

Although Albert's primary interest lay in how and why medicinal substances exerted their effects, his studies necessarily involved the preparation of myriad new and diverse heterocyclic compounds, which form the basis of nearly all modern ethical drugs. He and his colleagues became expert in the synthetic procedures required and in the physical chemistry associated with such products. Indeed, a high proportion of the original publications from his department involved pure chemistry and appeared in leading chemical journals. Albert sought unifying threads for this work in his substantial book *Heterocyclic Chemistry* (1959), of which the second edition (1968) proved invaluable as a specialised text for advanced students.

In 1973 Albert began an active retirement as visiting fellow, initially in the Research School of Chemistry and subsequently in the Department of Chemistry at the ANU, where he continued his research and writing with unabated vigour. He spent several periods as research professor in the department of pharmacological sciences at the State University of New York, Stony Brook, where his constantly updated lecture series on selective toxicity was especially valued.

A prodigious worker in the laboratory, Albert produced six books and more than 230 papers. He continually organised his own and his staff's time, but he disliked administration and its cessation was the only good aspect of retirement evident to him. Due to a gastrectomy, which followed a botched emergency operation in London during his postgraduate days, he was unable to get to work before 10 a.m., but he remained there until late at night, even on weekends. He was an excellent teacher of undergraduates, although he only made time for such activity in the late 1930s and in retirement.

Albert was a tall, thin person who invariably dressed carefully and, in his earlier days, fashionably. He had a very complex personality—even to his senior staff and colleagues he could be flatteringly courteous one day but tersely hypercritical the next. Thus, most co-workers appreciated his scientific acumen and integrity but only those who were willing to make many allowances ever classed themselves as friends. As a young man, he was mildly misogynistic, believing that a woman's place was in the home or in a secretarial role. He never married, having decided that a wife and family would use up too much valuable research time.

Providing there was a worthwhile conference or contact at the end of each journey, Albert was an inveterate traveller. He lectured in almost every country where medicinal chemistry was practised; he became reasonably proficient in German, French and Italian and had some knowledge of other European languages. Although research dominated his life, he was an accomplished pianist, a knowledgable music-lover, and a skilful cartoonist and photographer. He occasionally wrote poetry that was quite moving. Unusual plants and flowers fascinated him and overseas visitors were often taken on short bushwalks to admire Canberra's native flora.

Among his many honours and awards, Albert most appreciated being elected a fellow of the Australian Academy of Science (1958), appointed AO (1989), and invited to accept an honorary D.Sc. from the University of Sydney (conferred posthumously, 1990). He died on 29 December 1989 at Woden Valley Hospital, Canberra, and was cremated with Anglican rites. His memory is maintained by Adrien Albert lectures in London and New York, as well as in Australia; the medicinal chemistry laboratory at the University of Sydney was named after him.

Jnl of Chemical Education, vol 63, no 10, 1986, p 860; *Chemistry in Aust*, vol 57, no 4, 1990, p 116; D. J. Brown, 'Adrien Albert 1907-1989', *Hist Records of Austn Science*, vol 8, no 2, 1990, p 63, and for publications; Albert papers (Basser Lib).

D. J. BROWN

ALBRECHT, FRIEDRICH WILHELM (1894-1984), Lutheran missionary, was born on 15 October 1894 at Plawanice, County of Lublin, Russian Poland, eldest of ten children of German-speaking parents Ferdinand Albrecht, a farmer from Kroczyn, and his wife Helene, née Reichwald. Educated in the Russian language at a village school, Friedrich entered the Lutheran mission institute at Hermannsburg, near Hanover, Germany, in 1913. World War I interrupted his studies; lame in one leg from childhood, he served in the German medical corps on the Russian front. He was awarded the Iron Cross for tending wounded soldiers under fire. Returning to Hermannsburg, he completed his course in 1924 and received a call to work with the Finke River Mission, Hermannsburg, Northern Territory. He was sent to a seminary in the United States of America for five months to improve his English. Minna Maria Margaretha Gevers, whom he had met in Germany, joined him in Canada and they were married on 14 September 1925 at Winnipeg, Manitoba. The couple arrived in Sydney on 18 October and travelled on to South Australia.

Ordained a pastor in the United Evangelical Lutheran Church of Australia on 14 February 1926 at Nuriootpa, Albrecht reached Hermannsburg in April, replacing Carl Strehlow [q.v.12] as mission superintendent. In November Alfred Traeger, assisted by Rev. John Flynn [qq.v.12,8], installed a pedal wireless, which lessened the community's extreme isolation. In 1927-29 severe drought and scurvy led to an exceptionally high death rate in the mission; 85 per cent of infants died. Financed by public appeals in Victoria and South Australia, and helped by many friends

of the mission, including Violet Teague [q.v.12] and her sister Una, Albrecht set about piping water from a spring 5 miles (8 km) away. Construction work, undertaken by volunteers, was completed in 1935. With reliable water and adequate supplies of fresh fruit and vegetables assured, the child mortality rate dropped significantly. Albrecht later lamented: 'How many graves could have been left undug if we had had the water during those long years of drought'. An adept communicator, he contributed to church newspapers and fostered strong support among Lutheran clergy and lay people. He had been naturalised on 7 August 1931.

Envisioning that the Hermannsburg Christian community would develop into a fully fledged Indigenous church, Albrecht gave local elders and leaders responsibility for making decisions in areas of administration and congregational discipline, and he trained Aboriginal evangelists. He became fluent in the Arrernte language, supported the Bible translation and publication program begun by A. H. Kempe and Strehlow, and encouraged public worship and preaching in the local vernaculars. Although he held a deep respect for Aboriginal spirituality, he could find no way to reconcile traditional religion with Christian faith. His son Paul, who was to succeed him as field-superintendent in 1963, later noted that the Hermannsburg Christians affirmed the theological tenets of their faith but quietly retained ritual practices relevant to their continuing tribal and social existence.

While his missionary vocation remained paramount, Albrecht was always concerned with the Aborigines' material and social welfare. Arduous camel treks brought him into close contact with remnants of the Arrernte, Loritja and Pitjantjatjara peoples. He identified the destructive threat of European encroachment on fragile tribal lands and opposed the removal of part-Aboriginal children from their mothers. With Charles Duguid [q.v.] and T. G. H. Strehlow [q.v.16], he worked tirelessly for the establishment of more Aboriginal settlements (as at Areyonga and Yuendumu), and for secure reserves on tribal terrain. Keen to create employment opportunities for people within their communities, he and his wife promoted arts and crafts. They encouraged Albert Namatjira [q.v.15] and helped him to sell his paintings. Albrecht fostered a cattle-raising enterprise and established a tannery to supply hides for leatherwork products. By 1957 he was convinced that the church should facilitate integration of Indigenous people into the larger Australian society.

Of medium height and thickset, Albrecht possessed a robust constitution and had 'tremendous capacity for hardship and work'. His wife was a supportive and dedicated partner, but her health was often under strain and in 1952 the family moved to Alice Springs. There Albrecht ministered to urban Aborigines and visited workers on cattle stations. He was appointed MBE in 1958. In 1962 the Albrechts retired to Linden Park, Adelaide, where he continued to carry out pastoral duties. He was a co-author of a history of the mission, *Hermannsburg: A Vision and a Mission* (1977). The government of the Federal Republic of Germany awarded him the Officer's Cross of the Order of Merit in 1973. Survived by his three sons and two daughters, he died at Fullarton on 16 March 1984, four months after his wife, and was buried in Centennial Park cemetery.

S. Baldwin (ed), *Unsung Heroes & Heroines of Australia* (1988); B. Henson, *A Straight-out Man* (1992); P. G. E. Albrecht, *From Mission to Church* (2002); *People*, 5 Dec 1951, p 28; D1915, item SA1236 (NAA); Albrecht papers (SA Museum).

MAURICE SCHILD

ALEXANDER, HAL (1902-1990), dancer and trade-union official, was born on 21 June 1902 at Newcastle, New South Wales, and named Robert Alexander, son of Laura Williams, who was also born in that city. His father, whose name is unknown, left soon after his birth. When Robert was 4 years old a 'step-father', Bartholomew Bainbridge, 'arrived on the scene'; Bainbridge and Laura married in 1911. Robert Williams attended Cooks Hill School and Newcastle South School until he was 13 years old. He had discovered dancing at age 12. In 1919 his mother died and Bainbridge sent him and his half-sister, Laurel, to live with their maternal grandmother in Newcastle. As a teenager, Robert worked at many jobs, including 'sparrow starver' (required to walk behind horses and scoop their manure into bins), navvy at the steelworks and cook for gangers of the Main Roads Department. He met Madonna Irene Siostrom on a Newcastle dance floor early in 1924. They became dancing partners and married on 20 December 1924 in the district registrar's office, Merewether, but later divorced.

In Sydney Robert enrolled at Professor Alcorn's Pitt Street dance studio, where he was taught to 'buck'n'wing' (tap dance). His first professional engagement was in the chorus line of an Ernest C. Rolls production. During the Depression the Williams family was on the track—Robert danced where and when he could. In Adelaide, when he was hired as a dancer in a theatrical show which toured Port Augusta and Port Pirie, he adopted the name 'Hal Alexander' and teamed up with a 'cracker' tap-dancer, Jimmy Hart. They entered and won non-stop dancing contests, then hitchhiked east and were hired at the Tivoli Theatre, Melbourne, as the dancing team 'Alexander and Hart'.

By 1934 Alexander and his son, Bob, were a double act, specialising in soft-shoe song-and-dance routines, and comical patter. They appeared in identical black and white checked suits and bowler hats. Father and son danced across Australia for little money. During this period, stage performers were varied, itinerant and industrially unorganised. Alexander gained a reputation among employers as a 'stirrer and a firebrand' who demanded higher pay and better working conditions, but he won respect from other performers. In 1935 he joined the union, the Actors' Federation of Australasia.

When Alexander was in Sydney in a J. C. Williamson [q.v.6] show, he was sacked by the stage manager who, arguing that there were too many dancers, drew his name from a hat. After his dismissal, he and his supporters began to organise within their union, from 1936 called Actors' Equity of Australia. In the late 1930s, influenced by his experience of life rather than his reading of Marx and Lenin, he joined the Communist Party of Australia. In 1939 he stood for the position of general secretary of Actors' Equity. He was not elected, but claimed that the incumbent secretary, Bertie Wright, had rorted the election. Wright resigned and Alexander was appointed general secretary, a position, initially unpaid, that he held until his retirement in 1971.

Alexander's term as secretary of Actors' Equity of Australia (from 1945, Actors and Announcers' Equity Association of Australia) was a period in which performers gained standard contracts, rehearsal pay, sick leave, annual leave and minimum rates. Dedicated to his work and having a deep sense of class injustice, Alexander was a capable tactician. This quality was shown in the 1944 Equity strike on the issue of non-union theatre employees. After Actors' Equity members refused to perform in Williamson's productions and the striking performers launched their own well-attended show in Melbourne, the company agreed to 100 per cent union membership. As a union leader, Alexander imposed policy from above, rarely seeking a consensus. This approach led to conflict with others including his son. He was a strong advocate of Australian culture on the stage, screen and wireless. Actors' Equity awarded him honorary life membership.

On 29 October 1976 Alexander married June Margaret Humphrey at the registry of births, deaths and marriages, Sydney. In 1983 he was awarded the OAM. Brown-haired, light-footed and lean, Alexander throughout his long life retained the look of a dancer. Although baptised a Catholic, he was a lifelong atheist. He died on 20 June 1990 at Botany, and was cremated. His son, Bob, who had succeeded him as secretary of Actors' Equity, survived him.

Daily Telegraph (Sydney), 24 Nov 1946, p 27; Actors' Equity of Aust, *Equity*, Dec 1979/Jan 1980, p 27, Nov 1989, p 31, Nov 1990, p 1; *Hal Alexander* (film, 1980); private information.

DREW COTTLE

ALEXANDER, JOSEPH ALOYSIUS (1892-1983), journalist, was born on 27 June 1892 in Melbourne, son of Ernest Alfred Alexander, a labourer from Tasmania, and his Victorian-born wife Nelly, née Fitzsimon. From 1896 the family lived at Burnie, Tasmania. Joe entered St Patrick's College, East Melbourne, in 1905 but two years later his family's material circumstances ('straitened' at times) forced him back to Tasmania. He trained and worked as a journalist at Burnie and Launceston before returning to Melbourne, where, in 1923, he became a reporter for Sir Hugh Denison's [q.v.8] *Evening Sun*. In 1925 he gained a valuable patron when the Herald & Weekly Times Ltd, increasingly dominated by (Sir) Keith Murdoch [q.v.10], acquired Denison's newspaper interests in Melbourne.

Having conducted part of his research in Los Angeles, United States of America, in 1928 Alexander published a biography of the irrigationist George Chaffey [q.v.7]. On 29 January 1929 he married with Catholic rites Frances (Katherine) Broadwood, a café manageress, at St Patrick's College chapel. Three days later he took up the post of bureau chief for the *Herald* in Canberra where, within a decade, he was to own an impressive residence in Mugga Way, Red Hill.

In the hothouse atmosphere of Australia's infant 'bush capital' Alexander covered the fall of the Bruce-Page [qq.v.7,11] government. From October 1929 the impact of the Depression on the Labor government of James Scullin [q.v.11] was a source of dramatic news stories. As well as reporting on events, Alexander was involved in them. Following J. A. Lyons's [q.v.10] resignation from the Scullin cabinet, he attended meetings between Murdoch and Lyons which preceded the formation of the United Australia Party.

Alexander was responsible for the publication in March 1931 of the text of cables, sent by Scullin in London, which criticised a restive Labor caucus. He refused to disclose his source and in April the Speaker barred him from the House of Representatives. A privilege motion questioning the Speaker's power to do so was defeated only on the casting vote of the Speaker himself. The Senate repudiated the ban, enabling Alexander to continue to solicit information from its half of the parliamentary precincts. He was readmitted to the House in September.

When the UAP assumed office in January 1932, the ambitious Alexander exulted in a diary entry: 'Everyone is saying at Canberra that I have put Lyons in as Prime Minister. It is more than half true'. During the early years of the Lyons government, senior ministers and public servants kept him supplied with inside information. He wrote the news story announcing S. M. (Viscount) Bruce's mission to the Imperial Economic Conference, Ottawa, and his appointment to London as resident minister in 1932 before Federal cabinet had officially considered the matter. Alexander accompanied him to Ottawa as the Sun-Herald Cable Service representative. His elation at being at the hub of events ebbed as the intimacy between Lyons and Murdoch faded. Journalistic arrangements were also strained by the entry of (Sir) Robert Menzies [q.v.15] into the Lyons cabinet. According to Alexander, the imperious Menzies complained in 1936 that 'the *Herald* has clearly shown that it is opposed to the present Commonwealth Government—was indeed its worst enemy'.

While Alexander felt threatened by Menzies' 'towering ambitions', Canberra's long parliamentary recesses were also increasingly frustrating. He varied his workload, taking on the editorship (1937-44 and 1948-67) of *Who's Who in Australia*. His exemplary editorial vigilance guaranteed the publication's status as an invaluable and permanent work of reference. Alexander's uneasy relationship with Menzies never improved. In August 1941, on the eve of Menzies' resignation as prime minister, he was excluded from all interviews and press conferences with him. He was to rejoice when UAP candidates in the pro-Menzies National Service Group were seen to do poorly in the 1943 Federal election.

Alexander's strong private opinions did not detract from his personal and professional integrity. John Curtin [q.v.13], after becoming prime minister in October 1941, included him in the inner group of trusted senior journalists to whom he gave confidential wartime briefings. However, Alexander was too close to him to be an uncritical admirer. During the 1942-43 conscription controversy he wondered if the prime minister had the strength to overcome internal party opposition. He did not appreciate being sandwiched between Curtin and Murdoch, whose mounting public criticism irked the prime minister.

In 1944 Alexander, who relished nineteenth-century Russian literature, was named first secretary (public relations) to the Australian legation in Moscow. He admired the Red Army but felt uncomfortable with the Soviet political system during the three years—interrupted by a stint at the 1946 Paris Peace Conference—that he spent in the Soviet

Union. After being relocated to Murdoch's head office in Melbourne, he published *In the Shadow* (1949), a book full of adverse observations on Soviet communism. Anxious to return to Canberra, he applied personally to Menzies for a position as a press secretary following the coalition's electoral victory in 1949. He proffered loyalty and hoped that 'personal difficulties' would be forgotten. Menzies disdained the offer.

On his retirement from the full-time staff of the Herald & Weekly Times Ltd in 1957, Alexander was able to return to Mugga Way. Revering the abiding religious faith that he had seen in Russia, he became a generous benefactor when the Russian Orthodox Church of St John the Baptist was constructed at Narrabundah. Canberra's bracing winters forced Alexander and his wife to move to Buderim, Queensland, in 1967. He died on 7 January 1983 at Oxley, Brisbane, and was buried with Russian Orthodox rites in Canberra cemetery. His wife survived him; they had no children.

A 'brisk, short figure limping indomitably round the Canberra he loved', Alexander was Australia's top political journalist at the height of the Depression. Younger journalists later looked back on his news-gathering skills with awe, endowing him with near-miraculous powers of perception. They did not grasp the full extent of his heady intimacy with leading politicians, the key to his early sensational success in Canberra, which was later curtailed by the rise of Menzies.

Canberra Hist Jnl, no 29, 1992, p 10; *Canberra Times*, 16 Mar 1967, p 3, 8 Jan 1983, p 6, 28 Aug 1997, p 9, 4 Mar 2002, p 12; *Canberra & District Hist Soc Newsletter*, Feb 1983, p 11, Mar 1983, p 9; M. Pratt, interview with J. A. Alexander (ts, 1971, NLA); interview with J. A. Alexander (ts, 1977, NLA); J. A. Alexander, W. M. Hughes, R. G. Menzies, K. A. Murdoch papers (NLA).   Stephen Holt

ALLEN, CLABON WALTER (1904-1987), astronomer, was born on 28 December 1904 at Subiaco, Perth, third child of James Bernard Allen (d.1912), a South Australian-born lecturer in physics at Perth Technical School, and his wife Alice Hooper, née Aitken, a trained nurse who was born in New Zealand. Cla was educated at the High School, Perth, and the University of Western Australia (B.Sc., 1926; M.Sc., 1929; D.Sc., 1936). In 1926 he was appointed to a research fellowship at the newly established Commonwealth Solar Observatory at Mount Stromlo, Federal (Australian) Capital Territory, becoming an assistant there in 1928.

Allen's first considerable undertaking, a photometric study of the solar spectrum, established at once both his own reputation and that of the observatory. Besides providing a much better picture of the temperature structure and element abundances of the sun, it led to the development of the 'curve-of-growth' technique of analysing stellar spectra, which remained the standard method for many years. Observing the 1940 eclipse of the sun in South Africa, he obtained important results on the solar corona, among them measurements of its electron density which were to prove invaluable to radio astronomers.

During World War II Allen was asked to find a way of predicting intermittent interruptions to radio communications, known as 'fadeouts', which were understood to be related to disturbances on the sun. He did so in a remarkably short time and with conspicuous success. This work led him to foreshadow the identification of the solar wind—energetic particles emitted from featureless areas of the solar surface and constrained to move in streams by forces in the solar atmosphere.

After the war Allen worked closely with the solar group at the radiophysics laboratory of the Council for Scientific and Industrial Research, Sydney. The team was conducting its epoch-making studies of the radio emission from the sun. For several years he was the only optical astronomer in the world to take an active part in a radio astronomy program. He was particularly friendly with J. L. Pawsey [q.v.15], the leader of the group, who lent the Mount Stromlo observatory a 200-MHz receiver which Allen used to monitor solar 'noise' and to survey the radio emission from the southern part of the Galaxy. His final contributions from the observatory were two papers written with (Sir) Richard Woolley [q.v.], the definitive accounts of the structure and physical nature of the solar corona and the solar chromosphere as they seemed at that time.

In 1951 Allen accepted an invitation by (Sir) Harrie Massey to become Perren professor of astronomy at University College, London, and director of the University of London Observatory at Mill Hill. Within a few years he had built up his observatory into one of the best astronomical departments in England. In 1955 he published the first edition of *Astrophysical Quantities*, a compilation of numerical data of astrophysical interest. Universally known as '*AQ*', it is the most quoted book on the subject. A fellow (1936) of the Royal Astronomical Society, he held a number of positions in the society and other professional bodies. He retired in 1972 and returned to Canberra.

Twenty-five volumes of Allen's diary, started in 1922 as a means of improving his poor English expression, are held by the National Library of Australia. Concerned less with scientific matters than with social life and customs in early Canberra, its style is inimitable —only Cla could have written: (8 September

1929) 'I had a look into Pepys' diary this afternoon but thought it not as interesting as my own'. In 1977 he published *Hiking from Early Canberra*. He emerges from his writings as a man of good sense and integrity, with a talent for friendship. A staunch supporter of St Andrew's Presbyterian Church, Forrest, he sang in the choir, and in his younger years walked 10 miles (16 km) from Mount Stromlo to the Sunday service, then 10 miles back.

Allen was one of the finest Australian scientists of his day. He had a deep, almost intuitive understanding of physics and a talent for finding significant and rewarding problems. Survived by his wife Rose McKenzie, née Smellie, whom he had married on 25 May 1937 at the Baptist Tabernacle, Gisborne, New Zealand, and by their five sons, he died on 11 December 1987 at his Red Hill home and was cremated with Uniting Church forms.

Qtrly Jnl of the Royal Astronomical Soc, vol 14, no 3, 1973, p 311, vol 31, no 2, 1990, p 259; S. C. B. Gascoigne, 'History of Australian Astronomy', Astronomical Soc of Aust, *Procs*, vol 5, no 4, 1984, p 597; *Canberra Times*, 24 Dec 1987, p 10; Allen papers (NLA).   S. C. B. GASCOIGNE

ALLEN, LESLIE CHARLES (CLARENCE) (1916-1982), soldier, labourer and historical-artefact demonstrator, was born on 9 November 1916 at Ballarat East, Victoria, second son of Clarance Walter Allen, labourer, and his wife Ruby Ethel, née Robertson, both Victorian born. His early childhood was marred by domestic violence until he and his sister were abandoned and raised in an orphanage. At about 12 he started working, mostly as a farm labourer. On 19 April 1940 he enlisted in the Australian Imperial Force, giving his middle name as Clarence and his date of birth as 9 September 1918.

In September 1940 Allen embarked for the Middle East with reinforcements for the 2/5th Battalion. He was allotted to 'D' Company as a stretcher-bearer. Five ft 11 ins (180 cm) tall, with green eyes and black hair, he was physically imposing and strong. A keen sportsman with a wicked sense of humour, he was popular with all except perhaps officers, towards whom he displayed a certain disdain for authority. He acquired his nickname 'Bull' for charging through the opposition while playing Australian Rules football with the battalion.

Allen proved dependable during the Libyan campaign in January-February 1941, but was admitted to hospital with 'anxiety neurosis' in early April. Rejoining the battalion before the Syrian campaign, he came to notice on 10-11 July near Khalde when, under heavy shell-fire, he attended to casualties all night, and next morning, although fatigued, walked 6 miles (10 km) to get transport.

The 2/5th left the Middle East in March 1942, served in Ceylon (Sri Lanka) before returning to Australia in August, and sailed to Papua in October. Allen contracted malaria but was fit for the defence of Wau, New Guinea, in January-February 1943. On mountain tracks his strength, stamina, devotion to comrades and bravery were invaluable. He was awarded the Military Medal for rescuing wounded men under fire in the Crystal Creek area on 7-8 February. The citation noted that 'Private Allen's bearing and his untiring efforts in tending the wounded and helping with rations and stores were an inspiration'. Promoted to acting corporal in April (confirmed August), he received the United States' Silver Star for rescuing American casualties under heavy fire at Mount Tambu on 30 July. Although slightly wounded, he single-handedly carried to safety twelve men before collapsing from exhaustion. His gallantry, captured in a photograph by Gordon Short [q.v.16], evoked, according to the citation, 'the unstinted praise of all who witnessed his action'.

While Allen never showed fear in battle, it became clear after his return to Australia in September 1943 that he was badly affected. His behaviour became erratic and in February 1944 he struck an officer and was demoted. He was assessed as suffering 'constitutional temperamental instability' with 'anxiety symptoms', as well as malaria, and was medically discharged on 10 September.

Allen lived with an uncle while recovering, having temporarily lost the power of speech. At the Salvation Army Citadel, Malvern, Melbourne, on 23 April 1949 he married Jean Elizabeth Floyd, a former army nurse. He worked as a labourer and later as a theatre orderly at Ballarat Base Hospital. On his small acreage, he raised pigs and broke horses. Well known around Ballarat for his stature, booming voice and humour, he was also popular with tourists at Sovereign Hill, the re-created gold-mining town, where he demonstrated the horse-drawn Chilean mill used to crush quartz. For most Anzac Days he travelled to Melbourne and carried his unit association's banner in the march. Survived by his wife, and their daughter and three sons, he died of diabetes and myocardial infarction on 11 May 1982 at Sovereign Hill and was cremated.

D. Dexter, *The New Guinea Offensives* (1961); S. Trigellis-Smith, *All the King's Enemies* (1988); *Courier* (Ballarat), 13 May 1982, p 4; B883, item VX12513 (NAA); AWM 119, items 19 and US30 (AWM); private information.   JOHN MOREMON

AMADIO, CLIVE LYOFF (1904-1983), saxophonist and clarinettist, was born on 28 February 1904 at Darlington, Sydney, second son of New Zealand-born Harry Henville Taylor, furniture manufacturer and instrumentalist, and his wife Florence Ada, née Beer, who was from New South Wales. Harry had taken the surname of his stepfather, Henry Antonio Amadio. The flautist John Amadio, who was to marry Florence Austral [qq.v.7], was Harry's brother. One of Sydney's leading musicians, Harry played flute, oboe and clarinet for 'The Firm' (J. C. Williamson [q.v.6] Ltd), and also for the New South Wales State Conservatorium of Music orchestra. He gave Clive all his early training, first on the flute and oboe and then on the clarinet, and encouraged him to take the saxophone seriously. Having left school by the age of 13, Clive often practised for eight hours without a break. Eager to become an engineer, he began an apprenticeship but was, he claimed, 'forced into the musical world' by his father.

In his mid-teens, as well as playing in ensembles for silent pictures and musical comedies, Clive was solo clarinettist in both the New South Wales State Military Band and the Manly Municipal Band. At 19 he was touring as solo saxophonist on the Tivoli circuit, in, by his own account, one of the highest paid musical positions in Australia at that time, earning £15 a week. When 'the talkies' arrived, Amadio's popularity as solo saxophonist in the accompanying show bands blossomed. With slicked-back black hair and dark eyes, he was described in 1929 as 'that handsome sheik with the sax'. He had married Gwendolen Marjorie Morgan on 25 August 1928 at St Michael's Church of England, Rose Bay, but they were divorced after about a year. On 2 October 1935 he married Laurie Mary Walley at the registrar's office, Annandale.

Amadio played with groups such as the Royal Squadron Syncopators, Nigger Minstrels and Spanish Syncopators, and recorded with Quintrell's Tivolians. His show-band performances continued until the demise of the bands themselves after World War II, a frenetic period that included two years (1932-34) as principal clarinettist to the Australian Broadcasting Commission's studio orchestra; membership of an early light music broadcast ensemble, the New Note Octet; the formation of his own quintet, a group that was to survive the end of the war by thirteen years; and solo engagements that proliferated with his burgeoning popularity. He had performed on 1 July 1932, when the ABC assumed control of the national broadcasting service, as saxophone soloist on 2BL.

Late in 1939 the quintet that was to render him a household name across Australia and the South Pacific went to air for the first time. Usually billed in the early years as the Mode Moderne Quintet, its name was changed to the Clive Amadio Quintet after the war and the

group was given prime Sunday night listening time with recorded mid-week repeats. Reviews at the time reflected its popularity: 'the best light musical combination ever presented on the air in this country' and 'the finest small-ensemble music on the air'. It broadcast on the ABC for almost twenty years, sometimes featuring Australian compositions and guest artists.

Meanwhile Amadio was establishing a reputation as one of Australia's most accomplished clarinettists and its finest saxophonist. His public performances often included saxophone pieces that have since become standard repertoire: *Rapsodie* (Claude Debussy); *Concertino da Camera* (Jacques Ibert); *Saxo-Rhapsody* (Eric Coates); and works written especially for him by his three arrangers, Dulcie Holland, Henry Krips [q.v.] and Bruce Finlay. Employed by the State Conservatorium of Music (1942-45), he taught the saxophone.

In January 1954 Amadio played for Queen Elizabeth II at a royal banquet and was cited by the *Sun-Herald* as Australia's best-known serious musician after (Sir) Eugene Goossens [q.v.14]. He took part in the first of a series of chamber music concerts sponsored by the ABC in February 1954. Accompanied by his pianist Olga Krasnik, he left for an overseas tour of some months (1954-55). In Paris they recorded Holland's *Sonata for E♭ Alto Saxophone and Piano* and her *Musette and Gigue* for the United Nations Educational, Scientific and Cultural Organization. They gave recitals for the British Broadcasting Corporation and he performed Coates's *Saxo-Rhapsody* with the BBC Concert Orchestra conducted by (Sir) Charles Mackerras. Amadio and Krasnik also broadcast for the French, Austrian, Spanish and South African broadcasting services.

In August 1958 Amadio's contract was not renewed by the ABC. For a time he continued freelancing but by May 1959 he had bought the newsagency in Oxford Street, Woollahra, that, with Olga Krasnik, he would run for the next thirteen years. Divorcing Laurie, Clive married Olga, also a divorcee, on 28 July 1967 at the registrar-general's office, Sydney. In August 1972 they retired to Nelson Bay. They joined the part-time staff of the State Conservatorium of Music, Newcastle branch, where they taught and performed from 1973 until 1980. In that year he was appointed AM and awarded honorary life membership of the Clarinet Society of New South Wales, the first time this award had been made to an Australian. He collected rare guns, which interested him more for the workmanship displayed than for their performance. He died on 21 October 1983 at Randwick and was cremated. His wife, and the son and two daughters of his second marriage survived him.

15

D. Westlake, *From Me to You* (1999); *ABC Weekly*, 8 June 1946, p 5, 22 June 1957, p 9; *Sun-Herald* (Sydney), 31 Jan 1954, p 46; *Canon*, Oct 1956, p 93; SP613/1, item 7/4/10, pts 1 and 2 (NAA); private information.   DONALD WESTLAKE

ANDERSON, ARTHUR JEFFERY (1912-1985), gold refiner, soldier and intelligence officer, was born on 19 November 1912 at Boulder, Western Australia, fourth child of Australian-born parents Arthur Anderson, photographer, and his wife Florence Edith, née Basten. Educated at the local state school, he was remembered by a schoolmate as being a 'dapper little fellow' who often sported a bow tie. He moved into the mining industry and worked as a refiner in the gold room of the Lake View and Star mine. At the Cathedral of St John the Baptist, Kalgoorlie, on 28 September 1935 he married with Anglican rites Thyra Elizabeth Phillips, a nurse.

In 1938 Anderson was commissioned as a lieutenant in the Militia. On 1 May 1940 he was appointed to the Australian Imperial Force and posted to the 2/16th Battalion. Because he was prone to responding to complaints by troops with 'I'll fix it', he quickly earned the nickname 'Fixit'. Promoted to captain in September, he arrived in the Middle East in November. He was detached to the 21st Infantry Training Battalion, but rejoined the 2/16th in time for the final stages of the Syrian campaign in July 1941.

Anderson returned to Australia in March 1942 and two months later was posted to the 39th Battalion as a temporary major. Sent to Port Moresby in June, he fought with the Militia unit along the Kokoda Trail (July-September) and in the brutal battles for Gona and Sanananda (December 1942-January 1943). Back in Australia in March, he was transferred to the 2/3rd Battalion when the 39th was disbanded in July. On 20 October 1944 he was promoted to lieutenant colonel and given command of the 24th Battalion.

More aloof than his gregarious predecessor, Lieutenant Colonel G. F. Smith, Anderson has been remembered as an abrupt, sharp-tongued commanding officer. Although firm, his application of discipline was considered fair, and he worked hard for the welfare of his troops. When the battalion was sent to Bougainville in January 1945, he was assiduous in ensuring that the men received frequent mail deliveries, good food and regular periods of rest.

As a battlefield commander, Anderson was aggressive, but also thorough in his planning. He led from among his forward companies and effectively employed air and artillery support. A report compiled after the war noted that 'by training and temperament' he was most suited to the command of troops in the field. For his 'determined leadership, personal courage and outstanding organising ability' on Bougainville, he was awarded the Distinguished Service Order.

In December 1945 Anderson came home to Australia. Transferring to the Reserve of Officers on 28 September 1946, he returned to Kalgoorlie and resumed his previous occupation as a gold refiner. However, on 12 October 1948 he joined the Interim Army. In 1951 he attended the Staff College, Quetta, Pakistan. This equipped him for several postings on the headquarters of Western and Northern commands. His wife died in February 1956, and on 25 February 1957 at St George's Cathedral, Perth, he married Doris Emily Burke, née Bevan, a hotel proprietress and a widow.

Anderson retired from the Australian Regular Army in November 1959 and became a senior member of the Australian Security Intelligence Organization. His military career, however, seems to have been the formative influence on his character and he was known, by friends and family alike, as 'the Colonel' until the day he died. In retirement he retained an active interest in public affairs and his other great passion, sport. A keen shooter, he was a founding member of the Perth Gun Club and president of the Western Australian Field and Game Association. He also enjoyed fishing, football and racing. In his later years he suffered from ill health and blindness. Survived by his wife, two stepsons and a stepdaughter, and by the son of his first marriage, he died of self-inflicted shotgun wounds to his head on 30 March 1985 at his Sorrento home and was cremated.

M. Uren, *A Thousand Men at War* (1959); G. Christensen (ed), *That's the Way it Was* (1982); V. Austin (comp), *To Kokoda and Beyond* (1988); *West Australian*, 2 Apr 1985, p 40; *Pigeon Post*, June 1985, p 2; *Red and White Diamond*, June 1985, p 2, Dec 1985, p 7; AWM54, item 613/7/75 (AWM).
                                                    GARTH PRATTEN

ANDERSON, CHARLES GROVES WRIGHT (1897-1988), soldier, grazier and politician, was born on 12 February 1897 at Newlands, Cape Town, South Africa, third of five children of Alfred Gerald Wright Anderson, an English-born auditor and later newspaper editor, and his Belgian-born wife Emma (Maïa) Louise Antoinette, née Trossaert. In 1900 the family moved to the East Africa Protectorate (Kenya) and settled on a farm near Nairobi called Mount Margaret. After beginning his education at a government school in Nairobi, Charles was sent in 1907 to England, where he lived with an uncle and aunt before entering St Brendan's College, Bristol, in 1910.

On his return to Africa, Anderson enlisted in the local volunteers in November 1914, following the start of World War I. Next year he joined the Calcutta Volunteer Battery. On 13 October 1916 he was commissioned temporary lieutenant in the King's African Rifles. Serving with the 2nd Battalion, 3rd Regiment, he displayed outstanding leadership during fighting at Nhamacurra, Portuguese East Africa (Mozambique), in July 1918 and was awarded the Military Cross (1919). Before he was demobilised in February 1919, he was promoted to temporary captain.

Turning to farming, Anderson served as chairman of the Kenya Settlers' Association in the Rift Valley district. At the Anglican Cathedral of the Highlands, Nairobi, on 21 February 1931 he married Edith Marian Tout, a niece of (Sir) Frederick Tout [q.v.12], who came from Young, New South Wales, to tour Africa. During a subsequent visit to Australia, Anderson was impressed by his wife's home country. In 1935 they migrated to Australia with their daughter and twin sons. He purchased a 2200-acre (890 ha) grazing property, Fernhill, at Crowther, near Young.

On 3 March 1939 Anderson was appointed a captain in the 56th Battalion (Riverina Regiment), Militia. Promoted to major in October, he transferred to the Australian Imperial Force on 1 July 1940 as second-in-command of the 2/19th Battalion. Seven months later the battalion embarked for Singapore. On 1 August 1941 Anderson was promoted to command the battalion as a lieutenant colonel. Of medium height and slender build, softly spoken and bespectacled, he did not look the forceful and incisive commander he was about to prove himself. One of the few officers with experience of jungle fighting, he trained his men in bayonet use and snap shooting.

Following the Japanese invasion of Malaya in December, the 2/19th was sent to the Muar area on 17 January 1942. The unit arrived at Bakri next morning and by that evening was under fire from the guns of the Japanese Guards Division which, supported by tanks, was decimating the inexperienced 45th Indian Brigade and causing heavy casualties to the 2/29th Battalion already sent to reinforce it. When the brigade headquarters was bombed on the 19th, Anderson took command. After waiting to gather survivors into his perimeter, he decided on a fighting withdrawal to Parit Sulong. Joining his forward company the next morning, he destroyed two machine-gun posts with grenades and shot two enemy soldiers with his revolver, then personally led the assault that broke through the encircling Japanese.

Despite sustained air and ground attacks which caused further heavy casualties, the withdrawing troops covered 11 miles (18 km) carrying their numerous wounded. Nearing Parit Sulong, they learned that the Japanese

had already arrived in strength and seized the bridge there, cutting off the retreat. Anderson resolved to fight on and mounted further attacks on 21 January, but his weakened force was unable to achieve a breakthrough. At 9 a.m. next day, realising that relief was equally impossible, he ordered all personnel still capable of walking to destroy heavy equipment, including vehicles and guns, then slip away around the blocking enemy posts.

About five hundred Australians and four hundred Indian troops—a fifth of the force originally involved—reached British positions at Yong Peng on 23 January. Anderson was sent back to Johore Bahru to reconstitute his shattered unit from recently arrived reinforcements, but was hospitalised with dysentery on 8 February. He did not rejoin the 2/19th until 13 February, the day before it was announced that he had been awarded the Victoria Cross—the only Australian commander in World War II to be so honoured. On the 15th, despite his heroic efforts at Muar River (later considered a minor epic in an otherwise disastrous campaign), Anderson joined the rest of the Singapore garrison in captivity following the British surrender.

Appointed second-in-command of 'A' Force, the first group of 3000 Australians employed on the Burma-Thailand Railway, Anderson left Singapore in May. He took charge of a group of Allied prisoners working on the northern section of the railway. In negotiating to reduce the privations of his men, he frequently risked (and on at least one occasion received) a beating from Japanese guards. His personal conduct became legendary and helped to sustain prisoners' morale. Freed after Japan's surrender, Anderson was repatriated in November 1945 and next month placed on the Reserve of Officers. He returned to farming near Young and later took over a property, Springfield, that his wife had inherited.

At the 1949 Federal election Anderson won the House of Representatives seat of Hume for the Country Party. He became an advocate for rural issues and for improving the rehabilitation of service personnel. Defeated in 1951, he stood unsuccessfully in 1954 before regaining Hume next year; re-elected in 1958, he served until again defeated in 1961. During his second term, he was a member of the joint committees on the Australian Capital Territory (1957-61) and foreign affairs (1961).

In 1955 Anderson had revisited Kenya and Britain; in 1959 he returned to Thailand as special Australian representative during wreath-layings on war graves at the River Kwai. He retained his military links, becoming honorary colonel of the 56th Battalion (1956-57) and the 4th Battalion (1957-60), Citizen Military Forces. In 1968 he again visited Malaya as the guest of the British 17th Division, which was conducting a study tour of the

Muar battle. On 11 November 1988 he died in his home at Red Hill, Canberra, and was cremated with full military honours. He was survived by two daughters and a son; his wife and their other son predeceased him. A pencil drawing (1942) by Murray Griffin and a portrait (1956) by J. B. Godson are held by the Australian War Memorial, Canberra. Another portrait, by (Sir) William Dargie, entered for the Archibald [q.v.3] prize in 1948, is in the family's possession.

L. Wigmore, *The Japanese Thrust* (1957), *They Dared Mightily* (1963); R. W. Newton, *The Grim Glory of the 2/19 Battalion A.I.F.* (1975); *PD* (HR), 22 Nov 1988, p 2923; *Sabretache*, Oct-Dec 1983, p 10; *Canberra Times*, 15 Nov 1988, p 11; *Daily Telegraph* (London), 15 Nov 1988, p 29; B883, item NX12595 (NAA); private information.   CHRIS CLARK

ANDERSON, COLIN WARDEN (1901-1988), medical practitioner, was born on 26 January 1901 at Fremantle, Western Australia, son of Victorian-born Thomas Lynewolde Anderson, also a medical practitioner, and his wife Mary Jessie, née Warden, a nurse from Scotland. Colin attended local state schools and Scotch College, Perth. In 1915-18 the family lived in England and he completed his schooling at Highgate School, London. Back in Australia, he entered Ormond [q.v.5] College, and studied medicine at the University of Melbourne (MB, BS, 1924). After an internship at the Melbourne Hospital, Anderson gained further experience at Perth Public Hospital. In 1927, while medical officer at the Wooroloo Sanatorium, outside Perth, he was advised to go to the country for his health; he became a general practitioner at Dalwallinu. On 7 July 1928 at St John's Church of England, Northam, he married Constance Louisa Williams (d.1971), a nurse, who then assisted him in his practice. He was the local film projectionist, a keen horticulturist and an expert mechanic—later making parts for and maintaining his 1941 Daimler motorcar.

On 10 February 1941 Anderson was mobilised as a captain in the Australian Army Medical Corps. Posted as medical officer to the 5th Garrison Battalion at Swanbourne, he later served in military hospitals at Northam and Perth. In August 1944 he was appointed rehabilitation medical officer, Western Command, responsible for the care of returned servicemen and prisoners of war. He was promoted to temporary major in April 1945 and his appointment was terminated on 13 May 1946. Deputy-director of rehabilitation (1946-51) in the Commonwealth Department of Social Services, Perth, he was seconded to the Department of Post-war Reconstruction for three years. He became interested in occupational therapy and helped with the recovery

and retraining of both ex-servicemen and civilians. As part of his job he initiated a variety of community services in Perth, including the emergency housekeeper service.

In 1951 Anderson returned to general practice, in partnership with Dr Kenneth Aberdeen. Using the experience he had gained examining army personnel, he developed a clinical practice in which he conducted medical examinations for employees of insurance and mining companies and for the Metropolitan Passenger Transport Trust. A council member (1952-67) of the Western Australian branch of the British Medical Association (from 1962 the Australian Medical Association), he served as president in 1958 and permanent vice-president from 1968. He was a member (1955-63) of the federal council of the BMA and AMA and a director (1957-66) of the Australasian Medical Publishing Co. Ltd, publishers of the *Medical Journal of Australia*. Eager to promote postgraduate education for general practitioners, in 1956 he helped to set up the (Royal Australian) College of General Practitioners. He was chairman (1956-57) and provost (1956-62, 1973-74) of the Western Australia faculty of the college, and president (1963-66) of the federal body. Made a fellow of the RACGP in 1963, he continued to serve on the State board until 1988. Anderson was appointed OBE in 1981.

Survived by three of his four sons and his daughter, he died on 15 June 1988 at his East Fremantle home and was cremated. An obituarist praised his commitment to 'the traditions, values and ethics of medicine'.

Austn Medical Assn (WA), *Branch News*, July 1988, p 11; *WA Faculty & Family Medicine Programme Newsletter*, July-Aug 1988, p 1; WA Assn of Occupational Therapists, *Newsletter*, Aug 1988, p 1; B884, item W77 (NAA); M. Adams, interview with C. W. Anderson (ts, 1977, SLWA); private information.   CRIENA FITZGERALD

ANDERSON, GORDON ATHOL (1929-1981), musicologist and medievalist, was born on 1 May 1929 at Armadale, Melbourne, third child of Victorian-born parents Albert Anderson, minister of the Churches of Christ, and his wife Eva Violet, née Hallyburton. Gordon was educated at King's College, Adelaide, and was an accomplished jazz pianist. On 23 September 1950 at the Church of Christ, Maylands, Adelaide, he married Laurel Alice Heath, a typist.

Anderson's path to an academic career was hard hewn; most of his studies at the University of Adelaide (Mus.Bac., 1958; BA, 1959; M.Mus., 1971; Mus.Doc., 1977) were conducted part time. He was 29 before he completed the course at the Elder [q.v.4]

Conservatorium of Music for his first undergraduate degree. From 1957 to 1969 he taught languages and music at Pulteney Grammar School. In 1968 he enrolled as a research student in the musicology program at the university, where it soon became apparent that the quantity and quality of his scholarly output far exceeded the requirements for postgraduate awards. In his first year he published 'Notre Dame Bilingual Motets' (*Miscellanea Musicologica*), a ninety-page study of this neglected sub-genre of the thirteenth-century motet; and 'Mode and Change of Mode in Notre-Dame Conductus' (*Acta Musicologica*), his first foray into the theoretical intricacies of modal rhythm and its applicability to conductus. That year he also completed Part 1 of *The Latin Compositions in Fascicules VII and VIII of the Notre Dame Manuscript Wolfenbüttel Helmstadt 1099 (1206)*, (1968-76), his first critical edition of thirteenth-century manuscripts.

That Anderson should have chosen to specialise in Notre Dame repertoire, a shorthand term for the major musico-poetic genres of thirteenth-century (mostly Parisian) music, is understandable given his interests in Latin, philosophy, liturgy and music. His skills in philology and bibliography were ideally suited to the demands of researching this repertoire, characterised as it is by complex textual and musical interrelationships between pieces and their sources. One of his finest achievements, and his most frequently cited work, was his annotated guide to the vast corpus of paraliturgical Latin song. 'Notre Dame and Related Conductus: A Catalogue Raisonné' (*Miscellanea Musicologica*, 1972, 1975) represents the fruits of his period as a research fellow at Flinders University (1970-73). The catalogue and its taxonomy underpinned the volumes of transcriptions, *Notre-Dame and Related Conductus: Opera Omnia* (1979-88).

In a series of detailed articles, especially 'The Rhythm of *cum littera* Sections of Polyphonic Conductus in Mensural Sources' and 'The Rhythm of the Monophonic Conductus in the Florence Manuscript as Indicated in Parallel Sources in Mensural Notation' (*Journal of the American Musicological Society*, 1973, 1978), Anderson articulated the view that the prosody of conductus poetry, its accentual patterns, was the prime determinant of a piece's musical rhythm. Accordingly, all his transcriptions of this repertoire are given in rhythmicised versions, even where the musical notation is equivocal as regards rhythm. Anderson's view now represents the minority position.

As with his rate of publication, so with his career: the momentum once started proved unstoppable. Appointed as a lecturer in music at the University of New England, Armidale, New South Wales, in 1973, Anderson was pro-

moted to senior lecturer in 1975, to associate professor in 1977, and to a personal chair in musicology in 1979. In 1977 he became the first national president of the Musicology Society of Australia and a fellow of the Australian Academy of the Humanities. He also served (1977-80) on the editorial board of *Studies in Music*. In 1978 he joined the advisory committee of the Humanities Research Centre at the Australian National University, Canberra. Next year he took his only trip abroad to study at first hand the sources on which he had made himself an international authority. The focus of his leave was the most ambitious of his scholarly projects: a thematic index, complete concordance of sources, and critical edition of the entire corpus of medieval sequences.

Over thirteen years from 1968, Anderson produced four critical editions of major manuscripts, wrote more than two dozen articles and reviews, and completed nine of the projected eleven volumes of the monumental series *Opera Omnia*. A fine teacher and brilliant researcher, he was a down-to-earth, kindly man, keen on football, fond of jazz, and devoted to his family. At the height of his intellectual powers he died of myocardial infarction on 30 June 1981 at Armidale and was cremated. His wife, and their two daughters and son, survived him.

Gordon Athol Anderson (1929-1981): In Memoriam (1984); R. Jacobsson (ed), *Pax et Sapientia* (1986); *Musicology*, no 7, 1982, p 154; private information.   ROBERT CURRY

ANDERSON, JOHN CYRIL (1904-1983), road haulier and businessman, was born on 13 January 1904 at Toowoomba, Queensland, sixth of nine children of Queensland-born parents John Anderson, storekeeper, and his wife Clara Jane, née Harrold. Educated at Toowoomba South State School, Cyril worked in the family's grocery store before opening a motorcycle repair shop in the 1920s and becoming a successful speedway competitor (1929-32). On 16 December 1929 at the Presbyterian manse, Toowoomba, he married Doris Isabel Nairne, a clerk. In 1934 he acquired a Studebaker truck to fetch supplies from Brisbane for the grocery; the enterprise soon expanded into a general carrying business, later named Western Transport Pty Ltd.

On 4 June 1941 Anderson enlisted in the Australian Imperial Force. Posted to the 2/5th Armoured Regiment, he served in New South Wales, Western Australia and Queensland before being discharged as a sergeant on 20 April 1945. In 1950 he added a rival company, Maranoa Transport Pty Ltd, to his trucking business. Within ten years, with about five hundred trucks, and depots in all mainland capitals and fifty-three Queensland towns, the enterprise had become reputedly the largest road haulage company in Australia. It was closely challenged by two other Toowoomba hauliers: Bill Bolton's [q.v.Supp.] Cobb & Co. Ltd and (E. S.) Brown's Transport Pty Ltd.

From the early 1950s Anderson, Bolton and Brown argued about road taxes and licences with successive Queensland ministers for transport who had to deal with claims that they and other operators practised illegal discounting, avoidance of road tax (by 'border-hopping') and political patronage. A Privy Council decision in 1954 ruled that the system of licensing road transport contravened section 92 of the Australian Constitution. When the Liberal minister for transport, (Sir) Gordon Chalk, introduced a new Act in 1957-58, designed not only to comply with s.92 but also to protect Queensland Railways, the 'Toowoomba trio' launched a 'cataract of contumely' against Chalk and each other, and challenged the new legislation in the courts. Anderson's company, Western Interstate Pty Ltd, lost several cases in the State Supreme Court and the High Court of Australia, and failed in a subsequent appeal (1964) to the Privy Council.

After the war Cyril had established Anderson Agencies Pty Ltd (1947) and Westco Motors (1950) to import and distribute motor-cycles and motorcars. At Westco Motors he added the Mazda franchise for Queensland in 1963, subsequently acquiring those of other States; by 1980 the company was said to be Australia's largest importer of fully assembled motor vehicles. He ran (1963-79) Mack Trucks Australia Pty Ltd, which had an assembly line in Brisbane, and manufactured (1972-84) Leader trucks at Toowoomba. All the businesses were controlled by a family holding company, Great Western Pty Ltd, in which Anderson held 60 per cent of shares. He sold the haulage enterprise in 1972 and next year established Great Western Australasia Ltd to invest in mining shares and to provide funds for the Mazda franchises.

Appointed CBE in 1975, Anderson retired as chairman of the board in 1978. He then concentrated on running a pastoral property, Lakeland Downs, near Cooktown. In 1980 the company was reconstituted as GWA Ltd and thereafter focused increasingly on manufacturing; in 1982 it reported a turnover of $465 million. Anderson gave generously to churches, hospitals and charitable organisations, as well as to employees and business associates. Survived by his wife, and their three sons and three daughters, he died on 3 December 1983 in South Brisbane, and was cremated.

Cyril's brother, MERVYN JOHN REGINALD ANDERSON (1909-1971), was born on 4 April 1909 at Toowoomba. 'Curly' was also a champion speedway rider. He lost a leg in an accident in 1936. During World War II he managed Western Transport, which ferried troops between Toowoomba and Brisbane. Manager of the Maranoa and Western Transport companies to 1971, he was mayor of Toowoomba (1952-58) and, as a Liberal, represented Toowoomba (1957-60) and Toowoomba East (1960-66) in the Legislative Assembly. He was active in many local associations and was appointed OBE in 1970. Chosen Queensland Father of the Year in 1971, he died of myocardial infarction on 14 November that year at Toowoomba and was buried with Presbyterian forms in Toowoomba Garden of Remembrance. He was survived by his wife Ethel Roberts, née Nairne (the sister of Cyril's wife), and their daughter and two sons.

C. Hazlehurst, *Gordon Chalk* (1987); Great Western A'asia Ltd, *Annual Report*, 1974-80; *Courier-Mail* (Brisbane), 15 Nov 1971, p 3, 20 Dec 1983, p 23; *Chronicle* (Toowoomba), 23 Feb 1984, p 1, 24 Feb 1984, p 15; *Truckin' Life*, July 1990, p 36.
M. FRENCH

ANDERSON, KEITH STIRLING (1892-1986), businessman and community leader, was born on 8 May 1892 at Portland, Victoria, seventh of eight children of William Primrose Anderson, a Melbourne-born merchant, and his wife Euphemia Elizabeth, née Brown, who was born in Scotland. William's Scottish forebears Alexander and Cecilia Anderson had migrated to Australia in 1831 and settled at Portland in 1850. Keith, known as 'K. S.', was educated at Hamilton and Western District Boys' College. He worked as an accountant with the family firm and studied commerce in Melbourne.

On 2 February 1915 Anderson enlisted in the Australian Imperial Force. Posted to the 22nd Battalion, he served on Gallipoli, in Egypt and on the Western Front. In November 1916 he was commissioned and in May 1917 promoted to lieutenant. He was wounded in the leg in October, mentioned in despatches in May 1918, gassed in July and appointed adjutant in September. When the battalion mounted an attack on the night of 3–4 October near Péronne, France, he moved between headquarters and the front line, passing orders, directing the disposition of the men, taking command where necessary and controlling the firing line. He was awarded the Military Cross. His AIF appointment terminated in Victoria on 25 July 1919.

Anderson tried farming near Heywood in an attempt to recover from the effects of mustard gas. Returning to the family business at

Portland, he was the district representative (1922-34) of Dalgety [q.v.4] & Co. Ltd then secretary (1934-38) and managing director and chairman (1938-51) of the Portland Co-Operative Butter Factory. He served as honorary secretary of the local sub-branch of the Returned Sailors' and Soldiers' Imperial League of Australia (1918-19 and 1922-25) and as a borough councillor (1930-31).

With 'energy, drive and initiative', Anderson had campaigned from 1920 for a deep-water, all-weather port to be built at his home town. The Portland Harbor Trust Act was passed in 1949 and he was appointed chairman in 1950. It was widely held that the venture would fail. Financing the works proved a major challenge; at a critical time in 1952-53, the Australian Loan Council restricted public-sector borrowing, forcing the trust to obtain money from J. B. Were [q.v.2] & Son and other private sources. Inspired by Anderson's leadership, the trust developed two breakwaters enclosing a 250-acre (101 ha) artificial harbour, and built modern cargo berths, a rail system, a series of concrete bridges, a canal and roads. The harbour was officially opened in 1960. Anderson retired next year and wrote his account of the project, *A Port is Built* (1981).

Appointed CBE in 1961, Anderson won the Develop Victoria Council's first community service award that year and a Portland citizenship award in 1962. He was an elder of the Presbyterian Church, a life member of the Portland Agricultural and Pastoral Society, a charter member (1942) of the Rotary Club of Portland and a foundation member (1947) of the Masonic Lodge of Memories. He died on 12 May 1986 in the town of his birth and was buried in its cemetery. Obituaries praised his life of selfless community service and his friendly and gentlemanly nature. Unmarried, he left no descendants, but his name remains prominent in Portland: it is borne by a wharf and a scholarship for secondary students.

N. F. Learmonth, *The Story of a Port* (1960); *Official History: Portland Sub-Branch R.S.L. 1917-1992* (1992); *Age* (Melbourne), 17 Nov 1961, p 6; *Herald* (Melbourne), 17 Mar 1973, p 17; *Portland Observer and Guardian*, 14 May 1986, p 4.

GREG WALSH

ANDERSON, SIR KENNETH McCOLL (1909-1985), real-estate agent, property valuer and politician, was born on 11 October 1909 at sea off Adelaide, fifth of six surviving children of David More Anderson, an agent from Scotland, and his Sydney-born second wife Florence May, née McWhirter. David was to become an auctioneer and building contractor, an alderman and mayor of Ryde, and a member (1920-30) of the New South Wales Legislative Assembly. Educated at Ryde Public and Petersham Boys' Intermediate schools, Ken worked as an insurance clerk until his retrenchment during the Depression. He then followed his father into the real-estate business at Eastwood, later buying a larger agency, J. G. Stone & Co., at West Ryde and qualifying as an auctioneer and property valuer. At the Presbyterian Church, Meadowbank, on 17 June 1936 he married Madge Martha Merrion, a cashier.

Having served as a signalman in the Militia, Anderson enlisted in the Australian Imperial Force on 2 July 1940. Within fifteen months he was commissioned as a lieutenant in the 8th Divisional Signals, serving in Malaya until the fall of Singapore. As a prisoner of war from February 1942, he was held at Changi camp and later suffered severe hardship on the Burma-Thailand Railway. Released in September 1945, he returned to Australia next month and transferred to the Reserve of Officers on 4 December. His wife had run his business during the war.

Anderson's career continued to parallel that of his father. He was mayor of Ryde in 1949-50 and in June 1950 he was elected to the Legislative Assembly as the Liberal Party member for Ryde. In 1949-51 he also served on the Cumberland County Council, the statutory body formed to control the planning of a burgeoning postwar Sydney. At this time he disposed of his real-estate agency in order to concentrate on his political career. He was defeated at the 1953 State election, but on 9 May that year was elected to the Senate after defeating the incumbent senator J. P. Tate and the former New South Wales premier Sir Bertram Stevens [qq.v.16,12] at the Liberal Party preselection.

In the Senate Anderson was an active member of committees and served as chairman of the Select Committee on Road Safety in 1959-60. Ironically, he was later injured in two motor accidents. When Sir Robert Menzies [q.v.15] reshuffled his ministry on 10 June 1964, Anderson was appointed minister for customs and excise. On 28 February 1968, after (Sir) John Gorton became prime minister, Anderson replaced him as leader of the government in the Senate and was elevated to cabinet as minister for supply. He led an Australian parliamentary delegation to the Council of Europe in 1971 and was a member of delegations to the Inter-Parliamentary Union on three occasions.

Following the departure of L. H. E. Bury from the McMahon [qq.v.] ministry, on 2 August 1971 Anderson was made minister for health, a position he retained until the defeat of the government on 2 December 1972. He then continued as an Opposition Senator, serving on several standing committees before his retirement at the 1975 election. After the defeat of the coalition government in

New South Wales in 1976, he became president of the State division of the Liberal Party, with a mandate to restore harmony within the party. He held office for two years.

In his maiden speech to the Senate on 16 September 1953, Anderson had stated: 'I just want to do whatever is within my power to help my fellow man'. Although it seemed a disingenuous remark, it epitomised his character. Not a natural orator, he was nevertheless a competent public speaker, described by a colleague as 'quiet and persuasive'. He was one of those politicians whose career improved after making the transition from the State to Federal sphere, where he was unspectacular but assiduous in his parliamentary duties. Anderson had the rare distinction of holding ministerial office under five successive prime ministers—Menzies, Holt, McEwen [qq.v.14,15], Gorton and McMahon. This record was testament to his loyalty to his leader, as well as his detachment from any particular interest groups within his party.

Essentially Anderson was a conservative man, yet his Calvinist Presbyterian principles gave him a social conscience that led him to introduce measures for the liberalisation of censorship, to negotiate a new pharmaceutical benefits scheme and to devise new funding arrangements for nursing homes. Although these were contentious issues, he adroitly avoided public controversy. His integrity and reputation as a conciliator, assisted by his courteous demeanour and ability to interact with people from all social and ethnic backgrounds, earned the respect of both sides of politics at all levels of government.

Like his father before him, Anderson was president (1951-53) of the Ryde Bowling Club and chairman (1961-64) of the Ryde District Soldiers' Memorial Hospital board. He was also president of the Food for Babies Fund and Good Samaritan Association, and a member of the Returned Services League of Australia and the National and Union clubs. Knighted in 1970, he was appointed KBE in 1972.

A man of average height, with a dark complexion, black (later grey) hair and hazel eyes, Sir Kenneth was an undemonstrative, gentle man who enjoyed the time spent with his family and pet animals. They lived in his father's old home at Meadowbank, later moving to Eastwood. He bought a holiday house at Bilgola Beach, and a yacht, *Sinbad*, but did not prove to be an adept sailor. Never in robust health following his experiences as a prisoner of war, he succumbed to Alzheimer's disease and died on 29 March 1985 in a nursing home at Lane Cove; he was cremated after a state funeral. His wife and their daughter survived him.

PD (Senate), 16 Sept 1953, p 78, 16 Apr 1985, p 1019; *PD* (HR), 16 Apr 1985, p 1151; *SMH*, 2 Apr 1985, p 15; Liberal Party of Aust (NSW), Senate preselection papers, MSS 2385, box Y4691, items 3, 7 (SLNSW); M. Pratt, interview with Anderson (ts, 1977, NLA); private information.

PETER J. TYLER

ANDREWS, BARRY GEOFFREY (1943-1987), university lecturer and literary scholar, was born on 13 February 1943 at Auburn, Sydney, elder of twins and second child of Stanley Geoffrey William Andrews, store manager, and his wife Evelyn Jean, née McWilliam, both born in New South Wales. Barry attended Granville Central and Parramatta High schools. In 1960, supported by a Teachers' College scholarship, he joined the first group of students to enter the faculty of arts at the University of New South Wales (BA, 1964; MA, 1969). After graduating with honours in English, he completed a diploma of education (1965) at the University of Sydney. The subject of his master's thesis was the life and work of 'Price Warung' (William Astley [q.v.3]). During 1965-66 he was a junior lecturer at Teachers' College, Sydney.

In 1968 Andrews began a two-year appointment at Fort Street Boys' High School. On 10 May that year at the Methodist Church, Northbridge, he married Robyn Gwladys Turner, a schoolteacher whom he had met at Teachers' College. He joined the Royal Military College, Duntroon, Canberra, in 1970. As a lecturer in English in the faculty of military studies maintained at RMC by UNSW, he found congenial colleagues, notably W. H. Wilde and Joy Hooton. His first major publication was a selection of Warung's short stories, *Tales of the Convict System* (1975). It was followed by a critical study, *Price Warung (William Astley)* (1976). With Wilde he published *Australian Literature to 1900: A Guide to Information Sources* (1980), and with Wilde and Hooton he collaborated in editing (and writing much of) *The Oxford Companion to Australian Literature* (1985).

His love of factual detail and his encyclopaedic knowledge were demonstrated not only in books but also in numerous reviews and articles (including twenty-seven entries for the *Australian Dictionary of Biography*). He also wrote on popular culture, especially sport. In his own right, he was a talented cricketer. Quick of hand and keen of eye, he played with three clubs in the Australian Capital Territory: Woden, Western District and the Australian National University. He was also a passionate supporter of Parramatta's Rugby League team.

Andrews' enthusiasm for sport sat easily with his approach—forthright, informal, often exuberant—to all his personal and professional relationships. A demeanour which, in repose, could seem almost languid, masked an abundant energy. Any hint of humbug or false pretension would bring fire to his pale eyes; at any conference he attended he could be seen at the centre of debate or discussion, his face passionate beneath a crop of ginger hair. His capacity for friendship, generosity and inspirational leadership strongly influenced many of his generation of Australian literary scholars. As Ken Stewart, his UNSW classmate, recalled, the Association for the Study of Australian Literature was conceived over late-night conversations at a conference in Brisbane in May 1977. Frustrated by what they perceived as an inhibiting conservatism in the higher academic ranks of their discipline, Stewart, Andrews, Julian Croft and Mary Lord decided to set up their own organisation—relaxed, adventurous and exciting. The association held its first conference at Monash University, Melbourne, in 1978 and its second, under Andrews' leadership, in Canberra in 1979. He was president in 1985-86.

A senior lecturer from 1976, Andrews, with other RMC academic staff, transferred to the Australian Defence Force Academy in 1986. He died of cerebrovascular disease on 15 May 1987 at Royal Canberra Hospital and was buried in Gungahlin cemetery with the forms of the Churches of Christ. His wife and their three daughters and son survived him. With his death the literary community lost one of its most convivial and engaging personalities. He is commemorated by an annual memorial lecture at ADFA.

Notes & Furphies, Apr/May 1987, p 1; *Canberra Times*, 23 May 1987, p B12; *Island Mag*, Winter 1987, p 78; *Austn Book Review*, July 1987, p 39; H. Heseltine, 'Roost High and Crow Low', *Austn Literary Studies*, May 2000, p 313; Andrews papers (ADFA).   H. P. HESELTINE

ANDREWS, WILLIAM CHARLES (1908-1988), engineer, surveyor and town planner, was born on 20 November 1908 at Roslyn, Dunedin, New Zealand, eldest of six children of Sydney-born parents William Charles Andrews, printer, and his wife Claribelle Elsie, née Boaz. Bill spent his formative years in Sydney, matriculating in 1924 from Sydney Technical High School with an outstanding academic record. He qualified in local government engineering at Sydney Technical College while serving his articles with Dobbie & Foxall. Licensed as a surveyor in 1929, he was appointed assistant-engineer to Ku-ring-gai Municipal Council, and in 1934, from among sixty-two applicants, named as assistant-engineer and general inspector with the Tenterfield Shire Council, rising to shire engineer (1936). He gained certification from

the Royal Sanitary Institute, London, the town clerk's certificate and the first diploma of engineering surveying in the State. On 20 February 1937 at St Stephen's Presbyterian Church, Tenterfield, he married Lurline Patricia Ross.

In 1941 Andrews was seconded to the New South Wales Department of Public Works to provide essential engineering assistance and supervision for civilian and military projects. Enlisting in the Royal Australian Air Force on 29 March 1943 and commissioned in May as an engineer officer, he served at Tadji, New Guinea, and on Noemfoor Island, where he displayed outstanding ability in co-ordinating the construction of an airfield. He was mentioned in despatches and demobilised in 1945 as a flight lieutenant. Having returned to Tenterfield Shire as consulting engineer, Andrews was appointed senior planning officer (1946-50) with Cumberland County Council Regional Planning Authority headed by Sidney Luker [q.v.15]. Andrews held responsibility for the analysis and design phases of Australia's first statutory metropolitan plan. As city engineer and town planner with Parramatta City Council in 1950-58, he then designed and implemented a central traffic system and laid the foundations of the Parramatta Planning Scheme. He also lectured for the Sydney University Extension Board.

Growing status in his profession earned Andrews the first travelling scholarship in 1956 awarded by the New South Wales Foundation for the Technical Advancement of Local Government Engineers, enabling him to undertake a four-month study tour in North America. The substantial report he produced on his return, incorporating the latest and most innovative practices in all aspects of city and regional planning, further enhanced his reputation, and brought him to the notice of (Sir) John Overall, first head of the national Capital Development Commission, who, seeking proven professionals, recruited Andrews and Grenfell Rudduck [q.v.16] as associate commissioners in 1958. Andrews took special responsibility for all engineering design and construction work, which included such major projects as the construction of Lake Burley Griffin and its associated dam and bridgeworks; two further dams for Canberra's water supply (Bendora and Corin); Lake Ginninderra; major roads, including Anzac Parade; notable buildings such as the National Library of Australia; Russell and Campbell Park defence group offices; (old) Parliament House extensions; the Cameron offices, Belconnen; and the Canberra College of Advanced Education. His remit included planning and constructing the associated infrastructure for the new town centres of Canberra.

During these years when the commission experienced friction among government and non-government bodies in Canberra concerning areas of overlap and division of responsibilities, Andrews, with his equanimity and extensive background in local government, defused conflict and soothed competitive feeling and hostility. These qualities also proved invaluable inside the commission, his even temperament recalled by Overall as 'effective in moderating the wilder enthusiasms of people like myself'. Andrews took regular study tours to keep abreast of the latest and best overseas practices, which he incorporated into NCDC projects. He also provided professional advice at urban conferences in Hawaii and the Territory of Papua New Guinea. In November 1972 he succeeded Overall as commissioner. Although his period at the helm was brief, it was characterised by increased community consultation. On retiring in February 1974 he expressed disappointment that the plan to build a permanent parliament house was not more advanced. He favoured Walter Burley Griffin's Camp Hill site—envisaging Parliament Place as 'one of the great forecourts of the world'.

In retirement Andrews spent many years as a consultant in urban affairs and wrote a chapter on 'Roads and Bridges' in *Canberra's Engineering Heritage* (1983) which his colleague Peter Harrison called an enduring although impersonal testimony to his achievements. He was appointed OBE in 1967 and made an honorary fellow (1974) of the Institution of Surveyors, Australia, of whose Canberra division he had been president (1962). He also served as chairman (1960) of the Canberra division of the Institution of Engineers, Australia, foundation president of the Canberra division of the Royal Australian Planning Institute and federal president (1969-70) of the Australian Water and Waste Water Association. An active Rotarian, he enjoyed tennis and golf, and many memorable games of cricket with NCDC colleagues. Survived by his wife, and their two daughters and son, he died on 17 April 1988 at Woden Valley Hospital, Canberra, and was cremated. He was remembered by colleagues as the quintessential engineer, highly professional, extremely competent, responsible, unruffled—an absolute gentleman.

E. Sparke, *Canberra 1954-1980* (1988); *Austn Surveyor*, vol 34, no 3, 1988, p 323; *Australian*, 9 Nov 1972, p 6, 20 Feb 1974, p 8; M. Pratt, interview with Sir J. Overall (ts, 1973, NLA).   JUDY POULOS

ANDRZEJACZEK, TADEUSZ (1915-1987), architect, was born on 28 October 1915 at Czestochowa, Russian Poland, only son of Stanislaw Andrzejaczek, schoolteacher, and his wife Helena, née Schmidt. Orphaned at an early age, Tadeusz was brought up by his grandparents at Bydgoszcz, Poland, where he attended the local high school. He matriculated in 1934, and studied architecture at the Warsaw University of Technology until the outbreak of World War II. Interested in archaeology, he helped with excavations at the Iron Age settlement at Biskupin, and at King Stefan Bathory's sixteenth-century castle at Grodno. He produced precise survey drawings of the sites.

When Germany invaded Poland in September 1939, Andrzejaczek, a reservist, was mobilised. Wounded and taken prisoner, he spent the rest of the war in prisoner-of-war camps in Germany. He was released in May 1945, and on 5 July joined the II Polish Corps, part of the British Eighth Army, in Italy. On 18 December 1945 in the Polish army chapel, Altamura, he married Maria Stanislawa Rutkowska, an officer in the Polish Home Army. Moving to England, he resumed his architectural studies at the Polish University College, London (Dipl.Ing-arch., 1951). On 30 September 1949 he was discharged from the army as an officer cadet. After passing the professional practice examination of the Royal Institute of British Architects in 1951, he started work with the architectural division, London County Council. He was naturalised on 2 February 1953, and next year became an associate of the RIBA.

The Andrzejaczeks, with their daughter, Krystyna, and son, Krzysztof, migrated to Australia, arriving at Fremantle on 2 January 1954. They disembarked at Sydney and travelled directly to Canberra. Finding employment with the Department of Works, Andrzejaczek produced architectural plans for the Northbourne Flats and for educational buildings. By 1958 he was in Adelaide, where he worked for Sir Arthur Stephenson [q.v.12] and D. K. Turner, whose architectural practice specialised in the design of hospitals, and for Hassell, McConnell & Partners. On 4 January 1963 he was appointed principal assistant (design) in the Western Australian Public Works and Water Supply Department, Perth. He prepared development plans and designed buildings for the Royal Perth, Fremantle and King Edward Memorial hospitals. Other assignments included buildings for the Western Australian Institute of Technology, the astronomical observatory at Bickley and the Central Law Courts in St George's Terrace.

Convinced that Perth needed a cultural centre, Andrzejaczek fostered the proposal with energy and determination and served on the planning committee formed in 1967 to oversee the establishment of the centre. As project architect from 1972 he supervised the design and construction of new buildings, and the modification of existing structures, to house the State's art gallery, library and museum. The Perth Cultural Centre transformed the city and revitalised Northbridge and Forrest Place. Distinguished looking, socially motivated and highly cultured, he was described by his friend John Birman [q.v.] as 'a dreamer and an idealist' who would not 'compromise on deeply felt principles'. Andrzejaczek retired in 1980. Survived by his wife and their two children, he died on 18 February 1987 in Perth and was cremated.

O. Budrewicz, *Wśród Polskich Kangurów* (1982); *Kurier Zachodni*, Apr 1987, pp 8, 9; naturalisation certificate, item HO334/365 (PRO, UK); private information.   K. (CHARLES) SIERAKOWSKI

ANSETT, SIR REGINALD MYLES (1909-1981), aviator and businessman, was born on 13 February 1909 at Inglewood, Victoria, fourth of five children of Melbourne-born parents Charles John Ansett, cycle engineer, and his wife Mary Ann, née Phillips. Charles had a bicycle repair shop that evolved into a garage. When he joined the Australian Imperial Force in 1916, Mary closed the business and moved the family to Melbourne. After the war Ansett senior operated a small factory at Hawthorn (later Camberwell) that produced knitted woollen garments. Reg was educated at state schools in Essendon and Camberwell. Leaving at age 14 and entering his father's employment, he attended Swinburne Technical College and qualified as a knitting-machine and sewing-machine mechanic. In 1929 he cashed in a life assurance policy and took flying lessons. He was awarded Australian pilot's licence number 419.

Soon afterwards Ansett sailed for the Northern Territory, where he spent about a year, working as an axeman with a survey party. He briefly contemplated establishing a peanut farm but, deciding that he would not be able to bear the loneliness of such a life, returned to Victoria. With his savings of £70, he purchased a second-hand Studebaker car and used it to carry passengers and freight between Maryborough and Ballarat. Losing money, he shifted his base to Hamilton and from December 1931 ran between there and Ballarat. This venture was more successful. He hired employees, the first of whom, Colin MacDonald, was to remain with him and retire as a senior executive in 1974. Ansett also bought extra cars and established new routes in the Western District. On 1 October 1932 at Christ Church, Maryborough, he married with Anglican rites Grace Doreen Nicol, a clerk.

In 1932 the Victorian minister of railways, (Sir) Robert Menzies [q.v.15], introduced legislation that established the Transport Regulation Board. One of the board's functions was to protect the railways from competition. Refused a licence to operate between Hamilton and Melbourne by road, in 1935 Ansett registered Ansett Airways Pty Ltd and purchased a six-seat Fokker Universal; he already owned a small de Havilland Gipsy Moth. The Hamilton to Melbourne air service, begun in February 1936, proved to be unprofitable and Ansett made ends meet by taking people for 'joyrides', and by giving acrobatic displays and flying lessons. In December, piloting a Porterfield, he won the handicap section of the Brisbane to Adelaide air race; the prize was £500.

Backed by local graziers, Ansett had acquired an eight-seat Airspeed Envoy in August 1936. His aim, soon achieved, was to develop a network of air-routes linking Melbourne, Mildura, Adelaide, Sydney, Broken Hill and Narrandera. In 1937 he floated Ansett Airways Ltd and moved his headquarters to Essendon, Melbourne. While the road-transport side of his business was generating surpluses, the airline was not, a situation made worse by his decision to win over customers by high standards of service. Later that year he bought three Lockheed Electras for £50 000. The banks would only provide finance on the guarantee of his backers, which they gave in exchange for a substantial number of his personal shares.

By 1938 the value of £1 shares in Ansett Airways had dropped to 8s. 6d. The chairman, Ernest O'Sullivan, recommended that holders accept an offer by Australian National Airways Pty Ltd to buy the company for 8s. 10d. per share. At a meeting of shareholders the 29-year-old Ansett opposed his chairman and carried the day; the attempted takeover failed. In February 1939 a fire swept through the company's hangar at Essendon aerodrome and destroyed several aircraft, including one of the new Electras. Faced with this setback, Ansett summoned his senior staff and boldly announced that the firm would expand. With the aid of Commonwealth government subsidies—paid to all commercial airlines—Ansett Airways resumed its Melbourne-Sydney services, which had been stopped because of the fire, and quickly recovered lost ground.

During World War II Ansett's business expanded. All domestic services, other than the Hamilton-Melbourne run, were suspended and the aircraft diverted to charter-work for the Federal government and the American armed forces. Government aid helped the airline to double its hangar capacity and a manufacturing division (named Ansair Pty Ltd in 1945) was formed to make aircraft parts, including Beaufort gun-turrets. New hangars and engineering shops were built and by 1943 two thousand people were working for Ansett, mostly in production. Three years later, however, the airline was surviving on government subsidies and employment had declined to three hundred. Ansett restructured his business, forming Ansett Transport Industries Ltd as a holding company for Ansett Airways Pty Ltd, Pioneer Tourist Coaches Pty Ltd, Pioneer Tourist Hotels Pty Ltd, Ansair Pty Ltd, Air Express Pty Ltd and other subsidiaries.

Ansett's marriage had failed because of his absorption in his work and his affairs with other women. The couple were divorced in 1941; Grace remarried and moved to the United States of America with Ansett's two sons. On 17 June 1944 at Caulfield, Ansett married, with Presbyterian forms, Joan McAuliffe Adams, his 21-year-old private secretary.

At the end of the war Ansett expected that his airline would be the major competitor for ANA but the new government-owned Trans-Australia Airlines quickly assumed this position. Challenges in the High Court of Australia to the Chifley [q.v.13] government's airline policy removed restrictions against interstate operations and Ansett seized the opportunity to extend his services, particularly to holiday destinations in Queensland and Tasmania. This initiative complemented his growing coach and hotel businesses; by 1948 ATI was the largest operator of hotels in Australia. Yet Ansett believed himself to be at the crossroads and unable to topple ANA without the resources available to TAA. He offered to sell his airline to the Australian National Airlines Commission but the parties could not agree on a price and Ansett decided to stay in the industry.

Increased government charges in 1947 for the use of aerodromes and navigation aids forced Ansett into a more aggressive approach. His competitors sought to recoup these costs through higher fares. He responded by increasing the seating capacity of his planes and reducing cabin services. When the Commonwealth government attempted to force him to raise his prices in line with TAA and ANA, he refused, claiming that it was illegal for the government to dictate interstate fares; legal opinion supported his stand. In 1948 he negotiated a contract with Collier's Interstate Transport Service Ltd to carry its freight exclusively, enabling him to use his fleet of Douglas DC3s as freight carriers by night and passenger planes by day.

In 1952 the Menzies government introduced the Civil Aviation Agreement Act, which was designed to reserve the main interstate routes for the two major airlines. Ansett resolved to take business from ANA, the weaker of the two. He purchased new aircraft in 1954, gradually upgraded his cabin service and discounted fares. ANA could not compete. When the founder, Sir Ivan Holyman [q.v.14], died in January 1957, Ansett closed in. He approached the government and offered to take the place of ANA should it fail. In July the government refused financial help to ANA and next month its board reluctantly agreed to sell the company to Ansett for £3.3 million.

After he took over ANA, Ansett waged a brutal battle for control of his main regional rivals. The Commonwealth government wanted to stabilise the interstate airline industry and in 1958 introduced the Airline Equipment Act, which barred other companies from flying the main trunk routes. Under the two-airline policy Ansett-ANA (later Ansett Airlines of Australia) and TAA were made equal in the types of aircraft operated, seat capacity and scheduling. As a result there was little difference between them. Safety standards were excellent but customers complained of being taken for granted.

In the 1960s and 1970s Ansett's business empire expanded to encompass television stations in Melbourne and Brisbane, and interests in Diners' Club Pty Ltd and Biro Bic (Australia) Pty Ltd. Although he was firmly in control of the day-to-day management of his conglomerate, he owned only about 1 per cent of the shares in ATI. In April 1972 Thomas Nationwide Transport Ltd attempted to buy a controlling interest in ATI for $44 million. The Victorian State government of Sir Henry Bolte [q.v.] legislated to delay the takeover; TNT withdrew its bid and its managing director, Sir Peter Abeles, was elected to ATI's board. After he retired from parliament, Bolte also joined the board.

Other challenges confronted Ansett in the 1970s. In March 1975 air hostesses went on strike, prompting his regrettable remark that they were a 'batch of old boilers sitting on their executive'. His opposition to the recruitment of women as pilots ended with a decision of the High Court in 1979 ordering him to employ Deborah Wardley as a trainee. More damaging were the decisions of ATI to invest in two companies: Avis Rent-A-Car System Pty Ltd and Associated Securities Ltd. The purchase of Avis in 1977 sparked commercial competition and painful personal conflict between Ansett and his son Bob, who had earlier returned to Australia and become head of a rival firm, Budget Rent-A-Car System Pty Ltd. Bob successfully opposed his father's attempt to maintain monopoly rights to hire-car rental desks at airports. The collapse of ASL in February 1979 cut deeply into ATI's profits and rendered it vulnerable to takeover.

By April 1979 Robert Holmes à Court's Bell Group Ltd was buying large numbers of shares in ATI. TNT immediately acted to increase its stake in Ansett's company. Several other buyers entered the market, most importantly Rupert Murdoch's News Corporation Ltd. The ensuing fight for control ended in December and left ATI in the hands of Abeles and Murdoch. They persuaded Ansett to stay on as chairman.

Ansett had been appointed KBE in 1969 and awarded the (Walter) Oswald Watt [q.v.12] gold medal for 1975. He cultivated the image of the entrepreneur and industrialist. Addressed as 'R. M.' by his senior executives and other business intimates, he placed heavy demands on himself and his subordinates. At ATI headquarters he impressed his son Bob with 'his power, the confidence he projected that anything he wanted to happen would happen'. Each day he commuted by helicopter between his 113-acre (45.7 ha) property, Gunyong Valley, at Mount Eliza, and his office in Melbourne. He took a keen interest in the programming of his television stations. Espousing the interests and championing the virtues of private enterprise, he saw no contradiction in attacking the publicly funded, loss-making Victorian Railways—a competitor for his road-transport business—while his airtransport operation enjoyed the protection of the Federal government's two-airline policy. Yet he did not 'think that private enterprise should be allowed to go mad—some government control is necessary'.

According to John Hetherington's [q.v.14] description, Ansett in middle age was 'a lean and limber man, with an easy gait, five feet eleven and a half inches (182 cm) tall and weighing only eleven stone (70 kg). His face [was] long and narrow, with a lightly cleft chin and deep vertical creases beside the mouth'. His passion was breeding and racing thoroughbreds. He was a foundation member and sometime chairman of the Mornington Racing Club, and was president for some years of the Port Phillip District Racing Association. It was through racing that he cemented his friendship with Bolte, who in 1960 intervened on his behalf to prevent the State Rivers and Water Supply Commission from resuming 9.5 acres (3.8 ha) of Gunyong Valley for a dam.

Sir Reginald died on 23 December 1981 at Mount Eliza and was cremated. His wife and their three adopted daughters survived him, as did the sons of his first marriage. Ansett's estate was sworn for probate at $8 266 556. More than half of this amount was either bequeathed to his wife and daughters or held in trust for their benefit. There were also bequests to the Mornington Racing Club, and to the Peninsula Church of England School and Toorak College, Mount Eliza. His sons received $50 000 each. The remaining money was placed in a trust named after him and set up to support selected charities.

J. Hetherington, *Uncommon Men* (1965); B. Ansett with R. Pullan, *Bob Ansett* (1986); S. Brimson, *Ansett* (1987); P. Blazey, *Bolte* (1989); *Herald* (Melbourne), 18 Oct 1947, p 13, 3 Nov 1979, p 12; *People,* 11 Apr 1951, p 35; *Aircraft*, Mar 1961, p 30; *Sun News-Pictorial* (Melbourne), 13 July 1961, p 13, 9 June 1962, p 29, 13 Dec 1979, p 1, 11 May 1982, p 3; *Age* (Melbourne), 12 Dec 1962, p 8, 20 June 1979, p 10, 28 June 1979, p 16, 18 July 1979, p 1, 8 Aug 1979, p 1, 1 Nov 1979, p 1, 2 Nov 1979, p 3, 3 Nov 1979, p 1, 24 Dec 1981, p 1; *Australian*, 14 Apr 1979, 'Weekend Mag' p 1, 16 Apr 1979, p 7, 17 Apr 1979, p 7, 21 June 1979, p 6, 23 June 1979, p 4, 6 Nov 1979, p 10, 24 Dec 1981, p 1; *National Times*, 10 Nov 1979, p 73.
                                                   CHARLES FAHEY

ANSTEY, OLIVE EVA (1920-1983), hospital matron, was born on 9 August 1920 at Fremantle, Western Australia, youngest of three children of Terence Edwin Anstey, a sawmill benchman from Victoria, and his Western Australian-born wife Eva Annie, née Donovan. When Olive was eighteen months old the family moved to Sydney, where she completed her schooling. Returning to Western Australia in 1934, she learned commercial bookkeeping, shorthand and typing at Perth Technical College. At 15 she started work in a box factory at Fremantle while continuing her studies at night. She then worked as a bookkeeper with the soft goods manufacturers Creek, Petersen & Co. until becoming head bookkeeper at the shoe retailers Betts & Betts.

Against the wishes of her family, who wanted better things for her than the 'servitude' of nursing, Anstey began training at (Royal) Perth Hospital in 1941. She passed her final examinations in May 1944 and became a staff nurse; that year she was elected a council member of the local branch of the Australasian Trained Nurses Association. In 1946 she took part in the successful campaign waged by the Western Australian Nurses' Association for better pay and conditions, before moving back to Sydney to train for her midwifery certificate at the Royal Hospital for Women, Paddington. Registered as a midwife on 8 January 1947, she ran a small private hospital and, as organising secretary of the New South Wales Nurses' Association for a year, gained experience in industrial relations. In 1949, while a charge nurse in surgical wards at the Royal Prince Alfred Hospital, Camperdown, she served as founding honorary secretary of the New South Wales College of Nursing. She then worked in South Australia as a community health and school medical nurse for three years.

Back in Perth, Anstey was employed (1953-57) at the Perth Chest Clinic. After gaining a diploma in nursing administration at the College of Nursing, Australia, in Melbourne, and completing a short stint as matron of Collie hospital, Western Australia, in May 1958 she was appointed matron of the new Perth Chest Hospital. In 1963, renamed the Sir Charles Gairdner [q.v.] Hospital, it began admitting general patients and providing acute care. Under Anstey's leadership, it also became a community health centre. She initiated, encouraged and supported many innovative programs in various areas of nursing practice, education and administration.

Continuing to be an advocate for the nursing profession in Western Australia, Anstey was elected in 1958 to the council (president 1962-66) of the State branch of the Royal Australian Nursing Federation. She had helped to found the RANF Nurses' Memorial Centre of Western Australia, and was for many years also a member of the Florence Nightingale Committee and of the Nurses Registration Board of Western Australia. For four years she served on the nursing advisory committee, Western Australian Institute of Technology. Nationally, Anstey served as a council member (1964-71) of the College of Nursing, Australia, and sat on the nursing standing committee of the National Health and Medical Research Council for three years. As federal president (1971-75) of the RANF, she helped to establish the *Australian Nurses' Journal*. She completed her service to nursing as president (1977-81) of the International Council of Nurses. In 1978 she was made an honorary fellow of the New South Wales College of Nursing.

A sturdy and cheerful woman, Anstey was respected by her colleagues as an enthusiast and an optimist with an unswerving belief that anything was possible. On her retirement in 1981 Catherine Martin described her as 'having a natural simple manner', through which 'honesty, integrity and serenity' shone. When addressing an audience she had the power 'to touch the hearts of people'. Having been appointed MBE in 1969, in 1982 she was elevated to CBE. She died suddenly on the night of 18–19 August 1983 at Shoalwater, Perth, and was buried with Catholic rites in Karrakatta cemetery. An accommodation block for student nurses at Sir Charles Gairdner Hospital had been named after her in 1974; shortly after her death the hospital's board of management established the Olive Anstey Nursing Fund.

V. Hobbs, *But Westward Look* (1980); C. Polizzotto, *A Fair Sized Town* (1988); *Austn Nurses' Jnl*, Aug 1981, p 28, Oct 1983, p 9; *West Australian*, 19 Nov 1981, p 69; C. Jeffery, interview with O. Anstey (ts, 1977, SLWA); private information.

CRIENA FITZGERALD

ANTCLIFF, ALLAN JAMES (1923-1985), vine physiologist and breeder, was born on 21 December 1923 at Salisbury, Brisbane, son of Harry Herbert Antcliff, a Queensland-born public servant, and his English wife Kate Florence, née Filer. Allan was educated at state primary schools, Brisbane Grammar School (dux, 1940) and the University of Queensland (B.Sc., 1944). On 19 May 1944 he enlisted in the Royal Australian Air Force. Although he trained as aircrew, he did not see active service before being discharged in September 1945. He returned to the university to take honours in botany (1947).

After a short period at the Waite [q.v.6] Agricultural Research Institute, University of Adelaide, Antcliff was appointed in 1947 as a research scientist at the Commonwealth Research Station, Merbein, Victoria, controlled by the Council for Scientific and Industrial Research (later horticultural research section and then division of horticultural research, Commonwealth Scientific and Industrial Research Organization). Grapevine cultivation in the Sunraysia region was directed mainly towards the production of dried fruit and growers had long sought a research capacity devoted to their needs. Antcliff's early work on the physiology and yield of vines led to improved productivity and gained him a reputation for his understanding of the process of fruit-bud formation. He spent a year abroad in 1962, studying at the Imperial College of Science and Technology, London, and visiting vineyards and research institutions in Europe.

On his return Antcliff, as principal research scientist (1963) and senior principal research scientist (1967), took charge of CSIRO's vine improvement program, which gradually embraced wine as well as dried-fruit production. He supervised thousands of crosses of varieties and hybrids, searched for stock in old Australian vineyards and applied for permits to introduce varieties from abroad. Travelling frequently overseas, he gathered information and compared notes with fellow viticultural researchers. By 1983 more than forty thousand seedlings had been germinated and planted. Improved cloned variants of the Thompson Seedless Sultana were produced and valuable new drying varieties were bred, including the Carina (1975). Of the wine grapes developed, the red Tarrango (1975) and the white Taminga (1985) attracted the most commercial interest. Antcliff wrote *Some Wine Grape Varieties for Australia* (1976), *Major Wine Grape Varieties of Australia* (1979) and *Minor Wine Grape Varieties of Australia* (1983). These books were standard references for a generation and influential in promoting new varieties. In 1984 their author retired from the CSIRO. Illness prevented him from taking up a post-retirement research fellowship.

Antcliff was a mild-mannered but methodical, purposeful and substantially self-taught scientist who worked in often solitary conditions but who also collaborated successfully with his peers. His work proved valuable for an expanding and changing vine-growing industry. The University of Queensland awarded him a doctorate of agricultural science in 1980. Three years later he was appointed AM.

At St Margaret's Church of England, Mildura, Antcliff served as choirmaster and organist. He was (1979-85) on the council of the Sunraysia College of Technical and Further Education and supported numerous botanical and heritage-preservation projects. On 19 November 1951 at St John's Church of England, Merbein, he had married Freda Gwendoline Lowe, a teacher. Survived by her, and by their four daughters and son, he died of acute leukemia on 22 April 1985 at his Mildura home and was buried in the city's cemetery.

B. Collis, *Fields of Discovery* (2002); CSIRO, Division of Horticultural Research, *Report*, 1983-85; *Age* (Melbourne), 5 Jan 1982, p 13; *Sunraysia Daily*, 24 Apr 1985, p 2; *CoResearch*, June 1985, p 5; private information.   DAVID DUNSTAN

ANTILL, JOHN HENRY (1904-1986), musician, composer and broadcaster, was born on 8 April 1904 at Ashfield, Sydney, second child of English-born parents John Henry Antill, boilermaker, and his wife Marianne Elizabeth, née Baker. John was educated at St Andrew's Cathedral Choir School, Sydney, where his musical training began, then at Trinity Grammar School, Summer Hill. At the age of 16, he was apprenticed to the New South Wales Government Railways as a mechanical draftsman. One of his tasks was to help design a multi-toned steam whistle for the C-36 class locomotive.

Music was always in Antill's mind and while an apprentice he wrote several operas including *Endymion*, which was to be performed in 1953. Overcoming his father's reservations about the unreliable nature of a career in music, he left the railways and began studying with the organist Frederick Mewton. On Mewton's retirement he enrolled full time at the New South Wales State Conservatorium of Music, where Alfred Hill [q.v.9] taught him composition and Gerald Walenn was his violin mentor. Antill's practical experience included singing, as a tenor, in the chorus and playing second violin, and later bass clarinet, in the orchestra. After leaving the conservatorium he toured with the Williamson [q.v.6] Imperial Grand Opera company in Sydney, Melbourne and New Zealand from 1932 to 1934, singing in the chorus, conducting backstage and enjoying the experience of being a member of a professional company.

When the company was disbanded Antill formed a quartet, called the Mastersingers Male Quartet, for the Australian Broadcasting Commission. He also founded, and arranged for, other groups, among them the Melodymakers Male Quartet and the Choristers Male Quartet. In 1934-35 he participated in the (Sir Benjamin) Fuller [q.v.8] Opera Company as a member of the chorus, backstage conductor and player of the clarinet and the bass clarinet.

Antill joined the staff of the ABC in 1936 as assistant to the federal music editor and three weeks later was also appointed conductor of the Wireless Chorus. He was a member of the Sydney Symphony Orchestra simultaneously but found this commitment too much. In July 1939 he became the ABC's balance and control officer in Sydney and from October he worked as a presentation officer. On 2 February he had married with Anglican rites Constance Margaret Peaker, a clerk, at St Andrew's Cathedral, Sydney, where they had first met. They had a daughter in 1945; her twin was stillborn. John undertook considerable domestic duties in their home at Neutral Bay and then at Hunter's Hill, especially after Constance's death in 1957. He later lived at Cronulla.

As a child Antill had seen a form of corroboree performed at La Perouse. His memories of this experience stimulated an interest in writings on Aboriginal people and ultimately led to his composing the ballet *Corroboree*, which became his best-known work. Soon after the end of World War II the ABC made the SSO available to Antill for a 'read through' of the work, but took no further action. During his 1946 tour of Australia, (Sir) Eugene Goossens [q.v.14], having sought out Australian compositions, conducted the SSO in a symphonic suite of four excerpts from the ballet at a free Sunday afternoon concert in the Sydney Town Hall on 18 August. In October, his fare having been raised by public subscription, Antill attended a performance in London.

The presentation of *Corroboree* as a ballet proved more difficult than its performance as a suite. After a number of failed attempts, including one by (Sir) Robert Helpmann [q.v.] in London, Dorothy Helmrich [q.v.] arranged for its performance at Sydney's Empire Theatre, commencing on 3 July 1950, with choreography by Rex Reid and décor by William Constable; Antill conducted the SSO and the National Theatre Ballet Company provided the dancers. The season was a success, even financially, although there were critics who complained that it did not fully bring out the spiritual qualities of the Aboriginal ceremony. Antill said that he had attempted not a truly ritual corroboree but an entertainment that captured something of the idiom for a non-Aboriginal audience. A shorter version of *Corroboree* was staged in a gala performance for Queen Elizabeth II in 1954, with Beth Dean's choreography and with Antill as conductor.

Goossens later performed the music from *Corroboree* throughout the world. This work was authentically Australian, expressing something of the spiritual values of the original inhabitants of the country, and having an exhilarating percussive and rhythmic character. The work stimulated new approaches to composition among younger Australian composers.

During the four months from October 1946 that Antill had spent in London, the ABC had paid his salary and arranged for him to study orchestral and balance techniques with the British Broadcasting Corporation. He returned in February 1947 and became the ABC's music supervisor for New South Wales. A prolific composer, he wrote music for films, starting with *School in the Mail Box* in 1947 and extending to documentaries on Papua and New Guinea. He also wrote *Overture for a Momentous Occasion* (1957) and *Paean to the Spirit of Man* (1968), both commissioned by the ABC, *Music for a Royal Pageant* (for the royal tour in 1962) and *Symphony on a City* (1959) for the city of Newcastle. His operas included *The Music Critic* (1953) and *The First Christmas* (1969). Other works encompass an oratorio, *The Song of Hagar to Abraham the Patriarch* (1958), ballet music such as *G'Day Digger* (c.1955), *The Sentimental Bloke* (1955) and *Black Opal* (1961), and much vocal music. He wrote the music to precede Queen Elizabeth II's Christmas message in 1959. On his eightieth birthday he said that he wished that people would listen to the many other ballets that he had composed, not just to *Corroboree*. He decorated many of his scores with illustrations of set designs and costumes in watercolour.

Antill was slim in build and shy and diffident in manner. As music editor (1950-69) with the ABC, he was responsible for selecting compositions, and for encouraging Australian composers and promoting their work. Because of his reticence, he did little to seek performances or exposure of his own compositions. The Fellowship of Australian Composers conferred life membership on him in 1974. He was appointed OBE in 1971 and CMG in 1981 and was awarded an honorary doctorate in creative arts by the University of Wollongong in 1985. His portrait by Louis Kahan is held at the State Library of New South Wales and a bronze bust by Dawn Swayne is held at the Sydney Conservatorium of Music. The John Antill composition scholarship, offered annually to an outstanding conservatorium student, was established to honour him. Survived by his daughter, he died on 29 December 1986 at Caringbah and was cremated.

J. Hetherington, *Uncommon Men* (1965); R. Covell, *Australia's Music* (1967); F. Callaway and D. Tunley (eds), *Australian Composition in the Twentieth Century* (1978); B. Dean and V. Carell, *Gentle Genius* (1987); *Canon*, Apr 1955, p 353; *APRA: Mag of the A'asian Performing Right Assn*, Dec 1984, p 15; Antill papers (NLA).   HAROLD HORT

ARCHDALE, ALEXANDER MERVYN (1905-1986), actor, director and manager, was born on 26 November 1905 at Jhansi, India, second of three children of Theodore Montgomery Archdale, British soldier, and his wife Helen Alexandra, née Russel. Alexander returned to England with his mother as a young child and attended (1914-24) Bedales school, Hampshire. In 1925-27 he was enrolled at McGill University, Montreal, Canada, where he spent most of his time in the drama club, and did not complete his studies. Commencing his stage career in a company run by Henry Ainley, he then performed for five years in British repertory theatre and began producing for stage clubs. Archdale made his first London appearance in 1932, establishing a career as a West End supporting actor, mainly in light comedy. He married Lilian Patricia Dysart Wolseley on 25 March 1933 at the register office, St Martin, London; they were later divorced. Archdale served at sea and ashore in the Royal Navy Volunteer Reserve in 1940-45, and was demobilised as a temporary acting lieutenant commander.

Like other ex-service personnel Archdale could find little work, so he invested his gratuity in establishing in London the Services Sunday Society, a production company and agency which in 1946 presented Sunday performances by returned servicemen. From 1946 he performed in a variety of plays and also on radio and television. Nevertheless he felt out of sympathy with the contemporary theatrical style and left England at the end of 1951 to visit his sister, Betty Archdale, in Sydney. Joining the Mercury Theatre, he produced and acted in plays including Strindberg's *The Father,* in which he was judged to be the 'outstanding actor for 1952'. In 1953 Archdale led an extensive Arts Council of Australia tour in country New South Wales, and in 1954 performed in Alan Melville's light comedy *Dear Charles.* Later he was a director with the Young Elizabethan Players.

In the 1950s Archdale was associated with the Australian Broadcasting Commission: on the opening night of ABN-2 in Sydney in 1956 he played the lead in J. M. Barrie's *The Twelve Pound Look.* He had appeared in films in England and Australia including *House of Darkness* (1948), *Floodtide* (1949) and *His Majesty O'Keefe* (1953). He also provided commentaries for the Commonwealth Film Unit in Australia. In 1957 he returned to Britain, briefly revisiting Australia in 1960 for the Australian Elizabethan Theatre Trust. Next year in England he suffered a heart attack while working on the television series *Deadline Midnight.* This experience led to his decision to settle in Australia.

Beginning a new phase of his career with an appearance as the Earl of Warwick in George Bernard Shaw's *Saint Joan* at the Adelaide

Festival of Arts in 1962, Archdale achieved his main goal in 1965 when he founded the Community Theatre Company Ltd (Marian Street Theatre Company) on Sydney's North Shore. There was an echo of the approach of the nineteenth-century actor–manager in his conception of the company, with Archdale appearing in and directing many productions. His stated aims were to 'bring the theatre to the people', to provide work for actors and to teach. He planned to stage classics, being outspoken in his objection to the current experimental theatre. His productions received mixed reviews and the theatre suffered financial difficulties, even with a change to supposedly more popular works. Archdale was involved in the creative, technical and administrative aspects, and this broad engagement interfered with the performance of his designated artistic role. A car accident accelerated his retirement (1970) as artistic director. He continued to live on the 5-acre (2 ha) property at Galston which he had purchased with his sister early in the 1950s.

In 1972 Archdale again visited Britain but found little employment, and returned in 1974 to Australia, where he continued as a jobbing actor. Seeming dissatisfied, he was critical of the limited work available for older performers. He still had small parts in radio shows, local films and television series but had little success on stage. One of his last theatre appearances was in 1975 in the Old Tote's production of *Abelard and Heloise* by Ronald Millar. He also performed in a one-man show, *Time's Wing'd Chariot* (1977), at the Festival of Sydney.

Archdale was a tall, spare, rather gawky man, slightly precious in manner, with a shy giggle. He was a fine singer and classical musician and an adept sportsman. Although a loner and a perfectionist, he was sensitive and could be amusing, endearing and affectionate. He was a generous teacher who respected actors, and who saw 'the best thing in the theatre ... [as] the relationship between the performer and the audience'. But he also wanted his own way, liked to impress and could be argumentative. His wit could be cruel. Although skilled in his theatrical craft, he was too linked to pre-World War II British culture for the Australian ethos of his time. Survived by his two sons, he died on 13 May 1986 at Hornsby and was cremated.

B. Archdale, *Indiscretions of a Headmistress* (1972); D. Macpherson, *The Suffragette's Daughter* (2002); *Australian*, 18 July 1967, p 16, 7 Nov 1970, p 10; *TV Times*, 2 Dec 1972, p 44; *Daily Telegraph* (Sydney), 3 Oct 1975, p 57; *SMH*, 15 May 1986, p 9; SP1011/2, item 55 (NAA); Archdale and Community Theatre files (SLNSW); private information.

AILSA MCPHERSON

ARMSTRONG, JOHN MALET (1900-1988), naval officer, was born on 5 January 1900 at Elizabeth Bay, Sydney, younger child and only son of William George Armstrong [q.v.7], medical practitioner, and his wife Elizabeth Jane, née Garnsey. R. R. Armstrong and C. F. Garnsey [qq.v.3,4] were his grandfathers. John was educated at Sydney Grammar School and All Saints' College, Bathurst. In 1914 he entered the Royal Australian Naval College, Osborne House, Geelong, Victoria (relocated at Jervis Bay, Federal Capital Territory, next year). A natural leader and sportsman, he became a chief cadet captain and received colours for Rugby and swimming before graduating in 1917.

Appointed midshipman on 1 January 1918, Armstrong joined the battle cruiser HMAS *Australia* in April at Scapa Flow, Orkney Islands, Scotland. Back in Australia, he transferred to the light cruiser HMAS *Brisbane* in September 1919 and was promoted to sublieutenant in October. He was made lieutenant in March 1921 and sent to Britain, where he completed a series of courses, specialising in gunnery. On 7 July 1924 he married Philippa Suzanne Marett at the parish church, St Brelade, Jersey, Channel Islands. In the years that followed Armstrong was posted to a variety of sea and staff jobs in both Britain and Australia. He found the long and frequent absences from his growing family difficult and, as the pay of a junior officer was not high, he relied on financial support from his father and uncle. Nevertheless, his excellent professional performance continued and in 1927 he was the navy's guard commander for the opening of Parliament House in Canberra.

In March 1929 Armstrong was promoted to lieutenant commander while serving in HMS *Castor* on the China Station. He rose to commander in June 1935 and, as executive officer of HMS *Shropshire* in 1937, was involved in the evacuation of refugees from the Spanish Civil War. He briefly commanded the destroyer HMS *Broke* and her flotilla, which provided him with invaluable ship-handling experience. Returning to Australia in 1938, he was appointed executive officer of the RANC, which had moved to Flinders Naval Depot, Westernport, Victoria.

At the outbreak of World War II Armstrong was executive officer of the cruiser HMAS *Australia,* which escorted convoys of the Australian Imperial Force, patrolled Australian waters and participated in the Dakar operations against the Vichy French in July and September 1940. In October *Australia* went to the aid of a Sutherland flying boat which had come down in the North Atlantic in a vicious gale. The Sutherland capsized as the ship approached and Armstrong led a dozen sailors with bowlines over the side into the heaving, freezing ocean to rescue nine of the aircraft's thirteen crew. *Australia* spent much of 1941 escorting convoys and searching for raiders in the Indian Ocean. That year Armstrong was mentioned in despatches.

Recalled to Australian waters in December 1941, *Australia* operated from Noumea with United States forces. In March 1942 Armstrong left the ship to command (as an acting captain) the armed merchant cruisers *Manoora* (April-October) and *Westralia* (October-December). He was promoted to substantive captain on 31 December while chief of staff to the flag officer-in-charge, Sydney, and in November 1943 he was appointed naval officer-in-charge, New Guinea.

On 21 October 1944 a Japanese aircraft struck *Australia* at Leyte Gulf in the Philippines, wounding Commodore (Sir) John Collins [q.v.] and killing the commanding officer Captain E. V. F. Dechaineux [q.v.13]. Armstrong assumed command of the ship on 29 October. In January 1945 *Australia* supported the landings at Lingayen Gulf, Luzon. During the operation she suffered five kamikaze attacks, which killed forty-four and wounded sixty-nine of the ship's company. Extensively damaged, *Australia* sailed for Plymouth, England, in May for a refit. Armstrong was awarded the Distinguished Service Order (1945) for the Lingayen Gulf operation and the United States awarded him the Navy Cross (1946) for his 'gallantry and intrepidity' in the action.

Arriving in New York in June 1945, *Australia* embarked the New South Wales premier (Sir) William McKell [q.v.] for the passage to Plymouth. He was so impressed with Armstrong that he recommended that he succeed Lord Wakehurst [q.v.16] as governor of New South Wales but the Dominion Office rejected the nomination.

Armstrong relinquished command of *Australia* on 6 August with the jocular 'Goodbye you pack of bastards'. Selected to command Australia's planned postwar aircraft-carrier, he gained experience captaining HM ships *Ruler* and *Vindex*. On 3 April 1946 he was appointed second naval member of the Naval Board with the rank of commodore, second class. Unfortunately, a medical examination that year concluded that he was unfit for sea service; deteriorating eyesight and weak bones ended his prospects for further promotion. From 1948 he held staff appointments at Navy Office, Melbourne, and in London, before becoming the Department of Supply's liaison officer in Washington in 1955. He retired on 14 August 1958.

Known as 'Jock' from childhood and as 'Jamie' by his wife and his fellow naval officers, Armstrong was described by the *Bulletin* in 1954 as 'inevitably "Black Jack" to all hands, from hair, cliffy eyebrows and a dark general weathering burned-in over 40 years of naval service'. He was a good-looking man, standing six feet (183 cm) tall with a nose broken when playing Rugby. Armstrong had many friends and was able to move in all circles. He was dedicated to the naval profession and fearless under fire. Typical of many successful naval officers of the time, he preferred activity and practicality over staff work, which was his distinct weakness. A modest, humane and devoted family man, he took a progressive attitude to training, believing young naval officers to be poorly educated, too isolated and over-supervised and disciplined.

From 1962 Armstrong and his wife lived on Jersey. He trained the Jersey Sea Scouts, fished, tended his gardens and joined the Imperial Service Club and the Naval and Military Club, London. Survived by his wife, and their two sons and daughter, he died on 30 December 1988 in his home at La Haule and was cremated; his ashes were buried in the Marett family grave in the cemetery of the parish church, St Brelade.

F. B. Eldridge, *A History of the Royal Australian Naval College* (1949); A. Payne, *H.M.A.S. Australia* (1975); G. H. Gill, *Royal Australian Navy 1939-1942* and *1942-1945* (1985); *Bulletin*, 29 Sept 1954, p 10; *Sun* (Sydney), 16 Aug 1984, p 16, 8 Jan 1985, p 32; *Naval Hist Review*, Dec 1988, p 15, Mar 1989, p 7, June 1989, p 25; A6769, item Armstrong J M (NAA); Armstrong papers (NLA); private information.
J. S. SEARS

ARMSTRONG, ROBERT EDWARD (1911-1988), public servant, was born on 24 July 1911 at Erskineville, Sydney, fourth son of Sydney-born parents William Armstrong, grocer, and his wife Miriam Eleanor, née Baines. He was orphaned in 1919 when both parents were victims of the influenza epidemic. Educated at Erskineville Public and Petersham Boys' Intermediate High schools, he passed the Intermediate certificate in 1925. He worked briefly for the Mercantile Mutual Insurance Co. Ltd before joining the New South Wales Public Service in 1926 as a junior clerk in the Police Department. At the Methodist Church, West Maitland, on 28 March 1936 he married Gwen Isabel Jobson, a shop assistant.

On 3 June 1940 Armstrong enlisted in the Australian Imperial Force. Posted to 7th Division headquarters as a clerk, he served in Egypt, Palestine, Syria and Java, and was mentioned in despatches. He reached the rank of warrant officer, class two, and was discharged on 4 September 1942 to a reserved occupation at the request of the director-general of security, W. J. MacKay [q.v.10]. For the remainder of the war he was engaged in assessing the cases of aliens who had been interned and who had applied for release.

In 1945 Armstrong became private secretary to the newly appointed Federal minister for immigration, Arthur Calwell [q.v.13]. He travelled to Europe with Calwell in 1947 on a mission which, according to Armstrong, 'led to Australia for the first time in history accepting significant numbers of people other than British'. In 1949 he was appointed an assistant-secretary in the Department of Immigration. His responsibilities included the development of post-arrival services, which involved not only programs to assist migrants to adapt to their new circumstances but also measures—such as the establishment of Good Neighbour councils and the holding of citizenship conventions—to encourage the Australian community to welcome and support the newcomers.

Armstrong served as chief migration officer in London in 1954-57, heading an extensive operation which processed a great stream of applications for assisted passage. He led the Australian delegation to meetings of the Intergovernmental Committee for European Migration in Geneva (1959-61) and Washington (1959-64). In 1963 he was promoted to first assistant secretary in charge of the entry and citizenship division and later the planning and operations division of the department. By this time the emphasis was beginning to shift from an assumption that mass immigration was beneficial to the nation to a questioning of the scale of resources required by the program, the effects on employment and the issue of what was to be the optimum population for the country over the long term. In 1967 he was appointed OBE.

Accepting a second posting to London as CMO in 1969, Armstrong hoped that this would see him through to retirement. However, when the secretary of the department Sir Peter Heydon [q.v.14] suddenly died in 1971, he was recalled to Canberra to become permanent head. In 1974, after his department was merged with the Department of Labour, he retired. He was a council member (1975-77) of the Canberra College of Advanced Education and vice-president of the Young Men's Christian Association, Canberra.

Of middle height and stocky build, with brown hair and a ruddy complexion, Bob Armstrong was mild mannered and unpretentious, but strong in his convictions. He was described as a dedicated man with particularly strong powers of concentration, one who was 'wedded to his job' and who passionately believed the contribution the immigration program could make to the development of Australia. Remembered as being 'warm and helpful' and 'intensively family oriented', he died on 19 February 1988 in Canberra and was cremated with Anglican rites; his wife and their three daughters and son survived him.

A. A. Calwell, *Immigration* (1949), *Be Just and Fear Not* (1972); L. F. Crisp (ed), *Peter Richard Heydon 1913-1971* (1972); C. Kiernan, *Calwell* (1978); *Canberra Times*, 26 May 1971, p 1, 22 Feb 1988, p 8; Armstrong papers (NLA); private information.   ROBERT S. SWIFT

ARNOLD, VICTOR JULIUS (JOHN) CAUVAIN (CORVEIN) (1905-1982), actor, theatre manager and union official, was born on 6 July 1905 at East Dulwich, London, eldest child of John Julius Arnold, commercial traveller, and his wife Charlotte Maud, née Swindells. At 16 Vic ran away to sea; he worked in passenger and cargo vessels on the Atlantic run. In the late 1920s he left his ship at New York, and for a year toured the United States of America with vaudevillians. Finding himself in San Diego, California, he decided to sail to New Zealand. He was probably a communist by this time and had been drawn to theatre as a means of mobilising the working class.

After taking part in a militant maritime strike, Arnold was briefly gaoled in Wellington in 1932. By August he had crossed the Tasman to Sydney. Joining the Communist Party of Australia, he obtained the post of secretary of the Workers' Art Club. He became the organising genius of the drama section, which in 1936 adopted the name New Theatre League (shortened to New Theatre in 1945). Similar bodies were formed in other major Australian cities, drawing inspiration from the New Theatre League in the USA, the realist art movement in the Soviet Union and the Unity Theatre in Britain. The Sydney league became a focus for anti-fascist activism in Australia. Its emblematic production, *Till the Day I Die* by Clifford Odets, played more than a hundred times on Wednesday nights between 1936 and 1939, in defiance of a State government ban.

In 1938 Arnold argued for 'an Australian people's theatre with its roots in Australian soil', and produced Betty Roland's *War on the Waterfront*, a dramatisation of the strike (1938-39) by Port Kembla waterside workers over the export of pig-iron to Japan. Arnold organised a mobile unit, or 'living newspaper', to show the play in Port Kembla, but when the company tried to stage it in the Sydney Domain, he and four others, including Hal Alexander [q.v.], were arrested. The five were fined £5 each. On 21 January 1935 at Holy Trinity Church of England, Dawes Point, Arnold had married Sylvia Mary Lunn, a saleswoman; they were divorced in 1939. He moved to Perth, where he was involved with the Workers' Art Guild.

Enlisting in the Citizen Military Forces on 5 March 1941, Arnold understated his age by seven years to transfer to the Australian

Imperial Force in 1944. He served in Australia and New Guinea with detachments of the Australian Entertainment Unit, acted in plays produced by Peter Finch [q.v.14] and rose to sergeant before being discharged on 4 September 1946. Still active in the Communist Party, he worked in the Melbourne New Theatre and was secretary of the Realist Film Association. On 31 October 1951 at a civil ceremony in Melbourne, he married Joan de Hugard, a clerk.

From 1958 Arnold was Victorian State secretary of the Actors' and Announcers' Equity Association of Australia. He increased the membership, secured better conditions for members and led a successful campaign to establish a quota of domestically produced programs on commercial television—a turning point in the history of Australian culture. Arnold was a secretive but delightful man. Of middle height, he looked 'like a Spaniard', according to the journalist Jeanne Liddy. He worked almost until his death; Joan was also on the staff of Actors' Equity, serving for nearly four decades. Childless, but survived by his wife, Arnold died on 7 November 1982 at Box Hill and was cremated.

Austn Left News, Jan 1939, p 11; *Daily News* (Sydney), 1 June 1940, p 2; *Woman* (Sydney), 7 May 1945, p 20; Actors' and Announcers' Equity Assn of Aust, *Equity*, Nov 1982, p 7; A6119, item 1938, B883, item WX41277 (NAA); Actors' and Announcers' Equity Assn of Aust (Vic) records (Univ of Melbourne Archives); private information.

JANET MCCALMAN

ARNOTT, FELIX RAYMOND (1911-1988), Anglican archbishop, was born on 8 March 1911 at Ipswich, Suffolk, England, eldest son of Richard Girling Arnott, a sharebroker's accountant and later a solicitor, and his wife Daisy Flora, née Meadows. Felix attended the local grammar school and won a scholarship to Keble College, Oxford (BA, 1933; MA, 1941), where he studied classics and gained first-class honours in theology. A mission to the University of Oxford in March 1931, led by William Temple, archbishop of York (later Canterbury), convinced him of God's call to ordination, and he trained for the ministry at Cuddesdon College, Oxford. Made deacon (1934) at Wakefield, Yorkshire, he served his first curacy nearby, at Elland, in 1934-38 and was ordained priest in 1935. On 23 June 1938 in the parish church, Ashtead, Surrey, he married Anne Caroline Lane. Soon after, he took up an appointment as vice-principal of Bishop's College, Cheshunt, Hertfordshire.

College duties limited the time Arnott could spend at home with his bride, and he welcomed an invitation from the archbishop of Brisbane, William Wand [q.v.12], his former Oxford tutor, to be warden of St John's College, University of Queensland. The couple arrived in Brisbane in March 1939. Arnott was also rector of St Mary's, Kangaroo Point, in 1942-46. In 1946 he was appointed warden of St Paul's College, University of Sydney, and during the next few years oversaw its expansion. Recognised as a fine scholar and teacher, he had a special interest in seventeenth-century church history and in 1955 was awarded a Th.D. by the Australian College of Theology, Sydney. His lectures, addresses and sermons reflected a mind that was able to grasp complex ideas and convey them logically and simply. He served as president (1952-63) of Sydney University Settlement. From 1955 he was a regular participant in the Australian Broadcasting Commission's radio program 'Any Questions?'.

Appointed coadjutor bishop of Melbourne in 1963, Arnott was consecrated in St Andrew's Cathedral, Sydney, on 29 June. He was given particular oversight of the church schools, a portfolio that suited his interest in education. Chairman of the general synod's committee on theological education for some years and of the Australian College of Theology's board of delegates (1960-72), he was also president (1966-67) of the ecumenical Melbourne College of Divinity. He served as a council member (1964-70) of Monash University.

On 17 October 1970 Arnott was enthroned as archbishop of Brisbane in St John's Cathedral. He readily shared decision-making and responsibilities with senior clergy. An easy conversationalist and excellent after-dinner speaker, he put people at their ease and took a close interest in students, clergy and their families. He loved to cook, enjoyed fine wines and was a generous host. Interested in art, he was a founder (1951) and committee member of the Blake prize for religious art. There was, however, an eccentric edge to his personality: he never learned to drive; was not always able to conceal his irritability and even irascibility; and was known to communicate messages to ministers through their wives, from whom he seemed to evoke special affection.

During his archiepiscopate Arnott's ministry widened nationally and internationally. Inspired by Temple's vision of a united world through a united church, he was a member (1969-81) of the Anglican-Roman Catholic International Commission, work that he enjoyed immensely. He believed that the agreed statements on the Eucharist, on ministry and ordination, and on authority, made valuable contributions to the cause of church unity. With Justice Elizabeth Evatt and Anne Deveson, he was a member (1974-77) of the Commonwealth royal commission on human relationships, which he saw as a legitimate Christian concern. His critics regarded him as a dangerous theological liberal, and some of the resultant criticism hurt him. After speaking out at the annual diocesan synod in June 1978 against the erosion of civil liberties in Queensland, he was censured by the premier, (Sir) Johannes Bjelke-Petersen.

Arnott resigned on 31 July 1980. He was appointed CMG in 1981. While a member of the ARCIC he had grown increasingly fond of Italian culture and art, and he found a niche as honorary Anglican chaplain at Venice. After five years he and his wife retired to Chichester, Sussex, England, but by 1987 he was in failing health and they returned to Queensland to be near their family. Survived by his wife, and their two sons and two daughters, he died on 28 July 1988 at Taigum, Brisbane, and was cremated. One of his last acts was to choose a luncheon menu, with fine wines, for his family and selected friends to enjoy at the Brisbane Club after his funeral. It was a mark of his zest for gracious living and his generosity of spirit.

R. Wicks, *Felix Raymond Arnott* (1997); *Age* (Melbourne), 15 June 1978, p 9; Anglican diocesan archives, Brisbane.   JONATHAN HOLLAND

ASHBY, ALISON MARJORIE (1901-1987), botanical artist and plant collector, was born on 7 February 1901 in North Adelaide, youngest of four children of Edwin Ashby [q.v.7], a land agent from England, and his South Australian-born wife Esther Maria, née Coleman. In 1902 the family moved to Blackwood in the Adelaide foothills and, amid largely uncleared scrub, Edwin Ashby established Wittunga farm. Constrained by shyness and a severe stutter, Alison received most of her education at home. She shared her father's passion for native plants, and as a child vowed to paint every Australian wildflower. Gaining brief but valuable tuition from the artist Rosa Fiveash [q.v.8], she painted specimens from the surrounding bush in watercolours and on china. Later her activities were restricted by family responsibilities, including caring for her bedridden mother.

From about 1944, after both her parents had died, Ashby began to seek plants further afield. Besides painting, she collected cuttings and seeds for propagation at Wittunga or by fellow members of the South Australian Society for Growing Australian Plants, referring to plants which had never been cultivated before as her grandchildren. She also pressed thousands of specimens for the State herbaria in Perth and Adelaide. Her meticulous annotations demonstrated her powers of observation and knowledge of the flora. Two species —*Acacia ashbyae* and *Solanum ashbyae*—were named after her.

In 1957 Ashby transferred her portion of Wittunga to the National Trust of South Australia, of which she had been elected (1956) a founding council member. She wanted the 80-acre (32 ha) reserve, which was named Watiparinga, 're-clothed in Australian trees and shrubs' for the enjoyment of the public. Assisted by friends from SGAP and other organisations, she made it one of several planting projects. She had progressively lodged her completed watercolours with the South Australian Museum, and in 1958 nine paintings were reproduced as postcards, the beginning of a series that eventually included 240 of her 1500 paintings and led to widespread appreciation of her skills as a botanical artist. She was appointed MBE in 1960, and was awarded the Australian natural history medallion by the Field Naturalists' Club of Victoria in 1975.

Although suffering from hypothyroidism Miss Ashby travelled widely: every spring from 1963 to 1977 she drove alone to Western Australia, dividing her time between the Geraldton and Albany areas; each summer she went to the Australian Alps. She moved in 1972 from Wittunga to a home unit at Victor Harbor, a short drive from her nephew's farm, Mount Alma, near Inman Valley. In her eighties and walking with the aid of two sticks, she would work on 'Sandy Reserve', an area of partially cleared scrub on Mount Alma set aside for her plantings, and enjoy the 'bush air', which she believed had special therapeutic powers. She died on 12 August 1987 at Victor Harbor. A lifelong member of the Society of Friends, she was buried with a simple Quaker ceremony in the Inman Valley cemetery. The paintings which she had given to the museum are now held by the State Herbarium, South Australia.

E. L. Robertson, *Alison Ashby's Wildflowers of Southern Australia* (1981) and *Restoration of Grassy Woodland* (1999); *Friends of the Botanic Gardens Gazette* (Adelaide), Aug-Sept 1991, p 85, Oct-Dec 1991, p 113; private information and personal knowledge.
                                ENID ROBERTSON

ASHBY, SIR ROBERT (ROBIN) WILLIAM (1907-1981), bank officer and premier, was born on 4 April 1907 in Sydney, eldest of three sons of Adelaide-born William James Askin, sailor and later tram driver, and Ellen Laura Halliday, née Rowe, a widow, born in New South Wales. After spending his pre-school years with his mother in Stuart Town, young Askin (known as Billy) and his family moved to Glebe, where his parents married on 29 September 1916. Educated at Glebe Public School and awarded a bursary to Sydney Technical High School, he completed his Intermediate certificate in 1921.

At the age of 15, after a very short time in the electrical trade, Askin joined the

open the conference to the press; later, he and Bolte organised an 'emergency' premiers' conference, without Gorton, to publicise the plight of the States. After the 1969 election, Askin had helped to save Gorton; in 1971, he helped to defeat him.

The Sydney Opera House and the Eastern Suburbs Railway were the two landmarks for which Askin most wanted to be remembered. The first was initiated by Cahill and the second was completed under Neville Wran. Without the opposition from community groups, and the 'green bans' imposed from 1971 by the New South Wales branch of the Builders' Labourers' Federation, Askin might also have been remembered for the redevelopment of The Rocks, Kings Cross and Woolloomooloo, developments on parkland at Kelly's Bush and Eastlakes, and the building of a sports complex on parts of Moore and Centennial parks.

Askin's style was characterised by his deputy, (Sir) Eric Willis, as a 'slow, gradual, painstaking process of attacking one issue after another'. He was 'fanatically tidy'. An affable boss and gifted after-dinner speaker, he was a 'loner', but a happy one. Few of those who worked with him thought that they really knew him.

A law and order man, at least when there were votes in it, he told a luncheon in 1968 that when demonstrators ran out in front of the car in which he and Prime Minister Harold Holt [q.v.14] were travelling with President Lyndon Johnson in October 1966, he had said something like: 'It's a pity we couldn't run over them'. A journalist reported him as saying that he wanted the car to 'run over the bastards'. It was for that statement, more than any other, that he was remembered. He never corrected it because he thought it had done him no harm. His 'gravel voice, pugnacious presence and lack of kid gloves were trademarks'. He always wore his Returned Services League of Australia badge.

Although he attacked the Federal Labor Party in 1972 for advocating 'abortion on demand', 'homosexuality' and 'a soft approach to drug offenders and pornographers', and for wanting 'to flood the country with black people', Askin remained a pragmatist rather than an ideologue; he pushed such issues because, persuaded by Jack Kane [q.v.], he thought they might win votes. For expediency he had dropped his support for the reintroduction of capital punishment, for having Christian religion taught in schools, and for having communists barred from the public service; he had weakened his stand on the Summary Offences Act, 1970, targeted at 'rabid Communists' and 'professional agitators', after an adverse by-election result in 1973; and he had settled a power strike that year through 'talk, talk, talk', notwithstanding the pressure he was under to send in the police.

Askin's electoral focus was on the 'extreme centre'; this encompassed '80 per cent of the public'. Of the rest: the 10 per cent from 'big business', on the 'extreme right', had to vote for him; the 10 per cent of 'communists and radicals on the extreme left' would never vote for him. That the Liberals had to be a party of the 'middle' was also Carrick's view. None the less, relations with Carrick were strained; by the 1970s Willis deputised for Askin at meetings of the party executive. Carrick was uneasy with the 'burlesque' of the Liberal and Country parties presenting themselves as different but the same and insisted that Liberals should compete with the Country Party in three-cornered contests, albeit on a selective basis. He disapproved of Askin's taking money from business and directing it to Liberal candidates, to election advertising of his own, and to the Democratic Labor Party to help it win Labor and Catholic votes in particular seats and to deliver them, via preferences, to the Liberal Party. Askin refused to pass on the donations to the party for fear, he said, that they might be used for Federal rather than State purposes.

Askin's political skills included a 'phenomenal memory for faces', a feel for public opinion and a 'flair for manoeuvre'. Ahead of each election, he ensured that electoral boundaries were redistributed. He abolished compulsory voting in local elections, dismissed the Labor-dominated Sydney City Council and changed the city's electoral boundaries. Shrewdly, he refused to debate with the leader of the Opposition believing that it would put his 'weights up'. He was an astute manipulator of his cabinet, too. Sometimes he led his opponents to believe he was not going to do something he actually intended to do. At other times he misled his allies. After the ballot to determine his successor, he insisted that he had voted for Willis. But Askin had long thought Willis lacked political judgment: he supported Lewis.

At the height of Askin's popularity, candidates had to be restrained from dropping 'Liberal' from their publicity material and substituting 'Askin'. But towards the end of his career, an opinion poll reported that, of all the premiers, Askin was 'the most unpopular'. Elected in place of a Labor regime seen as 'worm-eaten' by 'graft, corruption, nepotism and general chicanery', the coalition was responsible for a police force widely seen as even more corrupt. According to David Hickie, while campaigning for office Askin had seen 'both the potential votes and finance available to him through the SP network'. Certainly Askin, who attended assiduously to inequities in police pensions, did little to encourage the enforcement of the laws on gambling, other than to call for police reports; he rejected demands for a racing control board; and rather than bet off-course through the Totalisator Agency Board, established in 1964, he maintained an account with one of the biggest SP firms in town. He 'almost entirely' ignored the recommendations of Justice Athol Moffitt's royal commission on allegations of organised crime in clubs.

In the week of Askin's funeral, under the heading 'Askin: Friend to Organised Crime', the *National Times* published the first of a series of articles by Hickie that accused Askin of wide-ranging corruption. Hickie was to expand on his claims in a book, *The Prince and the Premier* (1985). One of the most serious accusations, attributed to an 'impeccable' source, was that over the last seven years of Askin's premiership, Perce Galea [q.v.14], head of an illegal gambling empire, had paid him $100 000 a year in bribes. Another was that Sydney bookmakers had given Askin $55 000 on the eve of his retirement as a reward for his not doubling their turnover tax, a payment Askin described unapologetically as 'a gratuity from some members of the racing fraternity'. A third focused on the claim that businessmen had been buying knighthoods from Askin for $20 000 to $60 000 each.

According to Donald Horne, at the end of the 1965 campaign Askin had told one of his own staff that he was going to win, and to 'think of the money we'll make!' Even before his death Askin had been accused of being corrupt. But the sources turned out to be anonymous, as they were in Hickie's work, and defamation actions were settled out of court in Askin's favour. In 1993 the *Sun-Herald* took the extraordinary step of holding an inquiry, headed by a retired coroner, Kevin Waller. To the dismay of Evan Whitton, who organised the investigation, Waller believed that 'the evidence acceptable to a legal mind was miniscule'.

Throughout the Askin years, David Marr argued, a 'gullible press', with some 'very honourable exceptions', had 'much to answer for'. Askin's own view of the press was rather different. He always regarded journalists with suspicion, reducing the frequency of press conferences, and sometimes introducing controversial legislation late at night, allowing journalists little time to scrutinise it. John O'Hara recalled that, early in his premiership, Askin 'tried to bully journalists' whose writings displeased him, by cutting them off from news and by alluding to his close associations with their 'bosses'. To counter hostile reporting, his staff wrote to the press under assumed names.

In 1961 Carrick asked Askin not to appear on television without the party's permission. Brian White [q.v.] observed that, after Alan Green's death in 1970, Askin 'failed increasingly to get on with anyone in the press, radio or television'. Bill Peach wrote that when cornered, Askin 'resorted to a mixture of evasion, insult and threat'. Attacking journalists, Askin believed, added to his popularity. After 'needling programs' on illegal casinos and on police behaviour at moratoriums, in 1973 he accused those involved with the program 'This Day Tonight' of being 'extreme radicals' operating a 'subversive unit'; in September he transferred responsibility for the police from himself to Maddison.

Known since the war as Robert or Bob, Askin disliked the name Robin. Anticipating his appointment, on his own recommendation, as KCMG in 1972, he changed his name in 1971 to Robert; he was elevated to GCMG in 1975. The University of New South Wales had awarded him an honorary D.Litt. in 1966. The Antioch Orthodox Church gave him the Order of St Peter and St Paul (1972) for his services to ethnic minorities and he was appointed an Officer of the Lebanese Order of Cedars (1973). An executive member (1953-55) of the Food for Babies and Good Samaritan Fund, he was also a councillor, later a life patron, of the Royal Society for the Prevention of Cruelty to Animals, New South Wales; the RSPCA was to be a major beneficiary of Lady Askin's estate. A member of the University Club, an honorary member of the Royal Commonwealth Society (New South Wales branch) and (appointed by his government) a member (1966-77) of the Sydney Cricket Ground Trust, Askin was also chairman (1974) of the trustees of Randwick racecourse. In retirement, he joined (1976-80) the board of Thomas Nationwide Transport Ltd.

Askin died on 9 September 1981 at Darlinghurst and was cremated. Anticipating that questions might be asked about his estate, valued at $1.958 million, he had explained to his former press secretary, Geoffrey Reading, that for years he had been 'the highest paid public officer in the State', that 'his lifestyle was frugal', that he had 'taken out a series of maturing endowment policies', that 'he was a very successful punter', that he had benefited from the will of his brother, and that he was skilled in financial affairs and a most successful stock market investor. Though the Department of Taxation made no finding of criminality, it determined that a substantial part of Askin's estate was generated through undisclosed income from sources other than shares or punting and taxed it accordingly. Lady Askin, childless, and a devoted wife who almost certainly had no idea that he conducted a number of extramarital affairs, survived him and inherited most of his estate. Her estate was valued at $3.725 million; a substantial part of it, too, was taxed. A portrait (1968) of Askin by Judy Cassab hangs in the New South Wales Parliament.

B. White, *White on the Media* (1975); P. Tiver, *The Liberal Party* (1978); D. Hickie, *The Prince and the*

Premier (1985); A. Moffitt, *A Quarter to Midnight* (1985); G. Reading, *High Climbers* (1989); B. Peach, *This Day Tonight* (1992); E. Whitton, *Trial by Voodoo* (1994); D. Horne, *Into the Open* (2000); A. Curthoys, *Freedom Ride* (2002); *SMH*, 18 July 1959, p 1, 17 Feb 1968, p 2, 4 Mar 1970, p 2, 28 Jan 1971, p 6, 1 June 1974, p 8, 3 Jan 1975, p 6, 10 Sept 1981, p 14; *Bulletin*, 10 Feb 1962, p 14, 11 Jan 1975, p 23, 1 July 1986, p 53; *Nation*, 17 Apr 1965, p 4; *Austn Qtrly*, June 1967, p 36; *Austn Financial Review*, 2 Jan 1975, p 2; *Quadrant*, Jan-Feb 1975, p 37; *Daily Mirror* (Sydney), 10 Sept 1981, p 9; *National Times*, 13-19 Sept 1981, p 1, 29 Mar-4 Apr 1985, p 25; *Sydney Review*, May 1993, p 5; M. Pratt, interview with R. Askin (ts, 1976, NLA); private information.   MURRAY GOOT

ATKINSON, ROBERT LAMONT (1902-1986), grazier and cattle-breeder, was born on 31 January 1902 at South Yarra, Melbourne, fourth of five children of Robert James Atkinson, a pastoralist from North Queensland, and his Victorian-born wife Constance Charlotte, née Lamont. Educated at The King's School, Parramatta, New South Wales, 'Monty' helped to manage the family's Queensland properties including Cashmere, near Mount Garnet, and Wairuna, west of Ingham. On 12 March 1934 at St John's Church of England, Cairns, he married Ruth Dowse Collins. After his father's death in 1939 he acquired Cashmere, where he established the Glenruth Poll Hereford cattle stud. Four years later he bought Mungalla station at Ingham. One of the first graziers in North Queensland to grow improved pastures, he also produced some outstanding thorough-bred horses at Mungalla. As a young man he had been a successful amateur jockey.

Early in the 1930s Atkinson bought two cross-bred bulls, descended from a *Bos indicus* (Zebu or Brahman) bull that had been brought to North Queensland from the Melbourne Zoological Gardens about 1912. Aiming to produce cattle better suited to the tropics than British breeds (*Bos taurus*), he mated the bulls with Shorthorn, Devon and Hereford cows and assessed the various cross-breeds. He decided that red cattle were better adapted than beasts of other colours to both the humid coastal districts and the dry interior. In 1941 he purchased some calves which had resulted from breeding experiments initiated by J. A. Gilruth [q.v.9] of the Council for Scientific and Industrial Research, and continued crossing Shorthorns with Brahmans. By 1957 he had played a major role in producing a new breed which became known as the Drought-master. Generally red in colour, these cattle were highly resistant to ticks and tolerant of drought conditions and yielded a good quality beef carcass.

In 1952 Atkinson was founding president of the Australian Zebu-Cross Beef Cattle Breeders' Association (later the Australian Tropical Beef Breeders' Association). With Syd Staines in 1956 he took up a property at Gusap in the Markham Valley, New Guinea, and successfully grazed cattle there for several years. He was founding president (1962-63) and patron (1964-86) of the Droughtmaster Stud Breeders' Society and, as a classifier for the breed, travelled great distances to advise cattlemen. In 1963 he purchased the historic Valley of Lagoons station from the estate of J. S. Love [q.v.10].

Divorced in 1950, on 24 March 1951 at St Andrew's Presbyterian Church, Townsville, Atkinson had married Edna Grace Lillian Grant. After retiring to Townsville in 1966, he acted as a consultant to the family enterprises, and published three books: *Northern Pioneers* (1979), *Go West, Young Man* (c.1981) and *Bush Tales and Memoirs* (1984). He retained his life-long interest in horse-racing and was a life member of the Townsville Turf Club. Survived by his wife, and the elder daughter and two sons of his first marriage, he died on 2 July 1986 at Townsville and was cremated with Anglican rites. In 2002 the Droughtmaster breed was reputedly the second most numerous in northern Australia.

L. McDonald, *Cattle Country* (1988); *Procs of the Royal Soc of Qld*, vol 98, 1987, p 1; *Droughtmaster Digest*, no 3, 1986, p 6; *Townsville Bulletin*, 7 July 1986, p 4.   DAWN MAY

ATYEO, SAMUEL LAURENCE (1910-1990), artist, designer and diplomat, was born on 6 January 1910 at Brunswick, Melbourne, son of Victorian-born parents Alfred Vincent Atyeo, chauffeur, and his wife Olivia Beatrice Victoria, née Cohen. In childhood Sam suffered from bronchial illness and during prolonged periods of convalescence occupied himself with drawing. He studied architecture at the Working Men's College and attended the National Gallery schools (Grace Joel prize, 1930). His submission for the gallery's travelling scholarship was rejected because it lampooned the director, Bernard Hall [q.v.9]. The painting was controversially unveiled in the Collins Street shop of Frederick Ward [q.v.], a furniture and interior designer. Atyeo later replaced Ward as main designer at Cynthia Reed's [q.v.15 Nolan] shop in Little Collins Street, where, exhibiting his paintings, he met H. V. Evatt and his wife Mary Alice [qq.v.14]; they became lifelong friends.

At a time when Australian painters such as George Bell and William 'Jock' Frater [qq.v.7,8] were preoccupied with post-impressionism, Atyeo was impelled to explore emergent styles in European art. John and Sunday Reed [qq.v.] encouraged him and he joined their circle.

In 1934 he produced what is believed to be the first Australian abstract canvas, 'Organised Line to Yellow' (National Gallery of Australia, Canberra), in the style of Paul Klee. Atyeo's output over the next three years influenced the development of an Australian school of abstract painting. Applying his architectural training, he also designed façades and interiors, notably for Edward Dyason [q.v.8].

In October 1936 Atyeo sailed for Paris. There Louise Dyer [q.v.8] befriended him and he regularly attended her salon of artists and composers. Other than surrealism, which he regarded as stillborn, Atyeo delighted in the artistic movements of the day. His socialist views were strengthened by contact with refugees of the Spanish Civil War; he designed propaganda posters for the Republicans. In 1939 he bought a farm at Vence in the Alpes-Maritimes region of France. He moved there with Moya Dyring [q.v.14] after the German occupation of Paris in 1940. Atyeo and Dyring made their way to the Bahamas then to Dominica. They were married in a civil ceremony on Barbados on 29 May 1941 and later divorced.

Evatt, as minister for external affairs, personally recruited Atyeo into his service, probably in 1942. During a temporary appointment that was to last for about eight years, he enjoyed unhindered access to Evatt; this intimacy and Evatt's use of him to inform on officers in the Department of External Affairs caused many career diplomats to be suspicious and jealous of him. Atyeo was first attached to the office of the director-general of war supplies procurement in New York. Soon he was accompanying Evatt in both official and unofficial capacities as one of his few trusted advisers. Atyeo earned a reputation for gregarious bluntness and intemperate speech; (Sir) Winston Churchill is reported to have described him as the most foul-mouthed diplomat in the world.

By 1945 Atyeo was a second secretary with the Australian legation in Paris. He was often paired with a senior diplomat, John Hood, to handle briefs Evatt regarded as sensitive. In 1947 he assisted Hood, the chief Australian representative with the United Nations special committees on the Balkans and Palestine. Unlike Evatt, Atyeo opposed the partitioning of Palestine. Atyeo's selection in 1948 to succeed W. R. Hodgson [q.v.9] as Australian delegate on the Balkans committee was questioned by the Federal Opposition and the Commonwealth Public Service Clerical Association. With the fall of the Australian Labor Party government in December 1949, Atyeo lost Evatt's protection and was dismissed from the service on 1 April 1950.

Atyeo returned to his farm at Vence and grew roses and grapes. In November 1950 he married Anne Lecoultre. Having virtually ceased painting in the late 1930s, he returned to his easel about 1960. He rarely visited Australia and seldom exhibited after World War II; among his Australian exhibitions, one was organised by John Reed at George's Gallery (1963), Melbourne, and another by Jennifer Phipps at Heide Park and Art Gallery (1982-83). Survived by his wife, Atyeo died on 26 May 1990 at Vence.

The importance of Atyeo to the modernist movement in Australian painting and design is often neglected. He valued the sheer power of colour and its relationship with other arts such as music and poetry. His approach to modern interior design was premised on a fusion of utility and simplicity in keeping with contemporary social and economic conditions of domestic living. He championed greater use of natural light, brighter interiors and diversity of materials. In later life he disparaged his diplomatic career as mere 'international politicking'.

R. Haese, *Rebels and Precursors* (1981); J. Phipps, 'Atyeo', in *Atyeo: Heide Park and Art Gallery* (c1982); *Herald* (Melbourne), 3 Jan 1949, p 3; *Argus* (Melbourne), 4 Jan 1949, p 3; *Sun News-Pictorial* (Melbourne), 19 Aug 1963, p 23; *Age* (Melbourne), 13 Jan 1983, p 10; *Australian*, 10 Feb 1983, p 12; D. Mandel, Justice and Expediency (PhD thesis, Univ of Melbourne, 1999); G. Cuthbert, Changing the Landscape: The Life and Art of Moya Dyring (MA thesis, Univ of Melbourne, 2002); private information.   DANIEL MANDEL

AUCHMUTY, JAMES JOHNSTON (1909-1981), historian and vice-chancellor, was born on 29 November 1909 at Portadown, (Northern) Ireland, elder son of James Wilson Auchmuty, Church of Ireland clergyman, and his wife Annie Todd, née Johnston. James attended the Royal School, Armagh, and Trinity College, Dublin (BA, 1931; MA, 1934; Ph.D., 1935), from which he graduated with a first-class moderatorship in modern history and political science. He was elected to the position of auditor of the College Historical Society for the 1931-32 session. On 20 October 1934 in Creggan parish church, County Armagh, Northern Ireland, he married Mary Margaret Walters, an American who was a Vassar College graduate.

Abandoning thoughts of ordination after a single term at Ripon College, Oxford, Auchmuty returned to Dublin and pursued a career as a schoolmaster at Sandford Park School (1934-46), while lecturing in education at Trinity College (1938-43). He stood unsuccessfully for one of the university's three senate seats in 1943. A staunch internationalist and supporter of Allied engagement in World War II, he was unable to join the armed forces because of poor eyesight, and instead was recruited into the British Military Intelligence 6. He carried out intelligence work and pro-British cultural propaganda in Ireland. Denounced by Eamon de Valera as one of a number of persons working for non-Irish interests, he left after the war to avoid internment. A position of associate professor of history was found for him at Farouk I University at Alexandria, Egypt, where he taught and continued his work of political reporting and propaganda until obliged to leave the country, his savings confiscated, on the overthrow of King Farouk in 1952.

Through contacts in British intelligence, Auchmuty was recommended for the post of senior lecturer in history at the New South Wales University of Technology, Sydney (later the University of New South Wales), to which he moved in 1952. By this time he had ceased to be active as an intelligence operative. In 1954 the university's director, (Sir) Philip Baxter [q.v.], sent him, as associate professor, to head the school of humanities and social sciences at Newcastle University College. Promoted to professor of history and deputy-warden of the University College next year, he became warden in 1960 and foundation vice-chancellor when the college gained autonomy as the University of Newcastle in 1965.

Auchmuty had been elected a fellow of the Royal Historical Society in 1938. He was a foundation member (1956) and chairman (1962-65) of the Australian Humanities Research Council and a foundation fellow (1969) and member (1969-70) of the council of its successor, the Australian Academy of the Humanities. An active figure (chairman, 1969-71) in the Australian Vice-Chancellors' Committee, he was also a council member (1967-74) of the Association of Commonwealth Universities and was awarded its Symons medal in 1974. From 1973 to 1976 he chaired the Australian National Commission for the United Nations Educational, Scientific and Cultural Organization. He was appointed CBE in 1971 and in 1974 was awarded honorary degrees by the universities of Sydney (D.Litt.), Newcastle (D.Litt.), and Trinity College, Dublin (LL D). On his retirement from the University of Newcastle that year, the library and the sports centre were named after him, reflecting two of his particular interests. He and his wife then moved to Canberra.

Apart from his doctoral thesis on nineteenth-century United States government policy on Latin-American independence, Auchmuty's earliest publications were in Irish history, including a history of Irish education. A champion of the biographical approach to history, he wrote studies of the Irish historian William Lecky and the politician Sir Thomas Wyse. He turned himself into a historian of nineteenth-century Australia, concentrating on the Anglo-Irish influence. He was an early member of the national committee for the *Australian Dictionary of Biography*, being one of the few members of the group to have good relations with both Malcolm Ellis [q.v.14] and Manning Clark. Auchmuty wrote the *ADB* entries on John Hunter, D'Arcy Wentworth and Josiah Brown Pearson [qq.v.1,2,5]. Unusually for a vice-chancellor, he remained active in both teaching and research while carrying a heavy administrative load.

Of portly build and with a large head, Auchmuty was a man of perpetually ebullient character whose bluff manner sometimes alienated others. Accusations of overweening ambition had some foundation, though his rise to a vice-chancellorship was due as much to the patronage of Baxter and to the vagaries of good fortune as to his qualities of character. Once installed, however, he showed himself a shrewd and capable leader who won the admiration of his fellow vice-chancellors.

In 1969 Auchmuty was appointed to head a national advisory committee on the teaching of Asian languages and cultures. The committee reported in 1970; eventually the governments of both (Sir) William McMahon and Gough Whitlam agreed to implement its recommendations, leading to an expansion in the teaching of Asian studies in Australia. After his retirement, Auchmuty headed a national committee on teacher education (1978-80): its recommendations were largely overtaken by government cost-cutting and the amalgamations of universities and teachers colleges. The punishing schedule required for the preparation of the report may have adversely affected his health. He died on 15 October 1981 at Bloomington, Indiana, United States of America. His wife survived him, as did a son and daughter; their younger son had died in infancy. Auchmuty was cremated and his ashes were placed in the columbarium of Christ Church Cathedral, Newcastle, of which he had been a regular parishioner while vice-chancellor.

Though he would have wished to be remembered chiefly as a historian, his espousal of the 'Great Man' approach—as opposed to a concentration on broad social movements—put him at odds with the tendencies of his day, and he was not an influential figure in his field. His contribution to university administration, and notably his role in leading the University of Newcastle to autonomy, was Auchmuty's most significant achievement.

Trinity College (Dublin, Ireland), *Record Volume* (1951); D. Wright, *Looking Back: A History of the University of Newcastle* (1992); C. C. O'Brien, *Memoir* (1998); P. O'Farrell, *UNSW, a Portrait* (1999); K. R. Dutton, *Auchmuty* (2000); D. Rowe, interview with J. J. Auchmuty (ts, 1981, Univ of Newcastle Archives); J. J. Auchmuty papers (Univ of Newcastle Archives).   KENNETH R. DUTTON

AUSTIN, ALBERT GORDON (1918-1990), professor of education, was born on 20 September 1918 at Brunswick, Melbourne, son of Albert Ernest Austin, a New Zealand-born potter and lay preacher with the Churches of Christ, and his Victorian-born wife Minnie, née Plain. The Austins had adopted a daughter in 1908. Educated at Brunswick East State School, and at Coburg and Melbourne High schools, 'Bon' became a student-teacher in 1936 and that year joined the Melbourne University Rifles, Citizen Military Forces. After attending (1938-39) the Teachers' College, he was appointed to Murtoa Higher Elementary School.

On 15 June 1940 Austin enlisted in the Australian Imperial Force. A mature poem he published in the Teachers' College journal, *Trainee* (December), revealed the conflicting emotions with which he embarked for the Middle East. In June 1941 he was commissioned as a lieutenant and in March 1942 posted to the 2/24th Battalion. He led his platoon in the assault against Tel el Eisa Ridge, Egypt, on 22 July. His superior officers in 'C' Company having been hit, he took command. When ordered to withdraw his men, he remained behind and tended the wounded, becoming a casualty himself with a bullet in the leg. He was awarded the Military Cross.

Returning to Australia, Austin served with his unit in New Guinea from September 1943 to January 1944. He was promoted to captain (July 1944) and performed intelligence duties in Australia (1944-45) and on Bougainville (March-August 1945). On 12 February 1944 at Wesley Church, Melbourne, he had married Sylvia Amelia Smith, a stenographer. His AIF appointment terminated on 10 September 1945. War service had transformed him. Five ft 7 ins (170 cm) tall, he held himself erect and grew a moustache; his clear, confident speech left little trace of his austere upbringing and days as a student-teacher. He resumed teaching and attended the University of Melbourne (BA, 1948; Dip.Ed., 1949; B.Ed., 1954; M.Ed., 1956) on a Commonwealth Reconstruction Training Scheme scholarship.

In 1950 Austin was transferred to University High School and appointed part-time lecturer in method of social studies in the university's faculty of education. His marriage was amicably dissolved that year. At Scots Church, Melbourne, on 20 January 1951 he married Helene Iris Chalmers, a fellow schoolteacher. Although an inspiring classroom teacher, he resigned in 1956 and became a full-time university lecturer. His faculty was held in low esteem in the university and was torn apart by disagreements over educational theory. Austin, an empiricist, began researching the history of education to promote the academic respectability of the discipline and also to fill a gap in Australian history.

Despite a heavy teaching program, he produced *George William Rusden and National Education in Australia 1849-1862* (1958), *Australian Education 1788-1900* (1961) and *Select Documents in Australian Education 1788-1900* (1963). *Australian Education* was a meticulously researched and elegantly written account of the development of public education, concentrating on the tug of war between church and state. In 1963 he was awarded a senior Imperial Trust Fund fellowship, which took him to London. His edited volume *The Webbs' Australian Diary 1898* (1965) was an outcome of this visit. In 1966 he shared the Encyclopaedia Britannica award for education. Teaching, researching and writing brought him fulfilment.

In June 1966 Austin was appointed professor and dean of education. Endowed with neither taste nor talent for administration, he found this work an unwanted burden. He chaired the council of the Melbourne State College, the board of management of Melbourne University Press and the council of University High School. Within his faculty, he supported the establishment of the centre for the study of higher education (1967) and the introduction of Gwyn Dow's innovative 'Course B' for trainee-teachers. He was courteously formal in his professional relationships in the faculty, but wit and informality distinguished 'Bon's table' at University House.

Having suffered poor health throughout his tenure as head of education, Austin retired in 1978 and moved to Fairhaven. The academic board praised him for his humanity, helpfulness, tact and generosity, and affectionate minutes of appreciation from colleagues cheered him. He died on 20 August 1990 at Fairhaven and was cremated. His wife and their two daughters survived him.

S. Murray-Smith (ed), *Melbourne Studies in Education 1979* (1979); J. R. Poynter and C. Rasmussen, *A Place Apart* (1996); B. Falk, *The Figure in the Foreground* (2002); D. S. Garden, *Teacher Training in Carlton* (PhD thesis, Univ of Melbourne, 1992); private information.   BARBARA FALK

AUSTIN, MAURICE ('BUNNY') (1916-1985), soldier, was born on 15 December 1916 at Geelong, Victoria, son of Eugene John Austin, grocer, and his wife Helena Margaret, née Collins, both Victorian born. Educated at Christian Brothers' College, Geelong, he entered the Royal Military College, Duntroon, Federal (Australian) Capital Territory, in March 1935. He graduated as a lieutenant in December 1938 and was posted to the Darwin Mobile Force. On 1 May 1940 he was seconded to the Australian Imperial Force and appointed adjutant of the 2/27th Battalion. At St Roch's Catholic Church, Glen Iris,

Melbourne, on 26 September that year, before sailing to the Middle East, he married Enid Veronica, daughter of Joseph Lyons [q.v.10] and his wife Dame Enid [q.v.].

In February 1941 Austin was made brigade major of the 21st Brigade, but two months later he was sent to the Middle East Staff School, Haifa, Palestine, thus missing the Syrian campaign, and in August he was posted to the AIF (Middle East) Junior Staff School as an instructor. He was one of the officers despatched by air in February 1942 to General Sir Archibald (Earl) Wavell's headquarters in Java. It was closed on 25 February and he reached Broome, Western Australia, on the 27th. He became an instructor at the Staff School (Australia), Duntroon, in April. In March 1943, now a major, he moved to Advanced Land Headquarters, Brisbane, before going to the operations branch of headquarters, New Guinea Force, in August. Appointed brigade major of the 29th Brigade in December, he joined it at Lae. The brigade arrived on Bougainville in November 1944 and was involved in limited operations against the Japanese. In May 1945 Austin was transferred to the calm of RMC, Duntroon, as an instructor. He was mentioned in despatches, but in five years of war service had not been given a command.

Promoted to temporary lieutenant colonel in October 1946, Austin was posted to the Australian Military Mission, Washington. Four years in the United States of America on Australian pay was a trying experience for the Austins with four children. Returning to Australia in May 1950, he became general staff officer, 1st grade, of the 3rd Division. In June 1952 he was appointed commanding officer of the 2nd Battalion, Royal Australian Regiment, but on 20 October he was suddenly transferred to command 1RAR, fighting in Korea. A stranger to the battalion, he faced an aggressive enemy in mountainous country and bitter winter. For his successful conduct of operations, particularly in defending Hill 355, he was awarded the Distinguished Service Order. 1RAR left for home in March 1953 and in November Austin was sent to Western Command as chief administrative staff officer. Somehow in 1949-55 he qualified as an accountant.

As director of infantry (1954-57) at Army Headquarters, Melbourne, Austin rewrote the manual of infantry minor tactics and was promoted to colonel (June 1955). He commanded the Jungle Training Centre, Canungra, Queensland, in 1957-58. While colonel, general staff, Eastern Command (from July 1958), he was also commander (1960-61) of the 1st Logistic Support Force. This double task, in a period of reorganisation, 'required superhuman effort' which affected his health. He was appointed OBE in 1962.

Austin went to Army Headquarters, Canberra, in January 1962 as director of personnel services and devoted himself 'to the complex and often infuriating problems' of this appointment. He became deputy adjutant-general in November 1964 and rose to brigadier in February 1965. Travelling often to military stations at home and abroad, he worked to explain the Defence Forces Retirement Benefits Scheme to the soldier; as he put it: 'At all times we must watch his interests'. This concern for others, like the warmth and humour that endeared him to his family and his friends, illuminated Austin's service in the army. Always and to all he was a good companion.

Retiring from the army on 3 February 1971, Austin was appointed army historian. His passion for Australian military history was well known; now he could devote himself to it. In 1979 his research culminated in the publication of *The Army in Australia 1840-50*. A member of the armed services working party of the Australian Dictionary of Biography, author of articles for the *ADB* and service journals, editor (1981-83) of the *Journal of the Royal United Services Institute of Australia*, member (1982-83) of the Australian War Memorial's military historical atlas committee, and consultant (1981-84) to the Australian Heritage Commission, 'Bunny' Austin enjoyed 'retirement', but this was clouded by his failing health. He died of myocardial infarction on 13 October 1985 in Royal Canberra Hospital and was buried in Gungahlin cemetery; his wife and their two daughters and three sons survived him.

R. O'Neill, *Australia in the Korean War 1950-53*, vol 2 (1985); *Sabretache*, vol 26, no 4, 1985, p 45; *Austn Army*, 11 Feb 1971, p 8; Austin papers (AWM); private information and personal knowledge.

A. J. HILL

AVERY, ERIC NUGENT (1907-1986), oil company executive, was born on 8 May 1907 at Alford, Lincolnshire, England, son of Leonard Ray Avery, bank accountant, and his wife Florence Seaton, née Loweth. Educated at Sedbergh School, Yorkshire, where he was head student, Eric read law as an exhibitioner at St John's College, Cambridge (BA, 1930; MA, 1944). In 1928 he won a Henry P. Davison scholarship to study economics at Princeton University, New Jersey, United States of America. Joining the elite international service of the Royal Dutch/Shell Group, by 1930 he was on the staff of the subsidiary Asiatic Petroleum Co. (North China) Ltd, Shanghai. He acquired knowledge of Oriental philosophy and at the College of Chinese Studies, Peking, learned to speak and write Mandarin and to speak Cantonese. In addition, he spoke French and German fluently, knew some Italian, understood Spanish and read widely in Latin and Greek. He served (1936-37) in the Shanghai Municipal Police (Specials).

Transferring to the Shell Co. of Australia Ltd in 1939, Avery occupied executive positions in Melbourne. In 1940-41 he served part time in the Militia as a lieutenant with the 4th Provost Company. On 19 October 1944 at Christ Church, South Yarra, he married, with Anglican rites, Freda Marjorie (d.1983), daughter of Eric Connolly [q.v.8]; she had worked as a secretary. Avery was promoted to general manager of the Shell Co. of Australia in July 1947. When the conglomerate's head office in London appointed a local board in 1951, he became inaugural chairman. His determined vision for Australia led to Shell's building at Geelong the first major postwar oil refinery. After a prolonged and intricate business manoeuvre, in 1951 Shell surprised its competitors by introducing single-brand petrol retailing by service stations tied to the company. These initiatives changed the face of the industry in Australia.

In 1955 Avery was transferred to London. Three years later he resigned from Shell and returned with his family to Melbourne. As chairman and chief executive, he welded together a number of small exploration companies as the Associated Oil Group, dependent for capital on the good will of mainly small investors. In the Roma district of Queensland in the 1960s the group found several minor natural gas fields, which it developed to supply the Brisbane region. The group also discovered huge deposits of coal at Hail Creek, near Mackay, in 1968. As chairman of Claremont Petroleum NL from 1981, Avery helped build the company into a medium-sized petroleum producer and owner of pipelines. He was also a director of Jennings Industries Ltd, Dun & Bradstreet (Australia) Pty Ltd and other companies.

Avery had been a founder (later chairman and life member) of the Australian Petroleum Exploration Association, established in 1959 to give the exploration industry a united voice and to improve its reputation. His background, wisdom and standing helped advance the APEA's aims. He served on the board of the Alfred Hospital for nineteen years. In 1970 he was appointed CBE. A sportsman, he enjoyed polo in China and golf in Melbourne and ever rejoiced in his Hawks Club tie from Cambridge. In 1968 he became honorary consul for Brazil, a role that allowed full play to his gift for entertaining. He led a vigorous social life, lunching daily at one of his clubs, travelling extensively and offering hospitality to a wide circle of friends at his home in Toorak. Because of his fey sense of humour, English reserve and telling turn of phrase, his colleagues found it easier to respect him than to share the love for him of his close friends. He retired aged 77. Survived by his son and two daughters, he died on 8 January 1986 at Darlinghurst, Sydney, and was cremated.

R. Murray, *Go Well: One Hundred Years of Shell in Australia* (2001); *Herald* (Melbourne), 6 Feb 1974, p 2; *Age* (Melbourne), 13 Jan 1986, p 22; private information.   ROBERT MURRAY

AXFORD, THOMAS LESLIE ('JACK') (1894-1983), soldier, labourer and clerk, was born on 18 June 1894 at Carrieton, South Australia, son of Walter Richard Axford, an auctioneer from Tasmania, and his South Australian-born wife Margaret Ann, née McQuillan. The family moved to Coolgardie, Western Australia, when he was 2. Educated at the local state school, he worked as a labourer for the Boulder City Brewery Co. Ltd. On 19 July 1915 he enlisted in the Australian Imperial Force. Five ft 7¼ ins (171 cm) tall, with grey eyes, black hair and a dark complexion, he gave his religious denomination as Catholic. He arrived in the Middle East too late to serve at Gallipoli and in March 1916 joined the 16th Battalion at Tel el Kebir, Egypt.

Reaching France in June 1916, the battalion attacked towards Mouquet Farm, near Pozières, on 9 August. Axford was evacuated with shell-shock on the 11th, but he quickly rejoined his unit. A year later, on 10 August 1917, he suffered a shrapnel wound to his left knee at Gapaard Farm, Belgium. After treatment in hospital in England, he returned to his unit in January 1918 and next month was promoted to lance corporal. In March-April the 16th Battalion, as part of the 4th Brigade, stopped the German offensive at Hébuterne, France. Axford was awarded the Military Medal in May.

His most conspicuous hour came on 4 July 1918 at the battle of Hamel. The Allied barrage opened at 3.10 a.m. and when it lifted shortly afterwards the 16th Battalion attacked Vaire Wood. Axford's platoon reached the enemy defences but a neighbouring platoon was held up at the wire. Machine-guns inflicted many casualties among Axford's mates in the other platoon. He dashed to the flank, bombed the machine-gun crews, jumped into the trench and charged with his bayonet. In all, he killed ten enemy soldiers and captured six. Throwing the machine-guns over the parapet, he called the delayed platoon forward and then rejoined his own. In ninety-three minutes the victory of Hamel was complete. Axford's initiative and gallantry won him the Victoria Cross. 'I must have been mad', he commented later. On 14 July he was promoted to corporal.

In December 1918 Axford came home to Australia on furlough. Discharged from the army on 6 February 1919, he recommenced work as a labourer. At St Mary's Cathedral, Perth, on 27 November 1926 he married Lily Maud Foster, a shop assistant. They lived at Mount Hawthorn and had five children. Axford was employed by H. V. McKay [q.v.10] (Massey Harris) Pty Ltd and became a clerk. On 25 June 1941 he was mobilised in the Militia and posted to the District Records Office, Perth. Rising to sergeant in February 1943, he was discharged on 14 April 1947. In his leisure time 'Jack' regularly attended the races.

Axford attended the VC centenary celebrations in London in 1956. He was returning from a reunion of the Victoria Cross and George Cross Association when he died on 11 October 1983 on an aircraft between Dubai and Hong Kong. His wife had died three months earlier. Survived by their two sons and three daughters, he was cremated with full military honours. In 1985 his VC and other medals were presented to the Australian War Memorial, Canberra.

C. Longmore, *The Old Sixteenth* (1929); C. E. W. Bean, *The A.I.F. in France 1916* (1929), *The A.I.F. in France 1917* (1933), *The A.I.F. in France 1918*, 2 vols (1937, 1942); L. Wigmore (ed), *They Dared Mightily*, 2nd edn, revised and condensed by J. Williams and A. Staunton (1986); G. Gliddon, *VCs of the First World War: Spring Offensive 1918* (1997); *Listening Post* (WA), Summer 1983, p 29; B2455, item Axford T L (NAA).   P. L. EDGAR

B

BADCOCK, CLAYVEL LINDSAY (1914-1982), cricketer and farmer, was born on 10 April 1914 at Exton, Tasmania, second of three children of Tasmanian-born parents Lindsay Badcock, farmer, and his wife Lily May, née Cox. By the time 'Jack' left the local state school at 13 to work on the family farm, he was playing cricket for Exton, in the Westmorland association. Coached by his father, who had built a concrete pitch in the backyard of their home, in 1927-28 he attained the highest batting average in the association. He agreed two seasons later to play on turf for the Esk club in the Northern Tasmanian Cricket Association but, before he appeared for the club, he was selected in December 1929 for North (of Tasmania) against South. In February 1930 he joined the State team for a mainland tour. That month, aged 15 years 313 days, he played against Victoria at the Melbourne Cricket Ground.

Resuming his Tasmanian representation in 1931-32, Badcock experienced his best season in 1933-34, scoring 803 runs in five matches. In one innings, against Victoria at Launceston, he made 274 while severely bruised after falling off his motorcycle the day before. In March 1934 he was selected for an Australian second XI for a short tour of New Zealand, which was subsequently cancelled. To enhance his chances of playing for Australia, he moved to Adelaide in June and played first-class cricket for South Australia until 1941, while working in a furniture factory. Encouraged by (Sir) Donald Bradman, he soon ran up some large scores, including 325 against Victoria at the Adelaide Oval in February 1936.

Short and thickset, and possessing exceptionally strong wrists, Badcock excelled at playing cut and hook shots. He made his Test debut against England at Brisbane in December. At the MCG in February 1937 he scored 118 in the last Test of the series, and was selected to tour England in 1938. Although he enjoyed considerable success against county sides, he made only 32 runs in four Tests. In the seven Tests he played for his country he inexplicably averaged only 14.54, compared with a first-class average of 51.54 (97 matches, 7371 runs) over his career. Popular with his team-mates, he possessed an infectious laugh. He compiled a substantial record of the overseas trip with a movie camera.

Badcock continued to score heavily for South Australia, including 271 not out against New South Wales in December 1938 and 236 against Queensland in December 1939. After the Sheffield Shield competition was suspended in 1940 he participated in several first-class matches staged to raise money for the war effort. Suffering increasingly from sciatica, he returned permanently to the farm in Tasmania. On 6 April 1942 at St Matthew's Church of England, Prahran, Melbourne, he married Carol Dawn Cramond, a forewoman. He was a man of simple tastes who enjoyed fishing, shooting and playing golf. Survived by his wife, and their daughter and two sons, he died suddenly on 13 December 1982 at Exton and was cremated.

R. Finlay, 'Jack Badcock (1914-1982)', *Tasmanian Cricket Yearbook 1983/84*, p 52; *Examiner* (Launceston), 6 Dec 1929, p 3, 30 Dec 1933, p 7, 14 Dec 1982, p 39; *Mercury* (Hobart), 14 Dec 1982, p 36; *Sunday Tasmanian*, 22 Oct 1989, p 7; private information. RIC FINLAY

BADGER, HAROLD LINDSAY (1907-1981), jockey, was born on 10 October 1907 at Northcote, Melbourne, third of eight children and second son of Australian-born parents Ernest William Badger, boot clicker, and his wife Esther Kemp, née Moss. Two of Harold's brothers, Clarence and Eric, became jockeys. His great-grandfather, David Badger (1827-1890), had been a pioneering Baptist minister in South Australia. Harold grew up and attended school in semi-rural Montmorency. At 14 he was apprenticed to a Flemington-based trainer, Richard Bradfield, who proved to be an outstanding mentor. Bradfield often sent him to race in South Australia, where he did well, winning the Adelaide Cup on Stralia in 1925. When he finished his apprenticeship, Bradfield advised him to move to South Australia.

On 17 May 1928 at St Peters Church, Adelaide, Badger married Frances Augustus Newton, with the forms of the Churches of Christ. The couple returned to Victoria and lived near Mentone racecourse; they were to shift to Caulfield in 1938. As number-two jockey for the trainer Lou Robertson, Badger had few opportunities for major wins so in 1936 he turned freelance. That year he reluctantly accepted the mount on Northwind which duly won the Caulfield Cup at 66/1. His success with Ajax made Badger a household name. He rode the champion horse to 30 of his 36 top-class victories between 1937 and 1940. Even Ajax's loss, at 40/1 on, at Rosehill, Sydney, in 1939 perversely increased the fame of horse and jockey.

Clarence Badger had been critically injured in a race crash at Geelong on 13 April 1938. Harold rushed from Sydney to Melbourne

47

then, following his brother's death on the 14th, returned by air next day to keep his riding engagements at Randwick. On 20 April he rode three winners, only to be suspended for a month for careless riding. Over the five seasons from 1938-39 to 1942-43 he was Victoria's leading jockey.

A car accident in 1943 nearly killed Badger and kept him from the saddle for about five months. He vowed to secure another premiership and achieved this goal in 1947-48, helped by first-placings on Columnist in a number of races, including the Caulfield Cup. A fall from that horse affected his vision and he retired in November 1948. Next year he visited England for medical advice but the condition was inoperable. Over his career he had won nearly a thousand races; his victories in more than one hundred feature events included the Newmarket Handicap (three times) and the Doncaster and Epsom handicaps (twice).

In a sport tarnished with dubious dealings, Badger maintained a rare reputation for honesty. Not quite 5 ft (153 cm) tall, he had been rejected for army service in World War II despite his strength and tenacity: the press called him a 'pocket Hercules'. He rode at 7 st. 10 lb. (49 kg) with recourse to the steam baths, but never weighed more than 8 st. (51 kg). A private man who regarded racehorse-riding as a job, he disdained glamour and avoided publicity, so his achievements have been undervalued. He was happily inconspicuous in retirement, briefly leasing a hotel at Flemington, and farming at Romsey and Sunbury before settling in Melbourne at Mount Waverley. He died on 13 December 1981 at Cheltenham and was cremated. His wife survived him, as did their son, Harold, a distinguished musician.

M. Cavanough, *The Caulfield Cup* (1976); D. Badger, *David Badger* (1985); A. Lemon, *The History of Australian Thoroughbred Racing*, vol 2 (1990); *Argus* (Melbourne), 14 Apr 1938, p 1, 16 Apr 1938, p 22; *Turf Monthly*, Jan 1971, p 6, July 1980, p 18; *Age* (Melbourne), 16 Dec 1981, p 28; *Sun News-Pictorial* (Melbourne), 16 Dec 1981, p 88; private information.   ANDREW LEMON

BAILEY, HARRY RICHARD (1922-1985), psychiatrist, was born on 29 October 1922 at Picton, New South Wales, eldest child of Jack Nelson Bailey, railway night officer and later stationmaster, and his wife Ruth Kathleen, née Smith, both born in New South Wales. Educated at a Christian Brothers' college at Waverley, Sydney, Harry enrolled in science at the University of Sydney in 1940. Lacking money, he did not finish the course and found work as a pharmacist's assistant. On 19 January 1945 at the registrar general's office, Sydney, he married Marjorie Jocelyn Noonan,

a cashier. He studied medicine at the University of Sydney (MB, BS, 1951; DPM, 1954), winning the Norton Manning memorial prize for psychiatry and the Major Ian Vickery prize for paediatrics.

Psychiatry, then an unpopular specialisation, afforded opportunities for advancement for a bright, ambitious graduate from a modest social background. After twelve months at Royal Prince Alfred Hospital, Bailey became a medical officer at Broughton Hall Psychiatric Clinic, Leichhardt, in 1952. That year he was appointed assistant-director of psychiatric clinical services in the Department of Public Health. He had already come under the influence of such prominent advocates of surgical and pharmacological treatments for mental illness as (Sir) William Trethowan and Cedric Swanton [q.v.16]. From December 1954 he spent fifteen months on a World Health Organisation fellowship in the United States of America and Europe, closely observing the sedation techniques, psychosurgery and electroconvulsive therapy methods of Ewan Cameron in Canada, William Sargant in London and Lars Leksell in Sweden. On his recommendation, the Cerebral Surgery and Research Unit at Callan Park Mental Hospital was established in 1957. Bailey was named director. There he experimented with new ECT and psychosurgical methods, announcing significant developments in the successful treatment of mental illness.

His reputation high, in 1959 Bailey was appointed medical superintendent of Callan Park, a large institution suffering from years of neglect and a culture of confinement. He proved to be an impatient reformer. Within a few months he submitted a report to the Public Service Board with detailed allegations of staff cruelty, patient neglect and daily pilfering from hospital stores. Subsequent police and Department of Public Health investigations found nothing to substantiate the charges. Undeterred, Bailey 'blew the whistle', and dramatic newspaper headlines embarrassed the Heffron [q.v.14] government, particularly the responsible minister, William Sheahan [q.v.16]. The resulting royal commission report into Callan Park by J. H. McClemens [q.v.15] confirmed many of Bailey's allegations, while concluding that some were exaggerated. Laying partial blame on inadequate funding, it also noted 'problems of leadership' at the hospital. The findings forced future governments to take mental health policy more seriously but relations between Bailey and Sheahan were irrevocably damaged, leading to Bailey's resignation in September 1961 amid protests by members of the press and parliamentary Opposition.

Bailey moved to private practice in Macquarie Street. His high public profile ensured his success. He became a psychiatric consultant at Wollongong, Canterbury, Eastern Suburbs and Crown Street hospitals. A member of the Australian Medical Association (1951), the Australasian Association of Psychiatrists (later Royal Australian and New Zealand College of Psychiatrists) from 1952, the American Electroshock Research Association and the Pan-Pacific Surgical Association, he was president of the Sydney Biophysics and Medical Electronics Society.

In 1963 Bailey, with John Herron, and later Ian Gardiner and John Gill, began to treat patients at Chelmsford Private Hospital, Pennant Hills. There Bailey experimented with the combination of extended narcotic induced comas (deep sleep therapy) and ECT. Complications such as pneumonia, infections, dehydration, vomiting and respiratory problems were common. Within two years five patients had died as a result of this treatment. More deaths followed, although it was not until 1967 that a coronial inquest resulted. Impressed by Bailey's medical reputation and his justification for his therapeutic regime, the coroner did not consider him culpable. Apart from private mutterings in psychiatric circles and occasional published criticisms of Bailey's research, there were few efforts by the profession to control his methods. He continued to publish research papers on psychosurgery with reputable psychiatrists such as Cedric Swanton and John Dowling. By 1979, when Bailey's Chelmsford practice closed, at least twenty-four patients had died, others had committed suicide and many survivors suffered physical and mental complications arising from their treatment.

The veil of professional repute that protected Bailey began to unravel. From 1972 a Chelmsford nurse, Rosa Nicholson, documented treatment irregularities; she passed this evidence to the Citizens Committee on Human Rights, a branch of the controversial Church of Scientology. In 1978 the committee wrote to the attorney-general detailing the evidence of medical malpractice, and newspapers began to report their allegations. That year the suicide of the dancer Sharon Hamilton, a patient and lover of Bailey, and revelations that he was the beneficiary of her estate, further undermined his reputation.

In 1980 the influential current affairs program '60 Minutes' aired an episode on Chelmsford, containing details of the death of Miriam Podio in 1977. Five years later a coronial inquest into her death was held and in 1983 Bailey was charged with manslaughter. Although the charge was dismissed in 1985, the media siege was intense. Sick, tired, dispirited and facing years of litigation, on 8 September 1985 he drove to Mount White and parked on an isolated track. Next day police found him dead, the cause of death being barbiturate poisoning. Survived by his estranged wife and two adopted daughters, he was cremated.

A well-dressed, handsome and cherub-faced charmer, Bailey was charismatic, despite occasional drunken rages. A noted *bon vivant*, he was prone to exaggerating his achievements. Although he lapsed into periods of deep gloom, salved by drink and medication, he continued to assert that his methods were efficacious. He saw himself as a martyr, hounded by religious fanatics and ignorant critics. Bailey revelled in the trappings of professional power and exploited the vulnerabilities of those in his care, having sexual relationships with a number of female patients and some employees. Even when embroiled in controversy, he still managed to command intense loyalty and affection from his wife, former lovers and some close colleagues.

In 1988 the Greiner government established a royal commission into deep sleep therapy. The commissioner concluded that events at Chelmsford were deplorable, and found evidence of fraud, obstruction of justice and serious medical negligence. He condemned all the doctors involved but concluded that Bailey was central and that without him there would have been no deep sleep therapy. The New South Wales parliament banned the treatment and enacted stricter regulations governing the admission and treatment of mental health patients. For all the wrong reasons Bailey had again forced governments to improve the lot of the mentally ill.

Report of the Royal Commission into Deep Sleep Therapy (1990); B. Bromberger and J. Fife-Yeomans, *Deep Sleep* (1991); *Austn and NZ Jnl of Psychiatry*, vol 27, no 1, 1993, p 140; *SMH*, 8 Sept 1961, pp 1 and 2, 12 Sept 1961, p 1, 8 July 1978, p 5, 14 Sept 1985, p 1.
                                                    STEPHEN GARTON

BAKER, CLARENCE PATRICK (1898-1986), picture-show man and theatre proprietor, was born on 11 September 1898 at Matlock, Victoria, fourth of seven children of Victorian-born parents Henry Baker, an itinerant miner, and his wife Arabella, née Friel. Accounts of 'Paddy's' life before the 1940s vary, but it appears that in 1901 he moved with his family to Western Australia, living first at Gwalia and then at Yundamindera. His parents separated and at the age of 8 he went with his father to Mount Morgans on the Murchison goldfields, north of Kalgoorlie. Eventually the pair set up camp at Sandstone, where Paddy attended the local convent school and worked for fourpence a night at Charlie Hebbard's magic-lantern show. His father died in 1914 and he rejoined his mother and three sisters at Subiaco, Perth. Sent to board for two years at Christian

Brothers' College in the city, he learned 'a lot of Latin' and showed films to his fellow students.

By the summer of 1916 Baker was assistant-projectionist at the Coliseum picture garden at Subiaco. He and his sisters also sold tickets, 'lollies' and ice-creams. During the day he worked as a mechanic at a nearby garage; after the premises were destroyed by fire he repaired cars at customers' homes. Abstemious by nature, he saved £4 a week and in 1919 acquired a second-hand picture-show plant and motorcar. He named his enterprise Baker's Photoplays Deluxe, and headed for the bush. Screening at a different venue every night, he showed silent films from Esperance to Geraldton, then travelled south through the wheat-belt. Times were tough and his patrons paid either by coin or with produce. Baker assembled and dismantled his equipment in weatherboard halls, rough canvas tents and makeshift sheds. Sometimes he used a sheet for a screen, mounted the projector on the bonnet of his car, and ran the engine to generate light and power.

Endowed with characteristic Irish geniality, Baker was cheerful, energetic and innovative, but was also stubborn. His habitual dapper appearance and slight build belied a steely strength. After showing his first talking picture in the Bassendean Town Hall, he successfully tendered to show films at the Metro and Capitol theatres in Perth. He trained his projectionists; initially he developed his own sound equipment but later bought the best on the market.

In 1946 Baker purchased the Regal Theatre, built in 1938 on the site of the old Coliseum, to show 35-mm films. He continued to service regional cinemas, and from 1962 established a chain of drive-in theatres in country towns. In 1977 he renovated the Regal as a venue for live productions. Seven years later he restored the building to its original art deco elegance, but was careful not to make it 'too posh for Sir Les Patterson'. Widely known as 'Mr Showbiz', he lived on the top floor in 'a nice little flat with every convenience'. The Regal Theatre was reputedly the inspiration for Dorothy Hewett's play *Bon-Bons and Roses for Dolly* (1976). In May 1986 he formed the Baker Theatre Trust to administer the Regal in perpetuity. Baker, who had never married, died on 11 August that year in his theatre and was buried with Catholic rites in Karrakatta cemetery.

Sunday Independent (Perth), 10 June 1984, p 21; *West Australian*, 16 July 1984, p 20, 27 May 1986, p 2, 12 Aug 1986, p 12, 19 Aug 1986, p 18; *Sunday Times* (Perth), 8 June 1986, p 19; *Subiaco Post*, 19 Aug 1986, p 1; *Kino*, Dec 1986, p 22; P. Morris, taped interview with C. P. Baker (1978, SLWA); Baker memorabilia (Subiaco Museum, Regal Theatre Trust, Subiaco, Art Deco Soc of WA, West Perth).

WENDY BIRMAN

BAKER, HARRY FREDERICK (1904-1986), speedway motorcycle rider and aviator, was born on 29 July 1904 at Glanville, Port Adelaide, son of Western Australian residents Frederick George Baker, labourer, and his wife Evelyn May, née Smith. The family moved to Perth soon afterwards and Harry was educated at Maylands State and Perth Technical schools. From the age of 18 he was a keen speedway rider; his style earned him the nickname of 'Cannonball' and he was credited with being the first Western Australian motorcycle rider to reach 100 miles (160 km) per hour. In 1927 he won the first silver gauntlet at Claremont Speedway.

One of (Sir) Norman Brearley's [q.v.] early pupils at the Perth Flying School, established at Maylands in 1927, Baker qualified as an instructor, and started his own business. He then took employment with an importer of Lanz tractors, flying a Klemm monoplane to bring spare parts and service to customers in the wheat-belt. In October 1929 he competed in the Western Australian centenary air race from Sydney to Perth, piloting the Klemm, the smallest aircraft entered.

Joining Brearley's West Australian Airways Ltd in 1931, Baker initially flew to and from the North-West. On 24 November 1932 at St Mary's Church of England, West Perth, he married Lilian Gladys Henderson (d.1937). Next month he flew two prospectors to desert country near the South Australian border in quest of Lasseter's [q.v.9] reef. Engine failure forced him to land on a salt pan, 300 miles (483 km) from the nearest settlement, and the de Havilland 50 biplane was severely damaged. Baker made emergency repairs to the aircraft with such improvised materials as mulga saplings, and in a few days was able to fly to Forrest, on the trans-continental railway line. The site of the accident was later named Lake Baker. In another incident in October 1933, shortly after his Vickers Viastra took off from Maylands aerodrome on a commercial flight, the port propeller shattered, piercing the fuselage. With coolness and skill he nursed the plane down in a cabbage patch. One of the eleven passengers was slightly injured; the aircraft was a write-off.

When Australian National Airways Pty Ltd took over WAA in 1936, Baker became chief pilot on the Perth-Adelaide route. On 15 February 1938 at Christ Church, St Kilda, Melbourne, he married with Anglican rites Florence MacDonald, a typist. While flying company aircraft in support of Allied forces in World War II, he helped to evacuate to Perth (1942) refugees from the Netherlands East Indies who had reached Broome; on one flight he carried fifty-two people in a 21-seat Douglas DC-3. From 1946 he was ANA's representative at San Francisco, United States of America, and then in London. He returned to Western

Australia as State manager in 1951, and in 1955 was the airline's manager at Essendon airport, Melbourne.

Baker retired from ANA that year, having flown more than three million miles in 17 000 flying hours. He later worked in Perth for Lynas Motors Pty Ltd and Wormald Brothers (Australia) Pty Ltd. Divorced in 1969, on 11 July 1970 at the Church of Jesus Christ of Latter Day Saints, Como, he married Veronica May Bishop, née Baldwin, a security officer and a divorcee. He was incapacitated by a stroke in the 1970s and spent his final years in a nursing home at Como. Survived by his wife, and the daughter and younger son of his second marriage, he died there on 8 June 1986 and was buried in Karrakatta cemetery.

N. Brearley, *Australian Aviator* (1971); K. Brown (comp), *The All-Time Claremont Speedway Fact File* (2000); *West Australian*, 1 Sept 1927, p 6, 28 Dec 1932, p 7, 29 Dec 1932, p 7, 30 Dec 1932, p 9, 31 Dec 1932, p 9; *Far Horizons*, May-June 1986, p 18; B. Bunbury, taped interview with Fred Wayman (1987, SLWA); Jimmy Woods papers, Acc 4638A (SLWA); private information.
G. C. BOLTON
ANDREW MORANT

BAKEWELL, ROBERT DONALD (1899-1982), pastoralist and organiser of wool-growers, was born on 9 September 1899 at Unley Park, Adelaide, son of South Australian-born parents Edward Howard Bakewell, stock and station agent and later pastoralist, and his wife Octavia Eleanor, née Wilson. Educated at Kyre (Scotch) College, Adelaide, where he was dux and captain of the school, Don worked as a clerk with Goldsbrough Mort [qq.v.4,5] & Co. Ltd. In October 1918 he enlisted in the Australian Imperial Force but the war ended next month and he did not serve abroad. By 1922 he was overseer of Yalkuri station at Narrung. On 29 April 1929 at St Paul's Cathedral, Melbourne, he married, with Anglican rites, Ydonea Ridley Dale, an art student. Moving to Victoria about six years later, he was managing director in 1935-73 of Farnley Grazing Pty Ltd, a family farming enterprise near Benalla.

On 9 April 1938 a branch of the Graziers' Association of Victoria opened at Benalla. That day Bakewell was nominated as the branch's representative on the association's council; he was president (1943-46) of the GAV and a trustee, and was to remain on the executive committee until 1978. In 1940 he became a delegate to the two bodies that the State-based grazier organisations financed to represent their interests nationally: the Graziers' Federal Council of Australia, of which he was a member (to 1950), acting-president (1947) and president (1948-49); and the Australian Wool-growers' Council, of which he was chairman (1949-54) and a life member (1954).

Knowledgable and hard-working, Bakewell made an enormous contribution to the wool industry. In 1945-59 he served on the Australian Wool Realization Commission, which was responsible for the orderly sale, concurrently with postwar clips, of Australia's share of the stocks that had accumulated in British Commonwealth countries during World War II. Through clever and careful marketing, the commission disposed of the stockpile while protecting growers from serious falls in prices. Late in the 1940s Bakewell strongly supported Dame Jean Macnamara's [q.v.10] campaign to resume experiments with myxomatosis as a means of reducing rabbit numbers; the virus was used with good results in the summer of 1950-51. Bakewell was a member of the council of the Chamber of Agriculture of Victoria in 1940-50 and vice-president in 1946-48. He was appointed CMG in 1952.

In 1947 Bakewell had publicly condemned the Chifley [q.v.13] government's proposal to nationalise the banks, arguing that freedom and private enterprise were under attack. Four years later he opposed the Menzies [q.v.15] ministry's reserve price plan for wool, claiming that its real purpose was government control of the industry. Most graziers supported his conservative stance.

Bakewell was a quiet, likeable and helpful man who spent his spare time doing community work, the local volunteer bushfire brigade being a particular interest. He was a keen lawn bowler and earlier had enjoyed tennis and cricket. Survived by his wife and their daughter, he died on 11 July 1982 at Benalla and was buried in the local cemetery with Presbyterian forms.

F. E. Hitchins, *Tangled Skeins* (195-); *SMH*, 1 Nov 1945, p 3, 19 Aug 1947, p 5; Bakewell papers (SLV); personal knowledge and private information.
HUGH S. BEGGS

BALL, WILLIAM MACMAHON (1901-1986), professor of political science, diplomat, author, journalist and radio broadcaster, was born on 29 August 1901 at Casterton, Victoria, fifth and youngest surviving child of John Aubrey Ball, a London-born minister of the Church of England, and his wife Edith Laura, née McMahon, who had been born in Victoria. The family moved to Melbourne when the boy was 9. An indifferent scholar, he left Caulfield Grammar School seven years later, without matriculating. He became a student-teacher at New College, Box Hill, and qualified for entry to the University of Melbourne (BA Hons, 1923).

Until then Ball had remained strong in the Christian faith of his upbringing, and contemplated entering the ministry. Discussion with the head of one of the university's colleges revealed the depth of his underlying doubt and he was thenceforth an undogmatic rationalist. His academic results remained poor until he came under the influence of Mary Flinn, a tutor whose talents unlocked his latent brilliance. Graduating with first-class honours and several prizes, he was appointed research scholar in psychology. He taught a subject titled 'Psychology, Logic and Ethics'. On 24 May 1924 at the Congregational manse, Eagle Junction, Brisbane, he married Iris Shield, a journalist; she died childless in 1926. At St Paul's Church of England, Gisborne, Victoria, on 20 December 1928 he married Muriel Katrine ('Kay') Sandys Cliffe Anderson, a clerk.

In 1929 Ball won a Rockefeller travelling fellowship in political science, enabling him to study under Harold Laski at the London School of Economics and Political Science. On visits to Europe he observed the ferment that, following World War I, formed the seed-bed of fascism. In 1932 he returned to the University of Melbourne as lecturer (later senior lecturer) in political philosophy and modern political institutions. His classes were well attended, and he became a popular figure among the students, as he addressed their meetings and advised them. A left-leaning liberal, he raised eyebrows when he awarded an important academic prize to the prominent right-wing student B. A. Santamaria.

Ball's stature increased steadily throughout the troubled and emotional decade that led up to World War II: abroad were the Spanish Civil War, the regimes of Hitler, Mussolini and Stalin, and Japan's rampage in China; at home, the Depression, the dismissal of Premier J. T. Lang [q.v.9], and the New Guard. In such unquiet and strident times, Ball's voice was one of calm and reason. He was active in the adult education movement as a university extension lecturer, and he taught, in one capacity or another, an astonishing number of future Australian leaders. In this period, too, he began giving talks for the Australian Broadcasting Commission, a medium in which he shone. He also wrote articles on international affairs for the Melbourne *Herald*.

Working for disarmament and the peaceful settlement of international differences, Ball published his views in *Possible Peace* (1936). At first he supported the World Peace Congress but later denounced it as a communist front, and repented what he called his 'naïvety and folly' over disarmament. Yet he remained courageous and outspoken in defence of Australian democratic freedoms. In May 1938 he departed on another visit abroad. After witnessing the German occupation of the

Sudetenland, he was given a conducted tour of the notorious Sachsenhausen concentration camp—a horror which never left his memory. He returned via the United States of America where, with a Carnegie scholarship, he visited the political science departments of leading universities, arriving home in March 1939.

Invited by Prime Minister (Sir) Robert Menzies [q.v.15], in February 1940 Ball was appointed controller of broadcasting in the Department of Information. In June he became responsible solely for short-wave broadcasting. As well as heading a team that monitored overseas transmissions, he took charge of the nation's information and propaganda services directed to friendly, neutral and enemy countries in the region. Under Ball, the material disseminated abroad avoided blatant disinformation and crude hate, and thus gained credibility. His section was transferred to the ABC in July 1942. He resigned in protest when Arthur Calwell [q.v.13] moved it back to the department in April 1944. Ball remained with the ABC and added to his public laurels by chairing the popular radio debates, 'Nation's Forum of the Air'.

In 1945 'Mac' Ball returned to his university as senior lecturer-in-charge of the department of political science. He wrote an introduction to a book of speeches by H. V. Evatt [q.v.14], *Foreign Policy of Australia* (1945). That year he was part of Evatt's entourage at the United Nations Conference on International Organization in San Francisco, USA. Ball did not like his leader, nor approve his methods, and the two men jarred on each other. Nevertheless, Evatt sent him in November as special observer to report on the conflict in the Netherlands East Indies, where the Indonesians were throwing off colonial rule. His dispatches were undoubtedly penetrating and accurate, but not what Evatt wanted to read.

Ball's next assignment from Evatt was a surprise, and the matter may have been settled by Prime Minister J. B. Chifley [q.v.13]. Appointed British Commonwealth member of the Allied Council for Japan, and Australian minister to that country, Ball assumed office on 3 April 1946. His place on the council was a singular recognition of Australia's fighting role in World War II, and an acknowledgment of his personal qualities and standing. But it was not a happy time for him. General Douglas MacArthur [q.v.15], the dictatorial supreme commander for the Allied Powers, submitted little of importance for the consideration of the council; the British undermined their Commonwealth representative; and Evatt, as usual, was inconsistent and devious. Ball resigned in August 1947 and returned to Melbourne. Yet he agreed to carry out another job for Evatt in 1948, leading a mission of good will to South-East Asia. Newspapers reported an innocuous remark he made en route suggesting the possible future relaxation of the rigid White Australia policy. Ball was attacked in the Australian parliament and Evatt threw his man to the wolves.

For a short while Ball worked as a special foreign affairs writer on the Melbourne *Herald* where his elegant articles, largely on relations with South-East Asia, enhanced that newspaper's best traditions. But he liked the proprietor, Sir Keith Murdoch [q.v.10], little better than he had liked Evatt, and was glad to learn of his own impending appointment to the foundation chair of political science at the University of Melbourne. In 1949 he settled with contentment into the job which he was to retain until his retirement in January 1968. To be a teacher was his *métier*; in class or tutorial, in print or on radio, and in the 'cheerful flow of unguarded conversation' at the 'pub', he was a quiet teacher all his life.

Active in the general life of the university, Ball led the academic staff association. As chairman of the board of studies in journalism, he successfully resisted its elevation to degree status, maintaining that, while journalists should be as well educated as possible, theirs was essentially a craft to be learned on the job, and at risk of being degraded if it became 'academic'. On the board of management of Melbourne University Press he was usually influential. As chairman in 1961, against opposition, he persuaded the board and the university's council to make important changes in the press's management which were to endure for twenty-six years.

Ball was tall, straight-backed into oldest age, with handsome, strong features topped by a thick mane of silver hair. Although he well knew that he cut an imposing figure on campus, he was easy-going and readily approachable. (After a 'spat' on the professorial board, a defeated party was heard to grumble: 'the bloody trouble with Mac is that he looks like a Roman senator'.)

As well as innumerable articles, book reviews and radio broadcasts, his publications included the volumes *Japan: Enemy or Ally?* (1948); *Nationalism and Communism in East Asia* (1952); and an edited collection of documents and readings, *Australia and Japan* (1969). Alan Rix was to edit the diaries Ball kept in Indonesia and Japan as *Intermittent Diplomat* (1988). On Ball's retirement from the university, Sir Frederick Wheeler, chairman of the Public Service Board, invited him to give, over several years, a series of seminars for senior public servants in Canberra. He was appointed AC in 1978.

The Balls lived in a several-times-extended timber house in semi-rural Eltham, north of Melbourne. Here Kay's practical abilities and hard work maintained the 'bush and garden' small estate which provided fresh produce for the table and space for Mac to keep his horse. His relaxations included riding in the surrounding hills with younger friends, and assiduous (if modest) punting on the Victorian races. Aided by Kay's splendid table, Eltham saw much quiet but significant entertainment of leading figures in Australian and overseas affairs. Ball died on 26 December 1986 at Heidelberg and was buried in Eltham cemetery. His wife and their daughter survived him; their son predeceased him. Mac Ball's passing depleted the ranks of distinguished Australians who lived by the standards of 'gentlemen', and who combined high learning and genuine cultivation with a relaxed and authentic attachment to the ordinary citizens of their country.

K. S. Inglis, *This is the ABC* (1983); J. Hilvert, *Blue Pencil Warriors* (1984); P. Ryan, *William Macmahon Ball: A Memoir* (1990); H. de Berg, interview with W. M. Ball (ts, 1971, NLA); Ball papers (NLA).

PETER RYAN

BALLANTYNE, COLIN SANDERGROVE (1908-1988), theatre director and photographer, was born on 12 July 1908 at Wayville, Adelaide, second son of South Australian-born parents James Fergusson Ballantyne, corporation official, and his wife Emily Bbe, née Hack. Colin was educated at Westbourne Park Public and Adelaide High schools. His mother and her sister Stella Hack, both of whom read widely and were avid theatre-goers and professed Fabian socialists, influenced him and encouraged his interest in theatre. As a youth he acted in productions of the Workers' Educational Association of South Australia Dramatic Society's Little Theatre. At this time, as professional theatre began to decline under the impact of cinema, Adelaide's little theatre movement embarked on a 35-year period of often spirited and accomplished activity.

Another youthful interest, in photography, led Ballantyne in 1927 to join the *Register* as a staff photographer. In 1931 he established his own photographic studio, while also employed as pictorial editor of the magazine *Town Topics* and later, briefly, as a news cine-cameraman. During the 1930s he worked in repertory as both director and actor, sometimes playing opposite a talented young actress, Gwenneth Martha Osborne Richmond. On 25 October 1934 he and Gwenneth were married in the North Adelaide Baptist Church. He was chairman of WEA Little Theatre in 1934-39; in his report on its 1935 season he said that he believed the society had 'sufficient vitality to rise up and form the nucleus of a National Theatre'. In 1942-44 he served as a camouflage officer for the Department of Home Security in northern Australia. On his return to Adelaide he re-established his photographic business.

From 1945 Ballantyne worked hard to achieve a vigorous theatre life in South Australia. With John Bishop and John Horner [qq.v.13,14], he helped to found (1948) the Arts Council of South Australia to lobby for government subvention of performing arts. In 1948-52, at the Tivoli Theatre, he directed a celebrated series of large-scale Shakespeare productions for the council. The future Labor premier Donald Dunstan was one of the actors; he also participated in the campaign for a state-funded theatre. Ballantyne was a local consultant to the British theatre director (Sir) Tyrone Guthrie, who visited Australia in 1949 to advise the Chifley [q.v.13] government on the feasibility of a national theatre. In November that year the premier (Sir) Thomas Playford [q.v.] appointed Ballantyne South Australian representative on the board of the short-lived National Theatre Trust Fund.

Having read intensively during the war years about the Konstantin Stanislavsky method of acting, Ballantyne used it in directing more than sixty, mostly well-regarded, amateur and semi-professional productions of the classics and nineteenth- and twentieth-century European, American and Australian drama. The plays were mounted for a variety of incorporated theatre bodies, including the University of Adelaide Theatre Guild, Theatres Associated and the Adelaide Theatre Group, with which he founded the Sheridan Theatre in 1963. In 1960-68 he directed five major productions for the Adelaide Festival of Arts. Over the years he helped to train many actors, among them Keith Michell, Edwin Hodgeman and Leslie Dayman. His dream of a state-owned theatre company became reality in 1972 when the government took over the South Australian Theatre Company and began to build its home—the Playhouse—in the new Adelaide Festival Centre. As chairman of the board of governors (1972-78), Ballantyne helped to guide the company through its formation and many of its early successful productions. A Federal director (1966-74) of the Arts Council of Australia, he was president of the State division in 1972-73 and of the national organisation in 1974-77. He was founding chairman (1980-88) of the Performing Arts Collection of South Australia.

Ballantyne and his wife, a noted drama teacher and director, were dominant figures in an influential group of academics, writers, artists and actors, many of whom strongly supported Dunstan's rise in the Australian Labor Party. They held a monthly open house in their North Adelaide home. In 1971 Ballantyne was appointed CMG. Given to florid phrasing, large gestures and sometimes colourful personal exaggeration, he was described by Brian Medlin as 'maddening, rude, charming, pretentious, competent, dedicated and (by the hardy) lovable'. Dunstan said that he was 'the outstanding pioneer of theatre work when there was practically none in South Australia'. Survived by his wife, and their son and two daughters, Ballantyne died on 2 July 1988 at Walkerville and was cremated. His three children have pursued careers in theatre, film and television.

Arts Enquiry Ctte for SA, *Report* (1961); A. D. McCredie (ed), *From Colonel Light into the Footlights* (1988); P. Ward, *A Singular Act* (1992); W. Prest (ed), *A Portrait of John Bray* (1997); *Advertiser* (Adelaide), 24 May 1978, p 28, 21 Oct 1983, p 7; *Australian*, 5 July 1988, p 15; Ballantyne papers (Ballantyne Performing Arts Collection, Adelaide Festival Centre); private information and personal knowledge.   PETER WARD

BALLARD, BERTRAM CHARLES (1903-1981), diplomat, was born on 22 January 1903 at Toorak, Melbourne, eldest of three children of Charles William Ballard, a shorthand writer and accountant from London, and his Melbourne-born wife Ethel, née Whitham. He was educated at Scotch College (dux 1919-20) and at the University of Melbourne (BA, 1924; LL B, 1925; MA, 1926), where he graduated with first-class honours and the Dwight [q.v.4] prize in French. On 2 May 1927 he was admitted to practise as a barrister and solicitor of the Supreme Court of Victoria.

Moving to Horsham in 1928, Ballard managed the practice of the solicitor H. Balfour Cathcart and acquired considerable experience in the conveyancing of land. Next year he returned to Melbourne to practise at the Bar. His fluency in French and expertise in property law equipped him to become Australian government solicitor in the New Hebrides (Vanuatu). Arriving there in 1934, he handled the land claims of Burns, Philp [qq.v.7,11] & Co. Ltd, of Australian settlers and of the Presbyterian Church.

In August 1940 Ballard was appointed Australian official representative in New Caledonia. His instructions were to report on political and economic conditions in the colony and to encourage its continued wartime co-operation with both the British Empire and Australia. At that time most of the settlers in Noumea supported the Free French movement, while the governor and senior military officers remained loyal to Vichy. The Australian government instructed Ballard to discourage local efforts to overthrow the administration for fear that if Australia were asked to restore law and order, or establish a protectorate, the intervention might anger the Japanese and provide them with a precedent for seizing French Indo-China. Ballard contributed to a peaceful outcome in September when, countering the presence of a French sloop commanded by a pro-Vichy captain, the

Royal Australian Navy escorted Henri Sautot, a Gaullist official, to Noumea to take over the government.

By 1943 Ballard was anxious for a change and applied to join the fledgling Australian diplomatic service in the Department of External Affairs. After heading the department's international co-operation section in 1944-45, he was to serve continuously overseas for the rest of his career. He was political observer in Japan (1945-46), political representative and later Australia's first consul-general in the Netherlands East Indies (1946-47), counsellor in the Australian embassies in Paris (1947-48) and Moscow (1948-49), and Australian permanent delegate to the European office of the United Nations in Geneva (1949-51).

On 6 May 1952 Ballard presented his credentials as Australia's first minister to Thailand. In 1955 he was appointed minister to Israel, a country about which he presented consistently sympathetic reports during the Anglo-French effort, encouraged by Israel, to prevent the Egyptian nationalisation of the Suez Canal. While in Tel Aviv, he occasionally startled the local populace by riding a motor scooter with the Australian flag that usually adorned the embassy's car.

Aided by his fluent French, Ballard travelled extensively in West Africa as Australian high commissioner to Ghana in 1960-62. His last two postings were as high commissioner to Ceylon (Sri Lanka) in 1962-65 and as ambassador to Sweden from 1966. Although he retired in 1967, he later revised the British laws of the New Hebrides, where he was also employed as a consultant to the Department of Foreign Affairs on Australian land interests. He took up the church organ and was thereby able to fulfil his passion for baroque music. Ballard never married. He died on 15 July 1981 at Kew, Melbourne, and was cremated with Anglican rites.

P. Hasluck, *The Government and the People 1939-1941* (1952); A. Watt, *Australian Diplomat* (1972); *Documents on Australian Foreign Policy 1937-49*, vols 4, 5, 8, 10, 11 (1980-2001); J. Lawrey, *The Cross of Lorraine in the South Pacific* (1982); J. D. B. Miller, interview with Ballard (ts, 1975, NLA); Ballard papers (NLA); private information.   DAVID LEE

BANDT, LOUIS (LEWIS) THORNETT (1910-1987), motor vehicle designer and engineer, was born on 26 February 1910 at Moonta, South Australia, eldest of five children of Louis Seymour Bandt, butcher, and his wife Ethel, née Hobbs, both born in South Australia. After World War I the family moved to Adelaide. Encouraged by his father, in 1924 Louis junior began a fitting and turning apprenticeship with Duncan & Fraser Ltd.

This firm specialised in the modification and sale of T-model Fords, and Bandt spent most of his time designing custom-made bodies. In 1927 he moved to Victoria to work for the Melbourne Motor Body & Assembling Co. Pty Ltd. Two years later he was appointed a junior draughtsman at the Geelong plant of the Ford Motor Co. of Australia Pty Ltd. He became the first designer on the staff of Ford's Australian subsidiary. A job at the factory was arranged for his father, and the rest of the family moved from Adelaide.

Although he was to enjoy a 46-year career with Ford, Bandt's chief distinction, the design of the 'coupe utility', came early. In 1932 a Gippsland farmer's wife wrote to the company pointing out the need for a combined work and passenger vehicle, purpose-built for farmers who were having to make do with 'buck-boards': open-sided, soft-canopy T-model cars converted by adding a rear timber tray to carry loads. Bandt's innovation provided for an enclosed, protective and comfortable cabin at the front and a tray at the back, 5 ft 5 ins (165 cm) long and able to carry 1200 lb. (544 kg).

A sample body was made in 1933 and the first utilities, or 'utes', rolled off the production line next year. Dubbed 'the Kangaroo Chaser' by Henry Ford when Bandt displayed two examples in Detroit, United States of America, in 1935, the ute was quickly recognised as the ideal farmers' vehicle. Both the Ford and General Motors companies were soon manufacturing models for the American market. In World War II Bandt worked on the production of auxiliary fuel tanks for fighter aircraft. He won bronze medals in the annual British Empire motorcar design competitions in 1947-48. Among the most popular of Bandt's later designs were a station wagon conversion of the Mark II Zephyr in the 1950s and a right-hand drive version of the 1967 Fairlane. In the mid-1960s he spent some time at Ford's Canadian plant. Back at Geelong, he was manager of body engineering. He had several terms as chairman of the Geelong and South-West Victoria group of the Society of Automotive Engineers, Australasia.

On 6 September 1941 at Prospect North Methodist Church, Adelaide, Bandt had married Nellie Alice Rowe, a music teacher. A charity worker and, from childhood, a committed member of the Methodist (later Uniting) Church, he was an accomplished artist who painted Ford's nativity scene at Christmas. He retired in 1975. On 18 March 1987 he took part in an Australian Broadcasting Corporation television documentary about the utility. While driving his restored 1934 model home that day, he collided with a truck on the Midland Highway, near Bannockburn, and was killed. His wife and their three daughters survived him.

N. Darwin, *The History of Ford in Australia* (1986); G. Easdown, *Ford: A History of the Ford Motor Company in Australia* (1987); B. Tuckey, *True Blue* (2000); *Age* (Melbourne), 19 Mar 1987, p 3; *Geelong Advertiser*, 19 Mar 1987, p 1; *Herald* (Melbourne), 6 Apr 1987, p 11; Bandt papers (SLV).

DAMIAN VELTRI

BANKS, NORMAN TYRELL (1905-1985), radio broadcaster, was born on 12 October 1905 at Sandringham, Melbourne, fifth child of Victorian-born parents Charles Cecil Banks, a Hampton newsagent who had died six months earlier, and his wife Alice Mary, née Elliott. Alice went into business as a draper. After attending local state schools and Hampton Beach College, Norman studied for the Anglican priesthood in the mid-1920s. He did not complete his training but remained a regular communicant whose religiosity was to influence aspects of his broadcasting career.

While working for S. A. Cheney Motors (Victoria) Pty Ltd, Banks became a successful car salesman. The firm sent him to England and to the United States of America where, attracted to the booming radio industry, he gained some experience. Back in Victoria, and out of work at Colac, he dug onions for a farmer, Joseph Gilmore, whose daughter, Lorna May, he married with Anglican rites on 6 May 1930 at Christ Church, South Yarra. Desperate to find a job, Banks followed his mother's advice to try radio. 3KZ had just started broadcasting from the Melbourne Trades Hall, and he pestered the management until he was offered an announcer's position, starting on 4 July 1931.

Banks was an immediate success. His lucid and natural conversational speech and intimate on-air style challenged the practice by Australian commercial radio announcers of cultivating an artificial British Broadcasting Corporation accent. Known as 'the man with the smile in his voice', Banks became a celebrity. In 1932 he was paired with Naomi Melwit as 'Norm and Joan', and their 'Love Letter Competition' drew a flood of fan mail. Tall, good-looking and impeccably groomed, he was lionised by radio magazines. He quickly demonstrated his versatility, calling football matches, hosting beauty competitions, describing society weddings, covering the 1934-35 Melbourne and Victorian centenary celebrations, and recording voice-overs for Fox Movietone News, Val Morgan [q.v.Supp.] Pty Ltd cinema advertising and Commonwealth government films.

Soon Banks was Victoria's favourite announcer, and after a world trip in 1935-36 to study industry developments, he expanded his repertoire with American ideas, including the 'P[rofessional] and A[mateur] Parade' and 'The Voice of the Voyager' (shipboard interviews with famous visitors to Melbourne). 'The average housewife', he told *New Idea*, 'wants from radio what she gets from the talkies and novels—an escape from realities'. During 1938 Banks's week began on Monday around 4 a.m., when he rose to take the customs launch to an incoming passenger liner to broadcast at 8.30 a.m. 'The Voice of the Voyager'. Daily at teatime there was Norm and Kay's 'Kitchen Kapers', followed by theatre news, and the evenings were occupied by comedy shows ('Husbands and Wives', 'Stumbles') and music programs ('Masters of Melody', 'Crooners and Croonettes', 'Harmony Home'). Friday brought 'Sports Highlights', and Saturday was a veritable marathon with the 'Match of the Day' football broadcast (in summer, 'Musical Matinee' was substituted), then 'Voice of the People' (interviews with theatre-goers), before Banks compèred the 'Makin' Whoopee' cabaret, and rounded off the evening with an hour of dance music. In all, over six days Banks broadcast for almost fourteen hours, and on Sunday 'The Voice of the Voyager', his only pre-recorded program, was re-broadcast. Several colleagues, notably Doug Elliot [q.v.], assisted him on air with the variety shows and sports coverage, but mostly Banks did the research, selected the music and wrote the scripts.

His charity work was considerable: he conducted an annual Christmas Day appeal for the Austin Hospital and sought jobs for the unemployed with 'Help Thy Neighbour'. From 1938 he organised a festival of Christmas carols in the Alexandra Gardens; 'Carols by Candlelight' became a Melbourne institution and spread across Australia and abroad. That year his new long-term contract with 3KZ reputedly made him Victoria's highest paid broadcaster.

Banks had critics who considered risqué his conversations in 'Husbands and Wives', his suggestive banter with theatre crowds drawn to 'The Voice of the People' and his *doubles entendres* during department store broadcasts of 'The Voice of the Business Girl'. Such vulgarity, contrasting with the piety of his devotional programs, suggested hypocrisy. Banks's 75- to 80-hour working week damaged his health and then his marriage. He and his wife were reconciled, but he soon resumed his punishing schedule and in 1943 collapsed under the pressure of announcing six nights, and producing twelve large features, a week. In 1945, though badly injured in a motorcar smash, he recovered to mark the end of World War II, broadcasting the victory celebrations and a thanksgiving 'Carols by Candlelight'.

By the late 1940s Banks had rationalised his evening offerings to the top-rating program of popular classics 'Myer Musicale', two quizzes, and the devotional 'Hymns of Prayer and Praise' which in 1947 attracted one-quarter of

Melbourne's radio audience. But radio still curtailed his family life and disrupted his weekends. He had become a 'workaholic', addicted to success. The result was continuing marital disharmony from which he sought refuge in the occupation that in 1948 he branded 'the greatest single destroyer of normal social happiness'.

When differences with 3KZ management led to Banks's resignation in July 1952, he was quickly snapped up by the Macquarie Broadcasting Service Pty Ltd. On 3AW he duplicated most of his successes, including the quiz 'Party Line', the musical miscellany 'Your Music and Mine', the comedy show 'Rate Your Mate', and football, now uninterrupted by horse-racing. He also moved into public affairs, regularly travelling overseas to gather material for 'The World in My Diary'. Between 1952 and 1978 he made thirty-eight overseas trips. 'Views and Interviews' probed Melbourne issues; 'Children Make You Think' posed philosophical problems for clergy; and 'People I Meet' featured interviews with visiting notables. Listeners' views polarised: admirers lauded him as informed, erudite and polished, and praised his ease with eminent people; critics found him opinionated, overbearing and unctuous, and objected to his pedantry and name-dropping. Some divined a shift in his sympathies from the underdogs to the silvertails.

Certainly Banks's politics had changed. A Labor voter when he joined 3KZ, he grew cynical about trade union and machine politics and by 1949 supported the Liberals. The war had made him a pronounced Anglophile. He was inaugural president in 1944 of the Commercial Announcers' Club, which encouraged Empire loyalty. In 1946-47 he encouraged the revival of Empire Day by broadcasting Royal Empire Society addresses and hosting programs on the day. For services to broadcasting, including his radio appeals for charity, he was appointed MBE in 1953.

Banks covered the proceedings of the royal commission on espionage in 1954-55, complementing his daytime broadcasts with trenchant evening commentaries (later as 'Melbourne Diary'). In 1956 he became editor-in-chief of 3AW's world news coverage, with authority over the entire news division, including newsreaders and the sports department. Although the Macquarie Network contemplated broadcasting his programs nationally, he remained essentially a Melbourne figure, a towering and increasingly controversial one.

As an Imperial patriot Banks was dismayed by decolonisation. During an extensive tour of South Africa in 1957, he detected the spectre of communism behind African nationalism. By 1962 he supported the migration to Australia of white refugees from Kenya. In 1964 he investigated race relations in South Africa,

England and the USA, spending three weeks in South Africa as a guest of the Verwoerd government. On radio and television, he became an outspoken supporter of white supremacy and apartheid. 'The Norman Banks Program', seen on GTV-9 from 1963, brought him accusations of racism and anti-Semitism after he interviewed Eric Butler, director of the Australian League of Rights. Banks's retort, 'Some of my best friends are Jewish', and his continuing defence of the regimes in South Africa and Southern Rhodesia generated outrage and raised issues of media accountability. GTV-9 cancelled the program at the end of 1965. Embittered by the episode, Banks hardened in his defence of White Australia and apartheid. His opposition to miscegenation extended to declining an invitation to a mixed-race marriage.

Banks commanded a large audience that shared his obsessions and prejudices. In 1965 3AW, vaunting the 'Norman Conquest', attracted one-quarter of Melbourne's morning and early afternoon radio audience. In 1970 more than three hundred thousand listeners tuned to Banks for at least two hours each week. Unrivalled and unchallengeable, he was described by *Listener In-TV* in 1969 as 'almost a deity at the Macquarie Network'. The key to his supremacy was the talkback show 'Openline', which began with his ringing 'The top of the morning to you, ladies and gentlemen'. Talkback radio came just when his sight began to deteriorate as a result of two work accidents in the 1960s. Banks fudged football broadcasts for several years until 1971 and kept abreast of the news by relying on radio rather than print. He maintained his ratings with controversy, notably on-air brawling with the feminist Claudia Wright and the liberal-minded Ormsby Wilkins, who once labelled Banks 'a sanctimonious old hypocrite'. Railing against a hedonistic and permissive society, he denounced abortion, feminism and homosexuality, and extolled capital punishment. When ill health finally forced his retirement on 3 July 1978, there was standing-room only at the Windsor Hotel for his last broadcast. He signed off with thanks to 'the humble people, the little people … for your trust, loyalty and support'. Mrs Jennifer McCallum, former president of People Against Communism, wept.

In 1978 Banks's 47-year career in broadcasting was said to be the world's longest, but he had been more than a great survivor. He transformed the voice of radio in the 1930s, pioneered team broadcasting, became a master of talkback, and was for decades an influential spokesman for conservatism, bolstering the Liberal Party's long ascendancy in Victoria. Radio was the passion that consumed him. While extolling publicly the virtues of marriage, home and family, privately he was deeply unhappy. Although he claimed that any publicity was good publicity, he was dogged for years by the Melbourne 'scandal sheet' *Truth*'s coverage of his marital discord, and by popular innuendo about his alleged womanising. He feared for his and his family's privacy. On weekends he withdrew to a holiday house, and become dependent on male friendships. Even in the more sophisticated and questioning world of the 1970s, his audience remained substantial and loyal. His broadcasting style survived among those who revered his memory and emulated his delivery. His name and the causes he espoused continued to arouse passion among his admirers and detractors.

Near blindness and failing health made Banks's last years difficult. Survived by his wife and their two sons and two daughters, he died on 15 September 1985 at Malvern and was cremated two days later. Only then did the family announce his death.

R. R. Walker, *The Magic Spark* (1973) and *Dial 1179: The 3KZ Story* (1984); L. Johnson, *The Unseen Voice* (1988); Banks papers (SLV); family information and personal knowledge.   JOHN LACK

BARBER, NOLA ISABEL CONSTANCE (1901-1985), mayor and community worker, was born on 27 December 1901 at Woodend, Victoria, daughter of William Oswald Griffiths, a Melbourne-born 'student of electricity' and later estate agent, and his wife Elizabeth, née Dick, who was born in New Zealand. Nola was educated in Melbourne. Graduating from the (Emily McPherson) College of Domestic Economy, she taught at state schools in the city and suburbs, and in Geelong. She attended the University of Melbourne part time in 1926 and 1939 and ceased teaching in 1940. On 12 March that year at the office of the government statist, Melbourne, she married David Reaburn Barber (d.1971), a law clerk; they had three children and settled at Aspendale.

In 1948-57 and 1960-75 Mrs Barber served on Chelsea City Council, and in 1962-63 held office as mayor of Chelsea, the first woman to do so. As a councillor, she endeavoured to implement her vision of how a civilised society should provide for the needs of its members. Conservative colleagues often opposed her, but she persisted, sponsoring the appointment of a trained social worker, and the establishment of a home-help scheme, Meals on Wheels, kindergartens, a municipal library, a sewerage authority, a spastic centre at Aspendale, and elderly citizens' clubs. She attended the National Education Congress in Melbourne in 1963 and advocated increased Federal funding for schools.

Well organised and an efficient manager of her household, Barber found time for an extraordinary amount of community work. She was president of the Aspendale Technical School council and an executive member of the Technical Schools Association of Victoria. Among other organisations, she was active in the Aspendale Elderly Citizens Club, Chelsea Citizens Advice Bureau, Chelsea Community Health Centre, City of Chelsea Historical Society Girl Guides' Association, Chelsea Benevolent Society, Australian Red Cross Society and the Victorian Baby Health Centres Association. She also taught children to swim. The Royal Life Saving Society awarded Barber its recognition badge (1963), and the Rotary Club of Aspendale its community service award (1977). She was appointed OBE (1970) and included on the Centenary of Federation *Victorian Honour Roll of Women* (2001). A kindergarten at Aspendale was named after her. She was the Victorian Council on the Ageing's inaugural senior citizen of the year in 1983.

Barber had been a co-founder (1951) of the Australian Local Government Women's Association, which made her a life member (1966). Joining the Australian Labor Party in 1955, she presided over the women's central organising committee, broadcast regularly on radiostation 3KZ (until 1967) and, as a Victorian delegate, visited China and Japan in 1958. She contested as endorsed Labor candidate the Federal seat of Flinders (1958 and 1963) and the State seat of Mentone (1961 and 1967) at a time when prejudice in the party made it difficult for women to gain preselection.

A member of the Australian and New Zealand Congress for International Co-operation and Disarmament, Barber had served on the committee of the 1959 peace congress in Melbourne. She was also a member of the United Nations Association of Australia (Victorian division), the Union of Australian Women, and the Aborigines Advancement League (Victoria), and foundation president (1965) of the anti-conscription organisation Save our Sons. Barber sought peaceful solutions to conflict and fought strongly for human dignity and justice. Maintaining a positive outlook, she preferred to see the good in people. She was a skilled violinist who inherited a love of classical music from her mother. Survived by her daughter and two sons, she died on 29 December 1985 at Colac and was cremated.

S. Fabian and M. Loh, *Left-Wing Ladies* (2000); *Australian*, 10 June 1965, p 12; *VCOTA News Bulletin*, Feb/Mar 1983, p 3; Chelsea City Council, Minute books (held by City of Kingston, Melbourne); private information and personal knowledge.

IAN CATHIE

BARBOUR, LYNDALL HARVEY (1916-1986), radio actress, was born on 19 May 1916

58

in Cairo, eldest of four children and only daughter of Captain Eric Pitty Barbour (d.1934), Australian Army Medical Corps, Australian Imperial Force, and his wife Dora Frances Blanche, née Grieve (d.1930), who were both born in New South Wales. She was taken to live in Britain until the family returned to Sydney in 1919. Cared for by her grandmother, Lyndall was educated at Sydney Church of England Girls' Grammar School, Darlinghurst, and the University of Sydney (BA, 1938). She joined the Sydney University Dramatic Society and played leading roles under May Hollinworth's [q.v.14] direction.

After attending radio auditions in 1937, Barbour was engaged by Edward Howell [q.v.] to act as ladies-in-waiting in the serial 'Coronets of England'; she took drama lessons with his wife Therese Desmond. In January 1938 she was auditioned by the Australian Broadcasting Commission and given the leading role in the serial 'Into the Light'. Henceforth she starred in some three hundred plays and serials for the ABC. Possessing 'a fine clear voice, intelligence and wit, and a strong emotional drive', she developed her skills quickly. She worked regularly with George Edwards and Nell Stirling [qq.v.8,16]. In long-running serials she became well known as the intrepid Kay Lawrence in a wartime spy thriller, 'First Light Fraser', and as Elizabeth Blackburn in Max Afford's [q.v.13] 'Danger Unlimited', and co-starred with Peter Finch [q.v.14] in 'Crossroads of Life'. She accepted numerous leading roles for Lux Radio Theatre (broadcast successively on radio-stations 2GB, 2UW and 2UE), Macquarie Radio Theatre (2GB) and 'Library of the Air' (2GB).

Barbour found radio 'the most challenging medium for an actress' as 'you have to rely on only one skill, your voice'. At the microphone she was scared of doing a French accent, which she considered the most difficult to portray. Although adept at comedy, she preferred dramatic, emotion-charged roles such as prostitutes, female fiends, sex-motivated murderesses and psychiatric cases, 'the madder the better'. Lyndall loved books: P. G. Wodehouse was her favourite author. She also loved horses, and enjoyed attending race meetings, 'not particularly to bet, but just to see the glorious things'.

The late 1940s and early 1950s were her busiest times: she did forty or fifty serial episodes a week. Barbour won Macquarie awards for the best supporting actress in 1946 and 1948, and best actress in 1949 (in 'Genius at Home'). She played in the comedy show 'Gently Bentley' in the early 1950s, produced *Winterset* for the ABC in 1951 and took over 'Women's Week' on 2GB late in 1952 when Gwen Plumb went to England.

Her shoulder-length, honey-coloured hair waved naturally, framing a face 'alive with humour and intelligence'. Despite her good looks, Barbour took only stage roles that interested her. She won the Sydney Theatre Critics' Circle award for best actress in 1955-56 for her performance in Tennessee Williams's *The Rose Tattoo* (1956). After the introduction of television in 1956, she had 'to scratch a bit' to find radio work but managed to make a fairly comfortable living, helped by her title role as a brilliant lawyer in the long-running (1954-70) serial 'Portia Faces Life'. She visited England for six months in 1959 and starred in the West End, London, in *Detour After Dark*. Back in Sydney, she appeared in the television serial (1967) and film (1969) of Jon Cleary's novel *You Can't See Round Corners* (1948).

Dedicated to her career, Barbour did not marry. In her later years she became a recluse and spent much of her time in her North Sydney flat enthusiastically watching cricket on television, revelling especially in the batting of Greg Chappell. In the 1980s she recorded books for the Royal Blind Society of New South Wales. Lyndall Barbour died of cancer on 10 October 1986 at Wahroonga and was cremated. The National Film and Sound Archive holds recordings of many of her radio performances.

R. Lane, *The Golden Age of Australian Radio Drama* (1994); *ABC Weekly*, 26 May 1945, p 9, 15 Oct 1949, p 42; *SMH*, 7 Apr 1947, p 3, 14 Apr 1947, p 5, 21 Feb 1949, p 5, 6 Feb 1950, p 4, 9 July 1953, p 7, 13 June 1956, p 4, 24 Nov 1966, p 2, 13 Oct 1986, p 4; *Sun-Herald* (Sydney), 2 Apr 1967, p 90; Actors' Equity of Aust, *Equity*, Dec 1986, p 30; C1229, Artists cards—L. Barbour, and SP1011/2, item 151 (NAA).

MARTHA RUTLEDGE

BARCS, EMERY (1905-1990), journalist, was born Imre Bruchsteiner on 21 June 1905 in Budapest, son of James Julius Bruchsteiner, goldsmith, and his wife Ilka, née Matzner. Imre attended Bolyai College and the Royal Hungarian Faculty of Economics, completing his course in 1929. He worked as a journalist on *Esti Kurir* in 1925-26 and then as secretary to the president of the Chamber of Commerce and Industry for four years. After completing his degree, he returned to journalism, with the newspaper *Az Est*.

On 29 August 1931 in Budapest he married a 'childhood playmate', Eva Vica Somogyi. In 1933 he changed his name from Bruchsteiner to Barcs to conceal his Jewish origins. That year he was appointed to *Az Est*'s office in Rome. He reported on the Italo-Ethiopian conflict in 1935, and completed a doctorate in political science at the Royal University of Rome with a thesis comparing press laws in various countries. A committee member of the Foreign Press Association, he was expelled from Italy in 1938, possibly for his private criticisms of fascism.

On his return to Hungary Barcs continued to work on *Az Est* and became acting editor of *Pesti Naplo*. In a climate of rising fascism he was refused admission to the Hungarian Chamber of Journalists, which meant he could no longer follow his profession. He applied in December 1938 to migrate to Australia and arrived in Sydney next August. By this time he used the name Eméric, abbreviated to Em(m)ery. On 19 October 1939 his application to join the Australian Journalists' Association was accepted. At his request, the federal executive of the AJA had supported his application for entry into Australia. He was unusual in Australian journalism at that time for his university education, extensive background as a foreign correspondent and ability to speak five languages. He worked as a freelance journalist for Australian and overseas newspapers.

Barcs was asked to contribute to the Australian Broadcasting Commission's 'Notes on the News'; his commentaries were read by an announcer as his European accent was considered unsuitable for Australian listeners. These talks were broadcast from early 1941, but were interrupted when he was detained as an 'enemy alien' in December. In October 1939 he had tried to enlist in the Australian Imperial Force but was rejected. He was interned at Liverpool, New South Wales, and Tatura, Victoria, until February 1942. Called up for full-time duty in the Citizen Military Forces on 27 July, he served with the 3rd Employment Company before being discharged on 7 October 1944 because of a sinus condition. During this period he was asked to join the inaugural committee of the Association of Refugees (Association of New Citizens). Barcs was naturalised in 1946. He maintained an active interest in refugee issues through the Australian Council for International Social Service.

Having continued his freelance journalism while on military service, Barcs joined the staff of (Australian) Consolidated Press Ltd in November 1944 and worked on the *Daily Telegraph* under the editor Brian Penton [q.v.15]. Using pen-names (Esmond Barclay was one) he began with features on many themes, but quickly established himself as a specialist foreign-affairs writer at a time when commentary in this field was largely dominated by academics. He effectively became the *Telegraph*'s foreign editor in the mid-1950s, although he seems not to have held that title officially. During the 1950s Barcs travelled extensively on assignments including the Japanese Peace Conference in San Francisco (1951), the inaugural council meeting of the South-East Asia Treaty Organization in Bangkok (1955) and the Asian-African Conference in Bandung, Indonesia (1955). He also visited Africa and Europe. He had resumed work for the ABC and continued broadcasting into the 1980s. In 1945-46 he had lectured for the adult education branch of the University of Sydney.

Barcs also contributed a number of articles to the journal *Quadrant* and supported the organisation that published it, the Australian Committee (Association) for Cultural Freedom. He joined the Killara branch of the Liberal Party of Australia before the 1961 elections. Although he officially retired in 1975 he continued to write for the *Bulletin*, including sections of the 1976 series 'The Australian Family', and published his memoirs, *Backyard of Mars* (1980). He lived at Killara for forty years. Survived by his wife, Barcs died on 10 November 1990 at Castlecrag and was cremated. They had no children.

NY Times, 13 Feb 1938, p 6; *Bulletin*, 5 Sept 1989, p 23; *SMH*, 13 Nov 1990, p 10; A435, item 1945/4/4079, A12217, item L9170, B884, item N224856 (NAA); Barcs papers (SLNSW).

JOHN TEBBUTT

BARKER, CAROLINE (1894-1988), artist, was born on 8 September 1894 at Ascot Vale, Melbourne, second of ten children of Victorian-born parents Arthur Barker, journalist, and his wife Eliza, née Stribley. Caroline's great-grandfather was Henry Bone, a portraitist who exhibited at the Royal Academy, London; her mother, who painted privately, encouraged her to pursue a career as an artist. Educated at Ascot Vale State School, Caroline enrolled in 1912 at the National Gallery schools, where she studied painting with Bernard Hall and drawing with Frederick McCubbin [qq.v.9,10]. Among her contemporaries were M. Napier Waller, Adelaide Perry [qq.v.12,15], Sheila McCubbin, Marion Jones and Enid Dickson. Awarded second prize for monochrome painting in 1917 and given a year's free tuition, she completed her studies in 1919. Because of his health Arthur Barker moved the family in 1920 to Brisbane, where he established Barker's Book Store. Caroline taught art (1921-22) at Ipswich Girls' Grammar School and saved enough money for a trip to England. Accompanied by her mother, she set off in March 1923.

In London Barker met up with Perry and Jones, and Daphne Mayo [q.v.] from Queensland. Accepted into the Royal Academy schools, she studied under Cayley Robinson and Charles Sims. Next year at the Byam Shaw School of Art she learned painting from Rex Vicat Cole and drawing from F. E. Jackson and won a prize for portraiture. She visited the Continent and then spent a month in Cornwall sketching with Perry and Frances Hodgkins. Her painting 'Delphiniums' was included in the 1926 exhibition of the Paris Salon of the Société des Artistes Français. Returning to Brisbane that year, she initially painted in Vida Lahey's [q.v.9] and Mayo's studios, but soon established her own in George Street, where she was to remain until 1954. According to her sister Agnes Richardson, she would depart for her studio after breakfast and not return until the last tram at 11 p.m., except on Sundays, when she would appear for the evening meal. For some time the two sisters ran a gift shop in conjunction with the studio.

In 1928 Barker exhibited a portrait of W. A. Jolly [q.v.9], first lord mayor of Brisbane, at the Royal Queensland Art Society. That year she was elected to the council of the society. In the 1930s her studio became a significant meeting place for artists and was affectionately known as Grand Central Station. She held weekly life classes, and allowed the premises to be used for play rehearsals. During World War II Australian and other Allied servicemen and women, including Donald Friend [q.v.] and (Sir) William Dargie, frequented the studio and attended sketching classes. Dargie recalled in 1995 Barker's 'friendly bustling Queensland manner and her open-minded acceptance of all styles of artistic expression'. Barker taught art to schoolgirls at Somerville House (1935-46), where her students included Margaret Olley, Betty Cameron (later Churcher) and Margaret Cilento, and, at various times, at Loreto Convent, Clayfield College and St Margaret's Church of England Girls' School. She also taught privately at her Coorparoo home. Among those who benefited from her tuition were Dorothy Coleman, Lola McCausland, John Rigby, Gordon Shepherdson and Hugh Sawrey.

Barker exhibited portraits and still lifes with the RQAS in 1927-87. She served on the committee almost continuously in 1928-73 (life member 1964) and was a vice-president in 1945, 1953 and 1956-73. She rarely exhibited with other Brisbane groups and held her only solo exhibition in 1980. She took over the portraiture classes at the society in 1963 and three years later expanded her activities to include still-life painting. In 1974 three hundred people expressed their regard by attending her eightieth birthday party at the society's premises. She was appointed MBE in 1979. Still teaching two classes a week in 1986, she was quoted in the Brisbane *Daily Sun*: 'I love Queensland for the colours. The skies are such a vivid blue and the colours of the flowers are so sharp, so positive. I can't imagine myself living anywhere else'.

In 1986 Barker painted a portrait of Sallyanne Atkinson, lord mayor of Brisbane, who then became aware of her contribution to the local art community and arranged for the Civic Art Gallery, housed in City Hall, to acquire a substantial collection of her work.

That year Barker was named Zonta Club of Brisbane's woman of achievement. Through the joint effort of the Civic Art Gallery's advisory committee and the RQAS, the Caroline Barker prize for tertiary art students was first awarded in 1987. Barker died on 23 July 1988 in South Brisbane and was cremated with Anglican rites. A retrospective exhibition was held at Savode, Brisbane, the following year and in 1999 'A Tribute to Caroline Barker' was staged at the RQAS gallery.

K. Bradbury and G. R. Cooke, *Thorns & Petals* (1988); B. Larner and F. Considine, *A Complementary Caste* (1988); *Courier-Mail* (Brisbane), 11 Apr 1977, p 16, 10 Sept 1981, p 2, 21 Apr 1989, p 19, 28 July 1984, 'Great Weekend', p 4; *Telegraph* (Brisbane), 9 July 1980, p 60; *Daily Sun* (Brisbane), 11 Feb 1986, p 19; B. Blackman, taped interview with C. Barker (1986, NLA); private information.

GLENN R. COOKE

BARKER, LEWIS ERNEST STEPHEN (1895-1981), army officer, was born on 5 May 1895 at Mulgrave, Melbourne, fourth child of Victorian-born parents Richard Barker, market gardener and later dairyman, and his wife Edith Sibella Frances, née Irving. John Barker [q.v.3] was his grandfather. Educated at Brighton Grammar School (1909-13), Lewis entered the Royal Military College, Duntroon, Federal Capital Territory, in March 1914. Graduating sixth out of thirty-five, he was appointed as a lieutenant, Australian Imperial Force, on 4 April 1916. He was then 5 ft 10½ ins (179 cm) tall, with a fair complexion, blue eyes and fair hair.

Posted to the 8th Field Artillery Brigade, Barker sailed for England in May 1916. He served on the Western Front with this unit from December and with the 39th Battalion from June 1917. Twice wounded, he was promoted to captain in October and transferred to the 12th FAB in May 1918. In September, as a liaison officer with the infantry near Bellicourt, he bombed his way with grenades along a trench under heavy machine-gun fire and re-established an important post. He was awarded the Military Cross (1919).

In August 1919 Barker returned to Australia and the dispiriting life of a regular officer with its poor pay and limited prospects. On 28 April 1921 he married Alice Hope McEachern at the Presbyterian Church, Kew, Melbourne. It was to be a happy union and together they undertook the roundabout of postings to artillery brigades. He was recommended to attend the Army Staff College, Camberley, England, but the Scullin [q.v.11] government slashed defence expenditure, and he was denied the opportunity of training for senior operational planning appointments. While in Melbourne, he served under Lieutenant Colonel (Sir) Edmund Herring [q.v.], with whom the austere, abstemious Barker got on very well. Promoted to major in 1936, he commanded the fortresses at Newcastle, New South Wales, for a time in 1939. On 26 April 1940 he was seconded to the AIF and given command of the new 2/4th Field Regiment. He stayed with the regiment for only four months, but had an enduring impact on standards.

Arriving in the Middle East in August 1940, Barker shortly afterwards took over the 2/1st Field Regiment, 6th Division. His role was to retrain his unit with new 25-pounder (11 kg) guns. Again his forceful personality made an immediate impression. Quickly his men's attitude changed from apprehension to admiration and respect. In action he was known as 'Doag', his code name. He led from the front and ensured his guns were always well forward to give fire support. With rapid and sometimes daring advances, 'Barker's Bedouins' distinguished themselves in the capture of Bardia, Tobruk and Benghazi, Libya. For his bold leadership and technical proficiency, in 1941 Barker was awarded the Distinguished Service Order and mentioned in despatches.

Flown home to Australia in April 1941, Barker was promoted to colonel and made director of artillery. He oversaw organisational change in Militia units and the acceptance into service of a range of Australian-built equipment. In April 1942 he was appointed to command I Corps' artillery as a brigadier. With the Japanese threat growing, he was sent to Port Moresby in August, where he had a 'three-hatted' command of the artillery of the 7th Division, New Guinea Force and I Corps. Responsible for all artillery operations in New Guinea, he was the ideal man for the job.

Until February 1943, and again from August 1943 to May 1944, Barker was in New Guinea. In between he was the senior artillery brigadier of the First Army in Australia. Initially he had few guns, and these were of different calibre and capability. He moved them to the battlefields by barge, air or man-handling. As his resources increased, artillery proved decisive. Japanese prisoners said that artillery was one of the most potent factors in their defeat. Displaying 'coolness and courage' together with 'outstanding energy and efficiency', Barker was appointed CBE (1943).

There was one discordant note. To provide more effective artillery support, a lightweight Australian 'short' 25-pounder gun was developed. Barker strongly opposed its introduction, believing it offered no advantage. However, he accepted the contrary decision. It is doubtful that his attitude was the reason he gained no further promotion: his supporter, Herring, had ceased active service and, although Barker had served with distinction in his corps, top

appointments required broader experience. Again mentioned in despatches (1947), he finished the war in senior artillery appointments in Australia. In April 1946 he became commandant, 4th Military District (South Australia). He retired from the army on 12 March 1949.

Lewis and Alice lived at Bililla, a small mixed farm near Woodend, Victoria. They later moved to a peach orchard at Ourimbah, New South Wales, and finally settled at Corryong, Victoria. Barker died there on 13 December 1981 and was cremated with Anglican rites. His wife survived him, as did their two sons, one of whom, Trevor, graduated from Duntroon in 1946 with the King's medal. Lewis Barker was the model for one of the figures in May Butler-George's plaster relief 'Bringing Up the Guns', a bronze casting of which is in the sculpture garden of the Australian War Memorial, Canberra.

C. E. W. Bean, *The A.I.F. in France 1916* (1929), *The A.I.F. in France 1917* (1933), *The A.I.F. in France 1918*, 2 vols (1937, 1942); G. Long, *To Benghazi* (1952); E. V. Haywood, *Six Years in Support* (1959); D. McCarthy, *South-West Pacific Area—First Year* (1959); D. Dexter, *The New Guinea Offensives* (1961); D. Horner, *The Gunners* (1995); B883, item VX12777 (NAA); Barker papers, PR84/323 and PR01773 (AWM); private information.

S. N. GOWER

BARNARD, MARJORIE (MARJORY) FAITH (1897-1987), writer and historian, was born on 16 August 1897 at Ashfield, Sydney, only child of Sydney-born parents Oswald Holme Barnard, clerk, and his wife Ethel Frances, née Alford, and was baptised in the Anglican church. A delicate child devoted to her mother, Marjorie was stricken with poliomyelitis and was, at first, educated at home. Aged 10, she was enrolled at Florence Hooper's Cambridge School, Hunters Hill. In 1911 she moved to Sydney Girls' High School, where she completed the Leaving certificate, matriculating with a bursary in March 1916. She was pleased to leave school, but was 'in love with learning'.

At the University of Sydney (BA, 1920) Barnard graduated with first-class honours and the university medal in history. Well regarded by the history professor G. A. Wood [q.v.12], she was offered a scholarship to the University of Oxford. However her father, now a strict Presbyterian, prevented her from taking it up. In retrospect she thought he resented her abilities, and they were barely reconciled by 1940 when he died.

Barnard began work at the Public Library of New South Wales, where she topped library school examinations in 1921. Later she was transferred to Sydney Technical College, where she was librarian-in-charge from 1925. She pursued her writing at night. Her first book, short stories of childhood entitled *The Ivory Gate*, was published by H. H. Champion [q.v.7] in 1920.

On weekends, Barnard and Flora Eldershaw [q.v.14], a friend 'of the first importance' from student days, discussed collaborating on novels. A lucrative prize announced by the *Bulletin* in 1927 spurred them on. In 1928, as 'M. Barnard Eldershaw', they entered *A House is Built* (1929), a mercantile saga with a patriarchal theme set in nineteenth-century Sydney. To their astonishment, it was declared joint winner with K. S. Prichard's [q.v.11] *Coonardoo* (1929). Their book was acclaimed by no less a writer than Arnold Bennett and is now regarded as a minor classic. Barnard would later ruefully recall it as her most successful literary work, 'because it's ordinary'. At the time she asserted that the flawless collaboration was really quite simple: library research, agreed themes, allocation and exchange of chapters, and review.

Barnard and Eldershaw immediately embarked on a second novel, *Green Memory* (1931), with a similar setting and another patriarchal subject. It was less well received, and by 1932, Barnard's heart was set on short-story writing. But Harrap declined to publish her efforts, a verdict upheld by her recently acquired mentor Nettie (Janet) Palmer [q.v.11], and she had no success until 1936, when the first of numerous stories appeared in *The Home*. *The Persimmon Tree and Other Stories* (1943) came to be seen as one of her finest achievements, and a posthumous collection of stories by her and by M. Barnard Eldershaw, *But Not for Love*, appeared in 1988.

Photographs show the young Marjorie Barnard with high, wide cheek-bones and clear eyes behind thin-rimmed glasses. Shy but opinionated, she joined the main Sydney literary societies—the Society of Women Writers of New South Wales and the Henry Lawson Literary Society (1929), the Australian English Association (1930), the Sydney PEN Club (1931) and the Fellowship of Australian Writers (mid-1930s)—but without much enthusiasm. She also joined the Women's Club, and on occasion wrote speeches of feminist import for Flora Eldershaw, for example 'Contemporary Australian Women Voters'. When she first met Frank Dalby Davison [q.v.13], in 1934, she surprised him with her sharp remarks.

In 1933 Barnard had taken six months' leave and travelled overseas with her mother. She wrote 'The Conquest of Europe', an unpublished play, on the way home. In 1935 she resigned her job to write full time. Shipboard interactions provided the dynamic for Barnard Eldershaw's next novel, *The Glasshouse* (1936).

It was followed by *Plaque with Laurel* (1937), an acutely observed account of a literary gathering in Canberra.

As the world situation worsened, Barnard became more politically active. In 1935 she began a secret affair with Davison. With Eldershaw they were known as 'the triumvirate': they hosted literary soirées in a flat in King's Cross, and together with other dedicated writers, notably Jane (Jean) Devanny and Miles Franklin [qq.v.8], vigorously promoted writers' rights and opposed censorship. *Essays in Australian Fiction* (Barnard Eldershaw, 1938) evinced Barnard's concern for mature literary values. In 1939 Barnard Eldershaw contributed an essay on peace to the FAW's shelved 'Writers in Defence of Freedom'.

The onset of World War II caused Barnard 'horror and grief'. Her attempt at a manifesto, 'The Case for the Future', written for the Australian Peace Pledge Union, which she joined in 1939, and contributions to the local Council for the Unemployed's newsletter, show that an alleged indifference to politics has little basis in fact. In 1940 she joined the Australian Labor Party. But as a pacifist she was at odds with the times and, worse, with the Palmers.

Barnard's fifth novel in collaboration with Flora Eldershaw was written in 1941-43, when fear of invasion was intense. Censored in 1944 and published in expurgated form in 1947 as *Tomorrow and Tomorrow*, the complex and challenging futurist fiction fell flat, due to changed circumstances and the cuts. Its reception marked the end of the collaboration. Barnard never again published a novel (although she did complete one in 1969, 'The Gulf Stream', set in the Blue Mountains after 1945). When reissued in full by Virago in 1983 under its original title, *Tomorrow and Tomorrow and Tomorrow* was instantly recognised as a masterwork. Barnard deserves most credit for the writing and approach. However recent research suggests a true collaboration, despite emergent ideological differences and Eldershaw's move to Canberra in 1941.

For Marjorie Barnard, history was one of the creative arts. Before World War II Barnard Eldershaw had published three historical monographs of significance: the sesquicentennial *Phillip of Australia* (1938), dedicated to Wood; a fluent overview entitled *My Australia* (1939); and, in a luxury edition illustrated by Adrian Feint [q.v.14], *The Life and Times of Captain John Piper* (1939). Thereafter, as sole author, Barnard published seven historical works. In 1941 came *Macquarie's World*, dedicated to Davison. The book was a delight to generations of history students but displeasing to M. H. Ellis [q.v.14], whose charge of plagiarism was dismissed by the publisher. *Australian Outline* (1943), a striking miniature, and several deft minor works on Sydney history and biography which appeared over the next two decades, underpinned her *magnum opus*, *A History of Australia* (1962). But the *History* was another disappointment to her, due to drab presentation and grudging reviews; that she was the first Australian woman to meet the challenge of general history passed unnoticed. She was ahead of her times in highlighting social history and biography, and outstanding among the first generation of women historians trained in Australia.

With her turn to history, Barnard's reputation as a writer suffered an eclipse. However, she wrote lectures for the library school, and published short stories and a serial (in the *Australian Women's Digest*). In 1945 Barnard and Eldershaw delivered the Commonwealth Literary Fund lectures at the University of Sydney. Next year Barnard Eldershaw edited the short-story annual *Coast To Coast*, and later Barnard contributed reviews and critical essays to the literary journals *Southerly* and *Meanjin*. Notable outcomes of a long correspondence (1944-74) with the *Meanjin* editor Clem Christesen were articles on Miles Franklin (in 1955), on Patrick White (in 1956), and on the creation of *Tomorrow and Tomorrow* (in 1970).

The war had brought drastic changes to Barnard's personal life. She was now without regular contact with Eldershaw ('Teenie'); her relationship with Davison ended abruptly in mid-1942; and in that year, after stress-related ill health, she returned to work to support her widowed mother. As the librarian for the Division of Radiophysics and the National Standards Laboratory, Council for Scientific and Industrial Research (Commonwealth Scientific and Industrial Research Organization), Barnard earned the respect and affection of her staff. But 'housekeeping for scientists' and CSIR's failure in 1946 to publish her history of radar, 'One Single Weapon', affected her.

After Barnard's mother's death in 1949, a friend, Vera Murdoch, came to live with her in the family home at Longueville. Marjorie had met 'Vee' aboard ship in 1933 and they shared a passion for travel. Following Barnard's resignation from work in 1950, they embarked on extended and increasingly venturesome trips abroad, which punctuated sustained periods of research and writing. Barnard's last major work, a commissioned biography of Miles Franklin, appeared in 1967. Written with misgivings and before the release of Franklin's voluminous papers, it exhibited characteristic virtues, with insight and style making up for ambivalence and inevitable error.

In 1973 the State branch of the Society of Women Writers (Australia) gave Barnard a seventy-sixth birthday party and in 1989 it instituted a triennial award in her name for a published book. She had been appointed OAM in 1980. Three years later she received the Patrick White award, next year a New South Wales premier's special award. In 1985 the Lane Cove Library created the Marjorie Barnard local studies room to acknowledge her association with the area. The University of Sydney conferred on her an honorary D.Litt. (1986). She died on 8 May 1987 at North Gosford and was cremated.

L. E. Rorabacher, *Marjorie Barnard and M. Barnard Eldershaw* (1973); C. Baker, *Yacker 2* (1987); G. Giuffre, *A Writing Life* (1990); C. Ferrier (ed), *As Good as a Yarn with You* (1992); B. H. Fletcher, *History and Achievement* (1999); J. Roe, 'The Historical Imagination and Its Enemies: M. Barnard Eldershaw's *Tomorrow and Tomorrow and Tomorrow*', *Meanjin*, vol 43, no 2, 1984, p 241; *Hecate*, vol 17, no 2, 1991, p 9; *SMH*, 19 Nov 1983, p 43, 14 May 1986, p 9, 9 May 1987, p 6; R. Darby, While Freedom Lives (PhD thesis, ADFA, 1989); Barnard papers (SLNSW); private information.

JILL ROE

BARNES, JOHN HANDYSIDE (1922-1985), medical practitioner and toxinologist, was born on 2 April 1922 at Charleville, Queensland, younger child of Queensland-born Henry Edward Barnes, chemist, and his wife Vera Adeline, née East, who came from New South Wales. The family lived on a sheep station, Dungiven, about 100 miles (160 km) west of Charleville, and Jack was a pupil of the Queensland Correspondence Primary School. He became an expert horseman and an accomplished rifle-shooter. After boarding at Brisbane Grammar School for four years, he enrolled in 1940 as a medical student at the University of Queensland (MB, BS, 1946).

On 22 December 1941 Barnes interrupted his studies to enlist in the Australian Imperial Force. Posted to the 4th (2/4th) Independent Company, he served on Timor from September 1942 to January 1943. He suffered malnutrition, malaria and other infectious diseases, and returned to Australia weighing only 4 st. 6 lb. (28 kg). After recovering in hospital, he was discharged from the army on 24 April 1943 to resume his university course. On 23 May 1945 at Ann Street Presbyterian Church, Brisbane, he married Laloma Mavis Hudson, a physiotherapy student. He graduated next year and gained experience as a resident medical officer at Mater Misericordiae Hospital, South Brisbane. In July 1947 he was appointed medical superintendent of Thursday Island Hospital. Despite a heavy workload, he was able to pursue his interests in boating, fishing and vegetable-growing. In January 1953 he and his family moved to Cairns, where he set up in general practice.

Barnes was intrigued by Hugo Flecker's [q.v.14] research into *Chironex fleckeri* South-cott, a box jellyfish that caused potentially fatal stings to people swimming off North Queens-land beaches, and in 1958 agreed to a request from the local branch of the British Medical Association to investigate further. An innova-tive and incisive naturalist, he first sought to identify the different species of marine stingers found in the region. He focused his search on a small box jellyfish, associated with symptoms called 'irukandji syndrome'—head-ache, vomiting and joint pains—occurring about twenty-five minutes after a trivial sting hardly noticed by the victim. In 1961 he even-tually collected a specimen of this transparent jellyfish—the size of a finger nail—using an apparatus which incorporated a 'flour sifter and a rat trap'. To check the symptoms, he tested the venom on himself, his 9-year-old son Nick, and a young volunteer surf lifesaver, all of whom reported the delayed but excruciat-ing pain. His collaborator, R. V. Southcott, named the organism, which was new to science, *Carukia barnesi*. Barnes was appointed MBE in 1970.

In research into *C. fleckeri*, Barnes tried to determine the composition of its venom and how it was discharged, hoping that an antidote could be found. Discovering that the jellyfish would not discharge its venom against a synthetic surface, he donned pantihose when collecting specimens. This practice proved effective in preventing stings and was later adopted and adapted by surf lifesavers. Barnes mobilised a chain of medical practitioners and lifesavers from Mackay to Cape Tribulation to educate bathers about symptoms of enveno-mation, and to inform him when stingings occurred.

A close friend, Dr Graham Cossins, judged that Barnes was 'irritable and belligerent, ... demanding and critical, unsociable and rude' but that 'under that gruff exterior was a kindly and compassionate associate'. Survived by his wife, their two sons and one of their three daughters, he died of myocardial infarction on 11 August 1985 at Cairns, and was buried with Anglican rites in Martyn Street cemetery.

B. Kinsey, *Barnes on Box Jellyfish* (1986), *More Barnes on Box Jellyfish* (1988); J. Pearn (ed), *Pioneer Medicine in Australia* (1988); G. E. Lambert (comp), *Commando: From Tidal River to Tarakan* (1994); *MJA*, 17 Mar 1986, p 327; *SMH*, 30 Jan 1962, p 2, 11 Jan 2003, 'Good Weekend', p 14; personal knowl-edge.   JOE BAKER

BARNES, KATHLEEN HOPE (1909-1981), nurse, was born on 19 May 1909 at Cottesloe, Perth, fifth daughter of James Barnes, an Irish-born storekeeper, and his wife Agnes Kirkwood Burns, née Patrick, who came from Scotland. Educated at Methodist Ladies' College, Kathleen was head prefect in 1925. She commenced her nursing training at the Children's Hospital in July 1928 and graduated as a general nurse in February 1932.

On 20 December 1939 Barnes joined the Australian Army Nursing Service, Australian Imperial Force. The army recorded that she had blue eyes, brown hair and a fair com-plexion. Posted to the 2/2nd Australian Gen-eral Hospital as a staff nurse, she embarked for the Middle East in April 1940. She served at Gaza Ridge and Nazareth, Palestine, where she was seconded to a British hospital. Later rejoining the 2/2nd at Kantara, Egypt, she nursed casualties from the fighting in Greece, Crete and North Africa. From October 1941 to January 1942 she was attached to the 2/4th Field Ambulance at Tripoli, Syria. She returned to Australia in March and initially worked at the 109th AGH, Adelaide.

Sent to Port Moresby in October 1942, Barnes served with the 105th Casualty Clearing Station. A talented and experienced nurse, she was appointed lieutenant in March 1943 and promoted to captain in August. In February 1945 she took charge of the nursing contingent at Jacquinot Bay, New Britain. For her 'outstanding devotion to duty and solici-tude for soldiers' she was appointed (1947) an associate of the Royal Red Cross. She was also mentioned in despatches.

Back in Australia in September 1945, Barnes worked at the 110th Military Hospital, Perth. After five years of continuous active ser-vice, she was placed on the Reserve of Officers on 27 March 1946. She was a prominent mem-ber of Western Australian war-nursing organ-isations, including the returned sisters' sub-branch of the Returned Sailors', Soldiers' and Airmen's Imperial League of Australia. Treasurer of the War Nurses' Memorial Association from its formation in 1958 until her death, she was involved (from 1979) in the establishment of the war nurses' gallery in the Army Museum of Western Australia.

From 1947 the Silver Chain District and Bush Nursing Association employed Barnes as a district nurse. Within a year she was made assistant-superintendent and supervisor of the Cottage Homes. The Alfred Carson [q.v.7] Hospital was added to her responsibilities in 1950 and in 1955 she was appointed metro-politan nursing superintendent. Under her guidance, the organisation grew substantially. In July 1965 she resigned after a disagreement with management. Known for her leadership qualities and ability to inspire those around her, she had been appointed MBE in 1963 for her 'outstanding and meritorious service in the nursing profession, both in wartime and in peace' and was invested by Queen Elizabeth II during a royal visit to Perth. That year she was made a fellow of the College of Nursing,

Australia. Unmarried, she died on 4 July 1981 at her Nedlands home and was cremated with Presbyterian forms.

N. Stewart, *Little but Great* (1965); R. Goodman, *Our War Nurses* (1988); Silver Chain District and Bush Nursing Assn (WA), *Annual Report*, 1948-65; *West Australian*, 1 Jan 1963, p 8, 27 Mar 1963, p 24, 3 July 1965, p 22; *Listening Post* (WA), Spring 1981, p 43; Premier's Dept (WA), AN 2/10 Acc 1704, box 1, file 335/61 (SRWA); B883, item WX1543 (NAA); War Nurses Memorial Assn (WA) records (SLWA).

MELANIE OPPENHEIMER

BARNETT, HERBERT STANLEY (1896-1981), farmer and entrepreneur, was born on 3 June 1896 at Gordon, Tasmania, fourth child of Henry Ralph Barnett, storekeeper, and his wife Jane Taylor, née Lambert. Educated at Queen's College and The Hutchins School, Hobart, Stan trained as an electrical engineer and was employed in 1916-17 as a junior assistant-engineer in the Postmaster-General's Department. Having been mobilised in the Militia as a corporal in the 36th Fortress Company, Engineers, he enlisted in the Australian Imperial Force on 17 December 1917. He was posted to the Australian Flying Corps next month and commissioned in April 1918. Arriving in England in August, he had begun training as a pilot when the war ended. His AIF appointment terminated in Tasmania on 25 February 1920. On 10 December 1924 at Launceston he married with Methodist forms Annie Edith Humphreys. Combining farming with business, he was a director (1921-38) of the Hobart firm Barnett Brothers Pty Ltd, auctioneers and merchants, and part-owner in 1930-45 of two farms, one in the Huon district and the other at Randalls Bay. He was also involved in real estate development, particularly property subdivisions.

In the 1930s Barnett proposed forming a company to erect a toll bridge across the River Derwent at Hobart. (Sir) Allan Knight, then an engineer with the Department of Public Works, had conceived the idea and designed a structure. Despite opposition to construction of the bridge by private enterprise, criticism of the design (a curved arch made up of twenty-four reinforced concrete floating sections), and allegations that the real objective of the promoters was land speculation on the eastern shore, the Ogilvie [q.v.11] government approved the controversial project, estimated to cost £250 000. Barnett, managing director of the Hobart Bridge Co. Ltd, arranged the necessary finance (principally from City Mutual Life Assurance Society Ltd), and construction, under the supervision of officers of the Department of Public Works, began in April 1938. On 4 December 1943, shortly before the bridge was to open, an exception-ally intense storm caused damage to the structure. Repairs, costing less than £10 000, were carried out and the bridge opened for traffic on 22 December. Nevertheless the under-writers regarded the bridge as a total loss and paid the bridge company £250 000 in full settle-ment. In 1944 the government acquired the bridge and other company assets and paid an undisclosed amount of compensation. Barnett, who owned land on the eastern shore, sub-divided it into suburban housing blocks.

Sharp and shrewd, with a good head for business, Barnett was founding chairman (1951-76) of the Tasmanian board of City Mutual. He was for many years involved with the Legacy Club of Hobart, serving (1949-50) as president, and helping to raise much money for the organisation. In January 1947, with two partners, Barnett bought a property known as Bronte in central Tasmania. The land was resumed by the Hydro-Electric Commission in May, provoking extensive litigation. He and his wife and their son purchased Quamby, near Hagley, in 1956 and restored the historic homestead, at one time the home of Sir Richard Dry [q.v.1]. Barnett had no serious religious affiliations until the 1960s, when he became a regular worshipper at the Christian Brethren's Murray Street Chapel. Survived by his wife and their son and daughter, he died on 23 August 1981 in Hobart and was buried in Cornelian Bay cemetery.

A Dream is Realised (1943); E. G. Robertson and E. N. Craig, *Early Houses of Northern Tasmania* (1964); G. W. Cox, *Ships in Tasmanian Waters* (1971); P. C. Wickens, *The City Mutual Story* (1978); *Mercury* (Hobart), 25 Aug 1981, p 12; B2455, Barnett Herbert Stanley (NAA); private information.

BARON-HAY, GEORGE KINGSTON (1895-1989), director of agriculture, was born on 3 September 1895 at Kingston, Jamaica, son of George Herbert Baron-Hay, Methodist minister, and his wife Edith Mary, née Stuart. Educated at Kingswood School, Bath, England, young George migrated to Western Australia, arriving at Albany on 19 January 1914. As an 'assigned' migrant, he was placed at Narrogin State Farm. In 1915 he was one of the first students to enrol in the faculty of agriculture at the University of Western Australia (B.Sc. Agric., 1922). During his course, interrupted by World War I, he was awarded a Hackett [q.v.9] scholarship.

On 26 June 1916 Baron-Hay enlisted in the Australian Imperial Force. He served on the Western Front with the 51st Battalion from June 1917 but was sent to England for officer-training in October. Commissioned in May 1918, he rejoined his unit in France. On 4 August he held a defensive position during an enemy attack at Hourges, patrolled the area occupied by the enemy and helped to restore the line. For his 'coolness and prompt action' he was awarded the Military Cross. That month he was severely wounded in the right arm near Bray-sur-Somme and evacuated to England. Returning to his battalion, he was promoted to lieutenant in December. His AIF appointment terminated in Perth on 5 January 1920.

Following a brief period of farm work, Baron-Hay resumed his university studies. Employed from 1922 by the State Department of Agriculture as an agricultural adviser, he gained valuable experience dealing with problems encountered by British farmers who had settled in the lower south-west under the auspices of the group settlement migration scheme. He provided advice to wheat and dairy farmers, and published articles in departmental bulletins on such matters as suitable pasture grasses and legumes, and the kerosene method for eradicating zamia palm. After his promotion in 1930 to superintendent of dairying he wrote about practical aspects of milk production and of fattening pigs using a portion of the farmers' wheat crop. On 15 July 1933 at Wesley Methodist Church, Perth, he married Vera Robinson, née Cook, a medical practitioner and a divorcee.

In 1941 Baron-Hay was appointed under-secretary of the department. In 1948-52 he was seconded to the Department of Lands and Surveys as chairman of the Land Settlement Board. After his return to the Department of Agriculture as director, he filled both positions concurrently. Under his leadership the department was associated closely with the development of a diverse range of rural industries, particularly forestry, tropical crops in the north, dairying, wool and wheat. He had an enormous capacity for work and sought similar dedication from his staff. In 1960 he retired, and next year he was appointed CBE.

Baron-Hay was president (1936) of the State branch of the Australian Institute of Agricultural Science. He was also president (1935-36) and a life member (from 1946) of the Cottesloe Surf Life Saving Club, and a member of Perth Legacy and the Rotary Club of Perth. For recreation he spent time at his weekender at Glen Forrest. Survived by his wife, and their daughter and two sons, he died on 29 September 1989 at Claremont and was buried in Karrakatta cemetery.

Jnl of Agriculture of WA, Oct 1960, p 853; *Countryman*, 15 Aug 1985, p 13; *West Australian*, 6 Oct 1989, p 9; Perth Legacy, *Bulletin*, 31 Oct 1989, p 1; B2455, item Hay G K B (NAA).   CLEMENT MULCAHY

BARRACLOUGH, LESLIE BERNARD ('TOBY') (1922-1988), drover, was born on 30 June 1922 at Cunnamulla, Queensland, fifth child of William Arthur Barraclough, labourer and bullock-driver, who came from Wilcannia, New South Wales, and his Queensland-born wife Florence Ethel, née Reid. 'Toby' moved with his family to Cloncurry, where his father worked in a copper mine. Leaving school at the age of 12, he began droving at 18 and became a head stockman at 23. In World War II he tried to enlist in the armed forces but was not accepted because his droving skills were considered important to the war effort. He met Alma Douglas, a domestic whose mother was Aboriginal, when they were both working on Corella Park station, near Cloncurry; she was aged 17 when they were married on 15 October 1945 at the Cloncurry Presbyterian Church. About that time a horse fell on him and broke his right leg in several places, leaving him with the 'best set of bow legs south of the Gulf'. An accomplished horseman, he was head stockman at Corella Park for about twenty years. In the late 1950s he tried kangaroo-shooting in the Cloncurry district, before returning to droving.

Despite having a permanent home at Cloncurry, from 1974 the Barracloughs were mainly found as contract drovers, along stock routes in Queensland and the Northern Territory. Alma was the camp cook. Her father had been a fencer; as a child she had led an itinerant life and was used to camping. At first she and Toby took little more than their swags, but over the years conditions improved as they acquired well-equipped vehicles and a caravan. Eventually Alma travelled with a kitchen sink, gas stove, refrigerator, generator and sewing machine. Toby usually had a team of five men: three to tend the cattle, one to look after the horses (about forty), and a driver. On the Barracloughs' longest trip, in 1983, when they were accompanied by two of their children, they moved 1500 cattle in a five-month drive from Miranda Downs, near Normanton, to Bulloo Downs, south-west of Thargomindah. In 1987 on a journey lasting ten weeks, they drove 1500 bullocks from Rocklands, north-west of Mount Isa, to Tanbar station, south-west of Windorah, for the Stanbroke Pastoral Co. Pty Ltd. That year the journalist Lyndall Crisp described Barraclough as one of the few 'experienced boss drovers left in Australia'.

Thin and wiry, with a leathery complexion, Barraclough was a man who enjoyed life despite several falls which resulted in back and neck injuries. In 1986 he underwent major surgery for cancer. He died on 27 February 1988 at Cloncurry and was buried with Catholic rites in the local cemetery. His wife and their three daughters and two sons survived him.

Courier-Mail (Brisbane), 8 Aug 1987, p 5; *Times on Sunday* (Sydney), 20 Sept 1987, p 27; private information.   JONATHAN RICHARDS

BARTON, SIR CHARLES NEWTON (1907-1987), commissioner of main roads and co-ordinator-general of public works, was born on 5 July 1907 at Bowen, Queensland, eldest of three sons of Queensland-born parents John Barton, bank clerk, and his wife Louisa Burnett, née Pott. An outstanding student at Maryborough Grammar School, Charles studied civil engineering at the University of Queensland (BE, 1929). While at university, living in Emmanuel College, he represented the State in rowing. In 1929 he joined the bridge branch of the Queensland Main Roads Commission; three years later he transferred to the design staff of the new bridge board, under the direction of (Sir) James Holt [q.v.], who was then supervising the construction of Brisbane's Kangaroo Point (later Story [q.v.12]) bridge. With few opportunities for promotion, he resigned in 1935 to establish the firm of (J. A.) Pollock & Barton, consulting engineers, in Mackay; he was to remain a partner until 1959. On 6 August 1935 at St Thomas's Church of England, Toowong, Brisbane, he had married Enid Louisa Emily Wetherell, a clerk.

Having served in the Citizen Military Forces since 1925, Barton was appointed lieutenant, Corps of Australian Engineers, in 1931 and promoted to captain in 1935. On 28 October 1939 he was called up for full-time duty with the 42nd Battalion as a temporary major. Seconded to the Australian Imperial Force on 1 May 1940, he was made second-in-command of the 2/15th Battalion. He was captured in Libya in April 1941 and spent the remaining war years as a prisoner in Italy and Germany. Remembered as being a strong, quietly dependable presence, he occupied his time reading, becoming proficient in Italian and conducting courses for camp inmates in science and engineering. He was repatriated in June 1945 and transferred to the Reserve of Officers on 4 September. Rejoining the CMF, he commanded the 31st Battalion (Kennedy Regiment) in 1948-52 and the 42nd Battalion (Capricornia Regiment) in 1952-57 as a lieutenant colonel. In 1954 he was appointed OBE. He was honorary colonel of the 31st Battalion (1959-60), the Australian Cadet Corps, Northern Command (1961-66), and the Queensland University Regiment (1966-72).

When Barton was appointed commissioner of main roads on 1 January 1960, he moved back to Brisbane. Characterised as 'a strategic thinker and policy planner', he was the 'new broom' who introduced a private sector appreciation of the need for operational and attitudinal changes to achieve a more efficient, responsive department. Averse to centralised and bureaucratic empires, he delegated decision-making and accountability to district offices, and ensured that local authorities were consulted in the planning of public works. He emphasised the value of improving technical skills. Under his direction, the criteria for funding different road categories were revised and in 1963 the Road Plan of Queensland, a comprehensive classification of roads for forward planning and funding purposes, was completed. Barton again made organisational changes when implementing the recommendations of Wilbur Smith & Associates's 'Brisbane Transport Study' (1965) for an extensive metropolitan highway and freeway network. He was chairman (1961-63, 1968) of the Australian Road Research Board.

On 1 January 1969 Barton took up the position of co-ordinator-general of public works. Although he disliked the 'game' of politics, he was adept at it. The exhaustive background reports he commissioned from his professional staff gave him a strong information base, and he used his department's dominance of the wide-ranging inter-departmental committee system to advantage. In what was then criticised as a revolutionary change, he oversaw the devolution of the engineering design and construction function of the Department of the Co-ordinator-General to other government authorities, thereby returning it to its core planning and co-ordinating role. In 1971-72 he influenced new legislation which further loosened the department's previously pervasive control over State public works. His preference for decentralised planning gave rise to new entities administered by departmental co-ordinators. These regional co-ordination councils established under his direction proved, however, to be ineffectual and were disbanded soon after his retirement on 31 December 1976. Barton had been knighted in 1974.

Sir Charles was inaugural chairman of the Port of Brisbane Authority (1976-79) and of the Queensland Local Government Grants Commission (1977-79), and a member (1976-78) of the Great Barrier Reef Marine Park Authority. He was elected a fellow of the Australian Academy of Technological Sciences and of the Institution of Engineers, Australia, which awarded him the (Sir) Peter Nicol Russell [q.v.6] medal in 1978. In 1968-69 he was president (life member 1977) of the Queensland division of the Australian Institute of Management. He was a member (1969-77) of the University of Queensland senate. A tall, reserved man with a distinguished military bearing, he earned the respect and loyalty of friends, colleagues and staff.

Although dedicated to his work, Barton achieved a balanced life, keeping up sporting and other recreational interests and deriving particular enjoyment from topical, often spirited, discussions he had with fellow members of his clubs: the Queensland, Johnsonian and United Service, Mackay. President (1980-82) of the Boy Scouts' Association Queensland branch council and a trustee (1969-86) of the Queensland Cancer Fund, he was also active in the Rotary Club of Brisbane and in the Legacy clubs of Mackay and Brisbane. He served as president and national director of the Queensland branch of the Australia-Britain Society, and on the parochial council of St Andrew's Church of England, Indooroopilly. Afflicted by Parkinson's disease towards the end of his life, he died on 31 March 1987 at Auchenflower and was cremated. His wife survived him; there were no children.

G. Cossins (ed), *Eminent Queensland Engineers*, vol 2 (1999); *Qld Roads*, June 1969, p 1; Univ of Qld, *Alumni News*, July 1987, p 17; B883, item QX6198 (NAA); private information.   KAY COHEN

BARTROP, EDGAR JAMES (1903-1989), real-estate agent and community leader, was born on 11 February 1903 at Brighton, Melbourne, son of James Samuel Bartrop, a Victorian-born traveller (insurance agent), and his wife Blanche Caroline, née Tomkins, who was born in Sydney. Edgar attended Caulfield State School and Bendigo and Ballarat High schools. He left in 1921, wanting to become a Methodist minister, but was too young to enter training college. At the age of 18 he set himself up as a real-estate agent in Ballarat and soon discovered that this was his vocation.

Prospering, Bartrop took over a number of real-estate agencies. On 13 April 1927 at St Andrew's Kirk, Ballarat, he married with Presbyterian forms Madge Evelyn McArthur. In 1930 he purchased the long-established business of William Little & Co. at 54 Lydiard Street South. Bartrop's approach to his profession was entrepreneurial and innovative; in 1933 he sponsored Ballarat's first 'ideal homes show' to promote a residential development. He would later be involved in housing projects of various types, and prominent in schemes to accommodate workers and migrants.

Bartrop wished to establish ethical standards for his profession. After founding the Ballarat and District Auctioneers and Estate Agents Association in 1929, he took a leading part in forming the Real Estate and Stock (later Real Estate) Institute of Victoria in 1936. He was to be president (1943-44) and a life member (from 1971) of the institute and author of its history, *'50 Years On ...'* (1987). A pamphlet he wrote in 1941, *Real-Estate Multiple Listing*, led to the introduction of this system in Australia. His booklet *Co-operative Building Societies* (1944) influenced the framing of Victorian legislation to regulate these bodies.

Appointed Commonwealth controller of accommodation in World War II, Bartrop supervised the construction of new housing and the provision of hostels and other dwellings for munitions workers, and formulated plans to relieve the national housing shortage. Politicians noted his abilities, and in 1946 the Victorian government appointed him chairman of the Decentralization of Industries Committee and a member of the Central Planning Authority.

In 1937 Bartrop had brought together leading businessmen to found the Advance Ballarat (later Greater Ballarat) Association, which was effective in promoting industry, commerce and tourism in the city. After a study tour of Britain and Europe in 1949, he instigated the city's annual Begonia Festival in 1953. He was also foundation president of the Ballarat branch of both the National Safety Council of Australia, Victorian division, and the Good Neighbour Council of Victoria. In 1967 he was appointed OBE.

A small, wiry man of boundless energy, Bartrop was a teetotaller and pipe-smoker, an original thinker, an astute businessman and a tireless worker who championed his beloved city of Ballarat. He was a member of the Lydiard Street Wesleyan (later Uniting) Church, serving as choir member, lay preacher and elder. He died on 24 June 1989 at Ballarat and was cremated. His wife and their daughter and two sons survived him.

W. Bate, *Life after Gold* (1993); *Courier* (Ballarat), 7 Aug 1972, p 4; *Canberra Times*, 17 May 1988, p 25; *Ballarat News*, 29 June 1989, p 9; *Vic Real Estate Jnl*, Sept 1989, p 6; Bartrop Real Estate archives (Ballarat, Vic).   ANNE BEGGS SUNTER

BARWICK, DIANE ELIZABETH (1938-1986), anthropologist, historian and Aboriginal-rights activist, was born on 29 April 1938 in Vancouver, Canada, daughter of Ronald Bernard McEachern, forest worker, and his wife Beatrice Rosemond, née O'Flynn. She grew up in logging camps, sometimes housed on a log raft. Her father, nicknamed 'Bear Tracks', was a 'high rigger' and camp manager in an industry in which a personal reputation for bravery, skill and sheer survival secured his authority. Apart from one year at a Vancouver high school, Diane was schooled by correspondence before enrolling at the University of British Columbia (BA, 1959), where she graduated with first-class honours in anthropology. Based on five months' fieldwork in six camps, her thesis evoked the occupational subculture of the loggers of Englewood Valley.

In 1959-60 McEachern worked at the Provincial Museum of Natural History and Anthropology, Victoria, British Columbia, researching West Coast Indian material culture and ethnohistory. Awarded a postgraduate research scholarship in anthropology, she arrived at the Australian National University (Ph.D., 1964), Canberra, in 1960. Having been advised that the New Guinea Highlands were too dangerous for field-work, she studied the cultural adjustment of some three thousand Aboriginal people in Victoria. Her twelve months in the field between October 1960 and April 1962 included a stint in a fruit cannery and eight months visiting Aboriginal households in Melbourne. Victorian Kooris reminded her of Canadian lumbermen. Impressed by their independent sense of honour and warmed by their comradeship, she remarked in her thesis on the tension between her roles of 'friend' and 'observer'. Despite attempts to assimilate them, she argued, Kooris remained a self-conscious minority, divided by continuing ancestral attachment to home regions within Victoria, but united by unanswered grievances as a people dispossessed of land, harried by officials and despised by many non-Indigenous Australians. Koori memories persuaded her that historical scholarship must complement ethnography in understanding Aboriginality in the 1960s.

McEachern married a fellow Ph.D. student, Richard Essex Barwick, a zoologist from New Zealand, on 14 April 1961 at the registrar's office, Canberra. That year Diane Barwick attended the research conference that founded the Australian Institute of Aboriginal Studies. When the institute received its statutory charter in 1964, she was a founding member. In May 1978 she was the first woman to be elected to its council. From 1978 to 1982 she served on the institute's publications and social anthropology committees. In 1981, when she was invited to apply for the post of principal, she submitted an application that advocated training Indigenous researchers. She was not appointed. Partly at her urging, the institute set up a history committee in 1982; she participated in it during her second term as councillor, in 1982-86, and she chaired the publications executive committee in 1983-86. In May 1985 she accepted the institute's twelve-month honorary appointment to establish a national Aboriginal biographical register. Drawing in part on her own tireless combing of Victorian archives, the register comprised twelve thousand index cards by the time of her death.

The ANU was Barwick's other institutional home. However, as she was the pioneer in Australia of ethnohistory, her career suffered from the slow awakening of historians' interest in Aborigines and from anthropologists' tendency not to consider the historical dynamics of non-Western societies. From March 1966 to June 1972 she was a research fellow in the department of anthropology and sociology, Research School of Pacific Studies. Between April 1974 and December 1978 she was inter-mittently employed as a tutor and lecturer in anthropology in the Faculty of Arts, and in 1979-80 she was a temporary research fellow in the department of history, Research School of Social Sciences.

If Barwick's industry was not rewarded by tenured employment, she was none the less influential. In his formative historical and sociological survey *Outcasts in White Australia* (1971), Charles Rowley [q.v.] drew heavily on her unpublished thesis. It was through honorary work that she achieved much of her impact as a promoter of Aboriginal history and of Aborigines as historians. She was a founding editor of the journal *Aboriginal History* in 1977-82 and a co-editor of the *Handbook for Aboriginal and Islander History* (1979). In February 1981 at her instigation a 'Working Party of Aboriginal Historians' challenged 'Bicentennial' historians to consider the cultural biases of their notions of competent historical narrative. Australian historians must encourage diversity, she urged, in both the authors and the idioms of the narrated past. When two obituaries noted her strong dislike of 'dishonesty, misrepresentation and carelessness', they referred not just to her scholarly scruples but to her broader conviction that the truthful accounting of the past was a matter of justice.

Barwick's post-doctoral research amassed a detailed genealogical portrait of Victoria's surviving Aborigines. On this basis she developed arguments in historical demography (including an unpublished consideration of the impact of smallpox). In a series of biographical essays about Koori women she showed that families and congregations were the social units of Indigenous survival. The changing relations of gender and the utility of Christian faith were themes in her account of a remnant people's accommodation to the colonists' pressures in the period from 1870 to 1950. Her familiarity with Victorian administrative archives made her a formidable chronicler of governmental neglect and bad faith. When the traditional owners of Framlingham reserve demanded security of title in the late 1970s, Barwick's 1979 submission narrated more than a century of official indecision and Koori intransigence.

Her North American background acquired new relevance in 1980, when she involved herself in the Aboriginal Treaty Committee. Acknowledging her reservations ('I am by birth and conviction a Canadian', she wrote in 1983) about involvement in Australian politics, she was also proud to be descended from American Indians through her mother, a fact not evident in her publications. In 1960, fresh from Canada, she had been shocked to learn that Victorian Kooris were not protected by a treaty. Two decades later, her work for the committee urged that Australians rise, in this respect, to the standards of other British dominions.

Barwick died of a cerebral haemorrhage on 4 April 1986 at Royal Canberra Hospital and was buried in Gungahlin cemetery with Catholic rites. An obituarist, Nancy Williams, recalled her 'sense of humour, her sharp wit' and 'her infectious and hearty laugh'. She was survived by her husband and daughter; their editorial efforts ensured the posthumous publication of her manuscript *Rebellion at Coranderrk* in 1998. One friend, Ken Inglis, noted that its appearance had been delayed in her lifetime by 'two commitments': 'to other people's lives' and 'to perfection'.

Aboriginal Hist, vol 9, pt 1, 1985, p 4, vol 11, pt 1, 1987, p 1, vol 12, pt 1, 1988, p 2; *Canberra Anthropology*, vol 9, no 1, 1986, p 1; *Austn Aboriginal Studies*, no 2, 1986, p 70; *Oceania*, vol 57, no 2, 1986, p 81; *Canberra Times*, 7 Apr 1986, p 8; *ANU Reporter*, 9 May 1986, p 6; *Austn Hist Assn Bulletin*, June 1986, p 5; J. C. Kijas, An 'Unfashionable Concern with the Past' (MA thesis, Univ of Melbourne, 1993); private information.   TIM ROWSE

BASHAM, ARTHUR LLEWELLYN (1914-1986), professor of South Asian history, was born on 24 May 1914 at Loughton, Essex, England, son of English parents Arthur Abraham Edward Basham and his wife Maria Jane, née Thompson, who were both journalists. As a child he learned the piano and by the age of 16 had written several compositions; he continued to play throughout his life. In 1935 he published a collection of his poetry entitled *Proem*.

After achieving first-class honours in Indo-Aryan studies at the School of Oriental and African Studies, University of London (BA, 1941; Ph.D., 1950), Basham served in civil defence during World War II. In 1948 he was appointed lecturer in the history of India at the SOAS, becoming reader in South Asian history in 1953 and professor in 1957. He was director of the Royal Asiatic Society of Great Britain and Ireland in 1964-65. On 9 October 1942 he had married Violet Helen Kemp in the Rushall parish church, Norfolk; they were later divorced. He married Namita Catherine Shadap-Sen, a 34-year-old Indian research student, on 11 November 1964 at the register office, Hampstead.

In 1965-79 Basham was foundation professor and head of the new department of Oriental (Asian) civilisation(s) in the faculty of Oriental (Asian) studies at the Australian National University, Canberra. He served as dean of the faculty from 1968 to 1970. His inspiration and leadership contributed greatly to the expansion of Asian studies at ANU. Through his supervision of over fifty doctoral students, both at the SOAS and at the ANU, he exercised a broad influence in his field. As well as providing intellectual stimulus and concrete assistance, he showed kindness and personal concern to colleagues.

Basham's eminence as a historian of India had been established by the publication in London of his doctoral thesis *History and Doctrines of the Ājīvikas* (1951) and by his monumental *The Wonder that was India* (1954). In this book, which has been republished many times and translated into several languages, he tried to cover 'all aspects of Indian life and thought' before the arrival of the Muslims in the sixteenth century. His fine and demanding scholarship concealed itself in an easy and elegant style. This work showed him as a historian and humanist with wide interests, a discerning appreciation of art and literature, and an affection for the people and the land he made the focus of his life's work. After publishing *Studies in Indian History and Culture* (1964) and *Aspects of Ancient Indian Culture* (1966), Basham edited *Papers on the Date of Kaniska* (1968), *The Civilizations of Monsoon Asia* (1974) and *A Cultural History of India* (1975). He wrote about fifty research articles, a similar number of review articles, and numerous contributions to encyclopaedias.

In 1970 'Bash' became vice-president of the Australian Academy of the Humanities, of which he was a foundation fellow, and in 1976 he was elected vice-president of the Asian Studies Association of Australia. Due to his international stature and his efforts, the 28th International Congress of Orientalists was held at the ANU in 1971. Basham served as president. In 1979 he was president of the First International Conference on Traditional Asian Medicine, held in Canberra. This meeting led to the formation of the International Association for the Study of Traditional Asian Medicine.

In the 1960s and 1970s Basham held several visiting professorships in the United States of America and India. His contribution to scholarship was recognised by a D.Litt. from the University of London (1966), honorary doctorates from the universities of Kurukshetra (1965) and Nava Nalanda Mahavihara (1977), as well as the Bimala Churn Law gold medal of the Asiatic Society of Calcutta in 1975 and the Desikottama award from the Visva-bharati University in 1985. Survived by his wife and their son and daughter, Basham died of cancer on 27 January 1986 at Calcutta, India, and was buried in the Old Military Cemetery of All Saints Cathedral, Shillong.

S. K. Maity et al (eds), *Studies in Orientology* (1988); S. K. Maity, *Professor A. L. Basham* (1997); Austn Academy of the Humanities, *Procs*, 1984-86, p 141; Asian Studies Assn of Aust, *Review*, vol 9, no 3, Apr 1986, p 29; *ANU Reporter*, 28 Feb 1986, p 2; personal knowledge.   J. T. F. JORDENS

BATE, THELMA FLORENCE (1904-1984), community leader, was born on 3 August 1904 in Sydney, second surviving daughter of Olaf Olsen, a Norwegian seaman, and his Melbourne-born wife Florence Beatrice, née St Clair. In 1912 her mother married Carl Gustav Sundstrom, whom Thelma regarded as her father. She was close to Sundstrom, who believed that a good education was important for both girls and boys. A bright and talented student, unafraid to speak her mind, she attended the selective Fort Street Girls' High School and the University of Sydney (BA, 1928).

After teaching at Meriden Church of England Grammar School, Strathfield, and travelling abroad with her parents, Thelma married a grazier, Richard Falkner Harvey, on 20 June 1934 at St Philip's Church of England, Sydney. They lived on his property near Ivanhoe, where she was introduced to the Country Women's Association of New South Wales. Following the death of her husband in 1946, she was encouraged by members of the Country Party to stand as that party's candidate in the 1947 State election for the Labor-held seat of Dubbo. Although defeated, Mrs Harvey attracted attention as the first woman endorsed by the Country Party. A skilled and forceful debater, she developed a taste for politics. On 8 December 1949 at St John's Church of England, Darlinghurst, she married Kenneth Kirkby, who was a member of the Country Party State executive. They lived at Bellata, near Moree, and were later divorced. Thelma Kirkby ran unsuccessfully for the Senate in 1951 and 1953 on the combined ticket of the Liberal and Country parties. In December 1953 she was defeated in a by-election for the Federal seat of Gwydir, when the Country Party endorsed two candidates.

Increasingly based in Sydney, Kirkby made a considerable contribution to postwar Australia through organisations such as the Free Kindergarten movement, the Business and Professional Women's Club and the Air Ambulance Service (for which she was awarded life membership). A staunch anti-communist, she was secretary-general of the Australian Women's Movement Against Socialisation in the late 1940s. In 1953 she was the New South Wales representative to the Associated Country Women of the World conference, held at Toronto, Canada. In the 1950s, as part of these international women's networks, she was also involved in the Pan Pacific Women's Association (from 1955 Pan-Pacific and South East Asia Women's Association of Australia), including periods as national and international treasurer. During the Vietnam War, she organised a group that provided 'rest and recreation' for American servicemen in Sydney. She served as a committee member of the Freedom from Hunger Campaign. In 1975 she was the New South Wales representative on the United Nations Association of Australia International Women's Year national committee.

But it was as part of the State branch of the CWA that Kirkby really made her mark. For over forty years, she was an active member, serving as honorary secretary (1957-59) and, as Thelma Bate, president (1959-62). On 12 June 1958 at St Andrew's Presbyterian Church, Chatswood, she had married Henry Jefferson Percival (Jeff) Bate, long-standing Liberal member for the Federal seat of Macarthur and dairy farmer at Tilba Tilba. She had met him in conservative political circles and found him virile and charming. Their marriage ended in divorce in 1968. Her three marriages were childless.

Bate was probably best known for her passionate, and often defiant, stance on the inclusion of Aboriginal women in the CWA organisation and its branches. 'When we say we work for country women and children, where do we draw the colour line?', she asked CWA members as branches with mainly Aboriginal membership opened at Toomelah, Burnt Bridge-Green Hills and Copmanhurst-Baryulgil from 1956. In the 1960s she was treasurer of the Foundation for Aboriginal Affairs. She chaired the women's committee that, in partnership with Rotary, helped to establish International House at the University of Sydney and the University of New South Wales.

In 1969 the petite, energetic and enigmatic Thelma Bate was appointed CBE. She attributed her belief in equality and fair treatment for all, irrespective of colour, creed or sex, in large part to the enlightened influence of her stepfather. The significance of her contribution may have been partially lost through her name changes. She died on 26 July 1984 at Gordon and was cremated.

H. Mayer and J. Rydon, *The Gwydir By-election 1953* (1954); H. Townsend, *Serving the Country* (1988); *CWA* (NSW) *Annual Report*, 1961, p 9; *Jnl of Interdisciplinary Gender Studies*, vol 2, no 1, 1997, p 57; *SMH*, 23 Apr 1953, p 7, 27 Apr 1960, p 3, 27 Jan 1965, p 2; *Country Woman*, Mar 1960, p 5, May 1962, p 5; *Sun* (Sydney), 30 Jan 1969, p 34; H. de Berg, interview with T. Bate (ts, 1975, NLA).

MELANIE OPPENHEIMER

BATE, DAME ZARA KATE; *see* HOLT, DAME ZARA

BAXTER, SIR JOHN PHILIP (1905-1989), chemical engineer and vice-chancellor, was born on 7 May 1905 in Machynlleth, Montgomeryshire, Wales, younger child of John Baxter, a post-office engineer, and his wife

Mary Netta, née Morton. After moving with his family to England, Philip attended Hereford High School for Boys. He passed the Northern Universities' matriculation exam at age 14 and that of the University of London at age 16. Entering the University of Birmingham (B.Sc., 1925; M.Sc., 1926; Ph.D., 1928), he gained first-class honours in chemistry and was awarded the James Watt research fellowship. His Ph.D. thesis, on the combustion of carbonic oxide, was supervised by Professor F. H. Burstall. Baxter's degrees gave him professional standing as a chemical engineer, there being at that time no separate university courses in that field.

On Burstall's recommendation, Baxter joined Imperial Chemical Industries Ltd and began work as a research engineer at Billingham, County Durham. He became a member of the dramatic society in nearby Stockton-on-Tees, where he met Lilian May Thatcher, who was working as a stenographer. They married on 17 August 1931 in Stockton's register office. Following his appointment that year as research manager of the central laboratory in ICI's new general chemicals division, the Baxters moved to Widnes. His rapid rise continued when, in 1935, he was promoted to research manager of the whole division, which employed twelve thousand people. He served on the Widnes municipal council (1939-49) and chaired the Conservative Party organisation in the parliamentary constituency.

At Widnes Baxter concentrated on the development of new products involving chlorine and fluorine. This work led most notably to the new insecticide gamma benzene hexachloride (Lindane) and culminated in several patents bearing Baxter's name as sole inventor. The direction of his research changed when, early in 1940, the refugee physicists (Sir) Rudolf Peierls and Otto Frisch canvassed the possibility of a 'super-bomb' based on a nuclear chain reaction in uranium. Baxter's involvement began with a personal request from the physicist (Sir) James Chadwick at Liverpool for some uranium hexafluoride for research purposes, which Baxter duly produced. Chadwick later recalled that Baxter's help prepared the way for the wider participation of ICI. By the end of 1940, as a member of a panel responsible for chemical research, Baxter was immersed in the nuclear energy field, which was to dominate his subsequent career.

In 1944 Baxter was appointed to the position of research director for general chemicals. That summer he visited Oak Ridge, Tennessee, United States of America, for three months, to give advice on chemical engineering problems associated with the extraction of enriched uranium from the electromagnetic isotope plant. At the request of the Americans, he subsequently went back to Oak Ridge for the duration of the war, taking three colleagues with him.

On his return to England, Baxter took up his appointment as a delegate director of the general chemicals division at ICI. Early in 1947 the British government decided to build its own nuclear weapons, and planned an atomic pile to produce the necessary supplies of plutonium. Baxter and his team at Widnes assisted with the development of the chemical separation plant needed to extract the plutonium.

In 1949 Baxter accepted the post of foundation professor of chemical engineering at the New South Wales University of Technology, Kensington, Sydney. He arrived in Sydney in January 1950 and settled with his family at Enfield, where he remained until his death. The early years of the university were troubled by disputes over autonomy and academic independence. Baxter consistently stood apart from his disgruntled fellow professors and sided with the council, headed by the president, Wallace Wurth [q.v.16], who was also chairman of the New South Wales Public Service Board. Early critics were troubled by the association in the university's name of the concepts 'university' and 'technology', arguing that the limited educational scope implied by the latter term precluded the use of the former. The fact that the first professorial appointments were to the Department of Technical Education, rather than to an administratively autonomous institution, rankled with those who wanted to belong to a 'real' university.

In June 1951 these grievances were set out in a 'Prayer to the Council', signed by four of the foundation professors, which urged immediate discussions with a view to full autonomy from the Public Service Board by 1952. Baxter did not sign, and in his own later reflections praised the experience and wisdom of the president and council members who 'worked for autonomy at the proper time'. The authors of the prayer may have quoted Cardinal Newman to the effect that 'a university is not a school or a group of schools, but an atmosphere', but Baxter urged the advantages of allowing the State government to continue to provide such services as the library, purchasing, maintenance, accounts and building planning.

In February 1952 Baxter was appointed deputy-director of the university. Elected by council in December 1952 he became director, defeating the incumbent Arthur Denning [q.v.13], who was also the director of the Department of Technical Education. Denning had argued that the university should maintain close links with the department from which it had grown. Baxter's victory was thus a partial success for those advocating greater autonomy for the university, although in many ways he was at odds with his colleagues from a more traditional academic background. He had spent his working life in industry undertaking proprietary research and had little sympathy with traditional views on the functions and organisation of a university.

Autonomy was achieved on 1 July 1954, and the following year Baxter became vice-chancellor when the titles of senior positions were brought into line with those at other universities. Sir Keith Murray's committee on Australian universities recommended in 1957 that the State's second medical school be established at Kensington. This proposal prompted a name change in 1958 to the University of New South Wales, and a widening of the university's charter to permit the council to establish additional faculties.

Baxter remained vice-chancellor until 1969, at which time his successor, Professor (Sir) Rupert Myers, referred to him as the 'essential founder' of the university. Baxter had worked hard to build up the university in an attempt to achieve economies of scale. Some observers in the mid-1960s may have bewailed the joyless utilitarianism of the Kensington campus (in 1963, UNSW had ten thousand students), but Baxter's desire for growth also stemmed from a perception of the needs of postwar Australia. He often returned to the theme of the shortage of appropriately trained engineers and technologists, and saw the rapid expansion of technological training as holding out the only hope for the country's development. Believing that the task of universities was to train highly skilled people for industry, he sometimes expressed regret when good students returned to the academic fold after only a brief period outside. An innovation that reflected his background was the creation of Unisearch Ltd, a subsidiary company of the university that offered its expertise and resources to industry and government.

Baxter also lamented what he saw as excessive failure rates at UNSW, which, from an industrial point of view, amounted to wasted effort. His critics argued that as a result of his drive to build up the university, students were being admitted without satisfying normal matriculation requirements. In their view, these students pushed up the failure rates or required a disproportionate allocation of resources to get them through their courses. Baxter, on the other hand, stressed the deficiencies of academic administrative machinery, teaching and the examination process. By doing so, he fell foul of some of his colleagues.

Tensions also arose over differing views of university governance. Baxter favoured clear lines of executive authority, with the deans directly involved in the formation and implementation of university policy. In 1957 he set up a committee of deans which met weekly, with the bursar and registrar, under his personal chairmanship. By 1960 this body was reconstituted as the vice-chancellor's advisory committee, giving the vice-chancellor an administrative vehicle free from the constraints of formal faculty or board meetings. Baxter supported the system whereby deans were not elected by faculty, but appointed by council on the recommendation of the vice-chancellor. This form of governance did not sit well with the notion of a dean as the *primus inter pares* with his academic colleagues.

In 1950 Baxter had been appointed a member of the Industrial Atomic Energy Policy Committee, soon after it was established. In November 1952 the Australian Atomic Energy Commission, under the chairmanship of (Sir) Jack Stevens [q.v.16] and with Baxter as his deputy, was created as an administrative agency pending the passing of the necessary legislation in 1953. Baxter and (Sir) Frederick White of the Commonwealth Scientific and Industrial Research Organization left on a fact-finding tour of Britain, the United States and Canada in June 1953, returning three months later with a proposal for the establishment of research laboratories. After Baxter's next visit to England, in 1954, when he was accompanied by Stevens and Professor (Sir) Leslie Martin [q.v.] from Melbourne, the government approved the inclusion of a reactor project in the commission's proposed research program. The reactor was to be modelled on the E.443 heavy-water reactor at Harwell, England. The government also approved the commission's stated goal of developing means for the economic production of nuclear power and settled on Lucas Heights in Sydney's south as the site for the research establishment.

In August-September 1954 the New South Wales University of Technology hosted a symposium on 'Atomic Power in Australia'. It led to a confrontation between Baxter and Professor Harry Messel, head of physics at the University of Sydney, whose desire to build a low-power experimental reactor in his department was well known. In response to a question, Baxter told Messel that he favoured building a 'real reactor, not a low-power toy'. The symposium set the tone for Baxter's future involvement in Australia's push to join the 'nuclear club'. By 1954 he was both director of the New South Wales University of Technology, and at the centre of government involvement with nuclear power. From that time on, he combined the two roles, often explicitly trying to link the work of the university to the broader questions of national development which were the province of the commission. Even before Baxter became part-time chairman of the AAEC in 1956, on Stevens's resignation, it was clear that he was the driving force behind its research program. He became full-time chairman in 1969 when he retired from UNSW.

Baxter was attempting to realise his own vision of a technologically sophisticated and self-sufficient Australia, able to defend itself in what he saw as an increasingly hostile world. In practical terms, this vision took the shape of studies at Lucas Heights of two power reactor concepts: a high-temperature gas-cooled reactor system and a liquid metal fuel reactor system. Investigations into the first continued into the 1960s, despite increasing concerns about its economic viability. From the beginning, Baxter saw the military potential of nuclear power, and wanted Australia to have the capacity to build its own nuclear deterrent. These concerns were sharpened by events in Vietnam, and a mistrust of American willingness to defend Australia in the event of invasion from the north.

At a technical level, Baxter argued for Australia's first nuclear power station to be fuelled by natural uranium, to avoid any need to rely on enriched fuel from overseas. Further, reliance on overseas technology would also make Australia beholden to any safeguards and inspection regimes, such as those proposed under the Nuclear Non-Proliferation Treaty. Joining the Australian Association for Cultural Freedom in 1966, he adopted a more forthright public stance on nuclear and defence policy. His efforts behind the scenes accorded with the views of the prime minister (Sir) John Gorton. The Federal government decided to build a nuclear power station at Jervis Bay, New South Wales, but the project was deferred indefinitely by the McMahon government in 1971. Baxter was the Australian member on the International Atomic Energy Agency board of governors at its creation in 1957 and again in 1964-72. He was elected chairman for 1969-70.

On his retirement as chairman of the AAEC in 1972, Baxter was left with just one significant public role, that of chairman (1969-75) of the Sydney Opera House Trust. Throughout his life he had maintained an active interest in the theatre. He acted in and directed plays while at UNSW (including *The Devil's Disciple* by his beloved George Bernard Shaw), and succeeded in attracting the National Institute of Dramatic Art to Kensington. His own vision of the possible prospect for Australia in a new world order was set out in a play, 'The Day the Sun Rose in the West', written in the late 1960s or early 1970s. Although never published, it stood as a heartfelt if rather grim view of what its author saw as the consequences of the failure of his political masters to take the difficult decisions that were required for defence and national development.

Baxter was appointed OBE in 1946, CMG in 1959 and KBE in 1965 for services to science and engineering. He was elected a fellow of the Royal Australian Chemical Institute (1950), the Institution of Engineers, Australia (1952),

the Australian Academy of Science (1954) and the Australian Academy of Technological Sciences and Engineering Ltd (1976), and was an honorary corresponding member of the Royal Society of Arts (1969). He was a member (1973-75) of the council of the Australian Academy of Forensic Sciences. He also received a number of honorary doctorates from various universities: laws from Montreal (1958); science from Newcastle (1966), Queensland (1967) and New South Wales (1971); and technology from Loughborough (1970). The Institution of Production Engineers gave him the (Sir) James N. Kirby [q.v.15] award in 1965 and the University of Melbourne conferred on him the (W. C.) Kernot [q.v.5] medal in 1966.

By the early 1970s Baxter was the target of a great deal of animosity. His opponents regarded him as reactionary, autocratic and manipulative, perhaps even callously immoral. In April 1972 Bishop David Garnsey, the president of the Australian Council of Churches, branded as 'barbaric' Baxter's comments that Australia should consider using chemical and nuclear weapons to keep out refugees in the event of a global disaster. On the other hand, Baxter inspired feelings of loyalty from former students and colleagues, and was a close confidant of senior government figures for over twenty years. The tensions of his public career stemmed largely from his profoundly anti-democratic cast of mind. He argued that, in the event of a global crisis, it would be foolish to consult the wishes of the population at large, and that hard decisions must be left in the hands of those best equipped to make them.

An estimation of his career should not give too much weight to the controversy that dogged his later years in the public arena. His considerable achievements as a researcher, teacher and administrator, associated with some of the most significant events of the twentieth century, must also be added to the balance. That he was not a soulless technocrat is shown by his encouragement of attempts at UNSW and elsewhere to bridge the divide between C. P. (Lord) Snow's 'Two Cultures'.

Survived by three of his four children, Sir Philip Baxter died on 5 September 1989 at Haberfield and was cremated. His wife Lilian, whom he had described as giving him 'complete and loyal support on every occasion', had died six weeks earlier. UNSW holds portraits of him by Judy Cassab and William Pidgeon [q.v.]. Like others of his generation, he had placed his faith in the capacity of science and technology to address human problems, and maintained at best a tolerance of traditional religion.

M. Gowing, *Britain and Atomic Energy 1939-1945* (1964) and *Independence and Deterrence*, vol 2 (1974); W. J. Reader, *Imperial Chemical Industries,* vol 2 (1975); B. Martin, *Nuclear Knights* (1980); A. H. Willis, *The University of New South Wales: The Baxter Years* (1983); A. Cawte, *Atomic Australia 1944-1990* (1992); *Search*, vol 6, no 9, 1975, p 365; *Hist Records of Austn Science*, vol 8, no 3, 1990, p 183; P. Gissing, Sir Philip Baxter, Engineer (PhD thesis, UNSW, 1999); Baxter papers (UNSW Archives).

PHILIP GISSING

BAYLISS, CEDRIC ALFRED ('SYD') (1899-1983), hawker, whip-maker and saddler, was born on 27 July 1899 at Wangaratta, Victoria, fourth of seven children of Victorian-born parents Albert Ernest Bayliss, farmer, and his wife Florence, née Everitt. Nicknamed 'Shig' as a boy and known as Syd from about the age of 20, Cedric grew up on his family's Boorhaman station and attended Boorhaman State School. A good horseman, he often spent long periods alone in the bush, hunting, shooting and learning bushcraft.

Following the example of his two older brothers, Raymond and Ernest, both later killed in France, Cedric enlisted in the Australian Imperial Force on 13 March 1916; he was 16 years old, almost six feet (183 cm) tall and 10.5 stone (67 kg) in weight. He arrived in France in November with the 37th Battalion and was allocated to the 10th Machine-Gun Company next month. Gassed on 26 May 1918, he was hospitalised in France and England. He was discharged from the army, medically unfit, on 29 January 1919 in Melbourne. On 13 August he enlisted for seven years in the Royal Australian Navy. He served as a stoker, 2nd class, at HMAS *Cerberus*, Westernport, and in HMAS *Australia* before deserting on 14 April 1920 in Sydney.

Having been employed on properties in Victoria and western New South Wales and on Oaklands station near Urana, New South Wales, in 1921 Bayliss and a mate worked their way up the Queensland coast to Townsville and out to Dobbyn, north of Cloncurry. At Dalgonally station near Julia Creek he obtained a job as a ringer in mustering camps, taught himself plaiting and made rough greenhide whips and bronco ropes from cattle hides cured with salt and alum. After a few months in the Northern Territory in 1925, he worked his way south on various stations, including Connemarra and Mount Margaret in Queensland and Wingadee in New South Wales, and finally took delight in riding his horse onto the steps of the Melbourne General Post Office.

On 23 June 1927 at Sacred Heart Catholic Church, Cootamundra, New South Wales, Bayliss married Grace Margaret Dolan. They were to have two sons, one of whom died in infancy. In August, leaving his wife with relatives in Sydney, he returned north and for about two years worked on Brunette Downs station in the Northern Territory, where he learned the 'double American' plait. In 1931, after a fall from his horse, he went into business as a leather craftsman. Using a four-horse wagon with covered sides that opened down to make a display area, he hawked stockwhips, belts, hatbands, watch and knife pouches, together with tobacco and other items, from station to station. He also did saddlery and harness repairs. As he travelled he shot kangaroos and tanned the skins in casks of wattlebark liquor fitted to the sides of his wagon.

Bayliss's stockwhips, from 4 to 64 strands and from 5 ft (153 cm) to 50 ft (1530 cm) long, were popular in much of Australia. A consummate craftsman, he could plait the owner's name into the whip handle. After some years at Jerilderie, New South Wales, about 1940 he moved to Tumut, where he set up a tannery and saddlery store, the Valley of the Whites Trading Post, which he operated with his wife and their son John. He enjoyed teaching plaiting and boomerang-throwing and served on the Tumut rodeo committee. Craftsman, bushman and storyteller, Bayliss died on 1 February 1983 at Tumut and was cremated. His wife and their younger son survived him. A posthumous portrait by Howard Barron is held by R. Taubman, Murringo, New South Wales.

R. Taubman, *One of the Last* (1989); *Tumut and Adelong Times*, 8 Feb 1983, p 8; B2455, item BAYLISS C A (NAA).

G. P. WALSH

BEALE, SIR OLIVER HOWARD (1898-1983), barrister, politician, diplomat and company director, was born on 10 December 1898 at Tamworth, New South Wales, youngest of four surviving sons of Joseph Beale (d.1910), Wesleyan minister, and his wife Clara Elizabeth, née Vickery, both born in New South Wales. Ebenezer Vickery [q.v.6] was his great-uncle. Educated at Sydney High School and the University of Sydney (BA, 1921; LL B, 1925), Howard was admitted to the New South Wales Bar on 14 May 1925. His early career was interrupted by a life-threatening bout of rheumatic fever, which saw him bedridden for six months. Having recovered, he thrived on the drama, competitive camaraderie and what he called the 'polite brutality' of the barrister's profession. On 19 December 1927 he married Margery Ellen Wood, a history teacher and the daughter of a Presbyterian home missionary, in the manse at Bingara. They were to have two children; their daughter died in infancy.

Introduced to politics through his friendship with W. A. Holman [q.v.9], Beale joined a Sydney branch of the United Australia Party prior to the outbreak of World War II. However, he was impressed by few of his colleagues, other than (Sir) Robert Menzies [q.v.15], and welcomed the dissolution of the UAP. In 1944 he stood unsuccessfully as a Democratic Party candidate for Hornsby in the State election. Having joined the Royal Australian Naval Volunteer Reserve, he was appointed area skipper (sub-lieutenant) in the Naval Auxiliary Patrol on 7 August 1944. He led a patrol in his own motor cruiser around the entrance to Broken Bay.

A member of the first State executive of the Liberal Party from July 1945, Beale won the House of Representatives seat of Parramatta at the Federal election on 28 September 1946, succeeding Sir Frederick Stewart [q.v.12]. In Opposition he was an active parliamentary speaker, especially on issues relating to the Chifley [q.v.13] government's postwar controls over such activities as land sales, rationing, taxation and industrial relations. Reflecting later, he commented on his relishing the chance to be part of 'a sort of striking force', with (Sir) Percy Spender [q.v.], (Sir) Thomas White, (Sir) Eric Harrison [qq.v.16,14] and others, that helped to turn public opinion away from Labor. He was a member (1947-49) of the parliamentary standing committee on public works. In 1948 he visited Europe, including Berlin at the time of the Soviet blockade, an experience that confirmed for him the dangers of communism.

On 19 December 1949 Beale was given two portfolios in the new Menzies government, information and transport, which he restructured, at Menzies' request, to the extent of making them redundant. From 17 March 1950 he was minister for supply, a huge portfolio covering defence-related industries and including new ventures in aluminium production and uranium mining, atomic energy and weapons testing. He was also minister for defence production from 24 October 1956. His enthusiasm for atomic energy was shared by most of his colleagues, but historians have since criticised his dismissal of concerns about radiation fallout from the July 1956 Anglo-Australian atomic bomb tests in the Monte Bello Islands, and his recommendations that Australians produce weapons-grade enriched plutonium and work towards the production of their own atomic bomb. In 1950 he had been appointed KC.

Beale's relations with Menzies were uneasy, especially in the early years of his political career. He spoke often in cabinet, probably too often for Menzies' liking, and even dared to find better forms of words for his leader's policies and pronouncements. (Sir) Paul Hasluck's judgment was that he scored debating points too readily, to the irritation of others, but that he was one of the most valuable ministers in the Menzies governments of the 1950s, 'both for the contributions he made to Cabinet discussion and for the competence with which he administered his own departments'.

Although Beale might have waited for likely elevation to a more senior cabinet rank, he accepted the government's offer of the ambassadorship to the United States of America in July 1957 and resigned from parliament on 10 February 1958. He adjusted easily to the diplomatic whirl and multiple demands of Washington. Among the most prominent of Australian foreign policy issues during this time were the Indonesian claim to West New Guinea and then Confrontation, increasing levels of American involvement in preserving the Republic of Vietnam (South Vietnam), and the possible invocation of the Australia-New Zealand-United States treaty in relation to all of these.

Beale learned quickly the limits of ANZUS. In 1961 the new American administration of John F. Kennedy did not support the Dutch (and Australian) stand against prospective Indonesian control of West New Guinea, facilitating the passing of the territory to Indonesia in 1963. Beale pressed the Australian government to offer military assistance in support of the rapidly increasing numbers of American 'advisers' in Vietnam and, after some delay, the offer of a small Australian team of army 'observers' was accepted in 1962. The following year, however, he and the government struggled unsuccessfully to win an American assurance, under ANZUS, of assistance to Australian forces in Borneo if they were attacked during President Sukarno's Confrontation with Malaysia.

Beale's legal training and religious upbringing were influential in shaping his outlook and manner. He had a strong moral framework, a principled approach to policy-making, and a readiness to discredit hostile witnesses. His love of yachting was also a constant, and one of the highlights of his ambassadorship in the United States was the dinner he organised before the 1962 America's Cup challenge by the Australian yacht *Gretel*. President Kennedy and his wife were among the guests.

In 1961 Beale had been appointed KBE. On his return to Australia in 1964, he established himself as a businessman-consultant, serving on the boards of numerous companies, including the Occidental Minerals Corporation of Australia (as vice-president) and Clausen Trading & Investment Co. Pty Ltd (as chairman). He was president (1965-68) of the Australian Arts Council. Several American universities awarded him honorary doctorates. In 1977 he published his memoirs, *This Inch of Time*. He also enjoyed writing book reviews and opinion pieces for Australian newspapers on matters such as the role of the monarchy in Australia, the dismissal of Prime Minister Gough Whitlam in 1975, and the legacy of

Menzies, for whom he retained great admiration in spite of their strained relationship. Survived by his wife and their son, Sir Howard died on 17 October 1983 in his home at Darling Point, Sydney, and was cremated. His son, Julian, was a member of the House of Representatives in 1984-96.

G. Pemberton, *All the Way* (1987); A. Cawte, *Atomic Australia 1944-1990* (1992); P. Hasluck, *The Chance of Politics* (1997); W. Reynolds, *Australia's Bid for the Atomic Bomb* (2000); *Australian*, 18 Oct 1983, p 7; *Canberra Times*, 19 Oct 1983, p 7; NA1980/ 35 (NAA); M. Pratt, interview with O. H. Beale (ts, 1976, NLA); private information.   DAVID LOWE

BEATON, GORDON WILLIAM (1911-1988), motor mechanic and mycologist, was born on 14 June 1911 at Lismore, Victoria, only child of William Beaton, a Victorian-born boundary rider, and his wife Elizabeth, née Garrow, who had been born in Scotland. William was later a station manager and a shire overseer. Educated at Noorat and Terang State and Terang Higher Elementary schools, Gordon left after attaining the merit certificate. He subsequently read widely in philosophy and radical left-wing politics, becoming an atheist and in the 1940s a member of the Communist Party of Australia.

Working as a motor mechanic, Beaton rose to foreman with J. W. McKenzie Motors Pty Ltd, Terang. On 7 December 1935 at Waarre, near Port Campbell, he married, with Presbyterian forms, Katrine Campbell Owen, a bookkeeper. Mackenzie Motors manufactured military equipment under his supervision in World War II, the standard of work earning praise from the Department of Munitions. In 1948 he moved to Cobden, and ten years later to Camperdown, where he established a garage and dealership, Beaton & Son. He retired at Eildon in 1972. A keen rifle-shooter, he had won the Victorian junior King's prize (1936) and grand championship (1949), and represented the State three times.

Through Herbert Reeves, a fellow rifle-shooter and an accomplished nature photographer, Beaton became interested in photographing plants. He turned to fungi as subjects, because flowers would not keep still in the wind. Hoping to be told the names of different fungi, he contacted local experts but found that detailed knowledge was lacking, especially of the small disc variety which attracted his attention. He joined the Field Naturalists Club of Victoria, consulted Ethel McLennan [q.v.] at the University of Melbourne and James Willis at the National Herbarium of Victoria, and from the 1960s provided identifications to Willis and to field naturalists such as George Crichton, Bruce

Fuhrer and John Landy. Concurrently, Beaton sent his unknown fungal specimens to the Commonwealth Mycological Institute and the Herbarium, Royal Botanic Gardens, both at Kew, London.

Beaton's collections at the Kew herbarium provided novel and interesting material for a book on Australasian Pezizales by Mien Rifai (1968) and another on Australasian Helotiales by Brian Spooner (1987). Richard Dennis, at the Kew herbarium, encouraged Beaton to publish. In 1976-86 he produced thirty-eight papers, mostly in the *Transactions of the British Mycological Society*, introducing five new genera and forty-eight new species. Usually working with Gretna Weste of the University of Melbourne, he prepared descriptions and illustrations of the fungi, and Weste completed the papers for publication. He also collaborated with two London-based scientists, David Pegler and Thomas Young, in a series of papers on Australian truffles, published in the *Kew Bulletin*.

Beaton's contribution to the study of Australian fungi is significant not only for the volume and quality of his publications—a notable attainment for a person with no formal scientific training—but also for making his country the centre of that study, something which only Sir John Cleland [q.v.8] had achieved for native macrofungi. Beaton also had a key role in identifying the considerable diversity of truffles eaten by native mammals. He died on 2 April 1988 at Fairhaven and was buried in Eildon cemetery. His wife and two of their three sons survived him. Beaton's herbarium, stored in old ammunition boxes, was donated to the department of botany, University of Melbourne. The fungi *Microthecium beatonii* and *Underwoodia beatonii* commemorate him.

G. Forth (ed), *The Biographical Dictionary of the Western District of Victoria* (1998); *Vic Naturalist*, vol 105, no 4, 1988, p 90, vol 105, no 6, 1988, p 153; *A'asian Mycological Newsletter*, no 16, 1997, p 3; *Alexandra & Eildon Standard*, 1 June 1988, p 12; Beaton papers (Royal Botanic Gardens Melbourne archives).   T. W. MAY

BEECK, SIR MARCUS TRUBY (1923-1986), farmer, grains industry leader and company director, was born on 28 December 1923 at Gannawarra, Katanning, Western Australia, second of four sons of Gustav Edwin Beeck, a South Australian-born farmer of German descent, and his wife Martha Ellen, née Keast, who came from Sydney. Growing up in a Baptist family at Gannawarra, Marcus was educated through the Western Australian Correspondence School until his final year, when he rode on horseback each day to the Katanning State School. In his formative years he was much influenced by his mother, a schoolteacher and naturalist, who wrote on social issues under the pseudonym Cordelia Maskon in local newspapers, and was in regular contact with the journalist Muriel Chase [q.v.7]. He worked on his father's farm before enlisting in the Royal Australian Air Force on 5 May 1942. Exploiting his natural mechanical talent, he trained as a fitter and served as a leading aircraftman in the Northern Territory and Borneo, and on Morotai. He was discharged in Perth on 24 October 1945. Using his deferred pay from military service as a deposit, he acquired and began to develop a sheep and grain property, east of Katanning, which he called Coyrecup.

On 5 April 1950 at St Matthew's Church of England, Windsor, New South Wales, Beeck married Leonie Pamela Dale Robertson, a mothercraft nurse. Well educated, widely read, and a competent researcher, speech-writer and wily debater, she was to support Beeck in his many projects. A member (1947-51) of the Katanning Road Board, he was involved with many local organisations, including the Returned Sailors', Soldiers' and Airmen's Imperial League of Australia, pony and rifle clubs, and the historical society. He was active in agricultural societies at Nyabing Pingrup and at Katanning (where he was ringmaster), and as a council member (1966-86) of the Royal Agricultural Society of Western Australia, Perth. Councillor-in-charge of district displays, for some years he also organised the Great Southern District's entries. As president of the RAS in 1975-78 he was associated with the extension of the Claremont showground and the construction of the Silver Jubilee pavilion. He led Western Australian delegations to Canada, Jamaica and Wales for conferences of the Royal Agricultural Society of the Commonwealth. During the meeting held in Wales in 1975, fellow participants at a banquet at Ruthin Castle dubbed him 'The Baron', a 'sobriquet [that] subsequently stuck to him'.

In 1969 Beeck was elected a Growers' Council member of the Grain Pool of Western Australia. Chairman of the council in 1972-73, he was a trustee of the pool (1973-75), and president of the steering committee that arranged for amalgamation of the pool with the Western Australian Barley Marketing and Seed Marketing boards in 1975. In 1975-77 he was chairman of the reconstituted pool. He accompanied several trade missions to Europe, Japan, the Soviet Union and South-East Asia. Under the auspices of the Department of Overseas Trade, he led a materials-handling and warehouse-equipment trade mission to Indonesia in 1975. He was a director of Westralian Farmers Co-operative Ltd from 1977; as chairman (1983-86) he oversaw the company's restructuring and listing in 1984 as Wesfarmers Ltd. Awarded Queen Elizabeth II's silver jubilee medal in 1977, he was knighted in 1979.

Sir Marcus's recreations included rifle-shooting, flying, golf and tennis. Upstanding, approachable and sociable, he enjoyed meeting people and the conviviality and music of extended family gatherings. He was a member of the Western Australian, Weld and Katanning clubs. He died of cancer on 2 May 1986 in Perth and was buried in Katanning cemetery. His wife, their son, and two of their three daughters survived him.

R. Anderson (ed), *Katanning, a Century of Stories* (1988); M. Zekulich, *The Grain Journey* (1997); *Western Farmer and Grazier*, 21 June 1979, p 2, 8 May 1986, p 3; *West Australian*, 6 May 1986, p 11; *Countryman* (Perth), 8 May 1986, p 4; A9301, item 80385 (NAA); private information.

WENDY BIRMAN

BEETALOO BILL; see BILL

BEGG, PERCY RAYMOND (1898-1983), orthodontist, was born on 13 October 1898 at Coolgardie, Western Australia, and registered as Raymond Percy, eldest of three children of English-born parents Percy William Begg, accountant, and his wife Fannie Elizabeth, née Jacob. In 1900 the family moved to Adelaide. 'Tick' attended Pulteney Street School and the Collegiate School of St Peter, where he was a champion high-jumper. He spent a year as a jackeroo before enrolling in dentistry at the University of Melbourne (B.D.Sc., 1924). In 1924-25 he trained at the (E. H.) Angle College of Orthodontia, Pasadena, California, United States of America. Returning to Adelaide, he entered into practice as an orthodontist and lectured part time (1926-63) at the University of Adelaide. On 26 April 1928 at St Andrew's Church of England, Walkerville, he married Evelyn Ellen Hamilton.

Discarding the tenet, held by Angle, that a patient's full complement of teeth must be retained, in 1928 Begg began extracting selected premolars to correct dental crowding and in the early 1930s devised new techniques for repositioning teeth. The University of Adelaide conferred a D.D.Sc. on him in 1935. Begg went on to develop a new light-wire differential force method of treatment; his papers (1954, 1956, 1961) in the *American Journal of Orthodontics* established him as an orthodontist 'of international renown'. His light-wire appliance was made a permanent exhibit at the Smithsonian Institution, Washington, DC. In 1959-74 he lectured and conducted postgraduate courses throughout the world, demonstrating a series of technical and clinical innovations. He produced a textbook, *Begg*

Orthodontic Theory and Technique (1965); later editions (1971, 1977), written with P. C. Kesling, were translated into Spanish, Italian and French.

As an orthodontist, Begg was forward looking and innovative, consistently pushing at the frontiers of clinical advancement. Always immaculately groomed and dressed, he was 5 ft 11 ins (180 cm) tall with erect carriage, a straight profile, dark hair and eyes, and a piercing gaze. In his relationships with his students, staff and patients he was domineering and demanding. When lecturing, he communicated poorly, appeared vague and expressed intolerance of other clinical techniques. In many ways his manner seemed to be modelled on that of his teacher, Edward Angle. However, at every opportunity he invited dentists and students to visit his practice, to view his patients during treatment, and to examine the records of finished cases. He possessed a good sense of humour and had a fund of jokes for his patients.

A founding member (1927) of the Australian Society of Orthodontists and honorary member of the Australian Dental Association, South Australian branch, Begg was also a fellow of the International College of Dentists and of the (Royal) Australian College of Dental Surgeons. In 1977 the American Board of Orthodontics presented him with the Albert H. Ketcham memorial award. The Australian Society of Orthodontists' Foundation for Research and Education established the P. Raymond Begg award in 1978. Begg societies of orthodontics were formed in Europe, North America, Japan and the Philippines.

Begg retired in 1980 and next year was appointed AO. Survived by his wife, and their son and two daughters, he died on 18 January 1983 at Glen Osmond and was cremated. In 1986 the Begg Memorial Museum was established at the dental school, University of Adelaide. A portrait by Robert Hannaford hangs in the school's orthodontic clinic.

J. Healey (ed), *S.A.'s Greats* (2001); *American Jnl of Orthodontics*, vol 83, no 5, 1983, p 445; *Austn Orthodontic Jnl*, vol 8, no 1, 1983, p 39; *Advertiser* (Adelaide), 14 Nov 1980, p 7, 21 Jan 1983, p 13; private information and personal knowledge.

M. R. SIMS*
J. D. JENNER

BEILBY, RICHARD COURTNEY (1918-1989), author, was born on 18 July 1918 at Malacca, Straits Settlements (Malaysia), youngest of five children of Charles Victor Beilby, a Victorian-born rubber-planter, and his wife Ruby Isobel, née Devenish, who came from Western Australia. With his siblings away for schooling, Dick, who was tutored at home, had a solitary childhood, often invent-

ing stories about his toy soldiers. The Depression intervened and the family moved to Western Australia where Dick, aged 11, began formal education at Tambellup State School, south-west of Perth. Leaving at 15, he was variously employed as a driver, labourer, drover and insurance salesman. On 4 March 1940 he enlisted in the Australian Imperial Force, fulfilling a lifelong ambition to be a soldier. Posted to the 2/1st Field Company, Royal Australian Engineers, he served in North Africa, Greece and Crete in 1941 and Papua and New Guinea in 1942-45 before being discharged on 27 September 1945.

Back in Perth, on 26 January 1946 at the Wesley Methodist Church, Beilby married Agnes Joan Halliday, an insurance worker. While earning a living as a driver and then as a house-painter, he began writing short stories. A fascination with ancient Greece led to his first novel, *The Sword and the Myrtle* (1968). Paying close attention to style, he hunted 'painstakingly' for the correct word and structure. The complexity of his language reflected the theme: love, war and intrigue in the period before the Persian invasion in 480 BC. He had researched meticulously for fifteen years, creating indexes and cross-indexes, and maps of Athens and the surrounding countryside. His subsequent novels were to have a sparser style befitting their narrative.

In his second novel, *No Medals for Aphrodite* (1970), Beilby drew on his wartime experiences in Greece and Crete. He suffered a heart attack in 1968 but, despite chronic ill health, continued writing. Assisted by Commonwealth grants, from the early 1970s he wrote full time at his Mount Pleasant home. In *The Brown Land Crying* (1975) he described the struggle of Aborigines of mixed descent living in Perth to reconcile two very different cultures. He had prepared for this 'very effective and bitter novel' by talking at length with many Indigenous people. *Gunner* (1977) was based on the retreat by Allied forces from Crete in World War II. His last work, *The Bitter Lotus* (1978), set in Sri Lanka, reflected his interest in Buddhism.

In 1967 Beilby had joined the Western Australian section of the Fellowship of Australian Writers; he served on the executive in the 1970s and became an honorary life member in 1978. In 1972-81 he was regional vice-president of the Australian Society of Authors. A 'dark, nervously-energetic' man, he was gentle and unassuming, with a slight stammer. His hobbies were sculpture and, before his first heart attack, spear-fishing. In 1981 he underwent major heart surgery. Recurring strokes affected his writing but he continued to create detailed clay miniatures of soldiers, placing them in realistic historical dioramas. Survived by his wife and two sons, he died on 12 November 1989 in Canberra, a few days after attending an army reunion in Sydney, and was cremated.

Albany Advertiser, 25 Sept 1968, p 6; *Weekend News* (Perth), 28 Sept 1968, 'Weekend Mag', p 8; *West Australian* (Perth), 7 Feb 1970, p 12, 16 Nov 1989, p 9; *Overland*, Autumn 1976, p 56; Fellowship of Austn Writers (WA) papers (SLWA); R. Beilby papers (ADFA); J. K. Ewers papers (SLWA); H. de Berg, interview with R. Beilby (ts, 1976, NLA); private information.   TRISHA KOTAI-EWERS

BELL, HARRY JAMES (1913-1983), soldier and grocer, was born on 3 May 1913 at Northcote, Melbourne, fourth of six children of Charles John Bell, a baker's driver from New Zealand, and his South Australian-born wife Olive Ethelwyn, née Sampson. Educated at Helen Street State School, Harry worked as a grocer for Hales Bros. On 1 June 1940 he enlisted in the Australian Imperial Force. He arrived in the Middle East in October and was made acting corporal in January 1941. A fortnight later he reverted to private at his own request. He was posted to the 2/32nd Battalion in February.

In April 1941 Bell sailed to Tobruk, Libya, where he endured the siege. He sustained gunshot wounds to his right arm and buttock on 4 August and spent sixteen days in hospital. In September he travelled with his battalion to Palestine. After training and garrison duty in Syria in January-June 1942, the 2/32nd travelled to Egypt. Bell was promoted to corporal following the unit's involvement in the fighting near El Alamein in July. On the night of 30–31 October, during the battle of El Alamein, he led a successful attack on an enemy machine-gun and an anti-tank gun, and saved his platoon commander's life. Next day he showed inspiring leadership against enemy tank attacks. When a raid went awry on the night of 2–3 November, he refused to leave his wounded platoon commander behind, saying that '15 Platoon had never left one of its men, and they will not start now'. Bell was awarded the Distinguished Conduct Medal for his 'distinguished service and personal bravery'.

Returning to Australia in February 1943, Bell married Mildred Alice Robinson on 8 March that year at the Methodist Church, Northcote. In September-November he participated in the Lae-Finschhafen campaign in New Guinea as a sergeant. He took over his platoon on 14 September when the commander was wounded at the beginning of an attack on a village near Malahang. Moving into the open and ahead of his men, Bell destroyed an enemy machine-gun post that was holding up the advance from the flank. He was awarded the Military Medal. In November he was admitted to hospital with malaria, which affected him so severely that on 10 October 1944 he was discharged from the army. He was selected as a member of the Australian contingent to the Victory March in London in 1946.

As a soldier, Bell was a natural leader. Five ft 10 ins (178 cm) tall, with grey eyes and brown hair, he looked the part and was idolised by his men for his courage. According to one acquaintance, Bell wanted to be 'one of the boys', though he once told a comrade that he would have preferred a commission in the field to his decorations. After the war he lived in humble circumstances at Northcote. He resumed his career as a grocer and on Saturdays worked at Four'n Twenty Pies Pty Ltd, Ascot Vale. From the early 1960s he was employed as a storeman at Sigma (Pharmaceuticals) Pty Ltd, Clayton. He retired in 1978. President of his battalion association, he was a member of the Rats of Tobruk Association and the local sub-branch of the Returned Services League of Australia. He enjoyed horse-racing and music. A gentle, unassuming man, he was committed to helping others, especially his family and friends. He died of myocardial infarction on 3 January 1983 at Northcote and was cremated. His wife and their two sons survived him.

D. Dexter, *The New Guinea Offensives* (1961); S. Trigellis-Smith, *Britain to Borneo* (1993); B883, item VX501785 (NAA); private information.
MARK JOHNSTON

BENN, STANLEY ISAAC (1920-1986), political and social philosopher, was born on 16 September 1920 at Forest Gate, London, England, third of four children of Mark Benn, jeweller, and his wife Dora, née Prusansky. His father's surname was originally Bendkofski—that family was from Russia, his mother's from Poland. Both parents were Orthodox Jews by birth and practice. Stanley was educated at Stratford Grammar School, West Ham, while learning Hebrew at the synagogue. He studied political science at the London School of Economics and Political Science (B.Sc.Econ., 1941), graduating with first-class honours. By the time of his service as a lecturer in politics in the Army Educational Corps in World War II, he had largely given up religious belief, although not attachment to his cultural heritage.

In 1948 he was appointed lecturer in government at the University College, Southampton (University of Southampton). He married Joan Miriam Foster, née Embray, a lecturer in English and a divorcee, on 7 April 1951 at the register office, Southampton. Because of his increasing interest in political theory, he withdrew from doctoral study to write lectures on political and social philosophy for local government officers. He and the philosopher Richard Peters developed these lectures into the book *Social Principles and the Democratic State* (1959), which was well received and widely adopted as a university text. They discussed the institutions and principles needed by a modern democratic state to produce a rationally justifiable government rather than an arbitrary one.

In 1962 Benn moved to Canberra as senior fellow in the department of philosophy, Research School of Social Sciences, at the Australian National University, where, two years later, Miriam became lecturer in English, School of General Studies. Benn remained in the philosophy department, from 1973 as professorial fellow, until his retirement in 1985. A member (1965-71) of the Social Science Research Council of Australia and a fellow (1971-86) of the Academy of the Social Sciences in Australia, he was also elected a fellow of the Australian Academy of the Humanities in 1979.

Although Benn wrote many papers on such topics as power, human rights and freedom of action, his major and last work was *A Theory of Freedom* (1988). Completed shortly before his death, it was a closely reasoned inquiry into the concept of the person, the principle of respect for persons, and the kind of society most favourable to the development of free and self-governing moral agents. It was an ambitious attempt to make a substantial contribution to the literature on social ethics.

Benn was a stocky man of medium height with a leonine head of hair but an equable and benign disposition. In discussion he was unfailingly amiable and courteous yet indefatigable in pursuit of truth. His major relaxation was country life. Soon after his arrival in Canberra, he acquired the country property Tyira near Sutton, New South Wales. Survived by his wife and their two sons, he died there of cancer on 25 July 1986 and was buried in Woden cemetery, Canberra.

R. Brown, 'Stanley Isaac Benn 1920-1986', Austn Academy of the Humanities, *Procs*, 1984-86, p 145; Academy of the Social Sciences in Australia, *Annual Report*, 1985-86, p 42; private information and personal knowledge.   ROBERT BROWN

BENNETT, SIR ARNOLD LUCAS (1908-1983), barrister, was born on 12 November 1908 at Toowoomba, Queensland, third of four sons of George Thomas Bennett, a Brisbane-born commission agent, and his wife Celia Juliana, née Lucas, who came from London. Donald Bennett [q.v.] was his younger brother. Educated at Toowoomba and Brisbane grammar schools, Arnold started work in 1927 at the Public Curator Office. He studied part

time, graduating from the University of Queensland (BA, 1931) and completing the Barristers' Board examinations in May 1932. Admitted to the Bar on 7 June that year, he commenced practice in Brisbane. On 15 December 1934 at Albert Street Methodist Church he married Marjory Ella May Williams; they had two daughters and two sons before her death in 1942.

Early in his career Bennett became a skilled jury advocate. He thoroughly prepared every brief and carefully examined every precedent and piece of evidence. This attention to detail gave him confidence in arguments or hypotheses that he advanced to the court. A notable example was his defence in the retrial, in 1939, of E. C. Helton, who had successfully appealed against his conviction the previous year for the murder of a woman who had made a will in his favour. She had died of strychnine poisoning, probably from a large dose of Alophen pills. Hypothesising that self-administration was more likely than murder, Bennett stirred forty Alophen pills into a glass of water and sipped the liquid, demonstrating to the jury that the extreme bitterness of the poison could not have been concealed, and inviting them to try it. Helton was acquitted.

On 1 November 1940 Bennett began full-time duty as a captain in the Militia. Appointed to the Australian Armoured Corps, he transferred to the Australian Imperial Force on 15 May 1941. Serving in Australia, he was promoted to major in April 1942 and posted to the 2/7th Armoured Regiment, of which he became second-in-command and, for a time, acting commanding officer. His AIF appointment terminated on 13 October 1943. He returned to his legal practice, and on 17 June 1944 at St Andrew's Presbyterian Church, Brisbane, he married Nancy Margaret Mellor, a 21-year-old schoolteacher. They were to have three daughters and a son. Bennett took silk on 20 February 1947. He left his practice for two years from 1950, partly because he believed some judges showed unreasonable antagonism towards him, and went into business, mainly real estate. Commercial activities did not provide the intellectual rigour he had enjoyed at the Bar, and he returned to the law. Active in the Citizen Military Forces in 1951-55, he served in the 2nd/14th Queensland Mounted Infantry.

From his student days Bennett had had a particular interest in constitutional law. In two articles in the *Australian Law Journal* (1969, 1977) he expressed concern that, over a series of decisions, the High Court of Australia had diminished the power of the States. The Queensland government regularly briefed him in constitutional cases before the High Court and the judicial committee of the Privy Council, and, after he ceased appearing in court in the early 1970s, continued to seek his advice.

His last scholarly article, published in the *Australian Law Journal* in July 1982, dealt with proposed amendments to the Constitution.

President (1957-59) of the Bar Association of Queensland, Bennett was also chairman of the Incorporated Council of Law Reporting for the State of Queensland (1957-72) and of the Barristers' Board (1957-79), and a member of the Supreme Court library committee. He appeared before many royal commissions and conducted two inquiries on behalf of the Queensland government: into the Hendrikus Plomp rape trial (1962), and into the Brisbane City Council's handling of applications for building and land subdivision approvals (1966-67). In later years he practised from chambers at his residence, confining his work to providing legal opinions. For over fifty years his meticulous preparation of every brief and his resolute presentation of his cases in court had encouraged high standards at the Queensland Bar.

Having joined the Rotary Club of Brisbane in 1939, Bennett served as president in 1959 and district governor in 1972-73, and wrote a history, *Rotary in Queensland* (1980). He was a director (1955-80) of Sanders Chemical Ltd. For over thirty years he was a devoted Methodist Sunday school superintendent. He was a total abstainer, but nevertheless he believed that life could be lived with verve and delight. At his seventieth birthday celebration, held shortly after he obtained his unrestricted private pilot's licence, he offered to take each member of his family for a joy flight over the Gold Coast. A keen gardener, he was proud of the roses at Fairthorpe, the family home at Auchenflower, and of the avocadoes grown on his farm at Mount Tamborine. He enjoyed making home movies. Courteous but unbending in the formal atmosphere of court, he was charming, friendly and boyish when participating in the many other activities that engaged his mind and heart. He was knighted in 1975. Survived by his wife and his eight children, Sir Arnold died on 30 January 1983 at St Lucia and was cremated.

R. Johnston, *History of the Queensland Bar* (1979); *Courier-Mail* (Brisbane), 3 Mar 1939, p 2, 7 Mar 1939, p 1; *Qld Bar News*, Feb 1983, p 11, May 1999, p 10; B883, item QX19190 (NAA); private information.   ALAN DEMACK

BENNETT, DONALD CLIFFORD TYNDALL (1910-1986), aviator, air force officer, politician and company director, was born on 14 September 1910 at Toowoomba, Queensland, youngest of four sons of George Thomas Bennett, a Queensland-born stock and station agent and grazier, and his English-born wife Celia Juliana, née Lucas. (Sir) Arnold Bennett [q.v.] was his brother. Educated at Brisbane Grammar School, Don left without academic distinction to work on his father's cattle station. His move to Brisbane and attendance as an evening science student at the University of Queensland, together with his rank as a non-commissioned officer in the Militia, resulted in a successful application to become a cadet in the Royal Australian Air Force. He joined on 16 July 1930 and began flying training at Point Cook, Victoria. At the end of the course he came second in the theoretical examinations and top in practical flying.

Through his acceptance of a short-service commission in the Royal Air Force on 11 August 1931, Bennett began an association with England; he was to live principally in the Home Counties for the rest of his life. He served with No.29 Squadron, flying the Siskin, a biplane fighter aircraft, and with No.210 Squadron, equipped with flying boats, before becoming an instructor. In January 1932 he had been promoted to flying officer. He left the RAF and transferred to the RAAF Reserve on 11 August 1935, holding a first-class civil navigator's licence, a wireless operator's licence, three categories of the ground engineer's licence, a commercial pilot's licence and a flying instructor's certificate. On 21 August that year at the register office, Winchester, Hampshire, he married Elsa ('Ly') Gubler. With her co-operation, he wrote *The Complete Air Navigator* (1935), which became the essential textbook on the subject and remained in print for over thirty years.

Bennett joined Imperial Airways Ltd in January 1936 and was soon flying between London, Paris and Cologne, Germany. Posted to Egypt, he flew Handley Page 42s to India and Kenya, and Empire flying boats from Southampton, England, to Alexandria and South African ports. In 1938 he published *The Air Mariner*, which was concerned with the handling of flying boats. That year Imperial Airways decided to fly the North Atlantic mail using a small four-engined aircraft, *Mercury*, launched from the back of a larger flying boat. Bennett was placed in command of *Mercury* and in July he successfully made the first commercial trans-Atlantic flight employing this revolutionary combination. In doing so, he achieved a record east to west crossing of the North Atlantic. For these feats he was awarded (1938) the Johnston memorial trophy and the Oswald Watt [q.v.12] gold medal. In October he flew *Mercury* non-stop from Scotland to South Africa, setting a long-distance record for seaplanes. Next year he took part in proving the concept of air-to-air refuelling, designed to make possible non-stop trans-Atlantic commercial flights.

From July 1940 Bennett was flying superintendent of the Atlantic Ferry service, which was established to bring American aircraft to Britain. In mid-winter he personally led the first flight of seven Hudson aircraft to make the crossing. He rejoined the RAF on 25 September 1941 as an acting wing commander and became second-in-command of an elementary navigation school. In December he was given command of No.77 Squadron, which operated Whitley bombers; he consistently flew on operations. He became the commanding officer of No.10 Squadron, equipped with the Halifax bomber, in April 1942. Sent to attack the German battleship *Tirpitz* that month, his aircraft was shot down by ground fire over Norway. Bennett and several of his crew evaded capture and reached neutral Sweden. After release from internment, he returned to Britain and was awarded the Distinguished Service Order.

In July 1942, on promotion to acting group captain, Bennett was directed by Air Marshal Sir Arthur Harris to form and command the Pathfinder Force within Bomber Command. The establishment of a force to find and mark targets for night bombing raids was deemed essential if Bomber Command was to continue its offensive. Only one in three aircraft claiming to have attacked a target had got within five miles (8 km) of it. With a loss rate of between 4 and 5 per cent of the aircraft sent on each operation, Bomber Command was achieving very little at great cost. The appointment of Bennett with his superlative navigational skills and technical understanding was to be crucial to its success.

Harris later remarked that Bennett was the most efficient airman he had ever met. His Pathfinder Force, with its ability to guide bomber formations to their targets through the use of radar and pyrotechnics, greatly improved the accuracy and effectiveness of Bomber Command. Bennett saw the potential of the then underestimated Mosquito, and this magnificent aircraft, which could carry a 4000-lb. (1814 kg) bomb to Berlin, was used principally as the leading aircraft of Pathfinder marking forces. By May 1945 Bennett had eleven Mosquito squadrons. Frequently and against regulations he would fly a Mosquito himself to observe the marking of targets and the subsequent attacks.

In January 1943 the Pathfinder Force had become No.8 Group, Bomber Command, and Bennett had been promoted to acting air commodore. That year he was appointed CBE. In December he was promoted, at the age of 33, to acting air vice-marshal, becoming the youngest officer ever to hold such rank. Bennett was appointed CB and to the Russian Order of Alexander Nevsky in 1944. He was a fellow of the Royal Aeronautical and the Royal Meteorological societies.

The war had a sour ending for Bennett. Of all the senior RAF commanders he alone was not knighted. One explanation for such an omission lay in the reaction to his difficult personality. He possessed an impatient, dictatorial and pedantic style of command which, while sometimes most effective, inevitably made him enemies. Having had a strict Methodist upbringing, he never drank, smoked or was heard to swear and these strengths may have contributed to making him a difficult colleague in the masculine world of aviation. For example, he had left the Atlantic Ferry organisation after failing to reach amicable agreement with its executive, and during the war he had made an adversary of, among others, (Sir) Ralph Cochrane, who, when commanding No.5 Group, had become a rival in pioneering marking techniques for the main bomber forces. As Harris again said of Bennett: 'He could not suffer fools gladly and by his own high standards there were many fools ... Being still a young man he underrated experience and over-rated knowledge'. Bennett could be arrogant and abrasive. Yet many who served with him held him and his many skills in awe. His reputation for never asking anybody to do something he could not do himself was fully warranted.

Following the German surrender, Bennett was released by the RAF on 14 May 1945 so that he could contest a by-election for the House of Commons seat of Middlesbrough West as the Liberal Party candidate. He was elected unopposed, but was defeated at the general election in July and his brief period as a member of parliament ended with disillusionment and arguments. Bennett did not react sympathetically to party discipline. He stood unsuccessfully for North Croydon in 1948 and Norwich North in 1950.

Bennett had been appointed chief executive of the British South American Airways Corporation in 1945. He won his second Oswald Watt gold medal in 1946 for a survey flight to South America. His policy of using only British-made equipment, principally the Avro Tudor, and his conviction that the airline should return a profit, contributed to a series of tragic accidents. In 1948 the Tudor was grounded. Bennett publicly criticised the board of BSAA and was asked to retract his comments or resign. He refused to do either and was dismissed. During the Berlin airlift later that year he formed a profitable air transport company, Airflight Ltd, using two Tudors, which he later employed on equally profitable long-distance charter work as Fairflight Ltd until 1951. He then founded Fairthorpe Ltd, a company supplying sports cars in kit form, which he owned until 1983.

In 1958 Bennett published his memoirs, *Pathfinder*, a section of which resulted in a libel action. By the 1960s his political attitude had moved to the far right. He resigned from the Liberal Party in 1962 in opposition to its stand on the Common Market, and in 1967 stood as a National Party candidate in a by-election at Nuneaton, Warwickshire, and polled about five hundred votes. In 1969 he founded the Association of Political Independents, which had an aim of introducing a non-party parliament. He also gave support at times to the National Front and presided over the Independent Democratic Movement, which favoured the voluntary repatriation of immigrants. In 1970 he published a political tract, *Let Us Try Democracy*, which was critical of the then system of British government. Survived by his wife, and their daughter and son, he died on 15 September 1986 at Wexham Park Hospital, Slough, Berkshire, and was cremated. He is remembered as a superb aviator whose subsequent career was a disappointment.

A. Bramson, *Master Airman* (1985); A. S. Jackson, *Pathfinder Bennett—Airman Extraordinary* (1991); J. Maynard, *Bennett and the Pathfinders* (1996); *ODNB*, vol 5 (2004), p 124; *Times* (London), 17 Sept 1986, p 18; AWM65, item 292 (AWM); D. C. T. Bennett RAF record (RAF Personnel Management Agency, Innsworth, Gloucester, Eng).

JOHN MCCARTHY

BENNETT, ELLIOTT (1924-1981), boxer, was born probably on 3 April 1924 in south-east Queensland, son of Aboriginal parents Roger Bennett, bullock driver and athlete, and his wife Dolly, née Mitchell. 'Elley' was raised at Barambah (later Cherbourg) Aboriginal Settlement, near Murgon, and at Maryborough, where he attended primary school. At 13 he left school and became a rural labourer, cutting timber and sugar cane, digging vegetables and peanuts, and working with stock. He played football at first, but his shortness pushed him into boxing. From punching a bag of sawdust dangling from a mango tree, he graduated to tent bouts and preliminaries at Maryborough. Showing promise, he trained with 'Snowy' Hill in Brisbane and fought there from September 1946.

Bennett's eight-year career as a professional boxer, mostly as a bantamweight, spanned 59 fights for 44 wins (40 by knockout), 1 draw, 13 losses and 1 no-contest. During his busiest years (1947-51) he fought 33 times in east-coast capital cities. In April 1948 in Melbourne he won the Australian bantamweight title with a third-round knockout over Mickey Francis. Next year he knocked out the top French fighters Emile Famechon (twice) and Jean Jouas, and the leading world-title contender Cecil Schoonmaker, from the United States of America, before failing against Harold Dade, another American. In 1950 he twice defeated both Vic Eisen from the USA and Chai Sitphol from Thailand, but lost against Ernesto

Aguilar from Mexico. He won the national featherweight title from Ray Coleman in a thrilling bout in April 1951, becoming a dual title holder. Next month he lost his bantamweight title to Jimmy Carruthers [q.v.] after a tough fifteen rounds, and told Hill 'Thank heaven that's over. No more bantamweight starving for me. I feel like a free man'. He defended his featherweight title three times as a bantam, twice against 'Bluey' Wilkins. From December 1953 he fought as a featherweight, retiring in September 1954 with the crown.

An 'explosive' boxer, Bennett had lightning fists, strong counters and a big punch. His fights against Eisen, Wilkins and Coleman were rated as among the best ever between 'little men' by *Australian Ring Digest* and by the referee and sportswriter Ray Mitchell. *Ring*, an American magazine, rated him as pound for pound the hardest hitter in the world in his time. Local supporters lauded him as the best Australian fighter not to win a world title; he was unable to negotiate a world-title bout with the champion Manuel Ortiz of Mexico or, later, with Vic Toweel of South Africa. Many wins were tense and exciting as he reversed looming points losses with one punch. He won and defended his featherweight title against Coleman and Wilkins with last-round knockouts; Schoonmaker fell to one punch in the sixth round. Carruthers survived the fifteenth, but had to be led to his corner by a courteous and smiling Bennett. Bennett's power punching, however, was never accompanied by great evasive skills and he took punishment in his willing fights.

Journalists ascribed Bennett's decline after 1952 to an aversion to hard work, but weight increase, growing indifference and a lack of fitness were largely responsible. The boxing commentator Merv Williams [q.v.16] claimed that he 'fought only as hard as he had to'. Bennett, noted for his sportsmanship in the ring and for his flashing smile, confirmed this in 1973 when he stated, 'I never liked hurting anyone'. He retired, he said, because he was 'sick of it'. His career had netted at least £20 000 and in the late 1950s he worked as a railwayman, and then a carpenter's labourer, and owned his own home. Revered by his Aboriginal peers, he was a founding member in 1969 of the National Aboriginal Sports Foundation. He reportedly had a long battle with alcohol, and by 1973 was living on an invalid pension in a rented flat in Brisbane. Attributing his financial losses to gambling, he declared himself happy and remarked: 'I don't have any cauliflower ears or other effects from fighting. I'm fit but for my wonky leg'.

In the late 1970s Bennett moved to Bundaberg. He had never married but had had several relationships. Survived by his de facto wife Sheila Little and his two sons and two daughters, he died of pneumonia on 10 December 1981 at Bundaberg and was buried with Anglican rites in the local cemetery. In 1993 the boxing fraternity placed on his grave a plaque displaying the Aboriginal flag and his ring record. His elder son, Roger (1948-1997), commemorated his father's world in *Up the Ladder* (1995), a play about tent boxing.

R. Mitchell, *Great Australian Fights* (1965); *Sporting Globe*, 28 Apr 1948, p 1, 12 Aug 1959, p 5, 18 May 1968, p 7, 5 July 1969, p 17, 1 Aug 1973, p 28; *Austn Ring Digest*, Mar 1950, p 8, Apr 1950, p 28, July 1950, p 13, Sept 1954, p 4; *Daily Mirror* (Sydney), 20 Jan 1978, p 36, 13 Jan 1986, p 28; *Telegraph* (Brisbane), 18 Dec 1981, p 22.

RICHARD BROOME

BENNETT, PORTIA MARY (1898-1989), artist, was born on 28 January 1898 at Balmain, Sydney, daughter of William Albert Bennett, a mariner from London, and his wife Portia Bohannah Australia, née Booth, who was born in New South Wales. Captain Bennett was a harbour pilot who drowned while his daughter was still young; Portia was to have a lifelong fascination with water and boats. Educated at Fort Street Girls' High School, in 1914-16 she attended the Royal Art Society of New South Wales's school, where she was taught by Antonio Dattilo-Rubbo [q.v.11 Rubbo]. In 1915-18 she trained at the Teachers' College, Sydney, and studied art under May Marsden [q.v.15]. Awarded a third-year scholarship in 1917, she also took classes at Julian Ashton's [q.v.7] Sydney Art School. Fellow pupils included Dorrit Black, Rah Fizelle and Grace Crowley [qq.v.7,8,13].

In 1919-20 Bennett taught at Chatswood Intermediate and Darlington Public schools; in 1921-25 she was on the art staff at the Teachers' College. She exhibited with various groups, and in 1925 held a joint exhibition with Fizelle at Anthony Hordern [q.v.4] & Sons Ltd's gallery. On 26 August 1925 at St Stephen's Presbyterian Church, Sydney, she married William Henry James Wallace (d.1988), a marine engineer, and moved to Brisbane. She stopped painting until 1932, when the growing family of James-Wallaces (as they now styled themselves) settled in Perth. There she met Muriel Southern and Florence Hall, both of whom she had known at Ashton's. In 1933 the three women (with another local artist, Margaret Johnson) showed paintings, drawings and craft work in a Perth gallery, and next year Bennett's work was included in an exhibition, Women Artists of Australia, held in the Education Department Gallery, Sydney.

A founding member (1933) of the Perth Society of Artists, Bennett exhibited regularly with the society, as well as in smaller group exhibitions. She often stated modestly that her art was a hobby, and that her primary roles were those of wife and mother of four children, but she did nevertheless manage to make time for her painting. Her preferred medium was watercolour and, as she did not have a studio at home until late in life, she mainly painted out of doors. Many of her works feature boats moored on the Swan River, or are landscapes painted from sketches made on family holidays. Her favourite subject, however, was the rapidly growing city of Perth, and in particular the play of light on the city's built form. In the 1940s and 1950s she painted a highly regarded series of large, detailed images of the centre of Perth, featuring many buildings that have since been demolished. While these works focus on the architecture of the city, she was also interested in the everyday lives of people who passed through it, and often included vignettes of men and women going about their daily business.

In 1951 Bennett won the PSA's watercolour prize for 'Morning', and next year the (Sir) Claude Hotchin [q.v.14] prize for best watercolour for 'The Dinghy'. She continued to paint until the last few months of her life, and held solo exhibitions in 1953 and 1973. The University of Western Australia held a retrospective exhibition in 1986. Survived by her two sons and two daughters, she died on 1 May 1989 in her home at Nedlands and was cremated. A survey exhibition of her work opened at Hawks Hill Gallery, Perth, three weeks later. Her work is represented in the National Gallery of Australia, Canberra, the Art Gallery of Western Australia and the Holmes à Court collection, Perth.

J. Gooding, *Western Australian Art and Artists 1900-1950* (1987); M. Harpley, *Beyond the Image* (1990); J. Kerr (ed), *Heritage: The National Women's Art Book* (1995); *West Australian*, 18 May 1989, p 5; Bennett biog file (Art Gallery of WA).

MELISSA HARPLEY

BENNETT, WILLIAM ROBERT (1921-1988), air force officer and author, was born on 11 July 1921 at Durban, South Africa, son of Charles Henry Bennett, mechanical engineer, and his wife Daisy Violet, née Walters. The family migrated to Queensland and Bill was educated at Brisbane Grammar School and The Southport School. He became an apprentice to a fitter and turner and served as a gunner in the Militia before enlisting in the Royal Australian Air Force on 17 August 1941.

After completing pilot training in Australia, Bennett was commissioned on 23 July 1942. He arrived in England in November and six months later was posted to No.286 Squadron,

Royal Air Force, an army co-operation unit. From November 1943 he flew Spitfires with No.234 Squadron, conducting fighter sweeps over France, Belgium and the Netherlands, as well as anti-shipping sorties. In July 1944 he was promoted to temporary flight lieutenant. Next month he was transferred as a flight commander in No.453 Squadron, RAAF, to France, where he conducted numerous operations against varied targets. An aggressive leader, he won the Distinguished Flying Cross for his 'fine fighting spirit' and the 'inspiring example' he set by his 'courage and devotion to duty'. He was shot down on 24 December while leading a Spitfire flight against a V-2 installation at The Hague.

A prisoner of war in Germany until May 1945, Bennett was repatriated in July. At St Augustine's Church of England, Hamilton, Brisbane, on 4 August that year he married Florence June Barclay, a hairdresser; they were to have a daughter before being divorced in October 1954. Demobilised from the RAAF on 19 October 1945, he became a manager in his father's chain factory.

On 9 October 1950 Bennett rejoined the RAAF. He was in combat again in December 1951, flying Meteor jets in Korea with No.77 Squadron. In a total of 182 sorties, his fighting qualities again came to the fore with many aggressive and effective attacks on the enemy, frequently against strong opposition and superior numbers. In February 1952 he raided the marshalling yards at Sariwon, Democratic People's Republic of (North) Korea, which were protected by intense anti-aircraft fire. Next month he attacked enemy billets at Chinnamp'o at the 'dangerously low altitude of fifty feet [15 m]' in 'below marginal' weather. That year he was awarded a Bar to his DFC, and the United States' DFC and Air Medal. His 'valor, proficiency and devotion to duty' and 'outstanding leadership' drew special comment. As an acting squadron leader (February-September), he was temporary commanding officer of No.77 from June until the end of his tour in July 1952.

With a fine performance in Korea, Bennett's decision to rejoin the RAAF full time seemed vindicated, but this was not to be. Temperamentally unsuited to the peacetime air force, and with family distractions, he failed important training courses well within his ability to pass and eventually resigned from the RAAF on 31 January 1958. During the 1960s he drew on his wartime experiences to write twenty-eight short, action-packed novels based on flying and fighting in the air. While not great literature, the books had a ring of authenticity, taking the reader into the air battle with their technical accuracy and appealing style. Most were translated into other European languages. He also wrote two espionage novels in the early 1970s.

At the RAAF chapel, Williamtown, New South Wales, on 19 December 1955 Bennett married Moya Mahood Saunders, née Frederick, a widow. They were divorced in February 1963. He married Donal (Donna) Mary McNeill, a 24-year-old nursing sister, on 29 November 1965 at the general registry office, Brisbane; they had a son but were divorced in May 1976. Survived by his two children, he died of cirrhosis of the liver on 29 August 1988 at the Repatriation General Hospital, Greenslopes, and was cremated. His portrait (1952) by (Sir) Ivor Hele is held by the Australian War Memorial, Canberra.

J. Herington, *Air Power over Europe 1944-1945* (1963); R. O'Neill, *Australia in the Korean War 1950-53*, vol 2 (1985); D. Wilson, *Lion over Korea* (1994); A9300, item Bennett W R (NAA); private information.   DOUG HURST

BEOVICH, MATTHEW (1896-1981), Catholic archbishop, was born on 1 April 1896 at Carlton, Melbourne, second of four children of Matta Beovich, a fruiterer who was born in Croatia, then part of the Austro-Hungarian Empire, and his wife Elizabeth, née Kenny, from Victoria. Matthew, who was very close to his deeply pious mother, attended Christian Brothers' College, North Melbourne. Arthur Calwell [q.v.13] was a schoolmate and remained a lifelong friend. Beovich worked in 1912-17 as a clerk in the Postmaster-General's Department and continued his studies part time, gaining his matriculation. In 1917-23 he trained for the priesthood at the Pontifical Urban College of Propaganda Fide, Rome (Ph.D., 1919; DD, 1923); he was ordained on 23 December 1922. For the rest of his life his outstanding characteristic would be *Romanità*, defined by John Molony as 'unswerving loyalty to the office, and affection for the person of the Pope, acceptance of Rome and what it stands for as the centre and heart of Christendom, subservience to the Roman curia ... [and] a willing readiness to form and foster a local institutional Church according to Roman ideas'.

Returning to Melbourne in 1923, Beovich served for less than six months as assistant-priest at North Fitzroy before being appointed diocesan inspector of religious instruction. He established a central office, officially opened in 1932, to co-ordinate the Catholic education system and to liaise with the State education department. As director of Catholic education for the archdiocese of Melbourne in 1933, he worked on the production of a new catechism (1938), and also wrote *Companion to the Catechism* (1939). In 1925-33 he was secretary of the Australian Catholic Truth Society, and in 1932-39 he was a regular speaker on the radio program 'Catholic Hour'.

On 7 April 1940 Beovich was consecrated Archbishop of Adelaide. There he presided over a Catholic community that grew rapidly, largely due to the influx of migrants after World War II. He warmly welcomed the newcomers, many of whom were from Italy, and embraced their devotional processions and festivals. His pride and joy was St Francis Xavier Seminary, which opened in 1942. He fostered friendly relations with the State's civic leaders and, in an ecumenical initiative, with the heads of other mainstream Christian denominations.

In the 1940s and the early 1950s Beovich enthusiastically supported B. A. Santamaria and the lay apostolate, but he was disturbed by the Church's entry into the political field in its fight against communism. He realised that the bishops could not evade responsibility for the Church-funded Catholic Social Studies Movement, but refused to endorse its successor, the National Civic Council and the new Democratic Labor Party. Annoyed at the way Santamaria and his patron Archbishop Daniel Mannix [q.v.10] ignored the spirit, if not the letter, of the Vatican's directives in 1957 instructing 'the Movement' to cease its political activities, he nevertheless managed to remain close friends with other bishops, regardless of their views about the organisation.

In March 1962 Beovich was awarded the Order of Merit of the Italian Republic for his services to migrants. Returning that year to his beloved Rome for the first session of the Second Vatican Council, he was dismayed at the opinions voiced by some of the younger bishops: 'One wonders if they think the Holy Spirit was absent from some previous periods of the Church's history, but is helping them now'. He had no doubt, however, that the Holy Spirit guided the Pope, so when John XXIII and Paul VI supported reforms, he did so too. Thus he encouraged the development of the senate of priests, the diocesan pastoral council, parish pastoral councils and the vernacular Mass. While distressed by the negative reactions to the papal encyclical *Humanae Vitae* (1968), he none the less understood that adherence to the letter of the encyclical would cause pain to some Catholics and established a natural family planning section within the Catholic Family Welfare Bureau.

A man of deep personal piety, Beovich stressed the need for faith, hope, charity, humility and willing abandonment to God's will: 'Nothing less is sufficient in a Christian; nothing more is required in a saint'. He retired on 1 May 1971. Paying tribute to the quiet, calm way he usually faced difficulties, his secretary recalled that the only time he saw him excited was during World War II, at a meeting in the town hall to protest against the bombing of Rome. Although gentle and shy, he could appear remote and austere, but was affectionately remembered for his sense of humour and his 'jet-propelled' arrivals and departures from Catholic functions. Beovich died on 24 October 1981 in North Adelaide and was buried in West Terrace cemetery.

J. N. Molony, *The Roman Mould of the Australian Catholic Church* (1969); M. M. Press, *Colour and Shadow* (1991); K. Massam, *Sacred Threads* (1996); B. Duncan, *Crusade or Conspiracy?* (2001); *Southern Cross* (Adelaide), 2 Apr 1965, (entire issue), 29 Oct 1981, p 3; *A'asian Catholic Record*, July 1988, p 292; J. D. Laffin, Matthew Beovich (PhD thesis, Univ of Adelaide, 2006); Beovich papers (Adelaide Diocesan Catholic Archives). JOSEPHINE LAFFIN

BERG, CHARLES JOSEF (1917-1988), accountant and music administrator, was born on 28 March 1917 in Berlin, Germany, son of Jewish parents Richard Max Berg, merchant, and his wife Rosina, née Blaauw. His father, who had a senior training position in an opera company, died when Charles was 13. Educated at a gymnasium (secondary school), Charles also studied piano and violin. Following the family decision to leave Germany in 1936, Berg spent a year in England, where he worked as a commercial clerk. After arriving in Melbourne in 1937 he moved to Sydney and found employment as a clerk in 1938. On 23 January 1943 at the district registrar's office, Paddington, he married Greta Ladenheim, a typist; they were later divorced. He was naturalised in 1944.

While studying accountancy Berg worked for Murray Bros Pty Ltd, furniture manufacturers, from 1939. In 1940-41 he was admitted as an associate member of the Association of Accountants of Australia (from 1953 the Australian Society of Accountants). After the war he began private practice in the city, and later formed the company Charles J. Berg & Associates (from 1972, Charles J. Berg & Partners). The firm, which had a high reputation in formal accounting, audit and taxation, undertook work for many immigrant clients. A member of the Australian branch of the International Fiscal Association from 1957, Berg served as secretary of the Australian branch and a member of the general council and of the permanent scientific committee of the central organisation. He was later Australian representative of the Union Bank of Switzerland. In 1979-80 differences arising out of matters concerning this bank, between himself and his partners, Colin Borough and Robert Strauss, resulted in the dissolution of the partnership. He then operated his own private practice (1980-86), becoming a fellow of the Institute of Chartered Accountants in Australia in 1981.

Berg was also a director of various companies including Brown Boveri (Australia) Pty Ltd, Leighton Holdings Ltd and Zurich Australian Insurance Ltd. While a member of the council of the Association of New Citizens he had written a column on taxation for their publication *The New Citizen* in the late 1940s and early 1950s. He married 31-year-old Vera Spitz, née Matejv, a shop assistant and divorcee, on 3 October 1964; they were later divorced. On 15 March 1972 he married 31-year-old Robyn Annette Hains, née Spargo, a secretary and divorcee. Both marriages took place at the registrar general's office, Sydney.

Always interested in music, Berg joined the committee of the Musica Viva Society of Australia and later was appointed secretary (1954-68) and president (1968-74). He brought to Musica Viva the disciplines of sound administration and financial responsibility and his deep love of chamber music. As a member of the board of the Australian Opera from 1969 he was more prominent, especially as chairman (1974-86). His zealous pursuit of sponsorships assisted the Australian Opera to maintain its operations and his acquisition of premises for the company at Elizabeth Street, Surry Hills, increased its efficiency. He incurred criticism from the artists in 1985 when he announced that the company would have to become a part-time operation from 1987. Although the crisis was resolved by a rescue package from Federal and State governments in January 1986, amid further complaints by the company's singers, Berg resigned in February. He was made a life member of both the Musica Viva Society of Australia and the Australian Opera. His voluntary work also involved Jewish organisations: he was president (1976-86) of the board of Shalom College, University of New South Wales, governor of the Jewish Communal Appeal, auditor of Temple Emanuel, Woollahra, and life governor (1959) of the Sir Moses Montefiore Jewish Home, Hunters Hill.

Berg was an intense man, never finding it easy to relax. Although conservative by nature with a pessimistic strand in his make-up, once he settled on a course he acted with certainty —'there is no question about it' was a common statement. He was appointed OBE in 1972, awarded the Officer's Cross of the Order of Merit of the Federal Republic of Germany in 1973 and appointed AM in 1986. Following a heart attack which caused brain damage in 1986, he died of myocardial infarction on 6 February 1988 at his home at Point Piper and was buried in the Northern Suburbs Jewish cemetery, North Ryde. His wife and his son and daughter from his first marriage survived him.

M. Shmith and D. Colville (eds), *Musica Viva Australia* (1996); Musica Viva, *Annual Report*, 1988; *Bulletin*, May 1988, p 1; *Australian*, 25-26 May 1979, 'Weekend Mag', p 6, 11 Jan 1984, p 8; *Age* (Melbourne), 8 Feb 1988, p 14; private information and personal knowledge.   KENNETH W. TRIBE

BERGMANN, HEINRICH FRIEDRICH WILHELM (1899-1987), Lutheran missionary, was born on 10 November 1899 at Ostkilver, Westphalia, Germany, one of eleven children of Johann Heinrich Bergmann, farmer, and his wife Katharina Karoline Luise, née Ackermann. The devout family belonged to a Lutheran free-church. After eight years of schooling at the *Volksschule*, Willy returned home to become a farmer but in 1921, fulfilling a childhood desire, he entered the Lutheran seminary at Neuendettelsau, Bavaria, which prepared missionaries for the Neuendettelsauer mission in the Mandated Territory of New Guinea. A year later he was joined by his younger brother, Gustav, who was also to become a missionary in New Guinea. After six years' study, completed with honours, and a year learning linguistics and tropical medicine, Wilhelm left for Queensland, where he was ordained on 11 November 1928.

One of the first German missionaries permitted to enter New Guinea since World War I, Bergmann arrived at Finschhafen in December. On 14 October 1930 at nearby Sattelberg, he married his German fiancée Marie Luise Auguste Guetebier (d.1974), a nurse. Next year the first of their seven children was born and the Bergmanns began forty years' mission work in the populous New Guinea Highlands. They built their bush-material home and set up a small farm at Kambaidam, a temporary mission station founded to enable further extension of the mission inland. In 1933 they established a more convenient station at Onerunka, near Kainantu.

In August-October 1929 Bergmann had accompanied his fellow-missionary Georg Pilhofer on a trip inland to visit indigenous evangelists (then called 'helpers') already stationed through the Eastern Highlands. From that year, with colleagues and New Guinean carriers, he made annual visitation tours, which led to exploration of areas previously unseen by European missionaries and to contact with tens of thousands of highlanders. Such expeditions, notably one led by Wilhelm Flierl, eldest son of Johann Flierl [q.v.8], in 1930 and a second with Pilhofer in 1933, extended his knowledge of the Eastern Highlands. Following explorations by the Leahy [q.v.10] brothers and Jim Taylor [q.v.], and the consequent interest in the area shown by Father William Ross [q.v.16] and other Catholic missionaries, Lutheran officials decided on further expansion. In May-June 1934 a 43-day journey through the Chimbu and into the Western Highlands was jointly undertaken by the Finschhafen mission and its sister mission at Madang. Bergmann was part of a team of six missionaries and 110 New Guinean carriers and elders. Later that year the Bergmanns founded Ega station in the Chimbu and built an airstrip there.

Responding to pressure from the German vice-consul, Dr Walter Hellenthal, many of the Lutheran missionaries decided in 1936 to found a Nazi stronghold at Finschhafen. Bergmann applied for party membership but was rejected as the clergy were not eligible. The Finschhafen stronghold list, intercepted by the Australian Administration, became the basis for the internment, at the outbreak of World War II, of Bergmann and fifteen other members of the Lutheran Mission Finschhafen. Arrested in New Guinea on 21 September 1939, they arrived in Sydney on 9 October. They were taken to Tatura, Victoria, and placed in camp No.1, for single men. Luise Bergmann and her five children were evacuated in December 1941 and cared for by Lutherans at Tanunda, South Australia, until she, with other women of the LMF, managed to have themselves interned by insisting that they held 'the same beliefs as their husbands'. On 18 December 1942 the Bergmann family were reunited in Tatura 3, where their youngest child was born. Both camps were dominated by Nazis. Bergmann's camp dossier stated that his English was good, and that he was pro-Nazi. The family was at first listed for deportation to Germany but after a change in policy they were released from internment on 11 October 1946.

Next year Bergmann was one of the earliest German Lutherans allowed back to New Guinea. He and Luise continued their work at Ega station until 1968. That year he was awarded an honorary doctorate by the Friedrich-Alexander-University at Erlangen, West Germany. Bergmann had written grammars of local languages, translated the Bible into Kuman, and contributed articles to the mission press. In retirement, living with a daughter at Mutdapilly, Queensland, he completed his autobiography 'Vierzig Jahre in Neuguinea' (ten volumes in typed manuscript form) as well as a four-volume anthropological monograph, self-published in German and English: *The Kamanuku* (1971). Survived by four daughters and two sons, he died on 13 July 1987 at Mutdapilly and was buried in the local cemetery.

H. Fontius, *Mission-Gemeinde-Kirche in Neuguinea, Bayern und bei Karl Steck* (1975); H. Wagner and H. Reiner (eds), *The Lutheran Church in Papua New Guinea* (1986); R. Radford, *Highlanders and Foreigners in the Upper Ramu* (1987); C. Winter, 'The Long Arm of the Third Reich', *Jnl Pacific Hist*, vol 38, no 1, 2003, p 85; *Lutheran* (Adelaide), 17 Aug 1987, p 22; German consulate (Sydney), registration form; A6126, item 91 (NAA); Lutheran Mission correspondence (Mission archives, Adelaide and Neuendettelsau, Germany).

CHRISTINE WINTER

BERKELOUW, ISIDOOR (1913-1987), book-dealer, was born on 17 April 1913 at Rotterdam, the Netherlands, youngest of four children of Hartog Carel Berkelouw, bookseller, and his wife Henriette, née Engelsman. Isidoor entered his father's book-dealing business as an apprentice aged 19. The family enterprise had been established in 1812 by his great-grandfather Solomon Berkelouw, who carried his stock in a jute bag slung over his shoulder. Hartog opened a shop at Schoolstraat, for which Isidoor travelled (1931-36) through the Netherlands as a representative and buyer. On 7 July 1936 he married Francina Johanna Koet in Leiden. He worked in London in 1938-39, before returning to the Netherlands. World War II was catastrophic for the Berkelouw family. Their Rotterdam store was destroyed by bombs in May 1940. The business was re-established in that city for a short time and then in The Hague, only to be confiscated in 1942 by the occupying power. Isidoor's parents, sister and one brother perished in the Holocaust but he escaped from prison. On the liberation of Europe, he opened premises in Amsterdam for bookselling and auctions.

In 1948 Berkelouw decided on Australia as the land for his family's future, arriving in Sydney in March with Francina and their three children. Initially he was engaged in the clothing industry as a director of Leo's Store Pty Ltd, later called Leo's of London. Berkelouw was naturalised in 1955. In September 1950 he had issued from his home in Roseville his first Australian book list of thirty-one items. He opened a bookstore at 38 King Street in the city and held auctions there; in 1957 he moved to 114 King Street. After the redevelopment of that site in 1972, he conducted the business from Rushcutters Bay.

Berkelouw established himself as the pre-eminent dealer in rare, antiquarian and second-hand books in Australia. In 1949 he was the only member of the Antiquarian Booksellers' Association (International) listed as living in Australia. The press turned to him for comment on the book trade and matters of related interest. In November 1960 he scored a coup with his acquisition at auction of papers and manuscripts of Miles Franklin [q.v.8]: 'Going ... Going ... Gone—To Mr. B. Again!', headlined the *Daily Telegraph*. That collection was the subject of catalogue 47 issued to commemorate the 150th anniversary of the firm; one of Australia's leading bookmen, Walter

Stone [q.v.], contributed historical and bibliographical notes.

Bringing with him a profound knowledge of the book trade rooted in the European tradition, Berkelouw recognised on his arrival in Australia that there was a market for technical publications. Libraries, universities and other institutions acquired many components of their collection from him. He was an astute businessman ('you can't make a living by selling bargains') whose high standards, in terms of the quality of his stock and an efficient cataloguing system, won him the respect and admiration of fellow traders. Especially did he enjoy the loyalty and good will of bibliophiles and collectors. These responses were founded not merely in his engaging charm (he was a handsome man who even smoked with style) but also in his personalised conduct of that special trade in the most civilising of products.

In 1976 Berkelouw retired to the United States of America, first to Honolulu and then to Los Angeles, California. Yet he still worked, travelling with Francina throughout America and Europe seeking material for the Australian market. Francina died in 1981 and Isidoor's son Henry decided to join his father in Los Angeles. From 1977 his other son, Leo, operated the business at Bendooley, a historic house near Berrima. Isidoor's only daughter, Francis Haymes, independently established a bookshop in Woollahra, Sydney, which was owned and managed by her son Sam after her death in 1986. Isidoor Berkelouw died on 24 November 1987 at his home in Santa Monica and was cremated. The business of Messrs Berkelouw continued, conducted by the fifth and sixth generations of the family.

Miles Franklin's Manuscripts and Type-scripts [1962]; *The Golden Age of Booksellers* (1981); D. Levine, *The Isidoor Berkelouw Memorial Address* (1989); *Bulletin*, 9 Feb 1963, p 17; *SMH*, 29 Nov 1965, p 6; *Sun-Herald* (Sydney), 28 Nov 1971, p 116; *Austn Financial Review*, 17 Dec 1987, p 28.

DAVID LEVINE

BERNDT, RONALD MURRAY (1916-1990), social anthropologist, was born on 14 July 1916 at Rose Park, Adelaide, only child of South Australian-born parents Alfred Henry Berndt, jeweller, and his wife Minna, née Schulze. Ronald attended Anglican primary schools and Pulteney Grammar School, and developed an early interest in ethnology and Aboriginal culture. At his father's insistence, he began a course in accountancy. In 1938 he joined the Anthropological Society of South Australia and next year became an honorary assistant-ethnologist at the South Australian Museum, published his first ethnographic papers, and accompanied an expedition, mounted by the University of Adelaide's board

for anthropological research, to Ooldea in the western desert country. Encouraged by professors (Sir) John Cleland and T. Harvey Johnston, he studied anthropology under A. P. Elkin [qq.v.8,9,14] at the University of Sydney (Dip.Anth., 1943; BA, Research, 1951; MA Hons, 1954).

On 26 April 1941 at St Paul's Church of England, Adelaide, Berndt married New Zealand-born Catherine Helen Webb, a fellow anthropology student. The Berndts were to enjoy a very close professional partnership spanning five decades. They carried out field-work at Ooldea from July to November 1941 and published their findings in *Oceania* in 1942-45. Their book *From Black to White in South Australia* (1951) drew together their conclusions from work of 1942-44 in Adelaide, the Murray Bridge area and elsewhere in the State. In 1944-46 they investigated labour conditions on Vestey-owned cattle stations in the Northern Territory. Attached to the University of Sydney in 1946-51 and funded by the Australian National Research Council, they began studies of Aboriginal people in Arnhem Land that were to extend until 1979. In 1950 the Berndts were jointly awarded the Royal Society of New South Wales's Edgeworth David [q.v.8] medal. In 1951-53 Berndt undertook pioneering field-work, with his wife, in the Eastern Highlands of New Guinea. This research formed the basis for his doctoral thesis, submitted to the London School of Economics and Political Science (Ph.D., 1955), and his book *Excess and Restraint* (1962). In 1958 he was presented with the Wellcome medal by the Royal Anthropological Institute of Great Britain and Ireland.

Returning to Australia in 1956, Berndt took up a senior lectureship in anthropology in the department of psychology, University of Western Australia, and next year embarked on the first of a series of field-trips to the Balgo Mission, near Lake Gregory, that were to continue until 1981. He was promoted to reader in 1959 and to the foundation chair of anthropology in 1963, overseeing a rapidly growing department, especially in Aboriginal studies. Trained in a British structural-functionalist tradition, Berndt and his wife had eclectic interests and a holistic approach. Working among Aborigines whose first contacts with Europeans were relatively recent, and among those of mixed descent living under heavy acculturative pressures, they wrote extensively on social organisation, sexuality, social control, the life cycle, poetry and song, material culture, subsistence, religious life and sociocultural change. Ronald made a major contribution to the study of Aboriginal religion through his two studies of Aboriginal cults, *Kunapipi* (1951) and *Djanggawul* (1952), and his monograph *Australian Aboriginal Religion* (1974). Consummate field-workers, with an eye for detail, the Berndts cared less for anthropological theorising and cross-cultural generalisation than for the ethnographic and representational tasks they set themselves.

Berndt founded the Anthropological Society of Western Australia (1958) and the scholarly journal *Anthropological Forum* (1963), and was a foundation member of the Australian Institute of Aboriginal Studies in 1964. He was inaugural president (1962-64) of the Australian branch of the Association of Social Anthropologists of the Commonwealth. Concerned for the well-being of Aboriginal people, he was a prominent commentator and adviser, at both State and national levels, who took a keen interest in political developments. He served as an expert witness in early land claim cases in the Northern Territory, including *Milirrpum* v. *Nabalco Pty Ltd* (1971), advocated legal recognition and protection of Aboriginal sacred sites, and clashed in 1980 with the Liberal premier Sir Charles Court over the Noonkanbah dispute in the Kimberley region.

Usually seen puffing on one of his beloved pipes, Berndt was a larger-than-life character whose enthusiasm for his work was boundless and infectious. He was an unstinting supporter of graduate students. At UWA both anthropology and sociology prospered under his leadership; he recruited staff with an eye to maintaining both geographical and topical eclecticism in these disciplines. Known fondly as 'Prof', he ran his department on the 'God-professor' model, jokingly described as a 'paticipatory democracy' in which all staff participated while he made the major decisions.

Berndt was an avid and knowledgeable collector of Aboriginal and Asian art and artefacts. Although he and his wife seldom entertained at home—to be given a guided tour through their house-gallery was a great privilege—they were generous hosts, and Berndt loved to serve fine wines. In 1976 they set up an ethnographic museum at the university to accommodate, among other works, their collection of Aboriginal cultural materials. They took little time for recreation but shared a love of mystery novels. After Berndt's retirement in December 1981 he was named professor emeritus and continued to publish steadily. The Berndts' 1940s research into Aboriginal labour in the Northern Territory was written up as *End of an Era* (1987). Convinced of the necessity of communicating knowledge of Aboriginal Australian societies and culture to the public, they wrote children's stories and books for high school students, and in 1988 revised their introductory reference work *The World of the First Australians*, originally published in 1964. They also co-authored a treatise on Aboriginal narratives, *The Speaking Land* (1989), and, returning to their previously unpublished research on the culture of the Yaraldi people of the lower Murray River region, produced *A World that Was* (1993). In all, Ronald Berndt wrote or edited thirty-five books, fifteen of them in collaboration with his wife.

Elected a fellow (1948) and honorary fellow (1982) of the Royal Anthropological Institute of Great Britain and Ireland, and a member (1962) of the Social Science Research Council of Australia, Berndt served as president (1972-73) of the Royal Society of Western Australia, and received its medal in 1979. He became a fellow (1982) of the Australian and New Zealand Association for the Advancement of Science. The Anthropological Society of Western Australia awarded him its Silver Jubilee medal in 1983. In 1987 UWA conferred on him an honorary doctorate of letters. That year he was appointed AM. Survived by his wife (d.1994), he died on 2 May 1990 at Wembley, Perth, and was buried in Karrakatta cemetery. There were no children. The Berndts' contribution lives on through their endowment of the Berndt Research Foundation. In 1991 the museum of anthropology at UWA was named after them.

R. Tonkinson and M. Howard (eds), *Going It Alone?* (1990); V. Amit (ed), *Biographical Dictionary of Social and Cultural Anthropology* (2003); *Aboriginal History*, vol 29, 2005, p 77; *Australian*, 12 Aug 1995, p 9; Berndt papers (Berndt Museum of Anthropology, UWA); personal knowledge.

ROBERT TONKINSON

BERRY, THOMAS GEORGE (1920-1981), soldier and farmer, was born on 15 March 1920 at Foster, Victoria, elder of twins and sixth child of Victorian-born parents Thomas William Berry, farmer, and his wife Agnes Amelia, née Hoskins. Throughout his life he was known as George Thomas to distinguish him from his father. After leaving Foster State School at an early age, he worked as a farm labourer in the Korumburra district of south Gippsland. On 24 June 1940 he enlisted in the Australian Imperial Force; he was then 5 ft 7 ins (170 cm) tall, with blue eyes and brown hair. He was made an acting corporal just nine days after joining the 2/24th Battalion in August.

Arriving in the Middle East in December 1940, the 2/24th was sent to defend Tobruk, Libya, in April 1941. Active service did not begin well for Berry. Dysentery put him in hospital for three weeks in May and in August he received a bullet wound to his left hand in an accident. Hospitalised again, he returned to the 2/24th in late December and was immediately promoted to acting sergeant (confirmed June 1942). He was acting as a platoon commander in October when his unit fought at El Alamein, Egypt.

During an attack on the night of 25–26 October Berry's personal courage inspired his men to follow him unhesitatingly through heavy fire. He was awarded the Distinguished Conduct Medal for 'conspicuous gallantry and devotion to duty'. However, these prosaic words concealed the grim reality of close-quarter combat. Berry captured two enemy positions on his own and on reaching his company's objective, a strong enemy post, he 'carried out terrible execution with the bayonet' until his right arm was severely fractured. He was evacuated to Australia in February 1943. Declared unfit for active service because of his shoulder wound, he was transferred to the 2nd Movement Control Group, Melbourne, where he served from August 1943 to October 1944. After another period in hospital, he was invalided from the army on 17 January 1945.

Settling back into civilian life, Berry married Marie Catherine James, a nurse, on 25 August 1945 at St Paul's Church of England, Korumburra. He worked briefly as a tram driver, living at Camberwell, Melbourne, where his first child was born. In the early 1950s the family moved to Ranceby, south Gippsland, and Berry became a share-farmer. During this period two more children were born and he applied for a soldier-settlement block at Nyora. Granted a 140-acre (57 ha) property in 1958, he ran dairy cattle and involved himself in community activities, including the school council, a Masonic lodge and the local sub-branch of the Returned Sailors', Soldiers' and Airmen's Imperial League of Australia. He rarely missed an Anzac Day march.

Berry was a hard worker, a strong disciplinarian, a loving father, a competent public speaker and a sometimes fiery character. He had developed diabetes soon after his discharge and in 1973 ill health forced him to leave Nyora and move to Donvale, Melbourne, where he worked as a storeman. In 1980 he retired to Rosebud. He died of bronchopneumonia on 10 July 1981 at Southport, Queensland, while holidaying on the Gold Coast. Survived by his wife, and their daughter and two sons, he was cremated.

AWM 119, item A57, pt 1 (AWM); B883, item VX31716 (NAA); private information.

RUSSELL PARKIN

BERRYMAN, SIR FRANK HORTON (1894-1981), soldier, was born on 11 April 1894 at Geelong West, Victoria, fourth child of William Lee Berryman, engine driver, and his wife Annie Jane, née Horton, both Victorian born. Educated at Melbourne High School, he entered the Royal Military College, Duntroon, Federal Capital Territory, in March 1913; his record at both was impressive. He graduated from Duntroon in June 1915 and was appointed lieutenant in the Australian Imperial Force on 1 July. After brief artillery training, he was posted to the 12th Battery, 4th Field Artillery Brigade, 2nd Division. He arrived in France in March 1916 and became immersed in the artillery war that dominated the Western Front. In July he was made adjutant of the 4th FAB and promoted to captain. He obtained experience of infantry operations as a trainee staff officer with 7th Brigade headquarters from January 1917. Promoted to major in September, he was given command of the 18th Battery, 6th FAB. He commanded the 14th Battery, 5th FAB, in May-September 1918, a most demanding period, after which he was awarded the Distinguished Service Order. He was twice mentioned in despatches. Wounded in action in September, he returned to 7th Brigade headquarters as assistant brigade major, then as brigade major.

Back in Australia in August 1919, Berryman continued his service in the Permanent Military Forces as a lieutenant with the honorary rank of major. A two-year course in Britain in 1921-23 brought appointment as inspecting ordnance officer, followed by promotion to captain and brevet major in March 1923. On 28 November 1925 at St Stephen's Presbyterian Church, Sydney, he married with Congregational forms Muriel Alice Ann Whipp. He attended the Staff College, Camberley, England, in 1927-28. His report referred to his 'considerable strength of character'. He was 'very zealous and hard working', but 'highly strung' and 'might have done even better if he had not been almost over-anxious'. After two years in the Australian High Commission in London, he became army representative there in 1931.

When Berryman returned to Australia in 1932 in the depths of the Depression, the army was enduring cuts in personnel and pay. He remained on a captain's salary, but after two staff appointments was promoted to major in March 1935. Tensions in Europe and East Asia were preoccupying the Australian army. Berryman, promoted to brevet lieutenant colonel in May 1937 (substantive July 1938), was working so relentlessly in the operations branch at Army Headquarters, Melbourne, that his efficiency report in 1938 stated that he was 'under continuous mental strain' and recommended that 'it would be in the best interests of the Service and himself that he should be released for duty with troops'. This appears to have had its effect as in December he was posted to headquarters, 3rd Division, as general staff officer, 1st grade.

Seven months into World War II, on 4 April 1940, Berryman was appointed GSO1 of the 6th Division, AIF, with the rank of colonel. He established his reputation as a staff officer at Bardia and Tobruk, Libya, in January 1941, but was then transferred to the 7th Division to command its artillery. His former commander (Sir) Iven Mackay [q.v.15] considered that Berryman's outstanding ability and systematic planning had contributed largely to the successes at Bardia and Tobruk, and Lieutenant General (Sir) Richard O'Connor, commander of Western Desert Force, spoke to Lieutenant General Sir Thomas Blamey [q.v.13] 'in glowing terms of the way in which the staff work of the 6th Division was done'. Berryman was appointed CBE (1941). Good soldier though he was, he antagonised senior Militia officers; to him they were only 'weekend soldiers'.

In the brief campaign in Syria in June-July 1941 Berryman again distinguished himself. For a fortnight he commanded Berryforce, a mixed brigade fighting in the Merdjayoun sector until relieved by a British brigade. He planned and launched five attacks, using his guns well forward and aggressively. By the end of the campaign he was so exhausted that he went into hospital. The mention in despatches which followed was scant recognition of his performance.

Berryman became brigadier, general staff, of I Corps in August 1941. The corps being under orders to move to the Far East, Lieutenant General (Sir) John Lavarack [q.v.15], Berryman and others flew to Java, Netherlands East Indies, in January 1942, but disaster in Malaya and the swift advances of the Japanese put an end to Allied plans. Discussion of Japanese tactics with Colonel I. M. Stewart of the Argyll and Sutherland Highlanders enabled Berryman and Major General A. S. Allen [q.v.13] to prepare a paper on that subject for circulation within the Australian army. Berryman left for Australia late in February.

After the turmoil of events in February-March 1942, Berryman emerged in April as major general, general staff, of the First Army under Lavarack. In September he was promoted to substantive major general and made deputy-chief of the General Staff at Land Headquarters, Melbourne. At various times he was also in New Guinea as MGGS, New Guinea Force. He worked closely with Blamey, especially in the planning of the operations that cleared the Japanese from the Ramu Valley and the Huon Peninsula in 1943-44. Given command of II Corps (I Corps from April 1944) in November 1943, he was promoted to lieutenant general on 21 January 1944. As a staff officer then as a commander, Berryman was commended for 'his skilful planning, able supervision and vigorous leadership'. He was appointed CB (1945).

In July 1944 Berryman was relieved of the retraining of his corps on the Atherton Tableland, Queensland, to undertake work of critical importance as chief-of-staff, Advanced LHQ, Brisbane. He began with a Joint Planning Staff in Melbourne preparing for the proposed concentration in Australia of British forces to be used against Japan. Returning to Brisbane, his main task became liaison with Douglas MacArthur's [q.v.15] General Headquarters, which, with his forward echelon, he joined at Hollandia, Netherlands New Guinea, then on Leyte, the Philippines, and finally in Manila. Berryman was invaluable; he could get on with the Americans and they admired him, but he was there to 'safeguard Australian interests'.

Berryman continued in this role until the war ended. He was with Blamey at the surrender ceremony in Tokyo Bay on 2 September 1945 and when the Japanese Second Army surrendered at Morotai, NEI, on the 9th. Again mentioned in despatches, he was one of the officers Blamey recommended for a knighthood only to be rejected by the Australian government. The United States of America awarded him the Medal of Freedom with Silver Palm (1948).

His long service close to Blamey may well have prejudiced Berryman's standing in political circles, but senior officers respected him even if some did not like him. Lavarack considered him 'the best combination of fighting leader, staff officer, and administrator that I have met so far in our Army'. The 'soundest planner I saw in the AIF' was the verdict of (Sir) Horace Robertson [q.v.16]. He was indefatigable and could be as hard on others as on himself. An artillery commander writing after the Syrian campaign referred to 'the many occasions when your presence, effort and drive made all the difference between success and failure', but some called him 'Berry the Bastard'. He was so concerned about what appeared to have become his accepted image as 'the tireless dynamo of the staff' that he wrote to the army's assistant-director of public relations to complain, providing a lengthy account of his activities as a front-line soldier.

In March 1946 Berryman was given his final appointment, that of general officer commanding, Eastern Command, and commandant, 2nd Military District. At Victoria Barracks in Sydney in the postwar years, his policy was to raise the prestige of the army and to make it an integral part of the community. He worked to inculcate the spirit of community service in all ranks, himself setting an example by his public activities. Soldiers throughout Eastern Command sent thousands of food parcels to Britain, and war widows and crippled children were supported. Troops came to the aid of flood-hit Maitland and, on the Chifley [q.v.13] government's orders, mined open-cut coal during a miners' strike in 1949. Berryman delighted in military ceremonial, reviving the annual tattoo in 1947 and establishing the Eastern Command Band. He also began to improve army properties by planting trees, making lawns, gardens and playing fields, and by renovating buildings. A new nickname was heard—'Frank the Florist'.

Although Berryman did not attain the hoped-for prize of CGS in succession to (Sir) Vernon Sturdee [q.v.16], his skills as planner and administrator remained in demand. He was transferred to the Prime Minister's Department in February 1951 to be director-general of the Commonwealth Jubilee and of the royal visit planned for 1952. As the latter was postponed, he returned to Eastern Command in March, resuming duties as director-general in December 1953. After Queen Elizabeth II's tour early in 1954, he was appointed KCVO and was placed on the Retired List on 12 April.

Berryman was then the energetic director and chief executive officer of the Royal Agricultural Society of New South Wales until 1961. Other interests included Dr Barnardo's in Australia (president 1967-80), the Regular Defence Forces Welfare Association (president 1967-79), the Gowrie [q.v.9] Scholarship Trust Fund and the Remembrance Driveway committee (president 1952-81). He was a founder of the War Widows' Guild of Australia and a director of numerous public companies. He also found time for golf. In 1972 Lady Berryman was appointed CBE for her work with charities. Survived by his wife and their daughter and son, Sir Frank died on 28 May 1981 at Rose Bay, Sydney, and was cremated with full military honours. His portrait (1958) by Joshua Smith is held by the Australian War Memorial, Canberra.

G. Long, *To Benghazi* (1952), *Greece, Crete and Syria* (1953), *The Final Campaigns* (1963); L. Wigmore, *The Japanese Thrust* (1957); D. McCarthy, *South-West Pacific Area—First Year* (1959); D. Dexter, *The New Guinea Offensives* (1961); D. M. Horner (ed), *The Commanders* (1984); D. Horner, *High Command* (1992), *The Gunners* (1995) and *Blamey* (1998); *Bulletin*, 22 Mar 1961, p 47; Berryman papers (AWM); private information.

A. J. HILL

BEST, MARION ESDAILE HALL (1905-1988), interior designer, was born on 13 April 1905 at Dubbo, New South Wales, fourth and youngest child of Edmond Henry Burkitt, an English-born medical practitioner, and his Australian-born wife Amy Theodora, née Hungerford. Her sister Agnes Theodora (known as Dora) Sweetapple [q.v.Supp.] was a jeweller and painter. Marion attended Dubbo High School and Frensham, Mittagong. Connections she made there and on holidays at Palm Beach were to prove useful in later years. Nicknamed 'Youngie', she was influenced by the simplicity of life at Dubbo and by her mother's use of colour in the home.

Burkitt trained as a nurse at the Coast Hospital, Little Bay. On 19 December 1927 she married (Sir) John Victor Hall Best [q.v.13], a dentist, at St Mark's Church of England, Darling Point. In the late 1920s and early 1930s she attended classes in embroidery with June Scott Stevenson, who had lived in Chile, and in painting with Thea Proctor [q.v.11]. Marion Best's first decorating work was in 1929 at Farleigh, her mother's Palm Beach house, where she combined white walls and yellow ceilings with furniture of her own design.

The success of her adventurous design (1937-38) at the Elanora Country Club led to work at the Queen's Club, the Royal Exchange Club and the repatriation hospital Berida, at Bowral. She aimed at a three-dimensional translation of colour and was deeply impressed by the set designs of Colonel de Basil's Ballets Russes. Best attended lectures in architecture at the University of Sydney in 1938 and completed a correspondence course in interior design from New York. The skills gleaned from these courses enabled her to achieve a more professional standard in design presentation, including coloured isometric projections. She later employed architects in her business.

Following her family's move in 1934 to Queen Street, Woollahra, Mrs Best opened there a retail business, Marion Best Pty Ltd, in 1938, and added a small shop in Rowe Street, Sydney, in 1949. She won larger commercial commissions, the most significant of which was for the interiors of a new block of studio flats at 7 Elizabeth Street (1939). Commissions for the Lady Gowrie [q.v.9] Child Centre (1941), Erskineville, and the Rachel Forster Hospital for Women and Children (1942), Redfern, helped to keep the business viable during World War II. She also worked at the de Havilland Aircraft Pty Ltd factory during the war.

For an exhibition (1941) held by the Australian Red Cross Society (New South Wales Division), Best designed 'Classic Modern' and 'Young Modern' rooms. With a hypothetical client, ample publicity and no budget restrictions, she presented her most experimental work and reached an audience beyond her usual clientele. After the war her work was featured in home magazines, reaching thousands of readers. She ran the David Jones Art Gallery in 1947-48; helped to found the Society of Interior Designers of Australia in 1951; and addressed a conference of the Royal Australian Institute of Architects in 1956. Her domestic and commercial commissions completed in the 1960s and 1970s included the 'XXth Century' room for the Rare and Beautiful Things exhibition (Art Gallery of New South Wales, 1961), Moonbah Ski Lodge (with Bill Lucas, 1961), the 'Room for Mary Quant' (1967), the 'Room for Peter Sculthorpe' (1971) and many interiors undertaken for her major client, the Crebbin [q.v.] family.

An adventurous and sophisticated use of colour was always the hallmark of Best's work, which was influenced by Henri Matisse, the Fauves and, specifically, the colour wheels of Roy de Maistre [q.v.8]. She believed that colour in interiors was uplifting and adapted the techniques of Justin O'Brien to develop a method of glazing for walls and ceilings. Travelling widely from the late 1940s in Europe, Asia and North and South America, she negotiated at international trade fairs for import agreements with the makers of furniture, fabrics, lighting, wallpapers and accessories including Marimekko, Knoll, Herman Miller, Noguchi, McGuire and Jim Thompson. She also used many Australian designers and artists.

Following the death of her husband in 1972, she closed her Woollahra shop in 1974. The Darling Point flat of her widowhood, decorated in hot pinks, reds and oranges, with Saarinen chairs and Marimekko fabrics, showed that even in her seventies, she still set the standard for avant-garde design in Australia. A slim, smartly dressed woman, she was vivacious and generous, with tremendous energy. Survived by her daughter and son, Best died on 26 June 1988 at Elizabeth Bay and was cremated. Examples of her work are held by the Historic Houses Trust of New South Wales, Sydney, and the Australian National Gallery, Canberra.

C. Quinn, *Sydney Style* (1993); M. Richards, *The Best Style* (1993); *Herald* (Melbourne), 7 May 1970, p 18; *Mode Aust*, June 1984, p 26; *Art and Aust*, 1989, p 454, 1999-2000, p 88; *Bulletin*, 3 Aug 1993, p 36; Best archives (Historic Houses Trust of NSW, Sydney, and National Gallery of Aust, Canberra).

CATRIONA QUINN

BEYER, THOMAS DAVID (1906-1982), Anglican clergyman and air force chaplain, was born on 6 March 1906 at Lakes Entrance, Victoria, son of Thomas David Beyer, labourer, and his wife Victoria Ruth, née Dunk, both Victorian born. He attended Melbourne and Bairnsdale high schools. After working as a motorcar salesman in Melbourne, in 1931 he entered Ridley College (Th.L., Australian College of Theology, 1932). Made deacon on 18 December 1932, he was ordained priest on 17 December 1933 for the diocese of Gippsland. He served his curacy at Paynesville and was priest-in-charge at Drouin in 1934-35. At the Church of St John the Baptist, Bairnsdale, on 3 April 1934 he married Hazel Vera Johnston (d.1976). Next year he became rector of Morwell. There he contributed columns to the local newspaper under the pseudonym 'Inquisitas', played cricket and Australian Rules football, and participated in amateur theatricals.

Joining the Royal Australian Air Force as a chaplain, 4th class, on 11 November 1940, Beyer was posted to Laverton, then in December 1941 to Geraldton, Western Australia. He embarked for England in January 1943, travelling on escort duty via North America, and served for the remainder of the war at No.11 Personnel Dispatch and Reception Centre, located at Bournemouth and later at Brighton. This unit received RAAF personnel on arrival in England for further training or operational duties.

As sole unit chaplain, Beyer wrote hundreds of letters home to families of the airmen, conducted funerals, and produced a fortnightly magazine with a circulation of three hundred. In his office (christened 'Bludgers Bower' with the motto 'Abandon rank all who enter') men could talk over problems, read or write, receive comforts parcels from home or have a quiet yarn. His weekly services in local parish churches were always popular. A keen sportsman, he was responsible for arranging weekly matches against local teams. He was himself a handy cricketer who regularly played in or led RAAF teams against other service or county teams.

After VE Day Beyer worked with former prisoners of war. He arrived home in June 1946 and was posted to Point Cook, Victoria. In 1947-48 he served in Japan with the RAAF component of the British Commonwealth Occupation Force. Returning to Japan for a brief period in 1951, he spent a month in Korea during the war. In 1950 he had been appointed MBE. Official reports on his service both in England and Japan testified to his effectiveness as a chaplain. Dave Beyer's approach coupled a robust, practical Christianity with a rich sense of humour. Promoted to principal air chaplain (Church of England) on 1 January 1963, he was based at Penrith, New South Wales. This role required trips to yet another operational area, this time Vietnam. He transferred to the RAAF Reserve on 7 March 1965, but continued to serve, part time, in Melbourne as PAC until he was placed on the Retired List on 15 December 1967.

Having been prominent in service sporting administration, Beyer became executive officer of the South Pacific Games (1969) Trust in Port Moresby, where he stayed for three and a half years. Retiring to bayside Melbourne, he indulged his passion for 'catching fish, angling, boating, catching more fish' and supporting the Melbourne Football Club. Survived by his daughter, he died on 22 November 1982 at Frankston; after a military funeral he was cremated.

P. A. Davidson, *Sky Pilot* (1990); *RAAF News*, Apr 1965, p 7; private information.   P. A. DAVIDSON

BIALOGUSKI, MICHAEL (1917-1984), medical practitioner and intelligence agent, was born on 19 March 1917 at Kiev, Russia (Ukraine), and named Mykolo, younger son of Polish parents Gregorii Bialoguski, veterinary surgeon, and his wife Paulina, née Dudelzak, dentist. His father was a non-practising Jew, his mother a Christian; Bialoguski described his religion as Calvinist on his military papers but did not adhere to any religion later. In Wilno, Poland (Vilnius, Lithuania), he attended secondary school (1927-35), studied viola at the conservatorium of music from 1927 and enrolled in medicine at the Stephen Bathory University in 1935. He married Irena Vandos but they divorced in 1941. An account of his early life held by the Australian Security Intelligence Organization states that he was jailed briefly after protesting against some of the actions of the occupying Red Army.

Supposedly en route for Curaçao, he left Poland, travelled across Russia to Japan and in June 1941 arrived in Sydney. He copied music and worked for radio stations as a violinist and musical arranger. On 30 March 1942 he enlisted in the Australian Army Medical Corps, Militia. He served as an orderly at the 113th Australian General Hospital, Concord, before being discharged on 1 December to enable him, with Commonwealth government financial assistance, to study medicine at the University of Sydney (MB, 1947; BS, 1963). He married Agnes Patricia Humphry, née Ryan, a 35-year-old divorcee, on 17 May 1943 in the registrar general's office, Sydney; they were to be divorced in 1954. After a year (1948-49) in general practice at Thirroul, he set himself up in Macquarie Street, Sydney.

Hostile to communism and fascinated by spying, Bialoguski had offered his services to the Commonwealth Investigation Service in 1945. The CIS engaged him as an agent as did its successor, ASIO, in 1949. He was naturalised in 1947. At the Russian Social Club, Sydney, in 1951, he met Vladimir Petrov, a third secretary at the Soviet Embassy, Canberra. To Petrov, Bialoguski appeared an attractive prospect as a spy and he allocated him the code name 'Grigorii'. But the hunter was already the hunted and Bialoguski studied Petrov's every move. While working for ASIO Bialoguski had developed a left-wing persona, seeming to sympathise with the leftist Polish and Russian immigrants on whom he informed. As a doctor, he appeared as a respectable left-wing face for bodies such as the New South Wales Peace Council and the Save the Rosenbergs Committee.

ASIO had several code names for Bialoguski including 'Jack Baker' and perhaps most appropriately 'Diabolo', given both Bialoguski's physical appearance (he sported a devilish beard) and his infuriating manner. In 1952-53 Bialoguski and Petrov became close friends over drunken dinners at nightclubs. For a time Petrov gave 'Grigorii/Diabolo' some minor espionage tasks but Bialoguski's cultivation of him meant that they began to share a double life. Bialoguski played a key part in edging Petrov towards defection, suggesting a joint business with him, first a restaurant and later a chicken farm. He introduced Petrov to H. C. Beckett, an eye surgeon, for medical reasons. Beckett, on behalf of ASIO but without Bialoguski's knowledge, suggested explicitly to Petrov that he defect. After problems with their colleagues in the Soviet embassy, Petrov and his wife Evdokia did so in April 1954. At the royal commission on espionage which began hearings in May 1954, Bialoguski gave convincing evidence about Petrov's disenchantment with the Soviet Union despite claims by H. V. Evatt [q.v.14] that Bialoguski was part of a conspiracy to damage the Labor Party.

When extracts from Bialoguski's book *The Petrov Story* (1955) were published in the *Sun* (Sydney) and the *Herald* (Melbourne) in June, the *Telegraph* (Sydney) and *Argus* (Melbourne) released his ex-wife's version of his life and character. Patricia Bialoguski said that when she met Michael he had a 'strange—almost weird—personality' but that he had swept her off her feet. She described a clever, manipulative, self-absorbed and ambitious man, who could also be charming and entertaining. Even after discounting the bitterness of a former wife, this account accords with the perceptions of others. Bialoguski sued for libel and was to win his case in May 1961, the jury awarding him £1000 in damages.

In the late 1950s he was a minor press celebrity, subject to various public indignities. When he applied in May 1957 for a reduction in the alimony he paid to Patricia, the *Sun* reported: '"Spy" Doc Can't Pay!'. Bialoguski's counsel argued that his client's medical practice had suffered because of his public role. The registrar in divorce described Bialoguski as 'something of a showman, a free spender of money' but accepted that his book had netted him very little for film and television rights and reduced the alimony. While most public portrayals of him are unflattering, he had a more compassionate side. In a letter to the *Sydney Morning Herald* (2 June 1962) he noted:

The memories of my student days at the Sydney University still haunt me with the image of senior honoraries omitting to exchange greetings with the bedridden, neglecting to express regret when examining a man in pain, showing little consideration for the shy or courtesy for the old, often stooping to a display of witty sarcasm at the expense of a patient and for the benefit of an appreciative student gallery.

Bialoguski married 26-year-old Nonnie Frieda Peifer, a secretary, on 16 January 1957 at the registrar general's office, Sydney. Passionate about music, in the 1950s he had tried vainly to convince (Sir) Eugene Goossens [q.v.14] to teach him conducting and had played the violin in the Sydney Symphony Orchestra. In 1964 he and his wife moved to England and he continued to work as a medical practitioner. There he was able to realise some of his musical ambitions. He studied conducting, conducted the Royal Philharmonic Orchestra, and in 1969 hired the New Philharmonia Orchestra for a concert which he conducted at the Albert Hall. This performance was the start of a short but intense period of achievement, during which he formed the Commonwealth Philharmonic Orchestra and conducted in Westminster Abbey and the Albert Hall. Survived by his wife, and their two daughters and one son, he died of cancer on 29 July 1984 at Kingswood, Surrey, and was cremated.

R. Manne, *The Petrov Affair* (1987); D. McKnight, *Australia's Spies and Their Secrets* (1994); A6119, items 1-4, 325, 992-3, 2644-9, A6980, item S200513, B884, item N321158 (NAA); M. Bialoguski, diaries, 1953-55 (NLA); I. Boyle, The Divided Mind of Michael Bialoguski (ts, 1996, copy on ADB file); private information.   DAVID McKNIGHT

BIEUNDURRY, JIMMY (1938?-1985), Aboriginal leader, was born probably in 1938, near Lake Gregory, East Kimberley, Western Australia, son of Walmajarri (Walmatjarri) parents. As a child, Jimmy lived in a completely traditional way. He was among the last of the Walmajarri to come out of the desert regions into the cattle-station country of the Kimberley in the 1950s. While a young man he attended school at Fitzroy Crossing and learned to read. There, on 3 June 1967 at the People's Church, he married Olive Bent, a Bunuba woman who was to become a qualified translator and Bieundurry's partner in activism and leadership.

A committed Christian, Bieundurry studied at the United Aborigines Mission's Gnowangerup Bible Training Institute, and became a lay preacher at Fitzroy Crossing. He was politicised during the upheaval that followed the granting in 1968 of award wages to Aboriginal workers in the pastoral industry, as his people were evicted or, when owners and managers refused to pay the award, walked off the cattle stations on which they had lived and worked. In the early 1970s up to two thousand displaced people were camped in appalling conditions at Fitzroy Crossing. By 1977 Bieundurry was employed by Community Health Services at Looma. He was an inaugural member (1977-81) of the National Aboriginal Conference, rep-

resenting the West Kimberley, and a member (1978-80) of the Aboriginal Lands Trust. In 1978 he became a founding co-chairman of the Kimberley Land Council. Unlike its Northern Territory counterparts, the KLC was a non-statutory organisation. In its early years it was effectively supported by Bieundurry, from his NAC-resourced office at Derby.

In 1979 Bieundurry became involved in the conflict between the Yungngora (Yangngara) community of Noonkanbah station on the one hand, and, on the other, the Western Australian government and Amax Exploration (Australia) over plans to drill an exploratory oil well on sacred ground. Throughout the dispute he was a significant and eloquent advocate for the Aboriginal position. In 1980 he attended a World Council of Churches consultation on racism at Noordwijkerhout, the Netherlands, and was a member of the NAC delegation that took the Noonkanbah case to the sub-commission on prevention of discrimination and protection of minorities, United Nations Commission on Human Rights, in Geneva, Switzerland. He was appointed a founding member (1980-84) of the Aboriginal Development Commission.

Whether he was 'out bush' in the Kimberley, or in Canberra, or overseas, Bieundurry's charisma was evident. With a preacher's eloquence and passion, though not in the fire and brimstone vein, he was quiet but persuasive with a calm intensity. There was at times a tension between his twin roles of lay preacher and political leader. In the aftermath of the Noonkanbah dispute, he felt 'burnt out' and somewhat disillusioned. He largely withdrew from his political and leadership positions, and devoted considerable efforts to setting up an outstation at Jalyirr, in the desert country. Survived by his wife, and their three daughters and two sons, he died of ischaemic heart disease on 1 June 1985, ninety kilometres south-west of Billiluna station. His funeral, one of the largest ever seen in the Kimberley region, was held at Wangkatjunka. He was buried in Christmas Creek cemetery, near Fitzroy Crossing.

S. Hawke and M. Gallagher, *Noonkanbah* (1989); Cwlth Dept of Aboriginal Affairs, *Annual Report*, 1977-78; Kimberley Land Council, *Newsletter*, Jan 1979, p 2; private information and personal knowledge.   STEVE HAWKE

BILL, BEETALOO JANGARI (c.1910-1983), labourer and Aboriginal elder, was born probably between 1910 and 1915 at Beetaloo station (from which his English name derives), near Newcastle Waters, Northern Territory. His father, Roderick (Mirijilkari) Jampin, was Warumungu; his mother, Clara Parrangali

Nawurla, was Gurindji. Beetaloo Bill said that this proscribed marriage (Jampin-Nawurla) had arisen because a White man, Billy 'Cabby' or 'Cabbage' (perhaps Kirby), had taken his mother from the Camfield area to Tennant Creek. There, since Northern Territory law prohibited 'cohabitation', 'Cabby' engaged Roderick to give the appearance of the two Aborigines being a couple, which they later became. Beetaloo Bill was their first child; he had a younger brother and several younger sisters. His Aboriginal name was Wirinykari (Weingari).

As a child, Beetaloo Bill spoke his father's language, Warumungu, according to which his subsection was Jappangarti; in adult life his main language was Mudburra, of which his subsection was Jangari. He also spoke Warlmanpa, Warlpiri and Jingulu, and understood Gurindji. His main Dreaming (his father's father's but not his father's) was the Snake and Star story, which culminates along Hayward Creek. He was made a man in 'the year Phar Lap won the Melbourne Cup' (1930), and married Jessie (Jersey) Karnangkurrngali Nampijinpa. His exceptional knowledge of Aboriginal traditions was to assist numerous groups in land claims in 1980 and 1983.

During World War II Beetaloo Bill worked at camps along the Stuart Highway, including the Elliott staging camp, for the Department of the Army, the source of his nickname 'D. A.'. After the war he was employed by the Department of Works, eventually on full award wages, maintaining government bores on stock routes radiating for hundreds of miles from Newcastle Waters. A member of the Amalgamated Engineering Union, he was to retire on superannuation—rare for Aborigines — in 1975.

Beetaloo Bill wanted his children to have a good life. Early in the 1950s he paid a carpenter £500 to make a substantial iron shed in the Aboriginal reserve to the north-west of Elliott, and he lived there with his family until his death. His second wife, from the 1950s, was Biddy Judambi Nimarra; they were formally married at Elliott on 3 December 1961. In February 1962 the Northern Territory administration decided to integrate local Aboriginal children into Elliott Primary School rather than continue to bus them 18 miles (29 km) to Newcastle Waters. Beetaloo Bill's daughter Nita was one of the first to be transferred—a move that provoked a boycott by some European parents. The *Northern Territory News* reported that he wanted his girl to read and write and 'would not take her away from the school no matter what happened'. He told the writer Frank Hardy that he would be happy for his daughters to marry whom they liked; however, his children mostly married along traditional lines. He lobbied for the recognition of the entitlement of his wife's family to their country, which resulted in the establishment of an outstation near Powell Creek.

From his savings, Beetaloo Bill bought a good Holden utility truck, the first of several that he traded in regularly, long before other Aborigines owned vehicles in the region. He said that he would plan to run out of petrol when near a road camp or station where he knew he would get a welcome; his yarns, brilliant humour and comic repertoire would more than compensate for whatever favour he requested. Beetaloo Bill Jangari had a broad and deep knowledge of Aboriginal law, matched by an easy familiarity with Europeans, but largely unconstrained by convention, black or white. He died on 29 September 1983 at Elliott and was buried in the local cemetery. His wife, two sons and seven daughters survived him; a son and two daughters predeceased him. His family uses 'Bill' as a surname.

D. Lockwood, *Up the Track* (1964); F. Hardy, *The Unlucky Australians* (1968); F. Stevens, *Aborigines in the Northern Territory Cattle Industry* (1974); D. Nash, 'Beetaloo Bill Jangari', in D. Carment and B. James (eds), *Northern Territory Dictionary of Biography*, vol 2 (1992); *NT News*, 13 Feb 1962, p 1; F1, item 1952/837 (NAA); Banka Banka journals, 1929-30, 1934-36, 1941-58 (Univ of Qld Lib); W. E. H. Stanner notebooks and microfiche no 1 (AIATSIS).
DAVID NASH

BIN BIN, DOOLEY (c.1900-1982), Aboriginal community leader, also known as Winyirin, was born about 1900 in that part of the Great Sandy Desert of Western Australia traditionally occupied by Aborigines who spoke the Nyangumarta language. His mother was called Martukaninykaniny; his father's name is not recorded. Bin Bin's childhood coincided with a period when Western Desert groups from the interior were moving into neighbouring riverine and coastal country. When he was 9 or 10 he cleared spinifex from the recently constructed rabbit-proof fence, east of what was later known as Barramine station. After his preliminary initiation into manhood in 1911, he moved between stations throughout the de Grey River system and by the 1930s had established a reputation as a 'travelling Law-man' who merited respect.

One of several Nyangumarta who were generally attached to Warrawagine station on the confluence of the Oakover and Nullagine rivers, Bin Bin retained a view of the world and a system of values that were increasingly threatened. His commitment to his people's lore, his capacity to talk straight and his ability to stand up to the white man were discussed at a meeting of Aborigines from the Western Desert region held in 1942 at Skull Springs on the Davis River. There he was nominated, in his absence, to work with a non-Aboriginal social reformer, Don McLeod, as a representative of the inland's Aborigines. He and his kinsman Clancy McKenna [q.v.15] sought a minimum wage of thirty shillings per week for Aboriginal station-hands and planned a mass withdrawal of labour if the request were refused. The movement challenged pastoralists in the Pilbara and was to have wider repercussions for politicians, trade unionists and clergymen. To Bin Bin, who was impatient to act, and McKenna fell the tasks of co-ordinating the protest and of holding the waverers firmly to the cause. On 1 May 1946 workers from some two dozen Pilbara stations walked out. The initial wave of strikes lasted until late 1948.

While the issues of wages and working conditions were important in triggering the boycott, Bin Bin and other strikers such as Daisy Bindi [q.v.13] strove to dismantle wider social injustices which had been legally perpetuated by the Aborigines Acts of 1905 and 1936. The three strike leaders, Dooley, McKenna and McLeod, were arrested early in May 1946 (the two Aborigines being sentenced to three months' hard labour) for 'enticing' Aborigines from their places of employment. They received wide support when human-rights activists lobbied on their behalf. Amendments made to the Native Administration Act in 1954 were probably influenced by these events.

After his early release from gaol in June, Bin Bin was part of a group, led by McLeod and established as Nomads Pty Ltd, which attempted to set up Aboriginal mining and residential co-operatives in the Pilbara. Eventually it acquired Strelley station near Port Hedland; Bin Bin lived there as a senior member of the 'Strelley mob'. He remained a forceful, stubborn and single-minded advocate of the traditional values of his people, for whom he endeavoured to achieve social justice and economic security. Photographs reveal a person of strong purpose, and suggest the reserve and dignity that he embodied as a lawman of 'high degree'. Survived by his wife and son, he died on 24 December 1982 at Port Hedland and was buried in Strelley cemetery.

D. Stuart, *Yandy* (1959); R. M. Berndt (ed), *Australian Aboriginal Anthropology* (1970); C. D. Rowley, *The Remote Aborigines* (1971); P. Biskup, *Not Slaves Not Citizens* (1973); M. Brown, *The Black Eureka* (1976); K. Palmer and C. McKenna, *Somewhere Between Black and White* (1978); R. M. and C. H. Berndt (eds), *Aborigines of the West* (1979); D. W. McLeod, *How the West Was Lost* (1984); *Papers in Labour History*, no 3, 1989, p 18; personal knowledge.   JOHN BUCKNALL

BINGHAM, COLIN WILLIAM HUGHIE (1898-1986), journalist, was born on 10 July 1898 at Twenty Mile Camp, a Cobb [q.v.3] & Co. staging post near Richmond, Queensland, eighth of nine surviving children of Irish-born parents Henry Bingham, hotelkeeper, and his wife Ellen, née Cahill. Raised a Catholic, he was to abandon his faith as a youth. In 1907 the Binghams, who owned a tavern called the North Star, moved the ramshackle structure to Maxwelton, beside the Richmond-Cloncurry railway line then under construction. Colin was later to observe that 'the environment of a country pub was hard on a lad with fewer prosaic yearnings than most'. He received his early education from a 'staccato succession of governesses', and at the age of 12 wrote a novel on brown paper with a carpenter's pencil. Copied by his sister Martha, it was sent to a publisher in New York and never heard of again.

In 1912 Colin attended Townsville Central State School for boys, and in 1913-16 he boarded at Townsville Grammar School, where the headmaster, P. F. Rowland [q.v.11], encouraged his love of literature. Having been initially rejected by the army due to poor eyesight—caused by a childhood accident—he enlisted in the Australian Imperial Force on 24 May 1917 but was discharged because of cardiac weakness on 19 September. Back at Maxwelton, he helped at the North Star and wrote small pieces that he sent to the *Bulletin*. His mother died in 1918; next year he sold his beloved books to a passing commercial traveller and moved to Brisbane. Entering St John's College, University of Queensland, he enrolled in the faculty of arts in 1920. He befriended other 'scribblers', among them Jack Lindsay, Edgar Holt [qq.v.], Eric Partridge and P. R. Stephensen [qq.v.11,12], won the Ford memorial medal for poetry, and established the college magazine, *Argo*.

After eighteen months of lacklustre academic performance and unable to afford to continue at university, in June 1921 Bingham returned to Townsville and picked up work as a proofreader on the *Daily Bulletin*. In May 1922 he submitted and published his first leader column, on the League of Nations, thus beginning his career as a journalist. Later that year he went back to Brisbane and joined the staff of the *Telegraph*. In 1923 he began an evening course in journalism at the University of Queensland (Dip.Journ., 1925), and on 17 November at St George's Church of England, Windsor, he married Alexa Mary Strachan, a fellow student. Editor of the university magazine *Galmahra*, he won Ford medals in 1923 and 1924 and published two books of poetry.

At the *Telegraph* Bingham wrote theatre and concert notes, leaders, and the pseudonymous Middlemarch's 'Notes on the News', a mixture of editorial comment and poetry. He then edited the Saturday literary page, and in 1930 became the paper's literary editor. Seeking material that was not 'unintelligible to reasonably well-educated readers', he included poems by his friends James Picot [q.v.15] and 'Brian Vrepont' [q.v.16 Truebridge]. As a journalist, he worked hard and covered most fields except parliament and finance. In the 1930s, representing the Queensland branch of the Australian Journalists' Association, he helped to revise the university's diploma course in journalism.

In January 1940 Bingham was seconded to Australian Associated Press, London. Two years later he returned to Australia and took up a post on the *Sydney Morning Herald*; in 1943 he went back to London as a correspondent for that paper. His wartime reporting concentrated on political rather than military developments in Europe; he also travelled in the Levantine states, writing on such topics as the Jewish-Arab 'problem' in Palestine, the independence struggles in Lebanon, and negotiations between the Allied Military Mission and the Turkish government. In November 1943 he reported on the Allied leaders' conference in Cairo.

From March 1944 until the invasion of Normandy in June, Bingham was based in England, reporting on diplomatic events. Now an official war correspondent, he was accredited to the Supreme Headquarters Allied Expeditionary Force in London and in Paris, until the German surrender in May 1945. He covered the Potsdam conference in July that year. Continuing as a diplomatic correspondent, he returned to Sydney in 1948 as leader-writer and foreign affairs commentator for the *SMH*. He was appointed associate-editor in 1957 and editor in 1961. As editor he was able to balance his literary and diplomatic interests, and to inspire in journalists a broader appreciation of public affairs. After retiring in 1965 he published books of poetry and quotations, and an autobiography, *The Beckoning Horizon* (1983). Survived by his wife and their son and two daughters, he died on 24 February 1986 at Wahroonga and was cremated.

G. Souter, *Company of Heralds* (1981); *SMH*, 26 Feb 1986, p 2; *SMH* archives, Sydney; Bingham papers (NLA); personal information.

CHRIS LAWE DAVIES

BINNS, KENNETH JOHNSTONE (1912-1987), public servant, was born on 3 June 1912 at Rockdale, Sydney, eldest of three children of Kenneth Binns [q.v.7], a Scottish-born librarian, and his wife Amy Jane, née Higgins, who was born in Sydney. He lived in Melbourne from an early age and was educated at Melbourne Church of England Grammar School and the University of Melbourne (BA,

1933; B.Com., 1936; MA, 1936). Employed in 1934 by the Bank of New South Wales in Sydney as an economic assistant, he continued his studies by correspondence. Returning to Melbourne in 1936, he worked for the Commonwealth Grants Commission for two years and then as a stockbroker with Ian Potter & Co. until 1941. On 30 March 1940 at the Presbyterian Church, East St Kilda, he married Nancy Helen MacKenzie.

In 1942 the Tasmanian treasurer Edmund Dwyer-Gray [q.v.8] recruited Binns as an investigation and statistical officer and he moved to Hobart. Binns produced two reports: *Social Credit in Alberta* (1947) and *Federal Financial Relations in Canada and Australia* (1948), and was appointed deputy under-treasurer in 1948. Winning a Commonwealth Fund fellowship in 1950, he attended classes in economics at Harvard University, United States of America, and studied federal financial relationships in Canada. Back in Hobart, he often clashed with the under-treasurer H. D. Robinson in the advice he gave to the Labor premier (Sir) Robert Cosgrove [q.v.13]. At a politically difficult time the Cosgrove government was making many ad hoc decisions with which Binns did not agree. None the less, Cosgrove appointed him under-treasurer and State commissioner for taxes in 1952, positions he was to hold for twenty-four years.

An expert in intergovernmental financial relations, Binns successfully formulated Tasmania's cases for Commonwealth assistance. In 1943 Dwyer-Gray had argued, in a pamphlet widely thought to have been written by Binns, that Federal financial relations were misdirected in favour of the Commonwealth. Binns opposed the use of special purpose grants, on the grounds that they restricted the freedom of States to spend their funds on their priority areas, and argued for an increase in the amount distributed under the tax reimbursement formula. It was a theme raised in every annual financial statement while he was under-treasurer.

Binns was committed to the development of State resources through government funding. In the 1960s, serving under the Labor premier Eric Reece, he and (Sir) Allan Knight, commissioner of the Hydro-Electric Commission (1947-77), were responsible for obtaining additional loan funds for the continued hydro-industrialisation of the State. Knight played down claims that 'an old boys' network' consisting of Binns, himself, and later J. G. Symons, director of mines (1956-80), had a decisive influence over government policy. He asserted that they 'were simply putting into place the policies of the government of the day'. Involved in a range of other government-related duties directly concerned with State development, Binns served on the Australian Aluminium Production Commission (1955-60) and the board of Comalco Aluminium (Bell Bay) Ltd (1960-80). In 1960 he accompanied a Tasmanian investment mission to Britain, Europe and the USA. That year he was appointed CMG. Recognition of his expertise led to his appointment by the International Monetary Fund to the fiscal review commission in Nigeria (1964), and as an adviser to the Indonesian minister of finance (1968).

When southern Tasmania was ravaged by bushfires in February 1967 Binns, Knight and the commissioner of police formed a committee, responsible to the premier, to cope with the disaster. In 1972 he negotiated extra taxation revenue for the State from the operation of Hobart's Wrest Point casino and a new tobacco tax. In 1975 he helped to plan for reconstruction of the Tasman Bridge after its collapse in January that year, and to arrange the sale of the State's railway system to the Commonwealth government. Always at pains to make clear that he was subject to the decisions of 'his political masters', he met with the premier before each day's work began. He would proffer his advice, prefacing any disagreements with the phrase, 'with respect; with great respect'. If his view was not accepted he would request written instructions from the cabinet.

Membership of government bodies, such as the boards of the State Library of Tasmania (1943-78) and Tasmanian Government Insurance Office (1971-82), and the Retirement Benefits Fund Investment Trust (1976-83), was a source of much satisfaction for Binns; he thought his involvement contributed to the good standing of the Treasury, in which he took great pride. Despite these other activities, he maintained detailed control over agency funding and personally undertook a daily audit of payment vouchers for departments. He arranged for many of his senior Treasury officials to be appointed to boards, especially of State corporations. Some subsequently became heads of government departments and thus extended the influence of the Treasury across the whole public service.

The commitment to what Binns perceived as a public service ethic—providing fearless advice and maintaining political neutrality—led him, on his retirement in 1976, to criticise his fellow public servants. He questioned whether they were devoted to the best interests of the State, or were preoccupied with their own terms and conditions, and said, 'I leave depressed'. The Tasmanian Public Service Association launched a strong defence of its members, suggesting to him that if he had anything else to say he should 'say it soon so that we can digest it, dismiss it and get down to the serious business of forgetting all about you'. It was an unfortunate ending to a public service career dedicated to benefiting Tasmanians.

In 1976-80 Binns served on the State Grants Commission. He was a member of the Tasmanian and Athenaeum clubs. Apart from his work he enjoyed a weekly game of tennis, reading and, later, the occasional fishing trip from his holiday home on the east coast. He died on 1 November 1987 in South Hobart and was cremated. His wife survived him; there were no children.

W. A. Townsley, *Tasmania: From Colony to Statehood 1803-1945* (1991) and *Tasmania: Microcosm of the Federation or Vassal State 1945-1983* (1994); *Examiner* (Launceston), 31 Jan 1976, p 1, 6 Nov 1987, p 4; *Mercury* (Hobart), 10 Feb 1976, p 5, 8 June 1976, p 9; Tas Public Service Assn, *Service*, Feb 1976, p 1; Binns papers (TSA); private information.

R. J. K. CHAPMAN*

BIRMAN, JOHN (1913-1989), adult educationist, was born Chaim Jojna Birman on 11 February 1913 in Warsaw, Poland, eldest of three children of Abram Birman, clerk, and his wife Helena, née Abramczyc. Educated at the Lyceum Gymnasium and the Free University of Poland, Warsaw, where he studied social and political science, he became a freelance journalist. In 1933 he married Laja, a bacteriologist. Concerned about the international situation, he migrated to Australia. His wife stayed behind, intending to follow later. Arriving by ship on 6 December 1938 at Fremantle, Western Australia, he disembarked in Melbourne, travelled on to Sydney, and found employment as a timber-presser. He was befriended by members of the Fellowship of Australian Writers, who gave support when he received news that his entire family, including his wife, had been killed in the German invasion of Poland in September 1939.

On 5 January 1942 Birman enlisted in the Australian Imperial Force. Posted to the 17th Light Anti-Aircraft Battery and sent to Papua in May, he met Major Charles Rowley [q.v.], who secured his transfer to the Australian Army Education Service. He returned to Australia in October 1943 and proceeded to Western Australia, where he worked under Major Fred Alexander, soon proving himself a resourceful aide and beginning a lasting partnership. His varied experiences included persuading the Royal Australian Air Force to freight a small grand piano by DC-3 to Noonkanbah for a concert. He was naturalised on 23 September 1944. Discharged as a sergeant on 11 April 1945, he became readers' adviser at the State Library of Tasmania, Hobart.

In 1948 Alexander, professor of history and director of the Adult Education Board, University of Western Australia, attracted Birman back to Perth as assistant-director of the board, with the status of lecturer. Under Alexander's inspiration and Birman's management, the board ran courses during the year and an annual summer school, and organised events as diverse as a lecture in 1949 by (Sir) Anthony Eden (Lord Avon), concerts given in co-operation with the Australian Broadcasting Commission, and screenings of European films. The AEB helped to bring Musica Viva to the State in 1950 and next year sponsored a season of John Antill's [q.v.] ballet *Corroboree*, performed by the National Theatre Ballet Company. Profits subsidised country tours by classical musicians. Promoted (1952) to senior lecturer, Birman studied part time at UWA (BA, 1956). On 5 September 1952 at the Collegiate Chapel of St George, Crawley, he married with Anglican rites Frances Wendy Blake, a librarian. He was appointed executive officer of the AEB in 1954 and deputy director in 1975.

The AEB's summer school activities paved the way for the first Festival of Perth, in 1953. Featuring a series of three Beethoven performances and a production of *Richard III*, directed by an Englishman, Michael Langham, it set a precedent for future annual university-sponsored festivals. In 1954 Birman was appointed executive officer of the festival committee. He was to run the festival every year until 1976, except for 1957 and 1964, when he was overseas on study leave. A stocky figure with crisp, wavy, dark brown hair which greyed early, and an engaging grin, he brought to his task imagination, intelligence, energy and a lively appreciation of the cultural needs of Western Australia. Some, including officers of the Australian Security Intelligence Organization, were worried about his left-wing ideological tilt; others thought his genially cynical pragmatism at times tactless.

The number of people attending the Festival of Perth increased from 29 000 in 1953 to 154 000 in 1966, and to 330 000 in 1976. If this in part reflected the city's growth and prosperity, it also owed much to Birman's entrepreneurship. He obtained support from the State government, the Perth City Council, the Art Gallery of Western Australia and commercial promoters, and in 1966 the festival entered into partnership with the Adelaide Festival of Arts. Several much needed performance venues were constructed, among them the Playhouse (1956) and the Octagon theatres (1968). Birman was always in the thick of negotiations, using, as appropriate, charm, cajolery and devastating bluntness.

In 1966 Birman was made head of the UWA's Extension Service (which had separated from the AEB), and in 1972 he was appointed director. Next year he was named a Western Australian Citizen of the Year and in 1976 was appointed OBE. Inaugural president (1976) of the local branch of Musica Viva Australia, he was responsible for setting up a university FM radio station, which started broadcasting in 1977. He retired on 31 December 1978. In thirty years, largely due to his drive and managerial skills, Perth had advanced from a cultural backwater to a lively and diverse centre of the creative arts. In 1980-81 he published a history of the festival in *Studies in Continuing Education*. Survived by his wife and their three sons, he died on 23 August 1989 in Perth and was cremated.

F. Alexander, *Campus at Crawley* (1963); B. K. de Garis (ed), *Campus in the Community* (1988); *West Australian*, 13 Jan 1973, p 22, 30 Dec 1975, p 7, 26 Aug 1989, p 22; M. Adams and R. Hoare, taped interviews with J. Birman (1981, SLWA); A6126, item 601 (NAA).   G. C. BOLTON

BISHOP, JOHN ACKLAND (1908-1985), soldier and businessman, was born on 16 January 1908 at Malvern, Melbourne, second of three sons of Albert Adonis Bishop, an inspector of factories, and his wife Milly Emily, née Tate, both Victorian born. Educated at Box Hill State School and privately, John worked as a salesman and then as a manager with Ball & Welch Ltd. Having served in the senior cadets from 1924, he joined the 24th Battalion, Militia, in 1926. He was commissioned as a lieutenant in 1928 and promoted to captain in 1935.

On 13 October 1939 Bishop was seconded to the Australian Imperial Force and posted to the 2/7th Battalion. He attended a company commanders' course at the Command and Staff School, Sydney, before being appointed intelligence officer, 17th Brigade, in February 1940. Arriving in the Middle East in May, he became staff captain of the brigade in July. During the Libyan campaign of January-February 1941 he ensured that the brigade's troops were kept supplied with ammunition and that the men had hot meals whenever possible. He was also attentive to the needs of the wounded. For his 'continued devotion to duty and outstanding service' he was appointed MBE (1941).

Promoted to temporary major in April 1941 (substantive in June), Bishop took part in the disastrous Greek campaign that month. He was made brigade major in May. The 17th Brigade fought in the latter phases of the Syrian campaign, including the battle of Damour early in July. Bishop was mentioned in despatches for the superior performance of his duties in February-July. In the first half of 1942 he attended the Middle East Staff School, Haifa, Palestine. He returned to Australia in July and was made senior instructor at the senior wing of the Staff School (Australia), Duntroon, Canberra, as a temporary lieutenant colonel (substantive in September). In March 1943 he was appointed to command the

2/27th Battalion. Arriving in Port Moresby in August, the battalion flew to Kaiapit, New Guinea, and advanced up the Markham and Ramu valleys.

On 9 October 1943 the 2/27th took up a position astride the Japanese supply line north of Kumbarum, holding two features in the Faria River Valley. The battalion soon came under small-arms and artillery fire. The Japanese attacked four times on the 12th with more than a battalion supported by machine-guns and artillery. At this time the 2/27th was missing two of its companies and a platoon deployed on other duties. Though out-numbered and outgunned, the Australians repulsed all attacks. Bishop was faced with the possibility of having to withdraw when, with ammunition already low, he discovered that the ammunition supply party had been inter-dicted by the Japanese. By the evening, how-ever, the enemy broke contact, leaving about two hundred dead at the battalion perimeter. Bishop, who had 'fearlessly directed' his troops, setting them 'an excellent example of personal gallantry', was awarded the Dis-tinguished Service Order.

In November 1943 Bishop was appointed general staff officer, 1st grade, of the 6th Division. His divisional commander, Major General (Sir) Jack Stevens [q.v.16], com-mended him for his 'marked skill, efficiency and enthusiasm', which, together with his high-grade staff work and willingness to visit forward areas to keep himself appraised of tac-tical developments, contributed substantially to the success of the division. In May-July 1945 Bishop also administered command of the 19th Brigade, involved in mopping-up oper-ations in the Wewak area. Stevens noted that he directed operations with 'skill, courage and judgement'. For his command of the brigade and his earlier staff work, Bishop was elevated to OBE (1947).

After the war ended, Bishop worked with the co-ordinator of demobilisation and disposal (Sir) Stanley Savige [q.v.16], his former 17th Brigade commander. He transferred to the Re-serve of Officers on 4 July 1946. On 29 March that year at St Cuthbert's Presbyterian Church, Brighton, Melbourne, he had married Frances Marion Fowler, née Saunders, a divorcee; they had one daughter and were later divorced. They moved to Sydney in 1948 and Bishop joined Anthony Hordern & Sons [qq.v.4] Ltd as sales manager; he became general manager in 1962. Retiring from the firm in 1963, he was for a time managing director of Beard Watson [q.v.12 J. H. Watson] & Co. Ltd before going into private practice as a marketing consultant.

Resuming part-time duty in the Citizen Military Forces, Bishop commanded the 5th Brigade in 1951-55 and was promoted to brigadier in 1952. In 1956-59 he was an honor-ary aide-de-camp to the governor-general Sir William (Viscount) Slim [q.v.16]. As a tem-porary major general (substantive in July 1960), he commanded the 2nd Division in 1959-60. He was then given command of Eastern Command Troops before assuming control of headquarters, Communication Zone, in 1961. He transferred to the Unattached List in December that year and to the Retired List in 1965.

Bishop continued to serve the community in other capacities; he chaired the Vasey [q.v.16] Housing Association in 1969-80 and the New South Wales Council on the Ageing in 1975-79. His recreations included horse-riding and sailing. Survived by his daughter, he died on 8 October 1985 at Kirribilli and was cremated with Anglican rites and military honours.

G. Long, *To Benghazi* (1952), *Greece, Crete and Syria* (1953) and *The Final Campaigns* (1963); J. Burns, *The Brown and Blue Diamond at War* (1960); D. Dexter, *The New Guinea Offensives* (1961); *SMH*, 9 Oct 1985, p 18.

DAYTON MCCARTHY

BLACK, SIR HERMANN DAVID (1904-1990), economist, public-affairs commentator and university chancellor, was born on 15 November 1904 at Dulwich Hill, Sydney, younger son of Melbourne-born parents John Niven Black, an accountant of Scottish origin, and his wife Adele Ottilie, née Püttmann, granddaughter of Hermann Püttmann [q.v.5]. After her husband's death in 1914 Adele mar-ried Harry Shaw Clarke, also an accountant, who later suffered pecuniary losses. Hermann grew up in a happy and affectionate house-hold, attended Rockdale Public School and after failing to enter the navy at the age of 13, gained a bursary to Fort Street Boys' High School in 1918.

In 1922 Black won a Teachers' College scholarship to the University of Sydney (B.Ec., 1927; M.Ec., 1937). Ineligible for arts because he had studied Japanese rather than Latin, he enrolled in economics, from which he gradu-ated with first-class honours, sharing the medal with (Sir) Robert Madgwick [q.v.15]. He also won the Jones medal at Sydney Teachers' College in 1926. At school and university he stood out as a talented student with a capacity for friendship, and a wide range of interests including sport, debating and amateur dramatics. After teaching at Parkes Inter-mediate High School, Black was recalled to the college in 1927 by the principal, Alexander Mackie [q.v.10]. Postings to Nowra and Randwick Boys' Intermediate High schools followed.

Black was appointed as assistant lecturer in economics at the University of Sydney in 1933. Two years later he was promoted to lecturer and in 1937 he achieved first-class honours for his master's thesis. Awarded a Rockefeller Foundation fellowship, he spent 1936-38 in the United States of America and Europe. In 1939 he was invited by the New South Wales premier, (Sir) Bertram Stevens [q.v.12], to become adviser to the Treasury and, with the approval of the senate of the university, he served part time with the Treasury throughout World War II. His work for the government included reporting on matters relevant to decentralisation, loan council meetings, uniform taxation and loan raising for postwar graduates. He played a part in persuading the government to raise the school-leaving age from 14 to 15 and to appoint a permanent economic adviser. In 1944 he was promoted to senior lecturer and in 1951 he visited the USA under State Department auspices to study foreign and economic policy. He served as acting professor of economics in 1956. Retiring in 1969, he was made senior fellow in economics from 1970.

A self-confessed generalist who was influenced by Joseph Schumpeter, Black taught at all levels of the economics course from 1932 to 1989. Teaching, he believed, was intended less to instil knowledge than to develop the intellect. The lecturer, he observed, 'displays the processes of his own reasoning'. What was taught was 'not conclusion, but how to reason'. Some found his style discursive but his first-year introductory course was widely acclaimed and he was admired for infusing human values and colour into the 'dismal science'. Although he produced numerous papers and addresses, he was interested less in research and publication than in applying economic theory to practical issues.

This orientation underlay Black's remarkable capacity to bridge the gap between town and gown. He was an exceptionally talented orator, able to stimulate diverse audiences on an array of subjects. As a student he had taken part in community discussion groups and after graduating he lectured for the Workers' Educational Association of New South Wales. During World War II he spent his university vacations lecturing for the Australian Army Education Service. He also lectured for and chaired the University Extension Board and was a member (1939-79) of the joint committee for tutorial classes. It was, however, broadcasting that made 'H. D. Black' a household name. He first spoke on air in 1926 in a Sydney-Oxford university union debate. A news commentator for the Australian Broadcasting Commission from the 1930s and member of discussion panels such as 'Monday Conference', he also captivated generations of school children through his talks in series such as 'The World We Live In'. Black saw public speaking as an art form: 'graceful, educative and entertaining'. He possessed a phenomenal

memory, an unsurpassed command of language, an apt turn of phrase and a singular capacity to make telling use of anecdote. Solidly built, with a calm, dignified, reassuring presence, he spoke graciously but never condescendingly, lightening his words with touches of humour. Above all there was his voice—vibrant, cultivated and mellifluous; like everything else about him it was natural and unforced.

Black's experience of the University of Sydney's governing body began with his election to the senate in 1949. In December 1969 he was elected deputy-chancellor and five months later chancellor. This result was not universally welcomed and challenges were threatened before later elections, but none eventuated. As a member of senate he saw the university emerge from the overcrowded postwar years into the era of expansion made possible by the 1957 report of Sir Keith Murray's committee on Australian universities. While chancellor he was confronted by student unrest and financial stringencies in the 1970s and then by bureaucratic intervention, culminating in reforms of the late 1980s instituted by the Federal minister for employment, education and training, John Dawkins. His powers as chancellor were circumscribed, but he resolved to be more than a figurehead.

Universities, he insisted, must function 'without the claims of utilitarian philosophies laying their particular control over them'. They were not 'creatures of the market place' but centres of learning entrusted with responsibility for promoting knowledge and developing 'new truths, new horizons, new insights'. He encouraged change but, when basic academic values were threatened by militant students or intrusive governments, he responded with passion, threatening to resign in the late 1980s unless the State government abandoned moves likely to undermine the autonomy of the senate. Throughout, he provided courteous but firm leadership, blending deeply held beliefs with practical common sense and astute judgment sharpened by long experience in the world of affairs. His warm manner at graduation ceremonies affected the 60 000 students to whom he awarded degrees while chancellor. In 1978 he established the chancellor's committee to raise money for university-wide projects.

Black had married Katrina Mary Heyde on 29 December 1928 at the Pitt Street Congregational Church, Sydney. She later suffered an incurable mental breakdown, but their marriage could not be ended until, with Black's urging, the New South Wales divorce law was changed. The pain which this caused him was relieved by the happy years following his marriage to Edith Joyce Black, née Ritchie, who had taken his name, on 22 November 1963 at the registrar general's office, Sydney. She was a University of Sydney graduate (BA, 1939) and a talented organist and musician who worked as a secretary and a schoolteacher. Affectionately described by her husband as the 'better half of the Chancellor of the University', she worked unstintingly on the university's behalf and was made an honorary fellow in 1986.

A member of the Australian Round Table, Black was active in the Australian Institute of International Affairs, editing *Australian Outlook* (1953-58) and serving as president (1950-54) of the New South Wales branch. He was a member of the editorial board of the *Current Affairs Bulletin*, honorary secretary (1944) of a relief committee of the Australia-India Association and president (1958-60) of the Oriental Society of Australia. Active in business and financial circles, he was president (1961) of the State branch of the Economics Society of Australia and New Zealand. Appointment as chair of the newly established Australian Tax Research Foundation in 1982 reflected his long-standing interest in tax reform. He represented (1970-86) the university on the board of the Royal Prince Alfred Hospital.

Universities, Black remarked, 'are peculiar places', but to be in one was 'a kind of enrichment'. He derived great pleasure from his own university and participated in every aspect of its life. Fond of sport, he also loved theatre, art and music, played the violin, and wrote poetry and fascinating travel diaries. An extraordinarily well-rounded figure with a zest for life, he possessed a warm, gregarious nature and great charm. He described himself as a nineteenth-century liberal who had adapted to the twentieth century; he cared 'not one fig for any political party', viewing them as his 'servants' and not 'his spiritual home'. In his youth he had attended Anglican and Lutheran services, but while recognising the importance of religion he did not see it as a determining influence in his life. He was his own master, courting neither popularity nor advancement but enjoying both when they came. In 1982 the Rotary Club of Sydney gave him a vocational service award. He was honoured by the universities of Newcastle (D.Litt., 1971), New England (D.Univ., 1988) and Sydney (D.Univ., 1990). Knighted in 1974, he was appointed AC in 1986. Survived by his wife, Sir Hermann died on 28 February 1990 at St Leonards, a few miles from the Roseville home where he had lived for fifty years. He had no children by either marriage. Louis Kahan's portrait (1974) of Black is held by the University of Sydney.

W. F. Connell et al, *Australia's First*, vol 2 (1995); *Economic Record*, vol 66, no 194, 1990, p 266; *People* (Sydney), 16 Dec 1953, p 43; *Fortian*, 1969, p 64; Sydney Univ Economics Soc, *Economic Review*, 1969, p 6; *SMH*, 6 Mar 1990, p 2; Univ of Sydney, *Gazette*, Mar 1990, p 19, June 1990, p 4; Black papers and Senate minutes, 1949-90 (Univ of Sydney Archives).   B. H. FLETCHER

BLACK, JOHN RUSSELL (1908-1988), patrol officer and explorer, was born on 12 May 1908 in North Adelaide, eldest of five children of New South Wales-born parents Arthur Laughton Black, bank clerk, and his wife Beatrice Agnes, née Porter. He went to two primary schools, Auvergne in North Adelaide and Le Fevre Peninsula State School, and two secondary schools, Pulteney Street (1919-21) and the Collegiate School of St Peter (1922-25). In 1926 he began civil engineering at the University of Adelaide, paying his fees by working as a geology laboratory assistant under Sir Douglas Mawson [q.v.10]. He joined the 48th Battalion (later 43rd/48th Battalion), Militia, and by 1932 had passed his captain's examinations. In 1927 he left university and by 1928 was managing his father's farm at Mount Compass, near Adelaide. During the Depression he could not make it pay, and in November 1932 applied to be a cadet patrol officer in the Mandated Territory of New Guinea. He was the second accepted from 1659 applicants, his report recording that he was well built and strong, teetotal, and a good walker, bushman and horseman.

On 22 June 1933 Black arrived in Salamaua, headquarters of Morobe District. In July he joined Keith McCarthy's [q.v.15] exploring patrol into Kukukuku country. During a fight near Menyamya on 12 September he was wounded in the head by an arrow, and evacuated to hospital at Wau. After eight days he was billed 8s. 6d. for treatment and sent back to the patrol. He worked in Morobe until the prospector Bernard McGrath was killed near Finintegu in the highlands, when he went to help arrest the killers. He took a leading part in a five-hour battle against local people, and after they surrendered remained to enforce peace. In February 1935, following the killing of two missionaries, he was sent to Gorime, in the Central Highlands, to help restore order, but while there was ordered to attend a patrol officers' course at the University of Sydney. He fought off an ambush on the way out, and by March was in the classroom. In October he returned to work in Morobe until he went on leave in September 1937. He was marked as a leader, with a reputation as a brave, active and effective administrator, and a model report writer—several of his patrol reports were commended in Canberra.

In October 1937 Black was appointed second-in-command of Jim Taylor's [q.v.]

Hagen-Sepik Patrol, to explore the highlands between Mount Hagen and the Netherlands New Guinea (Indonesian) border. The patrol was the largest (271 people), longest (February 1938-July 1939) and best equipped in New Guinea's history. It walked over 1864 miles (3000 km), pioneered effective methods of supply from the air and reconnaissance, and made sense for the first time of the geography of the Western Highlands. From June 1938 Black held an independent command, during which he explored a large area of difficult country, and found the Porgera goldfield, among the largest in New Guinea. In 1939-40 he drew a large map of the patrol's route, then had it and Taylor's report suppressed, lest it give information to the Japanese in the war he knew was coming. After leave he was stationed on the Madang coast. While there, in February 1942 he began war service as a captain in the Australian New Guinea Administrative Unit.

When the Japanese invaded in December, Black remained to reconnoitre, lead patrols behind Japanese lines and write policy submissions calling for more enlightened postwar treatment of New Guineans. 'The breath of new ideas has been stirring the sleeping body of the controlled native population', he wrote in February 1944. 'It can no longer be ignored or denied.' Having transferred to the Australian Imperial Force in February 1943, he joined the Land Headquarters School of Civil Affairs, Canberra, in March 1945. That month Black and Zazahame of Ufeto, in the Eastern Highlands, had a daughter. On 21 June 1945 at the chapel of St Peter's College, Adelaide, he married Dawn Helen Reid Smith (d.1986). He was promoted to lieutenant colonel in October and served as military governor of Labuan, then Brunei, then Sarawak, in Borneo. On 19 March 1946 he was placed on the Reserve of Officers.

In June 1946 Black joined the civil administration of the Territory of Papua-New Guinea in Port Moresby. He found the capital's Europeans in two factions: an old guard yearning for pre-war days, and a 'pro-native' minority who sought more progressive treatment of local people. Appointed to the Department of District Services and Native Affairs as assistant-director of planning, effectively in charge of policy, he instructed that the administration's fundamental aim was to lead the Territory towards independence, and welcomed local leaders to his house to discuss the country's political and economic future. He thought this work the most important of his life: 'We stopped them putting the clock back'.

In March 1948 Black joined a syndicate to prospect the Porgera goldfield, and in May resigned from the administration to go into business. He took up importing, running transport and dealing in war surplus in Port Moresby, and made bitumen and plywood in Lae. In 1951 he stood unsuccessfully for the Legislative Council on a 'pro-native' platform, more in defiance than in hope. He left the Territory in March 1953 and, until late in life, farmed near Maitland and at Marion Bay, South Australia, though living increasingly in Adelaide. There he died on 6 April 1988 and was cremated. His two daughters and three sons survived him. Black lost neither his interest in Papua New Guinea, nor his ability to focus on policy, to probe ideas, to think clearly, to act decisively. In peace and war he was outstanding. He was what he aspired to be: 'an intellectual in action'.

B. Gammage, *The Sky Travellers* (1998) and for bib.   BILL GAMMAGE

BLACK, ROBERT HUGHES (1917-1988), professor of tropical medicine, was born on 20 December 1917 at Willaura, Victoria, son of Victorian-born parents Robert Nicol Black, bank manager, and his wife Margaret May, née Rountree. After attending many schools, Robert completed the Leaving certificate at Parramatta High School, Sydney. He studied medicine at the University of Sydney (MB, BS, 1939) and was awarded the university medal. In 1940 he was a junior resident medical officer at Royal Prince Alfred Hospital, Sydney, and in 1941 senior resident medical officer at Innisfail District Hospital, Queensland. He married Dorothy Rosemary Elsie Tandy, a medical practitioner, on 9 December 1941 at St Alban's Church of England, Innisfail; they divorced in 1952.

On 8 November 1941 Black had been appointed as a captain, Australian Army Medical Corps, Militia. He transferred to the Australian Imperial Force on 22 July 1942 and served with the 19th Field Ambulance and the 117th Australian General Hospital, Toowoomba. In June 1943 he was posted to the 106th Casualty Clearing Station and two months later embarked for New Guinea. At Lae he attempted to cultivate malaria parasites *in vitro* under very basic conditions. In July 1944 he was sent to the 2nd Blood and Serum Preparation Unit, Sydney Hospital, where he had some success in growing *Plasmodium falciparum* in red blood cells in the test tube. Returning to the tropics at the Land Headquarters Medical Research Unit, Cairns, Queensland, in December, he used this technique to show that anti-malarial drugs, as metabolised in the body, were active against cultured parasites.

Placed on the Reserve of Officers on 6 June 1946, Black worked that year as a bacteriologist at the Institute of Medical Research,

Royal North Shore Hospital, Sydney. He was awarded a doctorate of medicine by the University of Sydney (1947) for his study of the chemotherapy of malaria *in vitro*. After travelling to England as a ship's surgeon, he worked as a United Kingdom Medical Research Council fellow (1946-48) at the Liverpool School of Tropical Medicine (DTM&H, 1947). Returning to Australia to the School of Public Health and Tropical Medicine (Commonwealth Institute of Health), University of Sydney, he was appointed medical officer (1949), lecturer (1951), senior lecturer (1956) and professor (1963). He participated in international malaria surveillance, and wrote over two hundred papers and monographs, including a series of reports on eradication programs for the South Pacific Commission and the World Health Organization. From 1955 he served on the WHO expert advisory panel on malaria. In 1959 he was appointed consultant in tropical medicine at Army Headquarters as a temporary lieutenant colonel. Promoted to temporary colonel in 1964, he advised on the use of combined therapy for drug-resistant strains of malaria during the Vietnam War and championed the re-establishment of an army malaria research unit. He was placed on the Retired List in 1979. In Australia, as the public expert on malaria, he was active in practitioner education, surveys of receptive areas and, from 1969, in maintaining the central register of malaria cases. He retired from the university in 1982.

Black's early research was focused on the parasite and the mechanisms of the host response, but his experience in many areas, including New Guinea, the Pacific islands, South-East Asia, Africa and Australia, convinced him that narrowly based control strategies were inadequate. He vigorously supported ecologically based studies of insect vectors, while his own interests broadened to include anthropology. He undertook a study of life on a coconut plantation in the Solomon Islands as part of his training with the University of Sydney (Dip.Anth., 1963). Appreciating the critical role of social factors in effective control programs, he advocated training in social science for public health workers. He also urged national support for malaria research and surveillance in the face of drug-resistant disease in the Asia-Pacific region.

While in New Guinea during World War II, he had met Nora Heysen, who was working as a war artist. They married on 20 January 1953 at the registrar general's office, Sydney; the marriage ended in 1972. On 10 July 1976 he married 31-year-old Gail Lorraine Grimes, a nurse, at the registry office, Sydney. He was elected a fellow of the Royal Australasian College of Physicians in 1965 and was awarded the Darling Foundation medal and prize by the

WHO in 1986. Frequent travel abroad, coupled with a reserved manner and introspective temperament, sometimes impeded his professional collaborations and placed a strain on his personal relationships. He had a keen interest in amateur radio, writing several technical papers on the subject. Survived by his wife, and the son of his first marriage, Black died of cancer on 17 March 1988 in the ambulance carrying him from his home at Strathfield to the Repatriation General Hospital, Concord, and was cremated.

Malaria: Proceedings of a Conference to Honour Robert H. Black (1984); F. Fenner (ed), *History of Microbiology in Australia* (1990); *Roll of the Royal Australasian College of Physicians*, vol 2 (1994); T. Sweeney, *Malaria Frontline* (2003); *MJA*, 7 Aug 1989, p 171; *SMH*, 19 Dec 1963, p 13; PRO1437 (AWM).   YVONNE COSSART

BLACKBURN, SIR RICHARD ARTHUR (1918-1987), judge, was born on 26 July 1918 at Mount Lofty, South Australia, eldest of four children of Arthur Seaforth Blackburn [q.v.7], solicitor, and his wife Rose Ada, née Kelly, both born in South Australia. Richard, known as Dick, was educated at the Collegiate School of St Peter, Adelaide. At the University of Adelaide (BA, 1939), where he resided at St Mark's College, he won the Stow and John Howard Clark prizes, studied some law subjects and graduated with first-class honours in English literature. Developing a strong interest in the arts, especially drama, he appeared in a number of plays. He was named South Australian Rhodes scholar for 1940.

Having enlisted in the Militia on 4 September 1939, Blackburn deferred his scholarship. He transferred to the Australian Imperial Force in May 1940 and, commissioned as a lieutenant, embarked for the Middle East in November 1941. Posted to the 9th Division Cavalry Regiment, he served in Syria, Palestine and Egypt, before returning to Australia early in 1943. In August that year he was promoted to temporary captain (substantive August 1945) and sent to New Guinea with his division. By March 1944 he was back in Australia, where he performed instructional duties in staff schools. As a staff officer, from March 1945, with the 3rd Operational Report Team, he took part in the invasion of British North Borneo in June. He transferred to the Reserve of Officers on 8 November in Adelaide.

Taking up his Rhodes scholarship, Blackburn studied law at Magdalen College, Oxford (BA, 1948; BCL, 1949), where he became president (1948-49) of the junior common room. He won the Eldon scholarship and was called to the Bar of the Inner Temple on

17 November 1949. In 1950 he returned to the University of Adelaide as (Sir John Langdon) Bonython [q.v.7] professor of law. Against some opposition from the profession, he initiated changes to the curriculum and employed more full-time staff. An excellent teacher known for his clear exposition, he demanded high standards from his students. He took a positive interest in university life, as a member of the debating club, and as a councillor (1950-61) of St Mark's College, the constitution of which he helped to reform. Active (1950-57) in the Adelaide University Regiment, Citizen Military Forces, he commanded the unit in 1955-57 as a lieutenant colonel.

Blackburn had married with Presbyterian forms Bryony Helen Carola Curkeet, née Dutton, on 1 December 1951 at her family's home, Anlaby, at Kapunda, South Australia. As she was a divorcee, they had been unable to marry in the Church of England. The rift was healed in 1953 when the Bishop of Adelaide received them back into full communicant membership. Blackburn had been admitted to practise as a barrister and solicitor of the Supreme Court of South Australia on 23 October 1950. When he resigned from the university in 1957, he became a partner in an Adelaide law firm, Finlayson Phillips Astley & Hayward (Finlayson & Co.), specialising in commercial work. Resuming his CMF service in 1962 as a colonel, he commanded the 1st Battalion, Royal South Australia Regiment, until 1965. For leadership in his two commands he was appointed OBE (1965). He served as a governor (1965-66) of St Peter's College.

In 1966 Blackburn became resident judge of the Supreme Court of the Northern Territory. Conditions in the court were relatively primitive but he did not let that impair the quality or quantity of his judicial output. He wrote a new set of rules for the court, which was a busy one with a wide range of work. During this time he delivered his most famous judgment, *Milirrpum and others* v. *Nabalco Pty Ltd and the Commonwealth of Australia* (1971), the first major Australian superior court decision on Aboriginal land rights. Certain Aborigines claimed possession and a right to the enjoyment of parts of Arnhem Land. Sensitive to their claims, Blackburn found that they had a system of traditional law, highly adapted to the country and promoting a stable society. However, he felt bound by British precedent and held that the plaintiffs' law did not give them, in European terms, a proprietary interest in land. He was also unpersuaded that the claimed land was identified with that occupied by the plaintiffs' ancestors in 1788. The decision provoked legislation to give Aborigines access to land but stood until overruled by the High Court of Australia in *Mabo and others* v. *State of Queensland* (1992).

Blackburn also actively participated in Darwin community life. He was president of the Arts Council of Australia (Northern Territory Division) and of the Aboriginal Theatre Foundation. The first chancellor of the Anglican diocese of the Northern Territory, he wrote its constitution. He became patron of a number of organisations, including the Darwin Aero Club, the Darwin Sailing Club, the Northern Territory Basketball Association and the Historical Society of the Northern Territory. He and his wife were both pilots and often flew their Cessna 172 to remote places in the Territory. Blackburn maintained his private pilot's licence from 1963 until he sold the Cessna in 1979. Helen Blackburn, an expert on sea shells, published a book on the subject.

Appointed a resident judge of the Supreme Court of the Australian Capital Territory in 1971, Blackburn was also chairman (1971-76) of the ACT Law Reform Commission. During his tenure the commission produced eight reports, all carefully argued and researched. Many of the recommendations were implemented, not always promptly. Interested in the independence of the judiciary and in procedural reform, he also enjoyed the ACT court's wide range of legal cases, especially defamation proceedings. He presided over the ACT's long-running defamation action *Comalco Ltd* v. *Australian Broadcasting Corporation* (1986), which remains an important precedent for the damages payable to defamed companies.

In 1977 Blackburn was made a judge of the new Federal Court of Australia. In November he was appointed chief judge of the Supreme Court of the ACT and in 1982, when the position was renamed, became chief justice. He felt strongly about the institution of the judiciary and the separation of powers. In 1984 the Commonwealth government appointed the judge Donald Stewart head of the newly formed National Crime Authority. When the press reported that Stewart, who was obliged to resign from the New South Wales Supreme Court, would be appointed by the Commonwealth government to the ACT Supreme Court, Blackburn objected. Concerned at this apparent threat to the separation of powers, he took the unusual step of making a statement in open court that Stewart was not to be a judge of any court. The government legislated to give Stewart judicial status rather than an appointment.

Widely known for his courtesy on the bench, Blackburn retired on 31 March 1985. His judgments were scholarly and tightly reasoned but perhaps too legalistic. Chambers in Canberra and Darwin were named after him. The Law Society of the ACT established an annual lecture in his name; he delivered the inaugural lecture, 'The Courts and the Community', in 1986.

That year Blackburn was appointed with two other retired judges, Sir George Lush and Andrew Wells, to form a parliamentary commission of inquiry to consider whether any conduct of Justice Lionel Murphy [q.v.] of the High Court amounted to proven misbehaviour under section 72 of the Constitution. The commission identified forty-two allegations, twenty-eight of which it held lacked substance. It completed its report on the meaning of s.72 in August 1986 but the announcement on 31 July that Murphy had terminal cancer effectively halted the work of the commission.

Keen to educate practitioners appearing before him, Blackburn had chaired the committee of management of the Australian National University legal workshop. As pro-chancellor (1976-84) and chancellor (1984-87) of the ANU, he won respect for his fairness and commitment to the ideals of a university as a community of scholars. He maintained his wide interests in Canberra, joining (1972) the Australian Council for the Arts and becoming chairman (1983) of the Theatre ACT Patrons Organization. In 1977 he had declined election to the appellate tribunal of the Church of England, because he no longer regarded himself as a communicant member. Appointed commander of the Order of St John of Jerusalem in 1980, he was its patron in the ACT from 1979 to 1987. He was knighted in 1983. St Mark's College made him an honorary fellow in 1986. Still interested in military matters, he delivered the (Sir James) Harrison [q.v.14] memorial lecture at the Royal Military College, Duntroon, in 1986. Survived by his wife and their daughter and son, Sir Richard died of cancer on 1 October 1987 in Canberra and was cremated.

N. M. Williams, *The Yolngu and Their Land* (1986); *Austn Law Jnl*, vol 61, no 12, 1987, p 824; *Adelaide Law Review*, vol 11, 1988, p 364; *Canberra Times*, 2 Oct 1987, p 2; B883, item SX2747 (NAA); R. Blackburn papers (NLA).

RICHARD REFSHAUGE

BLACKWOOD, DAME MARGARET (1909-1986), botanist and geneticist, was born on 26 April 1909 at South Yarra, Melbourne, second of three children of Tasmanian-born parents Robert Leslie Blackwood, schoolteacher, and his wife Muriel Pearl, née Henry. (Sir) Robert Blackwood [q.v.] was Margaret's elder brother. Her mother had been a teacher before marriage, and from 1920 her father was classics tutor and sub-warden of Trinity College, University of Melbourne. Growing up in 'a scholarly environment', she attended Melbourne Church of England Girls' Grammar School, which emphasised academic attainment and encouraged scientific studies. Her biology teacher, Dorothy Ross [q.v.], was inspiring.

Margaret's father, who 'didn't think the university was a place for women', decreed a conventional domestic destiny for his daughter. His death in 1926 left her both free to choose her own future and needing to support herself. She qualified at the Associated Teachers' Training Institution, then taught at Lowther Hall and Korowa Church of England Girls' Grammar schools. In 1930 she enrolled in science at the University of Melbourne (B.Sc., 1938; M.Sc., 1939), completing the course part time while continuing to teach. A scholarship assisted her to write a thesis on die back of *Pinus radiata* for her master's degree, which was conferred with first-class honours. She then became a research scholar and demonstrator, working on plant cytology and genetics. The 1930s were a high point for women's participation in botany, and she found herself in a research environment in which women, notably Associate Professor Ethel McLennan [q.v.], were prominent.

World War II began before Blackwood had established herself at the university but she barely hesitated before volunteering to serve. On 15 March 1941 she enrolled in the Women's Auxiliary Australian Air Force. Commissioned twelve days later, she performed cipher duties and formulated policy and procedures for training recruits, mainly at Air Force Headquarters, Melbourne. She gained quick promotion, reaching the rank of temporary wing officer in January 1945. Her appointment ended on 8 January 1946. Returning to the university, she transferred to the new Mildura branch campus as lecturer in biology and dean of women. From her quarters, known as 'Mothering Heights', she maintained a firm but genial rule over her charges.

After a five-year break from science, Blackwood faced an uncertain academic future, dependent on further training. In 1948 she proceeded to Britain on a Commonwealth Reconstruction Training Scheme scholarship and entered the University of Cambridge (Ph.D., 1954), where she worked with David Catcheside on the B-chromosomes in *Zea mays*. Back in Melbourne, she was appointed at last to a permanent lectureship, becoming one of only two lecturers in genetics at the university.

Blackwood published little (five papers in 1953-68) and was promoted slowly, becoming a reader just before she retired in 1974. Her commitment to botany was nevertheless obvious from her obsession with tree planting, the detailed descriptions of local fauna she included in her travel diaries, and her refusal of job offers that would have taken her away from research. A Carnegie travelling scholarship (1958-59) had enabled her to study at the University of Wisconsin. There she met the American maize geneticist and future Nobel laureate Barbara McClintock, whom she described as 'my "Pin up" girl'.

Blackwood was first chairman (1961-75) of the council and a founder fellow (1966) of Janet Clarke [q.v.3] Hall, and first female fellow of Trinity College (1981) and the Genetics Society of Australia. She chaired (1957-58) the co-ordinating committee of Soroptimist Clubs of Australia and New Zealand and was a member of the Lyceum Club and the Australian Federation of University Women. In 1964 she was appointed MBE and in 1981 promoted to DBE. She was elected a member of the council (1975) and the first female deputy-chancellor (1980) of the University of Melbourne, which awarded her an honorary LL D in 1983.

Dame Margaret had been one of the few women of her generation to pursue a scientific career. She believed firmly in the equality of the sexes. As a geneticist she knew that only one of the forty-six chromosomes is different, therefore 'innate abilities and characters are common to both men and women'. In 1975 she convened the university assembly's working group on the position of women on campus, which found that their status was no higher than it had been in 1951. Despite this conclusion, she repudiated modern feminism, believing that 'it's no good having a chip on your shoulder. You don't get anywhere'. Blackwood died on 1 June 1986 in East Melbourne and was cremated.

F. Kelly, *Degrees of Liberation* (1985); H. Radi (ed), *200 Australian Women* (1988); J. A. Thomson, *The WAAAF in Wartime Australia* (1991); J. Carey, *Women and Science at the University of Melbourne* (1996); J. Thomson, taped interview with M. Blackwood (1984, AWM); Blackwood papers (Univ of Melbourne Archives).   JANE CAREY

BLACKWOOD, SIR ROBERT RUTHERFORD (1906-1982), businessman, professor of engineering and university chancellor, was born on 3 June 1906 at South Yarra, Melbourne, eldest of three children of Tasmanian-born parents Robert Leslie Blackwood, schoolteacher, and his wife Muriel Pearl, née Henry. Robert senior was later (1920-26) classics tutor and sub-warden of Trinity College, University of Melbourne. (Dame) Margaret Blackwood [q.v.] was Robert junior's sister. Educated at Melbourne Church of England Grammar School and the University of Melbourne (BEE, 1929; BCE, 1930; MCE, 1932), he obtained a post in 1928 as testing officer in the university's faculty of engineering. By 1929 he was senior demonstrator in strength and elasticity of materials. He wrote a thesis for his master's degree and several journal articles on the strength of electric arc welds, using statistics in ways that were new to his discipline. In 1930-33 he lectured in agricultural engineering.

On 5 November 1932 at the chapel of his old school, Blackwood married Hazel Levenia McLeod. Next year he was appointed a research engineer with the Dunlop Perdriau Rubber Co. Ltd; he was promoted in 1939 to technical manager. In 1946 he returned to the university as professor of mechanical engineering and dean of the faculty, but in 1948 was drawn back to industry as general manager of Dunlop Rubber Australia Ltd, a position he held until his retirement in 1966. He continued as a member of the board of Dunlop Australia Ltd and, as chairman in 1972-79, guided the company in its recovery after a lean period. Additionally, he was a director (1966-80) of Humes Ltd.

Blackwood had maintained his connection with the university through his membership of the council (1951-63) and several of its committees: buildings (1953-61), which he chaired in 1954-56; finance (1953-61); and future development. He took the visionary step of drawing up a budget for the university covering the years 1953-70, and played a key part in managing a substantial building program in the 1950s. His greatest contribution to academic life, however, came after the Victorian government announced in January 1958 his appointment as chairman of an interim council responsible for establishing the State's second university. Named after Sir John Monash [q.v.10], the institution officially opened in March 1961. Blackwood was knighted in June. When the permanent council assumed office next month, he became chancellor.

The Monash University Act of 1958 had made it clear that priority was to be given to the provision of courses in applied science and technology, these classes being seriously overcrowded at the University of Melbourne. Blackwood and his colleagues complied but from the outset saw the need to cater for all branches of learning; in particular, they identified a requirement for a faculty of education (established 1965). Their submissions to the Victorian government and the Australian Universities Commission were marked by the detailed compilation and analysis of data that typified Blackwood's working methods. Projections of student numbers and costs, building plans and the choice of a site for the university all benefited from this approach, as did the selection of the initial staff and the fixing of their conditions of employment.

Blackwood ensured that a master plan was prepared for the site and buildings; its main features, despite successive revisions, can be seen in the Monash campus at Clayton. The buildings lie for the most part inside a ring-road, and the faculties of medicine, science and engineering occupy contiguous positions. The older buildings are connected by a system of service tunnels—truly an engineer's university.

The interim council appointed (Sir) Louis Matheson as Monash University's first vice-chancellor. He had been a professorial colleague of Blackwood's at the University of Melbourne, and the ethos of the three engineers—Monash, Blackwood and Matheson—strongly influenced the development of the university. Blackwood stepped down as chancellor in 1968. That year he published *Monash University*, an account of the institution's first ten years. The university named its great hall after him and at the opening of the building in 1971 conferred on him the honorary degree of doctor of laws.

A trustee (from 1964) of the National Museum of Victoria, Blackwood was chairman of trustees (1968-70) and of the newly formed council (1971-78). He took part in archaeological digs conducted by the museum and established the Robert Blackwood Fund for Scientific Research, which he supported financially. In 1973-74 he was president of the Royal Society of Victoria. He helped to establish the Asian Institute of Technology, Bangkok, of which he was a founder trustee, in 1967; the university made him a life trustee and in 1978 awarded him an honorary doctorate of technology. His work as a member (from 1948) and president (1951-67) of the council of Sandringham Technical School, and as a trustee (from 1951) and chairman (1961-75) of the Dafydd Lewis Trust further expressed his commitment to education. He was a fellow (1968) of the Institution of Engineers, Australia, which awarded him the (Sir) Peter Nicol Russell [q.v.6] medal in 1964 for his notable contributions to the science and practice of engineering in Australia. In 1972 the University of Melbourne awarded him the (W. C.) Kernot [q.v.5] medal for distinguished engineering achievement.

Blackwood's associates described him as a friendly man who discharged his multifarious duties with skill and enthusiasm, but who was not one to show emotion. His interests were intense and varied. He prepared models for his engineering classes, travelled to archaeological sites in South-East Asia, gathered sea shells in remote locations, and drew maps for a guidebook, *Beautiful Bali* (1970), which he wrote about his favourite holiday destination. A feature of the book was the thoroughness with which it recorded distances, described the layouts of buildings and discussed social customs, thus providing an example in the public domain of the attention to detail that characterised his professional career. He painted, played the piano, worked in wood and metal, bound books in hand-tooled leather and tended his garden. 'Life doesn't mean much unless you take an interest in everything', he said in 1958 as he took up his Monash appointment; a friend commented later that he never did things by halves.

Sir Robert died on 21 August 1982 at Brighton and was cremated. His wife and their son and daughter survived him. On 10 September the Monash community gathered in Robert Blackwood Hall to commemorate his life and work.

J. R. Poynter and C. Rasmussen, *A Place Apart* (1996); *Robert Rutherford Blackwood, 1906-1982* (1982); *Jnl of the Instn of Engineers Aust*, vol 36, no 12, 1964, p N95; *Engineers Aust*, 1 Oct 1982, p 10; *Australian*, 19 Nov 1979, p 10; private information.

IAN D. RAE

BLAKENEY, FREDERICK JOSEPH (1913-1990), diplomat, was born on 2 July 1913 at Chatswood, Sydney, second child of Australian-born parents Frederick Joseph Blakeney, public accountant, and his wife Mabel Florence, née Bates. Educated at the Marist Brothers' High School, Darlinghurst, and at the Marist Brothers' juniorate at Mittagong, he entered the novitiate in 1931 and took his first vows on 2 July 1932. He adopted the religious name of Albeus and taught in schools at Forbes and at Bendigo, Victoria, before he left the Order in 1936. Enrolling at the University of Sydney (BA, 1942), he graduated with first-class honours in English and history, and won the university medal in history.

On 28 March 1942 Blakeney enlisted in the Royal Australian Air Force. He was 6 ft 1 in. (185 cm) tall and 12 st. 6 lb. (79 kg) in weight, with blue eyes and brown hair. Qualifying as an air observer, he was commissioned on 10 December. At St Patrick's Cathedral, Melbourne, on 11 January 1943 he married Marjorie Grosmont Martin, a photographer. He underwent further training in Canada and Britain and was promoted to flying officer in June. From October he served in North Africa, transporting anti-submarine aircraft. In January 1944 he was posted back to Britain as a navigator in No.271 Squadron, Royal Air Force. He dropped Canadian paratroops and towed a personnel-carrying glider over France on D-Day (6 June), and took part in the airborne operations at Arnhem, the Netherlands, in September. Promoted to flight lieutenant in December, he served with Transport Command in Canada from January 1945 and returned to Australia in July. His RAAF appointment terminated on 1 October.

Blakeney taught modern history at the University of Sydney before joining the Department of External Affairs in June 1946. He served in Paris from 1947 to 1949, the first of many European postings, and thereafter in Stalin's Moscow until 1951. From late 1953 to 1956 he was counsellor in Washington and between 1957 and 1959 he was minister in Indo-China. As a Catholic (which was unusual in the department at the time) and a staunch anti-communist (to a degree notable even among peers for whom such an orientation was customary), he appears to have encouraged Australia's nascent support for the South Vietnamese president Ngo Dinh Diem—a commitment that would lead to Australia's direct involvement in the Vietnam conflict.

Recalled to Canberra in 1959, Blakeney was appointed head of the department's South and South-East Asia branch, where he saw the end of the Menzies [q.v.15] government's policy of keeping West New Guinea out of Indonesia's hands. In 1962 he was dispatched again to Europe, and he remained there—with the exception of two more years in Canberra—for the rest of his career. He was appointed knight grand cross of the Order of St Gregory the Great by Pope Paul VI in 1964 and CBE in 1968. As ambassador in Bonn (1962-68), Moscow (1968-71) and The Hague (1974-77), and permanent representative to the European office of the United Nations in Geneva (1977-78), he reported widely on developments in East-West relations. But Australia also had more direct interests on the Continent. For example, in West Germany a major objective given to him was to achieve agreement that Australian exports would receive special treatment once Britain entered the European Economic Community; in the Netherlands Australia had significant concerns with regard to trade, finance and migration; and in the Soviet Union Blakeney negotiated something of a thaw in bilateral relations. This last step was part of Australia's attempt to take advantage of the growing split between the Soviet Union and China.

A heavy cigar smoker, Blakeney retired in June 1978 after a major heart attack. He had been well regarded among senior officers, one of whom described him as 'jovial in manner' and 'prudent and thoughtful in his approach to foreign policy issues'. However he was unpopular with subordinates, who perceived him as being overly conscious of his status, a man who did not suffer juniors gladly. Such a reputation earned him the sobriquets 'Blake the Snake' and 'Franz Joseph von Blakenburg'. His stiff and authoritarian manner appears to have sprung, at least in part, from two conservative beliefs: that his minions should be aware of their lowly place in the hierarchy and that subordinates should endure a series of trials in order to be prepared for greater responsibilities.

Blakeney's leadership, which sometimes extended to checking the fingernails of staff, had some positive features. His schoolmasterly approach is said to have accompanied a deep knowledge of old-style diplomatic skills that provided a valuable example for a career in the foreign service. In the more intimate surroundings of his home at Deakin, Canberra, and later at Mollymook, New South Wales, his family viewed him with affection and admiration. Survived by his wife and their daughter, he died on 16 June 1990 at Darlinghurst, Sydney, and was cremated.

Canberra Times, 21 June 1990, p 7; Canberra and District Hist Soc, *Newsletter*, Aug 1990, p 9; AWM 65, item 344 (AWM); A9300, item Blakeney F J, A6366, item MS1969/01T, A1838, items 3014/10/10/1 and 29/1/3, pt 4 (NAA); career details (Dept of Foreign Affairs and Trade, Canberra); Blakeney papers (NLA); private information.
STUART DORAN

BLAND, ROBERT HAVELOCK (1903-1989), sailor, was born on 5 May 1903 at Balmain North, Sydney, sixth child of Thomas George Bland, a locally born watchmaker and jeweller, and his wife Mary Hamilton, née Stewart, who came from Scotland. Bob was apprenticed to a blacksmith, but on 14 April 1921 he enlisted in the Royal Australian Navy as an assistant cook. He was 5 ft 7 ins (170 cm) tall with auburn hair, blue eyes and a fresh complexion. 'Rated' as a cook in the following year, he rose to leading cook in 1925 and to petty officer in 1927. On 4 December 1926 he had married Florence Alice Thomas, a dressmaker, at St Philip's Church of England, Auburn.

In October 1935 Bland was promoted to chief petty officer cook. Having served in HMA ships *Marguerite*, *Canberra*, *Vendetta*, *Australia* and *Adelaide*, he left for Britain, where he was among the commissioning crew of HMAS *Perth* in June 1939. The cruiser was at sea in the Caribbean when Australia declared war on Germany. 'Bob was Pusser built' recalled one of his peers, meaning that he embodied the highest standards of naval discipline and decorum. Another remembered a less punctilious chief cook who turned a blind eye when food was taken from the mess for the ship's cat.

Perth served in the Mediterranean from December 1940 and took part in the battle of Matapan in March 1941. During the evacuation of Greece in April, Bland 'worked untiringly and cheerfully throughout the night baking four batches of bread so that all troops onboard could be given plenty of bread and butter and jam which they appeared to regard as a special luxury'. He was mentioned in despatches. After evacuating 1188 troops from Crete in May, the ship endured numerous air attacks. A bomb blew away part of the ship's galley, killing thirteen men, including two cooks. Bland quickly supervised the restoration of the galley to working order and rallied the remaining members of his staff to provide within two hours a hot meal for the ship's company and the soldiers on board. For his 'zeal, patience and cheerfulness' he was awarded the British Empire Medal.

After refitting in Australia, *Perth* sailed for Java in February 1942. On 1 March she was sunk by the Japanese in a torrid sea battle in the Sunda Strait. Hauled from the ocean covered in black oil fuel, Bland and other survivors became prisoners of war. They were incarcerated first at Serang, Java, where Bland gave 'invaluable assistance' to medical staff. As the number of men with dysentery and chronic diarrhoea increased, he appealed to the Japanese to be permitted to cook the rice ration. This was allowed and, according to a fellow prisoner, 'not only was it then palatable, but our health improved'. From Changi camp, Singapore, he spent eighteen months working on the Burma-Thailand Railway. At Tamarkan, Thailand, he ran the camp kitchen. Repatriated in September 1945, he was again mentioned in despatches for his service in *Perth*. He elected to remain in the navy, but spent most of a year in hospital and was discharged medically unfit on 10 December 1946.

The ensuing years were difficult. Unable, because of dysentery, to continue in the trade he so enjoyed, he cooked only for the ex-POW reunions he could attend. He worked briefly as a storeman and as a gatekeeper, but recurring bouts of diarrhoea and malaria restricted his employment. Survived by his wife and their two sons, he died on 19 April 1989 at Concord, Sydney, and was cremated.

G. H. Gill, *Royal Australian Navy 1939-1942* (1957); A. Payne, *H.M.A.S. Perth* (1978); B. Whiting, *Ship of Courage* (1994); M. Gee, *A Long Way from Silver Creek* (2000); A6770, item Bland R H, B503, item Y19 (NAA); private information.

KATHRYN SPURLING

BLAXLAND, DAME HELEN FRANCES (1907-1989), conservationist, was born on 21 June 1907 at Neutral Bay, Sydney, sixth of seven children of (Sir) Robert Anderson [q.v.7], a Sydney-born businessman, and his wife Jean Cairns, née Amos, from Melbourne. Helen was educated at Bedales School, Hampshire, England; Frensham, Mittagong, New South Wales; and Julian Ashton's [q.v.7] Sydney Art School. On 8 November 1927 she married with Presbyterian forms Gregory Hamilton Blaxland (1896-1969), an engineer, at her parents' home in New South Head Road, Double Bay. They lived first at Bellevue Hill, then at Woollahra in a nineteenth-century house, Brush (named after Gregory Blaxland's [q.v.1] farm). Significant patrons of mainly Sydney artists, they collected works by (Sir)

Russell Drysdale, Donald Friend [qq.v.], (Sir) William Dobell, Loudon Sainthill [qq.v.14,16], Elaine Haxton, Paul Jones and others. The Blaxlands' only child, Antonia, was born in 1929.

From the outbreak of World War II Mrs Blaxland worked (1939-51) for the Australian Red Cross Society, New South Wales division, often dealing with special appeals such as the raffle for the 'Dream Home' and flower festivals. In 1946 she published *Flower Pieces*, on the art of flower arrangement, with photographs of her work by Max Dupain and Olive Cotton. *Collected Flower Pieces* (1949) presented arrangements by her friends. She gave special attention to their settings, often including paintings as backdrops. In 1953-54 she served on the council of the National Art Gallery Society of New South Wales. In 1957 she advised the architect J. L. S. Mansfield [q.v.15] on the decor for Kirribilli House. She contributed to numerous publications on architecture, decorative arts, entertaining and food.

In 1959 Mrs Blaxland joined the National Trust of Australia (New South Wales), a small group of conservationists led by Annie Wyatt [q.v.16]. Two years later she founded the women's committee to raise funds for the trust. She introduced the lucrative idea of 'house inspections' and initiated the exhibition No Time to Spare!, which was shown at the David Jones [q.v.2] Art Gallery in 1962 and later throughout the State for the New South Wales division of the Arts Council of Australia. On display were photographs by Dupain of early public buildings and houses.

Elected to the National Trust council in 1962, Mrs Blaxland was vice-president (1965-71), State representative (1969-71) on the Australian Council of National Trusts and an honorary life member from 1967. She had chaired (1964-71) the inaugural committee for Lindesay, Darling Point, a historic house which was given to the women's committee as their headquarters. The Lindesay committee furnished the house in period style and held trust events there, notably annual antique dealers' fairs and exhibitions of Australian decorative arts.

At Experiment Farm Cottage Helen Blaxland and K. Bernard-Smith had gathered in 1963 a collection of early Australian furniture for public viewing. In 1967 control of Old Government House, Parramatta, was vested in the National Trust by legislation; Mrs Blaxland was prominent on the Parramatta properties committee which presented to the public the home of the governors to 1855. She remained on the committee as honorary housekeeper—a self-chosen title—until her involvement with the trust ended when the Parramatta properties committee was abruptly disbanded in 1983.

In 1967 Helen Blaxland had been appointed OBE and in 1975 she was elevated to DBE. An honorary member (1970) of the Society of Interior Designers of Australia, she was also a foundation trustee (1970-89) of the National Parks and Wildlife Foundation (New South Wales), patron of the Eryldene Appeal (1971) for funds for E. G. Waterhouse's [q.v.12] home and garden at Gordon, and a member (1958-67) of the Sydney Fountains Committee. In 1978 she became foundation chairman of the Australiana Fund, set up to acquire Australian furnishings for the four official Commonwealth residences and, in 1979, an inaugural member of the Official Establishments Trust.

Tall and elegant, with grey eyes and brown hair which turned early to white, Dame Helen was confident, forthright and decisive. She had difficulty pronouncing the letter 'r': when asked about seeking grassroots members for the National Trust beyond the Eastern Suburbs and North Shore of Sydney, she replied, 'the only use I can think of for gwasswoots is for twamplin' on'. She was an educator with great foresight who set a standard of excellence among all those who worked with her.

Dame Helen moved to the Silchester apartments at Bellevue Hill in the late 1960s and in 1983 to a cottage at Camden Park. Grieving after her daughter's death four months earlier, she died on 17 December 1989 at Camden and was cremated. The Dame Helen Blaxland Foundation for the continued preservation of Experiment Farm Cottage, Old Government House and Lindesay was established to commemorate her. A portrait by Bryan Westwood is held by her family.

I. F. Wyatt, *Ours in Trust* (1987); *SMH*, 19 May 1962, p 9, 14 June 1975, p 1; *Sun-Herald* (Sydney), 4 Nov 1979, p 170; C. Simpson, 'Dame Helen Blaxland, DBE', *National Trust Mag*, Feb 1990, p 8; *Bulletin*, 17 June 2003, p 38; private information and personal knowledge.   CAROLINE SIMPSON*

BLUMANN, ELISE MARGOT PAULA RUDOLPHINA HULDA (1897-1990), artist, was born on 16 January 1897 at Parchim, Germany, youngest of three children of Paul Schlie, cavalry officer and civil servant, and his wife Elfrida, née Kunschmidt. After attending school at Hamburg, Elise was taught painting in 1914 by Baron Leo Lütgendorff-Leinburg at Lübeck. In 1917-20 she studied in Berlin under Max Liebermann and Lovis Corinth. Liebermann was an impressionist whose large, colourful, liquid brush strokes were to influence her lyrical interpretation of the Western Australian landscape. Lovis Corinth had made impressionism into a dramatic, highly expressive art, replete with the heritage of the art nouveau (*Jugendstil*) movement. In

local galleries she encountered a wide range of modernist art, including works by Marc Chagall, Wassily Kandinsky, Henri Matisse and Paul Cézanne. She worked as an art teacher, and in a Hamburg gallery in 1921 exhibited her paintings for the first time.

On 23 June 1923 at Lübeck Elise married Dr Arnold Blumann, a wealthy industrial chemist; they were to have three sons. After her marriage she travelled and painted but did not exhibit. For business reasons, and because he opposed the Nazi regime, Dr Blumann moved with his family to the Netherlands in 1934, and to England two years later. They migrated to Australia, arriving at Fremantle by ship on 4 January 1938. Dr Blumann was employed in Perth by Plaimar Ltd, manufacturing chemists, and the couple built a modernistic house, with a studio, at Nedlands. In the 1940s Elise Blumann executed a series of paintings of melaleucas by the Swan River, viewed from her studio window. Her first-hand experience of modern European painting was evident; for example, in 'On the Swan, Nedlands' (1942) she combined the decorative tendencies of *Jugendstil* with the flat expressive forms of early modernism to produce her vision of a primeval landscape.

At the time, Blumann's memory, artistic practice and advocacy were the only direct sources at hand for Western Australian painters who aspired to paint in the modern style. Her humanist, synthetic view of the style set the context for avant-garde patronage and taste in Western Australia. She was adamant that her work was never 'expressionist', and her treatment of the figure demonstrated that her ambition was far more lyrical: 'Charles, Morning on the Swan' (1939), for example, shows a close affinity to Cézanne, Matisse and the early Pablo Picasso. Even so, her paintings were too provocative for many people in Perth. In 1944, using the name Elise Burleigh, she held her first solo exhibition, at Newspaper House Art Gallery; it featured several nudes, including 'Summer Nude' (1939), and caused a scandal. Although avant-garde in her art, throughout her life she had no sympathy for social radicalism.

In 1945 Blumann travelled to the goldfields and to Broome, adding the outback and its inhabitants to her subjects. The art critic Charles Hamilton, in his review of her second Newspaper House exhibition (1946), noted that she had 'begun to abstract from our landscape its essential meaning': the banksia, the melaleuca, the blackboy and the zamia were 'survivals from the past'; her portrayal of desert Aborigines symbolised 'primitive man facing the encroaching forces of an alien civilisation'. In 'Gooseberry Hill' (1948) the modernist equation of abstraction with the primitive was to result in an eloquent, postimpressionist interpretation of the local flora.

A member of the Perth Society of Artists, Blumann lectured on Picasso and other topics, and held art classes for both adults and children for several years from 1945. In 1948 with Robert Campbell [q.v.13] and Salec Minc [q.v.], among others, she helped to found the Art Group to stimulate interest in modern art in Perth. From 1949 she visited Europe several times, and in 1950 she staged an exhibition of her work in Paris. Her career was interrupted for some years while she cared for her sick husband. After his death in 1970 she lived in Germany for five years. Back in Perth, she held exhibitions at local galleries in 1976 and 1979, and at the Art Gallery of Western Australia in 1984. Her work was included in the gallery's exhibition, 'Western Australian Art and Artists 1900-1950' (1987). Survived by two of her sons, she died on 29 January 1990 at Nedlands and was cremated. Her work is represented in the National Gallery of Australia, Canberra, the Art Gallery of Western Australia, and the University of Western Australia and Holmes à Court [q.v.] collections, Perth.

D. Bromfield (comp), *Elise Blumann, Paintings and Drawings 1918-1984* (1984); C. Polizzotto, *Approaching Elise* (1988); *West Australian*, 25 July 1946, p 3, 24 Sept 1984, p 10; *Art and Australia*, Winter 1993, p 511; B. Blackman, interview with E. Blumann (1986, NLA).   DAVID BROMFIELD

BLYTHE, LINDSAY GORDON (1908-1986), pastoralist and businessman, was born on 2 May 1908 at Derby, Western Australia, eldest of five children of Joseph William Blythe, a blacksmith who had been born at Bunbury, and his Queensland-born wife Ethel Marion, née Bell. The Blythe family's links with the Kimberley district dated from 1885 when Gordon's native-born grandfather, Joseph Blythe (1850-1919), arrived with his wife, daughter and seven sons to establish one of the first pubs at Derby, just in time to prosper from the Halls Creek gold-rush. Later, as manager of Noonkanbah station for the Emanuel [q.v.8] brothers, Joseph located good grazing country between the King Leopold and Phillips ranges. In 1894-97 he took a prominent part in conflict with its traditional occupants, the Bunuba people, who were led by Tjangamarra [q.v.12]. From that time he and his sons took up pastoral leases (more than thirty by 1900), sometimes individually, sometimes with partners, including (Sir) Sidney Kidman [q.v.9].

Educated at Guildford Grammar School, Perth, until 1926, Gordon followed commercial pursuits in the city. On 11 August 1934 in his old school chapel, he married with Anglican rites Mollie Gertrude Smith (d.1973). He enlisted in the Australian Imperial Force on 14 January 1942. Promoted to acting sergeant in March (confirmed 1944), he was posted to a succession of training, Volunteer Defence Corps and garrison battalions in Western Australia. In May-October 1945 he served on Bougainville, where he was attached to the 3rd Field Punishment Centre. He was discharged from the army on 16 November. His war experience alerted him to the potential of using aircraft for freight.

After the war Blythe took an increasing part in the running of the family's beef cattle stations. He and his brothers, Douglas and Keith, were responsible for managing the family's core properties, Mount House and Glenroy, covering 1 250 000 acres (505 862 ha) and capable of pasturing 20 000 cattle. Isolation from the nearest meatworks at Wyndham and Broome was a major impediment to marketing beef. Blythe took up the idea of killing cattle at an abattoir on Glenroy and air-freighting the carcasses to a meatworks, thus eliminating the loss of condition inevitable in droving cattle long distances. With Australian National Airlines Pty Ltd, MacRobertson-Miller [qq.v.11, 10 Sir Macpherson Robertson, H. Miller] Aviation Co. and a group of local pastoralists, he set up Air Beef Pty Ltd in 1948. He was managing director, and (Sir) Ivan Holyman [q.v.14] was the first chairman. Supported by the Western Australian government, and from 1951 helped by a Commonwealth subsidy, the Glenroy abattoir was soon slaughtering over four thousand cattle annually. The carcasses were flown out by Bristol freighter and processed at the Wyndham meatworks. Neighbouring cattlemen marketed stock through Air Beef, and serious thought was given to setting up killing centres at Halls Creek and Fitzroy Crossing.

Expansion ceased when the Federal government decided to concentrate its investment on providing all-weather roads to facilitate the transport of livestock. This initiative favoured Air Beef's competitor, the Broome meatworks. Blythe responded by sponsoring the opening of an abattoir in 1959 at Derby, in some ways a better location than Broome, but the completion of a beef cattle road to the Mount House-Glenroy region in 1962 spelt the end to freighting of beef by air. Blythe served (1964-65) on a six-man Commonwealth government committee chaired by Sir Louis Loder [q.v.15], investigating transport costs in northern Australia. In 1965 Air Beef was obliged to go into receivership.

Blythe was a director of Winterbottom Holdings Ltd (1967-78) and of the West Australian Trustee, Executor & Agency Co. Ltd (1970-79). He was a member of the Weld, West Australian and Royal Perth Yacht clubs. One of the foremost of that third generation of Kimberley pastoralists who brought innovative developments to the North-West, he died on 7 June 1986 in his South Perth home and was cremated. His two sons and two daughters survived him.

H. Pedersen and B. Woorunmurra, *Jandamarra and the Bunuba Resistance* (1995); *The Story of the Air Beef Project in North West Australia* (1951?); *Aircraft*, Feb 1950, p 12; *Weekend News* (Perth), 27 Oct 1962, p 14; *West Australian*, 6 May 1964, p 16; G. C. Bolton, A Survey of the Kimberley Pastoral Industry from 1885 to the Present (MA thesis, UWA, 1954); Blythe family papers (SLWA).

G. C. BOLTON

BLYTHE, SYDNEY WALLACE THOMAS (1905-1985), architect and town planner, was born on 13 November 1905 at Lewisham, London, and was registered as Sidney, second of four children of Sidney George Blythe, bank messenger, and his wife Annie Barnici, née Howalls. In 1918 he began architectural studies at the School of Building, Brixton; after his family moved to Tasmania in 1921 he was articled to Rudolph Koch [q.v.Supp.] and attended evening classes (1922-25) at the Hobart Technical College. He worked for three months in 1925 as an assistant-draftsman with Tasmania's Department of Public Works before taking a position with Electrolytic Zinc Co. of Australasia, Risdon. In 1927 he returned to the department. Retrenched in 1930, he travelled to London, where he worked for several architectural firms. It was a time of intense architectural debate in England, further stimulated by the arrival of leading European modernists fleeing Nazism. In 1933 he won second place in a Building Centre cottage competition. This enabled him to establish a private practice.

In September 1934 Blythe was invited to return to the Tasmanian Department of Public Works. He brought his wife Kathleen May, née Tarrant, whom he had married on 23 October at the Congregational Church, New Barnet, Hertfordshire. During the following fifteen years he was the department's chief designer of some sixty government buildings (not all were realised), including schools, technical colleges, hospitals, railway stations and law courts in most centres throughout Tasmania. He was responsible for major alterations and extensions to Tasmania's Parliament House, completing a new chamber for the Legislative Assembly in 1940. The quality of Blythe's modern architecture from this period was outstanding; the A. G. Ogilvie [q.v.11] High School (1936) at New Town was regarded as his masterpiece. He served as acting chief architect for several periods and in 1945 was named senior architect.

In 1949 Blythe became the first full-time head of the architectural department at the Hobart Technical College, gaining national and international accreditation for his program, which included diploma courses in quantity surveying and building and a postgraduate diploma in town and country planning. He also practised privately, but his later work did not reach the high design qualities of the earlier period and his most significant contribution was as joint master planner of the new University of Tasmania site, at Sandy Bay, in 1956. Taking a leading role in popularising planning, he promoted the cause of civic design in the community.

Active in professional affairs, Blythe had been admitted as an associate of the Tasmanian Institute of Architects in 1928 and of the Royal Australian Institute of Architects in 1930, the year in which he was registered. He served (1952-54) as president of the Tasmanian chapter of the RAIA and was elected (1970) a life fellow of the institute. Made an associate (1945) and fellow (1960) of the Royal Institute of British Architects, he was also a member (1952) and fellow of the (Royal) Australian Planning Institute from 1965. A dapper figure with his square-cut moustache, soft hats, tweedy suits and plain woollen waistcoats, he could have been mistaken for a country gentleman. His polite and courteous manner and traces of a refined English accent reinforced the image.

After retiring from teaching in December 1969, Sydney Blythe continued to practise privately, with his son, until 1979. He had an interest in liberal theology, and was disappointed that he could not find a publisher for his manuscript 'The Absolute and the Obsolete'. Survived by his wife and their son and two daughters, he died on New Year's Day 1985 in Hobart and was cremated.

B. McNeill and L. Woolley, *Architecture from the Edge* (2002); *Architecture Aust*, Jan-Mar 1953, p 18, May 1985, p 37; B. McNeill, 'SWT Blythe: The Early Works', *Tas Architect*, May 1966, p 37; *Fabrications*, Aug 1996, p 99; R. J. Blythe, Sydney Wallace Thomas Blythe (M.Arch. thesis, Univ of Melbourne, 1998).

BARRY MCNEILL

BOAS, WALTER MORITZ (1904-1982), physicist, was born on 10 February 1904 in Berlin, only child of German parents Arthur Abraham Boas, medical practitioner, and his wife Adele, née Reiche. Following studies at a technical high school, Walter studied applied physics at the Technische Hochschule Berlin (Dipl.Ing., 1928; D.Ing., 1930). The research project that formed part of his physics studies, an investigation of the influence of load and temperature on the plastic deformation of metals, was supervised by Professor Richard Becker. It led to a joint publication, and set the direction for his life's work in science. His doctoral degree was based on further work in this field conducted jointly with Erich Schmid at the Kaiser-Wilhelm-Institut für Metall-forschung at Berlin-Dahlem.

From 1933 to 1937 Boas worked in Switzerland, first at the University of Fribourg, and then at the Eidgenössische Technische Hochschule Zurich. While at Fribourg, he and Schmid published their book *Kristallplastizität* (1935), which continued to appear in German (and later English) for the next thirty-five years. Although he was a baptised Lutheran, Boas came from a Jewish family and so decided to leave Europe, taking an appointment at the Royal Institution in London, while he searched for a more permanent position, aided by the Society for the Protection of Science and Learning. In January 1938 he accepted a two-year appointment at the University of Melbourne, funded by the Carnegie Foundation, in preference to a position at University College, London. He married Eva Orgler, from Berlin, on 22 March at the register office, Hampstead, London, and arrived in Melbourne in May.

For the next nine years Boas lectured in the metallurgy department of the university, from 1940 as senior lecturer. His book *Introduction to the Physics of Metals and Alloys* (1947) was based on his lectures. Although initially classified as 'enemy aliens' during the war, he and his wife were soon accorded 'refugee alien' status and naturalised in 1944. Most of his research in this period was conducted in conjunction with the Council for Scientific and Industrial Research's section of lubricants and bearings, set up by F. P. Bowden [q.v.13]. Boas enjoyed a part-time appointment there from 1944. The section was renamed tribophysics under Bowden's successor, Stewart Bastow [q.v.13], who appointed Boas principal research officer in 1947. He succeeded, somewhat reluctantly, to the headship of the division of tribophysics in 1949, when CSIR was recast as the Commonwealth Scientific and Industrial Research Organization and Bastow joined the executive.

Boas was a friendly and hospitable man who fostered a family atmosphere in his division. He combined administration with strong leadership, nurturing the careers of his young scientists through joint research and publication, and promoting basic research into the structure and properties of materials. His international reputation grew. In 1956 he spent three months in the United States of America as visiting lecturer in metallurgy at Harvard University. He encouraged interaction between the University of Melbourne and CSIRO, lecturing to students of physics and engineering, serving on the faculty of science and accepting appointment as honorary senior associate in solid state physics. Late in the 1950s Boas established a Pugwash group in Melbourne. He represented Australia at the Oslo con-

ference (1961) against the spread of nuclear weapons and helped to organise the Pugwash regional meeting in Melbourne in 1967. These conferences brought together scholars and public figures who sought co-operative solutions to global problems.

A fellow of the Institute of Physics (1943), the Australian Academy of Science (1954) and the Australian Institute of Physics (1962), Boas was elected as a foreign scientific fellow (1965) of the Max-Planck-Institut für Metallkunde and a corresponding member (1972) of the Austrian Academy of Sciences. In 1966-72 he was a vice-president of the International Union of Pure and Applied Physics. After his retirement from the CSIRO in 1969, he was a hard-working honorary senior associate in metal physics at the university. He published his third book, *Properties and Structure of Solids* (1971), and was awarded an honorary doctorate of applied science by the university in 1974. Survived by his wife and their son and daughter, Boas died on 12 May 1982 at Prahran and was cremated. The Australian Institute of Physics established the Walter Boas medal to be awarded annually for excellence in research in physics in Australia. Royal Melbourne Institute of Technology, which he had served as an adviser, created an annual Walter Boas prize for the best final-year student in applied physics, and the University of Melbourne named in his honour the building in which he had worked.

D. W. Borland et al (eds), *Physics of Materials* (1979); R. W. Home, *Physics in Australia to 1945* (1990); *Hist Records of Austn Science*, vol 6, no 4, 1987, p 507; A12508, item 21/465 and A659, item 1943/1/7109 (NAA); Boas papers (Basser Lib, Canberra); private information.   IAN D. RAE

BOK, BART JAN (1906-1983), astronomer, was born Bartholomeus Jan Bok on 28 April 1906 at Hoorn, the Netherlands, elder son of Jan Bok, a sergeant major in the Dutch army, and his wife Gesina Annetta, née van der Lee. He attended school at The Hague, excelling at mathematics and science, before studying astronomy at the universities of Leiden and Groningen (Ph.D., 1932). In 1929 he was awarded a fellowship to Harvard College Observatory in Massachusetts, United States of America, under the astronomer Harlow Shapley. At Troy, New York, on 9 September 1929 Bok married Priscilla Fairfield (1896-1975), an astronomer who became not only his partner but his closest scientific collaborator. On completion of his doctorate, he joined the staff of the observatory and rose through its ranks to become a full professor in 1947. Naturalised as an American citizen in 1938, he shortened his first name to Bart.

Bok's principal research interest was the structure of the Milky Way. During the 1930s he studied the distribution and velocity of stars in the Galaxy in an attempt to determine its structure. He became an authority on the subject, even though the true spiral shape of the Galaxy was not revealed until the 1950s. With Priscilla he wrote *The Milky Way* (1941), widely acclaimed as one of the most successful astronomical books ever published. He also researched the small dark clouds in interstellar space that cause the absorption of starlight and showed that they consist of gas and dust that contract to form stars. The clouds are now known as 'Bok globules'.

In 1956, after applying unsuccessfully for the position of director of Harvard College Observatory, Bok accepted the post of director of the Mount Stromlo Observatory and professor of astronomy at the Australian National University, Canberra. His appointment was to have a significant impact on the development of Australian astronomy. At this time Australia was a world leader in radio astronomy, principally through the work of the Commonwealth Scientific and Industrial Research Organization group in Sydney led by Joseph Pawsey [q.v.15], but optical astronomy lagged behind. A 74-inch (1.9 m) optical telescope had been installed at Mount Stromlo in 1955 by the previous director, (Sir) Richard Woolley, but it was through Bok's endeavours that it became a major astronomical instrument. He forged close links with the Sydney radio astronomers and used his international contacts to attract prominent astronomers to Australia. By the early 1960s Mount Stromlo had become the leading centre for optical astronomy in the Southern Hemisphere.

Bok helped to establish the graduate program in astronomy at the ANU, the training ground for many Australian astronomers. He also recognised the need for a better observing site than Mount Stromlo and initiated a survey that resulted in the selection of Siding Spring Mountain, near Coonabarabran, New South Wales. Bok played a leading part in securing government funds for the telescopes and instruments for the new site, his efforts assisted by his friendship with Prime Minister (Sir) Robert Menzies [q.v.15].

Apart from his scientific achievements, Bok was an outstanding teacher and populariser of astronomy. He gave numerous public lectures, published articles in newspapers and magazines, and delivered radio broadcasts. His enthusiasm, exuberance and charisma conveyed the importance and excitement of his field to a generation of Australians. He became the public face of astronomy.

Bok worked long hours and expected others to show the same level of commitment. He believed in applying scientific principles to other areas of life and was a fierce critic of pseudo-sciences such as astrology. A pacifist and a firm advocate of international cooperation, he promoted scientific programs of the United Nations Educational, Scientific and Cultural Organization in developing countries.

In 1966 the Boks returned to the United States, where Bart was director (until 1970) of the Steward Observatory and professor of astronomy at the University of Arizona. He retired from the university in 1974. Bok received numerous awards for his contributions to astronomy: he was elected (1968) to the US National Academy of Sciences and awarded (1977) the Catherine Wolfe Bruce gold medal of the Astronomical Society of the Pacific, of which he was a board member in 1977-80. He served as vice-president (1970-74) of the International Astronomical Union and as president (1972-74) of the American Astronomical Society.

Survived by his son and daughter, Bok died on 5 August 1983 in his home at Tucson, Arizona; his body was bequeathed to the college of medicine, University of Arizona. His contribution to Australian astronomy is commemorated by the Bok prize, awarded jointly by the Astronomical Society of Australia and the Australian Academy of Science. In 1996 the Steward Observatory's 90-inch (2.3 m) telescope was named after him.

D. H. Levy, *The Man Who Sold the Milky Way* (1993); T. Frame and D. Faulkner, *Stromlo* (2003); *Sky & Telescope*, Oct 1983, p 303; *Jnl of the Royal Astronomical Soc of Canada*, vol 78, no 1, 1984, p 3; *Procs of the Astronomical Soc of Aust*, vol 5, no 4, 1984, p 608; *Qtrly Jnl of the Royal Astronomical Soc*, vol 28, 1987, p 539; *Hist Records of Austn Science*, vol 9, no 2, 1992, p 119; National Academy of Sciences (US), *Biog Memoirs*, vol 64, 1994, p 72.

PETER ROBERTSON

BOLTE, SIR HENRY EDWARD (1908-1990), farmer and premier, was born on 20 May 1908 at Ballarat East, elder son of Victorian-born parents James Henry (Harry) Bolte, miner, and his wife Anna Jane, née Martin. Harry was also a moderately successful handyman, shepherd and occasional prospector. His German parents had fled to England in 1847 and then migrated to Victoria in 1852. Anna's maternal grandparents were also of German origin. In 1892 her mother had married a second time, to William Warren. When Henry was born his parents moved to Skipton. The focal points of his childhood were the Ripon Hotel, owned by his father until 1921; the larger Skipton Hotel, owned by the Warrens until 1921, when they sold it to the Boltes; and the Skipton State School, where F. A. Moore, an Anglican churchman and Empire loyalist, was headmaster. Henry was conscious of the disadvantage of his German background during World War I; he later said that it had toughened him.

Harry Bolte was stern and prudent, a 'stand-over man' who in Henry's recollection 'ruled with a strap'. Although a publican, Harry was not 'a social drinker' and had little time for those who were. Henry weathered his father's bouts of anger, accepted his values and grew closer to him later in life. Anna was more tolerant, as were the Warrens, with whom Henry often stayed. Bill Warren's anti-socialist views influenced the boy. Henry's was 'an average, normal, happy family life consistent with [that of] country people'. Nicknamed 'Pudden' or 'Pud' for his stocky build, he was a gregarious youth who swam with friends in the 'Big Hole' of the Mount Emu Creek, and went shooting, fishing and camping on weekends.

At school Bolte played sport (captain of football and cricket), topped seventh grade in 1920 and next year attended Moore's extra classes for students seeking scholarships. In 1922, with the assistance of a junior technical scholarship, he became a boarder at Ballarat Church of England Grammar School. Now nicknamed 'Pot', he was better off than most of his peers and had money to lend. The school emphasised careers in the public service, the church and teaching. Its leading figures were the headmaster E. V. Butler and the 'character building' ex-army chaplain Alex Macpherson. A contemporary remarked that 'any polish Henry may have acquired he owed to Macpherson'.

Two of Bolte's schoolfellows, T. T. Hollway [q.v.14] and E. H. Montgomery, were to enter politics. When Bolte left school in 1924, he considered becoming a politician, clergyman, auctioneer or bank clerk. For the next ten years, however, he remained in the family circle and enjoyed small-town life. Harry Bolte sold the Skipton Hotel, purchased three small local sheep properties, and in 1925 started a haberdashery store at Skipton for his wife and elder son. It had failed by 1929. In the Depression Henry worked in his father's and other farmers' shearing sheds, joining the Australian Workers' Union.

Bolte acted in amateur theatricals and involved himself in the affairs of the Church of England. He played cricket and football for Skipton, and was 'a keen two-bob punter', secretary of the Skipton Racing Club and one of the first instructors appointed outside Melbourne in the *Herald* newspaper's Learn-to-Swim campaign. Sport honed his competitive instinct and brought him into contact with wealthy families who had powerful conservative political associations. Among his cricketing team-mates in the Western Plains side were (Sir) Rutherford Guthrie [q.v.], Geoffrey Street and (Sir) Chester Manifold [qq.v.12,15]. Bolte was later to extol the values of team sports as readily translatable to political life.

He met visiting politicians, including in 1931 (Sir) Robert Menzies [q.v.15].

With money his grandmother Warren gave him, in 1934 Bolte bought Kialla, a farm at Bamganie, near Meredith. The money also enabled him to marry his long-time sweetheart and Skipton neighbour, Edith Lilian 'Jill' Elder, on 24 November that year at Scots Church, Ballarat; the couple were to be childless. The run-down property to which they moved had 900 acres (364 ha) and 600 sheep, and, in Henry's estimation, 60 000 rabbits. He supplemented his income by trapping, poisoning and ferreting the rabbits. To support their community, the Boltes shopped locally even though Meredith was close to both Ballarat and Geelong.

On 20 August 1940 Bolte enlisted in the Militia as a gunner. He served with the 2nd and 3rd Field Training regiments, Puckapunyal, as an artillery instructor and a pay clerk. Promoted to acting sergeant in March 1942, he reverted to gunner in November and was discharged on 19 January 1943. He later lamented that he had been classified as medically unfit for overseas service. Compared with many of his future political peers, he had an undistinguished war record, involving numerous periods of leave without pay, and most weekends, home at Kialla.

In 1945 Bolte attended the Liberal Party's first State council as president of the minuscule Meredith branch. A paucity of candidates encouraged him to make an impromptu offer to stand for the Legislative Assembly seat of Hampden in the general election to be held in November. Manifold vouched for him as a popular and successful farmer whose wife, like her husband, was a good mixer, but the inexperienced Bolte ran a mediocre campaign and lost by nearly six hundred votes. Determined to secure a second opportunity, he took lessons in public speaking and, with friends canvassing for him, won preselection in 1947. At the State general election on 8 November the Federal Labor government's bank nationalisation proposal was a major issue. Bolte defeated the sitting Labor candidate, Raymond Hyett, by almost two thousand votes. He was to hold Hampden until retirement, although he won it by a margin of only seventy-two in 1952.

The parliament Bolte entered was one of 'unpredictably changing alignments within and between each of the three parties'. At first a Liberal and Country coalition governed under Hollway's leadership, but the alliance collapsed after only twelve months. On 3 December 1948 Hollway formed a minority Liberal administration in which his former schoolmate Bolte, a country member who spoke on rural issues, was given the portfolios of water supply, mines and (from December 1949) conservation. The Victorian Liberals renamed their organisation the Liberal and Country Party in 1949. Bolte rationalised the administration of the State Rivers and Water Supply Commission and provided for new dams. In May 1949 he introduced legislation establishing the Soil Conservation Authority. The Hollway government fell in June 1950. Bolte's brief ministerial experience was to put him ahead of future rivals for the leadership of the LCP.

Hollway obtained support from the party's executive for the '2 for 1' scheme, whereby every Federal electorate would be divided into two State electorates, ending an imbalance in the electoral distribution that grossly favoured country voters. But many members of the LCP, Bolte among them, had reservations, believing Labor would benefit. J. V. McConnell, (Sir) Arthur Warner [qq.v.15,16], and (Sir) John Anderson, an influential member of the party executive, moved against Hollway. They cultivated Bolte and introduced him to businessmen.

In December 1951 the parliamentary party dumped Hollway and his deputy T. D. Oldham [q.v.15] and elected L. G. Norman as leader and Bolte as his deputy. (Sir) Arthur Rylah [q.v.16] had polled successfully for the deputy-leadership but party convention stipulated that either the leader or deputy should come from a non-metropolitan area. Norman and Bolte then sought to reverse the party's commitment to the 2 for 1 scheme. Hollway and some followers were expelled from the LCP. In the general election held on 6 December 1952, Hollway stood against Norman for the seat of Glen Iris and defeated him.

Labor won the election and implemented the 2 for 1 plan. The LCP chose Oldham as leader and confirmed Bolte as deputy but in May 1953 Oldham was killed in an air crash. In the subsequent ballot for the leadership Warner's support proved crucial in gaining victory for Bolte and heading off Rylah, who became deputy. Bolte was now leader of the Opposition. His rise had followed the party's loss of three leaders in unusual circumstances in only eighteen months, and many believed that he was only a stopgap leader. But in 1955 the Australian Labor Party split and right-wing former members, many of them Catholics, established the Australian Labor Party (Anti-Communist), later renamed the Democratic Labor Party. This party's preferences were to flow overwhelmingly to the LCP and were to be a decisive factor in its future electoral success.

Using his 'cleanskin' image, the personable Bolte manoeuvred shrewdly behind the scenes, insisting that he, and not one of Labor's dissidents, move a no confidence motion against the government. It was carried on 20 April 1955 and a general election followed on 28 May. Winning a total of thirty-four seats in the Legislative Assembly, the LCP was able to govern narrowly in its own right. The pref-erences of ALP(A-C) candidates had secured the LCP nine of its Lower House seats, two of them being won by fewer than twenty votes.

Bolte promised a government of action. Besides being premier, he was treasurer and (to 1961) minister of conservation. In 1956 his government cleared the emergency housing settlement, Camp Pell, in Royal Park, raised rents for public housing and reorganised the Housing Commission. The abolition that year of quarterly cost-of-living adjustments to the wages of Victorian workers gave Bolte a personal victory over J. V. Stout [q.v.16] and earned him the enmity of the union movement. Accepting (Sir) Maurice Nathan's [q.v.] suggestion, Bolte formed the Victoria Promotion Committee, joined it himself, undertook the first of nine overseas missions promoting the State, and persuaded international companies to expand or establish in Victoria. He courted (Sir) John Williams [q.v.], managing director of the Herald & Weekly Times Ltd, in the hope of gaining that media group's support for his policies.

In Rylah, Bolte was fortunate to have a progressive, loyal and hard-working deputy. A disciplined cabinet, the LCP's majority in the Lower House and a steadily improving economy gave impetus to the government's program. In 1956 the Melbourne and Metropolitan Board of Works was made responsible for building freeways. Two years later the government established the National Parks Authority and ratified the Snowy Mountains hydro-electric scheme agreements. Notwithstanding Bolte's strong advocacy of private enterprise, public-sector authorities expanded under his premiership.

The parliamentary contest was made easier for Bolte with the death (1957) of the leader of the ALP, John Cain [q.v.13], whose forceful debating style he copied. At the general election on 31 May 1958, the LCP claimed that it had brought stable government to Victoria. The campaign was the first covered by television, which suited Bolte's direct and personal approach. He won an increased majority that included ten rural seats, preferential support from the DLP again proving vital. Seeking control of the Upper House, he tried to persuade the Country Party's parliamentary secretary, Dudley Walters, to accept the presidency, prompting the leader of that party, Sir Herbert Hyland [q.v.14], to describe the premier as 'a mongrel'. Bolte rode out attacks in 1958-60 by the leader of the Opposition, Clive Stoneham, on Warner's conflicts of interest between his commercial enterprises and ministerial responsibilities.

Bolte was a competent if necessarily parsimonious treasurer. Lucky to be in government at a time of prosperity, he nevertheless struggled to meet increasing demands for services due to the influx of capital and an expanding population, and ran deficits in his first four budgets. He asked the Commonwealth to return to the States the power, taken from them in 1942, to raise income taxes, and when his request was refused attempted to achieve his objective in the High Court of Australia. In 1959 the Commonwealth gave ground and introduced a new formula for financial support to the States but Bolte believed Victoria to be disadvantaged by the terms of the six-year arrangement. He also disliked tied grants from the Commonwealth, believing that they denied his government sovereignty.

The general election on 15 July 1961 was held in difficult circumstances due to the Federal treasurer Harold Holt's [q.v.14] 'credit squeeze' but Bolte won an extra Lower House seat. Once more, DLP preferences in marginal seats were of critical importance. Bolte's policy was to keep 'the DLP alive'. He helped find jobs for some of its members who had lost their seats, asked his business contacts to donate to DLP election campaigns, and maintained cordial relations with the Catholic Archbishop Daniel Mannix [q.v.10]. Although the Menzies government came close to defeat in the Federal general election in December, the Liberal Party lost comparatively few votes in Victoria. Party pundits and the press attributed Menzies' survival to the popularity of the Victorian premier, who now became a national figure.

In 1962 the standard-gauge railway from Melbourne to Albury was completed. The government legislated for Victoria's second and third universities, Monash (opened 1961) and La Trobe (opened 1967). Senior technical colleges were upgraded by the founding in 1965 of the Victoria Institute of Colleges. The completion of the La Trobe Library (1965) and the first stage of the Victorian Arts Centre (1968) had their origins in Bolte's 1955 campaign speech. Support was provided to provincial museums and galleries, and to William Ricketts, whose sculptures interested Jill Bolte.

Although the LCP's vote increased overall in the general election of June 1964, Bolte's victory came with the loss of one seat. Facing severe financial constraints, he proposed increased rail fares and freight charges and, in effect, a State income tax. But the government's briefly held Upper House majority disappeared following a by-election in October. When the CP threatened to combine with Labor to block supply, Bolte dropped his tax plan and the proposed increases in charges, and agreed to remove the words 'and Country' from the LCP's title. He also promised a redistribution (1965), which did away with the 2 for 1 principle and restored the favourable position of rural districts.

Bolte's deficits continued (1964, 1966 and 1968-70) and poor treatment by the Commonwealth became a standard complaint in his annual budget speech. With Menzies' support, he negotiated a deal for the supply of natural gas from the offshore Gippsland Basin, claiming that he and Menzies had gained the 'fuel bargain of the century'. Local supplies of oil and gas stimulated Victorian petroleum and petrochemical industries. In 1966 Bolte was appointed KCMG. An avowed monarchist, he went to London for the investiture at Buckingham Palace on 24 May and afterwards held court himself at the Hyde Park Hotel.

The Racing (Totalizators Extension) Act 1960 had legalised off-course betting. Bolte also favoured the liberalisation of trading hours for shops and hotels. (Sir) Philip Phillips's [q.v.15] report on the licensing laws, as expected, recommended ending the requirement that hotels close at 6 p.m. Bolte manoeuvred to change the Liberal Party's policy that the matter should be decided by referendum, and from 1 February 1966 hotels were permitted to remain open until 10 p.m. In 1965 a limit of .05 per cent blood-alcohol content had been set for motorists. From 1970 they and their passengers were compelled to wear seat-belts.

On other issues Bolte was a conservative brake. He opposed relaxing laws on abortion, censorship and sexual behaviour, favoured stiffer penalties for violent crimes, and advocated the death penalty. Nevertheless, his government had commuted fifteen sentences of death before refusing in 1962 to do so in the case of Robert Tait, a psychopathic and brutal killer. To allow consideration of submissions that Tait was insane, the High Court intervened and effectively thwarted Bolte. Despite this rebuff, his leadership was strengthened and his views were unchanged.

On 12 December 1966 cabinet decided not to commute the sentence of death imposed on Ronald Ryan [q.v.16] for killing a prison warder. Bolte's view was that the public's guardians had to be safeguarded and that there were no mitigating circumstances. Public and media opposition made the case one of national and international interest and Bolte complained about personal attacks on him. Tension increased as successive appeals failed. Ryan was hanged at 8 a.m. on 3 February 1967. A journalist asked Bolte what he was doing at the time. He retorted: 'One of the three Ss, I suppose'. When asked what he meant, he replied: 'A shit, a shave or a shower'.

The Liberal Party won the general election in April 1967 but not control of the Upper House. Although Bolte's leadership was under no challenge, he now had back-bench critics in the party room. Labor's new leader, Clyde Holding, promised a more combative approach. Drought and metropolitan water restrictions reminded people of Bolte's boast in 1964 that not 'one drop' of water would be taken from north of the Great Dividing Range to augment

Melbourne's supply. Inner city residents protested at the Housing Commission's forced evacuations and high-rise redevelopments, and the National Trust bemoaned the destruction of the city's heritage. Teachers, university students, do-gooders, unionists, anti-Vietnam War protesters and the *Age* newspaper opposed the government; all were the butt of Bolte's jibes at his morning press conferences. Fewer decisions were announced in parliament and the party room. The premier's homespun quips crystallised both his and his government's stance on many issues: 'More important than pollution of the air, soil and water is pollution of the mind'. 'Quality of life? It's peace of mind based on a home and garden'.

Bolte tried to prevent (Sir) John Gorton's election as federal Liberal leader in January 1968, mainly because of the latter's centralist views. Gorton soon roused Bolte's ire when he rejected Victoria's new 'stamps duty' as an income tax. Bolte was outraged at the premiers' conference in February 1970 when a decision was taken in his absence and Gorton reputedly vetoed an extra $35 million the Treasury had allocated to the States. After Gorton relinquished the leadership in March 1971, Bolte claimed that he had persuaded three Victorian Liberals to vote against Gorton. (Sir) William McMahon [q.v.] was elected and in June handed the States additional funds and allowed them to levy payroll tax, the proceeds from which enabled Bolte to balance his budget.

Staged election eve photographs of Bolte posing with local workmen, shearing, drinking in the local hotel, swimming in his dam at a time of drought, or kissing his aged mother, revealed no sense of self-parody. He could be ingenuous to a degree some found refreshing, others shocking. In 1968 he had said of militant schoolteachers: 'They can strike till they're black in the face. It won't make any difference'. The Liberals lost the seat of Dandenong at a by-election in December 1969 with a 10 per cent swing and suddenly Bolte looked vulnerable. A factor in the defeat was the scheme of the minister for lands, Sir William McDonald, to settle the Little Desert. Critics had challenged the viability of farming this marginal land. The government's back-down in December was a notable victory for environmentalists.

Opening his campaign for the 1970 general election, Bolte recited his government's achievements: prosperity for all, increased home ownership, industrial development, jobs and improvements in education. He now promised more national parks, environmental protection and a start on the Melbourne underground railway. The leader of the CP, George Moss, had derided Bolte's 'city-based financial henchmen' and indicated that his party's second preferences would go to the ALP at the election. But Labor's chances were damaged when the State executive overruled

Holding's support for the federal policy on state aid to non-government schools. At the election on 30 May the Liberals lost only two seats and gained control of the Upper House for the first time in six years.

Bolte planned to retire, like Menzies, with his party ascendant and a chosen successor in place. He made his last, and typically dramatic, political gesture in April 1972, when his government intervened legislatively to prevent for the time being a takeover of Ansett Transport Industries Ltd by Thomas Nationwide Transport Ltd. Support for his friend Sir Reginald Ansett [q.v.] was an evident motive but Bolte was also acting to protect a Melbourne-based company from a predatory Sydney raider. Criticism at this stage was irrelevant. On 10 July Bolte told cabinet of his intention to resign and he did so officially on 23 August. He was appointed GCMG that year but, despite his intense lobbying, failed in a campaign to be elevated to the peerage. His wife was appointed DBE in 1973; 'two working, one on the payroll', was Sir Henry's description of their partnership.

In retirement Bolte joined the boards of Australian companies and became a committeeman of the Victoria Racing Club and a trustee of the Melbourne Cricket Ground. The policies of the Whitlam government aroused his hostility and he flirted with an extreme right-wing organisation, People Against Communism. After 1982 Liberals in the Opposition would trek to Bamganie, whisky bottle in hand, seeking consolation and advice. (Sir) Joh Bjelke-Petersen, the premier of Queensland, adopted his political style and befriended him, but was unable to gain Bolte's endorsement of his prime-ministerial ambitions.

On 24 March 1984 the car Bolte was driving collided with another vehicle on a country road near his property and he suffered serious injuries. While he was in intensive care in hospital, the blood sample taken from him after the crash was switched by an unknown person who possibly thought it contained excessive alcohol, requiring Bolte's prosecution. No charges were laid. The sudden death of Dame Edith in 1986 affected him deeply. A compulsive talker to the last, he reminisced to journalists and to Mel Pratt for the National Library of Australia. Bolte died on 4 January 1990 at home and was cremated. A state memorial service was held at St Paul's Cathedral, Melbourne. His collection of memorabilia was left to Sovereign Hill, Ballarat.

According to Lindsay Thompson, Bolte had 'a warm natural manner and large expressive eyes which gave one an almost disconcertingly direct gaze'. He never allowed himself to be 'drowned in detail', rarely took files home and instead concentrated on 'issues that really mattered ... overall economic development, the attracting of big investors, early budgetary planning and major strategy for a forthcoming election'. Ministers were left to run their departments provided they kept within budgetary limits. He was 'a firm chairman [of cabinet] who insisted on members being concise and relevant'; once made, a cabinet decision was solid.

Although politics were Bolte's life, his pleasures and tastes were those of an ordinary Australian male of his time. He smoked, drank, followed sport, owned racehorses and bet on the races. Unlike his counterpart in New South Wales, Robin (Sir Robert) Askin [q.v.], whom he distrusted, he was never the subject of rumours of personal corruption. He admired Menzies but had little in common with him, save enjoyment of political success. A 'man's man', he nevertheless enjoyed time with his wife and went back to his farm at weekends.

Peter Blazey accurately represented Bolte as an accidental political leader given an easy run, a rural ingénue who justified the faith of hard-headed party organisers by maturing into a political ultra-realist and skilled tactician, whose drive, calculated appeals to the public, and refusal to be swayed by humanitarian motives, were his greatest strengths. Yet, despite his accomplishments, he 'lacked a developed philosophy of social justice and had little awareness of the problems of the family man'. Moreover, he was combative, defensive and insecure when he felt his position was under challenge. The public showdown, with manufactured overtones of a crisis, was his method of asserting authority. But he could also be pliant and accommodating when it suited him. His dismissal and ridicule of opposition, while effective and often entertaining, did little to elevate public debate or understanding.

To affectionate supporters Bolte well understood the concerns and desires of the average Australian. He was an uncut diamond, a plain talker and a good and canny leader, able to deliver pithy phrases and chart the right course by means that were often unconventional. With his fierce chauvinism in Commonwealth-State financial matters, close personal relations with local business elites, tours overseas to drum up investment, conservative stance on moral issues and crime, sensitivity to rural and non-metropolitan voters, and devotion to sport, Bolte refined the political model of an Australian State premier. His achievement was a Victorian record of seventeen years in power, although he never won as much as 40 per cent of the primary vote.

K. West, *Power in the Liberal Party* (1965); M. Harris and G. Dutton (eds), *Sir Henry, Bjelke, Don Baby and Friends* (1971); P. Blazey, *Bolte: A Political Biography* (1972 and 1989 edns); B. Muir, *Bolte from Bamganie* (1973); J. M. Powell, *Watering the Garden State* (1989); L. Thompson, *I Remember* (1989); T. Prior, *Bolte by Bolte* (1990); R. Wright, *A People's Counsel* (1992); M. Richards, *The Hanged Man* (2002); *PD* (LA, Vic), 6 Mar 1990, p 17; *PD* (LC, Vic), 6 Mar 1990, p 1; *Age* (Melbourne), 1 May 1967, p 5, 5 Jan 1990, pp 2 and 6, 12 Oct 1991, p 6, 10 Aug 2003, p 1; *Bulletin*, 7 Nov 1978, p 41; *Times on Sunday*, 17 May 1987, p 16; M. Pratt, taped interview with Bolte (1976, NLA).   DAVID DUNSTAN

BOLTON, BEULAH ALICE (1888-1982), Bush Book Club secretary, was born on 10 November 1888 at Wagga Wagga, New South Wales, fifth and youngest child of native-born parents Alexander Thorley Bolton, auctioneer, and his wife Martha Elizabeth, née Devlin. The family moved to Sydney in 1890 and in 1902-07 she attended Sydney Church of England Girls' Grammar School, Darlinghurst, where she also taught in 1909-10; later she was president (1925-28) of the Old Girls' Union.

After briefly working as a relieving governess at Government House, Sydney, in June 1911 she was appointed part-time, salaried secretary of the Bush Book Club of New South Wales, which had vice-regal patronage. Replacing Mrs Ida Mary Withers, who had founded the club in September 1909 with the object of providing sound reading for country people, Miss Bolton kept the club going for the next forty years. In 1917 she became secretary of the newly formed State branch of the Victoria League, whose aim was to unite the Empire through good fellowship, to educate children, and to extend hospitality to overseas visitors. In the 1920s, with other notable, independent women, she also belonged to the Zonta Club of Sydney.

Beulah Bolton was a handmaiden to Sydney's social elite, reflecting its prevailing conservative, loyalist British views. During World War I she had supported conscription and the book club refused to accept Marian Harwood's [q.v.Supp.] pacifist publications. Miss Bolton regarded most politicians of the left as 'bounders'. In 1930 she took eight months' leave to holiday in Britain and Europe and to represent the State at the annual meeting of the Victoria League in London. In 1939 she was honorary secretary of the Women's Voluntary National Register. During World War II the Victoria League helped to house and entertain visiting naval officers. In 1947 she joined the executive committee of the Australian Women's Movement Against Socialisation. Following another trip to Europe in 1951, Miss Bolton fell out with the committee of the Bush Book Club and resigned in February 1952; she was made a life member. She stayed on as secretary of the New South Wales branch of the Victoria League until July 1961 and in 1959-62 also served as honorary secretary of the national committee. In January 1962 she was appointed MBE.

Miss Bolton lived with her family, first at Randwick, then at North Sydney, before moving to a wisteria-garlanded home, Kareela, at Hunters Hill, which she shared with her mother (d.1931) and three sisters. She travelled each day to town with her sisters Constance and Nelly, arranged the flowers in Nell's tea-room in Bligh Street, then walked up to her office nearby. She became a firm friend of Lady Gowrie [q.v.9]. Tiny, with firm views and uncompromising standards, she was described as 'quirky without being quaint'. She loved cricket, enjoyed a bet on the horses and was a member of the Macquarie Club. A. E. Housman was among her favourite poets. Following a third trip to Europe, and the death of her last sibling in 1964, she lived alone at Kareela. She died on 9 July 1982 in a nursing home at Gordon and was cremated.

M. Lyons and J. Arnold (eds), *A History of the Book in Australia 1891-1945* (2001); *SMH*, 8 Sept 1909, p 5, 6 Apr 1910, p 6, 13 Dec 1930, p 9, 13 July 1961, p 4; *Daily Telegraph* (Sydney), 19 May 1917, p 7, 25 July 1917, p 8; Bush Book Club of NSW papers and Vic League (NSW) papers (SLNSW); private information.   CHRIS CUNNEEN

BONEY, LLOYD JAMES (1959-1987), labourer and prisoner, was born on 23 December 1959 at Walgett, New South Wales, son of Aboriginal parents Thomas James Boney, rural labourer, and Margaret (Maria) Murray. His birth was registered under his mother's surname. After his parents separated, he was raised by his father's sister Priscilla Boney and her partner Arthur Hooper, a shearer, at Goodooga until 1978 and then on the Aboriginal reserve known as Barwon Four, near Brewarrina. Aborigines, who constituted half of the population of Brewarrina by the 1980s, had earlier been subject to racial residential segregation and continued to experience high levels of unemployment. Lloyd was one of sixteen children raised in the Hooper/Boney household, though he remained in contact with his father. He attended Goodooga Central School in 1966-74, but did not acquire sufficient literacy to write a letter. While still at school he was convicted of breaking, entering and stealing, and released on probation.

On leaving school, Boney was intermittently employed as a rural labourer. In 1978 he fell foul of the law again—first for stealing (for which he incurred a good behaviour bond), and later for illegal use of a motorcar (for which he was incarcerated in Bathurst gaol). By this time he had become a binge drinker, exacerbating his epilepsy and causing episodic admissions to hospitals in the region. He was an unwilling patient whose hospital stays sometimes required police intervention.

In the 1980s he faced court on charges resulting from violence, property damage, assaulting police, driving under the influence of alcohol, and minor theft. He was also frequently detained by police for being intoxicated. During his long-term relationship with Grace Wilson (who bore their son Kelvin in 1985), he was sometimes violent. In 1986 he spent several months in prison. While he was on probation, his troubled domestic life and abuse of alcohol continued. In January 1987 he was charged with wounding Grace and released on bail. When he breached his bail conditions in June 1987 (after Grace and another woman had made further allegations of assault), his arrest in Brewarrina was a violent encounter with two policemen. These policemen and one other arrested him (again for breach of bail) on 6 August.

Boney's life attracted public attention by the way it ended. He died on 6 August 1987 in Brewarrina sometime in the ninety-five minutes after he was locked up at the police station. Police said that they found his body suspended at the neck by a football sock. A coronial inquiry, held at Dubbo in February-December 1988, found that he died of asphyxia by hanging and made several recommendations for future police procedure. After his funeral and burial at Brewarrina cemetery on 15 August, a violent clash occurred between some of Brewarrina's Aboriginal residents and the police.

Boney's death was one of a series in the 1980s in which police were suspected of murder or, at best, manslaughter. In April 1989 the Commonwealth government appointed a royal commission into Aboriginal deaths in custody. The commissioner, Hal Wootten, in his 1991 report on Boney's life and death, found no case of homicide for the police to answer, but criticised them for failing to monitor their prisoner and for their subsequent insensitive dealings with his family. Wootten also suggested that Boney's troubled life and evident suicide typified the conditions of many contemporary Aboriginal Australians.

J. H. Wootten, *Report of the Inquiry into the Death of Lloyd James Boney* (1991); *SMH*, 10 Aug 1987, p 1, 17 Aug 1987, p 1.   TIM ROWSE

BONNIN, KATHLEEN PATRICIA (1911-1985), army nurse, was born on 17 March 1911 at Hindmarsh, Adelaide, second of seven surviving children of Australian-born parents James Atkinson Bonnin, medical practitioner, and his wife Winifred, née Turpin, a trained nurse. Kath was educated at Creveen School, North Adelaide. Four of her five brothers were to become medical practitioners, but while she expressed a desire to also enter the medical profession, it was deemed more appropriate that she train as a nurse.

Completing her training at Ru Rua Private Hospital, North Adelaide, Bonnin qualified as a registered nurse in 1936. Soon afterwards she travelled to London, where she attended a midwifery course at Queen Charlotte's Maternity Hospital, becoming a registered midwife in January 1938. As a double-certificated sister, she returned to Australia and joined the staff of Australian National Airways Pty Ltd as an air hostess.

On 15 July 1940 Bonnin began full-time duty as a sister in the Australian Army Nursing Service. She was appointed to the Australian Imperial Force on 12 August. Initially stationed at the 52nd Camp Hospital, Wayville, Adelaide, she sailed for the Middle East in February 1941 with the 2/7th Australian General Hospital. She was attached to the 2/1st AGH at Gaza Ridge, Palestine, in March-May and later assigned to transport duties. In December she was made sister, group I. She served with the 2/11th Field Ambulance at Tripoli, Syria, in April-July 1942 before rejoining the 2/7th AGH at Buseili, Egypt, where she nursed casualties from the battle of El Alamein. A senior sister from December, she attained the rank of captain in March 1943.

Back in Australia in February 1943, Bonnin was sent to Port Moresby in October. Her unit moved to Lae in February 1944. She worked tirelessly and cheerfully, observing that 'the boys were so glad to see us, and so grateful for what we did, that no one minded working long hours'. The nurses needed to retain a sense of humour, especially when they received 'visits from all sorts of creatures, including rats, centipedes, and spiders'. Bonnin found that living under such conditions created 'a spirit of camaraderie and friendship' that more than compensated for 'the loss of the comforts and amenities of a more civilized existence'. She was admitted to hospital a number of times after she acquired sandfly fever in the Middle East and dengue fever in New Guinea.

In December 1944 Bonnin returned to Australia and joined the 105th Military Hospital, Adelaide. She was awarded the Associate Royal Red Cross (1945) for her 'devotion to duty and outstanding ability' and was mentioned in despatches. When hostilities ceased, she was posted to the 2/14th AGH and sent to Singapore to nurse returning prisoners of war. She transferred to the Reserve of Officers on 10 January 1946. That year she represented South Australian army nurses at the Victory March in London.

Becoming a senior sister (1947-64) in the cardiac unit at Royal Adelaide Hospital, Bonnin developed an expertise in interpreting electrocardiographs. One of her lifelong pleasures was fishing and she reputedly had a high level of success in the sport. Suffering from multiple sclerosis, she died on 14 September 1985 in North Adelaide, and was cremated with Anglican rites.

SA Trained Nurses' Centenary Ctte, *Nursing in South Australia* (1946?); R. Goodman, *Our War Nurses* (1988); *Advertiser* (Adelaide), 16 Sept 1985, p 11; B883, item SFX500278 (NAA); private information.   RUTH RAE

BOOTH, KENNETH GEORGE (1926-1988), schoolteacher, sportsman and politician, was born on 23 February 1926 at Kurri Kurri, New South Wales, second child of George Booth, member of parliament, and his wife Annie Elizabeth, née Payne, both born in England. He was educated at Kurri Kurri Public School and Maitland Boys' High School. From 1944 to 1946 he attended Armidale and Sydney Teachers' colleges (Dip.Phys.Ed., 1946). After teaching at Cessnock High School (1947-49), he was seconded to work in physical education and national fitness at the newly created Murrumbidgee area office at Wagga Wagga. In 1951 he lectured at Sydney Teachers' College. He returned to the Hunter as student welfare officer (1952-60) at Newcastle Technical and Newcastle University colleges. On 23 January 1954 he married Irene Margaret Marshall (d.1979), a teacher, at Christ Church Cathedral, Newcastle, with Anglican rites.

Ken's father was an Australian Labor Party member of the New South Wales Legislative Assembly, representing Newcastle (1925-27) and Kurri Kurri (1927-60) and serving as chairman of committees (1941-59). Ken joined the party at 16 and, following his father's death, became member for Kurri Kurri (1960-68) and then for Wallsend from 1968 until his own death. Father and son served for sixty-three years in the Assembly.

On the election of Neville Wran's government in 1976, Booth became minister for sport, recreation and tourism, although in opposition he had been shadow minister for education. When administering the first autonomous department of sport and recreation in New South Wales, he implemented a capital grants program and became popular with sporting organisations throughout the State. In 1980 he became assistant-treasurer while retaining his other portfolios; the following year he was appointed treasurer. He introduced significant reforms in the State's finances, including program budgeting and reorganisation of the parliamentary public accounts committee. Many changes were embodied in the Public Finance and Audit Act (1983).

Part of the loose left-grouping in the ALP caucus, Booth was also friendly with other members from the Hunter region. Jack Ferguson, deputy premier (1976-84) and a close friend, wanted Booth to succeed him as ALP deputy-leader in the Assembly when he retired, but divisions within the party's factions led to the victory of Ron Mulock. After Labor's defeat in 1988, Booth was appointed shadow minister for energy and mineral resources.

Throughout his life Booth was an enthusiastic sportsman. He played first-grade soccer in the Hunter region and in Sydney, first-grade cricket at Kurri Kurri and A-grade basketball at Newcastle, as well as Rugby League, Rugby Union, tennis and hockey. In the Newcastle district he was involved in sports administration. He also served on the councils of the University of New South Wales (1962-65), Newcastle University College (1963-64) and the University of Newcastle (1965-74), and on the board of the Hunter Valley Research Foundation (1962-68). On 21 February 1982 Booth married Gail Mary Mathieson, née Haigh, an office executive and a divorcee, in a civil ceremony at Redfern. Survived by his wife and by the daughter of his first marriage, he died of myocardial infarction on the night of 31 October–1 November 1988 at his home at Glendale and was cremated. As the plaque at the Ken Booth Gymnastics Centre at Glendale notes, he was 'highly respected for his modesty, honesty, integrity and fairness'.

PD (NSW), 8 Nov 1988, p 2877; *Australian*, 2 Nov 1988, p 4; *Newcastle Herald*, 2 Nov 1988, p 1; *SMH*, 2 Nov 1988, p 12; private information and personal knowledge.   JAN BURNSWOODS

BOSISTO, GLYN DE VILLIERS (1899-1990), lawn bowler and bank manager, was born on 15 February 1899 at Gawler, South Australia, youngest of eight children of Glyn de Villiers Bosisto, stock holder and horse dealer, and his wife Anna Letitia, née Davis, both born in South Australia. The Bosistos were of Cornish background and also had Welsh, Huguenot and Spanish forebears. Educated at Gawler District High School, young Glyn joined the National Bank of Australasia Ltd at age 16.

The family moved to Adelaide, where Bosisto senior won seven club titles for lawn bowls. Father and son practised on the Prospect club's green but at that stage tennis, golf and football appealed more to the younger man. Transferred to the country, he captained Kadina's Australian Rules football team and led a Yorke Pensinsula side against the Adelaide Metropolitan second XVIII. On 27 October 1928 at the Methodist Church, Kadina, he married Audrey Vida Winifred Davies (d.1986); she was later a keen bowls player and administrator.

After the bank transferred Bosisto to Melbourne in 1932, he took up competitive bowls, becoming the singles champion of the Glen Iris club in 1933-34. The bank moved him to Sydney in 1935. He won the singles title of the North Sydney club once and that of the City club seven times. In 1941 he was the skipper of the successful fours at the Metropolitan and State championships. Sent back to Melbourne in 1948, he joined the Victoria Bowling Club, where he was singles title holder in 1948-49 and (following a break with the Auburn club) 1954-56. He retired from the bank in 1955 as manager of the Western branch, Collins Street, and subsequently worked in insurance. Losing a vice-presidential election at the Victoria in 1956, he moved to the Kew club next year. Later he played for Camberwell and Auburn Heights.

Bosisto created so many records that he was dubbed the (Sir Donald) 'Bradman of bowls'. He won an unprecedented four successive Australian singles titles from 1949 and achieved another two national championships as skipper of fours in 1951 and 1957. In all, he won fifty-five major singles contests including five Victorian and seven Victorian champion of champions. He represented Australia, New South Wales and Victoria 256 times. At 67 he was considered too old to play against the top English player David Bryant, aged 35, but he defeated Bryant 21-17 in one exhibition match and led 9-6 when a second was abandoned. Bosisto achieved less success at the British Empire Games: he was selected for but unable to attend the Auckland games (1950) and found the greens in Vancouver (1954) too bumpy and those in Cardiff (1958) too heavy for his touch bowling.

A perfectionist, Bosisto never talked to an opponent during a game so that his 'intense, unsmiling concentration' was interpreted by some as surliness. He consulted frequently with greenkeepers to ensure the best possible playing surface. While his bowling style was unattractive, it was effective and honed by years of practice. He disapproved of bowlers who imbibed often during a match and commented: 'I will never understand why the absence of a bar should have ruled out play on the best greens at the Cardiff Empire Games'.

In 1977 Bosisto was appointed MBE and in 1985 inducted into the Sport Australia Hall of Fame. He published two books, *Bowling Along* (1963) and *Bowls by Bosisto* (1983), and raised money for charity through lectures and exhibition games. Reluctant to gain financial benefit from his name, he often coached in an honorary capacity. He died on 16 December 1990 at Centennial House, Royal Freemasons Home, Windsor, and was cremated. His daughter survived him, as did his son, Jon, who represented Victoria at bowls.

J. Pollard (ed), *Lawn Bowls—The Australian Way* (1962); J. Senyard, *The Tartan on University Square* (2001); *Bowls*, Sept 1975, p 16; *Age* (Melbourne), 22 Jan 1980, p 26.   R. I. CASHMAN

BOSTOCK, JOHN (1892-1987), psychiatrist, was born on 20 January 1892 at Glasgow, Scotland, son of Ralph Harry Frank Bostock, medical student, and his wife Helene Josephine, née Lambert. Growing up 'in a happy family with hard working parents' in Yorkshire, where his father was in general practice, John attended Scarborough College, and was to identify himself always as a Yorkshireman. He studied medicine at the London Hospital Teaching College, University of London (MB, BS, 1914). On 6 August 1914 he was appointed temporary surgeon, Royal Navy; he served at Gallipoli and in the Mediterranean and Atlantic before being demobilised in 1919. Back in London, he trained for a postgraduate diploma in psychological medicine awarded (1920) by the Medico-Psychological Association. On 17 January that year he married in Romania Anne Marie Stefenescu, whom he had met while on active service. They were to have two daughters and a son before being divorced.

Migrating to Australia in 1922, Bostock took up a post in Perth at the Hospital for the Insane, Claremont. Next year he moved to Sydney, and enjoyed a stimulating working environment at Callan Park Mental Hospital before becoming superintendent at Newcastle Mental Hospital in 1926. He wrote sixteen papers describing and classifying the physical and psychiatric illnesses of patients whom he treated in 1922-27. From 1927 he lived in Brisbane, working in private practice until 1953 as a specialist in nervous and mental disorders. He held honorary appointments at Brisbane and Mater Misericordiae Public hospitals, and with the War Pensions Assessment Appeal Tribunal. He and Dr L. J. Jarvis Nye put both their personal assets and their professional reputations 'on the line' to found (1930) the Brisbane Clinic, Wickham Terrace, a co-operative practice of specialists. In 1935 he was a member of the royal commission whose report damned Sister Elizabeth Kenny's [q.v.9] treatment of infantile paralysis. He voiced conservative social and political views about race and Australia's 'national decline', and with Nye published *Whither Away?* (1934) and *The Way Out* (1939).

In 1940 Bostock was appointed research professor of medical psychology at the University of Queensland. He established a child guidance clinic at the Hospital for Sick Children, Brisbane. In World War II he wrote leaflets for the Australian Army Education Service. He enjoyed lecturing and developed an innovative method of teaching psychology to medical students, using comics and cartoons to illustrate common psychological mechanisms. His major research interests were the history of Australian psychiatry— he wrote *The Dawn of Australian Psychiatry* (1951)—and the emotional and psychological needs and disorders of children. Enuresis (bedwetting) was a particular concern. Publishing widely, he collaborated with the kindergarten director Edna Hill in *The Pre-school Child and Society* (1946) and *Personality Deviations Occurring in Children of Pre-school Age* (1949). He gave many public lectures, talks and broadcasts on mental hygiene, alcoholism, child care and education, and published pamphlets giving advice on healthy living.

Bostock was a founding fellow in 1938 of the Royal Australian College of Physicians and in 1946 of the Australasian Association of Psychiatrists (Royal Australian and New Zealand College of Psychiatrists); he served as president of the AAP in 1948. He was president of the Royal Society of Queensland (1943) and of the Crèche and Kindergarten Association of Queensland (1943-44), chairman (1957-68) of the Lady Gowrie [q.v.9] Child Centre, president of the Australian-American Association and a supporter of the (Royal) Historical Society of Queensland.

Known as 'J. B.', Bostock was tall and austere, but sociable. He valued the friendship of other medical practitioners; William Forgan Smith [q.v.11] was also a close friend. Nevertheless, he could be intensely private and, according to Jarvis Nye's son John, 'hard to get to know, reserved and thoughtful', but 'warm and caring' with children. Retiring from his university post in 1962, he maintained a wide range of hobbies and pastimes, including fly fishing, boating, lawn bowls, gardening and stamp collecting, all of which, as in his professional life, he pursued with vigour. He had told his patients 'the one thing that matters is that you should have a passion for something'. On 1 March 1947 at St Andrew's Scots Church, Rose Bay, Sydney, he had married with Presbyterian forms Alice Dulcie Trout, a stenographer and sister of (Sir) Leon Trout [q.v.16]. Survived by his wife, and the three children from his first marriage, he died on 26 September 1987 at Clayfield, Brisbane, and was cremated with Anglican rites. In 1988 the psychiatry ward at Royal Brisbane Hospital was named after him.

R. L. Doherty (ed), *A Medical School for Queensland* (1986); J. H. Pearn, *Focus and Innovation* (1986); J. H. Tyrer, *History of the Brisbane Hospital and Its Affiliates* (1993); *MJA*, 5/19 Dec 1988, p 695; *Austn & NZ Jnl of Psychiatry*, vol 22, 1988, p 116; Bostock papers (Univ of Qld Lib); personal information.
                                        TOM O'BRIEN

BOTH, EDWARD THOMAS (1908-1987), inventor, was born on 26 April 1908 at Caltowie, South Australia, eldest of five children of South Australian-born parents James Alexander Both, miller, and his wife Lucy Victoria, née Thomas. He was educated at Caltowie Public and Jamestown High schools. A very able student, he became a technical assistant to (Sir) Kerr Grant [q.v.9], professor of physics at the University of Adelaide.

In 1932 Both built an electrocardiograph which attracted attention from leading Adelaide physicians. Grant, impressed with Both's abilities, set up a small medical equipment development and production facility, using rooms in the old mounted police barracks adjoining the university. That year Both's younger brother Donald joined the enterprise; together they were to produce a wide range of scientific instruments, including several versions of the electrocardiograph. Generating exceptionally accurate recordings, the machines allowed instant diagnosis and until 1942 were the only direct-wiring models marketed in the world. On 16 September 1937 at Christ Church, Essendon, Melbourne, Ted married with Anglican rites Lily Eileen Maud Naughton, a schoolteacher.

During the 1937-38 poliomyelitis epidemic Both designed a simple inexpensive respirator to replace an American 'iron lung' prototype, which was cumbersome and costly. Working day and night for a week he produced a portable model of laminated wood, known as a cabinet respirator, and the brothers began manufacturing. Machines were sometimes used by patients within an hour of production. Visiting England in 1938-39 during another poliomyelitis epidemic, Both produced some respirators in London and attracted the attention of Lord Nuffield, who financed the assembly of 1700 machines at the Morris car factory, Cowley, and donated them to hospitals throughout the British Empire. Appointed OBE in 1941, Both gained the popular title of 'Australia's Edison'. That year the brothers established Both Electrics Ltd.

In World War II Both worked on projects supported by the Army Inventions Directorate, producing medical equipment for the armed forces, and inventing instruments for the production and testing of armaments, including an electromicrometer (used to check the bore of a gun), cloth-cutting machines for army uniforms, and three-wheeled battery-operated vehicles. He helped with research into guided torpedoes, and designed and patented the 'visitel', an instrument that could transmit designs or drawings over long distances by wire or radio. It was a forerunner of the facsimile machine.

After the war Both moved to Sydney, where he set up a branch of the business (Both Equipment Ltd from 1952) and worked in association with Automatic Totalisators Ltd. The Boths designed an electric tennis scoreboard for use at the Davis Cup competition, held in Adelaide in 1952. Their scoreboards were subsequently used for the Melbourne Olympic Games (1956) and other major events. Other types of equipment developed were an automatic pen recorder, a humidicrib, foetal heart monitors and an electroencephalograph. In 1966 the brothers sold their firm to Drug Houses of Australia Ltd; they worked in DHA's Anax division until retiring in 1974. A quiet-living man, 'ET' Both was known for his total preoccupation with design problems and his exhausting capacity for work. He was a sports enthusiast who enjoyed swimming and playing tennis. Survived by his wife, he died on 18 November 1987 at Mount Beauty, Victoria, and was cremated. The couple had no children.

M. J. Both (comp), *The Both Family Story* (1981); *Austn Jnl of Instrumentation and Control*, Aug 1986, p 14, Dec 1988, p 15; *Advertiser* (Adelaide), 24 Nov 1987, p 15; private information.   PAULINE PAYNE

BOURCHIER, MURRAY GOULBURN MADDEN (1925-1981), diplomat, was born on 28 March 1925 at St Kilda, Melbourne, second of three children of Victorian-born parents (Sir) Murray William James Bourchier [q.v.7], grazier and politician, and his wife Minona Francis, née Madden. Sir Frank Madden was his grandfather; Sir John and Walter Madden were his great-uncles; and J. G. Francis [qq.v.10,4] was his great-grandfather. Educated at Geelong Church of England Grammar School and the Gordon Institute of Technology, young Murray enlisted in the Militia on 29 March 1943. He transferred to the Australian Imperial Force on 25 April and saw active service with the 2/16th Battalion in Borneo in 1945 before being discharged on 18 October 1946. He was then six feet (183 cm) tall with auburn hair and blue eyes. Next year he entered the University of Melbourne (LL B, 1951). On 8 December 1951 at Holy Advent Church of England, Malvern, he married Charlotte Ray Francis, a nurse.

In January 1951 Bourchier had joined the Department of External Affairs. A colleague remembered him as 'shy' with 'a rather abrupt way of speaking' and a 'quiet wit'. He studied Russian, but the hiatus in relations between Australia and the Soviet Union after the defection of the Petrovs in 1954 prevented him from serving in Moscow until 1965-68. In the meantime he served in London (1954-57) and in Colombo (1959-62), where he spent thirteen months as acting high commissioner and from which he was detached to act as high commissioner in Accra for two months. These responsible appointments in hardship posts marked his department's confidence not only in himself, but in the resilience and adaptability of his wife Ray.

Bourchier's first appointment as head of mission was to Seoul in 1971-75. It turned out to be a taxing assignment, calling on all his inner strengths of calmness and imperturbability. When Prime Minister Gough Whitlam suddenly decided to recognise the Democratic People's Republic of (North) Korea in 1973, the reaction of the president of the Republic of (South) Korea, Park Chung-hee, was sharp. Australia was the first of the sixteen countries that had provided forces to the United Nations during the Korean War to recognise the DPRK. Bourchier rode out the initial storm and loyally and effectively put the government's case for dialogue with the North. Political relations, which the South Koreans had threatened to downgrade, and trade promotion were kept on an even keel.

Promoted to first assistant secretary in charge of the department's legal and treaties division in 1976, Bourchier achieved his career ambition of being appointed ambassador to Moscow in 1977, succeeding Sir James Plimsoll [q.v.]. In his previous posting to Moscow, Bourchier had served as deputy to Australia's leading Sovietologist John Rowland, but Australia's role as a belligerent in the Vietnam War had limited what they could achieve. In 1977 bilateral relations were again under strain because of Prime Minister Malcolm Fraser's strongly anti-Soviet stance. It was to Bourchier's credit that Fraser considered a visit to the Soviet Union before it was ruled out by the invasion of Afghanistan. Bourchier was also accredited to Mongolia and enjoyed visiting Ulan Bator. In 1979 he was medically evacuated to London, where he was found to be suffering from a brain tumour. He relinquished his post in August 1980.

A member of the Royal Automobile Club, London, Bourchier listed his recreations as literature and fishing. In 1981 he was appointed AO. He died of a cerebral tumour on 3 July that year in his home at Deakin, Canberra, and was cremated; his wife and their two daughters and three sons survived him.

Austn Foreign Affairs Record, vol 48, no 8, 1977, p 434; *Canberra Times*, 5 July 1981, p 3; *Corian*, Apr 1982, p 83; A6119, item 737, B883, item VX141174 (NAA); private information.   GARRY WOODARD

BOURKE, JOHN MOUNTFORT (1916-1987), public servant, was born on 12 May 1916 at Petersham, Sydney, son of Richard Joseph Bourke, a tram driver born in New South Wales, and his Melbourne-born wife Cecilia, née Mountfort. Educated at De La Salle College, Ashfield, John completed the Leaving certificate in 1934. He took up an appointment with the New South Wales Department of (Works and) Local Government in October 1935. In 1937 he became secretary of the relief works regulation committee. He was later acting-secretary of the local committee of the Department of Labour and Industry and Social Services tradesmen training scheme.

Called up for full-time duty in the Militia on 4 December 1941, Bourke transferred to the Royal Australian Air Force on 22 April 1942 and trained as a telegraphist. He served in signals and radar units in northern Queensland from 1942 to 1944, and was discharged on 24 September 1945 as a temporary corporal. He resumed his public service career, moving to the Housing Commission of New South Wales, of which he became secretary in 1950. He also returned to the University of Sydney (B.Ec., 1949; Diploma of Town and Country Planning, 1951), where he had begun to study economics and public administration part time in 1936.

Bourke's time at the helm of the Housing Commission coincided with the formative years of Australian housing policy. In the immediate postwar period policy was directed at meeting pent-up demand from both returned servicemen and low-income groups, although policy makers were divided between supporting renters and assisting struggling home buyers. At first Commonwealth-State housing agreements directed Federal funding to bolster State rental housing stock, but after 1956 also assisted home buyers, the aim being to curb what the Menzies [q.v.15] coalition government saw as the rise of state landlordism. Between the mid-1950s and the early 1970s State governments of all political persuasions 'sold off' public housing stock in preference to supplying inexpensive rental properties.

From 1958 Bourke oversaw an expanding housing construction program. Remembering his own working-class origins, he was sympathetic to the plight of the 'battlers'. He helped to steer the commission away from austere paternalism and towards a dignified variety in the location and design of dwellings. The program ranged from ambitious housing estates on the outer fringes of Sydney—such as Green Valley—to the first tentative steps towards urban consolidation via slum clearance in inner city areas. By the early 1970s New South Wales faced a severe shortage of public rental housing, fuelled by a combination of the legacy of the Commonwealth-State housing agreements and spiralling land and building construction costs. Long convinced that rental assistance was more effective (and equitable) than home buyer support, in the years after his elevation to chairman in September 1970 Bourke expressed his views freely to the press in an attempt to angle housing policy in this direction, often to the annoyance of the Askin [q.v.] government, which gagged him in 1972 after he had spoken publicly about the housing plight of low-income earners.

By 1973, however, the Housing Commission was increasingly under attack for its overly 'bureaucratic' approach to managing public housing programs. The advent of both 'resident action groups' and trade union 'green bans', particularly those opposed to high-rise development in Woolloomooloo and Redfern-Waterloo, drew press attention to the commission. For Bourke such activism was an unfortunate by-product of 'gentrification' in inner-city areas, and while he resented the adverse impact on the commission's clients, he did ensure that community consultation occurred. By the time he retired in May 1981, he was seen as both a thorn in the side of organised residential protest and a staunch defender of the value of public housing.

Urban design issues and the quality of public housing administration loomed large in Bourke's life. He was a councillor of the Australian Institute of Urban Studies and a member of the Civic Design Society of New South Wales, and was elected to fellowships of the Royal Australian Planning Institute and the Australian Society of Senior Executives. At his own expense he travelled to many countries to investigate housing problems. In 1979 he was appointed ISO. Almost six feet (183 cm) tall and bald in middle age, he was described by a journalist as an 'emotional, generous man, capable of formidable toughness'. Affectionately known as 'Jack', he never married. He died of coronary artery disease sometime between 9 and 11 May 1987 in his home at Petersham, and was buried in the Catholic section of Rookwood cemetery.

Annual Report of the Housing Commission of NSW, 1960-81; *SMH*, 27 Sept 1955, p 2, 11 July 1972, p 1, 12 July 1972, p 1, 26 July 1972, p 1, 27 July 1972, p 3, 19 Feb 1973, p 3, 12 July 1973, p 7, 2 Nov 1973, p 6; *Sun-Herald*, 20 Sept 1970, p 106; *Sun* (Sydney), 31 Mar 1976, p 7.   MICHAEL DI FRANCESCO

BOURKE, MILES (1925-1982), farmer and organiser of primary producers, was born on 20 November 1925 at Warracknabeal, Victoria, second son of Michael Thomas Bourke, farmer, and his wife Lucy, née Powell, both born in Victoria. The Bourkes grew wheat and grazed sheep in the Areegra district between Donald and Warracknabeal, and Miles attended the local one-teacher primary school. He progressed to Donald Higher Elementary School (boarding during the week) then to Ballarat Church of England Grammar School, where he did well academically and at sport.

In 1939 Bourke's father died. His mother ran the farm with the help of hired labour and he joined her when he left school in December 1942. Through hard work and perseverance, they prospered. On 15 July 1953 at Canterbury Presbyterian Church, Melbourne, Miles married Ida Jean Brewster. He was a councillor (1955-76) and president (1959 and 1967) of Warracknabeal Shire, a member of Apex, a lay reader in the Church of England, a Freemason and a member of the Victorian Soil Conservation Authority's Northern Wimmera district advisory committee.

Active in the Victorian Wheat and Woolgrowers' Association, Bourke was elected to the State executive in 1963. This somewhat militant, non-party pressure group represented wheat growers and small wool producers, and became a rival of the Graziers' Association of Victoria, which bigger pastoralists dominated. Bourke was a member of the VWWGA's committees on bulk handling and on finance and administration. He was also a director of Farrer House Ltd, a company set up to rebuild the association's headquarters in Melbourne. The State government appointed him to the Wheat Advisory Committee and the Victorian Wheat Research Foundation. In 1965 he was gazetted a growers' representative on the Victorian Grain Elevators Board. He was elected to the Australian Wheat Board and appointed to the International Labour Organisation's advisory committee on rural development in 1974. Two years later he became senior vice-president of the Australian Wheatgrowers' Federation.

Earlier, Bourke's easy personality and negotiating skills had assisted efforts to amalgamate the VWWGA with the Victorian division of the Australian Primary Producers' Union to form the Victorian Farmers' Union; the merger took place in July 1968. As senior vice-president of the VFU, in the late 1970s he took a leading part in discussions with the Graziers' Association of Victoria and the United Dairyfarmers of Victoria, which were aimed at further unifying primary industry. These endeavours resulted in the formation in 1979 of the Victorian Farmers and Graziers Association (later renamed the Victorian Farmers' Federation).

Bourke's popularity with all parties led to his election as the first president of the new body. The position was demanding but he gave his time and energy without stint, travelling long distances to meetings. Drought added greatly to his workload in 1982. After collapsing at a wheat board meeting, he died of a dissecting aneurysm on 13 October 1982 in South Melbourne and was buried in Warracknabeal cemetery. His funeral was probably the largest ever seen in the town. A memorial service was held in a packed St Paul's Cathedral, Melbourne. Bourke was survived by his wife and their son and daughter. A wide circle of friends and colleagues remembered him with affection for his wit, humour and warm humanity. He was a wise and dedicated leader who did much to mould disparate factions into a united primary producers' organisation.

G. H. Mitchell (comp and ed), *Growers in Action* (1969); *Age* (Melbourne), 15 Oct 1982, p 5; Ballarat Grammar School records; Victorian Farmers' Federation records (Melbourne); private information and personal knowledge.

CAMPBELL CURTIS

BOURKE, WILLIAM MESKILL (1913-1981), lawyer and politician, was born on 2 June 1913 at North Carlton, Melbourne, son of William Bourke, boot clicker, and his wife Eileen Norah, née Meskill, both Melbourne born. Bill attended the Christian Brothers' school at Middle Park and St Kevin's College, East Melbourne. While studying at the University of Melbourne (BA Hons, 1934; MA, LL B, 1936), where he had a Newman College scholarship, he joined the National Trustees, Executors & Agency Co. of Australasia Ltd as a clerk. He was admitted to practise as a barrister and solicitor on 1 March 1938.

On 11 March 1942 Bourke enlisted in the Australian Imperial Force. He underwent artillery training before being posted to First Army headquarters, Toowoomba, Queensland, in May 1943. Promoted to corporal in January 1944, he was discharged on compassionate grounds on 1 March. At Newman College chapel on 14 July 1945 he married with Catholic rites Nancy Honor Maria Hanrahan, a schoolteacher. He worked as a solicitor in South Melbourne, the city and finally Prahran, while assisting his family's dry-cleaning firm, Bancrofts Pty Ltd. With his educated, well-to-do background, he was an atypical Labor candidate when he stood unsuccessfully for three State and Federal elections in 1946-48. On 10 December 1949 he won the House of Representatives seat of Fawkner. He was one of a new group of right-wing Victorians that included S. M. Keon [q.v.] and J. M. Mullens.

Bourke was an active member of parliament. A 'tall, reserved man', he shone as one of the few Labor intellectuals, speaking in his 'characteristic pained monotone' and showing so little emotion that he 'might have been reading a railway timetable'. He concentrated on economic and international issues. Although not a 'grouper' or a member of the Catholic Social Studies Movement, in his anti-communism Bourke displayed a rigidity of thought that helped to push the Australian Labor Party into its wilderness years. His running 'dead' in the 1951 referendum to proscribe communism was later used against him by the Labor left, as was his apparently having originally sought Country Party preselection.

Gradually Bourke became disillusioned with the Labor leader Dr H. V. Evatt [q.v.14]. He publicly opposed Evatt's pledge to remove the means test from pensions; he was disturbed by his erratic leadership; and he shared colleagues' concerns over the leader's 'softness' on communism. Bourke, Keon and Mullens were soon Evatt's main right-wing caucus critics. Years later it was revealed that Bourke was a key source for media stories about Labor's internal troubles.

On 22 September 1954 Bourke stunned caucus when he described Evatt as the communists' 'greatest asset'. In retaliation, on 5 October Evatt attacked 'the Movement', as well as the disloyalty of 'a small minority group of Labor members, located particularly in Victoria'. He subsequently named Keon, Mullens and Bourke as members who were grossly disloyal. Expelled from the party in April 1955, Bourke and six Victorian colleagues formed the Australian Labor Party (Anti-Communist), (Democratic Labor Party from 1957). For the remainder of his term he attacked 'the pathetic state' of the ALP, 'corroded and corrupted and split by Evattism'.

In the 1955 election Bourke led his ALP opponent and received most of his preferences, but lost to Peter Howson, the Liberal Party candidate, by 1757 votes. Bourke was defeated by much more in 1958 and slipped away from the political stage, though in 1959 and 1960 he publicly attacked B. A. Santamaria for attempting to control the DLP. In 1968 he ceased to practise law. He purchased a farm at Jamieson, which he ran with a son. His recreations included horse-riding in the bush, growing Australian plants and collecting Australian paintings for his substantial Toorak home. Survived by his wife, and their three daughters and two sons, he died of cancer on 22 May 1981 at Fitzroy and was buried in Melbourne general cemetery.

T. Truman, *Catholic Action and Politics* (1960); R. Murray, *The Split* (1970); D. Connell, *The Confessions of Clyde Cameron 1913-1990* (1990); R. Manne, *The Shadow of 1917* (1994); H. Myers, *The Whispering Gallery* (1999); *PD* (HR), 20 Apr 1955, p 37, 18 May 1955, p 861; B883, item VX73912 (NAA); private information.   SCOTT BENNETT

BOWRING, WILLIAM BRUCE (1916-1987), army officer and businessman, was born on 6 September 1916 at Mildura, Victoria, second child of Australian-born parents William James Bowring, merchant, and his wife Renee Elsie, née King. Educated, to matriculation, at Mildura High School and Wesley College,

Melbourne, young William entered the family business, William Bowring & Co. Pty Ltd, general merchants of Mildura, and of Wentworth, New South Wales. Commissioned as a lieutenant in the Militia in October 1937, he was promoted to captain in February 1940. At St John's Church of England, East Malvern, Melbourne, on 3 April that year he married Beryl Annetta Hill, a hairdresser.

On 4 July 1940 Bowring transferred to the Australian Imperial Force. Six ft 2½ ins (189 cm) tall, with a fair complexion, brown eyes and brown hair, he was posted to the 2/29th Battalion and made officer commanding 'C' Company. Arriving in Singapore in August 1941, the battalion trained and prepared defensive positions in the southern Malayan state of Johore. By mid-January 1942 the invading Japanese force had reached the northern border of Johore.

From 17 January the 2/29th Battalion was involved in bitter fighting between Bakri and Parit Sulong, south of the Muar River. The only company commander in the unit to survive the action, Bowring was awarded the Military Cross. The citation stated: 'at Bakri on 20 January 1942 after heavy artillery fire had caused the evacuation of part of our front, Captain Bowring immediately re-organised his Company and personally led a bayonet charge which captured the former position killing many Japanese'. Over the next two days he led further bayonet charges, and at one stage advanced under fire to engage enemy tanks with an anti-tank rifle. His 'personal leadership and courage greatly inspired all troops'. The Japanese commander Lieutenant General Tomoyuki Yamashita later described the fighting between Bakri and Parit Sulong as the most 'savage encounter' of the campaign.

On Singapore Island the 2/29th Battalion was reinforced by five hundred under-trained recruits. When the Japanese landed on the evening of 8 February, the battalion was in a reserve position. But by 10 February it was in the front line around Bukit Panjang village and that night it was broken up by a Japanese tank attack. On the following day Bowring was evacuated to hospital after being wounded by a bullet to the back of the neck while attempting to hunt down a sniper. After the capitulation of Singapore on the 15th, he was interned in Changi camp. In April 1943 he left Singapore as part of 'F' Force to work on the Burma-Thailand Railway. He was mentioned in despatches for his services while a prisoner of war. Returning to Australia in October 1945, he was placed on the Reserve of Officers on 24 November.

After the war he was general manager of Bowrings until 1969. He was strongly committed to Mildura and was active in a range of community organisations. Moving to Melbourne he became secretary of the Canners' Association of Australia and later worked for an import-export company. A keen golfer and billiards and snooker player, he also enjoyed boating and ballroom dancing. He died on 4 October 1987 at Doncaster, Melbourne, and was cremated. His wife and their daughter and two sons survived him.

L. Wigmore, *The Japanese Thrust* (1957); R. W. and R. Christie (eds), *A History of the 2/29 Battalion —8th Division AIF* (1983); A. B. Lodge, *The Fall of General Gordon Bennett* (1986); A. Warren, *Singapore 1942* (2002); J. Lack (ed), *No Lost Battalion* (2005); *Stand-To* (Canberra), May-June 1954, pp 1, 42; B883, item VX44362 (NAA); personal information.

ALAN WARREN

BOYD, GUY MARTIN à BECKETT (1923-1988), sculptor and potter, was born on 12 June 1923 at Murrumbeena, Melbourne, third child of William Merric Boyd [q.v.7], painter, and his wife Doris Lucy Eleanor Bloomfield, née Gough, a painter. Grandson of the painters Arthur Merric and Emma Minnie Boyd, nephew of the novelist Martin Boyd, cousin of the architect Robin Boyd [qq.v.7,13], and brother of the painters and potters Arthur and David Boyd, Guy never doubted his vocation as an artist. He chose sculpture, he said, because in painting he could not compete with Arthur, the brother he always revered. The à Beckett family fortunes, on which his father depended, dwindled to nothing in the Depression years. Guy and his brothers, for whom a Murrumbeena state primary school education had to suffice, took labouring jobs. In 1941-46 he served in the Militia. A committed pacifist, he refused to bear arms and worked at first as a draughtsman. Conflicts with his superiors were resolved when he was posted in 1944 to the 103rd Convalescent Depot, Ingleburn, New South Wales, to teach pottery to the patients.

Taking up a Commonwealth Reconstruction Training Scheme grant, Boyd enrolled in 1945 at the East Sydney Technical College, where he studied sculpture under Lyndon Dadswell [q.v.]. In 1946 at Neutral Bay he founded a commercial pottery which, confusingly, he called the Martin Boyd Pottery. With moderate prices, functional designs and Australian decorative motifs, his products were popular with postwar homemakers.

On 22 April 1950 at St John's Church of England, Darlinghurst, Boyd married 18-year-old Barbara Dawn Cooper, a secretary; they separated within a year. Divorced in 1952 and having sold his Sydney business, he moved back to Melbourne and, on 1 December at the office of the government statist, married Phyllis Nairn, an Adelaide-born graduate in social work. He moved into a disused pottery at his father's property in Murrumbeena. After twenty months of communal living with his parents, and with Arthur and his sister Mary Perceval and their families, Guy bought his first home, at nearby Oakleigh. While his second commercial venture, the Guy Boyd Pottery, flourished, with Phyllis as an active business partner, Guy began to sculpt part time. In 1964 he was confident enough to sell the pottery, move to Brighton, and start his career in sculpture. At a time when abstract sculpture prevailed, he was committed to figurative art, but he soon won high praise for his finely textured work in bronze and in aluminium overlaid with silver, and for the strength and delicacy of his female nudes. His first big commissions included wall sculptures for Tullamarine (1970) and Sydney (1971) airports.

Study in Europe and Asia, on a Churchill fellowship in 1969, persuaded Boyd to test his work internationally. In 1976 he moved to Toronto, Canada; his wife and their youngest four children accompanied him. With access to the big galleries of Chicago and New York, his sculpture flourished. It was a bonus that 'being a Boyd' was not an issue, as it was in Australia. However, it was family feeling that brought him home. On a visit in 1980 he could not resist buying his grandfather's house in Edward Street, Sandringham, because it held happy memories of childhood.

The Boyds returned to Melbourne in 1981 to restore the house and live in it. Continuing his career as a sculptor, with major works that expressed his Christian faith, Guy had also become a public figure who did not shirk controversy. A former president (1973-76) of the Port Phillip Bay Conservation Council, he remained active in environmental matters: he was arrested in 1983 while protesting against the damming of the Franklin River in Tasmania. With his wife and elder daughters he campaigned tirelessly to reverse Lindy Chamberlain's conviction for murdering her baby daughter, Azaria [q.v.13], at Ayers Rock (Uluru).

Conservative in his views on religion and family life, but ready to defy the law for his pacifist beliefs; ambitious to make his name in art, but selflessly dedicated to causes that depleted his energies, Boyd was a man of great charm, good looks and gentleness, with an inflexible will. In his remarkable family, he was never just 'another Boyd'. He died on 26 April 1988 from coronary artherosclerosis and was buried with Anglican rites in Brighton cemetery. His wife, and their five daughters and two sons, survived him. Boyd had held one-man exhibitions in all Australian capital cities and in London, Montreal, Chicago and New York. His work is represented in the National Gallery of Australia and in the State galleries of Victoria, New South Wales and Queensland.

A. von Bertouch and P. Hutchings, *Guy Boyd* (1976); B. Niall, *The Boyds* (2002) and for bib.
BRENDA NIALL

BOYD, JOHN à BECKETT PENLEIGH ('PAT') (1915-1981), air force officer and airline pilot, was born on 1 February 1915 at Brighton, Melbourne, first surviving child of Theodore Penleigh Boyd, an English-born landscape painter, and his Brisbane-born wife Edith Susan [qq.v.7], an artist and daughter of J. G. Anderson [q.v.3]. He was the first grandson of Arthur Merric and Emma Minnie Boyd [qq.v.7]. Martin Boyd was his uncle and Robin [qq.v.13] his younger brother. 'Pat' seemed destined for a career as a painter. After leaving Melbourne Church of England Grammar School in 1931, he studied at the National Gallery schools, where he won prizes in 1932-36. However, growing up in the Depression on the small income left after their father's early death, Pat and Robin knew that they had to enter the workforce. Pat, who loved and understood machinery of every kind, worked for a firm which made office equipment, but continued to paint with his grandfather and his cousin Arthur on the Mornington Peninsula. He exhibited landscapes with the Victorian Artists Society in 1939 and 1940.

On 13 October 1940 Boyd enlisted in the Royal Australian Air Force. After initial training in New South Wales, he was sent to Ontario, Canada, where he gained his wings and was commissioned on 29 May 1941. He arrived in England in July and in September joined No.125 (Newfoundland) Squadron, Royal Air Force, a night-fighter unit. Flying Defiants and Beaufighters, he was promoted to flying officer in November and temporary flight lieutenant in May 1943. He returned to Australia in January 1944 and in March was posted to No.31 Squadron, RAAF, based at Coomalie Creek, Northern Territory. In July he was made acting squadron leader. He was reserved and unassuming, and some thought him remote. Yet his friends appreciated his inventiveness and quiet humour. Five ft 9 ins (175 cm) tall and handsome, with dark hair and blue eyes, he was admired as well as liked. In war he found the gift of leadership.

Boyd's courage and organising ability were demonstrated in July 1944 when he led four Beaufighters on a long-range mission to Maumere, Flores, Netherlands East Indies. He destroyed two Japanese aircraft on an airstrip and made a single-handed attack on four twin-engined fighters in the air. Disregarding heavy anti-aircraft fire, he then attacked and damaged a 1500-ton ship in the harbour before leading his force safely home. He won the Distinguished Flying Cross, to which a Bar was added for an action over Timor in October.

Leading eight aircraft on a coastal sweep, he was at treetop height when his starboard motor was hit by enemy fire. With his aeroplane enveloped in smoke, he climbed out of the valley, cutting out the motor to prevent it catching fire. The port engine then gave trouble. Boyd dumped petrol to lighten the aeroplane, and when he landed after the 450-mile (724 km) return flight he had only enough fuel for a few more minutes in the air. He left the squadron in January 1945 and trained as a test pilot. From September he served with No.1 Aircraft Performance Unit. He had been mentioned in despatches.

Demobilised on 4 July 1946, Boyd joined the newly established Trans-Australia Airlines and later became senior captain of its test and performance unit. On 15 December 1947 at St John's Church of England, Toorak, Melbourne, he married Anne, daughter of T. A. L. Davy [q.v.8]. They settled at Balwyn in a modernist house designed by Robin. For Boyd, flying had become almost as essential as breathing, and when his age and health reduced him to a desk job, he hated the routine and endured it for less than a year before resigning in March 1973.

In 1974 Boyd and his wife joined their daughter Annabel at Penleigh Farm, a small property near Perth. He enjoyed using his mechanical skills in outdoor tasks. Although he did some painting, he was dissatisfied with the results: he had been away from it too long. After a long period of ill health, he died from bronchopneumonia on 8 March 1981 in the Midland Convalescent Hospital, Perth, and was cremated. His wife and their two daughters and son survived him. He is commemorated by a plaque at Springvale war cemetery, Melbourne.

G. Odgers, *Air War against Japan 1943-1945* (1957); G. Serle, *Robin Boyd* (1995); B. Niall, *The Boyds* (2002); A9300, item Boyd J A P (NAA); AWM 88, items RAAF I/26, RAAF I/32 (AWM); National Gallery of Vic Archives; private information.
BRENDA NIALL

BOYE-JONES, RUBY OLIVE (1891-1990), coastwatcher, was born on 29 July 1891 at St Peters, Sydney, fifth of eight children of English-born parents Alfred Jones, storeman, and his wife Emily, née Wild. Little is known of her childhood, except that she learned to play the piano. On 25 October 1919 she married Sydney Skov Boye at St Stephen's Church of England, Newtown. Her occupation was then listed as saleswoman, her husband's as laundry proprietor. They were to have two sons.

From 1928 to 1936 the Boye family lived at Tulagi, British Solomon Islands Protectorate, moving in the latter year to Vanikoro Island, in the Santa Cruz group, where Skov managed the Vanikoro Kauri Timber Co. At the outbreak of World War II, the operator of the company's teleradio left for Australia. Before his departure, he showed Ruby how to operate the radio and transmit weather reports in voice code. She taught herself Morse code, took over complete responsibility for the radio and became a member of Eric Feldt's [q.v.14] coastwatching service.

In May 1942 the Japanese occupied Tulagi and Guadalcanal. Invasion of the Santa Cruz Islands seemed imminent. Most European residents left for Australia, but Ruby and Skov elected to stay. Mrs Boye continued to operate the coastwatcher radio, sending her daily weather reports and acting as a relay station between coastwatchers further north and the naval intelligence office at Vila, New Hebrides. Five ft 10 ins (177 cm) tall, she was a dignified and imposing woman, with dark, wavy hair and a warm smile.

Being civilians, the coastwatchers risked execution as spies if captured by the enemy. To provide a measure of protection, the Royal Australian Navy had begun to grant them naval rank from March 1942. However, it was not until 27 July 1943 that Boye was appointed a third officer, Women's Royal Australian Naval Service. Her rank was honorary and carried no pay, setting her apart from her male contemporaries. The Japanese knew of her presence, having sent her a threatening radio message in 1942. She was unshaken. Feldt commended her courage and Admiral William F. Halsey, United States Navy, made a special flight to Vanikoro to meet her. When she fell ill late in 1943, he sent a US Navy aircraft to evacuate her for treatment. She returned to Vanikoro and in 1944 was awarded the British Empire Medal. Her WRANS appointment terminated on 30 September 1946.

Boye left Vanikoro only when her husband became seriously ill in 1947. He died shortly after they arrived in Sydney. On 19 June 1950 at St John's Church of England, Penshurst, she married Frank Bengough Jones (d.1961), a departmental manager and widower. Mrs Boye-Jones, as she became known, remained alone in her Penshurst home after Frank's death until she reached her late nineties. Survived by the two sons of her first marriage, she died on 14 September 1990 at Narwee and was cremated. An accommodation block at the Australian Defence Force Academy, Canberra, is named after her. The Ex-WRANS Association dedicated a page to her in the Garden Island Chapel Remembrance Book.

E. Feldt, *The Coast Watchers* (1975); *Naval Hist Review*, Aug/Sept 1984, p 7; *Austn Women's Weekly*, Feb 1988, p 229; A6769, item Boye R O, B3476, item 40A, B6161, item Boye/RO (NAA); AWM88, item O/C 3 Civil (AWM); private information.
ALAN POWELL

BOYER, RICHARD (1923-1989), pastoralist, public servant and Australian Broadcasting Corporation board-member, was born on 7 February 1923 at Charleville, Queensland, elder child of (Sir) Richard James Fildes Boyer [q.v.13] and his wife Eleanor (Elenor) Muriel, née Underwood, both born in New South Wales. Richard's early years were spent on his parents' property Durella, near Morven, Queensland. Having attended (1936-41) Brisbane Boys' College, on 10 March 1942 he enlisted in the Royal Australian Air Force. He served in Australia as a radio and radar operator, spending most of 1943 at Exmouth Gulf, Western Australia, and rising to temporary sergeant before being discharged on 26 September 1945. He married his teenage sweetheart Marjorie Hitchcock on 14 December 1946 at St Thomas's Church of England, Toowong, Queensland.

At the University of Sydney (BA, 1949), Boyer majored in economics. Lectures by Heinz Arndt 'brought the subject alive' for him. Boyer became manager and part owner of a sheep-grazing property, Aqua Downs, 80 miles (129 km) from Charleville. Bush life and its comradeship attracted him: 'because of the great distance from everything ... your neighbour will back you to the very hilt'. He believed that in so far as there was a distinctive Australian culture, it was to be discovered in the bush. Founder and chairman of a local community centre, he was also a member of the executive council of the United Graziers' Association of Queensland.

Leaving Aqua Downs under the management of a cousin, in 1956 Boyer went to Corpus Christi College, Oxford (BA, 1958; MA, 1962), to study philosophy, politics and economics. Following his return to Australia in 1959 he lived in Sydney. Unemployed, he began writing a strategy for the marketing of wool in the future. At a seminar at the Australian National University, Canberra, in July that year—part of Sir Keith Hancock's [q.v.] series on wool—he argued for a central wool marketing authority independent of government control. This paper was the beginning of Boyer's determined efforts to reform the economic system.

After appointment to the Tariff Board in 1959 Boyer moved to Canberra. He never again lived permanently at Aqua Downs, but holidays were spent 'going bush' until the property was sold in 1964. Aware of the entrenched resistance from both rural and industrial sectors to changes in the tariff regime, he called for discussion of the negative effects of Australia's high tariffs on the country's economic development. An exponent of the benefits of free trade for underdeveloped countries, in 1972 he succeeded Sir Leslie Melville as chairman of the Papua and New Guinea Tariff Advisory Committee. Boyer's mission was 'to entice more industry to Papua New Guinea'.

He contended that developing countries could gain substantial advantages from the export of labour-intensive goods, as their main economic asset was cheap labour. While countries like Australia protected industries with tariff walls, they restricted the export of goods from developing countries, which were thus made dependent on aid. Boyer argued for 'more trade, less aid' and 'more certain sources of foreign exchange' for Third World countries so they could be more independent.

In 1974 Boyer was appointed by the Whitlam government to the Industries Assistance Commission, successor to the Tariff Board. In a speech that year on 'Primary Production in a Harsh Environment—the Significance of the I.A.C.', at the Rural Management School, Charleville, he outlined what he saw as the way forward for the bush. He argued that assistance for primary industries had to be based on its benefits to the nation as a whole and advocated that small farms should be consolidated into large ones and more efficient technologies and production practices adopted.

A major dispute erupted after this address. The United Graziers' Association of Queensland said his views were contrary to those of the association. He resigned from its Warrego branch, deeply hurt by this response. In 1970 he founded Economic Wool Producers Ltd, which made a major contribution to the wool industry, introducing sale by sample and description, and developing a computerised selling system. At the Metal Trades Federation of Unions seminar on 'The Future of Australian Manufacturing' in 1977 at Bankstown Town Hall, Sydney, Boyer gave a paper on the role of the IAC, arguing that reduced protection would benefit not only the manufacturing sector but the economy and community as a whole. He felt keenly the opposition to his proposals expressed at the seminar.

The 1976 IAC inquiry into assistance to the performing arts, conducted by Boyer, supported 'some long term assistance' but could not assess the appropriate level. Boyer asserted that arts funding was little different from public subsidy in other areas of the economy and that the arts needed to demonstrate public benefit if they were to continue to receive public funds. Opera and classical ballet were not 'intrinsically more worthy' than other entertainments. He also suggested that State symphony orchestras had outlived their usefulness. For these attitudes he was branded a philistine. Gough Whitlam wrote in *The Whitlam Government* (1985) of his relief that the IAC's 'provocative, well-reasoned, widely misunderstood and in many ways salutary examination of the issues involved in public subvention for the arts finished up on [Malcolm] Fraser's desk rather than mine'.

In 1981 Boyer's term as commissioner expired. In twenty-two years with the Tariff

Board and the IAC, he had been noted for his outspoken and independent ideas, which were often contrary to government policy and which cut across powerful sectional interests fiercely resistant to change. However, many of the reforms Boyer advocated were later taken up. He served briefly as a special (economic) adviser to the Liberal minister for foreign affairs, A. A. (Tony) Street, and on the Pharmaceutical Benefits Remuneration Tribunal and the Paper Conversion Printing and Publishing Industry Council. He was senior partner of Boyer & Associates, economic planning consultants.

In 1983 Boyer was appointed to the Australian Broadcasting Corporation board for a three-year term. As principal author of a board paper, *The Role of a National Broadcaster in Contemporary Australia*, he argued, with his usual intellectual rigour, that the most pressing issues for the ABC were how to maintain independence from government while remaining accountable to parliament, and how to increase the range of ideas, interests and experiences available to the whole Australian community. The ABC was uniquely placed to articulate the reality of a changing, complex, pluralistic society and to strengthen Australia's democratic values of open-mindedness and tolerance by explaining and protecting diversity, even as it fostered unity.

Boyer's last major address, 'Australia—200 Years from Where I Sit', delivered at Murdoch University, Perth, in November 1987, warned against nihilism, corruption, and the abandonment of the traditional value system. Capitalism needed to be lubricated by a strong sense of national purpose and by the values of honesty and integrity.

A tall, handsome man, fearlessly committed to fundamental change, Boyer envisaged, and sought to win acceptance for, an open, competitive economic system with a strong ethical base. He was against special government handouts or protection for sectional interests, including the rural community from which he had come. Retaining the values instilled in him from birth, he strove for the common good. He was appointed AM in 1987. Survived by his wife and their two sons and three daughters, he died of cancer on 25 January 1989 in his home at Red Hill, Canberra, and was cremated.

G. Whitlam, *The Whitlam Government 1972-1975* (1985); *Oxford Mail*, 19 Jan 1956 and *Oxford Times*, 27 July 1956 (held by ADB); *Age* (Melbourne), 10 June 1983, p 7; *Canberra Times*, 6 Aug 1983, p 1, 27 Jan 1989, p 9; *SMH*, 9 Feb 1989, p 4; A9301, item 62676 (NAA); R. Boyer papers (NLA); private information.   MARION CONSANDINE

BOYLE, ALFRED BERTRAM (1914-1988), air force officer and reformatory supervisor, was born on 10 August 1914 at Springsure, Queensland, son of Robert Bertram Boyle, mailman and later farmer, and his wife Elizabeth Anna, née Frazer, both Queensland born. Educated at Westwood State School and at Rockhampton High School and Technical College, he gained the junior commercial certificate in 1932. He worked as a book-keeper, jackeroo and miner before enlisting in the Royal Australian Air Force on 8 November 1940.

'Paddy', as he was known, trained as a pilot in Australia and Canada, graduating with his wings in August 1941. He arrived in Britain next month. Serving with the Royal Air Force's Bomber Command, he undertook his first operational tour in 1942-43 with No.35 and No.51 squadrons, RAF, and No.460 Squadron, RAAF. He flew Whitley, Wellington, Halifax and Lancaster bombers and was involved in perilous night operations over enemy territory. In February 1943 during an attack on St Nazaire, France, Boyle's aircraft was hit by falling incendiary bombs that ignited the fuselage. He completed the attack before dealing with the fire. For this action he was awarded the Distinguished Flying Cross.

Commissioned on 14 March 1943, Boyle instructed aircrew at No.27 Operational Training Unit until June 1944, when he was posted to No.467 Squadron, RAAF. He won a Bar to his DFC for pressing home an attack on Stettin, Germany (Szczecin, Poland), at low level in August. Having completed fifty-one operational sorties by November, he ended the war as a temporary flight lieutenant (substantive September 1948) flying transport aircraft with No.511 Squadron, RAF, on shuttle runs from Britain to India and the Azores.

On 29 March 1945 at the parish church, Penn Fields, Wolverhampton, Boyle married Annie Woolley Hartill, a member of the Auxiliary Territorial Service. Back in Australia in 1946, he served as an air traffic control officer in Canberra until mid-1947, when he resumed flying duties. In 1950 he joined No.11 Squadron, a maritime reconnaissance unit equipped with Lincoln and later Neptune aircraft. Early in 1952 he piloted a Lincoln to the Cocos (Keeling) Islands to pick up a seriously injured airman. On the hazardous return flight to Perth, the aircraft's radios and two of its four engines failed but Boyle landed safely. For his leadership, initiative and flying skill he was awarded the Air Force Cross.

Boyle was promoted to squadron leader on 1 January 1953. After holding a number of staff appointments from 1954, he transferred to the Retired List on 11 August 1957. He worked as a senior officer at Riverbank, a Perth reform institution for boys, where he touched the lives of many young men before finally retiring in 1979. Five ft 10 ins (178 cm) tall and of medium build, with blue eyes and black hair, he was described by his superiors in the RAAF as 'a well balanced, dependable officer' and by his family as 'modest and compassionate'. He died on 29 May 1988 in Royal Perth Hospital and was cremated; his wife and their two daughters survived him.

P. Firkins, *Strike and Return* (2000); *West Australian*, 2 June 1988, p 20; A9300, item Boyle A B (NAA); private information.   MARK LAX

BRACK, THOMAS JAMES (1924-1984), conciliation and arbitration commissioner, was born on 16 September 1924 at Warburton, Victoria, second son of James Brack, land salesman, and his wife Frances Lillian, née Downey, both Victorian born. The family moved to the new national capital and Tom was educated at Canberra High School, where he passed the Intermediate certificate in 1939. Overstating his age he commenced full-time duty in the Militia on 15 July 1942. Five ft 8½ ins (174 cm) tall and solidly built, he had blue eyes, light brown hair and a fair complexion. He transferred to the Australian Imperial Force on 28 April 1943 and served as a cipher clerk in Australia, New Guinea and, for a few months after the war, on Morotai, Netherlands East Indies. Having risen to sergeant in December 1944, he was promoted to acting staff sergeant in November 1945. However, in January that year he had been described by a superior officer as 'a poor example' of a non-commissioned officer, one who had 'ability' but adopted 'an attitude of absolute disinterest' in the army.

At All Saints Church of England, St Kilda, Melbourne, on 10 July 1945 Brack married Elizabeth Eva Archer, a private in the Australian Women's Army Service. Demobilised from the army on 12 June 1946, he returned to Canberra and joined the Commonwealth Public Service in November as a clerk in the Department of External Affairs. In 1948 he transferred to the Department of the Interior, with which he served in Darwin for a time, and from 1950 he worked in the industrial and arbitration branch of the office of the Public Service Board, Prime Minister's Department. He rose steadily through the ranks before resigning from the public service in 1951 to become secretary of the Australian Capital Territory Employers' Association and the Canberra Chamber of Commerce. In 1954 he left these positions and moved to Sydney, where he worked as an industrial officer and personnel manager for the Nestlé Co. (Australia) Ltd. He was federal president (1963-67) of the Commonwealth Jam Preserving and Condiment Manufacturers' Association.

On 2 September 1968 Brack was appointed a commissioner of the Commonwealth Conciliation and Arbitration Commission. With long experience of industrial affairs in both the private and public sectors, he was well equipped for his new role, to which he adapted readily. He acquired a reputation at the commission for courtesy, efficiency and fairness, and for his ability to listen carefully to evidence and ask penetrating questions of witnesses. He enjoyed the respect of colleagues, employers and unions.

Brack was a horse-racing enthusiast and a keen lawn bowler. After his first marriage ended in divorce, he married Norma Gwen McKelvey, née Green, a divorcee, in a civil ceremony on 2 March 1980 at Baulkham Hills. Survived by his wife, and by the daughter and son of his first marriage, he died of a brain tumour on 7 June 1984 at Westmead and was cremated.

B883, item NX170457 (NAA); private information.
                                    FRANK BONGIORNO

BRADY, DONALD (1927-1984), Methodist pastor and Aboriginal leader, was born on 20 April 1927 at Palm Island Settlement, North Queensland, second child of Queensland-born parents Jim Brady, stockman, and his wife Grace, formerly Edmond, née Creed. Don was of Kuku Yalanji descent; his tribal name was Kuanji. As a boy at Palm Island he learned to perform traditional dances and to play the didgeridoo. He worked as a farm labourer and was a professional tent boxer for three years; in practice sessions he sparred with Jack Hassen, among others. A Christian from an early age, he trained as a missionary at the Men's Native Workers Training College of the Aborigines Inland Mission of Australia, at Karuah, near Newcastle, New South Wales, and graduated on 10 December 1949. After another year of study he was appointed to Brewarrina, but soon transferred to Walcha, and in 1952 to Moree. On 26 January that year he married a fellow missionary, Aileen Muriel Willis, at the AIM Church, Cherbourg, Queensland.

In 1962 Brady moved to Brisbane and, after attending the Methodist Training College and Bible School, began work as a lay pastor in July 1964 with the West End Methodist Mission, ministering to urban-dwelling Aborigines. A self-confessed former alcoholic, he was known as the 'punching parson' because of his ability to handle homeless inebriates frequenting Musgrave Park, South Brisbane. In 1965 he expanded his ministry to include the Christian Community Centre, based at the Leichhardt Street Methodist Church, Spring Hill. Providing not only spiritual guidance but also welfare assistance, the centre catered for some three thousand people. Brady established a sports club in a vacant church building in Upper Clifton Terrace, Red Hill, and set up a gymnasium where he instructed young men in boxing. Keen to foster in Aboriginal children an appreciation of their cultural heritage, he taught songs and dances, and formed the Yelangi dance group, whose performances he accompanied on the didgeridoo. He also showed local people how to make traditional artefacts.

Awarded a Churchill fellowship in 1968, Brady travelled to the United States of America to study the 'integration of indigenous people'. On his return he became active in the struggle for rights for Aborigines. Joining other Aboriginal militants, including Denis Walker and Cheryl Buchanan, he helped to form the Brisbane Tribal Council (from 1970 the National Tribal Council) to help Indigenous people to establish their own identity and to preserve their culture. In February 1970 he was elected founding vice-president of the Aboriginal Publications Foundation. On 12 April he led a silent street march to mourn the loss of Aborigines who died in defence of their country, and to demonstrate against 'the disruption of the aboriginal way of life by the white invasion'. After the protesters arrived at the Leichhardt Street church Kath Walker (later known as Oodgeroo Noonuccal) addressed them outside, and Brady conducted a service inside in memory of those 'thousands of our people who have died because of ignorance'. Aware that the procession had come to the attention of the police traffic and special branches, he assured the group of about sixty that this was a one-off event, and should be seen as similar to the annual Anzac Day remembrance service. He argued that the march was not intended as a demonstration of Black Power but rather as an assertion of Aboriginal rights.

In November 1971 Brady participated in a street march protesting against a bill before the Queensland parliament that extended governmental control of tribal and reserve councils. He and Denis Walker were arrested and charged with assaulting police. Using the media to highlight inequities in housing and employment opportunities, he inspired other Aboriginal people to join the battle for social justice. He encouraged young Queensland Aborigines and Torres Strait Islanders to protest at the Aboriginal 'tent embassy' set up outside Parliament House, Canberra, in January 1972. In July that year the board of the Brisbane Central Methodist Mission, which was reorganising the Christian Community Centre, asked for Brady's resignation. Following negotiations, he was released from responsibilities for spiritual care and in September was appointed to a new position, subsidised by the Commonwealth government, as liaison officer looking after the physical, social and political welfare of Aboriginal people. The centre, now independent of the mission, continued to use the Leichhardt Street premises.

Brady died of pneumonia complicating hypertensive cerebrovascular disease on 27 January 1984 in South Brisbane and was buried with Uniting Church forms in Mount Gravatt cemetery. He was survived by his wife, four sons and two daughters; two children predeceased him. More than five hundred people gathered at Musgrave Park to mourn his passing. Praising his leadership, Rev. Charles Harris described him as 'the Martin Luther King of the Aboriginal race'. His peers hailed him as a civil rights advocate who gave Aboriginal people a sense of pride and taught them to fight for their rights.

W. McNally, *Goodbye Dreamtime* (1973); *Sunday Mail* (Brisbane), 28 May 1967, p 2, 30 Mar 1969, p 31, 29 Jan 1984, p 2; *Courier-Mail* (Brisbane), 13 Apr 1970, p 5, 14 Sept 1972, p 10, 3 Feb 1984, p 5; *Identity*, Nov 1972, p 37.   YSOLA BEST

BRAIN, BRIAN WINTER (1910-1990), farmer, was born on 20 January 1910 at Battery Point, Hobart, only child of Tasmanian-born parents Charles Winter Brain, farmer of Risdon and later of Richmond, and his wife, Catherine Taylor, née McPhee. After ill health led to his father's early retirement, his mother took employment as a postmistress, at Richmond, at Kempton and at Sandy Bay, Hobart. Educated at Albuera Street State School and Hobart Technical School, Brian learned about farm machinery, irrigation equipment and electrical appliances while working for A. G. Webster & Sons Ltd, Hobart. He became a jackeroo on a property at Parattah and met Lorna Isobel Jessie Hyland (d.1988), whom he married on 31 March 1933 at St Peter's Church of England, Oatlands. They settled on a small farm at Andover.

Having been commissioned as a lieutenant in the Citizen Military Forces on 24 January 1939, Brain transferred to the Australian Imperial Force on 1 May 1940. In June he was posted as officer commanding the 7th Division Salvage Unit, which arrived in the Middle East in November. The unit reconditioned enemy equipment captured during the campaigns in North Africa and Syria. Appointed salvage control officer at I Corps headquarters in October 1941, Captain Brain returned to Australia in March 1942. Next month he was made deputy assistant controller of salvage at First Army headquarters as a temporary major; he served in Queensland and the Torres Strait. In August 1944 he was promoted to temporary lieutenant colonel (substantive 27 September 1945) and appointed director of salvage at Land Headquarters, Melbourne. He transferred to the Reserve of Officers on 31 May 1946. His continued concern for the men of the salvage service led him to help arrange annual reunions over the next forty years.

On his return to Tasmania, Brain was appointed by the Closer Settlement Board as manager of Lawrenny estate, Ouse, which had been acquired for subdivision from Henry Brock [q.v.7] and his brothers, under the war service land settlement scheme. Later, he bought part of Rotherwood, on the River Ouse, and some of nearby Shawfield, forming a 2501-acre (1012 ha) property that retained the name Rotherwood. Installing pumps to irrigate the run-down farm, he planted improved pastures. He co-operated with the Department of Agriculture in sheep-breeding trials and in 1961 started breeding Angus cattle. In 1963 he was one of the first producers in Australia to begin performance recording of livestock. With others in the district he formed the Angus Development Group in 1972; they achieved impressive genetic improvement in local herds.

Intent on optimising production in all aspects of rural enterprise, Brain made land and equipment available to the Department of Agriculture, and later to the University of Tasmania's faculty of agricultural science, for experimental work. Pasture improvement, corbie control, animal husbandry and trace elements were all subjects for trials at Rotherwood. In 1970, experiencing low wool prices and finding it difficult to sell hops, local farmers formed the Derwent Valley Development Association. Brain was active on the committee. His enthusiasm, careful research and analysis of the commercial potential of other crops suited to the district encouraged local farmers to undertake new initiatives such as growing poppies and pyrethrum, and producing essential oils. With the faculty of agricultural science, he conducted trials on peppermint and other essential oils at Rotherwood. Three of his sons had joined him on the farm; they grew peppermint and other specialty crops, including blackcurrants, dill, fennel and parsley. The mix of crops helped to maximise use of their harvesting machinery and the distillation equipment installed on the farm in 1975. Brain used his expertise to help other farmers to design and set up irrigation systems so that they too could grow high-yielding crops.

Brain was a member (1958-80) and chairman (1961-80) of the Ouse District Hospital board; he lobbied for a new hospital building in the 1970s. A volunteer fire-fighter (1947-87), and group captain (1968-87) of the Hamilton municipality's brigades, he was responsible for introducing two-way radios to co-ordinate fire crews in district emergencies. He was a member (1968-79) of the Rural Fires Board

and deputy-chairman (1975-80) of its equipment and technical sub-committee. In 1974-80 he served on the Tasmanian Grain Elevators Board, and in 1984-90 he was one of the university council's appointees on the faculty of agricultural science. He was appointed MBE in 1983, and next year received the Tasmanian rural promotions committee's award for outstanding service to Tasmanian agriculture. Survived by his four sons, he died on 19 April 1990 at Rotherwood and was buried in the cemetery of St John the Baptist Anglican Church, Ouse.

R. V. McNeice, *Knapsack Heroes* (1991); *Mercury* (Hobart), 29 Jan 1964, p 19, 28 Oct 1982, p 20, 27 Apr 1990, p 6; *Tasmanian Country*, 14 Sept 1984, p 3; *Derwent Valley Gazette*, 18 Mar 1987, p 5, 2 May 1990, p 6; personal information.   A. RAND

BRANDON, HUGH EARLE (1906-1984), musician and educationist, was born on 24 July 1906 in South Brisbane, seventh of eight children of Thomas William Brandon, a farmer from England, and his Queensland-born wife Mary Magdalene Fanny, née Anger. Raised on a farm near Allora, Hugh was educated at Berat, Wellington Point and Wynnum Central state schools. He learned piano first at Warwick from Ethel Hancock and, after 1917, in Brisbane from Hilda Foster. On leaving school he began work with a music retailer, G. J. Grice Ltd, Brisbane. He studied with Robert Dalley-Scarlett [q.v.8] and gained an associate diploma in pianoforte from Trinity College of Music, London, in 1925. Winning a three-year scholarship to Trinity College, in 1926-29 he studied piano with Charlton Keith and organ with Stanley Roper, who fostered his love of church music. George Oldroyd taught him music harmony and counterpoint. Brandon played the organ at several churches in London, including the Methodists' Central Hall, Westminster, and the Presbyterian Church, Bromley. In 1929 he qualified as a fellow of Trinity College and was awarded a licentiate of the Royal Academy of Music; next year he studied piano for nine months in Vienna with Otto Hinkleman.

Returning to Brisbane in 1931 Brandon taught piano and organ privately, and, with Eunice Cochrane, a singing teacher, staged a series of recitals, 'concerts intimes', sometimes with associate guests. On 19 December 1939 at Albert Street Methodist Church, Brisbane, he married Dorothy May Matters, a clerk. Deeply religious, he dedicated his musical gifts to the service of God. He was conductor of the Brisbane Bach Society (1931-46), and organist and conductor at city Presbyterian churches: Ann Street (1933-45) and St Andrew's, Creek Street (1945-78). During his long tenure at St Andrew's he was to conduct many fine performances of major choral works, including J. S. Bach's *B minor Mass* and *St Matthew Passion*, George Handel's *Messiah*, Antonin Dvorak's *Stabat Mater*, Johannes Brahms's *Requiem*, Gustav Holst's *Hymn of Jesus* and Edward Elgar's *The Light of Life*.

An examiner for the Australian Music Examinations Board in Queensland from 1942, Brandon travelled throughout the State in this role for forty-two years. In 1945 he gained an associate art of speech diploma from the AMEB, and the University of Queensland appointed him assistant to Sydney May [q.v.10], organiser in music. He revived the Queensland University Musical Society as a women's choir, adding men from 1947; he was to conduct the choir until 1965, when he became patron. On 1 January 1953 Brandon took over from May as organiser in music and was promoted to senior lecturer. Inaugural head (1955-66) of the department of music, he served as dean of the faculty of music in 1970. That year the university conferred on him an honorary B.Mus. Late in his career he developed a strong interest in Russian church music, and visited the Soviet Union in 1971 to explore this field. His publications included *Fifty Folk Songs* (1969), *12 Studies in Musicianship* (1969) for piano, and eight carols for four-part choir (1973). There were also some unpublished choral pieces. He retired from his university post in December 1973. In 1978-84 he was again choirmaster at Ann Street Presbyterian Church.

Brandon made a major contribution to raising standards in music in Queensland, introducing a generation of students to some of the best choral music in the repertoire. He particularly encouraged those singers whose potential he recognised early: some of his students later received national acclaim, notably Raymond McDonald, Janet Delpratt and James Christiansen. He also contributed to improving speech and drama in the State. President of the State branches of the Arts Council of Australia (1957-61) and of the Musica Viva Society of Australia (1964-66), he was also a member (1959-71) of the Queensland Conservatorium of Music advisory council.

Although Brandon suffered from diabetes for most of his life, he showed tremendous energy and determination in pursuing his goals. He was gentlemanly in manner with a bright demeanour, but occasionally he fell out with authorities when he held different views. His colleagues and friends, who valued his sincerity and generosity, set up the Hugh Brandon prize at the University of Queensland in 1980. Survived by his wife, and their daughter and son, he died on 19 April 1984 at his Moorooka home and was cremated after a funeral service at the Ann Street Church.

J. Dawson, *A History of the Queensland University Musical Society, 1912-1980* (1981); L. Schloss, Hugh Brandon (B.Mus. Hons thesis, Univ of Qld, 1983); N. Wilmott, A History of the Music Department, University of Queensland, 1912-1970 (MA Qual. thesis, Univ of Qld, 1986); Brandon papers (Univ of Qld Archives); private information.

GORDON D. SPEARRITT

BRAZILL, DAME JOHANNA (1895-1988), Sister of Mercy, nurse and hospital administrator, known as Sister Mary Philippa, was born on 24 December 1895 at Bosnetstown, Kilfinane, County Limerick, Ireland, daughter of Thomas Brazill, farmer, and his wife Julia, née Dwane. While still at school, Johanna responded to a recruiting drive in Ireland by the Victorian Institute of Our Lady of Mercy. She sailed with a party of novices and arrived in Melbourne aboard the *Omrah* on 23 September 1912. Sent immediately to the Sacred Heart convent, Newtown, Geelong, to complete her secondary education, she was professed as Sister Mary Philippa on 10 January 1918. Next year she studied at the Mater Misericordiae Novitiate and Training College, Ascot Vale, Melbourne, under the vibrant Sister Patricia O'Neill [q.v.15 M. M. O'Neill]. Sister Philippa taught at Coburg and in 1924 was principal of St Mary's School for Girls, West Melbourne.

During a school vacation Sister Philippa visited St Benedict's Hospital, Malvern, and met its administrator, Mother Francis Hanigan [q.v.14 Rose Hanigan], who asked her to switch to nursing. At first she resisted because she liked teaching but eventually agreed to the change. After completing a three-year training course at the Mater Misericordiae Hospital, South Brisbane, she returned to St Benedict's in January 1928. She accompanied Mother Francis on a six-month inspection tour of hospitals in the United States of America in 1930. With (Sir) Arthur Stephenson [q.v.12], the two women developed plans for a 'first-class' private hospital in East Melbourne. From the opening of the Mercy Private Hospital in 1935, Sister Philippa was its nursing director. She succeeded Mother Francis as hospital and community superior in 1948. During her tenure the Order reinvigorated its drive for a public maternity hospital to be built on a site adjoining the private institution.

In 1954 Mother Philippa transferred to Rosanna as provincial of the Order's Victoria-Tasmania region. Using her wide understanding of health care, she improved the diet and general welfare of all her communities. She returned to the Mercy as superior in 1959. Over the next decade, she was deeply involved with medical, nursing, university and government authorities in planning for the new

Mercy Maternity Hospital, which was to include a clinical teaching unit. It was formally opened on 11 February 1971.

Sister Philippa had stepped down as hospital superior in 1969. She was appointed DBE in 1979. The University of Melbourne awarded her an honorary doctorate of laws in 1981. Dubbed the 'Steel Maiden' by doctors, she saw herself as a woman who had 'been liberated all [her] life'. Her 'extremely directive' personality was tempered by a comprehensive insight into the care of patients, a 'delightful Irish wit', a 'rare sensitivity' and a deep compassion inspired by her faith. For recreation she read, listened to classical music and watched Australian Rules football on television. She died on 1 January 1988 at Newtown, Geelong, and was buried in Melbourne general cemetery, Carlton. Her Order established a foundation in her name to support research into and education in the ethics of health care.

M. G. Allen, *The Labourers' Friends* (1989); S. Priestley, *Melbourne's Mercy* (1990) and for sources; *Sun News-Pictorial* (Melbourne), 3 July 1979, p 12; *Austn Nurses Jnl*, Aug 1979, p 7; *Age* (Melbourne), 3 Aug 1981, p 5.

SUSAN PRIESTLEY

BREARLEY, SIR NORMAN (1890-1989), pioneer aviator, was born on 22 December 1890 at Geelong, Victoria, fourth of five children of Victorian-born parents Robert Hilliard Brearley, tanner, and his wife Mary Karen, née Petersen. Norman attended local schools before moving with his family to Western Australia in 1906. He studied mechanical and electrical engineering at Perth Technical College and at 18 acquired an apprenticeship at Hoskins [q.v.9] & Co. Ltd's foundry. Having developed an interest in the new technology of flight, he realised in World War I his ambition to fly. He took passage to England in April 1915 and was commissioned in the British Army on 12 October. Immediately joining the Royal Flying Corps, he began flying training at Thetford, Norfolk, later recalling inexperienced and nervous instructors, and aircraft ill-designed for training pilots. He was in action over the Western Front by June next year, and was awarded the Military Cross for destroying a German observation balloon in September. Two months later he attacked, with another pilot, seven enemy aircraft. Shot down in no man's land, he crawled back to the British trenches with bullet wounds that perforated both lungs. For his 'courage and determination' he was awarded the Distinguished Service Order (1917).

Back in Perth on sick leave, Lieutenant Brearley married with Anglican rites Violet Claremont Stubbs at Christ Church, Clare-

mont, on 5 July 1917. He was determined to fly again and swam in the Swan River baths to improve his lung capacity. On his return to England, he was declared fit for light duties but 'no stunts'. Captain Brearley became a staff instructor at the School of Special Flying, Gosport. In June 1918 he was given command of the Midland Area Flying Instructors' School at Lilbourne, near Rugby. Among those he trained at Gosport and Lilbourne were (Sir) Keith and (Sir) Ross Smith and A. H. Cobby [qq.v.11,8]. Promoted to major, Royal Air Force, in August, he was transferred to the Unemployed List on 26 June 1919. He was mentioned in despatches (1917) and awarded the Air Force Cross (1919). His brother Stanley George (1894-1979) won the Distinguished Flying Cross while serving with the Australian Flying Corps.

Already planning a peacetime career in aviation in Australia, Brearley brought back two war-surplus Avro 504 aircraft. Beginning with a series of demonstration and 'joyride' flights over Perth, he secured the support of Michael Durack [q.v.8], who represented Kimberley in the Legislative Assembly. He erected a hangar below Durack's house in Adelaide Terrace, and used the Esplanade, on the banks of the Swan River, as a runway. When, in 1921, he was awarded the contract to provide an airmail service between Geraldton and Derby, he imported six Bristol Tourer biplanes and formed Western (West from 1926) Australian Airways Ltd. Despite difficulties securing logistic support, he and his team of four pilots, including (Sir) Charles Kingsford Smith [q.v.9], began operating on 5 December 1921. The inaugural flight ended in tragedy when one plane crashed near the Murchison River, killing the pilot and his mechanic. Brearley blamed the accident on lack of suitable emergency landing strips. Urged on by Durack, he persuaded the director of the civil aviation branch, Department of Defence, H. C. Brinsmead [q.v.7], to organise upgrading of the airstrips, and then resumed flights.

With the north-west route established, in 1924 Brearley extended the service south to Perth. Three years later he set up the Perth Flying School at Maylands aerodrome. In 1928 WAA won the contract to carry mail between Perth and Adelaide. On this route, opened in June 1929, the airline used De Havilland 66 Hercules, which carried fourteen passengers, and Vickers Viastras. To ensure accurate navigation over the long distance, which pilots often flew at night, Brearley installed the American-designed Sperry rotating beacon system along the flight path. In 1934 WAA lost the north-west airmail contract to MacRobertson [q.v.11 Sir Macpherson Robertson]-Miller [q.v.10] Aviation Co. Ltd. Two years later Brearley sold the company and the rights to the Perth-Adelaide route to Australian National Airways Pty Ltd.

On 19 February 1940 Brearley was appointed temporary flight lieutenant, Royal Australian Air Force. Posted to various training schools as commanding officer, he rose to acting group captain in January 1942. He commanded No.4 Service Flying Training School, Geraldton, from October and RAAF Station, Tocumwal, New South Wales, from March 1944. His appointment terminated on 12 June. After the war Brearley served as a director of Sydney Atkinson Motors Ltd, Perth, played golf, and travelled overseas. He patented several inventions and published an autobiography, *Australian Aviator* (1971). Appointed CBE in 1965 and knighted in 1971, he was awarded the Oswald Watt [q.v.12] gold medal in 1974. He was founding president of the (Royal) Aero Club of Western Australia and a member (1926-89) of the Rotary Club of Perth. Predeceased by his wife, he died on 9 June 1989 at Nedlands and was cremated. His son and daughter survived him. A bust of Sir Norman by Gerard Darwin is displayed at the Perth International Airport.

N. Parnell and T. Boughton, *Flypast* (1988); B. Bunbury, *Rag Sticks & Wire* (1993); *Advertiser* (Adelaide), 5 Dec 1981, p 30; *Australian*, 5-6 Dec 1981, 'Weekend Mag', p 9; *Far Horizons*, Jan/Feb 1990, p 12; Brearley papers (SLWA); personal information.   BILL BUNBURY

BRENNAN, GLORIA FAY (1948-1985), Aboriginal community leader and public servant, was born on 12 September 1948 at Leonora, Western Australia, second child of Western Australian-born parents James Brennan, woodcutter, and his wife Myrtle, née Goodilyer. Gloria claimed Weebo as her *doogurr*, or country. As a small child she learned to speak the Wongi language fluently. Attending primary schools at Leonora, Laverton and Menzies, she and her siblings spent holidays with their Aboriginal grandmothers, camping in the desert country, finding bush tucker and listening to stories about their spirit ancestors. She topped the small one-teacher school at Menzies while assisting with grades one to three. Her parents worked and saved to send Gloria to high schools at Kalgoorlie and in Perth, refusing to accept a government scholarship. Not many knew of her talents as a classical pianist and as a singer. In 1966-71 she worked in programming for the Australian Broadcasting Commission in Perth.

At a University of Western Australia summer school in 1969, entitled 'Aboriginal Progress—A New Era?', the speakers Charles Perkins, John Moriaty, Margaret Valadian and David Anderson made Brennan aware of the need to address injustices experienced by Aboriginal people. Inspired to further her education, she enrolled in 1971 as a mature-age student in the faculty of arts at UWA (BA, 1978); she majored in anthropology, and also studied linguistics, English, history and music. A member from 1971 of the Aboriginal Advancement Council of Western Australia and of the New Era Aboriginal Fellowship, she was concerned about a range of issues, including the welfare of women and children, Aboriginal education and health, and the need for interpreter services. In the mid-1970s she helped to found the Aboriginal Medical Service in Western Australia, and joined the Aboriginal Women's Council and the Black Australian Women's Movement. As a casual field officer with the Aboriginal Legal Service of Western Australia, which she had helped to establish in 1973, she was involved with the domestic violence task force and in 1974-75 was an interpreter with the legal team investigating allegations of police brutality at Skull Creek, near Laverton. In 1975 she joined the Commonwealth Department of Aboriginal Affairs in Perth, becoming a senior research officer and a community adviser.

An advocate for Aboriginal land rights, Brennan co-authored (1975) a paper entitled 'No Land for the Soles of Our Feet', which was published in *Aboriginal and Islander Forum*. She travelled extensively, made contact with other indigenous people, and studied the Inuit of Canada. In 1977 she was a delegate to the World Black and African Festival of Arts and Culture in Lagos. Next year she transferred to the Canberra office of the DAA and prepared a report on interpreter services for disadvantaged Aborigines. In December 1980 she joined the Equal Employment Opportunity Bureau in the Public Service Board, as officer-in-charge of the Aboriginal Unit. She was president (1981-83) of the Aboriginal Publications Foundation. In 1983 she took up a six-month overseas study award and investigated how language and affirmative action policy were used to increase employment and education opportunities for minority groups.

A gregarious woman, with a big laugh, a big heart and a wicked sense of humour, Brennan was practically inseparable from her telephone. She loved life, people and conviviality. Challenging stereotypes of Aboriginal people, she became a highly respected bureaucrat, a forthright public speaker and an international traveller. She died of cancer on 2 November 1985 in Perth and was buried with Anglican rites in Kalgoorlie cemetery. The Gloria Brennan Memorial Honeywell Bull fellowship for promising Aboriginal students of Western classical music was first awarded in 1987; a scholarship for Indigenous undergraduates studying at public Western Australian universities was also named after her. The Gloria

Brennan Aboriginal and Torres Strait Islander Women's Centre was established in East Perth to provide health and childcare information.

K. Gilbert, *Living Black* (1977); S. Muecke, *No Road* (1997); *Canberra Times*, 6 Nov 1985, p 16; *West Australian*, 6 Nov 1985, p 36.   CHRISTINE CHOO

BRENNAN, KEITH GABRIEL (1915-1985), lawyer, public servant and diplomat, was born on 25 March 1915 at Hawthorn, Melbourne, youngest of five children of Victorian-born parents Henry Philip Brennan, journalist, and his wife Mary Teresa Cecilia, née Mackintosh. Keith, a nephew of Anna Teresa, Francis, Thomas and William Brennan [qq.v.7], was educated at St Patrick's College, East Melbourne, and at the University of Melbourne (LL B, 1943). While studying law part time he worked in 1934-38 as a clerk in the taxation branch, Victorian Department of the Treasurer, and in 1938-40 as associate to H. V. Evatt [q.v.14], then a justice of the High Court of Australia. He joined the Department of the Army in 1940. On 3 April 1945 at St Patrick's Cathedral, Melbourne, he married with Catholic rites Suzanne White, a stenographer. She and her parents had left the Soviet Union as Jewish refugees in 1920; arriving in Australia in 1922, they had later changed their family name from Vainshelbaum to White.

In 1947 Brennan transferred to the Department of External Affairs. His early assignments overseas were to New York, where he worked both at the consulate-general and at the Australian Mission to the United Nations (1950-54). After four years back in Australia, he was posted (1958-61) to Japan. In Canberra he is best remembered by his colleagues for his term (1963-70) as assistant-secretary, running the administration and personnel division of the department. He gave powerful support to two successive secretaries, Sir Arthur Tange and Sir James Plimsoll [q.v.]. He also displayed innate pastoral gifts in handling the workforce of the department and in dealing with the many, often delicate, personnel problems which are unavoidable in running a foreign service. The department benefited greatly from his time in the administrative division. Those who worked closely with him there remember him for his patience, kindliness and sense of humour.

Appointed ambassador to Ireland by the McMahon [q.v.] government, Brennan entered enthusiastically into his new duties in February 1972. He secured a chair of Australian history in the Australian Studies Centre, University College, Dublin, and took particular pride in mounting a successful exhibition of (Sir) Sidney Nolan's paintings in Dublin. His term was cut short when in April 1974 the Labor prime minister, E. G. Whitlam, decided for domestic political reasons to use Dublin as a post for Senator Vince Gair [q.v.14]. Brennan was moved at inconsiderately short notice to Berne, Switzerland. His wife, who was already suffering from cancer, died there in 1977. Yet Brennan still felt that Labor best embodied his hopes and ideals.

During his seven years in Berne, Brennan represented Australia at many international law conferences, most importantly the Third United Nations Conference on the Law of the Sea, which led to the conclusion of the Law of the Sea Convention in 1982. From 1977 he was leader of the Australian delegation. His work on this, and on Antarctica, earned him a formidable international reputation. The chairman of the Rio de Janeiro international conference on Antarctica in 1985, Christopher Beeby of New Zealand, said that Brennan had been 'the dominant figure' of the law of the sea negotiations and 'one of the most distinguished individuals ever to participate in Antarctic negotiations'. He noted in particular his contribution to reaching international agreement on the 1980 Convention on the Conservation of Antarctic Marine Living Resources. Brennan was later described as a pillar of the law of the sea conference. According to William Wertenbaker, writing in the *New Yorker*, he had 'worked informally and without credit on solutions to some of the most intractable of the seabed problems' and was 'trusted by everyone'. His work on international legal issues sprang from a sense of vocation, and from a belief that this work was of benefit to mankind.

In 1979 Brennan was appointed AO. He retired from the diplomatic service in 1981 and moved to Adelaide, but continued as Australia's chief negotiator for the Law of the Sea Convention. A devout Catholic, he was portrayed by Sir Walter Crocker as 'a splendid example of the convinced and unshakeable Christian—a man of solid Catholic values'. At the suggestion of a friend who was a priest, and encouraged by Archbishop James Gleeson, in February 1983 he entered St Francis Xavier Seminary, Rostrevor, to begin the requisite four years of training for the priesthood. Brennan was quoted in the press as saying that his new career came as an extension of his lifelong, unfaltering faith in Catholicism. He also said: 'As my daughter put it ... it's not everyone who can claim their father's a Catholic priest'. Before completing his studies he died of cancer on 16 January 1985 in North Adelaide and was buried in Centennial Park cemetery. His three sons and two daughters survived him.

M. Tsamenyi et al (eds), *United Nations Convention on the Law of the Sea* (1996); *Austn Law Jnl,* vol 59, 1986, p 357; *Sunday Mail* (Adelaide), 30 Jan 1983, p 3; *Age* (Melbourne), 9 Feb 1983, p 11; *New Yorker*, 1 Aug 1983, p 38; personal information.

P. G. F. HENDERSON

BRIDGES, ALFRED RENTON BRYANT ('HARRY') (1901-1990), trade union leader, was born on 6 July 1901 at Kensington, Melbourne, third child of Alfred Ernest Bridges, a newsagent who had been born in New Zealand, and his London-born wife Julia, née Dorgan. Educated at local Catholic and state schools, Harry left at 14 to work successively as a rent collector for his father, a clerk in a stationery store and a merchant seaman. He later attributed his radicalisation to the influence of his uncle Renton Bridges, who was a Labor Party activist, shipmates who were members of the Industrial Workers of the World, and the 1917 general strike. In April 1920 he landed at San Francisco and became a resident of the United States of America.

After two more years as a sailor, during which he was briefly a member of the IWW, Bridges sought work as a longshoreman on the San Francisco docks but, choosing to join the International Longshoremen's Association rather than the employer-sponsored 'Blue Book Union', was only employed intermittently. In 1924 he married Agnes Brown; they were later divorced. Family responsibilities forced him to enrol with the company union to get work in 1926-27, after which he found a steady job with a steel-handling gang until 1932.

As unemployment and industrial tensions increased in 1933, there was pressure to replace the company union. Several ILA factions sought control, including a small rank-and-file group, led by Bridges and called Albion Hall after its meeting place. During the bitter, 83-day maritime strike of 1934, Bridges played a prominent role in union strategy and negotiations. The strike ended with an arbitrated award that bolstered the union's role in the industry and delivered improved conditions for the members. Bridges emerged as an assertive, canny and incorruptible leader. To employers and political conservatives, his industrial militancy and truculent socialism personified the alien communist menace.

The unions were strengthened during a major strike in 1936. Next year Bridges and close colleagues established the International Longshoremen's and Warehousemen's Union, with Bridges as president. As his power increased, his political and industrial enemies launched repeated attempts to deport him to Australia, usually on the grounds—which he denied—that he was a member of the Communist Party of the USA. Government agencies brought criminal charges and civil suits against him, the Congress enacted laws specifically aimed at his deportation, and he twice appealed successfully to the Supreme Court. Although he had begun proceedings to become a US citizen in 1921 and 1928, it was not until 1945 that he completed the process. Efforts to strip him of his citizenship and expel him continued until 1955.

While consolidating on the West Coast, the ILWU had started organising the multi-racial workforce in Hawaii in World War II. This initiative confirmed the union's growing reputation as a champion of civil rights and added Hawaii's business elite to the burgeoning ranks of Bridges' enemies. He married Nancy Fenton Berdecio on 27 September 1946 at a civil ceremony in San Francisco. She divorced him in 1955, alleging, 'He's married to the union, not me'. On 10 December 1958 in a civil ceremony at Reno, Nevada, he married Noriko Sawada, a civil rights activist of Japanese heritage.

Despite his strong opposition to American Cold War politics, Bridges built his reputation as a charismatic labour leader on his skill and resolution as an organiser, strategist and negotiator. Eventually, his business opponents realised that they had to deal with a highly effective union chief rather than a communist conspirator. In 1960 the employers and union negotiated the Mechanisation and Modernisation Agreement, which facilitated technological change on the wharves while giving ILWU members greater security of employment and a generous pension plan. Although Bridges' legendary status as the leader who had transformed the longshoremen from 'wharf rats' to 'lords of the docks' was established, by the 1960s and early 1970s his power and influence were declining. Younger unionists saw the M&M agreement as an 'old man's' contract and radicals among them began to question his civil rights record. Industrial action in 1971 did not result in real improvements for ILWU members.

Described as 'rangy and thin, with a long, narrow head', a 'hawk nose' and 'sharp eyes under heavy lids', Bridges remained in office —some said for too long—until 1977, after which he lived comfortably in retirement as an elder statesman of the American labour movement. He died on 30 March 1990 in San Francisco and was cremated. His wife survived him, as did children from his first and third, and possibly second, marriages. Songs by Woody Guthrie and Pete Seeger, a plaza on the San Francisco docks and an endowed chair at the University of Washington commemorate him. Much of a growing body of writing about him and the ILWU has been published on the Internet by two educational foundations, the Harry Bridges Institute and the union-funded Harry Bridges Project.

C. P. Larrowe, *Harry Bridges* (1972); *Nation Review*, 19-25 May 1977, p 738; *San Francisco Chronicle*, 31 Mar 1990, p 1.   PETER LOVE

BRIGHT, SIR CHARLES HART (1912-1983), judge, was born on 25 November 1912, at Norwood, Adelaide, second child of Charles Bright, a 70-year-old English-born Baptist minister, and his second wife Annie Florence, née Hollidge, who was born in South Australia. Educated at Scotch College and the University of Adelaide (BA, LL B, 1934), Charles was admitted to the South Australian Bar on 15 December 1934. On 31 August 1940 at St Paul's Cathedral, Melbourne, he married with Anglican rites Elizabeth Holden Flaxman, a medical practitioner.

Having begun practising law in the firm of Shierlaw, Frisby Smith & Romilly Harry, in 1940 Bright entered into partnership with O. C. Isaachsen. Called up on 4 January 1943 for full-time duty as captain, Australian Army Legal Department, Militia, he transferred to the Reserve of Officers on 1 November 1944. In 1945 the law firm became Isaachsen, Bright & Zelling; after its dissolution in 1954, Bright joined D. B. McLeod in partnership. Bright, who specialised in commercial and taxation cases, took silk in 1960. He was president (1961-63) of the Law Society of South Australia and a councillor (1962-63) of the Law Council of Australia. In October 1963 he was appointed a judge of the Supreme Court of South Australia. He later became an associate of the International Commission of Jurists and an executive member of the World Association of Judges.

Involved in a wide range of community activities, Bright was a member (1950-67) of the council of governors of Scotch College and chairman of the council of Presbyterian Girls' College (1966-69) and of the Physiotherapists Board of South Australia (1953-63). He was president (1966-72) of Minda Home, Brighton, an institution for children and adults with intellectual disabilities, and vice-president of the South Australian division of the Australian Red Cross Society (1969-83) and of the State committee of the Musica Viva Society of Australia for some years. A foundation member (1966) of the council of the Flinders University of South Australia, he was its first pro-chancellor and chairman of the finance and buildings committee. In 1971 he succeeded Sir Mark Mitchell [q.v.15] as chancellor. He served until 1983 and guided the affairs of the council with 'skill and fairness' during an eventful period.

Bright had absorbed the values, though not the religious beliefs, of his liberal Protestant upbringing and admired what he saw as 'the spirit of independence and dissent which have always characterized the best South Australians'. He shared the new willingness of the Supreme Court in the 1970s, under Chief Justice J. J. Bray, to recognise that changed social attitudes should be reflected in the shaping and interpretation of law. A man of moderate and tolerant views, he was trusted by State governments of both main political parties. He was chairman (1969-78) of the Electoral (Districts Boundaries) Commission. In 1970 he was appointed royal commissioner to inquire into the anti-war demonstration organised by the Vietnam Moratorium Campaign, which, held in Adelaide in September of that year, ended in a violent confrontation with police. His recommendations formed the basis for an enlightened system of regulating assemblies and demonstrations in public places that was implemented through the Public Assemblies Act (1972) of South Australia.

In 1970-73 Bright chaired a committee of inquiry into the delivery of health services in South Australia. Its report made many suggestions for improvements and recommended the establishment of a statutory body, separate from the public service, to administer and co-ordinate all aspects of health care. As a result the South Australian Health Commission was created in 1977. In 1979-80 Bright was a part-time commissioner and special adviser to the government on health services. He also chaired (1976) a committee considering law and policy affecting persons with 'physical or mental handicaps' in the light of the United Nations declarations on their rights. Reports submitted in 1978 and 1981 proposed various measures to remove discrimination and to integrate people with disabilities into the community.

A short man, Bright was courteous and unassuming in manner, and always affable and self-controlled. He retired from the bench in December 1978 and was knighted in 1980. Enrolling in a postgraduate degree in history at Flinders University, he researched the life of Charles Flaxman, his wife's great-grandfather, who had migrated to South Australia in 1838 as the agent of G. F. Angas [q.v.1]. Following his resignation as chancellor because of illness, the university awarded him an honorary D.Litt. in May 1983. Three days later, on 16 May, he died of cancer at his North Adelaide home and was cremated. He was survived by his wife and their daughter and two sons. His book on Flaxman, *The Confidential Clerk*, was published later that year. In 1985 the Sir Charles Bright Scholarship Trust was established to provide scholarships for disabled South Australians undertaking post-secondary education. Flinders University holds a portrait of Bright by Robert Hannaford.

D. Hilliard, *Flinders University* (1991); *SA State Reports*, 1979, vol 20, p v; Flinders Univ, *Annual*

Report, 1983, p 4; *Advertiser* (Adelaide), 25 Oct 1963, p 3, 15 Dec 1978, p 10, 31 Dec 1979, p 1, 18 May 1983, p 32; B884, item S48836 (NAA); Bright papers (Flinders Univ Lib); private information.

DAVID HILLIARD

BRINDLE, KENNETH (1931-1987), community leader and Aboriginal rights campaigner, was born on 19 October 1931 in Sydney, son of Mary Brindle, who was born in New South Wales. Ken was raised from infancy in the United Aborigines Mission children's home, Bomaderry, and then in the brutal Kinchela Boys' Home, Kempsey (1942-44). Not allowed to attend high school, he worked 'about 80 hours a week' for a farmer near Tamworth. He ran away, picking up casual work and moving between Aboriginal reserves and stations, where his own people took him in. He said later 'in this business of helping one another along we [Aborigines] reckon we've got something pretty valuable that the white feller hasn't got'.

On 28 July 1952 Brindle enlisted in the Australian Regular Army. He served in the Republic of (South) Korea with the 1st Battalion, Royal Australian Regiment, in 1954-55 and was discharged on 27 July 1955. In the army he noticed that 'for the first time in my life white people were treating me as an equal. It made me realise that aborigines don't have to be inferior'. After living at Bega, New South Wales, and Dandenong and Lake Tyers Reserve, Victoria, he bought a house at Redfern, Sydney, where he lived with Mavis Goode, née Jacky, and their children. Young Aboriginal men from the country stayed there while adjusting to city life. Brindle worked for Peter's Ice Cream (New South Wales) Pty Ltd, the Metropolitan Water Sewerage & Drainage Board, the Foundation for Aboriginal Affairs and the Aboriginal section of the Department of Adult Education, University of Sydney.

In 1960 Brindle helped to re-establish the Redfern All Blacks Rugby League Club, seeking assistance with fund-raising from the Aboriginal-Australian Fellowship. Though initially suspicious of the AAF, which had both Aboriginal and white members, he became an executive member (1962-69). He participated in its ongoing campaigns against the New South Wales Aborigines Protection Act, 1909-1943, and the discriminatory police practices targeted at Aboriginal youths. Most of Brindle's involvement with the police was as an advocate for others, but occasionally he was prosecuted and fought the charges in court and won.

On 4 June 1963 a railway detective fatally shot an Aborigine running away from an attempted robbery. Brindle went to the Newtown police station seeking information; an exchange followed which ended with Detective-Constable Robert Armour charging Brindle with using insulting words. Brindle's claim that he was assaulted by Armour was not recorded. In court in January 1964 six prosecution witnesses supported Armour's evidence that Brindle was abusive and drunk but Rev. James Downing said that when he had inspected a wound on the inside of Brindle's mouth on his release there was not a trace of alcohol on his breath. This testimony, together with other inconsistencies in the prosecution case, led to Brindle's acquittal. The Council for Civil Liberties (New South Wales) supported a civil action against Constable Armour; the jury found in favour of Armour on the question of assault but awarded Brindle £400 damages plus costs for malicious prosecution. It was a significant victory for the Aboriginal community, which had rarely obtained redress through the legal system.

Brindle was of average height and build with a pleasant open face and striking blue eyes. As State secretary (1968-72) of the Federal Council for the Advancement of Aborigines and Torres Strait Islanders, he made an important contribution to the many campaigns and conferences that led to the removal of constitutional and legislative discrimination. With a philosophy of 'no charity, no handouts', he was particularly committed to providing educational opportunities for young Aborigines through the establishment of city hostels. He served (1969-74) as a trustee of the Aborigines Children's Advancement Society. His activism was characterised by an infectious energy and enthusiasm underpinned by intelligence, cunning and a sense of humour and he drew many converts to the Aboriginal cause. Those campaigning for Aboriginal civil rights were often branded as communists, but when Brindle was accused of being a 'red' he would laughingly reply, 'are you blind mate, I'm black'.

When Brindle considered writing a book on the lives of his Kinchela contemporaries, he found that the records of the Aborigines Protection (Welfare) Board were not easily accessible, so he indexed them to enable other Aborigines to research their past more easily. Soon after completing this task, he died of myocardial infarction on 10 April 1987 at his home at Waterloo, Sydney, survived by Mavis and their three daughters and two sons. He had been a foundation member (1963) and vice-president of the Aboriginal Education Council (New South Wales), which in 1989 created the Ken Brindle Memorial scholarships. The KBH Ken Brindle Memorial Shield is presented to the most promising player in the grand final of the annual New South Wales People's Knockout Rugby league competition.

K. Buckley, *Offensive and Obscene* (1970); F. Bandler and L. Fox (eds), *The Time was Ripe*

(1983); F. Bandler, *Turning the Tide* (1989); *Bulletin*, 8 Dec 1962, p 16; *Duran Duran*, May 1987, p 2; *Koorier* (Sydney), Dec 1987, p 5.

LYN BRIGNELL

BROCKHOFF, SIR JACK STUART (1908-1984), manufacturer and philanthropist, was born on 11 March 1908 in South Melbourne, third and youngest son of Victorian-born parents Frederick Douglas Brockhoff (1868-1961), manufacturer, and his wife Lola Landon, née Sleight. Frederick's father, Adolph, had migrated from Mecklenburg, Germany, to Victoria and started the biscuit-manufacturing firm A. F. Brockhoff & Co. Entering the business early in life, Frederick became governing director of the company, which was renamed Brockhoff's Biscuits Pty Ltd. Lola, who had been born into the Sleight family of undertakers, was a woman of strong social convictions. Jack attended Wesley College. He and his brothers, Harold Frederick (1902-1966) and Alan Bruce (1904-1989), were to spend most of their working lives with the family firm, controlling it after World War II.

In a felicitous spread of abilities and interests, Harold managed the marketing side, Alan the manufacturing operation and Jack the administrative, financial and corporate functions. This split of responsibilities enabled the brothers to work together harmoniously, while keeping their distance. Each was a director in charge of his sector. Jack was also managing director and later chairman. All three had a remarkable physical resemblance, though substantial differences of personality. Staff addressed them as 'Mr Jack', 'Mr Harold' and 'Mr Alan', and generally the atmosphere was friendly and paternal.

After 1945 the brothers anticipated a significant growth in demand for their products. Believing it to be economically imperative that they increase production, they purchased a large block of former market-gardening land at East Burwood in 1951 and opened an ambitious new factory there in 1953. The scale of operation allowed by the extra space and new plant gave their firm a competitive advantage and Brockhoff's share of the market expanded at the expense of its rivals T. B. Guest [q.v. Supp.] & Co. Pty Ltd, Swallow [q.v.6] & Ariell Ltd and Sunshine Biscuits Ltd.

Biscuit manufacturers mostly operated within one State but in the 1950s William Arnott [q.v.3] Pty Ltd of Sydney began buying out or merging with interstate firms. When the American-owned Nabisco Pty Ltd entered the Australian market, Arnott's, Brockhoff's and Guest's combined defensively, forming the Australian Biscuit Co. Pty Ltd, but at first keeping their operations separate. Nabisco sought to take over the publicly listed Swallow & Ariell in 1964 and Jack Brockhoff worked closely, shrewdly and courageously with Arnott's directors to beat Nabisco in a share-market battle, acquiring Swallow & Ariell for the Australian Biscuit Co.

Realising that the day of the medium-sized, one-State manufacturer was passing, Brockhoff then led his family firm into a full merger with Arnott's. The combined company became Arnott's Biscuits Pty Ltd in 1966 and the Brockhoff name gradually disappeared from supermarket shelves over the next few years. Arnotts Ltd was floated as a public company in 1970. Jack retired as chairman and managing director of the Melbourne operation, Arnott-Brockhoff-Guest Pty Ltd, in 1973 but was to remain a director of Arnotts Ltd until 1984.

Reserved, introverted and markedly shy, Brockhoff was nevertheless an astute businessman and investor who was also kind and honest. Much of his wealth came from private investment, an abiding interest. He could be very generous, but abhorred waste, show or pretence. He was a life governor of the Sandringham and District Memorial Hospital, the Royal Children's Hospital, the Burwood Boys' Home and the Victorian Civil Ambulance. In 1979 he organised a philanthropic trust, the Jack Brockhoff Foundation, and endowed it with $5 million. He was knighted that year. The foundation was dedicated to assisting 'the people of Victoria'. Most of its grants were of moderate amounts disbursed to a wide range of charities, but it gave priority to helping children and the elderly, and to funding medical research.

On 14 October 1933 at St John's Church of England, Toorak, Brockhoff had married Claire Cornelia Josephine Herd. The marriage was childless and broke down very quickly; the experience seemed to affect his personality, increasing his reserve. He lived modestly at Sandringham, a hard-drinking bachelor devoted to golf, bowls, sailing, fishing and business, and a member of numerous sporting clubs, including the Victoria Amateur Turf and the Victoria Racing clubs. Unexpectedly, on 27 June 1980 at Sandringham he married, with Uniting Church forms, Ursula Edith Lycoudis, née Hill, a widow who had recently been his housekeeper; the marriage was happy but short. Sir Jack died on 3 September 1984 at his home and was cremated. His will, sworn for probate at $7 455 835, provided the foundation with about $6 million in additional funds and almost $1 million more on the death of Lady Brockhoff in 1995.

Age (Melbourne), 14 Mar 1979, p 1, 15 Mar 1979, p 9, 4 Sept 1984, p 17; *New Idea*, 31 Jan 1981, p 10; *Sun News-Pictorial* (Melbourne), 4 Sept 1984, p 24; L. Sutherland, A Brief History of the Jack Brockhoff Foundation, 1979-1998, and of its Founder, Jack

Stuart Brockhoff, Kt. 1908-84 (ms, 1998, Jack Brockhoff Foundation, East Doncaster, Melbourne); private information.   ROBERT MURRAY

BROOKS, MARGARET STELLA; see LEE, M.

BROWN, CARTER; see YATES

BROWN, HENRY ALEXANDER (1900-1986), lay evangelist and Baptist pastor, was born on 12 April 1900 at Darjeeling, India, son of missionary parents Rev. Henry Ryland Brown and his wife June Halliday, née Symington. As a child of 6 Alex was gripped by the ministry of the evangelist Roderick Archibald, whose influence ultimately directed him towards a life similarly spent in children's evangelism. In 1913 his widowed mother took him to New Zealand, where she had family support. He worked on farms before going to Sydney in the early 1920s with a mission that became the Open Air Campaigners. Growing uneasy about their evangelistic methods, he left the group and took a farm job. In December 1923 Edmund Clark, the missioner of the Children's Special Service Mission (Scripture Union), invited him to join the interdenominational CSSM for three months. The letter of appointment mistakenly offered him a salary of £20 per annum; it should have read £200, but Brown's commitment was such that he accepted anyway. He studied in 1924 at the Melbourne Bible Institute, and resumed working for the CSSM in February 1925.

After conducting a CSSM camp at Cronulla, Sydney, that summer, Brown took charge of the children's meetings at the Katoomba Christian Convention, a major annual evangelical rally. He seemed to understand how children thought and felt. A tall, lean man, he used facial expressions to achieve particular effects. He was an individualist who was never discouraged by difficulties, as straightforward in his teaching as he was in his own faith. Bishop Graham Delbridge, an associate in youth ministry, described his style as 'effective, simple, childlike but not childish, and always directed at the needs of a person at his particular stage of development in life'.

For thirty-five years Brown travelled around the country setting up bush camps and beach missions, visiting schools and conducting services at local churches. His ministry extended to all States, but was concentrated on New South Wales and Queensland. On 25 February 1934 he married Joyce Samways (d.1974) at the Congregational Church, Sylvania, Sydney. She travelled with him until the birth of their first child in 1941, when they settled at Lewisham,

Sydney. In 1949 he was appointed as the Scripture Union's organising secretary and missioner in South Australia. A decade of solid effort in children's evangelism culminated in his work for the Billy Graham crusade of 1959.

Brown left the Scripture Union in 1960 to become pastor of the Burnside Christian Church, Adelaide. In 1967 he moved to Cootamundra, New South Wales, where he served as Baptist minister and superintendent of the Baptist churches of the State's south-west until 1975. He returned to South Australia, as pastor at Millicent (1976-79) and then at Peterhead, Adelaide (1979-80). Survived by his two sons and daughter, he died on 2 March 1986 at Norwood and was cremated.

J. and M. Prince, *Tuned in to Change* (1979); *SMH*, 6 Mar 1986, p 15; private information.
STUART BRAGA

BROWN, JOHN JOSEPH (1912-1989), trade unionist, was born on 4 April 1912 at Hawthorn, Melbourne, second child of Victorian-born parents Percy John Brown, carter and later a railwayman, and his wife Margaret Cathrine, née O'Halloran. Educated at St Brigid's School, North Fitzroy, Jack joined the Victorian Railways as a 'lad labourer' in 1926; he was employed in various roles, including carriage cleaner and boiler maker's help. In April 1931 he took leave and entered the Passionist Fathers' seminary at Goulburn, New South Wales, but he left next month. The Depression, he later explained, had a 'devastating effect' on him and in 1935 he joined the Communist Party of Australia. He was elected to the State council of the Australian Railways Union in 1936. Six years later he won the first direct election for the position of State secretary and, on taking office, suggested that his salary be reduced from £600 per annum to £500. From 1944 he also served as general (federal) president of the ARU.

In the campaign after World War II for improved wages and conditions, Brown was the most prominent trade union official in Victoria. He and C. L. O'Shea [q.v.] of the Australian Tramway and Motor Omnibus Employees Association led a transport strike in Melbourne in October 1946 that secured weekend penalty rates and three weeks' annual leave. Brown then supported the Amalgamated Engineering Union in its drive in 1947 for improved margins for skill. Further action by the tramways union in January 1948 resulted in the Hollway [q.v.14] Liberal and Country Party government's introducing the Essential Services Act. The legislation was proclaimed in November and officials of the railways and tramways unions were summonsed, but the prosecutions were withdrawn when the two unions agreed to submit disputes to the Trades Hall Council.

Brown clashed repeatedly with the moderate leadership of the THC. The press portrayed him as a commissar and a dictator; the red banner hanging in Unity Hall, the ARU's building in Bourke Street, was a particular affront. E. A. Drake-Brockman [q.v.8], the acting chief judge of the Commonwealth Court of Conciliation and Arbitration, condemned his 'irresponsible, loose demagoguery'. Communist officials also criticised Jackie Brown's lack of discipline, for he took his lead from the rank-and-file militants in the union. A robust six-footer (183 cm), non-smoker, teetotaller and fitness fanatic, he used the gymnasium of the Victorian Railways Institute to set world records in skipping; in September 1950 he achieved 30 111 turns in 155 minutes.

Brown withstood attempts by the Industrial Groups to defeat him until 1954, when he narrowly lost the ballot for secretary. The railways refused to re-employ him. Next year the Arbitration Court upheld an appeal against a new rule disqualifying him from contesting the secretaryship and he won it back in 1956—against the wishes of E. F. Hill [q.v.], the State secretary of the Communist Party. Brown sided with the group that opposed Hill's autocratic leadership and left the party in 1968. He remained State secretary and federal president of the ARU until 1975, when he was appointed to the board of the Victorian Railways. Once an exuberant, hard-working organiser, he had lost much of his fire.

On 19 October 1935 at the Catholic Church of Our Lady Help of Christians, East Brunswick, Brown had married Mabel Mary Dods, a machinist; they were divorced in 1944. At the office of the government statist, Melbourne, on 2 March 1946 he married Linda Victoria Chapple, a clerk and ARU official; she died in 1962. On 20 July that year, again at the government statist's office, he married Clara Ida Fraser, a housekeeper. He died on 25 July 1989 at Greenvale and was cremated. His wife survived him, as did the daughter of his first marriage and the son and two daughters of his second.

G. McDonald, *Australia at Stake* (1977); R. Gibson, *The Fight Goes On* (1987); T. Sheridan, *Division of Labour* (1989); T. Rigg, *John Joseph Brown* (2003); *Age* (Melbourne), 10 Oct 1942, p 2; *Sun News-Pictorial* (Melbourne), 31 Oct 1946, p 5; *Herald* (Melbourne), 26 May 1948, p 4, 26 Jan 1973, p 2; *Argus* (Melbourne), 29 May 1948, p 3; *Tribune* (Sydney), 2 June 1948, p 6.   STUART MACINTYRE

BROWN, THOMAS VICTOR STUBBS; *see* STUBBS-BROWN

BROWNE, FRANCIS COURTNEY (1915-1981), journalist, was born on 9 September 1915 at Coogee, Sydney, son of Courtney Browne, a tailor from New Zealand, and his Sydney-born wife Linda Veronica, née Heckenberg. Frank was educated at Christian Brothers' College, Waverley. After failing to win a bursary for university, he entered the Royal Military College, then at Victoria Barracks, in March 1934. He later claimed falsely to have won a 'gold pocket' for excelling in athletics, boxing, swimming and Rugby Union football. In August 1935 he was discharged as 'temperamentally unsuited to the military profession', though he later hinted that the real reason for his departure was his 'amorous activities' with an officer's wife. Events in Browne's life often received more than one explanation.

He spent a year as a cadet journalist on *Smith's Weekly*, then made his way as a ship's stoker to the United States of America, where he worked part time on the *Chicago Tribune* and boxed professionally as the featherweight 'Buzz Brown'. According to his own account, 'Buzz' fought twenty times for nineteen wins, losing only to Henry Armstrong, who later became world champion in three divisions simultaneously. Some have said that in 1937 Browne served with communist forces in the Spanish Civil War, was wounded, and received a Soviet decoration. Later in life he declined to confirm or deny this, but by then his political stance had become strongly anti-communist.

Between 1938 and 1941 Browne worked in Sydney as a publicist with film-distributing and advertising agencies, and as a greyhound racing writer for the *Daily Mirror*. Enlisting in the Citizen Military Forces on 23 January 1942, he served with anti-tank regiments and then, having been commissioned as a lieutenant in June, with the North Australia Observer Unit, a mobile group being prepared in Sydney for operational duty in the Northern Territory. Browne remained in Sydney and on 19 September 1942 at St Mary's Cathedral married with Catholic rites Marie Katherine Ormston (d.1963), a musician. Declared medically unfit for military service, he was placed on the Retired List on 10 February 1943.

Turning to politics, Browne stood unsuccessfully for parliament three times—in 1943 as the United Australia Party candidate for the Federal seat of Barton against Dr H. V. Evatt [q.v.14]; in 1944 as the Democratic Party candidate for the State seat of Bondi; and in 1947 as an Independent Liberal for the State seat of Vaucluse. He had become a branch president of the new Liberal Party in 1945, and had formed a Young Liberals' League which that party promptly disbanded.

These failures help to explain Browne's growing antipathy towards most politicians, with the notable exception of W. M. Hughes [q.v.9], of whom in 1946 he published a short, fulsome biography. Taller and heavier than his hero, Browne was bespectacled and prematurely balding, convivial and witty, but also bellicose. He was expelled from the Returned Sailors', Soldiers' and Airmen's Imperial League of Australia after throwing a Soviet flag at the State congress platform in 1946. Later he was charged with assault on several occasions.

By 1946 Browne had taken up his main vocation: the purveyance of political, business and personal information in a weekly newsletter for subscribers entitled *Things I Hear*. Disrespectful and sometimes scandalous, it was a gleaning of news, analysis and gossip. (Sir) John Gorton referred to it as 'Things I Smear'. Its gossip was sometimes maliciously unreliable, yet Browne could also be well informed and astute in political analysis.

Things I Hear managed to infuriate politicians of every party, particularly in Canberra, which Browne visited regularly. Thus it was not surprising, though the cause of some regret, that Federal parliament, in a unique exercise of its power under section 49 of the Constitution, called Browne and another defendant, Raymond Fitzpatrick [q.v.14], before the Bar of the House for breach of parliamentary privilege. The alleged breach had occurred in an article in a free advertising weekly, the *Bankstown Observer*, edited at the time by Browne and owned by Fitzpatrick, a wealthy haulage contractor known as 'Mr Big'.

In May 1955 the Labor member for Reid, Charles Morgan, had drawn parliament's attention to the offending reference which alleged his involvement in 'an immigration rackct'. The House of Representatives standing committee of privileges ignored advice from the clerk of the House, F. C. Green [q.v.14], that parliamentary privilege should not protect a member against allegations concerning his conduct outside the House, and that the proper place to seek requital was a civil court. Reporting no evidence of improper conduct by Morgan, the committee found Fitzpatrick and Browne guilty of a serious breach of privilege by publishing material intended to influence and intimidate a member in his conduct in the House.

Both men appeared before the Bar of the House on 10 June. 'Mr Big' spoke briefly and apologetically, but Browne gave as little ground as he might have done at a different kind of bar, talking vehemently about freedom of speech. During the ensuing debate Prime Minister (Sir) Robert Menzies [q.v.15] termed Browne's address 'an exhibition of unparalleled arrogance and impertinence', while the deputy-leader of the Opposition, A. A. Calwell (usually referred to in *Things I Hear* as 'Awful Arthur'), described Browne as 'an arrogant rat' and Fitzpatrick as 'an illiterate lout'. By 55 votes to 12 in the case of Fitzpatrick and 55

to 11 for Browne, the House resolved that both should be imprisoned for three months. And so they were, in Goulburn gaol, much to the disapproval of some press and public opinion.

On his release, Browne formed the short-lived Australian Party. In the 1960s he wrote a column for the *Daily Mirror* and exported sheep to Kuwait. He stood unsuccessfully for the Senate as an Independent in 1974. He produced *Things I Hear* until 1977, when he went to Rhodesia for sixteen months reputedly to fight terrorists and write speeches for the prime minister Ian Smith. Browne died of liver cirrhosis and meningitis on 14 December 1981 at Darlinghurst, Sydney, and was cremated. He had no children.

F. C. Green, *Servant of the House* (1969); G. Souter, *Acts of Parliament* (1988); *PD* (HR), 10 June 1955, p 1625; *SMH*, 24 Aug 1946, p 3, 11 June 1955, p 1, 16 Dec 1981, p 11; *People* (Sydney), 26 Apr 1950, p 18; *Observer* (Sydney), 5 Sept 1959, p 554; *National Times*, 24 Feb 1979, p 12; *Bulletin*, 9 Mar 1982, p 56; *Daily Mirror* (Sydney), 28 Feb 1984, p 20; A6119, item 83 (NAA).   GAVIN SOUTER

BUCK, VERA WINIFRED (1903-1986), composer and pianist, was born on 15 February 1903 at Kew, Melbourne, third daughter and fifth of nine children of William Buck, a Tasmanian-born accountant, and his wife Tessa Quinn, née Herberte, who was born in Victoria. Vera attended private schools in Melbourne. She played the piano from an early age and was said to have 'a prodigious memory', with one hundred solos at her command. On 18 November 1922 at the Methodist Church, Camberwell, she married Edgar Charles Wilson Burridge, an importer; they had two daughters and were to be divorced in 1937. She was radio-station 3AR's official accompanist in the late 1920s.

At age 15 Buck had written her first song, *Love of You*, which was performed at salon concerts in Melbourne. As a young woman she wanted 'to develop a real Australian spirit in her composing'. Allan [q.v.3] & Co. Pty Ltd published her early works. *Marche Orientale* (1928) and *Piper's Dance* (1931) sold well and were set for piano competitions and examinations. In 1930 she was awarded a scholarship to study composition with Fritz Hart [q.v.9], director of the Albert Street Conservatorium, East Melbourne. A gifted, driven woman who defied social norms by putting her career first, she placed her children in the care of relatives and moved to Britain later that year.

Buck's song *The Birds* (1932), with words by Hilaire Belloc, was sung by Florence Austral [q.v.7] and, in Australia, by Vera's sister, Consuelo (d.1933), a respected soprano and teacher of singing who promoted her music. Their sister Lilian (d.1928) had been a poet, and Buck set a number of her verses to music, including *Serenity* (1937). Her compositions published in London included *The Donkey* (1935), *Blue Bows* (1937) and *This Is My Prayer* (1938); the words were by G. K. Chesterton, Helen Taylor and Kenneth Ellis respectively. Under the pseudonym Pat Francis, she wrote light songs, two of which, *Across the Sands of Time* (1936) and *How Wonderful* (1937), used Bruce Sievier's lyrics. *Reminiscence* (1936), with words by Noel Cripps, and *Full Sail* (1937), with words by Perceval Graves, featured in musical events marking the coronation of King George VI in 1937; the British Broadcasting Corporation transmitted Peter Dawson's [q.v.8] recital of *Reminiscence* during the proceedings. She performed on stage and on radio and coached singers—including Jessie Matthews and Florence Desmond—for roles in musical comedies and films.

In 1938 Buck returned to Melbourne and continued to perform. Studio audiences for the Australian Broadcasting Commission's radio program 'Merry-Go-Round' watched her set to music lyrics, sent in by listeners, within ninety seconds of having seen the words. She married Bramwell John Gilchrist (d.1962), a manufacturer and a divorcee, on 15 February 1940 at Wesley Church, Melbourne. In World War II she gave recitals to raise funds and to entertain troops. The first movement of her *Concerto Impressionistique*, inspired by the campaigns in the Middle East, was performed in 1943; a reviewer described it as 'woven with definite skill and form'. Two songs published by Buck in 1943 used words by Toyohiko Kagawa: *A Hymn for Country* and *Take Thou the Burden, Lord. Until the Day I Die*, with words by A. D. Jones, appeared in 1945.

Buck was a vice-president of the Guild of Australian Composers. Talented and glamorous, she made a significant contribution to serious and popular music through her compositions and performances. Her songs were melodious and written with an economy of style, placing few demands on the piano accompanist, and allowing the singer to provide the dramatic interpretation. Survived by the daughters of her first marriage, she died on 2 January 1986 at Kew and was cremated.

G. R. Davies, *Music Makers of the Sunny South* (1934?); *Austn Musical News*, Nov 1925, p 37, 1 Jan 1929, p 25, Mar 1930, p 11, 1 Oct 1932, p 14, Mar 1933, p 2, June 1937, p 26, Mar 1938, p 22, 1 July 1938, p 18, 2 Aug 1943, p 25; *Musical Opinion*, Dec 1937, p 243.   GEORGINA BINNS

BUCKLEY, VINCENT THOMAS (1925-1988), poet, critic and professor of English, was born on 8 July 1925 at Romsey, Victoria, second son of Victorian-born parents Patrick Buckley, carter and sometime farm labourer, salesman and postman, and his wife Frances Margaret, née Condon, a librarian and school-teacher. Vincent spent his childhood in the Romsey district, an area of hilly farmland, much of it in the hands of Irish Australians. The poet was to celebrate this environment in his memoir, *Cutting Green Hay* (1983). His childhood straddled the Depression and his father's recurrent unemployment. Boarding in the city, he was educated by the Jesuits at St Patrick's College, East Melbourne. He said later, 'There's nothing like a boy of poor family given a Jesuit education. They're very faithful but uncomfortable colleagues'.

Buckley's Irish forebears had come to Australia from Cork and Tipperary, victims of 'the great emptying of Munster'. A century later he could still feel that 'the population was divided into Catholics and the others never actually seemed to *do* anything, except play football with us'. He was short and played as a rover before rheumatic fever and bad diagnoses put an end to sport. Illness helped to produce acute responses to physical sensation in his poetry.

After eight months as a clerk in the Commonwealth Department of Supply and Shipping, Buckley enlisted in the Royal Australian Air Force on 13 December 1943. He trained as a recorder but was invalided from the service on 5 February 1945. His later sequence of poems, 'Hospital Summer, Western Suburbs', reviewed a period of enforced reflection during which he had been confined in a military hospital in Sydney, a city whose poets were always reluctant to respond to him. In 1946 he enrolled at the University of Melbourne (BA, 1950; MA, 1954). He married Edna Jean Forbes, a salesgirl, on 12 July 1947 at St Patrick's Cathedral; they were to have two daughters before being divorced. From 1951 he taught in the university's English department. His teaching experience was recorded near the beginning of his career in a poem, 'Late Tutorial', and sardonically caricatured close to the end in another, 'Nightmare of a Chair Search Committee'. He always hated managerial bureaucracy.

Appearing in the same journals as the work of young avant-gardists of *Angry Penguins* descent, Buckley's poetry impressed with a lofty, hieratic idiom brushed by modernism: the passion of W. B. Yeats and Dylan Thomas, mollified here and there by the dandyism of John Crowe Ransom. His first collection, *The World's Flesh* (1954), did not wear well, and he came to realise its limitations as he moved into fluid idioms, a development reflected in his later essay 'Ease of American Language' (*New Poetry*, 1979).

In 1955-57 a Mannix [q.v.10] travelling scholarship enabled Buckley to live in England and work at the University of Cambridge on the moral criticism of Matthew Arnold,

F. R. Leavis and T. S. Eliot; *Poetry and Morality* (1959) resulted. He was in Cambridge at the same time as Ted Hughes, Sylvia Plath and A. S. Byatt. Over this period he began visiting the Ireland he had long imagined. Back at the University of Melbourne, he became the first Lockie fellow in creative writing and Australian literature, initiating the study of Australian writers and becoming one of the pioneers of the field.

The suasive eloquence of Buckley's critical prose came early. The pieces gathered in *Essays in Poetry: Mainly Australian* (1957) contain some of the most beautiful critical writing to have appeared in this country. Thus we have, memorably, of A. D. Hope, 'a heavy almost brooding mind consciously detaching itself in the act of poetry from what most exercises and torments it', and of Kenneth Slessor [q.v.16], 'there runs throughout his poetry a faint ground-bass of disgust with life'. These essays helped to establish a modern canon that included the works of Slessor, Hope, Judith Wright and James McAuley [q.v.15]. Such canon-formation was essential—then; there had to be books in print that could be set for the relevant courses.

Comparable stylishness was not to be found in Buckley's poetry until *Arcady and Other Places* (1966), which wedded his sense of presence with attachment to the solid world: the sturdy, or frail, objects surrounding our lives. He had now moved on and firmly grasped what the critic R. P. Blackmur described as 'behaviour'. In *Arcady*, the trees of his childhood had become tangible. 'Stroke', the first passionate suite, traced his father's hard passage toward death. Subsequent poems tilled two fields of behaviour: love and politics. The love poems in this volume were, no doubt, connected with the woman who would become his second wife; but they presented themselves as 'Versions from Catullus'. The persona left Buckley free to write such lines as:

When I, torment, feel my whole body
Lapse out at the first sight of you.
My mouth is drained of voice, my tongue
Stopped;

The collection also included 'Eleven Political Poems'. Here were angry satires against Stalinism and the shilly-shallying of 'fellow travellers'. These poems had been written after the fiercely divisive disarmament conferences of the 1950s. At this stage Buckley was deeply involved in politics, especially where the religious and secular overlapped. He became a leading 'public intellectual'. His schooling, membership of the Newman Society of Victoria and opposition to B. A. Santamaria's Catholic Social Studies Movement had forged his liberal Catholicism, but had also given it a debater's combative edge. When in the mid-1950s right-wing elements of the Australian

Labor Party—strongly anti-communist and largely Catholic—hived off and eventually formed the Democratic Labor Party, he remained in the thick of the conflict, balancing his hatred of totalitarianism with support of the ALP and its social policies.

For six years from 1958 Buckley intermittently edited the journal *Prospect*, many of whose contributors came from the Catholic centre-left. Politics was still in his blood in 1969 when he founded the Committee for Civil Rights in Ireland. In his later years, though, he was bitterly suspicious of the ways in which politics could debauch literature. Relations with the Church became more idiosyncratic as his career burgeoned. He remained part of a distinctive, Irish-Australian Catholicism, yet he grew less satisfied with what the hierarchy had to offer. On one social occasion he was bailed up by a 'literary bloke' who asked him about the Pope's reconfirmed ruling against contraception (1968). 'Silly old bugger panicked', was his gruff reply.

One of Buckley's most fascinating pieces was a 1970 essay in *Quadrant*, 'The Strange Personality of Christ'. Like Harold Bloom on the Torah, Buckley emphasised irony, absurdity and intellectual challenge. His Christ was oddly like the poet himself in making any question more difficult, any answer more paradoxical. This is a Jesus who 'shocks us into a kind of stillness not by what we recognize as his rightness but by what we sense as his strangeness'. Near the end of his life, in a short prose self-portrait, Buckley was to follow an admission that he watched sport on television 'as much as ever', and similar reflections, with a comment from Henry James: 'It is as impossible to avoid religion as it is to avoid morals'. He could not do so, but steadily refined it away to a subtle metaphysics.

The university had appointed Buckley to a personal chair in 1967. Like Hope, his friend and mentor, he became a distinguished example of that new figure, the poet-professor. In the title poem of *Golden Builders and Other Poems* (1976), Buckley paid tribute to formative meanings of Melbourne, much as Slessor had done for Sydney. He entered that city by way of William Blake's visionary London, his epigraph coming from 'Jerusalem' and including the vast question, 'What are those Golden Builders doing?'.

Buckley's third volume of criticism was *Poetry and the Sacred* (1968). In the essays which flock together there, the poet-critic addressed writers in whom the romantic impulse drives language toward mystery or transcendence. Of the critics in Australia whom John Docker characterised (negatively) as 'metaphysical', Buckley was perhaps the most romantic. Indeed, as Australian Leavisism split, many of its company veering into Marxism, he emerged as leader of the other party, standing out in his final decade as scorning 'theory'. He sought to retain 'the sacred' as a living concept, even as his relation to formal religion diffused.

Ancestral landscapes were always tugging at Buckley's poetry. His first, baroque response to that fabled country was the poem 'Walking in Ireland', his most profound the posthumously collected 'Hunger-Strike', which has been described in conversation by John Montague as the finest of all poetic accounts of the dark time in Northern Ireland. Indeed, many lyrics in Buckley's *Last Poems* (1991) were to be Ireland-based. An earlier, complete collection dealing with the Republic, its landscapes and its ways of life, was *The Pattern* (1979).

His Ireland was far more than a 'Celtic' dream. He visited or lived in that country on many occasions between the mid-1950s and 1986, haunted and often disappointed by its assortment of suggestions. He was pleased that the University of Melbourne awarded him the Dublin prize for 1977; it attached him to Ireland verbally. Observing its people years before the economic surge of the 'Celtic Tiger', he was seriously disturbed by what he saw as the country's 'virtual avoidance of play', its urban drug culture and its general aimlessness. For him, Ireland was a nation that had lost its memory, a loss that he was to struggle with in his late prose work *Memory Ireland* (1985), a discursive treatment of his relations with the Old World. The actual Republic distorts or effaces an Australian dream of Gaeltacht and benign ancestral voices. Much as William Wordsworth had borne witness to an England of beggars and crippled ex-servicemen, so Buckley would write of a mundane Ireland. As he put it in a later poem:

At dusk the sluttish children
Wandered down the Grand Canal
Where the soft lights lean over dark.
Who'll catch them when they fall?

Published simultaneously with *The Pattern*, his collection *Late-Winter Child* was a work that represented inner and outer, in a sense. Both books were made up of medium-short lyrics, or suites of the same. *Late-Winter Child* was remarkable for its capacity to celebrate, respondingly, a woman's body. At a time of pregnancy, he saw and felt the body of the mother-to-be as intimately as he so often did his own, in that poetry of vulnerability. On 18 September 1976 in a civil ceremony at Middle Brighton he had married Penelope Jane Curtis Buckley, a 33-year-old research student who had taken his name.

Buckley's last years as a professor were marked by continual illness, disillusion with universities ('The new broom may sweep cleanest, but what will clean the broom?'), and further visits to Ireland. He looked forward to a published entity entitled 'Poetry Without Attitudes', yet anxiety and dread trod close on his heels now. In 1985 he won the inaugural Red Earth poetry award, and he hoped that his retirement at the end of 1987 would bring him new imaginative freedom. As Peter Steele wrote of him, 'He regarded poetry as the great mediator or interpreter between the solitudes of the self and the bulking realities of the world'.

When he retired, Buckley had less than a year to live. Mortality lay all about him and in his third-last year he had lamented, thinking about a billabong near his suburban home, 'Who cares if I am dying if the banks are green'. He was working still at rhetorical freedoms, recalling the easy voices of William Carlos Williams and Galway Kinnell, away across the Pacific. His new anthology, *The Faber Book of Modern Australian Verse* (1991), developed in the teeth of his rapidly failing health. The introduction was never completed. Assembled by his widow from a manila palimpsest, it contained his characteristic plaint: 'All Australian poets are disadvantaged by the same comparative neglect ... They read poets who will never get the chance to read them'.

Buckley died of myocardial infarction on 12 November 1988 at Kew and was buried in Melton cemetery. His wife and their two daughters and the daughters of his first marriage survived him. Curiously, he had found questions about the relations between Aboriginal and non-Aboriginal Australians too hard to contemplate in his limited lifetime; perhaps Ireland occluded them, with its many centuries of colonial subjugation. His wonderful *Last Poems*, a book that crowned his achievement, was winnowed out from sheaves of remaining verse. The Vincent Buckley prize for poetry, which alternates between Irish and Australian poets, was first awarded in 1994. Much of his prose writing, especially, awaits collection and publication. But nothing, apart from scattered audiotapes, can recapture the remarkable soft authority with which he spoke and, above all, with which he rendered his poems to his willing listeners.

J. Davidson, *Sideways from the Page* (1983); C. Wallace-Crabbe, *Falling into Language* (1990); I. Hamilton (ed), *The Oxford Companion to Twentieth-century Poetry in English* (1994); *Meanjin*, vol 28, no 118, 1969, p 317; *Quadrant*, Aug 1976, p 26; Buckley papers (ADFA and NLA); private information and personal knowledge.

CHRIS WALLACE-CRABBE

BUGG, LEONARD FREDERICK (1918-1989), soldier, labourer, miner and tree feller, was born on 11 May 1918 at Wynyard, Tasmania, third child of Tasmanian-born parents

Frederick Henry Bugg, labourer, and his wife Laura Lavinia, née Williams. He worked as a labourer and miner before enlisting in the Australian Imperial Force on 16 May 1940. At that time he was 5 ft 11 ins (180 cm) tall, with a fair complexion, grey eyes and fair hair.

Arriving in Palestine in February 1941, Bugg served in Greece in March-April, probably with headquarters, I Corps. On 31 May he joined the 2/12th Battalion at Tobruk, Libya. The battalion left the fortress in August, but Bugg stayed until December. In March 1942 he returned to Australia with his unit. Sent to Papua in August, he took part in the battle of Milne Bay. He was hospitalised with malaria in October and with infected tinea in December. Brought home to Australia, he spent periods in hospital until April 1943, rejoining his battalion in Queensland in May. He embarked for New Guinea in August.

The high point of Bugg's military career came during operations in the Finisterre Range in January 1944. On the 22nd he commanded a section in an attack on a feature known as Prothero 2. A Japanese machine-gun and snipers hidden in trees were holding up the advance when Bugg, a Bren gunner, ran forward to a tree just 30 yards (27 m) from the enemy. Their bullets set alight his magazine pouches. Undaunted, he removed the webbing and continued firing. At his instruction, his men went round a flank while he covered them. He shot dead the enemy machine-gunner. His section then rushed and occupied Prothero 2. For his inspiring courage and aggression he was awarded the Distinguished Conduct Medal.

On 30 January Bugg was hospitalised with malaria. Two weeks later he was promoted to acting corporal. He returned to the 2/12th in March and that month his promotion was confirmed. Back in Australia, he was posted to the 24th Works Company in January 1945 and discharged from the army on 5 September. In 1946 he was a member of the Australian contingent for the Victory March in London.

Bugg's postwar life was peripatetic. At first he lived in Hobart, where a perceived slight led him to refuse to join the Returned Sailors', Soldiers' and Airmen's Imperial League of Australia. He did not join his battalion association, and marched in only one Anzac Day parade. In Melbourne during the war he had met Johanna Regina Joan Kennedy, whom he later married in Tasmania. They lived for some time at Table Mountain and Waratah. He undertook varied jobs, including mining and tree-felling, and travelled around Australia, doing some prospecting, before returning to Tasmania. Survived by his wife, their two daughters and two of their three sons, he died on 30 May 1989 at Burnie and was buried in Wynyard lawn cemetery. He had spoken little of the war, and at his funeral people who had known him for years were surprised to learn of his decoration.

D. Dexter, *The New Guinea Offensives* (1961); A. Graeme-Evans, *Of Storms and Rainbows*, vol 2 (1991); B883, item TX500138 (NAA); private information.   MARK JOHNSTON

BUICK, WILLIAM GEORGE (1923-1990), librarian and naturalist, was born on 29 June 1923 at Meldreth (Brooklyn) Park, Adelaide, eldest child of South Australian-born parents John Buick, motor painter, and his wife Clarice Ruby, née Wilson. Educated at Adelaide High School, George began work at 15 in a printer's shop. He gained a position as a junior library assistant at the Public Library of South Australia in 1940 and studied part time for matriculation. For nine months in 1944-45 he was librarian at the Adelaide Chemical & Fertilizer Co. Ltd; in July 1945 he was reappointed to the public library as a library assistant.

On 14 September that year Buick completed the registration examination of the Australian Institute of Librarians (from 1949 the Library Association of Australia). He had been active in the State branch of the association from 1943, first as a student member and then as an associate. Despite a slight speech impediment due to a harelip (generally concealed by a moustache), he addressed meetings, and gave his first paper, on postwar library planning, in 1944. After serving as branch secretary-treasurer from 1946 he was elected president in 1950. In his presidential address next year he spoke on 'Regional Planning and the Future of Libraries in South Australia'. At that time no local authority in South Australia was responsible for running a public library; Buick argued that a State-wide library service could be established, based on the regions identified in a 1946 report of the South Australian regional planning committee. His speech was published in 1952 in the *Australian Library Journal*.

In 1948-60 Buick was librarian-in-charge of the public library's country lending service. During this time he was a part-time student at the University of Adelaide (BA, 1956). On 13 September 1952 he married Barbara Laughton, a fellow librarian, in a civil ceremony at her Leabrook home. Awarded fellowships by the Carnegie Corporation of New York and the University of Chicago, United States of America, in 1957-58 he took a year's leave to study at the latter's graduate library school. He was awarded a master of arts degree in 1960 and, back in Adelaide, was promoted to assistant-principal librarian. The Libraries Board of South Australia published his thesis, *Population and Governmental Studies for the Provision of Public Libraries in South Australia* (1965).

Buick was appointed associate-librarian at the Institute of Advanced Studies, Australian National University, Canberra, in 1965. Still active in the LAA, he became a branch councillor, and representative (1965-66) for the Australian Capital Territory division on the general council. In 1966 he took up the post of librarian at the new University of Papua New Guinea, Port Moresby. He was inaugural president (1968-69) of the Papua and New Guinea branch of the LAA. A life member of the association from 1952, he was made a fellow in 1971. He left the Territory that year, having built up the university library's collection to over 100 000 volumes. Appointed (1972) founding librarian at Murdoch University, Perth, he again set about the task of establishing a university library from scratch, overseeing the construction of a new building and developing a collection of over 250 000 items. Throughout his career he had supported and promoted his profession; in addition to his committee work he served (1962-64) as an examiner for the LAA. He believed in fair play and social justice, opposed censorship, and thought that libraries should be freely accessible to all.

A keen naturalist, in 1969 Buick had produced a booklet on the indigenous flowers of the Territory of Papua and New Guinea. Over many years he pursued an interest in molluscs, forming a comprehensive collection and compiling a definitive citation index. He was a member of the Malacological Society of Australia and of the Royal Society of Western Australia, and president (1975-77) of the Western Australian Shell Club. In 1984 he retired from Murdoch in poor health and began work as a volunteer at the Western Australian Museum; in recognition of his efforts a new species of mollusc, *Splendrillia buicki*, was named after him in 1990. Survived by his wife and their son and daughter, he died of cancer on 8 December that year at Shenton Park and was cremated. He bequeathed his collection and his bibliographic records to the museum. In 1991 Curtin University named an award for academic excellence in a higher degree course after him. His wife Barbara, a founding member (1972) of the Women's Electoral Lobby, sat on the Western Australian Equal Opportunity Tribunal in 1985-94.

Austn Shell News, Jan/Apr 1982, p 7; *Murdoch Univ News*, 24 Feb 1984, p 2; *Jnl of the Malacological Soc of Aust*, 30 Nov 1990, p 92; Lib Assn of Aust, *Incite*, 11 Feb 1991, p 5.   G. A. STAFFORD

BULL, HEDLEY NORMAN (1932-1985), professor of international relations, was born on 10 June 1932 at Enfield, Sydney, third child of Sydney-born parents Joseph Norman Bull, fire insurance inspector, and his wife Doris Annie, née Hordern. Hedley attended Burwood Primary and Fort Street Boys' High schools, and the University of Sydney (BA, 1953), where he studied history and philosophy, gaining first-class honours in the latter. Throughout his life he acknowledged the intellectual influence of Professor John Anderson [q.v.7]. Having won a Woolley [q.v.6] scholarship, Bull went to England and read politics at University College, Oxford (B.Phil., 1955). He married Frances Mary Lawes, great-granddaughter of W. G. Lawes [q.v.5], on 13 March 1954 at the register office, Oxford; they adopted three children.

In 1955 Bull was appointed assistant lecturer in international relations at the London School of Economics and Political Science; he became a reader in 1963. After winning the Cecil peace prize (1956), he was awarded a Rockefeller travelling fellowship (1957-58), which took him to Harvard and other universities in the United States of America, and a North Atlantic Treaty Organisation fellowship (1959) to Paris. His book *The Control of the Arms Race* (1961), which gained him prominence internationally, showed that he had mastered the concepts and issues relating to nuclear weapons, while understanding the historical background of earlier attempts to limit other kinds of armament. An early member, he was later a councillor (1968-77, 1981-85) of the (International) Institute for Strategic Studies. In 1964 he accepted the post of director of the arms control and disarmament research unit of the British Foreign Office. Surveying the whole of his discipline, he often inflicted punishing blows on what he considered foolishness in its development, such as the 'scientific' pretensions of behaviourism. A notable example was his explosive article 'International Theory: The Case for a Classical Approach', published in 1966 in *World Politics*.

In 1967 Bull returned to Australia as professor and joint head of the department of international relations, Research School of Pacific Studies, Australian National University. He was also research director (1969-70, 1972-73) of the Australian Institute of International Affairs. In 1977 he went back to Oxford as the Montague Burton professor of international relations. He was a member (1968-71) of the Social Science Research Council of Australia and a fellow of both the Academy of the Social Sciences in Australia (1971) and the British Academy (1984).

One of Bull's major preoccupations was the nature of the international system and its potential for world order. He explored the implications of the great increase in the number of sovereign states since World War II. In particular, he asked whether Third World states would adapt themselves to what had been an essentially Eurocentric society. In his seminal work, *The Anarchical Society* (1977), he concluded that despite the brutalities of world politics, the historic system of sovereign states exhibited a degree of actual co-operation and the possibility of future extension of an international society. In 1984 he developed these themes further in *The Expansion of International Society*, which he edited with Adam Watson.

A formidable but always fair opponent in debate, Bull was a kind and patient teacher. He could be abrasive with both colleagues and students, but rarely caused lasting offence. Tall, slightly stooped and inclined towards portliness, he was serious but never solemn. Survived by his wife and their son and two daughters, he died of cancer on 18 May 1985 at Oxford and was cremated. He had been an atheist since 1949. The University of Oxford and the ANU created positions and scholarships in his honour.

R. O'Neill and D. N. Schwartz (eds), *Hedley Bull on Arms Control* (1987); J. D. B. Miller and R. J. Vincent (eds), *Order and Violence* (1990); *Balliol College Annual Record*, 1985, p 24; *Procs of the British Academy*, vol 72, 1986, p 395; *Times* (London), 20 May 1985, p 14; *SMH*, 21 May 1985, p 15; Bull papers (Bodleian Lib, Oxford, Eng); private information.

J. D. B. MILLER

BURBIDGE, BERYL EMMA (1902-1988), hospital matron, was born on 4 March 1902 at Gympie, Queensland, youngest of nine children of Victorian-born parents William Edward Burbidge, assayer, and his wife Maria Esther, née Wardle. Beryl's parents had moved to Gympie in 1893 during the gold rush. They became active members of the community and her father was mayor of the town in 1910. Educated at local state primary and high schools, Beryl left home at 19 to live with her sister at Charleville, where she worked as an assistant-nurse in a private hospital. In 1923 she began her training at (Royal) Brisbane Hospital; she obtained her general nursing certificate on 22 January 1927. Becoming a staff nurse, she was appointed sister in November. In 1929 she travelled to Hobart and in March next year gained her midwifery qualification at Queen Alexandra Hospital. She returned to Brisbane Hospital and in the 1930s took charge of medical, surgical and gynaecological wards. A senior sister from 1938, she worked in the operating theatre for four years.

On 12 January 1942 Miss Burbidge commenced full-time service in the Australian Army Nursing Service as a sister with the 6th Casualty Clearing Station, Ipswich. Appointed to the Australian Imperial Force on 2 November, she was promoted to senior sister next month (captain in March 1943). She served in general hospitals in Papua from September 1943 until January 1944, when she was recalled to take charge of the nursing staff at the Land Headquarters Medical Research Unit, Cairns, Queensland. There she supervised the care of volunteers exposed to malarial mosquitoes and oversaw the keeping of records of the secret experiments. She transferred to the Reserve of Officers on 14 November 1946.

In 1948 Miss Burbidge returned to Brisbane Hospital as a senior sister in the matron's office. In 1952 she was made deputy general matron and in this role she spent part of each day visiting wards to provide feedback to the matron. She transferred in August 1956 to the new South Brisbane (from 1959 Princess Alexandra) Hospital as acting-matron, but returned to Brisbane Hospital in March 1958 as general matron. Described as a 'large impressive woman', she lived in the nurses' quarters and was viewed by her staff as firm but approachable. She regularly toured the hospital to check everything from the organisation of ward staff to the cleanliness of the bathrooms. Helen Gregory observed that 'her military experience tended to reinforce both hierarchical structures and reliance on discipline'.

Miss Burbidge was president (1959-60) of the Queensland branch of the Royal Australian Nursing Federation, and a member of the State committee of the College of Nursing, Australia, and of the Centaur Memorial Fund for Nurses. Retiring on 28 February 1968, she was appointed OBE that year. She died on 27 November 1988 in her home at Stafford, Brisbane, and was cremated with Anglican rites. Her portrait (1945) by Nora Heysen is held by the Australian War Memorial, Canberra.

R. Goodman, *Our War Nurses* (1988); H. Gregory, *A Tradition of Care* (1988); H. Gregory and C. Brazil, *Bearers of the Tradition* (1993); North Brisbane Hospitals Bd, *Annual Report*, 1967-68, p 15; *Gympie Times*, 28 Mar 1987, p 3; private information.

MARIE COOKE

BURCHETT, WILFRED GRAHAM (1911-1983), journalist, was born on 16 September 1911 at Clifton Hill, Melbourne, youngest of four children of Victorian-born parents George Harold Burchett, builder and farmer, and his wife Mary Jane Eveline, née Davey. Wilfred spent his childhood in south-west Gippsland and Ballarat. He attended Ballarat Agricultural High School but his parents' indebtedness— resulting from the cost of medical treatment for his sister Amy (d.1921) and the failure of his father's building business—curtailed his formal education at age 15. While working in manual jobs during the Depression, he developed a hunger for knowledge, a flair for languages and a zest for travel.

In 1937 Burchett journeyed to London, where his proficiency in French and Russian secured him employment in the travel industry. He also frequented the London Linguists' Club. On 5 February 1938 at the register office, Hampstead, he married Erna Lewy, née Hammer, a divorcee and a Jewish refugee from Germany. In November 1938 he travelled to Berlin on behalf of his employers, the Jewish travel agency Palestine & Orient Lloyd Ltd, and arranged passages to Australia for thirty-six German Jews.

The Burchetts moved to Australia, arriving in July 1939. Disturbed by the locals' apathy towards Nazism, he sent letters and articles to Melbourne newspapers, warning of Hitler's planned European conquest. He also published accounts of his travels, and developed a working relationship with Andrew Fabinyi [q.v.14] of F. W. Cheshire [q.v.] Pty Ltd. Assisted by an advance from the publishers, and accredited with Australian Associated Press Pty Ltd, Burchett sailed to New Caledonia in early 1941. His book *Pacific Treasure Island* (1941), though essentially a travelogue, alerted Australians to Japanese designs in the Pacific.

Seeking a more active role as a journalist, Burchett headed for the Far East and in October 1941 reached the Chinese capital Chungking via the Burma Road. His reports on the Sino-Japanese War appeared in the Sydney *Daily Telegraph* and London *Daily Express*. After Japan entered World War II in December, he was appointed the *Express*'s Chungking correspondent. Early in 1942 he covered the rout of British forces in Burma then from June travelled extensively through Kuomintang-controlled China. Angered by the party's corruption and tendency to regard the communists and not the Japanese as the enemy, he left for India in October. While monitoring the British offensive in Arakan, Burma, in December, he was wounded. He courted Major General Orde Wingate and wrote *Wingate Adventure* (1944), an account of the Chindit operations in Burma.

In February 1944 the *Express* sent Burchett to the Pacific theatre. He sailed with the United States Navy's Third and Fifth fleets in their island-hopping advance on Japan. Although he wrote enthusiastically about the fire-bombing of Japanese cities, his attitude altered after atomic bombs were dropped on Hiroshima and Nagasaki in August 1945. He stole into Hiroshima in September, probably the first Western journalist to do so, and reported on the 'atomic plague' afflicting the inhabitants. Determined to suppress information about fall-out, the American authorities dismissed his story as pro-Japanese propaganda. The affair marked a watershed in his career and he began to question the morality of untrammelled American military might.

Burchett joined his family in London in November 1945. Soon afterwards the *Express* posted him to Berlin, where his dispatches turned stridently anti-American and pro-Soviet. He reported on the treason trial of Cardinal József Mindszenty in Budapest in February 1949. Convinced of Mindszenty's guilt, Burchett became an apologist for the Stalinist peoples' democracies emerging in Eastern Europe. His politics had moved away from those of the *Express* and he ceased writing for the paper in July. Having divorced his wife in 1948, on 24 December 1949 in Sofiya he married Vesselina (Vessa) Ossikovska, a Bulgarian communist.

In September 1950 Burchett returned to Australia and campaigned against the Menzies [q.v.15] government's Communist Party dissolution bill. Arriving in China in February 1951, he found the 'fullest flowering of humanity' in bloom under the communists. By July he was in Korea, covering the peace negotiations, from the North Korean and Chinese side, for the French communist newspaper *Ce Soir* and later for the radical New York *National Guardian* (*Guardian* from 1968). With the British *Daily Worker*'s Alan Winnington, Burchett accused the American-led United Nations negotiators of unnecessarily prolonging the talks while attempting to secure advantages on the battlefield. The pair also reported alleged atrocities by American soldiers.

The British Foreign Office secretly agreed with many of the concerns Burchett and Winnington expressed but did not believe their accusations (which were supported by material from left-wing sources) that American aircraft had conducted germ-warfare raids over North Korea and China in early 1952. The journalists were branded as traitors by their respective governments. By November 1953 the Australian government had collected evidence with a view to prosecuting Burchett for treason, but the director-general of the Australian Security Intelligence Organization, (Sir) Charles Spry, advised that the case against him was 'incomplete'. Burchett published his views on Korea in *This Monstrous War* (1953) and other works.

After a visit to Vietnam early in 1954, Burchett attended the Geneva Conference, which sought to resolve the Korean and Indo-Chinese conflicts. On 21 July delegates agreed to partition Vietnam. Five days earlier the US Far Eastern Command had sought the Australian government's concurrence in a plan to discredit Burchett and Winnington. Accompanying the request were statements by American pilots denying earlier admissions, made while prisoners of war in North Korea, that they had flown on germ-warfare missions. Repatriated, the airmen had recanted and claimed that Burchett and Winnington had extracted their confessions by force. The Australian government approved the request.

In 1955 Burchett lost the British passport on which he had always travelled. He applied for an Australian one and requested that his and Vessa's two children be registered as Australian citizens. At (Sir) Robert Menzies' direction, the government rejected both applications and asked the British Foreign Office not to grant him a new passport. In 1957 he was appointed the New York *National Guardian*'s correspondent in Moscow. He also resumed reporting (as 'Andrew Wilson') for the *Daily Express*; additionally, from 1960 he wrote for the London *Financial Times*. Although certain of communism's superiority over capitalism, he was beginning to question the nature of the Soviet form, which had stifled humanistic objectives. Moscow's self-assumed infallibility on communist affairs privately infuriated him. With the onset of the Sino-Soviet split, he sided with the Chinese; later he reversed his stance.

Burchett returned to Indo-China in 1962. Next year he travelled through territory controlled by the National Front for the Liberation of South Vietnam, reaching the outskirts of Saigon. The journey convinced him that the front, occupying vast tracts of the South, would determine the outcome of the Vietnam War, despite the presence of thousands of US military advisers helping South Vietnamese government forces. *My Visit to the Liberated Zones of South Vietnam* (1964) was one of several books he wrote on the conflict. In the mid-1960s he undertook three more treks through country under NLF influence. He moved from Moscow to Phnom Penh in 1965.

In 1966 the US government, via the British Foreign Office, sought Burchett's assistance in securing the release of captured American pilots held in Hanoi. He agreed on humanitarian grounds. Though little came of his representations, his efforts impressed the British and Americans. In 1968 he moved to Paris. He helped the Americans during the peace talks in the French capital that year, attempting to foster informal discussions between the delegations, and briefing British diplomats on the communists' negotiating tactics. Exploiting his increasing influence, he requested a British passport. The Foreign Office refused but permitted him to visit Britain that year. His autobiography, *Passport*, appeared in 1969.

Burchett was still barred from Australia. He had applied twice more for a passport, in 1960 and 1965. Buoyed by his entry into Britain, he tried again in July 1968. Prime Minister (Sir) John Gorton rejected his application but, following the deaths of his father (1969) and brother Clive (1970), the government allowed him to enter the country from Noumea aboard a private aircraft in February 1970. Unable to find evidence to support a charge of treason,

the Whitlam government finally granted him a passport.

In September 1971 Senator Vince Gair [q.v.14] had accused Burchett in parliament of being an operative of the Soviet KGB, tabling the testimony of a Soviet defector, Yuri Krotkov ('George Karlin'), who alleged Burchett's recruitment. An article reporting Gair's speech was published in the Democratic Labor Party organ, *Focus* (November), by his colleague J. T. Kane [q.v.]. Burchett sued Kane for defamation. At proceedings in the Supreme Court of New South Wales in 1974, it was revealed that Karlin's claim was based on supposition. Though the jury found Burchett had been defamed, it considered the *Focus* article a fair report of Senate proceedings and, therefore, protected by parliamentary privilege. Costs were awarded against Burchett, who appealed but lost. Unable to meet Kane's expenses, he was financially exiled from Australia.

Seemingly unbowed, Burchett covered the national liberation struggles in southern Africa, the genocide in Cambodia and the crumbling of China's socialist ideals. Only Vietnam had kept his revolutionary faith. With smears from the Kane case resounding in the press and right-wing journals, he wrote a second volume of autobiography, *At the Barricades* (1980), to tell his side of the story. By the time he settled in Bulgaria in 1982 he had published more than thirty books and countless articles. He died on 27 September 1983 in Sofiya. His wife, their daughter and two sons, and the son of his first marriage survived him.

Report of the International Commission for the Investigation of the Facts Concerning Bacterial Warfare in Korea and China (1952); *SMH*, 22 Oct 1974, p 1, 8 Aug 1985, p 9; *Australian*, 29 Sept 1983, p 9; A1838, item 131/6, item 3123/5/13, parts 1-3, and item 852/20/4/14, part 1, A6119, items 12-16, A6980, items S200614-S200616 and item S200619 (NAA); FCO 15/559, FCO 15/632, FCO 15/743-FCO 15/746, FO 371/186387 (PRO, London); Burchett papers (SLV); Burchett Passport Ctte papers (Univ of Melbourne Archives).   TOM HEENAN

BURGESS, FRANCIS PATRICK (1925-1989), journalist, was born on 14 March 1925 at Stanthorpe, Queensland, son of George Francis Burgess, a shearer from England, and his Queensland-born wife Ellen Mary, née Hickey. Pat's writing later showed the effects of his Catholic upbringing and schooling at Christian Brothers' College, Waverley, Sydney. On 30 November 1942 he was mobilised in the Royal Australian Navy. He was then 5 ft 9½ ins (177 cm) in height, with brown hair and eyes and a fair complexion; he later seemed taller. Physically robust, he was to be as at ease in the war environments of Vietnam and Cambodia as on the beaches of Sydney—particularly Manly—that he loved. After serving in HMA ships *Adelaide* and *Cowra*, he was discharged from the navy as an able seaman on 18 January 1946.

On 16 August 1947 at St Canice's Catholic Church, Elizabeth Bay, Sydney, Burgess married Una Elizabeth Oran, a stenographer. He studied arts and law at the University of Sydney in 1944-50: 'Went to university and wanted to be a writer. I didn't know what journalism was … and somehow I got the two confused', he later explained. His love of writing and sensitivity to detail would bring a rich poetic quality to his reporting.

Burgess's first jobs, beginning with the *Catholic Weekly*, were casual. He took up a cadetship with the Australian Broadcasting Commission and decided to become a foreign correspondent. Having served as a police roundsman for the *Daily Telegraph*, in 1962 he joined the *Sun* as senior feature writer. His copy was also used by other newspapers of John Fairfax & Sons [qq.v.4,8] (Pty) Ltd, especially the *Sydney Morning Herald,* and by News Ltd, in particular the *Daily Mirror*. His first foreign reporting experience was in Indonesia and in the early 1960s he reported from Timor for Fairfax and the London *Daily Telegraph*. Some material gathered during this time was used by Australian intelligence; he claimed that this was the only time he spied for his country. He also reported from Northern Ireland, Israel, Africa, Laos and Cambodia. In 1964 he won the Walkley [q.v.16] award for best newspaper feature story for despatches from the Territory of Papua and New Guinea.

In 1965 Burgess sailed for the Republic of Vietnam (South Vietnam) with the 1st Battalion, Royal Australian Regiment. He had chosen to chronicle the experiences of 6 Platoon, 'B' Company, trained by K. A. Wheatley [q.v.16] and known as the 'Scungees'. His reports varied from front-page news reports to cameo pieces such as 'Off-beat Vietnam'. He also wrote a series in *Pix* magazine entitled 'Where the Men Are'. Burgess was to be criticised by a British correspondent as a 'platoon reporter', but his response was that 'wars are finally won or lost at the sharp end'. He admitted to sometimes carrying a gun. His courage and his role in assisting two badly wounded Australian soldiers endeared him to many diggers.

Burgess again reported from Vietnam in 1966 and during the Tet offensive in 1968. He resigned from the *Sun* in 1970 and was sent by the *Daily Mirror* back to Vietnam, Laos and Cambodia. Although he generally reported sympathetically about the Australian soldier, he was still declared 'black' on occasion. In one incident Prime Minister (Sir) John Gorton 'turfed' him off an official aircraft in Singapore for his increasing criticism of the Australian government's stance on Vietnam.

In 1978 Burgess was awarded his second Walkley award, for the best television current affairs report: as a freelance journalist with a film crew, he documented Highway One from north to south in Vietnam. Perhaps this success owed something to his Churchill fellowship, awarded in 1968, to study at the British Broadcasting Corporation techniques for combining television documentary work with that of the newspaper correspondent. He published a novel, *Money to Burn* (1982), and an account of Australian reporters at war, *Warco* (1986).

Burgess loved the freedom of the foreign correspondent: 'It is, at last, very much his own barrow that he pushes'. His writings were full of lively and unforgettable images. Humour and colourful depictions of events and people often disguised the serious nature of the messages. Although he admitted to self-censorship to protect the 'gentle reader', he lamented that the public took little notice at times of significant issues: he believed that his reports on tuberculosis in Timor, for example, 'achieved exactly sweet nothing'. His legacy tells a different story—a rich and courageous life that sought individual freedom in areas of extreme conflict. Pat Burgess died of motor neurone disease on 23 January 1989 at Narrabeen, Sydney, and was cremated. He was survived by his wife and their daughter and three sons.

G. Souter, *Company of Heralds* (1981); T. Bowden, *One Crowded Hour* (1987); J. Hurst, *The Walkley Awards* (1988); *SMH*, 24 Jan 1989, p 8; *Australian*, 24 Jan 1989, p 3; *Canberra Times*, 3 Oct 1992, p C4; A6770, item Burgess F P (NAA); T. Payne, The Australian Press and the Vietnam War (paper given to AWM Hist Conference, 1986, copy on ADB file); T. Bowden, interview with F. P. Burgess (ts, c1978, copy on ADB file).   TRISH PAYNE

BURNET, SIR FRANK MACFARLANE (1899-1985), medical scientist, was born on 3 September 1899 at Traralgon, Victoria, second of seven children of Frank Burnet, bank manager, and his wife Hadassah, née McKay. Born in Scotland, Frank migrated to Australia as a young man; Hadassah was born in Victoria and also had Scottish forebears. Presumably to distinguish him from his father, the boy was known as Mac from an early age, and the sobriquet stuck. The family does not seem to have been close. Hadassah was busy looking after a handicapped daughter and Frank was a somewhat remote authority figure. A shy, serious child, Mac had a passion for reading. The family moved to Terang in 1909, and during rambles in the countryside the lad developed an avid interest in collecting and drawing beetles.

Following his primary education at Traralgon and Terang state schools, Mac went as a boarder to Geelong College on a scholarship. He later recounted that these years were not particularly happy, due in part to his retiring nature. Nevertheless he did well academically, winning a scholarship to Ormond [q.v.5] College, University of Melbourne (MB, BS, 1922; MD, 1924), where he continued to excel, coming second in a class that included (Dame) Jean Macnamara, (Sir) Roy Cameron, (Professor) Rupert Willis [qq.v.10,13,16] and (Dame) Kate Campbell [q.v.]. During his residency at the (Royal) Melbourne Hospital, he became fascinated with the intellectual challenges of neurology, but his superiors deemed him more suitable for laboratory than clinical work. He was appointed a senior resident in pathology at the Walter and Eliza Hall [qq.v.9] Institute of Research in Pathology and Medicine.

The institute's director, C. H. Kellaway [q.v.9], soon spotted Burnet's great promise and took him under his wing. Then, as now, it was thought that a young Australian medical researcher's training was incomplete without a spell abroad, so Burnet spent 1925-27 at the Lister Institute of Preventive Medicine, University of London (Ph.D., 1928). Back in Melbourne in 1928, he was made assistant-director of the Hall institute. On 10 July that year at Kew he married, with Presbyterian forms, Edith Linda Marston Druce. Linda was to prove a pivotal influence in his life, shielding him from mundane practical concerns, supporting his diligent work habits, acting as a sounding board for ideas and, later, as finances permitted, accompanying him on his many overseas trips. Theirs was a truly close union which produced two daughters and a son.

A major turning point in Burnet's career came when (Sir) Henry Dale, director of the National Institute for Medical Research, London, offered him a two-year fellowship (1932-33) to carry out research on viruses (Dale was later to nominate him for a Nobel prize). Viruses had been hard to work with and had not been clearly visualised, but, early in the 1930s, a series of advances, particularly the isolation of the influenza virus, made the field exciting. The next twenty-five years of Burnet's life were to be devoted to the study of viruses, principally influenza, that threaten people and animals. Dale wanted him to stay in London but he elected to return to his post in Melbourne.

In 1944 Kellaway left to become director of the Wellcome Research Institution in London. Burnet, too, had temptation thrown in his way. On his first trip (1943-44) to the United States of America, he was offered a chair at Harvard University. He refused and instead applied for the directorship of the Hall institute, despite the fact that Kellaway had advised him against it, fearing that his protégé might not be suited

to administration. Burnet's application was successful and he assumed office in March 1944; he was also appointed professor of experimental medicine at the University of Melbourne. In the event, he proved to be an inspiring leader of a team small by international standards but at the forefront of world virology.

While Kellaway and Dale strongly supported Burnet, neither was really a scientific mentor. In both Melbourne and London he forged his own path, initially authoring most papers by himself or with a research assistant. His first solid body of work had dealt with bacteriophage viruses, tiny parasites that infect and grow within bacteria. Having read in 1924 Félix d'Hérelle's *The Bacteriophage* (1922), Burnet soon established that many types existed, characterised by the different bacteria they could infect, their different patterns of growth, and the different kinds of antibodies they elicited when injected into laboratory animals.

Burnet studied how invisible virus particles attached themselves to the bacterial host cell and how they grew inside it, finally bursting the cell and releasing a brood of progeny into the growth medium. He noted how the genetic material of the virus appeared to integrate with the genetic material of the bacterium, and how certain metabolic shocks could extract it again, activating viral growth. In addition, he investigated genetic mutations in both bacteriophages and their bacterial hosts. This preoccupation produced thirty-two papers by 1937. As he would prove to be on other occasions, he was ahead of the times. His work preceded by about a decade the studies of the so-called 'phage club', the members of which, led by Salvador Luria and Max Delbrück, used generally similar experiments to lay the foundations of microbial genetics, and thus indirectly of molecular biology.

Burnet's interest in animal viruses had been stimulated at the National Institute for Medical Research. His first major contribution to the field was to improve and elaborate on Ernest Goodpasture's technique of growing these organisms in fertile hens' eggs. Burnet worked out how simple mouth or nasal washings could be injected into eggs as a convenient way of isolating a fresh virus. He learnt how to grow large quantities of a virus in eggs. The present method of producing enough influenza virus to mass-produce vaccines is based on this work. Burnet also carried out important studies into poliomyelitis (being the first to show that there was more than one strain, a crucial finding for the later development of a vaccine); many types of pox, including cowpox and mousepox; herpes; mumps; psittacosis; and numerous other viruses.

Microbe-hunting was not Burnet's main interest, however. He wanted to get close to the nature of viral reproduction, and thus to the secret of life. Making ingenious use of the membranes surrounding the chick embryo, he developed a novel method of quantifying virus numbers, giving his work a degree of precision akin to what had been achieved in the simpler bacteriophage systems. He and his colleagues, particularly Alfred Gottschalk [q.v.14], studied how the influenza virus attached to its target cell before entry and also how it detached from the cell surface prior to the invasion of a new batch of cells. In 1951 Burnet and Patricia Lind made the then heterodox finding that when a cell was infected with two different influenza virus strains, some of the progeny viruses that came out were recombinants with traits of each of the parent strains. It is now known that such reassortant viruses are potential precursors of major epidemics. A member of Burnet's team, Gordon Ada, was the first to show that the genes of the influenza virus consisted of ribonucleic and not deoxyribonucleic acid.

Though seemingly fundamental and reductionist, Burnet's work had important practical applications. Chief among these were his unsuccessful attempts to produce a live, attenuated, anti-influenza vaccine that could be administered intranasally. A significant contribution was his identification of a rickettsial organism as the cause of the serious typhoid-like disease of abattoir workers, 'Q' fever. This microbe is now known as *Coxiella burnetii*. A discovery of great importance, that he had made in 1928, was the cause of the deaths of twelve children at Bundaberg, Queensland, following their immunisation against diphtheria. He found that the bottle containing the vaccine had been contaminated with *Staphylococcus aureus* ('golden staph').

Thinking of himself as a naturalist and admiring Charles Darwin more than Louis Pasteur, Burnet sought to draw general biological and ecological truths from particular research findings. He examined specific problems from a broad biological and evolutionary viewpoint. Starting at his base in the ecology of human infectious diseases, he branched out into fields such as population genetics, human biology, cancer and ageing. His early, 'semipopular' books were immensely influential. Two such works were *Biological Aspects* (title changed in later editions to *Natural History*) *of Infectious Diseases* (1940), which ran into four editions and was translated into Italian, Japanese, Spanish and German; and *Virus as Organism* (1945), which was translated into Russian and Japanese. All of his books reflected his belief in the unity of biology and his conviction that natural processes needed to be understood in a holistic sense if useful human action were to follow.

The decision by Burnet in 1957 to switch his work, and that of his institute, to immunology has come to be seen as a master-stroke, though some senior virologists were dismayed at first. His fascination with the immune response to infection had begun in 1928, following the Bundaberg disaster. He rendered staphylococcal toxin non-poisonous by formalin treatment and studied the immune response of rabbits to the injection of this 'antigen'. A first injection evoked a very feeble antibody response, but a second dose a few weeks later gave a much faster and stronger boost to antibody levels, which rose in an exponential fashion for about five days. This outcome convinced him that 'something' must have been dividing as a result of antigen administration.

His interest thus piqued, Burnet investigated theories of antibody formation as part of his virus work. The central puzzle was the fact that animals and people can make so many antibodies, all different, in reaction to whatever antigen is presented. The prevailing explanation for this diversity was the direct template hypothesis, which held that, as the antibody molecule was synthesised, it fitted itself against a template of the antigen, much as metal is moulded against a die. With each passing year, Burnet became more convinced that this theory was wrong. In particular, it could not explain the booster response, the exponential increase in antibody levels, the observation that the quality of antibody improved with successive immunisations, and the fact that people and animals do not form antibody against their own tissues. Finding a better theory became a magnificent obsession.

Burnet published several monographs on the subject, at first reporting little progress. In his and Frank Fenner's *The Production of Antibodies* (1949), however, he made the prediction that was to win him the 1960 Nobel prize in physiology or medicine. Burnet argued that if a foreign substance were introduced into an embryonic animal, before its immune system had matured properly, the antigen would 'trick' the body into accepting the relevant molecule or molecules as 'self' rather than 'not-self'. As a result, no antibody would be formed, even when the antigen was introduced later in life. This phenomenon, which came to be termed immunological tolerance, was not supported by Burnet's own experiments, but was validated in 1953 by (Sir) Peter Medawar (who shared the Nobel prize with Burnet), Rupert Billingham and Leslie Brent.

In 1955 Niels Jerne published a paper arguing that antibodies pre-existed in the body before the antigen was introduced, and for Burnet 'the penny dropped'. The antigen merely had greatly to accelerate the production of this naturally occurring substance. Jerne said nothing about how such a vast range of natural antibody types could be fabricated, and the mechanism he proposed for the accelerated synthesis was clumsy. Burnet's clonal selection theory, published in the *Australian*

Journal of Science in 1957 after he became aware of a similar insight by David Talmage, postulated the idea of a large repertoire of spontaneously synthesised antibodies but located these as receptors on lymphocytes (white blood cells), each lymphocyte making only one antibody specificity. All an antigen had to do was to find the lymphocyte with a corresponding receptor, and to stimulate its repeated division, at the same time promoting accelerated antibody synthesis.

Burnet reasoned that the improvement in the quality of antibodies as immunisation progressed reflected the mutation and selection of cells with improved antibody on their surface. Immunological tolerance, he thought, was due to the deletion of antigen-binding cells if antigen (self-antigen) was encountered too early in life. Autoimmune diseases, where the body permits an immune attack against one of its own tissues, was seen as being due to 'forbidden clones', reflecting some failure of the tolerance mechanism. Both the booster response and the exponential rise in antibody levels were ascribed to sequential divisions of antibody-forming, clonally selected cells. Curiously, Burnet was not tempted to test his theory experimentally but it turned out to be essentially correct, and it set the agenda for much of immunology research over the next fifteen years. He considered clonal selection to be his most important scientific contribution.

There were other, less admirable reasons for Burnet's move away from virology. The subject was becoming more and more closely tied to molecular biology, which he detested. Virology also depended increasingly on the growth of viruses in test tubes and not in his beloved fertile eggs. Moreover, it was making greater use of high technology, for example in research involving radioisotopes, of which he had an exaggerated fear. Fortunately, the Hall institute's numerous contributions to cellular immunology vindicated his change in direction. In his last years as director he had much joy in examining disease progression in certain strains of mice genetically prone to autoimmunity.

Burnet's was a contemplative, almost solitary kind of genius. To forge his imaginative, synthetic constructs, he needed quiet and isolation. The thrust and parry of a vigorous discussion with a gifted colleague were not for him. He preferred the peace of his own small study at home—usually on the very evening of the day's experiment—when striving to accommodate a new finding into the constantly changing pattern of his speculative framework. For him, there was never a failed experiment. When the results did not pan out as expected, he believed that nature was trying to tell him something. He would simply force the uninterpretable data into some kind of order, designing the next experiment to test

the appropriately modified hypothesis. He published quickly, his critics accusing him of sloppy work. Although a talented and ingenious experimentalist, he left it for others to refine the results, preferring to move on to the next big problem.

Passionately committed to the world of ideas, Burnet had the extraordinary gift of being able to take apparently unconnected observations, forge a link between them, pose the next question and, during his heyday as a bench-scientist, design the next deceptively simple experiment to create a new paradigm. His originality was fed by wide and disciplined reading; in a sense the whole world was a laboratory waiting to confirm or refute the latest flight of his imagination.

Burnet served on numerous national and international committees, chairing the (Australian) Radiation Advisory Committee (1955-59) and the (British) Commonwealth Foundation (1966-69). Never afraid to speak out on public issues—such as the use of nuclear energy, which he first opposed then later supported—he assumed greater prominence after winning the Nobel prize. He worked extensively with publishers and the media to promote his blend of popular science, history, social and political theory and philosophy. To this endeavour, as previously to science, he brought originality, imagination, intuition, naïve honesty, conceptual breadth and daring, and an idealistic, impractical wisdom.

Showered with honours, Burnet won more than twenty major scientific awards, including the Copley medal (1959) of the Royal Society, London (to which he had been elected a fellow in 1942), the (American) Lasker award (1952) and the (German) Emil von Behring prize (1952). Thirteen Australian and overseas universities conferred honorary degrees on him. He was president of the International Association of Microbiological Societies (1953-57), the Australian and New Zealand Association for the Advancement of Science (1957), the Australian Academy of Science (1965-69) and other learned bodies, and was a fellow or member of many more. He was knighted (1951), appointed to the Order of Merit (1958), and appointed KBE (1969) and AK (1978). Between 1941 and 1978 he delivered some fifty named lectures, most overseas. In 1961 he was named Australian of the Year.

'Sir Mac' officially retired at 66, but, as guest professor in the University of Melbourne's department of microbiology, kept up a routine of daily work for the next twelve years. In this period he produced a remarkable thirteen books on a wide range of topics including virology, immunology, human biology, ethics and philosophy. His publications included an autobiography, *Changing Patterns* (1968), and a history, *Walter and Eliza Hall Institute, 1915-1965*

(1971). Some of his later books, among them *Genes, Dreams and Realities* (1971) and *Endurance of Life* (1978), received a critical reception; for example, his eugenicist and sociobiological views provoked controversy.

In 1973 Burnet suffered a severe loss: Linda died of a leukaemia affecting the very cells (lymphocytes) which he had been studying so assiduously. For a brief period he tried to cope alone in the small retirement house they had built at Kew, but he was not very good at looking after himself. Moving to Ormond College, he found himself out of tune with the younger generation there. On 16 January 1976 at Canterbury he married, with Presbyterian forms, Hazel Gertrude Jenkin, née Foletta, a widow who had been a singer and was a volunteer librarian in the microbiology department. They shared nine companionable years at her home in Canterbury.

Although he left his office and ceased his daily routines in 1978, Burnet continued to write, his last paper being published in 1983. He died on 31 August 1985 at Port Fairy and, following a state funeral, was buried in Tower Hill cemetery. His wife and the children of his first marriage survived him. Many consider him to be the greatest scientist Australia has produced, and it is noteworthy that his sixty years of sustained creativity were lived, almost continuously, in his homeland. No one who loves Australian science will ever forget his example.

A. M. Silverstein, *A History of Immunology* (1989); C. Sexton, *Burnet* (1999); G. J. V. Nossal, 'Sir MacFarlane Burnet (1899-1985)', *Nature*, vol 317, no 6033, 1985, p 108, and 'Frank Macfarlane Burnet', *MJA*, 9/23 Dec 1985, p 629; *Biog Memoirs of Fellows of the Royal Society*, vol 33, 1987, p 101; Burnet papers (Univ of Melbourne Archives).

G. J. V. Nossal

BURRELL, Sir HENRY MACKAY (1904-1988), naval officer, was born on 13 August 1904 at Wentworth Falls, New South Wales, only son and third of five children of Thomas Henry Burrell, a schoolteacher from England, and his Victorian-born wife Eliza Heather, née Mackay. He grew up in a family that was imbued with the values of patriotism and community service. His father, although aged 55, enlisted in the Australian Imperial Force during World War I and served in Egypt as a sergeant.

Educated at Parramatta High School, Burrell entered the Royal Australian Naval College, Jervis Bay, Federal Capital Territory, in January 1918. He gained colours for hockey and graduated in 1921. Becoming a midshipman in May 1922, he rose to sub-lieutenant in April 1925 and lieutenant in July 1926. He served in a number of RAN and Royal Navy ships in Australian and European waters in the 1920s before specialising as a navigator in Britain in 1930.

During the 1930s Burrell was navigating officer in, successively, a minesweeper, HMS *Pangbourne*; two destroyers, HMA ships *Tattoo* and *Stuart*; a cruiser, HMAS *Brisbane*; and, after qualifying from an advanced navigation course in 1935, two cruisers, HM ships *Coventry* and *Devonshire*. The captain of *Devonshire* criticised him for being too familiar with sailors, but he thought the ship 'would have been more efficient if officers and ratings had been in closer touch'. On 27 December 1933 at Scots Church, Melbourne, he had married with Presbyterian forms Margaret Isabel MacKay; they were to be divorced in November 1941. Burrell was promoted to lieutenant commander in July 1934. He completed the course at the RN Staff College, Greenwich, England, in 1938 and was posted to Navy Office, Melbourne, as staff officer (operations). War was looming and there was an urgent need for the RAN to build up its readiness. After the outbreak of hostilities, Burrell was concerned with the threat of enemy surface raiders in Australian waters and arrangements for convoying troop-ships to the Middle East. He was promoted to commander in June 1940.

Five months later Burrell went to Washington to join the Australian delegation headed by R. G. (Lord) Casey [q.v.13] at secret talks between Britain and the United States of America on the strategic situation in the Pacific. In January-April 1941 he served as the first Australian naval attaché in Washington. He participated in British-American staff conversations to develop a strategic concept for the still hypothetical entry of Japan and the United States into the war. The talks recognised that future priority would be accorded to the European theatre and, as a consequence, major US Navy units would be transferred from the Pacific to the Atlantic. Burrell's progress reports on the talks revealed increasing concern that the USA would be prepared to abandon the Far East, a realisation that perhaps affected his attitudes for the rest of his naval career.

Burrell took command of the new 'N' class destroyer HMAS *Norman* at Southampton, England, in September 1941. The ship's first duty was to convey a British Trade Union Congress delegation to northern Russia. *Norman* then joined Admiral Sir James Somerville's Eastern Fleet in the Indian Ocean. This fleet with its old capital ships was fortunate to avoid being annihilated by the overwhelming Japanese force of Vice Admiral Nagumo. In his memoirs, *Mermaids Do Exist* (1986), Burrell contested the British official history's assertion that Somerville was determined to avoid action with the Japanese, and regarded the survival of the Eastern Fleet as more good luck than good management. *Norman* was in action in the Mediterranean in mid-1942 during operations to resupply Malta. She was also engaged in escorting troop convoys in the Indian Ocean and was with the covering force at the capture of Diego Suarez and the assault force at Tamatave and Majunga, Madagascar. In February 1943 Burrell was mentioned in despatches for bravery and resource during the Madagascar operations.

In September 1943 Burrell was again at Navy Office, Melbourne, as director of plans. At the office of the government statist on 21 April 1944 he married Ada Theresa Weller, a mica specialist known by the surname Coggan. Much of his work at Navy Office involved planning for the use of British Commonwealth forces in the closing stages of the war against Japan and the basing of the British Pacific Fleet in Australia. In May 1945 he took command of the new Tribal-class destroyer HMAS *Bataan*. The ship joined the US Seventh Fleet and was in Tokyo Bay for the Japanese surrender ceremony in September, later assisting in the recovery of RAN prisoners of war from Sendai.

Promoted to captain in June 1946, Burrell was appointed deputy chief of Naval Staff in October. A major focus of his work for the next two years was to form the Fleet Air Arm and to introduce carrier aviation in the RAN. For twelve months from October 1948 he commanded the RAN's flagship, the heavy cruiser HMAS *Australia*. He completed the 1950 course at the Imperial Defence College, London, then became the assistant Australian defence representative in London. In December 1952 he assumed command of the light fleet carrier HMAS *Vengeance*.

Temporarily posted as DCNS in August 1954, Burrell was promoted to acting rear admiral in February 1955 (substantive in July) and made flag officer commanding HM Australian Fleet. In mid-1956 he was appointed to Navy Office to investigate a new officer structure for the RAN. The outcome was the General List of officers although Burrell himself was uncomfortable with the resulting additional authority for non-seaman officers. In September he became second naval member of the Naval Board (chief of naval personnel). He returned to the position of FOCAF in January 1958, flying his flag in HMAS *Melbourne*. On 24 February 1959 he was promoted to vice admiral and made chief of Naval Staff in Canberra. Appointed CBE in 1955 and CB in 1959, he was elevated to KBE in 1960.

As CNS, Burrell confronted critical force-structure dilemmas but, with a supportive minister for the navy in (Sir) John Gorton, won favourable decisions for the RAN, including approval to acquire Oberon-class submarines, Ton-class minesweepers, the survey ship HMAS *Moresby* and Wessex anti-submarine helicopters, and to commission the fleet tanker HMAS *Supply*. However, Burrell's greatest successes were to convince the government to reverse its 1959 decision to disband the Fleet Air Arm (at least as far as helicopters were concerned) and to buy three Charles F. Adams-class guided-missile destroyers from the USA. This purchase was a significant break from the tradition of acquiring British-designed warships. Burrell's alleged refusal to support efforts to retain fixed-wing naval aviation led some to suspect that he accorded it low priority. He retired from the RAN on 23 February 1962.

Sir Henry gained satisfaction from his farm, Illogan Park, on the Shoalhaven River near Braidwood, New South Wales. Diagnosed with heart problems soon after retirement, he suffered a major heart attack in 1980. In August 1981 his wife died. Survived by the two daughters and son of his second marriage, Burrell died on 9 February 1988 in Woden Valley Hospital, Canberra, and was buried with Anglican rites in Gungahlin cemetery.

Burrell had served with distinction at sea and had been an extremely able staff officer ashore. As CNS, he recognised the need for independence in Australian defence thinking and was prepared to step aside from unquestioning acceptance of principles inherited from the RN. Naturally friendly and approachable, he was an enthusiastic sportsman, excelling at Rugby Union football, tennis and hockey. He liked a bet and owned several successful racehorses. He was known for his common touch, his cheerful friendliness, a keen interest in the well-being of his men and an ability to bridge the generation gap between himself and younger people. With his egalitarian outlook and other qualities, he may well have been the first 'real' Australian to hold the office of CNS.

F. B. Eldridge, *A History of the Royal Australian Naval College* (1949); G. H. Gill, *Royal Australian Navy 1939-1942* (1957) and *1942-1945* (1968); Australian Naval Aviation Museum, Friends and Volunteers, *Flying Stations* (1998); D. Stevens (ed), *The Royal Australian Navy* (2001); *Navy* (Sydney), Nov 1947, p 20; *SMH*, 23 Feb 1962, p 2; *Canberra Times*, 10 Feb 1988, p 13; *Jnl of the Austn Naval Inst*, May 1988, p 11; A6769, item Burrell H M (NAA).

SAM BATEMAN

BURROW, KATHLEEN MARY (1899-1987), educator and community leader, was born on 18 April 1899 at Mudgee, New South Wales, elder daughter of English-born Elijah Richard William Graham, mining engineer, and his wife Catherine Mary, née Ray, who was born in New South Wales. From their dirt-floored cottage at the goldfield at Clarkes Creek, Kate attended the one-teacher Windeyer Public

School, and then boarded at St Matthew's Convent of Mercy School, Mudgee. Sponsored by the parish priest, she attended the University of Sydney (BA, 1922; Dip.Soc.Stud., 1944). A founding member of the University Catholic Women's Association, she was also a committee member of the Newman Association of Catholic Graduates. On 17 January 1925 she married Kenney William Noel Burrow (d.1954), a librarian, at St Mary's Catholic Church, Mudgee.

While teaching physical culture at North Sydney Girls' High School, she had undertaken voluntary work setting up physical education in Catholic orphanage schools. In 1926, with her sister Anne, who had trained in the United States of America, she founded the Graham-Burrow School of Physical Education, which provided exercise, deportment and dancing classes in Catholic schools throughout Australia for forty years. They organised St Patrick's Day sports, events for visiting dignitaries and celebrations such as the 'Living Rosary' display at the Sydney Showground for the Commonwealth Jubilee in 1951, all of which involved thousands of children. She completed a massage certificate (Dip. APA, 1936), and was a registered physiotherapist (1947-85) and, before 1950, a member of the Physiotherapists Registration Board.

Through her lucrative, wide-ranging business, Mrs Burrow moved to leadership in public life. President of the Legion of Catholic Women, Archdiocese of Sydney (1949-59), and of the Australian Council of Catholic Women (1957-59), she was the Australian representative (1957-65) on the World Union of Catholic Women's Organisations. Diplomatically mollifying the male hierarchy, she extended the influence of Catholic women's groups, initiating lasting co-operation with other religions and organisations concerned with justice, human rights, women's issues, migration, media and education. She served as international secretary (1954-60) and convenor for the mass media (1976-82) of the Australian National Council of Women (National Council of Women of Australia) and president (1969-72) of the Pan-Pacific and South East Asia Women's Association of Australia. Supportive of the State division of the United Nations Association of Australia for thirty years, she was chairman of its United Nations Educational, Scientific and Cultural Organization standing committee and a member of its executive committee. She travelled extensively, representing these organisations at international conferences.

A substantial figure, about 5 ft 10 ins (178 cm) tall, Mrs Burrow was a commanding presence. She was a charming hostess in her Ashfield home, a caring mentor, a highly principled and forthright advocate and a superb communicator and organiser who 'promoted social harmony often among divergent groups'. She was appointed MBE in 1956, awarded the Papal Cross *Pro Ecclesia et Pontifice* in 1977 and the United Nations peace medal in 1976 and 1986. Survived by her daughter and one of her two sons, she died on 20 May 1987 at Croydon. Following her funeral at St Vincent's Catholic Church, Ashfield, she was buried in the Catholic section of Rookwood cemetery.

H. M. Carey, *Truly Feminine, Truly Catholic* (1987); *Catholic Weekly*, 24 Feb 1949, p 21, 1 July 1987, p 24; *SMH*, 17 Apr 1962, p 21, 17 July 1963, p 15, 10 Feb 1976, p 8, 25 May 1987, p 7; *Sun-Herald* (Sydney), 27 May 1962, p 90; private information.

MARIANNE PAYTEN

BURTON, HERBERT ('JOE') (1900-1983), economic historian, university administrator and educationist, was born on 29 November 1900 at Chuwar, Queensland, eighth and youngest child of English-born Samuel Edwin Burton, farmer, and his Queensland-born wife Ada, née Pellatt. He was educated at Ipswich Grammar School and the University of Queensland (BA, 1922), where he studied modern languages, resided at St John's College and played both Rugby Union and League for the university. Selected as Rhodes scholar for Queensland in 1922, he went to Queen's College, Oxford (BA, 1925; MA, 1929), and gained first-class honours in modern history.

Returning to Australia, Burton taught first at Ipswich Grammar School and then at the Collegiate School of St Peter, Adelaide. He married Barbara McLennan, a kindergarten teacher, on 6 January 1928 at St Mary's Church of England, Kangaroo Point, Queensland. Barbara called him Joe, the name by which he came to be universally known. In 1930 he was appointed senior lecturer in economic history at the University of Melbourne. Five years later he was awarded a Rockefeller Foundation fellowship to study French economic history and thought. He published papers on the Australian economy, immigration and population. Promoted to associate-professor in 1946, he was head (1944-48) of the department of economic history. He accepted administrative responsibilities with alacrity, becoming chairman (1936-48) of the board of studies in public administration, sub-dean (1943-48) of the faculty of economics and commerce, chairman (1946-48) of the Union board of management, and academic staff representative (1947-48) on the council. Beyond the university, he served as foundation president (1936-40) of the (Australian) Council for Civil Liberties, president (1936 and 1947) of the Victorian branch of the Economic Society of Australia and New Zealand, and vice-president of the Victorian branch of the Australian League of Nations Union.

In November 1948 Burton was appointed inaugural principal and first professor (the chair was in economic history) at the Canberra University College, established in 1929 as a college of the University of Melbourne. Before taking the post he was awarded a Carnegie fellowship, to investigate the operations of small universities in North America and Britain. As principal, he was responsible for the transformation of the CUC—created to provide tertiary studies for public servants enrolled part time and dependent on part-time lecturers—into an institution of higher education respected throughout the nation for the quality of its staff and students. He recruited Manning Clark (history), L. F. Crisp [q.v.] (political science), H. W. Arndt (economics) and A. D. Hope (English). His leadership facilitated the amalgamation (1960) of the CUC and the Australian National University. He was appointed principal of the School of General Studies, ANU. As well as creating national undergraduate scholarships to attract the nation's top school leavers to the ANU, he built residential accommodation for its many interstate students.

After retirement in 1965, Burton served as the chairman of the committee of inquiry into the need for a college of advanced education in the Australian Capital Territory. This committee provided the blueprint for the Canberra CAE, later the University of Canberra, and for other colleges of advanced education in Australia. In 1977 he was made an honorary college fellow of the CCAE. He was also a councillor (1967-81) of the Royal Military College, Duntroon, and chairman (1969-80) of the Design and Siting Review Committee of Canberra. As secretary (1967-71) of the Social Science Research Council of Australia, he had guided its conversion into the Academy of the Social Sciences in Australia, of which he was the executive director (1971-73). As a member (1945) of the former, he automatically became a fellow of the latter.

Appointed CBE in 1962, and emeritus professor of the ANU on retirement, Burton was awarded honorary doctorates of laws by the University of Queensland (1967) and the ANU (1983), and an honorary doctorate of commerce (1983) by the University of Melbourne. A fellow (1964) of the Australian College of Education, he was an honorary life member (1971, honorary fellow from 1978) of the Australian Institute of Urban Studies. He had served on the editorial board of the *Australian Rhodes Review* and was a member of the Australian Round Table and the Commonwealth Club. His recreations included tennis, golf and trout fishing.

Burton was of medium height and stocky physique, with short, thick hair that turned grey prematurely. He was affectionate, sincere, tolerant and totally unpretentious. The citation for the honorary degree from the ANU referred to him as 'a good and gentle Australian'. A colleague, J. D. B. Miller, said that Burton's idea of a university was less austere than Cardinal Newman's, being 'centred more on personal contact than on the achievement of high discovery'. He was enthusiastic about the qualities of the young, and eager to seek out their views and ambitions. As an economic historian, he was an uncompromising advocate of economic growth, contending in a commencement ceremony address at the CUC in 1949 that 'learning and the discovery of new knowledge flourish most in countries where economic progress is taking place, and in their periods of most rapid economic progress'.

Predeceased by his wife (d.1981), Burton died on 24 July 1983 at Southport, Queensland, while visiting relatives and friends, and was cremated. Two sons, born prematurely, had died soon after their birth. Joe bequeathed his estate in equal shares to Canberra Grammar School and Burton Hall, ANU, which had been named after him. The University of Canberra established the Burton medal, an award for undergraduates, in his honour. A portrait by Louis Kahan hangs in the library of Burton and Garran halls.

Herbert 'Joe' Burton, 1900-1983 (1984); S. G. Foster and M. M. Varghese, *The Making of the Australian National University 1946-1996* (1996); *Canberra Times*, 30 July 1983, p 8; *ANU Reporter*, 12 Aug 1983, p 2; I. Hamilton, taped interview with H. Burton (1982, NLA).   SELWYN CORNISH

BURY, LESLIE HARRY ERNEST (1913-1986), banker, public servant and politician, was born on 25 February 1913 at Willesden, London, son of Ernest Bury, Anglican clergyman, and his wife Doris Elma, née Walgrave. Scholarships and financial assistance from an uncle enabled Leslie to attend Herne Bay College, Kent, and to matriculate at Queens' College, Cambridge (BA, 1934; MA, 1949). He rowed in Queens' third VIII, joined the Cambridge University Conservative Association, and obtained second-class honours in part I of the economics tripos and part II of the law tripos.

Recruited to the economic department of the Bank of New South Wales, Bury arrived in Sydney on 14 December 1935 and 'spent quite a number of months trailing round' with the royal commission on monetary and banking systems. He made useful contacts. Courteous and unhurried, he was 'very single-minded about things he wanted'. Close to his three sisters, he treated women with bantering gallantry and enjoyed dancing, although his lanky 6 ft 4 ins (193 cm) frame made him a challenging partner. On 23 August 1940 at St Mark's Church of England, Darling Point, he married Anne Helen Sise, daughter of C. E. Weigall [q.v.12].

Mobilised in the Citizen Military Forces on 22 January 1942, Bury transferred to the Australian Imperial Force on 23 August. He served with the Heavy Artillery, North Head, and with the 12th Radar Detachment before being posted to Alf Conlon's [q.v.13] Directorate of Research and Civil Affairs in January 1945. In January-February Sergeant Bury was detached to the Department of External Affairs, Canberra. He was discharged from the army as a warrant officer, class one, on 4 September and appointed second secretary in the economic relations division of the department on 10 May 1946. Accustomed to the 'ordered procedures of banking', he was dismayed by diplomatic administration, but acquired enduring respect for his colleagues' professionalism after working with them abroad in trade negotiations. He joined the Treasury in 1949, and moved to Washington in 1951 as Australian alternate executive director (executive director from 1953) of the International Monetary Fund and of the International Bank for Reconstruction and Development.

Bury had little experience of domestic policy-making and was decidedly ambivalent about politicians. Yet he spoke of politics as 'the prime profession' and returned to Sydney to seek Liberal Party preselection for the blue-ribbon House of Representatives seat of Wentworth, vacated through the resignation of Sir Eric Harrison [q.v.14]. At the by-election on 8 December 1956, three 'independent Liberals' opposed him. Denying claims that (Sir) Robert Menzies [q.v.15] had foisted him on the electorate, Bury scraped in on preferences, with 41 per cent of the primary vote.

In parliament, his trenchant criticism of economic management led journalists to link him with A. J. Forbes, H. B. Turner [q.v.] and W. C. Wentworth, and to dub these outspoken Liberal back-benchers the 'Oxbridge group'. Bury was closest to Forbes; both were less wilful, and steadier in judgment, than Turner or Wentworth. A fervent free trader, Bury regarded Adam Smith as 'the greatest economist', and attacked Australian Keynesians for failing to address the inflationary effects of their 'hyper-employment' policy, which disadvantaged professionals and the salaried middle class. On 22 December 1961 he was appointed minister for air and minister assisting the treasurer. His warm regard for the treasurer Harold Holt [q.v.14] scarcely compensated for the drudgery of acting as his 'punch boy'.

On 25 July 1962 Bury made headlines by contending that the economic consequences of British entry to the European Economic Community had been 'greatly exaggerated'. The *Sydney Morning Herald* opined that he was the tool of Holt and Treasury; Bury insisted that the views were his own. Menzies demanded his resignation from the ministry on 27 July after the leader of the Country Party and minister for trade, (Sir) John McEwen [q.v.15], claimed that the speech had weakened Australia's negotiating position and jeopardised its rural industries. Reported to be 'shocked and upset', Bury used his 'new-found freedom' to reiterate that the underlying issue was political: European integration was fundamental to Australian survival in a 'dangerous world'. He returned to the ministry on 18 December 1963 with the new housing portfolio. Promising no 'big, lurching changes', he introduced mortgage insurance and bonuses for first-home buyers.

When Holt succeeded Menzies on 26 January 1966, Bury was promoted to cabinet as minister for labour and national service. His removal of the 'marriage bar', which precluded the appointment of married women as permanent officers in the Commonwealth Public Service, was widely applauded, as was his resolute handling of industrial disputes. But growing public opposition to the Vietnam conflict dogged his administration of selective national service and tested his political skills. He was rebuffed by cabinet colleagues when he proposed an alternative form of civilian service, and he and the minister for the army (Sir) Phillip Lynch [q.v.] found themselves targeted by protesters, who occupied Bury's offices, and picketed his home, chanting 'lynch Bury, bury Lynch'.

An unsuccessful challenger for the Liberal Party leadership following Holt's disappearance in December 1967, Bury supported the new prime minister, (Sir) John Gorton, and on 12 November 1969 was appointed to succeed (Sir) William McMahon [q.v.] as treasurer. Unlike Holt and McMahon, Bury worked at the Treasury, rather than from his ministerial offices at Parliament House. In cabinet he proved no match for McEwen and Gorton as they pushed McEwen's Australian Industry Development Corporation proposal through against Treasury advice. Suffering from coronary atherosclerosis and hypertension, Bury looked 'very worn out', and appeared 'to waffle' and to lack concentration.

On 22 March 1971, twelve days after his swearing-in as Gorton's successor, McMahon shifted Bury to the foreign affairs portfolio. Bury was slow to engage with his new duties and continued to champion publicly a broad-based consumption tax. McMahon sacked him on 1 August, spreading rumours that the foreign minister was resigning because of serious illness. Bury himself announced, however, 'In good old words I have been sacked', prompting the *Australian* to brand the prime minister 'a nasty little twirp'. Bury declined to recriminate, commenting: 'Political life is full of hazards, even for Prime Ministers'. After losing preselection for his Wentworth seat, he retired from parliament at the 1974 election. He was appointed CMG in 1979.

A member of the Australian Institute of International Affairs (president of the Canberra branch in 1949-51) and of the Sydney group of the Round Table, Bury was also a fellow of the Australian Society of Accountants and an associate of the Bankers' Institute of Australasia. At various times he was a director of Duncan's Holdings Ltd, Legal & General Assurance Society Ltd, Lend Lease Corporation Ltd, Barclays Australia Ltd and Parkes Management Ltd. He belonged to the Union and Royal Sydney Golf clubs, and listed carpentry as his recreation. Survived by his wife and their four sons, he died on 7 September 1986 at his Vaucluse home and was cremated.

Bury's languid manner was redolent of pre-war Cambridge; like his charm and conviviality, it deflected attention from his sharp intelligence. He was a decisive, tough-minded departmental administrator. Although he was ill served by the increasingly important medium of television, on which he could appear laconic, wary and lacking in human warmth, colleagues recalled his candour, integrity and humanity.

P. Howson, *The Howson Diaries* (1984); P. Edwards, *A Nation at War* (1997); I. Hancock, *John Gorton* (2002); *PD* (HR), 19 Mar 1957, p 25, 15 Mar 1960, p 238, 14 Aug 1962, p 281, 16 Sept 1986, p 701, (Senate), 16 Sept 1986, p 438; *SMH*, 27 July 1962, pp 1 and 2, 28 July 1962, pp 1 and 2, 2 Aug 1971, p 1; *Bulletin*, 14 Mar 1964, p 13; *Australian*, 19 May 1967, p 7, 2 Aug 1971, p 8; M. Pratt, interview with L. H. E. Bury (ts, 1975, NLA); series SP1115 (NAA); private information.   DONALD BOADLE

BUSCH, ROLLAND ARTHUR (1920-1985), Presbyterian and Uniting Church minister, theologian and chaplain-general, was born on 26 October 1920 at Windsor, Brisbane, eldest of three children of Arthur Emil Busch, a pork butcher from Germany, and his Queensland-born wife Harriet, née Beck. 'Rollie' spent his childhood at Toowoomba, attending local state schools until he was 15 when, to assist his family financially, he became a telegram-boy with the post office. In 1938 he enlisted in the Militia. Commencing full-time duty with the 25th Battalion on 17 September 1941, he served in the signals platoon and rose to sergeant in March 1942. He transferred to the Australian Imperial Force in July and took part in the battle of Milne Bay, Papua, in August-September. On 2 July 1943 he was commissioned as a lieutenant. He was posted to headquarters, New Guinea Force, where he became staff captain (air maintenance). From January 1944 he served with various movement control groups. Mentioned in despatches,

he returned to Australia in March 1945 and was employed as a railway transport officer. He transferred to the Reserve of Officers on 1 May 1946 and worked briefly for the Queensland Department of Public Works.

Having decided to become a Presbyterian minister, Busch studied part time to gain his matriculation and in 1948 entered the University of Queensland (BA, 1951; MA, 1954). On 14 August 1948 at St John's Church of England, Penshurst, Sydney, he married Evelyn Mavis Smith, a nurse whom he had met in New Guinea. Graduating with first-class honours in philosophy, he lectured (1951-62) part time at the university in that subject while enrolled as an external student of Melbourne College of Divinity (BD, 1953). He studied divinity at the Presbyterian Theological Hall within Emmanuel College, University of Queensland (BD, 1955), gaining first-class honours in Old Testament and New Testament. On 16 February 1954 he was ordained and inducted into pastoral charge of St Giles's, Yeerongpilly, Brisbane. He spent a year at Union Theological Seminary, New York, graduating (1958) master of religious education.

Busch was professor of New Testament studies in the Presbyterian Theological Hall (1961-78) and in the Congregational, Methodist and Presbyterian Joint Faculty of Theology (1968-77). He also taught Biblical studies part time (1961-74) in the faculty of arts, at the University of Queensland. As principal of Emmanuel College (1962-78), he oversaw a 50 per cent increase in college membership and the admission of women in 1975. Theologically he was a liberal within the mainstream Protestant neo-orthodoxy. Although he was influenced by Rudolf Bultmann and other leading twentieth-century theologians, his thorough training in philosophy allowed him to assess critically both received and current theology. He gave a large degree of freedom of interpretation to both staff and students.

Convener of the Queensland Church's department of Christian education (1960-63) and board of local mission (1970-74), Busch was State moderator in 1972-73. He played a leading role in establishing the Uniting Church (1977), and served (1977-79) as moderator of the Queensland synod. In 1978 he supported the Aurukun and Mornington Island Aboriginal communities, who were resisting the Queensland government's efforts to bring them under State control. For his ongoing commitment to the Indigenous people's struggle for justice, the Uniting Aboriginal and Islander Christian Congress made him an honorary member in 1985. In 1979-85 he was foundation principal of Trinity Theological College, Brisbane. On 21 May 1982 he was installed as president of the national assembly of the Uniting Church for a three-year term. A leading ecumenist since the 1960s, he served as chairman (1985) of the Brisbane College of Theology.

In 1954 Busch had been appointed chaplain, 4th class, in the Citizen Military Forces. He was promoted to senior chaplain, headquarters, Northern Command, in 1963 and chaplain-general (Presbyterian) in 1968. From 1979 he was chaplain-general (Uniting Church in Australia). Placed on the Retired List in 1981, he served on the Religious Advisory Committee in the Services from its inception that year.

Believing in faith in action, Busch was an advocate of the Church's ministry to hospitals. He was Queensland branch chaplain to the Order of St John of Jerusalem (1973-85) and to the Order of St Lazarus of Jerusalem (1984-85). By the 1960s he was considered a national authority on bioethics. He supported the establishment (1984) of an in-vitro-fertilisation program at Wesley Hospital, Brisbane, and served on the hospital's ethics committee.

Busch was 5 ft 5 ins (165 cm) tall, with brown hair, increasingly silver in latter years. He had a warm personality; his face was open, engaging and quite handsome, with welcoming blue eyes. His analytical mind enabled him to see issues clearly and quickly, and on occasions he presented his point of view very forcefully. He was known for his humour: rejecting the sometimes too laudatory opinions of his admirers, he once told a colleague: 'Sainthood is all right for you Christians, but I have to be practical'. Appointed OBE (1978) and AO (1984), he appreciated the titles of office and the prominence of position. He could be anything but gentle if crossed, particularly by those whose opinions or motives he held in low esteem. Nevertheless, far outweighing such human idiosyncrasies were his great gifts as an administrator, a teacher, a communicator and a leader. He had also written a family history, *Emil's Children: The Story of a Saxon Immigrant Family in Australia* (1974).

Survived by his wife and their daughter and son, he died of myocardial infarction on 19 July 1985 in Sydney. After a funeral service with full military honours in Brisbane he was cremated. A portrait by Lola McCausland is held by Emmanuel College.

N. W. Wallis, *A Man Called 'Rollie'* (2001); *Life and Times*, 14-27 Aug 1985, pp 1 and 8; Busch papers (Univ of Qld Lib); Busch sermons and addresses (Trinity Theological College, Brisbane); private information and personal knowledge.

ANGUS A. EDMONDS

BUSH, CHARLES WILLIAM (1919-1989), artist, was born on 23 November 1919 at Brunswick East, Melbourne, son of Victorian-born parents Andrew Charles Thomas Bush,

signwriter, and his wife Alice Maude, née Rohsburn. Charles's younger brother Gordon was accidentally killed in 1929 and his mother was to die in 1936. He attended Coburg East State and Coburg High schools, and worked with his father but their relationship was not an easy one. At the age of 14 he gained a place at the National Gallery schools, where he won several prizes and met a fellow student Phyllis Paulina Waterhouse (1917-1989). His father disapproved of the trend his work was taking so he moved in with Phyl and her parents at Essendon. The two young artists rented a studio and began living together; they were to be married on 21 June 1979 at the office of the government statist, Melbourne.

In 1939 Bush held his first exhibition. Called up in July 1941 for full-time duty with the Militia, he served in an artillery survey unit, carried out camouflage work and helped produce service publications. By 1943 he was employed as a war artist. He painted in Papua and New Guinea and, after its liberation, on Timor. Having transferred to the Australian Imperial Force in 1943, he finished his service on 23 October 1946 as a lieutenant. A British Council grant in 1949 enabled him to travel to London and study with Bernard Meninsky. He exhibited at the Royal Academy and toured France, Spain, Italy and the Middle East.

Back in Melbourne, Bush was a drawing master at the National Gallery schools in 1953-54 and a member of the Australian cultural delegation to China in 1956. From 1959 to 1962 he hosted an afternoon television show, 'My Fair Lady', in which he commented, sometimes caustically, on the dress and appearance of women. In 1961 he visited Malaya to record on canvas the activities of the Royal Australian Air Force at Butterworth. He accepted commissions as an art critic and adviser. With Phyl Waterhouse and June Davies, he founded in 1962 the Leveson Street Gallery, North Melbourne (Carlton from 1979), which gave young artists encouragement and honest criticism.

Energetic and committed, Bush confidently and enthusiastically embraced painting and considered himself fortunate to be an artist. His knowledge of his profession was profound. One of the few to make a living at the easel, he endured with equanimity times of struggle and enjoyed his increasing success. He painted or drew in his North Melbourne studio nearly every day, and exhibited in Australia and overseas. As a watercolourist he had few equals. His paintings won more than fifty awards, including three (George) Crouch prizes (1945, 1952 and 1961) and two Wynne prizes (1952 and 1955). Examples of his work are in the National Gallery of Australia and the Australian War Memorial, Canberra, most State and regional galleries, and numerous corporate and private collections throughout the world.

Bush was excellent company and a great raconteur. With his sharp wit, flair for the apt word or phrase and forthright delivery, he delighted in deflating the pompous or the boring, but supported and encouraged the sincere. In addition to art, he expressed his passion for life through a love of the sea, the Australian landscape, literature and classical music. He had a very good voice and often sang while painting. Predeceased by his wife, he died of ischaemic heart disease on 13 November 1989 at Footscray and was cremated.

Charles Bush: Self-portraits 1936-1986 (1994); *Age* (Melbourne), 7 Apr 1962, p 18; *Independent* (London), 17 Nov 1989, p 14; National Gallery of Victoria, *Gallery*, Feb 1990, p 18; private information and personal knowledge.   DAVID KEYS

BUTCHER, ALFRED DUNBAVIN (1915-1990), biologist, manager of natural resources and public servant, was born on 4 June 1915 at Hamilton, Victoria, fourth child of Thomas William Butcher, Methodist clergyman, and his wife Grace Eliza, née Trevena, both born in Victoria. On leaving Geelong College, Alf began studying agricultural science but switched to science at the University of Melbourne (B.Sc., 1939; M.Sc., 1943). On 23 August 1940 at St David's Presbyterian Church, Newtown, Geelong, he married Bessell Carter Batten, a clerk.

In 1941 Butcher was appointed a biologist in the fisheries and game (later fisheries and wildlife) branch of the Victorian Department of the Chief Secretary. With rudimentary facilities he researched a variety of problems in fisheries management, including diseases of fish in hatcheries, the state of Quinnat salmon stocks, conservation of bream in the Gippsland Lakes, and the diets of Victorian freshwater species. His M.Sc. thesis was on parasites of fish. He was promoted to inspector of fisheries in 1947 and director of fisheries and game in 1949. His branch managed game birds and mammals and commercial fisheries, and attempted to meet the demands of sporting hunters, anglers and professional fishermen. Eager to educate the public, he produced material such as pamphlets, newspaper articles and chapters in books, and travelled extensively to consult fishermen and shooters. In 1954-55 he undertook a study tour of North America and returned strengthened in his belief that wildlife management and conservation must have a scientific foundation.

The prevailing view of conservation was a utilitarian one in which wise use of natural resources based on scientific investigation was the guiding principle. Butcher worked tirelessly to develop a strong research base. In the 1950s the staff was increased and facilities improved at the Snobs Creek Freshwater Fishery Research Station and Hatchery, near Eildon. The Arthur Rylah [q.v.16] Institute for Environmental Research was opened at Heidelberg, Melbourne, in 1970. Progressively under Butcher's direction, the branch expanded its role and addressed a wide range of issues, such as pesticides, pollution, land degradation and sustainable resource utilisation. He successfully blocked attempts to divide and 'rationalize' the organisation. In 1973 it was transferred to the new Ministry for Conservation, in which he was promoted to deputy-director.

In 1966 Butcher had been appointed the first biologist on the Land Utilization Advisory Council. This body became embroiled in the controversy over land use in the Little Desert, a significant issue in the rise of an environmental consciousness in Australia. Advice by the council in 1968 played a major part in convincing the government to halt development and convert the area into a national park. In 1971 the LUAC was replaced by the Land Conservation Council, on which Butcher served until 1973. Having acted (from 1968) as deputy-chairman of the co-ordinating committee which supervised a pioneering environmental study of Port Phillip Bay, in 1971 he was appointed chairman of the executive committee responsible for a similar investigation into Westernport Bay, which recommended the preservation of the natural values of the region and judicious planning for its development.

Butcher was a member of the Victorian State committee of the Commonwealth Scientific and Industrial Research Organization (1961-78), the National Parks Authority (1957-71), the Victorian Environment Protection Council (1971-73), the Australian Fishing Industry Research Committee (1970-72), the council of the Victorian Institute of Marine Sciences (1977-89) and numerous other scientific, conservation and resource-management organisations. He had attended the inaugural meeting of the Australian Conservation Foundation in 1964 and joined its executive committee in 1966, but he resigned in 1973 over what he perceived as a 'radical takeover' of the foundation. In 1971-72 he was president of the Royal Society of Victoria. He was a guiding force as a trustee of the World Wildlife Fund Australia in 1979-84.

Appointed an ex officio member of the Zoological Board of Victoria in 1947, Butcher became chairman in 1962 and held office for twenty-five years. He transformed the (Royal) Melbourne Zoological Gardens from a 'B grade' to an 'A grade' institution, replacing barred pens with spacious enclosures, setting up an excellent education service and inaugurating the Friends of the Zoos Society. The highlight of his work was the Butterfly House (opened in 1985 and named after him in 1990), which 'united all four objectives of the modern zoo': conservation, research, education and recreation.

Butcher retired from the public service in 1978. Six feet (183 cm) tall, he had been an imposing senior officer, 'absolutely devastating when he got into action'. In 1986 the University of Melbourne awarded him an honorary doctorate of science. He was appointed CMG (1978) and AO (1987). Although he listed gardening as his only hobby, he belonged to the Melbourne Club and also found time to support the Boy Scouts' Association. He died on 28 May 1990 at Heidelberg and was cremated. His wife and their two sons survived him.

C. de Courcy, *The Zoo Story* (1995); L. Robin, *Defending the Little Desert* (1998); B. Broadbent, *Inside the Greening* (1999); *A'asian Science*, vol 19, no 4, 1998, p 56; *Herald* (Melbourne), 22 June 1963, p 6; *Age* (Melbourne), 23 Feb 1978, p 4.

P. S. LAKE

BUTEMENT, WILLIAM ALAN STEWART (1904-1990), defence scientist and public servant, was born on 18 August 1904 at Masterton, New Zealand, eldest of five children of New Zealand-born William Butement, physician and surgeon, and his English-born wife Amy Louise, née Stewart. In 1912 the family moved to Sydney. Alan enrolled at Scots College in 1915 but the family moved again, to London. There he attended University College School (1917-22) and then studied at University College, University of London (B.Sc., 1926). After two years as a research student in physics, in 1928 he joined the War Office's signals experimental establishment at Woolwich as a scientific officer, where he helped to develop radio communication equipment for the British Army.

In 1931 Butement and a colleague, P. E. Pollard, succeeded in detecting radio signals reflected from a metal sheet at a distance of one hundred yards (91 m), thereby demonstrating the principle of what came to be known as radar. The War Office showed no interest, however, and the project was dropped; not until 1935 was official interest in such possibilities aroused, thanks to the advocacy of (Sir) Robert Watson Watt. In 1938 Butement joined Watson Watt's group at Bawdsey Manor research station in Suffolk as a senior scientific officer. There he played a major role in the development of the switched-beam technique that enabled targets to be located some twenty times more accurately than previously. The method was subsequently applied to detecting low-flying aircraft (these being undetectable by existing radar equipment), to directing fighter aircraft to their targets from the ground, and to locating submarines. Shortly after the commencement of World War II, he took charge of an army group that developed a highly successful radar control system for the searchlights used by Britain's coastal defence gun batteries. He also invented what became the standard method of controlling fire against shipping, using radar echoes from the splashes caused by shells hitting the sea. Later he was a senior principal scientific officer in scientific research and development (defence) in the munitions section of the Ministry of Supply.

Butement was primarily responsible for one of Britain's most important technical advances during the war, the proximity fuse: in effect, a tiny radar-set, built into a shell, that emitted radio signals and received reflections from the target causing the shell to explode at a predetermined range. The device dramatically increased the effectiveness of shell-fire. With the cavity magnetron that was the key to the development of microwave radar systems, it was one of the precious secrets the British passed to the Americans in August 1940 in exchange for the Lend-Lease agreement and on-going technical collaboration. In the later stages of the war, anti-aircraft shells fitted with proximity fuses played a major part in defeating both German VI flying-bomb attacks on London and Japanese kamikaze attacks on Allied shipping. He also invented and supervised the development of a secure radio-based method of battlefield communication using narrow beams of pulsed microwave signals, to replace the traditional telephone cable. His so-called 'Wireless Set No.10' was used with great success by Field Marshal Sir Bernard (Viscount) Montgomery.

In 1946 the British and Australian governments established a joint high-priority project to undertake research and development of guided missiles. The project included the development of extensive laboratory and workshop facilities in a wartime munitions factory complex at Salisbury, north of Adelaide, and a rocket testing range in the Australian outback supported by a new town, Woomera. Selected as deputy-chief of the project's scientific staff, Butement moved to Australia with other members of the British team early in 1947. He and his British colleagues provided the initial scientific core of what became the Long Range Weapons Establishment, based at Salisbury. Some months after his arrival, he was appointed chief superintendent of the project, succeeding A. P. Rowe [q.v.16].

In April 1949 Butement took up the new position of chief scientist within the Australian Department of Supply and Development (from 1950 Supply). The creation of this position was part of a major expansion of Australia's defence-related scientific services. This growth encompassed the union of aeronautics (previously within the Council for Scientific and Industrial Research), the Defence Research

Laboratories (later Defence Standards Laboratories) and installations at Salisbury and Woomera. Under Butement, these units collectively were known as the Australian defence scientific service. Part of the aeronautics group was transferred to Salisbury to form a high-speed aerodynamics laboratory, and new propulsion research and electronics research laboratories were established. All three were housed alongside the Anglo-Australian joint project, the research they undertook being closely linked to its needs. In 1955 the units on the Salisbury site, including the joint project facility, were merged to become a single entity, the Weapons Research Establishment, the head of which was answerable to Butement. Though ostensibly done for reasons of administrative convenience, the merger resulted in the joint project coming under Australian authority.

Under Butement's leadership, the defence scientific service became an important contributor to Australia's overall research effort, taking on a role analogous to that played in the civilian economy by CSIRO, which was now debarred from doing defence-related work. His position as a first-division officer, equivalent to head of a department, helped him to establish working conditions more suitable for scientific research than those prescribed by the normal Public Service Board regulations. Several hundred graduates were sent to Britain for research training.

By this time Butement himself was no longer a hands-on scientist but an administrator. He had not lost his flair for invention, however, and he continued to throw up ideas for others to pursue. Inevitably, many proved not to be feasible, prompting an only half-joking aphorism within the service: 'a think of Butey is a chore forever'. Others, however, succeeded. Among the developments that he claimed to have himself initiated were a rocket engine that used a semi-solid paste extruded into the firing chamber as propellant, and the Malkara anti-tank guided weapon that was in due course adopted by the British and Australian armies as standard equipment. He encouraged the WRE to establish working links with scientists and engineers at the University of Adelaide, and it was to this university (D.Sc., 1961) that he submitted a thesis describing his principal contributions to defence technology. His success as a leader of research teams and later as a science administrator owed much to his strong but engaging personality. Appointed OBE in 1946 in Britain, he was promoted to CBE in Australia in 1959.

At the earliest British atomic weapons tests, at the Monte Bello islands, Western Australia, in October 1952, and at Emu Field, South Australia, in 1953, Butement was one of three observers present on behalf of the Australian government. Although said in government press releases to have made an independent evaluation of the hazards, the group had no authority; their presence seems to have been intended merely to give an impression of Australian involvement and to reassure the Australian public on the safety of the tests. Butement led the party that identified Emu Field and Maralinga as suitable sites for atomic weapons tests on the Australian mainland, and was a member (1955-57) of the board of management responsible for co-ordinating the various government departments and civilian contractors engaged in the construction and management of the test range. During the same period, he was also a member of the atomic weapons tests safety committee established by the Australian government in preparation for the planned detonations at Maralinga.

Butement had married Ursula Florence Alberta Parish on 17 June 1933 at St Philip and All Saints Church, North Sheen, Surrey. When they moved to Australia in 1947, they lived at first in Adelaide, but following his appointment as chief scientist they settled in Melbourne. In 1966, not wishing to transfer to Canberra, he resigned his position to become, for a five-year term, director of research for Plessey Pacific Pty Ltd, the Australian subsidiary of the British electronics manufacturer. A journalist observing him at this time wrote: 'He is a quiet man. His well groomed greying hair and trim moustache give a first impression of unflappable calm, but the intense movements of his hands betray the nervous energy within'.

In 1969 Butement read a paper to the Australian Industrial Research Group, an association of managers of industrial research laboratories, advocating the formation of an Australian academy of applied science. His speech has been widely seen as the spark that led to the incorporation in 1975 of the Australian Academy of Technological Sciences. The new body arose out of widespread dissatisfaction among applied scientists and engineers about their effective exclusion from the Australian Academy of Science under the latter's electoral procedures, which put a heavy emphasis on scientific publications as the chief qualification for membership. Butement was a member of both the steering committee and the council of the new academy. A foundation fellow, he was appointed an honorary fellow in 1979.

Throughout his life, Butement loved working with his hands. In addition to his professional skills in electronics, he was an enthusiastic ham-radio operator and an adept carpenter, metalworker and mechanic. He was a convinced Christian, adhering to the Catholic Apostolic Church and later the Anglican Church. Survived by his wife and two daughters, he died on 25 January 1990 at Richmond, Melbourne, and was buried in Warrandyte cemetery.

Butement

J. G. Crowther and P. Whiddington, *Science at War* (1947); P. Morton, *Fire Across the Desert* (1989); B. Williams, *Dr W. A. S. Butement* (1991); J. Wisdom, *A History of Defence Science in Australia* (1995); *Hist Records of Austn Science*, vol 6, no 2, 1985, p 137; *SMH*, 20 Apr 1968, p 17.   R. W. HOME

BUTLER, STUART THOMAS (1926-1982), nuclear scientist, was born on 4 July 1926 at Naracoorte, South Australia, son of Welsh-born Ernest Butler, schoolteacher, and his wife Amy Victoria, née Wytkin, who was born in South Australia. Educated at Murray Bridge and Gumeracha primary schools and Birdwood High School, Stuart graduated from the University of Adelaide (B.Sc., 1945; B.Sc. Hons, 1947; M.Sc., 1948) achieving first-class honours in physics in 1947 and studying neurophysiology for his master's degree. He married Miriam Stella Silver, a trainee nurse and later a librarian, on 11 December 1948 at Holy Trinity Church of England, Adelaide.

Receiving a travelling scholarship from the Australian National University, Canberra, in 1949, Butler studied in England at the University of Birmingham (Ph.D., 1951) under the famous theoretical physicist (Sir) Rudolph Peierls. After two years (1951-53) in the United States of America at Cornell University, Ithaca, New York, he returned to the ANU as a senior research fellow (1953-54) in the department of theoretical physics, Research School of Physical Sciences. In 1954 he was appointed reader in physics at the University of Sydney, where he was to spend most of his career, becoming professor of theoretical physics in 1959. He was dean of the faculty of science (1970-73), and a member of the senate (1970-77, 1979-82) and its finance committee (1972-77, 1979-82), and of the council of Women's College (1970-79). The ANU had awarded him a D.Sc. in 1961. Having been elected a fellow of the Australian Academy of Science in 1969, he served on its council in 1970-73.

Butler published about fifty-five scientific papers. His thirty-one articles on nuclear physics were principally devoted to the theory of direct nuclear reactions, the so-called stripping reactions. The award of the (Sir Thomas) Lyle [q.v.10] medal by the Australian Academy of Science in 1966 and the Tom W. Bonner prize in nuclear physics by the American Physical Society in 1977 recognised his eminence in this field. In addition to his work in nuclear physics he published nine papers on the theory of superfluidity and superconductivity, and fifteen on plasma physics, stellar physics and atmospheric tides.

Butler was also involved in secondary education in New South Wales, serving as chairman (1966-77) of the science syllabus and science examination committees. He wrote physics textbooks and chaired a team of physicists who produced the *Senior Science for High School Students* texts (1966-67). He also published a large body of popular science for young audiences. Between 1960 and 1977 he edited and co-authored about twenty books or pamphlets arising from the vacation science schools for high-school students that he organised with Professor Harry Messel.

Believing that scientists have a responsibility to inform the general public, Butler acted as science correspondent for the *Daily Telegraph* (1958-61) and the *Sydney Morning Herald* (1972-74). He initiated and supplied the scientific information for a serial strip cartoon, 'Frontiers of Science', written by Robert Raymond and illustrated by Andrea Bresciani, which was printed from 1961 to 1979 in some Australian newspapers, syndicated widely overseas, and published in booklets. *Uranium on Trial* (1977), co-authored with Robert Raymond and Charles Watson-Munro, contributed to the vigorous contemporary debate about uranium. It was a tribute to his industry that he could do so much, but also to his modesty and his social conscience that he was willing to devote time to tasks that were intellectually humble.

In 1977 Butler became head of the nuclear science and technology branch of the Australian Atomic Energy Commission at Lucas Heights; his position was soon renamed director, research establishment. He wanted to broaden the research to all fields of energy. When a review committee recommended in 1979 that the AAEC be empowered to undertake non-nuclear research and development, he appeared to have succeeded. But in 1981, in what must have seemed like a governmental rebuff to the AAEC management, the research establishment at Lucas Heights was split, with some AAEC resources going to a new Commonwealth Scientific and Industrial Research Organization institute which would conduct non-nuclear energy research. While still director, research establishment, he was appointed chief executive officer of the AAEC in January 1982.

Butler was an accomplished pianist in his youth, a keen player of games ranging from football to bridge, and an enthusiast for all outdoor activities. Full of vitality, he was a genial and sociable man. Survived by his wife, and their two sons and daughter, he died of a cerebrovascular accident on 15 May 1982 at Royal Prince Alfred Hospital, Camperdown, and was cremated.

Hist Records of Austn Science, vol 5, no 4, 1983, p 83; *Austn Playboy*, May 1981, p 33; *Univ of Sydney News*, 1 June 1982, p 86; H. de Berg, interview with S. T. Butler (ts, 1972, NLA); private information and personal knowledge.   ARTHUR PRYOR

BUXTON, DAME RITA MARY (1896-1982), community worker, was born on 21 November 1896 at South Yarra, Melbourne, only child of Charles James Neunhoeffer (Neunhoffer), civil servant and later company director, and his wife Emma Alice, née O'Connor, both natives of Bendigo. Rita was educated at Sacré Coeur convent school, Glen Iris, and grew up in a privileged world that she never left, involving regular visits to Europe and North America and summers on the family's property at Mount Martha. Her father was a proprietor of Canada Cycle & Motor Co. (Victoria) Pty Ltd, motorcar importers; Rita later claimed that he gave her a 6-horse-power De Dion and allowed her to drive it at age 12. Other early adventures included becoming one of the first women to fly in an aeroplane over Melbourne.

On 22 November 1922 at St Joseph's Catholic Church, Malvern, she married Leonard Raymond Buxton (1896-1977). An uncle of Kathleen Fitzpatrick [q.v.], Leonard had worked for his family's real-estate agency but, on marrying, he chose to enter his father-in-law's business. He and Rita lived with the Neunhoffers in a mansion, Toronto, at 48 Hampden Road, Armadale. Leonard later became governing director of the company.

In 1927 Rita Buxton joined the Toorak auxiliary of St Vincent's Hospital, Fitzroy, an institution that was to provide her with a philanthropic outlet for her considerable energies and resources. By 1936 she was president of the central executive of the hospital's auxiliaries. She organised voluntary help for St Vincent's in World War II, and herself worked in the laundry. In 1947 she became the first woman (apart from the mother rectress) on the hospital's advisory council, and in 1958 she was a founding member of the council of St Vincent's School of Medical Research. As well as fund-raising, she donated large sums of money for studentships and research fellowships. She was often seen arriving at the hospital at 8 a.m.

For her service to St Vincent's, Buxton was appointed OBE in 1944, CBE in 1955 and DBE in 1969. Dame Rita was also a council member of the Victorian division of the Australian Red Cross Society for over twenty years. She was well known in Melbourne society, not least as an avid bridge player, golfer and racehorse owner. One of her horses, High Syce, won the Caulfield Cup in 1929 and another, St Razzle, was runner-up in 1949. The Victoria Golf Club instituted a cup in her name, awarded to the winner of an annual match-play tournament, in recognition of her contribution to the club as president (1937-49) of the associates. She was also a member of the Alexandra Club.

Following the death of her husband, Buxton retired from the bulk of her hospital work, although she remained a life councillor of St Vincent's and nominal president of the auxiliaries. Survived by her three daughters, she died on 22 August 1982 at the hospital and was buried in Mornington cemetery. Her estate was sworn for probate at $2 062 321. By the time of her death the importance to hospitals of voluntary fund-raisers and workers had declined dramatically.

B. Egan, *Ways of a Hospital* (1993); *Age* (Melbourne), 7 Nov 1934, p 13, 14 June 1969, p 15; *Herald* (Melbourne), 14 June 1969, p 2; *Sun News-Pictorial* (Melbourne), 1 Oct 1982, p 11; *Advocate* (Melbourne), 9 Sept 1982, p 4.   PETER SHERLOCK

BYRNE, LORNA (1897-1989), agriculture extension officer and broadcaster, was born on 27 December 1897 at Quirindi, New South Wales, youngest of ten children of James Byrne, schoolteacher, and his wife Margaret, née Crennan, who were both born in New South Wales. Ethel Byrne [q.v.13] was her sister. Lorna was educated at Currabubula Public, Quirindi Superior Public and West Maitland Girls' High schools, gaining a Teachers' College scholarship to the University of Sydney (B.Sc.Agr., 1921), where she was one of four women admitted to study agricultural science. Part of the practical training was at Hawkesbury Agricultural College. She and Margaret Brebner were the first women to graduate in this discipline at the University of Sydney.

From 1921 Byrne taught for the Department of Education in Sydney and Orange. With the growing recognition of the importance of women in rural life, she was invited in 1927 to join the New South Wales Department of Agriculture's 'Better Farming Train'. Equipped with machinery and farm animals, this train carried agriculture experts to selected venues where talks were given in tents. Byrne lectured on the importance of family life, leadership and community involvement, ideals to which she remained committed all her life. In August that year she was officially transferred to the Department of Agriculture as organiser, women's section, agricultural bureau, the first woman on the permanent professional staff of the department. She continued to travel, lecturing, advising and encouraging rural women. Attractive, enthusiastic and with an affinity for people on the land, she became well known and liked.

Byrne gave talks (1923-24) and made regular broadcasts (1932-36) for the department, and compèred two programs (1939-40) for the Australian Broadcasting Commission on radio-station 2FC. In 1935 she was awarded King George V's silver jubilee medal and in 1936 received a grant from the Carnegie Corporation to study rural extension education systems overseas. On her return, influenced by the Swedish model she had seen, she established leadership schools for young country people. The Department of Agriculture later adopted similar schools for its own staff-training program and other organisations followed. Byrne was to be prouder of having set up the schools than anything else she accomplished. Popular with young people, in 1941 she became Rural Queen in the Australian Red Cross Society (New South Wales division) Queen Competition and finished second overall, having raised £13 660.

In World War II Byrne had joined the Women's Australian National Services, acting in an advisory capacity to the land section in 1940. On 18 November 1941 she entered the Australian Women's Army Service. Appointed assistant-controller to Sybil Irving [q.v.14] in Melbourne, she held the rank of major from 28 January 1942. In May 1943 she was given her own command as assistant-controller, Western Australia. She transferred to the Reserve of Officers on 3 June 1944 and joined the AWAS Association (New South Wales), of which she was to become the 'much loved and esteemed' patron in 1981.

Following her army service Byrne spent six months assisting (Sir) Samuel Wadham [q.v.16] who, as a member of the Commonwealth Rural Reconstruction Commission, was writing reports on rural conditions. In 1945 she was appointed head of the women's extension service of the New South Wales Department of Agriculture. On 4 August 1948 at St Augustine's Church of England, Neutral Bay, Byrne married Stanley Ward Hayter, a 68-year-old retired master mariner. Devastated when he died in 1951, she travelled overseas extensively. She had given some talks for the Australian Broadcasting Commission in 1950 and resumed broadcasting as Lorna Byrne in 1953. Her 'Country Women's Session' ran for fifteen minutes one day a week, replacing the popular serial 'Blue Hills' for that day. For a while, she received 'the most insulting letters' for 'daring' to supplant 'Blue Hills'. Her voice was criticised as 'harsh and masculine', but with her outgoing personality and professionalism she soon developed a rapport with listeners. From 1964 the program was called 'Farm and Home'; she gave her last broadcast in 1966.

While with the ABC Mrs Hayter acted as public relations officer for the State division of the Australian Red Cross Society. In 1958 she led a delegation of Australian women on a tour of China. Describing the trip as 'one of the great experiences of [her] life', she visited factories and farms and met Mao Zedong. She worked as women's editor of *The Land* newspaper in 1961-71, then performed the same role with the *North Shore Times* for eight months. Later she spent several years carrying out historical research on country towns for the Bank of New South Wales. In 1975, as a member of the Farm Writers and Broadcasters Society, she represented rural journalists at an international conference in Milan, Italy.

Hayter was a member (1969-75) of the standing committee of the University of Sydney convocation, and president (1972-75) of the university's Agricultural Graduates Association. She was also a member of the State committee of the Australian Institute of Agricultural Science, of which in 1969 she became a fellow. In 1978 she was appointed a fellow of the Hawkesbury Agricultural College. She was involved in other organisations including the Country Women's Association of New South Wales, of which she had been an early member; the Young Women's Christian Association, for which she worked as general secretary for four years; the Society of Women Writers; and the Journalists' Club. Her publications included radio scripts and newspaper and journal articles.

Hayter helped to improve the lives of people in the farming community, especially women. In 1980 she was appointed CBE. She died on 15 July 1989 at Mona Vale and was cremated. On 24 September a memorial service was held at Hawkesbury Agricultural College, where trees were planted in her memory. Trees were also planted at her childhood home at Currabubula. The Australian Institute of Agricultural Science & Technology (Eastern New South Wales branch) sponsors the Lorna Byrne leadership awards for students in agriculture in New South Wales.

A. Lofthouse (comp), *Who's Who of Australian Women* (1982); J. Black, *The Country's Finest Hour* (1995); *Smith's Weekly*, 29 Oct 1927, p 20; *SMH*, 31 Jan 1936, p 9, 20 Mar 1937, p 11, 2 Apr 1937, p 5, 20 Nov 1958, p 63; Austn Federation of Univ Women (NSW), *Newsletter*, Nov 1989, p 14; H. de Berg, interview with L. Hayter (ts, 1978, NLA); B884, item N278216, SP1762/1, item 23/1 (NAA); private information.   AUDREY TATE

C

CAIRNS, KEVIN MICHAEL KIERNAN (1929-1984), dentist, economist and politician, was born on 15 May 1929 at Five Dock, Sydney, and registered solely as Kevin, only son of Michael Cairns, an English-born seaman and union official, and his wife Mary, née Jarvis, formerly Downey, who was born in Sydney. His working-class parents made great sacrifices to educate their intelligent son, sending him to the Christian Brothers' High School, Lewisham, then to St Joseph's College, Hunters Hill, where, at the age of 16, he won a bursary to the University of Sydney (BDS, 1953).

After registering as a dentist on 20 April 1953, Cairns practised briefly in Sydney, Melbourne and Broken Hill, New South Wales, before moving to Brisbane in 1955 and entering private practice at Stones Corner. Keen on a career in politics, he took up debating and joined the Young Liberal Movement. He stood unsuccessfully for the safe Labor seat of Brisbane in the House of Representatives in lively elections in 1955, 1958 and 1961. On 23 January 1957 at the Catholic Church of Saints Peter and Paul, North Broken Hill, he had married Tonia Maria Gainer, a dental technician.

At the 1963 Federal election Cairns won the marginal Brisbane seat of Lilley. While serving in parliament, he completed part-time studies at the University of Queensland (BA, 1964; B.Econ., 1965). He was made deputy government whip in 1967, but resigned the position in 1969 after a disagreement with Prime Minister (Sir) John Gorton, of whose leadership he had become intensely critical. On 22 March 1971 he was appointed minister for housing under (Sir) William McMahon [q.v.], becoming the fifth Catholic to serve as a Liberal minister. Losing his seat narrowly in 1972, he worked as an economic adviser in the Queensland Department of Industrial Affairs.

In 1974 Cairns regained Lilley. He visited Europe as a member of a parliamentary delegation in June 1975, chaired (1977-80) the House of Representatives standing committee on expenditure and served on various other parliamentary committees. Defeated again in 1980, he earned his living as a lecturer in economics, a member of the Independent Air Fares Committee, and a consultant to Mount Isa Mines Ltd and the Queensland Tourist & Travel Corporation. He also became president of the Queensland branch of the Economic Society of Australia.

Cairns was a man of medium height and stocky build, with hazel eyes and a fair complexion. Although sensitive, idealistic, modest and intensely serious, he displayed in private an impish sense of humour. Described as a voracious reader and a vigorous, determined debater, he brought to his political career a strong sense of social justice, conservative family and religious values, a free-enterprise approach to economics and an outlook so individualistic that within the Liberal Party he was sometimes seen as a 'boat rocker'.

An avowed anti-communist, he had become involved in controversies over the Vietnam War in 1966 and the boycott of the Moscow Olympic Games in 1980. He deplored Australia's falling birth rate and opposed the Family Law Act (1975). As a dentist, he favoured the fluoridation of water supplies, and as a humanitarian, expressed compassion for the disadvantaged, the aged and the unemployed. He campaigned to have Brisbane airport upgraded to international standard, pushed for state aid to independent schools and successfully promoted a plan to achieve better funding arrangements between the Queensland and Federal governments.

Cairns died of myocardial infarction on 6 July 1984 at Clayfield; he was accorded a state funeral and was buried in Nudgee cemetery. His wife and their four sons and three daughters survived him.

Courier-Mail (Brisbane), 7 July 1984, pp 1, 14; *Echo* (Brisbane), 11 July 1984, p 3; *Sunday Mail* (Brisbane), 15 July 1984, p 23; *Catholic Leader*, 15 July 1984, p 5; *News Weekly*, 18 July 1984, p 3; *PD* (HR), 21 Aug 1984, p 12, (Senate), 21 Aug 1984, p 31; private information.   ELAINE BROWN

CALDWELL, WILLIAM BLYTHE (1914-1983), army officer and public servant, was born on 26 March 1914 at Croydon, Sydney, third child of Newcastle-born parents Henry Blythe Caldwell, blacksmith, and his wife Fanny Florence, née Rigg. Educated at Flemington Public and Parramatta High schools, Bill played Rugby Union football and tennis. After studying land valuation, he joined the Newcastle office of the New South Wales valuer-general in 1935 as an assistant-valuer. Having risen to sergeant in the 30th Battalion, Militia, he was commissioned as a lieutenant in 1937.

Transferring to the Australian Imperial Force on 13 October 1939, Caldwell was posted to the 2/2nd Battalion as a captain. He married Elizabeth Mabel Roger on 28 October that year at St James's Presbyterian Church, Burwood, Sydney. In December he embarked for the Middle East with his unit's advance party. As officer commanding 'A' Company, he moved to Egypt in September 1940 and to Cyrenaica, Libya, in December. The 2/2nd took part in successful attacks on the Italian-held towns of Bardia and Tobruk in January 1941. Caldwell led his company ably during these operations, especially on 4 January, when it captured an important enemy gun post overlooking Bardia. He was awarded the Military Cross for 'his coolness and courage under fire' which 'set a stirring example to the men under his command'.

In March 1941 the 2/2nd Battalion was sent to Greece, but during April it was split into groups while withdrawing before the heavy German advance south. With nine others, Caldwell escaped daringly through the hills to the sea, reaching Crete on 25 April. He arrived in Palestine in June and was made officer commanding the battalion's Headquarter Company. In September he was promoted to major. Following periods of garrison duty in Syria and Ceylon (Sri Lanka), the 2/2nd returned to Australia in August 1942, with Caldwell as second-in-command. He was promoted to lieutenant colonel on 1 September and appointed to command the 14th/32nd Battalion in November.

Five ft 10 ins (178 cm) tall and heavily built, Caldwell was known by his men as 'The Bull'. He trained his battalion in Western Australia, Queensland, Papua and New Guinea before it sailed to Jacquinot Bay, New Britain, in November 1944. The 14th/32nd patrolled forward along coastal tracks towards Wide Bay, leading and preparing the way for the 6th Brigade's advance on Japanese-occupied positions in the Tol-Waitavalo area. Caldwell was designated commander, Wide Bay Force, in December. His battalion engaged in direct operations against the Japanese during February-March 1945. He was awarded the Distinguished Service Order for his leading part in 'tactical and administrative planning' before the initial landing, his 'careful and detailed work' in developing a series of bases along the coast and his command of his battalion during the final assault on Tol. His 'leadership throughout the whole operation' was 'an inspiration' to his unit. He moved the 14th/32nd from New Britain to Queensland in May and relinquished command in July. After a short period in charge of the Leave and Transit Depot in Sydney, he was placed on the Reserve of Officers on 1 February 1946.

Caldwell rejoined the New South Wales Valuer-General's Department. In 1947 he was appointed senior valuer in the land valuation branch of the Tasmanian Lands and Surveys Department in Hobart. He acted for the government in all its land acquisitions and advised on real-estate matters generally. During this period he arranged for the acquisition of land for Baskerville Raceway, which was opened in 1959.

Resuming his service in the Citizen Military Forces, Caldwell commanded the 40th Battalion in 1954-58 and served as an honorary aide-de-camp to the governor-general Sir William (Viscount) Slim [q.v.16] in 1956-59. Appointed OBE in 1958, he transferred to the Reserve of Officers in 1962. In his spare time he was involved in many family and community activities. President of the Sporting Car Club of Tasmania and the Motor Yacht Club of Tasmania, he competed in motorcar rallies and yacht races, and built and sailed small fishing boats. He was also an active member of Legacy and enjoyed art exhibitions.

In October 1970 Caldwell was appointed Tasmanian surveyor-general and secretary for lands (subsequently director of lands). His energy and efficiency always generated enthusiasm in his office, where he was referred to unofficially as 'The Colonel'. He lectured regularly at the Hobart Technical College, delivered papers at national and international conferences of valuers and in 1971 was elected a life fellow of the Commonwealth Institute of Valuers. In 1977 he retired from his post due to war-related back problems.

Although somewhat physically constrained, Bill Caldwell continued his active family life, playing croquet with his wife, taking caravanning holidays, exhibiting the family dog at shows, and playing the trombone, a skill he had learned from his battalion bandsmen in New Guinea. He died of complications arising from surgery for cancer on 6 December 1983 at Royal Hobart Hospital and was cremated. His wife and their son and two daughters survived him.

G. Long, *To Benghazi* (1952), *Greece, Crete and Syria* (1953), *The Final Campaigns* (1963); S. Wick, *Purple Over Green* (1977); K. Bilney, *14/32 Australian Infantry Battalion A.I.F. 1940-1945* (1994); *Mercury* (Hobart), 14 Oct 1970, p 3; *Valuer*, Apr 1984, p 138; B883, item NX92 (NAA); private information.
                                        KEITH D. HOWARD

CAMERON, CLAUDE EWEN (1894-1982), army officer, accountant and company director, was born on 13 September 1894 at Balmain North, Sydney, second child of Ronald John Cameron, 'gentleman' and later Anglican clergyman, and his wife Lilly Wafford, née Dempster, both born in New South Wales. Educated at Sydney Church of England Grammar School (Shore), Claude was employed by Dalgety [q.v.4] & Co. Ltd as a junior clerk. He served in the senior cadets and the Militia before enlisting in the Australian Imperial Force on 18 March 1915. Posted to the 20th Battalion, he was promoted to sergeant in May.

In August-December 1915 Cameron served at Gallipoli. Made company sergeant major in Egypt in February 1916, he arrived in France with his battalion next month. On 16 August he was commissioned. He was wounded in the shoulder near Flers on 15 November and next day promoted to lieutenant. Evacuated to England, he rejoined his unit on 1 September 1917, but was wounded in the thigh during the battle of Menin Road, Belgium, on 20 September. Again hospitalised in England, he returned to his battalion in December.

As a company commander, Cameron distinguished himself twice during the fighting near Amiens, France, in August 1918. On the morning of the 8th, with a non-commissioned officer, he attacked an enemy strong point, killing the occupants and capturing two machine-guns. Three days later, with only twelve men, he held his allocated company position against an enemy counter-attack. For his 'coolness and initiative' he was awarded the Military Cross. On 3 October, during a confused attack near Beaurevoir, he took charge of the forward elements of his battalion, directed tank fire on enemy positions and consolidated the flank of the brigade assault. He won a Bar to his MC.

Cameron returned to Australia in April 1919 and his AIF appointment terminated on 2 June. He attended Wagga Wagga Experiment Farm and began farming. In 1923 he joined Sydney Ferries Ltd as a pay clerk. At St James's Church of England, Turramurra, Sydney, on 14 August 1924 he married Aline Vindin (d.1964); his father performed the ceremony. Cameron qualified as an accountant and company secretary and in 1934 was appointed accountant with Sydney Ferries. He also served (from 1933) as chairman of Rozelle Lighterage & Storage Co. Ltd. An alderman of the Municipality of Ku-ring-gai, he was mayor in 1936.

Having rejoined the Militia in 1923, Cameron served in a variety of staff and regimental postings. A fit and soldierly figure, he rose to captain in 1924 and to major in 1929. In July 1933 he was promoted to lieutenant colonel and given command of the 18th Battalion. As a temporary colonel, he was appointed in May 1940 to command the 8th Brigade, which was responsible for protecting Sydney. He was made temporary brigadier in January 1941 and called up for full-time duty on 10 March. From July 1942 to September 1943 the brigade operated in the defence of Western Australia. Cameron adopted a mobile strategy, moving his units great distances and often. In August 1942 he transferred to the AIF.

After further training, the 8th Brigade deployed to Finschhafen, New Guinea, in January 1944 and pursued the Japanese fleeing westward. The formation advanced from Sio to link up with American forces at Saidor. Although untried in combat, it secured all its objectives at minimal cost. Cameron's men killed 734 Japanese, found 1793 dead and took 48 prisoners for the loss of three killed and five wounded. In April the brigade participated in the seaborne occupation of Madang. Advancing to the Sepik River, it encountered only the stragglers of the retreating Japanese army. Cameron relinquished command in August and then commanded the 2nd Brigade in New South Wales until December. On 27 February 1945 he was transferred to the Reserve of Officers with the rank of honorary brigadier. He was mentioned in despatches for his service in New Guinea.

Cameron returned to Sydney Ferries, but late in 1945 was appointed manager of the Port Jackson & Manly Steamship Co. Ltd. He became general manager in 1948 and managing director in 1949. From 1951 he was also managing director of Sydney Harbour Ferries Pty Ltd. He retired in 1964 and moved from Turramurra to Bayview. Honorary colonel of the 17th/18th Battalion (North Shore Regiment) in 1951-60, he was an active member of the Returned Services League of Australia and many other ex-service organisations. His recreations included motoring, fishing and golf. He was awarded the OAM in 1980. Survived by his son, he died on 10 September 1982 at Thornleigh and was cremated. He is commemorated by a park named Claude Cameron Grove at Wahroonga.

C. E. W. Bean, The *A.I.F. in France, 1918* (1942); D. Dexter, *The New Guinea Offensives* (1961); *SMH*, 31 Mar 1964, p 11; *North Shore Times*, 22 Sept 1982, p 8, 6 Dec 1989, p 27; B883, item NX110380 (NAA); private information.   ALAN RYAN

CAMERON, KATHLEEN (KAY) GORDON (1899-1987), rural community leader and environmentalist, was born on 7 May 1899 at Tambo, Queensland, only child of Victorian-born parents John Gordon Browne, grazier, and his wife Annie Emmeline, née Nicol. When Kay was 7, her father was left paraplegic by a farm accident. The family then moved to Malvern, Melbourne. While a comfortable income came from the Queensland property, Narada Downs, and from investments, Kay recalled a sense of isolation arising from her father's incapacity. At Lauriston Girls' School, she was dux and editor of the *Lauristonian*. After matriculation, and against her father's wishes, she attended lectures in biology and botany at the University of Melbourne, but finally bowed to family pressure and transferred to the National Gallery schools. She displayed a talent for watercolour landscapes. On 15 April 1925 at Malvern Presbyterian Church she married Neil Wilson Cameron, owner of Glenspean, a beef and wool property near Meredith, Victoria. The Camerons became active members of their community, known for their hospitality, and Kay had 'stacks of friends'.

When the Country Women's Association was founded in Victoria in 1928, Mrs Cameron established the first branch in her area. The CWA was an enduring commitment: as a member of State council, State president (1961-63) and national president (1963-65) she advocated the importance of addressing rural loneliness and arresting the drift of families to cities, and highlighted the need for educational and health facilities in the country. Holding office at a time when the CWA was broadening its focus, Cameron encouraged 'better citizenship' to fit women 'to take our true part in the life of the country and the world'.

In this spirit, she was drawn to the Associated Country Women of the World. Cameron was also CWA nominee and then president (1962-69) of the Pan Pacific Women's Association, and an energetic member of the British Empire League. Travel to international conferences, and to visit friends in the Philippines, Indonesia, Burma, Tonga and the United Kingdom, was a particular pleasure. Photographed in pearls and ornate glasses, Cameron had an open if formal official manner, reflecting a keen awareness of her responsibility to raise public interest in a wide range of causes.

Among them was a commitment to conservation, already evident in 1938 when Cameron offered prizes to the CWA branch that planted the most trees. Competition was fierce. In 1963 she presented a motion at the CWA national conference requesting that world governments reduce atmospheric testing of nuclear weapons. She was also a key supporter of the 'Garden State' movement in the 1970s, an early member of the Keep Australia Beautiful Council and, in 1974-75, president of the Natural Resources Conservation League of Victoria (the third woman of seventeen presidents since 1944). Concerned by 'the growing pressures of world population and modern science and technology', she urged campaigners to adapt imaginatively to changing circumstances. She was appointed OBE in 1970.

In the mid-1980s, widowed and afflicted with Parkinson's disease, Cameron moved to Sorrento, but returned to Meredith to be nursed by her family. Survived by her two sons, she died on 3 November 1987 at Ballarat and was buried in Western cemetery, Geelong.

CWA (Vic), *Years of Adventure, 1928-78* (1978) and *Official Annual* (1960-63); B. Stevens-Chambers, *The Many Hats of Country Women* (1997); C. Rasmussen, *Lauriston* (1999); Natural Resources Conservation League of Vic, *Annual Report* (1974-75); K. M. Crook, The Politics of Influence (PhD thesis, Univ of Melbourne, 1997); private information.

KAREN CROOK

CAMERON, LINDEN ARTHUR (1918-1986), army officer and farmer, was born on 17 March 1918 at Warracknabeal, Victoria, fourth of seven children of Australian-born parents Finlay Arthur Cameron, farmer and later member of the Legislative Assembly, and his wife Victoria May, née Marshman. Educated at Brim East State and Warracknabeal High schools, Linden entered the Victorian Public Service on 7 March 1938 as a clerk in the taxation branch, Department of the Treasurer. He also studied (1938-39) at the University of Melbourne.

On 3 November 1939 Cameron enlisted in the Australian Imperial Force and was posted to the 2/5th Battalion. He was 5 ft 10 ins (178 cm) tall, with hazel eyes and brown hair. In April 1940 he embarked for the Middle East. Sent to the Officer Cadet Training Unit, Cairo, in November, he was commissioned as a lieutenant on 30 March 1941. Next month he commanded anti-aircraft defences aboard the transport *City of London*, which evacuated the 2/5th from Greece. Thus reunited with his unit, he served as a platoon commander in the Syrian campaign in June-July. The 2/5th left the Middle East in March 1942 and arrived in Australia in August.

The battalion sailed for Papua in October 1942 and in January 1943 was transported by air to Wau, New Guinea. During the advance to Crystal Creek, Cameron and his platoon were ordered to clear a high ridge of troublesome enemy machine-guns. On 8 February he led his men in an assault up a steep slope into the centre of the Japanese position. Under heavy machine-gun and grenade fire, the party succeeded in capturing the ridge. Cameron himself shot ten of the defenders. For this action he was awarded the Military Cross. Next month he was promoted to captain. In July, while leading 'D' Company in an attack on Mount Tambu, he was wounded in the elbow and hospitalised. He rejoined his battalion in Queensland in February 1944. On 29 July that year at the Methodist Church, Kaniva, Victoria, he married Daphne Alice Grayling, a schoolteacher.

In November 1944 the 2/5th embarked for Aitape, New Guinea. The battalion's advance was barred by strong enemy opposition along a dominating razor-backed ridge at Perembil and Cameron, commanding 'C' Company, was sent forward to clear the heights on 3 January 1945. Again a frontal assault up a precipitous slope was required. Cameron displayed outstanding leadership skills, direction and personal courage and his company secured the position. He proved an inspiring leader over the next twenty-four hours during the defence of the newly won ground against repeated enemy counter-attacks and was awarded a Bar to his MC. Returning to Australia in October, he was assigned to the Directorate of Recruiting and Demobilization, Army Headquarters, Melbourne. His appointment terminated on 28 January 1948.

Cameron was a soldier's soldier, a combat officer who led from the front and set a powerful example for his men. On leaving the army he established a sheep farm, Ardroy, on a 604-acre (244 ha) soldier-settlement block at Dunkeld, Victoria. He became a leading figure in the Victorian Farmers' Union and unsuccessfully contested Western Province for the Country (National) Party in four Legislative Council elections in 1964-76. In 1972 he stood as an Independent for Malcolm Fraser's House of Representatives seat of Wannon, but was defeated. He was an active member of Hamilton Legacy and the Dunkeld sub-branch of the Returned Services League of Australia. A keen tennis player, he also liked fishing and supported the St Kilda Football Club. Survived by his wife, and their two sons and two daughters, he died suddenly of myocardial infarction on 19 March 1986 at Ardroy and was cremated.

D. McCarthy, *South-West Pacific Area—First Year* (1959); D. Dexter, *The New Guinea Offensives* (1961); G. Long, *The Final Campaigns* (1963); S. Trigellis-Smith, *All the King's Enemies* (1988); B883, item VX3347 (NAA); private information.

DALE BLAIR

CAMM, RONALD ERNEST (1914-1988), cane farmer and politician, was born on 22 July 1914 at Emerald, Queensland, second of eight children of Jonathan Robert Camm, locomotive fireman, and his wife Tassie, née Johnson, both Queensland born. Ron was educated at Rockhampton and Mackay primary schools and at Mackay State High School. From 1931 he worked as a labourer at Mackay and then at Bloomsbury, where his father had a small farm. On 17 June 1939 at St Joseph's Cathedral, Rockhampton, he married with Catholic rites Florence Alice Leech. Next year he acquired a cane farm at Mount Julian, near Proserpine. Director (1949-65) and chairman (1960-65) of the Proserpine Co-operative Sugar Milling Association Ltd, he was an executive member (1961-65) of the Australian Sugar Producers Association Ltd.

On 1 July 1961, following a by-election, Camm entered the Queensland parliament as Country Party member for Whitsunday. He was to serve in the Nicklin, Pizzey [qq.v.15,16] and Bjelke-Petersen Country-Liberal coalition governments. Best known as minister for mines (1965-80), he also held the portfolios of main roads (1965-74), electricity (1968-69), energy (1974-80) and police (1977-80). After unsuccessfully contesting the party's deputy-leadership against (Sir) Johannes Bjelke-Petersen in January 1968, he secured the post on 2 August when, following Jack Pizzey's

death, Bjelke-Petersen became leader. Two years later he almost gained the leadership when a group of Country Party politicians planned a coup against the premier, with Camm as their preferred alternative; Bjelke-Petersen survived by two votes. Camm was to remain deputy-leader until his retirement from parliament.

Throughout his political career, Camm espoused the ideology of development and progress that underpinned the Nicklin and Bjelke-Petersen governments. As Queensland's longest-serving minister for mines, he oversaw the dramatic growth of the State's mining industry and was a key figure in negotiations with major overseas companies, including the Utah Development Co. In his portfolios of main roads, electricity and energy, he played an important role in the development of infrastructure in Queensland. A self-proclaimed 'champion of free enterprise', he was an enthusiastic advocate of overseas capital investment. He judged virtually everything according to its contribution to Queensland's 'progress'.

Camm's commitment to resource exploitation and his promotion of the mining industry placed him in opposition to major environmental campaigns of the 1960s and 1970s. He supported oil drilling on the Great Barrier Reef and in 1967, with Bjelke-Petersen's help, persuaded the Nicklin government to zone most of Queensland's offshore territory, some 80 000 sq. miles (207 199 km²), into seventeen areas. Cabinet then secretly allocated prospecting rights to six companies. Responding in 1969 to concerns about the threat posed to the reef by drilling, he asserted in parliament that an oil spill would, if it occurred, have the positive outcome of providing an additional food source for fish. He appreciated the beauty of the State's natural attractions, including the reef, in terms of their potential for tourism. During the controversy in 1979 over the demolition of the historic Bellevue Hotel in Brisbane, he chided members of parliament for extending a debate that 'has not in any way been constructive or directed towards the development or progress of this State'.

In 1978 Camm unsuccessfully defied his leader in one of the most serious cabinet disputes of Bjelke-Petersen's coalition government. He and six of the seven Liberal Party ministers supported Millmerran as the site of a new power station against Bjelke-Petersen's preferred option of Tarong. The rift probably shortened Camm's parliamentary career; he retired from politics in July 1980 and later that month was appointed chairman of the Queensland Sugar Board, prompting Opposition claims of 'jobs for the boys'. He held the post until 1986.

A bridge over the Pioneer River at Mackay had been named in Camm's honour in 1980.

He was patron of the Port Denison Sailing Club and enjoyed fishing and playing bowls. Survived by his wife, and their son and two daughters, he died on 15 March 1988 at Auchenflower, Brisbane, and was buried with Uniting Church forms in Proserpine lawn cemetery. Bjelke-Petersen described him as 'one of my most loyal ministers' and his former colleague W. A. M. (Bill) Gunn acclaimed him as a team member, 'a big man and a very strong man'.

A. Patience (ed), *The Bjelke-Petersen Premiership 1968-1983* (1985); B. Galligan, *Utah and Queensland Coal* (1989); J. & M. Bowen, *The Great Barrier Reef* (2002); *PD* (Qld), 11 Sept 1969, p 498, 24 Sept 1974, p 996, 24 Apr 1979, p 4223, 17 Mar 1988, p 5295; *Morning Bulletin* (Townsville), 26 Mar 1980, p 27; *Telegraph* (Brisbane), 14 Aug 1980, p 6.

JOANNE SCOTT

CAMPBELL, ALAN JOHNSTON (1895-1982), grazier and political party organiser, was born on 31 July 1895 at Dubbo, New South Wales, fourth of five children of Charles Campbell, a grazier from Scotland, and his Victorian-born wife Sarah Ann Eliza, née Occleston. Alan's father owned a property near Nyngan, but sold up and in 1903 moved the family to Wallen station, near Cunnamulla, Queensland. Later he was to acquire Merino Downs, Roma. Educated by governesses and at Toowoomba Grammar School (1908-10), Alan worked on Wallen until 1914. On 14 December that year he enlisted in the Australian Imperial Force. He saw action with the 2nd Light Horse Regiment on Gallipoli (July to December 1915) and, as a lance corporal, in the Sinai and Palestine (from January 1916). Suffering from conjunctivitis and 'defective action of the heart', and blinded in the right eye by a bomb blast, he was admitted to hospital in May 1917. He was then employed on depot duties until repatriated in April 1919 and discharged on 16 June.

After the war Campbell managed Merino Downs and in 1929 acquired an adjoining property, Dalmally. He was chairman (1933-50) of the family's pastoral company Charles Campbell & Sons Pty Ltd and active in the Roma branch of the Maranoa Graziers' Association. Concerned about the declining profitability of wool, as founding president (1933) of the Australian Woolgrowers' Association he became convinced of the benefits of political representation. In 1935 he formed one of the first branches of the Queensland Country Party at Roma and in March next year was elected to the inaugural State council. The party was unsuccessful in the 1938 election; in protest against the central organisation an autonomous western division was set up in 1940, with Campbell as president.

Campbell objected to the merger next year of the parliamentary wings of the Country and United Australia parties. Both parties experienced a dramatic loss of members, and in October 1943 the parliamentarians agreed to return to the QCP; Campbell was elected president. After the party was restructured in June 1944 as the Australian Country Party—Queensland, the disharmony between the parliamentary and organisational wings evaporated. T. H. Thelander asserted: 'It was largely under the expert guidance of Campbell that a ... rejuvenation of the organization now took place'. Impressed by the Australian Labor Party's organisation, Campbell centralised power and rebuked parliamentarians whom he believed were neglecting their constituents. By 1951 the highly disciplined structure had attracted 35 000 members.

Due to poor health, Campbell resigned as president in 1951, but continued to occupy less strenuous executive positions at both State and federal levels, becoming a life member in 1956. Five years earlier he had liquidated his interest in the family company and moved to Brisbane. He travelled the world and was elected (1956) a fellow of the Queensland branch of the Royal Geographical Society of Australasia. Tall and handsome, he had been a committed bachelor until, on 19 August 1965 in the register office, Kensington, London, he married Barbara Jane Dunn, a 34-year-old registered nurse from Brisbane. In 1968 he resigned as a Country Party trustee when the Queensland central council insisted on using trustee account funds to meet the party's administrative debts. He was appointed CMG in 1973. A family history was published in 1974 and his memoirs of the Queensland Country Party in 1975. He was a member of the Queensland Turf and Queensland clubs. Survived by his wife, he died on 5 March 1982 at Auchenflower and was cremated with Presbyterian forms.

Qld Country Life, 11 Mar 1982, p 29; S. Walker, interview with A. Campbell (ts, 1974, NLA); T. H. Thelander, The Nature and Development of Country Party Organization in Queensland 1936-1944 (BA Hons thesis, Univ of Qld, 1974); Campbell papers (SLQ); private information.   KEITH MOORE

CAMPBELL, SIR JAMES KEITH (1928-1983), accountant and company director, was born on 4 March 1928 in Sydney, second of three children of Edward Colin Campbell, a bricklayer who was born at Braidwood, New South Wales, and his Victorian-born wife Amanda Maude, née Goodman. Keith was educated at Homebush Junior High School. Awarded a commerce scholarship, he attended the Australian Accountancy College Pty Ltd, run by (Sir) Keith Yorston [q.v.]. After working for Rettie & Vickery he joined the accounting firm D. M. Dixon (& Co.) in 1950, becoming a junior partner in 1952 at the age of 24. He gained a reputation for the restoration of ailing businesses. On 25 September 1951 he married Marjorie Elizabeth Burford, a bank clerk, at St Joseph's Catholic Church, Enfield.

As part of his work at Dixon's, Campbell was auditor for a home-building business, G. H. Thomas Pty Ltd, known as Thomas Homes, and he later joined the firm as a co-director. When the L. J. Hooker [q.v.14] Investment Corporation Ltd (Hooker Corporation Ltd from 1968) acquired Thomas Homes, Campbell worked for both firms part time. Hooker's reached the brink of bankruptcy following the Federal government's 1960 'credit squeeze', and Campbell came to the fore in restructuring the complex real estate and development business. In 1963 he was appointed general manager and from 1964 was called chief general manager. A director of the corporation from 1964, he was appointed chairman in 1974. During his time in charge of Hooker's the firm dealt with real estate, hotels, pastoral interests, retail and industrial developments and jewellery outlets. He selected able staff: he acknowledged that he was 'ruthless about transferring people if they don't fit', but ensured they were always treated with 'dignity'.

Campbell was a director of several companies including IBM Australia Ltd (1969-80), CitiNational Holdings Pty Ltd, later CitiNational Holdings Ltd and CitiNational Ltd (chairman 1971-80), and Network Finance Ltd (deputy chairman 1966-83). He relinquished his position with all but the last of these after the Fraser government appointed him chairman of a committee of inquiry into the Australian financial system. What the media termed 'the Campbell Inquiry' soon became a catch-phrase for economic reform. The lengthy submissions process provoked substantial debate about the antiquated Australian financial system. A perfectionist, Campbell closely supervised the committee. The 838-page report (1981) recommended a move from a fixed to a market-base currency exchange rate, permitting entry of foreign banks and deregulation of the banking sector. The Institute of Chartered Accountants in Australia, of which Campbell became a fellow in 1955, gave him the inaugural Chartered Accountant of the Year award in 1983. He had been appointed CBE in 1972 and knighted in 1982.

A tall, spare man with sandy (later greying) hair, Campbell commanded widespread respect. He held appointments in educational, charitable and government bodies, including the Australian Industry Development Corporation (1974-80) and (from 1981) the council of the University of New South Wales. He was also a member (1970-75) and then chairman

of the council of the Science Foundation for Physics at the University of Sydney, chairman of the Eastern Suburbs Railway Board of Review (1976) and a member of the committee of inquiry into the cost of housing in New South Wales (1977-78). He supported the Salvation Army and was a foundation director (1970-76) and chairman (1976-83) of the board of the Shepherd Centre for deaf children. In addition to his many other commitments he helped with the accounts at Santa Sabina Convent, Strathfield, where his children were educated: when one of the nuns chided him about smoking he jokingly replied that he would give up smoking when she changed her religion. The Campbell family lived at Strathfield until the mid-1970s and then moved to Mosman.

In April 1983 Campbell participated in Prime Minister Hawke's National Economic Summit, urging that unemployment and inflation must be addressed simultaneously; higher unemployment could not be tolerated because it caused great distress. His heavy workload took a toll on his health. Sir Keith died of ischaemic heart disease on 16 April 1983 at Concord. He had been playing golf which, with surfing, was his favourite recreation. Hundreds of mourners attended the requiem Mass for him at Santa Sabina Chapel, Strathfield. Survived by his wife and their three daughters and son, he was cremated. Financial commentators agreed that he had been both effective and intellectually flexible, an uncommon characteristic among accountants of his era. Though he was appointed to lead an inquiry under a Federal coalition government, most of his main recommendations were, ironically, not implemented until the Hawke Labor government, with Paul Keating as treasurer, came to power. According to an obituary he was regarded as 'unfailingly courteous' in a business climate where ideological posturing often took the place of reasoned argument.

R. Appleyard and C. Schedvin (eds), *Australian Financiers* (1988); *National Times*, 26 May 1979, p 36; *Australian*, 1 Jan 1982, p 2; *Chartered Accountant*, Feb 1983, p 3; *Austn Financial Review*, 18 Apr 1983, p 3; *Canberra Times*, 18 Apr 1983, p 3; *SMH*, 20 Apr 1983, p 6, 25 Apr 1983, p 11.

PETER SPEARRITT

CAMPBELL, JEAN MAY (McNEIL) (1901-1984), author, was born on 20 May 1901 in Melbourne, fourth child of Scottish-born John McNeil Campbell, bank manager, and his Victorian-born wife Louise, née Bollinger. Jean was educated at Presbyterian Ladies' College, East Melbourne, where she headed the debating team, edited the school magazine, acted in school productions, and achieved honours in the Leaving certificate. She briefly attended the University of Melbourne as a non-degree student, completed a licentiate of Trinity College of Music, London, and a teaching diploma from the London College of Music and then began instructing in the 'much abused art' of elocution.

In 1921 Campbell became the mistress of John Rose Gorton, businessman, whose son, John, was later prime minister of Australia. She was accepted into the family, often joining them at their property at Kangaroo Lake, near Kerang. While at Oxford the younger Gorton helped to place the manuscript of her first novel with Hutchinson & Co., London. *Brass and Cymbals* (1933) studied the strains experienced by a Jewish immigrant family in Melbourne, and was soon followed by three other novels: *Lest We Lose Our Edens* (1935), *Greek Key Pattern* (1935) and *The Red Sweet Wine* (1937). They were notable for detailed urban settings and (as observed in a review) their 'remarkable maturity' in handling 'racial and religious admixtures'.

In 1937 Hutchinson's offered Campbell a £60 advance for three novels but only *The Babe is Wise* (1939) appeared. The outbreak of war, the subsequent shortage of paper and the decline of circulating libraries put an end to her market. Yet between 1943 and 1945 she wrote 14 anonymous pulp-fiction romances (such as *Sailor's Sweetheart* and *Passion from Pekin*) while also working (1942-45) in the publicity censorship division of the departments of Defence and later Information. In 1947 she was awarded a £400 Commonwealth Literary Fund fellowship to work on a novel about a neglected Melbourne adolescent boy. The manuscript, entitled 'Runt', was praised by an American publisher in 1951 but never published.

Described by a journalist as 'tall and Junoesque', Campbell took pride in living by her wits. She performed in productions of the Little Theatre, Melbourne, and was later employed as its secretary. Active in PEN International and the Victorian section of the Fellowship of Australian Writers (secretary 1950; president 1954-55), in 1951 she was invited to prepare a script for a concert hastily convened to include Aborigines in the Commonwealth jubilee celebrations, following protests by the pastor, (Sir) Douglas Nicholls [q.v.], that no thought had been given to their representation. 'Out of the Dark' proved a great success. With Lina Bryans and Andrew Fabinyi [q.v.14], she organised the first Moomba Book Week in 1955, an event that became a feature of the annual Melbourne festival.

In 1958, in a court case that attracted considerable publicity, Campbell sued Bettina, the wife of Senator John Gorton, for shares (in the family company) then in Mrs Gorton's possession, which Campbell alleged had been given to her by Gorton senior before he died in 1936. Despite irregularities in the company minutes, the judge ruled in favour of Gorton, doubting Campbell's reliability as a witness, given her 20-year 'wait and see' attitude.

Over the following years Campbell continued to undertake freelance journalism, to teach English to immigrants and to visit relatives in Queensland. She appeared in five films, including three by Paul Cox, who also made a short documentary, *We Are All Alone My Dear* (1975)—with Campbell narrating—about life in the retirement village where she spent her last years. Campbell died on 10 December 1984 at East St Kilda and was cremated. The first of two portraits painted of her by Bryans, 'The Babe is Wise' (1940)—held by the National Gallery of Victoria—has been frequently reproduced. Wearing a hat insouciantly dipped over sardonic blue eyes, Campbell is presented (in Gillian Forwood's words) as 'an icon of the modern woman'.

G. Forwood, *The Babe Is Wise: The Portraits of Lina Bryans* (1995); *Herald* (Melbourne), 8 Nov 1933, p 18, 12 Dec 1938, p 16; *Australasian,* 4 Mar 1939, p 39; *People* (Sydney), 27 Jan 1954, p 30; *Age* (Melbourne), 25 Oct 1958, p 6; J. Campbell papers (NLA and SLV).   JOHN ARNOLD

CAMPBELL, JOHN STANISLAUS (1904-1984), Christian Brother and schoolteacher, was born on 20 May 1904 at Warwick, Queensland, and registered as Joseph John Bernardine, third of seven children of Joseph Campbell, a Queensland-born farmer, and his wife Catherine Elizabeth, née Shields, who came from New South Wales. Called John or Jack by his family, he began his education at Swan Creek State School. When he was 7 the family moved from the farm into Warwick, where he was taught first by the Sisters of Mercy and then by the Christian Brothers. He passed the senior public examination in 1920, and on 27 December entered the Christian Brothers' Training College, Strathfield, Sydney. There he was thought to be clever, with an Irish bent for arguing. Tall and heavily built, with jet-black hair, he had a ready smile and a sense of fun. He made his first profession on 17 March 1921, taking the name of Stanislaus.

For eighteen years Campbell taught at schools in and around Sydney. Heeding his mother's advice to teach the boys every day something that was not in the set texts, he embarked on a career in liberal education. In 1926-27 he lectured at Strathfield, while studying arts, majoring in English and Latin, at the University of Sydney (BA, 1929). He took his final vows and was professed on Christmas Day 1929. Sent to Queensland in 1940, he taught at St Joseph's College, Nudgee, Brisbane, and was headmaster at St Joseph's College, Rockhampton.

In 1943 Br 'Stan' transferred to St Joseph's College, Gregory Terrace, Brisbane; his main fields were senior certificate English and Latin. All his talents and experience came together in his vision for the school. With his simple but infectious piety, he was to shape generations of students, whom he called 'gentlemen of Terrace', in the mould of Christian humanists. Known as 'Doc', he enthralled the boys with his recitations of a wide range of verse, from Shakespeare to C. J. Dennis [q.v.8], instilling in them a love of literature. A former pupil observed: 'we saw a man falling in love with his subject every day'. A 'fanatical' follower of Rugby Union football, he was also sports master for many years. In 1959-64 Campbell served, unwillingly, as headmaster. Administration was not his *métier*; nevertheless, the school flourished under him, with much of the credit going to the talented staff.

A founding member (1959) of the Australian College of Education, Campbell was chairman (1964-66) of the Queensland chapter and was elected a fellow in 1967. In 1969-70 he sat on the W. C. Radford [q.v.16] committee which reformed secondary education in Queensland. Recognising that the world, and education, were changing, he feared that the humanism he had cultivated would be jettisoned and that the Christian element of the school would suffer. He was a vigorous contributor to the Conference of Catholic Education, Queensland. For thirty years a member of the local branch of the English Association of Queensland, he was president (1965) and patron (1972-84). He was appointed OBE in 1967.

That year Campbell became the first provincial of the new Queensland province of St Francis Xavier. Although he did not understand the personal problems of the younger Brothers, he set the province off to a good start. He saw teacher education as an important missionary activity and under his direction a novitiate at Helidon and teachers' colleges at Indooroopilly, Brisbane, and at Wewak, Territory of Papua and New Guinea, were established. The model of a true Christian Brother, in 1972-74 he lived with the novices at Helidon.

After he nominally retired in 1975 a Celtic melancholy sometimes clouded Campbell's innate optimism. Ill health curtailed his activities and he increasingly restricted himself to his literary and spiritual interests. He died suddenly on 9 November 1984 at Indooroopilly and, following a funeral in St Stephen's Cathedral, was buried in Nudgee cemetery. His panegyrist summed him up in a phrase he always used of himself, 'an incorrigible Christian Brother'. A portrait of him by Sir William Dargie, commissioned by Terrace old boys in 1982, is held by the school. Another portrait,

by Br Don Gallagher, hangs in provincial headquarters, Indooroopilly.

T. P. Boland, *Gentlemen of Terrace* (2000); Christian Brothers (St Francis Xavier province), *Our Life*, Dec 1984, p 1; *Christian Brothers Educational Record Necrology*, 1989, p 758; Campbell papers (Christian Brothers archives, Indooroopilly, Qld, and St Joseph's College archives, Gregory Terrace, Brisbane).
                                                              T. P. BOLAND

CAMPBELL, DAME KATE ISABEL (1899-1986), paediatrician, was born on 22 April 1899 at Hawthorn, Melbourne, third of four children of Scottish-born Donald Campbell, clerk, and his New Zealand-born wife Janet Duncan, née Mill, a former schoolteacher. The family had limited means, and the first two sons left school early despite their parents' reverence for education. Kate shone at Manningtree Road primary school and won a junior government scholarship that enabled her to attend the nearby Methodist Ladies' College. In 1917, supported by a senior government scholarship, she proceeded to the University of Melbourne (MB, BS, 1922; MD, 1924) and graduated from its medical school with (Sir) Frank Macfarlane Burnet [q.v.], (Dame) Jean Macnamara, Lucy Bryce, Rupert Willis and George Simpson [qq.v.10,7,16].

Even as a student, Campbell demonstrated acute powers of clinical observation and sympathy with patients. Having graduated within the top twelve, she and Jean Macnamara were grudgingly admitted to residencies (1922-23) at the Melbourne Hospital, where women residents were habitually restricted to less interesting cases and excluded from casualty duty. Deciding on private general practice, she believed she needed more experience in child and maternal health. The Children's Hospital, however, after taking women residents during World War I, was again claiming it lacked the facilities to accommodate female doctors. (Sir) William Upjohn [q.v.16] pleaded the special cases of Campbell and Macnamara with the hospital's board, and in later years would boast that his entry to heaven was assured by the fact that he 'got Jean Macnamara and Kate Campbell on at the Children's'. While holding the hand of a two-year-old girl at the hospital Campbell suddenly decided that she would specialise in children's health.

Further discrimination in the allocation of responsibilities prompted Campbell to resign from the Children's Hospital and accept a residency at the (Royal) Women's Hospital in 1924. She began working closely with Dr Vera Scantlebury Brown [q.v.11], who was pioneering aspects of child welfare in Australia. Together, they studied for their doctorates of medicine and in 1927, when Dr Scantlebury Brown was touring New Zealand to investigate the infant care methods of Dr Truby King, Campbell took over the training of infant welfare nurses. Thus began a lifelong association with the Victorian Baby Health Centres Association, for which she was medical officer until 1965. She visited centres throughout Victoria, saw 'all the difficult babies', lectured to nurses, and acted as examiner for the State Infant Welfare certificate. With Scantlebury Brown she wrote *A Guide to the Care of the Young Child* (1947), which remained the standard textbook for infant welfare sisters through seven editions to 1972.

Campbell had been appointed (1926) honorary paediatrician to the Queen Victoria Hospital, where she began work on newborn babies, an appointment she was to hold until 1965, after which she became a consultant. In 1927 she established a general practice at Essendon, but a decade later she moved to specialist paediatrics in Collins Street, and into a familiar routine that saw her conducting her hospital visits in the small hours and many of her consultations in the evening. She was also honorary paediatrician at the Women's from 1944 until 1960, when she was made consultant paediatrician. In 1929 she also began teaching neonatal paediatrics at the University of Melbourne (the first such appointment in Australia) after Professor Marshall Allan [q.v.7] heard her lecture at an Australian Medical Association meeting. It was an inspired appointment: until 1965 she trained generations of doctors in the intricate medicine of the newborn and their 'vocabulary', imitating their squeaks, snuffles and grimaces—all of which told her what the baby was feeling.

Through her private practice, her consultancies and her inimitable teaching, Campbell established an outstanding reputation as a diagnostician. She was remembered for spending hours late at night simply observing babies in special care wards. She developed her own tests for the reflexes and neurological function of the newborn long before such procedures were discovered by others and disseminated in the literature, and she chatted away to pre-term babies as fascinating fellow human beings. She was a pioneer of neonatal intensive care, and was respected by nursing staff for being one of the few senior doctors to treat nurses in special care wards as colleagues.

Campbell's unusual blend of clinical sensitivity, epidemiological curiosity and meticulousness translated into pioneering work on neonatal intensive care and a range of significant advances in the medicine of the newborn. This research led to major papers on infection control, neonatal feeding, jaundice in the premature infant, electrolyte and fluid tolerance in the newborn, and the effects of trauma in delivery. She also collaborated with medical scientists, in particular with Lucy Bryce and Rachel Jakobowicz of the Melbourne Red Cross Blood Bank, into Rh incompatibility of mother and child, the treatment of consequent haemolytic disease of the newborn and the development of exchange blood transfusion. Her most outstanding contribution in research was in establishing that excess therapeutic oxygen lay behind acquired retrolental fibroplasia —a condition that could lead to blindness among premature babies. For this work, she shared (with Sir Norman Gregg [q.v.14]) the inaugural Britannica-Australia award for medicine in 1964. By the end of her career she was publishing on sudden infant death syndrome. She was an honorary fellow (1961) of the Royal College of Obstetricians and Gynaecologists and the first woman president (1965-66) of the Australian Paediatric Association.

While irritating some colleagues with her intuitive gift of diagnosis and her tenacity in debate, Campbell was revered by most for her wisdom, diffidence, courtesy and sense of fun. She derived enormous pleasure from the human comedy, especially at the rougher end of public medicine. She was of a generation of women doctors who dressed impeccably and was rarely seen without a hat. She brought both diagnostic brilliance and clinical rigour to neonatal medicine in Australia, but also championed the virtues of maternal bonding and humane flexibility in an era beset by fads and lingering puritanism.

Campbell's singularity of character bordered on the eccentric. She never married and for 37 years her private life was well organised by Winifred Crick, a devoted housekeeper-companion. Appointed OBE in 1954, she was raised to DBE in 1971. The University of Melbourne conferred on her an honorary doctorate of laws in 1966. She was a member of the Lyceum Club. Dame Kate retired in 1976 and died on 12 July 1986 at Camberwell and was cremated. Her youngest brother, Donald Campbell, QC, was a distinguished and witty barrister who defended Frank Hardy in the *Power without Glory* trial.

P. Grimshaw and L. Strahan (eds), *The Half-open Door* (1982); *Austn Paediatric Jnl*, vol 10, no 2, 1974, p 48; *MJA*, 2 Feb 1987, p 161; *Age* (Melbourne), 21 Oct 1964, p 13, 11 Feb 1976, p 23; *Canberra Times*, 27 Jan 1965, p 23.   JANET McCALMAN

CAMPBELL, ROSS McKAY (1910-1982), journalist and humorist, was born on 26 December 1910 at Kalgoorlie, Western Australia, eldest of four children of Victorian-born parents Douglas McKay Campbell, insurance inspector, and his wife Alice Jean Nicol, née Paulin. The family moved to Melbourne, where Ross attended Scotch College. At the University of Melbourne (BA Hons, 1932), he was co-editor of the university newspaper *Farrago*. In

1933 he was awarded a Rhodes scholarship, which he took up in England at Magdalen College, Oxford (BA, 1935; B.Litt., 1937), but he felt that his degrees were poor preparation for the practicalities of life—a view reinforced by his inability to find a job on his return to Melbourne in 1937. He moved to Sydney, where he joined (Sir) Frank Packer's [q.v.15] *Daily Telegraph* as a journalist, subsequently writing for his *Australian Women's Weekly*, and for *Smith's Weekly*.

By 1941 Campbell was a public servant in the New South Wales Premier's Department. Serving in the Militia from January 1942, he was assigned to public relations duties in Sydney until boredom drove him to transfer to the Royal Australian Air Force on 5 December. After training in Canada and Britain, he flew (1944-45) with No.466 Squadron as a Halifax navigator. In 1945 he was awarded the Distinguished Flying Cross for courage and fortitude on operations, a fact he later omitted from his autobiography, *An Urge to Laugh* (1981). He was demobilised as a temporary flight lieutenant on 20 June 1946 in London.

After joining the *Sydney Morning Herald* in New York, Campbell married Ruth Hazel Seale, a journalist, on 11 December 1946 at Croton-on-Hudson, New York State. He continued to work for the *Herald* in Sydney, but found John Fairfax & Sons [qq.v.4,8] Pty Ltd staid and felt that his writing was undistinguished. In 1954 he rejoined the *Daily Telegraph* as a feature writer, book reviewer and columnist—and it was as a columnist that he found his voice. For more than twenty years, Campbell wrote 450-word articles about family life for the *Daily Telegraph*, *Sunday Telegraph* and *Australian Women's Weekly*. Set in his Sydney home, 'Oxalis Cottage', 'a suburban house of 15 squares, including myself', they featured his children under the pseudonyms of 'Theodora', 'Lancelot', 'Little Nell' and 'Baby Pip'. Many of these pieces—dealing with such subjects as television programs, children's expressions, advertisements—are gems of humour and social history. His originality lay in his persona of the bemused mid-century suburbanite. Unlike Lennie Lower [q.v.10], his view of suburban life depended on accurate reporting; unlike that of Barry Humphries, his satire was gentle.

Campbell also wrote ironic and witty articles for the *Bulletin*; at its best his wordplay bears comparison with that of James Thurber. He published collections of his writings in *Daddy, Are You Married?* (1962), *Mummy, Who is Your Husband?* (1964) and *She Can't Play My Bagpipes* (1970). He retired from journalism in 1978. In typical Australian fashion, he wore his learning lightly. His self-deprecating comment that 'I strove always for more profound superficiality' contradicts the care and pride he took in his craft. He died on 24 February 1982 in

his home at Greenwich, Sydney, and was cremated. His wife and their three daughters and son survived him. A further collection of his columns, *My Life as a Father*, was published in 2005.

Quadrant, Aug 1971, p 8; *SMH*, 25 Feb 1982, p 10; *Bulletin*, 9 Mar 1982, p 52; *Austn Women's Weekly*, 24 Mar 1982, p 22; *Daily Telegraph* (Sydney), 25 Oct 1989, p 48; A9300, Campbell Ross, B883, item NX79121, B884, item N388878 (NAA); H. de Berg, interview with R. Campbell (ts, 1974, NLA); Campbell papers (NLA).   JACQUELINE KENT

CAMPBELL, STUART ALEXANDER CAIRD (1903-1988), air force officer, aviator, administrator and businessman, was born on 27 March 1903 at Darling Point, Sydney, second son of Murray Aird Campbell, a man of independent means, and his wife Caroline Maxwell, née Caird, both Sydney born. Stuart was educated at Sydney Church of England Grammar School (Shore) and the University of Sydney (BE, 1926), where he studied mechanical and electrical engineering. On 26 April 1926 he enlisted in the Royal Australian Air Force. He completed flying training and was commissioned on 1 November. Promoted to flying officer in October 1927, next year he was posted to No.101 Flight, which was surveying the Great Barrier Reef. In 1929 he served in the seaplane-carrier HMAS *Albatross* before being selected as the senior pilot to the 1929-30 and 1930-31 British, Australian and New Zealand Antarctic Research Expedition, led by Sir Douglas Mawson [q.v.10]. With Pilot Officer G. E. Douglas [q.v.14], he pioneered flying in Antarctica in their Gipsy Moth seaplane. Campbell was promoted to flight lieutenant in July 1930. He was to be awarded the Polar medal in 1934.

Transferring to the RAAF Reserve on 7 March 1932, Campbell worked his passage to England in a tramp steamer. He joined H. Hemming & Partners Ltd, London, an air transport company, and returned to Australia as its field manager, undertaking aerial surveys of Western Australia, Victoria and New Guinea. On 2 September 1939 he was recalled to the RAAF's Active List. Made squadron leader in October, he served in a series of operational, training and command appointments and was promoted to wing commander in January 1941 and to acting group captain in January 1942 (substantive in December). Commanding No.42 Squadron from December 1944 and No.76 Wing from May 1945, he flew Catalina flying boats on long-range minelaying operations in the South-West Pacific Area. He was demobilised on 23 April 1946.

After working as acting-director of air navigation and safety, Department of Civil Aviation, Campbell was appointed director in June 1948.

Seconded as chief executive officer of the Australian National Antarctic Research Expeditions in May 1947, he led the group that established the Heard Island station in December. That year he was elected a fellow of the Royal Geographical Society, London. In 1951 he was attached to the International Civil Aviation Organization to set up a civil aviation organisation for the government of Thailand. After a successful two years, during which he had developed a love of the country, he was appointed (1954) commander of the Order of the Crown of Thailand. He soon returned as a private citizen and formed a successful importing business, Thai-Australia Co. Ltd. His books, *The Fundamentals of the Thai Language* (1957) —which he co-authored and which ran to five editions—and *A Guide to the Hard Corals of Thai Waters* (1980), were academically respected.

Campbell was 'a man of action, an adventurer and a hands-on administrator'. He listed his recreations as swimming, tennis, squash and shooting. On 17 December 1968 at the Australian Embassy, Bangkok, he married Shelagh Ann Nickson (d.1985), a registered nurse. In 1973 they retired to Townsville, Queensland. Stuart Campbell died on 7 March 1988 at his Melton Hill home and was cremated with Presbyterian forms. His portrait by Nina Orloff is held by the Mitchell [q.v.5] Library, Sydney.

H. Fletcher, *Antarctic Days with Mawson* (1984); C. D. Coulthard-Clark, *The Third Brother* (1991); D. Wilson, *Alfresco Flight* (1991); T. Bowden, *The Silence Calling* (1997); *West Australian*, 26 July 1935, p 23; Univ of Sydney, *Gazette*, Aug 1992, p 16; A9300, item Campbell S A C (NAA); Campbell diaries and papers (SLNSW).   DAVID WILSON

CANT, JAMES MONTGOMERY (1911-1982), artist, was born on 27 November 1911 at Elsternwick, Melbourne, only child of James Cant (d.1917), a mining agent from England, and his Melbourne-born wife Annie, née Montgomery. When James was 2 the family moved to Sydney, where he attended several schools including, for two terms, Sydney Grammar School. As a boy he studied art at Antonio Dattilo-Rubbo's Saturday morning class, and later at East Sydney Technical College and Julian Ashton's [qq.v.11 Rubbo,7] Sydney Art School. In 1934 he left for London where the modernist artist Roy (Roi) de Maistre [q.v.8], who had been an early influence in Sydney, introduced him to forward-looking art, artists and galleries.

In 1935-39 Cant produced the most adventurous art of his career. He experimented with the late cubist style of Georges Braque and Pablo Picasso—reflected in his paintings 'Still Life' (1935) and 'The Merchants of Death' (1938)—and the surrealism of Giorgio de Chirico and René Magritte, as revealed in 'The Deserted City' (1939). His most advanced works, however, were his 'Found Objects' and 'Constructed Objects', sculptures and assemblages that he exhibited in London in 1937 and 1938. Two three-dimensional creations, 'Surrealist Hand' (c.1936), and a collaged box of items entitled 'Welcome to Empire Day' (1938), survive from this period, and photographs exist of others such as 'The Caged Bunyip' and 'Scarecrow' (1937). These were the most avant-garde works of any Australian artist in the first half of the twentieth century. In 1937 Cant exhibited with de Chirico, Max Ernst and Paul Klee. He travelled to France and Spain and met many of the artists whom he admired including Braque, Picasso, Magritte and Joan Miró.

Cant returned to Sydney in October 1939 and next year held a one-man show at the Macquarie Galleries. Enlisting on 9 May 1941 in the Citizen Military Forces, he performed camouflage duties with the Royal Australian Engineers in New South Wales and Queensland, and rose to warrant officer, class two, before being discharged on 18 May 1944. On 4 March 1942 at the registrar-general's office, Sydney, he had married Noeline Woodard, a laboratory assistant. Seeking solace from the irrationality of surrealism and world events, he became interested in the more humanist and accessible imagery of social realism, particularly the powerful works of Mexican muralists such as Diego Rivera and José Orozco. Nevertheless, in later life he was to declare his religion as surrealist. With other artists, including Dora Cecil Chapman, he helped to form the Studio of Realist Art in 1945. Divorced that year, on 30 June he married Chapman at St James's Church of England, King Street. His major social realist works from this period include 'The Lunch Hour' and 'The Bomb' (1945). About this time both he and his wife joined the Australian Communist Party (Communist Party of Australia).

Employed by the Australian Museum as a display adviser, Cant also painted arid Australian landscapes and works influenced by Aboriginal art. At the suggestion of Charles Mountford [q.v.15], he produced reconstructions of Oenpelli rock art. In 1949 the Cants accompanied a display of these paintings to London. Remaining there for five years, Cant pursued a gentle form of social realism. Much of his work during this period was influenced by the populated streetscapes of L. S. Lowry; his wax-encaustic technique helped to give his paintings of London street scenes and industrial sites a subtle pearly tone.

Back in Australia in 1955, the Cants lived first in Adelaide, then in Sydney. Next year they settled permanently in Adelaide and Dora, who was to support her husband financially for most of their marriage, secured a teaching position at the South Australian School of Art. Cant's intimate grey and damp London scenes gave way to large sunny and dry South Australian landscapes—close-up images of local grasses and brush. These highly textured, almost calligraphic, works were successfully exhibited around Australia. They included 'Birds in the Bush' and 'The Yellow Hill' (1959), and his ultimate 'grass-scape', 'Dry Grass' (1964).

Afflicted with multiple sclerosis, in the mid-1960s Cant managed to execute broadly painted tree-scapes, but by the early 1970s he was unable to work. Survived by his wife but childless, he died on 26 June 1982 at Fullarton and was buried with Uniting Church forms in Willunga cemetery. The Art Gallery of South Australia staged a retrospective exhibition of his art in 1984 and a joint exhibition of his art and that of Dora Chapman in 1995. His work is represented in the National Gallery of Australia and all mainland State galleries.

R. Radford, *James Cant, 1911-1982* (1984); C. Chapman, *Surrealism in Australia* (1993); J. Campbell, *James Cant & Dora Chapman* (1995); H. de Berg, interview with J. Cant (ts, 1962, NLA); M. J. Murray, James Cant (MA thesis, Univ of Melbourne, 1994). 　　　　　　RON RADFORD

CAPELL, ARTHUR (1902-1986), linguist, anthropologist, ethnographer and Anglican clergyman, was born on 28 March 1902 at Newtown, Sydney, only child of English-born parents Henry Capell, commercial traveller, and his wife Sarah Ann, née Scott. Educated at North Sydney Boys' High School, Sydney Teachers' College (Dip.Mod.Lang., 1922) and the University of Sydney (BA, 1922; MA, 1931), he gained first-class honours in Latin and Greek and the university medal in classics. During the 1920s he taught at Canterbury Boys' Intermediate High and Tamworth High schools and collaborated on the preparation of a Latin primer. Made a deacon in the Church of England on 21 December 1925, and ordained priest on 21 December 1926, he worked in the Newcastle diocese as curate (1926-28) of St Peter's Church, Hamilton, and priest in charge (1928-29) of All Saints Church, Belmont.

As an undergraduate Capell corresponded with the English schoolmaster-linguist Sidney Ray, who used some of Capell's research notes for his book *A Comparative Study of the Melanesian Island Languages* (1926). Before the end of the decade Capell's papers were accepted for publication by the *Journal of the Polynesian Society*. His early work was based on material gleaned from private correspondence and missionary and other archival documents. The works of R. H. Codrington, Renward Brandstetter and Otto Dempwolff

inspired him to formulate his own theories on the genetic relationships between regional languages, the affinity between language and population movements, and suitable methods of modelling earlier language forms.

While teaching (1929-32) at Broughton School for Boys in Newcastle, Capell was introduced to A. P. Elkin [q.v.14]. In the following year, after a brief period as curate of Taree, Capell was appointed as curate (1932-35) at St James Church, Morpeth, where Elkin was rector. With his encouragement Capell studied at the School of Oriental and African Studies, University of London (Ph.D., 1938), writing a thesis, 'The Linguistic Position of South-Eastern Papua'.

On his return to Australia in 1938, Capell, at Elkin's behest, investigated the little-studied languages of the Kimberley region of north-western Australia. Helped by Howard Coate, a lay missionary with a knowledge of some of the languages, he interviewed many Aboriginal informants. A similar survey of Arnhem Land languages and dialects over the next few years was interrupted by his work on *A New Fijian Dictionary* (1941). In 1942 he returned to Sydney as curate in charge of St Paul's Church, Canterbury.

Capell was employed as a lecturer (1944-47) and a reader in Oceanic languages (1948-67) in Elkin's department of anthropology at the University of Sydney. From the 1950s, in collaboration with Professor George Shipp [q.v.16], he ran a separate linguistics course, for which he wrote *A Note Book of General Linguistics* (1963). Throughout his career he engaged in field work in Melanesia and Australia. He wrote pioneering linguistic surveys of Papua, New Guinea, the Solomon Islands, Fiji, the New Hebrides and Timor, and published *A Linguistic Survey of the South Western Pacific* (1954) for the South Pacific Commission. In *A New Approach to Australian Linguistics* (1956) he suggested that Australian Aboriginal languages had enough similar elements to suggest that most of them came from a common stock. Among some one hundred scholarly publications, which included contributions to social anthropology, his major works comprised a series on Austronesian languages, grammars of several Oceanic and Australian languages, and a major reformulation of his ideas about the structure and development of Australian Aboriginal languages, which was published in *Australian Linguistic Studies* (1979).

A shy person who never married, Capell seemed aloof to some students but was generous to serious linguistics scholars. He had a quiet sense of humour (being especially adept at the art of punning) and in later life enjoyed science fiction. He maintained an interest in Esperanto. In his priestly role he tried to care for youngsters in trouble. A prolific writer for church and missions publications, he studied ecumenical affairs, and the revolutionary theology movements in South and Central America. He was appointed honorary canon of the Cathedral of St Peter and St Paul, Dogura, Papua, in 1956.

Capell was president (1948-50) and vice-president (1950-52, 1958-59) of the Anthropological Society of New South Wales, a foundation member (1961-68) of the council of the Australian Institute of Aboriginal Studies and a patron of the Aboriginal Australian Fellowship. He was assistant editor (1945-85) of *Oceania* and a member (1977-83) of the editorial board of *La Monda Lingvo-Problemo*. Elected a fellow of the Australian Academy of the Humanities in 1979, he was awarded an honorary D.Litt. by the University of Sydney in 1981. He died on 10 August 1986 at Gordon and was cremated.

S. A. Wurm and D. C. Laycock (eds), *Pacific Linguistic Studies in Honour of Arthur Capell* (1970); P. J. F. Newton, 'Capell on Australia', in G. McCall (ed), *Anthropology in Australia* (1982); W. F. Connell et al, *Australia's First*, vol 2 (1995); Austn Academy of Humanities, *Proceedings*, vol 13, 1984-86, p 149; *Jnl of the Oriental Soc of Aust*, vol 17, 1985, p 5; *Austn Aboriginal Studies*, no 1, 1987, p 98; *Oceania*, vol 57, no 4, 1987, p 241; P. J. F. Newton, Movements and Structures (BA Hons thesis, Macquarie Univ, 1979); Capell papers and P. Money papers (NLA).

PETER J. F. NEWTON

CARNE, HAROLD ROY (1901-1990), professor of veterinary science, was born on 25 March 1901 at Hunters Hill, Sydney, second child of Joseph Edmund Carne [q.v.7], a Victorian-born geological surveyor, and his second wife Clara Grace, née Hudson, who was born in New South Wales. Roy attended Malvern Preparatory School and Sydney Grammar School. His childhood ambition was to go 'on the land' as a grazier and he decided to enrol in veterinary science as part of his preparation. He studied under Professor J. D. Stewart [q.v.12] at the University of Sydney (B.V.Sc., 1923; D.V.Sc., 1934) and was awarded first-class honours and the university medal. In 1922 he was president of the university's Veterinary Society. Next year he was appointed to the staff of the faculty of veterinary science, where he provided a practical course in materia medica, therapeutics and pharmacy, demonstrated in pathology and carried out the duties of assistant house surgeon. He resided at Wesley College and rowed in the Senior and College VIIIs.

In 1924 Carne became a research officer at the veterinary research station, New South Wales Department of Agriculture, Glenfield, serving under Herbert Seddon [q.v.16]. Gaining a Walter and Eliza Hall [qq.v.9] research

fellowship in 1926, Carne pursued his project, streptococcal mastitis of cattle, at the Laboratoire Central de Recherches Vétérinaires at Maisons-Alfort near Paris and completed courses in microbiology at the Institut Pasteur. He married Ursula Widmerpoole Starling (d.1989) on 10 October 1927 at St Nicholas parish church, Cuddington, England.

Appointed lecturer in veterinary pathology and bacteriology at the University of Sydney, Carne took up his duties in 1928. His sympathy for students who, in the absence of adequate textbooks, had to record verbatim the essence of lectures led to his preparing in roneo form extensive notes which he revised every couple of years. They were available to students at cost. Understanding the importance of parasitic diseases in grazing animals, he gave a comprehensive course in parasitology, which was subsequently expanded by (Sir) Ian Clunies Ross [q.v.13] and carried on for many years by Hugh Gordon. When the F. D. McMaster [q.v.10] Animal Health Laboratory was built for the Council for Scientific and Industrial Research in the grounds of the University of Sydney in 1931, Carne and Clunies Ross co-operated in planning and equipping it. A personal laboratory for Carne and new teaching facilities for veterinary students in practical classes were incorporated in the plans.

Carne's doctoral thesis was on corynebacterial infections of domestic animals. Having won a Rockefeller travelling fellowship, in 1934 he worked at the Lister Institute of Preventive Medicine in London, continuing his research on caseous lymphadenitis. He was appointed Hughes professor of veterinary pathology and bacteriology at the University of Sydney in 1947. As dean (1947-53, 1960-61) of the faculty he was concerned to develop veterinarians who, in addition to traditional skills with individual animals, had expert knowledge of the problems of the flock and herd. He advocated the expansion of existing facilities, but also wanted to create a rural centre to provide proximity to the animals needed as clinical teaching material. From the starting point of the McGarvie Smith Farm at Badgery's Creek he worked towards further developments, which led to the establishment of the university's rural veterinary centre at Camden. He supported the creation of departments of physiology and animal husbandry. His belief in the need for a corporate life within the university culminated in the building of the common room at the veterinary school.

Carne's vision of the requirements of veterinary science was broad and forward looking. As a teacher he was scholarly, devoted and stimulating, and his personal relationships were sincere, kindly and fair. President (1947-48) of the Australian Veterinary Association, he was elected a fellow in 1955. Five years later he delivered the first J. D. Stewart Oration. He served as honorary secretary (1940-50) of the Australian National Research Council, and member (1951-62) and chairman (1955-61) of the State committee of the Commonwealth Scientific and Industrial Research Organization. He was a fellow of the Australian and New Zealand Association for the Advancement of Science. Having reached the age of compulsory retirement from the University of Sydney in 1966 he moved to Cambridge, England, where he worked until 1986, researching and producing ten more papers on caseous lymphadenitis. Survived by his three daughters, he died on 11 February 1990 at Cambridge and was cremated.

Austn Veterinary Jnl, vol 67, no 5, 1990, *AVA News* supplement, 9 May 1990, p N168; H. Carne, autobiographical notes (ts, nd, copy on ADB file).
                                          ROBERT I. TAYLOR*

CARR, STELLA GRACE MAISIE (1912-1988), botanist, was born on 26 February 1912 at Footscray, Melbourne, eldest of six children of Victorian-born parents George Henry Fawcett, electrician, and his wife Ethel May, née Ward. In her parents' and grandmother's gardens, on nearby salt-marshes, and in nature study classes, Maisie developed an early love of plants. Dux of Footscray's Hyde Street State School in 1924, she attended Melbourne High School. Instead of accepting a university free place, she worked as a junior teacher in her old primary school and studied zoology and geology at night at the Austral Coaching College.

In 1932, with one of only twelve Teachers' College secondary studentships, Fawcett entered the University of Melbourne (B.Sc., 1935; M.Sc., 1936); she gained both degrees with first-class honours in botany and joined Teachers' College hockey and swimming teams. In the university's botany department she demonstrated to practical classes. With a succession of research scholarships and grants, and initially supervised by Ethel McLennan [q.v.], she studied Australian coral fungi and microscopic fungal and nematode diseases of plants. She also participated in the annual field-trips of the McCoy [q.v.5] Society for Field Investigation and Research. A severe head injury in 1940 precluded microscope work and her research grant was renewed in 1941 for ecological investigations.

Later that year Professor John Turner arranged for Fawcett's appointment, as a university research officer, to investigate soil erosion in the catchment of the Hume Reservoir for the Soil Conservation Board of Victoria. Living at Omeo, she monitored vegetation in two eroded areas that were fenced to exclude rabbits and stock. She covered long distances on horseback, investigated gully erosion and tested introduced grasses and fertilisers in pasture experiments. Her extensive, unpublished report documented widespread degeneration of vegetation and loss of soil due to over-grazing. She also contributed to Leonard Stretton's [q.v.16] 1946 royal commission into forest grazing. The locals called her 'Washaway Woman' and 'Erosion Girl'. A journalist commented on her 'strong independence' and noted her sturdy build and 'healthy weather-beaten appearance'.

Erosion on the Bogong High Plains posed a siltation threat to the Kiewa hydro-electric scheme. Appointed the SCB's first research officer, albeit temporary, in 1944, Fawcett set out to monitor the effects of grazing on the high plains. In January 1945 she selected for fencing a large area on the upper slopes of Rocky Valley that contained a range of vegetation—moss bed, snow grass, heath, scrub and woodland—and marked off reference plots of vegetation inside and outside the exclosure. The State Electricity Commission of Victoria later fenced one snow grassed acre (0.4 ha) adjacent to one unfenced control acre on the edge of Pretty Valley. Each summer for a decade Turner organised a university team to record the vegetation in Fawcett's plots. She was the SCB representative, and sole woman, on the Bogong High Plains Advisory Committee, which from 1946 determined the permissible number of cattle and the length of their stay each summer.

Fawcett accepted a temporary lectureship in Turner's botany department in 1949. Annoyed by the inadequacy of published floras, she organised the preparation of a botanical key, *The Families and Genera of Victorian Plants* (1949). She lectured on plant taxonomy and ecology to science and agriculture students, becoming senior lecturer in 1952. As the former beauty of Pretty Valley returned to its fenced acre, she and Turner documented the botanical changes in two papers (*Australian Journal of Botany*, 1959) that provided the first published scientific evidence of the destructive effects of grazing on the vegetation and soils of Victoria's high country.

On 9 February 1955 at Holy Trinity Church of England, Hampton, Fawcett married Denis John Carr, a fellow senior lecturer in the botany department. Their collaborative morphological and taxonomic work on eucalypts continued in Belfast (1960-67), where she was an honorary research fellow at the Queen's University, and then in Canberra, as a visiting fellow at the Australian National University. With Turner's university teams she re-surveyed the high plains plots in 1966 and 1979; she prepared a report on the region for the Victorian Land Conservation Council in 1977.

Maisie Carr was a perfectionist who loved books, art and music and had a 'dry and very Australian sense of humour'. Long interested in Australian history, with Denis she wrote articles for and edited *Plants and Man in Australia* and *People and Plants in Australia* (both 1981). A heavy smoker, she suffered from chronic bronchitis. She died on 9 September 1988 in Royal Canberra Hospital and was buried with Baptist forms in Gungahlin cemetery. Professor Carr subsequently provided funds to have her accumulated ecological data published. Her scientific legacy includes ecological ideas, some confirmed only recently, and a number of Australia's oldest vegetation records, exclosures and reference plots.

L. Gillbank, 'Into the Land of the Mountain Cattlemen', in F. Kelly (ed), *On the Edge of Discovery* (1993) and for sources; D. J. Carr (comp), *A Book for Maisie* (2005); *Austn Systematic Botany Soc Newsletter*, Mar 1989, p 21.   LINDEN GILLBANK

CARRUTHERS, JAMES WILLIAM (1929-1990), boxer, was born on 5 July 1929 at Paddington, Sydney, fifth of eight children of English parents John William Carruthers, labourer, and his wife Agnes Jane, née Allison. Jimmy attended Glenmore Road Public School, Paddington. His natural talent for boxing was recognised and encouraged at the Woolloomooloo Rotary-Police Boys' Club. He won the Australian amateur bantamweight title in 1947 and was included in the Australian team for the 1948 Olympic Games in London. After winning his first two bouts he was forced to withdraw because of a gashed eyebrow, a recurring injury that plagued him throughout his career.

As a wharf labourer and member of the Waterside Workers' Federation of Australia, Carruthers spoke out in favour of unionism and world peace in the 1950s, thereby earning himself an Australian Security Intelligence Organization file. Fellow 'wharfies' and officials supported his boxing career by arranging time off for him to train when he prepared for a major fight. He married his childhood sweetheart, Myra Louise Hamilton, a machinist, on 10 February 1951 at All Saints' Church of England, Woollahra.

After Carruthers had turned professional in 1950, his manager Dr John McGirr and trainer Bill McConnell shrewdly planned his professional campaign. In 1951, in his ninth professional fight, he won the Australian bantamweight title against Elley Bennett [q.v.]. In his fifteenth fight, in November 1952, he contested the world bantamweight title with Vic Toweel in Johannesburg, knocking him out after 2 minutes and 19 seconds.

Carruthers defended his title four months later, knocking out Toweel in ten rounds. He then defeated the American Henry 'Pappy' Gault in November 1953 despite slashed eyebrows and a tapeworm, which was discovered later. The bout, promoted by the Federation of New South Wales Police-Citizens Boys' Clubs, drew an Australian record boxing crowd of 32 500 at the Sydney Sports Ground. While some of the takings went to charity, Carruthers received £8625, the largest purse earned by an Australian boxer to that time. He successfully defended his title a third time, defeating Chamrern Songkitrat in Bangkok, in a ring soaked by torrential rain.

A southpaw, Carruthers was tall (168 cm) for a bantamweight with a long reach and broad shoulders. The boxing commentator Ray Connelly noted that his 'incomparable speed of hands and feet, exceptional balance, ... movement and anticipation' enabled him to demoralise opponents. The press saw Carruthers as a 'true sporting son of Sydney': there were stories of his waiting outside pubs while his wharfie friends drank inside and he was a star graduate of the police boys' clubs. His success enabled him to challenge the authority of Stadiums Ltd, the firm that dominated boxing in this period, and gain a greater percentage of takings.

When Carruthers retired on 16 May 1954, he was only 24 and at his peak physically and financially. He achieved the remarkable feat of retiring with a perfect record of nineteen wins in nineteen bouts. In four years of professional boxing he had grossed an estimated £64 500, enabling him to purchase homes for his family and his parents. He also bought the Bells Hotel at Woolloomooloo, close to where he had worked as a wharfie. In 1961, having sold his hotel, Carruthers made a comeback to boxing primarily to earn money: he had always regarded it as a business. He trained with the athletics coach Percy Cerutty [q.v.13] in the Portsea sandhills but lost four of his six bouts. For many years Carruthers officiated as a referee.

In the 1960s and 1970s he and his wife ran a fruit shop and milk bar at Avalon and a juice bar in the city. In later life Carruthers became a regular churchgoer and was baptised into the Churches of Christ. He died of cancer on 15 August 1990 at his home at Narrabeen. Survived by his wife and their two sons and two daughters, he was cremated. His portrait, painted by John Curtis, was presented to the State police commissioner, C. J. Delaney [q.v.13], in recognition of Carruthers's early association with the police-citizens boys' clubs.

T. Thomlinson (ed), *The Title Fight* (1955); J. Pollard, *Ampol's Australian Sporting Records* (1969); P. Corris, *Lords of the Ring* (1980); G. Kieza,

Australian Boxing (1990); *Bulletin*, 15 July 1961, p 6; *Australian*, 24 Sept 1973, p 9; *SMH*, 17 Aug 1990, p 46.   R. I. CASHMAN

CASEY, DANIEL (1899-1987), lawyer, was born on 26 September 1899 at Mitchell, Queensland, fourth of nine children of Queensland-born parents John Casey, acting-sergeant of police, and his wife Ada Frances, née Grogan. Dan's four grandparents had been born in Ireland and he was to retain pride in his Irish heritage all his life. The family moved to Inglewood when he was very young and then, about 1912, to Bundaberg. He attended Bundaberg State High School, passing the junior public examination in 1915, and joined the staff of the Queensland National Bank. In 1919 he was articled to his brother John, a solicitor at Ipswich, transferring next year to Frank Brennan [q.v.7], and finally to Leonard Power. Qualifying as a solicitor on 4 May 1926, he practised at Nanango until 1934. He moved to Brisbane and on 3 July that year was admitted to the Bar.

As a barrister specialising in criminal matters, Casey was busy from the start, and in 1936 a sensational murder trial attracting much publicity secured his reputation, even though he lost the case. His client Herbert Kopit had been accused of murdering a person on a train, and had confessed to police. The motive was apparently robbery, but there were no witnesses. A psychologist called by Casey to give evidence deposed that Kopit was insane at the time he struck the fatal blows. Casey sought unsuccessfully to have the record of Kopit's confession excluded from the evidence, which was fatal for the defence case.

Casey was an alcoholic who lost many briefs because of his problem. In 1947, encouraged by family and friends, he agreed to meet Lillian Roth, a founder of Alcoholics Anonymous in the United States of America, who was visiting Brisbane. Her effect on Casey was immediate: he stopped drinking and established a local branch of AA. He worked tirelessly for years supporting the organisation and encouraging hundreds to abstain and to embrace the twelve steps of the AA program. A supporter of Vince Gair and E. J. Walsh [qq.v.14,16] during the Australian Labor Party split, he unsuccessfully contested the seat of Brisbane for the Queensland Labor Party in the 1957 State election.

In 1959 Casey defended Neville Pressler, a Bundaberg cane-farmer, who was found guilty of murdering his neighbours Clifford and Marjorie Golchert. Shortly after, Pressler's uncle, Henry Edward Pressler, was found dead with a handwritten suicide note, confessing to the murders, and a rifle close by. Neville's mother, Enid Ethel Pressler, was charged with Henry's murder. Casey—with his junior (Sir) Gerard Brennan, later chief justice of the High Court of Australia—defended Mrs Pressler in what was to be his most famous case. The Crown asserted that, when her son was found guilty of murdering the Golcherts, Mrs Pressler forged the suicide note and killed her brother-in-law. It called expert evidence to establish that she was the author of the letter. Mrs Pressler claimed that Henry Pressler had dictated the 'confession', and signed it, on the day of his death. After a trial lasting nine days the jury returned a verdict of 'not guilty'. According to Kerry Smith, 'the end of the trial was a triumph for Mr Casey, one of the State's leading criminal advocates'. Brennan was later to refer to Casey as 'a legend in his own lifetime'.

Sir Dormer Andrews, chief justice of Queensland (1985-89), described Casey as 'a silver-tongued orator but with all the tradesman like virtues of a thoroughly efficient practising lawyer. Superb in cross-examination he was unerringly relevant and learned in the law'. His integrity was 'beyond question'. Sir Harry Gibbs, chief justice of the High Court (1981-87), observed that he was adept at identifying and exploiting any weakness in the Crown case and in skilfully using his eloquence to sway juries. Casey, who suffered from ill health from the 1960s, took few briefs after 1975. In 1984 the Queensland Bar Association honoured him with a dinner to mark the fiftieth anniversary of his admission. He was a devout Catholic who enjoyed horse-racing, Rugby League football and boxing. Unmarried, he died on 27 June 1987 at his Woolloongabba home and was buried in Hemmant cemetery.

K. Smith, *Dan Casey* (1987); *Courier-Mail* (Brisbane), 27 June 1936, p 15, 29 June 1987, p 9; *Telegraph* (Brisbane), 6 Nov 1959, p 1, 4 Nov 1960, p 3; *Daily Telegraph* (Sydney), 4 Nov 1960, p 1.   JAMES CROWLEY

CASEY, ETHEL MARIAN SUMNER (MAIE) (1891-1983), writer, artist and flyer, was born on 13 March 1891 at Brunswick, Melbourne, younger child of Victorian-born parents (Sir) Charles Snodgrass Ryan [q.v.11], surgeon, and his wife Alice Elfrida, née Sumner. Rupert Ryan [q.v.16] was her brother. Raised in Collins Street, Melbourne, where her father practised, she was educated privately by a Swiss governess and then with the four talented daughters of Sir Edward Mitchell [q.v.10]. One of them, Nancy [q.v.10 I. M. Mitchell], admired her chestnut ringlets, her large blue eyes and her delicate skin, invariably protected by a hat and veil. Maie's childhood was peopled by gifted artistic and professional relatives including her aunt, Ellis Rowan, her father's cousin Janet, Lady Clarke, and the Le Soeuf brothers, scientists and zoo-directors, as well as the Chirnside and Grice families [qq.v.11,3,10,7,9].

In 1907 Maie was sent to England to board at St George's School, Ascot. Her formal education was completed at a finishing school in Paris and she returned to Melbourne in 1910. To her disappointment, her father's colleague (Sir) Richard Stawell advised against a university education, as his brilliant sister Melian [qq.v.12] had suffered a breakdown at Cambridge. In England at the outbreak of World War I, Maie volunteered for work at (Sir) Douglas Shields's [q.v.11] Hospital for Wounded Officers and then with Vera Deakin's [q.v.16 White] Australian Wounded and Missing Inquiry Bureau. After the war she acted as hostess for Rupert in Germany, where he was working for the Interallied Rhineland High Commission.

Living in London from 1924, Maie Ryan renewed acquaintance with Richard Gavin Gardiner (Baron) Casey [q.v.13], whose family had been part of the same small Melbourne élite as her own, and who was working as Australia's liaison officer to the British government. They were married on 24 June 1926 at St James's parish church, Westminster. David Marr, the biographer of her friend Patrick White, described her wedding photograph as revealing 'a saucer jaw and the eager carriage of a pony about to bolt'. The Caseys' daughter was born in 1928 and their son shortly after their return to Melbourne in 1931. On 21 December that year Richard was elected member for Corio in the House of Representatives. More attuned to British than Australian politics, they opted to live in the capital rather than the electorate.

In Canberra, Mrs Casey, who had studied at the Westminster School of Art, London, found time to paint. Occasionally she attended classes at the art school run by Arnold Shore and George Bell [qq.v.11,7] in Melbourne. While in England in 1937 for the coronation of King George VI, both Caseys had their first experience of flying and, on their return, with characteristic whole-heartedness, took lessons, gained their licences, bought a primrose yellow Percival Vega Gull, and laid out an airstrip at Edrington, the property at Berwick, outside Melbourne, that Maie and Rupert had inherited from Chirnside relatives. With their new-found mobility they divided their time between Berwick, Canberra, where—following Casey's appointment as treasurer in 1935—they supervised the building of a ministerial residence, and East Melbourne, where they had bought a small town-house, once the home of Eugen von Guerard [q.v.4].

(Sir) Robert Menzies' [q.v.15] decision to send Casey in 1940 to the United States of America as Australia's first diplomatic representative was almost certainly the result of the intervention of Maie Casey, whom Menzies dubbed 'Lady Macbeth'. Ambitious for her husband, she had been disappointed when he failed to succeed Lyons [q.v.10] as prime minister. In Washington she was a popular hostess and a good ambassador for Australia, furnishing the legation with Australian timbers, fabrics by the Melbourne artist Frances Burke and paintings by Rupert Bunny [q.v.7] and her friends from the George Bell school, (Sir) Russell Drysdale [q.v.] and Peter Purves Smith [q.v.11]. When Casey was appointed British minister of state in Cairo in 1942, his wife's quick intelligence impressed the cavalcade of distinguished military and political visitors to their home. She threw herself into war work, visiting the wounded at the 9th General Hospital, Heliopolis, travelling with the Hadfield-Spears Mobile Hospital and chairing the St Dunstan's Unit, which helped blind servicemen. Casey's appointment as governor of Bengal, India (1944-45), brought his wife new duties as vicereine, which she ably fulfilled while collaborating with her husband to free the office of Imperial anachronisms.

Back in Melbourne from 1946, as her husband pursued his political career, Maie Casey found herself in demand as a public speaker. Acquaintance with the educated women of India had convinced her that Australian women should be more active in public life, and she said so to a wide range of audiences. When engagements permitted she indulged her passions for art and flying. As well as continuing to paint, she became a patron for young Australian artists such as (Sir) Sidney Nolan. She was delighted to be named in 1950 inaugural patron of the Association of Women Pilots of Australia and to be accorded in 1954 membership of the Ninety-Nines, an association of American women pilots founded by Amelia Earhart. In October 1953 she flew her Miles Messenger in Australia's first all-woman air race. That year a book on which she had collaborated with (Sir) Daryl Lindsay [q.v.10], her brother-in-law Dermot Casey and others, *Early Melbourne Architecture*, was published.

Lady Casey (her husband was made a life peer in 1960) won increasing recognition as a writer. Her account of her forebears, *An Australian Story 1837-1907*, was published in 1962; a book of her verse (with illustrations by Frances Burke) appeared the following year; in 1965 she collaborated with Margaret Sutherland [q.v.] on the creation of a one-act opera, *The Young Kabbarli*, based on the life of Daisy Bates [q.v.7], and in 1966 her memoir *Tides and Eddies* appeared. Her verse was kindly received, her libretto drew severe criticism, and her memoir, although rich in exotic settings and luminaries (she was an inveterate name-dropper), was superficial. Her best work was *An Australian Story*. In it, her love of her native land shone, and so did her capacity for evocative description and her artist's eye for the revealing detail.

Small and trimly built, with grey wavy hair and intense blue eyes, as wife of Australia's sixteenth governor-general (1965-69), Lady Casey performed her vice-regal duties with poise and élan. She converted Yarralumla into a salon for artists, musicians and writers while dutifully entertaining the dignitaries who came with the job. In retirement at Edrington, she continued to write verse, which she pressed on her friends, to correspond with the vast circle she had cultivated, to travel with her husband (the 'Casey season' in London remained an annual event), and, much to the alarm of her intimates, to fly her Cessna.

Maie Casey was a woman of paradoxes. Possessed of charm and wit, she could be manipulative and ruthless. A steadfast friend to many, she was a cold and inattentive mother. Although bohemian in her private life, she was a snob. Not conventionally beautiful, she attracted, and was attracted by, a host of men and women, but she remained a devoted wife to Richard Casey, channelling much of her formidable energy into promoting and supporting his career. A friend, Lady Drysdale, judged that she was 'napoleonic'.

After Lord Casey died in 1976, she withdrew into bereavement. She was made a fellow of the Royal Society of Arts in 1979 and was appointed AC in 1982, but she became increasingly absorbed in the past as she planned a book on her husband's life. She died on 20 January 1983 at Edrington and was buried beside him at the Church of the Good Shepherd, Macedon. Her children survived her. A memorial service was held at Christ Church, South Yarra, on Australia Day.

W. J. Hudson, *Casey* (Melbourne, 1986); D. Langmore, *Glittering Surfaces* (Sydney, 1997) and for sources; Maie Casey papers (NLA).

DIANE LANGMORE

CASEY, JOHN BRENDAN (1909-1985), Jesuit priest and educationist, was born on 3 February 1909 at Clarence Siding, New South Wales, eldest son of Irish-born parents Maurice John Casey, storekeeper, and his wife Hannah Maria, née Lyne. Educated at St Joseph's Convent School, Penrith, then by the Marist Brothers at Villa Maria, Hunters Hill, and at St Ignatius' College, Riverview, Casey worked in the retail grocery business while studying analytical chemistry at Sydney Technical College. He entered the novitiate of the Society of Jesus in 1930 at Loyola, Greenwich, and took his first vows in 1932. Casey was one of the 'new breed' of Jesuits trained entirely in Australia rather than in Ireland or elsewhere overseas. Following a home juniorate (1932-33) at Greenwich, he was sent to St Aloysius' College, Milsons Point, to teach science, economics and mathematics (1934-36). Though intelligent and natively shrewd, he never enjoyed robust health, and he was not encouraged to attend university—a fact that diminished his self-esteem throughout his life.

After studying philosophy at Loyola College, Watsonia, Melbourne, in 1937-38, and at Canisius College, Pymble, Sydney, in 1939, he taught at St Louis' School, Claremont, Perth, in 1940. He returned to Pymble for theological studies (1941-44), being ordained priest by Archbishop (Cardinal Sir Norman) Gilroy [q.v.14] in St Mary's Cathedral on 8 January 1944. After serving his tertianship at Watsonia during 1945, he worked at Riverview as division prefect and line teacher in 1946-48 and became rector of St Aloysius' College in April 1948. Next year he returned to Riverview as rector. This rich period of his administration (1949-54) was followed by another term as rector (1955-61) of St Aloysius'. He proved to be both a skilled builder and a far-sighted policy maker, very influential in times of educational reform and systemic change.

After his success in Sydney, Casey spent two quieter years at Campion College, Kew, Melbourne, the residence of Jesuit university students. From there he was sent back to St Louis', Perth, as rector (1964-66). When he returned to take charge (1967-68) of the house at Kew, his health was failing and he was suffering the effects of poorly controlled diabetes. In 1969 he went back to Pymble to recuperate but picked up sufficiently in spirits to resume living at Riverview in 1974. There he remained until his death, much loved and consulted by a wide variety of friends. A father-figure to many, he continued to perform his pastoral role. He died on 30 January 1985 at Darlinghurst and was buried in the Jesuit lawn cemetery, North Ryde.

In addition to holding high educational posts within the Jesuit Order, Casey was an important and respected figure in such professional bodies as the Australian College of Education (fellow 1961), the Headmasters' Conference of the Independent Schools of Australia and the National Council of Independent Schools (Australia). He was a strong advocate of per capita public funding for each student and he persistently advocated the political alliance of Catholic and other private schools in defence of the independent principle and in negotiations for a more favourable outcome from both State and Federal governments in the perennial and vexed question of state aid.

J. W. Hogg, *Our Proper Concerns* (1986); E. Lea-Scarlett, *Riverview* (1989); D. Strong, *The College by the Harbour* (1997) and *The Australian Dictionary of Jesuit Biography 1848-1998* (1999); *Jesuit Life*, Easter 1985, p 16; J. Casey personal file (Society of Jesus, Austn Province Archives, Melbourne).

J. EDDY

CASHMAN, ELLEN IMELDA (1891-1983), union organiser and arbitration inspector, was born on 19 November 1891 at Gladesville, Sydney, youngest of three daughters of Irish parents Edward Cashman, hotelkeeper, and his wife Ellen, née Manning. Mel was educated by the Sisters of St Joseph at Hunters Hill, before starting work at an early age. She was employed in the trades of meat preserving, upholstery, tailoring and bag-making before moving into printing, where she worked for William Brooks & Co. Ltd and W. C. Penfold [qq.v.7,11] & Co. While still under 21 she was told to 'put her hair up' as she was to be made forewoman.

President (1915-17) and secretary (1917) of the Printing Trades Women and Girls' Union, when that union amalgamated with the Printing Industry Employees' Union of Australia, New South Wales branch, she became organising secretary of the women and girls' advisory committee (section) on 31 March 1917, and from 1919 of the box and carton advisory committee (section). She was a member of the board of management, a federal councillor on several occasions, and regularly a delegate to the eight-hour (later six-hour) association and to Labor conferences. Appearing frequently as a witness before the Living Wage (Adult Females) inquiries, she worked on the union's case in 1918, and served as an employee representative for the inquiries in 1919, 1926 and 1927. In the printing trade's 44-hour-week case she appeared for the union in the Commonwealth Court of Conciliation and Arbitration. She had a column in the union's journals, the *Printer* and the *Printing Trades Journal*, and she helped organise a social club, which provided debating, excursions, and physical culture for women members. A fine mezzo-soprano, she also organised singing classes. She stood for the position of president of the union twice, losing narrowly in 1923 and again in 1940 despite leading on first preference votes.

Although Miss Cashman believed that men's wages should be sufficient to support a family, she objected to the 54 per cent rate for women. She was concerned about the readiness of men to work with non-union women when they would not work with men who refused to join. Her success in organising the women led to moves from other sections of the union to limit the voting rights of the women and girls. When another attempt to do so involved the union in proceedings before the Industrial Commission in 1940, she applied for the position of Commonwealth arbitration inspector. She was one of the six inspectors appointed in August 1940 from over six hundred applicants. A confidential report said she was 'a good type, moderate, and competent'. From 1940 to 1946, she was a member of the State board of the Women's Australian National Services, formed to mobilise and co-ordinate women's war effort. She was reprimanded for allowing attendance at WANS daytime meetings to interfere with her work as inspector. In December 1941 she was seconded to the Department of Labour and National Service to survey conditions in the clothing industry.

In April 1942 Miss Cashman was appointed to the Women's Employment Board, which regulated the conditions of employment for women in jobs which in peacetime were undertaken by men. After criticism by employers of her appointment as their representative, in June she was named as the Commonwealth's representative. When there was disagreement about the rates to be paid, she voted with the majority: in the State Electricity Commission of Victoria clerks' case she supported a rate of 85 per cent for women even though the employees' representatives wanted 100 per cent. The Women's Employment Board was disbanded in October 1944.

Miss Cashman's job as an arbitration inspector involved extensive travel. In 1952, after a period in hospital, she resigned. Retirement left her with 'time on her hands' and she returned to printing on a casual basis. Short, stout, intensely vital and a great talker, she had a fund of anecdotes about her union experience, which she had greatly enjoyed. Her philosophy was summed up in her statement: 'There is a lot of good in the best of us, and it would make up for the bad in the worst of us'. She died on 11 June 1983 at Bexley and was buried in the Catholic section of the Field of Mars cemetery.

Printing Trades Jnl, 8 May 1917, p 5, 17 Dec 1918, p 286, 11 Sept 1928, p 198, Aug 1983, p 83; *Printer* (Sydney), 26 Aug 1927, pp 120, 123, 31 Aug 1928, p 121, 7 June 1940, p 1, 16 Aug 1940, pp 92, 94; *SMH*, 7 Aug 1940, p 8, 18 Apr 1942, p 18; *Smith's Weekly*, 10 Oct 1942, p 5; MP239/2, item ST53/98, pt 1 (NAA); Printing Industry Employees' Union of Aust records (Noel Butlin Archives, ANU); private information.   HEATHER RADI

CAVANAGH, JAMES LUKE (1913-1990), politician and trade unionist, was born on 21 June 1913 at Paddington (Rosewater), Adelaide, youngest of three children of James Luke Cavanagh, boiler maker, and his wife Isobella, née Buckton, both Adelaide born. Educated by the Dominican Sisters at North

Adelaide and by the Christian Brothers at Ovingham, young Jim left school at 14 and eventually found work as a plasterer. He joined the plasterers' union and the Australian Labor Party, the local sub-branch of which he chaired at 17. His family's economic hardship during the Depression and his reading of the literature of social inequality made him a socialist, and his sympathy for the Republicans during the Spanish Civil War prompted him to leave the Catholic Church. When he married Alfreda (Elfrieda) Barbara Lamm on 11 October 1941, it was with Congregational forms at Stow [q.v.2] Memorial Church, Adelaide.

Secretary of the Plasterers' Society of South Australia in 1945-62, Cavanagh was to serve as president of the Operative Plasterers' and Plaster Workers' Federation of Australia in 1967-71. He was a militant and forceful workers' advocate in industrial tribunals. As a security precaution the Chifley [q.v.13] government barred him from visiting union members at the Woomera rocket range in the late 1940s. While serving as a commissioner of the South Australian Board of Industry in 1960-62, he won Labor preselection for the Senate. Elected comfortably at the 1961 election, he took his seat on 1 July 1962. His parliamentary speeches most commonly were on pensions, housing, migrants, repatriation and other matters affecting the disadvantaged. From the mid-1960s he also spoke against Australia's involvement in the Vietnam War and served on seven parliamentary committees.

When Labor regained government in December 1972, Cavanagh joined the Whitlam ministry. He was successively minister for works (December 1972-October 1973), Aboriginal affairs (October 1973-June 1975) and police and customs (June-November 1975). The most challenging twenty months of his career were spent in the Aboriginal affairs portfolio. He was chosen because his administrative skills and toughness were needed to sort out managerial and financial difficulties in the department that threatened to provoke an electoral backlash. Some commentators were surprised at his appointment because he had rarely spoken on Aboriginal issues previously, and Aboriginal groups were generally hostile to his appointment, which they interpreted as a sign of the government's timidity.

His most vociferous critics were Charles Perkins, a senior Aboriginal official within Cavanagh's own department, and the National Aboriginal Consultative Committee. Their conflicts with Cavanagh arose mainly from Perkins's wish to comment publicly on the government's Aboriginal policies. In February 1974 the departmental head Barrie Dexter charged Perkins with a breach of discipline under the Public Service Act for criticising the minister. Cavanagh himself fuelled the dispute by attacking Perkins and the NACC in a speech to the National Press Club in Canberra. At this point the prime minister intervened, ordering Cavanagh to drop the disciplinary charge against Perkins.

Despite such controversies, Cavanagh's achievements as minister for Aboriginal affairs were solid. He set in place a series of key policies, including the establishment of Aboriginal Hostels Ltd, the Aboriginal Loans Commission and the Aboriginal Land Fund Commission, and travelled widely to meet Aboriginal communities. At the same time his handling of the portfolio had exposed his limitations. He tended to be stubborn and inflexible, and his narrow assimilationist views on Aborigines were outdated. He had little appreciation of vexed issues such as Aboriginal identity and the psychology of dispossession that were critical to the Aboriginal political movement by the early 1970s. However, when Whitlam put him in charge of police and customs, it was because he wanted a competent, decisive minister to supervise the amalgamation of the Commonwealth, Australian Capital Territory and Northern Territory police forces. This was a goal Cavanagh was unable to achieve because the Whitlam government fell only five months later.

In Opposition again, Cavanagh served (1976-77) on the joint select committee on Aboriginal land rights in the Northern Territory and as parliamentary representative on the council of the Australian Institute of Aboriginal Studies. He remained a prominent spokesman on Aboriginal affairs. Retiring from the Senate on 30 June 1981, he returned to his home at Rosewater. Of medium height, he was thickset with brownish hair and a lined, craggy face. Eight months after the death of his wife, he died on 19 August 1990 at Woodville; he was accorded a state funeral and was buried in Cheltenham cemetery. His daughter and two sons survived him.

P. Read, *Charles Perkins* (2001); I. Howie-Willis, 'Cavanagh, J' in D. Horton (ed), *The Encyclopaedia of Aboriginal Australia*, vol 1 (1994); *National Times*, 4-9 Mar 1974, p 9; *Age* (Melbourne), 18 Mar 1974, p 7; *Advertiser* (Adelaide), 3 Apr 1974, p 5, 22 Aug 1990, p 4; T. Hannan, interview with Cavanagh (ts, 1985, NLA); private information.

IAN HOWIE-WILLIS

CAWTHORNE, CECIL HAMILTON (LESLIE ALLEN PERROT) ('JIM') (1906-1985), soldier, was born Leslie Allen Perrot Cawthorne on 1 April 1906 at Blackburn, Lancashire, England, son of James Radcliffe Cawthorne, master boot and shoemaker and town postman, and his wife Julia Sophia, née Bourne. Raised and educated in England, he went to New Zealand before joining his younger brother in South Australia in 1926.

Later their parents also migrated. During the Depression Leslie carried a swag and travelled the bush. He was a railway employee from 1937. Initially rejected by the army on medical grounds, he used a deceased brother's name, Cecil Hamilton Cawthorne, and enlisted in the Australian Imperial Force on 17 June 1940. Henceforward he was known as 'Jim'.

Joining the newly formed 2/43rd Battalion, Cawthorne was promoted to sergeant on 28 December 1940. Next day he embarked for the Middle East. After training in Palestine, the battalion, part of the 9th Division, deployed to Tobruk, Libya, which was besieged from April 1941. On the night of 27–28 July Cawthorne's patrol, seeking a German prisoner for interrogation, encountered an enemy working party some 1500 yards (1372 m) from the Australian lines. The patrol went to ground and awaited its approach. At 10 yards (9 m), Cawthorne stood up, approached the Germans and called for their surrender. They opened fire and wounded him in two places, then broke and ran after coming under Australian fire. Cawthorne pursued the Germans, killed one, and captured a corporal. Major General (Sir) Leslie Morshead [q.v.15], elated, recorded: 'a particularly good effort by a fighting patrol of the 43rd Battalion'. Cawthorne was awarded the Military Medal. He was in hospital until 19 August, then rejoined his battalion, which continued to serve at Tobruk until evacuated in October.

In July 1942 the 9th Division was in action in Egypt. Cawthorne was a platoon sergeant in the 2/43rd attack on Ruin Ridge on the 17th and ten days later commanded the platoon covering the start line for the 2/28th attack. As an acting warrant officer, class two, from July (substantive in October), he was for many weeks company sergeant major and on 17 August he volunteered to help his company commander search for a man missing from a patrol. For his actions in July-October he was awarded a Bar to his MM, the only such award to an Australian in the Middle East and the first of just five to Australians in World War II. Commissioned as a lieutenant on 22 January 1943 he returned to Australia with his battalion in February. He served on the Huon Peninsula, New Guinea, in 1943-44 and at Labuan and British North Borneo in 1945.

Demobilised on 18 April 1947, Cawthorne worked as a physiotherapist in Adelaide. At St Luke's Church of England on 18 September 1948 he married Alison Mary Peake (d.1960), a civil servant; they had no children and separated after several years. Employed for a time as a manufacturing chemist, by the mid-1960s he had set up as an antique and art dealer at Norwood. He was a small man with a large beard and a sparkle in his eye. A raconteur who elaborated his stories, he was intelligent, well read in esoteric and historical subjects, and interested in herbal medicines. He died on 1 September 1985 at Parkside and was buried in Centennial Park cemetery.

G. Combe et al, *The Second 43rd Australian Infantry Battalion 1940-1946* (1972); B. Maughan, *Tobruk and El Alamein* (1987); B883, item SX5399 (NAA); AWM76, item B93, AWM119, items A18, A62 (AWM); private information.

ANTHONY STAUNTON

CHADWICK, SIR ALBERT EDWARD (1897-1983), sportsman, businessman and sports administrator, was born on 15 November 1897 at Beechworth, Victoria, son of Andrew Chadwick, a London-born chemist, and his second wife Georgina, née Prater, who was born locally. Bert was educated at Tungamah State School. Following the family's move to Melbourne, he gained a scholarship to University High School but, his father having died, he was forced to enter an apprenticeship in electrical engineering to help support his mother and three sisters. On 12 February 1916 he added a year to his age and enlisted in the Australian Imperial Force, as an air mechanic. He served in the Middle East with No.67 Squadron, Royal Flying Corps (No.1 Squadron, Australian Flying Corps). In 1918 he was promoted to sergeant and next year mentioned in despatches and awarded the Meritorious Service Medal.

Discharged from the AIF on 20 March 1919 in Melbourne, Chadwick briefly worked as an electrical draftsman at the Cockatoo Island naval dockyard, Sydney. In 1920 he joined Robert Bryce & Co. Pty Ltd in Melbourne. Although he had played little sport as a child, he had taken up Australian Rules football and cricket while in Egypt. Starting to play in the ruck for the Prahran Victorian Football Association team, he wrote seeking a place with the Melbourne Football Club in the Victorian Football League. In the 1920 season he represented Victoria in an interstate side playing in Sydney, and by 1924 was Melbourne's captain. That year he was runner-up for the Brownlow medal, awarded to the VFL's best and fairest player. From 1925 to 1927 he captained and coached Melbourne in 58 games with a record of 42 wins and the club's first premiership (1926) since 1900. Playing at centre half-back, he was a 'rugged tear through player' with big hands, a great judge of a high mark and a brilliant strategist. In all, he played 142 games with Melbourne. He joined Hawthorn for 1929 as honorary captain and coach, but retained an enduring association with his old club. From 1950 to 1962 he was chairman of the MFC—a period in which they won five premierships.

On 24 January 1924 Chadwick had married Thelma Marea Crawley (d.1979) at St George's

Church of England, Royal Park, Melbourne. He began to develop a career in business management. In 1926 he moved to an engineering position with the Shell Co. of Australia Ltd but soon transferred to the commercial division. In 1935 he was appointed to the new post of controller of sales in the Metropolitan Gas Co. World War II broke out while he was on a study tour in the United States of America. In 1940-45 he served as an administrative officer in the Royal Australian Air Force, rising to acting group captain. Appointed director of recruiting in 1942, he was a vigorous advocate of mental and physical fitness, the 'national importance' of football in maintaining morale, and the urgency of increasing the enlistment of women.

Chadwick returned to the MGC in August 1945. When the government-owned Gas and Fuel Corporation of Victoria was formed in 1951, he was appointed its assistant general manager. Next year he was promoted to associate director and was general manager by 1962. As chairman following his retirement in 1963, he was involved in difficult and prolonged negotiations with the Broken Hill Proprietary Co. Ltd-Esso Australia Ltd partnership over the price consumers would pay for natural gas. He was responsible for the conversion of Melbourne's some four hundred thousand households to gas piped from fields off the Gippsland coast. Also chairman (1963-68) of the Overseas Telecommunications Commission, he oversaw Australia's investment in INTELSAT, a global satellite communications system.

As president of the Melbourne Cricket Club (1965-78), Chadwick approved the building of a new stand for the Melbourne Cricket Ground at a cost of $2.5 million, endorsed proposals to instal lighting for night cricket, and handled fraught negotiations with the VFL to ensure that the MCG was used throughout the football season. His last year as president was marked by deep dissension among members, who were asked to pay $5 to attend finals.

Six feet 1 in. (185 cm) tall and athletic, 'Big Bert' named 'all sports' as his recreations. He had been captain of the Riversdale Golf Club, a trustee and treasurer of the RAAF Women's Educational Fund and chairman of the RAAF Veterans Residence Trust. Appointed CMG in 1967, he was knighted in 1974. Sir Albert died on 27 October 1983 at his home in Toorak, Melbourne, and was cremated. He was survived by his son and daughter. The MCC holds portraits of Chadwick by Paul Fitzgerald and Louis Kahan.

E. C. H. Taylor, *One Hundred Years of Football* (1958); *Age* (Melbourne), 19 July 1958, p 3, 10 Nov 1966, p 3, 23 Aug 1978, p 27; *Herald* (Melbourne), 4 Oct 1966, p 17, 12 Nov 1966, p 12, 29 May 1969, p 7, 23 Mar 1973, p 23, 23 June 1973, p 36; *Sun* (Melbourne), 26 Oct 1968, p 11, 25 Feb 1969, p 33,

13 Feb 1973, p 2; B2455, item Chadwick, Albert and A9300, item Chadwick, Albert (NAA).

CHARLES FAHEY

CHAFFEY, WILLIAM ADOLPHUS (1915-1987), farmer and politician, was born on 18 February 1915 at Tamworth, New South Wales, second of six children of Frank Augustus Chaffey [q.v.7], farmer and politician, and his wife Amy Stella, née McIlveen. Bill attended Tamworth Public School and The King's School, Parramatta, and then gained a diploma of agriculture (1933) from Hawkesbury Agricultural College. After working on various farms, he acquired his own— Ardross, near Tamworth, which he owned for a decade before moving into town. On his father's death in 1940 Chaffey successfully contested, for the United Australia Party, a by-election for Tamworth, the electorate that his father had represented in the Legislative Assembly.

Enlisting in the Australian Imperial Force on 16 December 1941, Chaffey served in Papua and New Guinea in 1942-43 as a non-commissioned officer with the 2/5th Independent Company. In December 1943 he was promoted to lieutenant and in May 1944 seconded to 'Z' Special Unit, which conducted secret operations behind enemy lines. Landing from an American submarine in April 1945, he and a comrade blew up a train in occupied Indochina (Vietnam). Chaffey was in Borneo in July-October. On 8 December he transferred to the Reserve of Officers. He won the American Bronze Star Medal (1948) and was twice (1943 and 1947) mentioned in despatches for his service. In 1948-61 he served in the Citizen Military Forces, rising to major. He had married Patricia Ann Egerton-Warburton, a nurse, on 29 January 1946 at St Werburgh's Church of England, Mount Barker, Western Australia.

In 1941 Chaffey had refused to contest a preselection ballot and was returned as Independent UAP. He was elected, unopposed, as an Independent in 1944 but joined the Country Party the following year. In 1959 he stood against (Sir) Charles Cutler for the party leadership; he lost that ballot but became deputy-leader. As minister for agriculture (1965-68) in the Askin [q.v.] coalition government, Chaffey was responsible for a construction program that doubled the grain storage capacity of the State in five years. He supported the existing policy of production quotas for table margarine, apparently unconcerned that his attempts to protect dairying caused the oilseed industry to suffer and denied consumers a choice of spreads. After threatening to revoke the licence of Marrickville Margarine Pty Ltd if the company exceeded its quota, he was burnt in effigy by workers whose jobs were at risk. R. C. Crebbin [q.v.], chairman of the parent company Marrickville Holdings Ltd, accused Chaffey of waging a 'personal and private feud' against his company.

In 1968 Chaffey was defeated by (Sir) Davis Hughes in a ballot for the deputy-leadership; he also lost his ministerial portfolio. He resigned from the Country Party in 1972— ostensibly in protest against the government's refusal to allow him to move a motion on parliamentary security—and did not contest the 1973 election.

A councillor (1951-65) and vice-president (1966-79) of the Royal Agricultural Society of New South Wales, Chaffey became an honorary vice-president in 1979. He was forthright, occasionally volatile, but also humorous, in expressing his opinions. In 1940 he became a Freemason. Survived by his wife and their two daughters and son, he died on 4 March 1987 at Tamworth and was cremated. He and his father served a combined fifty-nine years and nine months in parliament. The Chaffey Dam on the Peel River is named after them.

R. Milliss, *City on the Peel* (1980); *SMH*, 10 Nov 1966, p 2, 16 Mar 1967, p 2, 1 Mar 1968, p 11, 21 Sept 1972, p 3, 16 June 1973, p 8, 11 Mar 1987, p 8; *Sun* (Sydney), 4 Dec 1968, p 21; *Northern Daily Leader* (Tamworth), 12 Oct 1979, p 4; *Tamworth Times*, 15 Apr 1987, p 6; Chaffey papers (UNE).

TOM CONNORS

CHALMERS, JOHN (1894-1982), surf life-saver and labourer, was born on 11 March 1894 in Wellington, New Zealand, son of Scottish-born John Chalmers, cooper, and his wife Louise, née Seager, who was born on the Isle of Wight. In 1906 Jack moved to Sydney with his family, and in 1908 to Queensland, where he worked as an engine driver. Enlisting on 5 October 1915 in the Australian Imperial Force, he served on the Western Front in 1916-18 with the 47th and 45th battalions. He married Jessie Alice Courtenay on 30 July 1917 at the register office, Wareham, Dorset, England. On 18 October 1919 he was discharged from the AIF in Australia.

Back in Sydney Chalmers joined the North Bondi Life Saving Club, winning (1919-22) the 'President's Pointscore'. In 1921 he won belt races at several beaches around Sydney. On 4 February 1922 a body surfer, Milton Coughlan, was attacked by a shark at Coogee beach. Lifesavers responded immediately. Chalmers tied a line around his waist, plunged into the water and raced to Coughlan, despite being dazed from a fall on the slippery rocks. (Sir) Frank Beaurepaire [q.v.7] joined Chalmers and helped to return the pair to the beach. Coughlan died at Sydney hospital soon after admission. Chalmers considered that as the

belt champion he had a responsibility to act: 'The fact is that I went in first and worried about it after, and am still worrying, for I shall never forget the shocking sight'.

The incident captured public attention. The *Sydney Mail* described the rescue as 'one of the most glorious deeds of gallantry ever recorded in Australia'. King George V awarded Chalmers the Albert Medal, then the highest bravery award for civilians. Chalmers and Beaurepaire received medals from the Royal Shipwreck Relief & Humane Society of New South Wales and the Surf Life Saving Association of New South Wales (Australia). In 1923 these two groups gave Chalmers's brother, Rob, the same honours for a rescue at North Bondi. Coogee and North Bondi Life Saving clubs honoured Chalmers and Beaurepaire with life memberships. Public testimonial funds raised at least £3000 for Chalmers. Proceeds from the *Referee* and *Sunday Times* and the North Bondi Life Saving Club appeals were used to pay off the debt on his home, while those from the citizens' committee appeal were used to pay a deposit on a truck, and to make investments. In 1972 at Buckingham Palace, London, Queen Elizabeth II conferred the George Cross on surviving Albert medallists including Chalmers. He later received the Surf Life Saving Association's twenty-five and fifty-year service awards.

Chalmers worked as an ironworker at the Balmain shipyards and later as a rigger. He died on 29 March 1982 at Bondi Junction, the suburb in which he had lived since 1939, and was cremated. Predeceased by his wife and son, he was survived by his daughter.

SMH, 6 Feb 1922, p 6, 2 May 1922, p 8, 17 Jan 1970, p 4, 8 July 1972, p 9; *Sydney Mail*, 8 Feb 1922, p 10; *Sunday Times* (Sydney), 19 Mar 1922, p 1; *Referee*, 3 May 1922, p 15; *Times* (London), 10 July 1922, p 13; *Daily Mirror* (Sydney), 26 Mar 1973, p 26; *Parade* (Sydney), May 1974, p 50; *Bondi Spectator*, 8 Apr 1982, pp 1, 5; B2455, item Chalmers John (NAA); private information.   DOUGLAS BOOTH

CHAMBERLAIN, FRANCIS EDWARD (1900-1984), Labor Party secretary, was born on 13 May 1900 at East Barnett, London, one of seven children of Frank Chamberlain, a pay sergeant in the Oxfordshire Light Infantry, and his wife Sarah Ann, née Willis. Nicknamed 'Joe' after the British politician, he was brought up at East Barnett in 'a terrible, drab two storey tenement, in [a] drab and gloomy street'. He was close to his mother, who died when he was 16. Educated at local schools, he was apprenticed at 14 to a copperplate printer, and was conscripted in 1918 to serve in the King's Royal Rifle Corps. After his discharge he could not find employment and in 1923 migrated to Western Australia. He took on jobs as a labourer, clearing timber and constructing roads and railways.

On 26 December 1927 Chamberlain married 18-year-old Gladys Lilian Burke at the Congregational Church, Busselton. For nine years they were group settlers on a dairy farm near Busselton before moving to Perth. Chamberlain worked (1936-42) for the Mines Department, first as a labourer and then as a watchman. Joining the Western Australian Government Tramways in 1942 as a conductor and later as a driver, he was secretary (1944-49) of the Western Australian Government Tramways, Motor Omnibus, and River Ferries Employees' Union of Workers, Perth. As union advocate, he became a skilled negotiator in the Court of Arbitration of Western Australia. In 1949 he was elected Australian Labor Party State secretary, a full-time, paid position wielding considerable influence. He soon dominated the party's industrial and political apparatus, serving as an ex-officio member of all State party committees, as secretary of the Trade Unions' Industrial Council, and as a delegate to the federal executive of the ALP and to the Australian Council of Trade Unions.

Chamberlain remained in office for a quarter-century, showing a resistance to change and an unwillingness to compromise that over the years caused many controversies. Among them was his opposition to the establishment of an independent Trades and Labor Council in Western Australia. On political grounds he objected to the increased influence of non-ALP members (especially communists) in the labour movement. He also recognised that moves to form a separate industrial body threatened the chief source of party funds, affiliation fees collected from unions. When in 1963 he could no longer prevent the TLC's formation, he controlled the process of creating the new body and of disbanding the ALP district councils.

In November 1953 Chamberlain had been elected one of two vice-presidents of the ALP federal executive. He strongly supported the parliamentary leader, H. V. Evatt [q.v.14], and regarded a leadership challenge in 1954 by Tom Burke [q.v.13], the member for Perth, as disloyal. At the federal conference in Hobart in March 1955, he moved the resolution to exclude the 'groupers', thereby clashing with other members of the Western Australian delegation who then withdrew from the conference. Afterwards dissidents in Western Australia associated with the 'grouper' faction split with the ALP and formed the Australian Labor Party (Anti-Communist), which became the Democratic Labor Party in 1957. As the ALP entered a period of repeated electoral defeats, Chamberlain reached the zenith of his power, as the party's federal president (1955-61) and federal secretary (1961-63).

Chamberlain's vision was militant in the 'old Labor Left' sense, setting him at odds with Labor conservatives and with communists. Repeatedly he warned party members of the need to maintain the principles on which the ALP was founded. His concept of democratic socialism was centred on the home. The male breadwinner worked 'usefully in the community' and was adequately remunerated while 'his wife [was] divorced from the drudgery of housekeeping [by] the application of modern science', and their children were educated to enable them to take their place as future citizens. Like Evatt, he warned against the 'enemy within'—those DLP sympathisers who remained in the ALP as part of a strategy to 'sow discontent with Labor leadership' and to 'undertake a steady campaign of reconciliation between the Labor Party and the breakaway groups'.

In 1964 Chamberlain attempted to stand against Senator Joseph Cooke, who had opposed him at the federal conference in 1955 but had remained in the ALP. Chamberlain withdrew his name from preselection after complaints that his nomination was contrary to 'a time-honoured practice' of not opposing a sitting member. During the State election campaign next year his continuing hostility to the DLP led to a major row with the ALP leader, Albert Hawke [q.v.], who publicly supported the idea of talks aimed at finding a basis of unity. Afterwards, when Chamberlain said Hawke's statement might have been a factor in the ALP losing the election, Hawke accused him of instigating 'a campaign of disruption and treachery'. The State secretary, however, had considerable support from both unions and ALP branches. Subsequently the federal executive censured Hawke and threatened him with 'more severe action' if he repeated his misdemeanour. Such was Chamberlain's power, even in 1965 when his only role on the federal executive was as a State representative.

While they were at odds over the DLP, Hawke and Chamberlain were united in their opposition to Australian involvement in the Vietnam War. In this they supported the federal leader, Arthur Calwell [q.v.13]. In June 1967 Chamberlain came into conflict with Calwell's successor, Gough Whitlam, and his deputy, Lance Barnard, over party policy in relation to the war. At the Western Australian State conference in July Whitlam and Chamberlain refused to speak to each other, until colleagues prevailed upon them to patch up their differences and to shake hands. Chamberlain took a prominent part in organising and leading anti-war rallies in Perth.

Despite ill health, Chamberlain continued as State secretary until December 1974. On the ALP federal executive for thirty years, he had given the State branch of the party unprecedented access to national politics. This, and the Cold War politics of the era, had brought the previously parochial Western Australian labour movement into the mainstream. However, Chamberlain left a party structure desperately in need of reform. His autocratic leadership and his quarrels with Federal and State parliamentary leaders had caused resentment and discord—he inspired intense loyalty among some Labor colleagues and deep enmity among others. A complex person with high principles, he was regarded as 'absolutely incorruptible'. Colin Jamieson [q.v.] assessed Chamberlain as a 'very genuine guy who liked to sail his ship straight. He didn't suit everybody, nor they him'. Other colleagues accused him of authoritarianism, inflexibility and sectarianism. The extent to which Chamberlain's motives and actions were misinterpreted is indicated by the fact that he was branded as 'extreme Left wing' by right-wing sections of the labour movement—especially those who formed the DLP—while communists regarded him as 'conservative'.

A tallish, fit man, impeccably dressed, usually in a light-coloured suit, 'Joe' Chamberlain liked to play golf, garden, and swim in the ocean in his spare time. Survived by his wife, their daughter and their younger son, he died on 20 October 1984 at Graylands, Perth, and was cremated. His autobiography, *My Life and Times*, was edited by his son Harold and published in 1998.

L. Hunt (ed), *Westralian Portraits* (1979); *SMH*, 16 Dec 1974, p 7; *West Australian*, 23 Oct 1984, p 15; S. Reid, taped interviews with K. Dowding (1991), R. A. Hartley (1988-90), C. Jamieson (1989), SLWA; R. Jamieson, taped interview with L. Elliott (1987), SLWA; P. Pendal, taped interview with A. R. G. Hawke (1971-73), SLWA; ALP (WA), State executive and State executive officers, minutes of meetings, 1949-74, SLWA; ALP (WA) metropolitan district council, correspondence, SLWA.

BOBBIE OLIVER

CHAMBERLAIN, SIR REGINALD RODERIC ST CLAIR (1901-1990), judge, was born on 17 June 1901 at Quorn, South Australia, youngest of ten children of Henry Chamberlain, a farmer of Wirrabara, and his wife Annie Parr, née Payne, both born in South Australia. A gifted student, Roderic won several scholarships at the Collegiate School of St Peter, Adelaide, and in 1918 was awarded the (Lord) Tennyson [q.v.12] medal for English literature. After studying law at the University of Adelaide (LL B, 1922) he was admitted to the Bar on 16 December 1922 and became associate to several judges of the Supreme Court of South Australia.

In 1926 Chamberlain joined the Crown Law Office. Crown prosecutor in 1928-49, he appeared in many criminal cases and developed a restrained style of advocacy, speaking quietly and relying on logic and the effective use of language. His acute appreciation of human nature enabled him to relate to jurors and formulate arguments which he knew would appeal to their common sense. Furthermore, he had no peer as a cross-examiner. This combination of skills made him a tough adversary. Chief Justice J. J. Bray was to recall in 1971 that Chamberlain was 'always courteous and considerate, and the more formidable for being so'. In the Supreme Court he was pitted against the doyens of the criminal defence Bar, including Francis Villeneuve Smith [q.v.11]. When Villeneuve Smith, who displayed flamboyance and theatrical rhetoric in court, was last to address the jury, Chamberlain would take comprehensive notes of his opponent's flowery prose and add to them deprecatory comments which he would have made, had he been given the opportunity to respond. Chamberlain drafted the South Australian Criminal Law Consolidation Act (1935).

Having taken silk in 1947, Chamberlain became assistant crown solicitor in 1948 and crown solicitor in 1952. He often appeared as counsel before the High Court of Australia and on three occasions before the Privy Council, but is most remembered for his role in the Stuart case. He prosecuted at the trial and represented the South Australian government at all later hearings. Rupert Max Stuart, an Aborigine, was found guilty in the Supreme Court in April 1959 of having raped and murdered a 9-year-old girl in December 1958, and was sentenced to death. After appeals to the Full Court, the High Court and the Privy Council had failed, claims of new evidence, which centred on Stuart's movements at relevant times and the authenticity of his alleged confession, cast doubt on his guilt; the Adelaide *News* and its editor Rohan Rivett [q.v.16] launched a campaign to reopen the case. A royal commission, chaired by Sir Mellis Napier [q.v.15], was appointed in 1959 to consider the new evidence. Although the verdict was upheld, during the proceedings Chamberlain announced that the Playford [q.v.] government had decided to commute Stuart's sentence to life imprisonment.

In November 1959 Chamberlain was appointed a Supreme Court judge. Given his ability and experience, his selection came as no surprise. His style on the bench was practical and direct; he was, in his own words, 'more interested in human problems than in the law as an intellectual exercise'. He was an ardent supporter of the jury system and the eligibility of women to serve as jurors. While he was required to preside in all jurisdictions, the criminal court was his preferred choice. His written judgments and directions to juries were lucid and succinct; his ability to persuade jurors remained, even though the judicial role demands a more moderate approach in order that jurors not be overawed by the bench. Although defence counsel often complained that he allowed himself to 'descend into the dust of the arena' when reviewing the evidence in favour of a conviction, it was difficult to demonstrate this by reference only to the words of the summing-up. In one appeal against a murder conviction, an attempt was made to give colour to the words through an affidavit chronicling Chamberlain's mannerisms and the inflection with which some of his words were spoken. The appeal failed.

Chamberlain presided (1963) over the State Electoral Commission, and in 1967-68 arbitrated in the dispute between the New South Wales government and the Snowy Mountains Hydro-electric Authority concerning the amount that the authority should pay in annual licence fees to help maintain the Kosciuszko National Park. He was founding chairman (1970-75) of the South Australian Parole Board. Knighted in 1970, he retired in 1971 and in 1973 revealed that Playford had told him at the time of his judicial appointment that cabinet had intended to name him chief justice after Napier's anticipated retirement. In the event Sir Mellis stayed on until l967, and Donald Dunstan's Labor government appointed Bray instead.

Commenting on the Stuart case after his retirement, Chamberlain told the journalist Stewart Cockburn that 'an attempt was undoubtedly made here to undermine some of our institutions'. Convinced that Stuart was rightly convicted, he expressed his view both in public statements and in his book *The Stuart Affair* (1973). He also spoke out several times in favour of capital punishment in certain circumstances. The case has continued to attract attention. A feature film, *Black and White* (2002), inaccurately portrayed Chamberlain as an urbane and wealthy lawyer whereas, in fact, he lived unostentatiously in a cottage at Glenelg.

Sir Roderic's interests outside the law reflected his love of the English language. He was a long-time vice-president of the State branch of the English Speaking Union and a member of the Modern Pickwick Club. Chairman for some years of the Anti-Cancer Foundation of the University of Adelaide, he was made a life governor of the fund. He was a member of the Adelaide Club and the Commonwealth Club of Adelaide, a golfer, a bridge player and an accomplished pianist. On 15 June 1929 at St Peter's Church of England, Glenelg, he had married Leila Macdonald Haining (d.1985), a clerk. Survived by his daughter, he died on 26 February 1990 at Glenelg and was buried in St Jude's cemetery, Brighton.

K. S. Inglis, *The Stuart Case* (1961, revised edn 2002); *SA State Reports*, 1971, p v; *Law Society Bulletin* (SA), May 1986, p 111; *Advertiser* (Adelaide), 17 June 1971, p 2, 29 Jan 1973, p 3, 27 Feb 1990, p 11; L. Arnold, interview with R. Chamberlain (ts, 1973, SLSA); private information.

KEVIN DUGGAN

CHAMPION, IVAN FRANCIS (1904-1989), patrol officer, naval officer and public servant, was born on 9 March 1904 in Port Moresby, eldest son of New Zealand-born Herbert William Champion [q.v.7], government storekeeper and later government secretary, and his wife Florence Louise May Mary Chester, née Foran. With his two younger brothers and a small band of schoolmates that included Jack Hides [q.v.9], Ivan had a 'larrikin' childhood at the Port Moresby European School (1911-14), before attending Manly Public School, Sydney (1915) and boarding at The Southport School, Queensland (1916-22).

Indifferent scholars, the Champion brothers excelled at sports, with Ivan showing great promise as a swimmer. His headmaster at Southport, James Dixon, instilled in him an enduring fascination with navigation but poor eyesight dashed his ambition, nursed from an early age, to enter the navy. Dissuaded by his father from becoming a patrol officer in impoverished Papua, he started work with the Union Bank in Sydney until a visit by (Sir) Hubert Murray [q.v.10] in 1923 enabled him to make a direct and successful appeal for a position. He was taken on as a cadet-clerk and appointed a patrol officer in May 1924. Aged 20, he was almost 5 ft 8 ins (173 cm) tall, well built and very fit. His calmness, application and modesty would see him establish a reputation as perhaps the most exemplary of Murray's 'outside men'.

Champion's first posting was to the relative quiet of Kerema but in 1925 he was transferred to Kambisi, a new police post run by the assistant resident magistrate Charles Karius. Impressed by Champion's composure under difficult circumstances, Karius chose him as his assistant for the North-West patrol, an ambitious attempt to cross the island of New Guinea at its widest extent. During the first attempt, from December 1926 to July 1927, Champion's keen sense of geography and his willingness to rely on local guides enabled him to identify a passage across the Central Range. This was the route they followed on their second, successful, expedition between September 1927 and January 1928—an exceptional patrol, among previously uncontacted communities, conducted without firing a shot in anger. Emulating earlier patrol officers, Champion published his account of the expedition, *Across New Guinea* (1932), a classic narrative of exploration. On 30 September 1929 at Ela Protestant Church, Port Moresby, he married Elsie May Sutherland Ross.

Between 1928 and 1935 Champion served again at Kambisi and at Ioma, Misima, the Trobriand Islands and Rigo. In April-December 1936 he led the major Bamu-Purari patrol to establish the remote Lake Kutubu patrol post, accompanied by the patrol officer C. T. J. Adamson. Champion was officer-in-charge there from November 1937 to January 1940. Subsequently he was acting resident magistrate at Kikori and then at Misima (1940), Rigo (1941) and Misima again (1941-42).

On 14 February 1942 Champion enlisted in the Militia. Twelve days later he was appointed sub-lieutenant in the Royal Australian Naval Volunteer Reserve, where his navigational skills and knowledge of local waters proved invaluable. As commanding officer of HMAS *Laurabada* (Murray's former vessel), he evacuated the survivors of the Rabaul garrison from Jacquinot Bay in April, a risky mission in Japanese-controlled seas. Promoted to lieutenant in June, he assumed command of HMAS *Paluma*, which surveyed the north-eastern Papuan coastline and landed coastwatchers, including J. K. McCarthy [q.v.15] and B. E. Fairfax-Ross [q.v.]. For much of the remainder of the war, Champion operated as a pilot and hydrographer over a wide area between Manus and the Torres Strait. His RANVR appointment terminated on 18 October 1945.

Champion returned to the newly amalgamated administration for Papua and New Guinea, serving as district officer for Western District (1945) before being appointed assistant-director (1946) and then acting-director (1949) in the Department of District Services and Native Affairs. He took charge of relief operations in the aftermath of the Mount Lamington volcanic eruption in 1951, and was installed that year as an official member of the Territory's Legislative Council. Overlooked for the position in which he had been acting, Champion moved to the Native Land Commission as chief commissioner in July 1952; he became senior commissioner of the new Land Titles Commission in 1963.

Leaving the public service in February 1964, Champion commanded the decommissioned *Laurabada* for private owners, and worked as a contract surveyor along the coasts of Australia and Bangladesh. In retirement he and Elsie lived first in Brisbane and then at Banora Point, New South Wales, before settling in Canberra. Survived by his wife and their daughter, he died on 12 August 1989 at Woden Valley Hospital and was cremated. He was appointed OBE (1953), and awarded two medals for exploration: the Gill memorial medal of the Royal Geographical Society (1938) and the John Lewis gold medal of the South Australian branch of the Royal Geographical Society of Australasia (1953).

J. Sinclair, *Last Frontiers* (1988); *Geog Jnl*, vol 96, no 3, 1940, p 190; Champion papers (Univ Qld Lib).
CHRIS BALLARD

CHANDLER, ARTHUR BERTRAM (1912-1984), science fiction writer and merchant navy officer, was born on 28 March 1912 at Aldershot, Hampshire, England, son of Arthur Robert Chandler (d.1915), soldier, and his wife Ida Florence, née Calver. Bertram attended Peddar's Lane Council School and Sir John Leman School, Beccles, Suffolk. He went to sea (1928-35) with the Sun Shipping Co., advancing from apprentice to third officer, and gaining his second mate's (1932, London) and first mate's (1935, Calcutta) certificates. While serving (1936-55) with the Shaw Savill & Albion Co. Ltd, he progressed from fourth officer to chief officer and obtained a master's certificate (1943, London). During World War II he was a gunnery officer in troop-ships and then chief officer in passenger liners.

On 25 May 1938 Chandler had married Joan Margaret Barnard at the parish church, Beccles, Suffolk. In New York during the war he met John W. Campbell Jr, the editor of *Astounding Science Fiction*, who urged Chandler to contribute to this and other science fiction magazines. Following the breakdown of his marriage he moved to Australia in 1956. Employed (1956-75) by the Union Steam Ship Co. of New Zealand, he started as third officer and advanced to master. After his divorce he married Susan Wilson, a designer, on 23 December 1961 at the registrar general's office, Sydney; they later divorced. Encouraged and bullied by his wife, he returned to writing. He published some forty novels and two hundred short stories, under his own name and the pseudonyms of Andrew Dunstan, S. H. M., Carl Lawrence, and, most frequently, George Whitley. Many of his books were translated into other languages, including Russian and Japanese.

Chandler, Jack to his friends and Bert to his fans, described most of his writings as essentially sea stories. His work was celebrated for the 'lived in' feel of the (space)ships in which his heroes travelled. He acknowledged his major character, John Grimes, to be a mix of C. S. Forester's Horatio Hornblower and a would-be Chandler. Australasia, the edge of the world, was Chandler's model for his Rim Worlds, the edge of the universe where disturbances in space-time allow for near arbitrary fantasy. Grimes's welcome most readily conjures up the Rim Worlds stories: 'This is Liberty Hall; you can spit on the mat and call the cat a bastard!'. Chandler's novel *Kelly Country* (1983), written with the help of a grant from the Literature Board of the Australia Council, was an alternative treatment of Australian independence. His short stories, notably 'Giant Killer' (1945) and 'The Cage' (1957), were considered his highest quality work.

Winning the Ditmar award for best Australian science fiction writer four times (1969, 1971, 1975, 1976), Chandler also won an American award in 1975 and the Seiun Sho award in Japan in 1976. The A. Bertram Chandler award, created in his honour and first presented in 1992, is for 'outstanding achievement in Australian science fiction'. A fellow (1947) of the British Interplanetary Society, he was guest of honour at the World Science Fiction Convention in Chicago in 1982. He died on 6 June 1984 at Darlinghurst, Sydney, and was cremated; the two daughters and son of his first marriage survived him.

N. Watson and P. E. Schellinger (eds), *Twentieth-Century Science-Fiction* (1991); P. Collins (ed), *The MUP Encyclopaedia of Australian Science Fiction & Fantasy* (1998); R. Blackford et al, *Strange Constellations* (1999); *Science Fiction*, vol 6, no 3, 1984, p 70; *Canberra Times*, 20 June 1984, p 22; *Locus*, Aug 1984, p 47; personal knowledge.

ALF VAN DER POORTEN

CHATTERTON, SIR PERCY (1898-1984), missionary and politician, was born on 8 October 1898 at Ashton-upon-Mersey, Chester, England, younger child of Henry Herbert Chatterton, commercial traveller, and his wife Alice, née Macro. He was educated in London at the Stationers' Company's School, (1906-12), and at the City of London School, from which he matriculated in 1916. World War I interrupted his studies for a science degree at University College; called up in June 1917 he served as a stretcher-bearer with the Middlesex Regiment in France. Percy returned to university in 1919 but did not complete his degree. From 1921 to 1924 he was master for science and physical training at the Friends School, Penketh, Lancashire.

Closely associated with the Ferme Park Baptist Chapel as a youth, Chatterton had taught Sunday School and formed a Boy Scout troop before experiencing 'a period of doubt common among those who undergo a scientific training'. Although he could claim no sudden conversion, he recovered his faith and, convinced that Christianity needed a 'stiffening of the backbone', applied to the London Missionary Society in 1923. He was accepted for service as a lay missionary teacher in Port Moresby. On 7 June 1924 at Aberdeen, Scotland, he married, with the forms of the United Free Church of Scotland, Christian Ritchie Finlayson, a teacher of domestic science. A fortnight later they embarked for Papua.

From 1924 to 1939 Chatterton ran the LMS school in the Papuan village of Hanuabada, Port Moresby, and his wife taught the infants. His letters to the *Papuan Courier* revealed his discomfort with racist aspects of the pre-war colonial regime. In 1939 they transferred to Delena, where Chatterton had been appointed district missionary. He was ordained into the Congregational Church in 1943. Returning to Port Moresby in 1957, he ministered at Koki to the migrants from other parts of Papua and New Guinea who were drifting to the town in search of work. In 1962 he played a major part in the transformation of the mission into the country's first wholly self-governing church, the Papua Ekalesia, and began a two-year secondment to the British and Foreign Bible Society to translate the Bible into Motu.

Reaching retirement age at the end of 1963, Chatterton embarked on a new career in 1964 as a member of the House of Assembly for the Central Special electorate. He was re-elected in 1968, defeating a formidable rival, J. K. McCarthy [q.v.15], for the Port Moresby Open electorate. In parliament he demonstrated the same concern for 'the unfortunate and underprivileged' as during his missionary career. Ahead of his time, he devoted his energies to 'lost causes', warning of the danger of 'economic colonialism', urging that certain occupations be reserved for indigenous employees, fighting for adequate low-cost housing, and advocating the appointment of an ombudsman. Many of his proposals were later adopted. He was more immediately successful in moving for the creation of a National Broadcasting Commission (1970) and the adoption of a Human Rights Ordinance (1972). Retiring from parliament in 1972, he was, that year, appointed OBE and awarded an honorary LL D by the University of Papua New Guinea. In 1974 his memoir, *Day That I Have Loved*, and his Motu translation of the Bible were published. He had been (1966-73) a regular columnist for *Pacific Islands Monthly*.

Short and stocky, Chatterton had a remarkably booming voice for his size. His infectious laugh signalled an ever-present sense of humour. Although he could be outspoken, impatient, caustic and controversial, expatriates and Papuans alike respected his wit and his wisdom. He was a passionate advocate for Papua, whose amalgamation with New Guinea he regretted, and a relentless critic of those aspects of Western civilisation that he believed harmful to the Papuan people. Yet he was scathing towards a sentimental attachment to the past. Energetic and alert, he continued to embrace new ideas and experiences but never compromised the personal integrity that had informed his life and work. In 1981 he was appointed KBE. Sir Percy died on 25 November 1984 in Port Moresby; after a state funeral he was buried at Delena. His wife had predeceased him; they had no children.

U.P.N.G. News, Mar 1972, p 3; *PNG Post-Courier*, 9 Aug 1974, p 9; *PIM*, Jan 1985, p 30, Feb 1985, p 23; Candidates' papers, Council for World Mission, second series, box 7 (School of Oriental and African Studies, Univ of London); personal knowledge.

DIANE LANGMORE

CHAUVEL, ELSA (1898-1983), actress and film maker, was born on 10 February 1898 at Collingwood, Melbourne, and registered as Elsie May, second of three children of Edward Wilcox, a tinsmith from New South Wales, and his Queensland-born wife Ada Marie, née Worrall. When Elsie was a child the family went to South Africa, where Wilcox (under the stage name Silveni/Sylvaney) formed a travelling troupe, which included both Elsie (Sylvaney) and her elder brother, whose stage name was Kyrle McAlister. Later, with her brother, she joined other theatrical companies in Cape Town and Johannesburg, and, after a successful tour of Basutoland under Kyrle's management, returned to Australia in 1924.

Elsie was petite and pretty, with dark hair, fair skin and blue eyes. While playing in the musical *Crackers* in Brisbane, she met the film director Charles Edward Chauvel [q.v.7], who cast her as the lead in his second feature film, *Greenhide* (1926). Elsa, as she became known, married Charles on 5 June 1927 at St James's Church of England, Sydney. Next year they sailed for the United States of America, seeking to further Charles's career in Hollywood. Elsa Chauvel returned to the stage at San Francisco and Los Angeles in *Mid-Channel*. On their return to Australia she performed only occasionally, appearing in Brisbane (1929), at Stanthorpe (1930-31), and in Sydney (1939). At Stanthorpe she contributed to their income by giving elocution and dancing lessons. Fourteen months after the birth (1930) of their daughter, they moved to Sydney, where they lived at Vaucluse, then Pymble and finally Castlecrag.

Women's role was to charm men, to love and to serve them, Elsa explained in a 1934 magazine article, and this role she played in her professional and personal partnership with Charles. They made a further seven feature films together, travelling to Pitcairn Island and Tahiti for *In the Wake of the Bounty* (1933) and to inland Australia for *Jedda* (1955). During World War II they produced documentaries and in 1956-57 they travelled through the outback filming a television series, 'Walkabout', for the British Broadcasting Corporation. Charles was the public face of the company, the name on the film credits as director–producer.

At first Elsa's contribution was uncredited. Then she was listed (as Ann Wynn) as production assistant for *Heritage* (1935), in which she played the minor character Mrs Macquarie, and as assistant-director of *Uncivilised* (1936). Named as co-writer with Charles on *Rangle River* (1936), *Forty Thousand Horsemen* (1940), *The Rats of Tobruk* (1944), *Sons of Matthew* (1949) and *Jedda*, she was also associate-producer of *Sons of Matthew* and dialogue director on *Jedda*. Referring to herself as 'Girl Friday', she did whatever was necessary behind the scenes: doubling for Margot Rhys on a camel in *Uncivilised*, coaching other actors, designing costumes, researching, and doing make-up and continuity.

After Charles's death in 1959, Elsa continued to promote Australian film, and collected prints of Chauvel films for preservation in the national film archive. Appointed OBE in 1964, she served as vice-president (1965-76), senior vice-president (1977-78) and patron (1979-82) of the principal committee of the Royal New South Wales Institution (Institute) for Deaf & Blind Children and worked for Dr Barnardo's in Australia. She wrote her memoirs, *My Life with Charles Chauvel* (1973). In 1977 she moved from Sydney to Toowoomba, Queensland, where she died on 22 August 1983 and was cremated. Her daughter survived her.

S. Carlsson, *Charles & Elsa Chauvel* (1989); *Austn Woman's Mirror*, 24 Jan 1933, p 13; *Telegraph* (Brisbane), 19 Apr 1933, p 17; *Woman's Budget*, 25 Apr 1934, p 28; *SMH*, 14 Oct 1939, 'Women's Supp', p 14, 26 Aug 1983, p 9; *Austn Women's Weekly*, 7 Aug 1957, p 7; C. Chauvel papers (SLNSW); Chauvel records (National Film and Sound Archive, Canberra).

PAM CRICHTON

CHEEK, DONALD BROOK (1924-1990), medical scientist and paediatrician, was born on 12 April 1924 in North Adelaide, third child of South Australian-born parents Royden Arthur Cheek, wholesale warehouseman, and his wife Olive May, née Brook. His father was later a well-to-do manufacturer of footwear. As a student at Prince Alfred College Donald developed a passion for science. At home he carried out chemical experiments, on one occasion accidentally spilling sulphuric acid on his bedroom carpet to the consternation of his mother. Keen on astronomy, he made a reflecting telescope. He became interested in biology and physiology, and studied medicine at the University of Adelaide (MB, BS, 1947; MD, 1953).

As a resident medical officer in 1947-50 at Royal Adelaide and Adelaide Children's hospitals, Cheek encountered his first patient with pink disease (acrodynia). This condition, usually occurring in infants aged 5-6 months, was characterised by pink extremities, irritability, profuse sweating, elevated blood pressure, a rapid heart rate, muscle weakness and refusal to eat. Cheek demonstrated for the first time that it was accompanied by excess loss of salt in the urine and observed that it improved when salt was administered. Professor Sir Stanton Hicks [q.v.14], with whom he discussed his work, enthusiastically accepted these findings, and proposed a hypothesis of defective adrenal cortical gland function. With Cheek he wrote a paper, 'Pink Disease or Infantile Acrodynia: Its Nature, Prevention and Cure', for the *Medical Journal of Australia* (1950). Cheek considered the paper premature and suffering from 'hyperbole', but failed to persuade Hicks to modify it. The paper attracted considerable press coverage but was much criticised by the medical community, with some damage to Cheek's local reputation. Later collaborations by Cheek, B. S. Hetzel and D. C. Hine, published in *MJA* (1951), revealed that there was no defect in adrenal cortical function. By this time researchers elsewhere had produced evidence that mercury poisoning was associated with pink disease. The incidence of the disease was to fall rapidly after 1954 when teething powders containing the element were withdrawn from the market.

Awarded a Rotary International medical and scientific fellowship, Cheek travelled to the United States of America in 1951 to work under Dr Daniel Darrow, an authority on water and electrolyte metabolism at Yale University, Connecticut. Cheek developed a successful method, using bromide, of measuring the extra-cellular water in the body. This immediately established his reputation at Yale. On 21 June 1952 at St Andrew's Episcopal Church, Norfolk, Virginia, he married Mary Ellen Whitmore, a nurse; they were to have two daughters. That year he took up a clinical appointment at the Hospital for Sick Children, Toronto, Canada, while continuing to investigate electrolytes at night.

In 1953-56 Cheek was on the staff of the Children's Hospital Research Foundation, University of Cincinnati, Ohio. The university awarded him a D.Sc. (1955) for his work on extra-cellular water and promoted him to associate-professor. In 1957-59 at the University of Texas (Southwestern) Medical School, Dallas, he carried out further studies on pink disease, using an animal model. He demonstrated a rise in blood adrenaline and confirmed that mercury-related damage to the kidney was the reason for the excessive salt loss. Returning to Australia, in 1959-62 he was senior research fellow and consultant at Royal Children's Hospital, Melbourne, where he pursued his work on water and electrolyte metabolism.

Cheek was back in the USA in 1962-73, at Johns Hopkins University's school of medicine, Baltimore, Maryland, as head of a unit studying growth disorders in children. Under his direction a group of clinical and laboratory scientists and mathematicians carried out systematic studies on growth and development. In 1967 the American Academy of Pediatrics awarded him the Borden prize. His book *Human Growth: Body Composition, Cell Growth, Energy and Intelligence* (1968) established his international reputation. During this period he and his family lived on Gibson Island in Chesapeake Bay, and entertained many Australian visitors.

In 1973 Cheek became director of the Royal Children's Hospital Research Foundation, Melbourne, and professor of paediatrics, University of Melbourne. This was not a happy period of his life. A poor administrator, he came into conflict with the foundation's board over expenditure, research priorities and recruitment of senior staff. He published a second book, *Fetal and Postnatal Cellular Growth: Hormones and Nutrition* (1975). Resigning in 1980 because of ill health, he returned to the University of Adelaide as visiting professor in obstetrics and gynaecology and continued his work on foetal development. On 3 April that year, following his divorce from Mary Ellen, he married in a civil ceremony at Crafers Wendy Elaine Langley, née Jones, a divorcee and a restaurant manager.

A special interest in Aboriginal health and nutrition had led Cheek to carry out fieldwork, in collaboration with scientists from the Commonwealth Scientific and Industrial Research Organisation's division of human nutrition, in the Kimberley region of Western Australia during the 1970s. He now pursued the question of zinc deficiency; work at the Yalata community in the western region of South Australia eventually demonstrated that the condition was associated with bowel infection. He retired from the university in 1988.

Cheek was short, quick-witted, warmhearted and lively, but he could be impulsive. He was a keen painter who had one-man exhibitions in Australia and the USA; the outback was his favoured subject. Many of his paintings were donated to the Children's Nutrition Research Center, Houston, Texas. Survived by his wife and the daughters of his first marriage, he died of cancer on 6 March 1990 in Adelaide and was cremated. His unpublished autobiography, 'Writing the Music' (1989), is held by the University of Adelaide library.

MJA, 4 Feb 1991, p 202; *Advertiser* (Adelaide), 7 Mar 1990, p 16; Cheek papers (Univ of Adelaide Lib); personal knowledge.　　BASIL S. HETZEL

CHERRY, WALTER JOHN (1932-1986), theatre director and professor of drama, was born on 10 May 1932 at Ballarat, Victoria, son of Victorian-born parents Walter Joseph Cherry, commercial artist, and his wife Vera Gladys, née White. Educated at St Patrick's College, Ballarat, and Geelong High School, in 1951 Wal entered the University of Melbourne (BA, 1954) and was soon active in student theatre. On 4 January 1956 at St John's Church of England, Geelong West, he married Marcelle Lynette (Peg) Mathieson, a schoolteacher. That year he was appointed manager of the Union Theatre at the university.

In 1956 Cherry became director of the Union Theatre Repertory Company. His productions were energetic, meticulous and stimulating, introducing audiences to Bertolt Brecht and contemporary British and American playwrights. He also began advocating a 'national drama', although he was critical of aggressively nationalist, under-prepared or poorly conceived work. In 1958 he returned from a study tour of Europe with renewed determination (as his successor, John Sumner, recalled) 'to raise the standard of his work and stretch the imagination of his audience'. For UTRC's next season he lengthened the runs of a challenging selection of plays—an initiative that failed to achieve commercial success. He resigned in 1959, becoming a freelance director and establishing his own Theatre Workshop and Actors' Studio.

After a series of ventures to develop an ensemble company, in 1962 Cherry and the actor, director and teacher George Whaley established the Emerald Hill Theatre Company. In the 1960s this company became Australia's most celebrated quasi-alternative theatre of ideas and style, recognised for its intimacy of space and actorly discipline, its left-progressive politics, its commitment to touring and reaching young people, and its exploration of connections with folk music, vaudeville, dance and film. It provided impetus for a 'new wave' of Australian plays, playwrights and performance that surged in Sydney and Melbourne from the late 1960s. Yet EHTC was unable to pay its way and the company closed in 1966.

In 1967 Cherry was appointed foundation professor of drama at Flinders University, South Australia. He began building a department based on his company-workshop model, integrating the teaching of theatre, film, radio and television under a broad concept of drama as 'a complex changing communal activity'. He was soon immersed in teaching and other university duties as chairman of the school of language and literature (later school of humanities) in 1968-70 and of the theatre management committee in 1968-78, and as dean of University Hall in 1970-74. His aspiration to link the drama program with a major theatre company escaped him: overtures to the South Australian Theatre Company were not reciprocated, although his work for New Opera,

State Opera of South Australia and the Festival Centre Trust—combining professionals, departmental staff and students—was of the highest standard. He formed the Australian Stage Company, an occasional ensemble including several now-famous performers.

Impatient with those 'owing their eminence to the flatness of the surrounding countryside', Cherry was a provocative figure for audiences, practitioners and students, and was often kept at arm's length by the professional mainstream for his visionary approach and personal style. Visits to the Berliner Ensemble and Schiller-Theater (Germany), the Theatre Royal Stratford East (Britain) and the Habima ensemble (Israel) inspired him to incorporate new ideas into his own innovative and eclectic work. He experimented with epic-presentational, naturalistic, expressionistic and absurd drama, masking and mumming traditions, theatre forms from 1930s Germany and contemporary America, and aspects of Australian vernacular style.

During his career Cherry directed at least eighty-six plays, revues, operas and music theatre pieces, wrote a novel and two plays, collaborated on film scripts, published incisive articles, delivered papers in Australia and the United States of America and served on over thirty university and industry committees. He won the 1958 and 1961 'Erik' awards in Melbourne and the 1959 Western Australian General Motors Holden [q.v.9] award for best production, and travelled to the USA on Fulbright fellowships (1972, 1976) and to Japan on a fellowship from the Cultural and Social Centre for the Asia-Pacific Region (1973).

In 1980 Cherry was appointed professor of theatre at Temple University, Philadelphia, and spoke of entering 'the most creative period' of his life. In 1985 he also became associate-director of the Boston Shakespeare Company. He enjoyed these new challenges too briefly. On 7 March 1986 he died of ischaemic heart disease at Boston and was cremated. He was survived by his wife and their two daughters, Kate and Anna, both of whom pursued careers in the theatre. The Wal Cherry play of the year award is sponsored by the Victorian Arts Centre.

G. Worby, 'Emerald Hill and the Ensemble Ideal', in P. Holloway (ed), *Contemporary Australian Drama* (1987); L. Radic, *The State of Play* (1991); J. Sumner, *Recollections at Play* (1993); G. Milne, *Theatre Australia (Un)Limited* (2004); private knowledge.
GUS WORBY

CHESHIRE, FRANK WALTER (1896-1987), bookseller and publisher, was born on 6 June 1896 in East Melbourne, second son of Victorian-born parents Thomas James Cheshire, journalist, and his wife Eliza, formerly Napper, née Holland. Educated at Blackburn, Balwyn and Glenferrie state schools, at 15 Frank was employed by George Robertson [q.v.6] & Co., booksellers, commencing with menial duties —dusting, unpacking, shelving—but quickly learning the rudiments of the trade. He also became active in the local Baptist church following the family's move to Canterbury about 1910. His Christian principles, developed as a lay preacher and member of the Christian Endeavour movement, at first prevented him from volunteering for active service in World War I. Between 1916 and 1918 he worked in firms supplying schools with stationery and materials. By 1918 the death of his brother in action in France and the war service of many friends prompted a reconsideration of his pacifism. Rejected for the Australian Imperial Force on medical grounds, he served briefly with the Young Men's Christian Association at the Point Cook base of the Australian Flying Corps.

Cheshire then returned to distributing educational supplies for Hutchinson's Pty Ltd, travelling extensively, selling directly to schools, newsagencies and bookshops, and building networks that would assist his own business venture. On 20 November 1920 at Canterbury Baptist Church he married Vera Mabel Worth; they had met as Sunday school teachers. In 1925 Hutchinson's was taken over and Cheshire negotiated the acquisition of its educational stock and equipment. On borrowed capital, F. W. Cheshire Pty Ltd, educational booksellers and stationers, opened for business on 1 April 1925 in a small office in Little Collins Street, with Frank and Vera at first the only employees. Schoolbooks remained its core business, particularly once Cheshire decided to publish his own editions of Shakespeare rather than import up to a thousand copies of set plays each year from England. He also took over the printing and distribution of arithmetic and mathematics texts compiled by a schoolteacher, Robert Wilson. According to Cheshire, Wilson's *Intermediate Certificate Arithmetic* (1933) 'formed the very foundations of the Cheshire Publishing enterprise'; the text sold in thousands and, by 1958, in twenty-two reprints.

Cheshire opened his first retail bookshop in 1932 and soon added a short-lived second-hand section. He promoted the bookshop by advertising on the back of tram tickets. The business moved to larger premises in 1938: a basement, at 338 Little Collins Street, which became 'a cultural landmark' (the *Age* recalled in 1975) and a 'gathering place for all interested in books and literature'. The company's first trade publication was Wilfred Burchett's [q.v.] *Pacific Treasure Island* (1941). Cheshire also published Burchett's *Bombs over Burma* (1944) and *Democracy with a Tommygun* (1946), although with increasing discomfort

at the author's left-wing sympathies. Another author, Alan Marshall [q.v.] offered him the manuscript of what was to become *These Are My People* (1944). 'Drawn to him immediately', Cheshire agreed to publication, sealing the deal with a handshake before reading the text. It was the start of a profitable relationship: the book sold nine thousand copies in its first month and by 1957 had gone into five editions. Cheshire published several other books by Marshall, including *I Can Jump Puddles* (1955).

In the transition from educational bookseller to major trade publisher, Cheshire was greatly assisted by Andrew Fabinyi [q.v.14], who had joined the company in 1939. As general manager of F. W. Cheshire Publishing Pty Ltd (formed in 1957), Fabinyi left a lasting mark on the Australian book trade, making Cheshire's notable for classics such as Robin Boyd's [q.v.13] *The Australian Ugliness* (1960). Through the 1950s, the original company also continued to expand, acquiring new premises in Little Bourke Street and a repository and trade counter in La Trobe Street. It opened a retail bookshop in Canberra and, by 1963, a trade room and office in Sydney. With efficient service and an established reputation, Cheshire's monopolised the school educational market. Its new Melbourne warehouse at Abbotsford was soon dispatching some 250 000 school texts each year.

Vera Cheshire died in 1955 after a long illness; on 18 August 1956 at St Paul's Church of England, Caulfield, Cheshire married Shirley Jean Moyes, née Mackay, a receptionist whose late husband had been a fellow Freemason and family friend. Jean's long interest in the Church of England's Girls' Friendly Society (world president, 1969) complemented Cheshire's commitment to the Burwood Boys' Home: he had joined its committee of management in 1946 and served as its president (1955-69). He was also an active member of the Victorian Booksellers' Association (president 1953-63) and the Australian Booksellers' Association (president 1959-60). As president of the VBA, in 1957 Cheshire supported the close scrutiny by the Literary Censorship Board of 'questionable' books, although in 1960 he protested at the police seizure of novels already cleared by the board.

In November 1964 Cheshire sold both companies (then with 130 full-time staff and 250 titles on the list) to a partnership of British and Australian interests, remaining as general manager until his retirement in 1967. Following yet another takeover, by the International Publishing Corporation, the name Cheshire began gradually to disappear from the Australian book trade.

Described by John Hetherington [q.v.14] as 'a quietly imaginative man', Cheshire was by nature conservative. He was a non-smoker, a teetotaller and a devoted father. His achievements were reflected in the title of his memoir, *Bookseller Publisher Friend* (1984). As Alan Marshall remarked, 'you'd search the world for a man to equal Frank Cheshire for honorable dealings'. In 1983 he and his wife were appointed knight and dame of the Order of St John. Survived by his wife, their three sons, and the two sons of his first marriage, Frank Cheshire died on 19 November 1987 at Balwyn and was cremated.

Herald (Melbourne), 30 Sept 1957, p 12, 22 July 1960, p 7, 28 Nov 1964, p 6; *Age* (Melbourne), 23 Feb 1963, p 18, 26 Nov 1964, p 3, 5 Apr 1975, p 23; *Sun News-Pictorial* (Melbourne), 11 Oct 1969, p 17; C. E. Sayers papers (SLV).   JOHN ARNOLD

CHIN, HOI MEEN (1917?-1982), photographer and businessman, was born probably on 28 January 1917 in Rabaul, Australian-occupied German New Guinea, son of Ah Chee, hotelkeeper, and his wife Kulasa. He attended a Methodist mission school before working for an Australian firm as delivery-boy, native overseer and truck driver, and then for the Department of Agriculture as a weather observer and clerk. In the evenings he collected tickets at the local cinema and practised photography. On 11 May 1935 at the Methodist Church, Rabaul, he married Wan Sit-Ying (Wan June Lan).

Early in 1941 Chin and other Chinese residents, determined to help defend Rabaul in the event of attack, had formed the Auxiliary Red Cross Ambulance Detachment. After the Japanese occupation in January 1942, they moved to Sum Sum plantation at Adler Bay on the south coast of New Britain and Chin began secretly collecting information for the Allied Intelligence Bureau. In 1943-44 he provided oral intelligence and drew maps of Japanese troop disposition and supply dumps in the Rabaul area for the AIB officers Major Charles Bates and Major Basil Fairfax-Ross [q.v.]. He also hid and guided to safety crashed American airmen. In 1946 Chin was awarded the King's Medal for courage in the cause of freedom, the citation stating: 'His work for the A.I.B. was voluntary and always at the risk of his own life'. In 1954 he was presented to Queen Elizabeth II in recognition of his heroism.

After the war Chin had resumed work with the Department of Agriculture. Later he established himself as a merchant and milk-bar proprietor and began a photography business. He served as the unofficial Administration photographer in Rabaul, acted as interpreter for Chinese residents (particularly in war damage compensation cases), helped to reorganise the ruined town and wrote again for the *Pacific Islands Monthly* magazine as he had before the war. A respected and trusted leader in the Chinese community, a councillor for the Rabaul Methodist Church, a promoter of sporting clubs as a means of breaking down social barriers, and a generous and usually anonymous donor to fund-raising activities, he served on the town advisory council.

Chin was one of the first New Guinea Chinese to be granted (1958) Australian citizenship. In 1964 he expanded his activities to Port Moresby with a prosperous business in photographic and electrical goods. He consolidated his interests in two companies: Territory Film Processing Pty Ltd (1966) and Chin Hoi Meen & Sons Pty Ltd (1967). Chin retained links with Rabaul and was proud that a street in Rabaul was named Ah Chee Avenue in honour of his father, who had been decorated by the Chinese and German governments. A gracious and humble man, Chin Hoi Meen was forced through ill health to retire in 1977 and settle in Brisbane. He died there of cerebral glioma on 31 March 1982 and was buried in Mount Gravatt cemetery. His wife and their two sons and three daughters survived him.

M. Wright, *If I Die* (1965); *South Pacific Post* (Port Moresby), 18 Sept 1967, p 7, 10 Nov 1967, p 7; *Times of PNG* (Port Moresby), 23 Apr 1982, p 27; P. H. Cahill, The Chinese in Rabaul 1914-1920 (MA thesis, UPNG, 1972) and for bib; AWM88, item O/C7 CIVIC (AWM); A1803, items EM(2)14251, EM(2) 14256, EM(2)14500 (NAA).   PETER CAHILL

CHINN, GEORGE ERNEST (1927-1981), army officer, was born on 28 October 1927 at Brunswick, Melbourne, eldest of three children of Australian-born parents Ernest Charles Chinn, fibrous plasterer, and his wife Marjorie Mary, née Marshall. On leaving St Brigid's School, North Fitzroy, George began his training as a cabinet-maker. In 1942 he overstated his age and joined the Volunteer Defence Corps. Discharged a year later when his real age was discovered, he became a member of the Air Training Corps while working as a cycle salesman.

On 4 April 1946 Chinn enlisted in the Australian Imperial Force. Serving in Australia, he rose to lance sergeant. He transferred to the Interim Army in July 1947 and joined the Australian Regular Army as a temporary sergeant in May 1948. Allotted to the 2nd Battalion, Royal Australian Regiment, in February 1950, he was promoted to temporary warrant officer, class two, in September (substantive in April 1956). In July 1951 he was posted to the 3rd Battalion, RAR, in Korea. The commanding officer of the battalion, Lieutenant Colonel (Sir) Francis Hassett, made him regimental sergeant major. He acted in this position for four months and was involved in the battle of Maryang San in October. Hassett later described him as 'one of a handful of the very best soldiers I have ever met'. Back in Australia in January 1952, Chinn married with Catholic rites Jean Margaret Malham, a telephonist, on 17 April that year at the Church of Our Lady of Lourdes, Devonport, Tasmania.

In 1952-60 Chinn was an infantry instructor at the Royal Military College, Duntroon, Canberra. Cadets of those times recall his influence and his inimitable style—regimental with a touch of humour. Appointed company sergeant major of the 1st Special Air Service Company, he was promoted to temporary warrant officer, class one, in October 1960 (substantive in April 1963). In March 1964 he arrived in Saigon and became a member of the Australian Army Training Team Vietnam. Three weeks later he was an observer on an operation which involved an air-mobile assault by two South Vietnamese ranger battalions. The force was opposed by the People's Liberation Armed Forces (Viet Cong) and Chinn changed from observer, taking command of a group to clear out the enemy. For his part in this operation he was awarded the Distinguished Conduct Medal. The Republic of Vietnam (South Vietnam) awarded him its Cross of Gallantry and Armed Forces Honour Medal.

Returning to Australia in March 1965, Chinn became RSM of the 6th Battalion, RAR, in June. He served a second year in Vietnam in 1966-67, taking a major part in the battle of Long Tan in August 1966. The commanding officer, Lieutenant Colonel C. M. Townsend, wrote: '6RAR owes a lot to RSM Chinn'. His presence, experience and inculcation of standards 'created a great esprit de corps'. The troops described him as a '3F man'—firm, fair and friendly.

In 1967 Chinn was posted to the Infantry Centre, Ingleburn, New South Wales, as an instructor. He was RSM of the Australian contingent that went to Paris in November 1968 for the fiftieth anniversary of the end of World War I. Commissioned lieutenant on 18 July 1969, he held various appointments at Army Headquarters, Canberra, and served in Singapore in 1972-74. He was promoted to captain in July 1973 and to major in July 1979. While commanding the army recruiting unit in Perth in 1981 he developed cancer. Survived by his wife and their three daughters, he died on 24 September that year in his home at Greenwood, Perth, and was buried with full military honours in Gungahlin cemetery, Canberra. His portrait by Wendy Kadell is held by the Long Tan Sergeants' Mess, Enoggera, Brisbane. The 6RAR museum, also at Enoggera, was named after him.

I. M. Williams, *Vietnam* (1967); I. McNeill, *The Team* (1984) and *To Long Tan* (1993); T. Burstall, *The Soldiers' Story* (1986); J. Rowe, *Vietnam, the Aus-* *tralian Experience* (1987); I. McNeill and A. Ekins, *On the Offensive* (2003); private information.

J. J. SHELTON

CHISHOLM, ALAN ROWLAND (1888-1981), professor of French, critic and commentator, was born on 6 November 1888 at Bathurst, New South Wales, fifth child of native-born parents William Samuel Chisholm, coach-painter, and his wife Eliza, née Heagren. Alan was to publish two volumes of memoirs: *Men Were My Milestones* (1958) and *The Familiar Presence* (1966). He recalled his childhood at Minore and Dubbo as 'a kingdom of dreams'. His earliest education was acquired at home and from 'Old Mr Ross', an erudite bush character. The family moved to Sydney and at Milsons Point and North Sydney Superior Public schools he showed a precocious joy in learning. He studied French and Latin at Fort Street Model School from 1905.

The University of Sydney (BA, 1911) was Chisholm's 'spiritual sanctuary'. He continued Latin and French, the latter under the exacting G. G. Nicholson, befriended Randolph Hughes [qq.v.11,14]—'the most memorable of all my milestones'—and graduated with first-class honours. Chisholm then taught at Fort Street and at Glen Innes. A scholarship enabled him to travel in 1912 to Berlin, where, at the Institut Tilly [q.v.12], he quickly mastered German. Moving to France in 1913, he attended the lectures of Gustave Lanson in Paris. That year he was awarded the German and French diplomas of the International Phonetic Association. He returned to Sydney in 1914 and joined the staff of the Teachers' College.

On 24 September 1915 at St Andrew's Scots Church, Rose Bay, Chisholm married with Presbyterian forms Laurel May Genge, a teacher; they were to have a son before being divorced in September 1923. The need to fight against Germany in World War I caused Chisholm acute anguish. Enlisting in the Australian Imperial Force on 22 December 1915, he served on the Western Front in 1917-18 at forward posts intercepting enemy communications. A diary and letters home told of staunch mateship in 'this land of lurking death', but also of private moments when he devoured French, German and Italian literary classics. He was demobilised as a lieutenant on 25 October 1919 in Sydney. Back at the college, he founded the *Modern Language Review of New South Wales* (1920-21).

The full impact on Chisholm of his friendship with Christopher Brennan [q.v.7]—a 'magic spell never since forgotten'—had come in 1919, when Chisholm, alerted to the links between German romanticism and French symbolism, began his lifelong devotion to the poetry of Stéphane Mallarmé. He was appointed lecturer-in-charge of French at the University of Melbourne in 1921 and senior lecturer in 1923. Nazar Karagheusian accepted his invitation to fill the role of native speaker; their happy collaboration was renowned. Chisholm married Lillian Norah Mulholland (d.1968) on 1 November 1923 at the Cairns [q.v.3] Memorial Church, East Melbourne; they had a daughter.

Chisholm's French course was bold and innovative. Almost from the start he promoted philological, medieval and Renaissance studies, as well as classical and nineteenth-century French literature, and pioneered the teaching of modern and contemporary authors. The historical bias was redressed by various 'special studies' that were critical, aesthetic and philosophical. His lectures attested to his idealism and his belief, as an educator, in the contact of minds. He encouraged co-operation between departments. On three occasions (1924, 1931 and 1937) he taught honours German courses during Augustin Lodewyckx's [q.v.10] sabbaticals.

After reading Schopenhauer, Nietzsche, Jules de Gaultier and Fritz Strich, Chisholm wrote his remarkable study *Towards Hérodiade* (1934), which situated Mallarmé in the broad sweep of nineteenth-century ideas and sensibility. Chisholm, always optimistic and objective, consciously rejected the Romantic subjectivism and Schopenhauerian pessimism that his study so beguilingly described. Promoted to associate-professor in 1930, he occupied the full chair from 1938.

His flirtation with the ideas of Charles Maurras, whom he met during a sabbatical in France in 1936, was redeemed during World War II by his fervent espousal of the Free French and *Italia Libera* causes, and by his numerous articles in the *Argus* newspaper aimed at restoring faith in fallen France. From 1943 onwards his nights were reserved for serious study as, unknown to students and most colleagues, Lillian's emotional health made their days a torment. Yet this was the time of Chisholm's spellbinding lectures on Baudelaire, Mallarmé and Valéry and of the increasing recognition in Europe of a 'Melbourne School' of scrupulous Mallarméan exegesis.

Chisholm was very short, tanned and dapper. His Australianness was free of both truculence and colonial cringe. After retiring in 1957, he revisited Europe, edited work by John Shaw Neilson [q.v.10] and Brennan, produced *A Study of Christopher Brennan's The Forest of Night* (1970), wrote volumes and articles on French poetry, reviewed regularly for the *Age*, and wrote poetry. In 1951 he had been appointed to the French Légion d'honneur; in 1961 he was appointed OBE. He died on 9 September 1981 at Armadale, Melbourne, and was buried in Springvale cemetery. The University of Melbourne holds his portrait by Clifton Pugh [q.v.].

Age (Melbourne), 25 July 1970, p 17, 7 Nov 1978, p 15; Chisholm papers (NLA and Univ of Melbourne Archives); personal knowledge. STAN SCOTT

CHRISTIE, CONSTANCE MARY CHARLOTTE (1908-1989), writer and illustrator of children's books, designer and photographer, was born on 31 January 1908 at Kidderminster, Worcestershire, only child of Thomas Robertson Christie, a Scottish-born jeweller and painter in oils, and his English wife Lizzie, formerly Wade, née Williams. From ages 6 to 15 Connie attended Our Lady and All Saints convent school, Stourbridge. At night she took classes at the town's art school and gained honours for every subject in the South Kensington examinations. She and her parents migrated to Australia, arriving in Melbourne in October 1923.

Studying at night at the Commercial Art School in Little Collins Street, Christie designed advertisements and cinema slides for Val Morgan [q.v.Supp.] Pty Ltd before joining G. J. Coles [q.v.13] & Co. Pty Ltd. She worked for eighteen years in the company's Swanston Street and Bourke Street stores as a ticket-writer and designer, and was known as the 'Coles Orchid'. Her designs included the company crest, the Embassy brand's emblem, Smart Girl cosmetics, toys, crockery, household gadgets and stationery. On 23 March 1931 at St Matthew's Church of England, Prahran, she married Winslow Richard Paul, an accountant; they were childless and were divorced in 1938.

In World War II Christie was invited to write and illustrate books for children. Her first, *The Adventures of Pinkishell* (1939), was the story of a mermaid, a character she invented. The book was an immediate success. She was to publish some fifty volumes, comprising stories, nursery rhymes, counting and alphabet-trainers, rag and painting books, and annuals. As Robert Holden has noted, her 'gentle, simple fantasy illustrations' used 'strong colours and definite outlines', avoiding 'over-decorative or unnecessary detail'. Her vibrant and lively artwork encapsulated the effervescence of childhood imagination. The *Bulletin* claimed in 1950 that two million copies of her works had been sold, but the lifting of import restrictions ended her career in the middle of the decade.

On 28 April 1945 at Scots Church, Melbourne, Christie had married with Presbyterian forms Maxwell Pemberton (d.1988), a manufacturer. Renting premises at Balwyn, near the family home, she set up a photographic studio with facilities for retouching, developing and hand-colouring, and with space for her to conduct classes in portraiture. A member of the Royal Photographic Society, she gave talks on retouching. In the 1960s she worked for Crawford Productions Pty Ltd as a photographer and appeared in television programs such as 'Consider Your Verdict'. Subsequently, she illustrated Murfett and Norcross greeting cards with paintings of Australian flora and fauna.

Christie's watercolours and later oils revealed her versatility. Her creations included portraits, landscapes, striking depictions of animals, ballet dancers in arresting poses, and naturalistic sketches of birds and children. She explained the challenge of illustration: 'unlike landscape artists and portrait painters, who are working from something they are looking at, we are illustrating something that doesn't even exist'. Although not a regular church-goer, Mrs Pemberton held Christian beliefs and was kind and tolerant. She made and embroidered clothes, and enjoyed the theatre, ballet, amateur dramatics, ballroom dancing and entertaining. Survived by the son of her second marriage, she died on 3 June 1989 at Brighton and was cremated.

R. Holden, *The Golden Age of Australian Fantasy* (1985); S. Lees and P. Macintyre, *The Oxford Companion to Australian Children's Literature* (1993); *Austn Women's Weekly*, 18 Feb 1950, p 26; *Bulletin*, 3 May 1950, p 18; biog notes on Connie Christie (ts, 1978?, copy on ADB file); private information.

PAM MACINTYRE

CHURCHILL, CLIVE BERNARD (1927-1985), footballer, was born on 21 January 1927 at Merewether, Newcastle, New South Wales, second son and fourth child of Herbert Hilton Churchill, clerk, and his wife Vera, née Fergusson, both native born. He was educated at St Joseph's Convent, Merewether, and at the Marist Brothers' High School, Hamilton. At primary school he learnt the rudiments of boxing from Fr Joseph Coady, an early mentor and patron of Les Darcy [q.v.8], the hero of the Hunter Valley. In his autobiography, *They Called Me the Little Master: Clive Churchill's Colourful Story* (1962), Churchill wrote that he thought he had a vocation to be a Marist Brother but, having failed the Leaving certificate, he became a tyre moulder.

As a schoolboy Churchill had excelled at Rugby League. Playing without boots, he kicked with either foot, though mainly the left, and developed a quicksilver elusiveness at five-eighth, occasionally at full-back. Known as 'Tigger', he played for Central Newcastle in 1945. Dark and dapper, he weighed 10 st. 7 lbs (67 kg), and was 5 ft 8 ins (173 cm) tall. Con-

centrating on full-back, in 1947 he played for Country Seconds against City, and so impressed the South Sydney Club that their patron, Dave Spring, signed him up for £12 10s. per match.

South Sydney, 'pride of the League', had won the first premiership in 1908 and by 1947 had won ten more, the last in 1932. It was embedded in a red-blooded working-class district, based on Redfern, with passionate and widespread supporters. Churchill moved to Mascot, on the southern fringe of the club's area. He fitted perfectly into the distinctive ethos of the club, and into the traditional free-flowing style of its team; he soon shone at full-back.

He was selected for the 1948-49 Kangaroos' tour of Britain, followed by a tour of France. This experience consolidated his exceptional talents. Despite his diminutive size Churchill honed a lethal tackling technique; based on exact timing and leverage, it enabled him to fell the beefiest of stampeding forwards, and could be adapted to smother skilful backs. In attack, instinctively reading the play, he transformed full-back tactics by limiting return kicks and running the ball to fuse with the three-quarter line; in these movements, his mercurial side-stepping, swerving and changing of pace were spiced with gibes and gestures at his opponents in the style later made famous by the boxer Muhammad Ali. When Churchill failed, he was buried under a swarm of tacklers, to emerge bloodied but defiant. The English regarded him as bad tempered and spiteful; to the Australians he was 'the little master', a will-o'-the-wisp with a sting.

In June 1950, aged 23, Churchill led Australia to its first 'Ashes' win against Britain since 1920. In September he played, under Jack Rayner's captaincy, when South Sydney regained the premiership. With J. P. Glasheen [q.v.14] as its president until 1954, Souths also won the Sydney competition in 1951, 1953, 1954 and 1955; its success was built on outstanding teamwork that noticeably incorporated Churchill's extraordinary ability and courage. On 13 August 1955 he broke a wrist at Redfern Oval, but played on, with a make-shift splint, to kick a goal after the final bell to win a game against Manly. Rejecting an offer from Wollongong, he had renewed his contract with Souths in 1953. On 19 June 1950 he had married Shirley Grace Berriman, a dressmaker, at St Francis's Catholic Church, Paddington. He needed to supplement his income, and in the 1950s he was variously a storeman, sports-store salesman, garage proprietor and taxi driver.

In July 1954 Churchill led Australia to another 'Ashes' win. After thirteen Tests against Britain, he was replaced as captain in 1956 by Ken Kearney for the ninth Kangaroo tour—his third; he was dropped after Australia lost the first Test. Playing against Britain,

France and New Zealand in Tests and World Cup matches, he represented Australia thirty-seven times. Throughout his tours, he had not only dominated on the field; he had also enlivened his team-mates with his mimicking, singing and telling of tall tales. Now the embers flickered. Divorced in June 1958, on 31 January 1959, as an insurance inspector, he married Joyce Ivy Martin in the registrar general's office, Sydney. He had turned to coaching, first with Souths as captain-coach in 1958. He coached and played with the Queensland team in a win over New South Wales in 1959, when he also trained the Australian team against New Zealand and France. In 1960-61 he was player-coach at Moree and in 1963-64 he prepared Canterbury. His career reignited; all the strands of his Rugby League primacy blended and triumphed nostalgically when he coached South Sydney to the premiership in 1967, 1968, 1970 and 1971. As Souths lost star players and games in 1972-74, Churchill was criticised and, amid recriminations, he resigned in 1975.

In January 1982 he was seriously injured when his liquor shop at Randwick was robbed; his assailants were ordered to pay him $5000 each. In December 1984 he was hospitalised with cancer. Next May a packed testimonial dinner raised about $50 000 for him and in June he was appointed AM. Survived by his wife and their son, he died on 9 August 1985 at Royal Prince Alfred Hospital, Camperdown. He was cremated after a requiem Mass at St Mary's Cathedral. The Clive Churchill Stand at the Sydney Cricket Ground is named after him, and the Clive Churchill medal is awarded to the best player in the grand final of the National Rugby League competition.

F. Hyde, *Straight between the Posts* (1995); G. Moorhouse, *A People's Game* (1995); I. Heads et al, *South Sydney* (2000); *SMH*, 20 Apr 1985, p 75, 1 June 1985, p 72, 10 Aug 1985, p 74, 11 Aug 1985, p 22.   BEDE NAIRN*

CILENTO, PHYLLIS DOROTHY (1894-1987), medical practitioner and journalist, was born on 13 March 1894 at Rockdale, Sydney, only child of New South Wales-born parents Charles Thomas McGlew, shipbroker and coal merchant, and his wife Alice Lane, née Walker. The family moved to Adelaide when Phyllis was a small child. She attended Tormore House school and studied medicine at the University of Adelaide (MB, BS, 1918), where she played hockey and tennis, captaining the women's tennis team for three years and winning a Blue. In 1918 she became engaged to (Sir) Raphael ('Ray') Cilento [q.v.], a fellow medical student. After graduating she worked as a house surgeon at the Adelaide Hospital.

In 1919 Dr McGlew accompanied her mother to Britain to be reunited with her father, who had served in France in World War I. Her parents separated soon after and she determined never to be economically dependent on her future husband. To further her education she enlisted as a clinical clerk at the Hospital for Sick Children, Great Ormond Street, London, where she first became interested in nutrition. She also attended the Marylebone Medical Mission Dispensary. Back in Adelaide, she married Cilento on 18 March 1920 at St Columba's Church of England, Hawthorn, and they briefly set up in general practice together at Tranmere.

In October that year the Cilentos sailed for Perak, Federated Malay States. While Raphael worked as a physician to the sultanate, Phyllis obtained a post as 'lady medical officer' in the British colonial service and took charge of a women's ward in a hospital at Teluk Anson (Teluk Intan). In February 1921 the first of her six children was born. In December she returned to Australia and next year, while her husband was studying in England, undertook a course in public health at the University of Sydney. Late in 1922 she joined him at Townsville, Queensland, and next year, shortly after the birth of their second child, they moved to Rabaul, Mandated Territory of New Guinea, where she worked (1924-27) in private practice.

The Cilento family settled in Brisbane in 1928. At the Hospital for Sick Children she was physician to out-patients (1931-33), and to in-patients (1935-38). She had a remarkable affinity with both mothers and children. For thirty-six years (apart from a year in Canberra in 1934 and three years in New York in 1948-50), Cilento was a general practitioner, with an active obstetric practice. Her surgery was attached to her Annerley home, allowing her to supervise her growing family. In 1939-46 and 1952-62 she was specialist lecturer in mothercraft at the University of Queensland. She sold her practice in 1964. Moving to Toowong in 1967, she continued to see patients until the early 1980s.

Throughout her career Lady Cilento (her husband was knighted in 1935) undertook advanced training in Australia, Britain, the United States of America and New Zealand, including a short course with Grantly Dick Read, a proponent of natural childbirth. In 1928 she had started contributing articles on mothercraft to *Woman's Budget*, and soon after began writing a weekly column under the *nom de plume* 'Mother M. D.' for the Brisbane *Daily Mail*, and from 1933 for the *Courier-Mail*. From 1950 her pseudonym was 'Medical Mother'. Later she wrote for *Woman's Day* and other magazines. She dealt with nutrition, the health of mothers and children, and all aspects of child care. In her writing she demonstrated her own remarkable facility to communicate complex medical facts to ordinary readers. Women came to quote her as a national oracle. As 'Mother M. D.', she conducted regular radio sessions for many years. She published her first book, *Square Meals for the Family*, in 1933; in all she wrote twenty-four books and monographs, including *The Cilento Way* (1984). In later years she controversially promoted the use of large doses of vitamins for good health. She wrote her last newspaper column in 1984. Her final work was an autobiography, *Lady Cilento M.B. B.S.: My Life* (1987).

Lady Cilento was involved in a wide range of medical and community organisations. She was inaugural president (1929) of the Queensland Medical Women's Society. In 1931 she founded the Mothercraft Association of Queensland, serving as president until 1946; she considered that the association was her 'greatest contribution to social welfare in Queensland'. Active for some years in the National Council of Women of Queensland, she was also president of the local branch of the Business and Professional Women's Association (1948) and of the Lyceum Club (1951-52). She was a member of the inaugural council of the Family Planning Association of Queensland, and also a member of the Crèche & Kindergarten Association of Queensland.

Some members of the mainstream medical profession disapproved of Lady Cilento's ideas, seeing them as alternative and unorthodox. Others, however, saw her as a woman ahead of her time. She stated in 1987 that much she had fought for, 'like natural childbirth, family planning, and permitting fathers to be present at the birth of their children', was now accepted. In 1971 the Brisbane City Mission publicly recognised her work with a citation signed by the premier and representatives of many churches and social organisations. She said later that it was the honour that she prized 'more than any other'. In 1974 she was selected as first Queensland Mother of the Year. In 1977 an award established by the Nutritional Foods Association of Australia and a resource centre for parents in Brisbane were named after her. She was elected (1978) a fellow of the International Academy of Preventive Medicine and a life member (1980) of the Australian Medical Association. First Queenslander of the Year (1981) and Queensland Senior Citizen of the Year (1987), she was awarded a medal of merit by the Australian chapter of the Legion of Frontiersmen of the Commonwealth, and was named (1982) Loyal Australian of the Year by the Assembly of Captive European Nations.

Widely known as 'Lady C.', Phyllis Cilento was 5 ft 7 ins (170 cm) tall, with smooth, olive skin, brown eyes and a direct gaze. She had a strong presence, an outgoing, warm and friendly personality, an immense enthusiasm for life, her work and her family, and a lively sense of humour. In her autobiography she described her children as 'Ray's and my greatest achievement': four became doctors, one a noted artist, and her youngest daughter, Diane, an actor. Her husband died in 1985 after an enduring, although sometimes turbulent, partnership of sixty-five years. Survived by her children, she died on 26 July 1987 in Brisbane and was buried in Albany Creek cemetery. Several portraits were painted of her, including one by John Rigby (1973) which is held by the Queensland Art Gallery, Brisbane.

J. H. Pearn, *Focus and Innovation* (1986); A. Mackinnon, *The New Women* (1986); F. G. Fisher, *Raphael Cilento* (1994); M. Mahoney & D. Gordon, 'Obituary: Phyllis Dorothy Cilento', *MJA*, 18 Apr 1988, p 415; *Sunday Mail* (Brisbane), 15 Mar 1987, p 12; *Australian*, 27 July 1987, p 2; Cilento papers (Univ of Qld Lib); private information.

MARY D. MAHONEY

CILENTO, SIR RAPHAEL WEST (1893-1985), medical practitioner and public servant, was born on 2 December 1893 at Jamestown, South Australia, second of five children of South Australian-born parents Raphael Ambrose Cilento, stationmaster, and his wife Frances Ellen Elizabeth, née West. His paternal grandfather, an Italian migrant, had run a shipping business in Adelaide. After attending Jamestown Public School, 'Ray' became a pupil-teacher in 1908. He taught at Port Pirie in 1910-11. Completing his secondary education at Adelaide High School and Prince Alfred College, he studied medicine at the University of Adelaide (MB, BS, 1918; MD, 1922). On 26 November 1918 he was appointed captain, Australian Army Medical Corps, Australian Naval and Military Expeditionary Force. Next month he arrived in Rabaul. There he became acquainted with the field of tropical medicine and sent reports on medical conditions in New Guinea to senior administrators in Rabaul and Melbourne. Failing to secure a continuing role, he returned to Australia in September 1919 and his military appointment terminated in Adelaide next month.

On 18 March 1920 at St Columba's Church of England, Hawthorn, Cilento married Dr Phyllis Dorothy McGlew [q.v. Cilento, P. D.], who had been a fellow student. Later in the year he obtained a post as a physician to the sultanate of Perak, Federated Malay States, where he gained expertise in tropical medicine and acquired a lifelong interest in the countries of the Asia-Pacific region. In 1921 he was offered employment back in Australia, as medical officer for tropical hygiene with the Commonwealth Department of Health, based at the Australian Institute of Tropical Medicine, Townsville, Queensland. His appointment entailed study at the London School of Tropical Medicine (DTM&H, 1922), which he completed with distinction. Next year he was elected a fellow of the Royal Society of Tropical Medicine and Hygiene. He became a leading figure in the field; appointed director of the AITM in 1922, he was seconded in 1924-28 to Rabaul as director of public health for the Mandated Territory of New Guinea. Developing a research interest in the survival of Europeans in tropical environments, he published *The White Man in the Tropics* (1925), in which he defended the White Australia policy.

With J. H. L. Cumpston and J. S. C. Elkington [qq.v.8], Cilento helped to shape policy and practice in the development of quarantine and tropical disease management. In 1928 he succeeded Elkington as director of tropical hygiene and chief quarantine officer, Brisbane. The division closed in 1934 and he transferred to Canberra. In September that year he accepted an appointment as the first State director-general of health and medical services in Queensland and returned to Brisbane. Knighted in 1935, he threw himself into the task of creating a new public medical system, writing legislation for general medicine and for mental health. To help him with this work, he studied law and was admitted to the Bar on 29 April 1939. Not opposed to private practice, he nevertheless endorsed a salaried health service; his ideas, published privately in *Blueprint for the Health of a Nation* (1944), provoked serious conflict with other members of the medical profession. He advocated the establishment of a medical school at the University of Queensland. The university awarded him an honorary MD in 1935. In 1937-46 he was honorary professor of social and tropical medicine and he served (1935-46, 1953-56) on the university senate. Active on the new National Health and Medical Research Council, he supported the establishment in 1945 of the Queensland Institute of Medical Research. He also pursued his own research, especially into the state of Aboriginal health.

In World War II Sir Raphael was prevented from contributing to the war effort when he came under suspicion from the Commonwealth security services because of his Italian name and rumours about his associations with the Italian government and with organisations such as the Dante Alighieri Society. His commitment to public service found a new outlet when his expertise in preventive medicine resulted in his engagement in May 1945 with the United Nations Relief and Rehabilitation Administration. He worked first in the Balkans on malaria control and then in Germany. In July he was the first civilian doctor to enter Belsen concentration camp. Next month he was appointed UNRRA director, British zone,

occupied Germany, a post requiring administrative capacities of a high order to manage the refugee problem and to prevent the outbreak of disease. In 1946 he joined the UN Secretariat as head of the division of refugees in its department of social affairs. The following year he became director of its division of social activities based in New York. In 1948, as director of disaster relief in Palestine, he declared his sympathies with the dispossessed Palestinian refugees. He resigned from the UN in 1950.

In spite of his distinguished international service, Cilento failed to obtain a significant appointment on his return to Australia. Eventually he resumed private medical practice part time, while pursuing other public activities. He made two unsuccessful attempts to enter the Commonwealth parliament: he stood as a Democratic Party candidate for the Senate in the 1953 election and, as an Independent Democrat, challenged Sir Arthur Fadden [q.v.14] in the seat of McPherson in 1954. His mix of progressive social policy, free trade and internationalism did not help his political ambitions. He was an early advocate of the importance of Australia's Asia-Pacific context. An active historical researcher, he was president of the (Royal) Historical Society of Queensland (1933-34, 1943-45, 1953-68) and of the National Trust of Queensland (1966-71).

Critical of 'idealistic socialism' for lowering 'vitality in a national sense', Cilento otherwise remained a forceful advocate of state medicine. A man of his time in his fascination with the interaction of population and resources, he conceived of 'the conquest of climate' as 'primarily, essentially, the conquest of disease'. His difficulty in finding suitable appointments in later life was matched by his failure to develop beyond his earliest ideas. His history of Queensland, *Triumph in the Tropics* (1959), written with Clem Lack [q.v.15], regurgitated arguments of the 1920s, but added offensive commentary on Aboriginal societies. The book's language reflected attitudes that emerged strongly in his private correspondence. Yet his research on Aboriginal health in the 1920s and 1930s, the state of which he regarded as threatening the 'survival of the race', had prompted severe criticism of government policy and administration. In later years he was tempted to embark on moral rearmament enterprises, and allied himself with the extreme right of Australian politics, including the Australian League of Rights.

In a long marriage over more than six decades, Cilento's occasional infidelities were forgiven by the loyal and supportive Phyllis. Survived by his wife, and their three sons and three daughters, Sir Raphael died on 15 April 1985 at Oxley, Brisbane, and was buried with Catholic rites in Pinaroo lawn cemetery, Aspley.

H. Gregory, *Vivant Professores* (1987); R. Patrick, *A History of Health & Medicine in Queensland 1824-1960* (1987); D. Denoon, *Public Health in Papua New Guinea* (1989); R. MacLeod and D. Denoon (eds), *Health and Healing in Tropical Australia and Papua New Guinea* (1991); F. G. Fisher, *Raphael Cilento* (1994); R. Kidd, *The Way We Civilise* (1997); *Ethnic and Racial Studies*, vol 23, no 2, 2000, p 248; *MJA*, 16 Sept 1985, p 259; Cilento papers (Univ of Qld Lib). MARK FINNANE

CLANCY, PATRICK MARTIN (1919-1987), trade unionist, was born on 21 January 1919 at Redfern, Sydney, third of four children of Denis Edward Clancy, grocer, and his wife Olive, née Kitchen, both born in New South Wales. Pat was educated at St Peter's De La Salle School, Surry Hills. He left at 14 and, after working in a boot pattern factory, began an apprenticeship in the printing industry, but it was terminated. He was then employed in a battery factory. He played Rugby League with the Balmain juniors in 1936 and had some success as an amateur boxer.

In 1937 Clancy contested a professional fight at Leichhardt that netted him 22s. 6d., which covered his fare to Port Kembla to take up an apprenticeship as a bricklayer with Australian Iron & Steel Ltd. He began to represent other apprentices in disputes with management. His political consciousness was raised in 1938-39 by the dispute over the export of pig-iron to Japan, and further in 1940 by the strike called by the Australasian Coal & Shale Employees' Federation which led to the closing of the Port Kembla steel works and to his sacking. When the works reopened he returned to a job there.

Early in 1941 Clancy joined the United Operative Bricklayers' Trade Society of New South Wales. After the bricklayers and carpenters amalgamated at State level in 1942, he was elected to the committee of the new organisation. In February 1943 he became secretary of the South Coast district council of the Building Workers Industrial Union of New South Wales. On 10 August 1940 Clancy had married Alma May Thomas, a machinist, at St Francis Xavier's Catholic Church, Wollongong. He studied Marxism with the intention of converting Alma, whose family were committed socialists, to Catholicism. Instead he became a Marxist and in 1943 joined the Communist Party of Australia. Elected as a delegate to the South Coast branch of the Labor Council of New South Wales, he soon became a vice-president. He later served on the parent body in Sydney for many years until he moved to the federal sphere.

In 1944 Clancy was elected an organiser in the New South Wales branch of the BWIU, a paid position which necessitated a move to Sydney in January 1945. He settled with his family at Revesby. Known as the 'boy organiser' because of his youthfulness, he led the struggle for full daytime trade training for apprentices. In Sydney he met Tom McDonald, with whom he soon had close links through the union and the CPA. They also played Rugby League in a Eureka Youth League team. Through the Eureka league Clancy also organised sporting events for children.

A 'craggy, bespectacled, soft-spoken, affable man', Clancy became assistant secretary (1947) and secretary (1953) of the New South Wales branch of the BWIU, then acting federal secretary (1971), and federal secretary (1973) after the death of Frank Purse. At a time of intense rivalry between the building unions, he served (1970-73, 1975-79) as the building group's representative on the executive of the Australian Council of Trade Unions, losing one election to Norm Gallagher of the Australian Building Construction Employees' & Builders' Labourers' Federation. Under Clancy's leadership the first national building trades construction award was processed through the Australian Conciliation and Arbitration Commission in 1975. This development was important not only in reflecting market rates in an award but also because its first renewal, in 1976, under the so-called Ludeke formula foreshadowed the process of award restructuring in the late 1980s. Permanent employment for building workers was also won under his leadership. He retired from the federal secretary's position in 1985 and became the honorary chair of the union's international department, developing fraternal relations with overseas unions—a continuation of his work through his representation of the union on the executive of the communist-aligned World Federation of Trade Unions. Since 1980 he had been completely blind, as a result of diabetes, but, through a combination of tenacity, prodigious memory, sharp intelligence and the assistance of other union staff, had continued to work effectively.

After returning to Sydney Clancy had been elected to the Sydney district committee of the CPA in 1947 and to the central (national) committee of the party in 1958. He had stood unsuccessfully as a Communist candidate for the Federal seat of Banks in 1954. He sat on the executive of the central committee at the time of the split in the CPA after the 1968 Soviet invasion of Czechoslovakia. The party's attitudes to industrial policy and its relationship with the trade unions had long been a source of conflict: he regarded his first obligation as being to the interests of union members. He resigned from the CPA in 1971. The Socialist Party of Australia was formed in December that year; although he was cautious initially he became president. The party was pro-Moscow in its outlook and he was fondly referred to as 'Clansky'. Because of differences among members he was removed as president in 1983 and resigned from the party. In 1984 he formed the Association for Communist Unity in an attempt to reunify the communist Left.

A choir boy in his youth, Clancy had been appointed as the trade union representative (1973-78) on the board of the Australian Opera as a result of his interest in classical music. He had always followed the South Sydney Rabbitohs; he continued to do so by listening to the radio when he could no longer see them. Although he presented a gruff exterior at times, he was a man of integrity, concerned for the welfare of workers and for world peace. The Soviet Union awarded him the Order of People's Friendship in 1979 and the New South Wales Labor Council included him on its list of leading unionists in 1980. After suffering a heart attack, he died on 24 July 1987 at Bombay (Mumbai), India, on his way home from a peace conference in Mongolia. He was survived by his wife and their two sons.

The BWIU (1985); G. Mitchell, *On Strong Foundations* (1996); *SMH*, 17 Feb 1979, p 15, 17 Oct 1985, p 2, 27 July 1987, p 7; *Bulletin*, 10 Apr 1979, p 76; *Mercury* (Hobart), 10 Aug 1983, p 8; R. Raxworthy, interviews with P. Clancy (ts, 1985-86, NLA); A6119, item 133 (NAA); Building Workers' Industrial Union records (Noel Butlin Archives, ANU); private information.   SUZANNE JAMIESON

CLARK, ANNIE EVELYN (1903-1983), netball administrator, was born on 16 August 1903 at Waterloo, Sydney, third of five children of Victorian-born parents George Cornelius Clark, sewerage labourer, and his wife Martha, née Doidge. Anne, as she preferred to be called, attended Redfern Superior Public School, leaving aged 14. From 1919 she worked at the W. D. & H. O. Wills (Aust.) Ltd cigarette factory, becoming a welfare assistant (1938), and then assistant to the personnel officer (1940). Participating in a range of sports, she was very involved in the company's physical culture 'Vice Regal Club' from 1921, which she served as president for twelve years. After breaking her ankle in her first season of women's basketball (netball), she decided to concentrate on umpiring and coaching. She joined the Sydney City Girls' Amateur Sports Association in 1924. When this organisation changed its name to the New South Wales Women's Basketball Association (from 1970 New South Wales Netball Association) in 1929, she became a vice-president. She lived with her parents in Waterloo until the late 1930s.

During World War II, a member of the Women's Australian National Services, Clark used her sewing and knitting skills for the war effort. She assisted with many charities throughout her life. On 29 September 1941 she enlisted in the Women's Auxiliary Australian Air Force but she was discharged on 12 November on compassionate grounds. Her mother died that year. She returned to W. D. & H. O. Wills, and worked as a welfare officer until 1963. After retirement she fulfilled her wish to live on the North Shore.

From 1950 to 1979 Clark was president of the New South Wales Women's Basketball (New South Wales Netball) Association, as well as manager, coach and selector for State teams. She advocated acquisition by the association of its own premises and encouraged in 1968 adoption of a new constitution which established district associations throughout the State. She was required to step down in 1979. The termination of her twenty-nine-year term as president signalled the end of an era of amateur leadership and the beginning of a more businesslike and strategic approach to netball administration. Clark was five times (1955, 1960, 1966, 1972 and 1978) concurrently national president of the All Australia Women's Basket Ball Association (from 1970 the All Australia Netball Association).

Through her training of umpires, Clark had made a major contribution to women's basketball and netball. She conducted numerous umpires' camps beginning at Lithgow in 1949. Keen to help with the development of the game in the Territory of Papua and New Guinea, she made four umpiring tours there, the first in 1966. She was an international umpire, officiating at world tournaments in 1967 and 1975.

Nicknamed 'Little Anne', she was a diminutive but stalwart figure, who believed that netball taught its participants the essentials of teamwork, which translated into lessons of good citizenship. She was awarded the British Empire Medal in 1975. Her many honours from netball included the All Australia umpire badge (1931) and service award (1964). She was granted life membership (1968) and named patron (1979) of the State association. The Anne Clark service award was established in 1975 and the Anne Clark centre, New South Wales Netball Association headquarters complex, was officially opened on 11 October 1980. Unmarried, she died on 12 June 1983 in Singapore while attending the Sixth World Netball Tournament and was cremated in Sydney.

D. Hyland, 'Little Anne' (1987); J. Dunbar (comp), *1929-1989: 60 Years of Netball in New South Wales* (1989); M. Duncan, *Conversations with Netball Players and Administrators* (1994); *SMH*, 30 Aug 1972, p 19; A9301, item 92516 (NAA).
                                                      TRACY TAYLOR

Clark

CLARK, COLIN GRANT (1905-1989), economist and public servant, was born on 2 November 1905 in London, son of James Clark, a merchant who had lived in Queensland, and his wife Marion Nellie, née Jolly. Colin was educated at the Dragon School, Oxford; Winchester College; and Brasenose College, Oxford (BA, 1927; MA, 1931; D.Litt., 1971). As an undergraduate he studied chemistry. In 1928 he won the Royal Statistical Society's Frances Wood memorial prize. In 1928-29 he worked on social surveys of London and Liverpool as a research assistant before joining the Economic Advisory Council, set up by the government in 1930 to examine unemployment in Britain. Next year, on the recommendation of J. M. (Baron) Keynes, also a member of the council, he was appointed a lecturer in statistics at the University of Cambridge. He unsuccessfully stood as a Labour Party candidate in British parliamentary elections of 1929, 1931 and 1935. On 27 July 1935 at the parish church, Carbrooke, Norfolk, he married Marjorie Tattersall, a secretary. In the late 1930s he converted to Catholicism, the tenets of which, according to some critics, were to influence his ideas.

On leave from Cambridge in 1937-38, Clark took up visiting appointments at the universities of Sydney, Melbourne and Western Australia. In Brisbane he met the Queensland premier, William Forgan Smith [q.v.11], who offered him the posts of director of the Bureau of Industry, government statistician and financial adviser to the Treasury, vacant after the resignation of J. B. Brigden [q.v.7]. He accepted and commenced duties in May 1938. In 1940 he produced his seminal work, *The Conditions of Economic Progress*. Reviewers recognised the immense energy and labour involved in amassing the vast amount of statistical data that enabled Clark to compare real product over time and across nations, but criticised his reluctance to use the material to develop theoretical constructs. The absence of theorising, however, reflected his conviction that 'economics should be based on the empirical observation and classification of what has actually been happening'. He believed that there was limited room for theorists and that the majority of economists should be content to build a structure of ordered knowledge through the constant testing and retesting of economic theories against observed facts.

In *The Economics of 1960* (1942), Clark produced a twenty-year econometric forecasting model for the world economy. Analysing capital investment as a determining factor in growth, he first used the terms 'capital hunger' and 'capital satiation'. Not surprisingly most of his long-range estimates proved to be wrong, but his prediction of a long and sustained period of postwar growth based on 'capital hunger' was correct.

Clark promoted rural development and population decentralisation in Queensland, goals that had dominated that State's economic policy since the 1930s and had much in common with Catholic social thought at the time. His policy advice reflected his vision of the 'good' society in which a type of democratic capitalism prevailed, offering maximum opportunities for economic independence through small-business activities. In 1947 he was appointed under-secretary of the newly formed Department of Labour and Industry, but following differences of opinion with the premier, Vince Gair [q.v.14], he resigned in 1952.

Returning to England Clark became director of the Institute for Research in Agricultural Economics, University of Oxford. His previous work on international comparisons of real income, which focused attention on the classical problem of economic growth, was a starting point for the study of economic underdevelopment by drawing attention to the wide disparities in real income between countries. He traced the changing sector balance between agriculture, secondary industry and services as real incomes rise, while his particular interest in economic underdevelopment led him to a study of agricultural productivity and the economic consequences of population growth. Addressing the need for rapid development in poor countries, he opposed neo-Malthusianism and stressed the economies and benefits arising from a dense population. He claimed that there was enormous potential for growth in labour productivity within agriculture. His cursory treatments of very low income countries, however, perhaps a result of the relatively limited data available at the time, served to weaken his argument; furthermore, in many densely populated countries, subsistence farming has shown little capacity to increase output per head. In 1964-66 Clark served on Pope Paul VI's Commission on Population and Birth Control.

Retiring from his post at Oxford in 1969, Clark became a fellow (1969-78) at Monash University, Melbourne, and a research consultant in economics (1978-89) at the University of Queensland. He returned to the study of the relationship of capital investment to long-term economic growth, first analysed in *The Economics of 1960*. The burst of high investment, he now argued, was the up-swing of a fifty-year cycle which came to an end in the 1970s and was followed by a period of much slower economic growth as the world economy entered an age of 'capital satiation'.

Over the course of his career Clark produced more than fifty pioneering and influential contributions to applied economics. They included studies of rural national product; a questioning of capital investment as a determining factor in economic growth; and a study of the limits on taxation and proposals for its reduction. Opposed to big government, he believed that with lower taxation people generally would be better able to make provision for their own welfare needs. He has been described as the first economic statistician, but it could equally be argued that he was very much a political economist, since he regarded economics as subservient to political science, and ultimately dominated by moral philosophy. Perhaps this somewhat old-fashioned approach to economics, with his attitude to economic theorising, explains why he did not receive the recognition that his work deserved. To some extent the Economic Society of Australia redressed this in 1967 when it named him, with Trevor Swan [q.v.], an inaugural distinguished fellow. Earlier Clark had received honorary degrees from Tilbury University, the Netherlands, the University of Milan, Italy, Monash University and the University of Queensland.

Quiet and good-humoured, Clark had a remarkable memory that could always be called upon to settle an argument. He lived simply on a small farm by the Brisbane River at Kenmore, and often looked unkempt. Survived by his wife, who had been a constant support throughout their marriage, and their eight sons and one daughter, he died on 4 September 1989 at Auchenflower, Brisbane, and was buried in Mount Gravatt cemetery.

D. Sills (ed), *International Encyclopedia of the Social Sciences: Volume 18, Biographical Supplement* (1979); G. M. Meier and D. Seers (eds), *Pioneers in Development* (1984); A. G. Kenwood, 'The Use of Statistics for Policy Advising', in D. Ironmonger et al (eds), *National Income and Economic Progress* (1988); *Economic Record*, vol 16, Dec 1940, p 262, vol 65, no 190, 1989, p 296, vol 66, no 195, 1990, p 329; *Economic Jnl*, vol 51, Apr 1941, p 120; *People* (Sydney), 10 May 1960, p 32; *Times* (London), 5 Sept 1989, p 16; Clark papers (Univ of Qld Lib).

A. G. KENWOOD*

CLARK, ELLEN (1915-1988), naturalist, was born on 25 March 1915 at Geraldton, Western Australia, third of four children of Scottish-born parents John Clark [q.v.13], car builder, and his wife Maggie, née Forbes. Ellen's family moved to Melbourne in 1926 when her father, an authority on Australian ants, was appointed entomologist with the National Museum of Victoria. Ellen had helped with her father's work since childhood and, in 1933—without having completed her school Leaving certificate—she was employed to assist him at the museum. She also began developing an independent research program on Australian crustacea, in the course of which she revised the genus *Euastacus*. Clark's most significant scientific contribution was to describe and name many of Australia's freshwater crayfish ('yabbies'). In 1936 she became the first woman to publish in *Memoirs of the National Museum of Victoria*, with an article on Australian freshwater and land crayfishes. She published seven other papers from this research and in 1937 was appointed a temporary museum assistant under a grant from the Carnegie Corporation.

According to the *Herald*, Miss Clark had 'that intense and exclusive devotion which distinguishes the born scientist'. Her enthusiasm extended to teaching natural history to children through the Royal Victorian Institute for the Blind and, from 1940, writing occasional columns for the *Argus* and the *Australasian*. That year, having failed to gain a permanent position, she resigned from the museum. She moved to the Walter and Eliza Hall [qq.v.9] Institute, where, although formally employed as secretary of the virus department, she continued her work on crustacea, adapting it to serological and immunological fields; she also investigated influenza strains. Clark co-authored several papers on these topics and, with (Sir) Macfarlane Burnet [q.v.], a monograph, *Influenza* (1942), which surveyed the history of the virus from the 1889 pandemic in the light of modern knowledge. Having completed her secondary education at night school, in 1941 she enrolled in science at the University of Melbourne, but completed no subjects.

The extent of Clark's scientific contribution was unusual given her lack of formal qualifications and her sex. While the nineteenth-century tradition of amateur participation in science survived to some extent in museums, and the 1930s and 1940s were a high point for women's participation in Australian science, both remained largely male domains. As Clark once quipped, 'I feel I should have a beard'.

In 1945 Clark left WEHI to work with her father at their home at Box Hill (later Mooroolbark), specialising in the physiology of bull ants. In 1947, after testing the reactions of ants to air travel, she accompanied 4500 specimens on a three-week round-trip to the United States of America. In 1950 she delivered blood samples gathered by the Australian National Antarctic Research Expedition from animals on Heard Island to the Serological Museum of Rutgers University, and commenced a year's study there on a Rockefeller Foundation grant. While in the USA she married Alex Guba, a serologist, and worked as a scientist with Cooper Laboratories (later Cooper Vision). Survived by her husband, she died on 2 May 1988 at her home at Santa Clara, California, and was buried in Mission City memorial park.

Herald (Melbourne), 27 Aug 1937, p 13; *Sun News-Pictorial* (Melbourne), 'Women's Mag', 30 July 1947, p 3; *Sun News-Pictorial* (Melbourne), 25 Aug 1947, p 6; *Argus* (Melbourne), 8 May 1950, p 12.

JANE CAREY

CLARK, SIR GORDON COLVIN LINDESAY (1896-1986), mining engineer and company director, was born on 7 January 1896 in South Melbourne, eldest of six children of Victorian-born parents Lindesay Colvin Clark, civil engineer, and his wife Jessie Taylor, née Meekison. Young Lindesay spent most of his childhood in northern Tasmania, where he had a governess until he was 12. He then attended Launceston Church Grammar School and the University of Tasmania (B.Sc., 1916). On 2 February 1916 he enlisted in the Australian Imperial Force. While serving (1917-18) on the Western Front with the 2nd Field Company, Australian Engineers, he was commissioned and promoted to lieutenant. He won the Military Cross for skilful and courageous work near Rosières, France, on the night of 22-23 August 1918.

Back in Australia, Clark was demobilised on 9 May 1919. He studied at the University of Melbourne (BME, 1921; MME, 1923) and gained experience at the Sulphide Corporation Ltd's lead smelter near Newcastle, New South Wales. In 1922 he returned to Melbourne to work with his father, who was then a consulting mining engineer. On 5 April that year in Hobart he married with Congregational forms Barbara Jane Crosby Walch. For the next decade he lectured part time at the University of Melbourne and during this period set up his own consultancy. He examined mining properties in remote parts of Central Australia, Queensland, Papua and the Mandated Territory of New Guinea.

Clark's 1930 report on a gold prospect in Tasmania impressed W. S. Robinson [q.v.11], who offered him a job as a mining engineer with Gold Mines of Australia Ltd. Thus began Clark's forty-eight-year association with the Collins House group of companies. He was appointed manager of GMA in 1931 and technical managing director of Western Mining Corporation Ltd on its formation in 1933. He was later to chair a number of GMA's and WMC's subsidiaries. Working for Robinson, Sir Colin Fraser and Sir Arthur Robinson, and subsequently for Sir Walter Massy-Greene [qq.v.8,11,10], Clark recalled that 'to have come under the influence of these men, as well as my father, was a very fortunate thing for a young man'.

The GMA-WMC group acquired and redeveloped numerous gold mines in Queensland, Victoria and Western Australia. Clark's enthusiasm for scientific exploration was evident in WMC's decisions to engage eminent geologists from Harvard University, Massachusetts, United States of America, and to conduct an aerial survey of the eastern gold-fields of Western Australia. In World War II he was the Commonwealth's deputy-controller of minerals production, responsible for the supply of strategic minerals. His initiatives resulted in new mining ventures, including one to extract scheelite on King Island. He joined the boards of Broken Hill Associated Smelters Pty Ltd, Broken Hill South Ltd and North Broken Hill Ltd in 1944. After the war, he directed the expansion of the WMC group's gold-mining operations at Kalgoorlie, Norseman, Bullfinch, Reedy and Coolgardie, Western Australia, and at Newstead and Woods Point, Victoria.

Appointed chairman of WMC in 1952, Clark initiated a program of diversification that led to the proving in 1958 of bauxite deposits in the Darling Range, Western Australia, the formation of Alcoa of Australia Pty Ltd in 1961 (chairman 1961-70), and the establishment of an integrated aluminium industry; the exploitation of an iron ore deposit in the Koolanooka Hills, and the signing of the first long-term contract for the export, beginning in 1966, of iron ore to Japan; the discovery that year of nickel deposits at Kambalda, and the development of an integrated nickel industry; the finding of uranium at Yeelirrie in 1972; and the discovery of an extensive copper-uranium-gold mineralisation at Roxby Downs, South Australia, in 1975. As chairman of BH South from 1956, he advocated that this company should also diversify; it began mining phosphate near Duchess, Queensland, and copper at Cobar, New South Wales, and Kanmantoo, South Australia.

Clark was president (1956-58) of the Australian Mines and Metals Association, a councillor of the chambers of Mines of Western Australia and Victoria, a councillor of the Australian Mineral Industries Research Association, a member (1967-73) of the executive committee of the Australian Mining Industry Council and a foundation fellow (1975) of the Australian Academy of Technological Sciences. His achievements gained him an honorary doctorate of engineering (1961) and the W. C. Kernot [q.v.5] medal (1964) from the University of Melbourne, and an honorary doctorate of laws (1975) from Monash University. He was a councillor and president (1959) of the Australasian Institute of Mining and Metallurgy, which awarded him its medal (1962) and honorary membership (1973). The Institution of Mining and Metallurgy (London) also recognised him with honorary membership (1971). He was appointed CMG (1961), KBE (1968) and AC (1975).

Sir Lindesay insisted on the use of the best available technology. He encouraged innovative thinking and inspired people to bring out the best in themselves. When required, he had the courage to make difficult and unpopular decisions. His enthusiasm was inspirational. Above all, he showed a deep interest in the welfare of others, particularly those in remote mining areas, whose problems and hopes were always of concern to him. The WMC-Lindesay Clark Trust Fund was established

(1979) to benefit communities in areas where WMC operates. Clark was generous with his advice and liberal with his praise. Although quietly spoken he was persuasive without being dominant, and he commanded attention through good leadership rather than position. He had a lasting influence on the metallurgical industry and on the lives and attitudes of many of its subsequent leaders.

In 1974, at the age of 78, Clark stepped down from a number of directorships and from the chairmanship of BH South and WMC. He remained on the board of the latter company for a further four years, during which he wrote *Built on Gold: Recollections of Western Mining* (1983). For the most part, his life was his work and his work his life. He played tennis with enthusiasm and golf more for exercise than competition. He was skilful at billiards and enjoyed walking. Classical music gave him much pleasure and few people knew of his talent for painting. His gift (1971) to Monash University of the Lindesay Clark window by Leonard French in the Robert Blackwood [q.v.] Hall was one indication of his generosity and love of the visual arts.

Survived by his wife and their two daughters and son, Clark died on 3 January 1986 in his home at Kooyong, Melbourne, and was cremated. His estate was sworn for probate at $1 037 595. A bequest to his old school enabled it to build an administration centre. Alcoa holds a portrait of him (1973) by Clifton Pugh.

G. M. Ralph, 'Sir Lindesay Clark: An Appreciation', in *Technology in Australia 1788-1988* (1988); A'asian Inst of Mining and Metallurgy, *Supplement to the Bulletin*, no 254 (1963) and no 375 (1974); A. Hodgart, taped interview with Sir Lindesay Clark (1974, NLA); J. A. L. Matheson, citation for Sir Lindesay Clark's honorary doctorate of laws, 1975 (Monash Univ Archives); A'asian Inst of Mining and Metallurgy records, Melbourne; Western Mining Corp Ltd archives, Melbourne; private information and personal knowledge.   GILBERT M. RALPH

CLAYTON, ERIC ELWIN SAMUEL (1896-1987), commissioner of soil conservation, was born on 27 July 1896 at Orange, New South Wales, elder child of Robert Ashton Clayton, storekeeper, and his wife Alice Eliza, née Smith, who were both born at Orange. Raised by his widowed mother, Sam was educated at Hurlstone Agricultural High School. He graduated from Hawkesbury Agricultural College in 1914, and in 1915 joined the State Department of Agriculture at Cowra Experiment Farm.

On 22 August 1916 Clayton enlisted in the Australian Imperial Force. In 1917-18 he served with the 6th Mobile Veterinary Section in Palestine and Egypt. Following his return to Australia in February 1919, he was discharged from the army in April. He resumed civilian life at Wagga Experiment Farm and then became an agricultural instructor on the New South Wales north coast. On 15 February 1922 he married Marjorie Ella Molesworth Oxley at St John's Church of England, Wagga Wagga.

Clayton next moved to the State's southwestern district, where he rose in 1927 to senior experimentalist; the challenges of growing wheat in semi-arid lands led him to fear the effects on the thin topsoil. In the *Agricultural Gazette of New South Wales* (volume XLII) in 1931, he called soil erosion a 'serious problem' that threatened to degrade thousands of fertile properties into 'barren wastes'. Two years later the government established a soil erosion committee. Clayton, a tall, lean, outspoken member with a distinctive toothbrush moustache, cultivated support from land users and newspaper readers. His first political sponsor was Roy Vincent [q.v.12], Country Party secretary for mines and minister for forests (1932-41) in the State government, who sent him abroad in 1936 to study erosion remedies.

The eight-month tour incorporated Britain, Europe, and North America, where the Federal Soil Conservation Service, Washington, under the charismatic Hugh Bennett, left a lasting impression. Back in Australia, Clayton published *The Problem of Soil Erosion* (1937), demanding 'forthright, determined, nationwide action' to rectify 'yesterday's failure to look more carefully to our land'. His approach emulated Bennett's combination of central publicity and decentralised action.

Clayton drafted the Soil Conservation Act, 1938, which passed with strong support from (Sir) William McKell [q.v.]. The new Soil Conservation Service, with Clayton as director of a very small founding staff, was based first in the Department of Mines and from 1944 in the Department of Conservation. McKell, while premier, travelled with him through the Snowy Mountains to discuss controls over high-country grazing. Such connections cushioned Clayton from the protests of other agencies when he rode roughshod over them or poached their best technicians. Although Clayton saw erosion as a national menace, Australian responses remained State based.

In 1949 the Soil Conservation Service was brought under the aegis of the new Conservation Authority of New South Wales, and Clayton's position was redesignated as commissioner. He filled this post until his compulsory retirement in 1961. Continuing to live at Cremorne, he enjoyed fishing and bowls. In 1975 he was appointed AM and in 1984 he received the inaugural Sir William McKell medal for his contribution to soil conservation. Predeceased by his wife, he died on 4 January

1987 at Broadbeach, Queensland, and was cremated. His two daughters and son survived him.

R. Breckwoldt, *The Dirt Doctors* (1988); *PD* (NSW), 14 July 1938, p 388, 28 July 1938, p 690; *Jnl of Soil Conservation, NSW*, vol 43, no 1, 1987, p 49; *SMH*, 27 Apr 1927, p 4; *Smith's Weekly*, 4 Oct 1947, 'Monthly Country', p 6; S. M. Powell, Mothering, Husbandry and the State (PhD thesis, Monash Univ, 2000); Clayton papers (SLNSW).
STEPHEN M. POWELL

CLEARY, HELEN AGNES (1914-1987), air force matron-in-chief, was born Helena Agnes Cleary on 28 March 1914 at Petersburg (Peterborough), South Australia, fifth child of Michael Augustine Cleary, labourer, and his wife Mary, née Fitzgerald, both born in South Australia. Educated at St Joseph's convent school, Peterborough, she trained at the Broken Hill and District Hospital, New South Wales, qualifying as a general nurse in 1941 and as an obstetric nurse in 1942.

After working for a year at Calvary Hospital, North Adelaide, Cleary joined the Royal Australian Air Force Nursing Service as a sister on 15 November 1943. She served at No.2 RAAF Hospital, Ascot Vale, Melbourne, and at No.7 School of Technical Training, Geelong, before being posted in April 1945 to No.2 Medical Air Evacuation Transport Unit, Morotai Island, Netherlands East Indies. Along with other RAAF nurses, she took part in evacuations throughout New Guinea and Borneo. These 'flying angels' were known as the 'glamour girls' of the air force, but they slept in nurses' quarters with corrugated iron roofs and hessian doors and sometimes rose at 2 a.m. for their long flights. Cleary survived an aeroplane crash with only a broken arm. Following the surrender of Japan in August, No.2 MAETU began bringing thousands of Australian and British servicemen, as well as Dutch civilians, from prisoner-of-war camps in Java, Sumatra and Thailand to the evacuation base in Singapore. Cleary was one of the first RAAF nursing sisters to arrive there. On board overloaded Dakota aircraft, she and other nurses cared for patients suffering from malnutrition and dysentery.

In 1946-49 Cleary nursed at air force hospitals and stations in Victoria, South Australia and New South Wales. Posted to No.6 RAAF Hospital, Laverton, Victoria, in April 1950, she tutored on medical air evacuation courses. She served at RAAF Station, Pearce, Western Australia, from April 1951, and was promoted to senior sister in September. In January 1952 she took part in a risky flight across the Indian Ocean to Cocos Island to retrieve a seriously injured airman. On the return flight to Perth, one engine of the Lincoln bomber failed and

another was faltering but Flight Lieutenant A. B. Boyle [q.v.] successfully landed the aircraft in a crosswind of 20 knots (37.04 kph).

During the Korean War, Cleary was charge sister (1952-53) of the RAAF hospital at Iwakuni, Japan. She organised medical evacuations of Australians from Korea, fought for better conditions for the critically wounded, and nursed recently exchanged prisoners of war. After the war she served at various bases in Victoria and South Australia. She was matron (1957-63, 1964-66) of No.3 RAAF Hospital, Richmond, New South Wales, and in 1962 completed a diploma in nursing administration at the New South Wales College of Nursing. Sent to Malaysia, she was senior sister (1963-64) and then matron (1966-67) at No.4 RAAF Hospital, Butterworth.

On 18 August 1967 Cleary was promoted to acting group officer (substantive 1 January 1968) and appointed matron-in-chief, RAAFNS, in Canberra. She was also made honorary nursing sister to Queen Elizabeth II. Having been appointed an associate of the Royal Red Cross in 1960, she was elevated to member in 1968 for her contribution to the training of medical staff and for maintaining 'the high ideals of the nursing profession'. She retired on 28 March 1969. Five ft 5 ins (165 cm) tall, with short brown hair and blue eyes, she was handsome and energetic. Within the service she was known for her sense of humour and camaraderie. Unmarried, she died on 26 August 1987 at Toorak Gardens, Adelaide, and was buried with Catholic rites in Centennial Park cemetery.

A. S. Walker, *Medical Services of the R.A.N. and R.A.A.F.* (1961); G. Halstead, *Story of the RAAF Nursing Service* (1994); *Advertiser* (Adelaide), 22 Nov 1961, p 27; *Herald* (Melbourne), 16 Aug 1967, p 23; *Canberra Times*, 19 Aug 1967, p 8; *SMH*, 28 Mar 1969, p 18; A12372, item N4452 (NAA); private information.
LINDA BOWMAN

CLIFF, GEOFFREY JOHN (1907-1988), civil engineer and naval officer, was born on 14 August 1907 at Beecroft, New South Wales, son of Richard Charles Cliff, a Sydney-born engineer, and his wife Adelaide Gertrude Orontes, née Goss, who had been born at sea. Jack attended Sydney Church of England Grammar School (Shore) in 1922-24. He later became a civil engineer, working for Coolah Shire Council in 1934-38 and the Snowy River Shire in 1939-40.

On 1 January 1941 Cliff was appointed probationary sub-lieutenant, Royal Australian Naval Volunteer Reserve, under the Yachtsmen Scheme. He was then 5 ft 7½ ins (171 cm) tall, with fair hair and blue eyes. Sent to England for training at HMS *King Alfred*, he was promoted to provisional lieutenant in April and posted to the Admiralty's land incident section, which disarmed and disposed of German magnetic and acoustic mines dropped by parachute across the British Isles. He used his engineering skills to defuse mines that had penetrated deep below ground, thus earning the nickname 'Contractor Jack'. Peter Firkins described him as slightly eccentric, a confirmed bachelor with a remarkable capacity for drinking beer. He was a bright and jovial man with a hearty laugh.

In May 1941 Cliff made his way through the debris of a two-storey building at Bermondsey, London, to reach an unexploded parachute mine. A nearby mine or bomb detonated, nearly burying him in wreckage. Realising that the explosion had probably started the clockwork fuse of the parachute mine, he extricated himself and rendered it safe. On another occasion he dealt with a mine buried in 24 ft (7.31 m) of clay at Leysdown, Kent. This weapon was even more dangerous than usual as it had been badly damaged in its fall and was fitted with an anti-handling device operated by a photoelectric cell. For his 'gallantry and undaunted devotion to duty' in these and other operations, both on land and under water, he was awarded the George Medal in June 1942.

Cliff won a Bar to his GM for defusing mines in Belfast at the sewerage works and in the town reservoir in June 1942. For 'great bravery and steadfast devotion to duty' in other actions he was appointed MBE in September 1943. That month he was promoted to acting lieutenant commander. He was elevated to OBE in April 1944. In October he and his colleague L. V. Goldsworthy were transferred to the Pacific as liaison officers with the United States Navy's Mobile Explosives Investigation Unit No.1. Cliff's RANVR appointment terminated on 29 January 1946. That year he returned to London as a member of the Australian contingent for the Victory March.

After the war Cliff resumed his career as a civil engineer with various shires of New South Wales. In 1955-58 he was the chief roads engineer for the British protectorate Brunei, Borneo. A member of the Imperial Service Club, Sydney, and the Dee Why sub-branch of the Returned Services League of Australia, he enjoyed the company of friends at the Collaroy Services Beach Club on Sunday mornings. He listed golf as his recreation. In later years he was devoted to his dogs and garden. He died on 14 October 1988 at the Repatriation General Hospital, Concord, and was buried in the Field of Mars cemetery, Ryde.

G. H. Gill, *Royal Australian Navy 1942-1945* (1968); P. Firkins, *Of Nautilus and Eagles* (1983); C. M. Fagg, *George, Albert and Edward Medals to Australians 1887-1984* (1988); *Naval Hist Review*, Summer 1972, p 5; A6769, item Cliff G J (NAA); PR89/184 (AWM); private information.

BILL BILLETT

CLIFFORD, WILLIAM (1918-1986), criminologist, was born on 6 October 1918 at Bradford, Yorkshire, England, son of Thomas Clifford, printer's labourer, and his wife Elizabeth Hilda, née Humphreys. Educated at St Bede's Grammar School, Bradford, he found work as a gas inspector. On 17 May 1940 he enlisted in the Royal Air Force. Posted to the RAF Police, he was sent to the Middle East in March 1941. At the Chapel of the English School of the Immaculate Conception, Cairo, on 22 July 1944 he married Margaret Mary Sillitto, a sergeant in the Auxiliary Territorial Service; their only child was stillborn.

Returning to England in 1945, Clifford was discharged from the air force on 19 July 1946. He joined the Birkenhead Police Force, Cheshire, but finding his inclination more towards prevention and reform, transferred to the probation service, training recruits at Wallington, Surrey. At night he studied at the London School of Economics and Political Science (B.Sc. (Econ.), 1952) and the University of London (LL B, 1957; LL M, 1963).

In 1952 Clifford became the British colonial service's director of social development in Cyprus, charged with bringing Cypriots closer to administrative independence. He promoted ethnic integration policies and founded Greek and Turkish children's homes around the island. Transferred to Northern Rhodesia (Zambia) in 1958 as director of social welfare and probation services (later commissioner of social affairs), he worked for greater racial integration and in 1962 became the founding principal of the Oppenheimer College of Social Service, the first multiracial college in central Africa. In 1964 he moved to the United Nations, organising refugee services in the Congo (Zaïre). He went to Japan in 1966 as a senior adviser to the UN Asia and Far East Institute for the Prevention of Crime and the Treatment of Offenders.

From 1968 Clifford was in New York as UN director of social defence. He was executive secretary for the Fourth UN Congress on the Prevention of Crime and the Treatment of Offenders at Kyoto, Japan, in 1970. Made head of the UN's crime prevention and criminal justice services, he was also an adjunct professor in criminology at New York University. He wrote numerous articles and influential monographs on prisoner rights, preventive criminology and crime control, including *An Introduction to African Criminology* (1974), *Crime Control in Japan* (1976) and *Planning Crime Prevention* (1976). In 1974 he accepted an invitation to become the first permanent director of the newly established Australian Institute of Criminology.

Clifford arrived in Canberra in 1975 with a determination to ensure that Australia did not succumb to the racial tensions of the United States of America, which he believed underpinned rising crime rates. An energetic researcher and enthusiastic reformer, he noted the high rate of imprisonment of Aborigines and sought to train Aboriginal social workers. Clifford believed in prisoner rights, opposed the death penalty and pioneered fields such as white-collar criminology and victimology. He argued forcefully that crime was sociological, a product of social and economic disadvantage rather than individual pathology.

A tall, heavy-set, balding, red-haired, fresh-faced man, Bill Clifford was challenged by the public-service culture of the institute, possible police corruption and the perennial conflicts between the States and the Commonwealth. He was vice-president (1978-80) of the Australian Academy of Forensic Sciences. In 1980 he founded the Asian and Pacific Conference of Correctional Administrators. He retired in August 1983 and next year advised on law and order in Papua New Guinea. Survived by his wife, he died of ischaemic heart disease on 6 June 1986 at Royal Canberra Hospital and was buried with Catholic rites in Gungahlin cemetery. In 2002 his wife had his body moved to the mausoleum at Woden cemetery.

Austn Inst of Criminology, *Annual Report*, 1975-83; *Austn Law Jnl*, vol 49, no 2, 1975, p 106, vol 57, no 11, p 655, vol 60, no 9, p 538; *Canberra Times*, 15 Oct 1974, p 3, 23 Jan 1975, p 3, 10 June 1986, p 10; *Sun* (Sydney), 31 Oct 1974, p 24; Austn Inst of Criminology, *Reporter*, June 1986, p 1; *Reform* (Sydney), Oct 1986, p 217; Clifford papers, series M3548 (NAA); private information.

STEPHEN GARTON

CLINCH, LINDSAY (1907-1984), newspaper editor, was born on 13 December 1907 in New York, eldest child of Australian-born Leslie John Clinch, clerk, and his English wife Alice, née Levy. The family moved to Australia; Lindsay was educated at North Sydney Boys' High School, where he excelled at football. He began his newspaper career as a copy-boy at the *Sun* in Sydney. On 22 July 1932 he married Bessie Edna Macpherson (d.1940), a nurse, at the Northbridge Presbyterian Church; they had a son before divorcing in 1936. Clinch joined the *Daily Telegraph and Daily News* (Sydney) as a news and court reporter, and rose to become chief sub-editor and news editor (1938-41). As a correspondent for the *Telegraph* he returned to his birthplace in 1941. He married Melbourne-born Norah

Marie McCarthy on 4 October 1944 at St Patrick's Catholic Church, New York, but they soon separated.

When he returned to Sydney after World War II, Clinch became editor (1947-53) of the *Sunday Sun*. In 1953 he was appointed executive editor of the *Sun*. During the next few years circulation figures of the paper overtook those of its competitor, the *Daily Mirror*. After years of rivalry between the two newspapers, in 1959 Clinch was seconded as editor-in-chief of the *Daily Mirror* and the *Sunday Mirror* by the new owner, O'Connell Pty Ltd, which was financially backed by John Fairfax & Sons [qq.v.4,8,q.v.] Pty Ltd. When Mirror Newspapers Ltd was sold in 1960, Clinch returned to New York as editor and manager of Fairfax's office. In 1961 he was recalled to Sydney as executive editor of the *Sun*, where he tried to keep circulation buoyant against competition from the *Mirror* and the new medium, television. He used sensational headlines and front-page stories to attract attention but had a more balanced approach with editorials and features.

Throughout his career, Clinch rejected management interference in editorial policy. This approach led to several arguments with Fairfax management, one in 1962 over a headline relating to the policy of the United States of America on Netherlands New Guinea. In 1965 he asked unsuccessfully for an increase in his salary of £5000. His services as editor were terminated by the Fairfax company in mid-1965 and he left in 1966. He was general manager of Infoplan Pty Ltd (1967-69) and a consultant with the public relations firm William Love & Co. Pty Ltd for some years but his health was failing and his memory loss worried his family. After he and Norah were divorced in 1971, on 18 June he married at the registrar-general's office, Sydney, Eena Dale (Sally) Baker, née Young (a journalist and former wife of Sidney Baker [q.v.13]), with whom he had lived since the early 1950s.

Stocky and short, with curly hair which turned white in middle age, Clinch walked with a slight swagger and puffed on a pipe or Senorita cigar. He liked to boast that he could jump from his bed straight into his shoes. Energetic, enterprising and competitive as a journalist and editor, his nicknames were 'Little White God' and 'Little Caesar'. His lifelong recreations were yachting and boat-building. Survived by his wife and the son of his first marriage, he died on 27 August 1984 at Ashfield and was cremated.

G. Souter, *Company of Heralds* (1981); *Daily Mirror* (Sydney), 23 Jan 1959, p 3; *Sun* (Sydney), 27 Aug 1984, p 3; *Journalist* (Sydney), Oct 1984, p 8; Clinch personal file (John Fairfax Holdings Ltd archives, Sydney); private information.

VALERIE LAWSON

CLUFF, FLORENCE AMY (1902-1990), trade unionist, communist and pensioner activist, was born on 4 November 1902 at Chillagoe, Queensland, fifth of nine children of Frederick William Davis, an English-born railway carpenter, and his Victorian-born wife Florence Emma, née Nightingale. Flo attended primary schools at Chillagoe and Einasleigh, and Cairns District High School from 1917, returning home to Einasleigh in 1919 as a pupil-teacher. After her father's death in a railway bridge accident in 1921, she left teaching to look after her mother and brothers, but within months her mother also died. Unable to return to teaching, she married Robert Dawson Kershaw, a labourer, on 29 November 1921 with Anglican rites at Einasleigh. In 1931 she went to Brisbane, where she worked in hotels to support herself and her two youngest brothers; in 1932 she and Kershaw divorced.

Moving to Sydney in 1935, Flo worked at a Pitt Street café, sometimes for thirteen or fourteen hours a day, for a weekly wage of about £2. During the Depression union membership had dropped dramatically, award conditions were seldom observed, and activists were dismissed. At meetings of the Hotel, Club, Restaurant, Caterers, Tea Rooms & Boarding House Employees' Union of New South Wales, she met the communists Topsy Small and Vic Workman. Flo, 'a friendly pretty woman with a gentle air who, in the past had been more interested in dancing than in union affairs', returned to part-time work after the birth of her daughter and, in February 1937, joined the Communist Party of Australia. On 29 November 1940 at the registrar general's office, Sydney, she married Geoffrey Davis, soldier, former waiter and father of her child. They later divorced.

In 1940 Flo Davis was elected to the HCRU executive. She then became an organiser, assistant secretary (1941) and secretary (1945). One of the first women elected as secretary of a union, through her leadership she radicalised the HCRU. Equal pay was achieved for women cooks in the larger hotels; later the five-day working week in the catering industry, sick leave, and weekend penalty rates for club workers were won. The HCRU endorsed the 1946 boycott of Dutch ships during the Indonesian independence struggle; supported the 1949 miners' strike; worked with other left-wing unions in 1948 to fund a full-time country organiser; protested against encroachment on Aboriginal land for nuclear testing at Maralinga, South Australia; opposed the Menzies [q.v.15] government's Communist Party dissolution bill (1950) and the Korean War; and helped establish the New South Wales Peace Council in 1949. Davis stood unsuccessfully for the Senate on the Communist Party ticket in 1955 and 1958. Following absorption of the HCRU into the Federated Liquor & Allied Industries Employees' Union of Australia, New South Wales branch, in 1961, she was assistant secretary until 1968. On her retirement she was named Woman of the Year by the Australian International Women's Day Committee.

A delegate to the State Labor Council and the Australian Council of Trade Unions for over thirty years, Davis was also prominent in the campaign for equal pay for women. She represented the HCRU on the Council of Action for Equal Pay which Muriel Heagney [q.v.9] had helped to establish in 1937. Davis became the council's assistant-secretary and also served on the Labor Council equal pay committee established in 1941. As vice-president of the New South Wales section of the Union of Australian Women, she participated in a delegation attending a Women's International Democratic Federation congress in Denmark in 1953, returning through the Soviet Union and then China, where she spent a month as a guest of the Chinese women's movement.

Flo Davis married Eric James Richard Cluff, a retired cleaner, on 9 October 1975 at the registrar general's office, Sydney. After travelling around Australia, they joined the Petersham group of the Combined Pensioners' Association (of New South Wales). Mrs Cluff enjoyed the social activities, but her skills were again in demand: in 1979 she became assistant-secretary and in 1980 secretary of the State branch. She worked long days, lobbying State and Federal governments for better pensions, health and welfare services, utility rebates and transport concessions. In 1983 she led the campaign against the assets test on pensions.

Mrs Cluff was awarded the OAM in 1984. After a lifetime working for social justice, she resigned as secretary of the Combined Pensioners' Association in 1988. Survived by her husband and her daughter, she died on 20 September 1990 at Kogarah and was buried in the independent section of Rookwood cemetery.

A. Johnson, *Bread & Roses* (1990); *Sun-Herald* (Sydney), 17 Mar 1968, p 115; *Sixty Years of Struggle*, vol 1, 1980, p 35; *Pensioners Voice*, Nov-Dec 1982, p 1, Oct 1990, p 2; *SMH*, 30 Sept 1983, p 3, 16 Mar 1985, p 3, 22 Sept 1990, p 6; *Tribune*, 3 Oct 1990, p 11; R. Raxworthy, interview with F. Cluff (ts, 1985, NLA).   DANNY BLACKMAN

COBLEY, JOHN FREDERICK CLAIR CAMPHIN (1914-1989), physician and historian, was born on 3 August 1914 at Newcastle, New South Wales, only child of Joseph Will Camphin Cobley, clerk, and his wife Ada Craig (Creagh), née Robertson, both born in New South Wales. He attended Abermain Public and Katoomba Intermediate High schools and won a scholarship to the University of

Sydney (MB, BS, 1937). After travelling to England as a ship's surgeon, in 1938 he obtained a diploma in anaesthetics issued jointly by the Royal College of Physicians, London, and the Royal College of Surgeons of England. He also qualified as a member (1939) of the RCP.

Back in Sydney he became a tutor in medicine at St Paul's College, University of Sydney, and practised as a physician at Sydney Hospital and privately in Macquarie Street. Commissioned on 1 July 1940 as a captain, Australian Army Medical Corps, Australian Imperial Force, he served in the Greek campaign (1941) with the 2/3rd Casualty Clearing Station, and in the occupation of Syria (1941) and the battle of El Alamein, Egypt (1942), with the 2/8th Field Ambulance. He married Margaret Sanbrook, a member of the Australian Women's Army Service, on 9 March 1943 at St Paul's College, Sydney, with Anglican rites. In 1943-45 he was in New Guinea as a major with the 111th CCS and during this period was mentioned in despatches, probably for his work on scrub typhus. He returned to Sydney, where he was demobilised in February 1946. In 1948-54 and 1958-60 he was active in the Citizen Military Forces, rising to lieutenant colonel (1951).

Cobley's chief interest was diabetes: he held appointments at the Royal Hospital for Women, the diabetic clinic at Royal Prince Alfred Hospital and the Blue Mountains District Anzac Memorial Hospital. A member (1940) and fellow (1978) of the Royal Australasian College of Physicians, he was also a councillor (1957-60) of the State branch of the British Medical Association. For many years he was an accredited medical examiner of airline pilots and, in 1966-68, as 'Dr John', he appeared on the television program 'Casebook' on Channel 7 in Sydney.

Convivial and hospitable, Cobley was an avid reader and book collector, with interests ranging from poetry to Antarctica. He became a member of the Royal Australian Historical Society (1961) and the Society of Australian Genealogists (1963). Between 1962 and 1986, with the assistance of his wife, he published a series entitled *Sydney Cove*. The five volumes recorded daily events in the settlement from 1788 to 1800, in the words of contemporary writers. He also produced *The Convicts 1788-1792* (1964), *The Crimes of the First Fleet Convicts* (1970) and *The Crimes of the Lady Juliana Convicts, 1790* (1989). The noted medical historian Dr Bryan Gandevia believed that Cobley's works introduced 'a new dimension and new techniques to Australian historiography'. Through his publications he played an important role in popularising Australian history. Survived by his wife and their three daughters, he died on 4 January 1989 at Wahroonga and was cremated.

Roll of the Royal Australasian College of Physicians, vol 2 (1994); *SMH*, 6 Jan 1989, p 5; B883, item NX35128 (NAA); private information.

K. A. JOHNSON

COCHRANE, DONALD (1917-1983), economist and university administrator, was born on 27 May 1917 at East Malvern, Melbourne, youngest of three sons of Victorian-born parents Arthur Cochrane, manager, and his wife Elsie May, née Turvey. Leaving Melbourne High School in 1933, Don worked as a clerk for Goldsbrough Mort [qq.v.4,5] & Co. Ltd and studied accounting part time. In 1939-42 he was a student at the University of Melbourne (B.Com., 1945). Enlisting in the Royal Australian Air Force on 14 August 1942, he qualified as a navigator, flew with No.36 Squadron and No.107 Squadron, and rose to flight lieutenant, before being demobilised in Melbourne on 23 September 1945. That year he was appointed to a lectureship in economics at the university.

On 28 November 1946 at Scots Church, Melbourne, Cochrane married with Presbyterian forms Margaret Jean Schofield, a well-known pianist and a divorcee. In 1947 he travelled to England and entered Clare College, Cambridge (Ph.D., 1949), where he completed his doctorate in minimum time under (Sir) Richard Stone. With Guy Orcutt, he wrote two path-breaking papers in econometrics, published in the *Journal of the American Statistical Association* (1949); the 'Cochrane-Orcutt transformation' remains a standard reference.

Although Cochrane returned to the University of Melbourne in 1949 as a senior lecturer in mathematical economics, he began to move away from the technical side of the discipline. An invitation from the United Nations department of economic affairs gave him an opportunity to spend twelve months (1951-52) in New York, working in the field of social accounting. In 1955 he was appointed to the Sidney Myer [q.v.10] chair of commerce at the University of Melbourne. Interested in applied economics, he continued the practice of his predecessors, (Sir) Douglas Copland and Gordon Wood [qq.v.13,16], of maintaining strong links with business and government. He established a summer school of business administration for senior executives, a venture other Australian universities later emulated. His was a commanding presence in the lecture theatre, especially in front of large classes of first-year undergraduates; wearing his gown, he would sweep in, position his notes at the rostrum, quickly brush back his forelock, and begin.

Cochrane found that the departmental structure at Melbourne limited his scope for integrated teaching and research. In 1961 he moved to Monash University as professor of economics and foundation dean of the faculty of economics and politics. His vision for the Monash faculty was that it should have a single department of economics that trained professional economists; accounting and the more commercial subjects were to play a relatively subservient role. Reflecting his Cambridge experience, he required students in economics to take subjects taught by the faculty's department of politics.

The faculty's structure gave way over time in response to student demands to study accounting and the full range of business subjects. In 1974 Cochrane reluctantly oversaw the splitting of economics into five smaller departments. The economics department had quickly become equal to the best in Australia and was well known internationally. As dean, according to Professor Joe Isaac, on the big issues he 'knew what he wanted and he pursued it skilfully', but he delegated much responsibility to the professors he had appointed. His public demeanour was 'composed, matter-of-fact'; his capacity for kindness and compassion was revealed only to his closest friends. The vice-chancellor Sir Louis Matheson described him as a 'persuasive speaker on the Professorial Board, always well-informed and cogent in argument'.

In 1961 Cochrane had been appointed a commissioner of the State Savings (State) Bank of Victoria; he was to serve as its chairman in 1971 and 1974-83. He became deputy-chairman of the associated merchant bank Tricontinental Holdings Ltd in 1978. He was a member of the Commonwealth Bureau of Roads (1966-74), the Defence Business Board (1968-76) and the Defence Industry Committee (1977-79). Federal and State governments selected him to inquire into such diverse matters as wool sales at Portland, Victoria (1962), rural wages in the Territory of Papua and New Guinea (1970), and the cost of electricity supplied to smelters owned by Alcoa of Australia Ltd in Victoria (1981). In 1974 he chaired the committee of inquiry into labour market training which led to the establishment of the National Employment and Training Scheme. He headed the Australian Trade Union Training Authority from 1978.

Cochrane was appointed CBE in 1975. His professional honours included a fellowship (1974) of the Academy of the Social Sciences in Australia and the first honorary doctorate of economics (1982) awarded by Monash University. He was a golfer and a member of the Melbourne Club. The Cochranes lived at Kew and in 1973 bought a cattle farm at Tanjil South as a hobby and holiday retreat. Retiring in 1981 because of illness, he died of cancer on 31 March 1983 at Richmond and was cremated. His wife and their son and daughter

survived him. Monash University holds a portrait of Cochrane by Clifton Pugh [q.v.].

'Preface', in M. L. King and D. E. A. Giles (eds), *Specification Analysis in the Linear Model* (1987); *Herald* (Melbourne), 27 Dec 1973, p 9, 31 Mar 1983, p 9; R. L. Martin, citation for D. Cochrane's honorary doctorate of economics, 1982, and L. Matheson, J. Isaac and J. A. Hancock, eulogies at Cochrane's memorial service, 1983 (Monash Univ Archives); Univ of Melbourne Archives; private information and personal knowledge.   ROSS WILLIAMS

COLAHAN, COLIN CUTHBERT ORR (1897-1987), painter and sculptor, was born on 12 February 1897 at Woodend, Victoria, fifth of six children of John Joseph Aloysius Colahan (1836-1918), an Irish-born, retired surgeon major general in the British Army, and his wife Eliza Newton, née Orr (1861-1899), who was born in Australia. Colin attended Xavier College, Melbourne, and contributed humorous cartoons to the *Xaverian* and *Bulletin* magazines. In 1916 he enrolled in medicine at the University of Melbourne but he left next year to study painting and drawing at the National Gallery schools. He soon moved on to Max Meldrum's [q.v.10] school, adopting his teacher's practice of tonal realism, and editing *Max Meldrum, His Art and Views* (c.1919), to promote the latter's theories. Colahan's work was first shown publicly as part of an exhibition by 'Meldrumites' at the Athenaeum Gallery in 1919.

On 19 August 1921 in the office of the registrar of marriages, Melbourne, Colahan married Violet Winifred Lester; they were to have a son, David (d.1945), before being divorced in 1931. In 1921-27 the couple lived and travelled in England, France and Spain. Colahan studied the classical masters and developed his technique, showing his work in London and Paris. He returned to Melbourne, where his reputation grew and his work matured. His subjects included landscapes, streetscapes, portraits and nude studies, and his exhibitions generated favourable reviews and good sales. Quick, skilful and full of Irish wit and charm, physically he was small and attractive to women. One of these was Mireille Wilkinson, the French wife of an Australian economist, Launcelot Wilkinson; she and Colahan had two sons. In 1931 Colahan was shaken by the brutal murder of another of his lovers, the model Mary ('Mollie') Dean, and further distressed by the inquest and publicity that followed.

In 1935 Colahan suddenly departed for England, where he built a reputation as a portrait painter. His more notable subjects included George Bernard Shaw, Charmian Clift [q.v.13] and Sir Malcolm Sargent. At the register office, London, on 21 November 1939 he married 23-year-old Ursula Nora Winifred Marx. They had two daughters and lived in the White House, Tite Street, Chelsea, formerly owned by James McNeill Whistler. The Australian War Memorial, Canberra, appointed Colahan an official war artist in 1942 and directed him to cover the activities of his country's armed services, especially the Royal Australian Air Force, in Britain and Europe. This commission (terminated in 1945) resulted in some of his best paintings, such as 'Ballet of Wind and Rain' and 'Waterloo Station'; these two and eighty-eight more of his works are held by the AWM. He became the first president of the Australian Artists' Association, London, in 1952.

Moving to Italy in 1958, Colahan built a house at Mortola Superiore, near Ventimiglia. He continued to paint portraits and landscapes, but much of this work is inferior. He was divorced from Ursula in 1967. On 29 September that year at the British Consulate, Nice, France, he married Monique Eliza Bornoff, née Hazelden, a 52-year-old divorcee. Around this time he turned to sculpture, producing over thirty works, including the 'Sircna' fountain for the Italian town of Bordighera, and a head of Victor Smorgon, bought by the National Gallery of Victoria. His work is represented in the State galleries of Melbourne, Adelaide and Brisbane. Colahan died on 6 June 1987 at Ventimiglia and was buried locally. His wife and four of his five children survived him.

G. Kinnane, *Colin Colahan* (1996) and for sources; file 205/002/030, parts A1, A2 and B, file 89/0857, file 97/0347 (AWM); private information.

GARRY KINNANE

COLES, SIR ARTHUR WILLIAM (1892-1982), businessman, politician and philanthropist, SIR KENNETH FRANK (1896-1985), businessman and philanthropist, and SIR EDGAR BARTON (1899-1981), businessman and philanthropist, were the sixth, eighth and tenth children of Victorian-born parents George Coles, storekeeper, and his first wife Elizabeth Mary, née Scouler (Scoular); their half-brother SIR NORMAN CAMERON (1907-1989), businessman and philanthropist, was the only son of Coles and his second wife Ann Cameron, née Topp, also born in Victoria.

Arthur was born on 6 August 1892 at Newtown, Geelong, Victoria, and educated at a local state school and Geelong College. He then worked in branches of the chain of general stores that his father had established across rural Victoria until, in 1909, he joined the National Bank of Australasia in Melbourne as a clerk. In 1912 he resigned to assist as storeman in another of his father's operations at Wilmot, Tasmania. In April 1914, following the return of his eldest brother, (Sir) George James Coles [q.v.13], from a tour of the United States of America (during which he had investigated F. W. Woolworth's 'five and dime' stores), the brothers Arthur, George and Jim together opened a store in Smith Street, Collingwood, under the slogan 'nothing over 1/-'; this venture marked the beginning of a revolution in Australian retailing.

Arthur enlisted in the Australian Imperial Force on 17 August 1914 and landed on Gallipoli with the 6th Battalion on 25 April 1915. He was wounded in action in May and, again, in May 1916 while serving on the Western Front. Commissioned and posted to the 8th Battalion in August, he suffered a third wound later that month and was repatriated in November. Following the termination of his AIF appointment on 20 December 1917, he returned to the Smith Street store, but with George's discharge in 1918 the two brothers decided to begin a new partnership. On 20 June 1919 they opened another store in Smith Street, now boasting 'nothing over 2/-' (commercial pressures soon pushed the limit to 2/6d, achieved sometimes by pricing shoes per foot, and pyjamas by tops and bottoms). On 27 September 1919 at the Gardenvale Presbyterian Church, Arthur married Lilian Florence Knight, a stenographer.

With their business identities increasingly conveyed by their initials, in 1921 the brothers began trading as G. J. Coles & Co. Pty Ltd with G. J. as managing director and A. W. as director. Kenneth—K. F.—soon joined them, also as a director. In 1922 A. W. became manager of store 'Number 2' in Chapel Street, Prahran. The following year, returning from a business tour of the USA, he argued that a greater variety in merchandise would attract more diverse patronage. From 1928 Coles 'Number 12' in Bourke Street demonstrated this initiative, gaining fame for its art deco detailing and in-store cafeteria. In that year A. W. went to Sydney to manage store Number 10.

Seeking further capital, the brothers floated the firm as a public company in 1927, A. W. becoming managing director, K. F. and Edgar Coles (E. B.) directors, and Norman (N. C.) its secretary. Its shares, released at £1, quickly rose by 220 per cent. Yet expansion fostered strain between the brothers, particularly as A. W. increasingly challenged G. J.'s caution as chairman of the board. G. J. objected to the lack of disclosure to shareholders regarding bonuses and share-issues granted to directors through an initiative introduced by A. W. In August 1936, A. W. engineered his own appointment as chairman. Negotiations over the following weeks, including a petition from managers and staff, saw G. J. restored to the chair and A. W. named managing director, a position he held until 1944. After the resolution of the 'big trouble', as it became known, G. J. made notes about each of his brothers: A. W., he recorded, was a 'good organiser, hard worker, quick thinker & speaker and honest' but 'conceited, over ambitious, dictatorial, difficult to work with and bears a grudge'.

By the early 1930s A. W.'s interests extended beyond the family firm, reflecting a commitment to public service: 'to give some return'. In 1930 he joined the council (chairman, 1939-69) of Geelong College, supporting the ambition of its headmaster, (Sir) Frank Rolland [q.v.11], for new buildings to match his educational ideals (the school's new science block was later to be named in Arthur's honour). From 1938 Arthur was a trustee (chairman 1952-78) of the Northcote [q.v.11] Trust's Children's Emigration Fund, which administered a farm school for British children at Bacchus Marsh. In August 1934 he was elected for Latrobe Ward to the Melbourne City Council. Impressing fellow councillors with his business acumen, A. W. was elected lord mayor in 1938, and re-elected unopposed in 1939 and 1940. He promised a 'healthy, well-built city' with efficient administration and priorities of slum clearance and child welfare.

Coles's mayoralty was marked by major appeals to raise funds to support the victims of devastating Victorian bushfires in January 1939 and, after the outbreak of World War II, to aid those affected by the bombing of British cities. Other initiatives ranged from hosting a Christmas party for over 1500 children of unemployed workers in 1938 to modernising the town hall's offices and processes. As lady mayoress, Lilian Coles supported the free kindergarten movement, helped to form the National Women's Register to co-ordinate women's skills in wartime, and worked to establish the Australian Comforts Fund.

During 1940 Coles became increasingly disturbed by Australia's 'apathetic' response to the war. On 24 September he was elected to the House of Representatives as the Independent member for Henty (resigning as mayor although remaining a councillor). He undertook to work towards a 'government of all parties', the nationalisation of resources, and the widening of social services (including national insurance, child endowment and public housing provision). In February 1941 he funded his own 'unofficial mission' to the USA and Britain to survey shipping difficulties and air-raid precautions. Returning in April, he presented a 23-point plan of action to (Sir) Arthur Fadden [q.v.14], the acting prime minister, centring on the expansion of central government powers over taxation, trade and employment. When (Sir) Robert Menzies [q.v.15] returned from London in May, also emphasising the need for national unity, Coles committed his support to the United Australia Party. This trust was soon eroded by the circumstances of Menzies' resignation—or 'lynching', as Coles saw it—as prime minister. On 3 October Coles resigned from the UAP and voted against the Fadden government with another Independent, Alexander Wilson [q.v.16], with whom he shared the balance of power.

On taking office, John Curtin's [q.v.13] Australian Labor Party recognised Coles's strength and experience. He was appointed to the Commonwealth War Workers' Housing Trust (1941-45), the War Damage Commission (chairman, 1942-48) and the Commonwealth Rationing Commission (chairman, 1942-50). Beginning work in the Coles boardroom, the CRC was charged with organising a rationing schedule for six million Australians, to be implemented in six weeks. In this massive task, as H. C. Coombs, director of rationing, recalled, A. W.'s retailing experience was directly relevant.

In January 1946, having decided not to contest another election, Coles acceded to a request from the treasurer, Ben Chifley [q.v.13], with whom he had a close working relationship, that he become the first chairman of the Australian National Airlines Commission. At the same time he was named chairman of British Commonwealth Pacific Airlines. As an advocate of free enterprise, in 1945 he had opposed the Chifley government's commitment to providing a nationalised airline service. Yet his appointment to ANAC was to lead to an unprecedented venture in building a commercially competitive and accountable government-owned business. Within a year, he and a small team of executives had purchased and converted wartime aircraft, selected new aircraft, built hangars, established a commercial pilots' training scheme and formed a network of offices throughout the country. By 1949 Trans-Australia Airlines' fleet had grown to thirty-five, including the only pressurised aircraft on interstate routes. Resigning in April 1950, amid rumours of political pressure from the new Menzies government, Coles claimed, instead, simply that his job was done. He had donated his chairman's salary to Geelong College.

In 1952 Coles was appointed chairman of the finance and organising committee for the 1956 Melbourne Olympic Games. Warned of the stresses of the job, he replied, 'I don't get ulcers, I give them'. In May 1953, however, he resigned in protest at the Victorian government's reneging on promises he had personally conveyed to international Olympic officials. By contrast, his appointment (1956-65) to the executive of the Commonwealth Scientific Industrial and Research Organization (member of advisory council 1965-70) was a more harmonious experience, reflecting his interest in the application of science in the cause of public service. In 1949 he was a foundation member of the Commonwealth Immigration Planning Council.

Described as 'tall, slim and fair with the bullet head and the rapid, incisive speech of the man of action', Coles was regarded as a 'human dynamo'. He was a gregarious man, dogged in his principles, stern, impatient, even ruthless in business, but warm and affectionate in family and personal contexts. His interests included music (he was a keen chorister), golf, tennis and photography. He was an active Presbyterian, in Toorak where he worshipped, as a member of the board of management (1933-50) and Kirk Session (1954-82), and on the trusts corporation of the Church in Victoria (1951-76). Knighted in 1960, Sir Arthur died on 23 June 1982 at Kew and was cremated; his wife (d.1985) and their three daughters and two of their three sons survived him. A portrait of A. W.—as of K. F., E. B. and N. C.—was painted by (Sir) William Dargie; all four paintings are held by the National Portrait Gallery, Canberra.

All of the Coles brothers, as Kenneth Frank Coles remarked in 1960, were 'bred behind a counter'. Frank was born on 19 April 1896 at St James, Victoria, where his father had bought a shop in 1892. Gaining his first business experience in the Wilmot store, he studied accountancy and book-keeping at night. Having been declared unfit for military service, he worked in New Zealand (1918-19) before returning to join G. J. Coles & Co. as a storeman. His apprenticeship was short. He was appointed a director (1921-76) and through the early 1920s managed stores at Prahran and Collingwood. On 22 July 1925 at All Saints' Church of England, St Kilda, he married Marjorie Evelyn Tolley, a stenographer. In 1926 they sailed for London, where he became the European buyer in the new Coles office at Cheapside. Returning in June 1928, he ran the Melbourne office before becoming general manager (1932) and then State director (1933) in New South Wales. During World War II he chaired the Lord Mayor of Sydney's Appeal that organised food for Britain.

K. F. was not as ambitious as his brothers. He provided a moderating influence during the 'big trouble', being (in G. J.'s assessment) 'addicted to compromise'. None the less, he rose to deputy-chairman (1946-56) and chairman (1956-63) of the company. His business skills were recognised in a wide range of corporate appointments: board member of the Equitable Life & General Insurance Co. Ltd, the Permanent Trustee Co. of New South Wales, and the Australian Oil & Gas Corp. Ltd; deputy-chairman of Rothmans of Pall Mall (Australia) Ltd (1961-69); and chairman of Beard, Watson & Co. Ltd (1958-59) and Bankers & Traders Insurance Co. Ltd (1963-71). He was president (1955-57) of the Associated Chamber of Manufacturers and in 1963 was appointed to the Decimal Currency Board, which co-ordinated Australia's transition to a new currency three years later.

From 1939 to 1969 Frank was a director of the New South Wales Society for Crippled Children. He served as chairman of its welfare committee and board before succeeding Sir Henry Braddon [q.v.7] as president (1947-69) during a period of remarkable expansion in the society's services. He was world president (1957-60) of the International Society for the Rehabilitation of the Disabled and co-author with James Donaldson of a history of the society (1976). Knighted in 1957, Sir Kenneth, as he chose to be styled, was also awarded— by King Paul of Greece—the Gold Cross of the Order of the Phoenix (1962). He served on the board of the Sydney Hospital (1960-68) and as president of Sydney Rotary Club (1944-45).

Of slight build but with a quick sense of humour, K. F. enjoyed golf, tennis and swimming. He took classes in public speaking to overcome a natural shyness, and conveyed (and sought) integrity in business and social dealings. Survived by his wife and their two daughters and a son, he died on 2 April 1985 in Sydney Hospital and was cremated.

Edgar Barton Coles was born on 3 June 1899 at St James. Educated there and at Wilmot, he completed his secondary education at Scotch College, Launceston, where he was dux (1915). In 1916 he joined the Bank of New South Wales, Hobart, and (after a transfer to Albury, New South Wales) began studying accountancy by correspondence and teaching himself typing and shorthand. He started work at the family's Smith Street store in 1919 and was soon managing the office. He formed the partnership into a proprietary company and in 1921-34 served as its secretary. In 1925 it was his turn to tour the USA, and he returned advocating streamlined procedures in management. At St Andrew's Cathedral, Sydney, on 15 October 1927, E. B. married with Anglican rites Mabel Irene Christian, a typist.

With the formation of the public company in 1927, E. B. was appointed a director (assistant managing director, 1938). In 1940 E. B. joined A. W. as joint managing director, and from 1944 he was sole managing director, taking charge of an expanding chain of stores represented in all States of Australia. After World War II he pursued a vigorous take-over program, targeting retailers such as Selfridges (New South Wales) in 1950, F. & G. Stores (Victoria and southern New South Wales) in 1951 and Mantons (Melbourne) in 1955, and next year merging with Penneys in Queensland and northern New South Wales.

Further travel to the USA (1955, 1957) convinced E. B. that the future of the company lay in suburban food retailing; accordingly, he acquired the supermarket chains of S. E. Dickens (Victoria), Beilby's (South Australia) and Matthews Thompson (New South Wales). The first full-scale Coles supermarket opened in North Balwyn, Melbourne, in 1959 and by 1962 E. B. had captured popular enthusiasm for the 'space race' by naming these stores 'New World' and decorating them with model rockets. He also seized the opportunities of television advertising, in 1960 launching the 'Coles £3,000 Question' (later $6000) quiz show on Channel 7. From 1961 his title was controlling managing director. At his retirement in 1967 he could survey 570 stores with annual sales of $280 million and net profit of $8.9 million; he could also envisage the complete transformation of food retailing to self-service.

E. B., six feet (183 cm) tall, was a 'big man' in every sense, feared by many of his staff. He mellowed in later life and, living at Mount Eliza, joined the Mornington Baptist Church following a Billy Graham crusade. Throughout his business career his restless drive had expressed itself in civic and charitable work through his service as a Kew city councillor (1936-38), as chairman (1958-62) of the Lord Mayor's Fund appeal committee and numerous other charitable appeals, as councillor (1956-76) and life councillor (1976-81) of the Royal Agricultural Society of Victoria and as a director (1956-60) of the Melbourne Moomba Festival. He was also president of the Retail Traders Association of Victoria (1946-48, 1951-54) and the Australian Council of Retailers (1952-54) and a leading member of several amateur sporting associations. E. B. was knighted in 1959. His wife was appointed CBE (1965) and DBE (1971) for her community service, especially to the Royal Women's Hospital (president, 1968-72).

An avid sportsman (Australian 'B' Grade singles tennis champion in 1922 and a champion golfer at the Commonwealth Golf Club in 1932), Sir Edgar also enjoyed contract bridge and 16-mm cinematography. Survived by his wife (d.1993) and their two daughters and son, he died on 19 February 1981 at Mornington and was cremated. In addition to the portrait by Dargie, another—by Paul Fitzgerald—is held by the family.

Inevitably seen as the 'youngster', Norman Cameron Coles was born on 17 September 1907 at St James and educated at Launceston Grammar School, Tasmania, and Trinity Grammar School, Kew, Melbourne. Joining G. J. Coles & Co. as a storeman at Smith Street in 1924, he transferred to the accounting area of head office in 1926. He became an associate (1933), member (1953) and fellow (1983) of the Federal Institute of Accountants.

Having gained first place in the Chartered Institute of Secretaries' Examination in 1931, he was elected to the institute's council in 1938.

On 7 April 1932 at St John's Church of England, Toorak, Norman married Dorothy Verna Deague and was then transferred to Coles's first Queensland store in Brisbane. His overseas tour focused on the investigation of accounting procedures. While serving as a lieutenant in the Militia (1942-43) and the Australian Imperial Force (1943-44), he performed administrative duties in Melbourne. He returned to his post of company secretary (1934-50) and joined the board (1949). Over the following years, he concentrated on the financial and legal operations of the company as director of personnel (1950), superannuation and housing (1958), and finance (1963). Made deputy-chairman in 1961, he became managing director in 1967 and succeeded E. B. as chairman in 1968. His retirement from that position on 16 November 1979 saw the end of the brothers' leadership of the company.

Norman's major contribution to the empire was Coles's joint venture with S. S. Kresge Co. Ltd in 1968 to introduce K mart discount stores in Australia. The first opened in Burwood, Melbourne, in 1969; by 1978 K-Mart (Australia) Ltd had become a wholly owned subsidiary of Coles. In 1971 N. C. oversaw the introduction of a store-wide discount policy into New World supermarkets, marking the beginning of competitive price matching in supermarkets. Under his guidance, in 1975 Coles became the first Australian retailer to achieve sales exceeding $1 billion in a twelve month period.

An imposing figure of 6 ft 2 ins (188 cm) with a bellowing voice, but known for his kindness, courtesy and humanity, Norman described himself and his four brothers as 'just ordinary shopkeepers'. Even so, in May 1973 he joined the Whitlam government's first trade mission to China. Knighted in 1977, Sir Norman was a member of the Retail Traders Association of Victoria, the Australian Retailers' Association, the finance committee of the Victorian Liberal Party, and the board of the Multiple Sclerosis Society (1977-83). He enjoyed golf, music and gardening and, like all his brothers, was a devoted family man. Survived by his wife and their son and daughter, he died on 24 November 1989 at Windsor, Melbourne, and was cremated. At his death, G. J. Coles & Co. was the world's eleventh largest retailing network.

W. Ives, *Arthur William Coles* (1982); J. McLaughlin, *Nothing over Half a Crown* (1991); B. Kingston, *Basket, Bag and Trolley* (1994); J. Gunn, *Contested Skies* (1999); *Age* (Melbourne), 27 Aug 1936, p 12, 25 Jan 1968, p 13; *Herald* (Melbourne), 11 Oct 1938, p 6, 18 Sept 1940, p 5; *Sun News-Pictorial*

(Melbourne), 30 Aug 1939, p 13; *Argus* (Melbourne), 19 Apr 1941, p 11; *People* (Melbourne), 16 Aug 1950, p 33, 1 July 1953, p 34; *Sunday Telegraph* (Sydney), 7 Aug 1960, p 75; *Australian*, 25-26 Nov 1989, p 3; S. Barber, Struggle for Supremacy (ms, 1996, Coles Myer Ltd, Melbourne); M. Pratt, interview with A. W. Coles (ts, 1971, NLA); A. W. Coles papers (NLA).   STELLA M. BARBER

COLLINS, SIR JOHN AUGUSTINE (1899-1989), naval officer and diplomat, was born on 7 January 1899 at Deloraine, Tasmania, fourth son of Michael John Collins, a medical practitioner from Ireland, and his English wife Esther, née Copeland. C. Q. D. Collins [q.v.8] was his brother. Michael, who had spent many years as a merchant navy doctor, died seven months before John was born. Educated at Christian Brothers' College, East Melbourne, he entered the Royal Australian Naval College, Osborne House, Geelong, with the first intake in 1913. The college relocated to Jervis Bay, Federal Capital Territory, in 1915. Collins became a cadet captain, gained colours in Rugby and athletics, and graduated in 1916 with prizes for seamanship and engineering (theory) and 'maximum time gained', which accelerated his eventual promotion to lieutenant.

Appointed as a midshipman on 1 January 1917, Collins was sent to Britain for training with the Royal Navy. His first sea posting was to the battleship HMS *Canada*, a unit of the Grand Fleet. He was promoted to sublieutenant in September 1918 and, as World War I drew to a close, he joined the destroyer HMS *Spenser*, becoming her gun control officer. After serving in the destroyer HMAS *Stalwart* and rising to lieutenant in December 1919, he returned to Australia in 1921 to join the cruiser HMAS *Melbourne*.

In 1922 Collins went back to Britain to undertake the long gunnery course. He topped his class, winning the Commander Egerton prize, and completed the advanced course before coming home in 1925 to rejoin *Melbourne*, this time as her gunnery officer. *Melbourne* soon deployed to the Mediterranean Fleet as part of an exchange program with the RN. On his return to Australia, Collins was appointed naval liaison officer for the 1927 visit of the Duke and Duchess of York. He accompanied the royal party at the opening of Parliament House in Canberra and in their passage in the battle cruiser HMS *Renown* back to Britain.

Promoted to lieutenant commander in December 1927, Collins joined the new heavy cruiser HMAS *Australia*, which was fitting out at Clydebank, Scotland. After serving in her for two years as squadron gunnery officer, he

was placed in command of the destroyer leader HMAS *Anzac* in 1930. This appointment was a clear recognition of his potential for higher rank and the navy's desire to round out his professional development. At St Mark's Church of England, Darling Point, Sydney, on 3 June that year he married Phyllis Laishley McLachlan.

Collins was posted as first lieutenant of Flinders Naval Depot, Westernport, Victoria, in 1931. He attended the staff course at the RN College, Greenwich, England, in 1932 and was promoted to commander in June. In 1933 he joined the Admiralty's Plans Division, where he was responsible for Imperial port defences. While on leave at Portwrinkle, Cornwall, in 1934, he rescued a girl swept away by a rip. Phyllis assisted by manning an improvised lifeline. The Royal Humane Society, London, awarded Collins a testimonial on parchment for his actions.

In 1935 Collins was appointed executive officer of the new light cruiser HMAS *Sydney*. His commanding officer was the at times brilliant, but unpredictable Captain J. U. P. Fitzgerald, RN, who made Collins's duties even more of a challenge. *Sydney* was attached to the Mediterranean Fleet in response to the Abyssinian crisis and did not arrive in Australian waters until August 1936. Promoted to captain in December 1937, Collins became assistant-chief of Naval Staff and director of naval intelligence at Navy Office, Melbourne, in February 1938. He played an important staffing role in the procurement of much-needed anti-submarine escorts; the successful Bathurst-class corvettes were the result. Another pressing issue was the production of naval mobilisation plans and procedures.

The period at Navy Office and his earlier service in the Mediterranean prepared Collins well for his most memorable operational appointment, that of commanding officer of *Sydney*. He had a good grasp of the strategic environment and knew his superiors from Prime Minister (Sir) Robert Menzies [q.v.15] down. Collins assumed command in November 1939 and in May 1940 *Sydney* once again joined the Mediterranean Fleet, commanded by the redoubtable Admiral Sir Andrew (Viscount) Cunningham. Cunningham's leadership style was based on broad direction with the expectation that subordinates would use common sense and initiative to achieve the strategic aim. Captain Hec Waller [q.v.16] and the 10th ('Scrap-Iron') Destroyer Flotilla flourished under this approach. The less flamboyant but highly competent and astute Collins was to prosper equally.

In June-July 1940 *Sydney* took part in the bombardment of Bardia, Libya, sank the Italian destroyer *Espero* and fought in the battle of Calabria. On 18 July *Sydney*, with the destroyer

HMS *Havock*, conducted a sweep off the Cretan coast while at the same time providing support to four other British destroyers. Collins used the freedom provided by Cunningham to remain close to the smaller ships while they remained vulnerable to attack in the Aegean Sea. Next morning the destroyers encountered two Italian cruisers, the *Bartolomeo Colleoni* and the *Giovanni delle Bande Nere*. Collins decided to maintain radio silence while closing for battle. This tactic proved decisive. *Sydney*'s appearance caught everyone by surprise, including Cunningham, and in the ensuing engagement *Colleoni* was stopped and subsequently sunk by torpedoes from two destroyers. Outnumbered, *Bande Nere* escaped using her superior speed.

The battle of Cape Spada was the first substantial naval victory in the war against Italy. It catapulted Collins and the *Sydney* into the world's headlines. Appointed CB (1940), Collins became a national hero and was to wear that mantle for the remainder of his life. *Sydney* returned to her namesake port in February 1941 to a tumultuous welcome. Collins had only three months remaining in command, but in that time *Sydney* took the first naval member Admiral Sir Ragnar Colvin [q.v.8] to a conference in Singapore. There it was decided that Collins would be appointed assistant chief of staff to Vice Admiral Sir Geoffrey Layton, commander-in-chief, China (based in Singapore).

Collins took up his duties in Singapore in June 1941, accompanied by his wife and daughter. His immediate task was to plan for the employment of Allied air and naval forces. He established a good rapport with Layton and was disappointed when Admiral Sir Tom Phillips relieved him. On news of the sinking of the British capital ships *Prince of Wales* and *Repulse* and the death of Phillips in December, Collins had the presence of mind to rush to the departing *Dominion Monarch* to recall Layton to duty. So began a gruelling period for Collins. Having arranged for the evacuation of his family, in January 1942 he became commodore commanding China Force, which consisted of RN and RAN cruisers and destroyers based in Batavia (Jakarta). It was a significant command and Collins, who was made commodore, second class, was junior for the post.

Exercising his authority within the complex and unwieldy Australian-British-Dutch-American Command, Collins employed his forces escorting shipping to and from Singapore or assigned them to a Dutch-led striking force. After the surrender of Singapore and the Allied defeat in the battle of the Java Sea, it was clear to him that Batavia would fall. Collins organised evacuations of civilians and military personnel to Australia and India and embarked in one of the last departing ships.

He was mentioned in despatches and appointed a commander of the Netherlands' Order of Oranje-Nassau (1942).

On his arrival at Fremantle in March 1942, Collins became senior naval officer, Western Australia. During his tenure he was involved in the controversial decision to relieve his RANC classmate Acting Commander Paul Hirst of his command of the corvette HMAS *Toowoomba*. In Hirst's assessment the ship was not in a fit material state to take to sea. This view was not shared by his superiors including Collins. Late that year he proceeded to Britain to take command of the heavy cruiser HMAS *Shropshire*, commissioned in the RAN in April 1943. He took *Shropshire* to the Pacific theatre, where she joined other RAN ships attached to the United States Seventh Fleet.

In May 1944, on Prime Minister John Curtin's [q.v.13] insistence, Collins was appointed commodore, first class, and given command of the Australian Squadron. His force took part in the New Guinea and Philippines campaigns and on 21 October at Leyte Gulf his flagship, *Australia*, was struck on the bridge by a Japanese dive-bomber. Thirty men, including Captain Emile Dechaineux [q.v.13], were killed and Collins was seriously wounded. After convalescence he returned to command the squadron in July 1945 and was the RAN representative for the Japanese surrender on board USS *Missouri* in Tokyo Bay on 2 September. The US government appointed him an officer of the Legion of Merit (1946).

A rear admiral from January 1947, Collins attended the Imperial Defence College, London, that year. On 24 February 1948 he became the first Australian-trained officer to become chief of Naval Staff. He considered himself too young for the post, but Prime Minister Ben Chifley [q.v.13] was adamant that an Australian should lead the RAN. Promoted to vice admiral on 10 May 1950, Collins was to remain in the appointment for seven years. This long tenure was partly the result of the war losses suffered by his generation of officers.

Collins proved to be a shrewd and capable administrator who enjoyed the respect of the higher echelons of defence and government. These qualities were much needed as he reshaped the navy to meet changing strategic, social and fiscal circumstances. Collins oversaw the introduction of aircraft-carriers into the fleet as well as the involvement of the RAN in the Korean War and the Malayan Emergency. He instigated co-ordinated strategic and operational planning by the RAN, RN and Royal New Zealand Navy, and followed this success with similar arrangements with the US Navy. The resultant Radford-Collins Agreement (1951) came to symbolise the postwar primacy of the RAN's relationship with the USN. Appointed KBE in 1951, he relinquished his post on 23 February 1955 and retired from the navy on 16 March.

In 1956 Collins accepted the appointment of high commissioner to New Zealand. By virtue of his wife's New Zealand heritage and his frequent naval visits, he was well acquainted with his host nation. He proved to be a sensitive observer of national affairs and developed an unrestrained love for the natural beauty of New Zealand. Travelling throughout the country, he especially enjoyed angling. His travels were further extended when in 1957 he also became one of the Australian members of the South Pacific Commission. He retired in 1962. Settling at Rose Bay, Sydney, he kept in regular contact with his former naval comrades, particularly at the Royal Sydney Golf Club. He wrote his memoirs, *As Luck Would Have It* (1965), and further pursued his hobby of bookbinding. In 1965 Menzies offered him the governor-generalship, but he refused the honour.

From the outset of his brilliant naval career, it was clear that Collins was a clever and ambitious officer. The reports by his superiors on his performance are striking in their consistently glowing assessments. Most notable in their estimation were his professionalism, cool head and keen sense of judgment, attributes he was to demonstrate in the battle of Cape Spada. As a leader he was brave and forceful. Conservative by nature, he actively maintained the traditions of the service. His patience would occasionally be tested by poor performances from subordinates, which probably led to his being viewed with more respect than affection by ships' companies.

Collins was handsome and always well turned out. He was for a generation the public face of the Australian navy. Unlike most naval officers, he was very aware of the importance of the media and some of his peers accused him of self promotion. Whatever the case, his contribution to the positive public image of the navy was considerable. There are numerous portraits of Collins, including one by Dennis Adams (1945) and another by (Sir) William Dargie (1958) held by the Australian War Memorial, Canberra. Survived by his wife and their daughter, Sir John died on 3 September 1989 at St Luke's Hospital, Darlinghurst, and, following a funeral conducted with full naval honours and Anglican rites at St Andrew's Cathedral, Sydney, he was cremated. In 1993 Lady Collins launched HMAS *Collins*, the lead ship of a new class of submarines.

F. B. Eldridge, *A History of the Royal Australian Naval College* (1949); G. H. Gill, *Royal Australian Navy 1939-1942* (1957) and *1942-1945* (1968); D. Stevens (ed), *The Royal Australian Navy in World War II* (1996) and *The Royal Australian Navy* (2001); *People* (Sydney), 28 Mar 1951, p 22; *Salute*, July 1989, p 9; *Navy News*, 15-29 Sept 1989, p 4; *Naval Hist Review*, Dec 1989, p 9; A6769, item Collins J A, MP1185/8, items 2026/3/351 and 2026/7/457 (NAA); Collins papers (NLA); private information.

PETER D. JONES

COLLINS, PERCY ALFRED (1905-1990), sailor, was born on 22 January 1905 at Murwillumbah, New South Wales, fourth child of William Walter Thomas Collins, a Sydney-born hairdresser, and his wife Ellen Frances, née Foley, who came from Wales. The family settled at Stanmore, Sydney, and Percy attended Stanmore Public School and joined the choir of the local Anglican church. Moving to Rose Bay, he excelled at State amateur athletics while employed as a clerk. He married Mary Lilian Wilson on 24 May 1933 at St Paul's Catholic Church, Dulwich Hill.

On 10 August 1927 Collins had joined the Royal Australian Navy as a stoker, 2nd class. Before World War II he served in HMA ships *Canberra*, *Tattoo*, *Voyager*, *Waterhen*, *Swan*, *Yarra* and *Adelaide*. He was promoted to leading stoker in 1935 and petty officer in 1939. Invariably, he was known to his shipmates as 'Jumper'. In 1940 he was posted to Britain as a member of the commissioning crew of HMAS *Napier*, the first of the new 'N' class destroyers and the lead ship of the 7th Destroyer Flotilla.

Napier arrived in the Mediterranean in May 1941 and, during the battle of Crete that month, evacuated troops to Alexandria, Egypt. For his 'gallantry, fortitude and resolution' Collins was awarded the Distinguished Service Medal. Another sailor on board, Bernard McCarthy [q.v.15], also won the DSM. They were to become the only two RAN sailors to receive the DSM and Bar. Collins's citation noted that he 'was in charge of No.1 Boiler Room. A heavy blast was felt, half the lights went out [and] the boiler water level surged violently'. Collins 'took the necessary precautions, reduced sprayer output until the water level steadied and then worked up to nearly full power, taking the increased load caused by the failure of No.2 Boiler'. His 'steadiness contributed largely to the general effort of keeping the ship mobile'.

Promoted to temporary chief stoker on 1 January 1942, Collins served in HMAS *Maitland* from June 1943 to March 1944. He then joined the Bathurst-class corvette HMAS *Strahan*, which operated mainly in the South-West Pacific Area. In October 1945 he was awarded the Bar to his DSM for the 'courage, endurance and skill' he displayed while the *Strahan* performed escort duties 'under hazardous and trying conditions between the coast of Australia and the Philippines'. He was demobilised on 12 February 1946.

After the war Collins became a purchasing officer for a Sydney optical company and devoted his time to his family. He was a charming and courteous man who was modest about his wartime achievements. In retirement he lived at Lawson and later at Katoomba. His wife died in 1987. Survived by his two daughters and two sons, he died on 28 January 1990 at Leura and was buried in the Catholic lawn cemetery, Kemps Creek. His medals were presented (1991) to the Australian War Memorial, Canberra, which also holds his portrait (1956) by Alfred Cook. In 1995 he featured in a series of Australia Post stamps commemorating Australians whose war service was outstanding.

M. Fogarty, 'The Navy's "Other" Collins', *Defence Force Jnl*, no 63, 1987, p 48; A6770, item Collins P A (NAA); PR87/122 (AWM); private information.

MIKE FOGARTY

COLLINSON, LAURENCE HENRY (1925-1986), poet and playwright, was born on 7 September 1925 at Leeds, Yorkshire, England, only child of David Collinson, speciality salesman, and his wife Sara, née Lewis. The family moved to the antipodes when Laurie was 2, and endured 'frequent periods of comparative poverty' in Auckland, Melbourne and Sydney, before settling in Brisbane about 1937. As a student at Brisbane State High School Laurie helped to found *Barjai*, which between 1943 and 1947 developed from a crudely produced school magazine into a sophisticated national cultural organ for 'youth'. His contributions revealed a combative and melancholy personality. The music critic Charles Osborne, also a *Barjai* alumnus, remembered the 17-year-old Collinson saying that 'those born in a great Depression and growing up into a World War would not ever have much humour'. Such pessimism was exacerbated by Collinson's feelings as an outsider—Jewish, homosexual and communist—and by what Barbara Blackman later described as an 'unprepossessing' physical appearance.

Collinson and the co-editor, Barrie (Barrett) Reid, organised a '*Barjai* group' that met regularly and forged links with both the southern avant-garde and an older group of Brisbane writers surrounding Clem Christesen, the founder of *Meanjin*. In 1944 Collinson's poem 'Myself and the New Year, 1944', published in the 'Ern Malley' edition of *Angry Penguins*, was mentioned in the indictment for indecency launched against the editor Max Harris in Adelaide.

Collinson was also an aspiring painter: in 1944 he studied at the Central Technical College, Brisbane, and next year at the Julian Ashton [q.v.7] School, Sydney. In December 1945 he led a group of young artists away from the conservative Royal Queensland Art Society and formed the Miya Studio, which, for a few years, had its own premises and ran exhibitions. The Miya group cultivated a loosely expressionistic style, evident in Collinson's own canvases, that was remarkably advanced in the Brisbane art scene of the time. The communist-led New Theatre, which had close links with some members of the Miya Studio, performed Collinson's one-act plays *Friday Night at the Schrammers* in 1948 and *No Sugar for George* in 1949. After the theatre merged in 1949 with remnants of Miya, Collinson painted stage sets, wrote and produced plays, and sometimes acted in them. Jewish identity, the psychological outcomes of war, homosexual relationships, social justice issues, the family, and education were recurring concerns in his poems, plays and stories.

Moving to Melbourne in 1950, Collinson wrote while supporting himself in various jobs. On 3 January 1955 at the Temple Beth Israel, St Kilda, he married Ray Green, a stenographer; they later divorced. Also in 1955 he gained a teaching diploma at Mercer House. He worked for the Victorian Education Department, in 1956-61 as a schoolteacher and in 1961-64 in the publications branch. In 1957 his first major book of poems, *The Moods of Love*, was published by Overland. A member in the 1950s of the Communist Party of Australia and of the Australasian Book Society, he was State president (1960) of the Fellowship of Australian Writers. He won an award in 1961 for a stage play, *The Zelda Trio*, and contributed to the anthology *Eight by Eight* (1963), which featured the work of an 'unorganised group' of Melbourne poets, including Vincent Buckley [q.v.] and Chris Wallace-Crabbe. In 1963 the Australian Broadcasting Commission produced his television play *Uneasy Paradise*.

Inspired by these achievements, Collinson left for London in 1964, hoping to earn his living as a writer. Although he had some success—he published a book of poetry, *Who is Wheeling Grandma?* (1967), a children's book, *The Lion Who Ran Away* (1969), a novel, *Cupid's Crescent* (1973), and a stage play, *Thinking Straight* (1975)—he remained reliant on his work as a sub-editor for a magazine publisher. Portraying himself as an outsider in London's literary circles, he remained emotionally linked to Australia and contributed regularly to such Australian journals as *Overland* and *Westerly*. The Literature Board of the Australia Council awarded him a grant in 1974-75 and he spent six months in France writing most of the poems for a collection entitled *Hovering Narcissus* (1977).

From the mid-1970s Collinson found job satisfaction and a measure of financial security through his work as a practitioner of 'transactional analysis'. While dismissed by some literary friends as a faddish obsession, his fascination with psychotherapy was consistent with his long interest in the psychological economy of the family. Throughout his adult life he campaigned for homosexual law reform. He suffered from hepatitis and died of cirrhosis of the liver on 10 November 1986 in London and was cremated.

M. Helmrich, *Young Turks and Battle Lines* (1988); D. Foster (comp), *Self Portraits* (1991); B. Blackman, *Glass after Glass* (1997); *Overland*, Mar 1987, p 48; M. E. Anderson, Barjai, Miya Studio and Young Brisbane Artists of the 1940s (BA Hons thesis, Univ of Qld, 1987); Collinson papers (NLA); Meanjin papers (Univ of Melbourne Lib).

WILLIAM HATHERELL

COLLISSON, MARJORIE CHAVE (1887-1982), lecturer and feminist, was born on 5 February 1887 at Muncie, Indiana, United States of America, one of four children of Rev. Reginald Kingsmill Collisson, a London-born Anglican clergyman, and his Irish wife Katherine Elizabeth, née Gamble. The family returned to England in 1887, and came to Australia in 1896. After incumbencies in Tasmania, Marjorie's father served in South Australia from 1908 until his death in 1932. Marjorie was educated privately and at the Collegiate School, Hobart.

In 1913, aged 26, Collisson (often known as Chave) enrolled at the University of Sydney (BA, 1916), where, after winning two Women's College scholarships, Professor George Arnold Wood's history prize (1914 and 1915) and the Frazer [qq.v.12,4] scholarship (1916), she obtained first-class honours in history. In 1915 she was president of the Sydney University Women Undergraduates' Association. Writing to Meredith Atkinson in May 1916, F. A. Todd [qq.v.7,12] described her as a 'pestilential feminist' whose influence upon her fellow undergraduates was 'almost wholly bad' and who had been chiefly responsible for 'bringing the Pankhurst [q.v.12 Thomas Walsh] female to the University to address the women undergraduates and spread the gospel of vandalism'. Collisson was accused of throwing two hockey sticks at male undergraduates who were protesting at Adela Pankhurst's lecture, but another woman owned up. A prominent supporter of conscription during the plebiscite campaign in October 1916, next month she helped form a women's national organisation, which, she asserted, was 'not an anti-man' group.

After graduation Collisson taught in the department of tutorial classes at the university, organised a short-lived women's department of the Workers' Educational Association of New South Wales, and joined the staff of Methodist Ladies' College, Burwood. In July 1918, accompanied by Rose Scott's [q.v.11]

niece Mollye Shaw, Collisson suddenly left Australia to lecture in the United States of America. Next year, on a bursary, she wrote a thesis—on the evolution and economic policies of the Australian Labor Party—at Columbia University, New York (MA, 1919); she taught history (1919-20) in its extension school. She also lectured for the City of New York Board of Education, and for the New York State government, for which she toured promoting the victory loan.

Collisson moved to London, where she was associated with the City Literary Institute and studied at the London School of Economics and Political Science. She joined the international campaign for equal citizenship. With Bessie Rischbieth [q.v.11], whom she had known as a girl in Australia, she was a co-founder of the British Commonwealth League, formed to promote equal citizenship throughout the Empire. Appointed organising secretary at its first conference (London, July 1925), she addressed economic discrimination against women workers in Australia. In 1927, having been presented at Court, she visited India in support of its feminists, and early in 1928 returned to Australia as advance agent for the Australasian tour of the English preacher Maude Royden, which she financed and managed for the BCL.

Briefly owner-manager of an experimental picture theatre in London in 1930, Collisson was living with Mollye Shaw, now Menken, when Miles Franklin [q.v.8] encountered her in 1931 running conferences for the BCL. Although 'the big woman' was 'not one of my favourites', Franklin deemed a lecture on the White Australia policy 'brilliant and comprehensive'. By 1939 Collisson worked for the Imperial Policy Group.

Chave Collisson was a member (from 1949) of the board of the International Alliance of Women, and hard-working chair (from 1952) of its Equal Moral Standard Committee, focusing on prostitution. Between September 1949 and 1960, when she resigned after 'a stupendous fight' against the Street Offences Act, 1959, she served as secretary to the Association for Moral and Social Hygiene (Josephine Butler Society). This organisation was the British branch of the International Abolitionist Federation; she also chaired the IAF's international committee. In 1966 she delivered the Alison Neilans memorial lecture on 'Prostitution Today, The International Scene'. In this period Collisson's main interests were prostitution from a feminist perspective, the rights of deserted or separated wives and persons born out of wedlock, the age of consent and marriage, and female genital mutilation.

Commemorated by colleagues for 'her brilliant mind, dedication to fighting injustice, booming voice, warm sense of humour and infinite compassion', Collisson campaigned for equal moral rights for women and men into her eighties. Her only sister, Nora, had died in Australia in 1963. In her later years Collisson lived in hotels and finally at the Nightingale Home, Twickenham. She died on 14 April 1982 at Isleworth, London, and was cremated.

J. Roe (ed), *My Congenials*, vol 1 (1993); R. Annable (comp), *Biographical Register: The Women's College Within the University of Sydney*, vol 1 (1995); A. Woollacott, *To Try Her Fortune in London* (2001); *SMH*, 10 Oct 1916, p 5, 25 Nov 1925, p 8, 13 Feb 1928, p 5, 14 Feb 1928, p 5; *Daily Telegraph* (Sydney), 18 Nov 1916, p 18; *International Women's News*, Sept 1982, p 42; Collisson personnel file, and Minutes of the Joint Committee of Tutorial Classes and the WEA (Univ of Sydney); Collisson papers (Women's Library, London Metropolitan Univ).

JILL ROE

COLQUHOUN, ARCHIBALD DOUGLAS (1894-1983), artist and teacher, was born on 26 October 1894 at Heidelberg, Melbourne, second of four children of Scottish-born Alexander Colquhoun [q.v.8], artist, and his London-born wife Beatrice Helen, née Hoile, also a painter. Archie later recalled meeting many of the 'Bohemian friendly crowd' with whom his parents associated. His art training began at home as a 'chief amusement' before he attended the National Gallery schools in 1911. He studied drawing under Frederick McCubbin [q.v.10] but, restless with his progress, left to join the *Herald* as a staff artist, while also briefly taking classes with C. D. Richardson [q.v.11]. When he met Max Meldrum [q.v.10], who had recently returned from France, Colquhoun found a mentor. He studied with him for several years before building a studio and exhibiting with other Meldrum students. By 1924 he realised that 'I'd bust unless I got [abroad] and saw for myself'.

For the next three years Colquhoun travelled in France, Spain, Italy and England. His paintings were hung at the Société des Artistes Français, Paris (1924, 1925, 1926), and the Royal Institute of Oil Painters, London (1925). He returned to Melbourne in 1926 and established a studio and art school at 125 Little Collins Street. With 'a high ideal' and 'unquenchable zest for attainment', the *Age* noted in 1929, he became a prominent painter and a dedicated, influential teacher. In 1933 he won the Crouch [q.v.8] prize, and in 1934 the Newman prize for Australian historical painting. His pre-eminent students included (Sir) William Dargie, Harley C. Griffiths, Rex Bramleigh and Hayward Veal.

AMALIE SARAH FEILD (1894-1974), born on 20 March 1894 at Murtoa, Victoria, daughter of Australian-born parents Alfred Francis Feild, blacksmith, and his wife Louisa Caroline, née Degenhardt, was among Colquhoun's early students. Amalie ('Millie') commenced private art tuition as a child and, after teaching at Sebastopol State School for several years, studied drawing and design at the Ballarat Technical School. Recognising her abilities, the Victorian Education Department supported her study of pottery and stained glass at Sydney Technical College. On return to Ballarat, Feild initiated the teaching of pottery at the school and designed windows for St Andrew's Presbyterian and Lydiard Street Methodist churches. In 1927 she was appointed an instructor in art at the Working Men's College, and soon after began studying with Colquhoun. On 21 November 1931 they married in a civil ceremony in Melbourne. Amalie resigned from the college in 1933 to concentrate on portraiture and teaching at Colquhoun's school. In 1934, in the first of their many joint exhibitions, her 'graceful rhythmic fluency' was praised as complementing his 'directness of treatment'.

In 1936 the Colquhouns travelled to London. They rented a studio in Bloomsbury and held a successful exhibition at the Arlington Gallery in Old Bond Street. Portraits were commissioned and others shown in the 8th Annual British Empire Society of Arts Exhibition; their floral studies were hung in the United Society of Artists' Exhibition. Already a foundation member of the Australian Academy of Art, Archie dismissed the 'big noise' of modernism. Returning to Melbourne in 1937, they both resumed teaching and painting. Over the following years Archie's better-known commissioned portraits included those of the prime minister, J. B. Chifley, the chief justice of the High Court of Australia, Sir Owen Dixon, and the archbishop of Brisbane, (Sir) James Duhig [qq.v.13,14,8]. Amalie gained increasing recognition for her sensitive portraits of children.

In 1950 the Colquhouns closed the school, and in 1954 moved from the city to Kew, establishing a studio and occasional gallery in their home. Their painting—including landscapes and seascapes reflecting summer and autumn travels—remained intensive. Archie, with goatee beard and usually wearing a tartan beret, was the more extrovert of the two; Millie, her hair always tied neatly back, the more disciplined and reflective. She died on 16 June 1974 in East Melbourne and was buried in Boroondara cemetery, Kew, with Anglican rites. Archie died on 14 May 1983 at Fitzroy, and was buried beside her. In November that year a memorial exhibition of their paintings was held at Adam Galleries, Melbourne.

The Colquhouns' work is represented in the National Gallery of Australia, the State galleries of New South Wales, Queensland, Victoria and Western Australia, and many regional galleries.

P. and J. Perry, *Max Meldrum and Associates* (1996); *Age* (Melbourne), 13 Feb 1929, p 11, 3 July 1934, p 6; *Herald* (Melbourne), 17 July 1936, p 6; H. de Berg, interview with A. D. and A. Colquhoun (ts, 1965, NLA).   PETER W. PERRY

COMMINS, JOHN BEDE (1913-1987), political journalist, was born on 10 June 1913 at Parkes, New South Wales, second child and only son of Francis Bede Commins, solicitor, and his wife Nora, née Byrnes, both born in New South Wales. His father was killed in action in France in 1917 while serving with the 53rd Battalion, Australian Imperial Force. The family moved to Sydney and Jack was educated at Christian Brothers' High School, Lewisham. At the age of 21 he joined the *Sydney Morning Herald*, later moving to the *Daily Mirror*. In December 1941 he was appointed to the news staff of the Australian Broadcasting Commission. Next month he was transferred to the parliamentary press gallery in Canberra. He took over as head of the ABC's Federal parliamentary bureau in 1945, becoming one of the pioneers of the ABC's independent news service which began on 1 June 1947.

During thirty-five years in the Canberra press gallery Commins gained a reputation, according to the politician Fred Daly, for 'impeccable honesty, trustworthiness and impartiality'. He reported on major events under prime ministers from John Curtin [q.v.13] to Malcolm Fraser, mingling with and enjoying the friendship of a number of political leaders. Curtin he regarded as 'a superb wartime leader' and J. B. Chifley [q.v.13] as the 'greatest of Prime Ministers'. He believed that (Sir) Robert Menzies [q.v.15] despised the press: he 'thought we were on a lower intellectual level, and in the end he didn't think he needed us. Well, let's be frank, he didn't'. But on trips away with a relaxed Menzies, journalists 'couldn't have had better company'. Commins was a member of the press contingent on several prime ministerial visits overseas.

When he retired in June 1977 Commins was the second-longest-serving member of the Canberra press gallery, yet his name was little known outside Parliament House. His reputation among his peers had developed when the ABC, in keeping with the impersonal style of its news bulletins, did not use reporters' names. Anonymity suited him. He saw his job as getting the news and getting it to the public quickly. When Curtin died in the early hours of 5 July 1945, Commins ran from Civic to Parliament House to get the story. In those days he was never off the job: he recorded picking up a lead to an important story on the links at the Royal Canberra Golf Club.

Commins remained an old-style journalist steeped in the habits of radio. His tall figure was visible at televised news conferences but he never became a 'talking head'. At the beginning of 1966 the ABC gave him a chief of staff, Ray Aitchison, part of whose brief was to increase the ABC's television coverage of political events and issues. According to Aitchison, in Commins's last decade as chief of bureau, 'rarely did he find a news story that hadn't been obvious' and he did not develop new contacts. However, his skill in smoothing the way for executives visiting Canberra to meet ministers or give evidence at parliamentary committees ensured that he remained an asset to ABC management. Throughout, he ran the ABC's parliamentary news room with a light hand, confident that reporters would work well without obtrusive supervision. He was appointed MBE in 1977.

Jack Commins lived at Braddon with his wife Joan, née Raven (d.1982), whom he had married with Catholic rites on 2 August 1941 at St Mary's Cathedral, Sydney. They had no children. Both were devoted to their dogs and were enthusiastic golfers. He died between 5 and 7 August 1987 at his home and was cremated. Fred Daly described him as a 'quiet man', 'compassionate and gracious'.

Canberra Times, 12 Aug 1987, p 7; *Journalist*, Sept 1987, p 7; *Canberra & District Hist Soc Newsletter*, Oct 1987, p 10; M. Pratt, interview with Commins (ts, 1971, NLA); Ray Aitchison papers (NLA); personal knowledge.   PATRICIA CLARKE

CONNELLAN, EDWARD JOHN (1912-1983), aviator, pastoralist and businessman, was born on 24 June 1912 at Donald, Victoria, eldest of seven children of Victorian-born parents Thomas Peter Connellan, farmer, and his wife Lucy, née Glowrey. Eddie completed his secondary education at Xavier College, Melbourne, in 1927-29. He joined the Victorian Education Department in 1930, but resigned in July 1933 to go into business for himself. Neither of his firms, Rural Radio Pty Ltd and London Aero Ads Pty Ltd, was successful, but his involvement in the latter encouraged him to learn to fly and he gained his private pilot's licence on 8 July 1936.

Flying became an obsession, as did the Northern Territory, where he saw business opportunities. Connellan made two aerial surveys of the Territory in 1938, to assess opportunities for an air service and to select a cattle station. Afterwards, he negotiated a Federal government subsidy for a mail service between Alice Springs and Wyndham, Western Australia, and a contract with the Australian Aerial Medical Service (Royal Flying Doctor Service of Australia). His friend Damian Miller, a grandson of Henry 'Money' Miller [q.v.5], helped to finance additional aircraft and staff and joined him as a pilot. Connellan flew the first medical flight from Alice Springs in July 1939, with his new business, Survey & Inland Transport, conducting the inaugural official mail run in August. On 29 August 1940 at the Catholic Church, Alice Springs, he married Evelyn Mary Grace Bell; they were to have a daughter who died in infancy and two sons.

During World War II the authorities considered Connellan's work essential to the war effort and he continued the mail run with charter work throughout the Territory. He registered the name Connellan Airways in July 1943, but his postwar plans for his aerial service conflicted with the Federal government's two-airline policy, which prevented him from competing on routes serviced by the major airlines. Nevertheless, with station people as shareholders, he incorporated his business as a limited company in February 1951.

'E. J.' was about 5 ft 11 ins (180 cm) tall with light auburn hair and fair skin, which meant that he frequently wore a wide-brimmed hat. He was a man of immense energy and sharp intellect who possessed an unshakeable self-belief. A prominent figure in Central Australian affairs, he was a natural choice as chairman of the provisional committee of the Northern Territory Development League in June 1944. He resigned in November after some members sought to use the proposed organisation to remove the administrator C. L. A. Abbott [q.v.13], but served on the executive when the league was formed early in 1945.

Connellan had realised his dream of developing a pastoral property. Having selected in 1938 the preferred site for his station, about 100 miles (160 km) north-west of Alice Springs, he acquired the lease in partnership with others in 1942 and registered the Narwietooma Pastoral Co. in September 1943. The deaths of his partners during the war enabled him to acquire all shares in the property in 1946; he sank the first bore next year and grazed cattle on the station from 1948. He became successful and served on the executive of the Central Australian Pastoral Lessees' Association (Centralian Pastoralists' Association) for ten years and as president in 1950-51. He moved his family to Narwietooma in 1955 and supervised all station work. His interest in pastoral improvement was evident when he published a pamphlet, *Drought Management and Pasture Protection in Central Australia* (1965).

Other business ventures included a partnership with the former policeman Ted Morey [q.v.] in Wildman River Safaris in March 1948. Morey pulled out in 1949 and the project lasted only one more season. In addition, Connellan became the chief promoter and inaugural chairman of Alice Springs Commercial Broadcasters Pty Ltd, the Centre's first commercial radio station, which was established in February 1969. In December 1965 the Federal government had appointed Connellan as one of three non-official members of the Northern Territory Legislative Council. However, he resigned in November 1967 after elected members questioned his objectivity because of his receipt of a Commonwealth subsidy for his aerial service. The Federal government later appointed him as a member (1974-78) of its Transport Industries Advisory Council.

Meanwhile, Connellan Airways Ltd grew, although never to the extent that E. J. would have wished because of government-imposed limitations: the price of a guaranteed fifteen-year subsidy from 1965 was a government appointee to the Connellan board. Also, his reluctance to share authority or entertain the idea of his airline (renamed Connair Pty Ltd in July 1970) becoming a public company restricted access to ready sources of credit for purchase of newer and larger equipment.

Other circumstances hampered growth. The Royal Flying Doctor Service acquired two Connellan aircraft for its own use in 1965 and ceased using company pilots in 1973. The effects of Cyclone Tracy at Christmas 1974 disrupted schedules, although the company escaped damage to staff or aircraft and played a part in Darwin's relief. Then Connair lost its 'plum' route from Alice Springs to Mount Isa and Cairns, Queensland, following a pilots' strike in September 1976. The biggest setback was the death of Connellan's eldest son, Roger (b.1944), when a former employee deliberately crashed an aeroplane into Connair's offices at Alice Springs in January 1977. Connellan had groomed Roger as his successor and was forced to increase his involvement in airline management again, although he had been treated for cancer.

Connair finally received permission to become a regional airline in September 1977, but it remained handicapped by its lack of capital. This ultimately persuaded Connellan to sell his company to East-West Airlines Ltd in March 1980. He used a large proportion of the sale proceeds to establish the Connellan Airways Trust to provide educational opportunities for outback people. The deputy prime minister Doug Anthony launched the trust in February 1983.

Connellan had received several awards in recognition of his services to aviation. They included Queen Elizabeth II's coronation medal in 1953, his appointment as OBE in 1957, and the 1964 (Walter) Oswald Watt [q.v.12] gold medal. He was elevated to CBE in 1976 and appointed AO in 1981. Survived by his wife, and their younger son, he died on 26 December 1983 at Narwietooma station; he was accorded a state funeral and was buried in Alice Springs memorial cemetery. Before his death he had completed *Failure of Triumph:*

The Story of Connellan Airways, which was published in 1992.

N. Parnell and T. Boughton, *Flypast* (1988); P. Donovan, 'EJ Connellan—a Brief Biography', in E. J. Connellan, *Failure of Triumph* (1992); D. Carment and B. James (eds), *Northern Territory Dictionary of Biography*, vol 2 (1992); *Australian*, 3 Mar 1977, p 11; *Sun-Herald* (Sydney), 28 Oct 1979, p 16; *Bulletin*, 27 Dec 1983/3 Jan 1984, p 46; *Canberra Times*, 29 Dec 1983, p 7; *Age* (Melbourne), 29 Dec 1983, p 6; *Centralian Advocate*, 30 Dec 1983, p 1; *Northern Territory News*, 28 Jan 1984, p 13; private information.   PETER DONOVAN

CONNOLLY, SIR WILLIS HENRY (1901-1981), electrical engineer and public-utility manager, was born on 25 November 1901 at Benalla, Victoria, only surviving child of Victorian-born parents Joseph John Connolly, farmer, and his wife Adelaide May, née Little. Young Willis's uncle E. A. Connolly [q.v.8] and maternal grandfather, Willis Little, were horse-racing identities and Little was also a member (1903-16) of the Legislative Council. Horses, gambling and politics did not interest young Willis. He attended Benalla High School and the University of Melbourne (BEE, 1923; Dip.Com., 1936; B.Com., 1947), and while a student gained practical experience at the Carlton workshop of E. Campbell & Son Pty Ltd and at the Richmond power station of the Melbourne Electric Supply Co. Ltd.

In 1921 Connolly joined the wages staff of the State Electricity Commission of Victoria at Yallourn. Next year he transferred to the commission's electric supply branch, Melbourne, as a junior engineer. On 20 April 1927 at St Bede's Church of England, Elwood, he married Mary Milton Clark, a stenographer. After a secondment (1927-29) to the SEC's briquetting and research branch under Hyman Herman [q.v.9], he gained a solid reputation as assistant-manager of two branches: electrical sales (1929-31), in which he formulated new tariffs; and metropolitan electricity supply (1932-37), in which he furthered the conversion of the supply to three-phase.

Appointed manager of the State-wide electricity supply department in 1937, Connolly satisfied the SEC's political (mostly Country Party) masters, extending rural electrification and taking the first steps towards uniform tariffs. His key role in conserving electrical energy during the postwar shortages brought his work to the attention of the commissioners, who in 1949 appointed him assistant to the general manager. He had not been as popular with the public: people had put up with various inconveniences and had seen one of their footballer heroes, Jack Dyer, successfully prosecuted for ignoring power restrictions. As assistant general manager, Connolly helped increase generating capacity to meet the requirements of Victoria's expanding secondary industries.

In September 1956 Connolly was appointed chairman and general manager of the commission. His term of office was marked by his close personal involvement in power and fuel policy. Within the organisation he cultivated the 'family' spirit that had been absent since the death of Sir John Monash [q.v.10]. Connolly's biggest problem was poor industrial relations in the La Trobe Valley, including the rise of white-collar militancy. He fared much better in his dealings with the premier, (Sir) Henry Bolte [q.v.], with whom he developed a close relationship based on mutual regard. The government underwrote the construction of new power stations. But Connolly watched with resignation the almost total switch from brown coal (briquettes) to oil in the domestic fuel market.

Connolly brought to his tasks meticulous preparation and scrupulous attention to and memory for detail. He often personally intervened in conflicts, disarming hostility by well-placed humour or by a drink and talk. He anticipated technical, planning and personality difficulties, but was occasionally indecisive in dealing with individuals. He delegated effectively, supporting subordinates and monitoring their progress. By example and exhortation he promoted teamwork. He endeavoured to enhance the reputation of the SEC by being accessible and sociable—for example, lunching with engineers or businessmen at the Australia Club—and by allowing himself to become a public figure, although he did not crave personal recognition for its own sake.

Retiring in 1971, Connolly continued as a consultant with the SEC and retained his place on State and national power committees. He was a member of the Barbarians (a brown-coal industry fraternity), the Australian-German Association, the Australian Club of Rome, and the board of trustees of the Thomas Alva Edison Foundation in the United States of America. His principal interests were the World Power (Energy) Conference, of which he was president in 1962-68, and education; chairman (1961-65) of the State Advisory Council on Technical Education, he was interim chairman (1965-67) and first president (1967-74 and 1978-80) of the Victoria Institute of Colleges.

Connolly was awarded numerous professional honours, including the (W. C.) Kernot [q.v.5] medal (1957) by the University of Melbourne, an honorary doctorate of engineering (1967) by Monash University, and the (Sir) Peter Nicol Russell [q.v.6] medal (1968) by the Institution of Engineers, Australia. He was appointed CBE in 1962, knighted in 1971 and awarded the knight commander's cross of the Order of Merit of the Federal Republic of

Germany in 1980. Sir Willis's chief hobby was photography. He enjoyed regular overseas travel from 1950, mainly to Germany and the USA. A 'tall, brawny man', he played tennis competitively for Elsternwick and socially at Kooyong, where he was a member of the Lawn Tennis Association of Victoria. He died on 13 February 1981 at his East St Kilda home and was cremated. His wife and their daughter and son survived him.

A. Spaull, 'Willis Connolly—a Biography', in J. T. Woodcock (ed), *Victoria's Brown Coal* (1984) and for sources; A. D. Spaull, The Origins and Rise of the Victorian Brown Coal Industry 1835-1935 (MCom thesis, Univ of Melbourne, 1967).

ANDREW SPAULL

COOK, CECIL EVELYN AUFRERE (1897-1985), medical practitioner and administrator, was born on 23 September 1897 at Bexhill, Sussex, England, son of James Whiteford Murray Cook, medical practitioner, and his wife Emily, née Puckle. The family migrated to Australia in 1899. 'Mick' grew up at Barcaldine, Queensland, where his father was in general practice, and attended The Southport School (dux 1914). In 1915 he began medical studies at the University of Sydney (MB, Ch.M., 1920; MD, 1929; DPH, 1931). After a residency at Brisbane General Hospital, he practised with his father at Barcaldine, in hospitals at Mount Morgan and Longreach, and as a general practitioner at Hughenden. Working his passage to London as a ship's medical officer, he attended the London School of Tropical Medicine (DTM&H, 1923) and won a Wandsworth scholarship.

On the advice of J. H. L. Cumpston [q.v.8], Cook used his scholarship to survey Indigenous health in tropical Australia in 1924-25, visiting Aboriginal people in Queensland, Western Australia and the Northern Territory. He received his MD for his report *The Epidemiology of Leprosy in Australia* (1927). On 4 March 1924 at Coreena station, Barcaldine, he had married with Anglican rites Jessie Winifred Miller (d.1978). In December 1925 he joined the Commonwealth Public Service. At the Australian Institute of Tropical Medicine, Townsville, he surveyed hookworm in the Cairns region and sometimes doubled as Townsville's quarantine officer.

In March 1927 Cook became the chief medical officer and chief protector of Aborigines in North Australia (Northern Territory from 1931). He served as Darwin's only medical practitioner for six months before he was able to focus on developing a public health system. In 1929 he set up a training school for nurses and a tuberculosis clinic at Darwin Hospital, and a medical benefit fund. Next year, after founding the Nurses' Board of North Australia,

he took leave in Sydney to study anthropology (under A. R. Radcliffe-Brown [q.v.11]) and public health. He established general hospitals at Katherine (1931), Tennant Creek (1936) and Alice Springs (1939), and a hospital for lepers outside Darwin (1931). In 1934 he began to subsidise his colleague Dr Clyde Fenton's [q.v.] private Gipsy Moth aeroplane and the two men established the Northern Territory Aerial Medical Service. His admiration for this venture softened his initial scepticism towards John Flynn's [q.v.8] (Royal) Flying Doctor Service. In 1936 Cook was founding chairman of the Northern Territory Medical Board. Becoming aware of the high rate of infant mortality in the Aboriginal population, he commenced infant welfare services at the new Bagot Reserve, Darwin, in 1937. He had been appointed CBE and awarded the Cilento [q.v.] medal in 1935.

Worried that the fertility of Asians and 'half-caste' Aborigines exceeded that of Europeans, Cook encouraged young European families to settle in the Territory, and he searched for ways to 'uplift' the morality and standard of living of 'half-castes' so that they might inter-breed with Whites. He was proud to report in 1934: 'Practically all half-caste children of both sexes, formerly left to live with aboriginals in compounds and bush camps ... have been re-moved to half-caste institutions under Government control'. 'Half-caste' women were crucial to his 'uplift' strategy. He would not allow them to marry unless they were worthy (in his eyes) of a European or 'half-caste' partner who met his standards. Lest they be 'removed', he defined as 'European' the children of such unions. His phrase 'breed out the colour' had as much to do with reclassifying individuals of Aboriginal descent as with skin pigment in the literal sense.

Cook championed 'full bloods' by prosecuting unauthorised visitors to reserves, and he defended Woolwonga Reserve from covetous settlers. In 1936 he appointed T. G. H. Strehlow [q.v.16] as a patrol officer, based at Jay Creek, to protect Aboriginal interests. Generally critical of the social impact of Christian missions, Cook threatened with loss of subsidy any that did not meet his standards in sanitation, nutrition and education. He made it mandatory for licensed employers of Aborigines to report their employees' illness or injury. Because the pastoral economy had subverted the tribal economy, he argued, rural employers must provision their employees' many relatives. His relationship with Alice Springs townsfolk was strained when he urged them to admit Aboriginal patients to their proposed hospital in 1932 and when he allowed a Catholic mission to the Arrernte in that town in 1936.

Cook was not embarrassed by his unpopularity among many Europeans. His intellectual arrogance no doubt contributed to their dislike and to his disdain. Tall and thin, with one glass eye, he had a fastidious self-assurance as a scientific improver that sometimes spilled over into comical prolixity. Notwithstanding these tensions of manner and policy, his methods were grounded in his underlying support for northern 'development'. When miners flocked to Tennant Creek in 1934, he 'protected' the local Aborigines by banning them from the newly settled zone. His ambitions for his protectorate sometimes exceeded his administrative resources and legal capacities. Against his advice, the Commonwealth separated Aboriginal and public health functions in 1939. He returned to the University of Sydney, where he taught in the School of Public Health and Tropical Medicine.

Having been appointed provisional captain, Australian Army Medical Corps, in 1937, Cook transferred to the Australian Imperial Force on 11 August 1941 as a major. Posted to the 2/12th Australian General Hospital, he served as a pathologist in Ceylon (Sri Lanka) from October that year to December 1942. From March 1943 he was deputy assistant director of hygiene for, successively, II Corps, New Guinea Force and I Corps. His analysis of case records identified sources of infections such as typhus, dysentery and cholera. In November 1944 he was promoted to lieutenant colonel and made assistant director of hygiene at Advanced Land Headquarters, located first at Hollandia, Netherlands New Guinea, then at Morotai. He developed hygiene protocols in which officers and men could be instructed, and reported on the operations in Borneo in 1945. On 22 March 1946 he transferred to the Reserve of Officers.

As Western Australia's commissioner of public health from March 1946, Cook offered a swingeing critique of the poor performance of local government in that State. His interest in perinatal and infant health resulted in State legislation requiring the notification of premature and still births. In November 1949 he was recruited to the Commonwealth Department of Health, Canberra, as a senior medical officer. From 1958 until his retirement in September 1962 he was the inaugural director of the division of public health. Traffic injuries, skin cancer, native health, food standards and tobacco's carcinogenic properties were among his many concerns. He also continued his involvement in the National Health and Medical Research Council, six of whose advisory committees he was to chair, including its public health committee. In the latter role he contributed heavily to Australia's campaign against poliomyelitis.

Cook never lost his interest in 'native affairs'. From 1964 to 1972 he was a member of the human biology advisory committee of the Australian Institute of Aboriginal Studies, of which he was a founding member. He complained in 1969 that a once necessary paternalism had been maintained by a public service 'seized with the importance of precedent', inducing a psychology of dependency among Aborigines. Meanwhile, he believed, Aborigines were being tempted by an irresponsible mass media to blame whites for all their misfortunes. In that way, he argued in 1971, racial hatred was being fostered to an unprecedented degree.

In retirement Cook lived in Sydney and then at Burleigh Heads, Queensland. Survived by his two sons and daughter, he died on 4 July 1985 at Wahroonga, Sydney, and was cremated.

A. S. Walker, *Clinical Problems of War* (1952) and *The Island Campaigns* (1957); D. Snow, *The Progress of Public Health in Western Australia 1829-1977* (1981); S. Baldwin (ed), *Unsung Heroes & Heroines of Australia* (1988); D. Carment et al (eds), *Northern Territory Dictionary of Biography*, vol 1 (1990); A. Markus, *Governing Savages* (1990); J. Pearn and M. Cobcroft (eds), *Fevers and Frontiers* (1990); T. Austin, *Never Trust a Government Man* (1997); NT Administration, *Annual Report*, 1927-39; Cwlth Dept of Health, *Health*, June 1962, p 53; A2749, item Cook C E A PS729 (NAA); H. Giese, interviews with C. E. A. Cook (ts, 1981, NTA).   TIM ROWSE

COOK, KENNETH BERNARD (1929-1987), novelist and film-maker, was born on 5 May 1929 at Lakemba, Sydney, and named Bert Kenneth, third and youngest child of Herbert Warner Cook, inspector for a time-payment firm, and his wife Lily May, née Soole, both born in New South Wales. His father left the family soon after. Kenneth attended Fort Street Boys' High School, then became a cadet on the *Richmond River Express* at Casino while also writing essays, stories and plays. He worked as a journalist in country towns and in Sydney for some years. Acting with the Genesian theatre company in Sydney, he met a librarian and researcher, Irene Patricia Hickie, whom he married on 17 March 1951 at St Canice's Catholic Church, Elizabeth Bay.

In 1952-54 Cook worked for the Australian Broadcasting Commission, at Broken Hill—a town he loathed—and then at Rockhampton, Queensland. There he wrote a novel which, initially accepted, was later considered libellous and pulped. After six months in Brisbane, he returned to Sydney in November 1954. He resigned from the ABC in 1961 and that year published his best-known novel, *Wake in Fright*, which drew on his experience in Broken Hill. The novels *Chain of Darkness* (1962) and *Stormalong* (1963) followed; royalties together with successful real-estate speculation enabled him to take his family overseas for an extended holiday, described in *Blood Red Roses* (1963). Back in Australia, he, Philip Hickie and John Crew set up Patrician

Films Pty Ltd to make television films, mainly for children.

Cook stood for Federal parliament twice, unsuccessfully: in 1966 for the seat of Parramatta on behalf of the Liberal Reform Group on an anti-conscription ticket, and in 1969 for Bennelong as an Australia Party candidate. A Catholic of liberal views, he opposed the Church's stand on the Vietnam War. He expressed his passionate opposition to the war in the novel *The Wine of God's Anger* (1968), and—couched as government oppression at Eureka—in the musical play *Stockade*, first performed in 1971. *Stockade* and *Wake in Fright* were released as films that year.

Continuing to write with the aid of Commonwealth literary grants, Cook published many novels including *Tuna* (1967) and *Pig* (1980), two of his best books. He separated from Patricia; they were later divorced. The butterfly farm that he had established on the Hawkesbury River failed; in 1983 he was declared bankrupt after personally guaranteeing a film project. Ill and depressed, he wrote *The Killer Koala* (1986), the first of three collections of comic bush stories, contrasting the heroic image of the Australian bush and the stark reality: the amusing obverse of *Wake in Fright*. Sales of 30 000 copies helped to restore his confidence, as did his marriage to Jacqueline Frances Kent, a writer and editor, on 5 January 1987 in a civil ceremony at St Leonards, Sydney.

Survived by his wife and the two daughters and two sons of his first marriage, Cook died of myocardial infarction on 18 April 1987 at Narromine. He was buried in Frenchs Forest lawn cemetery. A consummate professional, he wrote novels, plays, songs, screenplays, and radio and television scripts. At heart he was a storyteller, and he knew how to treat serious, even tragic, themes with compassion and a light touch. Probably because of his popular success, he was an underrated Australian writer.

Westerly, no 3, 1977, p 75; *Bulletin*, 15 Dec 1973, p 43; *SMH*, 27 June 1985, 'Northern Herald' supp, p 1, 21 Apr 1987, p 4; J. Kent, 'Jacqueline Kent Remembers Kenneth Cook', *Austn Author*, July 1987, p 3; H. de Berg, interview with K. Cook (ts, 1972, NLA); personal knowledge.

JACQUELINE KENT

COOK, SIR PHILIP HALFORD (1912-1990), psychologist and public servant, was born on 10 October 1912 at Benalla, Victoria, fourth child of Victorian-born parents Richard Osborne Cook (d. 1924), Methodist clergyman, and his wife Elinor Violet May, née Cook. William Glanville Lau Cook [q.v.] was his brother. After attending Caulfield North Central School and Wesley College, Mel-

bourne, Hal worked in a bank. While studying philosophy at the University of Melbourne (BA Hons, 1937; MA, 1938), he was attracted to the embryonic area of clinical psychology. Interested in the work of J. K. Adey at Royal Park Mental Hospital, he conducted research for his master's degree assisting Peter Bachelard at the pioneering Travancore child guidance clinic. His postgraduate studies in the field of abnormal psychology, specialising in the training of mentally retarded and maladjusted children, began at University College, London. He moved to New York when World War II began. After a brief enrolment at Columbia University, he transferred to the University of Kansas (Ph.D., 1941). His doctoral work appeared as *The Theory and Technique of Child Guidance* (1944).

Returning to Melbourne early in 1942, just as psychology was being recruited to the war effort, Cook was 'manpowered' into the Department of Labour and National Service as the senior industrial psychologist in the newly established industrial welfare division. The psychological testing that his team developed, initially for the allocation of women to munitions factory tasks, was gradually extended to a range of industrial occupations. After he became a permanent officer in 1946, he rose to assistant secretary (1952), first assistant secretary (1962), and permanent head (1968), replacing Sir Henry Bland. In 1965 he was appointed OBE. With the election of the Whitlam government in 1972, Cook was removed by the incoming minister for labour, Clyde Cameron, who later claimed that Cook had 'put too much time and enthusiasm into preparing evasive answers' to parliamentary questions. Cook's leadership in the department had helped to shape the development of the Commonwealth's vocational guidance and employment services, and the field of personnel management in Australia.

Given the job of a special labour adviser, with ambassadorial status, in Europe, Cook was attached (1972-77) to the Australian Mission to the United Nations in Geneva until his retirement from the public service. In 1975-76 he chaired the executive council of the International Labour Organisation. He was knighted in 1976. Energetic and Anglophile, he remained thoroughly committed to notions of civil service in the British tradition.

Cook also played a significant role in the professionalisation of applied psychology in Australia. He practised as an honorary (consultant) psychologist at Prince Henry's Hospital. His distinctive contribution was the advocacy and application of Rorschach tests. Having attended the Rorschach Institute while studying in New York, he co-founded the Australian Rorschach Society in 1942. On his way home he had visited Samoa to apply these tests to study the interaction of personality and culture. His advice was sought on the interpretation of tests completed by Nazi leaders on trial at Nuremberg in 1945. He wrote *The Productivity Team Technique* (1951), reporting an investigation undertaken at the Tavistock Institute of Human Relations, London, of communication processes within industry. His articles appeared in journals of industrial relations and occupational psychology. A fellow (1943) of the British Psychological Society and chairman (1960-61) of its Australian branch, he encouraged the emergence of the Australian Psychological Society.

On 6 October 1945 at Queen's College chapel, University of Melbourne, Cook had married, with Methodist forms, Myra Victoria Bellman, née Dean, a clerk and a widow. A 'neat, spry man' of 5 ft 6 ins (168 cm), he enjoyed playing, later watching, football, and walking. Survived by his wife and their daughter and son, Sir Halford died on 4 January 1990 at Box Hill and was cremated. In 1992, to celebrate his contribution to Queen's College as student, fellow (1972-90) and council member (1978-90), the friends of its library established the biennial Sir Halford Cook lecture.

M. Nixon and R. Taft (eds), *Psychology in Australia* (1976); C. Cameron, *The Confessions of Clyde Cameron 1913-1990* (1990); S. Cooke, *A Meeting of Minds* (2000); *Smith's Weekly*, 16 Oct 1943, p 11; *Australian*, 8 Dec 1967, p 3, 19 Dec 1972, p 2; *Herald* (Melbourne), 27 Jan 1968, p 16; *Nation*, 25 May 1968, p 5; *Age* (Melbourne), 19 Dec 1972, p 1; *Bulletin of the Austn Psychological Soc*, June 1990, p 21; A. Turtle, interview with P. H. Cook (ts, 1988, copy in Austn Psychological Soc papers, Univ of Melbourne Archives). 						HELEN BOURKE

COOK, WILLIAM GLANVILLE LAU (1909-1983), rationalist, was born on 7 June 1909 on the island of Lakemba (Lakeba), Fiji, son of Victorian-born parents Richard Osborne Cook (d.1924), Methodist clergyman, and his wife Elinor Violet May, née Cook. (Sir) Philip Halford Cook [q.v.] was his brother. Bill's parents were Australian missionaries and they returned home soon after his birth. At Melbourne High School, he gained his Leaving certificate with honours in English, rowed, and captained the lacrosse team. He became a candidate for the Methodist ministry but found that he could not accept the notion of eternal damnation and, with 'a great sense of freedom and relief', turned away from religion.

After training at the Faraday Street State School, Carlton (1927-28), and the Teachers' College (1929), Cook was posted to Bamawn, where he broadened his reading, particularly in philosophy, and expanded his already good understanding of religious writings. On 17 January 1931 at Malvern, Melbourne, he married with Methodist forms Ida Lowell Madder, a

secretary. In 1930 he had joined the Rationalist Society of Australia. Back at Faraday Street in 1937, he carried out voluntary and paid work for the society. In 1940 he was appointed the RSA's full-time secretary and lecturer, and editor of its journal, the *Rationalist*; he was also assistant-secretary of the RSA's business arm, the Rationalist Association of Australia Ltd. He resigned from the teaching service in April.

The RSA had been through a turbulent period. Cook revitalised the organisation. He gave lectures, arranged conferences, took part in public debates, wrote essays for the *Rationalist*, contributed letters and articles to newspapers, and mounted public campaigns. The battle against state aid to church schools was to be lost but, among other successes, a crusade to increase the availability of secular marriage resulted in his appointment as a civil registrar of marriages in 1946. A fine debater, he took on such opponents as Arnold Lunn, a visiting English propagandist for the Catholic Church, and he regularly challenged local church leaders to meet him at the rostrum.

Cook was a talented radio and later television broadcaster. In 1946 he participated in a series of talks on radio-station 3XY, entitled 'What the Four Freedoms Mean to Me'. He argued that social justice and equality were needed before all people would be able to enjoy the freedom of religion and speech and the freedom from fear and want that Franklin D. Roosevelt had called for in 1941. Always at the forefront of socially progressive activity, he played an important part in the establishment of the Humanist Society of Victoria and the Australian Council for Civil Liberties.

Over five decades Cook developed a wide range of contacts and friends in Australia and overseas, particularly in the British Rationalist Press Association. To improve the standing of rationalism, he solicited the support of public figures. Alfred Foster, Sir John Latham, (Duncan) Max Meldrum, (Edward) Vance Palmer, Brian Fitzpatrick, Norman Haire [qq.v.8,10,11, 14] and (Sir) Macfarlane Burnet [q.v.] were among those whom he invited to associate their names with rationalism, speak at RSA conferences, give lectures and contribute articles to the *Rationalist*. The RSA could not afford to pay his salary from 1952 but he remained in office until 1978 and received occasional honorariums for his work. He was president in 1979-83. To make a living after 1952, he had tried to start several businesses and then taught (1957-72) at state schools in Melbourne.

A gregarious and sometimes rumbustious man, Cook combined his intellectual pursuits with a great enjoyment of life. His 'lusty interest in good food and wines' (his words) found expression in stimulating Saturday lunches that he hosted at the Café Latin. Ralph Biddington described him as 'a short, thickset man with a quizzical look, very quick in both movement and comment'. Cook's health was never good and it declined further in his last years. He suffered from a number of illnesses and lost several toes due to complications of diabetes, but his spirit never flagged.

Cook was fortunate in his wife Lowell, a woman of intelligence and strong character 'who created an atmosphere of calm where his tempestuous spirit could regenerate'. He died on 11 May 1983 at his Malvern home and, after a Rationalist ceremony, was cremated. His wife and their daughter survived him. His library became part of the Rationalist collection in the Victoria University Library.

R. Biddington, *The Supremacy of Reason* (2001); *Austn Rationalist Qtrly*, July-Sept 1983, p 3; *Austn Rationalist*, Spring 2003, p 1; *Herald* (Melbourne), 24 June 1972, p 6; personal knowledge.

LESLEY VICK

COOK, WILLIAM HENRY (1910-1985), jockey, was born on 12 January 1910 at Hornsby, Sydney, second of five surviving children of William Edward Cook, butcher, and his wife Mary Ella Louise, née Adam, who were both born in New South Wales. Billy learnt to ride on an Arab pony, delivering his father's meat orders, and became familiar with horse-racing as a result of family trips to race meetings. In 1923-24 he was apprenticed to the Sydney trainer John Donohoe. His first ride was on Little Marg, which finished unplaced in a race at Canterbury on 24 July 1925. Two months later he rode his first winner, Pigeon Pie, also at Canterbury.

In the 1929 Sydney Cup, riding Crucis, Cook achieved his first major victory. Subsequently he won two Melbourne Cups, on the 3-year-old colt Skipton in 1941, and on the mare Rainbird in 1945. Other important triumphs included two Victoria Racing Club (1942, 1954) and two Australian Jockey Club (1940, 1946) Derbies, two VRC Oaks races (1941, 1946), three AJC Metropolitans (1939, 1949, 1953), three Mooney Valley Gold cups (1936, 1940, 1945), a Caulfield Cup (1930), a Doomben Newmarket (1937), and one further Sydney Cup (1953). His dominance of New South Wales racing, in particular, was reflected in the fact that he won the Sydney jockeys' premiership six times between 1931-32 and 1946-47. His achievements included riding a record-breaking 126 metropolitan winners in the 1939-40 season.

Cook also enjoyed success overseas. He visited India three times, beginning in 1932, to ride for the Maharajahs of Kolhapur and Baroda, and for Alec Higgins. In Britain in 1949 he had forty-two winners in a three-month period. Returning there in 1951, he again tasted success and such was his reputation that he was invited to ride for King George VI. His dislike of travelling and cold weather prevented an extended career in England in the mould of another outstanding Australian jockey, Edgar Britt.

Much to Cook's surprise, he had been initially rejected for military service in World War II because of flat feet. He enlisted in the Militia on 25 June 1942 and worked in the accounts office, Sydney. On 2 August 1944 he was discharged with the rank of corporal. Although short, he possessed the physique of a prizefighter, but it was not his strength that earned him the nickname of 'the Champ'. Rather, he was renowned for his sense of timing and for his ability to nurse a horse through a race and to drive it to the front in the last few yards. At Randwick racecourse, owing to the steep rise in the straight, this tactic proved particularly successful. Although Cook rode for royalty and rajahs, he never lost a sense of obligation to average racegoers, and he tried as hard on a midweek hack as he did on a fine thoroughbred in a Group 1 race. Because of his uncanny knack of winning the last race on the program, and in the process restoring the seemingly lost 'banks' of many small punters, he was also known affectionately as 'Last-race Cookie'.

Although he enjoyed a career of some thirty-five years, winners came less frequently in the late 1950s. After a training accident in which he broke a leg, and faced with increasing weight problems and fewer opportunities for good rides, he decided to retire in 1959. Thereafter, he dabbled in training and owning racehorses. His greatest pleasure was his son Peter's triumph on Just A Dash in the 1981 Melbourne Cup, in part because father and son had plotted together the tactics to be employed in the running. Peter won the Melbourne Cup again in 1984.

On 19 October 1933 at St Aloysius' Catholic Church, Caulfield, Melbourne, Cook had married Ray (Rae) Estelle Sybil Fisher, an actress who had played Doreen in Francis (Frank) Thring's [q.v.12] screen version of *The Sentimental Bloke*, produced in the previous year. For years Cook helped to raise money for St Margaret's Hospital, Darlinghurst. Survived by his wife and their three daughters and three sons, he died on 29 January 1985 at the Gold Coast, Queensland, and was buried in the Allambe Garden of Memories cemetery, Nerang. In his career Cook won virtually every major race in Australia, the Epsom and Doncaster standing out as the only significant exceptions. The journalist Bill Whittaker remembered Cook as 'the most immaculate rider ... to don racing colours in Sydney'.

N. Penton, *A Racing Heart* (1987); J. Pollard, *Australian Horse Racing* (1988); *People* (Sydney),

13 Sept 1950, p 40; *Sun-Herald* (Sydney), 26 July 1959, pp 3 and 64; *Daily Mirror* (Sydney), 1 Dec 1978, p 56, 14 Aug 1979, p 51; *Age* (Melbourne), 4 Nov 1981, p 1, 30 Jan 1985, p 34; *SMH*, 30 Jan 1985, p 36, 2 Feb 1985, p 71; N. Bennetts, interview with W. Cook (ts, 1980, NLA).

RICHARD WATERHOUSE

COOKE, MAXWELL GREAYER (1898-1989), insurance manager, was born on 31 December 1898 in Perth, son of William Ernest Cooke [q.v.8], government astronomer, and his wife Jessie Elizabeth, née Greayer, who were both born in South Australia. In 1912 Maxwell moved with his family to Sydney and completed his schooling at Sydney Grammar School. From 1917 to 1920 he studied economics at the University of Sydney (B.Ec., 1921).

Cooke devoted his entire life to the insurance industry. He began work with the Mutual Life & Citizens' Assurance Co. Ltd in Sydney in 1917 and after appointments as branch manager of the Commonwealth General Assurance Corporation Ltd in Adelaide and of Commonwealth Life (Amalgamated) Assurances Ltd in Perth in 1928, he was appointed branch manager of the Prudential Assurance Co. Ltd in Adelaide in 1933. In New South Wales the government had been involved with insurance in a small way from 1911 through its Treasury Fire Insurance Board (from 1917 Treasury Insurance Board). The Government Insurance Office was established in 1926 to cater for the business generated by the Workers' Compensation Act, 1926, which had been bitterly opposed by private insurance companies. The Government Insurance (Amendment) Act, 1941, introduced by the McKell [q.v.] Labor government, allowed the GIO, as a corporate body, to expand its business to include all forms of insurance. Cooke became general manager on 16 November 1942.

Bringing to the GIO an extensive knowledge of all types of insurance, Cooke helped the organisation to enter the life assurance field. The GIO was less successful, however, in the contentious field of third-party (motor vehicle) insurance that private firms generally shunned. Between February 1943 and December 1953, after underwriting nearly 70 per cent of the State's third-party business, it lost £1.1 million. Blaming this loss on the four-person jury system that made disproportionately high awards for 'pain and suffering' and press publicity of these large awards, Cooke advocated 'some sort of stability' in the scale of awards so that insurers could fix premiums with some notion of how much they could expect to pay claimants. By mid-1959, with 82 per cent of the State's third-party business, the GIO had an accumulated loss of £4.5 million. Cooke's view

was that 'if motorists were careless in the control of their vehicles, they must expect to pay compensation. If this compensation exceeds the total of insurance premiums, the premiums must be increased'. The government substantially increased premiums in late 1959. Cooke claimed that the GIO was not less efficient in its claims settlements than other insurers and ran its third-party business at an expense rate of 3-4 per cent, 'by far the lowest in Australia'. In June 1959 he opposed any change in the law that prevented husbands and wives from suing each other.

The losses, however, on third-party were more than offset by profits in other types of insurance, and Cooke could justly claim to have 'constantly done everything possible to keep down the costs of all classes of insurance'. On his retirement on 31 July 1962, GIO had 91 per cent of the third-party business and was one of Australia's leading life companies with total assets under management exceeding £50 million. Later that year he became general manager of Security Life Assurances Ltd. He had been appointed OBE in 1959.

A director of Coal Mines Insurance Pty Ltd, and a member of the Mine Subsidence Board and the Actuarial Society of Australasia, Cooke was also involved in the management and regulation of the insurance industry; in 1954 he was president of the Insurance Institute of New South Wales. A fellow of the Australian Insurance Institute, he served as president in 1962. Tennis and bowls were his main recreations; he belonged to the Double Bay Bowling Club, the Royal Sydney Yacht Squadron and Tattersall's Club, Sydney.

Cooke had married Georgina Liggins Rankin, née Denning, a divorcee, on 21 April 1928 at North Unley, Adelaide. Following her death he married with Anglican rites Dulcima Gladys Anthony, a secretary, on 8 October 1954 at the Church of St John the Baptist, Milson's Point. There were no children of either marriage. Survived by his wife, he died on 7 June 1989 at Surry Hills and was cremated.

A. C. Gray, *Life Insurance in Australia* (1977); *SMH*, 27 Aug 1942, p 4, 15 Dec 1953, p 3, 16 Dec 1953, p 10, 5 June 1959, p 1, 9 June 1959, p 13, 1 Oct 1959, p 6, 7 Nov 1959, p 2, 10 Oct 1961, p 2, 24 May 1962, p 11, 1 Aug 1962, p 8; *Security*, June 1945, p 4, Jan 1950, p 47; Inc Austn Insurance Inst, *Jnl*, vol 40, 1962-63, p 5; *Daily Telegraph* (Sydney), 13 June 1989, p 34.

G. P. WALSH

COOMBE, REGINALD JOSEPH (1899-1985), magistrate, was born on 7 August 1899 at Gawler, South Australia, second of three sons of Joseph Coombe, engineer, and his wife Emily Avis, née Cheek. The family was renowned for its passion for music and its strong Methodist faith. Reg was educated at Gawler

Public and Adelaide High schools and Prince Alfred College, Adelaide. Winning a scholarship to study the organ, he began a music course at the Elder [q.v.4] Conservatorium of Music, University of Adelaide, but in 1920 transferred to the faculty of law (LL B, 1923). Articled (1919-23) to A. J. McLachlan [q.v.10], he was admitted as a barrister and solicitor on 13 December 1923. In 1924-30 he practised as a solicitor at Waikerie. On 2 July 1927 at East Adelaide Methodist Church he married Adelaide Hilda Headland (d.1981).

The Depression forced Coombe to return to the city and he entered into partnership with Howard Vaughan [q.v.12]. In 1935 he was appointed a stipendiary magistrate, to preside over the Adelaide Juvenile Court. Awarded a travelling fellowship by the Carnegie Corporation of New York, in 1939 he toured the United States of America and Europe observing a variety of juvenile justice systems. Following the trip he drafted the Juvenile Courts Act, 1941, and made other recommendations, focusing on crime prevention, that became the foundation of the current juvenile justice framework in South Australia. He was an advocate for the humane treatment of young offenders and he emphasised a rehabilitation process to support the courts in their work. Seeing the need to recruit suitably skilled professionals, he helped to establish the academic study of social work in Adelaide. From 1950 he was also a magistrate in the Adelaide Police Court.

A firm believer in the benefits of physical activity, Coombe was a board-member of the local Young Men's Christian Association (president 1942-45) and chairman (1945-49) of the Boys' Brigade, Adelaide. He helped to establish many organisations, including the South Australian Board of Social Study and Training (1935), National Fitness Council of South Australia (1939), South Australian Council of Social Service (1947) and Marriage Guidance Council of South Australia (1950). Inaugural president (1949-51, 1963-65) of the Good Neighbour Council of South Australia, he was active on its executive for twenty-six years, encouraging newcomers 'to retain their love for their land of birth, its language and culture'.

Coombe's humanitarianism was a logical expression of his deep religious faith; he practised what T. H. Green called a 'simple, religious citizenship'. He played the organ at various Adelaide churches and found time to train choirs and occasionally to preach. In the report on his Carnegie tour he had remarked that the methods of American judges were 'a lesson in courtesy, patience and friendliness'; these qualities defined Coombe also. He was appointed MBE in 1956, and raised to OBE in 1968. Tall and thin, he was always well groomed. He read voraciously and maintained an active sporting life, playing cricket and lawn bowls. Generous with his time, after retirement in 1964, he worked as a relieving magistrate, and as a volunteer at the Glenside Hospital. He was named South Australian Father of the Year in 1969. Survived by a son and a daughter, he died on 18 May 1985 at Toorak Gardens and was cremated.

News (Adelaide), 4 Aug 1964, p 24; *Advertiser* (Adelaide), 7 Apr 1983, p 7; L. Arnold, taped interview with R. J. Coombe (ts, 1969, SLSA); L. E. Ardlie, *Australianization to Melting Pot* (BA Hons thesis, Univ of Adelaide, 1967); Good Neighbour Council of SA records (SLSA); private information.

BRENDAN MORAN

COOPER, ARTHUR GEORGE STENING (1899-1986), radiologist, was born on 28 November 1899 at Mosman, Sydney, only child of Henry Kingsbury Cooper, a woolbroker's clerk from South Australia, and his Sydney-born wife Harriet Priscilla, née Stening. After attending Sydney Grammar School, Arthur studied medicine at the University of Sydney (MB, Ch.M., 1923), where he represented Wesley College in rifle-shooting. He travelled to Britain and in 1923-24 was a house surgeon and physician at Royal Hampshire County Hospital, Winchester. On 30 October 1924 at St Peter's Church of England, Belsize Park, Hampstead, London, he married Marguerite Henry (d.1982).

Back in New South Wales, Cooper worked (1925-37) as a general practitioner at Denman, in the Hunter Valley. He was interested in X-rays and, after two years of postgraduate study at the Royal Cancer Hospital, London, was awarded (1938) a diploma in medical radiology by the University of London. He was radiologist at New Plymouth Hospital, New Zealand, until 1940, when he was appointed radiological supervisor at (Royal) Brisbane Hospital. His offer to join the Australian Army Medical Corps, Australian Imperial Force, was not accepted and in 1941 he was commissioned honorary captain in the Reserve of Officers. With one registrar, he experienced long days, especially early in 1942, with units of Allied forces requiring radiological services. In 1944, through contacts in the United States Army, he obtained radioactive phosphorus and reputedly was the first in Australia to use this material. That year he became full-time radiotherapist-in-charge of the new Queensland Radium Institute, and in 1946 was made director.

Under Cooper, the institute gained the respect of colleagues in Australia and overseas. Annual reports disclosed outcomes of therapy as measured by percentages of cancer patients surviving five years. Quiet, determined and thoughtful, Cooper led his staff by example and created a happy, though very busy, team. He treated his patients with kindness and courtesy, as well as with skill, setting the standard at that which he would wish to experience if he were a patient. In 1961 he helped to found the Queensland Cancer Fund; he was a trustee (1965-85), and a member of its anti-cancer council (1962-67) and its medical and scientific advisory committee (1962-66). In 1965 the fund named a hospital for country patients at Hamilton, Brisbane, after him. He was appointed CBE in 1963.

Cooper served (1951-66) on the radio therapy advisory committee of the National Health and Medical Research Council. A foundation fellow of the (Royal) College of Radiologists of Australasia, he was elected president (1965-66) and became a life member in 1971. He was an honorary member of the Japan Radiological Society. After retiring as director of QRI in 1965 he continued in private practice for ten years. A keen gardener, he also played tennis until his retirement and then took up bowls. He enjoyed fishing and relaxing at his beach house by Currimundi Lake on the Sunshine Coast. Survived by his two daughters and son, he died on 14 March 1986 at Brookfield, Brisbane, and was cremated.

H. R. Woolcock and M. J. Thearle, *A History of the Queensland Cancer Fund* (1991); *A'asian Radiology*, vol 30, no 4, 1986, p 294; *MJA*, 17 Nov 1986, p 545; personal information.   BRUCE KYNASTON

COOPER, GARRIE CLIFFORD (1935-1982), racing car designer, manufacturer and driver, was born on 22 December 1935 at Glenelg, Adelaide, only child of South Australian-born parents Edwin Henry Clifford Cooper, motor-body builder, and his wife Phyllis Gerder, née Taylor. Educated at St Leonards Public and Goodwood Boys' Technical High schools, Garrie acquired skills in mechanical drawing and metalwork and became passionately interested in motor-racing. Using Austin 7 and A30 components, he designed, built and raced a Cooper-Austin 'special'. In 1958 his father gave him control of the family business, Cooper Motor Bodies, at Edwardstown. On 21 November next year at Trinity Methodist Church, Glenelg, he married Lorraine Joy Chynoweth, a clerk. Shortly after, he produced a small batch of a model named Streamliner, based on the British-made Lotus Eleven.

Renaming the firm Elfin Sports Cars Pty Ltd, Cooper manufactured more Streamliners and a string of other models, including the Clubman, and established his reputation as a designer and manufacturer. Although he lacked professional qualifications, his solid technical background, manual expertise, dedication and enthusiasm, together with a small but highly skilled work team and the backing of his father, ensured a steady flow of sports or racing cars that compared favourably with imported models. The Elfin Mono, introduced at the 1964 Melbourne Racing Car Show, was particularly competitive.

Success on the track, however, did not translate into sales. Ever resilient, Cooper designed the space-framed Type 600 and in April drove it to victory at the Singapore Grand Prix. The resultant publicity and prize money of $5000 revived Elfin's fortunes, which were further consolidated when Cooper jointly won the Australian Formula 2 Championship with Max Stewart. The 600 proved to be a world-class car, and a Formula Ford variant provided aspiring young drivers with the opportunity to compete overseas.

In 1971 Cooper was fitted with an artificial valve to correct a congenital heart condition. Next year Ansett [q.v.] Transport Industries Ltd became the Elfin team's sponsor. In 1978 Cooper was awarded the Confederation of Australian Motor Sport's membership of honour. Competing later that year in the Australian Grand Prix at the Sandown International Motor Racing Circuit, Melbourne, he was severely injured when, due to mechanical failure, his Elfin Formula 5000 car crashed at high speed. After battling CAMS medical advisers he renewed his competition licence and finished seventh in the 1980 AGP. He completed manufacture of a new model, the MR9, before the loss of Ansett's support in mid-1981 threatened Elfin's financial viability and Cooper's driving opportunities. Turning his attention to building a clubman road car, he scaled down his racing activities.

Tall, quietly spoken, unassuming, and habitually dressed in faded jeans and a checked shirt, Cooper could be stubborn but was never arrogant. Survived by his wife and their son and daughter, he died of a ruptured aortic aneurysm on 25 April 1982 in Adelaide and was cremated. Elfin Sports Cars had produced over 240 cars since 1959 and was considered the most successful racing car constructor in the Southern hemisphere. Cooper's family and friends remembered his optimism in the face of adversity, and especially the perennial end-of-season promise to his wife, 'next year will be the year, Lor'.

J. Blanden and B. Catford, *Australia's Elfin Sports and Racing Cars* (1997); *Advertiser* (Adelaide), 27 Apr 1982, p 10; personal knowledge.
                                        PETER STRAWHAN

COOPER, GLEN ALBERT (1915-1986), air force officer, was born on 20 November 1915 at Glenferrie, Melbourne, second child of Victorian-born parents Leslie Claude Cooper (d.1934), carpenter and later butcher-shop proprietor, and his wife Nellie, née McDowell. Baptised into the Churches of Christ, Glen was educated at state schools at Mitcham, Kew and East Kew, and to Intermediate certificate level at Melbourne High School, before finding work as a manchester salesman. As a boy he had learned the trumpet. Family tradition has it that the money earned in competitions and in dance bands enabled him to remain in school.

On 16 July 1934 Cooper enlisted in the Royal Australian Air Force as an aircraft-hand. He remustered as a clerk and bandsman, and in 1936 began flying training, an unusual privilege for a man of his rank in the 1930s. Graduating as a sergeant in December, he spent five months with No.1 Squadron at Laverton before being recalled to No.1 Flying Training School, Point Cook, as an instructor, another indication of rare ability.

Cooper was commissioned in the Permanent Air Force on 1 June 1939. On 24 June that year at St Patrick's Cathedral, Melbourne, he married with Catholic rites Doreen May Freeland, a hairdresser. He resigned his commission in August and the couple moved to Adelaide, where he was appointed chief flying instructor with the Royal Aero Club of South Australia. In July 1940, however, he was recalled to the Active List of the Citizen Air Force. Promoted to flying officer in August, he filled instructional posts at Parafield, and at Camden and Narromine, New South Wales. In July 1942 he was posted to No.2 Operational Training Unit, Mildura, Victoria, where, by this time a flight lieutenant, he trained as a fighter pilot.

From October 1942 Cooper flew for short periods with Nos 23, 83 and 86 squadrons, gaining operational experience with the last of these at Merauke, Netherlands New Guinea. Finally, in September 1943 he assumed command of No.80 Squadron at Townsville, Queensland, as a temporary squadron leader. Flying Kittyhawks, the unit was based successively from February 1944 at Nadzab, Cape Gloucester, Aitape, Hollandia, Biak and Noemfoor, advancing with the army as it occupied New Guinea and the nearby islands. For the 'utmost daring' with which he led his squadron in many dive-bombing and strafing attacks on the enemy throughout the campaign, Cooper was awarded the Distinguished Flying Cross.

Relinquishing his command in July 1944, Cooper returned to Australia and in October was posted to No.2 OTU as an instructor. In January 1945 he was promoted to temporary wing commander. He converted to Spitfires and in March succeeded Group Captain Clive Caldwell as officer commanding No.80 Wing at Morotai, Netherlands East Indies, where the RAAF was concentrating for the forthcoming invasion of Borneo. After the war ended, he was promoted to acting group captain in September and given command of No.81 Wing, equipped with Mustang fighters, which arrived in Japan in March 1946 as part of the occupation forces. He returned to Air Force Headquarters, Melbourne, in June 1947.

In September 1948 Cooper received a permanent commission as an acting wing commander. Although lack of seniority prevented promotion to the highest ranks, his talents were rewarded with an unusual number of commands: No.1 FTS (1949-50); No.21 Squadron, one of the first Australian squadrons to fly jet fighters (1950-52); North-Western Area, Darwin (1952-54); No.78 Wing when the Sabre aircraft were deployed from Australia to Malaya for active operations (1957-60); and the RAAF Base, Williamtown, New South Wales, during the introduction of the supersonic Mirage fighter (1966-70). For his leadership at No.78 Wing, Cooper was awarded the Air Force Cross (1959).

Cooper was superintendent of the RAAF at the Weapons Research Establishment, Woomera, in 1962-63. Between 1963 and 1966 he was air attaché in Paris, where he was involved in planning for the introduction of the Mirage into RAAF service. For this work he was appointed a commander of the National Order of Merit by the French government in 1967. Having risen to group captain in January 1957, he was promoted to acting air commodore in November 1966 (substantive October 1968). He retired in 1970 to bayside Melbourne and the challenges of the Victoria Golf Club. That year he was appointed CBE.

Compact and athletic, gentlemanly in manner and appearance, with fair hair and a clipped moustache, Cooper epitomised the contemporary ideal of a fighter pilot. He commanded with generosity and good humour, expecting high self-discipline from his pilots but encouraging them to enjoy the adventure and high spirits he associated with flying fighters. Survived by his wife, and their son and daughter, he died of cancer on 6 April 1986 in East Melbourne and was cremated with Anglican rites and full air force honours.

G. Odgers, *Air War against Japan 1943-1945* (1957) and *The Royal Australian Air Force* (1965); A. Stephens, *Going Solo* (1995); *Units of the Royal Australian Air Force*, vol 2 (1995); J. H. Harding, *It Had to B.U.* (1996); F. Morton, taped interview with Cooper (1980, NLA); private information.

DON LANCASTER*

COOPER, JANET PIERSON (1891-1984), medical practitioner, mayor and community worker, was born on 25 February 1891 at Elmsvale, Nova Scotia, Canada, daughter of William James Cooper, who ran a farm and a wood-lot, and his wife Margaret, née Ervin.

Her father died when she was 4 and her sister still a toddler. Janet attended school at Middle Musquodoboit. The family had connections in the United States of America and at 16 she left for Boston, Massachusetts, intending to enrol as a nurse. Rejected because of her youth, she advertised for a position and went to the household of Dudley Page at Stoneham as companion for his adult daughter who was suffering from complications of diabetes. After her death, Page advised Janet to study medicine rather than nursing, and offered to pay her expenses. She completed the course, then based on homoeopathy, at Boston University (MD, 1917).

Through a Methodist minister, Seth Cary, brother-in-law of W. K. Bouton [q.v.7], Cooper learned of a call from Melbourne Homoeopathic (Prince Henry's) Hospital for resident medical officers, and was accepted for a three-year term. According to Jacqueline Templeton, the arrival of the 'Yankee girl' in October 1917 as the hospital's first female doctor created a stir, but her vivacity and energy, and her skill as 'a particularly fine anaesthetist', won over her colleagues. She was on the honorary medical staff in 1921-48, and from 1928 was honorary anaesthetist. Convinced that homoeopathy's benefits lay not in 'drugs but humanity', she embraced its melding with standard medicine during the 1920s.

On 22 October 1918 at Collingwood she married with Congregational forms Robert Jensen (d.1934), a 42-year-old musician. They moved to the USA in 1923 but a scarcity of jobs forced their return. King O'Malley [q.v.11], one of her many friends from widely divergent backgrounds, assisted her to secure a bank loan and she set up in private practice at 6 Kerferd Road, Albert Park. She married Frank Royden Beauchamp Swifte (d.1968), an inspector, on 6 April 1939 at Holy Advent Anglican Church, Malvern.

To ameliorate social problems affecting her patients, particularly women and children, Dr Cooper helped to invigorate local community support groups. In 1944-46 she was unsuccessful but polled well as an Independent in elections for South Melbourne City Council. Her backing was based on her membership of the League of Women Voters of Victoria (president 1967), the Melbourne Business and Professional Women's Club (president 1959), the Lyceum Club, the Penguin Club of Australia (Victorian branch), the Woman's Christian Temperance Union of Victoria, and numerous other community and charitable organisations.

In 1950, standing again as an Independent, Cooper was elected South Melbourne's first female councillor. Defeated in 1953 but returned in 1956, she again broke new ground by serving as mayor in 1958-59. She lost to Doris Condon [q.v.13] in 1962, but was re-elected in 1963 and had a second mayoral term in 1965-66, before retiring. As councillor and mayor she had maintained her strong social focus, founding the South Melbourne Women's Auxiliary, whose gatherings featured speakers and musicians, combined with fund-raising for local youth programs.

Cooper had been appointed OBE in 1959. In the early 1970s she moved to Hawthorn but continued to practise at Albert Park. To her intense satisfaction, she returned there for care at the South Port Community Nursing Home, which she had helped establish. She died on 6 June 1984 at the home and was cremated with the forms of the Uniting Church. Her daughter and adopted daughter survived her.

J. Templeton, *Prince Henry's* (1969); S. Priestley, *South Melbourne* (1995); *Age* (Melbourne), 10 Aug 1944, p 3, 3 Sept 1958, p 8; *Herald* (Melbourne), 2 Sept 1958, p 15, 18 Oct 1965, p 3, 21 Feb 1970, p 38, 22 Dec 1978, p 11; *Sunday Press* (Melbourne), 3 May 1981, p 13; private information.

SUSAN PRIESTLEY

COOPER, REVEL RONALD (1934?-1983), artist, was born of Nyungar descent, probably in 1934, at Katanning, Western Australia. As a young boy Revel was declared a ward of the state and placed in the Carrolup Native Settlement (from 1948 Marribank farm school). Amid conditions of poverty and degradation, in 1945 the school headmaster, Noel White, and his wife, Lily, established educational programs in art and music. Art produced by Carrolup children, including Revel, was widely exhibited: at Boans [q.v.7] Ltd department store, Perth (1947); at Mysore, India (1949); and, through the auspices of a visiting Englishwoman, Florence Rutter, in New Zealand, Britain and the Netherlands (1950). Revel's work appeared in *Child Artists of the Australian Bush* (1952), written by (Dame) Mary Durack Miller in association with Rutter.

The Whites intended that the training provided at Carrolup would serve a vocational role and Cooper was employed for a short period by J. Gibbney & Son Pty Ltd, commercial artists, Perth. When Marribank closed in 1951 he worked locally as a farm labourer and as a railway fettler. In November 1952 he was convicted of manslaughter and sentenced to four years' imprisonment. Cooper subsequently served several prison sentences in Western Australia and Victoria. Nevertheless he succeeded in forging a career as an artist. In the mid-1950s he was employed briefly at Bill Onus's [q.v.15] Aboriginal Enterprise Novelties, and he became a role model for the young aspiring artist Lin Onus and a formative influence on later generations of Nyungar artists.

With help from an art collector, James Davidson, and the Victorian Aborigines

Advancement League, Cooper exhibited regularly during the 1960s in Victoria and elsewhere, gaining recognition for his landscapes and corroboree scenes. In a review in the Melbourne communist weekly, the *Guardian*, of 28 March 1963, Noel Counihan [q.v.] spoke of Cooper's 'strongly original artistic talent'. Working from Fremantle Prison, Cooper undertook several commissions, among them illustrations for the second edition of Mary Durack's book *Yagan of the Bibbulmun* (1976), and images of the stations of the cross for the Sacred Heart Church, Mount Barker, Western Australia. With emerging Aboriginal self-determination he assumed a new cultural voice. While in gaol at Geelong, Victoria, he wrote an article, 'To Regain Our Pride', for the July-September 1968 issue of the *Aboriginal Quarterly*. In an interview for a documentary, 'The Broken Covenant', broadcast posthumously by Australian Broadcasting Corporation television on 1 September 1983, he recalled his experience of discrimination and injustice and, in a passionate affirmation of his Aboriginality, attacked the materialism of a 'white', 'machine' world.

Cooper was of medium height with a slim build, a broad smile and an open, friendly disposition. His struggle with alcoholism and his itinerancy contributed to both the achievements and the tragedy of his life. About April 1983 he died from the effects of head injuries received when he was attacked with a heavy instrument. His body was found on 28 December 1985 at Buxton, after Matthew DeCarteret confessed to the murder. He was buried on 30 January 1987 in the Catholic section of the Fawkner cemetery. Cooper is regarded as a leading figure of a distinctive Nyungar landscape tradition that is the heritage of Carrolup. His work is represented in the Berndt [q.v.] Museum of Anthropology (University of Western Australia), the Art Gallery of Western Australia, and Fremantle Prison, Fremantle Hospital and Holmes à Court [q.v.] collections.

J. E. Stanton, *Nyungar Landscapes* (1992); S. Kleinert, 'Aboriginal Landscapes', in G. Levitus (ed), *Lying about the Landscape* (1997); S. Kleinert and M. Neale (eds), *The Oxford Companion to Aboriginal Art and Culture* (2000); *West Australian*, 27 Nov 1952, p 12, 29 Nov 1952, p 7; *Age* (Melbourne), 14 Nov 1985, p 21; private information.

SYLVIA KLEINERT

CORBOULD, HAROLD EDWARD (1909-1989), pastoralist and philanthropist, was born on 9 February 1909 at Bellevue Hill, Sydney, younger of twin sons of Victorian-born William Henry Corbould [q.v.8], mining engineer, and his wife Una Robina, née Dodds, from New South Wales. Two sisters had preceded the boys, one dying in infancy. After earlier years near a copper mine at Burraga, New South Wales, their mother became 'resolutely urban'. Their father, who was to found Mount Isa Mines Ltd, was usually in north-west Queensland or travelling abroad, raising capital for his mining ventures. 'Ted' and his brother, Eric ('Bill'), were educated at Tudor House, Moss Vale, and The King's School, Parramatta.

On leaving school in 1926 Ted Corbould worked as a jackeroo, woolclasser and overseer. In 1934, assisted financially by his father, he acquired Avon Lake, a property near Cooma. Although primarily a commercial wool-grower, from about 1951 he also maintained merino sheep and Aberdeen Angus cattle studs. Intensely hard-working, he was nicknamed 'Daylight' by station hands, who had to use all of it. In the 1940s he accumulated more land in the Monaro region, which he sold in the wool boom of the early 1950s, making a substantial profit. Moving to the New England area in 1955, he bought several properties, including Springfield, near Wallangra, north-west of Inverell, and in 1960 Avon, near Tenterfield. In 1956 he acquired a group of leases amounting to 4540 sq. miles (11 759 km^2) of 'good cattle breeding country' north-west of Coen, Cape York Peninsula, Queensland. Headquarters were at Rokeby station. Amid a flurry of further negotiations Corbould began improvements, including cattle yards, an airstrip, and housing for Aboriginal stockmen, and bought stock. He sold the enterprise in 1959, for a time retaining a minor interest.

About 1960 Corbould studied for a short while at the Julian Ashton [q.v.7] Art School, Sydney. Ill health saw him return to New England, and by late 1963 he was in semi-retirement at Eagle Heights, Tamborine Mountain, Queensland. From 1966 he mostly lived on a small farm called Wilga, at Bunya, north of Brisbane (with two years back in the Tamborine district in 1980-82). He bought up smallholdings in south-east Queensland, some from dairy farmers leaving the industry, others in pockets that had been little developed by previous owners. At times a tree planter, from about 1975 he donated twenty properties to the Queensland government for conservation purposes. According to an official of the State's Environmental Protection Agency, Tim Ellis, it was the single most important contribution to the conservation of south-east Queensland by any non-State organisation or individual.

In 1977 Corbould, suffering from emphysema, became distressed when his favourite cattle dog died. His housekeeper contacted the Salvation Army. An officer came to the house, buried the dog, and consoled the household. Corbould commented: 'if the Salvos will do this for a dog, what do they do for people?'. Over the next twelve years he gave the Salvation Army more than $2.5 million and donated generously to charities such as the Blue Nursing Service. In 1980 he sold land at Caloundra cheaply to the Landsborough Shire Council for what was to become the Corbould Park racecourse. He provided $50 000 to the Astronomical Association of Queensland in 1987 for research projects.

Corbould was appointed MBE in 1987. Shy but polished in manner, frugal to a fault and at times litigious, despite increasing illness he spent his later years pursuing his interests in painting, in conservation and, above all, in donating to charities that he considered the most practical. He died on 10 June 1989 at Everton Park, Brisbane, and was buried with Salvation Army forms at Pinnaroo lawn cemetery, Aspley. Corbould had never married. His will, after personal legacies and a bequest of $10 000 to the 'Infinite Way' movement founded by Joel S. Goldsmith, directed that the income from continuing trusts be distributed predominantly to the Salvation Army, and the remainder to other charities that he had supported. In 2002 Perpetual Trustees Queensland Ltd, on behalf of the Harold Edward Corbould Charitable Trust, distributed $537 240 to the Salvation Army, Queensland, and $143 789 to other good causes. Properties that he had given to the Commonwealth in his lifetime were transferred in 1994 to the Queensland government; they are now nature reserves named for Edward Corbould and Una Corbould.

W. H. Corbould, *Broken Hill to Mount Isa* (1981); K. W. Lawrence, *The Background to the Sunshine Coast Turf Club and the Development of Corbould Park 1975-1985* (1985); J. Broinowski, *A Family Memoir* (1993); *Daily Sun* (Brisbane), 30 May 1986, p 1; *Sunday Mail* (Brisbane), 18 June 1989, p 3; Supreme Court of Qld, file 2980/96, Re: Perpetual Trustees Qld Ltd (Supreme Court of Qld archives); personal information.   S. J. ROUTH

CORDER, ADA ELIZABETH (1895-1987), pianist and music teacher, was born on 20 March 1895 at Ararat, Victoria, daughter of James Charles Freeman, railway guard, and his wife Ada, née Byrne, both Victorian born. For her sixth birthday Ada was given a piano; by 8 she had won an under-13 piano championship, her early musical development being fostered by Mother Mary Agnes (also known as Madame Stewart) during her education (1906-12) at the Faithful Companions of Jesus' Vaucluse convent at Richmond, Melbourne. In 1910 Ada was selected as solo pianist for concerts given in Melbourne by the Australian tenor Walter Kirby, and in 1911 she was awarded an Australian Natives Association scholarship. That year she attained licentiates of the Royal School of Music (piano) and of Trinity College of Music, London (piano and

teaching). At 17 she entered the University of Melbourne's conservatorium of music (B.Mus., 1917), where, after completing a diploma in music, she was admitted to the third year of the bachelor of music degree. Studying (1913-16) piano under Edward Goll [q.v.9], she won an Ormond [q.v.5] exhibition each year and graduated with honours.

Miss Freeman was 'constantly before the public', as solo pianist, accompanist and performer with orchestras. She introduced Australia to works by Elgar, Prokofiev and Ravel then regarded, she later said, as 'weird music'. But it was as a teacher that she made her greatest contribution. Her students were regularly celebrated for their 'excellent grounding' and ability, and she taught and promoted many young pianists of exceptional talent, among them Stephen McIntyre, Geoffrey Saba and Raymond O'Connell. Nancy Weir was her most renowned pupil, and in 1930 Freeman travelled with her 14-year-old protégée to Berlin, where they both studied with Artur Schnabel. Freeman proceeded to further study in London with George Woodhouse, returning to Australia in 1931. On 26 January 1937 she married Henry Corder, a clerk, at Our Lady of Victories Basilica, Camberwell.

Mrs Corder took great pride in her teaching, trusting—as she put it—in 'some intuitive feeling' that she could 'get out of [pupils] what is in them'. In 1965 she joined with Weir to found the Australian Musicians Overseas Scholarship, which (to 1976) commissioned original works for piano by Australian composers and enabled Australian pianists to study abroad. She was an honorary life member of the Victorian Music Teachers Association and a member of the Royal Overseas League (London and Melbourne) and the Lyceum Club, Melbourne. In 1974 she was appointed MBE. She retained a 'tremendous enthusiasm' for teaching into her eighties, although her playing was by then inhibited by arthritis. Predeceased (1965) by her husband, and childless, she died on 27 September 1987 at Camberwell and was buried in Box Hill cemetery.

A. Lofthouse (comp), *Who's Who of Australian Women* (1982); M. C. O'Connor, *The Sisters, Faithful Companions of Jesus in Australia* (1982); *Austn Musical News*, Oct 1923, p 25, Oct 1928, p 15, Feb 1931, p 9, Nov 1931, p 10; *Herald* (Melbourne), 24 June 1975, p 19.   EMMA MATTHEWS

CORDNER, GEORGE DENIS PRUEN (1924-1990), footballer and businessman, was born on 28 June 1924 at Diamond Creek, Victoria, third of four sons of Edward Rae Cordner (1887-1963), a Victorian-born medical practitioner, and his English wife Margaret Constance, née Pruen. Educated at Melbourne

Church of England Grammar School, Denis enlisted in the Royal Australian Naval Reserve on 6 May 1942. He served in the South-West Pacific in HMA ships *San Michele, Kapunda* and *Barcoo*, and was promoted to sub-lieutenant in 1944. Demobilised in 1946, he was to be active in the naval volunteer reserve until 1964, rising to lieutenant commander (1957). He studied metallurgy at the University of Melbourne (B.Sc., 1949; M.Sc., 1951) under the Commonwealth Reconstruction Training Scheme. On 15 January 1947 at St John's Church of England, Darlinghurst, Sydney, he married Patricia Shirley Bowes, a stenographer.

Standing 6 ft 4 ins (193 cm), Cordner played once for the Melbourne Football Club in 1942 and for the University Blacks in 1946-48, gaining a Blue in the first season. In 1947 he was awarded a Blue for cricket and a half-Blue for athletics. As his final examinations approached in 1948, he was reluctantly persuaded to play at centre half-back for Melbourne in the Victorian Football League grand final against Essendon. The game was drawn and Cordner was named one of Melbourne's six best. He took part in the rematch, which his team won. Thereafter, he was a ruckman. Playing 152 games for Melbourne, he captained the side in the 1951-53 seasons and won its Best and Fairest trophy in 1950 and 1954 before retiring in 1956. That year he led a team comprising VFL and Victorian Football Association amateurs that defeated a Victorian Amateur Football Association side in an exhibition match at the Olympic Games. He had represented Victoria in 1949, 1951, 1952 and 1955.

In 1951, calling himself 'an industrial chemist and spare-time footballer', Cordner had started working for Wunderlich Ltd. Six years later British Nylon Spinners (Australia) Pty Ltd (later Fibremakers Ltd), a subsidiary of Imperial Chemical Industries (Australasia) Ltd, appointed him production superintendent. Selected in 1964 to be general manager of Fibremakers (New Zealand) Ltd, he moved to Auckland and started a synthetic-fibre factory, despite protests from the wool industry. By 1968 he was back in Australia as general manager of ICI's alkali-chemical group. In 1970 he became an executive director of ICI Australia Ltd, and in 1972 managing director of Fibremakers Ltd. The following year he was posted to Britain as joint deputy-chairman of ICI Fibres Ltd, returning to Australia in 1977. He was a managing director of ICI Australia Ltd and chairman of Australian Fertilisers Ltd and Consolidated Fertilisers Ltd from 1979.

Appointed by the Fraser coalition government to a three-year term as Australian consul-general, New York, Cordner stepped down from his directorships and took office in March 1982. The Hawke Labor government recalled him after two years. His candid disappointment at what he considered an 'unearned' dismissal did not impress the government. He joined the boards of AMI Toyota Ltd (chairman from 1985), British Petroleum Co. of Australia Ltd, Plessey Pacific Pty Ltd and John Holland Holdings Ltd (chairman from 1986).

Cordner studied naval history in his spare time. In 1978-80 he was Australian co-ordinator of Operation Drake, a 'discovery voyage' for young people organised by the (British) Scientific Exploration Society. Later he was active in the Queen Elizabeth II Silver Jubilee Trust for Young Australians. He encouraged the restoration of the schooner *Alma Doepel* in Melbourne. Prints of sailing ships adorned his office walls, and he was able to observe the vessels entering Port Phillip heads from the Cordner family holiday house at Point Lonsdale, where he and his three brothers, Edward, Donald and John, spent many happy times with their families. The rangy brothers were renowned as 'brainy' sportsmen. Ted and Don became medical practitioners and John a chemist and company director. All played football for the Melbourne club, as had their father and his brother Henry (Harry) before them, and Ted's son David after them. The family's collective sporting ability was acknowledged in the naming of the Cordner Entrance at the Melbourne Cricket Ground in 1993.

Good looking with fair, wavy hair, Denis Cordner was quiet, straightforward, unassuming and popular. In later life he played tennis and golf and allowed himself the extravagance of a succession of red Jaguar cars. He died of coronary heart disease on 17 October 1990 at his East Kew home and was buried in Point Lonsdale cemetery. His wife and their two daughters survived him.

R. Holmesby and J. Main, *The Encyclopedia of AFL Footballers* (2002); *Herald* (Melbourne), 4 July 1972, p 2; *Age* (Melbourne), 7 Dec 1978, p 17, 25 Mar 1990, p 4, 18 Oct 1990, p 28; *Sunday Press* (Melbourne), 18 Oct 1981, p 8; private information.

GILLIAN M. HIBBINS

CORKHILL, ELIZABETH PEARL (1887-1985), nurse, was born on 11 March 1887 at Tilba Tilba, New South Wales, second of three children of William Henry Corkhill, grazier, cheesemaker and photographer, and his wife Frances Hawtrey, née Bate. Samuel Bate [q.v.1] was her great-grandfather. Pearl grew up on her father's property, Marengo, received her early education from a governess and later attended Tilba Tilba Public School. After training at Burilda private hospital, Summer Hill, Sydney, she graduated as a general nurse in 1914. On 4 June 1915 she joined the Australian Army Nursing Service, Australian Imperial Force, as a staff nurse. She was 5 ft 8 ins (173 cm) tall, with grey eyes and brown hair.

Posted to the 1st Australian General Hospital, Corkhill arrived in Egypt in July 1915. From August to January 1916 she was at the Choubra Military Infectious Hospital, where she tended sick troops from the Gallipoli campaign. Reaching France in April, she served at the 2nd British General Hospital, Le Havre. A notable occasion for her was the AIF's first celebration of Anzac Day. To mark the event she and two other Australian nurses wore green gum leaves with the inscription 'Dardanelles 1915'. She rejoined the 1st AGH at Rouen in June 1916.

In June-August 1918 Corkhill was attached to the 38th British Casualty Clearing Station, near Abbeville. On one night in July the CCS suffered an air raid during which Corkhill 'continued to attend to the wounded without any regard for her own safety'. For her 'courage and devotion' she was awarded the Military Medal, becoming one of only seven Australian nurses to receive that award during World War I. Her only comment was that she would have to face 'old George and Mary [King George V and Queen Mary] to get the medal' and that it would cost her a new mess dress as her old one was worn out. Transferred to the 1st Australian Auxiliary Hospital, Harefield, London, in August, she was promoted to sister in October.

Corkhill returned to Australia in March 1919 and her AANS appointment terminated on 22 June. She held various private nursing positions both in Australia and overseas until, in 1951, she was appointed as senior sister at Bega District Hospital, New South Wales. In 1961 Sister Corkhill, as she was always known, retired to Akolele, overlooking Wallaga Lake. Greatly respected in the district, she was often asked to preside at local occasions. A skilful horsewoman, she also led the parade for the centenary of the Cooma Show in 1975.

A major achievement of Corkhill's old age was the donation to the National Library of Australia of about one thousand glass plate negatives of photographs taken by her father in the Tilba Tilba area between 1890 and 1910. Apart from family photos, William Corkhill's images documented with astonishing clarity the people and the social and economic life of this remote dairying area. The library was able to print some 840 of the plates and in 1976 produced an engagement calendar, *Coast and Country*, using fifty-three of them. In 1983 the library published *Taken at Tilba*, a selection of seventy-eight of these photographs. Pearl Corkhill's knowledge of the history and people of Tilba Tilba assisted greatly with the captioning of the collection and she took much satisfaction in knowing that her family had added to the nation's historic collections.

Corkhill died on 4 December 1985 at Dalmeny and was buried with Anglican rites in Narooma cemetery. She had never married.

Her MM and other service medals are held by the Australian War Memorial, Canberra.

R. Goodman, *Our War Nurses* (1988); *SMH*, 25 Apr 1984, p 7; B2455, item Corkhill P E (NAA); PR88/165 (AWM); private information.

RICHARD E. REID

COUCHMAN, DAME ELIZABETH MAY RAMSAY (1876-1982), political organiser and activist, was born on 19 April 1876 at Geelong, Victoria, second surviving child of Scottish-born parents Archibald Tannock, confectioner, and his wife Elizabeth, née Ramsay. The family was of limited means, but May's education to matriculation at Geelong prepared her for employment as a teacher at Methodist Ladies' College and Tintern Girls' Grammar School. Her political interests, aroused early by discussions between her mother and grandmother, drew her to the politically conservative Australian Women's National League in 1910. Ambitious to pursue further study, May left for Perth in 1913 to enrol at the University of Western Australia (BA, 1916), where tuition was free. She founded the Educational Association, of which she was also president, and returned to teaching. On 9 January 1917 at St George's Cathedral, Perth, she married Claude Ernest Couchman (d.1931), an architect and engineer with the Victorian Public Works Department, and a widower with one adult child.

Back in Melbourne, Mrs Couchman embarked on a career of political activism in support of the Nationalist Party through the AWNL. She joined its St Kilda branch and became a vice-president (1918-27). By 1922, alive to the imminence of generational change in the leadership of the league, she accepted appointment to the central executive, becoming its honorary secretary later that year. At the annual conference soon after, she spoke in favour of deleting from the preamble of the AWNL constitution the statement 'we do not wish to send women to Parliament'. Her concern was not for 'the "battlesome" female who talks of sex war' but for women who put 'public good before personal ambition'. The motion was defeated but tapped a current of interest among younger members.

Over the following years Couchman worked to reassure those who may have doubted her suitability for leadership by energetically engaging in organisational and educational work at branch and central levels, and representing the league's views to government ministers on issues ranging from the conservation of timber, a colony for sterilisation of the intellectually disabled, segregation of 'sex-perverts' and the need for more policewomen. The AWNL organ *The Woman* praised her efficiency, 'sound university training' and her gifts as a 'charming and brilliant speaker'. In 1922 she had been unanimously elected secretary (president 1927) of the AWNL Debating Society; in 1925 she became metropolitan vice-president and in 1927 AWNL delegate to the National Council of Women, of which she later became a vice-president and life member. She had also been elected to the executive of the Victorian Women Graduates' Association, the common interests committee of the English Speaking Union, and the council of the Australian Federation of University Women.

In 1927 Couchman was elected president of the AWNL. Although she assured the league that she 'intended to follow in the footsteps of those who had gone before', Couchman also saw new opportunities. She launched the Tasmanian branch of the AWNL in 1928 and sought unsuccessfully to federate the Nationalist Party's women's organisations under AWNL leadership. She also reopened the issue of women's election to parliament. Declaring that 'principles do not alter, but the means by which we attain them change', early in 1931 she nominated for the Senate, commenting acerbically that 'all political wisdom does not lie under the hats of men'. Endorsed only as the emergency United Australia Party candidate, she was not elected. The league's support, however, was unreserved. Its 1932 annual conference finally passed a resolution in favour of 'women candidates for parliament', recognising 'the important part women have taken in political, financial and public matters in the State'.

Couchman's public profile expanded rapidly: she was one of four NCW representatives at the Industrial Peace Conference in Canberra in 1928 and she was made a Victorian justice of the peace the following year. Already vice-president of the Children's Cinema Council, in 1932 she was the first woman appointed a member of the Australian Broadcasting Commission, on which she served to 1942. In 1933 she was elected to the NCW centenary council executive. She helped to plan an international conference of women held in Melbourne in 1934 (at which she spoke of the 'great reservoir of citizenship' contained in women's voluntary organisations). That year she was granted leave to investigate and report on public broadcasting, first in Canada, then in New York and finally in London, where she was a guest of the director-general of the British Broadcasting Corporation, Sir John Reith. She represented Australia at an International Council of Women conference in Paris, and addressed a meeting at the Sorbonne in French.

Within weeks of leaving Australia, Mrs Couchman was also asked by the Commonwealth government to travel on to Geneva as alternate delegate to the League of Nations. There she took particular interest in the issue of the nationality of married women, a major concern of the NCW and the Australian Federation of Women Voters. Following her return in November, she addressed many women's organisations on her impressions of the strength of women in diverse areas of responsibility, the need for opportunities for the young, the importance of broadcasting as an educational medium, and the challenge of balancing authority against the 'freedom to develop as individuals'.

From 1931 Couchman saw the need to bring the AWNL—the membership of which was declining—into closer relations with the UAP, acknowledging that it was effectively the women's branch of its extra-parliamentary structure. Couchman's own parliamentary ambitions were repeatedly frustrated: she ran for Senate preselection for the UAP in 1937 but was endorsed only as the emergency candidate, and for the 1943 Federal election was preselected for the safe Labor seat of Melbourne. But with the disintegration of the UAP and the regrouping of conservative forces after 1943, Couchman was prepared to drive a hard bargain for the league's co-operation and the recognition of her own skills.

When representatives of conservative political organisations met in Canberra in October 1944 to discuss the formation of a new party, the *Argus* observed the 'marked attention that was paid to Mrs Claude Couchman': prospective candidates for parliament would be 'indulging in a crude form of political suicide if they neglected to enlist the active support of [the AWNL]'. Couchman was convinced by (Sir) Robert Menzies' [q.v.15] arguments that the league should merge with the proposed Liberal Party as a distinct women's section, even at the cost of its disbandment. In return, she secured equal representation for women at all levels of the Victorian division—thus giving them unprecedented political power and influence—while preserving their separate identity within the party.

Couchman chose not to stand for election as chair of the women's section but used her experience and political acumen behind the scenes to support new office-bearers, consolidate the branches, and ensure women's continuing influence on Liberal policy and strategy. In August 1949, however, she was elected unopposed as a metropolitan vice-president of the State party, a position she held until 1955, after which she served on the State council until well into her eighties. She frequently reiterated the view first articulated in 1931 that 'what women think in politics today, men will think tomorrow', and put her energies into gaining Senate preselection for (Dame) Ivy Wedgwood [q.v.16] and, later, (Dame) Margaret Guilfoyle. Her influence on Menzies remained considerable: she was, he once remarked, 'the greatest statesmen of them all', and he rarely took action in the State party without first consulting her.

Slender, ascetic and, to some, aloof in manner, Couchman was a fine conversationalist and an omnivorous reader. Colleagues respected the incisiveness, logic and directness of her political style, Julia Rapke [q.v.16] noting her 'rapier thrusts' of wit. A woman of modest means, according to Rapke she trimmed her own hats and dressed with 'simple elegance'. She loved dancing, was a proficient pianist and was for many years a member of the faculty of music, University of Melbourne. Appointed OBE in 1941, Couchman was elevated to DBE in 1960. Dame Elizabeth died on 18 November 1982 at Camberwell, and was cremated. Appropriately, her death certificate gave her occupation as 'retired politician'.

H. Radi (ed), *200 Australian Women* (1988); D. Sydenham, *Women of Influence* (1996); M. Fitzherbert, *Liberal Women* (2004); *Woman* (Austn Women's National League), Nov 1922, p 261, June 1923, p 101, Jan 1924, p 326, Apr 1924, p 38, Jan 1927, p 328, Apr 1927, p 42, May 1927, p 79, Aug 1927, p 186, June 1928, p 115, Dec 1931, p 282, Nov 1932, p 203; *Sun News-Pictorial* (Melbourne), 20 May 1931, p 3; 26 Nov 1982, p 32; *Herald* (Melbourne), 12 July 1934, p 24, 18 Nov 1937, p 6; *Argus* (Melbourne), 20 Nov 1934, p 12, 22 Nov 1934, p 12, 21 Oct 1944, p 11; *Age* (Melbourne), 30 Nov 1934, p 15; J. Rapke papers and Couchman papers (NLA).

JUDITH SMART

COUNIHAN, NOEL JACK (1913-1986), artist and revolutionary, was born on 4 October 1913 at Albert Park, Melbourne, and registered as Jack Noel, second of three sons of Victorian-born parents John Henry Counihan, salesman, and his wife Jessie Pritchard, née Evans. Conflict between his Catholic father and Protestant mother, caused in part by differences over religion and in part by his father's drinking habits, resulted in an unhappy childhood. In 1921-27 he attended St Paul's Cathedral School and sang in the choir. A year at Caulfield Grammar School followed, after which he found work as an office boy.

At age 16 Counihan joined the evening classes at the National Gallery of Victoria's drawing school. He became associated with the left-wing 'painters, writers, journalists, musicians, teachers, medical students and doctors' who met in the workshop of William Dolphin, a talented stringed-instrument craftsman; the group included Herbert McClintock, Judah Waten [qq.v.], Roy Dalgarno and Brian Fitzpatrick [q.v.14]. Counihan later described the circle as 'the final expression of old Melbourne's bohemia'. He recalled that as a chorister he had been required to sing on special occasions, 'Let us now praise famous men, and our fathers that begat us'. Because

he was on the worst possible terms with the father who had begotten him, Noel came to regard Bill Dolphin as his 'spiritual father', and he absorbed the older man's 'profound hatred of all that was mercenary and predatory in society'.

Young Counihan read Nietzsche, Dostoevsky, Balzac, Gorky, Bukharin, Marx and Engels. Appalled by his politics, his father burnt many of his books. Noel left home and his job, and 'dossed down' in the Workers' Art Club. He drew pencil-portraits and caricatures for a living, joined the Communist Party of Australia as Noel Cunningham, and took part in political demonstrations. On the evening of 19 May 1933, locked in a cart to impede arrest, he addressed shoppers in Sydney Road, Brunswick, on the sufferings of the unemployed. Arrested and convicted, he appealed, won on a technicality and was released. The event became legendary in the fight for free speech during the Depression.

In 1938 Counihan was a foundation member of the Contemporary Art Society (Australia). Next year he sailed for New Zealand intent on selling drawings to the press and saving for a trip to Europe. He obtained employment as a clerk and, following the outbreak of World War II, became involved in the local anti-conscription campaign. On 21 May 1940 at the registrar's office, Wellington, he married Percivale Mary Patricia (Pat) Edwards, a graduate of Victoria University College and a fellow communist. In June he was arrested and deported to Australia. Between November that year and Easter 1941 he was a patient at the Gresswell Sanatorium, near Melbourne, recuperating from tuberculosis.

Encouraged by Josl Bergner, Counihan began to paint. Early works, such as 'The New Order' (1942), carry a potent, anti-fascist message. But, dissatisfied with such a direct approach, he turned to personal recollections of the Depression, as portrayed in his masterly 'At the Corner of Nightingale Street' (National Gallery of Victoria). His 'Miners working in Wet Conditions' (National Gallery of Australia, Canberra) won first prize in a major exhibition, Australia at War, held at the National Gallery of Victoria in 1945. Next year he, Bergner and Victor O'Connor exhibited at the Myer [qq.v.10, 15] Art Gallery as 'three realist artists', seeking to affirm their social realist position and their discontent with trends then prevailing in the Contemporary Art Society.

In 1949 Counihan was an Australian delegate at the World Congress of Peace held in the Salle Pleyel, Paris. He arranged for a message, signed by Picasso, Pablo Neruda, J. D. Bernal, Frédéric Joliot-Curie, Marcel Gromaire and André Fougeron, among others, to be sent to Australian intellectuals urging them to support the conference. Addressed to E. V. (Vance) Palmer [q.v.11], it was never received.

Counihan assumed that it had been intercepted by Australian intelligence authorities and destroyed. Between May and October he visited Czechoslovakia, Hungary and Poland, where he worked for some months as a graphic artist and befriended the American artist William Gropper. Moving to London, he lived with his wife and their two boys for two years at the Abbey Art Centre, New Barnet. He drew caricatures for the *Daily Mail* and, later, cartoons for *Public Opinion*. He also produced a notable series of linocuts, published—with related poems by Jack Lindsay [q.v.]—as *War or Peace* (1950?). In 1951 Counihan held an exhibition of his drawings at the Irving galleries, Leicester Square.

Back in Victoria from 1952, Counihan lived in the Dandenongs and painted in Tom Roberts's [q.v.11] former studio at Kallista. In 1956 he visited the Soviet Union. While there he met many younger Soviet artists and criticised the older academicians for vulgarising realism. Home again, he and his family settled at Canterbury, Melbourne. He won the (George) Crouch prize for 1956 with 'On Parliament Steps' (Ballarat Fine Art Gallery). Two years later he started painting local 'pub' life, winning (1958) the John McCaughey memorial prize with 'After Work' (National Gallery of Victoria). In 1960 he visited the Soviet Union again, for an exhibition of Australian realist art which also included work by McClintock, O'Connor and James Wigley. During the 1960s he painted many pictures based on the condition of Australian Aboriginal people. He also produced a series of mother-and-child paintings, an image he used to express his opposition to the Vietnam War. In 1969 he toured North America and Europe; in Mexico he met the artist David Siqueiros and in Poland found new inspiration in folk carvings.

On returning to Australia in 1970 Counihan began a series of self-portraits. These and his 'Laughing Christ' paintings brought a new expressive force to his work as revealed in a major exhibition at the Commonwealth Institute Gallery, London, in 1973. Earlier that year Eric Westbrook, director of the National Gallery of Victoria, had mounted a large retrospective of his oeuvre in the face of criticism from the staff and trustees either that it was insufficiently 'modern' or that its subversive nature might bring the gallery into disrepute. Westbrook found an ally in Professor (Sir) Joseph Burke, who opened the exhibition and whose opinion carried weight with most trustees. Counihan's acceptance as a major Australian artist was further enhanced by the decision of Melbourne University Press to publish (1974) Max Dimmack's monograph on him.

In 1980 Counihan and his wife spent some months at Opoul, near Perpignan, France. There he produced a memorable series of drawings of peasant life, later transformed into lithographs. The Opoul work, exhibited in September 1981 at Realities Gallery, Toorak, demonstrated that his realism had lost none of its force and had gained greater subtlety of expression. During the show he was asked to talk about his art: 'My work is ... my personal response to life and it involves response to shape, form, colour, living people, human relations, nature in toto ... my problems became more and more complex as I went on'.

John Hetherington [q.v.14] described Counihan as a tall, slender, active man who gave the 'appearance of wiry strength'; he had 'searching blue eyes, a long upper lip, a tight mouth, and a chin with an aggressive tilt'. Counihan died on 5 July 1986 at Canterbury and was cremated. His wife (d.2001) and their sons survived him. Over three hundred friends attended his memorial service at the Camberwell Civic Centre. The Moreland City Council established the Counihan Gallery at Brunswick in 1999.

M. Dimmack, *Noel Counihan* (1974); R. Smith, *Noel Counihan Prints, 1931-1981* (1981); B. Smith, *Noel Counihan* (1993); *Age* (Melbourne), 3 Mar 1962, p 18; Counihan papers (NLA); private information and personal knowledge.

BERNARD SMITH

COWPER, SIR NORMAN LETHBRIDGE (1896-1987), solicitor and army officer, was born on 15 September 1896 at Roseville, Sydney, second son of Australian-born parents Cecil Spencer de Grey Cowper, solicitor, and his wife Alice Mary, née Dodd. Descended from Governor Philip Gidley King, and from Rev. William and Sir Charles Cowper [qq.v.2, 1,3], Norman attended Chatswood Preparatory School and then Sydney Grammar School, where he was a prefect and won the Salting [q.v.2] exhibition for 1915. At the University of Sydney (BA, 1918; LL B, 1923) he excelled at debating and won a Blue for hockey.

Rejected by the Australian Imperial Force, Cowper worked as a jackeroo on several outback stations to overcome the residual effects of rheumatic fever. He succeeded in enlisting on 17 June 1918 but was discharged, medically unfit, two months later. Returning to the university in March 1919, he was articled to his father (d.1919) then to Alfred Hemsley, partners in Allen, Allen [qq.v.1,3] & Hemsley. On 6 June 1923 he was admitted as a solicitor; he became a partner in Allens in 1924.

At St Mark's Church of England, Darling Point, on 17 June 1925 Cowper married Dorothea Huntly ('Honey'), daughter of the poet Hugh McCrae [q.v.10]; they lived at Wivenhoe, Wahroonga, for sixty-two years.

Honey was one of Ethel Anderson's [q.v.13] 'Turramurra Wall Painters'.

In the late 1920s Cowper joined the Wahroonga branch (president, 1930) of the National Party. In 1930 he was a delegate to the State and National conventions and a founder of the '1930' Club. Next year he was elected to the council of the State branch of the party. He also joined the Old Guard. As a joint candidate for the United Australia Party, he stood unsuccessfully for the Federal seats of North Sydney (1931) and Wentworth (1940). In March 1932 he helped to draft the constitution of the UAP and in 1933-37 served on its standing committee on policy, chaired by (Sir) Bertram Stevens [q.v.12]. A superb mimic, Cowper told 'devastating anecdotes' and belonged to Justice H. V. Evatt's [q.v.14] lunch club.

Cowper and his wife visited Britain and the United States of America in 1935; he made many friends and business links, including the Dulles brothers, partners in the big New York legal firm Sullivan & Cromwell, which later sent work to Allens. Liberal-minded, he was outraged by the Commonwealth government's treatment of Mrs Mabel Freer, who was alleged to have committed adultery with an Australian army officer serving in India. After she failed a dictation test in Italian, the minister for the interior, Thomas Paterson [q.v.11], refused her admission to Australia in December 1936. Cowper lodged a writ of habeas corpus on her behalf in the High Court of Australia. Justice Evatt dismissed the writ but made plain his disapproval of the minister's executive decision. In June next year cabinet countermanded the minister's action.

On 26 May 1939 Cowper was commissioned as a lieutenant in the Militia; he rose to major and carried out part-time duties. He transferred to the AIF in May 1941 and served with the Armoured Division at home. Joining the Australian Provost Corps (military police) in March 1942, he served as army provost marshal, New Guinea Force (September 1943-May 1944) and Northern Territory Force (July-November 1944). As a lieutenant colonel from 20 November he held the same position at Advanced Allied Land Forces Headquarters, Hollandia and Morotai (January-May 1945). Back in Sydney, with, according to John Wilkes, 'a fund of stories about his experiences', he was placed on the Reserve of Officers on 11 July 1945.

Abandoning his political ambitions, Cowper concentrated on rebuilding his career and rehabilitating Allen, Allen & Hemsley, which had suffered attrition of personnel and business. He discouraged nepotism, sought to recruit talent and tolerated no carelessness. Cowper wrote in clear, concise English and encouraged its use in the drafting of legal documents. His ability to reduce issues to non-threatening proportions enabled him to reassure his clients.

A specialist in commercial law, Cowper looked after the firm's most important client, the Bank of New South Wales. In 1947 the Chifley [q.v.13] government announced its intention to introduce legislation to nationalise the trading banks. Cowper immediately retained as many counsel as possible (to deprive the government of their advice) for the impending challenge in the High Court, and briefed (Sir) Garfield Barwick and (Sir) Frank Kitto. The case was won in 1947. The Cowpers spent nine months in London while the case was before the Privy Council, which eventually upheld the High Court's decision.

Through professional connections Cowper was a director of many companies including Gilbert Lodge (Holdings) Ltd (chairman, 1950-79), Australian Fixed Trusts Pty Ltd, New Guinea Goldfields Ltd, Development Finance Corporation Ltd and Permaglass Ltd (chairman, 1969-77). Essentially 'a man who believed in professional and public service', he was a council-member (1940-41 and 1945-60), office-bearer, and president (1958-59) of the Incorporated Law Institute of New South Wales. From 1951 Cowper virtually ran Allens; he succeeded A. D. Allen [q.v.13] as the senior partner in 1963. His important clients included Kaiser Walsh Perini Raymond, one of the consortiums that constructed the Snowy Mountains hydro-electric scheme. When he retired on 30 June 1970 he had done much to modernise Allens.

Hoping to promote a more rational understanding of public questions, Cowper was a foundation director (1932-69) and chairman (1933-37) of the Australian Institute of Political Science. He contributed numerous papers to its summer schools in Canberra, chaired its conferences (notably on the Territory of Papua and New Guinea in 1958 and 1968), and wrote pamphlets, and articles and book reviews for the *Australian Quarterly* and the *Sydney Morning Herald*. A councillor of the State branch of the Australian Institute of International Affairs in 1933-41 and intermittently thereafter, he was a delegate to its Commonwealth council (president 1949-50). From 1964 he served as chairman of the Council on New Guinea Affairs; in 1968 he attacked the government's 'equivocating policies' on independence for the Territory.

Appointed CBE in 1958 and knighted in 1967, Cowper was president (1969-72) of the Australian Club and a member of the University Club. He remained a major influence behind the scenes in non-Labor politics. In 1959 he sat on the Richardson committee of inquiry into the salaries and allowances of members of the Commonwealth parliament; the committee's recommendation for increased payments raised a storm of protest. On 29

October 1975, during the political crisis triggered by the Senate's refusal of supply to the Whitlam government, Cowper wrote to the *SMH*: for 'a constitutional lawyer, it is the most interesting confrontation since Federation'. He believed that 'the power of removal (the reserve power of the Crown) may be the only safeguard against the destruction of democracy'. The letter impressed the governor-general Sir John Kerr by its 'acuity'.

As a young man Cowper had immersed himself in the Old Sydneians' Union; from 1932 he was an elected trustee of Sydney Grammar School, serving as chairman in 1951-74. In the 1960s he advised the headmaster to allow students to protest against the Vietnam War while wearing school uniform. He maintained a close interest in legal education and training. In 1955-74 he was a member of the council of the Australian National University, Canberra.

Known for his ability to resolve disputes, Cowper joined the board of Angus & Robertson [qq.v.7,11] Ltd (chairman, 1960-70); he led the successful fight against a threatened takeover by Consolidated Press Ltd. In similar circumstances, he was appointed (1962) to the national committee and editorial board of the Australian Dictionary of Biography at a time when there were great differences over policy. He contributed articles to the *ADB* on the Allens, and on Georgiana and George Gordon McCrae [qq.v.2,5]. Although he produced no major book, all that Cowper wrote was elegant.

Even in his late seventies Cowper 'was a vigorous and skilful tennis player'. Nevertheless, he preferred more scholarly pursuits. Bookshelves overflowed every room in the house. 'His garden was a great passion & solace all of his life'. Its charm lay in the balance achieved between Honey's philosophy of 'letting plants grow into their natural shape' and Norman's 'urge for order & discipline'. He confessed that his wife believed him to be 'a murderer where trees and shrubs are concerned'. Distinguished looking, he was 5 ft 10 ins (178 cm) tall, with blue eyes and brown hair. He invariably wore a suit and smoked a pipe. With his confidence, impish humour and easy command, he frequently did and said the unexpected.

Sir Norman died on 9 September 1987 at Hornsby and was cremated. His wife and their three daughters survived him. Obituarists remarked on his 'tremendous generosity of mind and spirit, the breadth of his vision, his appreciation of the place of both the traditional and the unconventional and his ability to communicate with people of all kinds'. June Mendoza's portrait of Cowper is held by the Australian Club.

R. Fitzgerald (comp), *The Letters of Hugh McCrae* (1970); V. Lawson, *The Allens Affair* (1995); *Austn Law Jnl*, vol 7, no 12, 1934, p 462, vol 61, no 11, 1987, p 758; *Austn Quarterly*, vol 59, nos 3 & 4, 1987, p 438; *Law Soc Jnl*, vol 26, no 1, 1988, p 71; *Jnl of the Royal Austn Hist Soc*, vol 86, pt 1, 2000, p 74; *SMH*, 2 Apr 1959, p 2, 31 July 1965, p 12, 29 Oct 1975, p 7, 12 Sept 1987, p 15, 14 Sept 1987, p 8; *National Times*, 24-29 Oct 1977, p 11; *Sydneian*, Mar 1988, p 20; A432, item 1936/1360 and A2998, item 1951/696 (NAA); private information.   MARTHA RUTLEDGE

CRAIG, CLIFFORD (1896-1986), surgeon, radiologist, author and collector of antiques, was born on 3 August 1896 at Box Hill, Melbourne, third of five children of Victorian-born parents Walter Joseph Craig, medical practitioner, and his wife Jane, née Hughston. Educated at Scotch College, in 1915 he was captain of the school and of the first XI. On 17 February 1916 he enlisted in the Australian Imperial Force. He served in the Middle East in 1916-18 as a medical orderly with the 14th Australian General Hospital and the 4th Light Horse Field Ambulance, from which he was detached to the mobile Desert Mounted Corps Operating Unit led by Lieutenant Colonel John Storey. Almost immediately after his discharge on 14 April 1919 in Victoria, he began medical studies at the University of Melbourne (MB, BS, 1924; MD, 1926; MS, 1930), where he won a cricket Blue. He was a resident medical officer at the (Royal) Melbourne Hospital (1924-25) and at the (Royal) Children's Hospital, Melbourne (1925-26).

In 1926 Craig was appointed surgeon-superintendent at the Launceston General Hospital, shortly after the resolution of a damaging eight-year dispute between the State government and the local branch of the British Medical Association, which had banned its members from working in Tasmanian hospitals. Supported by some very capable medical practitioners now free to undertake duties in an honorary capacity, he built up the hospital into an excellent regional medical and teaching facility. He envisioned it as 'the spiritual centre of a medical community'. To improve nurse training, in 1927 he published a handbook of hospital technical procedures that served as a text for nurses in all Tasmanian and some mainland hospitals for many years. He was made a fellow of the Royal Australasian College of Surgeons in 1930. Next year he entered private practice and became an honorary surgeon at the hospital. He was again surgeon-superintendent in 1941-49. In World War II he held the rank of squadron leader as a part-time specialist surgeon with the Royal Australian Air Force.

From 1927 Craig contributed many articles to medical journals, mostly on clinical aspects of medicine. Always an innovator, in the early 1940s he attempted to cure diabetes by transplanting foetal pancreatic tissue, considering that such tissue was less likely to be rejected

—a concept well before its time. He was president (1941) of the Tasmanian branch of the BMA and chairman (1949-52) of the State committee of the RACS. In 1951 he was appointed CMG.

Forced to give up surgery in 1951 because of a soap allergy that affected his hands, Craig studied at the University of Melbourne for a diploma in diagnostic radiology (1954). He worked as a radiologist in private practice and at the Launceston hospital until he retired in 1977; he was a member (1961), State chairman (1966-76) and life member (1975) of the (Royal) Australasian College of Radiologists. President (1953-65) of the Medical Council of Tasmania, he was chairman (1951-76) of the Tasmanian Cancer Committee and president (1970-73) of the Australian Cancer Society.

Craig shared a keen interest in early Tasmanian homes and colonial furniture with his wife EDITH NANCE, née Bulley (1905-1978), whom he had married with Anglican rites at All Saints Pro-Cathedral, Bendigo, Victoria, on 14 July 1927. Edith was born on 3 July 1905 at Bendigo, Victoria, youngest of four daughters of Victorian-born parents Charles Edward Bulley, commercial traveller, and his wife Clara Jane, née Collings. In 1960 Mrs Craig, assisted by a lawyer, R. M. Green, established the National Trust of Australia (Tasmania) and arranged for it to purchase its first property, The Hollies (since renamed Franklin House), on the outskirts of Launceston. Mrs Craig was a leading member of the house's furnishings committee and later that of another trust property, Clarendon House. In collaboration with E. Graeme Robertson [q.v.16] she published *Early Houses of Northern Tasmania* (1964). She died on 26 June 1978 at Launceston and was cremated.

Clifford was also a founding member (1960) of the Tasmanian branch of the National Trust, and chairman in 1963. He helped to raise community awareness of the beauty and value of the State's colonial buildings, and to prevent the destruction of many. When the Hobart City Council proposed to allow demolition of early houses in Davey Street to permit construction of a petrol station, he remarked: 'no one will ever visit Hobart to see a petrol station'. He edited the trust's newsletter from 1965 to 1986, apart from a break in the early 1970s. With his wife he had accumulated a collection of colonial furniture that came to be considered one of the best of its kind in Australia. Having amassed an extensive assortment of early Tasmaniana, comprising documents, books, maps and prints, he sold 2350 items at a three-day auction at Launceston in 1975. In 1979 he donated over 450 books on the history of medicine to the Launceston hospital.

At 65 Craig began a new phase of his life as author of eight books including *The Engravers*

of Van Diemen's Land (1961), *The First Hundred Years* (1963)—a history of the Launceston hospital—and *Early Colonial Furniture in New South Wales and Van Diemen's Land* (1972), co-authored with Kevin Fahey and E. Graeme Robertson. His last book was published shortly after his death. A member of the Royal Society of Tasmania and of the Tasmanian Historical Research Association, he also contributed papers to their proceedings.

Craig maintained a lifelong interest in cricket and enjoyed playing tennis and golf. He was president of the Launceston Rotary Club in 1950. Rather slightly built and a little stooped, he had eyes that were alert and searching, but that twinkled when he was amused. He spoke with certainty and authority. Survived by his daughter and two sons, he died on 5 September 1986 at Launceston and was cremated. In 1992 the Clifford Craig Medical Research Trust was set up to aid research at Launceston hospital. A portrait of him by Audrey Wilson is held by the Queen Victoria Museum and Art Gallery, Launceston.

T. Jetson, 'In Trust for the Nation' (2000); J. Morris, Dr Clifford Craig (2002), and 'Pioneer Attempts to Cure Diabetes by Pancreatic Transplantation', MJA, 5/19 Dec 1988, p 634; A'asian Radiology, vol 31, 1987, p 224; Examiner (Launceston), 10 Sept 1986, p 35; Craig papers (TSA) and collection (Queen Victoria Museum and Art Gallery, Launceston).   JOHN MORRIS

CRAIG, SYBIL MARY FRANCES (1901-1989), artist, was born on 18 November 1901 at Southgate, London, only child of Australian-born parents Matthew Francis Craig, architect and surveyor, and his wife Winifred Frances, née Major. The family returned to Melbourne and Sybil was educated at a small St Kilda school. She recalled a childhood in a 'suburban bohemian household' frequented by musicians and artists. The Craigs resided first at Brighton, and after 1914 at Caulfield, in a house designed by Sybil's father, which remained her home for the rest of her life. In 1920 she began private art tuition with John Shirlow [q.v.11]. She then studied (1924-31) at the National Gallery of Victoria's school of painting with Bernard Hall, William McInnes and Charles Wheeler [qq.v.9,10,12]. A beautiful young woman with Titian hair, she was painted by Rupert Bunny [q.v.7] in 1928. Her enthusiasm for design drew her to classes with Robert Timmings at Melbourne Technical College in 1935.

Craig's first solo exhibition, at the Athenaeum Gallery in 1932, included subjects ranging from still lifes to portraits. Accomplished in oils, watercolours and pastels, Craig also applied her talent for design to line-drawings for book-plates and emblems. She was a foundation member of the New Melbourne Art Club and, during the 1930s and 1940s, exhibited with the Melbourne Society of Women Painters and Sculptors, the Victorian Artists Society, and the Twenty Melbourne Painters. Between 1936 and 1951 she maintained a Collins Street studio; numerous seascapes reflected the time she spent at the family's beach house at Canadian Bay on the Mornington Peninsula. Yet her life remained centred at home, particularly as she began to withhold her more innovative works—or 'exercises'—from sale, doubting their quality but, as 'an advantaged child', also lacking (she later conceded) the stimulus to 'earn a living'.

In March 1945 Craig became an official war artist, commissioned by the Australian War Memorial (under pressure to appoint modernist artists) to record work at the Commonwealth Explosives Factory at Maribyrnong. Her admiration for women munitions workers is evident in the seventy-nine works held by the AWM. Describing herself as an 'instinctive' artist, Craig was becoming more exploratory in her media and style. Her second solo exhibition was held at Georges Gallery in 1948. Thirty years later Jim Alexander, director of the Important Woman Artists Gallery, East Malvern, persuaded her to present a retrospective (1978) of her work. It inspired renewed critical appreciation and the purchase of several paintings by major public galleries. Another exhibition was held in 1982.

A diminutive woman with a remarkable memory and a keen sense of fun, Sybil Craig remained, according to Mary Eagle, 'devastatingly direct' and 'almost overwhelmingly vital'. In 1981 she was awarded the OAM. She died on 15 September 1989 at Surrey Hills and was buried in St Kilda cemetery. Her work is represented in the National Gallery of Australia, the NGV, the State Library of Victoria, the Art Gallery of South Australia, and Victorian regional galleries.

Lip, 1978-79, p 16; *Argus* (Melbourne), 28 June 1932, p 5; *Age* (Melbourne), 7 Apr 1978, p 17; *Herald* (Melbourne), 21 Apr 1982, p 27; B. Blackman, interview with S. Craig (ts, 1987, NLA); Craig papers (SLV).   DIANNE REILLY

CRANLEY, ALISON HILMA BARBARA VICTORIA (1910-1987), schoolteacher and unionist, was born on 20 April 1910 at Fitzroy, Melbourne, daughter of Victorian-born parents Robert William Cranley (d.1920), confectioner, and his wife Alison, formerly Friend, née Tuck (d.1932). Inspector James McRae [q.v.10] was Hilma's uncle by marriage; while in her teens she lived with the McRae family. After attending Fitzroy North State School and Melbourne High School, she started work in 1926 as a student-teacher. She trained at the Teachers' College in 1929. During her career she rose to infant mistress (head of the infant department in a primary school), her main appointments being to North Melbourne (1933-47), Moreland Central (1947-54) and Brunswick North (1966-75).

Active in the Victorian Teachers' Union, Miss Cranley joined its council in 1947 and served as president in 1965-67, only the second woman to be elected to that position. As a union leader she worked hard to improve her colleagues' conditions of service, opposing especially discrimination against women. She led campaigns for equal pay (implemented over four years from 1967); for the establishment of a common roll of men and women primary teachers (achieved in 1972); and for women to become eligible for promotion to the rank of principal. Seeking to abolish sectional branches of the VTU, and believing in a single union for teachers, according to a colleague she suffered 'a bitter blow' when some of her members defected to the Victorian Secondary Teachers' Association in 1967.

Cranley was one of six Victorian delegates to the Australian Teachers' Federation, which she represented at conferences in Britain, Europe and Asia. She was a union member of the Education Department's standing committee for the revision of the curriculum in primary schools. Additionally, she was involved in educational television, the children's library movement and the education of immigrant children. After ceasing paid employment in 1975, she played a prominent part in the affairs of the Victorian Retired State Teachers' Association, and of the Council of Adult Education, Victoria, which she chaired in 1975-77.

A tall woman, Cranley dressed quietly and wore her hair in a bun. She loved the VTU and was formidable as a union advocate. In retirement she was kind and approachable, never losing her interest in young children. She had lived at Parkville for many years with an older teacher, Meron Downes. Formerly a Baptist, Cranley became a Presbyterian after meeting Downes. The two were active in the ecumenical movement and protagonists of unity between the Presbyterian, Methodist and Congregational denominations. Cranley was an elder at College Church, Parkville, from 1975 and a member of the Presbyterian and later the Uniting churches' education consultative committees.

In 1970 she had been appointed MBE and elected a fellow of the Australian College of Education. Three years later she won the Lillian Horner prize for the best infant teacher in Victorian state schools. The CAE named one of its two overseas travelling fellowships after her in 1981. By then she was a life member of the VTU. Miss Cranley died on 29 August 1987 in East Melbourne, and was cremated.

Her friend Rev. Dr J. D. McCaughey, governor of Victoria, addressed a service of thanksgiving at her beloved College Church.

Sun News-Pictorial (Melbourne), 28 Jan 1965, p 12, 1 Jan 1970, p 21, 6 Mar 1974, p 15; *Age* (Melbourne), 12 Dec 1975, p 35; *VTU Jnl*, 10 Sept 1987, p 7, 16 Mar 1989, p 8; *Newsletter of the Victorian Retired State Teachers' Association*, 1987? (copy on ADB file); A. D. Spaull, Teachers and Politics (PhD thesis, Monash Univ, 1972); G. M. Griffin, biog notes on Cranley (copy on ADB file); J. D. McCaughey, address at Cranley's thanksgiving service, 1987 (copy on ADB file).   ANDREW SPAULL

CRAVEN-SANDS, COLIN DE CLOUET (1917-1987), Anglican seamen's missioner, was born on 13 April 1917 in North Sydney, son of Adelaide-born George Colin Craven-Sands, ironmonger, and his wife Rachel Marguerite, née de Clouet, born in Sydney. After studying at Moore Theological College (Th.L., 1940), Colin was made deacon on 2 March 1941 and ordained priest on 8 March 1942. He served as an Anglican curate at St Stephen's Church, Port Kembla (1941-42), and as an assistant at the Missions to Seamen, Sydney (1942). An honorary curate (1942-46) at St John's Church, Rockdale, he married Beryl Ruth Knox, daughter of the rector, there on 3 October 1942. On 16 September he had been appointed as a temporary chaplain in the Royal Australian Navy, an event which he described as the determining factor in his future ministry. He served in HMAS *Australia* (1942-44) and in shore establishments before being demobilised in February 1946. Moving to England, he was appointed as curate (1946-47) at Chadderton, Lancashire, and as vicar (1947-51) at Lannarth, Cornwall. He returned to Sydney, where he was rector at Castle Hill for two years.

In 1953 Craven-Sands joined the Missions to Seamen, Sydney, as senior chaplain, leading a team who worked for the spiritual and social welfare of seamen. The chaplains visited men on board their ships, in hospital and in gaol, and provided recreational activities for them. The Sydney, Newcastle and Port Kembla branches amalgamated in 1966 to form the Missions to Seamen, New South Wales. Continuing as senior chaplain in Sydney, Craven-Sands also became State secretary. He began researching conditions at sea as containerisation was reducing the time merchant ships spent in port and increasing the seamen's isolation. Chinese comprised the largest non-English-speaking group and he appointed the first Chinese chaplain. Later, chaplains from Japan, Korea, Pakistan, the Netherlands and Denmark worked in the mission. He visited nautical colleges, unions and government departments worldwide, and undertook relieving duties in major international seaports, including Yokohama, Japan, where he learned the language. A popular speaker at home, he visited clubs, churches and schools, and attended overseas conferences. He gained media exposure for the mission, partly through his appearances on the television programs 'Captain Fortune' and 'A Visit to the Flying Angel'.

Following the death of his wife in 1969, Craven-Sands married on 6 June 1970 at St Paul's Church of England, West Tamworth, Maaike Lafebre, a 23-year-old secretary born in the Netherlands. In 1977 the mission moved to larger premises, Flying Angel House, in Macquarie Place, Sydney. Craven-Sands had been appointed MBE in 1975 and in 1980 the Japanese minister for foreign affairs presented him with a letter of appreciation. A tall, bearded, athletic man, he was later described by colleagues as a dominant, dynamic and flamboyant missionary-minded Christian of great vision and enthusiasm, who achieved monumental work. Yet he himself lamented the limited influence that he exerted in the Church, especially locally.

In 1980 Craven-Sands travelled to England, where he worked as chaplain at Great Yarmouth, Norfolk. On retirement from the mission in 1982 he became priest-in-charge at Holbrook, Ipswich, Suffolk. He died of thrombosis of the vena cava on 16 August 1987 at Ipswich. His wife and their four sons and daughter survived him, as did the two daughters of his first marriage.

Missions to Seamen (NSW), *Annual Report*, 1966-80; *Sunday Telegraph* (Sydney), 7 Aug 1966, p 11; *SMH*, 19 Apr 1977, p 16, 19 Jan 1980, p 6; *NSW Flying Angel*, Sept 1987, p 1; A6769, Craven-Sands (NAA); private information.   VILMA PAGE

CRAWFORD, ALEXANDER (ALISTAIR) CAMERON (1907-1987), army officer and engineer, was born on 3 June 1907 at Forteviot, Perthshire, Scotland, son of Andrew Crawford, carter, and his wife Elizabeth, née Cameron. After migrating to Australia when he was about 17, he worked with bullock teams on the construction of roads in Gippsland, Victoria, becoming an overseer. At the Methodist Church, Pakenham, on 3 December 1932 he married Beryl Victoria Waterhouse; he had adopted the forename Alistair, which he used before, after or instead of Alexander. The Crawfords had a son who died in infancy and were later divorced.

On 26 October 1939 Crawford enlisted in the Australian Imperial Force. Posted to the 2/2nd Field Company, Royal Australian Engineers, as a sapper, he arrived in the Middle East in May 1940 and rose to sergeant next month. During the battle of Bardia, Libya, on

3 January 1941 he and his section constructed a series of crossings over anti-tank ditches while exposed to heavy enemy fire. For his 'courage and coolness', he was awarded the Military Medal. He was made company sergeant major as a warrant officer, class two, in March. In April he was responsible for some outstanding demolitions in the withdrawal of the 6th Division in Greece. He was mentioned in despatches and, in August, was promoted to warrant officer, class one.

In November 1941 Crawford was commissioned as a lieutenant and posted to the 2/8th Field Company. He served in Syria and Ceylon (Sri Lanka) before returning to Australia in August 1942. By October the 2/8th was at Milne Bay, Papua, supporting the 17th Brigade. In January 1943 the company flew to Wau, New Guinea, as part of Kanga Force, initially in close support of the infantry but later doing roadworks. Crawford was again mentioned in despatches. Back in Australia in July, he became engineer instructor at the 1st Commando Training Battalion. In October he joined headquarters, 6th Divisional Engineers, as a field engineer and was promoted to captain. He reached Aitape, New Guinea, in October 1944 and in the next few months accompanied many infantry patrols through enemy-held territory, garnering engineering intelligence to open a route to Wewak. For this work he was appointed MBE (1946). He finished the war as second-in-command of the 2/8th Field Company. His AIF appointment terminated on 29 November 1945.

A forceful leader and strict disciplinarian, Alex Crawford was 5 ft 9 ins (175 cm) tall and powerfully built, with hazel eyes, brown hair and a fair complexion. He settled in Melbourne after the war and was employed by Malvern City Council as a senior supervisor of road construction. In 1949 he joined John Holland & Co. Pty Ltd as a superintendent of construction projects. (Sir) John Holland had served in North Africa and Greece with Crawford and held him in high regard. Recalling Crawford's service with his own company, Holland stated that his 'man management skills were very much in evidence during a period which could be described as industrially aggressive'. Crawford later became general manager of Bayview Quarries Pty Ltd and a road construction company, and then worked for the Department of Defence. In his spare time he enjoyed gardening. On 22 May 1978 in a civil ceremony at East Malvern he married Alice Frances Cummins. Survived by his wife and one of their two sons, he died on 3 August 1987 at South Caulfield and was cremated.

G. Long, *To Benghazi* (1952) and *Greece, Crete and Syria* (1953); R. Davidson, *With Courage High* (1964); R. McNicoll, *The Royal Australian Engineers* *1919 to 1945* (1982); B883, item VX1305 (NAA); private information.   P. J. GREVILLE

CRAWFORD, DOROTHY MURIEL TURNER (1911-1988), radio and television producer, was born on 21 March 1911 at Fitzroy, Melbourne, daughter of Victorian-born parents William Henry Crawford, commercial traveller, and his wife Charlotte, née Turner, a contralto and organist. Dorothy attended schools at Fitzroy and East St Kilda. She later claimed that at age 16 she had been the youngest elocution licentiate in Victoria, and that at the same age she had begun teaching the subject at home. The Congregational and Australian churches influenced her early musical and dramatic activities. She sang contralto in their choirs and ran their amateur drama groups.

After winning a scholarship to the Albert Street Conservatorium, East Melbourne, Crawford graduated in voice and piano, but chose a career in speech rather than music. On 19 December 1931 at the Congregational Church, East St Kilda, she married Maxwell James Balderson, a salesman and church organist; they had one child, Ian, who lived with his maternal grandparents while Dorothy pursued her career. She acted in radio dramas and in 1939 had the title role in a popular live comedy series on radio 3UZ, 'Little Audrey', in which, at age 28, she played the naughty child 'who laughed and laughed'. In March 1942 she became one of the Australian Broadcasting Commission's first three female announcers in Victoria and by August was talks presentation officer. As the ABC's policy was not to employ married women, she kept her marriage and child secret.

Divorced in 1944, Crawford left the ABC and joined her brother Hector in the radio-production firm Broadcast Exchange of Australia Pty Ltd. In 1945 the siblings founded Hector Crawford (later Crawford) Productions Pty Ltd. While her brother managed musical, administrative and sales matters, Dorothy worked on production: chiefly script-editing and casting. She produced many successful radio series, beginning with Hector's outdoor concerts, 'Music for the People', broadcast by 3DB.

In 1946 the Crawfords developed 'Opera for the People', which was broadcast on 3DB and interstate networks. Local singers performed the principal arias from each work and actors presented the story linking the songs. 'Melba', a dramatisation of the life of Dame Nellie Melba [q.v.10], was broadcast from early 1946. Similarly combining music and speech, with the soprano Glenda Raymond and the actress Patricia Kennedy sharing the title role, it captured a large audience. More musical biographies followed, including 'The Blue Danube' (on the Strauss family) and 'The Amazing Oscar Hammerstein'. Interstate and overseas sales boosted the company's profits. Dorothy also produced serials, plays and crime series, such as 'D24' and 'Consider Your Verdict', the second of which was later adapted for television (1961-64).

Two years before the introduction of television into Australia in 1956, she initiated the Crawford TV Workshop, a school for young people interested in careers in the medium; it was to run until 1966. In mid-1956 she went abroad to study television. She and her brother made the transition to production for the small screen, starting with the ubiquitous quiz and game shows. By 1964 their persistence with drama had been rewarded with the success of the ground-breaking 'Homicide' (1964-75). They produced other popular police dramas such as 'Division 4' (1969-75) and 'Matlock Police' (1971-76); then a number of serials, including 'The Box' (1974-77), 'Cop Shop' (1977-80) and 'The Sullivans' (1976-83). Eventually the company benefited from Commonwealth government tax incentives that financed mini-series, among them 'All the Rivers Run' (1983), and 'The Far Country' (1987), both of which sold well domestically and internationally.

Although Dorothy Crawford's marriage to Donald Ingram Smith had been announced by the press in 1945, the couple had not married but had enjoyed a close relationship since 1942. On 23 December 1948 at the Collins Street Independent Church, Crawford married with Congregational forms Roland Denniston Strong, a fellow radio producer; they were childless and were divorced in 1968.

Known as 'D. C.' by her staff, she was at the centre of the Crawford family business, able to predict trends in popular culture and supply entertainments that appealed to listeners and viewers. Of boundless energy and erudition, both literary and musical, and with a brilliant technical flair, she was described by former colleagues as 'a woman ahead of her time'. Scriptwriters later recalled her creative advice on writing 'soap operas'. Crawford developed Parkinson's disease in the 1960s. People remember her as a tiny, lively woman who, even when confined to a wheelchair, was still a sparkling dinner-party companion. Honoured in 1973 by the Australian Writers' Guild with a special award for encouraging Australian writers, she continued working until 1978. She died on 2 September 1988 at Camberwell and was cremated. Her son, who had changed his name to Crawford when he joined the family firm in the 1960s, survived her. The AWG commemorated her with the annual Dorothy Crawford award for outstanding contribution to the profession.

K. S. Inglis, *This Is the ABC* (1983); *Commonweal*, 1 Apr 1931, p 7, 1 Jan 1936, p 14, 2 Jan 1939, p 13, 1 June 1940, p 3; *Vic Independent and Jnl of the Congregational Churches*, 1 Sept 1931, p 176, 1 Aug 1934, p 159, 1 June 1935, p 119; *ABC Weekly*, 23 June 1945, p 9, 26 July 1947, p 2, 12 Nov 1949, p 37; *Listener In*, 16-22 Sept 1939, p 1, 2-8 Feb 1946, p 11; *Herald* (Melbourne), 22 May 1954, p 22, 7 July 1973, p 18; Melba Conservatorium of Music Archives; Univ of Melbourne Archives; private information.

MIMI COLLIGAN

CRAWFORD, SIR JOHN GRENFELL (1910-1984), economist, public servant and academic administrator, was born on 4 April 1910 at Hurstville, Sydney, tenth of twelve children of Henry Crawford, stationmaster, and his wife Harriet Isabel, née Wood, both born in New South Wales. T. S. Crawford [q.v.8] was his uncle. His elder brother Raymond Maxwell Crawford (1906-1991) was to become professor of history at the University of Melbourne.

Jack was educated at Bexley Public and Sydney Boys' High schools. He left the latter in 1926 because of his father's unemployment and joined the Government Savings Bank of New South Wales. Returning to school in 1927, he achieved brilliant results in the Leaving certificate and won an exhibition to the University of Sydney (B.Ec., 1932; M.Ec., 1940), which allowed him to be employed by day as a junior clerk in the Department of the Attorney-General and of Justice. At the beginning of his third year he left the public service and gained a Teachers' College scholarship; he did the training course by day while continuing his economics studies at night. He obtained first-class honours.

As a young man in the Depression, Crawford had a few months of unemployment before a year of school teaching at Stanmore and Temora. From 1933 to 1935 he held a Walter and Eliza Hall [qq.v.9] research fellowship at the University of Sydney and from 1934 to 1942 he was a part-time lecturer in rural economics there. He was also a highly successful tutor in economics and international affairs for the Workers' Educational Association of New South Wales, and economic adviser (1935-44) to the Rural Bank of New South Wales. On 18 May 1935 at the Presbyterian Church, Bexley, he married Jessie Anderson Morgan, a clerk. The chronic illness, undiagnosed until her eventual death, of their intellectually gifted daughter profoundly distressed him.

In the 1930s Crawford was concerned for the state of Australian agriculture and vitally interested in international affairs, both in Asia and Europe. He published widely on trade. His book *The National Income of Australia* (1938), co-authored with Colin Clark [q.v.], was a pioneering effort, as was his courageous chapter, 'Australia as a Pacific Power', in *Australia's Foreign Policy* (1938), edited by W. G. K. Duncan [q.v.]. That paper stands out still as a precursor of later attempts to analyse and foreshadow Australian relations with Asia, especially Japan; it looked forward to a more effective peace in Asia.

Perhaps the decisive element in Crawford's development was the award of a Commonwealth Fund fellowship in 1938, which enabled him to study in the United States of America until 1940. He spent time at the Brookings Institution, the US Department of Agriculture and Harvard University. Crawford retained a long-standing affection for the USA and for the teachers and friends he had met there, and he was proud that he had learned to drive in Washington, DC. He was to be foundation president (1960-62) of the Canberra division of the Australian-American Association.

After returning to Sydney, Crawford obtained first-class honours and the university medal for his master's thesis on tariffs, an issue that would concern him throughout his future career as a public servant. In 1942 he was appointed as rural adviser to the Commonwealth Department of War Organization of Industry, and next year director of research in the Department of Post-War Reconstruction. In this capacity he advised J. B. Chifley [q.v.13] wisely on postwar soldier settlement. He moved to Canberra in 1944.

A milestone in Crawford's career was the establishment in 1945 of the Bureau of Agricultural Economics. As its founding director he made this agency an indispensable part of the Commonwealth's resources, before becoming secretary of the Department of Commerce and Agriculture in 1950. Known as one of the 'seven dwarfs'—senior public servants short in stature and influential in policy-making—he held that office until 1956, when, with a reorganisation of departments, he was made secretary of the new Department of Trade. In this role he supervised the negotiation of agreements with Britain and Japan. The first of these, concluded in 1956, greatly modified the 1932 Ottawa Agreement and its Imperial preference arrangements, leaving Australia free to eliminate preference to British goods. The second, the Australia-Japan Agreement on Commerce of 1957, provided for the expansion of trade with Japan, and, for the first time, most-favoured-nation treatment of Japanese imports. Awarded the Farrer [q.v.8] Memorial medal in 1957, Crawford was president of the Australian Agricultural Economics Society in 1958.

Having been appointed CBE in 1954, Crawford was knighted in 1959. In 1960 he left formal government service, and became professor of economics in, and director of, the Research School of Pacific Studies at the Australian National University, Canberra, while stipulating that he must be free to undertake government inquiries and international commitments. The school had been in some disarray because of personal conflicts, doubts about purposes and concerns about regional emphases. Crawford took firm control. He re-established the department of international relations, instituted regular faculty board meetings, set up a department of economics specialising in Indonesia, founded the Strategic and Defence Studies Centre and encouraged the New Guinea Research Unit, thus giving the school a strong regional focus while not preventing units and departments from venturing further afield. His work led to the development of the Contemporary China Centre, the North Australia Research Unit and the Australia-Japan Research Centre. The school attained much international attention and respect under his leadership.

Crawford's association with the ANU, of which he had become fiscal adviser soon after his arrival, did not prevent his involvement in wider activities. He was chairman (1962-64) of the Australian Wool Industry Conference. In 1964-65 he took part in the World Bank's economic mission to India; he then made regular visits to assist in the implementation of his strategy for Indian agricultural development. From his earlier concern with local agriculture he had moved on to international considerations in the same sphere, his work on India being the most comprehensive and effective. It was the initiative of which he was most proud, contributing as it did to the making of a world where people would have enough to eat. His Roy Milne memorial lecture of 1961 for the Australian Institute of International Affairs entitled 'International Aspects of Feeding Six Billion People' set out his position as a 'Malthusian optimist' (Lloyd Evans's expression) who sought to falsify the 'Malthusian expectation' of population growth outstripping the means of subsistence. In his association with the World Bank and with the Food and Agriculture Organization of the United Nations he pursued that aim to the end of his life.

In Australia Crawford served on a variety of government inquiries. The most significant was (Sir) James Vernon's committee of economic inquiry (1963-65), of which he was vice-chairman and the most active member; the government's rejection of its main recommendations was one of Crawford's greatest disappointments. The state of the Australian economy was his continuing concern, and he was to chair a study group on the structural adjustment of manufacturing industries, which reported to the government in 1979. His interest in Australian trade policy also persisted; his last major work was *Australian Trade Policy 1942-1966* (1968), in which he was assisted by Nancy Anderson and Margery Morris.

Sir John's appointments as vice-chancellor (1968-73) and chancellor (1976-84) of the ANU were logical culminations of his career. To his years as vice-chancellor he brought his intense managerial style and his capacity to identify issues and confront them. He weathered the years of student revolt with careful strategic preparation, improved communication between the university's administration and student bodies, and increased student involvement in university government. He also sought to promote the intellectual unity of the university and to strengthen relations between the Institute of Advanced Studies and the School of General Studies, while maintaining the existing structure.

As chancellor, Crawford perhaps overdid his part; but always his initiatives were for perceived purposes, such as the concern about the deterioration of the environment that had led to his creation of the Centre for Resource and Environmental Studies. Its establishment also furthered his aim of bringing the IAS and the SGS closer together. His approach to university management and funding was constant; allied with this was his close interest in scientific discovery and the effect it might have on the environment and on human prosperity. President of the Australian and New Zealand Association for the Advancement of Science in 1967-68, he was awarded the ANZAAS medal in 1971.

Crawford continued to be in demand internationally. One of his more challenging roles at this period was that of chairman (1971-76) of the technical advisory committee of the Consultative Group on International Agricultural Research. During his term he persuaded the group to establish several new research centres; he was to be a driving force behind the formation of the Australian Centre for International Agricultural Research in 1982. He demonstrated his concern for Papua New Guinea by serving as chancellor of its university in 1972-75 and chairman of the Development Bank of Papua and New Guinea in 1972-74. At the invitation of Prime Minister Malcolm Fraser and Prime Minister Masayoshi Ōhira of Japan, he convened in September 1980 the Pacific Community Seminar, which charted the course for the later establishment of Asia-Pacific Economic Cooperation, and he became a close adviser of Prime Minister Bob Hawke on the first steps towards that initiative. In 1972 he had been appointed to the Japanese Order of the Sacred Treasure and in 1984 he won a Japan Foundation award. Appointed AC in 1978, he was named Australian of the Year for 1981. He received honorary doctorates from the ANU and the universities of Newcastle, New England, Tasmania, Sydney, Papua New Guinea and Orissa, India.

A small man with a big head, Crawford joked about having trouble buying shirts because of his short arms. He also became somewhat deaf. None of these characteristics reduced his impact on those with whom he worked. Russell Mathews, a colleague and friend, listed his qualities as 'authority, persuasiveness, reason, fairness, humanity, integrity, stubbornness, fiscal acumen, a background of scholarship and public service, academic vision and administrative capacity'. G. V. Portus [q.v.11], who had taught him, remembered him as 'wise, kindly, humorous, lovable'. To these qualities should be added loyalty, pragmatism and personal dignity combined with good-humoured self-deprecation; he was also a 'workaholic'.

Sir John pursued the public good, both nationally and internationally. He was not dogmatic, nor a follower of any political party. The ministers whom he admired most were Chifley and (Sir) John McEwen [q.v.15], from opposite sides in politics: he found that both had visions of a future Australia and both could be persuaded to courses of action which went beyond immediate pressures and considerations. Well aware of how different interests pulled in different directions, he looked for consensus and for the best level of agreement that could be achieved, which made him a remarkably effective committee chairman.

Crawford's pragmatism was not opportunism. Given a particular problem, in a committee or an inquiry, he would often begin with the desired outcome and would pursue it in the debate. Maintaining respect for other points of view, he yielded to them if he was persuaded of their validity, while making clear his own original position if he thought it vital. He operated in terms of principle, yet also had a natural politician's awareness of the plurality of opinion and of the bounds of possibility. His basic reasonableness and his persuasiveness, combined with his sense of fairness and his humorous nature, meant that he often got what he wanted. When he did not, as with the unhappy outcome of the Vernon committee and the unsuccessful attempt in the early 1970s to retain a somewhat privileged position in government funding for the ANU, he accepted the result and did not repine.

Although Crawford was among the earliest Australian economists to gain general respect, he did not find the development of the subject, or of the social sciences at large, entirely to his liking. H. W. Arndt related that Crawford thought of himself as 'an economist, but very much a practising applied economist'. He had a poor opinion of 'what passes for economics' at universities, so much of it being, he believed, 'exercises in mathematical logic'. He was a policy man. His natural bent and his experience in government led him to the view that, while knowledge might well be pursued for its own sake, the resources available might be better spent when they had practical purposes.

Survived by his wife, Crawford died on 28 October 1984 in Royal Canberra Hospital and was cremated. He was universally mourned by those who had known and worked with him. His final illness had brought letters from Indira Gandhi, Pierre Trudeau and Lord Home. Bryan Westwood's portrait (1973) of Crawford is held by the ANU, where a building and a prize for postgraduate students are named after him. A memorial lecture, sponsored by the Australian government, is held at annual CGIAR meetings. The Crawford Fund, established by the Australian Academy of Technological Sciences and Engineering in 1987, promotes international agricultural research.

Sir John Crawford 1910-1984 (1986); L. T. Evans and J. D. B. Miller (eds), *Policy and Practice* (1987) and for publications; S. G. Foster and M. M. Varghese, *The Making of the Australian National University 1946-1996* (1996); *The Australia-Japan Agreement on Commerce 1957* (1997); *Economic Record*, vol 61, no 173, 1985, p 507; *ANU Reporter*, 11 May 1984, p 2, 9 Nov 1984, p 2; *Canberra Times*, 31 Oct 1984, p 2; Crawford papers (NLA).   J. D. B. MILLER

CREBBIN, RICHARD CHARLES (1913-1989), businessman, was born on 21 November 1913 at Paddington, Sydney, younger son of Victorian-born Thomas George Crebbin, police constable, and his wife Maude Alice Alma, née Farindon, who was born in New South Wales. Richard attended Sydney Boys' High School, leaving aged 15. He enjoyed rowing at school, later became a State champion and continued to coach as an adult. His first job was at Copmanhurst on a peanut farm that belonged to Marrickville Margarine Pty Ltd. Charles Abel had founded this company in 1908 with his sons, one of whom, Albert, had married Richard Crebbin's aunt Frances Farindon in 1912. After a year or two on the farm Richard returned to Sydney and, by the mid-1930s, was a master butcher, with two retail shops. He studied accounting at night and joined Marrickville Margarine as an accounting clerk.

Enlisting in the Citizen Military Forces in 1941 and employed as a pay clerk, Crebbin transferred to the Royal Australian Air Force on 18 July 1942. In May 1943 he was commissioned as a pilot. He served in Australia with No.107 Squadron and in New Guinea with No.8 Communication Unit, whose commanding officer described him as 'an excellent officer of outstanding personality'. Crebbin was demobilised as a flight lieutenant on 15 October 1945.

Returning to Marrickville Margarine as a senior executive, Crebbin took on other business roles. In 1949 he became chairman of Kork-n-Seal (Aust.) Pty Ltd, a cork-manufacturing business. A publicly listed company, Marrickville Holdings Ltd, was created with Crebbin as a foundation (1951) director;

from 1955 he was managing director, and from 1957 chairman. That year he became a director, and in 1968 chairman, of Waugh & Josephson Holdings Ltd, importers of Caterpillar products.

On 7 January 1954 at St Mark's Church of England, Darling Point, Dick Crebbin had married Joan Hazel Cridge, widow of his wartime friend Keith Cridge, and adopted their daughter. They lived at Castlecrag, a residential estate designed by Walter Burley Griffin [q.v.9], and their home was furnished by Marion Hall Best [q.v.]. Crebbin acquired a collection of Australian art that included paintings by (Sir) William Dobell [q.v.14], (Sir) Sidney Nolan, Charles Blackman and (Sir) Russell Drysdale [q.v.], and sculptures by Robert Klippel, Gerald Lewers [q.v.15] and Clement Meadmore. In 1966 the *Sydney Morning Herald* reported that he had two Drysdale paintings on the wall of his office, which had also been decorated by Best. His chauffeur drove him to work each day in a 1962 maroon Cadillac with the number plate RC 900. He arrived at the office at 9 a.m., and was rarely home before 7.30 p.m.

Marrickville Holding's brands included Mother's Choice flour, Eta peanut butter and cooking margarines derived from animal fats. The growth of the market for table margarine based on vegetable oils was blocked by State-government-imposed quotas to protect the politically powerful dairy industry. Marrickville Margarine tested the New South Wales Dairy Industry (Amendment) Act, 1951, by producing table margarine without a licence. In 1955 the High Court of Australia found in *Grannall* v. *Marrickville Margarine Pty Ltd* that, while section 92 of the Australian Constitution guaranteed freedom of trade between the States, the manufacture of margarine was distinct from interstate trade in margarine and hence not protected.

The Cahill [q.v.13] government did increase the quotas and reallocate licences in 1955. Marrickville Margarine was given a quota of 2166 tons of table margarine but felt that its market position was threatened as Allied Mills Ltd acquired other quota-holding table margarine companies. When Marrickville later manufactured above its quota, the Country Party members of the subsequent coalition government, led by William Chaffey [q.v.] the minister for agriculture, insisted on enforcing the New South Wales Dairy Industry (Amendment) Act, 1955. Crebbin's counsel argued that Marrickville's production above quota was only for interstate orders and therefore was protected by s.92. In 1966 in *Beal* v. *Marrickville Margarine Pty Ltd* the High Court upheld its earlier ruling. The company launched an advertising campaign devised by 'Sim' Rubensohn's [q.v.16] advertising agency, Hansen Rubensohn-McCann Erickson Pty

Ltd, and featuring the margarine-buying housewife Mrs Jones.

The quotas had become a potent symbol of Country Party protection of farming interests at the expense of Australian consumers and taxpayers, and Crebbin had become one of the best known proponents of change. He argued for the removal of both the quotas for table margarine made from Australian fats and oils and the restrictions on the use of Australian vegetable oils in the manufacture of cooking margarines. The journalist Maxwell Newton [q.v.], a vehement economic rationalist who became a friend and business associate of Crebbin, assisted the campaign against the quotas.

By the late 1960s Crebbin had close connections with the Australian Labor Party, which he had long supported. Following the success of the party in the 1972 Federal election, the Whitlam government announced in 1974 that it would phase out quotas on margarine production in the Australian Capital Territory over two years. The New South Wales government increased quotas in 1973 and 1975. Following the abolition (1976) of quotas in South Australia, those in New South Wales were withdrawn by the Wran Labor government in the Dairy Industry (Amendment) Act, 1977. Mrs Jones had won. Through energetic appeal to public opinion and political alliances and persistent pressure, Crebbin had succeeded in removing the Country Party's restrictions on the production of margarine. He achieved a victory for competition and market deregulation in the Australian economy.

In the 1970s the Marrickville business attracted the interest of Melbourne's Liberman family, which controlled Southern Packers Pty Ltd. Despite Crebbin's opposition, Southern Packers and associated interests acquired just over half of the shares in Marrickville Holdings in October 1977. He resigned from the company in November.

One of Crebbin's major interests was arts administration. The Whitlam government had appointed him chairman of the interim board of the Australian National Gallery in September 1974. Under the Fraser government, he chaired (1976-82) the permanent council. He also chaired (1980-83) Artbank, a government agency that bought works by Australian artists and leased them to public and private clients. Survived by his wife, their daughter and two sons, he died on 23 August 1989 at Wahroonga and was buried in Northern Suburbs cemetery.

S. Newton, *Maxwell Newton* (1993); *SMH*, 27 Sept 1966, p 6, 8 Nov 1966, p 1, 11 Nov 1966, p 5, 16 Mar 1967, p 9, 26 Aug 1989, p 11; *Age* (Melbourne), 12 Feb 1977, p 14; A9300, item Crebbin Richard (NAA).   JOHN EDWARDS

CRISP, LESLIE FINLAY (1917-1984), professor of political science and public servant, was born on 19 January 1917 at Sandringham, Melbourne, son of Leslie Walter Crisp, hardware salesman, and his wife Ruby Elizabeth, née Duff, both Melbourne born. 'Fin' was educated at Black Rock State School (1924-28), Caulfield Grammar School (1929) and the Collegiate School of St Peter, Adelaide (1930-34). Graduating from the University of Adelaide (BA, 1938; MA, 1948) with first-class honours in political science and history, he was selected as South Australian Rhodes scholar for 1938. Next year he enrolled at Balliol College, Oxford (BA, MA, 1948). On 22 June 1940 at the register office, Oxford, he married Helen Craven Wighton, whom he had met at university in Adelaide. Crisp chose not to complete a wartime degree and, rejected on medical grounds for military service, sailed with his wife for Australia. Their wedding had been brought forward to enable them to share a cabin home.

Joining the Commonwealth Public Service in 1940, Crisp worked first in Melbourne with the Department of Information then in Canberra in the reconstruction division of the Department of Labour and National Service (Department of Post-War Reconstruction from 1942). His work was interrupted in 1947-48 when he and Helen returned to Oxford, where he gained first-class honours in philosophy, politics and economics. In 1949 he was appointed director-general of postwar reconstruction.

Next year Crisp took up his appointment as the first professor of political science at Canberra University College. Despite having been a member (1949-50) of the interim council of the Australian National University, he later opposed what he called the 'shotgun wedding' of the college and the research-only ANU in 1960. After the amalgamation, however, he worked hard to give a sense of permanence to the reshaped university. He helped in the development of a student union, served as president of the staff association, did his share of committee work and endeavoured to ensure that the teaching of undergraduates received its due recognition. Unfailingly helpful to younger staff and students, he encouraged them in their research and writing, and enjoyed entertaining them at home. Crisp was a distinctive figure on campus. He was one of the last to lecture in a gown and, until his retirement, continued to line up to receive his fortnightly pay in cash. His lecturing style was deliberately theatrical: chin tucked into his chest, he peered at the class over the top of his glasses, addressing them in his deep, rumbling voice. Students enjoyed the performance.

Crisp spoke of how growing up in the Depression years shaped his world view, which included a lifelong membership of the Australian Labor Party. This coloured his teaching.

Generations of students were told that the 'anti-Labour' parties (the 'parties of town and country capital') 'lifted' most of their social policies from the ALP, that the Australian federal system was a 'constitutional confection', and that a 'formidable' case could be mounted for the abolition of the Senate.

Crisp's teaching focused heavily on political and governmental institutions, and was interlarded with what a colleague described as 'a wealth of political history'. He believed that students could comprehend Australian government only if they understood it as an ongoing development of the Westminster model. His introductory course therefore began with an analysis of British government before moving to the Australian example. This approach could also be seen in his writing. In 1949 his University of Adelaide master's thesis had been published as *The Parliamentary Government of the Commonwealth of Australia*, a work expanded and renamed *Australian National Government* in 1965. This textbook was ground-breaking in Australia and was a staple of many reading lists, going through numerous editions and remaining in print for some years after his death. The book made few concessions to contemporary events, which limited its usefulness as a pedagogical tool, and it was eventually superseded by works less rooted in the past. Crisp's other major works were a history of the ALP (1955) and a fine biography of J. B. Chifley [q.v.13] (1961), both of which showed his skills in historical analysis.

During the 1960s Crisp became disillusioned with changes in Australian universities. He was a vocal critic of the emerging 'institutions versus theory' divide in political science; he regretted the push to continuous assessment; and he deplored burgeoning student demands for some say in their course structures and assessment, claiming in his John Curtin [q.v.13] lecture of 1974 that the 'middle-class sprigs of this post-Spock generation' were more interested in political power than in hard study. Crisp stepped down from the departmental headship in 1970. In his words, he 'pulled up the drawbridge' on most of his colleagues, abandoned his undergraduate work in Australian politics and shifted his teaching focus to United States politics. He retired in 1977.

Appointed by the ANU to an honorary research position, Crisp enjoyed the opportunity to study the views of some of his heroes of the Federation story. Sir George Dibbs, Sir George Reid, Albert Piddington, Thomas Price, Henry Bournes Higgins, Sir Isaac Isaacs and Charles Kingston [qq.v.4,11,9] were for him men who stood apart from 'the narrowly conservative and provincialist federalism' of men like Sir Samuel Griffith, Sir Edmund Barton and Andrew Inglis Clark [qq.v.9,7,3]. Between 1979 and 1984 he wrote five self-published booklets dealing with these men's concerns over how Australian Federation had been shaped. The essays and his Federation bibliography were published as *Federation Fathers* (1990) after his death. Crisp also remained active as chairman of the Commonwealth Banking Corporation, a position he had held since 1975.

Life in the national capital suited Crisp—he spoke of 'forty years' happy residence in Canberra'. He served as a long-term, active member of the local branch of the ALP, worked on the Canberra Community Hospital board (chairman 1951-55), assisted the push for Australian Capital Territory parliamentary representation and enjoyed his golf at the Royal Canberra Golf Club. Survived by his wife (d.2002), and their two daughters and son, Fin Crisp died of myocardial infarction on 21 December 1984 in Canberra and was cremated. He is commemorated in the city by the Finlay Crisp centre and by the L. F. Crisp building on the ANU campus.

D. Aitkin (ed), *Surveys of Australian Political Science* (1985); S. G. Foster and M. M. Varghese, *The Making of the Australian National University* (1996); T. Rowse, *Nugget Coombs* (2002); Austn College of Education, *Unicorn*, vol 20, no 4, 1994, p 59; *Canberra Times*, 14 June 1969, p 1, 22 Dec 1984, p 7; *ANU Reporter*, 22 Mar 1985, p 6; Crisp papers (NLA); private information.   SCOTT BENNETT

CRISP, SIR MALCOLM PETER (1912-1984), judge, and **PATRICK GUY** (1917-1988), solicitor and magistrate, were born on 21 March 1912 and 10 April 1917, eldest and youngest of four children of Tasmanian-born parents Thomas Malcolm Crisp, solicitor, and his wife Myrtle May, née Donnelly. Both boys were born in Tasmania: Peter at Devonport, and Patrick at Ulverstone. They were descendants of Samuel Crisp who had arrived in Tasmania as a convict in 1826. Several family members, including Sir Harold Crisp [q.v.8], had been prominent in Tasmanian legal circles.

Peter was educated at the Burnie convent school, St Ignatius' College, Riverview, Sydney, and the University of Tasmania (LL B, 1932). He joined the staff of the Supreme Court and Sheriff's Department, and on 22 March 1933 was admitted to the Bar. On 27 September 1935 in Hobart he married with Catholic rites Edna Eunice Taylor, a nurse. In 1936 he was appointed a solicitor with the Solicitor-General's Department. Having served as an artillery officer in the Militia, on 1 January 1940 he was appointed captain, Australian Imperial Force, and posted to the 1st Anti-Tank Regiment. Arriving in Britain in June, he was seconded to AIF Headquarters then to the

Australian Army Staff, United Kingdom. He rose to lieutenant colonel (1944) before returning to Australia in March 1945. Promoted to temporary colonel in July, he was posted to Morotai as staff officer, convening authority, for the military courts that tried Japanese war criminals. On 26 February 1946 he transferred to the Reserve of Officers.

Resuming his legal career in Hobart as a crown solicitor, in 1951 Crisp became solicitor-general. In 1947-52 he lectured in law at the University of Tasmania and in 1948-55 served on the university council. He took silk on 5 July 1951 and next year was appointed a judge of the Supreme Court. Held in high esteem by his colleagues and other members of the legal profession, he showed himself to be a master of all branches of the law, particularly criminal and administrative. Among the criminal cases, his judgment in *Regina* v. *Vallance* (1960) set a benchmark on the subject of intent and the mental element in crime. In *Hitchens* v. *The Queen* (1962) he addressed the problems of insanity in relation to criminal responsibility, and in *Haas* v. *The Queen* (1964) he delivered an outstanding judgment concerning attempts to commit a crime. These judgments had a lasting impact on the development of the criminal law in Tasmania, and helped to focus attention on the provisions of the State's criminal code.

In the field of administrative law, Crisp gave two especially valuable judgments. First, in *Gerard* v. *Hope and others* (1965), with considerable erudition and at some length, he dealt with a case (involving fourteen days' wrongful imprisonment) that others might have disposed of more summarily, and in which he awarded damages against the State. Secondly, in *St Leonards Municipality* v. *Brettingham-Moore* (1968) he extended the boundaries within which the courts could interfere in administrative action affecting individual rights. He also brought a breadth of learning to other areas of the law, especially in cases involving medical or scientific expertise. On the occasion of Crisp's retirement, in 1971, Chief Justice Sir Stanley Burbury described his judgments as significant 'examples of incisive, clear, imaginative and original legal reasoning'.

Both publicly and privately Crisp espoused a view, which he called 'his creed', that any charter of human rights should be accompanied by a corresponding charter of social duties. Never one to suffer fools gladly, he was compassionate when the occasion called for it; for example, in 1970, he went out of his way to discharge his duties beyond the strict requirements of his office when he settled a claim for damages from his hospital bed. In 1966-68 he was royal commissioner investigating fluoridation of public water supplies; his report achieved nationwide respect at a time when debate on the subject was often heated. He was knighted in 1969.

Interested in libraries, Crisp served (1956-77) as chairman of the Tasmanian Library Board, overseeing extensive development of the State's library administration. He represented Tasmania (1958-82) on, and was chairman (1973-82) of, the Australian Advisory Council for Bibliographical Services. A founding member (1960-71) of the council of the National Library of Australia, he was chairman in 1971. He was president (1964-66) of the Library Association of Australia. In 1963 he visited North America on a Carnegie Corporation of New York travel grant to study specific aspects of law and library administration. The LAA presented him in 1977 with the Redmond Barry [q.v.3] award for outstanding service. In 1980-83 he was on the interim council of the (National) Museum of Australia, Canberra.

Crisp had been captain of the university's Rugby Union football club in 1933, and later became patron of the club and of the Tasmanian Rugby Union. A keen cruising yachtsman and fly fisherman, he acted as consultant to various anglers' associations, and collected rare books on fishing which he eventually donated to the National Library. He was interested in classical music and a supporter of the Friends of Music, a group which from 1958 arranged concerts in Hobart in association with the Musica Viva Society of Australia. Survived by his wife and their two daughters, Sir Peter died on 13 February 1984 in Hobart and was cremated.

His brother Patrick attended Burnie convent school, St Ignatius' College, Riverview, Sydney, and The Friends' School, Hobart. Enlisting in the AIF on 10 November 1939, he sailed to Britain, where he trained in ciphering. In April-August 1941 he served at Tobruk, Libya, with the 9th Division's Intelligence Section. He returned to Australia in March 1942 and was commissioned as a lieutenant in June. On 15 January 1943 at St Mary's Cathedral, Hobart, he married with Catholic rites Margaret June Seager, a schoolteacher. From July 1943 he was a cipher officer in the Northern Territory. His AIF appointment terminated on 7 September 1944. He studied law at the University of Tasmania (LL B, 1948) and was admitted to the Bar on 3 September 1948. After working in private practice with Page, Seager, Doyle & Bethune, Hobart, in 1952 he joined the family firm Crisp, Crisp & Hudson, at Burnie.

In 1967-80 Crisp was a magistrate for the north-western division of Tasmania. He simplified procedures in the Burnie Children's Court. Held in high esteem as a humane and just magistrate, he often gave those appearing another chance, especially if they were first offenders, and sought help for them from agencies outside the legal system. He served on committees of the local tennis and athletic clubs and on the North Western Football Union. A devout Catholic, he was active in local church affairs. Among his interests were painting and making 8-mm movies. In 1978 he helped to establish the Burnie Art Gallery. He was appointed OBE in 1988. Survived by his wife and their son and three daughters, he died on 2 February 1988 at Swansea and was buried in Burnie lawn cemetery.

Tasmanian State Reports (1971), p vii; *Mercury* (Hobart), 15 Feb 1984, p 2; *Examiner* (Launceston), 16 Feb 1984, p 26; *Advocate* (Burnie), 15 Feb 1984, p 3, 1 Feb 1980, p 4, 3 Feb 1988, p 2; private information.   H. A. FINLAY*

CROLL, HOPE (1901-1982), army and hospital matron, was born on 17 March 1901 at Bungwahl, New South Wales, fourth child of James Croll, sawmill proprietor, and his wife Jessie Sarah, née Souter, both born in New South Wales. Raised in the Anglican faith and educated privately, Hope held a long-cherished ambition to become a nurse. She completed her general nursing training at Marrickville District Hospital, Sydney, in 1927 and obtained her midwifery certificate at the Royal Hospital for Women, Paddington, in 1930. Having gained experience at the Forbes and Maitland hospitals, she became matron at Moree District Hospital in 1935. Five years later she moved to the Armidale and New England Hospital.

On 1 February 1941 Croll was appointed matron, Australian Army Nursing Service, and posted to the 113th Australian General Hospital, Concord. She took charge of the new hospital's nursing staff, which eventually numbered more than two hundred. Five ft 5¾ ins (167 cm) tall, with grey eyes and brown hair, Matron Croll was described as 'forthright', 'very professional' and 'imposing'. She was appointed major, Australian Imperial Force, in March 1943.

In April 1944 Croll was made matron of the 2/9th AGH, then at Tamworth. Promoted to temporary lieutenant colonel in April 1945 (substantive in September), she arrived on Morotai Island, Netherlands East Indies, with her nurses in June. By early July the hospital held some 770 patients. Tropical campaigns meant that patients suffering from diseases such as dysentery, dengue fever and malaria outnumbered the wounded. On Morotai the lives of the nursing staff were very restricted. Owing to the enemy presence on the island, nurses were permitted to leave the hospital only in groups of six or more, accompanied by armed escorts. There were other challenges too—rain, mud, insects and floods which brought snakes into sleeping quarters. The nurses themselves were not immune to the tropical diseases that ravaged their patients. For the professionalism she exhibited at Morotai, Croll was awarded the United States' Bronze Star in 1945. She returned to Sydney in March 1946 and transferred to the Reserve of Officers on 2 October. In March 1947 she was awarded the Royal Red Cross for her 'example and inspiring leadership' at Morotai.

Miss Croll's dedication to the nursing profession continued into peacetime. She was matron of the Rankin Park chest unit of the (Royal) Newcastle Hospital in 1947-51 and of Maitland Hospital in 1951-55. As matron of the Prince Henry Hospital, Little Bay, in 1955-66, she played an important part in its development as a teaching hospital. There she was seen as an 'intelligent, hard working, competent administrator' who was 'approachable and enthusiastic but never familiar'. A foundation fellow (1952) of the New South Wales College of Nursing, she was president of the college in 1956-58. At various times she also presided over the Australasian Trained Nurses' Association, the Institute of Hospital Matrons of New South Wales and the Maitland branch of the Australian Red Cross Society. In 1959 she was appointed MBE. Retiring to her home at Mosman in 1966, she spent much of her leisure time supporting returned nurses' organisations. Her favourite hobby was gardening. She died on 7 March 1982 at Hornsby and was cremated.

J. Crouch, *A Special Kind of Service* (1986); R. Goodman, *Our War Nurses* (1988); M. Cordia, *Nurses at Little Bay* (1990); *SMH*, 'Women's Section', 10 Mar 1966, p 8; B883, item NX138748 (NAA).
KATHRYN SPURLING

CROOKS, LOUISE WARDEN; *see* MCDONALD

CROSBY, GEORGE WALLACE DONALD (1924-1985), actor and actor's union president, was born on 29 October 1924 in Sydney, fifth child of Adelaide-born parents Joseph Alexander ('Marshall') Crosby [q.v.13], vaudeville artist, and his wife Teresa, née King. Don first appeared on stage, aged 1, in a burlesque operetta, *His Royal Highness*, in Perth with his father, and his father's friend George Wallace [q.v.12], after whom he was named. Wallace introduced him to the audience as 'Marshall Crosby's latest production'. From the age of 12, he took part in children's radio sketches for the Australian Broadcasting Commission. He left school after the Intermediate certificate and combined minor acting roles with a job as an insurance agent. Enlisting on 16 February 1943 in the Royal Australian Air Force, he trained as an air gunner and from October 1944 to March 1945 flew with No.460 Squadron in operations over Europe. He was demobilised on 27 February 1946 in Sydney as a flying officer.

Late in 1945 Crosby had worked as an assistant stage manager in London's West End. Awarded a Commonwealth Reconstruction Training Scheme scholarship in 1946, he studied at the Royal Academy of Dramatic Art, London. He then spent several months in English repertory in Morecambe, Lancashire, and High Wycombe, Buckinghamshire, before returning to Sydney. On 8 October 1949 at Holy Cross Catholic Church, Woollahra, he married Elizabeth Teresa Glover, an actress. He played (1950) in Sydney and Melbourne in *Dark of the Moon*, produced by (Dame) Doris Fitton [q.v.]. His role as Christy in J. M. Synge's *The Playboy of the Western World* at the Little Theatre, Melbourne, in 1951, was followed by a long tour for J. C. Williamson [q.v.6] Ltd in Hugh Hastings's *Seagulls over Sorrento*.

From 1949 Crosby also had a successful radio career as actor and director. After the advent of television in Australia in 1956 he appeared in several ABC plays, including 'Murder Story', 'The End Begins', 'Shadow of Heroes', 'Bodgy' and 'One Bright Day'. He and his wife Betty both appeared in Hector Crawford's police dramas of the 1960s and 1970s on commercial television. His craggy face—which bore some resemblance to that of John Mills—was an asset for television. He also produced the long-running ABC radio serial 'Blue Hills' and its successors in the 1 p.m. slot.

Continuing to work on stage, in the mid-1960s Crosby had toured in the J. C. Williamson production of *Camelot*. He claimed that the first time he played an Australian on stage was in 1971 in his role as Sergeant Simmonds in David Williamson's *The Removalists*. A celebrated role, and a personal favourite, was a dignified Dad in George Whaley's production (1979-80) in Sydney of *On Our Selection*, by 'Steele Rudd' [q.v.8 A. H. Davis]. Also appearing in several films, Crosby was nominated for the Australian Film Institute's award of best supporting actor for his roles in *Newsfront* and *The Chant of Jimmie Blacksmith* (1978).

Crosby was president (1976-85) of the Actors' (and Announcers') Equity (Association) of Australia. He urged the use of Australian actors where possible and spoke out against cuts in ABC funding. In 1980 he was awarded an OAM and in 1985 he received the AFI Raymond Longford [q.v.10] award. Survived by his wife and their three sons and one daughter, he died of myocardial infarction on 3 December 1985 at his home at Potts Point.

His children were involved in the entertainment industry, as actors, film director and federal secretary of Actors' Equity.

R. Lane, *The Golden Age of Australian Radio Drama. Volume 2* (2000); *SMH*, 17 July 1949, p 9, 4 Dec 1985, p 23; *Sun* (Sydney), 2 Feb 1967, p 47, 27 Apr 1967, p 75; *Daily Telegraph* (Sydney), 3 May 1973, p 49, 21 Dec 1979, p 31; *Advertiser* (Adelaide), 6 May 1976, p 34; Actors Equity Aust, *Equity*, Mar 1986, p 3; A9300, Crosby George (NAA).

MARK McGINNESS

CROWLEY, SIR BRIAN HURTLE (1896-1982), grazier, horse-breeder and racing administrator, was born on 18 February 1896 at Waverley, Sydney, only son of New South Wales-born parents Charles Brian Crowley, grazier, and Agnes Moore. Brian Crowley grew up with his five sisters at Waverley, Sydney, and rode his pony daily to Scots College. Leaving school in 1910, he worked on his father's stations and on 1 August 1916 enlisted in the Australian Imperial Force. From February 1917 he served on the Western Front as a gunner with the 7th Field Artillery Brigade. On 4 October at Passchendaele, Belgium, while acting as telephonist to the forward observing officer during an attack, he set a 'splendid example of courage and determination', ensuring that vital messages were transmitted. He was awarded the Military Medal. Sent to England for officer training in June 1918, he was commissioned on 3 January 1919 and promoted to lieutenant in April. His AIF appointment was terminated in Australia on 17 June.

On 5 July 1922 Crowley married Dorothy Ida Sweet at St Stephen's Presbyterian Church, Phillip Street, Sydney. His father transferred to him the family property, Oreel, at Merrywinebone, west of Moree, in 1926. On 27 000 acres (10 927 ha) he bred horses and ran some 15 000 medium-fine-woolled merino sheep, buying his rams from Eulalie station. Almost 6 ft (183 cm) tall, he had blue eyes with a twinkle, and wavy auburn hair. He suffered badly from sunburn and always wore a solar topee when working outside. With his self-taught store of knowledge, Crowley travelled many miles to treat horses for neighbours. He played cricket for the Collarenebri club and was a good tennis player. In 1954 he set up the Oreel Pastoral Co. Pty Ltd.

Interested in pony-racing from his school days, after the war Crowley won many races in Sydney with his chestnut mare Ellinga. He joined the Australian Jockey Club in 1921 and later the Sydney Turf Club. In the early days he trained his own racehorses and Dorothy, a notable horsewoman, rode track-work for him

(Brian always rode 'steady stock horses'). He recorded the breeding, dates of birth and death, sex and colour 'of every horse he ever owned'. For many years his dark blue and orange colours 'were carried successfully in the north-western districts'. His first Sydney winner was Blue Blood in the 1936 Corinthian Cup at Rosehill.

Widely known as an authority on blood lines, Crowley paid sixty guineas at William Inglis & Son Pty Ltd's sale in 1942 for an unkempt Royal Step-Lambent filly and named her Flight. Trained by F. J. Nowland, she won 24 races out of 65 starts and £31 185, becoming the greatest stake-winning mare of her time and an idol of Sydney turf patrons. From Flight's Daughter by Star Kingdom Crowley bred Skyline, winner of the Golden Slipper Stakes and AJC Derby in 1958, and Sky High, winner of the Victoria Derby and the Golden Slipper in 1960.

A committee member (1944-74) of the AJC, Crowley was elected chairman on 17 August 1962. He repeatedly urged the government to introduce off-course betting through the totalisator and claimed that racing in New South Wales 'would be of little consequence', as the AJC could not match the spectacular increases in prize money offered in Victoria, where the totalisator had already been introduced. In 1964-66 he was the AJC member of the Totalizator Agency Board. Chairman of the third Asian Racing Conference, held in Sydney in 1963, he represented Australia at the fourth conference, in Manila, and the seventh, in New Zealand. Under his guidance, the AJC committee preferred to distribute increased prize-money in a well-balanced program 'to giving very big prizes for two feature events'. Despite the success of the totalisator, Crowley believed that on-course bookmakers 'gave a great deal of atmosphere to race meetings'. Knighted in 1969, he retired as chairman in 1974 and was appointed a life member of the AJC in 1979.

From 1961 Crowley had lived in Sydney: at Collaroy until he moved to Darling Point in 1971 (his wife preferred to live at Moree, but entertained for him in Sydney). One who 'liked to get things done properly', he 'always dressed meticulously'. He belonged to the Union and Australian clubs, and enjoyed taking his grandchildren (at boarding schools in Sydney) to lunch on Sundays at Elanora Country Club. A music lover, he 'spoke with an unusual lilting, slightly raspy voice'. Sir Brian still had several horses he had bred in training with Albert McKenna at Randwick when he died on 25 July 1982 at his Darling Point home. He was buried in South Head cemetery. His wife and their son and two daughters survived him.

D. M. Barrie, *The Australian Bloodhorse* (1956); *SMH*, 15 Apr 1944, p 8, 25 Aug 1944, p 5, 18 Aug 1962, p 1, 15 Apr 1963, p 5, 24 Sept 1963, p 26, 25 Sept 1964, p 16, 2 Oct 1966, p 46, 14 June 1969, p 10, 26 July 1982, p 24; *Moree Champion*, 27 July 1982, p 16; private information.   MARTHA RUTLEDGE

CROWLEY, DESMOND WILLIAM (1920-1984), adult educator, was born on 11 October 1920 at Invercargill, New Zealand, third surviving child of William Gladstone Crowley, cabinet-maker, and his wife Eva, née Murdoch, both born in New Zealand. Desmond was educated at Southland Boys' High School, the University of Otago (BA, NZ, 1941; MA, 1947; Dip.Ed., 1948) and Dunedin Training College. He married Jessie Nora Gertrude Gibson on 1 February 1941 at the Church of Christ, North East Valley, Dunedin. In 1941-45 he served at home with the New Zealand Military Forces, rising to staff sergeant. He was appointed assistant lecturer at the University of Otago in 1947. As a Leverhulme research student, he attended the London School of Economics and Political Science (Ph.D., 1952). He became assistant lecturer (1951-54) in history at the University of Aberdeen and lecturer (1954-58) in adult education and extra-mural studies at the University of Leeds.

While in Britain Crowley had written a history of the development of the New Zealand labour movement from 1894 to 1913 (*Historical Studies*, 1951). His book *The Background to Current Affairs* (1958) derived from his teaching at Leeds. He sought to identify the main historical forces operating in contemporary affairs, beginning with Britain and the postwar world, and including descriptions of the Commonwealth. The book covered issues such as racial divisions, the emergence of new nations and power blocs, and the existence and spread of nuclear weapons.

Moving to Australia in 1959, Crowley worked as assistant-director in adult education at the University of Adelaide. In 1964 he was appointed director of the department of adult education at the University of Sydney. The boom in higher education under the Menzies [q.v.15] government had led to new universities and colleges supplanting the University of Sydney's outreach. Crowley concentrated on developing tutorial classes in Sydney, and took up the challenge of infusing Aboriginal adult education with a new vigour. In 1966 the Australian Universities Commission submitted a proposal (later rejected by the Gorton government) to divert funding for adult education from the universities to the new colleges of advanced education after the 1967-69 triennium. Crowley printed ten thousand copies of a pamphlet, 'The Challenge to University Adult Education', and posted them to adult students and parliamentarians. In 1968 he spoke on 'The Role of Colleges of Advanced

Education in Australian Adult Education'. He again emphasised the gravity of the triennium crisis in a chapter in Derek Whitelock (ed.), *Adult Education in Australia* (1970).

Abreast of developments in educational technology, Crowley sought new modes of communication for adult education. He contributed to radio programs and television and became a regular contributor to the Australian Broadcasting Commission's 'Notes on the News'. He was 'Guest of Honour' on the ABC in 1972, and the following year he endorsed a proposal for the creation of a new Australian open university. After speaking at a conference on lifelong education, he edited the proceedings, *Educating the Whole Person* (1975). In his paper entitled 'Progressive Alternatives to Trendyism', he argued that the question of standards in academic subjects confronted both progressive and conservative educationists.

As editor (1964-82) of the *Current Affairs Bulletin*, Crowley coaxed academic authors to write incisive accounts of issues of interest to serious readers of the news. An increasing number of subjects were opened up for discussion, and changes in style and format gave the bulletin a modern appearance. When Crowley retired as editor, Sir Hermann Black [q.v.] commended him for having adhered to the 'academic faith' that 'all issues are open to scrutiny' and that 'reasonable discourse' could be sustained by adults through the printed page. This achievement, he added, was simply one facet of Crowley's long period of devotion to the cause of adult education. He had been founding secretary (1960-63), editor (1963-65) and chairman (1965-67) of the Australian Association of Adult Education, a trustee (1968-80) of the Museum of Applied Arts and Sciences, and a member (from 1974) and deputy chairman (from 1979) of the New South Wales Board of Adult Education. He was admitted as a fellow of the Australian College of Education in 1975.

After his retirement from the university in 1982, Crowley lived quietly at his home in Willoughby. His recreations were camping and writing and, despite declining health, he worked on a history of adult education. Survived by his wife and their two sons and daughter, he died of a cerebrovascular accident on 7 January 1984 at Cammeray and was cremated. He had known before he died that he was about to be appointed AM.

SMH, 2 Jan 1967, p 20, 31 Jan 1972, p 16; *Current Affairs Bulletin*, Oct 1982, p 17; *Austn Jnl of Adult Education*, Apr 1984, p 4; Crowley papers (Univ of Sydney).　　　　　　　　　　FRANK FARRELL*

CROWTHER, SIR WILLIAM EDWARD LODEWYK HAMILTON (1887-1981), medical practitioner, collector and bibliophile, was born on 9 May 1887 in Hobart, second of six children of Edward Lodewyk Crowther [q.v.3], surgeon, and his second wife Emily Ida, née Hamilton. W. L. Crowther and John Hamilton [qq.v.3,4] were William's grandfathers. He was educated at Buckland's and The Hutchins [q.v.1] schools, Hobart, and Ormond [q.v.5] College, University of Melbourne (MB, BS, 1910). In 1911 he sailed as a ship's doctor to London to further his medical training at Bolingbroke Hospital. Much to his regret this phase was cut short when he was called home because his mother was seriously ill. He became junior house surgeon at Hobart Public Hospital and joined the Australian Army Medical Corps in 1913.

Formidable in both physique and personality, Crowther transferred to the Australian Imperial Force on 26 March 1915. On 17 March, shortly before leaving on active service, he had married with Anglican rites Joyce Nevett Mitchell (d.1965) at St David's Cathedral, Hobart. He spent a month on Gallipoli with the 7th Field Ambulance before being evacuated sick in October. By December 1915, convalescent in Italy, he was enjoying visits to Rome, Florence and Siena, broadening his education. On the Western Front from April 1916, he served successively with the 8th FA, the 1st Casualty Clearing Station and the 14th FA, showing leadership and determination in adversity and a talent for organisation. In October 1917 he was promoted to lieutenant colonel and placed in command of the 5th FA. He was mentioned in despatches and awarded the Distinguished Service Order (1918). Always modest and reticent about his war experiences, he returned to Tasmania with a fine reputation and a profound respect for the Australian soldier. His AIF appointment was terminated on 9 April 1919.

Back in Hobart, Crowther worked as deputy quarantine officer in a community confronting a severe influenza epidemic. He then entered into a general and obstetrics practice and held long-time honorary positions at (Royal) Hobart and Queen Alexandra hospitals. Kind, compassionate and practical, he inspired confidence, loyalty and affection in both patients and staff. He was medical adviser (1933-45) to the governor Sir Ernest Clark [q.v.8]. He served on the Hobart Public Hospitals District Board (1943-46), and the Millbrook Rise Hospital (1934-66) and Midwives Registration boards. A fellow (1946) of the Royal Australasian College of Physicians, he was president of the Tasmanian branch of the British Medical Association (1934-35, 1942-43) and of the Medical Council of Tasmania (1952-54). In 1955 he was appointed CBE.

Keen on natural history from boyhood, Crowther was chairman (1924-28) of the

Tasmanian Field Naturalists' Club and an enthusiastic member of the Royal Australasian Ornithologists' Union. He had joined the Royal Society of Tasmania in 1911; on the council (1919-58) he was closely involved in its campaign to establish a wildlife sanctuary on Macquarie Island in 1933. The society awarded him its medal in 1940 and elected him a life member in 1962. Crowther was a trustee (1919-73) of the Tasmanian Museum and Art Gallery.

Anthropology was another of his many interests. The shame and notoriety brought to the family in 1869 when his grandfather had mutilated the body of an Aborigine, William Lanney, did not deter him from conducting his own research: as a medical student in 1908, he had helped to remove Aboriginal remains from Oyster Cove. Twenty years of holidays spent investigating Aboriginal camp-sites throughout Tasmania resulted in a series of papers published (1921-50) in *Papers and Proceedings of the Royal Society of Tasmania*. In 1933 in Canberra he delivered the Halford [q.v.4] oration on 'The Passing of the Tasmanian Race'. Predicting damage to Australia's reputation if Aboriginal people were not treated with more compassion and respect, he recommended a national approach to their welfare, to be administered by culturally sensitive officials trained in anthropology. He believed that tribes on their lands should be as autonomous as possible and that it would be a tragedy if the Tasmanian experience were to be repeated elsewhere in Australia. In 1963 he donated his family's collection of Aboriginal skeletal remains to the Tasmanian Museum.

Although Crowther's scientific, professional and community interests ebbed and flowed over time, his passion for Tasmanian history was always at the centre of his intellectual life. From the 1920s he collected books and manuscripts, artwork and artefacts, shipping logs, photographs and other historical documents. Tenacious and determined in the pursuit of a rarity, he nevertheless retained the respect of other competitors in the field. He was modest about his own collection and generous in his praise and encouragement of others. His early focus on Tasmania broadened into an emphasis on Australia, New Zealand and the South Pacific. The subjects covered included medical and maritime history, anthropology, natural history and Antarctic exploration. His particular interest was the history of the Tasmanian whaling industry. Fired as usual by a family connection (his grandfather W. L. Crowther owned whaling ships), he had had the foresight in the 1920s to save every record he could find. He was founding chairman (1956-69) of the Van Diemen's Land Memorial Folk Museum (from 1998 the Narryna Heritage Museum).

In 1964 Crowther began handing over his collection, eventually to comprise some 15 000 items, to the State Library of Tasmania. That year he was knighted. He supported the public campaigns to protect the wilderness in southwest Tasmania and to halt woodchipping. All his life he lived up to his family's motto: *Carpe diem* (seize the day). In old age he continued to write prescriptions for long-standing patients. Survived by his son, Sir William died on 31 May 1981 in Hobart and was cremated. In 1985 the Crowther collection of Aboriginal remains was cremated at Oyster Cove. The State Library of Tasmania holds portraits of Crowther by Sir William Dargie and Florence Rodway.

N. Cree, *Sir William Crowther* (1987); C. von Oppeln, 'Sir William Crowther', in G. Winter (ed), *Tasmanian Insights* (1992); *MJA*, 6 Feb 1982, p 142; *Sat Evening Mercury* (Hobart), 11 Apr 1964, p 5, 13 June 1981, p 30; *Mercury* (Hobart), 1 June 1981, p 2; *Tas Mail*, 7 May 1985, p 4; personal knowledge.
C. A. VON OPPELN

CROXFORD, ALAN HUMPHREY (1922-1985), barrister, cattle-breeder and works administrator, was born on 22 September 1922 at Wangaratta, Victoria, fourth of seven surviving children of Victorian-born parents Charles Reuben Croxford, farmer, and his wife Irene Mabel, née Dunlop. Educated at Port Fairy Higher Elementary and Warrnambool High schools, he developed an early enthusiasm for stock-breeding, winning the Port Fairy Young Farmers' Best Young Farmer award in 1937 and next year judging stock himself. In 1940 he began work as a law clerk in Port Fairy and on 6 October 1941 enlisted in the Citizen Military Forces. He transferred to the Australian Imperial Force in September 1942 but remained in Australia, serving with the 3rd Motor Brigade. Commissioned as a lieutenant in October 1945, he served in New Guinea with the Australian New Guinea Administrative Unit from November 1945 to May 1946 and then at No.1 Internment Camp, Tatura, Victoria.

Immediately on leaving the AIF on 5 March 1947, Croxford entered the University of Melbourne (LL B, 1950). Admitted to the Bar on 1 August 1950, he built a thriving practice in Melbourne as a thorough advocate and forceful cross-examiner. He relished criminal law but also worked in liquor licensing law, common law and Equity.

On 16 August 1947 at All Saints Church of England, St Kilda, Croxford married Eleanor Pearl Willis, an army nurse whom he had met at Tatura. 'A farmer at heart', Croxford moved his family to 50 acres (20 ha) at Warrandyte in the mid-1950s, and commuted daily to

Melbourne to attend his practice. At Warrandyte and later at Malmsbury and Nagambie (with the help of his daughters) he developed a highly successful Aberdeen Angus stud cattle-breeding program.

The lack of services and poor planning on the outer suburban fringes of Melbourne drew Croxford into local politics. Outgoing, friendly, with an imposing, handsome presence, a good sportsman and a family man who comfortably bridged the urban-rural divide, he soon emerged as a natural leader in the district. The local schools, sports clubs and Civic Association grew to rely on his analytical and organisational skills as well as his knowledge of the law. In 1961 he was elected to Doncaster and Templestowe Shire Council. As chairman (1961-66) of the Warrandyte Waterworks Trust, he set about improving services to his riding. His fellow councillors were quick to recognise his abilities: in 1962 he was appointed their delegate to the Melbourne and Metropolitan Board of Works, a body representing all Melbourne's municipalities in co-ordinating water and sewerage provision.

In 1966 the MMBW commissioners prevailed on Croxford to give up his law practice —and a higher income—to accept the full-time chairmanship of the board, the responsibilities of which now included drainage, urban planning, major roads and freeways, foreshores, river management and metropolitan parks. This position, encompassing the role of chief executive officer, was one of great power but with it went a heavy workload, particularly given the pressures of urban expansion. Croxford proved an able, if sometimes abrasive, administrator with an ability to digest masses of detail. Above all he was decisive, tackling head-on anyone who disagreed with his plans.

Croxford had a clear vision of what the board must do. The population of Melbourne was predicted to double over the next two decades; accordingly it would be necessary to double water storage and sewage-processing capacity as well as extending services to old and new suburbs. In an increasingly tightly regulated capital market, Croxford cajoled unprecedented levels of finance from both State and Federal sources. Despite his Liberal leanings, in 1973 he struck up a strong working relationship with Tom Uren, minister for urban and regional development in the Whitlam Federal government. The resulting funding did much to clear the backlog of work on Melbourne's sewerage system, laying the foundations for an infrastructure that served the city to the end of the twentieth century.

The board found Croxford an inspiring leader after his indecisive predecessor, Raymond Trickey, and appreciated his willingness to defend the organisation when attacked publicly, as it often was over issues ranging from rate increases to the concrete lining of creeks. During his first decade at the MMBW its workforce doubled in size and a massive building program began; it included the construction in Spencer Street of a forbidding bluestone 'fortress' as head office, complete with a sumptuous twenty-second floor office to which the chairman allegedly summoned State government ministers. An enthusiast for new technologies such as computers, he encouraged innovation. His uncanny ability to remember the names of workers, and of wives and children, and his zeal for social events that brought the workforce together, made 'Big Al' popular with the rank and file—despite his insistence on conservative dress codes and his anti-union stance on industrial relations. Some commissioners, however, particularly those representing the more environmentally active local governments, were unimpressed by the autocratic way he ran meetings. Discontent with the MMBW forced the government of (Sir) Rupert Hamer to establish a public inquiry in 1977, the report of which affirmed Croxford's 'enlightened dictatorship' (as the *Age* put it) by replacing the fifty-four quarrelsome commissioners with a board of seven.

As one of Victoria's best known and powerful public bureaucrats, Croxford was dogged by controversy including a 1972 inquiry into his land dealings (during which he stood down as chairman, and which exonerated him). His relations with the press were always wary, often hostile, and coloured by its perception of his arrogance. In some respects he was an environmental pioneer although not widely recognised as such. His credentials were evident in the sewering of Melbourne's postwar suburbs and in a change in philosophy on metropolitan drainage that led to the revitalisation of many suburban creeks. The associated system of metropolitan parks owed much to his strategic flair. On the other hand, the freeways built by the board as well as its attempts to deposit treated sewage into Port Phillip Bay and to dam the lower Yarra River were attacked by environmentalists.

The State Labor party was a constant critic of Croxford's style and policies, and its election in April 1982 prompted his resignation in July —pre-empting likely dismissal. Open-heart surgery in 1978 had slowed him somewhat, but in retirement he maintained his active engagement with family, friends and cattle-breeding, and his commitment to a range of community organisations. A Freemason from 1943, he was master of his Lodge (Chatham) in 1953 and past senior grand warden from 1981. In 1967 he had been a founding board member and councillor of the Australian Institute of Urban Studies, and was twice (1983 and 1984) elected its chairman. Embarking on a third term, he died of a heart attack on 13 November 1985 in

Hobart, and was cremated. His wife and their five daughters survived him.

T. Dingle and C. Rasmussen, *Vital Connections* (1991); Austn Inst Urban Studies, *Bulletin*, Dec 1985, p 3; *Age* (Melbourne), 31 Jan 1973, p 9, 18 Mar 1978, p 10, 7 July 1982, p 11; *Sun News-Pictorial* (Melbourne), 1 Apr 1977, p 3, 29 June 1982, p 3; *Sunday Press* (Melbourne), 3 Sept 1978, p 9; private information.   CAROLYN RASMUSSEN
                                    TONY DINGLE

CUGLEY, ROBERT CECIL (1902-1987), printer and publisher, was born in 1902 at Daylesford, Victoria, son of Australian-born parents Thomas Frederick Cugley, miner, and his wife Agnes, née Rowling. In 1914 the family moved to Port Melbourne, where Bob attended a local primary school. He left at 14, to join Specialty Press, a city-based printer and occasional publisher.

Due to wartime manpower shortages, Cugley did not undertake a formal apprenticeship but quickly learnt the rudiments of the trade. By the 1920s he was printing music and concert programs for J. C. Williamson [q.v.6] Ltd and (after 1932) the Australian Broadcasting Commission, meeting many notable musicians and performers. In the 1930s his networks extended to include large corporate advertising accounts. At St Joseph's Catholic Church, Port Melbourne, on 26 August 1926 he married Rose Marie Hooper.

In 1938, deciding to be 'the sole judge of the people I dealt with', he purchased a struggling printery, National Press, at 34 Lonsdale Street, Melbourne; he was to run the business from this address for forty years. Sympathetic towards and, he confessed, 'a sucker for protesters', Cugley printed magazines and leaflets supporting left-wing causes at or near cost: 'every ratbag in Melbourne', he once remarked, 'sooner or later finds his way here'. He printed *Angry Penguins* from its fifth number (1943), including the infamous 1944 Ern Malley issue; from 1947 he handled the annual *Melbourne University Magazine*; and from 1972 he printed *Overland*. Regular fare for the press also included high school annuals and journals such as *The Secondary Teacher*.

National Press also published books—mainly novels and poetry—and some political pamphlets, all selected by Cugley not so much on literary merit but through his assessment of whether the author was 'a good sort of bloke who deserved a go'. His major venture was Frank Dalby Davison's [q.v.13] *The White Thorntree* (1968), which, owing to its length, complexity and focus on sexual relationships, had been rejected by other publishers.

In 1975 Cugley was honoured by the inaugural National Book Council's Bookman's award. Forced to vacate his Lonsdale Street premises because of fire regulations, in 1978 he moved the business to Abbotsford. By 1983 his age, and competition from new technologies, forced him to close the press. The last book appearing over the National imprint was an autobiographical memoir by Frank Cheshire [q.v.], a fellow publisher whom Cugley had known since the 1920s.

Short, usually dressed in a dark blue suit and always with a hat when outdoors, Bob Cugley was described by Max Harris as 'the Unknown Great Australian'. Lunch at the Florentino, Bourke Street, was a regular pleasure for him: he celebrated his eightieth birthday there with women-only companions, one of whom, the artist Mirka Mora, recalled him as a much-loved man although one with a 'fierce judgement of people'. Survived by his wife and one of their two sons, he died on 24 June 1987 at Preston and was cremated.

M. Harris, *The Unknown Great Australian* (1983); M. Mora, *Wicked but Virtuous* (2000); *Secondary Teacher*, Nov 1978, p 19; personal information.
                                    JOHN ARNOLD

CULICAN, WILLIAM (1928-1984), archaeologist, was born on 21 August 1928 at New Barn Farm, Great Harwood, Lancashire, eldest son of Alfred Culican, farm labourer, and his wife Louisa, née Richardson. Educated at the Catholic College, Preston, Bill intended to study classics and medicine. His national military service (1947-49) in the Royal Army Medical Corps included a posting to Germany.

At the University of Edinburgh (MA, 1953) Culican read classics and archaeology. Graduating with first-class honours in the latter, he won a scholarship to Queen's College, Oxford, to start a B.Litt. on the Western Phoenicians; he also studied Egyptian, and joined the Oxford excavation at Motya in Sicily in 1955. On 4 February 1956 he married with Catholic rites Elisabeth ('Dinny') Frances Badenoch, a secondary schoolteacher, at the Church of Saint Edmund and Saint Frideswide, Oxford. He travelled to Jerusalem as a scholar at the British Institute of Archaeology before returning to Edinburgh, learning Sumerian and Akkadian and winning the Tweedie scholarship to examine Syro-Hittite monuments in Turkey.

After applying for many jobs, Culican was appointed lecturer in Semitic studies at the University of Melbourne in 1960 and promoted to senior lecturer in 1964. Transferring to the department of history in 1966, he became reader in 1972. He was a foundation member of the Humanities Research Council (1966) and the Australian Academy of the Humanities (1969). Through these years he immersed himself in academic and extra-mural commitments with tireless energy. Although he classed himself as an art historian, his field-work was extensive. In 1965 he founded the Archaeological Society of Victoria (its members largely drawn from his devoted Council of Adult Education students), which evolved into the Archaeological and Anthropological Society of Victoria (president 1982-83). With the architect John Taylor he branched into industrial archaeology, directing the excavation of nineteenth-century cement works at Fossil Beach, Mornington, Victoria (1966-69); their book (1972) covering the project won several prizes. During the 1970s he worked in Iran, the Levant, Sicily, Africa and Europe, and became an indispensable participant in Oriental congresses. He was the pottery expert in Honor Frost's excavation of a Punic ship at Marsala, Sicily (1972), and director of the Melbourne excavations at el Quitar, Syria (1982), and the excavation of an Aboriginal ochre mine at Mount Gog, Tasmania (1983).

Iran and Phoenicia were Culican's two central fields of research. His main scholarly output comprised articles in learned journals on both; those on the Phoenicians were collected in his *Opera Selecta* (1986). Otherwise he is remembered for *The Medes and Persians* (1965) and *The First Merchant Venturers* (1966), both volumes demonstrating his mastery of descriptive prose and art history. His definitive chapter on Phoenician colonisation appeared posthumously in the *Cambridge Ancient History* (1992). He also planned books on Persian cities and Iranian metal work.

Culican taught 'Biblical Archaeology' and 'Pre-Classical Antiquity'. His lectures were daunting to first-year and uncommitted students, but inspiring to more advanced scholars. Striking in his manner and use of colour, notably in his dress and the many shades of his ink, Culican was also an engaging raconteur, drawing on the many eccentrics of the archaeological world, pretending with conscious irony not to be one of them, and embellishing his stories with a high-pitched, spluttering laugh. He loved to perform, presiding over one interdepartmental lunch wearing an apron on which he had drawn a giant escutcheon above the motto 'Ich diene' ('I serve'). A prodigious memory gave his discussions of artefacts their vital contexts, and he ranged with ease over the Mediterranean world and as far east as India.

Survived by his wife and their five sons and two daughters, Culican died of myocardial infarction and diabetes on 24 March 1984 at his home in South Box Hill. He was buried in Templestowe cemetery. At the time of his death he had been nominated for the personal chair he richly deserved.

Austn Academy of the Humanities, *Procs*, 1982-83, p 119; *Archiv für Orientforschung*, vol 31, 1984, p 231; *Artefact*, vol 9, nos 1-4, 1984, p 2; private information and personal knowledge.

RONALD T. RIDLEY

CULOTTA, NINO; *see* O'GRADY, J.

CUMING, MARIANNUS ADRIAN (1901-1988), industrial chemist and company manager, was born on 26 November 1901 at Footscray, Melbourne, the last of five surviving children of American-born James Cuming [q.v.8], general manager of Cuming Smith & Co., chemical fertiliser manufacturers, and his Victorian-born wife Alice Louisa, née Fehon. 'Mac', as he was known from his initials, was educated at a small private school in Footscray, then at Camberwell Grammar and (from 1917) Melbourne Church of England Grammar schools. He graduated from the University of Melbourne (B.Sc., 1924) and, after investigating superphosphate production in the United States of America, completed a diploma in chemical engineering at the Imperial College of Science and Technology, London. Joining Cuming Smith, Mac became an expert on acid plants and allied factory procedures. At the Chapel of St Peter at Melbourne Grammar, on 20 April 1926 he married Wilma Margaret Isles Guthrie.

In 1930 Cuming moved to Perth as works manager (general manager, 1933) of Cuming Smith & Mt Lyell Farmers Fertilisers Ltd (later CSBP & Farmers Ltd). He returned to Melbourne in 1936. A director since 1933 of Commonwealth Fertilisers & Chemicals Ltd (formed in 1929 from a merger of Cuming Smith & Co. Pty Ltd and three other companies) he was groomed to succeed his uncle, William Fehon Cuming (d.1933). In 1945 he was appointed general manager (chairman, 1957-80) of Cuming Smith & Co. Ltd, and became managing director (1948) and chairman (1956) of CF&C.

As the central figure in Australia's postwar chemical fertiliser industry, Cuming was chairman of CSBP & Farmers (1943-71), ACF & Shirleys Fertilizers Ltd (1964-65), and a director of almost every major fertiliser company in Australia. He was also a director of Imperial Chemical Industries of Australia and New Zealand Ltd and the Broken Hill Proprietary Co. Ltd. In 1949-76 he was deputy-chairman of the Victorian board of the Australian Mutual Provident Society. He took quiet pride in his family's industrial origins as working proprietors, recalling with pleasure their reputation as 'the manure Cumings', and had a paternal affection for employees he had known since the 1920s. In 1978 he was disquieted by the take-over bid for Cuming Smith by a corporate raider, which led to its acquisition by Westralian Farmer's Co-operative Ltd in 1979. Valuing history, Cuming secured the public deposit of the business and family records.

An active member of many societies and charities, Cuming served (1945-77) on the board (vice-president 1975-77) of the Alfred Hospital, as a trustee (1965-76) of the Baker Medical Research Institute and as a governor (1977-78) of the Ian Clunies Ross [q.v.13] Memorial Foundation. He was made a fellow of the Australian Institute of Management (1957) and appointed CMG (1962). His clubs were the Melbourne, Weld and Australian, and his hobbies were golf, fishing, and working in the gardens designed for him by Edna Walling [q.v.16]. A dedicated composter, Mac Cuming was delighted to be taken for a jobbing gardener. He died on 26 February 1988 and was cremated; he was predeceased by his wife (d.1984) and survived by their three sons and daughter.

His nephew, WILLIAM JAMES CUMING (1912-1986), engineer and manager, was born on 3 February 1912 at Footscray, eldest son of William Fehon Cuming and his wife Annie, née Jordan. Bill was educated at MCEGS and the University of Melbourne (B.Min.Eng, 1935). While employed by North Broken Hill Ltd (1936-39), he obtained a mine manager's certificate and published *Mine Drainage System* (1938). On 27 June 1940 at Broken Hill he married Grace Laurette Dunstan.

In 1939, encouraged by his uncle Sir Alexander Stewart [q.v.12], Cuming joined Commonwealth Fertilisers as technical assistant, and soon was engaged in vital war work, including the construction of three sulphuric acid plants. He was successively works engineer (1946), works manager (1952) and technical manager (1958). His executive advancement, however, was blocked. After ICIANZ acquired Chemical Fertilisers in 1961, he became technical (1962) and special assignments (1968) manager of the fertiliser division. Retiring in 1972, Cuming was appointed a consultant to Boral Ltd and a director (1974-80) of Cuming Smith and of CSBP & Farmers.

Through the 1950s Cuming became increasingly interested in technical and tertiary education. The industry's face in Melbourne's western suburbs, he was a member of the council from 1953 (vice-president 1959-65; president 1965-69) of Footscray Technical College (renamed Footscray Institute of Technology in 1968), which, in 1982, named a building after him. He served the Australasian Institute of Mining and Metallurgy as councillor (1957-86), vice-president (1963-66), president (1970), honorary treasurer (1975) and acting chief executive officer (1983-84), and as its representative on the University of Melbourne's engineering faculty (1959-74).

Quiet and direct in manner, and possessed of a dry wit, he was made an honorary member (1982) of the AusIMM and declared its 'elder statesman in residence'. Survived by his wife and their son and two daughters, Bill Cuming died on 15 January 1986 at Canterbury and was cremated.

K. P. Smith, *A Bunch of Pirates* (1984); C. Rasmussen, *Poor Man's University* (1989); J. Lack and I. D. Rae, 'Many Happy Returns', in E. Richards and J. Templeton (eds), *The Australian Immigrant* (1998); A'asian Inst of Mining and Metallurgy, *Procs*, no 284, 1982, p 4, vol 291, no 1, 1986, p 35; Cuming Smith & Co. Ltd papers (Univ of Melbourne Archives); private information and personal knowledge.
JOHN LACK

CUMMINGS, ROBERT PERCY (1900-1989), architect, was born on 11 September 1900 at Kelvin Grove, Brisbane, third child of Victorian-born Frank Percy Cummings, warehouseman, and his wife Catherine Elizabeth, née Brown, who came from England. At 14 Robert left Eagle Junction State School to work in the timber-manufacturing firm of Brown & Broad Ltd as office-boy and then draftsman. His contact with structural prefabrication and his ability to prepare meticulous working drawings encouraged an interest in architecture. From 1916 he took evening classes at the Central Technical College (Dip.Arch., 1923). Articled at various times to L. L. Powell, F. R. Hall [qq.v.11,9] and H. G. Kirkpatrick, he was employed (1919-23) as an architectural draftsman by the Commonwealth War Service Homes Commission. He had enlisted in the Australian Imperial Force on his eighteenth birthday, two months before World War I ended, but was not called up.

In 1924 Cummings won the Queensland Wattle League's architectural scholarship, enabling him to study for three years at the Architectural Association School, London, and to obtain its diploma of architecture (1928). Awarded (1927) the Rome scholarship in architecture, he was in residence for two years at the British School at Rome. He became (1928) an associate of the Royal Institute of British Architects. After further professional and teaching experience in London, late in 1930 he returned to Brisbane. On 17 April 1933 at his father's house at Clayfield, he married with Methodist forms Mavis Mifanwy Williams, a schoolteacher. In 1934-36 he was in charge of the architecture course at the Central Technical College. He formed a partnership with F. Bruce Lucas in 1936, a time when architectural work was scarce. Two notable commissions were the First Church of Christ, Scientist, on North Quay (1939), reminiscent of the Dutch public buildings of the (Willem) Dudok school and ingeniously planned on a restricted site, and extensions (comprising a self-effacing group of slab and local stone buildings) to Binna Burra Lodge, in Lamington National Park.

When the University of Queensland's faculty of engineering introduced a part-time diploma course in architecture in 1937, Cummings was appointed lecturer. In World War II he assumed additional tasks, including working with erstwhile students and artists for a unit researching and implementing military camouflage systems in south-east Queensland and northern New South Wales. He and his wife held a regular 'open house' at their Alderley home on Sundays for visiting servicemen and women. Their guests included the official war artists Douglas Annand [q.v.13] and Donald Friend [q.v.]. This custom of domestic hospitality was later to extend to successive waves of students.

In 1948 the university established a faculty of architecture, having instituted a degree course the previous year. Cummings was awarded (1948) an honorary bachelor's degree, and was appointed foundation professor in February 1949. He and his colleague Bruce Lucas provided a sound framework of theoretical, practical and professional knowledge, retaining always the affection and esteem of colleagues and students. On retiring in December 1966 he was made emeritus professor. In 1987 the university conferred on him an honorary doctorate of letters.

President (1948-50) of the Queensland chapter of the Royal Australian Institute of Architects, Cummings was made a life fellow in 1959. Fulfilling other public roles, he was a trustee of the Queensland (National) Art Gallery (1939-67) and of the Royal Queensland Art Society (1944-69), and a member (1958-68) of the Greater Brisbane Planning Committee. He was a skilful photographer and a keen gardener. In retirement he lived at Currumbin on the Gold Coast. Survived by his son and two daughters, he died on 27 September 1989 at his home and was cremated. His wife had predeceased him. A portrait of Cummings by his daughter Elisabeth is held by the department of architecture, University of Queensland. His stocky figure also appears in a gallery of sculptures of founding professors, in the guise of grotesques, on the walls of the cloisters of the Great Court.

I. Sinnamon and M. Keniger, *Ideas into Practice* (1987); *Courier* (Brisbane), 21 June 1924, p 6; *Qld Architect*, Nov 1989, p 4; Cummings papers (Univ of Qld Lib); private information and personal knowledge.   IAN SINNAMON

CUMMINS, JOHN EDWARD (1902-1989), chemist and science administrator, was born

on 21 October 1902 in Perth, son of Australian-born parents Ambrose Michael Cummins, tailor's cutter, and his wife Elizabeth Mary, née Hamilton. Jack attended Perth Modern School and the University of Western Australia (B.Sc., 1923). He was officer-in-charge of chemical investigations with the Western Australian Forests Department from 1924 to 1927 before taking up a Council for Scientific and Industrial Research (Commonwealth Scientific and Industrial Research Organization) research studentship in forest products at the University of Wisconsin (M.Sc., 1932), United States of America. On 4 January 1927 at St Mary's Church of England, West Perth, he had married Elizabeth Margaret Lamborne (d.1983).

Back in Australia in 1929, Cummins was appointed to the staff of CSIR's division of forest products, at first on a senior studentship. In 1940, after the outbreak of World War II, he was moved to the information section, and in March 1943 he became assistant-director of the Scientific Liaison Bureau in Melbourne, under (Sir) Eric (Baron) Ashby. The bureau's major function was to co-ordinate scientific and manufacturing objectives as part of the war effort. Cummins became full-time director in June and held that post until 1945.

In 1948 Cummins was transferred to London as chief scientific liaison officer, a position which gave him access to visiting Australian scientists and students. His responsibilities included handling enquiries for CSIRO, procuring equipment, attending conferences, maintaining close links with overseas scientific developments and facilitating the exchange of information. The CSIRO executive arranged in 1954 for him to be sent to Washington to take charge of the Australian Scientific Liaison Office there; he assumed control in August 1955. That year he became a member of the United Nations Educational, Scientific and Cultural Organization's committee on scientific documentation.

Cummins was granted leave without pay in 1958 to become director of the division of scientific and technical information at the International Atomic Energy Agency, Vienna. Returning to Australia in January 1961, he retired from CSIRO in October 1962 but continued to work in a consultative capacity. In 1965 he acted as scientific attaché in Washington for six months pending the appointment of a full-time replacement. Having helped to set up the Ian Clunies Ross [q.v.13] Memorial Foundation in 1959, he served at various times as treasurer, executive officer, secretary and governor.

Cummins was described by colleagues as enthusiastic, loyal and hard working, and as a man of simple tastes. In his youth he had been a keen rower, cricketer and golfer, and he maintained passions for fishing and gardening throughout his life. He was elected a fellow of the (Royal) Australian Chemical Institute (1940), the Royal Institute of Chemistry, London (1949), and the Royal Society of Arts (1974). In 1970 he was appointed OBE. Survived by his daughter, he died on 7 October 1989 in his home at Kew, Melbourne, and was cremated.

D. P. Mellor, *The Role of Science and Industry* (1958); C. B. Schedvin, *Shaping Science and Industry* (1987); M. C. O'Dea, *Ian Clunies Ross* (1997); *Chemistry in Aust*, vol 57, nos 1 and 2, 1990, p 17; *Smith's Weekly*, 27 Mar 1943, p 11; CSIRO Archives, Canberra.   BARRY W. BUTCHER

CUMPSTON, JOHN STANLEY (1909-1986), diplomat, geographer, historian and publisher, was born on 3 June 1909 in Perth, eldest of seven children of Victorian-born parents John Howard Lidgett Cumpston, medical practitioner, and his wife Gladys Maeva Cumpston [qq.v.8,13], née Walpole. He was educated at Wesley College, Melbourne, and the University of Melbourne (BA Hons, 1930; LL B, 1932; Dip.Pub.Admin., 1939). At university he was a prominent sportsman. Commissioned as a lieutenant in the Melbourne University Rifles in May 1932, he continued to serve in the Citizen Military Forces and was named 'the best shot in the militia force in Australia'.

On 1 May 1933 Cumpston was admitted as a barrister and solicitor of the Supreme Court of Victoria. He joined the Commonwealth Public Service in June 1934 as one of the first group of graduate appointees. After working in the Crown Solicitor's Office in Sydney, he transferred in November 1935 to the Department of External Affairs, Canberra. At the Anglican Church of St John the Baptist, Reid, on 31 May 1940 he married Helen Ida Dunbar, a librarian.

Seconded to the Australian Imperial Force on 1 October 1940, Cumpston was posted to the 2/23rd Battalion and made a liaison officer at 26th Brigade headquarters. He served at Tobruk, Libya, in April-May 1941, was promoted to captain in September and was mentioned in despatches. From December to February 1942 he was officer commanding the 9th Division Ski Company in Lebanon. In February 1943 he returned to Australia and in April joined the Allied Geographical Section at General Headquarters, South-West Pacific Area. He transferred to the Reserve of Officers on 25 April 1945. Rejoining the Department of External Affairs, Cumpston was first secretary in Santiago (1946-49), official secretary in Wellington (1950-53), and consul in Noumea (1953-58) and Dili (January-March 1963). In 1960 he had become departmental historian, a position he held until he retired in July 1969.

In 1939 Cumpston had assisted in the preparation and publication of the first reliable map of Antarctica. This led in 1940 to his being elected a fellow of the Royal Geographical Society, London. The University of Melbourne awarded him a doctorate of letters (1949) for his studies in the geography of Antarctica and of the Pacific area. In 1966 his contribution to the knowledge of Antarctica was marked by the naming of the Cumpston Massif. His book on Macquarie Island, published in 1968, has remained the basic work of reference.

Although Cumpston wrote other books—on Tobruk, on Bass Strait sealers, and on Kangaroo and King islands—publishing became his main retirement occupation. He set up and funded a publishing company, the Roebuck Society, to 'provide an outlet for books of merit on Australian historical subjects not otherwise published'. Before his death, it had produced over thirty publications.

Cumpston demonstrated public spiritedness in other ways. He helped to establish the Sir Leslie Morshead [q.v.15] War Veterans' Home, Lyneham, St Luke's Church of England, Deakin, and the Brindabella Gardens retirement home, Curtin. He served as president of the Canberra and District Historical Society (1973-75) and of the Australian Capital Territory branch of the Rats of Tobruk Association (1958-67 and 1983). In all these activities, as during his earlier career in the department, Cumpston's enthusiasm and good nature did much to achieve whatever the common goal happened to be. He encouraged people to make an effort, and they liked him for it. Injuries sustained in a motorcar accident in 1984 resulted in serious health problems. Survived by his wife and their two daughters and two sons, he died on 6 August 1986 at Royal Canberra Hospital and was cremated.

Canberra Times, 2 July 1969, p 10, 3 Apr 1979, p 1, 14 Aug 1986, p 15; Canberra and District Hist Soc, *Newsletter*, Sept 1986, p 10; *Tobruk Times*, Sept-Oct 1986, p 1; B883, item NX70393 (NAA); private information.   P. G. F. HENDERSON

CURLEWIS, SIR ADRIAN HERBERT FREDERIC (1901-1985), judge and surf lifesaving administrator, was born on 13 January 1901 at Mosman, Sydney, second child of Sydney-born Herbert Raine Curlewis, barrister and later judge, and his English-born wife Ethel, née Turner [qq.v.12], author of children's stories. Educated at Sydney Church of England Grammar School (Shore), Adrian studied law at the University of Sydney. He worked in a law firm, then served as clerk first to Sir William Cullen and then to (Sir) Philip Street [qq.v.8,12], chief justices of the Supreme Court of New South Wales. Admitted to the

Bar on 11 March 1927, he practised in Sydney. A founding member of the Palm Beach Surf Life Saving Club, he was club captain (1923-28) and president (1929-33). He married Beatrice Maude Carr on 12 December 1928 at St Philip's Church of England, Sydney.

Commissioned in the Militia on 6 June 1939, Curlewis transferred to the Australian Imperial Force in September 1940. By February 1941 he was a general staff officer, 3rd grade, at the headquarters of the 8th Division in Malaya. Twelve months later, when it was obvious that Singapore would fall to the Japanese, he was included in a plan to evacuate the divisional commander, Major General H. G. Bennett [q.v.13], and some staff officers. However, Curlewis considered it improper to leave 'the men at this critical time, even if it did mean the chance of getting home'. Following his capture, for eighteen months his family did not know whether he was alive or dead. He helped organise the 'Changi University' education scheme and kept two secret diaries. One, written during his eight months (April-November 1943) constructing the Burma-Thailand railway, became the basis of a report (co-authored with Lieutenant Colonel C. H. Kappe) detailing the activities of 'F' force and its experience of Japanese atrocities. His diaries and letters, compiled by his daughter, were published as *Of Love and War* (1982). Following his release in September 1945, Curlewis was a key witness before the commission of inquiry into Bennett's escape from Singapore. On 26 January 1946 Captain Curlewis transferred to the Reserve of Officers.

In 1948 Curlewis was appointed a District Court judge. He served on a number of government inquiries, including the State shark menace advisory committee (1934-35), the royal commission (1950) on Claremont Hospital for the Mentally Insane, Western Australia, and the commission of inquiry (1973-74) into privately operated omnibus and tourist vehicle services in New South Wales. Always interested in young people, he sat on the councils of his old school, Shore, and Wenona School.

Juvenile delinquency and crime after World War II worried Curlewis. Delivering the Roentgen Oration to the sixth annual meeting of the College of Radiologists of Australasia, in 1955, he 'charged' the community with 'gross neglect of its duties to youth ... by failing to give proper instruction' and 'by placing false values before [them]'. He urged the minister for justice to 'appoint an Advisory Committee to inquire into the causes of delinquency'. The State government eventually heeded the call and appointed Curlewis chairman of the youth policy advisory committee in 1960. He did not claim to have the solutions to juvenile crime, but believed that his experiences as a prisoner of war, 'learning and practising every con-

ceivable form of dishonesty in order to remain alive', and observing youth involved in surf lifesaving placed him 'in a better position ... than any of my brother judges' to understand the issues confronting young people. The committee's report (1962) bears his imprimatur, especially his faith in the ability of established youth organisations to train young people in 'responsibility' and thus combat misbehaviour.

Very active in public life, Curlewis held leadership roles in numerous associations. He was chairman (1949-71) of the New South Wales National Fitness Council, founder (1956) of the Outward Bound movement in New South Wales, national co-ordinator (1962-73) of the Duke of Edinburgh's Award in Australia, and president (1968-84) of the Royal Humane Society of New South Wales. In 1960 he chaired an international convention on life-saving techniques that led to widespread adoption of the 'kiss of life'. As president (1934-41, 1945-75) of the Surf Life Saving Association of Australia, he saw the association enter a period of crisis in the 1960s as young men left the clubs en masse and took up surfboard riding. Their pursuit of what he regarded as selfish personal interest troubled him. He was appointed CBE in 1962 and CVO in 1974, and was knighted in 1967. In 1971 Sir Adrian retired from the bench. Survived by his wife and their son and daughter, he died on 16 June 1985 at his Mosman home and was cremated.

H. J. H. Henchman, *A Court Rises* (1982); S. Brawley, *Beach Beyond* (1996); D. Booth, *Australian Beach Cultures* (2001); Surf Life Saving Assn of Aust, *Annual Report*, 1974-75, p 2; *Austn Law Jnl*, vol 59, no 9, 1985, p 581; *Austn Women's Weekly*, 14 Sept 1955, p 12, 17 Feb 1971, p 4; B883, item NX70316 (NAA); N. Bennetts, interview with A. Curlewis (ts, 1976, NLA); Curlewis family papers (SLNSW).   DOUGLAS BOOTH

CURRAN, BERNARD AUGUSTINE (1908-1983), stockbroker, was born on 24 August 1908 at Balmain, Sydney, second of eight children of Joseph Charles Curran, a clerk born in New South Wales, and his Queensland-born wife Catherine Mary, née Barbeler. Bernard attended Christian Brothers' School, Balmain. His career began as a clerk (1923-39) with the stockbrokers (Charles) Titmus & (Claudius) Quinan (later C. B. Quinan & Cox). He then worked (1939-47) for another stockbroker, Stanley R. Johnson. Curran's business acumen was well known in the financial world from the 1930s, when he encouraged (Sir) Norman Rydge [q.v.16] to buy controlling interests in cinema companies that ultimately became the Greater Union Organisation Pty Ltd. In July 1947 Curran's assets were estimated to be £28 630, including £18 176 in shares and securities, largely in cinema-related enterprises.

When Curran applied in 1947 for membership of the Sydney Stock Exchange, the committee suggested that he withdraw his application and resubmit it in twelve months' time: this rejection may have been due to his Catholicism or to his relative youth and aggressive style of business. Evan Whitton later described the SSE as a 'rather WASP-ish club', although from the beginning it had included a few Catholics. Prominent businessmen, who had given Curran references, probably lobbied in support of his candidature and the intervention of his brother-in-law, Senator John Armstrong [q.v.13], a minister in the Chifley [q.v.13] government, may have led the committee to reconsider its decision rather than face the threat of regulation of the Exchange. On 23 October 1947 Curran was elected a member.

Next year Curran became a sole trader. James McHugh worked for him from 1950 and when he became a partner in 1955 the firm was named Bernard Curran & Co. In 1965 it was renamed Bernard Curran, McHugh & Co. Curran succeeded in overcoming interstate rivalries in order to float companies from outside New South Wales on the Sydney market. Through his association with the accountant Raymont Moore, (Sir) Reginald Ansett [q.v.] and Rydge, Curran was often engaged in company flotation and underwriting issues, bringing some twenty companies, including Gilbert Lodge (Holdings) Ltd and Woolcord Fabrics Ltd, to the lists of the SSE. He resigned as senior partner of Bernard Curran, McHugh & Co. in 1982 but continued as a consultant.

A director of Metropolitan Theatres & Investment Co. Ltd (National Properties Ltd) from the 1930s, Curran was closely associated with other companies (including National Investments Ltd for twenty-five years), which benefited from his financial skills. Curran, who never married, played bowls for recreation. He died on 25 March 1983 in an ambulance on the way from his Lindfield home to the Mona Vale District Hospital and was buried in the Catholic section of Northern Suburbs cemetery. A benefactor of numerous charities, he provided in his will for the Bernard Curran Foundation to distribute funds to the Hornsby hospital and other medical and charitable institutions.

S. Salsbury and K. Sweeney, *Sydney Stockbrokers* (1992); *SMH*, 23 Apr 1977, p 33, 29 Mar 1983, p 12; *Austn Financial Review*, 17 July 1979, p 1; private information.   W. J. MURRAY

CURRIE, SIR GEORGE ALEXANDER (1896-1984), agricultural scientist and university vice-chancellor, was born on 13 August 1896 at Windyhills farm, Grange, Banffshire, Scotland, second son of George Currie, a black-smith journeyman and later a tenant farmer, and his wife Mary, née Craib. The family belonged to the Free Church of Scotland and George was to remain a devout Presbyterian. He attended the local school and won a scholarship to Keith Grammar School, where he was dux of the intermediate school (1911) and science medallist (1912 and 1914). Through living and working on the farm he developed an interest in agriculture. After the outbreak of World War I, he enlisted in the 6th Battalion, Gordon Highlanders. He served in France in 1915-16, but was invalided to Britain suffering from diphtheria. In 1919 he was discharged from the army as a sergeant instructor.

Government assistance for ex-servicemen and a grant from the Carnegie Endowment for International Peace enabled Currie to study at the University of Aberdeen (B.Sc., 1923; B.Ag.Sc., 1923; D.Sc., 1936). He graduated with first-class honours in zoology and geology. On 5 April 1923 at the United Free Church, Inverurie, he married Margaret Smith, his geology lecturer. They migrated to Queensland and joined a cousin of Margaret at Koumala, near Mackay, where in 1923-26 Currie managed a sugar plantation.

Joining the Queensland Department of Agriculture and Stock as an assistant-entomologist in 1926, Currie carried out investigations into cotton pests. Three years later he took a post in Canberra with the division of economic entomology, Council for Scientific and Industrial Research. His work on the biological control of noxious weeds established his reputation as a research scientist and in 1935 he was made officer-in-charge of the weeds investigation section. In 1937, while on a trip to Britain, Europe and the United States of America, he visited Algeria and collected seeds of a grass, *Dactylis glomerata*. It would later be grown widely as pasture in New South Wales and Victoria and become known as Currie cocksfoot. That year he was promoted to principal research scientist.

In 1939 Currie was appointed Hackett [q.v.9] professor of agriculture and director of the institute of agriculture at the University of Western Australia. Succeeding H. E. Whitfield [q.v.12], he took on additional administrative duties as part-time vice-chancellor in September next year. In 1945 he reported on rural training for returned service personnel for the Commonwealth Department of Post-war Reconstruction. As full-time vice-chancellor from 1945, during a period of rapid growth for the university, he formed a good relationship with the Liberal premier, (Sir) Ross McLarty [q.v.15], who was also State treasurer. The under-treasurer, (Sir) Alexander Reid [q.v.16], was another member of the university senate. Supported by the chancellor, (Sir) Walter Murdoch [q.v.10], and the registrar, Colsell Sanders, Currie was, according to the historian Fred Alexander, 'peculiarly well placed to turn immediate difficulties into continuing opportunities'. In 1950 the relationships with McLarty and Reid were put to the test when proposals for university expansion caused the premier and under-treasurer to assert that the government should decide how additional funds would be spent. Currie insisted that the senate retain the right to determine university policy, including its fields of growth, and rejected the premier's proposal that university budgets be reviewed in a similar way to those of government departments. The degree of government interference was reduced; Alexander observed later that 'the outcome was a tribute both to the firmness of Dr Currie's stand on this issue of University autonomy and to the moderation and responsiveness of Mr McLarty'.

Through his administrative skills and his genial, outgoing personality, Currie improved the university's public relations. He relished contacts with people in all walks of life. With his wife, he frequently held open house for staff and students at their official residence, Tuart House. Despite his abstemiousness, these occasions were always convivial. He was chairman (1949-51) of the Australian Vice-Chancellors' Committee, and a member of the executive council (1949-61) of the Association of Universities of the British Commonwealth.

In 1952 Currie was appointed vice-chancellor of the University of New Zealand, which then comprised four university colleges. His office was located in Wellington. Devolution had already been proposed, the constituent colleges were in agreement but the university senate was divided on the issue. In 1954-57 he prepared a series of analyses which enabled the senate to devise a new system, based on autonomous universities and a university grants committee to administer matters of common concern and to negotiate with the government on their behalf. The reorganisation eventuated in 1961. Currie was knighted in 1960 and next year, at its final congregation, the University of New Zealand conferred on him an honorary LL D. He had previously been awarded honorary doctorates from the universities of Aberdeen (1948), Western Australia (1952) and Melbourne (1954), and Dalhousie University, Nova Scotia, Canada (1958).

In 1960-62 Currie chaired the commission on education in New Zealand. His amiability, tact and courtesy, as well as his skills as a chairman, made it easy for all to have their views heard and considered. The commission's recommendations, almost all of which were adopted, were the blueprint for educational development in schools and universities for a quarter of a century. Currie had a broad-ranging mind; in his J. M. Macrossan [q.v.5] lecture (1947) he had confessed that he shared 'with all other scientists the charge that we have been too devoted to science and too little concerned with that humanity which is more important than science'.

Sir George retired in 1962 and he and his wife settled in Canberra. In 1963-64 he chaired a commission on higher education in Papua and New Guinea that led to the establishment there of a university; it awarded him an honorary LL D in 1967. He was chairman of the Canberra Theatre Trust (1964-68), of the Literature Censorship Appeal Board (1964-67), and of advisory committees of the Canberra Public Library Service (1963-70) and the local hospital. Engaged in 1964 by the Commonwealth Scientific and Industrial Research Organization's executive as a consultant on the development of its archives, he wrote *The Origins of CSIRO* (1966) with the assistance of John Graham. In 1966-67 he chaired a working party that inquired into education in the Australian Capital Territory; its report set the basic principles and patterns for the ACT Schools Authority. Survived by his wife and their two sons, he died on 4 May 1984 in Canberra and was cremated.

F. Alexander, *Campus at Crawley* (1963); *Dictionary of New Zealand Biography*, vol 5 (2000); *Canberra Times*, 8 May 1984, p 12; UWA Archives.

D. E. HUTCHISON

CUSACK, ELLEN DYMPHNA (1902-1981), author, was born on 21 September 1902 at Wyalong, New South Wales, third of six surviving children of James Cusack, storekeeper, and his wife Bridget Beatrice, née Crowley. Nell's parents, of Irish-Catholic stock, were born in New South Wales. She was a frequently ill and fractious infant; her mother's childless sister, also called Nell, and her husband Tom Leahy, took over her upbringing in 1905. She lived at Cooma, Narrandera and Guyra and attended St Ursula's College, Armidale, as a boarder. In 1920 she won an exhibition and Teachers' College scholarship to the University of Sydney (BA, 1925; Dip.Ed., 1926); her academic mentors included George Arnold Wood and Henry Tasman Lovell [qq.v.12,10]. Sydney University Drama Society took Cusack into the world of 'little theatre'. Her début play script, 'Safety First'—a feminist drama with themes of illegitimacy, middle-class hypocrisy and the liberated 'New' woman as heroine—was one of the final dozen selected in the 1927 competition of the magazine *Triad*.

After teaching (1926-27) at Neutral Bay Girls' Intermediate High School, in 1928 Cusack was posted by the Department of Education to Broken Hill High School, where she wrote her first (unpublished) novel, 'This

Nettle, Danger', a rite-of-passage, Joycean-inspired, 'portrait of the artist' as a young woman. Cusack returned to 'the drama', convinced that her true talent lay there, and her plays *Shallow Cups* (1933), *Anniversary* (1935), and *Red Sky at Morning* (performed 1935; published 1942) were well received.

After six years' country service, teaching at Broken Hill, Goulburn and Parramatta, Cusack was posted in 1935 to Sydney Girls' High School. Her second novel, *Jungfrau* (1936), about three young women and their views on abortion, was runner-up in 1935 for the *Bulletin*'s S. H. Prior [q.v.11] memorial prize. In 1938 she was recruited to the executive of the Fellowship of Australian Writers (president 1968-69). Her controversial radio documentaries challenged social orthodoxies. By 1939, when Angus & Robertson [qq.v.7,11] published *Pioneers on Parade*—her first collaboration with Miles Franklin [q.v.8] and an irreverent pasquinade of Australia's celebrations of 150 years of British colonial settlement—she had taken on too many 'sacred cows' for the liking of the Department of Education. Moreover, after a fall two years earlier, she was pursuing a workers' compensation case against the department. In December she was summarily transferred to Bathurst High School. Appointments at Parkes and Newcastle followed.

Her revenge in exile was the prize-winning play *Morning Sacrifice* (1943), set in an all-female staffroom in a girls' high school. Another play, *Comets Soon Pass* (1943), was her personal catharsis and artistic reprisal for the defection of her former lover, the novelist Xavier Herbert [q.v.], and payback to the 'asparagus king' Gordon Edgell [q.v.8], who had tried to damn her publicly for her activism on behalf of unemployed youth. She also indulged in another satirical collaboration with Miles Franklin in the play *Call up Your Ghosts* (1945).

In 1944 Cusack's always perilous health broke down and she was pensioned out of the Department of Education. To economise she pooled resources with a friend and fellow-writer, Florence James, with whom she shared a cottage in the Blue Mountains. They worked together on a children's book, *Four Winds and a Family* (1946), before rigorously planning and writing their classic wartime epic of Sydney, *Come In Spinner* (1951), which won the £1000 prize in the novel competition run by the Sydney *Daily Telegraph* in 1946. *Come In Spinner*'s satirical exposé of low life and 'high' society in wartime Sydney bordered on the carnivalesque. The potential for libel action, latent in the authors' descriptions of locations, the vice industries specific to them, and the rich caricatures of those who had profited through wartime corruption, caused the *Daily Telegraph* to hesitate about publication. The authors reclaimed their manuscript with the aid of the solicitor Marie Byles [q.v.13], and published it in London. *Come In Spinner* was a best-seller.

Late in 1948 Cusack consolidated a long-term if intermittent relationship with Norman Randolph Freehill, then chief-of-staff of the Communist Party of Australia's newspaper, the *Tribune*. As the Cold War gained momentum, the Australian political situation became increasingly dangerous for communists. In 1949 Cusack, and later Freehill, sailed for Europe. When health permitted, she worked on the manuscripts that she had taken to London, including *Say No to Death* (1951), about a young woman with tuberculosis, *Southern Steel* (1953), set in Newcastle, and *Caddie* (1953), the autobiography of a barmaid which Cusack edited and introduced. She wrote *The Sun in Exile* (1955), based on the racism she had witnessed on her voyage through the Caribbean and in London. Freehill negotiated her publishing and publicity schedules. From 1951 to 1956 they travelled each winter to the south of France as London's cold exacerbated Cusack's illness. After several months of near-paralysis in 1954 Cusack dictated *Pacific Paradise* (1955), a play protesting against atomic weapons. It made her reputation in countries of Asia, Eastern Europe and the Pacific, and led to an invitation to Peking (Beijing), where she and Freehill stayed for eighteen months. While in China Cusack researched and wrote a collection of social documentary pen-portraits, *Chinese Women Speak* (1958).

In the winter of 1958-59, en route to London from Peking, Cusack happened to witness a Nazi SS officers' reunion and the beginnings of the neo-Nazi cult in Germany. The result was *Heatwave in Berlin* (1961), also widely published and translated. From 1959 her works had found a popular audience overseas: in eastern European countries she was given untransferable royalties. This resulted in a nomadic annual schedule as, with Freehill, she lived on literary earnings and wrote, out of the cultural experiences, books including *Holidays among the Russians* (1964) and *Illyria Reborn* (1966).

On 21 June 1962 Cusack married Freehill, then a 70-year-old widower, in the register office at Crowborough, East Sussex, England. They returned to Australia as *Picnic Races* (1962), a small-town comedy, was published. Cusack became friendly with Faith and Hans Bandler of the Aboriginal rights movement, and wrote *Black Lightning* (1964), in which she experimented with free indirect style and multiple voices.

Heatwave in Berlin was staged and televised across the Soviet Union as part of the 1965 celebrations of the twentieth anniversary of victory over fascism, at which Freehill and

Cusack were official guests. During the next few years Cusack researched and wrote *The Sun Is Not Enough* (1967), which was thematically linked to *Heatwave in Berlin*. She returned to Australia in 1967, the year of the referendum that gave citizenship rights to the Aboriginal people. *The Half-Burnt Tree* (1969) incorporated themes of deracination, misguided paternalistic social welfare policies, the Vietnam War and individual emotional isolation.

Cusack's experiences of a sister's battle with alcoholism resulted in *A Bough in Hell* (1971). In 1973 the Australian Council for the Arts awarded her a literary pension. An International Women's Year grant seeded the production of *Caddie* (1976) as a film. Freehill wrote a biographical travelogue, *Dymphna Cusack* (1975), based on years of taped dialogues which they recorded as they travelled. Although frail they continued to travel and write—Fiji and Noumea (1976), Hong Kong (1977), South-East Asia (1979) and finally South America (1980)—using their preferred mode of transport, the cargo ship.

In 1978 medical tests had confirmed that Cusack's lifelong 'dog's disease' was multiple sclerosis; by December 1980 she was completely paralysed. She had refused appointment as an OBE earlier because of her republican beliefs, but was appointed AM in 1981. She was small, with a fine-boned face framed by a coronet of braided hair. A committed social reformer, she interpreted history through the lives of ordinary people and used various forms of popular culture to entertain, inform and educate. She regarded herself, in Jean-Paul Sartre's phrase, as an *'écrivain engagé'*—one for whom the pen was mightier than the sword. Despite constant illness, she was a brave and prominent anti-nuclear activist in the World Peace Movement during the Cold War era. Survived by her husband (d.1984), she died on 19 October 1981 at Manly and was cremated.

M. North (ed), *Yarn Spinners* (2001); R. Nile and B. York (eds), *Workers and Intellectuals* (1992); *Meanjin Qtrly*, vol 24, no 3, 1965, p 317; *Independent Austn*, vol 3, no 4, nd, p 3; H. de Berg, interview with D. Cusack (ts, 1964, NLA); V. H. Lloyd, Conscience and Justice (MA thesis, Univ of Qld, 1986); D. Adelaide, Australian Women's Literature (PhD thesis, Univ of Sydney, 1991); A6119, items 315, 1555, 2486 (NAA); Cusack papers (NLA).
MARILLA NORTH

CUTHBERT, EDITH MARY (1891-1988), community worker, was born on 12 December 1891 at Rochester, Victoria, sixth of ten children of Victorian-born parents James Robison Chapman, bank manager, and his wife Ada, née Valentine. In 1895 the family moved to Albury, New South Wales, where Edith went to school; they later transferred to Hobart. During World War I Edith served in the voluntary aid detachment of the Tasmanian division of the British (Australian) Red Cross Society. In 1925 she worked as a journalist for nine months on the Hobart *News*, and next year wrote for the women's and children's pages of the Melbourne *Leader*. On 21 October 1926 at All Saints' Church of England, St Kilda, she married 47-year-old Charles D'Arcy Cuthbert, a barrister and solicitor, and returned to Hobart. The couple had two sons, whom she raised alone after her husband's death in 1942.

Retaining her literary interests, Edith Cuthbert had several poems included in the 1935 publication of the Hobart Lyceum Club's literary circle, of which she was secretary. She joined the local branch of the Victoria League in 1936; as its acting-secretary (1938-44) she helped to organise Empire Day celebrations and the collection of metals for munitions. At the league's national conference in Canberra in 1939 she spoke on the ways in which the Hobart group assisted British migrants. Secretary of the Tasmanian Women's Non-Party League for twenty-five years (1948-51, 1953-74), she wrote to State and Federal ministers, to the Hobart City Council and to the *Mercury*, with suggestions on aged care, social welfare, health, the environment, the promotion of tourism and the registration of rest homes. With a friend she ran a monthly British newcomers' club in the 1950s and early 1960s, and helped migrants to find jobs and housing. She pleaded for a subsidised housekeeper service for persons in need and for more convenient transport amenities, and held monthly at-home days for lonely old people in her suburb. In 1967 she was made a life member of the WNPL.

After seeking advice from Doris Taylor [q.v.16], Cuthbert began a meals-on-wheels service in 1955, delivering hot midday meals from a commercial kitchen at a nominal cost. The Meals on Wheels Association of Tasmania was formed next year and in 1956-58 Cuthbert, as organising secretary, arranged car rosters. Honorary secretary in 1958-62 and vice-president in 1962-65, she was made a life member in 1971. That year she completed a social welfare course but was unable to find a position in a citizens' advice bureau as she wanted.

Cuthbert spent her last twelve years, active physically and mentally, in the Queen Victoria Home for the Aged, Lindisfarne. Her friends and family considered her a 'character' for her forthright, down-to-earth attitude and many idiosyncrasies; a premier is reputed to have refused to consider her for an Imperial honour because she was 'much too troublesome a person'. At 91 she arranged the manufacture of a prototype of an inflatable bedpan and promoted its use to the Commonwealth Department of Health. The 'Cuthbert Comforter' received serious consideration but was not taken up. Survived by her sons, Mrs Cuthbert died on 8 September 1988 at Lindisfarne and was cremated.

G. N. W. MacFarlane, *The First Twenty Years* (1989); *Mercury* (Hobart), 16 Dec 1971, p 21, 2 May 1974, p 12, 14 May 1983, p 8; Victoria League (Tas), Minutes, 1936-44 (Hobart); Tas Women's Non-Party League, Minutes, 1948-74, and Meals on Wheels records (TSA); private information.   A. RAND

CUTHBERT   BROWNE,   GRACE JOHNSTON (1900-1988), medical practitioner, was born on 2 January 1900 at Port Glasgow, Scotland, fifth (fourth surviving) and youngest child of John Cuthbert, shipmaster, and his wife Mary, née Ross. Grace came to Australia at the age of 1, when her father was appointed chief marine surveyor for a group of insurance companies in Sydney. Raised a Presbyterian, she was educated at Ravenswood, Gordon, and the University of Sydney (MB, Ch.M., 1924). She worked in the pathology laboratories of Royal Prince Alfred Hospital, Camperdown, and Royal North Shore Hospital, St Leonards, becoming resident medical officer (1924-25) at the latter. Her years in general practice at Pambula and Eden (1926-29) on the New South Wales south coast and at Wollstonecraft, Sydney (1929-37), fired her enthusiasm for obstetrics and infant welfare. From 1929 to 1937 she served as an honorary medical officer at the Rachel Forster Hospital for Women and Children, the Royal Society for the Welfare of Mothers and Babies (Tresillian) and the Lane Cove Baby Health Centre.

In 1937 Dr Cuthbert was appointed director of maternal and baby welfare in the Department of Public Health of New South Wales. She promoted meticulous antenatal care and established free baby-health centres. During her 28-year incumbency maternal and infant mortality declined dramatically, from 4.91 to 0.35 mothers, and from 40.68 to 20.29 infants, per thousand live births. Her drive and organisational ability contributed much to this improvement. The programs she developed became models nationally and were recognised internationally.

Cuthbert's influence was felt through her work on innumerable committees, including the Child Welfare Advisory Council of New South Wales and the maternal and child health committee of the National Health and Medical Research Council, as well as through her teaching (1946-69) in maternal and child health in the school of public health and tropical medicine at the University of Sydney. Medical secretary of the committee investigating maternal mortality in the State in the 1950s, she wrote a report on the subject which was published in the *Medical Journal of Australia* (1960). On her retirement as director in 1965 she was appointed to Grosvenor Hospital for handicapped children and remained there until her second retirement in 1970.

In 1950 Grace had met Francis James Browne, a visiting distinguished obstetrician and gynaecologist whom she had admired since reading his 1935 text on antenatal and postnatal care. While in England on a World Health Organization travelling scholarship, she married the 71-year-old widower on 15 February 1951 at the Scotch National Church, Westminster, London, and they returned to Sydney. Settling at Wollstonecraft, she and 'F. J.' had a happy marriage based on mutual love and respect and close professional interests; he died in 1963.

One of Grace Cuthbert Browne's commitments was to encourage women in the professions. In 1952, while president of the Australian Federation of Medical Women, she was elected vice-president of the Medical Women's International Association. She was president (1952-54) of the Australian Federation of University Women, Australian convenor of the standing committee on public health for the Australian National Council of Women for many years, and a member of Soroptimist International from 1961. When she was awarded an honorary doctorate of medicine (1986) at the University of Sydney, John Ward [q.v.], the vice-chancellor, described her as 'a distinguished graduate who has contributed notably to the advancement of public health and to community appreciation of the status of womanhood generally'.

Appointed MBE in 1959, Cuthbert Browne was elected to fellowships of the Royal College of Obstetricians and Gynaecologists (1959), the Australian Medical Association (1971) and the Australian College of Obstetricians and Gynaecologists (foundation fellow 1978). She was also active in numerous cultural and community organisations and was a member of the Avondale Golf and Queen's clubs. A modest woman who generously acknowledged her teachers, colleagues and husband, she devoted her working life to the well-being of infants and their mothers. Warm, even sentimental, and childless, she was a loving 'second mother' to the children of her close circle of women friends and to the younger members of her extended family. She died on 17 December 1988 at St Leonards and was cremated.

S. Blackall et al (eds), *The People Who Made Australia Great* (1988); Report of the Director-General of Public Health, *PP* (NSW), 1937-64; *SMH*, 26 Sept 1986, 'Northern Herald' supp, p 21, 19 Dec 1988, p 4; H. de Berg, interview with G. Cuthbert

Browne (ts, 1972, NLA); W. G. McBride, proposal for Dr Cuthbert Browne's candidature for an honorary Doctorate of Medicine, and G. C. Browne, Curriculum Vitae (Univ of Sydney Archives); private information.   ELSPETH BROWNE

CZULAK, JÓZEF KAROL (1915-1985), bacteriologist and cheese technologist, was born on 18 April 1915 at Miedzybrodzie, Cracow, Austria-Hungary (Poland), son of Leon Czulak, gentleman farmer, and his wife Maria, née Wallus. After matriculating in 1935 from the gymnasium at Kepno, Poznan province, Józef enrolled at university but was soon called up for military service. He graduated from the Polish cavalry college as a second lieutenant in 1938. Posted to the 12th (Podolian) Lancers Regiment, he fought on horseback against German tanks at Mokra on 1 September 1939 and was wounded. Two weeks later, when the Russians entered Poland, he fled into Romania and was interned. He escaped in December and travelled through Yugoslavia and Italy to France. Joining the 10th Polish Armoured Cavalry Brigade, he saw action near Dijon late in May 1940. In June, following the surrender of France, he was evacuated to England.

After spending time in hospital, Czulak rejoined remnants of his unit in Scotland. In 1942 he attended the Polish Army Staff College, Peebles, and was promoted to captain. Serving in the 1st Polish Armoured Division, he participated in the invasion of Europe in July 1944 and was awarded the Polish Cross of Valour for his part in the battle of the Falaise Gap in August. Back in Britain, he entered the University of Reading (B.Sc.Agric., 1948) in October 1945. He was naturalised on 28 July 1948 and on 9 December at the register office, Reading, he married Agnes Gillespie Swales, née Brough, a Scottish medical practitioner; she was a divorcee who had a daughter. Next year he completed a postgraduate diploma in bacteriology at Reading and began work with United Dairies Ltd, London, as a research bacteriologist, investigating cheese starter cultures.

Appointed research officer with the dairy research section of the Commonwealth Scientific and Industrial Research Organization, Czulak arrived in Melbourne with his family on 2 April 1951. He was located at first at the Victorian Department of Agriculture's School of Dairy Technology, Werribee, transferring to the CSIRO laboratory at Fishermens Bend in 1953 and to Highett in 1955. Within three years he had designed a system for preparing freeze-dried starter cultures, which were distributed to cheese factories through State departments of agriculture. He then led a team that worked on mechanising the making of cheddar cheese, and by 1957 had produced a pilot plant that encompassed all stages of the process: cheddaring, milling, salting and hooping. The machines, commercially developed in collaboration with James Bell Machinery Pty Ltd (later Bell Bryant Pty Ltd), became known as Bell-Siro cheesemakers. They revolutionised cheddar cheese manufacture and were sold overseas. For this work Czulak won the Australian Society of Dairy Technology's gold medal in 1960.

In 1962 Czulak visited India under the auspices of the Colombo Plan. At the Kaira District Co-operative Milk Producers' Union Ltd, Anand, Gujarat, he succeeded in developing methods for manufacturing cheddar and gouda cheese from buffalo milk. Sardar Patel University, Anand, awarded him an honorary doctorate of science in 1973. In the 1970s he introduced the 'factory-derived system' for propagation and management of cheese starter cultures. This gave greater reliability and predictable performance in large-scale manufacture of cheese, factors which were important in meeting the stringent requirements of developing export markets, particularly Japan. A dynamic and at times volatile leader, who did not suffer fools gladly, Czulak commanded great respect and loyalty from his teams, both in Australia and in India. Colleagues protected him from the effects of heavy drinking. He was promoted to chief research scientist in 1973 and retired from CSIRO in 1976. Elected a fellow (1976) of the Institute of Biology, London, he then worked as a consultant to the Australian Dairy Corporation, and in 1978 chaired the new technology session at the International Dairy Congress in Paris.

Czulak had been divorced in 1968. On 22 April that year at the registrar general's office, Sydney, he married Jeannette Durham, née Burgoyne, a broadcaster; she was a granddaughter of Thomas Burgoyne, a great-granddaughter of Thomas Cotter [qq.v.7,1], and a divorcee with a daughter. Survived by his wife, Czulak died of myocardial infarction on 5 August 1985 in his home at Mount Eliza, Victoria, and was cremated. The biennial Joe Czulak award for excellence in dairy technology was established in 1997 and is administered by the Australian Starter Culture Research Centre.

A. McKay et al, *Surprise and Enterprise* (1976); B. Collis, *Fields of Discovery* (2002); CSIRO, *Food Research Qtrly*, vol 36, no 4, 1976, p 82; *Austn Dairy Foods*, Dec 1996, p 24, June 2002, p 32; A8520, items PH/CZU/1, pts 1 and 2, PH/CZU/1B, pts 1 and 2 (NAA); private information.   GAIL CLEMENTS

D

DADSWELL, LYNDON RAYMOND (1908-1986), sculptor and technical college teacher, was born on 18 January 1908 at Stanmore, Sydney, elder child of Sydney-born parents Arthur Raymond Dadswell, accountant, and his wife Maysel Cobcroft, née Pidgeon. Educated at Sydney Church of England Grammar School (Shore), Lyndon attended Julian Rossi Ashton's [q.v.7] Sydney Art School (1924-25) and East Sydney Technical College (1926-29). Trained under Rayner Hoff [q.v.9], Dadswell moved away from an early interest in commercial art to specialise in sculpture and modelling. His student work, such as 'Untitled Classical Relief' (Art Gallery of New South Wales, Sydney), reveals the strong reliance on British traditions shared by most Australian sculptors until the 1960s. This orientation was modified by European ideals of postwar reconstruction and Hoff's notion of 'modernising' British classicism through the stylistic devices of art deco, in order to produce sculptures appropriate to a modern Australia.

In 1929 Dadswell left the technical college to work as an assistant to Paul Montford [q.v.10] in Melbourne on the sculptural project for Victoria's memorial to World War I, the Shrine of Remembrance. Dadswell produced twelve huge relief panels in Hawkesbury freestone illustrating all sections of the Australian armed services. He married Elza Antoinette Ruth Stenning on 24 May 1930 at Windsor, Melbourne, with Congregational forms; they later divorced.

Returning to Sydney in 1932, Dadswell completed a number of commissions, such as a plaque of Bertha McNamara [q.v.10 Matilda McNamara] (1931, Sydney Trades Hall) and a bust of E. W. Knox [q.v.9] (1933, Colonial Sugar Refining Co. Ltd). When he won the Wynne prize for 1933 with 'Youth' (AGNSW), Dadswell was only the fifth sculptor to win this prize in its forty-year history. With the proceeds he travelled to London in 1935 to further his studies, enrolling at the Royal Academy schools. Frequently impoverished, he moved away from the academic dictates of the live model, although his art remained firmly tied to the human figure. The preoccupation of the British sculptors Henry Moore and Barbara Hepworth with the dictum 'truth to materials' (the view that materials possess intrinsic qualities which must be respected) influenced Dadswell. He was also inspired by the stylised figures of the Swedish sculptor Carl Milles, and by the work of Britain's greatest modern portrait sculptor, Jacob Epstein, and the British figurative artist Frank Dobson.

Dadswell remained at the Royal Academy until 1937, when he returned to Australia to take up a teaching position at East Sydney Technical College. He participated in academic causes such as the inaugural Australian Academy of Art exhibition (1938) and joined the Society of Artists' executive and hanging committees. On 16 December 1939 at Mosman, he married with Congregational forms Audrey Margaret Herbert, a secretary.

On 29 April 1940 Dadswell enlisted in the Australian Imperial Force. Posted to the 2/3rd Battalion, he fought in North Africa and Greece. He was seriously wounded in Syria in June 1941; the injury permanently impaired his vision. In September he was commissioned as a lieutenant and appointed a war artist. For six months he worked in a studio at Heliopolis, Cairo, completing about a dozen sculptures. These abstracted figurative works, a significant development for him, were the most stylistically innovative of any Australian war sculptures. Several were included in the touring exhibition (1943-44) of works by Australian official war artists, before being placed in the Australian War Memorial collection, Canberra. He returned to Australia in March 1942 and resigned his AIF commission on 18 December.

In 1943 Dadswell returned to East Sydney Technical College (later the National Art School), where he became head of the division of fine arts in 1966. Due to his commitment to sculptural experimentation, his skills as a modeller and his belief in fostering the artistic growth of each student, the school became a nationally respected institution for sculpture training. His work was exhibited in Sydney and Melbourne. Dadswell's contribution to Australian sculpture was three-fold: through his own substantial and varied body of studio work; through his activities and innovations as a teacher of two generations; and through his public role as a sculptor, and promoter, of major civic commissions. He created sculptures for the Maritime Services Board building, Sydney (1952); Commonwealth banks in Hobart and Sydney (1954) and Perth (1960); the Newcastle War Memorial Cultural Centre (1957); the R. G. Menzies Library, Australian National University (1964); the Jewish War Memorial, Maccabean Hall, Sydney (1965); and the Campbell Park defence establishment, Canberra ('The Tree of Life', 1977).

Dadswell was a foundation member (1951) and later president of the Society of Sculptors and Associates, a group that lobbied for the greater presence of sculpture in the Australian public environment. He served as an adviser to the National Capital Development Commission, Canberra. While travelling through the United States of America, Britain and Europe in 1957, supported by Fulbright, Smith Mundt and Carnegie grants, he studied art school education.

Remaining influenced by Henry Moore, from the 1950s Dadswell became increasingly receptive to various forms of sculptural abstraction. By the early 1960s he was almost exclusively interested in abstract sculpture—from welded constructivist assemblages to organically modelled and built-up forms that are among his most significant works. Preoccupied by teaching from 1955 to 1965, he enjoyed renewed commitment to his own sculptural practice following his retirement from the college in 1967. He virtually ceased work, due to ill health, in the late 1970s.

In 1967 Dadswell had been awarded the International Co-operation Art Award and the Britannica Australia award for art, and in 1973 an Australian Council for the Arts award. He was appointed CMG in 1978. That year the Art Gallery of New South Wales devoted a major retrospective exhibition to his work. In 1967 Laurie Thomas [q.v.16] described him as 'a man forever on the move'. Dadswell was committed to the concept of ceaseless experiment and change in the development of individual creativity. Survived by his wife and their daughter and son, he died on 7 November 1986 at Elizabeth Bay and was cremated. His work is represented in the Australian War Memorial, the National Gallery of Australia and most State galleries.

D. Edwards, *Lyndon Dadswell 1908-1986* (1992); B883, item NX13548 (NAA); Dadswell biog file (NGA); H. de Berg, interview with L. Dadswell (ts, 1960, NLA); Dadswell papers (SLNSW).

DEBORAH EDWARDS

DALE, WILLIAM ARTHUR CHARLES (1904-1982), air force officer, civil engineer and town planner, was born on 18 November 1904 at Petersham, Sydney, eldest of four children of Henry John Dale, schoolteacher, and his wife Agnes, née Roan, both Australian born. Bill was educated at Armidale High School and at the University of Sydney (BE, 1927), where he studied civil engineering. He served in the senior cadets and the Citizen Military Forces, reaching the rank of lieutenant in the Australian Engineers. In December 1925, while still at university, he resigned his army commission to enlist in the Citizen Air Force, Royal Australian Air Force. Five ft 9½ ins (177 cm) tall and weighing 9 st. 6 lb. (60 kg), he had brown hair and grey eyes.

Completing flying training at Point Cook, Victoria, Dale graduated as a pilot officer in April 1926. He served with No.3 Squadron at Richmond, New South Wales, before transferring to the Unattached List in July 1928 as a flying officer. On 26 May that year at the Presbyterian Church, Kogarah, he had married Edna May Westaway, a schoolteacher. After leaving the air force, he worked in local government, notably as Wingadee shire engineer at Coonamble.

Dale was called up on 9 October 1939 for full-time duty as a temporary flight lieutenant in the Directorate of Works and Buildings at RAAF Headquarters, Melbourne. He was appointed assistant-director in February 1941. Promoted to temporary wing commander in April 1942, he was attached to the United States 1st Marine Division in July for the landings at Tulagi and Guadalcanal next month. In July 1943 he assumed command of the RAAF's No.62 Works (Airfield Construction) Wing at Port Moresby. Displaying 'exceptional qualities of leadership', he was largely responsible for vital engineering works—runways, taxiways, revetments, buildings, supply dumps, roads and waterworks—completed under great hardship at Milne Bay, on Goodenough and Kiriwina islands, and in the Markham Valley.

In April 1944 'W. A. C.' Dale was appointed task force engineer for the Allied landings at Aitape, in command of all Australian and American engineer troops, a force of some 2500 men. He showed 'complete disregard for his personal safety by landing with the earliest wave of assault troops and making a personal reconnaissance of the airstrip in the face of enemy opposition'. Within two and a half days Allied aircraft were flying from the airstrip at Tadji that Dale's men had prepared.

Two months later Dale again led from the front during a hazardous assault at Noemfoor, Netherlands East Indies, starting his survey while parts of the airfield were still held by the enemy. Working day and night, his engineers built a new runway 6000 ft (1829 m) long and 100 ft (30 m) wide in seven days, a remarkable achievement which enabled a squadron of Thunderbolt fighters to fly in on the eighth day. Promoted to temporary group captain in July 1944, he was awarded the Distinguished Service Order (1944) and mentioned in despatches (1946) for his leadership. In 1945 the air officer commanding the RAAF's First Tactical Air Force, Air Commodore (Sir) Frederick Scherger [q.v.], formally noted Dale's 'magnificent record'.

Remaining in the RAAF after the war, Dale was appointed director of works and buildings in January 1946 and made substantive group captain in March 1950. As the air force's senior civil engineer, he was responsible for an ambitious Cold War development program. His construction squadrons built strategically important airfields in Japan, at Woomera, South Australia, on Cocos and Manus islands, and in Malaya and Darwin, invariably working in tough conditions. Popular and highly respected, the unassuming Dale consistently demonstrated professional excellence, initiative, an ability to finish demanding jobs on time and a deep concern for the welfare of his staff. He was a 'wonderful listener', believing he could learn from anyone, regardless of his or her rank. In 1957 he was appointed CBE. Because of limited career prospects within his branch, he remained a group captain until he retired on 18 November 1959 with the honorary rank of air commodore.

From 1959 to 1969 Dale was (town) clerk for the shire (municipality) of Blacktown, Sydney, and in the process 'possibly held the record in the number and variety of local government qualifications he held'. He was a fellow of the Institution of Engineers, Australia, the Royal Australian Planning Institute and the Institute of Municipal Administration. In 1962 he obtained a diploma in town and regional planning at the University of Melbourne. From his home at Manly he pursued a wide range of interests including philately, Japanese art, languages, woodwork, the Boy Scouts' Association and writing. In his spare time he had studied arts at the University of Melbourne (BA, 1949). Survived by his wife, and their daughter and son, Dale died on 31 August 1982 at Armidale and was cremated. His portrait by Geoffrey Mainwaring is held by the Australian War Memorial, Canberra.

G. Odgers, *Air War against Japan 1943-1945* (1957); D. Wilson, *Always First* (1998); A. Stephens, *The Royal Australian Air Force* (2001); *Shire and Municipal Record*, Dec 1982-Jan 1983, p 413; A9300, item Dale WAC (NAA); private information.

ALAN STEPHENS

DALEY, EDWARD ALFRED (1901-1985), air force officer and medical practitioner, was born on 23 January 1901 at Bendigo, Victoria, fourth son of Charles Daley, schoolteacher, and his wife Caroline Rose, née Bromfield, both Victorian born. C. S. Daley [q.v.8] and F. S. Daley [q.v.] were his brothers. Ted attended (1915-19) Caulfield Grammar School, Melbourne, where he became a prefect, gained honours in matriculation physics and made his mark as a tennis player.

After studying at the University of Melbourne (MB, BS, 1925), Daley worked at Warrnambool and at the Austin Hospital, Melbourne, then spent a further two years in private practice. At Scots Church, Melbourne, on 21 July 1927 he married with Presbyterian forms Katharine Grace Wright-Smith (d.1984); they had no children. On 16 July 1928 he joined the Royal Australian Air Force as a flight lieutenant. One of only three doctors in the Permanent Air Force, he served at Laverton and Point Cook. In 1930 he qualified as a pilot to improve his assessment of candidates for flying training, and to estimate flying fatigue. He was promoted to squadron leader in November 1933. In 1936 he went to England on exchange.

Believing that any coming war would involve action in the tropics, Daley completed a diploma in tropical medicine (1937) at the University of Liverpool. He enjoyed his two years in England and gained considerable insight into Royal Air Force medical administration. When he returned to Australia in July 1938, he was appointed deputy-director (director from January 1939) of medical services (air) with the rank of wing commander. He immediately introduced RAF methods of organisation and documentation, which proved invaluable after the outbreak of World War II and allowed RAF and RAAF medical units to operate together with precision.

In June 1940 Daley was promoted to temporary group captain and made deputy-director (deputy director general from January 1943) of medical services under (Sir) Victor Hurley [q.v.14]. That year Daley initiated the building of No.1 RAAF Hospital, Laverton, where intensive training of medical staff took place. He introduced No.1 Air Ambulance Unit to the Middle East in 1941. Appointed honorary physician to King George VI (Queen Elizabeth II from 1952) in 1940, he was elected a fellow of the Royal Australasian College of Physicians in 1943. In July 1944 he visited Normandy to observe the British practice of flying casualties home rather than setting up hospitals in France.

Promoted to acting air commodore in August 1945 (substantive January 1947), Daley was made director-general of medical services in December. He rose to air vice-marshal in March 1952 and that year was appointed CBE. In 1956 he formed the RAAF School (later Institute) of Aviation Medicine at Point Cook and served on the medical committee for the Melbourne Olympic Games. He had established (1949) the special group on aviation medicine of the British Medical Association in Australia and was its first chairman. In 1954 he was elected a vice-president of the Aero Medical Association.

Daley retired from the RAAF on 31 March 1961. Recognised as an outstanding administrator, he became national director (1961-75) of the St John Ambulance Association. He supervised the rewriting of the first-aid manual to reflect Australian conditions and was appointed (1962) a knight of grace of the Order of St John. In 1965-68 he was president of the Victorian section of the Royal Flying Doctor Service of Australia. Though seemingly austere, with a piercing gaze and toothbrush moustache, he was a kind and gentle man with a keen sense of humour and a love of music and tennis. He died on 15 March 1985 in his home at East Malvern. His body was bequeathed to the department of anatomy, University of Melbourne.

A. S. Walker, *Medical Services of the R.A.N. and R.A.A.F.* (1961); I. Howie-Willis, *A Century for Australia* (1983); G. Halstead, *Story of the RAAF Nursing Service 1940-1990* (1994); J. C. Wiseman and R. J. Mulhearn (eds), *Roll of the Royal Australasian College of Physicians*, vol 2, 1976-90 (1994); Royal Flying Doctor Service of Aust, *Vic Section Bulletin*, July 1970, p 4; D. Thomson, 'The Flying Doctor', *Labora*, July 1982, p 13.

D. S. THOMSON

DALEY, FRANCIS STANLEY (1891-1983), mechanical engineer, was born on 1 November 1891 at Bendigo, Victoria, third son of Victorian-born parents Charles Daley, schoolteacher, and his wife Caroline Rose, née Bromfield. C. S. Daley [q.v.8] and E. A. Daley [q.v.] were Frank's brothers. Having attended Stawell State School and Geelong College, he was apprenticed in fitting and machining at the Vulcan Foundry of Humble [q.v.4] & Sons, Geelong. He studied at the Gordon Technical College and then at the University of Melbourne (B.Mech.E., 1918), where he won Bage [q.v.7] and Dixson scholarships and became a member of the Students' Representative Council. After graduating, he travelled to England and worked in armament production at the Royal Arsenal, Woolwich, and in the factories of Armstrong Whitworth & Co. Ltd and Vickers Ltd. Back in Melbourne, he was an assistant manager at the Commonwealth government's Ordnance Factory, Maribyrnong. In 1920 he joined the Institution of Engineers, Australia, as a foundation associate member.

On 21 May 1927 at All Souls' Church, Sandringham, Daley married with Anglican rites Eleanor Gladys Tweddle, a masseuse; they had a daughter before divorcing in 1949. In 1931 he had joined General Motors-Holden's [q.v.9] Ltd as senior staff engineer, responsible for modernising the company's plant at Woodville, South Australia, to prepare for the manufacture of steel bodies for motor vehicles. The company began fitting Australian-produced all-steel bodies to GM chassis in 1937. Next year Daley's paper 'Beyond the Yield Point' described original research into the pressing of sheet steel (*Journal of the Institution of Engineers Australia*, October 1942). He also lectured part time in industrial organisation at the South

Australian School of Mines and Industries. His work with GMH involved travel throughout Australia and abroad.

From the mid-1930s leading industrialists, including (Sir) Laurence Hartnett [q.v.], managing director of GMH, fostered aeroplane manufacturing in Australia. Daley became involved in 1938 as a member of a committee investigating aircraft for defence. After World War II began, the Commonwealth government appointed (June 1940) Hartnett director of ordnance production and he immediately engaged Daley as his second-in-charge (controller). Hartnett later affirmed that there was no man 'better qualified [than Daley] for the job', as he was 'a top production engineer'. Daley eventually succeeded Hartnett as director. He also chaired the Department of Postwar Reconstruction's optical industry advisory panel.

After the war, Daley transferred to GMH's plant at Fishermens Bend, Victoria, and worked with Hartnett during the initial development of the Holden car. His role remained that of a production engineer, and included executive support until Hartnett left GMH at the end of 1946. On 30 April 1949 at St Stephen's Presbyterian Church, Caulfield, Daley married Annie Adalene Verna Walsh, née Gray, a widow. About 1951 he became general technical manager of Kelvinator Australia Ltd in Adelaide. In 1956 he entered practice as a consulting engineer in Melbourne. A member of the Royal Historical Society of Victoria, he published 'The Holden Saga' in the *Victorian Historical Magazine* (February 1967). He was a hard-working and studious man whose recreations included motoring, writing and handicrafts. Daley died on 20 July 1983 at Forest Hill, Melbourne, and was cremated. His wife and the daughter of his first marriage survived him.

D. P. Mellor, *The Role of Science and Industry* (1958); L. Hartnett, *Big Wheels and Little Wheels* (1981); N. Darwin, *100 Years of GM in Australia* (2002); *Smith's Weekly*, 16 Dec 1939, p 7; private information.

BRIAN LLOYD

DALEY, MICHAEL JOSEPH (1940-1982), science journalist and television producer, was born on 23 October 1940 at Christchurch, New Zealand, son of Matthew Patrick Daley, baker, and his wife Mary, née Walsh. From an early age Michael displayed a journalistic bent: at high school he wrote and edited the *Daley Weekly*. Starting with general journalism, he developed an interest in science, which flourished when he moved to Sydney in the early 1960s to work on the *Sydney Morning Herald*. In 1964 he became the inaugural science and medical correspondent for the *Australian*. At

St Mary's Catholic Church, North Sydney, on 25 November 1961 he had married Anne Elizabeth Rogers, a nurse.

In 1968 the Australian Broadcasting Commission's science unit, led by Peter Pockley, launched 'The World Tomorrow', one of the first science magazine programs on radio in the country. Its essence was journalism and Daley was recruited to report on major issues. Although reporters were not yet favoured as on-air presenters, he soon took over from the designated announcer and made the show his own. Before long, tensions emerged as his uninhibited style clashed with leading scientists' views on everything from ozone depletion and supersonic flight to radiation hazards. Scientific institutions were unused to dealing with truculent journalists who would not give up. During this period he maintained his print journalism, notably with the *Bulletin*.

Late in 1972 Daley moved to ABC television. As executive producer, he established a television science unit that made a series of programs, and documentaries including 'Vela X: The Supernova Story', which he wrote, produced and directed. Other subjects covered were Sir Mark Oliphant and his particle accelerator at the Australian National University in Canberra; Papua New Guinea; and, presciently, babies and their genes. By 1982 the unit had made over seventy programs ranging from half-hour portraits of Australian scientists to 'Genesis', a series on evolution on which Daley worked as executive producer until just days before his death.

Daley's work was always 'edgy' and questioning. He was one of the first to stress the centrality of politics in scientific affairs. He was as uncomfortable with the ABC hierarchy as with the scientific establishment. But his insistence on the importance of science in public affairs placed it at the centre of the broadcasting schedule, where it has remained ever since. He was a 'journo's journo' who relished all the convivial distractions of the traditional reporter, but who barely missed a beat however hard he played. A robust physique and gruff tones contrasted with his boyish demeanour. His work was his life; holidays were dismissed as unwelcome interruptions. Diagnosed with acute leukaemia during the compulsory medical examination for one of his trips to Antarctica, he virtually ignored his condition, working with undiminished intensity right until the end.

Survived by his wife and their son, Daley died on 6 May 1982 at Royal North Shore Hospital and was cremated. The Michael Daley award for science journalism, established by the Federal government, commemorated his pioneering work. His son, Jonathan, who followed him into television as a cameraman, was later killed when he fell from a helicopter during a shoot.

K. S. Inglis, *This Is the ABC* (1983); ABC, *Annual Report*, 1967-82; *Australian*, 8-9 May 1982, p 9; *Age* (Melbourne), 13 May 1982, p 6; ABC, *Scan*, 31 May-20 June 1982, p 15; personal knowledge.

ROBYN WILLIAMS

DALLAS, KENNETH MCKENZIE (1902-1988), historian, was born on 11 September 1902 at Detention River, west of Wynyard, Tasmania, son of Robert Dallas, a Tasmanian-born farmer, and his wife Margaret Jane, née Robinson, formerly a schoolteacher from Victoria. Brought up on a farm at Rocky Cape, Ken advanced through the local school to Launceston State High School (1916-19). Entering the State education service, he spent 1921 in Hobart at the University of Tasmania and Philip Smith [q.v.2] Training College. His chief mentor then was J. A. Johnson (and later J. B. Brigden) [qq.v.9,7]; he became a socialist about this time. He taught in rural areas, mainly at South Riana's one-teacher school, and studied externally for a commerce degree at the university (B.Com., 1928), achieving outstanding results. In 1925-30 he taught at Launceston High, friendship there with A. L. Meston [q.v.10] stimulating his interest in Tasmanian (notably Aboriginal) history.

In 1930 Dallas became tutor at Devonport for the Workers' Educational Association, which was then linked with the university. On 31 January 1931 at St George's Church of England, Burnie, he married Margaret Cecilia Hogarth, a schoolteacher. That year he worked with the WEA at Newcastle, New South Wales. In March 1932 he was appointed as Pitt Cobbett [q.v.8] lecturer in the commerce faculty in Hobart, a position that entailed both university duties and directorship of the WEA. Dallas embodied the ideal WEA type: while of an intellectual cast, he focused on the action of social and economic forces. His discourse was always positive and informed, often enthralling, sometimes overbearing. Powerful in body as in mind, he was a rower and yachtsman, with compelling presence. He deliberately followed L. F. Giblin [q.v.8] in simplicity of dress and style.

Although sensitive to the radicalism of Depression-time Newcastle, Dallas moved sharply to the left only with the burgeoning of fascism. He was commissioned in the Royal Australian Navy Volunteer Reserve on 1 January 1941, before Hitler's invasion of the Soviet Union. Sent to Britain for service in landing ships of the Royal Navy, he expected 'a rendezvous with death'. He rose to lieutenant, saw action in the Mediterranean, took part in the first wave of the assault against Normandy on D-Day (6 June 1944) and won his superiors' approbation. His appointment terminated on 19 March 1945 in Hobart.

Back at the university, Dallas taught many socially conscious undergraduates. He formed friendships with, among others, Polish migrants and Asian students. Cultural interests included the Australasian Book Society and European films. He was divorced in 1945, and on 11 June 1948 at the registrar-general's office, Hobart, married Ina Freund, a photographer. In 1951 he was promoted to senior lecturer. Committed to the WEA, he felt bitter distress as it lost centrality in Tasmania's adult education. He supported the university's Labor Club and the Australian Peace Council, but never joined the Communist Party of Australia. In 1954, on the advice of the Australian Security Intelligence Organization, the government refused him a passport. An ASIO memo reported that Prime Minister (Sir) Robert Menzies [q.v.15] 'had a good opinion of Dallas', and next year the ban was reversed, allowing him to take up a Rockefeller fellowship for a year's study leave in Britain.

Dallas's contempt for Professor S. S. Orr [q.v.15] separated him from colleagues who challenged Orr's dismissal in 1956, and he became isolated in an ever more specialised faculty. By contrast, his retirement in 1967 saw rare flowering. A 'Dallas' issue (September 1968) of the *Papers and Proceedings* of the Tasmanian Historical Research Association comprised three articles: a study of the 'tyranny of distance' concept, Dallas counter-arguing that 'remoteness' offered bounty and opportunity; 'Slavery in Australia—Convicts, Emigrants, Aborigines'; and 'Commercial Influences on the First Settlements of Australia'. This last subject also formed the basis of a monograph, *Trading Posts or Penal Colonies* (1969). Questions raised by Dallas were to provoke much scholarship, some more detailed than his, but never more probing. *Horse Power* (1968) celebrated the economic importance of horses. Vividly evoking childhood on the family farm, this essay merits recognition as an Australian classic. *Water Power—Past and Future* (1970), prefigured 'slow-growth' themes in subsequent writing about British industrialisation: old-style water-power remained significant far into the nineteenth century, he argued, and then hydroelectricity intensified that story.

Divorced in 1967, on 29 January 1971 at the Scots Presbyterian Church, Hobart, Dallas married Janet Mary Tarbath, née Lorimer, a schoolteacher. He died on 6 August 1988 at New Town and was cremated. His wife, the son of his first marriage and two daughters and a son of his second marriage, survived him.

A6119, items 979 and 980 (NAA); Dallas papers (Univ of Tas Archives); private information and personal knowledge.   MICHAEL ROE

DALY, JEAN MARY (1897-1986), women's rights activist, was born Jane May on 10 December 1897 at Strathfield, Sydney, eldest of six children of Walter Edmunds [q.v.8], barrister, and his wife Monica Victoria May, née McGrath, both born in New South Wales. Jean was educated at Santa Sabina College, Strathfield, and the University of Sydney (BA, 1918). While studying law, she was associate (1919-21) to her father, then a judge of the Court of Industrial Arbitration of New South Wales. On 6 October 1921 at St Martha's Catholic Church, Strathfield, she married Harry John Daly (d.1980), a medical practitioner and later a specialist anaesthetist. She did not continue her law degree after her marriage.

In her early forties and childless, Jean Daly became the secretary and then president of the Navy Club of the Catholic United Services Auxiliary New South Wales. In 1943 she was one of a small number of Catholic women, mostly graduates, who formed the discussion group Altair to present the viewpoint of Catholic women. Their first task was to make a submission to the Department of Post-war Reconstruction stressing the importance of family structures in population policy. Wanting to present women's perspectives to the Church as well as the government, Altair criticised Catholic Action's *The Family: Social Justice Statement, 1944* because it lacked 'the woman's point of view'.

With Mary Tenison Woods [q.v.12] and other members of Altair, in 1946 Mrs Daly founded the New South Wales branch of the St Joan's Social and Political Alliance to encourage women to play a more active part in public affairs as Catholic citizens. Cardinal (Sir) Norman Gilroy [q.v.14] advised Catholic women that membership was contrary to his wishes; the *Catholic Weekly* refused to advertise its functions. The alliance, with Mrs Daly as president, joined the revived Liaison Committee of Women's International Organisations Australia Group, a body sympathetic to countering communist influence in women's organisations. She served as treasurer (1948) and secretary (1950-52) of the liaison committee. After the Federal government had established the Australian National Committee for the United Nations, she was elected treasurer of the New South Wales council in 1948.

In 1949 Mrs Daly accompanied her husband to the United States of America, and used the opportunity to attend UN sessions, to inspect the UN's work in Paris and Rome, and to participate in conferences and meetings in Amsterdam, New York and London. On her return she organised the Australian delegation to the Pan-Pacific Women's Association conference at Christchurch, New Zealand, in 1952. She represented Australia on the UN

Commission on the Status of Women in 1951 and 1955. In 1954 she was elected president of the Australian Association for the United Nations, New South Wales Division. She attended the International Federation of University Women regional meeting in Manila in 1955 as an observer, and remained for the PPWA conference. In 1957 she was an observer at the UN seminar, held in Bangkok, on civic responsibilities and increased participation of Asian women in public life.

Though staunchly anti-communist, Mrs Daly was opposed to B. A. Santamaria and the Catholic Social Studies Movement, which she criticised in a letter published in July 1956 in the English magazine the *Tablet*. She saw 'the Movement's' penetration of the political sphere as disastrous and considered that some of its methods 'were not dissimilar' to those used by the communists. Her letter referred to articles by Santamaria published in June 1955 in the *Examiner* newspaper of Bombay (Mumbai), India, in which he had claimed the authority of the Church for his organisation. She received 'abusive' correspondence from Melbourne, but some Sydney clerics, including Cardinal Gilroy, privately commended her. In December the *Catholic Worker* also criticised Santamaria for his statements in the *Examiner*. Mrs Daly did not want the St Joan's Alliance to become part of Catholic Action; she feared membership would mean an unhealthy loss of autonomy.

In the late 1950s and the 1960s Mrs Daly spoke frequently at schools and university seminars, and contributed a regular column, 'The Things That Matter', to the *Catholic Weekly*. Her theme was usually the importance of women taking their place in public life. She argued to a colleague that women should be seen as 'human persons together with men rather than placed in the narrow category that stems from medieval philosophy and canon law'. In 1967 she was appointed OBE. A woman of courage, energy and intellect, she was encouraged by her education and experience to work for social justice. Described by her friend Edmund Campion as 'redoubtable', she was supported by strong family ties and a loving marriage. She died on 23 November 1986 at Bayview and was buried in the Catholic section of the Northern Suburbs cemetery.

S. Kennedy, *Faith and Feminism* (1985); E. Campion, *A Place in the City* (1994); B. Duncan, *Crusade or Conspiracy?* (2001); *SMH*, 17 Apr 1951, p 4, 27 Nov 1986, p 4; *Sun-Herald* (Sydney), 26 Sept 1954, p 68, 1 Jan 1967, p 64; private information.

ANNE O'BRIEN

DALY, DAME MARY DORA (1896-1983), charity worker, was born on 24 August 1896 at Cootamundra, New South Wales, eldest child of Australian-born parents Thomas Patrick MacMahon, solicitor, and his wife Mary Ellen, née O'Donnell. 'May' was educated at the Loreto convent at Normanhurst, Sydney, and Loreto Abbey, Ballarat, Victoria. She then worked in her father's law firm and became active in the State division of the Australian Red Cross Society and the Voluntary Aid Detachments. Her immediate family provided formidable examples of professional success and social service: her father was an alderman of the municipal council, justice of the peace, deputy-coroner and member of the local hospital committee; several of her sisters and brothers (including John Stephen MacMahon [q.v.15]) pursued careers in law or medicine. These family characteristics were reinforced when, at St Canice's Church, Darlinghurst, on 3 January 1923, she married John Joseph Daly (d.1953), medical practitioner, whose family included five aunts involved in charity work in Melbourne. One of them, Mother Berchmans [q.v.8 Anne Daly], was the influential founder of St Vincent's Hospital: May's son and daughter carried Berchmans as their second name.

Settling with her husband in Melbourne, Mrs Daly became increasingly engaged in charity work: as honorary secretary (1927-29) of the Hawthorn-Kew auxiliary for St Vincent's Hospital; member (1930) of the executive committee of St Anne's Hall, a hostel for girls in Carlton; and president (1927-29) of the Loreto Old Girls' Association. To raise funds for the Loreto Kindergarten Association, she wrote and self-published a children's book, *Marie's Birthday Party*. Under her guidance as honorary president (1933-36) of the St Vincent's Hospital committee, £1300 was raised in two years to build a new ward. 'Zest and thoroughness are distinguishing marks of her service', the *Advocate* commented, wondering how she found time 'to engage in the exacting and multifarious range of activities which absorb her interest'. Even so, Daly assured the press, 'my children come first'. 'I always try to spend my mornings at home, and whatever happens I have lunch with them'. She was awarded a silver jubilee medal in 1935 and, in 1937, appointed OBE.

With the outbreak of World War II, Daly was the only woman on the executive of the Catholic Welfare Organisation, founded in 1939 by Archbishop Mannix [q.v.10]. She became its president in 1941 as—among its many activities—the CWO established the first canteen in Melbourne for servicemen and women. 'The Hut', as it became known, provided food and 'wholesome' company to those facing 'grave moral dangers in the somewhat hysterical wartime atmosphere'. Over all, eighteen 'huts' were placed at service camps across Victoria. The CWO raised £253 450 for the welfare of Australian and Allied troops, and sent over 350 000 tins to the Food for Britain Appeal and 40 000 knitted garments to the Allied forces. The organisation also worked closely with the Prisoners of War Service Bureau, co-ordinated through the Vatican, and substantially funded religious pastoral care for Catholics in active service. Mrs Daly was president until her death. In recognition of her work, she was elevated to CBE (1949) and DBE (1951); in 1952 Pope Pius XII awarded her the Papal Cross *Pro Ecclesia et Pontifice* (she was the first woman to be so invested by Archbishop Mannix).

Conforming to the Catholic culture of the time, Dame Mary rarely took a public stand on women's issues, although in 1949 she had defended Catholic women who wanted smaller families, quipping that 'it must be remembered that the holiest of all families was one in which there was only one Child'. After nursing her husband through a terminal illness she threw her energies into new causes, as fund-raiser for the Caritas Christi Hospice, first woman president (1966-75) of Australian Catholic Relief and a foundation member (president 1975-77) of the Ryder-Cheshire Foundation (Australia). She remained prominent in the Australian Red Cross Society as a member of the national council and the State executive. She also served on the State councils of the Girl Guides Association and the National Heart Foundation, as well as the Victorian Anti-Cancer Council. In 1961 she returned to writing children's books, now in support of the Yooralla Hospital School for Crippled Children. *Cinty and the Laughing Jackass*— illustrated by seventeen leading artists including twelve Archibald [q.v.3] prize winners— raised $25 000 to build a therapy pool; *Timmy's Christmas Surprise* (1967) provided over $800 annually towards its maintenance; and *Holidays at Hillydale* (1974) generated additional funds.

According to the *Herald*, Daly could 'organise people with the ease of a field marshal'—a skill evident when she chaired the hospitality committee for the International Eucharistic Congress held in Melbourne in 1973. Her final years were spent at Kew, living with her daughter. Survived by her children, Dame Mary died on 11 June 1983 at Fitzroy and was buried in Melbourne general cemetery.

Catholic Welfare Organisation (1948); *Advocate* (Melbourne), 14 Nov 1935, p 27, 17 Dec 1936, p 13, 23 June 1983, p 2; *Herald* (Melbourne), 3 Feb 1937, p 9, 22 Nov 1966, p 6, 6 Feb 1973, p 13, 10 Dec 1974, p 23; *Sun News-Pictorial* (Melbourne), 8 Feb 1949, p 16; *Argus* (Melbourne), 21 Aug 1951, p 17; private information.   ELLEN WARNE

DANAYARRI (DANAIYARRI), HOBBLES (c.1925-1988), Aboriginal lawman and community leader, was born about 1925 at Wave Hill station, Northern Territory. He was a Mudburra man; his name has been also spelt as Daniari, Danaiari and Danayari. His spiritual history began with a barramundi. His father speared the fish, his mother ate it, and the spirit became the baby who grew into the man known as Hobbles Danayarri. On his right temple he had a small mark said to be where his father speared the fish. He grew up partly in his own country along Cattle Creek, and partly on Wave Hill station.

As a boy, when Danayarri's father took him to see Aboriginal men and women constructing a dam under the direction of a European overseer, he became aware of the injustices his people suffered. He realised that the workers did not receive adequate wages for their back-breaking labour, and that they continually encountered discrimination. Although constrained by the requirements of the Wave Hill and Victoria River Downs cattle stations where he worked, and by his status as a ward of the state, he learned the songs, visited the sacred places and performed the rituals of the country into which he had been born. He became a respected lawman.

In 1966 Danayarri was among the Aboriginal pastoral workers on Wave Hill who went on strike, demanding land rights and fair wages. Afterwards he went with his wife Lizzie Wardaliya, a Ngarinman woman, to her country, and helped to found the Yarralin community. By this time he had become a senior lawman and ceremony leader and, with citizenship, travelled widely in the Northern Territory and the Kimberley on law business.

Danayarri devoted his later years to the analysis of race relations since European settlement. He was a deep thinker who could pull together isolated facts to link past and present. Expressed primarily in the form of stories, the oral narratives were set in historical rather than Dreaming time. They were a blend of political exhortation, parable, history, myth and legend. In his saga of Captain Cook [q.v.1], for example, he described how, following the arrival of the Europeans (represented by Cook) in the Victoria River district, some Indigenous people were murdered and others were dispossessed of their land, captured and forced into work on the cattle stations, for little or no pay. There was an added dimension to his account: British law was seen as lacking the moral basis that characterised 'true' (Aboriginal) law.

Although generally sensitive and thoughtful, Danayarri occasionally erupted into action. He was particularly concerned about the continued presence of Pentecostal missionaries among his people, despite requests from community leaders to stay away. On one occasion he chopped up a Bible with a butcher's knife, shouting, 'Strike me dead, God, if this is your book, strike me dead!' Turning to the people who had witnessed his action, he exhorted them to follow their own law.

A moral rather than a political leader, Danayarri had no time for regret, nostalgia or recrimination. Rather, he had a passionate desire to see Aborigines achieve a better future, based on social equality. This could only come with understanding of the processes of European power and control. He believed that greater unity would enable Indigenous people to make choices. His vision of the nation's future was both compassionate and challenging. He urged all Australians to develop a sense of shared lives and of shared potential. Encouraging settler Australians to make peace with Aboriginal people, he said:

> We're not trying to push you back to London and big England, but what's your feeling? You the one been making lot of mistake, but we can be join in, white, and black, and yellow. This a big country, and we been mix em up [people]. We're on this land now. We can be friendly, join in, be friends, mates, together.

Survived by his adult children, Danayarri died of cancer on 24 March 1988 in Katherine Hospital and was buried at Wave Hill. His adult children include some community leaders; all of them are knowledgable in Aboriginal law, as are many of his grandchildren, and all have been active in acquiring land rights. Danayarri expected that his spirit would go the way of those of his ancestors: that he would become a shooting star, a set of bones, a spirit that would become new life and another spirit that would stay forever in its own country.

C. Healy, *From the Ruins of Colonialism* (1997); D. B. Rose, *Hidden Histories* (1991), and 'The Saga of Captain Cook', *Austn Aboriginal Studies*, no 2, 1984, p 24, and 'Danayarri, Hobbles', in D. Carment and H. J. Wilson (eds), *Northern Territory Dictionary of Biography*, vol 3, 1996.   DEBORAH BIRD ROSE

DARBY, EVELYN DOUGLAS (1910-1985), teacher and politician, was born on 24 September 1910 at Lowestoft, Suffolk, England, son of Percy Charles Darby, estate agent, and his wife Jessie, née Ainslie. Douglas attended Portsmouth Council Southern Secondary School. In 1926 he visited Australia while working as a ship's steward. Returning to New South Wales two years later, he attended Sydney Teachers' College (1928-29). He taught at Bannister Provisional (1930-33) and Mosman Public (1934-40) schools, and enrolled at the University of Sydney (B.Ec., 1938).

Medically unfit for war service, in 1939 Darby founded the British Orphans Adoption Society—which sponsored the formation, in 1940, of the Help the Children of the Allies Campaign—to bring orphans to Australia. He extended this charitable work to include children in Australia and, after the war, from Europe. At Mosman he met ESME JEAN McKenzie (1908-1997), a teacher, who helped with the City–Country Holiday Exchange Scheme for children, which he had started while at Bannister. They were married with Salvation Army forms on 30 August 1941 in their home at Mosman. During the war Esme served as secretary of BOAS.

As a Liberal Party candidate, Darby won the State seat of Manly in a by-election in 1945. During a wharf-labourers' strike in 1947, he encouraged volunteer labour in Sydney to unload a ship carrying potatoes, an episode that became known as the 'Potato Blue'. At a rowdy meeting at the Domain, he and some colleagues were assaulted. During transport strikes he arranged for car-pooling to circumvent the effects on his constituents, earning the enmity of the labour movement but the affection of his community. Although an energetic and popular local member, he was less well liked in the party room. He unsuccessfully stood for the leadership of the State parliamentary Liberal Party in August 1954 and in April and July 1959. After losing preselection for Manly in 1961, he resigned from the party. He successfully contested the seat in the 1962 and 1965 elections as an Independent, and was readmitted to the party in August 1966. The split was at times bitter and Darby did not advance past the back-bench when he returned, although he continued to represent Manly until he retired in 1978.

Darby had railed against the 'prospects of communist-socialist influence' from the 1930s. After World War II he made contacts with European émigrés escaping communist regimes. This led to his work for the Captive Nations Council of New South Wales, of which he was president. From the late 1960s to the mid-1970s he was a delegate to World Anti-Communist League conferences. He attended an Anti-Bolshevik Bloc of Nations conference in London in 1982 and a Captive Nations Committee meeting in Washington in the following year. He was sympathetic to the extreme-right activists with whom he worked in these organisations and he published several polemical anti-communist tracts. By 1973 his main focus had changed to support for Taiwan and he formed the Australia—Free China Association.

A Freemason from 1941, and a professed puritan, Darby was prominent in campaigns against gambling and Sunday trading. He was also concerned about mental health, penal reform, pollution and transport. In 1968 he advocated developing Bathurst as the new State capital. Although he was an indefatigable campaigner who believed in his own rectitude, he failed to find wide support for his causes. He died on 22 August 1985 at Wahroonga and was cremated.

Esme had been born on 1 November 1908 at Redfern, Sydney, daughter of James Alexander Oliver McKenzie, carpenter, and his wife Ada Maria, née Daniel, both born in New South Wales. She attended Fort Street Girls' High School (1922-26), Teachers' College, Sydney (1927-28) and the University of Sydney (BA, 1934) and worked as a teacher (1928-41, 1943-44). Living with her family in the Manly area, she supported local community groups and children's charities including the New South Wales Society for Crippled Children.

In 1961 Mrs Darby was unsuccessful in her attempt to gain preselection for the seat of Wakehurst. She represented the Australian Housewives' Association on the Captive Nations Week committee in the late 1960s and later accompanied her husband on several trips to World Anti-Communist League conferences and to Taiwan. She worked in the office, and on the committee, of the Australia—Free China Association, which effectively offered the services of a consulate. Committed to youth welfare, she was appointed MBE in 1975. A few years after her husband's death she moved to Adelaide, where she died on 19 November 1997 and was cremated. She was survived by two sons and four daughters.

J. Power (ed), *Politics in a Suburban Community* (1968); S. Moran, *Reminiscences of a Rebel* (1979); *SMH*, 15 Nov 1968, p 6, 23 Mar 1979, p 6, 25 Aug 1985, p 5; H. de Berg, interview with E. D. Darby (ts, 1975, NLA); Darby family papers (SLNSW).

PETER HENDERSON

DARBYSHIRE, BEATRICE DEAN (1901-1988), artist, was born on 31 March 1901 in Perth, eldest of three children of Benjamin Harvie Darbyshire, a Uruguayan-born barrister, and his wife Agnes, née Campbell, who came from Victoria. Beatrice was educated at Miss Jobson's school, Perth, and at Geelong Church of England Girls' Grammar School (the Hermitage), Victoria (1915-17). As a child she had shown talent at drawing and, encouraged by her parents, had begun Saturday classes with Henri Van Raalte [q.v.12] about 1913. After returning from Geelong, she continued to study and work with him. She frequently visited Netherton farm, Balingup, the home of her aunt Jean Lukis. Her young cousin Mollie Lukis was a constant companion and model and the landscape of tall trees was to inspire some of her best work.

In 1921 Darbyshire exhibited with the Western Institute of Artists at the Museum and Art Gallery of Western Australia. Advised by Van Raalte, in 1924 she travelled to London and enrolled at the Royal College of Art, where she studied engraving under Malcolm Osborne. Among her fellow pupils were Eric Ravilious, Iain Macnab and Charles Tunnicliffe. In 1924 and 1925 two of her dry-points, 'The Cowshed, Balingup', and 'In the Blackwood Country', were chosen for the British Empire Exhibition at Wembley. On both occasions she received a certificate of honour and a bronze medal. After graduating in 1927 with a diploma from RCA she returned to Perth and had an etching press made to the same specifications as that of Van Raalte.

Darbyshire's first solo exhibition was held in 1933 at Newspaper House Art Gallery. That year she met (Dame) Mary Durack and visited her and her family at their stations in the Kimberley region. She made numerous portraits of Aborigines that were later developed into dry-points and etchings. In 1937 her work was included in the Exhibition of Western Australian Art 1826-1937, at the Western Australian Museum and Art Gallery. Later that year she showed her work jointly with J. W. R. Linton [q.v.10] at Newspaper House. She exhibited with the Perth Society of Artists in 1938 and 1939.

Reputedly the finest etcher working in Western Australia in the 1920s and 1930s, Darbyshire suddenly gave up printmaking in 1940. Her seemingly inexplicable decision appears to have been due in part to her natural reticence, combined with the loneliness of working in isolation and the desire for a more active life. Also, the artists she most admired and wished to emulate—Charles Meryon, Jean-Baptiste Camille Corot and members of the Barbizon school of painter-etchers—were being supplanted in the public imagination by the modernists. She joined the Women's League of Health and moved to Sydney in 1940 to train as an instructor. Next year she displayed her work at the league's headquarters. Back in Perth in 1944, she ran the State branch for about twelve years. She wrote occasional articles for, and illustrated, the league's quarterly publication *Movement*, and gave several art lectures. In 1970 she donated her long unused press to Perth Technical College.

In the 1970s Hendrik Kolenberg rediscovered Darbyshire's work and mounted an exhibition, A. B. Webb [q.v.16], Edith Trethowan and Beatrice Darbyshire: Western Australian Printmakers of the 1920s and 1930s, which toured Australia in 1979-81. In 1987 the Art Gallery of Western Australia included her in Western Australian Art and Artists, 1900-1950. She died unmarried on 31 July 1988 at Mosman Park, Perth, and was cremated with Anglican rites. Her work is held by the National Gallery of Australia, Canberra, Art Gallery of New South Wales, Art Gallery of Western Australia, National Trust of Australia

(Western Australia), Royal Western Australian Historical Society, and in private collections.

A. B. Webb, Edith Trethowan and Beatrice Darbyshire (1979); J. Gooding, *Western Australian Art and Artists, 1900-1950* (1987); B. Chapman, *Beatrice Darbyshire* (1990); *Westerly*, no 1, Mar 1982, p 89, no 4, Dec 1986, p 53; *West Australian*, 3 Aug 1988, p 44.   BARBARA CHAPMAN

DARIAN-SMITH, DOUGLAS; *see* SMITH, D.

DARK, ELEANOR (1901-1985), author, was born on 26 August 1901 at Croydon, Sydney, second of three children of Sydney-born parents Dowell Philip O'Reilly [q.v.11], schoolteacher and author, and his wife Eleanor Grace, née McCulloch, who died in 1914 after an unhappy marriage and a period of ill health. Small, dark and elfin, 'Pixie', as she was known to her family, attended several private schools before boarding at Redlands, Neutral Bay, from 1916 to 1920. She became very fond of her stepmother, Marie (Mollie) Miles, whom her father had married in 1917.

Although Pixie had written verse from the age of 7, as the family's finances grew tighter her hopes of university and a writing career faded. After attending Stott & Hoare's Business College, she worked as a stenographer for a firm of solicitors, Makinson, Plunkett & d'Apice, for eighteen months. She married Eric Payten Dark [q.v.], a medical practitioner and a widower with an infant son, John, on 1 February 1922 at St Matthias's Church of England, Paddington. Eric and Eleanor shared many interests: literature, history, tennis, bushwalking, mountain-climbing and gardening. Next year they moved to Katoomba. In the relative isolation of the Blue Mountains she resumed writing. Eric enthusiastically encouraged her. They were absorbed in each other; John moved back and forth between them and his mother's family and later boarded at Sydney Grammar School, visiting the Darks for occasional weekends. Their son Michael was born in 1929; Eleanor was and remained a devoted mother to him.

Dark used the pseudonyms 'P. O'R.' and 'Patricia O'Rane' for the verse which she wrote in the 1920s and early 1930s. It was published in Australia by journals including the *Triad*, *Bulletin* and *Woman's Mirror*, but was not very significant. Her short stories were also published in these journals and in *Motoring News*, *Home* and *Ink*. She wrote most of her ten novels in the 1930s and 1940s. Seven had contemporary themes; the others formed a historical trilogy.

In *Slow Dawning* (1932), Dark explored the social and professional restrictions on a young woman doctor. This, her first published novel and by her own admission a 'pot-boiler', made little impact. However, she twice won the Australian Literature Society's gold medal—for her second and third novels, *Prelude to Christopher* (1934) and *Return to Coolami* (1936). The former raised the issues of eugenics and insanity; the latter was a more conventional, romantic domestic drama. Both novels demonstrated her skills in the methods of psychological modernism. Her two novels set in the Depression, *Sun across the Sky* (1937) and *Waterway* (1938), in which she attempted to assimilate techniques of social realism, were less successful.

The first volume of Dark's trilogy, *The Timeless Land* (1941), brought her acclaim both at home and overseas, especially in the United States of America, where it was the Book of the Month Club's selection for October. A generation of Australian students learned the history of their country through her fictionalised account of the beginnings of European settlement; the book was for a time set on the school syllabus in New South Wales and Victoria. Her historical trilogy proceeded unevenly. The second book, *Storm of Time* (1948), matched the first in critical reception and, arguably, surpassed it in quality. The third, *No Barrier* (1953), did not find an American publisher and was the poor relation of the earlier two.

The Little Company (1945), a novel set in wartime Australia, was a manifesto from a writer alienated from all that she saw as petty, shallow and coarse in society. It disappointed most readers. But *Lantana Lane* (1959) surprised and pleased the critics with its sunniness and light-hearted wit. Set in small-town rural Australia, it was based on the community at Montville, Queensland, where the Darks lived on a hobby farm for part of each year in the 1950s. It proved to be her last published work.

Most of Dark's novels were initially published by Collins. The advent of the feminist Virago Press in the mid-1980s rescued two of them from oblivion. Among several short non-fiction pieces were an essay on Caroline Chisholm for *The Peaceful Army* (1938), edited by Flora Eldershaw [qq.v.1,14], and two travel articles for *Walkabout*. She regarded literary criticism as loathsome and parasitic, and refused to engage in it. An unpublished novel, 'Pilgrimage', and three unpublished plays are among her papers.

Although Dark experimented across a range of genres well into her seventies, the novel was her principal medium. She had a facility for popular romances that she exploited fully when her artistic conscience allowed her. She experimented widely with technique, and was among the pioneers of modernist writing in Australia. Her best writing derived from intimate knowledge of her material and first-hand experience of the characters and worlds she created. She knew educated middle-class Australia from the inside, and could capture its nature with a few strokes of the pen. Mostly disapproving of suburban values, she disassociated herself from the middle class by reserving for it her most scathing social comments.

Psychology fascinated Dark, and the bush was her physical and spiritual solace. She drew compelling landscapes of the mind and of the Australian natural environment. In 1959 the Australian poet John Manifold [q.v.] caught the confluence of these two streams in her work:

It was not principally for their human characters that I used to read and re-read these early novels of Eleanor Dark, but for the feel of sunlight and the smell of boronia. The characters were living such intensely inward lives, so wrapped in reminiscence and self-analysis, that I didn't find them very good company ... But the landscape, the Australianism of the background, that was dinkum!

Dark loathed publicity. She wrote to her American literary agent, Nellie Sukerman: 'If I could arrange the literary world to my satisfaction writers would never be photographed, and would be known by numbers instead of names!' In 1942, at the height of her career, an American academic, Bruce Sutherland, wrote requesting a brief biographical sketch. She was willing to help, but explained that 'there's hardly material for such a thing, as my life has been uneventful to the point of being humdrum!' She sought futilely to deflect attention from the personal to the work, partly because of a firm conviction that the text was all and partly to protect her privacy. Her life may not have seemed one of high drama but it had elements of tragedy that influenced her writing. Her mother died aged 43, her brother at 26, and her father at 58, and her stepmother committed suicide.

Although not heavily involved in the politics of her profession, Dark joined the Fellowship of Australian Writers in 1939. She also became a vice-president of the Australian Council for Civil Liberties that year. In 1951 she signed a petition supporting Frank Hardy when he was prosecuted for criminal libel for his novel *Power without Glory*. She contributed a chapter to the unpublished FAW volume 'Australian Writers in Defence of Freedom', criticising Nazi Germany's back-to-the-kitchen directives to women. Dark had socialist views but was not a member of any political party.

It was fitting that Dark's most celebrated novel should have been the artist's rendition of the essence of her Australia: the timeless land. Unlike most of her fellow writers, she did not pine for other lands and cultures. Australia was not only her physical, but also her spiritual, home. A residential writers' centre was established in her memory at Varuna, the spacious, solid, brick home in the Blue Mountains that she had designed in 1939 and lived in for most of her adult life. She was appointed AO in 1977 and next year was given the Alice Award by the Society of Women Writers (Australia). Survived by her husband and their son, she died on 11 September 1985 at Katoomba and was buried in the Anglican section of Blackheath cemetery.

A. G. Day, *Eleanor Dark* (1976); B. Brooks and J. Clark, *Eleanor Dark* (1998); *Overland*, July 1959, p 39; M. Wyndham, Eleanor Dark (BA Hons thesis, ANU, 1987); M. Wyndham Luther-Davies, A 'World-proof Life' (PhD thesis, ANU, 1995); Eleanor Dark papers (SLNSW and NLA). MARIVIC WYNDHAM

DARK, ERIC PAYTEN (1889-1987), medical practitioner and activist, was born on 23 June 1889 at Mittagong, New South Wales, youngest of three children of Rev. Joseph Dark, an Anglican clergyman born in England, and his third wife, Adelaide, née Goodwin, who was born in Sydney. His father had three older children from his first marriage. After private tutoring, Eric attended Sydney Grammar School and the University of Sydney (MB, Ch.M., 1914). He worked briefly as a resident radiographer at Sydney's Royal Prince Alfred Hospital.

Appointed a temporary lieutenant in the Royal Army Medical Corps on 15 March 1915, Dark sailed to England. He was sent to the Western Front, where he spent five months with the 18th General Hospital and two years with the 9th Field Ambulance. As a temporary captain (1916), he was awarded the Military Cross for evacuating the wounded under fire at Boesinghe (Boezinge), Belgium, on 31 July 1917. In October he was temporarily blinded and badly affected by gas, having removed his mask better to attend to casualties. Invalided to England, he recovered and was posted to a general hospital in Macedonia. He returned to Australia in July 1919.

While on leave in Australia Dark had married Kathleen Aphra ('Daidee') Raymond, a nurse, on 25 January 1918 at St Philip's Church of England, Sydney. Next year they moved to Bungendore, where he worked in general practice. Following the birth of their son in 1920, Daidee died of septic peritonitis. Devastated, Dark returned to Sydney, where he became a demonstrator in the anatomy department at the University of Sydney. On 1 February 1922 at St Matthias' Church of England, Paddington, he married Eleanor O'Reilly [q.v. Dark], twelve years his junior; they were to have a son. They moved to

Katoomba and bought a house named Varuna in 1923 and he took over a general practice. Dark published his innovative and successful *Diathermy in General Practice* (1930). He enjoyed reading and listening to classical music. A 'small, wiry, energetic, extremely fit' man, with 'reddish hair, a small moustache and flying eyebrows', Eric shared with Eleanor an enjoyment of gardening, tennis, golf, bush-walking and rock-climbing. He became a director of the Katoomba Colliery Ltd and Katoomba Hotels Pty Ltd.

Initially a political conservative, Dark witnessed the impact of the Depression on his patients. He realised that their health was influenced as much by political and economic factors as by viruses and bacteria. An advocate of the nationalisation of medicine, he published a collection of his articles, *Medicine and the Social Order* (1943). By the end of the 1930s Dark was an active member of the Australian Labor Party, later serving as vice-president of the local branch. In the 1940s he stood twice, unsuccessfully, on the Labor ticket in council elections. He was involved in obtaining local community improvements such as a children's library, healthy 'Oslo' lunches at the school, childcare facilities and a current affairs library.

In protest against government censorship and the banning of the Communist Party of Australia in 1940, the Darks purchased shares in the People's Printing & Publishing Co. In 1941 he became vice-president of the Russian Medical Aid & Comforts Committee. He wrote *Who Are the Reds* (1946) and *The World against Russia?* (1948). His concern for freedom of speech led to his becoming a vice-president of the Australian Council for Civil Liberties and found further expression in *The Press against the People* (1949). In 1942-45 he had served part time in the Volunteer Defence Corps, rising to lance sergeant. He was commended for his work of training men in the skills of bushcraft and exploring the Blue Mountains for suitable guerrilla bases in the event of a Japanese invasion.

Although he was never a member of the Communist Party and was insistent that his political philosophy was 'democratic socialism not communism', his left-wing views and association with known communists resulted in suspicion of him in the 1940s and 1950s. In 1947 the charter of the Katoomba branch of the ALP was revoked and the Darks were named in Federal parliament as underground workers for the CPA. He supported the Lithgow coalminers during the 1949 strike. Under surveillance by the Commonwealth Investigation Service (Australian Security Intelligence Organization), he received threatening letters and was expelled from the Returned Sailors', Soldiers' and Airmen's Imperial Services League of Australia in 1950.

His joining of the Australian Peace Council that year precipitated his resignation from the ALP. Next year he and Eleanor opposed the Federal government's attempt to proscribe the Communist Party.

After selling the practice, in 1951 the Darks bought a farm at Montville, Queensland, where Eric pursued a new interest in sustainable agriculture. The political climate relaxed somewhat and in 1957 he was appointed school medical officer in the Blue Mountains. Enjoying this kind of social medicine, he worked until forced by government regulations to retire, aged 85. He was awarded life membership of the Doctors' Reform Society of New South Wales (1981) and the Sydney Rock-Climbing Club. A man of moral rectitude and courage, he died at Wentworth Falls on 28 July 1987, two years after Eleanor, and was cremated. His sons survived him. An oil portrait painted by Brian ('Bim') O'Reilly hangs at Varuna.

B. Brooks and J. Clark, *Eleanor Dark* (1998); *New Doctor*, June 1984, p 11; *Hummer*, July-Aug 1987, p 7; *Blue Mountains Gazette*, 12 Aug 1987, p 21; *Rock* (Glebe, NSW), Jan-June 1990, p 18; J. Boyd, That Dark Lady's Husband (BA Hons thesis, Univ of Western Sydney, 1992); B884, item N347269, A6119, items 82 and 1482 (NAA); Dark files (Blue Mountains City Lib); E. Dark papers (SLNSW).

JOHN LOW

DART, RAYMOND ARTHUR (1893-1988), anatomist and anthropologist, was born on 4 February 1893 at Toowong, Brisbane, fifth of nine children of Samuel Dart, a Queensland-born storekeeper, and his wife Eliza Ann, née Brimblecombe, who was born in New South Wales. Raised mainly on a dairy farm near Laidley, Raymond attended Toowong and Blenheim State and Ipswich Grammar schools. He graduated from the University of Queensland (B.Sc., 1914; M.Sc., 1916) with first-class honours in biology, and studied medicine at the University of Sydney (Ch.M., MB, 1917; MD, 1927), where he came under the influence of J. T. Wilson [q.v.12]. Resident in St Andrew's College, he was acting vice-principal in 1917. He was a medical officer at Royal Prince Alfred Hospital; as a captain (1918-19) in the Australian Army Medical Corps, he served in England and France but saw no action.

Demobilised in England, Dart took a post at University College, London, as senior demonstrator in anatomy, under (Sir) Grafton Elliot Smith [q.v.11]. He spent a year (1920-21) on a Rockefeller Foundation fellowship in the United States of America, mostly at Washington University, St Louis, Missouri. On 3 September 1921 at Woods Hole, Falmouth, Massachusetts, he married with Congregational forms Dora

Tyree, an instructor in anatomy, and a divorcee. He worked for eighteen months at University College, London, before moving in January 1923 to South Africa, as professor of anatomy, University of the Witwatersrand, Johannesburg. Helping to build up the infant medical school, he served (1925-43) as dean of the faculty.

In November 1924 Dart was handed a fossil skull that had recently been discovered at Taungs (later Taung), 100 miles (160 km) north of Kimberley. He extracted the fossil from the hard matrix and found that the skull was that of a child possessing a mixture of apish and human features. The child had held its head on a nearly vertical spinal column; its teeth, especially its little canines, were human-like. Although the brain was small, like that of an ape, its form seemed to be hominoid. Thinking that its blend of traits might characterise the supposed missing link between humans and non-human animals on the old notion of a chain of being, Dart named the species *Australopithecus africanus* and published his findings in *Nature* in February 1925.

For over twenty years most scholars rejected Dart's claims. Critics asserted that the Taung child was on the wrong continent, was too young at death to make predictions about its likely adult form, and belonged to a geological epoch too recent. With its apish small brain and human-like posture and teeth, the skull belonged to a form antithetical to the kind of ancestor many theoreticians had envisaged, namely one in which the brain enlarged early in human emergence, and the posture and teeth 'humanised' later. Some held that Dart was too inexperienced for his arguments to be taken seriously; others disliked the name *Australopithecus*, because it was a hybrid of Latin *(australis)* and Greek *(pithecus)*. In time more fossilised hominid remains were found in Africa, and Dart's theory was generally accepted. The palaeontologist Robert Broom considered that Dart had made 'one of the greatest discoveries in the world's history'.

Another of Dart's research contributions had major consequences for evolutionary science. From Makapansgat, an archaeological site 174 miles (280 km) north of Johannesburg, there emerged a few dozen fossil remains of *Australopithecus*, and tens of thousands of broken animal bones. In thirty-nine papers, published between 1949 and 1965, and in his book *The Osteodontokeratic Culture of Australopithecus Prometheus* (1957), Dart developed his hypothesis that some of the bones had been wilfully shaped by the ape-men and used, with teeth and horn-cores, to kill animals for eating. A fierce debate ensued as opponents advanced other possible reasons for the collections of modified bones, horn-cores and teeth. His ideas gave impetus to a new branch of science, taphonomy, the study of the impact upon bones of physical and biotic agencies.

Fair haired and blue eyed, with firm and richly modulated speech, and kindly and forthright in manner, Dart had a charismatic personality. He stimulated many students to pursue careers in biomedical science before his retirement, as emeritus professor, in 1958. His other interests included swimming and music and, with Dennis Craig, he wrote an autobiography, *Adventures with the Missing Link* (1959). He was elected (1930) a fellow of the Royal Society of South Africa and was awarded honorary doctorates from the universities of Natal (1956) and the Witwatersrand (1965). In 1966-86 he spent six months each year teaching and researching at the Institutes for the Achievement of Human Potential, Philadelphia, Pennsylvania. Divorced in 1934, on 28 November 1936 he had married Marjorie Gordon Frew, a librarian, at her parents' home in Johannesburg. Survived by his wife and their daughter and son, he died on 22 November 1988 in Johannesburg and was cremated.

C. K. Brain, *The Hunters or the Hunted?* (1981); P. V. Tobias, *Dart, Taung and the 'Missing Link'* (1984), and 'In Memory of Raymond Arthur Dart FRSSAf', *Nature*, vol 337, no 6204, 1989, p 211; F. Wheelhouse and K. S. Smithford, *Dart* (2001); *Trans of the Royal Soc of South Africa*, vol 48, pt 1, 1992, p 183.
                                    PHILLIP V. TOBIAS

DARWEN, DOUGLAS JAMES (1906-1988), newspaper owner and editor, was born on 12 April 1906 at Bowen, Queensland, fifth of thirteen surviving children of William Henry Darwen, journalist, and his wife Caroline, née Christofferson, both born in Bowen. Jim was educated at the local state school and, as a boy, worked on his father's newspaper, the *Bowen Independent and Proserpine Agriculturalist*. On publication nights (Monday and Friday), the Darwen children were responsible for 'flying' the paper, taking the printed sheet from the cylinder of the printing machine as each of the four to five hundred copies was run off. At daylight they delivered the papers, sometimes running late for school. They also brought the 'smoko billy' of tea prepared for the staff by their mother.

Although Jim wanted to become an apprentice carpenter, at 14 he was 'pressed into service' at the newspaper office by his father. Overcoming his resentment, he became proficient at hand-setting type. After four years of this monotonous routine, he persuaded his father to buy a Linotype, a mechanical typesetter. He received a fortnight's tuition from a skilled Linotype user and, in the first week, amazed his father by setting the copy for the

Independent's two issues and for all the commercial printing jobs, tasks that normally occupied three hand-setters.

On their father's death in 1931, the five sons took over the firm, with Jim as editor and Linotype operator. Despite his lack of journalistic experience, he was to fulfil his new role with distinction, tirelessly promoting the needs of the district through his editorials. Under an impressive masthead the newspaper also covered State, national and world news, although it later became more parochial. After his younger brother Henry became editor in 1950 Jim continued to typeset copy until June 1976, remaining a senior partner. On 1 January 1986 the family sold the business to the North Queensland Newspaper Co. Ltd.

As editor, Darwen had followed his father's dictum of 'you've got to get out and get into things to run a country newspaper'. He was secretary of the progress association and the 1937 Back to Bowen celebrations; a long-time member and sometime president of the local town band; and a committee-member of the show society. A sailor for fifty years, he held every office in the Port Denison Sailing Club. He was twice elected a member of Bowen Town Council.

On 27 April 1932 at St Mary's Catholic Church, Bowen, Darwen had married Mary Reynolds (d.1970). At Holy Trinity Church of England, Fortitude Valley, Brisbane, on 15 December 1973 he married Glennie Brushe, née Blinco, a widow. Survived by his wife, and the son and one of two daughters of his first marriage, he died on 17 March 1988 at Bowen and was buried in the local cemetery.

R. Kirkpatrick, *Sworn to No Master* (1984); *Bowen Independent*, 13 Apr 1988, p 5, 16 July 1993, 'special edn' (whole issue); private information.

ROD KIRKPATRICK

DAVIDSON, SIR CHARLES WILLIAM (1897-1985), politician, army officer and farmer, was born on 14 September 1897 at Toowong, Brisbane, third child of Alexander Black Davidson, a Scottish-born sugar-planter, and his wife Marion, née Perry, who had been born in England. Leaving Townsville Grammar School in 1914, Charles worked as a stockman in North Queensland. On 14 February 1916 he enlisted in the Australian Imperial Force and from November served with the 42nd Battalion on the Western Front. He was commissioned in December 1917, promoted to lieutenant in July 1918 and wounded in action in September. His AIF appointment terminated in Australia on 31 October 1919.

Back in North Queensland, Davidson tried dairying on the Atherton Tableland then in 1925 bought a farm near Carmila, some 60 miles (97 km) south of Mackay, where he grew sugar cane. On 21 December 1929 at St Thomas's Church of England, North Sydney, he married Mary Gertrude Godschall Johnson, a nurse. He was active in cane-growers' organisations and in the 1930s took a leading part in moves to persuade the Queensland government to revise the peak-year scheme by which sugar farmers' production quotas were determined. In February 1939 he was appointed as a lieutenant, 42nd Battalion, Militia. Mobilised for full-time duty as a major on 20 September 1941, he transferred to the AIF in August 1942. Next month he was promoted to temporary lieutenant colonel and given command of his battalion.

In January 1943 the 42nd sailed for Milne Bay, Papua. Moving to Tambu Bay, New Guinea, in August, the unit took part in the successful final stages of the Salamaua campaign then in further operations around Lae. Davidson performed well, gaining the confidence of higher commanders as well as his own officers and soldiers. He knew his responsibilities, spoke decisively and authoritatively, gave clear orders and, in action, frequently visited the troops at the front. According to S. E. Benson, he was 'firm but not severe' and 'strict but just' towards his subordinates, qualities the men respected. The battalion returned to Australia in May 1944, Davidson having departed from New Guinea earlier in the month to attend a senior officers' course. Suffering from malaria, he relinquished his command in September and transferred to the Reserve of Officers on 2 December. He was appointed OBE (1945) and twice mentioned in despatches for his service. After the war he was to become honorary colonel of the 42nd Battalion (1955) and patron of its association.

Continuing his efforts to promote the interests of cane-growers, Davidson was appointed assistant-secretary of the Australian Sugar Producers' Association in November 1945. Next year he stood as the Country Party candidate for Capricornia in the House of Representatives. At the general election on 28 September he defeated the sitting member Frank Forde [q.v.]. Davidson switched to the newly created seat of Dawson in 1949 and was to hold it comfortably until his retirement. A member of the parliamentary delegation to Japan in 1948, he was to lead the visit to South-East Asia in 1963. He served on the Joint Committee on Broadcasting of Parliamentary Proceedings in 1950-55. His party chose him as its whip (1950-56) and deputy-leader (1958-63) under (Sir) John McEwen [q.v.15]. On 11 January 1956 he joined (Sir) Robert Menzies' [q.v.15] ministry as postmaster-general. Between October that year and December 1958 he held the additional portfolio of the navy.

Davidson assumed responsibility for posts and telegraphs at a time of rapid development in telecommunications technology. He effectively managed the political aspects of the changes. In 1959 he presided over the introduction of the teleprinter reperforator switching system that 'mechanised the public telegraph service', and the same year announced plans for an automated telephone service that eventually would be capable of handling subscriber-dialled trunk calls. His selection in 1961 of F. P. O'Grady [q.v.] as director-general, posts and telegraphs, assisted the department to keep abreast of the technological revolution. The Australian Broadcasting Commission was included in his portfolio. Sir Richard Boyer [q.v.13], the ABC's chairman until 1961, considered Davidson to be 'one of the best ministers who had been responsible for national broadcasting'. He retired on 18 December 1963, the longest-serving postmaster-general since Federation.

A good-natured, able and sensible man, Davidson had given dependable service as a middle-ranking army officer, advocate for sugar producers, and Commonwealth government minister. To Sir Arthur Fadden [q.v.14] he was 'a staunch and reliable mate'. (Sir) James Darling found him 'pleasant and friendly', as did many people. Of middle height, slim and with thinning, sandy hair, Davidson dressed neatly, wore a trim military moustache and had a staccato way of speaking. He was president (1964-73) of the Asthma Foundation of Queensland, and a director of Magellan Petroleum Australia Ltd and Telephone & Electrical Industries Pty Ltd. In 1964 he was elevated to KBE. Sir Charles lived at Yeronga, Brisbane, in retirement. His tastes were simple: he liked fishing, playing bowls, growing roses and eating Queensland mud crabs. He died on 29 November 1985 at his home and, following a state funeral at St Paul's Presbyterian Church, Brisbane, was buried in Mount Gravatt cemetery. His wife and their two daughters and son survived him.

S. E. Benson, *The Story of the 42 Aust. Inf. Bn.* (1952); G. C. Bolton, *Dick Boyer* (1967); A. Fadden, *They Called Me Artie* (1969); J. R. Darling, *Richly Rewarding* (1978); A. Moyal, *Clear across Australia* (1984); R. Thomas, *42nd Infantry Battalion* (1996); *PD* (HR), 11 Feb 1986, p 238; *Austn Sugar Jnl*, 15 Nov 1945, p 369; *Sun-Herald* (Sydney), 16 Sept 1956, p 22; B2455, item Davidson C W, B883, item QX33882 (NAA).   DARRYL BENNET

DAVIDSON, JAMES (JIM) HUTCHINSON (1902-1982), band leader, was born on 6 August 1902 at Balmain, Sydney, second son of Alexander Davidson, a restaurant cook from New Zealand, and his English-born wife Mabel, née Walker. Jim described his father, of Scottish descent, as hard, stern and unsmiling. His maternal grandfather encouraged his interest in music, taking him to hear the American bandmaster John Philip Sousa on his Australian tour of 1911. Davidson took up the cornet, joining his school cadet band and a local church band. After leaving school at 14, he found work with the soap manufacturer Lever Bros Pty Ltd. His days, however, were a means to an end and nights were given over to music. Replacing his cornet with a drum kit, he played in dance band and cinema pit ensembles.

On 8 February 1928 Davidson married Gertrude Madeline Kitching at St Thomas's Church of England, Rozelle; they were to be divorced in 1935. He had joined Jimmy Elkins's dance orchestra in the mid-1920s and after it disbanded in 1928 he played at the Ambassadors restaurant until it was destroyed by fire in 1931. Following engagements at the Ginger Jar and a significant concert at Hillier's Café in August 1932—sometimes described as the first jazz concert in Sydney—Davidson opened the winter season of 1933 at Sydney's Palais Royal dance hall, which drew crowds of 10 000 a week. Further successful seasons followed in 1934 and 1936. A regular Thursday evening 2UE live radio broadcast from the Royal augmented his audience. The Columbia recording company made sound recordings of his most popular pieces; Davidson claimed that a 78-rpm disc of 'Shuffle Off to Buffalo' and 'Forty Second Street' sold 95 000 copies. He and his orchestra also played a six-month season at the Palais de Danse at St Kilda, Melbourne, in 1933. At a formal 'Dress Night', when patrons were encouraged to dress as elegantly as the musicians, who routinely wore evening dress, Davidson met Marjorie McFarlane, an artist. They were married with Presbyterian forms at Scots Church, Melbourne, on 7 June 1935.

While in Melbourne, having signed a contract with the Australian Broadcasting Commission, Davidson enlarged his orchestra and performed over the national network to all States. Broadcasting from Sydney from 1936, Jim Davidson's ABC Dance Band, with the trumpeter Jim Gussey, the vocalist Alice Smith and the trombonist and arranger George Trevare, became the most popular in the country. It presented dance programs on Friday and Saturday evenings and played for other ABC shows including 'Out of the Bag' and 'A.B.C. Parade'. In 1937-39 the band made three interstate tours, with a variety of artists including Bob Dyer, Tex Morton [qq.v.] and Gladys Moncrieff [q.v.10]. Davidson was a strict but encouraging leader who inspired great loyalty in his players.

On 30 May 1941 Davidson was appointed an honorary lieutenant in the Australian Imperial

Force. He produced, directed and led the orchestra in variety shows staged for troops in the Middle East and the South-West Pacific Area. From 1943 he was in charge of the AIF's concert parties. Rising to temporary lieutenant colonel, he transferred to the Reserve of Officers in October 1947. He applied for the position of director of light entertainment at the ABC but was unsuccessful. Stung by his rejection, he made use of management skills developed in his military command, taking up an offer of work as director of productions for the Tivoli circuit and, soon after, for Harry Wren Enterprises. He managed Australian tours for performers such as Will Mahoney [q.v.15] and Evie Hayes [q.v.] and for the British comedian Tommy Trinder.

In 1947 Davidson joined the British Broadcasting Corporation. He arrived in London with his wife the following January. Starting as assistant-head of variety (music), he rapidly advanced to become the second-in-charge of the light entertainment unit. His most important contributions included support for what became the 'Goon Show', which went to air against some resistance on 28 May 1951. Davidson estimated that he had produced 3500 live shows on radio, among them a historic Beatles concert at the Royal Albert Hall in April 1963. He was given a farewell concert there before his retirement in September.

Returning to Australia in 1964, Davidson was disappointed that although Australians remembered his success as a band leader, they were unaware of his achievements in England. He served briefly as a consultant to the ABC but found that old 'ghosts' continued to haunt its corridors. The Davidsons turned to house renovation and gardening, first in Sydney and then in the southern highlands of New South Wales. Survived by his wife, Jim Davidson died on 10 April 1982 at Bowral and was cremated. His memoir, *A Showman's Story* (1983), was published posthumously.

A. Bisset, *Black Roots, White Flowers* (1979); K. S. Inglis, *This Is the ABC* (1983); *Wireless Weekly*, 13 Jan 1939, p 16; *ABC Weekly*, 2 Dec 1939, p 75, 18 Jan 1941, p 7, 6 Jan 1951, p 4; *SMH*, 30 May 1946, p 4, 12 Apr 1982, p 2; *Jazz* (Sydney), May-June 1982, p 33; Australian Performing Arts Collection (Callaway Centre, UWA); Jim Davidson papers (National Film and Sound Archive).

JEFF BROWNRIGG

DAVIES, ALAN FRASER (1924-1987), political scientist, was born on 25 September 1924, at St Kilda, Melbourne, son of Australian-born parents, George Vernon Davies, physician, and his wife Ruth, née Fraser. George Schoen Davies [q.v.4 Sir John Davies] was his grandfather. Educated at a Wangaratta state school and at Geelong College, Alan proceeded to Ormond [q.v.5] College at the University of Melbourne (BA Hons, 1945). There he was appointed a lecturer in political science in 1946. He commenced doctoral research in sociology at the London School of Economics and Political Science in 1949, assisted by an overseas scholarship from the Australian National University, but withdrew in 1950 to accept a senior lectureship at Melbourne. He was universally known as 'Foo'. Perhaps the nickname originated when, after an absence, he overheard colleagues speculating about his return and announced, 'Foo is here'. Graffiti of the time represented an elusive, never present figure ('Foo *was* here'). It may have stuck because it rendered the aloof Davies more approachable. He was appointed reader (1960) then professor (1968), and became one of Australia's most creative political scientists. Over forty years he drew on art, film, fiction, history and psychoanalysis in his exploration of political behaviour, at a time when cautious positivism was the norm.

His first monograph, *Local Government in Victoria* (1951), based on an MA thesis completed with first-class honours in 1947, traversed issues of municipal finance and reform. *Policies for Progress* (1954), edited with Geoffrey Serle for the Victorian Fabian Society, revealed his initial interest in what he called 'practical' socialism. *Australian Democracy* (1958), his first book to make a broad impact, combined analysis of politics with speculation about underlying attitudes, and offered incisive aphorisms (such as: 'The characteristic talent of Australians ... is for bureaucracy'), for which some of his peers never forgave him. A gem of conscientious detail and inspired hunches, it remained a standard text for years. In 1961 he published a collection of short stories, *A Sunday Kind of Love*.

In *Australian Society* (1965) Davies, with his co-editor, Sol Encel, drew together a range of contributors to provide a pioneering, integrated sociological introduction to Australian society. In 1965 he was elected a member of the Social Science Research Council of Australia. Increasingly, Davies found his *métier* in the analysis of personal politics, and in the use of psychoanalytic theory as a means of relating the individual and personal to the social and cultural. This interest had taken shape in his undergraduate years and grew during a period at the Tavistock Institute of Human Relations in 1958. While there he began analysis with Hedwig Hoffer, who had come from Vienna with Freud in 1936. On returning to Melbourne Davies began to teach a course on interpreting dreams and to apply psychoanalytic frameworks to political research. The first fruit of this approach was *Private Politics* (1966): case studies of activists used to illustrate the formation of political outlooks, what they owed to the psyche and what they meant for social adaptation. This study was followed by *Images of Class* (1967), which traced links between self-perceptions (including class perceptions) and political socialisation.

Despite his preoccupation with individual experience, Davies never overlooked the dialectic between individual and society. After a visiting professorship at the University of Alberta (1967), he drew together *Essays in Political Sociology* (1972), demonstrating his catholic vision by covering topics including biography, Rousseau and modern sensibility, migrants, suburban political styles, intellectuals, and political and literary criticism. 'A sounder man', he quipped, 'would surely have started less [*sic*] hares, but caught a couple'. Two monographs, *Politics as Work* (1973) and *Political Passions* (1975), then foreshadowed his masterwork, *Skills, Outlooks and Passions* (1980), which took three elements—how individuals work, think and perceive, and feel—and considered them as the integral components of politics. Lapidary, intensely detailed, multi-layered and elegant, it was a brilliant synthesis of others' insights in juxtapositions that shed new light on them and suggested fresh directions that transcended them. It reviewed applied psychoanalysis, rescued classic paradigms, mapped new uses of theory and was an annotated bibliography of life-history and politics.

Davies' influence extended as much through conversation as through his publications. In a small reading circle on Freud he shaped the thinking of younger scholars. He was central to the groups of academics who, from the 1950s, gathered in Carlton pubs where, according to Chris Wallace-Crabbe, Davies practised 'the enchanting legerdemain of new ideas'. By the 1970s he had formed the 'Melbourne Psychosocial Group', which combined academics from many disciplines with practising psychoanalysts. Davies' influence can also be traced in the texts and footnotes of biographies and histories written by his contemporaries, including the work of his closest successor, Graham Little, who, not only as an academic but as a journalist and broadcaster, kept Davies' legacy in the public eye.

Within his department, Davies' interest in psychoanalysis—coupled with his self-description 'social psychologist' rather than political scientist—was treated with scepticism by some and opposed by a few. He had no 'talent for bureaucracy', and no gift for or interest in institutional politicking. He simply disdained critics, allowing diversity to flourish. In contrast to the conversational brilliance that garnered a following of those keen to savour his latest *bon mot*, his lectures were delivered with a diffidence demanding a committed audience. His characteristic mode was an affable courtesy; he could, however, be quietly ruthless and coruscating when provoked (the more devastating because so witty).

Davies encouraged people to articulate their projects and to discover their own potentials and impediments, while also suggesting fresh insights, different angles, apposite readings. Driven by an unquenchable curiosity, he was a pioneer of interdisciplinary dialogue. His capacity to bring together novelists, poets, psychoanalysts, literary critics, journalists and historians, as well as political scientists, gave his department a distinctive élan—but it was a quality largely dependent on his own enthusiasm.

In 1978 Davies became a founding member of the International Society of Political Psychology, serving on its governing council (1979-80) and regularly attending its meetings. He maintained close links with British and North American colleagues, and extended these networks in 1980-81 as fifth visiting professor of Australian studies at Harvard University. Davies hoped to retire early to concentrate on writing but before he could do so he died of cardiac arrest on 18 August 1987 at North Carlton; he was cremated. He had been married twice: to Judith Humphries Wise, at St James' Old Cathedral, West Melbourne, on 15 January 1946 (divorced 1967); and to Helen Margaret Hughes, whom he had married in Edmonton, Alberta, Canada on 3 January 1968 (divorced 1983). His son, from his first marriage, survived him.

Two books remained uncompleted: a study of dreams was one; a fragment of the other had been published as an essay, 'Small Country Blues' (*Meanjin*, June 1985). Here Davies returned to an enduring concern that Australia must contend with the limits imposed by a small pool of talent and a denial of scale and complexity in politics. The essay reflected his sense of being a metropolitan in a peripheral country. A posthumous collection of essays, *The Human Element* (1988), captured his quizzical, allusive, provocative voice, 'blending', as Little observed, 'the free enjoyment of curiosity with the responsibilities of knowledge'.

J. Damousi, *Freud in the Antipodes* (2005); *Age Monthly Review*, Oct 1987, p 21; J. Walter, 'A. F. Davies', *Austn Book Review*, Oct 1987, p 17; *Age* (Melbourne), 22 Jan 1980, p 1, 19 Aug 1987, p 2; C. Wallace-Crabbe, The Foo Scene (ts, copy on ADB file).   JAMES WALTER

DAVIES, ARTHUR THOMAS ('CLARENCE THE CLOCKER') (1912-1984), racecourse clocker and television personality, was born on 26 March 1912 at Rockdale, Sydney, fourth child of Ernest Edward Davies, a carpenter born in New South Wales, and his Victorian-born wife Constance, née Hall. Arthur grew up in Redfern and worked as a bread carter and a milkman in the 1930s.

A small man, barely five feet (153 cm) tall, Davies wanted to be a jockey but did not obtain a licence. Instead, in 1942 he formed a working association with the future champion horse-trainer Tommy Smith. Davies became a racecourse clocker, timing the pre-dawn gallops of horses in training for Smith and others. Sharp-eyed clockers were in demand from sporting newspapers and radio stations as tipsters. Davies' prowess as pundit and his flair for the wry and telling phrase earned him a following on a racing preview program, 'First with the Latest', on radio 2KY. In 1957 he was co-opted into television for station TCN-9, owned by the racehorse owner and media entrepreneur (Sir) Frank Packer [q.v.15]. Davies' sobriquet 'Clarence the Clocker' came from Bing Crosby's song *The Horse Told Me*, which was regularly used at the opening of the show.

Racing in the 1950s continued to attract wide media attention, and broadcasters—notably Ken Howard [q.v.14] in Sydney, and Bert Bryant and Bill Collins in Melbourne—were celebrities. As with football broadcasting, racing gave an opportunity for the airing of untutored Australian accents, and Clarence's earthy humour struck a chord. He soon became a great favourite in Sydney, appearing on Saturday morning television as 'Clarence the Clocker'. His racing segment grew to be a half-hour program. He was the cheeky battler talking to 'the girls' or 'the ladies', his main audience. 'Okay, girls, down with the brooms and up with the skirts' was his opening sally. Howard and his successor as race-caller, Johnny Tapp, were regulars on Clarence's show, with the former make-up artist Pam Burling (née Bunyan) his perfect foil.

In 1977 Davies suffered the first of two strokes that affected his movement and speech, but his television appearances continued until 1982. He was upset by his forced retirement. Clarence's program was described as 'the longest-running, locally-produced show in Australia'. He also wrote racing columns for newspapers.

Davies had married Edna May Mitchell, a machinist, on 8 December 1936 at St Patrick's Catholic Church, Kogarah. They lived at Dolls Point (Sans Souci) until about 1970, when they separated. A journalist claimed that Edna 'intensely disliked horse racing and every manner of person associated with it'. Davies dressed as the racecourse 'spiv', with sharp clothes and inevitable hat. Survived by his wife and their daughter and son, he died on 4 August 1984 at Kanwal and was cremated.

J. Tapp, *Tappy* (1999); *Austn Women's Weekly*, 26 Oct 1960, p 70; *Sunday Mirror* (Sydney), 3 June 1975, p 27; *SMH*, 6 Aug 1984, p 28; *Sydney Review*, May 1994, p 10.   ANDREW LEMON

DAVIS, FLORENCE AMY; *see* CLUFF

DAVIS, NEIL BRIAN (1934-1985), cameraman and war correspondent, was born on 14 February 1934 in Hobart, youngest of four children of Tasmanian-born parents Geoffrey Crocker Davis, farmer, and his wife Marjorie Elaine, née New. Brought up on subsistence farms at Nala and then at Sorell, Neil was educated at Sorell State and Hobart High schools. At 15 he joined the Tasmanian Government Film Unit as an office-boy. Although nicknamed 'Tiny' as a child, he was by this time a wiry six-footer (183 cm) playing as a ruckman in the Sorell district senior Australian Rules football competition. Intensely competitive, he became a professional footballer while still a teenager, partly to augment his paltry salary at the film unit, and took up middle-distance running. In 1952, shortly after completing national service training, he contracted poliomyelitis. Through willpower and intensive exercise, he was back playing football in four months.

Davis had acquired the basics of photography while taking still pictures with flash powder at the film unit. He was introduced to news cinema-photography in the late 1950s when the unit was making 35-mm segments for Cinesound Productions and Fox Movietone News. Film footage was scarce and expensive, and he learned to be economical with his coverage and to 'edit' in the camera, a practice allowing the quickest possible processing of stories. In 1961 he became a staff cameraman with the Australian Broadcasting Commission. Three years later he was a roving news correspondent in South-East Asia for the British Commonwealth International Newsfilm Agency, known as Visnews. He quickly established a reputation for his fast, accurate and daring reporting of the two wars then taking place in the region: Indonesia's confrontation with Malaysia, and the growing conflict between the Democratic Republic of Vietnam (North Vietnam) and the Republic of Vietnam (South Vietnam). His simple upbringing in rural Tasmania had created, he believed, an instinctive empathy with the peasant farmers whose lives were damaged by war.

In Vietnam Davis realised that, as a lone operator, he could not match the resources of the United States of America's networks, which were covering only American military action. He accompanied soldiers of the Army of the Republic of Vietnam, staying out in the field for up to a week at a time, eating local food and drinking paddy water. Using a spring-loaded Bell & Howell 16-mm camera, and with a cassette recorder strapped to his waist, he employed a mix of intuition and experience to bring distinctive Asian images of the war to television screens around the world. In February 1973 he was the first Western cine-cameraman to cross into South Vietnamese territory held by the People's Liberation Armed Forces (Viet Cong), surviving a savage aerial attack by Allied helicopter gunships.

Recording front-line combat in Laos and Cambodia (Kampuchea) as well as in South Vietnam, Davis was wounded many times. He was seriously hurt on 11 April 1974 in Cambodia when an exploding mortar shell almost severed his right leg just below the knee. A transfusion of fluid from a green coconut kept him alive until he reached medical help. He was back at work within three months, despite having no feeling below his right knee. Early in 1975 he began working for the USA's National Broadcasting Corporation. On 30 April he achieved his greatest scoop—filming the last act of the Vietnam War, a North Vietnamese tank breaking down the gates of the presidential palace in Saigon. Because of his reputation as a fair and honest reporter, the North Vietnamese regime allowed him to stay in Saigon (Ho Chi Minh City) for three months. He then moved to Bangkok, to cover from the Thai border the tragic events unfolding in Cambodia.

Davis made friends with many of the leading politicians in the region. He was generous with his expertise, giving information and background to print journalists on stories he could not record on film. Never cynical, he retained his compassion and often risked his life to portray the human tragedy of war. He was particularly moved by the plight of Asian children, and supported charities that assisted them. Specialising in his 'one-man-band' operation—shooting pictures and standing in front of his camera while recording his own commentary—he also worked in Africa and the Middle East. He achieved iconic status in his profession, and his later nickname of 'The Old Fox' belied his blond hair, slim frame and perennially boyish good looks. In 1980 David Bradbury's documentary *Frontline*, a portrait of Davis, was released to international acclaim.

A compulsive and successful womaniser, on 29 January 1977 Davis had married Chou Ping (Julie) Yen, in Taipei. They had no children and later separated. He was killed by tank fire, covering a failed Thai coup in Bangkok on 9 September 1985. A professional to the last, he had filmed his own death as his locked-on camera captured the continuing action. As he had requested, a Buddhist cremation was carried out in Bangkok. His wife survived him. In the front of every one of his meticulously kept work diaries he had inscribed lines from the English poet Thomas Osbert Mordaunt that summed up his philosophy of life:

One crowded hour of glorious life
Is worth an age without a name.

T. Bowden, *One Crowded Hour* (1987); *Daily Telegraph* (Sydney), 14 June 1971, p 15; *SMH*, 1 May 1975, p 1; *Mercury* (Hobart), 10 Sept 1981, p 1; Davis collection (AWM).   TIM BOWDEN

DAWBARN, MARY CAMPBELL (1902-1982), biochemist and nutritional physiologist, was born on 5 January 1902 at Ballarat, Victoria, elder child of English-born Gilbert Joseph Dawbarn, a lecturer at the local school of mines, and his second wife Mary Isabella, née Macdonald, born in Victoria. The family moved to South Australia in 1907 when 'Mollie's' father took up a post at the Wallaroo smelter. She won a scholarship to Methodist Ladies College, Adelaide; she was dux in 1918 and next year came second in the higher public examination of South Australia. Winning a government bursary, she entered the University of Adelaide (B.Sc. Hons, 1923; M.Sc., 1928; D.Sc., 1958). She began her working life in 1924 as a demonstrator for Professor T. B. Robertson [q.v.11] in the department of physiology and biochemistry, while researching the composition of a synthetic diet suitable for mice.

In February 1927 Dawbarn joined the Animal Products Research Foundation of the University of Adelaide, which was associated with the Council for Scientific and Industrial Research's division of animal nutrition. Working under the direction of the charismatic H. R. Marston [q.v.15] for her entire career, she first carried out chemical analyses for a survey of the iodine content of the thyroid glands of sheep. Marston's criticisms could be most hurtful and Dawbarn was especially vulnerable. Contemporaries have suggested that she worshipped him and hence did not marry. Granted study leave in 1933-34, she travelled to Europe to work at the Lister Institute of Preventive Medicine, London, and the University of Strasbourg, France.

During World War II Dawbarn investigated the nutritional requirements of the Australian armed forces, in particular, problems of supplying vitamin C to troops fighting in areas remote from sources of fresh fruit and vegetables. Marston thought highly of her research, telling CSIR's chief executive officer Sir David Rivett [q.v.11] in 1944 that she was 'the only professional nutritional person in Australia who is really well based scientifically'. In 1948 he asserted that she was the leading authority on human nutrition in Australia, having perfected methods for the estimation of thiamine (vitamin B_1) in bread. Her work on producing an assay for B_{12} was perhaps her most important achievement; in 1950-51 she carried out further research into the vitamins of the B complex at the University of Cambridge, England. In 1954 she officially transferred to the division of biochemistry and general nutrition, Commonwealth Scientific and Industrial Research Organization, and was appointed a principal research officer.

Dawbarn took early retirement in 1963 and over the next few years travelled to some exotic locations, including South America. An expert photographer, she produced her own black-and-white enlargements. She was an active member of the Adelaide Lyceum and Soroptimist clubs. Treasurer (1965-69) of the South Australian Ornithological Association, she enjoyed bird-watching trips into the outback. A vibrant personality, she had a wide circle of friends. Throughout her life she was modest about her achievements; she said that she could 'never have got the D.Sc. without [the] unflagging help' of the young women researchers whom she had trained. She died on 24 May 1982 in Adelaide and was cremated.

Animal Products Research Foundation, *Annual Report*, 1924-29, 1933-35, 1940-46; *The News* (Adelaide), 10 Oct 1932, p 1; A8520, item PH/DAW/5, pts 1 and 2 (NAA); Dawbarn papers (Univ of Adelaide Archives); private information.

ROGER CROSS

DE BERG, HAZEL ESTELLE (1913-1984), oral history pioneer, was born on 21 March 1913 at Deniliquin, New South Wales, third child of George Robert Holland, Methodist clergyman, and his wife Ann, née McIntosh, both born in New South Wales. Hazel's early childhood was spent in a succession of country parsonages. In 1928 the family moved from Kempsey to Sydney, where she was to live for the rest of her life. She attended the Methodist Ladies' College, Burwood, gaining the Leaving certificate in 1932. Trained as a photographer at Paramount Studios, she later worked in the studio of Noel Rubie. She lived with her parents until her marriage to Woolf (William) de Berg (d.1981) on 15 May 1941 at the Great Synagogue, Sydney. Born in Lithuania, then part of the Russian Empire, de Berg was a company director and a leading figure in the Jewish community. Hazel converted to Judaism before the marriage. By the 1950s, as their three children grew older, she was able to take on new activities, completing a course in radiography, studying Indonesian and providing hospitality to Colombo Plan students.

Hazel de Berg first used a tape recorder in 1957, when she undertook voluntary work for the Blind Book Society. She persuaded Dame Mary Gilmore [q.v.9] to make some intro-ductory comments about her book *Old Days, Old Ways* (1934) and this recording, lasting 1 minute, 26 seconds, marked the beginning of de Berg's extraordinary career as a recorder of life histories. In the next three years, encouraged by the writers Douglas Stewart [q.v.] and John Thompson [q.v.16], she recorded about seventy poets, as well as novelists and playwrights. In 1960 she turned to artists and, with advice from Hal Missingham and Daniel Thomas, eventually recorded about 250 painters and sculptors.

Although de Berg occasionally spoke of retiring, her recordings gradually became longer and the subject range more diverse. Armed with her tape recorder, she travelled to every State and also to Britain and the United States of America, sometimes making two or three recordings in a day. Writers and artists formed the largest groups, but she also recorded composers, actors, theatre and film directors, architects and scientists, as well as smaller groups of politicians, public servants, journalists and churchmen. Most of her subjects were prominent or rising figures in their fields, but in her later years she also became interested in local history and carried out interviewing projects in Tamworth, Cowra and Young, New South Wales. Over a period of twenty-seven years she recorded 1290 individuals.

The originality of the enterprise attracted attention and de Berg's work was praised and publicised by many participants. In 1968 she was appointed MBE. She began donating the tapes to the National Library of Australia in 1960 and the library funded the transcriptions and from 1972 paid her an annual grant. By the 1970s she was recognised as the pioneer of oral history in Australia, yet it was not a term that she favoured. She regarded herself not as an interviewer, but as a recorder of the voices, recollections and ideas of Australians of diverse ages, backgrounds and talents. She brought to this work great energy, enthusiasm, charm and perseverance, often managing to record individuals who were notoriously reticent or reclusive. Her practice of excluding her own voice from the tapes has been criticised, while the brevity of the earlier recordings limits their value. Taken as a whole, however, the de Berg tapes provide a unique record of the voices and memories of hundreds of Australians born between 1865 and 1956.

Hazel de Berg died suddenly of myocardial infarction on 3 February 1984 at her Bellevue Hill home and was cremated. She was survived by her two daughters and son. Her collection of recordings forms the basis of the National Library's oral history collection.

The Hazel de Berg Recordings from the Oral History Collection of the National Library of Australia

(1989); *Oral Hist Assn of Aust Jnl*, no 18, 1996, p 29; *SMH*, 2 Jan 1968, p 6, 14 June 1972, p 12, 17 Feb 1984, p 12; *Australian*, 24 July 1971, p 9; H. de Berg papers (NLA); private information.

GRAEME POWELL

DEEGAN, ALLEN THOMAS (1924-1987), businessman, was born on 29 January 1924 at Drummoyne, Sydney, sixth child of John Michael Deegan, insurance agent, and his wife Elsie Grace, née Adam, both born in New South Wales. Educated at Eastwood and Stanmore Commercial schools, Allen joined Standard Telephones & Cables Pty Ltd in 1939. The 5 ft 4 ins (163 cm), neat and respectful costing clerk, with 'nose somewhat flattened', enlisted in the Royal Australian Air Force on 11 May 1942. He trained as an electrician (later electrical fitter) and served in Australia, New Britain and Borneo, before being discharged as a leading aircraftman in May 1946. Returning to his job at STC, he married Violet May Phillips, a machinist, on 14 December 1946 at the Presbyterian Church, Ryde.

Noted for his business acumen and ability to break complex problems down to a simple set of questions, Deegan rose steadily through STC to become managing director in 1970. Fiercely Australian, he refused to allow his wife to buy other than Australian products, and believed passionately that Australia should develop a strong manufacturing base and should export aggressively. He could be pugnacious in business dealings and lobbying politicians. Although not an engineer, he was alert to the need for research and development and for a highly skilled workforce. His ability to select the right people was a particular strength. He walked the factory floor regularly. Competition in the telecommunications industry was keen, but the STC prospered under Deegan's forceful leadership. The company produced electronic switchboards, the Commander telephone system for small businesses, wiring harness for the first AUSSAT satellite, and repeaters used in the Australia-New Zealand-Canada coaxial submarine cable project.

An 'elder statesman' in the industry, Deegan was an active member of the Australian Telecommunications Development Association from 1963. Chairman (1980-81) of the Australian Electronics Industry Council, he was also president (1981-84) of the Australian Electronics Industry Association. In the 1970s and 1980s he served on the Metal Trades Industry Association of Australia, the Australia-New Zealand Businessmen's Council Ltd, and the Chamber of Manufactures of New South Wales. He held directorships in Nationwide Food Service Pty Ltd, Bly's Indus-tries Pty Ltd and some companies in the telecommunications industry.

Deegan also had several government advisory roles. A member of the Manufacturing Industries Advisory Council (1972-77), he was deputy-convenor of the Multilateral Trade Negotiations Industries Consultative Group (1975-79). He was on the Electronics Industry (1976-81) and the Electrical and Electronics Industries (1981-83) advisory councils. In 1983 he received the Australian World Communications Year award. Next year he retired as managing director of the STC and was appointed AM. He chaired the company from 1977 until his death.

Tennis, golf and surfing were his recreations, but he had little time to indulge in them. Occasional retreats to the family house at Avoca Beach were prized, and the STC donated several boats, one of which bore Deegan's name, to the Avoca Beach Surf Life Saving Club. Survived by his wife, their daughter and two sons, he died of cardiomyopathy on 17 January 1987 at Darlinghurst and was cremated.

J. Murray, *Calling the World* (1995); *Bulletin*, 25 Oct 1983, p 123; *Austn Financial Review*, 19 Jan 1987, p 17; *SMH*, 19 Jan 1987, p 5; A9301, item 64469 (NAA); private information.   IAN CARNELL

DELANDRO, FRANCIS PHILIP (1889-1982), motorcar retailer, was born on 6 October 1889 at Millers Point, Sydney, son of an Italian immigrant Francisco D'Landro, labourer, and his English-born wife Ellen, née Smith. Frank later modified his name to Delandro. After spending his early childhood near Brooklyn at the mouth of the Hawkesbury River, where his father farmed oysters, he completed his education at Fort Street Superior Public School. In May 1900 he witnessed the unloading of the first motorcar (a De Dion Bouton) in Sydney. Fascinated, he spent much of his spare time washing and repairing early imports. In 1904 the Columbia Cycle & Motor Agency hired him as an apprentice motor mechanic. Advancement came quickly in the fledgling motor trade. Before he was 20, he was manager of Empson's motor works.

In 1912, with £28 capital, Delandro opened his own garage in North Sydney, a propitious location. He proved an astute businessman, establishing another branch at Manly. The modern service station that he built in 1938, near the northern end of Sydney Harbour Bridge, was reputed to have the greatest volume of passing traffic of any in Australia. He was best known as a motor retailer, however; in 1921 he established his own motor company, which included the first suburban

Ford dealership in Australia. The company was later registered as Frank Delandro Motor Services Pty Ltd and he became managing director.

Involved in many activities related to the motor industry, Delandro was chairman (1930-32) of a State government apprenticeship committee and a long-term chairman of the North Sydney Technical Education District Committee. He was president of the Motor Traders' Association of New South Wales in 1931 and 1955-57. During his second term, he fought unsuccessfully to limit the growth of 'single-brand' service stations. For some years he served on the council of management of the Road Safety Council of New South Wales; he chaired its first congress in 1959. He helped to found, and was an executive member of, the Australian Automobile Chamber of Commerce.

Delandro had married Nina Enid Wilson on 2 March 1916 at St Stephen's Church of England, Newtown. Financial security enabled him to buy a large home overlooking Middle Harbour, and later one at Roseville. He enjoyed racing both motorcycles and cars. Active in community and civic affairs, in 1930 he joined the Rotary Club of North Sydney (president 1935; district governor 1952-53). In 1932-41 he was an alderman of the North Sydney Municipal Council. During World War II he served in the Volunteer Defence Corps, and, using his own motor cruiser, took part in organised patrols of Sydney Harbour. He was appointed MBE in 1959.

After fifty years as a dealer, Delandro retired in 1971. In retirement he fished and continued to work for Rotary. He died on 28 August 1982 at Chatswood and was buried in Northern Suburbs cemetery. Predeceased by his wife and a daughter, he was survived by another daughter and three sons.

J. Maitland (comp), *The Presidents 1910-1982* (1983); *M.T.A. Official Jnl*, Jan 1955, p 7, Mar 1962, p 9; *SMH*, 29 Apr 1971, p 16, 3 Sept 1982, p 8; *Sun-Herald* (Sydney), 2 May 1971, p 29; A463, item 1958/2095 (NAA).   JOHN KNOTT

DEL PIANO, JAMES ANDREW (1916-1981), businessman and community leader, was born on 17 November 1916 at Kalgoorlie, Western Australia, younger child of Italian-born parents Giovanni ('Jack') del Piano, labourer, and his wife Maria, née Fazzina. He was named Giacomo, but was later known as James Andrew. Educated at primary schools at Widgiemooltha and Kalgoorlie, Jim completed his secondary education in Italy after his family moved to Castello dell'Acqua, Valtellina, in 1930. He worked as a clerk in Italy before returning to Australia with his widowed mother in 1935. Next year he enrolled in engineering at the University of Western Australia. Failing to complete his course, in 1940 he joined the works and services branch of the Commonwealth Department of Interior as an engineering draftsman. On 27 March 1942 he was interned, on equivocal evidence, because of alleged fascist sympathies; after spending time in Fremantle Prison, in Parkeston (Kalgoorlie) and Harvey camps, and at Loveday, South Australia, he was released on 6 January 1944.

Back in Perth, in 1946 del Piano established an immigration and shipping agency, representing Lloyd Triestino, and a real-estate business. His interests were to diversify in the 1960s into timber-milling and finance. On 11 September 1948 at St Brigid's Catholic Church, West Perth, he married Armida Nizzola, an Italian-born schoolteacher. Committed to aiding and supporting Italian migrants, he was president (1947-65) of the Western Australian Italian Club, formerly La Casa D'Italia. During his tenure he saw the membership increase from just fifty to more than three thousand. He served on the executive of several other organisations, notably as president of the Azzurri Soccer Club (1950-52, 1956-57) and of the Italian Australian Businessmen's Association (1967-69), and as vice-president (1969-72) of the Italian Chamber of Commerce and Industry. He also helped to establish a kindergarten at North Perth and an aged-care centre and hospital for Italian migrants in Wanneroo Shire. Although he was assertively Australian, he remained proud of his Italian heritage and advocated policies of integration rather than assimilation. He was awarded the Italian Star of Solidarity, second class (1955), and appointed officer (1969) and commander (1978) of the Order of Merit of the Italian Republic.

As well as his work for Italian migrants, del Piano had a remarkable record of service to the community at large. Made a justice of the peace in 1963, he sat (1967-77) on the Perth City Council and was deputy-mayor in 1974-75. He was inaugural deputy-chairman (1970-75) and chairman (1975-81) of the Keep Australia Beautiful Council (Western Australia); he was also vice-chairman (1975-77) of the organisation's national body. In 1979 he was appointed OBE. Survived by his wife and their son, he died of cancer on 13 July 1981 at Subiaco and was buried in Karrakatta cemetery.

Keep Aust Beautiful Council (WA), *Annual Report*, 1981-82, p 3; *Daily News* (Perth), 8 Aug 1967, p 12; *West Australian*, 15 July 1981, p 13; WA Italian Club, *Bulletin*, Sept 1981, p 38; A367, item C79928, A463, item 1964/2410, MP1103/1, item W15213, A1838, item 1535/18/46 (NAA); private information.   MATHEW TRINCA

DERHAM, SIR DAVID PLUMLEY (1920-1985), lawyer and vice-chancellor, was born on 13 May 1920 at Armadale, Melbourne, second son of Victorian-born parents Alfred Plumley Derham [q.v.13], medical practitioner, and his wife Frances Alexandra Mabel Letitia [q.v.], née Anderson. Enid Derham [q.v.8] was his aunt. After attending Trinity Grammar School and Scotch College, David entered the University of Melbourne (BA Hons, 1941) in 1938 and resided at Ormond [q.v.5] College. He joined the Melbourne University Regiment on 1 November 1940. Rejected by the Royal Australian Air Force because of asthma, he enlisted in the Australian Imperial Force on 28 July 1941 and served as a trooper in an armoured regiment before being commissioned as a lieutenant in April 1942. From 1943 he performed air liaison and support duties at headquarters in New Guinea, the Netherlands East Indies and Borneo, and for brief periods with American forces in the Solomon Islands and the Philippines. He was appointed MBE (1947) for this work. A temporary major from December 1944, he transferred to the Reserve of Officers on 27 November 1945.

At St John's Church of England, East Malvern, on 22 January 1944, Derham had married Rosemary Joan Brudenell, daughter of General Sir Brudenell White [q.v.12]. Now determined to be a lawyer, he returned to the university in 1946 under the Commonwealth Reconstruction Training Scheme, and graduated LL B (1947) and LL M (1948) with first-class honours, the Supreme Court prize, and the E. J. B. Nunn scholarship. Articled to his uncle F. P. Derham [q.v.13], he was admitted to practice as a barrister and solicitor on 3 November 1948; he signed the Bar roll on 5 August 1949. That year, already a tutor in law at Queen's College, he became an independent lecturer in constitutional law in the university. He gained a reputation as an outstanding teacher.

In 1951 Derham succeeded (Sir) George Paton [q.v.] as professor of jurisprudence, lecturing also in constitutional law. He spent six months as a visiting fellow at Wadham College, Oxford, in 1953. Although impressed by the high standards achieved in British professional practice and postgraduate research, he detected little interest in studying the aims and methods of legal education. In the United States of America as a Carnegie travelling fellow (1953-54), he found at Harvard University 'the best law school in the common law world', and admired (not uncritically) many others for their vigour, standards and experimentation. Their libraries made the Melbourne law school's seem 'hopelessly inadequate'. He maintained contacts made during this trip, promoting staff and postgraduate exchanges and visits and returning himself in 1961 (as senior research fellow and visiting lecturer, University of Chicago, and visiting professor, Northwestern University). Working with Professor (Sir) Zelman Cowen, Derham adapted the US case method and moot court for Melbourne, despite limitations imposed by under-funding and increasing student numbers.

The numerous bodies in which Derham was an active participant included the Victorian Council of Legal Education (1951-68), Victorian Chief Justice's Law Reform Committee (1951-68), Medico-Legal Society (1967-82; president 1963-64), Royal Melbourne Hospital board of management (1958-83), and Overseas Service Bureau (chairman, 1964-81). He occasionally gave legal advice within the university, was a member of its council (1961-63) and vice-chairman of the professorial board (1962-63). He had also retained a right of private practice. He regularly gave advice as a barrister and sometimes appeared in court. He was briefed as counsel (1962) in the Supreme Court of Victoria action to stay the execution of the convicted murderer Robert Peter Tait on grounds of insanity. Derham also served as constitutional law consultant to the Indian Law Institute (1958-59), and in 1960 investigated the administration of justice in the Territory of Papua and New Guinea for the minister for territories, (Sir) Paul Hasluck.

Meanwhile Derham was learning about the funding and functioning of Australian universities through membership of Commonwealth committees of inquiry into teaching costs in hospitals (1961-65), academic salaries (1964), and the future of tertiary education (the Martin Committee, which he joined in 1962 and for which he drafted the section of its report dealing with legal education). These committees provided guidance to the Australian Universities Commission, of which he was a member (1965-68).

In 1960 Derham wrote of the need for a second law school in Victoria and in 1964 became foundation dean and Sir Owen Dixon [q.v.14] professor of law at Monash University. To mitigate the disadvantages of Monash's distance from the facilities and professional contacts of the city, he sought full-time academic staff, a tutorial system, and the integration of practitioners into teaching and examining, and service on the faculty board. His initiatives achieved a staff/student ratio 'more than twice as good' as Melbourne's. Non-legal courses to 'open more windows to the legal mind' were included in a three-year bachelor's degree in jurisprudence, which was followed by a two-year bachelor's degree in laws leading to admission to practice. Provision was made for specialisation, honours and postgraduate research, and combination with other disciplines was encouraged. Derham planned the law school building to accommodate his preferred maximum number of staff and students, with a spacious and well-organised library as its heart. He enlisted Emeritus Professor Frank Beasley [q.v.13] to assist in developing the collection.

Derham edited the third (1964) and (with Paton) fourth (1972) editions of G. W. Paton's *A Textbook of Jurisprudence* and was joint author with F. K. Maher and P. L. (Louis) Waller of *An Introduction to Law* and *Cases and Materials on Legal Processes* (1966). He contributed chapters to books and articles to Australian and overseas journals on law and legal education. In 1967 he was elected a member of the Social Science Research Council of Australia.

With 'great qualms', Derham admitted, he accepted the invitation to succeed Paton as vice-chancellor of the University of Melbourne, taking up the post in March 1968. He knew of the administrative and financial problems besetting his old university, and of the dissatisfaction with which the AUC (through which the university had to negotiate for much of its funding) regarded its deficiencies. Their extent, and in particular that of the budget deficit, nevertheless shocked him on his arrival. Assuming these new responsibilities 'the elegant professor' (as a *Herald* journalist described him) determined to restore confidence in the university's management, while also seeking additional funds, personally surveying departmental practices and needs, and pressing the case for cuts in expenditures wherever possible. For the longer term, with the support of senior colleagues, he decentralised aspects of academic administration and financial responsibility while also improving centralised recording, accounting and management. A personal priority was the adoption of a master plan to bring order and beauty to the campus. Yet the pressures of budget reductions were rarely stayed, and he spoke forcefully against universities' increasing uncertainty and vulnerability to 'intervention', especially after 1974, when they became dependent on Commonwealth funding.

Derham freed himself as much as possible from direct management to concentrate on such matters with his characteristic mastery of detail, but constraints on delegation until late in his term ensured long evenings of paper work. Student activism added to his concerns. He saw this unrest as largely derivative, distinguishing the 'planned attack' from 'youthful enthusiasm'. Though prepared to discuss issues affecting students, Derham was uncomfortable with large confrontational groups and found little common ground with many individual radicals. He believed that universities must retain intellectual freedom and some autonomy in order to serve society by pursuing and disseminating knowledge and maintaining high academic standards. Fortified by his own courage, foresight, perception of the

university's purpose, knowledge of the law and support of like-minded colleagues, Derham resisted both violent interference in the university's affairs and the delegation of its defence to outside bodies. He preferred to invoke internal disciplinary procedures while not hesitating to call the police to the campus when he judged it necessary. His manner of dealing with these and other matters touching the university's welfare, sometimes termed 'legalistic', was not supported by all.

On becoming vice-chancellor Derham had relinquished most outside activities. University-related committees, including the Melbourne Theatre Company (chairman 1972-82), the board of management of the Walter and Eliza Hall [qq.v.9] Institute of Medical Research (1968-82), and the Australian Vice-Chancellors Committee (deputy chairman 1972-74; chairman 1975-76), replaced them. Increasingly, however, the pressures of office caused him to withdraw from much informal contact in the university. He could appear remote, to the regret of those who knew him not only as a hard-working, strong and effective executive, but as a charming and witty companion, a wise counsellor and a kindly man.

Having long experienced ill health, Derham retired in May 1982, receiving an honorary LL D from the University of Melbourne and the T. H. B. Symons award from the Association of Commonwealth Universities. In 1968 he had been appointed CMG and, in 1977, KBE. Monash had earlier recognised his achievements with an honorary LL D and by naming its law school after him. Survived by his wife and their two daughters and son, Sir David died of a chronic obstructive airways condition on 1 September 1985 at home in Toorak, and was buried in Templestowe cemetery. The University of Melbourne holds his portrait by Sir William Dargie. His last article, published posthumously, on the dismissal of the Whitlam government, won the 1986 Rogers Legal Writing Award.

J. Poynter and C. Rasmussen, *A Place Apart* (1996); *Law Inst Jnl*, vol 56, no 12, 1982, p 1024, vol 57, no 1, 1983, p 79, vol 59, no 11, 1985, p 1166; *Monash Univ Law Review*, vol 12, no 1, 1986, p 1; *University Gazette*, 30 June 1954; *Australian*, 25 Nov 1966, p 13, 18 Sept 1985, p 13; *Age*, 18 June 1975, p 12; *Herald* (Melbourne), 29 July 1982, p 4; D. Beswick, interviews with D. Derham (1982), and Derham papers, and Univ Council Minute Books and official papers (Univ of Melb Archives); L. Waller papers and official files (Monash Univ Archives).   CECILY CLOSE

DERHAM, FRANCES ALEXANDRA MABEL LETITIA (1894-1987), artist and art educator, was born on 15 November 1894, at Malvern, Melbourne, daughter of Irish-born parents Joshua Thomas Noble Anderton, engineer, and his wife Ellen Mary, née White-Spunner. Her father's work often took the family to remote locations, limiting Frankie's access to formal schooling. Educated by governesses, she first attended art classes when the Andersons moved to Dunedin, New Zealand, in 1902, and continued them while living in Belfast, Ireland, after 1905. Three years later the family settled at Narbethong, near Healesville, Victoria. Frankie completed her Merit certificate at the local school and assisted her father with drafting. Impressed by her ability, he encouraged her to further study: in 1911 she enrolled in the National Gallery schools, Melbourne, also taking courses at the Eastern Suburbs (Swinburne) Technical College, where she qualified as a teacher and taught briefly. On 10 July 1917 at St Mary's Church of England, Caulfield, she married Alfred Plumley Derham [q.v.13], a medical student.

People who influenced Frankie Derham's art included Walter Burley and Marion Mahony Griffin [qq.v.9], for whom her father was consulting engineer, and Mary Cecil Allen and George Bell [qq.v.7], with whom she studied. During the 1920s while raising four sons—among them (Sir) David [q.v.]—she became an active member of the Arts and Crafts Society of Victoria (vice-president, 1928-31). While lecturing in art (1928-64) at the Melbourne Kindergarten Training College, Derham also joined the Nursery School Committee in 1931 and later taught at the Associated Teacher Training Institution (1949-61). Her commitment to 'child art' developed after 1935 when she accepted an invitation from Margaret Lyttle [q.v.15] to teach at Preshil school.

Increasingly associated with 'progressive' education, Derham was an energetic advocate for the value and significance of art in children's lives. After 1937 she worked with Christine Heinig [q v 14] towards establishing the Lady Gowrie [q.v.9] child centres, advising on their design and the materials to assist in developing 'visual thinking'. Following correspondence with the anthropologist C. P. Mountford and the artist Rex Battarbee [qq.v.15,13], in 1938 she visited Hermannsburg mission in the Northern Territory (and later Aurukun, Queensland) to study the art of Aboriginal children. Her awareness of Indigenous culture complemented modernist themes developing in her own art. Derham frequently exhibited a rapidly growing collection of children's art, and became a foundation member (1956) and president (1959-61) of the Art Teachers Association of Victoria, Australian delegate (1960, 1963) to congresses of the International Society for Education Through Art, and visiting lecturer (1963) at Columbia University, New York. Her practical

guide *Art for the Child under Seven* (1961) was widely used by parents and teachers through seven editions to 2003.

As a 'courageous and indefatigable' pioneer of creative art education (according to Bernard Smith), Derham remained a prominent speaker for the cause into her retirement. For her community service, particularly in establishing an emergency housekeeping service during World War II, she was appointed MBE (1950). She was a foundation (1968) and life (1984) member of the Advisory Council for Children with Impaired Hearing. In 1976 her collection of nearly ten thousand children's drawings and paintings was acquired by the Australian National Gallery. Survived by two sons, Frances Derham died on 5 November 1987 at Kew and was buried in Boroondara cemetery. Exhibitions of her art work were held at the Jim Alexander gallery, East Malvern (1986), and the Lyceum Club (1970, 1982, 2003). The National Gallery of Australia, Canberra, the National Gallery of Victoria and the Ballarat Fine Arts Gallery hold samples of her prints.

J. H. L. Cumpston and C. M. Heinig, *Pre-school Centres in Australia* (1945); B. Smith (ed), *Education through Art in Australia* (1958); M. White and C. Stevenson, *Drawing on the Art of Children* (1997); *Childhoods Past* (1999); P. Alexander (ed), *Frances Derham in Retrospect* (2003); *Austn Jnl of Early Childhood*, vol 18, no 1, 1993, p 3; Arts and Crafts Soc of Vic, *Recorder*, June 1929, p 8; S. Lunney, interview with F. Derham (ts, 1975, NLA); B. Blackman, interview with F. Derham (ts, 1984, NLA); F. Derham papers (Univ of Melbourne Archives).

MARGARET H. WHITE

DEXTER, NANCY NUGENT (1923-1983), journalist, was born on 16 February 1923 at Coburg, Melbourne, elder child of John (Jack) Hanks, iron-moulder, and his wife Hilda Evelyn, née Barratt. During the Depression Jack resettled the family at Wagga Wagga, New South Wales, where he built a successful foundry business. An energetic, cantankerous man, he gained prominence in 1948 when he closed the foundry for several months after the communist-influenced Federated Ironworkers' Association of Australia signed up his workforce.

Nancy was educated at Wagga Wagga High School until the age of 15, and then—encouraged by her strong-willed mother to vocational study—at the local commercial college. Attracted to journalism, she obtained her first job in newspapers in 1941 as a copy-typist for the Wagga Wagga *Daily Advertiser*, and then moved to Sydney to monitor radio news for the *Daily Telegraph*. In 1946 she became a copy-typist at the Melbourne *Herald*, and in 1950 a cadet on its social pages, but she was retrenched amid economic uncertainty in 1951.

On 17 September 1951 at St Andrew's Presbyterian Church, Box Hill, Melbourne, Nancy married Harry Norman Dexter (d.1979), a locally based sports and racing correspondent for the Sydney *Sun*. Harry was twenty-two years her senior and from a well-known family of racing writers. The couple worked for the same public relations firm until, in 1960, Nancy Dexter returned to the *Herald* women's section as a journalist. By 1964 she had inherited responsibility for a banal column of shopping and social news, which she began spiking with substantial commentary on consumer and women's issues: articles on 'working wives escaping from boredom' followed notes on seaweed diets and the 'frazzle' of Christmas shopping.

Dexter resigned from the *Herald* in 1966, frustrated, she said later, by its 'stifling' editorial atmosphere. Graham Perkin [q.v.15] then offered her work with the *Age*, and from 1967 her column 'Nancy Dexter Takes Note' appeared in Accent, the women's section. A few years before Women's Liberation emerged, she discussed such issues as the fight for equal pay, domestic violence and abortion-law reform. In 1968, for example, she encouraged women who had terminated pregnancies to tell their stories, and received many responses. She was to clash repeatedly with the Right To Life Association, Victoria.

As the women's movement gained momentum in the 1970s, Dexter documented its agendas and debates with 'guts and substance' (so recalled Beatrice Faust, a founder of the Women's Electoral Lobby) while also normalising discussion of controversial subjects: 'a drip wearing away a stone' was Dexter's favoured metaphor. Her middle-aged, middle-class appearance and down-to-earth demeanour were at odds with popular stereotypes of second-wave feminism, and part of her appeal. Always an advocate of equal opportunity, she offered a perceptive, sometimes prescient, occasionally caustic analysis of women's issues that was shaped by her own experiences, including her years as a working mother relishing a measure of financial independence. As editor of Accent (1972-79), she maintained a balance between its traditional fare and hard coverage of women's issues. A resourceful cook, she also happily turned her hand to cookery writing for Accent in addition to her column.

In 1979 Dexter became the *Age*'s travel editor, embracing this task with typical energy. She died suddenly on 21 April 1983 while on assignment at Jaipur, India. Her two sons survived her. The newspaper established a prize in her name at Royal Melbourne Institute of Technology's school of journalism.

J. Larkins and B. Howard, *A Tribute to Australian Women* (1980); S. Morris, *Wagga Wagga* (1999); *Lip* (Melbourne), 1980, p 24; *Age* (Melbourne), 20 May 1987, p 18, 29 May 1987, Accent, p 1; R. Smallwood, Guts and Substance (BA Hons thesis, RMIT, 1985); E. Owen, taped interview with N. Dexter (SLV); N. Dexter papers (Univ of Melbourne Archives); private information.   SYBIL NOLAN

DIAMOND, RICHARD FRANK (1906-1989), trade union official, dramatist and journalist, was born on 27 July 1906 at Walthamstow, Essex, England, son of Simeon Barnett Diamond, farrier, and his wife Annie Thirza Caroline, née Smiley. In 1914 the family migrated to Victoria, settling in South Melbourne. After a basic formal education, Dick worked as a journalist on minor magazines, developing interests in film, theatre and left-wing politics. On 14 July 1934 he married Lilian Frances Rembelinker, a clerk, in a civil ceremony in Melbourne. They both joined the Communist Party of Australia and became active in the Youth Theatre of Action, an agitprop group that performed sketches at street meetings and factory gates. In 1936 they graduated to the Workers' Theatre Group (New Theatre Club after 1937), which staged Diamond's first satirical play, *Soak the Rich* (1941). He also wrote for the *Communist Review* on the role of theatre in 'dramatising the worker's problems'.

From 1945 to 1955 Diamond was Victorian State secretary of the Actors' and Announcers' Equity Association of Australia. John White later remembered his 'casual but aware approach' as an effective union advocate, and his 'roguish' chuckle. In 1948 moderates in the Victorian division challenged the powerful, militant committee, making concerted attempts to exclude communists from office, and in 1949 the royal commission into the Communist Party of Australia investigated claims that Diamond had used his position to stack meetings. These allegations were deemed not proven, although Diamond, who denied current membership of the party, was judged 'very well disposed' towards it.

Diamond's political pantomime, *Jack the Giant Killer*, produced by the NTC in 1947, was followed in March 1953 by his most successful play, the folk musical *Reedy River*. Based on the shearers' strike of 1891, it incorporated traditional bush ballads. The Sydney version, opening in December and running for eight months, introduced the Bushwackers' Band, including lagerphone and bush bass. In the *ABC Weekly* Geoffrey Thomas praised it for being as 'unmistakably Australian as a bluegum'. A mainstay of New Theatre repertoire across Australia, *Reedy River* played to an estimated 450 000 people over the next four years and helped to revitalise Australian folk music. It has been frequently revived—an achievement not matched by his second musical, *Under the Coolibah Tree*, first produced in Brisbane in 1955.

In 1956 Diamond travelled to Vietnam. He lived in Hanoi and edited the English short-wave broadcast service, taught English and wrote the pro-Viet Minh novel *The Walls Are Down* (1958). Joined by Lilian in 1957, he then moved to China before returning to Australia in 1962, settling in Sydney and taking what work he could find in public relations and editing. He left the Communist Party about 1963. A photograph of Diamond reading the militant play *Waiting for Lefty* from the back of a truck in 1939 shows him to have been of medium height with short, dark hair, his almost non-descript appearance belying a life lived through drama and politics. Predeceased by his wife (d.1988), and childless, he died on 9 February 1989 at Balgowlah and was cremated.

Notes on the History of New Theatre Australia (1959); J. White, *Alan Marshall and the Victorian Writers' League* (1987); *Australian*, 25 Oct 1969, p 44; G. Lobl, taped interview with R. Diamond (1989, NLA); A. O'Brien, The Road Not Taken (PhD thesis, Monash Univ, 1989); New Theatre Melbourne Archives (Performing Arts Museum, Victorian Arts Centre); 'Mr Justice Lowe's Findings on Royal Commission into the Communist Party in Victoria, 1949', Actors' Equity of Aust (Vic), Acc 84/44, box 30, folder 52/2, Univ of Melbourne Archives; private information.					ANGELA O'BRIEN

DICKSON, ELLEN (1895-1984), community worker, was born on 26 July 1895 at St John Timberhill, Norwich, Norfolk, England, daughter of Robert Edward Hare, upholsterer-journeyman, and his wife Margaret, née Ryan. While working as a Red Cross nurse at the Norfolk War Hospital, Norwich, she fell in love with a patient, Roy Sinclair Dickson, a Tasmanian gunner with the Australian Imperial Force. On 19 October 1918 they married in the parish church at Cholderton, Wiltshire. Roy returned to Tasmania and Ellen soon followed. They settled on the Dickson family farm, Glen Ayr, near Richmond, and had three children.

Forced to sell the farm in the early stages of the Depression, the Dicksons moved in 1930 to Lindisfarne, on Hobart's eastern shore, and started a small clothing business. Roy produced machine-knitted fabrics that Ellen made into fashionable garments. She also managed a shop that stocked her clothes in a Hobart arcade. Roy, who had never fully regained his health since being gassed during the war, died in 1938; Ellen ran the business until 1954.

In 1958 Mrs Dickson founded the Riverside Arts Club; the inaugural committee appointed her life patroness. The group's meeting-place was an old barn in her garden at Lindisfarne. With the help of donations, hard work and ingenuity, members refurbished in a rustic manner what came to be called the Barn, and began popular social and cultural activities. Beginning with an alfresco production of *Alice in Wonderland* (1959), directed by Dickson, who also designed and made the costumes, the club gradually focused on drama. It became one of greater Hobart's most respected amateur theatre groups, staging forty-six full-length plays in 1959-92, as well as numerous variety and charity performances. Dickson loved acting, directing, designing sets, and creating spectacular costumes out of remnants from bargain stores. Her infectious enthusiasm inspired many people, but some avoided her lest they be inveigled into one of her projects against their will. She was particularly adept at inducing reluctant men to accept roles in her productions.

Dickson arranged for the Adult Education Board of Tasmania to conduct classes in a variety of arts-related subjects in the Barn from 1958 until the building was demolished in 1971. She was active in the Australian Red Cross Society, first at Richmond, then at Lindisfarne, where she staged concerts and propagated and sold hundreds of plants for its funds. A supporter of the 'Little Shop', which raised money for St Aidan's Church of England, Lindisfarne, she was a stalwart of local branches of the Penguin Club of Australia and the Royal Overseas League, and of the committee of the Queen Victoria Home for the Aged.

Small and slightly built, Dickson was fair, charming and vivacious, with an innate elegance. She related easily to all types of people but concealed her age, even from her family. Late in life she discovered a talent for painting in oils and also produced hundreds of 'character' rag dolls with expressive hand-painted faces. Survived by her daughter and two sons, she died on 10 June 1984 in her home at Lindisfarne and was cremated.

S. Spargo, *Recollections of the Riverside Arts Club* (1997); *Mercury* (Hobart), 16 Dec 1981, p 32, 28 May 1982, p 2, 12 June 1984, p 16; private information and personal knowledge.					SHEILA SPARGO

DIMMICK, SAMUEL GUY McLAREN (1922-1984), public servant and college warden, was born on 15 January 1922 at Canterbury, Melbourne, eldest of three sons of Victorian-born William (Roy) Dimmick, estate agent, and his wife Myrtle Elvira, née Monie, who came from New South Wales. After attending Carey Baptist Grammar School, Sam worked as a clerk with the Melbourne and

Metropolitan Board of Works. He served part time (1940-41) in the Militia then, having enlisted in the Royal Australian Naval Reserve on 27 June 1941, saw active service (1943-45) in the Pacific as a leading supply assistant in HMAS *Shropshire*. After demobilisation in 1946, he enrolled at the University of Melbourne (Dip.Soc.Stud., 1951; BA, B.Com., 1953).

At university Dimmick was a towering figure on the Students' Representative Council (secretary 1950-51; president 1951-52) and a forceful advocate for new welfare and commercial services. As SRC housing officer he became particularly aware of the needs of the increasing numbers of Asian students. With fellow students Abinash Jerath and Rajaratnam Sundarason, and the backing of the Rotary Club of Melbourne, he campaigned successfully to establish the first International House at an Australian university.

After graduation, Dimmick joined the Commonwealth Office of Education—in which he arranged the training of overseas students—before transferring to the Department of External Affairs in 1954. He was posted as cultural attaché (1956-59) to Jakarta, where his duties included liaison with universities and Colombo Plan matters. In March 1960 he was appointed second warden of IH. He proceeded to raise its academic standing, attract distinguished Australian and overseas visitors, and secure funds for new building. He also chaired (1961-66) the Australian committee of World University Service.

In July 1970 Dimmick resigned, protesting at a rise in student fees but also frustrated in his ambitions for further expansion. He never visited IH again. By December he had been appointed the foundation chairman of the Land Conservation Council, a small body charged with devising a system for the planning and use of all public land in Victoria. His appointment as an outsider, with no background in conservation, initially concerned others on the council. Yet his commitment soon won approval, as did his skills in harnessing external resources, managing an excellent research staff and gaining ministerial support to consolidate the council's independence and circumvent vested interests. The establishment of Victoria's extensive system of conservation reserves owed much to his efforts.

Socially well connected, Dimmick used his networks effectively. He enjoyed opera and ballet, and was a generous and entertaining host. Tall and heavily built, with a powerful voice, he was a hard taskmaster at the LCC and a stickler for hierarchy and discipline at IH. He never married but adopted Boniat Slamet in Jakarta, sponsoring his move to Australia in 1962. Boniat, with his wife and their two children, became his family.

Dimmick died of myocardial infarction on 9 July 1984 at home at Toorak and was cremated. His contribution to IH is commemorated by the Dimmick dining hall, in which hangs his portrait by June Mendoza, and the Dimmick flats, opened in 1998.

L. Robin, *Defending the Little Desert* (1998); L. R. Humphreys, *Wadham: Scientist for Land and People* (2000) and *Of Many Nations* (2004); *Farrago*, 29 July 1952, p 6, 28 July 1953, p 11; *Satadal*, 1959, p 25, 1984, memorial issue; *Sun* (Melbourne), 11 Dec 1970, p 13; private information.

CHARLES A. COPPEL

DINTENFASS, LEOPOLD (1921-1990), industrial chemist and research biomedical rheologist, was born Lieb Ben Isser on 29 April 1921 at Tarnow, Poland, son of Jewish parents Isser Dintenfass, attorney, and his wife Anna, née Katzner. After his secondary education he wanted to study medicine but his family persuaded him to enrol in engineering first. Conscripted, he was sent for training near Poland's eastern border. He completed his studies in chemical engineering at the Lviv (formerly Lvov, Poland) Polytechnical Institute, Soviet Union (Ukraine), gaining a Dipl.Ing. (Chem.) in 1946. Having learned of the deaths of his family as a result of the German occupation, he left Poland in 1946 and, via a displaced persons' camp in Salzburg, Austria, reached Munich, Germany, later that year.

In Munich Dintenfass worked as a clerk and interpreter for the American Jewish Joint Distribution Committee and gave lectures on chemistry for a Jewish vocational school that helped jobless and homeless refugees. He hoped to go to America but, encountering Australian migration officials, made a snap decision to apply for Australia. Knowing no English, he arrived in Sydney on 19 February 1950. After a meeting with the technical manager of Imperial Chemical Industries of Australia & New Zealand Ltd, with whom Dintenfass could converse in German, he was appointed in 1950 to a research laboratory of the ICI subsidiary BALM Paints Pty Ltd at Concord, where he worked on the formation and flow of paint. He married Irene Kurzer, an interpreter typist, on 26 September 1954 at the Mizrachi Synagogue, Bondi, and was naturalised on 29 September 1955. While working for BALM, he studied at the University of Technology (University of New South Wales) (M.Sc., 1958). In 1956 he moved to Taubmans Industries Ltd, where he was paid a full salary to undertake research for a thesis on the radiorheology of surface coatings, which earned him a Ph.D. (1962) from UNSW.

Shortly after submitting his thesis he was asked by Bernard Bloch, an orthopaedic surgeon at Prince of Wales Hospital, Randwick, to undertake some studies on synovial fluid from normal and inflamed joints. Dintenfass later described this work as 'like going into a field to pick flowers that had been growing completely undisturbed'. Made an honorary associate of the department of medicine, University of Sydney, in 1962, he received grants from the National Heart Foundation (1963-69), the National Health and Medical Research Council (1969-75) and drug companies to support his research. His work centred on blood flow and its use in the diagnosis and prevention of disease. In 1967-75 he was an honorary senior research fellow at the Kanematsu Memorial Institute of Pathology, Sydney Hospital, and in 1976 he was appointed its director of haemorheology and biorheology. He relocated his laboratory to the Rachel Forster Hospital, Redfern, when the Kanematsu was dismembered in 1982, and retired four years later.

Dintenfass published approximately 280 research papers and six books, the most significant of which were *Blood Microrheology* (1971) and *Rheology of Blood in Diagnostic and Preventive Medicine* (1976). He was a persistent, if self-interested, and remarkably successful lobbyist of politicians, press reporters and commercial firms. His great strength, apart from what his University of Sydney colleague Professor C. R. Blackburn called his 'tenacity of purpose', was his skill in designing a variety of instruments, 'viscometers', for making his pioneering measurements. These were crucial to his success in having an Australian experiment (number MPS77/F113) with blood samples accepted in 1977 by the United States of America's National Aeronautical and Space Administration for use in their space shuttles of 1985 and 1988. He was an elected fellow of the Royal Australian Chemical Institute, the Royal Society for the Promotion of Health and the International College of Angiology. Serving as secretary (1958-63) and president (1963-65) of the State branch of the British Society of Rheology, he was also secretary (1969-75) for Australia and New Zealand of the International Society of Biorheology.

Although Dintenfass had a significant international reputation, and was a regular visitor to international conferences and laboratories, in Australia his standing was not so assured. Possibly he was seen as an interloper into medicine but his thick accent, together with a reluctance to make any intellectual concessions to his audiences, did not help him. Many people were sceptical about his concept of a 'viscoceptor' (a shear-detecting mechanism in arteries and veins that contributes to the stability of blood viscosity), while others believed that a poor understanding of 'biological variation' led to his erroneous view that it was not necessary to do more than a single experiment (or even to do them at all) in reaching his conclusions.

A small, bald and bespectacled man, 5 ft 6½ ins (169 cm) tall, Dintenfass reminded one colleague of the actor Peter Lorre. He was one of the earliest Jewish-European scientists to strengthen intellectual life in Australia. In addition, he was in the vanguard of the move of physicists, engineers and mathematicians into biomedical research. Survived by his wife, he died of myocardial infarction on 4 August 1990 at Darlinghurst and was buried in the Jewish section of Rookwood cemetery.

R. Brasch, *Australian Jews of Today* (1977); *SMH*, 16 Aug 1966, p 9, 11 Oct 1966, p 8, 15 Oct 1968, p 8, 18 June 1977, 'Weekend Mag', p 14, 6 June 1978, p 6, 30 Oct 1979, p 19, 30 Apr 1981, p 14, 31 Mar 1983, 'Life & Home', p 4, 16 Feb 1985, p 13, 4 Oct 1985, p 5, 8 Aug 1990, p 8; *Sun* (Sydney), 9 Dec 1977, p 19, 26 Nov 1981, p 5, 1 Dec 1981, p 4, 4 Dec 1984, p 4; *Austn Jewish News*, 10 Aug 1990, p 8, 17 Aug 1990, p 48; SP244/2, item N1950/2/2637, A446, item 1955/12289 (NAA); Dintenfass papers (Univ of Sydney Archives); private information.

JOHN CARMODY

DIPLOCK, LESLIE FRANK LOUIS (1899-1983), schoolteacher and politician, was born on 16 September 1899 in South Brisbane, eldest child of Louis Diplock, a Queensland-born house-painter, and his wife Louisa May, née Lucas, who came from New South Wales. Educated at Rockhampton State and Grammar schools, in 1914 Les became a pupil-teacher in the Department of Public Instruction, at Rockhampton. He taught (1918-24) at schools there and at Toowoomba and Bribie Island, and on 20 December 1920 at Taroom married with Anglican rites Olive Constance Becker. From 1925 to 1953 he was head teacher successively at Bribie Island, Emu Park, Pinelands (Crow's Nest), Finch Hatton, Warwick East and Dalby. He was acting district inspector of schools, south-west region, in June-December 1952. On 7 March 1953 he was elected to the Legislative Assembly as Australian Labor Party member for the seat of Condamine.

A cabinet reshuffle in June 1956—forced by the resignation of T. A. Foley less than a month after the third Vince Gair [qq.v.14] ministry was sworn in—led to Diplock's appointment as minister for public instruction. On 21 March next year he introduced into parliament a bill which, among other things, provided for the establishment at the University of Queensland of a new appointments and promotions appeal board to be chaired by a government appointee. This clause incurred the wrath of the Opposition and of university staff members, who viewed it as an assault on academic integrity and university self-government, especially in relation to the appointment of staff. Despite a storm of protests, a deputation of students to the minister and a public petition with 30 000 signatures, the legislation was passed. Next year (Sir) Frank Nicklin's [q.v.15] new Country Party-Liberal Party coalition government repealed the controversial provisions.

In the aftermath of the Labor split in 1957, Diplock supported Gair. He joined the Queensland Labor Party and in the election that year retained his seat. In 1960 he transferred to the Dalby-based electorate of Aubigny, defeating the sitting Country Party member (Sir) James Sparkes [q.v.16]. Advertisements in the early 1960s used catch-phrases such as 'It's the Proven Stimulant Diplockium: Containing All the Vitamins Essential to Growth and Development'. The QLP's electoral support dwindled, and by 1963 Diplock was its sole representative in State parliament. The party had formally aligned with the Democratic Labor Party in 1962, but he continued to stand as a QLP candidate until the 1969 election, when he represented the DLP. In an electoral redistribution two years later Aubigny was abolished and he did not contest the poll in April 1972.

Unusually for a DLP politician, Diplock was a staunch Anglican and a Freemason. He had a slightly dour face, reminiscent of the actor Noel Coward, and his political persona was that of a fatherly teacher or family physician. In 1972 he was appointed CMG. Living in retirement at Scarborough, near Redcliffe, he played bowls and golf. He was chairman (1962-75) of Napier Bros Ltd, Dalby. Survived by his wife and their two sons and two daughters, he died on 6 November 1983 at Sandgate, Brisbane, and was cremated.

C. Lack (comp), *Three Decades of Queensland Political History* (1962); M. I. Thomis, *A Place of Light & Learning* (1985); R. Fitzgerald and H. Thornton, *Labor in Queensland* (1989); *PD* (Qld), 1956-57, vol 216, pp 1572, 1609, 1957-58, vol 219, p 1463, 1983-84, vol 292, p 29; Diplock personal file (QSA).   SIMON PATON
KIERAN MCCONVILLE

DI SALVO, GIUSEPPE (1902-1988), merchant naval captain, labour movement activist and immigrant advocate, was born on 19 April 1902 on the island of Lipari, off Sicily, Italy, first of eight children of Italian parents Sebastiano Di Salvo, builder, and his wife Annunziata, née Virgona. In 1928-32 he lived in the United States of America. Di Salvo had dreamed of going to sea: as a teenager, he had stowed away aboard an English merchant vessel and worked as 'ship's boy' before returning to Italy,

where he qualified for merchant ship command at the Istituto Nautico di Palermo, Sicily.

At the helm of cargo ships, Di Salvo travelled the globe. On 30 October 1934 he married Elena Maria Rampolla, daughter of a wealthy Palermo family, at the Church of Santa Lucia in that city. On the outbreak of World War II, his anti-fascism cost him his command and he became a target for harassment by blackshirts. Exiled to Lipari, he joined the Resistance and fought alongside American forces in their 1943-44 landings at Salerno and Anzio.

Returning to sea following the war, Di Salvo visited Australia and become convinced of its opportunities. In 1951 he moved his family to Melbourne, trading their comfortable home in Lipari for accommodation above a Richmond barber's shop. Multilingual, he obtained work teaching English to immigrants but in 1954, when plans to establish an Italian-Australian newspaper stalled, and short of money, he accepted command of an Italian merchant ship. In 1957 he arrived back as abruptly as he had departed. Naturalised the following year, he was then managing his own travel agency.

Di Salvo soon became active in the labour movement and with the early representation of 'New Australian' interests in the Australian Labor Party. Credited with founding (1956) *Il Progresso (Italo-Australiano)*, the official organ of the Italo-Australian Labour Council in Melbourne, he was the newspaper's first editor, and its director and driving force for the remainder of his life. With the assistance of several unions and the Melbourne Trades Hall Council he also became a full-time liaison officer between the unions and Victorian migrant workers. A friend of the Labor politicians Arthur Calwell [q.v.13] and Jim Cairns, in November 1966—as Captain Joseph Di Salvo —he contested a Senate vacancy for the ALP. Although he was unsuccessful, the local Italian community proclaimed him as its first candidate for the national parliament.

In 1972, working from home in Thornbury, Di Salvo founded the Istituto Nazionale Assistenza Sociale, an Australian offshoot of the welfare division of one of Italy's peak trade union confederations. His efforts were recognised in 1975 when he was appointed officer of the Order of Merit of the Italian Republic. By the time he retired as its national co-ordinator in 1986, INAS was an Australia-wide network.

Di Salvo's stocky appearance was enhanced in later life by a thick shock of white hair. Headstrong and impulsive, he was also compassionate and an uncompromising enemy of discrimination. The call of the sea never left him; in old age he would wistfully recite John Masefield's 'Sea Fever': 'I must go down to the sea again'. Survived by his wife and their two daughters, he died on 27 August 1988 at

Thornbury and was buried with Catholic rites in Preston cemetery. 'Addio, Comandante!' *Il Progresso* declared.

J. Jupp, *Arrivals and Departures* (1966); *25th Anniversary Almanac INAS-CISL Australia*, 1999; Austn Soc for the Study of Labour His, *Recorder*, Oct 1988, p 3; *Age* (Melbourne), 5 Nov 1966, p 5; *Herald* (Melbourne), 11 Feb 1977, p 12; *Il Progresso* (Melbourne), July 1988, p 1; Sept 1988, p 1; private information.   PAUL STRANGIO

DOBSON, AGNES MAY (1901?-1987), actor, theatre director and writer, was born, possibly on 30 December 1901, at Glebe Point, Sydney, only child of New Zealand-born parents Collet Barker Dobson, actor and travelling theatre manager, and Harriet Agnes Thornton, née Meddings, an actor whose stage name was Harrie Collet. Agnes's birth was not registered. Collet Barker [q.v.1] was her great-great-uncle. As a child, Agnes performed with her father's theatre company—first as a baby in a cradle—and received most of her education from her father. The family's fortunes fluctuated.

During World War I, Agnes lived for a time in Brisbane, where her mother had purchased a tearoom with a library attached. She developed into a beauty; Hal Porter [q.v.] described her as a 'slender reddish-brunette, five feet five inches [165 cm] tall, with green eyes'. At 15 or 16 she acted the lead role in *Camille* with (Sir) Benjamin Fuller's [q.v.8] stock company. In 1917 she made her silent film début as a young sideshow dancer in *The Hayseeds' Backblocks Show*; in 1919 she appeared in *The Face at the Window* and *Barry Butts In*. On 18 April 1921 at the district registrar's office, Newtown, Sydney, aged 19, she married a widower, Frederick Stanley Holah, who was an actor and playwright known as Ronald Riley. Their son, William John, later known as Bill Barclay (d.1970), was born in December that year. Three months later she was touring again, to Adelaide, Melbourne, Sydney and New Zealand, acting with Fuller's Dramatic Players and Hugh J. Ward's, J. & N. Tait's and J. C. Williamson's [qq.v.12,6] companies.

Having divorced Holah, on 16 February 1924 at Christ Church, Enmore, Sydney, Dobson married with Anglican rites George Oliver Clapcott Barclay, a motor salesman. She wrote poetry and a dramatic sketch, 'The Secret of the Confession' (1924). In 1931 she settled in Adelaide. Divorced that year, on 27 January 1932 at the office of the registrar-general, Adelaide (claiming her age to be 26), she married Wilfred Thornton, branch business manager. This marriage was dissolved in 1934. She acted, directed and produced plays for Ab Intra Studio, Adelaide Repertory and Workers' Educational Association Little

theatres, and the Esmond George Players. Co-founder (1936) of the Independent Group, she ran the Stage-Craft Studio for the Development of Individuality in Stage Work and Voice Production and briefly taught drama at the Wilderness School. She wrote plays: *The Immortal Road*, *Legend*, *The Halfcaste*, *My Own Land*, and *Dark Brother*, which was runner-up in the South Australian Centenary play competition (1936). She regularly performed on radio, for both the Australian Broadcasting Commission and commercial stations.

In 1940 Dobson moved to St Kilda, Melbourne. Using the pseudonym Agnes Grey, she presented talks and book reviews for the ABC. She wrote scripts for radio plays and school broadcasts, and played parts in serials, including that of the tyrannical Mrs Sharpshott in 'The Village Glee Club'. In the 1950s and 1960s she freelanced as an actor, appearing in films and television dramas, mainly for Crawford Productions Pty Ltd. She was principal (1953-57) of the Crawford School of Broadcasting. Eventually incapacitated, she lived in a nursing home at Oakleigh, supported by the Actors' Benevolent Fund. She died there on 26 February 1987 and was cremated with Churches of Christ forms. Colin Ballantyne [q.v.] later recalled that he had 'never met anyone with her vitality or anyone with a better grasp of the fundamentals of theatre'. An unpublished autobiography is held by the Performing Arts Collection of South Australia.

H. Porter, *Stars of Australian Stage and Screen* (1965); A. D. McCredie (ed), *From Colonel Light into the Footlights* (1988); *Jnl of Austn Studies*, no 71, 2001, p 45; *Age* (Melbourne), 6 Feb 1981, p 14; *Advertiser* (Adelaide), 3 Mar 1987, p 14; SP767/1, Dobson (NAA); Dobson papers (NLA and Performing Arts Collection of SA).   ROSE WILSON

DOBSON, RUTH VIOLET LISSANT (1918-1989), diplomat, was born on 5 October 1918 at Neutral Bay, Sydney, elder daughter of Austin Arthur Greaves Dobson (d.1926), an English-born draughtsman, and his wife Marjorie, née Caldwell, from Victoria. The granddaughter of the English poet and essayist Austin Dobson and sister of the Australian poet Rosemary Dobson, Ruth was educated at Frensham School (1929-36), Mittagong, New South Wales, and the University of Sydney (BA, 1940). She tried various jobs including teaching briefly and acting as secretary to the principal of Women's College, where she had resided as a student. In 1942 she joined the Sydney office of the Commonwealth Department of Munitions as a records clerk.

Interested in international affairs, Ruth applied for a cadetship with the Department of External Affairs in 1943. Although her application was unsuccessful, she was employed as a temporary research assistant. Within the department she faced the institutionalised discrimination that hampered many women of her generation in the public service. Regarded as too old (over 25) for appointment as a graduate and eager for an overseas posting, she resigned from the department in 1946 and went to London. In June she joined the Australian High Commission as a locally engaged temporary employee in the external affairs office.

Miss Dobson acted as adviser to Australian delegates at many sessions of the United Nations, and at the Paris Peace Conference in 1946. In February 1949 she was appointed third secretary (temporary). This work led to her selection for the Geneva office of the Australian UN Delegation in 1950. Attending UN conferences and meetings of the General Assembly and participating in the committee meetings of various international and specialised agency conferences, she also served on the third committee of the UN General Assembly, which dealt with social, cultural and humanitarian matters and drafted the Convention on the Status of Women.

Dobson's status as temporary and locally engaged dogged her until 1953 when the rules were relaxed and she was appointed as a clerk, third division, in Canberra. This change was not intended to encourage aspirations to a position in the diplomatic service. Another attempt to gain a cadetship in 1953 was unsuccessful, but she was officially appointed to the diplomatic staff in 1957. Two years later Miss Dobson was included in the Australian delegation to the UN General Assembly, again sitting on the third committee. She went to New Zealand as second secretary in 1961 and while there was promoted to first secretary. From 1964 she was the department's international conference officer in Canberra until appointed as first secretary to Brazil in 1965. She did not take up the position because in September that year she was seconded to Government House, Yarralumla, as private secretary to Lady (Maie) Casey [q.v.].

On her return to the department in 1967, Miss Dobson was posted as first secretary in Manila but fourteen months later was invalided home after contracting pneumonia. In 1968 she became first secretary, later counsellor, in the Europe, Africa and Middle East branch in Canberra and again represented Australia at the UN General Assembly. She was counsellor (1971-74), and, briefly, chargé d'affaires at the Australian embassy in Athens. The acme of Miss Dobson's career was in 1974, when she became the first woman career diplomat to be appointed as an ambassador. She went to Denmark as the first resident Australian ambassador and, in 1978, to the

Republic of Ireland, where she remained until her retirement in 1981. Next year she was appointed OBE.

Indomitable despite ill health, Miss Dobson continued to travel and to serve in many organisations, including the Australian Capital Territory branch of the Royal Commonwealth Society (councillor 1982-85), the Canberra branch of the Australian Institute of International Affairs, the Immigration Review panel (1984-88), the Additional Rhodes Scholarship selection committee (1981-84), Winifred West Schools Ltd, Mittagong (1982-87), and the Australian Federation of University Women. She died on 14 December 1989 in Canberra and was cremated.

Austn Foreign Affairs Record, Mar 1974, p 213, Dec 1989, p 733; *SMH*, 28 Mar 1974, p 3; *Age* (Melbourne), 9 May 1981, p 26; I. Hamilton, taped interview with R. Dobson (1984, NLA); A6371 and M3072, item 4 (NAA); private information.

SYLVIA MARCHANT

DODD, ALAN PARKHURST (1896-1981), entomologist, was born on 8 January 1896 at Upper Ithaca Creek, Brisbane, fifth of eight children of Frederick Parkhurst Dodd, a Victorian-born clerk who was to become a well-known naturalist, and his wife Jane Gertrude, née Dempsey, who came from Ireland. The Dodds moved to Townsville in 1899 and shortly after to Kuranda. From childhood Alan was involved in the family business of collecting and preserving insects for sale worldwide. Educated at Kuranda State and Townsville Grammar schools, in 1912 he was appointed assistant-entomologist with the Bureau of Sugar Experiment Stations, Gordonvale. He worked under A. A. Girault, writing up to eight scientific papers a year on *Microhymenoptera*, in particular minute scelionid wasps. Tall and gangly, he had dark hair and a long thin face with a somewhat morose expression.

Enlisting in the Australian Imperial Force on 26 February 1916, Dodd served on the Western Front in 1917-18 as a medical orderly with the 15th Field Ambulance and took three months' leave in 1919 to study natural history at the British Museum, before being discharged in Brisbane in October. He returned to his position at Gordonvale, and in 1921 became a laboratory assistant with the new Commonwealth Prickly Pear Board, Commonwealth Institute of Science and Industry, under T. Harvey Johnston [q.v.9], who had attempted unsuccessfully to control the weed with the moth *Cactoblastis cactorum*. In 1924-25 Dodd, now senior entomologist, directed the board's investigations in North and South America. With the assistance of an Argentinian, E. E. Blanchard, he collected live specimens of

Cactoblastis from Argentina and arranged for their shipment back to Queensland. In his report he thanked Blanchard for 'his ever-willing assistance'. The insects, reared and host-tested in Brisbane by John Mann, had by 1930 destroyed the prickly pear, which had spread over an estimated 65 million acres (26.3 million ha), but Dodd never again publicly acknowledged the roles played by Blanchard and Mann.

The successful control of prickly pear established Dodd as a leading scientist, and in 1925 he was named officer-in-charge, prickly pear investigations. In 1939 he was appointed MBE. He published *The Biological Campaign against Prickly Pear* (1940). When the Prickly Pear Board was wound up in 1939, its facilities at Sherwood, Brisbane, and remaining staff were taken over by the Queensland government to form a biological section within the Department of Public Lands, with Dodd as director. Although an excellent naturalist with a wide knowledge of insects, he was difficult and autocratic, and distrustful of scientists with degrees. As a result the biological section achieved very little under his leadership. He retired in 1962 and that year was appointed OBE.

Dodd was a founding member (1923) of the Entomological Society of Queensland, serving as president in 1938 and 1945, and becoming an honorary life member in 1962. A bachelor whose only interest was his work, he lived alone or with siblings in his house near the research station. Many Australian insects, and a second species of *Cactoblastis*, were named after him. Dodd died on 3 July 1981 at Chelmer and was cremated with Presbyterian forms.

SMH, 7 July 1981, p 8; Entomological Soc of Qld, *News Bulletin*, July 1988, p 43; R. E. McFadyen, The Harrisia Cactus Eradication Scheme (M.Pub. Ad. thesis, Univ of Qld, 1990) and for bib.

R. E. McFadyen

DODS, Sir LORIMER FENTON (1900-1981), physician and professor of child health, was born on 7 March 1900 at New Farm, Brisbane, elder child of Robert Smith Dods, an architect born in New Zealand, and his American-born wife Mary Marian, née King. Moving to Sydney with his family when he was 14 years old, Lorimer attended Sydney Church of England Grammar School (Shore), North Sydney, and St Paul's College, University of Sydney (MB, Ch.M., 1923; MD, 1936). After working as a resident medical officer at Newcastle Hospital in 1923-24 and at Royal Alexandra Hospital for Children in 1925, he entered general practice at Edgecliff, where his interest in paediatrics grew over the next

ten years. He married Margaret (Margot) Kathleen Walsh on 26 February 1927 at St Alban's Church of England Chapel, The Southport School, Queensland.

Appointed to the Royal Alexandra Hospital for Children, Camperdown, in 1928 as a temporary honorary relieving medical officer, Dods became an honorary assistant physician in 1937. The previous year he had gone overseas for further studies in England at the Birmingham Children's Hospital under Professor (Sir) Leonard Parsons, and had gained the diploma in child health issued jointly by the Royal College of Physicians, London, and the Royal College of Surgeons of England. He had also visited the Hospital for Sick Children, Toronto, Canada. On returning to Sydney he commenced consultant practice in Macquarie Street and was appointed medical tutor in clinical paediatrics by the University of Sydney. His papers in publications such as the *Medical Journal of Australia* were to remain models of concise scientific prose.

Dods had enlisted in the Australian Imperial Force in 1918 but had seen no action. On 13 October 1939 he was appointed major, Australian Army Medical Corps, AIF. He sailed in January 1940 with the first convoy transporting Australian troops to the Middle East, where he was attached to the 2/1st Australian General Hospital. From March 1942 he served in hospitals in Australia, except for the period January-May 1943, when he was in Port Moresby. Demobilised on 20 March 1945 as a lieutenant colonel, he returned to the Royal Alexandra Hospital and became a full physician in 1948. His wartime friendships helped the hospital in later years when comrades in arms who had achieved distinction in the business life of Sydney became directors and benefactors.

In 1947 Dods was awarded a Carnegie travelling fellowship that enabled him to visit the Children's Hospital, Boston, in the United States of America. On returning to Sydney he shared his knowledge and insights, and encouraged young doctors to investigate childhood diseases using the newest research tools. Medical associates quickly became his friends and he used this network to ensure that his registrars were able to obtain appropriate experience overseas to complete their training. His interest in and affection for his young colleagues was envied by others.

Australia had no university chairs in paediatrics. After the war the Commonwealth government responded to this need by establishing the Institute of Child Health within the School of Public Health and Tropical Medicine of the University of Sydney. In 1949 Dods was appointed as the founding director of the institute and the first professor of child health in the country. Subsequently he worked successfully for the establishment of chairs in other Australian medical schools. He retired from his own chair in 1960 to concentrate his energies on promoting and facilitating research at the hospital. With Dr John Fulton, general medical superintendent of Royal Alexandra, and Douglas Burrows, honorary treasurer of the board and later president, he had marshalled public support to establish the Children's Medical Research Foundation in 1958. For the next twenty years he guided and nurtured the foundation as honorary director and chairman. He retired on his eightieth birthday, leaving the foundation with a sound financial base.

Dods's association with the hospital had spanned fifty years. He was elected to the board of management in 1959. His influence was immense and little happened at the hospital without his involvement. During his time there could be no greater accolade than to be medical registrar to the professorial unit— Lorimer's registrar. He had a very busy practice but he knew everyone and greeted all at the hospital with a cheerful salute. To walk the corridors with him was like a royal progress. In later years he became a prodigious letter writer, although his handwriting was often indecipherable. His work with children extended beyond Camperdown. He was an honorary consulting paediatrician to the Royal North Shore Hospital, the Royal Hospital for Women, Paddington, and the Tresillian Homes run by the Royal Society for the Welfare of Mothers and Babies, and he served on the board of the New South Wales Society for Crippled Children from 1955 to 1962.

A foundation fellow (1938) of the Royal Australasian College of Physicians, Dods was a councillor (1956-65) and chairman (1957-63) of the research advisory committee. In 1965 he was made an honorary fellow of the (Royal) Australian College of General Practitioners. The respect he engendered greatly helped to establish the new specialty of paediatrics. A founding father of the Australian Paediatric Association (later the Australian College of Paediatrics), he became its secretary-treasurer (1950-51), vice-president (1953-54) and president (1954-55). He was chairman (1965-68) of the publication board of the *Australian Paediatric Journal*, and on his seventieth birthday an issue of the journal was dedicated to him. Appointed MVO in 1947, he was knighted in 1962. He received an honorary doctorate of science from the University of Sydney in 1974 and was further honoured when the title of Lorimer Dods Professor was conferred on the director of the Children's Medical Research Foundation.

At university he had been a rowing Blue and had excelled at skiing. In 1968 he listed his interests as gardening, surfing and antiques. Well read, he enjoyed making literary allusions in his medical writings. He was a warm and charming man whose wisdom and knowledge continued to pervade paediatrics through the many who were influenced by his teaching and his example. Above all, he was kindly Dr Dods, the children's friend, or, as Sir Edward Ford [q.v.] dubbed him, 'the ambassador for the children'. Sir Lorimer died on 7 March 1981 at Potts Point and was cremated. His wife had died in 1977; their daughter and son survived him. A portrait (1964) by Vladas Meskenas is hung near the Lorimer Dods lecture theatre at the Children's Hospital, Westmead, and one (1968) by Judy Cassab is located in the foyer of the research facilities of the Children's Medical Research Institute, Westmead.

D. G. Hamilton, *Hand in Hand* (1979); R. Manchester, *Beloved Physician* (1989); *Austn Paediatric Jnl*, vol 6, no 1, 1970, p 3; *SMH*, 9 Mar 1981, p 11; *AMA Gazette*, Apr 1981, p 27; *MJA*, 2 May 1981, p 441; Royal A'asian College of Physicians, *College Newsletter*, Aug 1981, p 1; H. de Berg, interview with L. Dods (ts, 1968, NLA); B2455, item Dods Lorimer, B883, item NX35 (NAA).   JOHN YU

DOHERTY, MURIEL KNOX (1896-1988), nurse and air force principal matron, was born on 19 July 1896 at Prahran, Melbourne, eldest of three children of Victorian-born parents Robert Knox Doherty, clerk, and his wife Elizabeth Mary, née Mendell. Taught at home by a governess until the family moved to Wollstonecraft, Sydney, about 1909, Muriel completed her education at Woodstock private school, North Sydney. In 1914 she was employed as the school nurse and an unqualified teacher at Abbotsleigh, Wahroonga. That year she gained the St John Ambulance Association's first aid and home nursing certificate. In 1915-21 she was a member of the Australian Red Cross Society's No.6 Voluntary Aid Detachment, North Sydney, working at the Sydney, Mater Misericordiae and Royal Prince Alfred hospitals. She left Abbotsleigh in 1917 so that she could be a full-time VAD while helping her mother at home.

In 1921 Doherty commenced nursing training at RPAH. She passed her final examination in November 1925, winning the Sir Alfred Roberts [q.v.6] medal for general proficiency, and was registered on 10 February next year. Becoming a charge nurse in the gynaecology ward, she was promoted within six months to sister-in-charge. She sailed for England early in 1930, took up a number of private nursing positions in Britain and on the Continent, and travelled extensively. In 1932 she enrolled in the sister tutor course offered by King's College for Household and Social Science, University of London. Returning next year to RPAH, she was appointed a tutor sister. In 1936 she introduced a preliminary training school for nurses at the hospital. She transferred to Prince Henry Hospital, Little Bay, in 1937. Active in the New South Wales Nurses' Association, she was treasurer (1935) and a member of the executive council.

Doherty had been appointed a staff nurse in the reserve of the Australian Army Nursing Service in August 1935. Following the outbreak of World War II, in October 1939 she was called up for full-time duty. On 16 September 1940 she transferred to the two-months-old Royal Australian Air Force Nursing Service as matron of No.3 RAAF Hospital, Richmond, New South Wales, and principal nursing officer for No.2 Training Group and all units in New South Wales and Queensland. Her rank on entry was squadron leader. She assisted the matron-in-chief Margaret Lang [q.v.] to organise the new service in the region for which she was responsible. Doherty was promoted to principal matron (wing commander) in March 1943 and was acting matron-in-chief at Air Force Headquarters, Melbourne, in January-July 1944. Concurrently she was a member (1943-44) of a State government committee for reorganisation of the nursing profession (in New South Wales), and co-author of a textbook, *Modern Practical Nursing Procedures* (1944). Awarded the Royal Red Cross in 1945, she was demobilised from the RAAF at her own request on 22 May that year.

Keen to work in war-devastated Europe, Doherty immediately joined the United Nations Relief and Rehabilitation Administration and was appointed matron to the recently liberated Bergen-Belsen concentration camp, Germany. A London newspaper of the time described her as 'a practical-looking woman with a kindly smile'. After a year she was sent to Poland to assist in the rehabilitation of nursing education there. In October 1946 she was back in Sydney. At the inaugural meeting in December of the National Florence Nightingale Memorial Committee of Australia she and Agnes Walsh [q.v.16] were elected vice-presidents; Doherty was also elected convener of the education sub-committee. She helped to establish and became a foundation fellow (1949) of the New South Wales College of Nursing.

In 1955-56 Doherty travelled widely in Europe studying developments in geriatrics. She wrote a number of reports on her findings and a small monograph, *Caring for the Elderly* (1956). In 1958 she organised the first 'Old People's Week' for the Old People's Welfare Council of New South Wales.

Doherty lived in England in 1961-68. Back in Sydney, she took up residence in the Queen Mary Nurses' Home at RPAH so that she could undertake research for a history of 'her' hospital. She died on 29 September 1988 at West Ryde and was cremated. Throughout her career she had kept a record of her experiences and had collected documents and other nursing memorabilia. She had arranged for most of her papers to be placed in the archives of the New South Wales College of Nursing. Other material was deposited in the State Library of New South Wales, the National Library of Australia, the Australian War Memorial, Canberra, and the Yad Vashem Holocaust Martyrs' and Heroes' Remembrance Authority, Jerusalem. Her autobiography, *Off the Record*, and her history, *The Life and Times of Royal Prince Alfred Hospital* (both edited by Lynette Russell) were published in 1996. *Letters from Belsen 1945*, edited by Russell and Judith Cornell, appeared in 2000.

R. Pratt and R. L. Russell, *A Voice to be Heard* (2002); *Lamp*, Nov 1988, p 32; A9301, item 501020, B884, item N60136 (NAA); Doherty collection (SLNSW, NLA, AWM, College of Nursing, Burwood, Sydney).   R. LYNETTE RUSSELL

DOIG, EDNA NELL (1915-1988), army matron-in-chief, was born on 21 June 1915 at West End, Brisbane, youngest of three children of Joseph Lindsay Doig, labourer, and his wife Jessie Margaret, née Clark, both Brisbane born. Although a Presbyterian, Edna was educated at All Hallows' convent school. In 1937 she completed her general nursing training at Brisbane General Hospital.

Joining the Australian Army Nursing Service, Australian Imperial Force, as a staff nurse on 15 December 1939, Doig embarked for the Middle East in May 1940 but the convoy was diverted to Britain. She was sent to the 2/3rd Australian General Hospital at Godalming, Surrey, which was in the path of German bombers attacking London during the Blitz, and she later recalled the difficulty of sweeping floors while wearing outsized 'tin' helmets.

Doig arrived at the 2/2nd AGH at Kantara, Egypt, in December 1940. She was promoted to sister, group I, in December 1941. Returning to Australia with her unit in March 1942, she served in Queensland at Watten and on the Atherton Tableland. She was appointed as a lieutenant in March 1943 and promoted to captain in August. Her fondest memory of her nursing career was repatriating Australian prisoners of war from Singapore in September-November 1945 with the 2/14th AGH.

From 1946 to 1949 Doig served in Japan as deputy-matron of the 130th AGH, nursing Australian members of the British Commonwealth Occupation Force and their families. Back in Australia, she transferred to the Reserve of Officers on 23 April 1949. She trained in midwifery at the Women's Hospital, Melbourne, and in infant welfare at the Berry

Street Foundling Hospital, East Melbourne, before working at the Repatriation General Hospital, Heidelberg.

On 3 December 1951 Doig 'surprised herself' by joining the Royal Australian Army Nursing Corps, Australian Regular Army, as a major. Her first appointment was matron of the 1st Camp Hospital, Yeronga, Brisbane. Her experience and skills ensured rapid promotion. Rising to temporary lieutenant colonel in May 1956 (substantive August 1960), she was assistant-director, army nursing service, of Northern Command, Southern Command and Eastern Command successively. In 1959 she gained a diploma in nursing administration at the College of Nursing, Australia. Succeeding E. J. Bowe [q.v.13], she became matron-in-chief and director, army nursing service, on 23 May 1961 with the rank of honorary colonel. That year she was made honorary nursing sister to Queen Elizabeth II. Appointed an associate of the Royal Red Cross in 1953, she was elevated to member in 1963 for her 'outstanding ability as an administrator' and for being 'devoted and untiring in her efforts' as a nurse. In November 1964 she was promoted to colonel. On overseas duty tours she travelled widely, visiting seven countries in 1967 and the Republic of Vietnam (South Vietnam) three times. On 21 June 1970 she retired.

Five ft 1 in. (155 cm) tall, of medium complexion with brown hair and green eyes, 'Teddy' was praised in a citation for her 'tact and devotion to duty', while her sound judgment, dignity and friendliness won the affection of those with whom she served. In retirement she was involved in many returned nurses' and ex-service organisations; she was president of the Returned Nurses' Club, Melbourne (1973-76), and the returned sisters' sub-branch of the Returned Services League of Australia (from 1987). She had been awarded the Florence Nightingale medal and elected a fellow of the College of Nursing, Australia. She died on 24 November 1988 at Manly, Queensland, and was cremated. The Colonel Edna Doig Memorial Trust Fund contributes to cancer research.

R. Goodman, *Queensland Nurses* (1985); J. Bassett, *Guns and Brooches* (1992); *Herald* (Melbourne), 29 May 1961, p 17, 20 June 1970, p 2; *Courier-Mail* (Brisbane), 21 May 1970, p 14; J. Bassett, taped interview with E. N. Doig (1986, AWM); private information.   JANETTE BOMFORD

DOLAN, JOHN (1901-1986), schoolteacher, Australian Rules footballer and politician, was born on 25 December 1901 at Victoria Park, Perth, third child of Cormick Dolan, an Irish-born carrier, and his wife Ellen, née McMahon, who came from Victoria. Brought up on the goldfields, 'Jerry' was educated by the Christian Brothers at Kalgoorlie. In 1920 he became a monitor at North Kalgoorlie State School and next year joined the Australian Labor Party. He trained (1922-23) at Claremont Teachers' College, Perth, and in March 1924 was posted to Fremantle Boys' Central (High) School. On 31 December 1932 at St Patrick's Catholic Church, Fremantle, he married Eileen Margaret Foley, a shorthand-typist. They were to live at Fremantle all their married life. He was active in the State School Teachers' Union of Western Australia and coached football at Aquinas College, Manning. From 1956 until June 1963 he held senior positions at John Curtin [q.v.13] Senior High School, Fremantle.

Dolan was a champion Australian Rules footballer; 6 ft 3 ins (191 cm) tall and slender, he was a centre half-forward and ruckman. In 1923-38 he played sixteen seasons in the Western Australian National Football League, eleven with East Fremantle and five with East Perth. He participated, often as team captain, in twenty-two finals games and nine grand finals: 1923-25, 1928-31, 1933 and 1936. A club coach for seventeen years, he took East Fremantle to a WANFL record of thirty-five straight wins, including an unbeaten 1946 season. In 1946-49 he coached Western Australia to three successive wins against Victoria.

Secretary of the East Fremantle ALP branch for many years, Dolan seldom missed a party meeting. He had frequent contact with John Curtin and as early as 1933 was campaign manager for John Tonkin. After twice unsuccessfully seeking preselection, he was elected the member for West Province in the Legislative Council in a by-election on 29 June 1963. In his maiden speech on 14 August he called for greater investment in education and presented a strong case for the benefits of smaller class numbers. He also underscored his teetotal approach to life, complaining that Australian spending on liquor consumption greatly exceeded outlays on education. In 1965-74 he represented South-East Metropolitan Province.

Tonkin became premier of a new Labor government in March 1971 and appointed Dolan to the police and transport portfolios. In October Dolan took on railways as well. As police minister he caused a furore, and was censured by the ALP State executive, when he crossed the floor in December to vote for an Opposition amendment to the parliamentary commissioner bill exempting police from investigation by the Ombudsman. Leader of the government in the council from 7 February 1973, and minister for education, transport and railways from 30 May that year until 8 April 1974, he did not stand at the general election on 30 May. He was reported as saying, 'I've never really been a politician in the true sense of the word', and was not pleased that a woman, Grace Vaughan [q.v.], succeeded him in his seat and then lost it after only one term.

Throughout his life Dolan was a devout Catholic, rarely missing Mass at 7 a.m. on Sundays. His legendary status as a footballer was recognised in 1986 with his induction into Western Australia's sporting 'Hall of Fame'. Survived by his wife and their son and two daughters, he died on 26 December 1986 at Bicton and was buried in Fremantle cemetery.

M. Glossop (comp), *East Perth, 1906-1976* (1976); D. W. Black (ed), *The House on the Hill* (1991); J. Lee, *East Fremantle Football Club* (1998); *PD* (LC, WA), 14 Aug 1963, p 270, 3 Dec 1971, p 822; *Daily News* (Perth), 22 May 1967, p 19; *West Australian*, 27 Dec 1986, p 30; R. Jamieson, taped interview with E. Dolan (1989, SLWA).   HARRY C. J. PHILLIPS

DONALD, COLIN MALCOLM (1910-1985), agricultural scientist, was born on 21 March 1910 at Colchester, Essex, England, one of six children of William Donald, corporal in the Royal Field Artillery, and his wife Julia Jane, née Bloxham. He spent his childhood on a small farm, receiving his early education at the Dover County School. In 1926 he travelled to Australia under the auspices of the Wembley scholarship scheme and began a course at Hawkesbury Agricultural College, Richmond, New South Wales (Dip.Ag. Hons, 1929). Awarded a further scholarship, he graduated with first-class honours at the University of Sydney (B.Sc.Agr., 1933, D.Sc.Agr., 1963). In 1932 he was appointed as an assistant-agrostologist in the New South Wales Department of Agriculture. On 12 November 1935 at St Peter's Church of England, Neutral Bay, he married Margaret Clare Voysey, a secretary.

In 1934 Donald had joined the Council for Scientific and Industrial Research's pasture research group, based at the Waite [q.v.6] Agricultural Research Institute, University of Adelaide. He worked initially on strain variation in grasses and clovers, then on mineral nutrition of pastures and in 1936-37, with David Riceman, made the first discovery of a trace element deficiency in Australia. After gaining a master's degree in 1939 from the University of Adelaide and winning the Pawlett scholarship from the University of Sydney the same year, Donald studied pastures for two years in Britain, the United States of America and New Zealand. On his return to Australia he transferred to the CSIR's division of plant industry, Canberra. In 1942-45 he was seconded to the Department of War Organization of Industry, Melbourne, first under (Sir) John Crawford [q.v.], and later as assistant-director in charge of the rural division. He then undertook research into competition among annual pasture plants in the Mediter-

ranean environment of southern Australia. In 1951, sponsored by the Organisation for European Economic Co-operation to assist with a survey of grasslands in Mediterranean countries, he also led an Australian plant-collecting expedition in that region. He became assistant-chief of his division in 1953.

In 1954 Donald was appointed professor of agriculture and head of the department of agronomy at the Waite Institute. During his nineteen-year tenure he expanded the departmental academic staff to seventeen, and attracted a rapidly rising number of post-graduate students. He was dean of the faculty in 1955-59 and 1962-64. In later years he found expression for his strong social conscience by becoming increasingly involved with agricultural improvements in the less-developed countries of South-East Asia. He led missions to various countries and surveyed agricultural faculties at universities in Malaysia, Thailand and the Philippines.

A lucid writer, Donald generated sixty-seven scientific publications, three of which gained him international recognition. The first, written with C. G. Stephens, was 'Australian Soils and Their Responses to Fertilisers' (*Advances in Agronomy*, 1958). It drew attention to the antiquity of Australian soils, their severe nutritional limitations for plant growth, and the scope for amelioration through the use of superphosphate, trace elements and subterranean clover. In the second, 'Competition among Crop and Pasture Plants' (*Advances in Agronomy*, 1963), he summarised the factors that influenced yields of plants growing at high densities in crops and sown pastures. The third, 'Phosphorus in Australian Agriculture' (*Journal of the Australian Institute of Agricultural Science*, 1964), highlighted the trends in Australian cereal yields: the initial reduction due to progressive exhaustion of soil nutrients, and subsequent increases associated first with the introduction of superphosphate and fallowing, and later with better crop rotations and the use of legumes to increase soil nitrogen content.

Donald had a profound influence on pasture and crop development in Australia. Recognised for his important contributions to discussions on the most recent discoveries in the plant sciences, he was also able to talk easily with farmers. Often dressed in the farmers' attire of a tweed jacket, he had a friendly, equitable and considerate approach and a ready availability which provided great stimulus to farmers, students and staff alike. He was elected a fellow of the Australian Institute of Agricultural Science (1961) and of the Australian Academy of Science (1968), and was a section president at the 1962 meeting in Sydney of the Australian and New Zealand Association for the Advancement of Science. In 1964 he was awarded both the Farrer [q.v.8] memorial medal and the Australian medal of agricultural science. He retired in 1973 and served (1973-75) on the Wheat Industry Research Council. In 1979 he was appointed CBE.

During his final years Donald suffered from Alzheimer's disease. Survived by his wife and their son and daughter, he died on 14 March 1985 at Parkside, Adelaide, and was cremated.

V. A. Edgeloe, *The Waite Agricultural Research Institute* (1984); *Hist Records of Austn Science*, vol 10, no 1, 1994, p 51; personal file, PH/DON/1 (CSIRO Archives, Canberra).

JOHN C. RADCLIFFE

DOUGAN, ALAN ABERNETHY (1909-1982), Presbyterian minister, was born on 4 March 1909 at Ashfield, Sydney, second son of Stewart Abernethy Dougan, grocer, and his wife Mary Jane, née McCook, both born in New South Wales. Alan was educated at Canterbury Boys' Intermediate High and Sydney Boys' High and the University of Sydney (BA, 1930; MA, 1960). At the Presbyterian Theological Hall of St Andrew's College, within the university, he completed his studies for the ministry, winning the Mitchell prize (1932).

In March 1933 Dougan accepted the call to the pastoral charge of Balranald and was ordained and inducted by the Murrumbidgee presbytery. On 10 January 1935 he married Elsie Stewart, a schoolteacher, at St Stephen's Presbyterian Church, Sydney. He was appointed minister at Blayney in 1936 and at St Stephen's Presbyterian Church, Bathurst, in 1939. His keen interest in worship and liturgy, to which most of his fellow Presbyterian clergy were unsympathetic, caused him to be regarded as a ritualist. He served in New South Wales as a chaplain in the Militia (1940-42) and in the Royal Australian Air Force (1942-45). Committed to pastoral ministry, he worked among migrant communities and served as the foundation chairman of the Scots School, Bathurst.

Dougan was elected moderator of the Presbyterian Church of New South Wales in 1956. Next year he was appointed principal of St Andrew's College, where he remained until 1974. He completed a master's thesis on religion in the department of anthropology and served (1964-69) on the senate of the university. Interested in the links between art and religious faith, he was a committee member and judge for the Blake prize for religious art. The corporate trustees of the Presbyterian Church and various boards and committees of the Church also engaged his interest.

Dougan was a member of the Joint Commission on Church Union, which wrote the 1964 *Proposed Basis for Union* of Presbyterians, Methodists and Congregationalists in Australia, which envisaged bishops and further links with the Church of England in Australia. He supported this ideal with the emphasis on the fullness of the catholic faith in the proposed 'Uniting Church'. Because of a dislike of episcopacy in all three denominations, but especially among Presbyterians, a second, revised basis of union in 1971 dropped this objective. Dougan wrote that the second version was a repudiation of the catholic faith, was deliberately vague in essential matters of doctrine, and did not contain a clear confessional statement. When the Uniting Church of Australia was formed in 1977, he remained a Presbyterian although distressed by divisions within his Church and the growing fundamentalist emphasis among Presbyterian clergy after the union.

Author of fourteen entries for the *Australian Dictionary of Biography*, Dougan published reflections on historical and liturgical issues and a book on the controversies generated by the theological views of Professor Samuel Angus [q.v.7]. In 1979 he declined nomination as moderator-general of the Presbyterian Church of Australia because of poor health. Survived by his wife and their daughter and two sons, he died on 22 May 1982 at Mona Vale, Sydney, and was cremated.

R. I. Jack, *The Andrew's Book* (1989); R. J. Willson (comp), *Reverend Principal Alan Dougan, M.A.* (2004); *Minutes of Proceedings of the General Assembly of the Presbyterian Church of Aust in the State of NSW*, 1933-82; H. Clements, The Presbyterian Struggle 1970-1977 (PhD thesis, Univ of NSW, 1983); personal knowledge.   ROBERT WILLSON

DOUGLAS, JAMES ARCHIBALD (1917-1984), judge, was born on 14 August 1917 at Townsville, Queensland, second of five children of Queensland-born parents Robert Johnstone Douglas [q.v.14], barrister, and his wife Annie Alice May, née Ball. Jim's grandfather was Premier John Douglas [q.v.4]. Educated locally and at St Joseph's College, Nudgee, Brisbane (1929-34), he became an associate to his father, who was then northern judge of the Supreme Court of Queensland at Townsville.

On 15 March 1940 Douglas was appointed as a lieutenant, Australian Imperial Force. He joined the 2/12th Battalion in Britain in August. Next year he took part in the defence of Tobruk, Libya, as a platoon commander. In May he and his men withstood a strong German attack on their section of the fortress's perimeter. His comrades believed that he should have been decorated for his part in the action. He served with Northern Territory Force in 1942-43. On 1 February 1943 at Holy

Spirit Catholic Church, New Farm, Brisbane, he married Marjorie Mary Ramsay, a civil servant. From August 1944 he assisted with the repatriation of Australian prisoners of war as a major with the AIF Reception Group, United Kingdom. This work took him to Russia and Poland in February-June 1945. His AIF appointment terminated in Australia on 15 October.

Completing his law studies, Douglas was admitted to the Bar on 25 November 1946. He set up chambers in Brisbane; his practice was mainly in the common law jurisdiction but he was a capable practitioner in all fields, including appellate work in the High Court of Australia. For three months in 1956-57 he was an acting-judge of the Supreme Court of the Northern Territory. In 1960 he was appointed QC. He appeared (1963-64) for the Queensland Police Union of Employees at the royal commission into allegations of police corruption in relation to the National Hotel, Brisbane.

President (1963-65) of the Bar Association of Queensland, he helped G. L. Hart [q.v.14] to develop the Inns of Court as a home for the Brisbane Bar. He was an executive member (1963-65) of the Law Council of Australia and vice-president (1964-65) of the Australian Bar Association. On 11 February 1965 he was appointed a Supreme Court judge. Conscientious and careful, he was outstanding in his ability to conduct trials in both criminal and civil jurisdictions. He could appear stern but his overriding concern was to ensure litigants were given a fair hearing and appropriate representation. Members of the profession whom he considered had not properly discharged their duty to the court or to the client were reprimanded. He served (1968-71, 1973-74) on the law faculty board, University of Queensland, and chaired (1972-82) the Central Sugar Cane Prices Board.

When Sir Charles Wanstall, the chief justice, and George Lucas, the senior puisne judge, retired on the same day in February 1982, Douglas, as the next most senior judge, had the support of the attorney-general, Samuel Doumany, and of the Bar to replace Wanstall. He was passed over for both offices by (Sir) Johannes Bjelke-Peterson's cabinet in politically controversial circumstances—reputedly because he had voted at the 1972 State election for the Australian Labor Party.

A devout Christian, Douglas was chairman (1967-83) of the advisory board of Mount Olivet Hospital, Kangaroo Point, and Queensland president for some ten years of the St Vincent de Paul Society. In the latter role he helped to serve Christmas lunch to the poor before returning home to his own family's festivities. He was made a knight of the Sovereign Military Order of Malta in 1975. A modest collector of Australian art, he also retained a love of ballet that had developed in Russia in 1945. He enjoyed gardening,

served as patron of the Queensland Hibiscus Society, relished convivial meals and fine wines with colleagues, family and friends, and often attended reunions of his World War II battalion. Douglas was a member of the Queensland, United Service, Johnsonian, Tattersall's and Queensland Turf clubs, and of the Wine and Food Society. Amply proportioned, he was known affectionately as 'Big Jim' or 'Jumbo'. He was noted for his courtesy, integrity and moral courage.

Survived by his wife, and their daughter and three sons, he died of cancer on 2 February 1984 in Mount Olivet Hospital and was buried in Nudgee cemetery. In his valedictory, the president of the Queensland Bar, Bill Pincus, described him as 'one of the last of the great Civil jury advocates in Queensland'. All three sons became barristers and took silk. Two, Robert Ramsay (d.2002) and James Sholto, were appointed judges of the Queensland Supreme Court in 1999.

A. Graeme-Evans, *Of Storms and Rainbows*, vol 1 (1989); *Austn Law Jnl*, vol 38, 1965, p 428, vol 58, 1984, p 477; *Sunday Sun* (Brisbane), 6 Dec 1981, p 19; *Telegraph* (Brisbane), 3 Feb 1984, p 1; *Courier-Mail* (Brisbane), 4 Feb 1984, p 15, 7 Feb 1984, p 2; *Australian*, 17-18 Sept 1994, 'Magazine', p 46; valedictory ceremony speeches (ts, 1984, copy on ADB file); personal information.   M. W. D. WHITE

DOWD, ERIC RONALD (1914-1990), tenor, was born on 23 February 1914 at Camperdown, Sydney, third surviving son of Victorian-born Robert Henry Dowd, railway fitter, and his wife Henrietta, née Jenkins, a pianist who was born in New South Wales. Thin as a boy (belying the strong physique that he later developed), Ronald sang as a chorister at Holy Trinity Church of England, Erskineville. He appeared in radio broadcasts and competitions, with many successes, including the City of Sydney and the Railway and Tramway eisteddfods. After what he called a 'robust' education at Cleveland Street Boys' Intermediate High School, Redfern, he worked at the National Bank of Australasia Ltd from 1930. Taught singing by his inspiring mentor Richard Thew, organist at Rockdale Congregational Church, he performed in hotels, music clubs and Masonic lodges. He married Elsie Burnitt Crute, a flag maker, on 8 October 1938 at St Clement's Church of England, Marrickville.

Enlisting in the Australian Imperial Force on 9 March 1942, Dowd served as a lance sergeant with the 1st Advanced Reinforcement Depot in Papua and New Guinea and on Morotai, before being discharged on 16 January 1946 in Australia. He began a singing career, travelling to Japan with a civilian entertainment unit. In 1948, following a chance meeting with Henry Krips [q.v.], he sang the title role in Perth in Offenbach's *The Tales of Hoffmann*; he performed it again in 1949 in Melbourne with Gertrude Johnson's [q.v.14] Australian National Theatre Movement. He later sang successfully with Clarice Lorenz's [q.v.] National Opera of New South Wales (Australia) in Sydney, in *La Traviata, Fidelio, Tannhäuser* and Arthur Benjamin's *The Devil Take Her*. In 1954 and 1955 he sang and broadcast in New Zealand. Late in 1955 he left for Britain and joined the Sadler's Wells Company.

Dowd's first British appearance, as Canio in *Pagliacci* in January 1956, was the beginning of a formidable European career, marked by a fierce determination to master new and demanding works. His forthright willingness to challenge managements earned him the nickname 'Rowdy Dowdy', but he was commonly the person whom younger Australians sought when they needed help. Music critics applauded his personal and musical integrity and intelligence. After his performance in the title role of Vaughan Williams's *Hugh the Drover*, one reviewer said that 'Dowd shows that he can sing with quiet lyricism yet appear manly'; other critics noted that he could sound virile, especially in heroic roles such as Aeneas in Berlioz's *The Trojans*. Another English success (repeated later at the Aix-en-Provence Festival, France, and for the Victoria State Opera in Melbourne) was Mozart's then seldom performed *Idomeneo*. After hearing those performances one London critic wrote: 'He imbued the character with a personality that vibrated with human sensibility and his interpretation carried conviction from first to last', while another thought that 'his singing and phrasing were a joy to hear'.

When in 1970 he sang with his compatriot Marie Collier [q.v.13] in *Wozzeck* as the 'flamboyantly confident' Drum Major, his 'sheer animal exuberance' was appreciated. His performance as Claudius in the première of Humphrey Searle's *Hamlet* in Hamburg in 1968 (where a year earlier he had sung in the première of Alexander Goehr's *Arden Muß Sterben*) moved the critic in *The Times* to enthuse about his 'strength and authority'. While his Wagnerian performances were highly praised (especially in *Lohengrin*), Benjamin (Lord) Britten's *Peter Grimes* was his greatest achievement. Experienced judges considered him the finest exponent ever of that tortured role, in Australia on stage (1958) and on Australian Broadcasting Commission television (1964), and in London at Covent Garden (1961) and Sadler's Wells (1963). Other London roles included Manrico (*Il Trovatore*), Florestan (*Fidelio*) and Rodolfo (*La Bohème*); his performance of the title role in *Oedipus Rex* earned the high regard of its composer, Stravinsky. Praise for the clarity

of his singing gained him the sobriquet 'Diction Dowd'. In concerts he performed pieces by Berlioz, from Wagner's *Tristan und Isolde*, and—with a peerless profundity—from Elgar's *Dream of Gerontius*.

In 1972 Dowd returned to Australia. He joined the Australian Opera and next year at the new Sydney Opera House sang Pierre in Prokofiev's *War and Peace*. Subsequently he made a number of appearances there, notably in *Fidelio*, but his relations with the Australian Opera were inharmonious and an opportunity was lost by its decision not to mount *Peter Grimes* for him. A fighter for singers' rights, Dowd unsuccessfully sought election to the board in 1978 and 1980, causing the chairman Charles Berg [q.v.] to seek a senior barrister's opinion to thwart him.

When his contract with the Australian Opera was not renewed after 1979, Dowd channelled his energies into teaching, supporting musical ventures in the deprived western suburbs of Sydney and founding, at Bathurst in 1988, an annual summer school for singers. Averse to 'careful' singing, he advised students: 'Be well prepared but prepared to take risks'. He had been appointed AO in 1976. Survived by his son, he died on 15 March 1990 at Darlinghurst, Sydney, and was cremated; his wife and daughter predeceased him.

B. and F. MacKenzie, *Singers of Australia* (1967); *Woman's Day and Home*, 22 Jan 1951, p 10; *SMH*, 15 Oct 1955, p 7, 26 Jan 1956, p 3, 2 July 1980, p 3, 17 Mar 1990, p 82, 5 Jan 1991, p 10; *Opera Australia*, Aug 1982, p 7, Sept 1982, p 5, Apr 1991, p 1; B883, NX91611 (NAA); Royal Opera House (Covent Garden, London), English National Opera (London), and Hamburgische Staatsoper (Hamburg) Archives; private information and personal knowledge.

JOHN CARMODY

DOWNER, SIR ALEXANDER RUSSELL (1910-1981), politician and diplomat, was born on 7 April 1910 in North Adelaide, son of Australian-born parents Sir John William Downer [q.v.8], solicitor and member of the Legislative Council, and his second wife Una Stella Haslingden, née Russell. Alick, as he was commonly known, was 5 when his father died, and the boy received his early education at The Hutchins School, Hobart. From 1924 he boarded at Geelong Church of England Grammar School, winning several prizes, earning a reputation for debating and, in his final year (1927), obtaining honours in five subjects, including a first in British history.

In 1928 Downer went up to Brasenose College, Oxford (BA, 1932; MA, 1947), where he studied philosophy, politics and economics, and took a diploma in economics and political science (1932). After reading law in London, he was called to the Bar at the Inner Temple in 1934. He returned to Adelaide and was admitted to the South Australian Bar on 24 April 1935, but he spent much of his time as a grazier on his estate, Arbury Park, near Bridgewater in the Adelaide Hills. There he built a two-storey Georgian-style mansion, attached a deer park and, after his mother died in 1955, added a chapel in her memory.

Downer had grown into a handsome, fit-looking man, almost six feet (183 cm) tall. With the outbreak of World War II, he was mobilised in the Militia on 22 July 1940. He transferred to the Australian Imperial Force on 30 November and was posted to the 2/14th Field Regiment. Arriving in Singapore in August 1941, he served as a gunner with head-quarters, 8th Divisional Artillery, and was captured by the Japanese in February 1942. He spent the rest of the war at Changi. As an acting sergeant, he helped to pass the time by assembling a library, holding classes in law and politics for his fellow prisoners, and giving them elocution lessons. Captivity taught him to value comradeship, reflection and spiritual nourishment. Although he later expressed wonder that so many had survived Changi and were 'able to live useful lives', his own inner strength ensured that he was numbered among them.

After the war Downer returned to South Australia and was discharged from the army on 15 November 1945. At the Church of the Epiphany, Crafers, on 23 April 1947 he married with Anglican rites Mary Isobel Gosse, daughter of (Sir) James Gosse [q.v.14]. Securing Liberal Party preselection for the rural seat of Angas, he was elected to the House of Representatives as part of the Liberal-Country Party victory in 1949, and retained the seat until his retirement in 1964. He sat on the back-bench for over eight years: Prime Minister (Sir) Robert Menzies [q.v.15] was in no hurry to elevate the younger, so-called 'forty-niners', many of them idealistic ex-servicemen. During this time Downer was a member of the parliamentary delegation to the coronation (1953) of Queen Elizabeth II, and of several parliamentary committees, most notably those concerned with constitutional review and foreign affairs. Menzies eventually appointed him minister for immigration on 20 March 1958 and next year brought him into cabinet.

Downer's appointment coincided with a growing campaign by immigration reform organisations to modify the White Australia policy. The new minister contributed to change in 1959 by removing the notorious dictation test, which he described as 'an archaic, heavy-handed piece of machinery' whose 'clumsy, creaking operation has evoked much resent-ment outside Australia, and has tarnished our good name in the eyes of the world'. In its place he introduced 'the neat, simple expe-

dient of an entry permit'. He also piloted an amendment to facilitate naturalisation of non-European spouses and unmarried children of Australian citizens. Simultaneously, he removed arbitrary ministerial powers to deport, extended the legal rights of potential deportees and, citing his experience as a detainee in a prisoner-of-war camp, provided for non-criminal deportees to be held in deten-tion centres rather than gaols. The object was to impart 'justice, tolerance, and humanity in accord with liberal principles', and thus to give Australia 'in many respects ... the finest immi-gration charter that the world has yet seen'.

He may have presided over a minor liber-alisation of the White Australia policy, but Downer was determined to preserve Aus-tralia's 'predominantly homogeneous popula-tion'. He remained unmoved when the Student Action movement—formed just before the 1961 Federal election—harassed him at politi-cal meetings. Believing that the large major-ity of Australians wanted to maintain the existing restrictive policies, he argued that every country had the right to choose its own racial mix, that homogeneity was the best defence against the disharmony that affected all mixed-race societies, and that Australia's Asian neighbours understood and accepted Australia's stand. He was equally adamant on another issue: although he welcomed migrants from continental Europe, he asserted in 1959 that he favoured attracting 'our kinsfolk' from Britain to ensure that Australia remained essentially 'a British country'.

While Downer could successfully resist demands for change in immigration policy, he could not—on a personal matter—sway Sir Thomas Playford's [q.v.] State Liberal govern-ment. Playford had approved plans in 1962 to construct a freeway through the Adelaide Hills, bisecting Arbury Park and passing within 200 yards (183 m) of the house. Downer sought a compromise by offering to cede land on the edge of the estate. Advised that divert-ing the highway would be too expensive, Playford rejected the offer. After Menzies invited Downer at the end of 1963 to succeed Sir Eric Harrison [q.v.14] as Australian high commissioner in London, Alick decided to settle the issue and sold Arbury Park to the South Australian government. When Menzies also recommended him for a knighthood—he was appointed KBE in 1965—the news came as 'sunshine after rain' (Mary's mother had recently died) and the recommendation was even more welcome coming from a man who could 'always count upon my loyalty, friend-ship, and affection'.

Sir Alexander, his black hair having turned into a distinguished grey, looked and sounded the part in representing Australia in a post he obviously enjoyed, not least because the posi-tion involved a special relationship with British ministers of the day. In October 1965 the Downers acquired Oare House in Wiltshire, built in the 1740s—but, according to Alick, 'more Queen Anne than Georgian'—where visitors from Australia and Britain were warmly and informally entertained. The Downers moved easily through the upper political and social world, but it was a difficult time for an Anglophile and a passionate Commonwealth man to be high commissioner. The fact that Britain had a Labour government (1964-70) was not itself a problem, although he did have reservations about Prime Minister (Sir) Harold (Baron) Wilson. Downer had good personal relations with several Labour ministers and a high regard for many whose politics were far removed from his own. What he found disturbing and saddening was the prospect of Britain joining the European Economic Community and of ending its military commitments east of Suez. He feared that 'our British connections would recede', while noting that the majority of migrants going to Australia were of British stock and that, despite the 'occasional rumblings of the avant-garde, no country has shown itself more loyal to the Sovereign'.

Alick left the London post in October 1972 and in 1975 the Downers settled on their new rural property north-east of Adelaide. Full retirement was not an option. He had promised to speak out: 'Though I'm nominally a diplomat ... substantially I'm a politician'. Downer wanted to be a link between Britain and Australia, and he and Mary travelled frequently between both. Made a freeman of the City of London in 1965, he was elected a fellow of the Royal Society of Arts in 1968. In 1973 the University of Birmingham conferred on him an honorary LL D. He served on the boards of several societies and, despite the illness of his final years, completed a manuscript entitled *Six Prime Ministers*, which was published posthumously (1982). It dealt, in part, with the prime ministers he knew well: Menzies, Harold Holt [q.v.14] and John Gorton of Australia; Wilson and (Sir) Edward Heath of Britain; and Viscount Brookeborough of Northern Ireland. His account was invaluable as a corrective to conventional wisdom: Downer was one of the first to clear Menzies of the charge of being a dictator in cabinet. The book also reveals much about the writer: a shrewd judge of character with a cultivated mind and a readiness to temper criticisms of political friends and foes in the light of the pressures placed on politicians.

Unfailingly courteous, Downer had what Menzies once described as 'an uncommon capacity for getting on with people'. William Hayden, as leader of the Labor Opposition, called him 'an extraordinarily decent man'. A tribute in *The Times* referred to his 'sheer goodness' and his 'stern sense of public duty'.

He believed that a privileged background imposed obligations. It was easy enough—if unfair—to typecast him as an unreconstructed Tory, and as a member of the Adelaide Establishment who spoke in the accents of southern England and who steadfastly maintained positions even as they were becoming anachronistic. Downer—correctly—saw himself as 'a mixture of the conservative and the radical'. The man who continued to support the White Australia policy was the one who spoke out against censorship, applauded the changes in sexual mores in the late 1960s, entertained notable Labor leftists such as Eddie Ward [q.v.16] and Clyde Cameron at his home, and praised Donald Dunstan, the Labor premier of South Australia, for helping to propel the State out of its 'intellectual desert'.

Downer died on 30 March 1981 at his home and was cremated. He was survived by his spirited wife and their three daughters and son, Alexander, who led the federal Liberal Party in 1994-95 and who, in 1996, was appointed minister for foreign affairs in the Howard government. A portrait of Alick by (Sir) Ivor Hele is held by the family.

H. I. London, *Non-White Immigration and the 'White Australia' Policy* (1970); B. O'Neil et al (eds), *Playford's South Australia* (1996); *PD* (HR), 1 May 1958, p 1396, 1 Apr 1981, p 1159; *Canberra Times*, 19 June 1964, p 2; *Australian*, 1 May 1971, p 17, 13 Jan 1972, p 2, 14 Jan 1972, p 9; *Corian*, July-Aug 1978, p 306, Oct 1981, p 74; *Age* (Melbourne), 1 Apr 1981, p 15; *Times* (London), 4 Apr 1981, p 14, 6 Apr 1981, p 14; Sir Robert Menzies papers (NLA); private information.   I. R. HANCOCK

DOWNES, RONALD GEOFFREY (1916-1985), agricultural scientist and public servant, was born on 3 January 1916 at Ascot Vale, Melbourne, third surviving child of Victorian-born parents Albert John Downes, salesman, and his wife Florence Maude, née Davis. Geoff was educated at Essendon and University High schools, and at the University of Melbourne (B.Agr.Sc., 1937; M.Agr.Sc., 1939) under (Sir) Samuel Wadham [q.v.16]. On 20 July 1940 he married Gwenyth Edith Dodds at Caulfield Methodist Church.

Between 1939 and 1950 Downes was a research officer in the division of soil of the Council for Scientific and Industrial Research (Commonwealth Scientific and Industrial Research Organisation), conducting surveys across Australia. He was seconded to advise the United States air force on the preparation of airstrips in Papua and New Guinea in 1942-43. In 1950 he returned to Melbourne as one of the first three members appointed to the Soil Conservation Authority, established to address extensive erosion in Victoria. He rose to deputy-chairman in 1953 and chairman in

1961. A shy but confident man, he carried the trappings of office with dignity. While reluctant to forgo applied work, he became a respected and effective manager, allowing his staff to work with considerable freedom. His unemotional and objective approach to problems made him a useful committee-man.

In the 1950s and 1960s the SCA consolidated its role in what Downes preferred to term 'land conservation': 'the devising of stable and therefore sustainable systems of land-use', irrespective of the form of use (whether grazing, forestry or wildlife reserve). Under his guidance the SCA gained a national and international reputation for the conservation of land. Downes also acted as a consultant to the Food and Agriculture Organization of the United Nations on dryland farming in Israel (1960, 1965), Iran (1967), Algeria (1972-73), Morocco (1981) and Brazil (1982). He used his knowledge of soils, ecology, hydrology and land management to help in attempts—mostly highly successful— to make the deserts bloom.

From 1961 Downes also chaired the Land Utilisation Advisory Council, an interdepartmental committee dealing with increasingly controversial issues of land alienation and development. He took pride in the LUAC's 'unique' level of expertise, but his emphasis on science over consultation, and his commitment to an overarching public interest, led to LUAC's influence waning with the Victorian minister for lands Sir William McDonald. By 1970 LUAC had effectively lapsed.

In 1973, under (Sir) Rupert Hamer's reform-minded government, Downes was appointed director of conservation and permanent head of a new Victorian Ministry of Conservation. He again sought to bring a 'hard-headed' approach to environmental and development issues. Distrusting the slogans and emotionalism entering debates over conservation, he none the less used his 1974 Meredith Lecture, *Environment, Conservation and People*, to urge critical attention to questions of 'life-style', population pressure and resource strain from a 'spiritual' as much as a social perspective. On his retirement in 1979 he was farewelled as 'a quiet champion' of the environment. That year he was appointed CB.

Downes served as a vice-president (1966-73) of the Australian Conservation Foundation, president (1961-63) of the Australian Society of Soil Science, and president (1971-72) of the Australian Institute of Agricultural Science. He was a fellow of the AIAS, the Soil Conservation Authority of America, the Australasian Academy of Technological Sciences and Engineering, and the Australian Institute of Management. Awarded a doctorate in agricultural science by the University of Melbourne in 1972 in recognition of his work, he received other honours including the Prescott medal of the ASSS (1976), the Australian medal of agricultural science of AIAS (1977) and the Hugh Hammond Bennett Award (1981) of the Soil Conservation Society of America—the first to a non-American. In 1984-85 he was deputy-chancellor of the University of Melbourne.

In his private life Downes played first division lawn bowls and sang in the choir of the Ivanhoe Methodist Church. After a long illness, he died of cancer on 2 May 1985 at home at Eaglemont, Melbourne, and was buried in Eltham cemetery. He was survived by his wife and three sons.

G. Thompson, *A Brief History of Soil Conservation in Victoria, 1834-1961* (1979); L. Robin, *Defending the Little Desert* (1998); *Age* (Melbourne), 6 May 1985, p 7; private information.   NICK UREN

DOYLE, ALEC BROUGHTON (1888-1984), naval officer, was born on 5 October 1888 at his family's property, Invermien, Scone, New South Wales, youngest of five children of James Henry Doyle, grazier, and his wife Rebekah, née McDonald, both born in New South Wales. Alec was educated at Scone Grammar School and at The King's School, Parramatta, where he excelled at sport and served as school captain (1907). At the University of Sydney (BE (Mech. & Elec.), 1911), he studied engineering, boxed, rowed and played cricket and Rugby. He went to England to gain further industry experience.

On 23 March 1912 Doyle was commissioned in the Royal Australian Navy. After training in Britain, he returned home in 1913 as an engineer lieutenant in the new battle-cruiser HMAS *Australia*. When World War I broke out in August 1914, he was engineer officer of HMAS *Parramatta*. The ship sailed immediately to German New Guinea, then patrolled South-East Asian waters. During the deployment Doyle became bored by inactivity and disdainful of his superiors' competence. He was senior engineer of *Encounter* (1917-18) and *Australia* (1919-20) before being appointed as engineer officer of Williamstown Naval Depot, Melbourne. Athletic and dapper, he married Charlotte Madge Lillies on 18 December 1917 at St George's Church of England, Malvern. Much of their married life was spent in naval lodgings, though in 1950 the couple settled at Vaucluse, Sydney.

As Doyle's career flourished he spent most of his time ashore in shipbuilding and repair installations. In December 1923 he became engineer commander at the refit and repair establishment on Garden Island, Sydney Harbour. Later he worked at Cockatoo Island Dockyard, where he was overseer for the building of the sea-plane carrier *Albatross*, in which vessel he served (1929) as engineer officer. Having been fleet engineer officer in *Sydney* in 1925, he was squadron engineer officer in *Australia* and *Canberra* in 1929-32. From 1933 he was engineer manager at Garden Island. He was promoted to captain in 1934 and appointed CBE in 1937. On the night of 31 May 1942, when Japanese midget submarines penetrated Sydney Harbour, he was awakened in his married quarter on the island by gunfire from USS *Chicago*. A Japanese torpedo ran aground, without exploding, on a small beach beneath the bedroom in which his wife remained sleeping.

In September 1942 Doyle was appointed to Navy Office, Melbourne, as director of engineering (naval). Twelve months later he was promoted to rear admiral and named third naval member of the Naval Board and chief of construction. He retired from the navy on 5 October 1948. In December 1950 he was appointed to a Commonwealth government manpower allocation committee. The Institution of Engineers, Australia, awarded him the (Sir) Peter Nicol Russell [q.v.6] medal in 1953.

Doyle's politics were conservative and sometimes clandestine. Although there was a ban on serving Commonwealth defence personnel joining paramilitary groups, during the Depression he was apparently connected with The Country (Northern Division), part of the secretive Old Guard. His trenchant anti-communism and his belief that apathy permeated Australian political life inspired his prominence in The Call to the People of Australia, a Cold War project announced on Armistice Day 1951. This movement called for a spiritual renaissance against the 'moral dry rot' and lassitude that had reputedly overtaken the country. Doyle became deputy-chairman of the State standing committee of The Call in 1953, and chairman in 1957. Co-trustee of The Call's funds in New South Wales, he belonged to a discreet policy committee that devised ways and means of collecting money.

After he retired, Doyle's many projects included the family pastoral company, Dr Barnardo's Homes (Dr Barnardo's in Australia), the Royal Society of St George, and the Institution of Engineers, Australia. He was a regular letter writer to the *Sydney Morning Herald*, pontificating on themes such as the need for enhanced civic amenity and active citizenship, and the importance of coastal shipping, local shipbuilding and defence planning, while denouncing the perils of communists undermining Australia's maritime industry and its universities. An article of his, published in the *Sydney Morning Herald* on 28 April 1955, argued that Middle East oil lines were the weak link in Australian security, creating vigorous debate. He became a competent family historian and genealogist, between 1956 and 1960 preparing a manuscript on the

descendants of his ancestor Andrew Doyle, an Irish rebel transported to New South Wales for his part in the 'troubles' of 1798 and 1801. Alec Doyle's belief in participatory citizenship and active engagement in the democratic process accorded with the principles of his forebear. His work *How Shall I Vote?* (1952), with which he was assisted by his friend M. H. Ellis [q.v.14], was a passable history of political parties in Australia intended for working-class readers.

Doyle was active in Liberal Party circles in the Eastern Suburbs of Sydney, a member of preselection committees in the seat of Wentworth and occasionally a campaign manager. Though he was enthusiastic, many of his proposals reflected a lack of political experience. His insistence that The Call remain wedded to the White Australia policy did not assist that organisation's longevity.

Bespectacled and trim, Alec Doyle remained physically active, playing tennis twice a week at the Royal Sydney Golf Club until well into his seventies. In 1963, Doyle, aged 75, left Vaucluse to manage Invermien. He served as chairman of the Scone branch of the Graziers' Association of New South Wales and delegate to the district council. After Charlotte died of cancer in 1951, he enjoyed the companionship of his friend and housekeeper, Hilda Lomax. Following her death, Invermien was sold in 1973 and Doyle lived with family at Boggabilla, where he died on 30 June 1984. Survived by his two sons, he was cremated.

Doyle had a self-effacing streak and was quick to acknowledge his foibles. In 1970 he reflected:

> for one of a nervous and unadventurous nature, painfully and foolishly self conscious and shy even up to an advanced age, and not overgifted with brains, one whose main assets were robust health and vigour allied with persistence and good fortune, I feel that, superficially at least, it was a modestly successful career.

I. Chapman, *Sydney University Regiment* (1996); *Navy* (Sydney), Sept 1947, p 19; *Jnl of the Inst of Engineers, Aust*, Dec 1953, p 253; *King's School Mag*, Dec 1984, p 116; E. Ulacco, A Call to the People of Australia 1951-1959 (BA Hons thesis, Univ of Wollongong, 1992); A6769, item Doyle A B (NAA); Doyle papers (SLNSW); King's School Archives (Parramatta, Sydney); private information.
                                                 ANDREW MOORE

DREW, SIR FERDINAND CAIRE (1895-1986), public servant, was born on 1 May 1895 at Norwood, Adelaide, second of three sons of Charles Henry Drew (d.1911), an English-born harness-maker, and his wife Edith

Eleanor, née Eaton, who was born in South Australia. Charles Drew ran a saddlery shop in Currie Street, Adelaide, and the family lived at Dulwich. Educated at Rose Park Public School and Muirden [q.v.10] College for Business Training, as a lad 'Fred' learned to play the flute and earned good money accompanying entertainers such as 'Stiffy' and 'Mo' (Nat Phillips and Roy Rene [q.v.11]). On 1 July 1911 he joined the South Australian Public Service as a junior clerk in the Survey Department, under the commissioner of crown lands and immigration; his salary helped to support his widowed mother and younger brother.

Over the next twenty years Drew worked in the departments of Irrigation and Reclamation Works, Highways and Local Government, and Industry. He studied accountancy, becoming an associate (1929) and a fellow (1947) of the Commonwealth Institute of Accountants. He was also an associate of the Australian Institute of Cost Accountants. On 6 June 1934 at the Church of the Epiphany, Crafers, he married with Anglican rites Crissie Avis McGowan, a civil servant.

As an 'efficiency officer' in the audit section of the Chief Secretary's Department, Drew came to the attention of the auditor-general, J. W. Wainwright [q.v.12], and in 1936 was appointed assistant auditor-general. Next year he became a founding board-member of the South Australian Housing Trust. He approached the Treasury Department for the necessary £25 000 start-up funds, inspected land, collected rents, assessed future needs at Port Pirie and Leigh Creek, and used his public service contacts to have buses re-routed and water supplied to the new houses. Site inspections were a regular weekend outing for the Drew family. Although he left the board in January 1940 he maintained an interest in the trust; after A. M. Ramsay [q.v.16] became general manager in 1949, he and Drew kept in close contact.

In 1939 Drew had transferred to the Treasury Department and begun working for the premier and treasurer (Sir) Thomas Playford [q.v.]. That year he was appointed assistant under-treasurer and in 1946 under-treasurer. He and Playford shared offices, meeting at 9.30 each morning to discuss the business of the day. Playford told him: 'You manage the money, Fred. I'll manage the politics'. Drew was not only Playford's chief financial adviser but also his friend and confidant, having power of attorney and control of the premier's cheque-book when he left the country. Chairman of the South Australian Grants Committee from 1939, he became an authority on Commonwealth-State financial relations. He was also a member of the Supply and Tender Board (chairman 1943-49), the Farmers Assistance Board (1939-43) and the Industries Development Committee (1942-50).

In 1948-73 he served on the State Bank of South Australia board; he was chairman in 1961-63.

Implementing Playford's industrialisation program, Drew arranged loans and Commonwealth grants to develop the Leigh Creek coalfields, build the Morgan-Whyalla water pipeline and fund the expansion of the housing trust. He managed the sale of the Adelaide Electric Supply Company to the government in 1946 and worked out the compensation system for shareholders. In 1949 he became chairman of the Electricity Trust of South Australia. His instructions from Playford were to extend electricity to as many houses as possible as quickly as possible and to maintain good industrial relations. He defused potential disputes in amicable discussions over his parents-in-law's fence with the Australian Labor Party deputy-leader Francis Walsh [q.v.16] and ran ETSA with such efficiency that the charges were not increased for twenty years.

Drew was renowned for his sound judgment and for his picturesque vocabulary—according to Stewart Cockburn he was 'an artist in profane language'. Shrewd and irascible, he took a tough stance on demands on the public purse, tossing proposals that failed his feasibility test on top of a large cupboard in his office. At home he paid attention to his children's development and insisted that they receive the university education he had missed. Appointed CMG in 1951, he was knighted in 1960 and retired as under-treasurer that year. Sir Fred sat on several boards, including those of Cellulose Ltd (1950-69), Adelaide Steamship Co. Ltd (1961-70) and Chrysler Australia Ltd (1962-74), and remained chairman of ETSA until 1970. Survived by his wife and their son and two daughters, he died on 23 May 1986 at his Glenelg home and was cremated.

S. Cockburn, The Patriarchs (1983), and Playford (1991); Auditor-General's Report, PP (SA), 1946-60; S. Marsden, interview with F. Drew (ts, 1981, SLSA); Advertiser (Adelaide), 7 June 1951, p 3, 11 June 1960, p 3; personal information.   KATHRYN GARGETT

DRIVER, ARTHUR ROBERT ('MICK') (1909-1981), civil engineer, administrator and immigration official, was born on 25 November 1909 at Albany, Western Australia, youngest of five surviving children of Australian-born parents Henry Driver, packer, and his wife Mary Ann, née Hicken. Educated at the High School, Perth, and at the University of Western Australia, 'Mick' entered the Western Australian Public Works Department in 1928 as an engineering cadet. He was appointed engineer on the permanent staff in 1937. On 8 August 1936 at St Mary's Church of England, West Perth, he had married Hazel Freda Kelly.

Called up for full-time duty as a lieutenant, Royal Australian Engineers, Militia, on 16 October 1940, Driver transferred to the Australian Imperial Force on 10 April 1941. He was 6 ft 2 ins (188 cm) tall, with blue eyes and auburn hair. Posted to the 2/4th Pioneer Battalion, he served in the Northern Territory and underwent staff training. In March 1943 he was promoted to temporary captain. As brigade major of the 23rd Brigade from September, he was sent to Papua and New Guinea, and then to Bougainville. He was promoted to temporary major in February 1944. In September 1945 he was made general staff officer, 2nd grade (operations), at Advanced Land Headquarters, Morotai, Netherlands East Indies. He transferred to the Reserve of Officers on 5 December.

Driver returned briefly to the Public Works Department and in 1946 became an associate-member of the Institution of Engineers, Australia. On 1 July that year he succeeded C. L. A. Abbott [q.v.13] as administrator of the Northern Territory, becoming the fifth to administer the Territory on behalf of the Commonwealth government. In 1947 the Legislative Council was created to manage Territory affairs locally; next year Driver was named its first president. The council comprised seven appointed members (senior public servants) and six elected members, thereby maintaining Federal hegemony. Driver participated vigorously in council proceedings and debate.

Presiding over the postwar reconstruction of Darwin, Driver supervised the conversion of freehold land titles to leasehold. He reorganised the administration and police force, developed stock routes to open up pastoral lands, promoted agriculture and mining, expanded education facilities, including the School of the Air, and ensured that these aspects of the Territory were widely publicised throughout Australia to attract new residents. On 18 October 1949 (ten days after he was divorced), at St Leonard's Presbyterian Church, Brighton Beach, Melbourne, Driver married Marjorie ('Mardi') Campbell, née Leighton, a secretary who had previously changed her surname to Driver by deed poll.

Frustrated at the slow rate of progress, Driver resigned as administrator with effect from 30 June 1951. He joined the Commonwealth Department of Immigration and served as chief migration officer in Italy (1951-54) and in Central-Northern Europe (1954-55). In 1956-61 he was chief of the department of operations, Intergovernmental Committee for European Migration, Geneva. On returning to Australia, he briefly resumed engineering work in Melbourne and became director of the

resources development branch of the Victorian Employers' Federation (1963-70).

Driver moved to Buderim, Queensland, and from 1970 was managing director of Communicator Public Relations (Queensland) Pty Ltd and Mirrabooka Rural Resources Pty Ltd. His recreations included tennis, squash and golf. Survived by his wife and their daughter, and by the son and daughter of his first marriage, he died on 18 May 1981 at Buderim and was cremated. A suburb of Palmerston, Northern Territory, was named after him.

P. F. Donovan, *At the Other End of Australia* (1984); D. Carment and B. James (eds), *Northern Territory Dictionary of Biography*, vol 2 (1992); P. A. Rosenzweig, *The House of Seven Gables* (1996); E. Gibson, *Bag-huts, Bombs and Bureaucrats* (1997); A2065, item A R Driver (NAA).

PAUL A. ROSENZWEIG

DRYSDALE, SIR GEORGE RUSSELL (1912-1981), artist, was born on 7 February 1912 at Bognor Regis, Sussex, England, son of George Russell Drysdale, a gentleman of private means and Scottish ancestry, and his wife Isobel, née Gates, who was English. George Russell Drysdale [q.v.4] was his grandfather. Having relinquished a commission with the Black Watch, his father returned in 1919 to Pioneer, the family's sugar farm on the Burdekin River in northern Queensland. The family moved to Melbourne in 1923 and 'Tas', as he was known, went to Geelong Church of England Grammar School. When his father acquired Boxwood Park in the Riverina district in 1926, Tas was introduced to the inland plains that had been memorialised by novels of Tom Collins [q.v.8 Furphy] and Marcus Clarke [q.v.3], by the work of the nineteenth-century Aboriginal artist Tommy McCrae, and by Tom Roberts's [q.v.11] paintings 'Shearing the Rams' and 'The Breakaway'.

A detached retina was discovered in Drysdale's left eye in 1929. In his final year at Geelong Grammar, possibly as a form of therapy, he had five sessions a week in drawing, including perspective, three-dimensional form, the art of memory, and design in plant forms. Eye exercises introduced Drysdale to art and perhaps determined his career; moreover, his great images—remarkable for their depth of space—were to be produced by one who had effective vision in one eye only.

During the spring of 1930, with a school friend, 'Bunny' Reed, Drysdale oversaw the shearing and farm work at Boxwood Park in his father's absence, then worked for some months at Pioneer with his uncle Cluny Drysdale. After accompanying Cluny to Britain on family business in 1931, he returned to Boxwood Park. Plans to be a farmer receded in 1932 when he was recovering in a Melbourne hospital from an eye operation. Julian Smith, his surgeon and a gifted photographer, showed Drysdale's drawings to (Sir) (Ernest) Daryl Lindsay, who suggested that he take lessons from George Bell [qq.v.11,10,7]. During the first few months that Drysdale attended his classes, Bell advised him against mere illustration and unreflective imitation, advocating the study of 'form' in modern art. The reproductions he showed to Drysdale had no meaning for the young man, who made an appointment to see (Sir) Keith Murdoch [q.v.10]: the press baron squashed his aspirations to be an illustrator. Travelling in Europe in 1932-34, Drysdale took note of works of modern art and began to change his mind about its appeal.

In 1934, while working at Boxwood Park, Drysdale did some painting, including an oil of the foothills east of Albury similar in style to landscapes of the region painted concurrently by Bell and Rupert Bunny [q.v.7]; and he courted Elizabeth (Bon) Stephen of Albury. She was knowledgeable about modern art, having travelled through Europe in 1930 with Lucy Swanton [q.v.], who was to become Drysdale's art dealer in Melbourne and later at the Macquarie Galleries in Sydney. On 8 February 1935 Drysdale and Bon married in a civil ceremony in Melbourne.

After undergoing surgery on his eye that year, Drysdale re-enrolled at the Bell-Shore [q.v.11] school, Melbourne. Bell's teaching was towards the intellectual marriage of form and idea. In May 1937 Peter (Charles Roderick) Purves Smith [q.v.11] arrived and for seven months shared Drysdale's working space, spurring him on in friendly rivalry. The period was decisive for both young artists. Following Tas's first solo exhibition in April 1938, the Drysdales went to London, where he took some lessons at Iain Macnab's Grosvenor School of Modern Art. For a time Drysdale shared Purves Smith's studio in Paris, and bought day tickets for life drawing at the Grande Chaumière; his paintings over the next two years paid luscious homage to the School of Paris. With war threatening, the Drysdales retreated to London in October, and in April 1939 sailed for home.

In Melbourne Drysdale shared Bell's home studio and was unwillingly drawn into acrimonious politics within the Contemporary Art Society. To his dismay he was not accepted for military service because of his eye. Doubly frustrated, he retreated with his family to Albury in mid-1940 and offered to manage Boxwood Park: its new owner, Bunny Reed, was absent on military service. Having supervised the shearing, he admitted the gesture was 'ridiculous ... one of the stock and station agents could do it far better', and moved to Sydney.

According to his biographer Lou Klepac, 'Drysdale felt that it was only when he got to Sydney that he really began to paint'. In his country themes, from 1941, Drysdale produced significant art. The major paintings of the next forty years commenced with 'The Crow Trap', 'Man Reading a Paper' and 'Man Feeding His Dogs' (1941). The back-country theme evolved through 'Home Town' (1943), 'The Drover's Wife' (1945), 'Sofala' (1947), for which he won the Wynne prize, 'The Cricketers' (1948), the group portraits of Cape York Aborigines in the early 1950s, 'Native Dogger at Mount Olga' and 'Basketball at Broome' in 1958. His characteristic image throughout was the figure-in-landscape. In 1959 figures and background melded together suggestively in paintings such as 'Snake Bay at Night'. The culminating work, 'Man in a Landscape' (1963), was the image of an Indigenous Australian who, as Drysdale explained to the owner, Queen Elizabeth II, was trying to hold on to his land. Unlike his contemporaries (Sir) Sidney Nolan and Arthur Boyd, Drysdale did not incorporate literary subjects and characters from external sources into the Australian scene but sought to represent people in their places. His memorable achievement was to suggest that certain types of country Australians (from 1950 the types tended to be Aboriginal) represented a foundation for national identity.

Drysdale joined the board of Pioneer Sugar Mills (Pty) Ltd in 1947; he established strong ties with Pioneer, calling it his 'spiritual home'. Through painting he expressed something of his, his father's and grandfather's love of the land, while retaining a wider choice than was available to those whose lives were tied to it. His art reflected the British-Australian experience, representing Australia to British as well as to Australian audiences; thus he resolved the so-called 'provincial' dilemma of whether to look for meaning within Australia or outside.

The repertoire of Australian types that he developed was at a level of myth too well understood by Australians to engender a sense that they were his personal creation. At inception his successful figures already had the stamp of myth. In sequence, exaggerated renditions of life on a country farm followed tall-story sessions with Purves Smith; images of wartime's dislocated domesticity (cocooned soldiers sleeping uncomfortably at Albury railway station) followed his recognition of the symbolism in Henry Moore's drawings of Londoners in underground shelters; drought and erosion subjects followed a trip to western New South Wales with the journalist Keith Newman of the *Sydney Morning Herald*; images of deserted mining towns were stimulated by George Farwell's [q.v.14] evocation of ghost towns; and a six-month journey through the north of Australia with his son, Timothy, led to totemic beings that melded human and animal. Characteristically, Drysdale remained in touch with his subjects, his mode being the daydream and the doodle by which key characters took on a life of their own. Thus the drover's wife 'Big Edna', for example, had several incarnations in Drysdale's art. By 1950, his practice when planning an exhibition was to use a few completed paintings to 'seed' the titles of other works, which he would then produce.

Drysdale's career was international although, unlike other major Australian artists of his generation, Nolan and Boyd for example, he did not choose to live abroad. He was a regular exhibitor in London (at the Leicester Galleries in 1950, 1958, 1965, 1972), where he attracted critics and buyers. Like other internationally successful artists of his generation, he did not have to depend largely on public patronage. In 1941 the Metropolitan Museum of Art, New York, acquired 'Monday Morning' (1938) from the Art of Australia 1788-1941 exhibition then touring the United States of America, and the Tate Gallery, London, bought 'War Memorial' (1950) from Drysdale's first London exhibition, but many of his major works were sold privately, with Sir Kenneth Clark, Captain Neil McEacharn, Kym Bonython and Edgar Kaufmann among notable collectors. Between 1942 and 1962 he had nine exhibitions at the Macquarie Galleries, Sydney. The first of many monographs about him appeared in 1951, written by (Sir) Joseph Burke, who held the Herald chair of fine art at the University of Melbourne. In 1960 a retrospective of Drysdale's work was organised by the Art Gallery of New South Wales. The creativity of his colour photographs was recognised when Jennie Boddington organised a posthumous exhibition at the National Gallery of Victoria.

Tragedy entered Drysdale's life in the early 1960s with the suicide of his son, Timothy, in July 1962 and of Bon in November 1963. On 20 June 1964 at Holy Trinity Church of England, Millers Point, Sydney, he married Maisie Joyce Purves Smith, a librarian and the widow of his friend. They lived at Bouddi Farm, near Gosford, from 1966. A member of the board of trustees of the Art Gallery of New South Wales (1962-76) and of the Commonwealth Art Advisory Board (1963-76), he was knighted in 1969 and appointed AC in 1980. Three months after a major exhibition of drawings at Joseph Brown's gallery, Melbourne, Sir Russell died of cancer on 29 June 1981 at Westmead and was cremated. He was survived by his wife and the daughter of his first marriage.

G. Dutton, *Russell Drysdale* (1964); M. Eagle and J. Minchin, *The George Bell School* (1981); L. Klepac,

The Life and Work of Russell Drysdale (1983); J. Boddington, *Drysdale Photographer* (1987); G. Smith, *Russell Drysdale 1912-81* (1997); Drysdale papers (SLNSW).   MARY EAGLE

DUGUID, CHARLES (1884-1986), medical practitioner and Aboriginal rights campaigner, was born on 6 April 1884 at Saltcoats, Scotland, eldest of seven children of Charles Duguid (pronounced Dogood), schoolteacher, and his wife Jane, née Kinnier. He attended the High School of Glasgow, and studied arts and medicine at the University of Glasgow (MA, 1905; MB, Ch.B., 1909), where he won twenty-one prizes. A full Blue, he represented the university in quarter-mile and half-mile events, his red hair earning him the nickname 'the Scarlet Runner'. After graduating he practised medicine at Glasgow.

In 1911 Duguid travelled to Australia as a ship's medical officer. On board he met and became engaged to Irene Isabella Young, an Australian returning home from England, and decided that his future lay in Australia. Back in Scotland he assisted in a practice that served four mining villages; his observations of poverty and suffering there were to influence his later concern for social justice. Next year he migrated to Australia, again working his passage as a ship's doctor. On 23 October 1912 he and Irene married with Congregational forms at the Collins Street Independent Church, Melbourne. He practised in the Wimmera township of Minyip before moving to Adelaide in 1914.

On 5 February 1917 Duguid was appointed captain, Australian Army Medical Corps, Australian Imperial Force. He treated casualties in the Middle East (March-July) before returning to Australia in a hospital ship. His AIF appointment terminated on 5 October. He wrote about his war experiences in *From the Suez Canal to Gaza with the Australian Light Horse* (1917?) and *The Desert Trail* (1919). After a trip to Scotland in 1919 for postgraduate study he bought a house at Magill, Adelaide, where he set up practice, while also working as a surgeon at the Memorial Hospital, North Adelaide. He became active in local branches of the Returned Sailors' and Soldiers' Imperial League of Australia, Legacy and Toc H.

Duguid undertook further medical study in Britain in 1927. His wife, returning home separately with their son, died suddenly at sea. In 1929 he met Phyllis Evelyn Lade, daughter of Rev. Frank Lade [q.v.9] and an English teacher at Presbyterian Girls College, of which he was a councillor (1922-34). They married on 18 December 1930 at the Kent Town

Methodist Church. That year he was elected a fellow of the Royal Australasian College of Surgeons. A patient, who was a missionary in the Northern Territory, had told Duguid of abuses suffered by Aborigines there. In 1934 he decided to visit Darwin and look into the situation himself. Arriving by train at Alice Springs in July, he was asked to perform emergency surgery and, having missed his connection to Darwin, stayed in the area for over three weeks. He was appalled by the treatment that he saw meted out to Aborigines, and by their poor living conditions. At Hermannsburg Mission he visited Pastor F. W. Albrecht [q.v.] and met Albert Namatjira [q.v.15], with whom he became friends.

In 1935 Duguid was elected the first lay moderator of the Presbyterian Church in South Australia and president of the Aborigines Protection League. Albrecht had suggested that he investigate conditions in the Musgrave Ranges, in north-western South Australia. In June, with R. M. Williams, he journeyed to Ernabella, a pastoral lease, and for the first time met Pitjantjatjara people—thus beginning a relationship with them that was to last for fifty years. Gilpin, a part-Aboriginal youth, guided him farther west. Duguid was again disturbed by his observations of discrimination and of abuse of Aboriginal workers and women, and by evidence of increasing health problems. He discussed with his wife the possibility of establishing a Christian mission to serve as a 'buffer between the Aborigines and the encroaching white man'. They decided that there should be 'no compulsion nor imposition of our way of life on the Aborigines, nor deliberate interference with tribal custom' and that the vernacular language should be used, medical care offered, and responsibility passed to the local people as soon as possible. In 1936 he visited Haasts Bluff, west of Hermannsburg, with Albrecht. That year, despite opposition from some influential members, including Rev. John Flynn [q.v.8], the general assembly of the Presbyterian Church of Australia approved Duguid's proposal to establish a mission in the Musgrave Ranges. With support from the government of South Australia, Ernabella Mission was founded in 1937.

Duguid and his wife also took an interest in the children of mixed descent living in Colebrook Home, Quorn, run by the United Aborigines Mission. For six weeks over Christmas 1935 thirty-four had stayed at the Duguids' home. Duguid was to maintain contact with them into adulthood and to assist their struggle for equality with White people. In 1939 he toured the Aboriginal reserves west of Ernabella with Albrecht, T. G. H. Strehlow [q.v.16] and Rev. Harry Taylor, the superintendent of Ernabella. From the Petermann Ranges they travelled on camels, guided by a Pitjantjatjara man, Tjuintjara, who became Duguid's close friend and later lived at Ernabella.

Appointed a founding member (1940) of South Australia's Aborigines Protection Board, Duguid inspected reserves throughout the State, noting abuses against Aborigines on pastoral properties and discrimination in education. The Duguids, with their two children and their fostered Aboriginal son, Sydney James Cook, visited Ernabella in 1946. Soon afterwards they heard of the British proposal to test guided weapons over South Australia from a base to be built at Woomera. Concerned about the impact of the rocket range on the inhabitants of the Central Australian reserves, Duguid criticised the scheme at public meetings in Adelaide and, with Donald Thomson [q.v.16], in Melbourne. Duguid resigned from the Aborigines Protection Board when it approved the proposal, but as a result of the protests a patrol officer, Walter MacDougall [q.v.15], was appointed at Woomera.

During a measles epidemic at Ernabella in 1948 Duguid helped to care for the sick. In 1951 he reported on health needs of Aborigines in the Northern Territory. President (1951-61) of the Aborigines Advancement League of South Australia, in 1953 he arranged a meeting in the Adelaide Town Hall at which five Aborigines spoke of their experiences. One told of discrimination against young Aboriginal women applying for entrance to nursing training at Royal Adelaide Hospital. The Duguids supported moves to break down this barrier. Another outcome of the meeting was the establishment in 1956 by the AAL of Wiltja Hostel at Millswood, to accommodate Aboriginal country girls attending secondary schools in Adelaide.

Duguid was president (1944-60) of the District and Bush Nursing Society of South Australia. Following a motorcar accident in 1956 he retired as a surgeon and took up an interest in geriatric medicine. Under the auspices of the AAL, he published *The Central Aborigines Reserve* (1957). He and his wife were leaders of a campaign that in 1958 resulted in the repealing of a clause in the Police Offences Act which had enabled police to arrest Aborigines for consorting with non-Aborigines. That year he was elected inaugural president of the Federal Council for Aboriginal Advancement. The Duguids continued to visit Ernabella, and welcomed the mission's choir to Adelaide in 1954 and 1966. He wrote *No Dying Race* (1963) and an autobiography, *Doctor and the Aborigines* (1972).

Stubborn in defence of the rights of the under-privileged, and sometimes impetuous, Duguid fought for justice and fiercely opposed hypocrisy and incompetence in the administration of Aboriginal affairs. His concerns and actions were motivated by his Scottish Presbyterian faith and by his conviction that in this changing world one thing remains unchanged—'the astonishing power of selfless love'. By the 1960s, however, Aboriginal leaders in organisations such as the FCAA were objecting to the assimilationist approach of Duguid and other white campaigners, considering it paternalistic. For his part, Duguid was dismayed by the emergence of the 'Black Power' movement.

In 1971 Duguid was appointed OBE. Next year he received what he considered his greatest honour: a letter from the Ernabella people requesting that when he died, his body be buried at the mission, 'so that the Aboriginals will always remember that he was one of us and that he faithfully helped us'. The Pitjantjatjara people called him Tjilpi, or 'respected old man'. In 1980 he attended a meeting in Adelaide at which Pitjantjatjara people met with members of parliament to press their claim for recognition of their land rights, which was granted in 1981. The Ernabella choir made a special visit to Adelaide to sing at his hundredth birthday. He died on 5 December 1986 in his home at Kent Town and was buried in the Ernabella Mission cemetery. His wife (d.1993), their son and daughter, and the son of his first marriage, survived him.

N. Barnes, *Munyi's Daughter* (2000); S. Taffe, *Black and White Together* (2005); *People* (Sydney), 14 Feb 1951, p 42; *Advertiser* (Adelaide), 2 Dec 1981, p 4; S. Kerin, 'Doctor Do-good'? Charles Duguid and Aboriginal Politics, 1930s-1970s (PhD thesis, ANU, 2004); Duguid papers (NLA, SLSA); private information.   W. H. EDWARDS

DULDIG, KARL (1902-1986), sculptor, was born on 29 December 1902 at Przemysl, Austria (Poland), and named Karol, son of Marcus Duldig, businessman, and his wife Eidla (Eydl), née Nebenzahl. In 1914 the family moved to Vienna, where his interest in sculpture emerged spontaneously, leading to study at the Kunstgewerbeschule (1921-25) under Anton Hanak, and the Akademie der Bildenen Künste (1925-29). He then shared a studio in Vienna with Arthur Fleischmann, exhibiting widely and obtaining steady commissions. Through the 1920s and 1930s he also gained prominence as a sportsman of international standard in soccer, tennis, and table tennis (Austrian national champion, 1923).

On 15 December 1931 in Vienna Duldig married Slawa Horowitz, herself an artist (who had also invented and patented the first foldable umbrella). Her middle-class, Polish-Jewish origins were similar to his. Their only child, Eva, was born shortly before the 1938 *anschluss*; in March German troops entered Austria just as Duldig sent sculptures to Paris for exhibition (where they remained unpacked until discovered in 1961). The Duldigs left for Switzerland, and then for Singapore, where a niece had organised visas. He established a studio there and gained wealthy patrons, but in September 1940 the family was deported to Australia as enemy aliens and interned at Tatura camp, Victoria. Released in April 1942 to enlist in the Militia, Duldig was posted to the 8th Employment Company but was discharged on medical grounds in September. The family then settled at St Kilda, Melbourne (moving later to East Malvern), and were naturalised in 1946.

After working in various commercial art positions, Duldig was appointed art master (1945-67) at Mentone Grammar School, while also establishing a small ceramics business with Slawa. Gradually he gained recognition as a sculptor. He exhibited regularly with the Victorian Sculptors' Society (winning their annual prize in 1956) and in private galleries; his work featured in the Catholic Centenary Art Exhibition (1948), the arts festival associated with Melbourne's Olympic Games (1956), the early Mildura Sculpture Triennials (inaugurated 1961) and the first Adelaide Festival of Arts (1960). Commissioned glazed ceramic relief murals made a significant contribution to contemporary taste in Melbourne. His figurative expression was tempered by modernism, monumentality and—in works such as the 'Progress of Man' mural (1960, now destroyed), St Kilda Road, and the Kadimah relief (1972) and 'Kore' (1976), Elsternwick—a capacity to cast philosophic and mythic light on the everyday world of Melbourne's streetscapes.

As a leading figure among the generation of European-trained sculptors who arrived with the diaspora before and after World War II, Duldig affirmed the place of sculptural practice in Australian public and cultural experience. An advocate for artists' support groups and for his profession, he was foundation president (1962) of the Ben Uri Society for the Arts, which became the Bezalel Fellowship of Arts in 1964. He was president (1977) and an honorary life member (1982) of the Association of Sculptors of Victoria. After retirement from Mentone Grammar, he worked in more diverse media and on larger commissions, and travelled widely. Slawa died in 1975; on 13 February 1983 at Elwood Synagogue he married Rosia Ida Dorin, née Goldman, a Belgian-born widow.

Strong and energetic, Duldig continued to take commissions into his eighties: his last work was the Raoul Wallenberg monument (1985) at Kew Junction. He died on 11 August

1986 at Malvern and was buried in Chevra Kadisha cemetery, Springvale. His wife and the daughter of his first marriage survived him. Several retrospective exhibitions—including a centenary exhibition (2002-03) that travelled to Kraków, Vienna and Melbourne—explored his work. In 1986 the National Gallery of Victoria established an annual lecture on sculpture in his name. His studio at East Malvern is preserved as a house museum and public gallery. Duldig is represented in the National Gallery of Victoria, the McClelland Gallery and Sculpture Park, Langwarrin, and the Newcastle Region Art Gallery, New South Wales.

P. Ruskin, *Karl Duldig: Sculpture* (1966); K. Scarlett, *Australian Sculptors* (1980); *Karl Duldig: Survey* (1982); H. Bond, *The Duldig Ceramics* (1988); K. Bandman, *A Palette of Artists* (1989); P. Stasny (ed), *Karl Duldig: Sculptures, Drawings* (2003); *Age* (Melbourne), 3 Feb 2003, p 12; Archives (Duldig Studio, East Malvern, Melbourne).

JULIET PEERS

DUNBAR, RANDOLPH EDWARD ('RANDAL') (1909-1989), technical educator, was born on 4 March 1909 at Wellington, New South Wales, eldest of five sons of Edward Auburn Dunbar, railway fireman, and his wife Dolby (Dolly), née Lees, who were both born in New South Wales. Randal was educated at Dubbo High School and, holding a Teachers' College scholarship, enrolled at the University of Sydney (B.Sc., 1929; Dip.Ed., 1930). He played tennis and gained awards from the Royal Life Saving Society. Although he had been an active member of the Sydney University Regiment, during World War II he was declared to be in a reserved occupation and was unable to enlist.

His first appointment as a mathematics and science teacher with the Department of Education was to Hurlstone Agricultural High School in 1930. He later taught at Temora Intermediate High School, where he met Marjorie Ellen Griffin, a bank clerk, whom he married on 14 December 1935 at St Stephen's Presbyterian Church, Sydney. In 1938 he was seconded to the technical education branch and appointed teacher of pre-apprenticeship classes at Central Technical School, Ultimo. In 1939 he became head teacher of the preparatory trade classes at Sydney Technical College. His ability as an administrator was revealed in this new area of responsibility.

In February 1941 Dunbar was officially transferred to the technical education branch. He remained at STC until 1946, when he was appointed principal of the Canberra Technical College. Concurrently, he was deputy-director of industrial training in the Australian Capital Territory. After two years in Canberra, he moved, as principal, to Wollongong Technical College, where he remained until his appointment in 1951 as assistant-director of the Department of Technical Education.

With the support of the director, Arthur Denning [q.v.13], in 1954 Dunbar won a six-month Fulbright grant to participate in a foreign-teacher education program in the United States of America. His specialisation was vocational training with emphasis on the administration and supervision of technical education. For his Fulbright studies he was attached to Ohio State University. He then spent a month in England to observe technical education. On his return to Sydney he produced two reports: 'Vocational Education in U.S.A.' and 'Technical Education in the U.K.'.

In November 1956 Dunbar was appointed senior assistant-director of the Department of Technical Education. He acted as deputy-director from 1958 with substantive appointment in July 1960. In March 1962 he was promoted to the post of director. During his nine years in the position he oversaw an expansion of certificate and diploma courses and an increase in the number of technical colleges throughout the State. In 1965-68 he was also the foundation director of the New South Wales Institute of Technology. With the registrar he spent three months touring the USA, Europe and Britain to study the organisation and administration of institutions of higher technological education. His wife had died in 1964; on 23 September 1966 he married Gertrude Annie Williams at the register office, Brent, London.

As the Institute of Technology gained increasing autonomy, Dunbar was a member of the new council from 1967. He also served on the council of the University of New South Wales from 1963 to 1971, and on the State's Board of Secondary School Studies. In 1967-68 he helped to manage the transformation of the Bathurst Teachers' College into the Mitchell College of Advanced Education, establishing its interim council in 1968.

An ambitious man, Dunbar was extremely diligent, prepared to work very long hours and to take holidays only rarely. Within the department he was regarded as a firm and uncompromising leader, insistent on high standards and attention to detail. He believed passionately in the importance of tertiary education. His main adult recreational interest was gardening. He retired in 1971 and next year settled in Dorset, England. Survived by his wife and by the two daughters and son of his first marriage, he died on 15 February 1989 at St Leonards, Dorset, and was cremated.

Dept of Technical and Further Education (NSW), Information Services Division (comp), *Spanners,*

Easels & Microchips (1983); *SMH*, 5 Aug 1954, p 7, 25 Jan 1965, p 19, 8 Apr 1967, p 9, 16 July 1969, p 13, 1 Sept 1969, 'Careers Supp', p 1; R. Dunbar personnel file, 13/9331 (SRNSW); private information.

RACHEL GRAHAME

DUNCAN, WALTER GEORGE KEITH (1903-1987), adult educator and political philosopher, was born on 11 July 1903 at Leichhardt, Sydney, youngest of four children of New Zealand-born parents George Henry Duncan, plumber's clerk, and his wife Clara, née Walton. A boy from a working-class neighbourhood, Keith was educated at Fort Street Boys' High School and the University of Sydney (BA, 1924; MA, 1926). While an undergraduate he gave some extramural tutorials in psychology. He graduated with first-class honours and university medals in both history and philosophy, then took his master's degree in philosophy, again gaining first-class honours and a medal. Awarded a James King [q.v.2] of Irrawang travelling scholarship in 1926, he set off for the London School of Economics and Political Science (Ph.D., 1930), where he heard lectures by Bertrand Russell, Arnold Toynbee, Sidney Webb and George Bernard Shaw. His thesis, supervised by Harold Laski, was on 'Liberalism in England 1880-1914'. As a Commonwealth Fund fellow he spent two years in the United States of America, visiting the universities of Chicago, North Carolina, and California at Berkeley, and undertaking a study of population and migration.

Returning to the University of Sydney, Duncan became assistant-director (1932-34) and director (1935-51) of the department of tutorial classes. He wrote and edited works on immigration, social services and the Workers' Educational Association. A founding director (1932) of the Australian Institute of Political Science, and the first editor (1942-50) of the *Current Affairs Bulletin*, he helped to develop the Australian Army Education Service during World War II. Contemporaries knew him as a left-wing liberal; although not a communist, he was impressed by the Soviet regime, and was a hostile critic of capitalism, imperialism and religion.

Duncan was seconded in 1944 to the Universities Commission to investigate adult education in Australia. He believed that lifelong learning 'should cater for all the interests and problems of adult life'. His report recommended that 'adult education ... should be organised as a nation-wide service; and that responsibility for it (both moral and financial) should be accepted and shared by Commonwealth, State and Local Governments'. The report was neither adopted nor published. Duncan was told that J. B. Chifley [q.v.13],

prime minister from 1945, did not wish 'to buy into a fight with the States' about it. In 1973 the University of Adelaide's department of adult education published the main text, with fifteen commentaries, as *The Vision Splendid*. The editor, Derek Whitelock, introduced it as 'the Magna Carta of Australian adult education', and asserted that it was 'the most substantial, comprehensive and thoughtful document on adult education in this country'.

In 1951 Duncan moved, by invitation, to the chair of history and political science at the University of Adelaide. The department was to be divided and, when the professor of history arrived in 1954, Duncan became head of politics, but without change of title for some years because the premier, (Sir) Thomas Playford [q.v.], forbade the university to have a professor of politics. Besides his departmental work and teaching, he chaired (1957-65 and 1967-68) the university's board of adult education. He gave the Australian Broadcasting Commission's 1962 Boyer [q.v.13] lectures, published as *In Defence of the Common Man*. He retired in 1968, but in 1973 completed a commissioned centenary history of the University of Adelaide that had been left unfinished by R. A. Leonard.

As a child, Duncan had thought that his mother dominated and diminished his father, and that he should beware of 'bossy' women. Christina Stead [q.v.], a fellow student at the University of Sydney, fell in love with him. He wrote regularly to her from London, but when in 1928 she arrived, uninvited, he did not make her welcome. She wrote to her sister: 'He has a thorough-going indignation for (what he conceives to be) all forms of oppression, depression, impression, repression, suppression, compression and (irrational self-) expression, in short for all forms of everything which does not represent (what he conceives to be) Liberty and Justice'. Long afterwards she published a savage portrait of him as Jonathan Crow in *For Love Alone* (1944). Duncan thought it a misrepresentation that confirmed his worst expectations of women.

Despite those expectations, on 27 September 1934 at the district registrar's office, Chatswood, Sydney, Duncan had married Dorothy Mary Anderson, a lecturer whom he had met in England. Dorothy was a submissive partner in their marriage. They were quietly and intelligently helpful to colleagues whom they liked or admired. Duncan died on 18 December 1987 in North Adelaide and was cremated. Having no children, the Duncans bequeathed their estates to a trust fund for needy students. Bequests of $87 000 in 1987, and $255 000 at Dorothy's death in 1990, grew to $1 163 500 in 2003, with the fund's income helping a hundred or more distressed students every year.

H. Rowley, *Christina Stead* (1993); *Adult Ed News*, May 1988, p 19; *NLA News*, Aug 2003, p 7; N. K. Meaney, taped interview with G. W. K. Duncan (1986, NLA); personal knowledge.

HUGH STRETTON

DUNCAN-KEMP, ALICE MONKTON (1901-1988), author, was born on 3 June 1901 at Charleville, Queensland, second of four children of Scottish-born William Duncan, station-manager, and his wife Laura [q.v. Supp.], née Davis, daughter of a Sydney solicitor. Alice's father appears to have been well educated, with interests in comparative religion and anthropology. After their marriage the Duncans had bought the lease for Mooraberrie, a cattle property of 340 square miles (881 km²) west of Windorah, south-west Queensland. In 1903 their eldest child and only son died. After William's death in 1907 his widow, with her three daughters, stayed on in the isolated desert country, raising 'baby beef' Shorthorn cattle. Her help came from local Aborigines and hired stockmen, and from her daughters as they grew older. Alice's friends were the Aborigines who lived on the station. Her mother described her as ' "mad" on horses, and fairly "cracked" on the blacks'.

Mostly educated at home, Alice boarded for a few years at Spreydon College (from 1917 Fairholme Presbyterian Girls' College), Toowoomba. On 12 November 1923 at St Andrew's Church of England, Longreach, she married Frederick Clifford Kemp, a New Zealand born grazier. They were to have five children. Her husband soon became a manager with the Bank of Australasia, and while they moved around country towns, mainly in Queensland, they retained interests in pastoral properties, with Alice actively involved in stock work and management.

Writing under the name Alice Duncan-Kemp, she published a memoir, *Our Sandhill Country* (1933). She drew on her childhood experiences, her father's diaries and day books, and information from a Karuwali man named Moses to cover the usual themes of bush life—droughts and floods, musters and race meetings, pastoralists and stockmen—all interwoven with lyrical and knowledgable descriptions of landscape, flora and fauna. Her open mind and observational skills led her to beliefs then rarely accepted in Queensland: that Aborigines were the true owners of the land and a moral community whose culture was based on obedience to an elaborate and unwritten system of law; that the introduction of cattle had brought severe food shortages to Black communities, leading them to spear stock; and that pastoralists could not have established themselves without Aboriginal labour and advice. Duncan-Kemp saw pastoralists and Aboriginal clans as equal protagonists in the management of a cattle station. The operational needs of the property adapted to and, in turn, forced changes on Aboriginal values and social responsibilities. She discussed the importance of women's ceremonies and women's country, the cultural differences between language groups, and the techniques employed to increase the natural stock of available food.

In 1947-58 Duncan-Kemp corresponded with Dr L. P. Winterbotham [q.v.16], providing him with detailed descriptions of Aboriginal cultural practices as she remembered them. Her later books—*Where Strange Paths Go Down* (1952), *Our Channel Country* (1961) and *Where Strange Gods Call* (1968)—contained the same themes as in *Our Sandhill Country* but had a less systematic structure and an uncertain time-frame. Despite reflecting her generally liberal attitudes, they were not free of Imperial rhetoric. Although Duncan-Kemp stood in contrast to her times, she was still a woman of them. In retirement she lived at Oakey. She died there on 4 January 1988 and was cremated. Predeceased by her husband, she was survived by two of her three sons and one of her two daughters.

P. L. Watson, *Frontier Lands and Pioneer Legends* (1998); *Jnl of Austn Studies*, no 67, 2001, p 37; Y. Steinhauer, A. M. Duncan-Kemp: Her Life and Work (MA thesis, Southern Cross Univ, 1998); L. P. Winterbotham papers (SLQ).

PAMELA LAKIN WATSON

DUNK, SIR WILLIAM ERNEST (1897-1984), public servant, was born on 11 December 1897 at Morgan, South Australia, fifth of six children of Albert Landseer Dunk, clerk, and his wife Winifred Jane, née Gibbs, whose grandfather, Thomas Young Cotter [q.v.1], had been South Australia's first colonial surgeon. Bill's childhood was spent in this small, busy river port until, supported by his elder brothers, he moved from the local two-room school to Kapunda High School. In 1914 he took the Commonwealth Public Service clerical entrance examination and was appointed to the Commonwealth Auditor-General's Office in Adelaide.

As a junior customs clerk, Dunk endured the tedium of bureaucracy. He enlisted in the Australian Imperial Force on 26 April 1918 and served in Egypt from November. Back in Australia, he was discharged in May 1919. Marriage to Elma Kathleen Evans, great-granddaughter of George Fife Angas [q.v.1] on 20 April 1922 at St Matthew's Church of England, Kensington, Adelaide, brought fresh ambition. In 1924 he completed a correspondence diploma in accountancy with the Federal

Institute of Accountants and in 1928 secured appointment as government auditor for the Mandated Territory of New Guinea. Intended to enhance Dunk's prospects of promotion, this experience exerted an enduring influence, impressing on him the challenge (as he later put it) of achieving 'self-respect all round' in colonial and Indigenous development.

On his return to Adelaide in 1930, exposure to the strains of economic depression stimulated Dunk's expanding interests in the role of government. Frustrated by a lack of advancement, in 1934 he was transferred to the London office to audit the Commonwealth Bank. Often assisting that shrewd negotiator, the Australian high commissioner S. M. (Viscount) Bruce [q.v.7], Dunk was also unravelling the residual financial legacy of World War I and auditing an extensive registry of public borrowing. When, in 1938, he returned to the bank's central office in Sydney, his friends included the young economists Leslie Melville and H. C. ('Nugget') Coombs.

Recruited to the Treasury in 1939, Dunk moved to Melbourne in September to assist the Board of Business Administration in bringing the expertise of senior consultants (initially Essington Lewis, (Sir) Norman Myer and Sir George Pearce [qq.v.10,15,11]) to bear on defence expenditure. Given the lack of clear procedures, and the need to adjudicate shifting, competing demands and to wage war 'on the cheap', this work required endurance and versatility. Dunk's adaptability, which impressed J. B. Chifley [q.v.13] when he became treasurer in 1941, led to his appointment to the defence division of Treasury, as liaison officer overseeing expenditure in the Department of Defence.

With the entry of the United States of America into World War II, the support of Allied operations in the Pacific added to these responsibilities. In 1942 Dunk was appointed director of reciprocal Lend-Lease finance, managing the cash-free supply of American munitions, equipment, machine tools and fuel in exchange for food, clothing, ammunition and facilities. Overall, Lend-Lease achieved an effective division of labour of which Dunk was proud, but he was also aware of its implications for future balances of economic power. Observing meetings in Ottawa and Washington in 1944, Dunk marvelled at the skill of Baron Keynes in gaining support for British and Commonwealth reconstruction from legalistic and competition-minded Americans. He was soon to engage in similar wrangling with US officials, who required strict accounting for any equipment remaining in Australia at the end of the war.

Dunk insisted that the war economy offered opportunities to pursue aggressive policies of national development, denouncing as 'dangerously soporific' any focus on 'juggling budgets' when ventures in industry, trade and population expansion beckoned. Surprised to be offered the job of secretary of the Department of External Affairs in 1945 by its minister, H. V. Evatt [q.v.14], he hoped to advance linked economic and diplomatic initiatives. Instead he felt cast as the 'glorified staff manager' for a rapidly expanding and strained department, attending to personnel questions and marginalised from Evatt's clique of policy advisers. Tensions with his choleric minister increased, but Dunk twice declined the offer of appointment as chairman of the Commonwealth Public Service Board, only accepting it in March 1947 under personal pressure from Chifley—and immediately questioning his decision when offered a more lucrative executive position in Vacuum Oil Co. Pty Ltd.

Having come up 'through the ranks' of the public service, Dunk was highly qualified for the chairmanship. Most recently, at External Affairs he had become concerned that the privileges of training accorded to diplomatic cadets should be extended to officers in other departments similarly charged with expanding the charters of government (but not all, presumably, to be invited to the Sunday teas Elma hosted for new cadets). Equally, having shared an austere flat in Canberra with Coombs, or camped in Evatt's house while the minister was travelling, Dunk also insisted that the quality of government would only improve with the conditions under which its 'servants' lived and worked in the 'bush capital'. He soon advised Chifley that the national bureaucracy was 'run down and out of date', showing the strains not only of war, but of the Depression and even World War I before that. 'Civilisation is management' was a brash aphorism, but it expressed Dunk's priorities for the board: recruitment to address generational and skill imbalances; advanced training methods; salaries to attract and hold the 'sound, plain-speaking intelligent man'; improvement of allowances and amenities; and, overall, efficiency and economy.

Dunk promoted modern methods such as the use of film in training and 'geometric' office design. Beyond these ideals, he was soon dealing with harder political and industrial constraints. Scrutiny of the size of the public service intensified after the change of government in 1949 and in response to the inflationary pressures of the early 1950s. With no consultation, in 1951 Prime Minister (Sir) Robert Menzies [q.v.15] announced the retrenchment of ten thousand Commonwealth employees 'as an example', just as departmental heads complained of understaffing and as under-represented groups, such as women, gained employment, often in temporary positions. These pressures also emerged in marginal wage claims, leading to bitter disputes and, in 1956, crippling stoppages. While Dunk sought to be open, consultative and devolutionist in style, he was uncomfortable with strong unionism and faced departmental resistance to change. Confidentially, he feared 'institutional protection' was replacing 'individual responsibility'; publicly, he held firm to a lean diet of 'standards', striking the gruff pose of balancing conflicting interests.

These demands aside, Dunk remained committed to introducing competitive entry and promotion opportunities, enabling the best candidates to advance to senior administrative positions. By 1959 the report of the Boyer [q.v.13] committee of inquiry into public service recruitment consolidated arguments that Dunk had made through each of his three terms of appointment—although still encountering suspicions of creating an elite. Reservations had also met Dunk's advice to Menzies in 1955 on departmental amalgamations, following his dictum on 'the maximum use of firm unbroken lines' in policy. The creation of an 'embracive' Department of Trade in 1956 was, however, a source of satisfaction, as was the increasing recognition of Canberra as the appropriately planned and developed centre of national government.

A conscientious chairman, Dunk admitted to sometimes feeling 'tensed-up' but prided himself in never using leave entitlements and took comfort from the prestige of the job. Stocky, brisk in manner and clipped in speech, he lacked the prominence of other senior public servants but exerted considerable influence through personal networks. In 1948 he advised, with Coombs, on the restructuring of the Council for Scientific and Industrial Research to address security concerns; into the 1950s he regretted the polarisation of Cold War politics, feared nuclear annihilation, and urged Sir Percy Spender [q.v.] to strengthen the ANZUS alliance through pre-positioning American weaponry in Australia. He lobbied hard for ambitious mining and pastoral development in the Northern Territory, declaring it 'crazy' that Aboriginal reserves should interfere with mineral exploration. Conversely, he pestered (Sir) Paul Hasluck, as minister for territories, to transfer 'the main elements of government to the natives' of the Territory of Papua and New Guinea as soon as possible. He noted the decline of Labor policy into 'soft social service philosophy' but worried that Liberal governments lacked the imagination for ambitious public works programs.

In 1959 Dunk announced his intention to retire and began grooming the steely (Sir) Frederick Wheeler as his successor. When he left the board at the end of 1960 its status was enhanced, and the public service in general transformed, relative to 1947. Appointed CBE in 1953, knighted in 1957, and flattered to be nominated to the Melbourne Club by Lord Casey and W. S. Robinson [qq.v.13,11], Dunk declared 'Australia is my hobby'. Having retired to Toorak, Melbourne, he became chairman of Sitmar Line (Australia) Pty Ltd and of General Television Corporation Pty Ltd, and Australian representative (1962-70) on the British and Christmas Island Phosphate Commissions. Always self-conscious about his 'grim visage', he remained active, playing bowls, savouring cigars, and publishing characteristically laconic memoirs, *They Also Serve* (1974). Survived by his wife and their daughter and son, he died on 12 January 1984 at Prahran, Melbourne, and was cremated.

Nation (Sydney), 20 June 1959, p 9, 4 July 1959, p 14; B2455, item Dunk W E (NAA); M. Pratt, interview with W. Dunk (ts, 1971, NLA); Dunk papers (NLA).   NICHOLAS BROWN

DUNPHY, MYLES JOSEPH (1891-1985), architect and conservationist, was born on 19 October 1891 in South Melbourne, eldest of seven children of Irish-born Myles Arthur Dunphy, draper, and his wife Margaret Mary, née Johnson, who was born in Tasmania. The family moved frequently through Victoria and New South Wales in search of new business opportunities. Myles's education was disrupted but his formative schooling occurred at Kiama Superior Public School from 1903 to 1906. When the family moved to Annandale in 1907, he attended evening classes in architecture at Sydney Technical College, and worked by day as an office-boy and messenger with the Art, Painting & Decorating Co. The burden of work and school was made more difficult by the fact that his father left the family home. Dunphy continued at Sydney Technical College in 1912-13; his meritorious passes in 1912 earned him a scholarship in model-drawing. While maintaining his studies, he took jobs with W. C. Penfold [q.v.11] & Co. and the architectural firm of H. E. Dakin, before working as a draughtsman (1912-22) for a civil engineer, Arthur Hart.

A temporary assistant teacher of trades drawing in 1915-16 and of constructional drawing from 1916, Dunphy was appointed a full-time teacher of architectural engineering at Sydney Technical College in 1922. He was registered formally as an architect in 1923, but never practised professionally, although he did design his own home forty years later. In 1916 he had been engaged to be married to Hazel Matheson but she died of tuberculosis in that year. He married 21-year-old Margaret Tinsley Peet, a clerk, on 19 December 1925 at Manly Methodist Church. They lived at Mortdale before settling at Oatley. His skill as a teacher marked his contribution to the field of architecture. He taught at the college until 1953, the

New South Wales University of Technology from 1953 to 1958, and under its new name, at the University of New South Wales from 1959 until he retired in 1963, aged 71. Elected a fellow of the Royal Australian Institute of Architects in 1951, he became a life fellow in 1970.

While architecture framed Dunphy's professional life, he found personal solace in the natural world. Walking in bushland around Sydney and Kiama as a child was a source of both relaxation and intellectual stimulus. In 1907 he formed the Orizaba Tourist and Cricket Club (named after Mexico's highest peak, Pico de Orizaba) so that weekends could be devoted to exploring the area between North Annandale and Glebe Point. In 1914, after the Orizaba group was disbanded, Dunphy, with his friends Roy Rudder and Bert Gallop, formed the Mountain Trails Club. Membership was by invitation only and required a stiff initiation ritual of a twenty-mile (32 km) walk.

Resolved to achieve his aim of 'self-sufficiency in rough country', he camped and lived on food rations during extended walks through the region surrounding the Kowmung River. Many of his expeditions were in the Blue Mountains, but in 1920 he and Rudder canoed the length of the Murray River from eastern Victoria to its mouth in South Australia. Dunphy's exploits were in largely uncharted territory and the exertion often taxed his health. As a child he had contracted typhoid fever and while his convalescence at the Dame Edith Walker Hospital on the Parramatta River at Concord provided him with an idyllic setting for reading, fishing and exploring nature, his body was weakened by the illness. He was exempted from military service in World War I as a consequence and in his forties suffered heart problems, probably cardiomyopathy.

Dunphy's association with formal walking clubs reflected his search for a recreational area free from the constraints of urbanisation. He later wrote that people needed a space to rid themselves 'of the shackles of ordered existence', and this belief sustained his approach to conservation. Even when married with children, Dunphy would often go on long treks alone, but he and Margaret together managed a fifteen-day trek from Oberon to Mount Kanangra in the Blue Mountains by pushing their 20-month-old son, Milo, in a pram.

Through his association with the Mountain Trails Club, he drew a series of maps for newly developed trails within the greater Blue Mountains area. His maps were idiosyncratic; they not only provided topographical information but also named a series of peaks, valleys and rivers to reflect the difficulties of the walks. Map references in the Gangerang area to Paralyzer Steeps and Murdering Gully left little to the imagination for those who followed. His nomenclature revealed his appreciation for Aboriginal life, with names such as Mount Moorilla (meaning thunder). It was also influenced by his own life, with Dex Creek, for example, named after his dog Dextre. These maps established the Mountain Trails Club as an unofficial authority on trails in the greater Sydney region and the organisation gained added credibility from 1923 when the New South Wales Government Tourist Bureau directed travellers to it for information and guidance on walks in the Blue Mountains.

As the Mountain Trails Club did not admit women as members, in 1927 the Sydney Bush Walkers club was formed, with Dunphy as a foundation member. Through this club, he focused on protecting bushland from development. He helped to negotiate the purchase of the lease of the Blue Gum Forest on the Grose River in 1931-32 to save the area from being logged. Similarly, an area of the Garawarra coastline in Sydney's south was reserved as parkland in 1934 after Dunphy directed a lobbying campaign aimed at the under-secretary for the Department of Lands.

In 1933 Dunphy had helped to form another group, the National Parks and Primitive Areas Council, which sought the reservation of scenic areas for recreation. He looked enviously on the development of national parks in the United States of America and hoped to encourage similarly protected environments in New South Wales for bushwalkers. As secretary of the NP&PAC, in 1934 Dunphy publicised a proposal for a Blue Mountains national park that had been submitted in 1932, but it was not until 1959 that lobbying resulted in a government gazettal of 155 676 acres (63 000 ha). This park was only a quarter of the size envisioned by Dunphy but with subsequent additions, such as the Wollemi National Park in 1979, the eventual Greater Blue Mountains Park fulfilled his original proposal. Other parklands, for example the Warrumbungle National Park in 1953, were created as a result of NP&PAC lobbying and his maps. In 1967, with the establishment of the National Parks and Wildlife Service, the lobbying role of the NP&PAC diminished but Dunphy served on the Blue Mountains National Parks Trust and in his retirement successfully fought the Geographical Names Board of New South Wales, of which he was an honorary counsellor, to retain the names he had chosen in the Blue Mountains region.

Displaying a lifelong commitment to connecting urban residents with the natural world, Dunphy made a profound contribution to the conservation cause. 'Whether we like it or not', he had commented in 1934, 'we hold our land in trust for our successors'. His skill as a cartographer and his role as a lobbyist ensured that land was preserved for his successors to enjoy. His trail (literally) can still be followed. He was appointed OBE in 1977 and was given the Fred M. Packard International Parks merit award by the International Union for Conservation of Nature and Natural Resources in 1982. Survived by his wife and their two sons, he died on 30 January 1985 at Peakhurst and was cremated. Some of his writings have been published in P. Thompson (ed), *Myles Dunphy* (1986).

D. Hutton and L. Connors, *A History of the Australian Environment Movement* (1999); P. Meredith, *Myles and Milo* (1999); *SMH*, 2 Feb 1985, p 10; Dunphy papers (SLNSW).   RICHARD GOWERS

DUNSTAN, DOUGLAS AVON (1906-1987), printer and book designer, was born on 29 September 1906 at York, Western Australia, eleventh of thirteen children of Victorian-born parents Richard Dunstan, Methodist minister, and his wife Martha Euphemia, née Cock. In 1907 the family moved to Rockhampton, Queensland; Douglas's father died ten years later. Educated at Toowoomba and Maryborough schools and at Brisbane Grammar School, Douglas was apprenticed to a compositor in Brisbane. He finished his training with Green Press Ltd, Sydney, under his brother-in-law Percy Green [q.v.9], whose influence on Dunstan as a typographer and book designer was profound. By 1929 he was production manager. On 6 September 1930 at the Methodist Church, Concord, he married Winifred Kate Thompson (d.1961). Active in trade associations, he wrote *The Typography of Letterheads* (1934).

In 1938 Dunstan was appointed manager of the Advertiser Printing Office, a department of the Adelaide *Advertiser*. Supported by the paper's managing director, (Sir) Lloyd Dumas [q.v.14], he insisted on the highest standards of craftsmanship and service. Despite wartime difficulties, in 1944 he embarked on a seven-month overseas trip investigating postwar business opportunities. He recommended that the office install offset printing and die-stamping presses to enable it to compete in the fine printing field. In 1947 he travelled abroad again, to assess the potential for book production in Australia. The company entered the market seriously, confident that few competitors could match the required investment. Dunstan successfully fought for machinery capable of producing work economically and to the highest standard. He was president of the South Australian Master Printers and Allied Trades Association (1948-50) and of the Printing and Allied Trades Employers' Federation of Australia (1949-50). His presidential address (1948) to the State association was entitled *Printing for Profit and Pleasure*.

The printing office became Griffin Press in July 1954. Books were a speciality, and over one thousand different titles were produced in Dunstan's time; he was responsible for establishing and maintaining excellence in typography and design. He secured commissions for four books from the Limited Editions Club, New York, including *The Explorations of Captain James Cook in the Pacific* (1957), edited by (Sir) Archibald Grenfell Price [q.v.16]. All were designed by Dunstan, and printed and bound by the press. On 4 August 1962 at Wesley Methodist Church, Norwood, he married Una Betty Macdonald, a schoolteacher.

Dunstan retired in 1967. He continued to design books, and wrote *The Story of the Griffin Press* (1977). A committee-member (1955-84) of the Friends of the Public (State) Library of South Australia, in 1978 he donated his collection of rare and special editions to the library. He was president (1974-75) of the Rotary Club of Adelaide and, for over a decade, a member of the South Australian working party of the *Australian Dictionary of Biography*. The journalist Stewart Cockburn described him as an enthusiast: 'a coiled spring of energy seeking outlet and self-expression, with an instinctive passion for excellence and a compulsive desire to help others'. A teetotaller and non-smoker, he was a member of the congregation of Beaumont Uniting Church and editor of its history (1980). In his later years he became a proficient wood-carver. He was appointed OAM in 1986. Survived by his wife and the son and two daughters of his first marriage, he died on 14 April 1987 at his Hazelwood Park home and was cremated.

P. G. Green, *I Am Evergreen* (1967); *Advertiser* (Adelaide), 28 Oct 1967, p 11, 1 July 1983, p 6, 16 Apr 1987, p 8; *News* (Adelaide), 29 June 1983, p 23; *Mortlock Lib Newsletter*, June 1987, p 3; J. Robertson, interview with D. A. Dunstan (ts, 1973, SLSA); private information.   MICHAEL TRELOAR

DYASON, DIANA JOAN (1919-1989), university lecturer and historian of medicine, was born on 10 July 1919 at Sandringham, Melbourne, second child of Victorian-born parents Edward Clarence Evelyn Dyason [q.v.8] and his wife Anne Elizabeth, née McClure. Her family was wealthy and her parents were, she recalled, 'sophisticated, free-thinking and rather unusual people'. Her childhood was shaped by her father's trust in the power of reason and was often spent in diverse company, including that of several professors of the University of Melbourne; (Sir) Ernest Scott [q.v.11] was an uncle by marriage. 'Ding' appreciated the academic rigour of her education (particularly in science) at Melbourne Church of England Girls' Grammar School. However, her lack of respect for authority was regularly reported, and was a characteristic she never entirely lost.

At the University of Melbourne (B.Sc., 1943; M.Sc., 1945), Dyason majored in physiology and bacteriology. She entered into life at the recently established University Women's College with enduring enthusiasm (she was to be a member of its council in 1945-52 and a governor in 1961). Her postgraduate research in the physiology department (completed with first-class honours and an exhibition) was on malaria as a problem in general physiology. Through it she began to work closely with Professor (Sir) Douglas Wright [q.v.], as his research assistant and, from 1947, as senior demonstrator in physiology. Wright's strong belief that students should understand the history of their subject and the elements of scientific method led to the establishment of a department of general science in 1946. In 1950 Dyason became a lecturer in the renamed department of history and methods of science. The remainder of her career was devoted to the development of this pioneering Australian venture in a relatively new academic field.

Dyason began by lecturing to first-year medical students, leaving a memorable impression on many despite her frustration that the subject was compulsory but unexamined. Feeling under-equipped in both history and philosophy, she applied for leave to investigate teaching and research overseas. In Britain and the United States of America (1952-53), she attended relevant lectures and seminars wherever she could find them, including those by Karl Popper at the London School of Economics and Political Science. When she returned (after extended absence due to a skiing injury), the department had begun to grow: in 1954 Stephen Toulmin, on exchange from the University of Oxford, noted the vigour of cross-faculty discussions and, in an influential memorandum, recommended an expansion of staff, teaching and resources. In 1957 the department was renamed history and philosophy of science, and Dyason, now a senior lecturer, succeeded Gerd Buchdahl as its head.

Under Dyason's leadership, student numbers increased, new courses were established and the department's position within the university was consolidated. Her major teaching and research interests were in public health and germ theory, as displayed, for example, in her article on William Gillbee in the *Journal of Australian Studies*, 1984. While her publications were few, she was an inspiring teacher, innovative in her extensive and energetic use of primary sources, as in her resoundingly popular continuing education course 'Glorius Smelbourne', in which she collaborated with the folk singer Danny Spooner. Although she often seemed to be acting amid barely controlled chaos, students appreciated Dyason's dedication and generosity. Determined, forceful and outspoken, she could seem formidable but nobody could be kinder to someone in trouble. Her wit and hospitable nature fostered a sociable, collegial atmosphere in HPS.

Beyond the department, Dyason was active in national and international scholarship, giving papers at conferences in Australia and overseas, and providing leadership in securing the professionalism she sought for her field. She was foundation president (1967) of the Australasian Association for the History and Philosophy of Science, a founding member of the Australian Academy of Science's national committee for history and philosophy of science, and a delegate to the general assemblies (Tokyo, 1974; Edinburgh, 1977) of the International Union of the History and Philosophy of Science. As her successor Professor R. W. Home noted, 'more than anyone else in the country', Dyason 'helped bridge the gap' between the 'untutored enthusiasm of medicos' for the history of their discipline and the 'illiteracy, scientifically speaking, of most social historians'.

Appointed reader in 1965, Dyason continued as head of department until 1975. She published an autobiographical piece in P. Grimshaw and L. Strahan (eds), *The Half-open Door* (1982). Retiring in 1984, she was awarded an honorary D.Litt. (1985) by Deakin University. Outside the university, she wrote poetry, painted in watercolours and enjoyed bush-walking. She died of myocardial infarction on 30 September 1989 at Heidelberg and was buried in Andersons Creek cemetery. A portrait by Wes Walters hangs in the departmental library, which is named after her.

Metascience, vol 8, no 1, 1990, p 6; D. Dyason papers (Univ of Melbourne Archives); private information and personal knowledge.

MONICA MACCALLUM

DYER, ROBERT NEAL (1909-1984), radio and television performer, was born on 22 May 1909 at Hartsville, Tennessee, United States of America, son of Heywood Leaman Dies, a poor share-farmer, and his wife Delia, née Bell. Bob's mother taught him the harmonica, guitar and ukulele. The musically inclined lad did not finish high school, dropping out when he secured a song and dance engagement at a Nashville theatre. At 17 he left home. He spent the next few years hitchhiking around the USA, doing odd jobs when there was no theatrical work. Returning to Tennessee at the beginning of the Depression, he eked out an existence, often performing for showboats and carnivals, before joining the *Marcus Show* in 1932.

In 1937 Bob Dyer, as he wished to be known, travelled to Australia with this vaudeville troupe. Billed as 'the Hill Billy', he achieved immediate rapport with Australian audiences. Radio and theatre work followed, including a tour with Jim Davidson's [q.v.] ABC Dance Band. In 1938 he went to England, where he appeared in music halls, and on radio for the British Broadcasting Corporation. Returning to Tennessee in 1939, he was rejected for military service because of a duodenal ulcer. He came back to Australia in 1940 following an offer from Tivoli Circuit Australia Pty Ltd. In July he opened in Melbourne with George Wallace [q.v.12] in *The Crazy Show*. That year Dyer met Thelma Phoebe McLean, known as Dorothy (Dolly) Mack, a 19-year-old Tivoli dancer. He proposed after a nine-day courtship and the couple married nine days later, on 5 September 1940, at St John's Church of England, Darlinghurst, Sydney. In front of the microphone and camera, and behind the scenes, Dolly was an indispensable partner in his subsequent career. Late in World War II, Dyer toured the South-West Pacific Area with a show for service personnel.

Dyer's conquest of different entertainment media was remarkable. He achieved wireless celebrity as the host of programs such as 'The Last of the Hillbillies' (1940), 'Bob Dyer's Variety Show' (1944), 'Can You Take It?' (1946), 'Pick-a-Box' (1948), 'Cop the Lot' (1951) and 'It Pays to Be Funny' (1955). His radio days are especially remembered for his mock rivalry with Jack Davey [q.v.13], though the relentless search for stunts that this broadcast battle entailed was later described by Dyer as 'soul destroying'. In 1957 Dyer launched television versions of 'It Pays to Be Funny' and 'Pick-a-Box'. The latter continued on Channel 7 until he retired in June 1971. He claimed that the show was the 'longest-running continuous prime time TV program in the world': on radio and then television, the quiz show ran for twenty-three years, fifty-two weeks a year, without a break. Dyer was unusual among radio personalities in transferring so successfully to television. 'Howdy, Customers', his raucous opening line, and his trademark question 'The money or the box?' were recognised across the country. Despite his Tennessee accent, he became a national institution. In the first decades of Australian television, he represented both American dominance and the quest for Australian content within that hegemony.

Although Dyer was a smart businessman and a warm, clever and consummately professional performer, he had none of Davey's gift for unscripted repartee. His shows were formulaic and carefully planned. The skills learnt in vaudeville served him well since audience participation was crucial to all his shows. He was a good actor whose booming voice contributed to radio success while his imposing physical presence was helpful on television. Dyer attributed the longevity of 'Pick-a-Box' to his ordinariness, but his claims to represent the average Australian were illusory. A wealthy man, he owned luxury homes and pursued an obsession with deep-sea fishing that took him round the world. He and Dolly held numerous world and Australian fishing records, many of their exploits filmed by Dyer, a skilled photographer.

Dyer drew a sharp line between the public and the private. The best-known contestant on 'Pick-a-Box', Barry Jones, described the private Dyer as an 'old-fashioned liberal' who detested racial and religious intolerance. Dyer had been awarded Logies in 1961 and 1968; he and Dolly received one jointly in 1971. That year he was appointed honorary OBE and Dolly was appointed MBE. Shunning publicity after retirement, and heavily bearded, he spent his final years reclusively with Dolly on the Gold Coast, Queensland. He died on 9 January 1984 at Southport and was cremated. His wife (d.2004) survived him; they had no children.

J. Kent, *Out of the Bakelite Box* (1990); C. Jones, *Something in the Air* (1995); *People* (Sydney), 13 Sept 1950, p 11, 20 Feb 1984, p 4; *Sun-Herald* (Sydney), 5 Apr 1959, p 29, 15 Jan 1984, p 15; *Bulletin*, 14 Sept 1963, p 13; *Sun* (Sydney), 17 Mar 1971, p 1, 22 Mar 1971, p 3, 23 Mar 1971, p 12, 24 Mar 1971, p 12, 25 Mar 1971, p 12, 26 Mar 1971, p 12; *Courier-Mail*, 11 Jan 1984, p 4; *Daily Mirror* (Sydney), 22 Jan 1985, p 18; A12508, item 2/2183 (NAA).

DIANE COLLINS

DYKE, LEWIS GLANVILLE HOWARD (1900-1984), army officer, was born on 6 August 1900 at Fort Glanville, Adelaide, youngest of three children of South Australian-born parents Lewis Dyke, and his wife Marion Alice, née Abbott. An enthusiastic volunteer artilleryman, Dyke senior was then a major in the State's Permanent Military Force. L. G. H. Dyke was educated at the Collegiate School of St Peter. While not academically inclined, he excelled at cricket and Australian Rules football. He left at 17 and was indentured to a solicitor. Service as a gunner in the Citizen Military Forces possibly influenced him towards a military career. He entered the Royal Military College, Duntroon, Federal Capital Territory, in March 1919. On graduation in December 1922 he was described as being 5 ft 10½ ins (179 cm) tall, of dark complexion with brown hair and eyes, and as having achieved an average performance in both military and academic subjects.

Dyke's first posting as a lieutenant, Staff Corps, was to Fort Queenscliff, Victoria. On 20 September 1924 at All Saints Church of England, St Kilda, Melbourne, he married Maude Josephine ('Bobbie') Preece. During overseas training with a Royal Artillery field battery in 1926-27, he saw service in India and China. He returned to Australia in 1928 to a succession of appointments with responsibility for the training and administration of Militia artillery units in New South Wales, Victoria and Western Australia. He was promoted to captain in 1930 and major in 1938.

Following the outbreak of World War II, Dyke was seconded to the Australian Imperial Force on 13 October 1939 as a battery commander in the 2/2nd Field Regiment. He arrived in the Middle East in May 1940 and was second-in-command of the regiment during the 6th Division's advance to Benghazi, Libya, in January-February 1941. A man of military mien, he was quick to react and somewhat explosive at times. Active, energetic and practical, he gave clear orders and delegated well. He was interested in and stood up for his troops. They returned his loyalty and called him 'Gunner Dyke'.

In April 1941 the 2/2nd took part in the Greek campaign and the subsequent withdrawal to Crete. There the regiment fought as infantry until, in the face of overwhelming odds, the survivors were evacuated to Egypt. Dyke was acting commander of the 2/2nd until appointed Australian liaison officer at Creforce headquarters early in May. For his calmness under fire and 'profound sense of duty' during these trying days, he was awarded the Distinguished Service Order and mentioned in despatches.

Return to Egypt in June 1941 brought promotion to temporary lieutenant colonel and command of the Artillery Training Regiment in Palestine. He took over the 2/3rd Field Regiment in October. With the threat from Japan materialising in December, the regiment returned to Australia in March 1942. In June Dyke was promoted to temporary brigadier as commander, Royal Australian Artillery, of the 2nd Division, which soon moved from Sydney to defend Western Australia. Faced with considerable challenges, he applied himself with good humour coupled with criticism born of experience, and welded the artillery units of the division into an effective force. In mid-1943 he made a short familiarisation tour of New Guinea.

In November 1943 Dyke was appointed commander, Corps Royal Australian Artillery, II Corps. He arrived in New Guinea as the corps was pushing the Japanese from the Ramu Valley, clearing the Huon Peninsula and advancing to Madang. With the completion of this phase, he returned to the Atherton Tableland, Queensland, in May 1944. For his work in ensuring the best use of artillery support and his 'outstanding devotion to duty' during this campaign, he was appointed CBE (1945). The months that followed involved the resting, refitting and retraining of the artillery units of the corps (now redesignated I Corps) before deployment to Morotai to provide fire support for the landings and operations during the final campaigns at Tarakan, Labuan and Balikpapan, Borneo.

The capitulation of Japan saw Dyke take the surrender of Japanese forces in Timor in September 1945. As commander of Timor Force, he was responsible for the recovery of prisoners of war, the disarming and concentration of Japanese troops, the welfare of the civil populace, and liaison and negotiation with the Portuguese authorities in East Timor. Dyke tackled these problems with his usual drive. In April 1946 he was appointed brigadier (later director), Royal Australian Artillery, at Army Headquarters, Melbourne. He was Australian army representative in Washington from 1950 to 1952 and then deputy quartermaster general back at AHQ. Promoted to temporary major general in September 1954 (substantive 30 October), he commanded Western Command until his retirement on 6 August 1957.

In 1957-65 Dyke was employed as personnel manager by Austral Bronze Pty Ltd, Sydney. He maintained an interest in gardening, trees and the environment, and played a little golf. After a few years in Melbourne, he and his wife (d.1976) returned to Sydney. Survived by his son, Dyke died on 23 November 1984 at Royal North Shore Hospital and was cremated.

W. Cremor (ed), *Action Front* (1961); G. Long, *Greece, Crete and Syria* (1953) and *The Final Campaigns* (1963); D. Horner, *The Gunners* (1995); L. Bishop, *The Thunder of the Guns!* (1998); Dyke personal file (Royal Military College Archives, Canberra); private information.   J. WHITELAW

E

EASTICK, SIR THOMAS CHARLES (1900-1988), engineer and army officer, was born on 3 May 1900 at Hyde Park, Adelaide, eldest of six children of Charles William Lone Eastick, plumber, and his wife Agnes Ann, née Scutt. Tom was educated at Goodwood Public School but left at the age of 12½ to look after his sick mother and his younger brothers and sisters while his father struggled to support the family. He became a junior purchasing officer with the hardware firm Colton [q.v.3], Palmer & Preston Ltd, where he developed the managerial skills which were a feature of his later life. He married Ruby Sybil Bruce, a saleswoman, on 31 October 1925 at the Baptist Church, Richmond, and they set up their home in the new suburb of Reade Park. He was a fair but firm father to his five sons, and a strict teetotaller who was never known to swear.

In 1927 Eastick was invited to manage temporarily an engineering company in Adelaide for twelve months. This career change was so successful that he co-founded a small engineering business, Angas Engineering Co. (Pty Ltd), with a friend who was a first-class mechanic. Business prospered until the Depression but thereafter times became progressively harder. During the night he would ride his bicycle to the factory to check on the case hardening of automotive components.

Having served four years in the senior cadets, Eastick had enlisted in the Australian Field Artillery, Militia, in 1918. Commissioned as a lieutenant in 1922, he set about his duties in the 13th Field Brigade with energy and efficiency and quickly developed a reputation as a sound trainer of men. He was given command of the 50th Battery in 1924 and promoted to captain in 1926. That year he demonstrated for the first time in Australia the use of survey procedures to predict gun data to engage targets without ranging. A second innovation with which he was associated was the control of artillery fire from aircraft: in 1927 a Royal Australian Air Force pilot adjusted the fire of Eastick's battery during field firing. Eastick rose to major in 1930 and in 1938 his battery was awarded the Mount Schanck trophy for being the most efficient Militia field battery in Australia. In 1939 he was promoted to temporary lieutenant colonel and appointed commanding officer of the brigade.

Early in 1940, after the outbreak of World War II, Eastick embarked on a rigorous three-month training regime with his brigade. In April he was selected to raise and command the 2/7th Field Regiment, Australian Imperial Force, as a substantive lieutenant colonel. His unit was ultimately allotted to the 9th Division

and embarked for the Middle East in November. Deployment on operations in North Africa followed from May to October 1941, after which the 2/7th became depot regiment at the British Army's Middle East School of Artillery at Almaza near Cairo for three months. This honour was in recognition of the efficiency which Eastick had brought to his regiment and for which he was mentioned in despatches (1942). In February-June 1942 the regiment performed defensive duties in Syria and Lebanon.

For the 'forcefulness' and 'determination' with which he commanded his regiment in Egypt, first at Tel el Eisa in July and then during the battle of El Alamein in October-November, Eastick was awarded the Distinguished Service Order. He returned to Australia in February 1943. In June he was promoted to temporary brigadier and posted as commander, Royal Australian Artillery, 7th Division. From August 1943 to April 1944 he served in Papua and New Guinea.

Appointed to command the 9th Division's artillery in June 1944, Eastick served in Australia, Morotai and Borneo. During his command of Kuching Force (September-December 1945), he took the surrender of Japanese forces in southern Sarawak. He administered command of the 9th Division from December 1945 until February 1946. On 28 February he transferred to the Reserve of Officers with the honorary rank of brigadier. He was appointed a companion of the Order of the Star of Sarawak (1946).

Eastick resumed his civilian occupation and joined the Colonel Light Gardens sub-branch of the Returned Sailors', Soldiers' and Airmen's Imperial League of Australia (Returned Services League from 1965); he was State president in 1950-54 and 1961-72. A Freemason, a justice of the peace and a leading participant in 'A Call to the People of Australia', he was also federal president of the Australia Day Council (1963-65, 1976-80). He served in an honorary capacity in some twenty-five other organisations, most of which were ex-service related.

On 28 January 1950 Eastick was recalled to the army as a brigadier and appointed commander, Headquarters Group, Central Command. Additionally, he was an honorary aide-de-camp to the governor-general Sir William McKell [q.v.] in 1950-53. He again transferred to the Reserve of Officers on 1 October 1953. From 1955 to 1960 he was a colonel commandant of the Royal Australian Artillery. Having been appointed CMG in 1953, he was knighted in 1970. He remained with Angas Engineering Pty Ltd until 1977.

Lady Eastick died suddenly in 1980. A few years later Sir Thomas moved to the Masonic Nursing Home at Somerton Park, where he died on 16 December 1988. Survived by his sons, he was cremated. His son Bruce was Speaker (1979-82) and leader of the Opposition (1972-75) in the South Australian parliament.

Integrity, professional competence, steadfastness, self-discipline and self-reliance had been instilled in Eastick at an early age. He inspired the officers and men he commanded with his proficiency and resolution. He was a valued and trusted businessman and servant of the many organisations with which he was involved. Despite the hardships of his early life and war service, he remained a kindly and charitable man who was tough and forceful when those attributes were required. He was not flamboyant, but a consistent performer who lived by the dictum with which he had been brought up—'near enough is never good enough'.

D. Goodhart, *We of the Turning Tide* (1947) and *The History of the 2/7 Australian Field Regiment* (1952); G. Long, *The Final Campaigns* (1963); B. Maughan, *Tobruk and El Alamein* (1966); S. Cockburn, *The Patriarchs* (1983); D. Brook (ed), *Roundshot to Rapier* (1986); D. Horner, *The Gunners* (1995); T. Roberts, *Will We Be Disappointed—After?* (1995); Returned Services League of Aust (SA), *Annual Report*, 1969, 1972; *Advertiser* (Adelaide), 17 Dec 1988, p 17; Eastick papers (AWM); private information.   DAVID N. BROOK

EBERT, MAX; *see* McCLINTOCK

EDGAR, GRAHAME (1901-1985), veterinarian and public servant, was born on 25 May 1901 at Petersham, Sydney, fourth of five children of Thomas Ferdinando Edgar, an English-born commercial accountant, and his Victorian-born wife Grace Littler, née Meeking. Grahame was educated at Sydney Grammar School and the University of Sydney (B.V.Sc., 1924). Following a year spent in China, the Philippines and North Borneo, he joined the New South Wales Department of Agriculture in 1926 as a junior veterinary officer, working in the field at Tamworth and Albury and at head office. He also served (1924-42) in the Australian Army Veterinary Corps (Militia), rising to provisional captain. On 28 November 1928 at St Paul's Church of England, Burwood, Sydney, he married Mary Barnes Elliott.

As the inaugural McGarvie Smith Institute research scholar, in 1927 Edgar had transferred to the Glenfield Veterinary Research Station. He concentrated first on soil infections and anaerobic infections of sheep and cattle. In 1928 he proved that black-disease microbes were soil-borne in certain districts and that the bacilli remained dormant in sheep livers until activated by liver fluke infestation. Control of black disease—the cause of great economic loss to the State's sheep industry—now rested on better control of liver fluke. In 1929 Edgar was promoted to senior research officer and in 1936 to senior veterinary research officer. He continued his work on diseases caused by anaerobic organisms (blackleg, enterotoxaemia and botulism) and began research into infectious diseases of sheep, and into parasites (mainly of sheep and cattle). In 1946 he travelled extensively overseas to investigate the latest research into animal diseases and to attend international conferences.

Back at Glenfield, in 1947 he was appointed director of veterinary research. In 1949 his long-term research into toxaemic jaundice in sheep identified the two causes as being heliotrope ingestion and chronic copper poisoning. He made a major contribution to the Commonwealth's large-scale pasture-improvement program of the 1950s and 1960s in the form of rabbit control. The Glenfield strain of the myxomatosis virus proved more virulent than others and was distributed free on request to New South Wales graziers from 1951 (and interstate from 1961).

From the 1950s overseas scientists visited the Glenfield station, which also hosted scholars under United Nations Food and Agriculture Organization and Colombo Plan fellowships. In 1952 Edgar was seconded for four months by the FAO to advise the government of Burma on an animal health laboratory. He also visited Britain to observe research on foot-and-mouth disease. When he accepted the position of assistant under-secretary of the department in 1959, his research activities ended, after seventy-two published papers. In 1962 he was awarded a doctorate in veterinary science by the University of Sydney for thirty-three of these research papers collectively titled *Some Contributions to Problems of Animal Health and Production in New South Wales*.

In 1961 Edgar had become director-general of agriculture, the first veterinarian to be in charge of the department. He remained a strong proponent of quarantine vigilance against the introduction of exotic disease, of rabbit control, and of Glenfield. From 1959 the department promoted and distributed the poison sodium fluoroacetate, '1080', to supplement myxomatosis. In 1960 Edgar was a member of the Australian delegation to the 11th General Session of the United Nations Educational, Scientific and Cultural Organization, and in 1963 he attended international veterinary conferences and visited research institutions in Europe, Britain and the United States of America. He retired in 1966.

Edgar gave long service to the Australian National Science Committee of UNESCO

(1948-72; chairman 1957-61) and to the Australian Veterinary Association, culminating in his presidency of the State (1938) and federal (1948-49) branches. He was elected (1952) fellow of the AVA and the Australian College of Veterinary Scientists (1971) and was appointed (1963) an honorary associate of the Royal College of Veterinary Surgeons, London. Awarded the Farrer memorial medal in 1966, he was also appointed OBE that year. He received the Gilruth [q.v.9] prize from the AVA in 1967. Active in retirement, he became chairman (1967-85) of the McGarvie Smith Institute. He continued his involvement with the University of Sydney as a member of the faculty (1960-79) and the postgraduate committee (1962-78) of veterinary science, and as a fellow (1966-78) of the senate. A councillor from 1959 and treasurer from 1968 of the New South Wales Sheepbreeders' Association, he was elected a life governor in 1980. He was a member of the council of the World's Poultry Science Association (1962-70) and a director (1966-76) of William Cooper & Nephews (Australia) Pty Ltd (Cooper Australia Ltd).

Edgar's colleagues praised him as a 'public spirited, responsible and energetic' scientist, whose expertise was imparted with an 'infectious gusto and characteristic warmth'. He was remembered by Sir Hermann Black [q.v.] as a 'big, sparkling brown-eyed man, wholesome, learned yet with the common touch ... constructive, cheerful, companionable'. Survived by his wife and their daughter and son, he died on 9 August 1985 at Killara and was cremated.

U. M. L. Bygott, *A History of the McGarvie Smith Institute, 1918-1992* (1994); Dept of Agriculture (NSW), *Annual Report*, 1926/27, 1960/61, 1963/64, 1965/66; *SMH*, 15 Oct 1928, p 9, 24 July 1963, p 10; *Pastoral Review and Graziers' Record*, 18 Dec 1961, p 1015; *AVA News*, 7 Feb 1986, p 14, in *Austn Veterinary Jnl*, vol 63, no 2, 1986; Sir Hermann Black, A Tribute to Dr Grahame Edgar, (ms, 1985, Univ of Sydney Archives).   PATRICIA HALE

EDIS, MARGARET DOROTHY (1890-1981), nurse, was born on 19 April 1890 at Kyabram, Victoria, second child of John Edwin Edis, a London-born house-painter, and his wife Hannah, née Menzies, from Scotland. The family moved to Kalgoorlie in 1896. Educated at local state and high schools, 'Dot' began training as a nurse at Coolgardie Hospital in 1911. On her first day the matron told her 'you'll never make the grade' and next morning forced her to remain in the nurses' dining room until she had eaten her porridge. Finding herself often in strife as she rebelled against the discipline and the Spartan environment, she transferred to Kalgoorlie Hospital and completed her training in December 1914.

On 10 August 1915 Edis was appointed a staff nurse in the Australian Army Nursing Service, Australian Imperial Force. Sailing immediately for the Middle East, she was attached to an auxiliary hospital in Egypt before moving to the Western Front in April 1916. She worked in British and Australian hospitals and the 2nd Australian Casualty Clearing Station and rose to the rank of sister in October 1918. Her AIF service ended in Perth on 9 December 1919.

After working for five years at the Anzac Hostel for repatriated soldiers at Freshwater Bay, Edis commenced a refresher course in the nursing of women and children at Fremantle Hospital. One night she assisted in the delivery of a premature baby, who subsequently died. Shocked by the experience, she embarked on training in midwifery and child welfare under Matron Agnes Walsh [q.v.16] at King Edward Memorial Hospital for Women, Subiaco. She took charge of the postnatal ward and specialised in caring for premature babies. In 1938 she adopted an undersized boy to whom she had taken a 'grand fancy' and named him Reginald.

Called up in July 1940 for full-time duty in the Citizen Military Forces (and later in the AIF), Edis served as principal matron, Western Command (Western Australian Lines of Communication Area) until April 1943. Under wartime manpower regulations she returned to KEMH. In January 1948 she was appointed matron of the Home of Peace, Subiaco. Finding that conditions were deplorable, she confronted the home's all-male management committee and insisted on urgent and sustained improvements. She promised to stay for two years but remained for eighteen.

Small (5 ft 2½ ins or 159 cm), with fine features and a clipped voice, Edis was remembered by a wartime colleague as 'brisk, eager and capable'. Her nurses considered her 'a strict disciplinarian' but 'fair'. As president (1945-50) of the Western Australian branch of the Australian Trained Nurses' Association, Edis helped to establish (1949) the College of Nursing, Australia. She was also State president of the Trained Nurses' Guild (1947-49) and of the Australian United Nurses' Association (1949-53), and served (1943-53) on the Nurses' Registration Board. In 1953 she was presented with Queen Elizabeth II's coronation medal and in 1954 was appointed MBE. The International Committee of the Red Cross awarded her the Florence Nightingale medal in 1965. Next year she retired. She eventually moved to Swan Cottage Homes, Bentley, and then to the Home of Peace. Survived by Reginald, she died there on 14 August 1981 and was cremated with Anglican rites.

D. Popham (ed), *Reflections* (1978); *Weekend News*, 22 Dec 1962, p 27; *West Australian*, 29 May

1965, p 22, 24 Sept 1966, p 25; V. Hobbs and S. Gare, interview with M. D. Edis (ts, 1975, SLWA).

                                          DEBORAH GARE

EDOLS, JENIFER; *see* WHITECROSS

EDWARDS, CHARLES AUGUSTUS ('BILL') (1905-1990), pharmacist, businessman and sports administrator, was born on 11 August 1905 at Copeville, Marian, near Mackay, Queensland, elder child of Queensland-born parents Arthur Codrington Edwards, farmer, and his wife Agnes Ouleva, née Gabriel. Educated at Devereux Creek and Marian state schools and Mackay State High School, he began a pharmacy apprenticeship at Mackay, and played Rugby League football. He moved to Brisbane to attend the Queensland College of Pharmacy, where he won a medal. He decided to call himself 'Bill' and, taking up tennis, was a competitive A-grade player, particularly in doubles, until he became a 'nimble 17-stoner' (108 kg). Six ft 2 ins (188 cm) tall, he was eventually to weigh about 21 stone (133 kg) and to be known as 'Big Bill'.

Registered in 1926, Edwards opened his first suburban pharmacy at Greenslopes next year, and added a city shop in 1930. For forty years from 1934 his base was at 236 Edward Street; with an adjunct lottery agency, he was said to dispense both 'health and wealth'. During his career he acquired and sold other pharmacies. On 7 July 1934 at St Andrew's Church of England, Lutwyche, he married Ruth Henrietta Barr (d.1983), a dressmaker. They had three sons and from late 1942 lived on 12 acres (4.8 ha) at Alderley.

In World War II, as well as running his by then well-known pharmacy, Edwards operated four motor launches in Moreton Bay as transport for the armed services. He came close to one theatre of combat: after vicious brawls in Brisbane between Australian and American soldiers in November 1942, a local woman wrote that her American husband, who was in danger of being kicked to death, was protected inside the pharmacy, by the chemist, 'a very big man'. Edwards stood as the Labor candidate in two mayoral elections, in 1943 and 1946, but failed both times to unseat (Sir) John Chandler [q.v.13]. He was also unsuccessful as a Queensland Labor Party candidate for State parliament in 1957, having stood 'because of my friendship with Vince Gair [q.v.14]'.

Edwards's wartime purchase of two Jersey cows led to the formation of his Benvue stud at Samford. He also bought two established Jersey studs, Grasmere, near Kilcoy, and in 1953 the celebrated Trecarne, Lockyer, but sold his dairy cattle interests in 1954. A breeder of stud ponies, with Percy Skinner he revivified the Royal National Agricultural and Industrial Association of Queensland's annual exhibition of thoroughbred horses. He was a councillor (1954-81) of the association, and a hands-on ring committee chairman (1956-80). As ringmaster, he dwarfed the golf-cart in which he darted about the arena. In 1959-81 he was on the committee of the Queensland Turf Club; of his many racehorses, some owned in partnership, the best were probably Urgona and Refulgent.

From the 1930s Edwards was a committee-member of the Queensland Lawn Tennis Association and its constituent bodies. As vice-president (1946-51) and president (1952-65), he oversaw the transformation of the courts at Milton into a venue for international competitions. Gregarious, he was a man of wide acquaintance and superabundant energy. He planned carefully and then led, and at times drove, contractors, a few permanent staff, and large numbers of volunteers to the successful completion of projects. A succession of new stands and headquarters were built, and in 1955 the Queensland Lawn Tennis Club was issued with the first liquor licence for a principal sporting club in the State. Milton hosted Davis Cup matches from 1952, its first Australian championships in 1956, and the Davis Cup challenge round in 1958.

Edwards was elected president (1965-69) of the Lawn Tennis Association of Australia, the first to come from outside Victoria. In 1966 he placed his casting vote against the introduction of open tournaments to Australia, but the recruiting power of professional promoters and the contradictions inherent in 'shamateurism' saw the Australian Open championship inaugurated in 1969. His vote had reflected his consciousness of the support that local tennis associations had given junior and regional tennis; the era of large television revenues and sponsorships had not yet arrived.

In the expansion of Queensland hospitals after World War II, Edwards was often on their boards, as deputy-chairman and chairman of works committees. He showed imaginative foresight and drive during the implementation and building stages. A member of the Brisbane and South Coast Hospitals Board from 1955, he resigned from the successor (from 1959) North Brisbane, South Brisbane and Redcliffe boards in 1967 'due to pressure of business', but rejoined North Brisbane for 1970-76. Princess Alexandra, Chermside (Prince Charles), Royal Brisbane, Royal Children's, (Royal) Women's, Redcliffe and Southport hospitals were all built or much developed during his tenure. He was a committee-member (1976-87) of the Queensland Anti-Cancer Council.

Directorships in the hotel and entertainment industries became an increasing preoccupation for Edwards in the 1960s. From 1960 he was a director of Lennons Hotel Ltd, Brisbane, and of Lennons Broadbeach Hotel Ltd, which were taken over by The Federal Hotels Ltd in 1961. On the Federal Hotels board from 1964, he was chairman in 1967-69. He was also chairman of Northstate Tenpin Bowling Ltd (1963-77), the Crest International Hotel, Brisbane, the committee that organised Brisbane's first Warana Festival (1962) and, in the early 1970s, of the Australian National Travel Association (Queensland council).

Appointed CBE in 1959, Edwards was voted many life memberships. In his spare time he enjoyed deep-sea fishing. Ill health, particularly diabetes, marred his later years and he became a gaunt 'Big Bill'. Survived by his sons, he died on 8 August 1990 in Brisbane and was cremated.

A Century of Queensland Tennis (1988); F. Mills, *The Ekka* (1990); J. H. Tyrer, *History of the Brisbane Hospital and Its Affiliates* (1993); P. A. Thompson and R. Macklin, *The Battle of Brisbane* (2000); *Qld Country Life*, 19 Mar 1953, p 4, 9 Aug 1973, p 5; *Aust Financial Review*, 22 Dec 1960, p 18, 6 Nov 1967, p 8, 5 Aug 1969, p 15; *Qld Racing Calendar*, 1 Apr 1961, p 477; *Telegraph* (Brisbane), 24 Oct 1968, p 16; *Sunday Australian*, 15 Aug 1971, p 33; *Sunday Mail* (Brisbane), 20 Nov 1977, p 26.   S. J. ROUTH
VIVIAN E. EDWARDS

EDWARDS, SIR HUGHIE IDWAL (1914-1982), air force officer, businessman and governor, was born on 1 August 1914 at Fremantle, Western Australia, third of five surviving children of Welsh-born parents Hugh Edwards, farrier, and his wife Jane Ann, née Watkins. Called Idwal by his family, he was to be known as Eddie in the Royal Air Force and Hughie to his Australian aircrews. He attended White Gum Valley State School and Fremantle Boys' School, which he had to leave, reluctantly, after gaining his Junior certificate because the family finances could no longer support him.

After working in a shipping agent's office, a racing stable and a factory, Edwards enlisted in the Permanent Military Forces in March 1934 and served with the 6th Heavy Battery, Royal Australian Artillery, which manned the defences of Fremantle. Six ft 1½ ins (187 cm) tall and about 12 stone (76 kg) in weight, he played Australian Rules football for South Fremantle and cricket for the Fremantle garrison team. His stay in the army was brief as, much to his surprise, he was accepted as a cadet in the Royal Australian Air Force on 15 July 1935 and sent to No.1 Flying Training School, Point Cook, Victoria. He was not a natural pilot but on graduation was rated as 'above average'.

The Royal Air Force was seeking recently graduated officers such as Edwards; he and six others arrived in England and were granted short-service commissions on 21 August 1936. Edwards loved the club-like atmosphere of the pre-war RAF. He soon became proficient on the new Blenheim bombers and was promoted to flying officer in May 1938, but in August he flew into a cumulo-nimbus cloud and his aircraft iced up and went into an uncontrollable spin. After baling out his crew, he managed to escape at low altitude but his parachute caught on the radio aerial and he 'rode' the aircraft to the ground. He was critically injured and spent much of the following two years recovering, afraid that he would be unable to take part in World War II, which had broken out in September 1939.

By sheer determination and constant pressure on the medical authorities, in April 1940 Edwards finally gained permission to resume flying. Promoted to flight lieutenant, he sustained only minor injuries when he crashed in October after becoming lost in a nationwide blackout. In February 1941 he joined No.139 Squadron, again flying Blenheims. The squadron was engaged in the dangerous task of attacking German convoys off the coast of Europe as well as bombing nearby targets on land. Edwards had another accident but survived unscathed. With the heavy loss of crews, life expectancy being only a few weeks, promotion came quickly to the survivors and in April he was made acting squadron leader.

In May Edwards became the commander of No.105 Squadron as an acting wing commander. Demoralised by the mortality rate and poor results, the squadron rallied to his determination to make it the best in the group. Edwards was almost worshipped by his crews. He was severe but fair and outstandingly courageous, while admitting that he was as frightened as his men. On 15 June he led a formation of aircraft against enemy merchant shipping off the Dutch coast. He attacked one ship from mast height, severely damaging it, and for his 'great leadership, skill and gallantry' was awarded the Distinguished Flying Cross.

On 4 July 1941 a group of twelve Blenheims led by Edwards made a daylight attack on the German city of Bremen. His bombers had to fly under high-tension wires, through a balloon barrage and into intense anti-aircraft fire. The surviving aircraft were riddled with holes. Four of the attacking force were shot down and Edwards' own Blenheim returned with a wounded gunner, a smashed radio rack and a large part of the port wing shot away. For this gallant action Edwards was awarded the Victoria Cross. Later that month he took his squadron to the besieged island of Malta to attack Italian convoys on their way to Libya. To his chagrin he was not allowed to fly; after two months only three of his crews survived out of the eighteen that had arrived.

Following a propaganda tour of the United States of America in October-December, Edwards married Cherry Kyrle ('Pat') Beresford, née Kemp, the widow of a friend, on 21 January 1942 at St Mary's Church of England, Bryanston Square, London. A few days later he took command of No.22 Operational Training Unit. In August he was posted to the command of No.105 Squadron, flying his favourite aircraft, the Mosquito. The squadron took part in many successful attacks, including the destruction of the Philips factory at Eindhoven, the Netherlands, in December and the submarine-engine plant in Copenhagen in January 1943. In most of these attacks Edwards played the leading role. He was awarded the Distinguished Service Order for his part in the Eindhoven raid.

In February Edwards was promoted to acting group captain and placed in command of the large RAF station at Binbrook, Lincolnshire, which became the base from which No.460 Squadron, RAAF, operated until the end of the war. Edwards found his first substantial command—of a large number of Australian ground and air crews—a challenging task. He soon started operations on Lancaster bombers, almost certainly doing more trips than he was allowed. Losses were heavy in the battle of the Ruhr and the battle of Berlin, but morale never faltered, due in large part to his example. He was very popular with his crews, provided they did not have to fly with him: he was a poor pilot with more enthusiasm and courage than ability.

Edwards was sent to Ceylon (Sri Lanka) as group captain, bomber operations, in December 1944 and as senior air staff officer at Lord Louis Mountbatten's headquarters, South-East Asia Command, in January 1945. He was engaged first in supporting the 14th Army in Burma and then, after being posted to Malaya and to Batavia (Jakarta), in the rescue of prisoners of war and Dutch civilians from the troubled Netherlands East Indies. Having been mentioned in despatches, he was appointed OBE (1947).

Returning to England in May 1947, Edwards attended the RAF Staff College, Bracknell, Berkshire. He spent the following years flying jet aircraft and instructing. In 1956 he was posted to command the large RAF station at Habbaniyah, Iraq, which was besieged during a military coup in 1958. He acquitted himself well in a tense situation and withdrew the force without casualties. In October that year he was made commandant of the Central Fighter Establishment, West Raynham, Norfolk, as an acting air commodore (substantive 1 July 1959). He was appointed CB in 1959 and an aide-de-camp to Queen Elizabeth II next year. In 1961 he attended the Imperial Defence College, London. Director of organisation (establishments) at the Air Ministry from January 1962, he retired from the RAF on 30 September 1963.

Edwards took up a post in Sydney as resident director of a large mining firm, Australian Selection (Pty) Ltd. His wife died in 1966. At the registrar-general's office on 11 September 1972 he married Dorothy Carew Berrick, née Nott, a divorcee. On 7 January 1974 he was sworn in as governor of Western Australia. He was appointed a knight of grace of the Order of St John in May and KCMG in August. Impeded by chronic ill health, Sir Hughie resigned on 2 April 1975 and returned to Sydney. Survived by his wife, and by the son and daughter of his first marriage, he died suddenly of subdural haematoma after a fall on 5 August 1982 at Darling Point and was cremated. The most highly decorated Australian of World War II, he had been respected by all with whom he came in contact and revered by those with whom he served. The Australian War Memorial, Canberra, holds his medals, his portrait (1944) by Stella Bowen [q.v.7] and a painting (1982) by Ray Honisett of the episode in which he won his VC. A bronze statue of him by Andrew Kay was erected in Kings Square, Fremantle, in 2002.

P. Firkins, *Strike and Return* (1964) and *The Golden Eagles* (1980); C. Bowyer, *For Valour* (1978); A. Hoyle, *Sir Hughie Edwards VC KCMG CB DSO OBE DFC* (2000); A. Staunton, *Victoria Cross* (2005); Edwards papers (AWM).   ARTHUR HOYLE

EHAVA, GABRIEL; *see* KARAVA

EINIHOVICI, AVRUM (1895-1988), medical practitioner and Esperantist, was born on 6 March 1895 at Balti, Bessarabia, Russia, son of Ghers (Hirsch) Einihovici, merchant, and his wife Mirlia (Miriam), née Langman. Avrum received a traditional Jewish education until the age of 11 before attending a state primary school for two years. He matriculated in 1916 from a Jewish high school where he developed an interest in Yiddish theatre. In 1916-17 he served briefly in the Russian Army.

Subjected to persecution, Einihovici's parents escaped to Romania; he joined them in 1920 and enrolled in the faculty of medicine at the University of Jasi. After anti-Semitic riots at the university, he moved to Italy in 1922 and graduated (1924) in medicine from the University of Pavia. He worked as a general practitioner in a rural town before studying at Milan to become an ear, nose and throat surgeon. In time he became a consultant to opera singers at La Scala. On 22 July 1934 at Milan he married with Jewish rites Idyss Kleyman, a clerk from Warsaw.

Legislation in 1938 revoked Italian citizenship granted to Jewish persons after 1 January 1919, and in January 1939 Einihovici and his family travelled to Palestine. Unable to practise his profession, he migrated to Australia, arriving at Fremantle on 8 August 1939. His sponsor was Cyrus Caldera, a Perth doctor who had been his professor at the University of Pavia. Registered next month, he entered into general practice at Corrigin. He acted as interpreter for the local council and for Italian prisoners of war who were working on farms in the area. On 26 January 1949 he became an Australian citizen.

Einihovici moved to Perth after the war and resumed his career as an ear, nose and throat surgeon. An ardent supporter of Esperanto, which he valued as a promoter of world peace, he was awarded (1950) the diploma of the British Esperanto Association and later, the upper diploma of the Australian association. He was very active in the Esperanto League of Western Australia, and until 1987 regularly attended annual world congresses. Known as 'Tim', he was a member, freeman and dais president (1957) of Western Australian Rostrum, an adjudicator for the Western Australian Debating League and president in the early 1960s of the Dante Alighieri Society. He was founding president (1947-72) of the Perth section of Friends of the Hebrew University. Keen to maintain a creative Jewish arts group in Perth, he produced many Yiddish plays. He was associated with the local Bahá'í community, the Society of Friends (Quakers), the Moral Rearmament movement, Amnesty International and the Freemasons. People appreciated him for his gentle and encouraging manner and sound common sense.

Five ft 5 ins (165 cm) tall and of light build, Einihovici enjoyed sports—soccer and skiing in his youth, and later tennis, golf, swimming and bowls—and attributed his longevity to healthy food and physical fitness. Survived by his wife and their daughter, he died on 7 March 1988 at his Floreat home and was buried in Karrakatta cemetery. In 1990-92 the Perth Friends of the Hebrew University raised money for a scholarship named in his honour.

Australian Esperantist, Mar-Apr 1988, p 137; *Dante Society's News*, no 3, 1988, p 2; *Maccabean*, 1 Apr 1988, p 10; *WA Rostrum Informer*, July 1988, p 1; PP302/1, WA17052 (NAA); personal knowledge.

LAURA RAITER

ELLIOT, DOUGLAS GEORGE (1917-1989), radio and television broadcaster and politician, was born on 12 February 1917 at Armadale, Melbourne, son of New Zealand-born John Pollock Elliot, importer, and his Australian-born second wife Laurel Agnes Monica, née Hickey. Doug was educated at Scotch College, where he sang with the Glee Club, until the Depression forced him to leave school. He worked briefly for Dimmeys department store and then for the stockbrokers J. B. Were [q.v.2] & Son, and in his spare time performed with the Gregan McMahon [q.v.10] Players. Outgoing and versatile, he then joined the chorus of J. C. Williamson [q.v.6] Ltd. While touring in Queensland he broke his leg and was forced to quit. He made his way back to Melbourne, reputedly by singing on streets and in pubs with a one-string fiddler.

In 1934 Doug joined Melbourne radio-station 3AW. He performed bush ballads as 'Kanga' on the children's show 'Chatterbox Corner', with 'Nicky' (Cliff Whitta [q.v.16]) and 'Nancy Lee'. In 1938 he moved to 3KZ, where he worked with Norman Banks [q.v.] and hosted popular variety programs. He subsequently transferred to 3UZ, on which he presented programs for Leyshon Publicity Services Pty Ltd. At St Mark's Church of England, Fitzroy, on 12 January 1940 he married Heather Bernice Pearce, a salesgirl. Enlisting as an equipment assistant in the Royal Australian Air Force on 27 May 1943, he later joined a concert party that performed in Northern Australia and New Guinea. He was discharged in September 1945. Elliot returned to radio and worked at 3XY, 3UZ, 3KZ and 3AK as compère, announcer and 'King of the commercials'. He most enjoyed 'Sports Parade' on 3KZ—with the comedian Max Reddy and the former Victorian Football League players Lou Richards and Jack Dyer—and 'Fifty and Over', an interview series on 3UZ.

Almost 6 feet (183 cm) tall and rotund, with a strong, fruity voice, Elliot also had a long and successful career in Melbourne television. In 1957 he joined HSV-7, and gave live introductions to the popular American children's show 'The Mickey Mouse Club'. He regarded this as the highlight of his career, recalling shortly before his death: 'The kids, they loved me and boy I loved them. There were 12 000 of them'. On the show he became known as 'Uncle Doug', a nickname that stuck. In 1959 he produced a sports review on Saturday mornings, moving it in 1960 to time he had bought from the station on Sundays. As 'World of Sport', hosted by Ron Casey, the program ran for a record twenty-nine years, each week featuring Elliot's unrivalled 'Big Sell' advertisements ('Leather Lungs' becoming another nickname).

In 1958 Elliot unsuccessfully contested the Federal seat of Maribyrnong for the Australian Labor Party, but in a 1960 by-election he was elected to the Victorian Legislative Council for the province of Melbourne. The combination of politician and television spruiker (with interests in land, motels, racehorses and greyhounds) was uneasily regarded by some colleagues, yet Elliot's directness and enthusiasm won respect. As shadow minister for State development, decentralisation and tourism, he showed a remarkable knowledge of water resources; he was also committed to improving welfare, particularly for the elderly. A self-confessed 'bag-man' for the ALP, his commercial links and investment advice benefited the union movement and an embattled party.

Elliot lost preselection in 1977, but before leaving parliament in 1979 he was elected to the Essendon City Council. He served as mayor (1982-83) and then retired to Murabit to live close to his 'great mistress', the Murray River. Survived by his wife and their two daughters and son, he died on 25 March 1989 at Kerang and was buried in the local cemetery with Catholic rites, having recently converted to that faith.

R. R. Walker, *Dial 1179* (1984); J. Main and L. Richards, *Sports Screamers* (1995); *PD* (Vic), 11 Apr 1989, p 167; *Herald* (Melbourne), 17 Feb 1977, p 4, 14 Aug 1980, p 4; *Sunday Press* (Melbourne), 20 Feb 1977, p 8, 26 Mar 1989, p 3; *Age* (Melbourne), 15 Dec 1978, p 9; private information.

DERHAM GROVES

ELLIOTT, ELIOT VALENS (1902-1984), trade unionist, was born on 12 September 1902 at Huntly, New Zealand, and named Victor Emmanuel, son of New Zealand-born parents James Elliott, wheelwright, and his wife Helena, née Gray. After the deaths of his father and stepfather in mining accidents, Vic's schooling was cut short. In his teens he worked on the New Zealand railways and went to sea as a ship's fireman. He joined the Federated Seamen's Union of Australasia (Seamen's Union of Australia) in 1919. By 1922 he was chiefly domiciled in Australian ports, where he earned a reputation as a trade union delegate capable of holding his own with the toughest colleagues in grim conditions. After he campaigned for improved working conditions in 1924 he was blackballed by the Commonwealth Government Shipping Line.

Under the name Eliot Valence Elliott McPherson, on 26 August 1930 he married Violet Muriel Uhr at the district registrar's office, Rockdale, Sydney. During the Depression he walked from their home at Five Dock to the city wharves in search of work, watched sculling competitions on the harbour, bet on racehorses and bred greyhounds. He came to prominence in the waterfront labour movement during the 1935 seamen's dispute as assistant-secretary of the Sydney strike committee. That year he unsuccessfully challenged the constitutionality of the controversial anti-union Commonwealth Transport Workers Act (1928-29) in the High Court of Australia.

Elliott was elected Queensland branch secretary of the FSUA in 1937. He claimed that he began his career as a union official in order 'to earn a quid so I can eat' after being blacklisted for employment by shipping companies. In office he displayed a talent for negotiation and organisation absent in his predecessors. He regularly produced a union journal, *Seamen's Voice*, as a vehicle for policy formulation and expressions of solidarity. Becoming a member of the Communist Party of Australia, he attended the party's classes and theatre groups to develop his communication skills. Like his fellow CPA member and maritime trade unionist James Healy [q.v.14], Elliott was a moderniser in touch with national issues, who was able to combine a radical vision of socialist progress with realistic and successful bargaining tactics.

After a bitter contest with old guard rivals burdened by the failures of the Depression years, Elliott became general secretary of the FSUA, based in Sydney, in 1941. During World War II he maintained a balance between militancy and support for the productivity aims of the war economy. In 1942 when the Curtin [q.v.13] government created the Maritime Industry Commission, shipping's wage-setting and regulatory body for the next ten years, he was appointed as the representative of the seamen. After a spat with other unionists on the commission over penalties, he withdrew in June 1943. Ten months later he rejoined the MIC but his socialist hopes were disappointed when it failed to sponsor the postwar nationalisation of the shipping industry.

In the 1940s Elliott established a reputation in the international labour movement, sponsoring union recruitment and organisation among Australian and visiting seamen in the closing stages of the war, and promoting collective action by Chinese, Greek and Indonesian shipboard workers. He became a member of the central committee of the CPA and in 1949 accepted the vice-presidency of the maritime section of the Moscow-backed World Federation of Trade Unions. The Australian Council of Trade Unions decided later that year to withdraw from the WFTU but the Seamen's Union did not disaffiliate until September 1952, and even then continued some involvement. Elliott was removed from the central committee of the CPA in 1969. Maintaining his pro-Moscow orientation, he joined the new Socialist Party of Australia in 1971. Press photographs revealed him as groomed in the style of Trotsky with a clipped moustache and, later in life, a goatee. According to one journalist he had 'a face fierce with concentration and zeal, and capped by a shock of white hair. He looked the part. He spoke the part. He acted the part. About his public image there was a touch of the larrikin'.

Elliott's work demanded sophisticated planning and tactical skills. He worked long hours, attending political party meetings at night as well as numerous ad hoc meetings with union faction members to consider industrial action. The union's public role in opposition to wars in Korea and Vietnam embroiled him further in arguments with conservative politicians and journalists. But, industrially, conditions continued to favour high wages and generous provisions for his members. Australian shipping, and indirectly the jobs of Australian seamen, remained subsidised and protected. Believing that 'it is easier to walk down the gang plank than walk back up', he tried to avoid costly strike action and relied on negotiating acumen to win benefits for his members.

In the later years of his general secretaryship, Elliott continued to defend his members' rights in vigorous campaigns against shipowners including Broken Hill Proprietary Co. Ltd and the American mining conglomerate Utah Development Co. A Senate select committee in 1958 inquired into indemnity payments made by shipowners when Australian crews were not used, and in 1974 a royal commission into alleged payments to maritime unions examined money given to the unions in respect of the use of permit vessels. Both reports deemed that the unions were acting improperly in demanding payments from shipowners. Elliott's retirement in 1978, after thirty-seven years as general secretary, was marked by the unveiling of a portrait by Graeme Inson in March 1979.

On 24 September 1982 Elliott, by then a widower, married a 64-year-old divorcee, Kondelea (Della), née Xenodohos, a journalist and accountant, at their home in Roseville. Her father owned a café at Circular Quay that had been frequented by the seafaring fraternity since the 1920s. Elliott's long-standing relationship with Della, who was politically active, had given him support both in the office and at home. Survived by his wife and his son from his first marriage, he died on 26 November 1984 at Hornsby and was cremated.

B. Fitzpatrick and R. J. Cahill, *The Seamen's Union of Australia* (1981); R. Morris, 'The Maritime Industry Commission, 1942-52', *Great Circle*, vol 20, no 1, 1998, p 46; *Smith's Weekly*, 10 May 1941, p 7; *SMH*, 21 May 1966, p 14, 7 Sept 1974, p 24, 21 Oct 1978, p 6, 27 Nov 1984, p 17; *Age* (Melbourne), 28 Dec 1978, p 21; *Seamen's Jnl*, June/July 1979, p 131, Dec 1984, p 428; A6119, items 138 and 139, SP1714/1, item N41557 (NAA); Elliott papers (Univ Wollongong Archives); private information.

RICHARD MORRIS*

ELLIS, NANCY LORNA; *see* LEEBOLD

ELLIS, ULRICH RUEGG (1904-1981), journalist, author, political organiser and activist, was born on 23 July 1904 at Mount Morgan, Queensland, sixth surviving and youngest child of Thomas James Ellis, an Irish-born miner, and his English wife Constance Jane, née Ruegg. When Ulrich was 3, the patrician Constance left her feckless husband and moved with her children to Tingalpa, Brisbane, where, despite proximity to the city, Ulrich enjoyed a rough-and-tumble bush childhood. After attending Kelvin Grove Road (Boys) and Brisbane Grammar schools, aged 16 he became a cadet journalist. In 1921-22 he was employed in Melbourne by the Press Bureau, which served Victorian provincial newspapers. Next he worked as a galleryman and political roundsman for several metropolitan dailies, including the Melbourne *Morning Post*, launched by the Victorian Country Party in 1925.

In 1927 Ellis moved to Canberra as one of the first permanent press correspondents to live in the 'bush capital'. Next year he became private secretary to (Sir) Earle Page [q.v.11], leader of the Australian Country Party. A competent and energetic assistant, Ellis organised Page's daily working life and focused his employer's ideas about the role of the Country Party. Though Page was a hard and often erratic taskmaster the pair became friends. On 19 December 1930 at Trinity Presbyterian Church, Camberwell, Melbourne, Ellis married RAY ARNOT (1897-1987), daughter of George Maxwell [q.v.10] and his wife Jean Russell, née Ross. Born on 21 October 1897 at St Kilda, Ray had graduated from the University of Melbourne (BA, 1921; Dip.Ed., 1923), and taught at Telopea Park Intermediate High School, Canberra.

In 1936 Ellis joined the Commonwealth Department of Commerce as a commercial intelligence officer. Four years later he moved to the Department of Munitions in Melbourne, where he became assistant-controller (administration) in charge of a staff of some six hundred officers. Between 1944 and 1946 he served as deputy-director of public relations in the Department of Post-war Reconstruction, Canberra. Never entirely comfortable with the constraints of the public service, in 1945 he had publicly criticised the practice of the minister for the interior in allocating housing. For contravening public service regulations he was fined £2. After a year in the Department of Information he resigned from the public service in 1947 and established a rural lobby group, the Office of Rural Research (and Development), which worked closely with the Country Party.

Bald, wiry and indefatigable, Ellis attached himself to causes on the periphery of the political mainstream. As a Canberra resident he was a passionate advocate of local self-government, and of the need to improve Canberra's amenities and to attract tourism to the national capital. After helping to establish the Kangaroo Club in 1931 to 'keep Canberra hopping', he was founding chairman (1937-40) of the Canberra Tourist Bureau. He was an elected member (1947-51) of the Australian Capital Territory Advisory Council and was prominent in the Turner Progress Association (ACT).

Labelled the 'arch-priest' of the Australian New State movement by the grazier P. A. Wright, in 1933 Ellis had been publicity officer for the secessionist Riverina Movement of Charles Hardy [q.v.16,9]. That year he wrote *New Australian States*, a polemical historical survey of the need for constitutional review and further decentralisation. In 1934 he presented evidence to H. S. Nicholas [q.v.11], the royal commissioner on new states. In 1948 he joined the executive of the New England New State movement and from 1960, having moved with Ray to Armidale, he oversaw 'Operation Seventh State'. Not even defeat in the 1967 New State referendum caused his enthusiasm to wane. He was named a life member of the movement in 1970 and patron in 1972.

Another of Ellis's passions, related and equally enduring, was for the Country Party. In the 1950s he had been publicist, valet, chauffeur, nursemaid and baggage handler for the Country Party leader, Sir Arthur Fadden [q.v.14]. Ellis was a foot-soldier whose energy and dedication compensated for his lack of sparkling intellect. His two pioneering historical works, *The Country Party: A Political and Social History of the Party in New South Wales* (1958) and *A History of the Australian Country Party* (1963), were unscholarly and partisan. His pen was sharpest as a pamphleteer. *Farewell to Democracy* (1947) was an eloquent diatribe against the denial of democratic rights to Canberra residents. *Zoo-Centralisation* (1953), in which he employed the memorable pseudonym of Violet Lavender Skunk, was a lively parody of centralisation and socialisation. He also wrote for the *Australian Encyclopaedia* (1958) and helped both Page and Fadden to write their memoirs.

In addition to supporting her husband's 'causes', Ray Ellis was active in philanthropic groups, serving as president (1950-52) of the National Council of Women of the Australian Capital Territory and as a councillor (1954-58) of the Canberra University College. A member (1958-60) of the Commonwealth Literature Censorship Board, she was appointed MBE in 1961.

Ellis is sometimes remembered as less reactionary than his brother Malcolm [q.v.14]. None the less, his argument that the New State movement was 'the only permanent safeguard against extremist domination in indus-try and government', and his warnings that lax security in Canberra public service offices was assisting communist espionage, echoed his brother's concerns. Survived by his wife and two sons, Ellis died on 4 December 1981 at Tamworth and was cremated. Ray died on 17 November 1987.

B. B. Schaffer and D. C. Corbett, *Decisions* (1965); C. J. Ellis, *I Seek Adventure* (1981); P. Wright, *Memories of a Bushwhacker* (1982); *SMH*, 8 Feb 1958, p 14, 27 Feb 1958, p 5, 13 Apr 1967, p 8; *Canberra Hist Jnl*, 10 Sept 1982, p 16; N. Brown, Possess the Time (PhD thesis, ANU, 1990); A463, item 1960/6068 (NAA); Ellis papers (NLA).

ANDREW MOORE

ELPHICK, GLADYS (1904-1988), Aboriginal community leader, was born on 27 August 1904 at Wright Court, Adelaide, daughter of John Herbert Walters, gas-meter inspector, and Gertrude Adams. Her maternal great-grandmother was Kudnarto, a woman of Kaurna-Ngadjuri descent, who had married English-born Tom Adams in 1848. At 8 months Gladys Adams was taken to live with relations at Point Pearce Mission Station, Yorke Peninsula. Educated at the local school, as a child she rode horses, swam, played sports and taught herself the organ. Leaving school at 12, she worked at the station dairy. Women Elders trained her as a midwife.

On 13 June 1922 at the Point Pearce Church Gladys married with Methodist forms Walter Stanford Hughes, a shearer. They had two sons. Her husband died in 1937; two years later she moved to Adelaide and found work as a domestic. On 2 December 1940 at St Ignatius' Catholic Church, Norwood, she married Frederick Joseph Elphick (d.1969), a soldier. They resided first at West Thebarton and later at Ferryden Park. Employed during World War II at the South Australian Railways' Islington workshops, producing munitions, she won an award for a shop-floor invention.

In the 1940s Mrs Elphick joined the Aborigines Advancement League of South Australia and in the 1960s served on its activities committee, which organised social and sports events. As founding president (1964-73) of the Council of Aboriginal Women of South Australia, she worked to raise the status of Indigenous people in the community. The council employed a social worker, set up various sports clubs and arts and crafts groups, and encouraged women to learn public speaking so that they could confidently express their ideas. Members campaigned for the 'Yes' vote in the 1967 referendum that ensured Federal responsibility for Aborigines, and lobbied for the franchise and Aboriginal rights generally. They established a women's shelter and health service in Adelaide, and took steps to set up a legal aid service and a kindergarten. In 1973 the women's council changed its name to the Aboriginal Council of South Australia and included men in the organisation. That year the Aboriginal Community Centre was established to house the various services; Elphick was elected treasurer and was later made a life member of the centre. She was a founder (1977) of the Aboriginal Medical Service.

In 1966-71 Mrs Elphick was a member of the South Australian Aboriginal Affairs Board. She was appointed MBE in 1971. An advocate of adult education courses for Aborigines, in the 1960s she had helped to arrange evening art classes, conducted at Challa Gardens primary school by John Morley. These and other programs led to the establishment in 1973 of the College of Aboriginal Education, as part of the Underdale campus of the South Australian College of Advanced Education.

Known as 'Aunty Glad', Elphick, according to Kevin Gilbert, possessed a 'lively sense of humour' and 'a shrewd personality' that pierced through 'humbug'. A highly respected elder, in 1984 she was named South Australian Aboriginal of the Year. She died on 19 January 1988 at Daw Park, Adelaide, and was buried in Centennial Park cemetery. Her elder son, Timothy Hughes [q.v.14], had predeceased her; her son Alfred survived her. In 2003 the Aboriginal women's group advising the International Women's Day Committee (South Australia) presented the inaugural Gladys Elphick award.

K. Gilbert, *Living Black* (1977); J. Healey (ed), *S.A.'s Greats* (2001); *Advertiser* (Adelaide), 9 July 1981, p 3, 21 Jan 1988, p 14; private information and personal knowledge.   E. M. FISHER

ELSE, ALICK (1916-1985), soldier and farmer, was born on 20 August 1916 at Taringa, Brisbane, eighth child of Thomas Else, farmer, and his wife Emily Mary, née Bycroft, both Queensland born. Alick, who followed his father onto the land, enlisted in the Australian Imperial Force on 30 May 1940. Five of his brothers also served in the army, Alick and Cyril being posted to the 2/15th Battalion. The unit arrived in Egypt in February 1941 and took part in the defence of Tobruk, Libya, in April-October. Else was promoted to corporal soon after the beginning of the siege.

Having been stationed in Palestine and Syria, the 2/15th Battalion returned to Egypt in July 1942. On the night of 4–5 August Else was a member of a fighting patrol ordered to secure a prisoner in the coastal sector of Tel el Eisa. Going well behind enemy positions, the group encountered heavy fire from a German machine-gun post. The Australians rushed the post, killing at least five enemy soldiers and capturing a prisoner. Further fire killed the prisoner, and the patrol's commander, Captain W. W. Cobb [q.v.13], was twice wounded. Else took charge and extricated the patrol, with Cobb over his shoulder. For his 'conspicuous bravery' and 'outstanding leadership', he was awarded the Military Medal. The success of the 2/15th Battalion in this sector led to its deployment next month in a highly successful feint, Operation Bulimba. In October-November the battalion fought in the battle of El Alamein.

Back in Australia in February 1943, the 2/15th played an important role in the battle for Finschhafen, New Guinea, in September-October. On 13 October Else, who had been promoted to acting sergeant in September, was a platoon commander in an attack in dense jungle near the village of Kumawa. In a sustained action of grenade and bayonet charges, his men overcame a series of Japanese posts in well dug-in positions that had seemed impregnable. Five men were killed and ten wounded of a platoon of twenty-six, while Japanese dead numbered thirty-nine. Else led his platoon with 'a total disregard for his own safety and with soldierly resolution'. His voice 'could be heard clearly and distinctly giving directions to his section leaders', including his brother Cyril, who was killed storming a strong post. The padre later commented that 'it was terrible that the sergeant had to tell his own brother to go and get killed'. Else was recommended for the Distinguished Conduct Medal, but was awarded a Bar to his MM. He was promoted to staff sergeant in November. In March 1944 the battalion returned to Australia. Following several severe bouts of malaria, Else was discharged from the army on 27 October.

Else typified the easy-going, devil-may-care digger, with a nonchalant exterior behind which lay steely determination. An engaging, friendly man, he was esteemed by his battalion for his outstanding courage and ability to lead at critical moments. After a brief stint at the fruit and vegetable market at Haymarket, Sydney, he returned to Queensland, working first at Harlin then on a dairy farm at Moggill, Brisbane. On 1 August 1946 at St Andrew's Presbyterian Church, Gladstone, he had married Joan Isabel Mylrae. He farmed at Lower Cressbrook from 1950 until 1963, when he bought another property at Colinton. Survived by his wife and their two sons, he died of Parkinson's disease and pneumonia on 21 September 1985 at Esk and was buried in Kilcoy lawn cemetery.

D. Dexter, *The New Guinea Offensives* (1961); B. Maughan, *Tobruk and El Alamein* (1966); R. J. Austin, *Let Enemies Beware!* (1995); B883, item QX5495 (NAA); AWM 52, item 8/3/15 (AWM); private information.   STUART BRAGA

ENGLAND, JOHN ARMSTRONG (1911-1985), farmer and grazier, politician, and administrator of the Northern Territory, was born on 12 October 1911 at Clayfield, Brisbane, third of five children of New South Wales-born parents Sidney Willis England, accountant, and his wife Jane McLelland, née Fisher. Raised at Murwillumbah, New South Wales, John was educated at the local public school and at Brisbane Boys' College. He worked (1928-35) for the Commercial Banking Co. of Australia Ltd, in Sydney and at Forbes. In 1936-41 he managed Wilga, a sheep and wheat farm near Grenfell. On 16 December 1939 at Holy Trinity Church of England, Grenfell, he married Polly Wills Wheatley.

From 1929 England was also a citizen-soldier, serving in Militia artillery and cavalry units and being commissioned in 1931. Called up for full-time duty on 23 June 1941, next year he was promoted to lieutenant colonel and placed in command of the 110th Light Anti-Aircraft Regiment. In August he transferred to the Australian Imperial Force. He commanded two composite anti-aircraft regiments: the 52nd (1943-45) at Merauke, Netherlands New Guinea, and the 2/3rd (1945-46) in north Borneo. As commander of North East Borneo Force in October 1945, he oversaw the surrender of Japanese in the region. He was transferred to the Reserve of Officers on 28 February 1946 and mentioned in despatches for his service in Borneo.

England returned to Wilga, and bought it in 1947. At a by-election in November 1960 he entered Federal parliament as the Country Party member for the formerly Liberal seat of Calare. Party whip in 1972-75, he did not contest the general election in December 1975. On 1 June 1976 he took up the appointment of administrator of the Northern Territory. Darwin was then recovering from the devastation wreaked by Cyclone Tracy in December 1974, and the Territory was pursuing political autonomy from Canberra. He assumed presidency of the Legislative Assembly, a fully elected body from 1974, and oversaw ceremonies marking the proclamation of self-government on 1 July 1978. Respected by local politicians, and using his contacts among Commonwealth ministers and senior public servants, he alleviated Darwin-Canberra tensions from behind the scenes. However, some, including the chief minister, Paul Everingham, saw him as a legacy of the Commonwealth era

at a time when the Northern Territory was asserting its independence. In 1977 he was appointed commander brother of the Order of St John and made inaugural patron of the St John Council for the Northern Territory.

Appointed CMG in 1979, England retired in December 1980 and settled at Grenfell. Six ft 4 ins (193 cm) tall, he was naturally diplomatic and had a good sense of humour. He was remembered in the Territory for maintaining the dignity of his office. In 1981 he was elected secretary of the federal council of the National Country Party of Australia. Survived by his wife and their daughter and three sons, he died on 18 June 1985 at Grenfell and was cremated. At his funeral he was described as 'a man of integrity ... upright and forthright; who no doubt used his physical stature to good advantage. Yet he was humble of character and regarded duty as a privilege'.

A. Heatley, *The Government of the Northern Territory* (1979), and *Almost Australians* (1990); C. J. E. Rae et al, *On Target* (1987); D. Carment and B. James (eds), *Northern Territory Dictionary of Biography*, vol 2 (1992); P. A. Rosenzweig, *The House of Seven Gables* (1996).   PAUL A. ROSENZWEIG

ENGLISH, PETER BEDE (1904-1984), ophthalmologist and army medical officer, was born on 11 March 1904 at Goonengerry, near Lismore, New South Wales, youngest of nine children of James English, a New South Wales-born dairyman, and his wife Catherine Jane, née Buckley, who came from Ireland. In 1908 Peter's father, lured by the stands of red cedar on the Atherton Tableland, North Queensland, moved the family to Malanda. With his older sons he established a dairy farm and a sawmill. In 1911 he built the Malanda Hotel.

Peter was educated at Malanda State School, Mount Carmel College, Charters Towers, and the University of Sydney (MB, BS, 1927). Back in Queensland, he was a general practitioner, first at Capella and then at Cairns. On 13 May 1929 at St Patrick's Catholic Church, Sydney, he married Mona Elliott, a nurse; they had two daughters and a son. Interested in local politics, he served on the Cairns City Council and the Barron Falls Hydro-Electricity Board (1933-35).

After the death of his wife in 1935, English left his children in the care of his sister Mary and sailed, as a ship's doctor, to London. He enrolled in an ophthalmology course at Moorfields Eye Hospital and gained the diploma of ophthalmological medicine and surgery (1935), awarded by the Royal colleges of Physicians and Surgeons, London. After travelling on the Continent he returned to Australia and set up an ophthalmology practice in Wickham Terrace, Brisbane. On 6 June

1940 at St Agatha's Catholic Church, Clayfield, he married Evelyn Twiss (d.1961), a secretary. They were to have three sons and a daughter.

Appointed a captain, Australian Army Medical Corps, Militia, on 23 January 1942, English began full-time service as a temporary major in July. He worked in army hospitals in the Northern Territory, New South Wales and Queensland. In Brisbane in 1945 he and another ophthalmologist, James McBride White, performed the first recorded corneal graft in Australia. English transferred to the Retired List on 30 April 1946, returning to private practice and work as a consultant at the Mater Misericordiae Public Hospital, South Brisbane. In 1945 he had become a fellow of the Royal Australasian College of Surgeons. Maintaining his interest in corneal surgery, he established an eye bank (1953) and a glaucoma unit (1956), both among the first of their kind in Australia. He practised medicine until 1984.

English served on the council of the Ophthalmological Society of Australia for many years and was president in 1956. Chairman of the fund-raising appeal for the new Holy Spirit Hospital, Brisbane, he was also president of the Catholic Medical Guild of St Luke. He enjoyed fishing, shooting and racing, and published a family history, *North to the Timbers* (1964). Five ft 11 ins (180 cm) tall, with hazel eyes and a fair complexion, he wore a moustache. He was appointed MBE in 1970. Survived by the three children of his first marriage and the three sons of his second, he died on 3 July 1984 in Brisbane and was buried in Nudgee cemetery.

A. S. Walker, *Clinical Problems of War* (1952); *Malanda* (1995); *Austn Jnl of Ophthalmology*, vol 12, no 3, 1984, p 299; *MJA*, 13 Oct 1984, p 542.

RONALD WOOD

ERWIN, GEORGE DUDLEY (1917-1984), politician, was born on 20 August 1917 at Winchelsea, Victoria, fifth of nine children of Victorian-born parents Herbert Edward Erwin, farmer, and his wife Alfreda Mary Elizabeth, née Blake. The Erwins owned a small property near the mining town of Wensleydale. Reared in a strict but caring family of strong religious convictions, Dudley milked the cows, rode horses when he could and attended the local state school. He left school at 13 to work on the farm, at the same time taking a correspondence course in Morse code, and acquired a lifelong taste for the bread and dripping that his family gave to passers-by during the Depression.

After two years in Sydney at the Marconi School of Wireless and a period in Melbourne as a student-lecturer, Erwin enlisted in the Royal Australian Air Force on 8 January 1940. Training first as a radio operator, he was a navigator with No.25 Squadron in 1941-43 and No.31 (Beaufighter) Squadron in April-September 1943. He had been commissioned in October 1942. Subsequently he served as an area navigation officer and a navigation instructor. Promoted to flight lieutenant (October 1944), he was considered keen and conscientious, although his commanding officer described him as an 'unimpressive officer' who 'lacks personality'.

On 8 January 1944 at St Clement's Church of England, Mosman, Sydney, Erwin married Alma Betty Cleburne. After demobilisation on 1 October 1945, he bought a 360-acre (146 ha) farm adjoining his father's and, later, a property at Lethbridge, Victoria, which produced fine wool. Abandoning teenage socialist inclinations, he joined the Country Party, then switched to the Liberal Party, which preselected him for the Labor-held seat of Ballaarat in the House of Representatives. He was elected in 1955 with the support of Anti-Communist Labor Party preferences. A well-organised man who 'loved people', he assiduously cultivated his electorate and held it until he retired in 1975. He also became part-owner and, eventually, sole owner of Ballarat's historic Craig's Royal Hotel.

Although the Canberra press gallery dubbed him 'Deadly Dudley', his career prospered in the 1960s. He chaired the committee which produced the government style manual and in February 1967 Harold Holt [q.v.14] appointed him government whip. Involved in the speculation about Holt's faltering leadership, Erwin actively supported (Sir) John Gorton's successful campaign to become prime minister after Holt disappeared in the surf at Portsea in December. Gorton rewarded Erwin by appointing him minister for air and leader of the House on 13 February 1969, but dismissed him after the October election, claiming he was 'hopeless'. Erwin's late-night explanation of his banishment, delivered on the telephone to a journalist, entered political folklore: referring to Gorton's 23-year-old principal private secretary, he said 'it wiggles, it's shapely, and its name is Ainsley Gotto'.

After divorcing his wife in 1957 on the grounds of desertion, Erwin married with Methodist forms Virginia Joan Burrows, née Eagan, an American divorcee, on 9 June 1962 at Fishkill, New York State, United States of America. Following another divorce, and having retired to Canberra, at the registrar's office there, he married Gwendolyne ('Gwenda') Phyllis Potter, née Pennant, a 38-year-old trained nurse and a divorcee, on 22 June 1977.

A strong supporter of small business, Erwin was the foundation president of the Australian

Association of Independent Businesses Ltd. Living intermittently at Caloundra, Queensland, he managed a block of units with Gwenda. In 1979 he stood, unsuccessfully, as an Independent for the Australian Capital Territory House of Assembly, after originally being placed fourth on the Liberal Party ticket. Suffering for years from heart problems, he died of a cerebrovascular accident on 29 October 1984 in Canberra and was cremated. He was survived by his wife, their son and his stepson, and by the daughter of his first marriage; the son of his first marriage predeceased him.

PD (HR), 21 Feb 1985, p 25, (Senate), 21 Feb 1985, p 30; *Canberra Times*, 19 Feb 1969, p 13, 30 Oct 1984, p 1; A9300, item Erwin G D (NAA); R. Linford, interview with G. D. Erwin (ts, 1984, NLA); Sir John Gorton papers (NLA); private information and personal knowledge.   I. R. HANCOCK

EVANS, SIR BERNARD (1905-1981), army officer, lord mayor and architect, was born on 13 May 1905 at Manchester, England, son of Isaac Evans, builder, and his wife Lucy, née Tunnicliffe. In 1913 the family migrated to Melbourne and settled at St Kilda, where Bernard attended primary school, later moving to Hampton. After completing secondary education at Prahran Technical School, he studied architectural drawing at the Working Men's College at night while working for his father and then as a designer and builder for Albert Weston, a timber merchant at Box Hill. In 1928 he established Hampton Timber & Hardware Pty Ltd and the Premier Building Co. Pty Ltd. At Hampton Church of England on 21 September 1929 he married Dorothy May Ellis.

By the late 1920s Evans had begun building speculative villas at Brighton and Hampton; his 'Arts and Crafts' bungalow 'Bunyip Lodge' (c.1930) was commissioned by his father-in-law. He also designed and oversaw the construction of houses for the State Savings Bank of Victoria and hospitals for the Victorian Bush Nursing Association. The Depression saw Evans and his father head for Perth to establish a branch of their timber and hardware business. Claude Albo de Bernales [q.v.8] engaged them to construct foundries and mining buildings at Kalgoorlie and Wiluna. In 1935 he contracted Bernard—now styling himself a 'designer and master builder'—to replace decrepit mansions in St Kilda and Queens roads, Melbourne, with *moderne* or period revival-style flats, and, in 1936, to design the Tudor Revival London Court Arcade in Perth. His eclectic designs were made in response to his clients' wishes. After working for other clients, Evans sold his interests for £20 000 and travelled with his family to London for the completion of Westralia House (1937-39), another de Bernales project. While in Britain he was accepted into the Incorporated Association of Architects and Surveyors (1937); on return to Australia, he registered (1940) as an architect in Victoria.

Having been commissioned in the cadets (1923) and the Militia (1924), Evans had become a major in the 46th Battalion by 1934. On 1 July 1940 he was appointed to the Australian Imperial Force as a temporary lieutenant colonel and ordered to form and command the 2/23rd Battalion, 'Albury's Own'. He was then the youngest battalion commander in the AIF. Sent to the Middle East, his unit was engaged in the defence of Tobruk, Libya (April-October 1941), where Evans's 'solid leadership and total disregard of personal danger' were 'an inspiration to all ranks'; he was awarded the Distinguished Service Order. On 1 November 1942, during the Battle of El Alamein, Egypt, he assumed command of the 24th Brigade as a temporary brigadier.

The brigade trained in Australia in 1943 and in September took part in the capture of Lae, New Guinea. During these operations Evans clashed with his divisional commander, (Sir) George Wootten [q.v.16], arguing that his troops lacked the support of sea transport. Next month Wootten criticised Evans's tactics in a Japanese counter-attack at Finschhafen, considering that a retreat ordered by Evans had unnecessarily sacrificed vital ground. Sir Leslie Morshead [q.v.15] and (Sir) Frank Berryman [q.v.] agreed. Evans was relieved of his command and posted as chief instructor (later commander) of the Land Headquarters Tactical School (School of Tactics and Military Intelligence), Beenleigh, Queensland. On 23 October 1945 he transferred to the Reserve of Officers as an honorary brigadier. He had been mentioned in despatches three times.

Returning to civilian life, Evans formed Bernard Evans & Associates, which became one of Victoria's largest architectural firms, developing shared-ownership buildings and the 'own-your-own' concept in flats. In 1958 it won the State Housing Commission tender for Emerald Hill Court, South Melbourne: a mixed high-rise and low-level development, combining open space and economical slip-form construction. Major office buildings handled by the firm included AMPOL House, Carlton, the CRA and the Legal and General Assurance buildings in Collins Street; it also built the Sheridan apartments and office buildings in St Kilda Road. Evans's private companies were responsible for large suburban subdivisions, such as Witchwood Close, South Yarra, and industrial estates at Moorabbin.

As a Melbourne city councillor for Gipps ward (1949-73), Evans gained further prominence. His service on council committees included terms as chairman of building and town planning (1956-58, 1964, 1966-70), town hall and properties (1957-58) and finance (1961); he was twice elected lord mayor (1959, 1960). He was a commissioner of the Melbourne and Metropolitan Board of Works (1956-73). Citing European examples, Evans argued for taller buildings and more people living in the city. He advocated greater open space and new buildings set back from the street to save the city from becoming 'a dull, dusty jungle'. For many years he campaigned for the creation of a city square. His other causes included a radial corridor plan to balance growth, an underground railway and an international airport. He was knighted in 1962 and appointed to the Order of the Star of Italian Solidarity in 1971.

Evans's reputation suffered in 1970 when his public role and private interests were alleged to have been in conflict. Companies he controlled had benefited through the purchase of properties near the West Gate bridge project and along the proposed underground rail loop, and through the sale of buildings to the Royal Melbourne Institute of Technology (of which Evans had been a councillor in 1950-60 and president in 1959-60). In 1971 he resigned from his firm—by then Bernard Evans, Murphy, Berg & Hocking Pty Ltd—and in 1973 from the city council.

Of medium height, moustached, and silver haired in later life, Evans was always well-dressed, courteous, persuasive, laconic in speech and disciplined in manner. He was an associate (1947) and fellow (1960) of the Royal Australian Institute of Architects, and foundation national and State (1960-77) president of the Royal Commonwealth Society of Australia. In 1973 he provoked the resignation of David Wang [q.v.16] from the latter by his racist remarks. Sir Bernard was a self-made, hardworking and innovative professional designer-builder, a courageous if controversial military leader, and an effective, influential, but again controversial architect-businessman, active in city planning and community affairs. His career was marred by his acquisitiveness and his neglect of principle. In retirement in his Walter Butler [q.v.7] home, Warrawee, at Toorak, he indulged his enthusiasm for painting, and continued to manage his investments. Survived by his wife and their two daughters and son, Evans died on 19 February 1981 at Toorak and was cremated. A portrait by John Frawley is held by the family.

D. Dexter, *The New Guinea Offensives* (1961); B. Maughan, *Tobruk and El Alamein* (1966); L. Sandercock, *Cities for Sale* (1975); *Building & Construction*, 10 July 1936, p 5; *Architecture Australia*, vol 70, no 3, 1981, p 66; *Vic Hist Jnl*, vol 63, nos 2-3, 1992, p 50; *Herald* (Melbourne), 1 Sept 1966, p 5, 28 May 1969, p 21; *Newsday* (Melbourne), 6 Oct 1969, p 11; *Sunday Observer* (Melbourne), 1 Nov 1970, p 1; *Sun* (Melbourne), 9 Dec 1970, p 1; A. Willingham, Brookwood (ts, 1989, SLV).

DAVID DUNSTAN

EVANS, HARRY LINDLEY (1895-1982), pianist, was born on 18 November 1895 at Cape Town, South Africa, eldest of five children of English parents Harry Evans, chemist, and his wife Edith, née Killingbeck. The family was musical. At St George's Grammar School Lindley sang in the choir; he also enjoyed sport. Aged 15, he came to Sydney with his family and made some attempts to follow his father as a chemist but, already playing the piano and the organ in public, looked to a future in music. While taking lessons with Frank Hutchens [q.v.9] at the New South Wales State Conservatorium of Music, he taught piano privately to earn some money. He later had further lessons from Tobias Matthay in England, but otherwise was self-taught.

The role of accompanist suited Evans, who was modest and free of driving ambition. A successful collaboration with John Lemmone led to an introduction to Dame Nellie Melba [qq.v.10]. He accompanied her in England in 1922-23 and on her later tours of Australia. On 2 September 1926 he married, with Presbyterian forms, Marie Florence Stewart at Strathfield, Sydney.

In 1920-29 Evans taught at Presbyterian Ladies' College, Croydon. He developed music appreciation classes, which were given the same status in the curriculum as other subjects, an innovation at the time. At the invitation of the Australian Broadcasting Co. (Commission) he adapted these lectures for a program later called 'Adventures in Music'. When the headmaster at PLC was removed in 1929, Evans resigned. From 1930 to 1946 he was a visiting teacher at Methodist Ladies' College, Burwood. He also taught (1928-68) at the State conservatorium, and served (1966-74) on its board.

Forming a duo-piano team, Evans and Hutchens worked together for forty-one years until Hutchens's death following a car accident in 1965. They performed staples of the classical repertoire (such as works by Mozart and Francis Poulenc) and contributed their own original material. Their programs and personal tastes ran generally to a soft kind of impressionism mixed with an English pastoralism. The duo played from memory, as did Evans for his song accompaniments. They performed at concerts and recorded programs for broadcast by the ABC.

Evans's compositions included piano solos, many (such as *Tally Ho!* and *Vignette*) written for student use, while some (such as *Rhapsody* and *Berceuse*) were more showy or suited to the concert platform. He wrote music for two pianos, and for two pianos with orchestra; *Idyll* was much played and was one of the earliest larger-scale Australian works recorded by the ABC, with Evans and Hutchens performing. Evans, who had a rapport with the voice, also composed part-songs and choral works. His compositions were not the music of passion or tragedy but, rather, of well-crafted affability.

After he had written the score for Charles Chauvel's [q.v.7] film *Uncivilised* (1936)—one of Australia's earliest full-length soundtracks—Evans visited Hollywood in 1936-37 to learn more about film-making. He composed the music for Chauvel's *Forty Thousand Horsemen* (1940) and *The Rats of Tobruk* (1944). He also wrote music for films of Cinesound Productions Ltd, such as Ken Hall's *Tall Timbers* (1937).

From 1939 the ABC employed Evans in its children's sessions on radio; he became nationally renowned as the 'Melody Man' in the 'Argonauts Club' which ran until 1969. Revealing a relaxed, charming personality on air, he often featured as guests young Argonauts who sang and played. An interest in public and youth education led to his involvement in the National Music Camp Association as piano tutor, administrator, director and councillor. He worked with the Australian Youth Orchestra from its inception in 1957. Throughout his career he was an adjudicator at eisteddfods and an examiner for the Australian Music Examinations Board. He was three times president and a life member of the Musical Association of New South Wales, and a composers' representative (1951-71) on the board of the Australasian Performing Right Association.

Tall (6 ft 4 ins or 193 cm) and lean, Evans was a keen sailor who built his own boat in the 1940s. He was president (1947-59) and a life member of the Sydney Savage Club. In 1963 he was appointed CMG. He died on 2 December 1982 at Greenwich and was cremated. His wife survived him; they had no children. *'Hello, Mr Melody Man'*, his autobiography, was published in 1983.

Sun (Sydney), 6 Mar 1927, p 21; *ABC Weekly*, 27 July 1957, p 44; *Bulletin*, 9 May 1964, p 27; *SMH*, 3 Dec 1982, p 12; H. de Berg, interview with L. Evans (ts, 1972, NLA); A463, item 1963/2685 (NAA); Evans papers (SLNSW); personal knowledge.

LARRY SITSKY

EVANS, HENRY JAMES (1912-1990), exploration geologist, was born on 7 November 1912 at Greymouth, New Zealand, third of six children of New Zealand-born parents Henry David Evans, carpenter, and his wife Eva Lillian, née Lawn. When Harry was a boy, his father drowned while attempting to rescue people from a rip off the west coast. His mother subsequently married James William Patterson, who encouraged Harry's interest in ore deposit geology by taking him to prospect for gold in the Reefton district. Harry attended the Waitahu and Reefton District High schools, and at 16 began work at the nearby Alexander gold mine. After severely damaging his left arm in a shotgun accident, he went back to school, obtained the New Zealand Public Service entrance certificate, and gained employment as an assistant-assayer at the Reefton School of Mines. His duties included assaying ore samples for gold, and standing in for lecturers who were temporarily absent. He completed his qualifications as an assayer about 1934.

In 1936 Evans took employment with the Geological Survey Branch, Department of Scientific and Industrial Research, mainly exploring for gold in South Westland. On 27 March 1937 at Knox Presbyterian Church, Reefton, he married Helen McLean Watson, a shop assistant. Next year he joined New Zealand Petroleum Co. Ltd, which was searching for oil and gas, particularly in the Taranaki area.

In 1946 Evans moved to Melbourne to work for Zinc Corporation Ltd, under (Sir) Maurice Mawby [q.v.15], then director of exploration and research. Seconded to the Frome-Broken Hill Co. Pty Ltd oil exploration consortium, he travelled widely in Queensland and the Northern Territory. In 1949-50 he was sent to Britain to investigate potash deposits in Yorkshire. He joined the Australasian Institute of Mining and Metallurgy as an associate-member in 1953 and was also a member of the Geological Society of Australia.

While exploring for oil on Cape York Peninsula in 1955, Evans came across the extensive bauxite deposits at Weipa, assumed since their discovery in 1902 to be low grade. He recognised their potential; simple and inexpensive screening to remove the matrix improved the alumina content to ore grade and triggered the development of the deposits. Evans worked in the aluminium industry until 1968, as field superintendent (1956-60) with Commonwealth Aluminium Corporation Ltd during the Weipa construction years, and as chief geologist (1960-67) with Comalco Industries Pty Ltd. He was appointed OBE in 1965. Chief research geologist with the exploration section of Conzinc Rio Tinto of Australia Ltd from 1968, he later became chief geologist. Evans was a director of the Australian Mining & Smelting Co. Ltd in 1962-72. He retired in 1975, staying on at Brighton, Melbourne, where he had lived for some years.

Quiet, slim and unassuming, with a ready smile, Evans was known for his practical bushcraft skills and for his enthusiasm for all areas of natural science. In 1988 he received the president's award of the AusIMM. Survived by his wife and their daughter and son, he died on 9 November 1990 in South Melbourne and was buried in New Cheltenham cemetery.

AusIMM Bulletin and Procs, Dec 1988, p 13; private information and personal knowledge.

D. A. BERKMAN
G. W. PATTERSON

EVATT, CLIVE RALEIGH (1900-1984), barrister and politician, was born on 6 June 1900 at East Maitland, New South Wales, sixth and youngest surviving son of Indian-born John Ashmore Hamilton Evatt (d.1901), a licensed victualler of Irish descent, and his Sydney-born wife Jane (Jeanie) Sophia, née Gray, who was to be the dominating influence on his early life. Herbert Vere ('Bert') Evatt [q.v.14] was Clive's brother. The family moved to Sydney about 1905 and Clive attended Fort Street Boys' High School. Two older brothers were killed in World War I and Clive, deterred by the family from enlisting, enrolled in the Royal Military College, Duntroon, Canberra, graduating with the King's medal in 1921. But in April 1922, as a lieutenant, he resigned from the army and followed Bert to the University of Sydney (LL B, 1926) and the Bar (admitted 6 May 1926).

While at the university he resided at St Paul's College. His uninhibited and outgoing personality found outlets in the Sydney University Dramatic Society and in the Sydney University Union, of which he was an executive member from 1923 to 1926. He represented the university (1922-25) and the State (1922-24) in Rugby League, playing as hooker. On 28 January 1928 he married Marjorie Hannah Andreas at St Stephen's Presbyterian Church, Sydney. Appointed KC in 1935 at an exceptionally early age, he specialised in workers' compensation and personal injury cases, in which, with other like-minded practitioners, he enlarged the concept of negligence in the interest of employees injured in industrial accidents. One of the celebrated cases in which he appeared was the 1935 'Shark arm case' (*Ex parte Brady; re Oram*).

In March 1939 Evatt won a by-election for Hurstville for the Industrial Labor Party and took his place with R. J. Heffron as part of a splinter group opposing J. T. Lang [qq.v.14,9]. On 5 September (Sir) William McKell [q.v.] defeated Lang to become party leader. When Labor won government in May 1941 Evatt was elected to cabinet and became minister for education. His administration of the portfolio was distinguished by ambitious plans for reform of the inspection and examination systems. But his tendency to act impulsively without consultation did not endear him to the premier, and relations soon deteriorated. Several times McKell overruled his minister, including one occasion when Evatt outlawed corporal punishment in public schools. McKell won the May 1944 election and tried to exclude Evatt from his second cabinet. Caucus elected the maverick, however, but the leader then humiliated him by making him an assistant-minister. Evatt had charge of the State government's 'Yes' campaign in the unsuccessful Federal powers referendum of 1944. In May 1946 he was appointed minister-in-charge of tourist activities and immigration.

Evatt played a crucial role in James McGirr's [q.v.15] defeat of Heffron in the leadership contest to replace McKell in February 1947; he was rewarded with the portfolio of housing and from May 1947 to 1953 held the position of assistant-treasurer. He was colonial secretary in 1950-52, minister for housing in 1952-54 and minister for co-operative societies in 1950-54. In March 1954 he was forced to resign from cabinet by Premier J. J. Cahill [q.v.13]. Expelled from the Labor Party in July 1956, for voting against party measures in parliament (to increase fares on public transport), Evatt stood as an Independent for Hurstville and was defeated at the election of February 1959.

Returning to the Bar, Evatt developed an enormous practice, appearing usually for impecunious plaintiffs in damages claims for personal injury or for more affluent clients in defamation actions. The latter included politicians, among them Arthur Calwell [q.v.13], Tom Uren, Bill Rigby (Evatt's former private secretary, who succeeded him as member for Hurstville), and other notables such as Shirley Bassey, Dawn Fraser, Junie Morosi and Gretel Pinniger. Although regarded by some as essentially a trial lawyer, Evatt enjoyed a very substantial practice before appellate courts. In the Uren litigation he prevailed over his adversary's appeal in the Privy Council. He was the plaintiff, albeit unsuccessful in the appeal to the Privy Council, in the leading case of *Mutual Life & Citizens' Assurance Co. Ltd* v. *Evatt* (1971), where he asserted negligence on the part of the appellant and which is now recognised as a *locus classicus* for negligent advice and negligent misstatement.

Evatt's style of advocacy before juries in civil litigation resulted in many victories for his clients, although it did not always find favour with members of the judiciary or his professional colleagues. A certain eccentricity in manner, which he cultivated as part of his courtroom style, became almost habitual as he aged. Sir Richard Kirby, former president of the Commonwealth Conciliation and Arbitration Commission, described him as 'one of the most dazzling personalities I've ever met. He was good-looking and a marvellous actor, and, I think, a much better lawyer than he is given credit for'.

An honorary member (1943) of the Royal Australian Historical Society, he was also president (1951-52) of the Royal Society for the Prevention of Cruelty to Animals and a vice-president of the Australia-Soviet Friendship (Australia-USSR) Society. After he left parliament, the practice of law was his life, but he maintained an enthusiastic interest in sport and a deep love of music, serving as president of the Musica Viva Society of Australia. A supporter of democracy in Greece at the end of the civil war in 1950, and the leader of the Australian committee for the self-determination of Cyprus, Evatt was appointed a commander of the Royal Order of the Phoenix by King Paul of the Hellenes in 1958. The decoration was not conferred until November 1964 because the Australian government delayed before recommending to Queen Elizabeth II that he should be permitted to accept and wear it.

Evatt was tall, with an outspokenness and lack of caution unusual in a government minister. Although his electorate, Hurstville, was located in Sydney's south, he lived at Wahroonga, on Sydney's North Shore. A house at Leura in the Blue Mountains was a much-loved family retreat. Predeceased by three months by his wife, Evatt died on 15 September 1984 at Darlinghurst and was cremated with Anglican rites. He was survived by his son, Clive, also a barrister, and daughters Elizabeth, foundation chief judge of the Family Court of Australia, and Penelope, an architect and the wife of Harry Seidler.

B. d'Alpuget, *Mediator* (1977); P. Crockett, *Evatt: A Life* (1993); C. Cunneen, *William John McKell* (2000); *Austn Law Jnl*, vol 58, no 11, 1984, p 682; *Unicorn*, vol 15, no 2, 1989, p 120; *Smith's Weekly*, 8 Nov 1941, p 15; *People*, 11 Feb 1953, p 14; *SMH*, 1 Apr 1954, p 3, 14 July 1956, p 1, 10 Mar 1959, p 13, 17 Sept 1984, p 3; *Australian*, 17 Sept 1984, p 2; private information.   CHRIS CUNNEEN
JOHN KENNEDY MCLAUGHLIN

EVERETT, MERVYN GEORGE (1917-1988), lawyer, politician and judge, was born on 7 October 1917 at Sandy Bay, Hobart, third of four children of William George Everett, clerk, and his wife Cecilia Vida, née Bumford. After leaving Hobart High School, Mervyn was a reporter on the *Mercury*, then private secretary to Eric Ogilvie, the Tasmanian attorney-general and minister for education.

He studied at the University of Tasmania (BA, 1942; LL B, 1947), winning the James Backhouse Walker [q.v.6] prize. At Wesley Methodist Church, Hobart, on 11 July 1940 he married Anna Constance Fraser, a typist; they were to have two children before being divorced in May 1953.

On 3 March 1942 Everett enlisted in the Australian Imperial Force. He performed intelligence duties in Hobart then served with field security sections in Victoria and Queensland, and at Balikpapan, Borneo, and Morotai. Rising to sergeant, he was discharged on 1 March 1946 and became a clerk to the Tasmanian solicitor-general. Admitted as a barrister and solicitor of the Supreme Court of Tasmania on 2 April 1948, he next practised in a firm which included (Sir) Reginald Wright [q.v.]. In 1951 he established his own practice; he was to take silk in 1964. On 3 July 1953 at Scots Presbyterian Church, Hobart, he married Jenny Murray Taylor, née Williams, a divorcee; they had two children and were divorced in December 1961.

Elected to the House of Assembly in 1964 as an Australian Labor Party member for Denison, Everett was minister for health under Eric Reece until the Labor government was defeated in 1969. He had married Daphne Grace Hall, matron of Royal Hobart Hospital, on 10 December 1965 at the office of the government statist, Melbourne. On Reece's return to power in 1972, Everett became deputy-premier, attorney-general and minister for the environment, racing and gaming. He was notable for his 'voracious appetite for work', being 'always at his best when heavily engaged with legal and legislative business'.

In July 1972 the Lake Pedder Action Committee sought the fiat of Everett as attorney-general to allow litigation to proceed to test whether the inundation of parts of the South-West National Park was contrary to the proclamation establishing it. Reece refused to accept the legitimacy of this request, but Everett disagreed and resigned from the ministry. His duty 'was not to decide whether Lake Pedder should be flooded or not, but whether there was a legitimate legal question in the situation which should be resolved in the courts'. Everett returned to office in August, once legislation validating the flooding had been passed, but his relationship with Reece was permanently damaged. In 1975 he was to support a retiring age for Labor members of parliament that was to see Reece resign his office.

Fellow politicians were surprised when Everett stood for the Senate in 1974, the *Mercury* marvelling at this decision by 'the man who has greatly dominated State politics for a decade'. He was elected and, showing the self-confidence of one who had held ministerial office and who believed himself intellectually superior to most colleagues, he quickly settled into the Senate. Of medium height, with thinning hair and bulging eyes, he had various interests, with many of his questions relating to foreign affairs. Unusually for a new senator, he played a major part in the passage of legislation, contributing much insight to debates on trade practices, the family law and the Administrative Appeals Tribunal. He also worked on numerous committees.

Everett chaired the Senate Standing Committee on Legal and Constitutional Affairs that reported in July 1975 that the Whitlam government's national compensation bill contained 'significant deficiencies', and recommended that it be reconsidered. A furious Whitlam attacked Everett, declaring his government's determination to proceed with the legislation, though the bill died with the dissolution of parliament in November. During intense Tasmanian Labor preselection activity, a Senate ticket deadlock was avoided by Everett's quixotic offer to run in the fifth, and probably doomed, position. He had attacked coalition threats to supply as 'the nadir of political perversity', and his bitterness was evident after his narrow election defeat.

Returning to private practice, Everett was appointed in 1978 a judge of the Supreme Court of Tasmania. He resigned in 1984 to become president of the Inter-State Commission and that year was also appointed to the Federal Court of Australia. In addition, he was chairman (1985-88) of the Constitutional Commission's advisory committee on trade and national economic management. He retired from the Federal Court and the Inter-State Commission in 1987. In 1988 he was appointed AO.

Merv Everett died on 27 October 1988 in Singapore after a history of heart trouble. He was survived by his wife, the daughter and son of his first marriage and the two daughters of his second marriage. An obituarist in the *Australian Law Journal* reflected that it was 'difficult to think of any other Tasmanian who, with such distinction, served both his State and the Commonwealth of Australia in such a variety of fields, judicial, political, administrative and academic'. The University of Tasmania awarded him a posthumous Ph.D. (1992) for his research on the Nuremberg war trials.

M. Harris and G. Dutton (eds), *Sir Henry, Bjelke, Don Baby and Friends* (1971); D. Lowe, *The Price of Power* (1984); W. A. Townsley, *Tasmania* (1994); *PD* (Senate), 21 Oct 1975, p 1302, 1 Nov 1988, p 1681; *PP* (Cwlth), 1975, vol 11, paper no 142; *Austn Law Jnl*, vol 52, no 12, 1978, p 714, vol 63, no 2, 1989, p 143; *Mercury* (Hobart), 2 May 1974, p 1, 15 Dec 1975, p 10, 28 Oct 1988, pp 1, 9; *Examiner* (Launceston), 29 Oct 1988, p 9, 7 Nov 1988, p 7.

SCOTT BENNETT

EVERIST, SELWYN LAWRENCE (1913-1981), botanist, was born on 22 April 1913 at Tewantin, Queensland, third child of William Allen Everist, a Queensland-born mechanic, and his wife Mary Emily, née Pearson, who came from Melbourne. Selwyn was educated at New Farm and Toowong state schools and at the Commercial High School, Brisbane. In January 1929 he joined the Queensland Public Service as a cadet clerk in the Department of Public Works. Fifteen months later he transferred to the botany section of the Department of Agriculture and Stock. Encouraged by the government botanist C. T. White [q.v.12], he studied science as an evening student at the University of Queensland (B.Sc., 1937).

On 27 March 1937 at the Toowong Methodist Church Everist married Margaret Sybilla Douglas. That year he was appointed assistant research officer at Blackall, where he developed a love for western Queensland and the arid country. His work focused on the impact of grazing on Mitchell [q.v.2 Sir Thomas] grass (*Astrebla*) pastures. Enlisting in the Royal Australian Air Force on 4 April 1942, he served as a meteorological officer in Australia and Papua before being demobilised in January 1946. He returned to the department; although based in Brisbane, he continued to work in western Queensland. Economic botany was his strength and his early interest in the management of pastures expanded into studies of poisonous plants, edible trees and shrubs, and weeds and weed control. He pioneered research into the use of mulga as drought fodder and played a major role in identifying the poisonous plants causing Birdsville horse disease and Georgina River and St George diseases of sheep and cattle. On 1 July 1954 he succeeded W. D. Francis as government botanist. While maintaining his interest in economic botany, he oversaw the modernisation of the Queensland Herbarium. He retired in 1976.

Everist was active in several scientific societies; he was president of the Queensland Naturalists' Club (1958-59) and of the Royal Society of Queensland (1961). An unforgettable character, irrepressible and at times overpowering, he had great enthusiasm and energy and a prodigious memory for scientific facts. Of his many publications, *Poisonous Plants of Australia* (1974) was his greatest achievement, and has remained a definitive work. In 1977 the University of Queensland conferred on him an honorary Ph.D. For his work on the effects of poisonous plants on livestock, he was made an honorary fellow of the Australian College of Veterinary Scientists.

Much of Everist's spare time was taken up with his involvement in the Boy Scouts' Association. He was scoutmaster and later rover scout leader (1946-63) of the 1st Taringa scout group, and in 1963-66 was State commissioner for rover scouts. Very sociable, he liked to be the centre of attention and loved performing on stage in the scouts' annual 'Gang Show'. He also enjoyed the outdoors and was a keen photographer. Survived by his wife and their daughter and two sons, he died of ischaemic heart disease on 22 October 1981 in South Brisbane and was cremated.

R. W. Johnson, 'Obituary: Selwyn Lawrence Everist 1913-81', *Austn Weeds*, vol 1, no 2, Dec 1981, p 42, and 'Selwyn Lawrence Everist 1913-1981', *Qld Naturalist*, vol 24, nos 1-4, 1983, p 68; *Qld Country Life*, 24 June 1976, p 5; personal knowledge.

R. W. JOHNSON

EYRE, FRANK (1910-1988), publisher, is believed to have been born on 21 November 1910 at Manchester, England. He was reticent about his early life but claimed to be the son of Stanley Eyre, army officer, and his wife Berenice. Following a public school education, Frank bowed to paternal pressure to become an articled law clerk; as soon as he qualified, however, he ran off to London to be a poet, supporting himself as a freelance journalist and researcher. In 1935 he published *The Naiad and Other Poems*, the first of several collections to his name. He joined the London Auxiliary Fire Service in 1938 and next year was conscripted into the National Fire Service. With E. C. R. Hadfield he wrote *The Fire Service Today* (1944) and *English Rivers and Canals* (1945), a guide reflecting his enthusiasm for long-distance canoeing. In 1942 Eyre was recruited by Oxford University Press and in 1945, after demobilisation, he joined its children's book department as editor, soon becoming manager. He greatly improved editorial and production standards. At the register office, Hampstead, on 28 August 1948, he married Muriel Erskine Hatfield Cribb, a production assistant at OUP.

In 1949 Eyre was sent to Melbourne as editorial manager (general manager, 1952-75) for OUP's Australian branch, with responsibility for developing the local publishing component of what was, until then, primarily a sales office. When in 1951 OUP decided to terminate its representation of other British publishers in Australia, Eyre skilfully managed the transition. He started to train editors and, with his wife, herself a skilled typographer and book designer, built a strong team that brought, and demanded of printers and paper manufacturers, new standards in Australian book production.

As recalled in his *Oxford in Australia 1890-1978* (1978), Eyre's innovative approach forged enduring links with academic and arts communities. He built up a list of significant books on Australian subjects, among them Alexandra Hasluck's *Portrait with Background* (1955), Russel Ward's *The Australian Legend* (1958), Judith Wright's *The Generations of Men* (1959) and Bernard Smith's *Australian Painting* (1962). His love of poetry was revealed in anthologies such as Wright's *A Book of Australian Verse* (1956) and James McAuley's [q.v.15] *A Map of Australian Verse* (1975). The *Australian Pocket Oxford Dictionary* (1976, edited by Grahame Johnston [q.v.14]) was the first OUP dictionary to appear in a local edition and a major undertaking reflecting Eyre's close personal support. He was also responsible for the fourteen-volume *Oxford English Course for Papua and New Guinea* (1954), produced with the guidance of the Territory's director of education, W. C. Groves [q.v.14].

Eyre quickly became a leading figure in the Australian book trade, serving as Victorian vice-president (1952-63) and national president (1961–63) of the Australian Book Publishers Association, and foundation chairman (1955-59) of the Publishers Association Committee in Australia. He proved an effective negotiator between the English Publishers Association and the Australian Booksellers Association over the importation of British books. Committed to increasing the professionalism of Australian publishing, he encouraged young artists to become designers and illustrators, played a leading part in establishing (1952) the ABPA's Book Design award, and gave lectures to the (Royal) Melbourne Technical College printing department and at the Caulfield Institute of Technology on copy editing. He was a member of the committee that produced the Australian government's *Style Manual for Authors, Editors and Printers* (1966).

Children's literature remained Eyre's special interest. He served as president (1964-67) of the Victorian branch of the Children's Book Council of Australia and as vice-president (1960-66) and president (1966-68) of the national body, and published award-winning books by Australian authors, among them Nan Chauncy [q.v.13], Eleanor Spence and H. F. Brinsmead. A small survey that he had made in 1952 was expanded into *British Children's Books in the Twentieth Century* (1971).

In the 1950s Eyre participated frequently in Australian Broadcasting Commission talks programs and became the witty chairman of the popular radio (later television) forum 'Any Questions'. He also chaired (1968-70) the ABC's Victorian State advisory committee. In 1974 he was awarded an honorary MA by the University of Oxford. After he left OUP the following year, he established an editorial and publishing consultancy service. He was chairman (1976) of the Plain English Committee, which produced a style manual for the Victorian government, and lay observer (1981) to Victoria's solicitors' and barristers' disciplinary tribunals.

Strong, energetic and forthright, Frank Eyre was an exacting master. Some thought him too demanding, some abrupt. As the *Age* noted, he 'personified the image of the tall English gentleman, taking great pride in the English language'. He belonged to the Melbourne and the Beef and Burgundy clubs, and enjoyed reading and writing poetry and listening to music. Yachting was an enduring passion. On 6 March 1988 Eyre died on board his boat *Pegasus* in Port Phillip Bay; he was cremated. He was survived by his wife (d.2001) and their son and daughter.

J. Nicholson and D. Thorpe, *A Life of Books* (2000); *Age* (Melbourne), 27 Dec 1975, p 12; 9 Mar 1988, p 20; Eyre papers (NLA); private information and personal knowledge.   DAVID F. ELDER*

F

FACEY, ALBERT BARNETT (1894-1982), soldier, farmer, tram driver and autobiographer, was born on 31 August 1894 at Maidstone, Melbourne, youngest of seven children of Joseph Facey, quarryman, and his wife Mary Ann, née Carr. Bert's parents, who were born and raised on the Victorian goldfields, had moved from Barkers Creek, near Castlemaine, to Melbourne in 1890. With the collapse of the building boom in the 1890s, Joseph Facey and his two eldest boys went to the Western Australian diggings. When Joseph died of typhoid in 1898, his wife left Bert and the other children with her parents at Barkers Creek and set out to bring her sons home. Instead of returning she remarried, and her new husband refused to take in the younger children. Bert stayed with the Carrs until his grandfather died in 1901. His grandmother then took him, his two brothers and a sister to Kalgoorlie, Western Australia, where her daughter Alice and son-in-law Archie McCall were living. With the McCalls he became a pioneer on a farm at Wickepin, in the wheat-belt.

Aged 8, Bert was sent to work on neighbouring properties. He learnt bush skills but was badly treated by some employers. At 14 he moved to Perth to live with his mother and stepfather—who now accepted him because he could pay board—but he soon struck out on his own, droving in the North-West. He led a roving life, prepared to 'have a go' at anything: 'I have always believed if you want to do something you usually can'. Returning to the wheat-belt, at 16 he was managing a property. He fenced dams, lumped wheat, cleared scrub, laid railway sleepers and travelled with a boxing troupe. On 4 January 1915 he enlisted in the Australian Imperial Force. He served on Gallipoli with the 11th Battalion until August, when he was diagnosed with 'heart trouble' and repatriated. Discharged on 3 June 1916, he attributed later health problems to a bullet wound and the effects of a shell blast that blew bags of sand on him.

Back in Western Australia, on 21 August 1916 at St David's Church of England, South Bunbury, Facey married Evelyn Mary Gibson (d.1976), a domestic. Employed on Perth trams until 1922, he then took up a soldier-settler block at Wickepin but had to abandon it in the Depression. He went back to driving trams. Active in the Western Australian Government Tramways, Motor Omnibus and River Ferries Employees' Union of Workers, he was elected president in 1945.

When he was 86 Facey published *A Fortunate Life* (1981), the autobiography that made him and his life famous. His ordinariness and decency, and the enjoyment he took from a life that by the usual standards was far from fortunate, endeared him to his fellow Australians. The style of the book passed beyond plainness into an elemental purity. The chapters are short, each one like a yarn. Facey's only harsh judgment was that his mother deserted him. Critics have suggested that the book had been heavily edited, but surviving manuscripts of his several versions refute this contention. The final version reveals considerable artifice. He was uncertain about dates and the book contains some factual errors. It won the New South Wales Premier's Literary Award for non-fiction and a National Book Council prize and was made into a play and a television series. Facey's success as an author was the more remarkable because he had had little schooling and had taught himself to read and write.

Six feet (183 cm) tall with blue eyes, as a young man Facey had dark brown hair. He always kept his promise to his grandmother that he would not drink alcohol. Survived by his three daughters and three of his four sons, he died on 11 February 1982 at Midland and was buried in the local cemetery. His eldest son, Albert Barnett, had died on 15 February 1942 while on active service in Singapore during World War II.

J. Hirst, *The World of Albert Facey* (1992); *Australian*, 8-9 Mar 1986, 'Weekend Mag', p 9; B2455, item Facey, A. B. (NAA); A Fortunate Life (ms, UWA); Facey papers (SLWA).   J. B. HIRST

FAGAN, ROY FREDERICK (1905-1990), politician, was born on 28 December 1905 at Waratah, Tasmania, eldest child of James Fagan, a Victorian-born hotelkeeper, and his Tasmanian wife Annie Theresa, née Breheney. The family moved to a farm at Wynyard and Roy's mother, a strict Catholic, sent him to St Virgil's College, Hobart. He was later an agnostic who never went to Mass after he was out of his mother's sight. Leaving school at 16, he worked in the Commonwealth Bank of Australia at Burnie. On 8 December 1925 at the Catholic Presbytery, Wynyard, he married Gertrude Estelle Cooney (d.1946), a shop assistant. He 'did the right thing' by Miss Cooney, who was pregnant, and, although they never lived together, she refused to grant him a divorce.

Transferring to Hobart, Fagan studied part time at the University of Tasmania (LL B, 1934; BA, 1935). Meeting individuals of like mind, including W. H. Perkins and K. M. Dallas [qq.v.], he was a member of what was known as the 'Fabian branch' of the Australian Labor Party. He was president (1931-33) of the Tasmania University Union. A fellow student, Mavis Isabel Smith, became his partner for the rest of his life. Regarding themselves as progressives, the couple were particularly interested in the writings of G. B. Shaw and Aldous Huxley.

Admitted as a barrister and solicitor on 8 August 1934, Fagan felt a strong sense of injustice on behalf of his clients when representing farm workers from the Midlands region who were treated like serfs by landowners and often paid in kind. In 1941-46 he lectured part time in law at the university. The premier (Sir) Robert Cosgrove [q.v.13] asked him to stand in the November 1946 election for the ALP in the seat of Wilmot, which covered more than half the State. Under Tasmania's Hare-Clark [q.v.3 A. I. Clark] proportional representation system he was elected second, after the leader of the Liberal Party, Neil Campbell. Immediately appointed attorney-general, he sold his law practice as the premier expected him to be a full-time politician. He became a mentor to two other new members of parliament, W. A. Neilson [q.v.] and E. E. Reece; Neilson was later to describe him as a man to whom 'colleagues could always turn for friendship and wisdom'. On 23 January 1947 at Corpus Christi Catholic Church, Bellerive, Roy, now widowed, and Mavis, a schoolteacher, were married.

As attorney-general, Fagan was involved in several political crises. In December 1947 he indicted Cosgrove on a conspiracy charge; Cosgrove, who stood down as premier, was acquitted by the Supreme Court of Tasmania in February next year and reinstated. The Legislative Council denied supply over the issue and the government was forced to an election in August 1948. At the elections in 1950 and 1955 neither party gained a clear majority but Labor remained in power. In September 1956 when the minister for housing C. A. Bramich defected to the Liberals, Fagan was credited with saving Labor, by moving and gaining an adjournment of the House. This action prevented the Liberals from exercising their newly gained majority and becoming the government. Fagan then worked all night preparing the case for dissolving parliament; the governor Sir Ronald Cross [q.v.13] agreed to an election and Labor, able to go to the people with the advantage of incumbency, won narrowly.

In 1958 allegations of bribery and corruption were made against Cosgrove and his treasurer R. J. D. Turnbull over the granting of a lottery licence. As attorney-general, Fagan laid charges against both to enable a court determination. Turnbull's animus made it impossible for Fagan to remain in cabinet and he resigned his portfolio in July. He sat on the back-bench until May next year, when he again became attorney-general, in the Reece ministry. While it is generally accepted that he was not ambitious, many believed that if he had been in cabinet at the time of Cosgrove's retirement, he would have succeeded him as premier. He was deputy-leader of the Labor Party (1948-58), deputy-premier (1959-69), minister administering the Industrial Development Act 1954 (1959-69), deputy-leader of the Opposition (1969-72) and, when Labor returned to power, minister for industrial development and forests (1972-74). In 1970-74 he lectured part time in constitutional law at the University of Tasmania.

Although a man of quiet disposition, in parliament Fagan spoke with such intellectual authority and deep moral conviction that members listened to him in silence. Thoroughly preparing his arguments, he often destroyed his opponents with devastating logic. He was a persuader rather than a fighter. In 1970, while in Opposition, Fagan inveigled the Liberal government into abandoning plans to build a fence around Risdon Prison. However, a more combative Labor colleague, M. G. Everett [q.v.], intervened and the government reverted to its former position. A Liberal member, F. A. Marriott, said: 'I just wouldn't take him on because if I did, I knew I'd get a roasting'. Marriott recalled that he always played the game 'extra decently'. Although he judged Fagan 'one of the best debaters' of his time, he 'never once heard him indulge in personalities'.

Fagan regarded his greatest achievement in politics as the abolition of capital punishment. Owing to the conservatism of the Legislative Council, the reform was rejected in the Upper House twelve times before Fagan succeeded on the thirteenth, in 1968. It is testament to his stature in the parliamentary Labor Party that he was authorised to pursue the measure to this extent. His speech on capital punishment is regarded as one of the finest ever given in the House of Assembly, but because there was no Hansard in the Tasmanian parliament at the time, it was unrecorded.

In 1973 Fagan told one of his sons: 'the acceptance of responsibility is what life is all about'. He advised him to be kind but firm, to give praise where it was deserved and never to lose his temper 'for your dignity is lost with it'. Fagan retired from parliament at the 1974 election. His old age was marred by the development of Alzheimer's disease. He died on 18 July 1990 in Hobart and was cremated. His wife and their three sons, and the daughter of his first marriage, survived him.

A. Ferrall, *Notable Tasmanians* (1980); *PD* (HA, Tas), 21 Aug 1990, p 2151; *Sunday Examiner Express* (Launceston), 20 July 1974, p 4; *Mercury* (Hobart),

19 July 1990, p 8, 13 Mar 1993, p 37; private information and personal knowledge.

MICHAEL FIELD

FAIR, RICHARD EDWARD (1907-1982), actor and radio compère, was born on 17 November 1907 at Mosman, Sydney, son of Richard Edward Fair, a Canadian-born general contractor, and his second wife Emily Gertrude, née Kennedy, from Victoria. Brought up in his father's North British Hotel, Circular Quay, he was educated at St Aloysius' College (in 1916-23), and at St Ignatius' College, Riverview. Dick recalled that his parents 'were great theatregoers'; he studied voice production with Laurence Campbell and Scott Alexander, and attended Andrew McCann's acting school.

At 19 Fair made his first stage appearance in the walk on (and off) role of a police photographer in *The Terror*. He played for about three years with the Maurice Moscovitch Company until it returned to New York. Finding work hard to get, he went on the road with Bert Bailey [q.v.7] in *The Patsy* then joined a touring stock company. Back in Sydney he appeared with J. C. Williamson [q.v.6] Ltd's companies. He played in two films for Ken Hall, *On Our Selection* (1932) and *The Squatter's Daughter* (1933), using the screen name 'Grant Lyndsay' in the latter. At St Mary's Basilica, he married with Catholic rites Agnes Margaret McLeod on 23 September 1933.

In 1935 Fair joined radio-station 2SM. He soon took over the breakfast session and infused it with friendly humour, his 'impromptu conversations with that plaintive cow, Strawberry, ... being an especial delight'. Moving to 2GB in 1937, Fair sang in the Jack Davey [q.v.13] show. He and Harry Dearth [q.v.13] were released in 1939 at the request of the advertising agency J. Walter Thompson (Australia) Pty Ltd to handle the Sunday night Lux Radio Theatre and 'Australia's Amateur Hour' on 2UE (later on 2UW). When Dearth joined the air force in 1942, Fair took over as producer.

Originally made in Sydney, 'Australia's Amateur Hour' was later broadcast from all major cities; Fair with a staff of six travelled for eight months a year to audition some five thousand people and to rehearse the ten needed for each Thursday performance. His 'deep, friendly, confident and confidential voice' calmed 'the fears of thousands of amateur performers', according to *People* magazine. Six feet (183 cm) tall, 'strongly built and maturely handsome', he could cajole audiences into doing what he wanted. The show was immensely popular. He journeyed to Sydney to present the Lux Radio Theatre every Sunday night until Dearth returned in January 1946. Finding the travelling increasingly arduous, Fair resigned in 1950 and moved to 2UW.

From 1952 to 1955 Fair produced 'Australia's Hour of Song' for 2UE; it was relayed over forty-nine stations. Famous guests, including Gladys Moncrieff and Peter Dawson [qq.v.10, 8], were paid £300 or £400 to sing; after some rehearsing, the audience sang the choruses. Fair continued at 2UE as an announcer with a mid-morning program of serials, commercials and 'nattering'. From 1960 he produced freelance for 2CH for ten years before returning to 2GB in mid-1971 for a night music session.

Fair's landlady had taken legal action in 1958 to evict him from the flat in her Vaucluse home on the grounds that he was 'frequently drunk and disorderly', that he lived at one time with a woman 'not his wife' (Mrs Peggy Pollock), that he had twice set fire to his bedding, and that he played the radio late at night 'at full belt'. Emerging from court 'battle-scarred but triumphant', he remained in the flat until 1963. He shared his father's interest in harness-racing and recalled often having driven for him, 'in professional company'. Although he had lived mostly in the Eastern Suburbs, he supported the South Sydney ('Rabbitohs') Rugby League team. In about 1974 he moved to the Methodist retirement village, Normanhurst. He died there on 20 July 1982 and was cremated. His daughter survived him, as did his mistress Dorothy White.

N. Bridges, *Wonderful Wireless* (1983); *Wireless Weekly*, 11 Dec 1936, p 39; *ABC Weekly*, 5 Aug 1950, p 43; *People* (Sydney), 13 Jan 1954, p 29; *Truth* (Sydney), 16 Feb 1958, p 44, 9 Mar 1958, p 41, 6 Apr 1958, p 7; *Daily Mirror* (Sydney), 6 Mar 1958, p 6; *Sun* (Sydney), 19 July 1972, p 45; *SMH*, 26 July 1982, p 11; SP1762/1, items 83/1, 83/2, 84/1 (NAA).

MARTHA RUTLEDGE

FAIRFAX, SIR WARWICK OSWALD (1901-1987), newspaper proprietor, was born on 19 December 1901 at Fairwater, Double Bay, Sydney, only child of Sydney-born parents (Sir) James Oswald Fairfax [q.v.8], newspaper proprietor, and his wife Mabel Alice Emmeline, née Hixson. Warwick was educated privately in Sydney and spent a year at Warden House School, Kent, England, before returning to Australia in 1914. The following year he entered Geelong Church of England Grammar School. He edited the school magazine, and although he passed the Leaving certificate in 1917, he took it again with further subjects in 1918 and 1919. The shy, industrious youth studied Greek and Latin at the University of Sydney in 1920 before going to England and reading philosophy, politics and economics at Balliol College, Oxford (BA, 1925).

On Fairfax's return to Australia, he joined his family's company, John Fairfax [q.v.4] &

Sons Ltd. A contributor of numerous articles, particularly on foreign affairs and history, to the *Sydney Morning Herald*, he worked as a sub-editor before becoming a director in 1927. He married Marcie Elizabeth ('Betty') Wilson on 27 March 1928 at St Mark's Church of England, Darling Point. They were honeymooning overseas when Fairfax's father died. Following other sudden deaths within John Fairfax & Sons, 28-year-old Warwick became managing director in 1930; he personally held 35 per cent of shares in the group. He edited *A Century of Journalism* (1931), a rather grandiloquent celebration of the *Herald*'s 'unremitting service to the public'. Slender and 6 ft 2 ins (188 cm) tall, with a long face, blue eyes and brown wavy hair, the quietly-spoken Fairfax struck one of his editors, J. D. Pringle, as 'rather like a sensitive, intelligent, slightly neurotic don'.

In 1934 John Fairfax & Sons Ltd acquired the *Home*, notable for its graphic modernity, and *Art in Australia*, a champion of modern and Australian art. Fairfax installed his friend Peter Bellew, also the *Herald*'s art critic, as editor (1941-42) of *Art in Australia*. In an unwarranted attack in 1942, Howard Ashton accused Fairfax ('a playboy proprietor') and his 'boy friends' of setting out to belittle 'all established artists'. In the *Herald*, Fairfax staunchly defended the award of the 1943 Archibald prize to (Sir) William Dobell [qq.v.3, 14] for his portrait of Joshua Smith, as well as works by (Sir) Sidney Nolan, Lloyd Rees [q.v.] and Sali Herman. A ballet enthusiast, he backed the Kirsova [q.v.15] company and, donning the hat of a dance critic, compared the chorus of the rival Borovansky [q.v.13] Ballet to a row of sheep.

Fairfax usually attended the *Herald*'s daily editorial conferences and was unconcerned when the meetings of directors and editorial executives were stridently interrupted by the general manager, R. A. G. Henderson [q.v.]. The pair had first met in the early 1920s, and Fairfax allowed Henderson to modernise the company in the second half of the 1930s as it faced a resurgent *Daily Telegraph*. Fairfax and 'Mr Henderson' usually lunched together, sometimes with others. For all his love of tradition, Fairfax rarely feared change. He supported the proposal (realised in 1944) to banish advertisements from the front page.

In the 1940 Federal election the traditionally conservative newspaper urged readers to vote in certain electorates for outstanding men irrespective of party allegiances; (Sir) Robert Menzies [q.v.15] held the press partly responsible for his downfall in 1941 and there were stories of Fairfax's being cut in the Union Club. In 1943, as the *Herald* renewed its fervent appeal for 'outstanding men', Fairfax contributed articles under the byline of 'A Political Observer'. He looked to a government unshackled by party loyalties, which would develop the greatest possible opportunities for every citizen, and wrote lively, penetrating profiles of leading politicians. Reprinting the *Herald*'s articles in *Men, Parties and Politics* (1943), Fairfax observed that 'the difficulty about politics is that when it does matter at all, it matters desperately and tremendously'.

During World War II Fairfax experienced bouts of ill health and his marriage disintegrated. He was determined to explore the fundamentals for 'reconstruct[ing] our national life'. 'Ethics and National Life', published in the *Herald* in December 1944, argued that the Christian message must be given in its original simplicity, purged of all theological fogginess. Henderson was disturbed by the suggestion of a 'personal crusade' and tendered his resignation. In the end Henderson stayed, and did much to consolidate ownership of John Fairfax & Sons Pty Ltd in the hands of Warwick and his cousin (Sir) Vincent Fairfax.

Divorced in 1945, Warwick Fairfax married Hanne Anderson, née Bendixsen, a 32-year-old Danish divorcee, on 1 May 1948 at St Paul's Church of England, Cobbitty. Some disquiet developed about Fairfax's increasing absences from the office as he restored Harrington Park, a property at Narellan, and began breeding Poll Hereford cattle. The motoring enthusiast, whose garage housed a Phantom V Rolls Royce, enjoyed driving a tractor and riding a pony around the property. He was also preoccupied with self-publishing *Metaphysics of the Mystic* (1947) and writing a book on science, religion and philosophy, eventually published as *The Triple Abyss: Towards a Modern Synthesis* (1965). He wrote three plays—*A Victorian Marriage*, *Vintage for Heroes* and *The Bishop's Wife*—which were performed in Sydney in the 1950s, and served as a director (1954-69), vice-president (1969-74) and governor (1975-85) of the Australian Elizabethan Theatre Trust.

In 1956, in the midst of a period of aggressive expansion—including the acquisition of Associated Newspapers Ltd and one of Sydney's first television licences—overseen by Henderson, John Fairfax Ltd was incorporated as a public company and Fairfax became chairman. In 1959 Hanne obtained a divorce; on 4 July at his home Barford, Bellevue Hill, Fairfax married a 30-year-old Polish-born businesswoman, Mary Symonds, née Wein. Her former husband, Cedric, had issued a Supreme Court writ against Fairfax alleging that he had induced her to leave him. In January 1961 Fairfax resigned as chairman in order to avoid embarrassing the company; he was reinstated in March when the case was settled out of court.

The episode did little to improve relations with James, the son of his first marriage and now a director, and Henderson, who resented

Mary's influence on her husband. Fairfax's health improved and he began to involve himself more closely in the daily concerns of the office. At the 1961 election, apparently concerned at the impact of the Menzies government's credit squeeze on the *Herald*'s volume of classified advertising, he threw the company's resources behind Arthur Calwell [q.v.13] and the Australian Labor Party. In 1964 Fairfax unhesitatingly accepted Henderson's decision to retire. When Fairfax proposed weekly meetings with executives, the new managing director, A. H. McLachlan, objected, believing that Fairfax was acting like an executive chairman.

Knighted in 1967, Fairfax served (1963-74) on the council of the Australian National University. On McLachlan's retirement in 1969, Fairfax argued for his own appointment as executive chairman. James Fairfax brokered a compromise whereby his father was constituted a 'Committee of One' and the position of managing director was abolished. Although denied the title, 68-year-old Fairfax relished the opportunity to wield practical power. Presiding over a period of steady growth rather than omnivorous acquisition, he kept a careful eye on the *Herald*'s editorial page and appeared intolerant of criticism at board meetings. He suspended his overseas jaunts, choosing instead to investigate outback Australia, and, with Mary, hosted lavish parties at Fairwater, their home at Double Bay.

In 1976 Fairfax tabled a proposal to increase the general manager's salary, with the implication that his own should also be increased. In Sir Vincent's view the time had come for a new generation to assume the chairman's responsibility; Sir Warwick's executive authority was terminated and, in March 1977, he reluctantly resigned as chairman. At the first board meeting under James's chairmanship, his father was accused of having engaged in discussions with David Syme [q.v.6] & Co. Ltd, publisher of the *Herald*'s sister paper, the Melbourne *Age*, concerning the possible takeover of John Fairfax Ltd. It did not eventuate and Sir Warwick resigned from the Syme board. After disagreeing with other directors on the matter of managerial succession, he accepted several changes approved by the board, although he opposed plans to raise extra capital without a specific project in mind. He retained an office and the services of a secretary and driver, resumed normal relations with James, and in 1984 wrote a statement of principles on the *Herald*'s traditions and policy.

Fairfax died on 14 January 1987 at Double Bay. At his funeral at St Andrew's Cathedral, Sydney, mourners heard extracts from his unfinished book 'Purpose': 'Existence for us is best defined as PURPOSE ... I prefer an incomprehensible God to a meaningless world'. Sir James Darling paid tribute to his integrity, honour, intelligence and courage. Buried in South Head cemetery, Fairfax was survived by his wife, his son and daughter from his first marriage, the daughter and stepson from his second marriage and the son and adopted daughter and son from his third marriage. His son Warwick soon made a disastrous attempt to take over the company, which, within a few years, was lost to the family.

J. D. Pringle, *Have Pen: Will Travel* (1973); G. Souter, *Company of Heralds* (1981), and *Heralds and Angels* (1991); J. Fairfax, *My Regards to Broadway* (1991); *Daily Telegraph* (Sydney), 2 June 1945, p 12; *People* (Sydney), 11 Mar 1953, p 5; *SMH*, 15 Jan 1987, p 1, 31 Jan 1987, p 2; *Australian*, 15 Jan 1987, p 2; W. O. Fairfax and R. A. Henderson files (John Fairfax Holdings Ltd archives, Sydney).

BRIDGET GRIFFEN-FOLEY

FAIRFAX-ROSS, BASIL EDWARD (1910-1984), coastwatcher and businessman, was born on 4 April 1910 at Springwood, New South Wales, second child of Sydney-born parents Basil Fairfax-Ross, who described himself as of independent means, and his wife Doris Riverstone, née McCulloch. He was a descendant of both John Fairfax and Rev. Robert Ross [qq.v.4,2]. Educated at The Kings School, Parramatta, Basil hoped to study law, but the means were not available. After some time as a jackeroo, realising that, without further education or funds to buy a property, he would have to look abroad for advancement, he turned to the Mandated Territory of New Guinea. About 1931 he obtained work with Burns, Philp [qq.v.7,11] & Co. Ltd as a plantation assistant. By 1940 he was an assistant plantation inspector at Rabaul.

On 19 January 1940 Fairfax-Ross enlisted in the Australian Imperial Force. Commissioned in July, he served in the Middle East with the 18th Brigade. In March 1942 he returned to Australia and in August joined the Allied Intelligence Bureau (later 'M' Special Unit). Sailing to Papua in the *Paluma*, he carried out coastwatching duties at Oro Bay. Early in 1943 he led a party attempting to relieve two coastwatchers on New Guinea's Rai Coast. 'Fax' (as he was known) was wounded but he and other survivors escaped over the mountains to Bena Bena. In 1944-45 he commanded (as a temporary major from January 1945) a force of fifteen coastwatchers and some two hundred local men engaged in guerrilla operations against the Japanese in southern New Britain. On 6 April 1946 he transferred to the Reserve of Officers. He was awarded the American Medal of Freedom (1948) and twice mentioned in despatches for his service.

On 25 April 1946 at St Sebastian's Catholic Church, Yeronga, Brisbane, Fairfax-Ross married Jessie Agnes Dalton, a secretary. That year he returned to Burns Philp as plantation inspector before becoming assistant general manager of the British New Guinea Development Co. Ltd, the largest of the planting companies in Papua. In 1951 he was appointed general manager of the company in Port Moresby. He served as president (1949-71) of the Planters' Association of Papua, member (1951-73) and chairman (1971-73) of the Copra Marketing Board of Papua and New Guinea, and chairman (1956-74) of the Copra Industry Stabilisation Board. His directorships included Burns Philp (NG) Ltd, Bougainville Copper Ltd, South Pacific Post Ltd, South Pacific Brewery Ltd and several plantation companies. In 1964 he was appointed CBE.

A nominated member of the Legislative Council of the Territory of Papua and New Guinea from 1951, Fairfax-Ross also sat (1961-63) on the Administrator's Council. In him the planting community had an articulate representative, one whose interests extended well beyond the concerns of trade and commerce. As a leading planter conveniently resident in Port Moresby and with a long memory of the country before, during and since the war, Fairfax-Ross held considered opinions on most issues and presented them with characteristic self-assurance. In 1959 he led the opposition of the three elected and the nine non-elected members in the Legislative Council to the introduction of an income tax bill. He continued to advocate special representation for the expatriates, who, he argued, contributed disproportionately to the economy, although he conceded that there should be an indigenous majority in a reformed system. His perspective was eclipsed by the creation of the House of Assembly in 1964 and he did not seek to continue his political career. In 1965-71 he was a member of the interim and inaugural councils of the University of Papua and New Guinea.

The determination of the Australian government to move towards a rapid transfer of power to a self-governing indigenous majority caused planters to reassess their position. Fairfax-Ross resigned from BNGD Co. Ltd in 1971 and retired to Mosman, Sydney, where he maintained an active interest in Papua New Guinea affairs as a director of both Bougainville Copper and Burns Philp. In Papua he had indulged a fondness for horse-racing that went back to his jackerooing days; in Sydney he joined the Australian Jockey Club and was frequently seen at Randwick and Rose Hill. He also belonged to the Imperial Service and Union clubs. Trim in build, highly articulate and courteous, Fairfax-Ross possessed a conspicuous ability that readily drew respect and disarmed potential foes. He died on 9 November 1984 at St Leonards, Sydney, and was cremated. His wife and their two daughters survived him.

E. Feldt, *The Coast Watchers* (1946); D. Dexter, *The New Guinea Offensives* (1961); D. G. Bettison et al (eds), *The Papua New Guinea Elections 1964* (1965); I. Downs, *The Australian Trusteeship* (1980); *SMH*, 14 Nov 1984, p 17; *PIM*, Jan 1985, p 36; AWM54, 433/9/31 (AWM); private information and personal knowledge.   D. C. LEWIS*

FARMER, KENNETH WILLIAM GEORGE (1910-1982), Australian Rules footballer, was born on 25 July 1910 in North Adelaide, elder son of South Australian-born parents William Thomas Farmer, labourer, and his wife Ethel Ann, née Sitters. Educated at North Adelaide Public School, Ken started work at 14 as a junior storeman with Swallow [q.v.6] & Ariell Ltd.

Selected in 1929 as centre half-forward for North Adelaide, in his first South Australian National Football League game on 27 April Farmer kicked four goals against West Torrens. In 224 league and eighteen interstate appearances between 1929 and 1941 he was never held goalless in a completed game. On thirty-seven occasions he scored ten goals or more in a match, including thirteen at Unley Oval on a wet day on 7 September 1935 and twenty-three goals and six behinds against West Torrens on 6 July 1940. The first South Australian footballer to kick one hundred goals in a season, he continued to do so for eleven consecutive seasons, a feat unparalleled in senior Australian football. In 1936 he booted 134 goals from nineteen matches to establish a South Australian record that stood until 1969. During his career he kicked 1417 goals for North Adelaide and seventy-one for South Australia; he was dubbed 'football's Bradman'. Nevertheless he failed to win a Magarey [q.v.2] medal for best and fairest player in the league. His rewards were North Adelaide team premierships in 1930 and 1931.

On 21 December 1935 at St Cuthbert's Church of England, Prospect, Farmer married Floris Edna Craig, a shop assistant. He retired from league football in 1941. Enlisting in the Royal Australian Air Force on 28 April 1942, he was employed as a service policeman in Australia (1942-44) and England (1944-46) before being discharged in Adelaide on 3 July 1946 as a temporary sergeant. He played in RAAF football teams; in England he captained a side that included the cricketer Keith Miller against an army team led by Lindsay Hassett.

In 1948 Farmer coached the reserves at North Adelaide. Next year he became league coach, winning premierships in his first season and in 1952. Always well prepared and analytical, he studied the styles of opposing players and teams, and emphasised fitness. He had a professional approach to football in an amateur age; his intensity and attention to detail bordered on the obsessive. In 1954 he trained the State side. That year he wrote about football for the *Sunday Advertiser* and, with the advent of television, gave commentaries on the game. The North Adelaide Football Club named gates at Prospect Oval after him in 1980, and next year the SANFL instituted the Ken Farmer medal, presented each season to the leading goal-kicker.

Farmer, who had worked as a sales representative, chiefly for G. & R. Wills & Co. Ltd, retired in 1970. A complex personality, he could be witty and charming but suffered from depression for long periods. He died on 5 March 1982 at Modbury and was cremated. His wife and their son survived him. In 1998 he was inducted into the Australian Football Hall of Fame.

B. Whimpress, *The South Australian Football Story* (1983); P. Depasquale, *The Farmer Files* (2002).   BERNARD WHIMPRESS

FARRELL, FRANCIS MICHAEL (1916-1985), footballer and policeman, was born on 19 September 1916 at Surry Hills, Sydney, second child of Sydney-born Reginald Farrell, jeweller, and his Scottish-born wife Margaret Theresa, née Wynne. Frank was educated at the Patrician Brothers' school, Redfern, and at Marist Brothers' Boys' School, Kogarah. His nickname, 'Bumper', originated in high school, where he surreptitiously smoked cigarette butts, known as 'bumpers'. He played junior Rugby League for Marrickville. Graded in 1936, he made his début for the Newtown Rugby League Football Club's first-grade team in 1938.

On leaving school, Farrell had been an apprentice boilermaker. He worked at Garden Island Dockyard, but felt he could better himself by joining the police force. His first post, in 1938, was that of a probationary constable at Darlinghurst, where 'sly grog', illegal gambling and prostitution were rife. Soon the enemy of crime leaders such as Matilda ('Tilly') Devine and Kate Leigh [qq.v.8,10], Farrell joined the vice squad in 1943. He married Phyllis Dorothy Mary Read (d.1981), a draughting assistant, on 11 November 1944 at St Brigid's Catholic Church, Marrickville.

A tough, inspirational front-row forward, Farrell had been appointed captain of Newtown's first-grade side in 1942. He led Newtown to the semi-finals consecutively from 1943 until 1948; the team won the grand final in 1943 and was runner-up in 1944. Between 1946 and 1951 Farrell served as Newtown's captain-coach. On his retirement from football in 1951, he had played 250 matches for the club, 205 of them in first grade.

Controversy befell Farrell's playing career on 28 July 1945. A St George front-row forward,

Bill McRitchie, who sustained an ear injury which required extensive skin graft surgery, accused Farrell of biting. Farrell faced an official inquiry before the New South Wales Rugby Football League and a disciplinary hearing at the Police Department. He pleaded not guilty, explaining that he wore false teeth and that he had left them in the dressing room. Both tribunals exonerated him. Nevertheless, the incident coloured his career, overshadowing even the four Test matches he played for Australia in 1946 and 1948, and his twelve appearances for New South Wales between 1939 and 1950.

Farrell's toughness was equally apparent in his profession. He developed a reputation as an uncompromising plain-clothes policeman. With the rank of detective sergeant, he was appointed chief of the vice squad in the Darlinghurst division in May 1965. After the squad was disbanded, he moved to suburban uniform duty at Collaroy in October 1966. He then worked at Eastern Suburbs, Manly and Central police stations. His return to Darlinghurst in January 1973 as inspector third class (second class from August), resulted in more visible policing and fewer violent crimes. In 1976 he was awarded the Queen's Police Medal for Distinguished Service. He retired in September, an inspector first class in command of 230 officers.

Involved with the Newtown club in an administrative capacity since his playing days, Farrell helped to establish the Newtown Leagues Club Ltd. His imposing, bulky frame, cauliflower ears and oversized hands were the delight of Sydney newspaper caricaturists. Survived by his two daughters and two sons, he died of myocardial infarction on 23 April 1985 at Warriewood and was buried in the Catholic section of Mona Vale cemetery.

T. Williams, *Out of the Blue* (1993); A. Whiticker and G. Hudson, *The Encyclopedia of Rugby League Players* (1999); L. Writer, *Razor* (2001); *SMH*, 5 Feb 1946, p 8, 26 May 1965, p 4, 20 Jan 1973, p 8, 25 Aug 1976, p 2; *Sporting Life*, Aug 1948, p 14; *Daily Mirror* (Sydney), 22 Apr 1970, p 83, 15 July 1974, p 11, 24 Apr 1985, p 58; *Herald* (Melbourne), 10 Aug 1974, p 21; *Daily Telegraph* (Sydney), 28 Jan 1981, p 1, 24 Apr 1985, p 4; *NSW Police News*, Aug 1988, p 19; private information.   ANDY CARR

FAVELL, LESLIE ERNEST (1929-1987), cricketer, was born on 6 October 1929 at Arncliffe, Sydney, second child of Ernest Hastings Favell, postal assistant, and his wife Amelia Doris, née Saunderson, both born in Sydney. Les attended local schools and played his early cricket in the A. W. Green and Poidevin [q.v.11]-Gray Shield competitions. At 18 he began his first-grade career with the St George District Cricket Club.

In 1951 Favell moved to South Australia and joined the East Torrens team. A right-hand batsman, he made his State début later that year, scoring 86 and 164 against New South Wales, and in 1952-53 played in his first Sheffield Shield winning side. In nineteen Test appearances starting in 1954-55 he made 757 runs, averaging 27.03. He toured the West Indies, South Africa, New Zealand, India and Pakistan with Australian teams. His only Test century was 101 at Madras, India, in 1959-60. He lost his place after proving susceptible to the speed of the West Indies' fast bowler (Sir) Wesley Hall in 1960-61. In 1953 and 1954 he had also made the All-Australian baseball team.

As captain of South Australia in 1960-70, Favell played ninety-five games and led the State to Sheffield Shield wins in 1963-64 and 1968-69. In a record-breaking opening partnership in November 1967 he and John Causby made 281 runs against New South Wales. He played 202 first-class matches, amassing 12 379 runs at an average of 36.62, with 27 centuries. Of compact build, he was a great crowd pleaser whether opening the batting or in the middle order. He believed that the ball was there to be hit, and regularly peppered the short side-boundaries on the Adelaide Oval with hook and cut strokes. His aggression sometimes cost him his wicket and undoubtedly had limited his Test appearances, but his habitual striking of the first ball for four often set the foundation for 300-plus runs in a day, excellent for the era.

A South Australian selector in 1965-76, Favell was also a radio commentator for the Australian Broadcasting Commission after retiring as a player in 1970. For many years he conducted coaching clinics for junior cricketers and footballers in South Australia. He was appointed MBE in 1969. Sir Donald Bradman stated in 1970 that he had 'set an example in sportsmanship that has never been bettered by anyone who had played the game'. That year Favell published a memoir, *By Hook or by Cut*.

First employed as a clerk with Philips Electrical Pty Ltd, Favell moved on to work for the Myer [qq.v.10,15] Emporium, Adelaide Sports Depot Pty Ltd and Berri Fruit Juices Co-op Ltd, as a sales representative. From 1965 he was a promotions manager at the Adelaide *Advertiser*. He had made what he described as 'the best partnership in his life' when, on 24 September 1955 at Burnside Christian Church, he married Berry Clare Shepley, a florist. Survived by his wife and their son and daughter, he died of cancer on 14 June 1987 at his Magill home and was cremated. Next year the Les Favell Foundation was established with the support of the South Australian Cricket Association to create opportunities for talented young players from country areas. In 1998 the indoor cricket centre at Adelaide Oval

was named after him and Neil Dansie. Alan Tucker's naïve portrait of Favell hangs in the Adelaide Oval Museum.

C. Harte, *SACA* (1990); R. Cashman et al (eds), *The Oxford Companion to Australian Cricket* (1996); G. Sando and B. Whimpress, *Grass Roots* (1997); *Canberra Times*, 14 Feb 1970, p 33; *Age* (Melbourne), 16 June 1987, p 52.   BERNARD WHIMPRESS

FAWCETT, STELLA GRACE MAISIE; *see* CARR

FEATHERSTONE, SYDNEY ('DON') (1902-1984), ambulance officer and amateur cinematographer, was born on 16 November 1902 at Darlington, Durham, England, second of six sons of Joseph Featherstone, railway shunter and ambulanceman, and his wife Eliza Dorothy, née Moody. In 1911 the family migrated to Toowoomba, Queensland. Educated at Harrowgate Hill School, Darlington, and Toowoomba East State School (1912-14), Sydney left aged 12. He worked for a year as a boot delivery-boy before securing an apprenticeship as a coach-trimmer and signwriter in his uncle's paint shop, where he was nicknamed 'Don' to avoid confusion with another apprentice. In 1924 he moved to a larger firm in Brisbane but, made redundant by the introduction of spray painting, returned to Toowoomba. He was self-employed until 1927, when he found work as a machinery painter at the Toowoomba Foundry.

Tall and lanky, in his youth Featherstone had moderate local success at swimming, tennis and rifle-shooting and, learning to play the steel guitar, participated in two local entertainment groups, the Bohemian Club and the Merry Makers. An early member (1927) of the Toowoomba Art Society, he won prizes for his paintings at the Royal Adelaide Show and the Brisbane Exhibition. On 25 February 1933 at St James's Church of England, Toowoomba, he married Emmie Gillam, a shop assistant.

At the foundry Featherstone initiated a benevolent fund and started first-aid training under his father, gaining the St John Ambulance Association instructor's certificate in 1939. Rejected in 1942 for active service in the Royal Australian Air Force, he worked as a medical orderly in the Civil Constructional Corps at Wallangarra, Drayton and Canungra, and at Truscott, Northern Territory. In January 1946 he became an ambulance officer and honorary instructor at the Toowoomba station of the Queensland Ambulance Transport Brigade. From late 1961 to June 1968 he was a nurse and, from 1965, a first-aid instructor at Toowoomba Mental (Baillie Henderson)

Hospital, Willowburn. On 27 July 1966 he was awarded the insignia of the serving brother of the Order of St John.

Featherstone's great love was film-making. He had bought a second-hand 16-mm Kodascope camera in 1926 and had begun experimenting with home and holiday films. By 1980 he had made fifty-five films including fictional stories, travelogues, and historical epics and documentaries—mainly about the Darling Downs, including the only surviving footage of the royal visit there in 1954. He was a foundation (1952) and life member (1961) of the Darling Downs Amateur Cine Society. Widely acknowledged as the best amateur film-maker in Australia, he won several national and international prizes for his work. He was awarded the BEM in 1978.

Infrequently irascible, Featherstone was noted for his enthusiasm, humility and charity, and his joy in the small pleasures of an 'amateur' artistic life. In retirement he taught painting at adult education classes and introduced art therapy at Baillie Henderson Hospital. He handed over his film collection to the Heritage Building Society for preservation in 1982. Survived by his wife and their daughter, he died on 6 May 1984 at Toowoomba and was buried in the local cemetery. His autobiography, *Brush, Camera and Memories*, was published in 1985.

Toowoomba Chronicle and Darling Downs Gazette, 28 July 1966, p 10; *Chronicle* (Toowoomba), 31 Dec 1977, p 1, 16 Apr 1982, p 4, 9 May 1984, p 17.

M. FRENCH

FELGATE, RHODA MARY (1901-1990), speech and drama teacher and theatre director, was born on 31 July 1901 at Stoke Newington, London, daughter of Gordon Felgate, commercial traveller, and his wife Alice Maude, née Willson. The family migrated to Australia when Rhoda was 18 months old and settled in Brisbane in 1910. Educated at Brisbane Girls' Grammar School, she studied speech and drama under Barbara Sisley [q.v. Supp.], gaining qualifications from Trinity College, London (ATCL, 1922; LTCL, 1923; FTCL, 1928). She taught elocution at BGGS in 1923-48. A founding member (1925) of Brisbane Repertory Theatre Society, she directed her first production, *A Happy Family* by Vance Palmer [q.v.11 E. V. Palmer], in 1926. During the next ten years she directed fourteen more plays for the society, three of them Australian. In 1931 a review in the *Telegraph* congratulated her on her production of George Bernard Shaw's *You Never Can Tell*: 'Her judgment, her sense of stagecraft and the fruits of her coaching were everywhere apparent'.

By 1936 Felgate had her own speech and drama studio. Believing that she could help her pupils by forming another theatre society, she organised a new group of amateurs, the Twelfth Night players. In its first year the company presented nine 3-act and four 1-act plays by playwrights such as Maurice Maeterlinck, J. M. Barrie, Clemence Dane, J. B. Priestley and A. A. Milne. Felgate produced twenty-one plays for Twelfth Night Theatre during its first three years. In December 1936 A. H. Thomas, the *Telegraph*'s theatre critic, praised the 'solidity and strength' of Twelfth Night's productions. Felgate attracted outstanding talent: her 1937 production of Shakespeare's *Twelfth Night* included Stanley Hildebrandt as Feste and Lorna Forbes [q.v.14] as Olivia.

Travelling overseas in 1939 and 1947, Felgate studied trends in stage production and secured the rights of plays, many of which had never been performed in Brisbane, including Shaw's *In Good King Charles's Golden Days*; *George Washington Slept Here*, by Moss Hart and George Kaufman; *I Remember Mama*, by John Van Druten; *Dear Ruth*, by Norman Krasna; and *Gaslight*, by Patrick Hamilton. Felgate acted and directed, sometimes in the one production, to widespread acclaim. In May 1940, for example, a review in the *Telegraph* of Emlyn Williams's *The Corn Is Green* described her performance as the schoolteacher Miss Moffatt as the 'characterisation which will live longest in the memory'. Elsewhere the play was said to be a 'persuasive and touching piece of work'.

In 1948 TNT obtained the lease of a large two-storey building on Wickham Terrace. The upper floor became a rehearsal and play-reading space, and the lower housed speech teachers, including Felgate, and their studios. The Twelfth Night Speech and Drama School contributed to the strength of TNT, at times providing economic stability. A senior speech examiner for the Queensland section of the Australian Music Examinations Board (1948-75), Felgate planned theatre productions around her examination tours of country centres and her teaching duties. In 1949 she hosted in Brisbane a visit of the English theatre director (Sir) Tyrone Guthrie, who was advising the Chifley [q.v.13] government on the feasibility of a national theatre, for which he had campaigned. An advocate for Australian playwrights, she produced many of their works and supported Eunice Hanger [q.v.14] in particular.

Felgate was appointed MBE in 1955. Next year TNT acquired Gowrie Hall on Wickham Terrace, a church hall that was converted into a little theatre to complement the Albert Hall, where major productions were staged. Felgate marked her retirement from the theatre in

1962 by directing and playing the leading role in a twenty-fifth anniversary production of *I Remember Mama*.

Described in 1948 as a 'poised, easy-to-talk-to woman, with greying hair and sparkling eyes', Felgate was 'a quiet, determined personality'. A commissioner (1960-72) of the Australian Broadcasting Commission, she expressed concern about the diction of some ABC newsreaders, but made her main contribution through her knowledge of theatre, her commitment to the performing arts and her encouragement of Australian television drama. She was a member of the Library Board of Queensland (1961-75) and of the Lyceum Club, Brisbane. In 1976 the AMEB (Queensland) named an annual scholarship after her. She continued to teach until the 1980s at her Kangaroo Point home, and was patron of Twelfth Night Theatre and of the Speech and Drama Teachers' Association of Queensland. The University of Queensland awarded her an honorary MA in 1983. Never married, Felgate died on 14 September 1990 at Auchenflower and was cremated with Uniting Church forms.

Telegraph (Brisbane), 12 Sept 1931, p 13, 12 Dec 1936, p 20, 13 Mar 1937, p 7, 14 May 1940, p 12; *Courier-Mail* (Brisbane), 5 Feb 1936, p 25, 18 Sept 1990, p 22; *Modern Times*, Dec 1948, p 23; J. J. Radbourne, Little Theatre (MA thesis, Univ of Qld, 1978); B. Blackman, taped interview with R. Felgate (1986, NLA); Felgate papers (Univ of Qld Lib).

JENNIFER RADBOURNE

FELTHAM, PERCY VICTOR (1902-1986), solicitor and politician, was born on 24 May 1902 at Footscray, Melbourne, youngest of six children of Victorian-born parents Charles Edward Feltham, iron moulder, and his wife Annie, née Clarke. Both parents died before Percy was 14. Raised by an aunt, he was educated at the local Geelong Road State and Melbourne High schools before attending the University of Melbourne (LL B, 1923; LL M, 1938), where he graduated with the Supreme Court prize and shared a final honours exhibition. He was admitted as a solicitor on 1 May 1925 and became an associate to Justice (Sir) Hayden Starke [q.v.12] of the High Court of Australia. On 16 November 1929 at St Paul's Church of England, Ascot Vale, he married Sylvia Josephine Box.

Feltham then joined, and later bought, a solicitor's practice at Shepparton, and became prominent in a wide range of professional and community organisations. He was a director (1938-39) of the Shepparton Fruit Preserving Co. Ltd, a board-member of the Mooroopna and District Hospital, and founding president of the Shepparton Rotary Club and the Goulburn Valley Law Society. On 7 September 1940 he was commissioned in the Militia but, wishing to serve overseas, transferred to the Royal Australian Air Force in April 1941. Employed as an intelligence officer in RAAF Command, he became probably the Allies' leading authority on the Japanese air order of battle. In 1943-45 he attended conferences in London and Washington and worked for periods at General Douglas MacArthur's [q.v.15] headquarters. He was appointed MBE (1944) and demobilised in October 1945 as an acting wing commander.

Returning to his practice, Feltham joined the Country Party, serving (1947-58) on its central council and as the McDonald [q.v.15] government's nominee as a director (1950-53) of the Gas and Fuel Corporation of Victoria. In 1955 he was elected to the Legislative Council for Northern Province and, as a dutiful backbencher, impressed colleagues with his keen mind, 'puckish' character and wry sense of humour. He was a member (1959-67) of the council of Monash University.

In September 1965 the premier, (Sir) Henry Bolte [q.v.], offered Feltham the presidency of the Legislative Council, promising a pairing arrangement to protect the balance of power held by the CP. Feltham put the proposal to his colleagues, who rejected it. The CP leader, George Moss, issued a statement which Feltham interpreted as an accusation of disloyalty. Stating angrily, 'I refuse to sit under a man I cannot trust', he resigned from the party, thereby gaining the balance of power himself.

For the next two years Feltham voted as an Independent, typically not revealing his intentions until late in his speeches. Liberal-minded, he sponsored a progressive indecent publications bill in October 1965, and in November supported a move to abolish the death penalty. He campaigned for the 1967 election with the slogan 'better the devil you know', but he was soundly defeated by the CP's Stuart McDonald.

A vigorous man although slight, with 'a countryman's ruddy skin', Feltham continued to practise and to work on a farm he acquired at Wyuna, before retiring to Point Lonsdale. Survived by his wife, and their son and daughter (both of whom had distinguished legal careers), he died there on 24 October 1986 and was buried in the local cemetery. A tribute from E. H. Walker, the minister for agriculture and rural affairs, described him as 'a true Independent'.

PD (Vic), 28 Oct 1986, p 683; *Age* (Melbourne), 29 Sept 1965, p 1; *Canberra Times*, 29 Sept 1965, p 4; *Herald* (Melbourne), 29 Sept 1965, p 1, 22 Apr 1967, p 7; *Sun News-Pictorial* (Melbourne), 30 Sept 1965, p 13.   B. J. COSTAR

FENTON, CLYDE CORNWALL (1901-1982), flying doctor, was born on 16 May 1901 at Warrnambool, Victoria, second of four surviving children of George Augustus Frederick Boyd Fenton, a Victorian-born bank manager, and his wife Kathleen Mary, née Clarke, from England. Educated at Natimuk State School and Xavier College, Melbourne (dux 1917), Clyde acquired an early reputation as a wit and an expert with machinery and mathematics. He proceeded to Newman College, University of Melbourne (B.Sc., 1922; MB, BS, 1925).

After working as a resident medical officer at St Vincent's Hospital, Fitzroy, and practising privately at Geelong, Fenton attempted to drive across Australia in record time with his younger brother Frederick. A motor accident in South Australia terminated this escapade and in 1927 he ended up at Wyndham, Western Australia, as district medical officer. There he purchased a small single-engine, single-seater aircraft, assembled it and taught himself to fly. After crashing his aeroplane, he sailed for Melbourne in 1928, calling at Darwin on the way. He was persuaded by the chief medical officer, C. E. A. Cook [q.v.], to remain; he spent five months in North Australia's health service, becoming very aware of the communication problems there.

Fenton subsequently made his way to England and in October 1929 joined the Royal Air Force as a flying officer (medical). He gained navigation qualifications, but resigned in February 1930 after disputes over regulations. On 11 November 1932 at the register office, St Martin, London, he married Eve Ryan-Gallacher; they were later divorced. Back in Australia next year, he took various short-term posts while seeking flying medical positions. He maintained contact with Cook and in March 1934 was appointed medical officer, Katherine, Northern Territory. There the attraction was the offer of mileage for the small Gipsy Moth aircraft he had acquired. Operating as pilot as well as doctor (unlike those of what was to become the Royal Flying Doctor Service), with Cook's support he formed the Northern Territory Aerial Medical Service.

Over the next six years Fenton, tall, lean and bespectacled, became well known and respected by communities, pastoral properties and missions throughout the Top End. His kindness and determination to help became legendary. He also received attention from the media, both local and national, for his daring rescues, escapades, and occasional pranks, which often brought him into conflict with aviation regulatory authorities. Cook remarked on his 'resolute devotion to duty', his 'compulsive acceptance of challenge' and his 'wilful disregard of personal hazard'. Fenton's solitary, resilient figure contributed much to an enduring Northern Territory self-image.

His other historical contributions to the Territory were to demonstrate the usefulness of aircraft as a means of communication in the difficult terrain and to press for the construction of rural landing strips. Awarded King George VI's coronation medal (1937) and the Oswald Watt [q.v.12] gold medal (1937), he was appointed OBE (1941).

On 17 June 1940 Fenton was called up for active service as a pilot officer in the Royal Australian Air Force. He completed a flying instructor's course at Camden, New South Wales. Posted to the Northern Territory in February 1942, he was appointed commanding officer of No.6 Communication Unit in December. His group of aircraft, known as 'Fenton's Flying Freighters', provided transport and rescue services to military bases as well as unofficial medical support to missions. In August 1943 he was promoted to temporary squadron leader. His RAAF appointment terminated on 11 January 1946.

That year Fenton joined the Commonwealth Department of Health in Brisbane. While he was there he wrote a lively and popular account of his pre-war years in the Territory, *Flying Doctor* (1947). At the registrar-general's office, Sydney, on 10 October 1949 he married Sheila Ethyl Young, née Pigott, a trained nurse and a widow; they were to be divorced in October 1959. Transferring to Melbourne in 1949, he remained with the department until his retirement in March 1966. On 29 March 1963 he married Lavinia Florence Catalano, née Robinson, a divorcee, at the Presbyterian Church, Winchelsea. He was awarded the Cilento [q.v.] medal in 1971. Survived by his wife, he died on 27 February 1982 at Malvern, Melbourne, and was cremated. He had no children.

E. Hill, *Flying Doctor Calling* (1948); S. Baldwin (ed), *Unsung Heroes & Heroines of Australia* (1988); D. Carment et al (eds), *Northern Territory Dictionary of Biography*, vol 1 (1990); E. Kettle, *Health Services in the Northern Territory—a History 1824-1970*, vol 1 (1991); Cwlth Dept of Health, *Health*, June 1966, p 27; A1928, item 716/9, A9300, item Fenton C C (NAA); Cwlth Dept of Health, staff file, 1936-46 (NTA); interviews with L. Lockwood, C. E. A. Cook, C. C. Fenton and B. A. Fenton (ts, 1980-83, NTA).   BRIAN REID

FERGUSON, IAN BRUCE (1917-1988), soldier, was born on 13 April 1917 in Wellington, New Zealand, only child of D'Arcy Stuart Ferguson, a Sydney-born manager, and his Melbourne-born wife Ethel May (later known as Helen), née Rattray. His parents divorced when he was about 10 and his mother married Sydney Wren, a journalist with Reuters Ltd.

Educated in Wellington, Melbourne, London, Paris and Dunedin, New Zealand, Bruce began his working life as a cadet journalist in Wellington and was with the Sydney *Sun* when World War II was declared. On 3 November 1939 he enlisted in the Australian Imperial Force. Allotted to the 2/1st Battalion, he was soon transferred to the intelligence section of headquarters, 16th Brigade. In February 1940 he arrived in the Middle East and was promoted to sergeant. He was commissioned probationary lieutenant on 27 June. As brigade intelligence officer, he was active in the capture of Bardia and Tobruk, Libya, in January 1941. He joined the 2/2nd Battalion in May and served with it in Egypt and Syria.

In March 1942 Ferguson arrived with his unit in Ceylon (Sri Lanka) and was promoted to temporary captain (substantive in September). He took over command of 'B' Company from Major Charles Green [q.v.14] and returned to Australia in August. The battalion sailed to Port Moresby in September and Ferguson led his company across the Owen Stanley Range to Sanananda in October-December. The 2/2nd began the crossing with 550 all ranks and mustered only eighty-eight when it came out of the line. Ferguson spent the next nine months in and out of hospitals due to malaria and dengue fever. He was awarded the Military Cross for his leadership in the hard-fought action at Templeton's Crossing on 20 October.

Appointed liaison officer at headquarters, 6th Division, in September 1943, Ferguson was promoted to temporary major that month (substantive May 1945). He attended the junior wing of the Staff School (Australia) at Cabarlah, Queensland, and in October 1944 was posted to the 1st Australian Combined Operations Section. Attached to headquarters, 7th Division, to assist in the planning of amphibious landings, he served on Morotai and was at Balikpapan, Borneo, when the war ended in August 1945. He was mentioned in despatches. Volunteering for service in the British Commonwealth Occupation Force, Japan, he commanded a company of the 67th Battalion at Kaitaichi, near Hiroshima, and then on Eta Jima island. In 1947 he was appointed second-in-command of the battalion. He was attached to headquarters, BCOF, in 1948. On 26 June that year he married Alice Elizabeth (Betty) Browne, from the staff of the Canadian Legation, Tokyo.

Ferguson displayed his organisational skills when the battalion, now designated the 3rd Battalion, Royal Australian Regiment, was ordered to the Republic of (South) Korea in 1950 to join what was later to be the 27th British Commonwealth Brigade. That there was a structured unit re-equipped and organised for war when Green, the new commanding officer, arrived only a fortnight before the battalion embarked for Korea in September was mainly due to Ferguson's drive.

On 8 November Ferguson was appointed to command 3RAR as a temporary lieutenant colonel (substantive October 1957) after Green was mortally wounded in the Democratic People's Republic of (North) Korea. During his command he led the battalion through all the phases of war, beginning with the withdrawal from North Korea to south of Seoul during the bitter winter months, the advances and attacks across the 38th Parallel and the battle of Kapyong in April 1951, for which he was awarded the Distinguished Service Order and his battalion a United States Presidential Unit Citation. Then followed a further withdrawal to the Han River and another arduous advance across mountains and in rain, and finally a move north-west to the Imjin River. His command of 3RAR officially ceased on 5 July.

Ferguson had a good eye for terrain and was an excellent map reader. His orders were clear and concise. He was invariably close to the action, with his tactical headquarters behind the leading company. The battalion was always balanced and ready for the next orders from brigade headquarters. Those close to him in the field knew that his somewhat brusque manner was a mask for a sensitive nature. He cared deeply for the battalion that had been his home for more than five years.

After Korea, Ferguson commanded the 1st Battalion, RAR, and the 13th National Service Training Battalion, served (1952-53) in Japan, instructed (1959-62) at the Royal Military College, Duntroon, Canberra, and performed (1963-66) staff duties with the South-East Asia Treaty Organization in Bangkok. On 14 April 1967 he retired from the army and was granted the rank of colonel. He was secretary of the Union Club, Sydney, in 1969-74. Survived by his wife and their three sons, he died on 21 December 1988 in Canberra and was cremated with Anglican rites.

A. J. Marshall (ed), *Nulli Secundus Log* (1946); D. McCarthy, *South-West Pacific Area—First Year* (1959); S. Wick, *Purple Over Green* (1977); R. O'Neill, *Australia in the Korean War 1950-53*, vol 2 (1985); A. Argent, 'The Next Leader: Bruce Ferguson', in D. M. Butler et al, *The Fight Leaders* (2002); private information.   A. ARGENT

FERRIER, JAMES BENNETT ELLIOTT (1915-1986), golfer, was born on 24 February 1915 at Manly, Sydney, son of John Bennett Ferrier, an insurance clerk born in Shanghai, China, and his Sydney-born wife Louisa, née Elliott. Educated at Sydney Grammar School, Jim began his playing career at Manly Golf Club, of which his father was secretary. In 1931, aged 16, Ferrier won the New South

Wales amateur title, and was runner-up to Ivo Whitton [q.v.12] in the Australian Open. Very tall and solidly built, 'Big Jim' won the Australian amateur title on four occasions (1935, 1936, 1938, 1939), as well as numerous State titles. In Britain in 1936 he lost the final of the British amateur at the Royal and Ancient Golf Club of St Andrews, Scotland, but won two other significant titles. He married Norma Kathleen Jennings (d.1979) on 12 January 1938 at All Saints Church of England, Woollahra, Sydney. An ungainly but powerful hitter with an accurate short game and a strong will, he won the Australian Open title in 1938 and 1939.

The amateur rules were applied in Australia in a manner that allowed Ferrier to earn his living by writing about golf. In 1940 he went to the United States of America to contest open and amateur championships and to cover the professional circuit for the *Sydney Morning Herald* but, after the United States Golf Association deemed that his small manual *Jim Ferrier's Golf Shots* (1940) breached his amateur status, he became the club professional at Elmhurst Country Club, Chicago. From March 1944 to November 1945 he served in the United States Army, rising to staff sergeant. He became an American citizen in 1944.

In 1947 Ferrier won the Professional Golfers' Association of America championship, the first Australian-born golfer to win one of the four major tournaments. He achieved second place in another 'major', the US Masters at Augusta National in 1950. That year he won several titles including the Canadian Open (won again in 1951) and finished as the second-highest money winner on the US tour. In 1960, aged 45, he finished second in the American PGA. Winner of eighteen US tour titles, he also earned substantial income by endorsing golf equipment and clothing and by being paid appearance money. He contributed to *The Golf Clinic* (1949).

From 1954 Ferrier eased his playing schedule, taking a position as golf professional at the Lakeside Golf Club, Hollywood. His yearly retainer there matched his 1950 winnings. Returning to Australia occasionally, he contested the 1948 Australian Open (which he lost in a play-off), the 1973 New South Wales Open, and a veterans' event at Manly in 1978. His combination of force, finesse and focus had earned him grim nicknames: 'the Undertaker' was the most common, 'the Wolf' another. On 11 September 1980 he married Lorraine Ruth Sheldon, née Devirian, a divorcee, with Presbyterian forms at Los Angeles. Survived by his wife, he died on 12 June 1986 at Burbank, California, and was cremated.

C. H. Bertie, *A History of the Manly Golf Club* (1946); A. Barkow, *The History of the PGA Tour* (1989); J. Pollard, *Australian Golf* (1990); P. Mitchell, *The Complete Golfer Peter Thomson* (1991); *SMH*, 25 June 1947, p 10, 3 Oct 1973, p 17; *Daily Mirror* (Sydney), 7 Apr 1972, p 34; *Sun-Herald* (Sydney), 6 July 1986, p 66.   BRIAN STODDART

FETHERS, GEOFFREY ERNEST (1897-1988), veterinarian, was born on 2 April 1897 at Malvern, Melbourne, son of Victorian-born parents William Fethers, accountant, and his wife Edith Mary, née Clarke. Educated at Caulfield Grammar School, Geoff spent a year at Longeronong Agricultural College before attending the University of Melbourne (B.V.Sc., 1918). He was registered to practise veterinary science in Victoria on 5 August 1918. On 29 July he had been appointed a captain in the Australian Army Veterinary Corps, Australian Imperial Force. He arrived in Egypt on 19 October and was attached to the 5th Light Horse Regiment before returning to Melbourne, where his appointment terminated on 25 November 1919. His four brothers had also joined the AIF. In 1921-37 he served in the Militia, rising to major (1929). On 6 November 1924 at St John's Church of England, Camberwell, he married Annie (Nancy) Browne Cassady.

Fethers' first veterinary practice was a partnership at Box Hill. In 1925 he opened his own practice at Mont Albert. Until his retirement in 1958 he provided a conventional emergency service for horses, cats and dogs. He also—unconventionally for that era—visited farmers in all States except Western Australia to perform surgical procedures and offer appraisals of farm management, with a particular interest in feeding and breeding regimes as they related both to the health of stock and the profitability of the enterprise. He was a pioneer in the tuberculin testing of dairy herds.

Simultaneously with his thriving practice, Fethers became closely involved with the development of his profession, as a member (1924-42) and president (1933-39) of the Veterinary Board of Victoria, and honorary secretary (1924-29) and president (1932-33) of the Veterinary Association of Victoria. He was a part-time lecturer (1927-40) at Dookie Agricultural College, a founding council member (1961-69) of Marcus Oldham Agricultural College, Geelong, and a veterinary consultant to the Royal Agricultural Society, the Melbourne Zoological Gardens, the Sir Colin MacKenzie [q.v.10] sanctuary at Healesville, and the Victorian Graziers Association. He strongly supported the reopening in 1962 of the University of Melbourne's veterinary school, which had closed in 1928.

Agricultural and veterinary journalism provided Fethers' most public face: for decades he offered valued advice, tailored to the animal-loving urban community as well as to the dairy, sheep and cattle industries. He wrote a regular column for the *Weekly Times* for fifty-five years, a selection of which was published as *An Elephant in My Garden* (1980); he also provided much material to six editions of the *Weekly Times Farmers Handbook* (1934-78) and for fifty years contributed to the *Pastoral Review and Graziers Record*. His many radio appearances included frequent items on the Australian Broadcasting Commission's 'Country Hour'.

In 1980 Fethers was awarded the Gilruth [q.v.9] prize by the AVA. He had also received King George VI (1936) and Queen Elizabeth II (1953) coronation medals. In 1942-57 he was a member of the Royal Society of Victoria. He was also a member of the Australian Club, the Rotary Club of Melbourne (president 1936), and the Peninsula Country and Metropolitan Golf clubs. In his later years he was a lawn bowls enthusiast at the Glenferrie Hill Recreation Club, where he was president, superveteran and honorary life member. A modest man of conservative bearing, Geoff Fethers died on 26 September 1988 at West Heidelberg and was cremated. Predeceased by his wife (d.1983), he was survived by two sons and a daughter.

Austn Veterinary Jnl, vol 56, no 9, Sept 1980, p 450; *Weekly Times* (Melbourne), 5 Oct 1988, p 2; *AVA News*, 9 Dec 1988, p 5; private information and personal knowledge.   D. C. BLOOD

FIDGE, SIR HAROLD ROY (1904-1981), solicitor, mayor and community leader, was born on 24 December 1904 at Warracknabeal, Victoria, fourth and last child of South Australian-born parents Edward Fidge, farmer, and his wife Beatrice Alice, née Triplett. Roy was educated at Beulah East State and (to matriculation) Geelong High schools. Excelling in athletics and as a scholar, he won scholarships to Geelong College and then Ormond [q.v.5] College, University of Melbourne (LL B, 1928), where he obtained a half-Blue in athletics (1926). In 1929 he joined a practice in Geelong (from 1954 Price Higgins and Fidge). He soon became solicitor to the Shire of Corio (1932-64), and secretary-treasurer (1932-54) of the Geelong Law Association. On 3 November 1934 at East Malvern Presbyterian Church he married Mavis Melba Jane Burke (d.1948), a masseuse.

In 1939 Fidge's election to Geelong City Council began a long career in local government, during which he made outstanding contributions to the community. Having joined the Royal Australian Naval Reserve in 1923, he resigned from the council to serve with the RAN (1940-45), performing administrative duties ashore in Australia and Papua and rising to acting paymaster lieutenant commander. Re-elected to the council in 1946, he remained

a member until his death, serving six terms as mayor (1954-56, 1964-68) and at some time chairing most committees, as well as the Geelong Promotion Committee, the Transport Advisory Board and the city band. He became, as (Sir) Henry Bolte [q.v.] saw him, 'Mr Geelong': a powerful, colourful personality, whose forthright, even blunt, manner underscored his commitment to Geelong's development.

Fidge advocated the creation of a Greater Geelong by the amalgamation of the city, Geelong West and Newtown, and supported the official Liberal policy of industrial decentralisation, but he was frustrated by a lack of progress. His many initiatives included the transformation of the Geelong Free Library into a regional municipal library while his strong support for the local historian Dr Phillip Brown bore fruit when the Geelong Historical Records Centre opened in 1979. As a member (1954-57, 1964-81) of the executive of the Municipal Association of Victoria, he bewailed the low level of interest in community development and local government.

There was scarcely a voluntary organisation in Geelong and district with which Fidge was not associated. An active founding (1932) member of the local Apex Club, he served as secretary-treasurer (1935-40, 1946-47) of the Apex national council and in 1940 was appointed a life governor. In 1931 he had helped to establish the Navy League Sea Cadet Corps in Geelong; in 1953-54 he assisted in creating the Geelong Community Chest; and the following year he organised the observance of Commonwealth Youth Sunday. He chaired many funding and charitable appeals, for causes ranging from flood relief to anti-cancer research, and supported local schools, the Australian Red Cross Society, and the Legacy and Rotary clubs. President of the Geelong Law Society in 1959-61, he retired from his legal practice in 1964.

Fidge received the Victorian Community Services award in 1966, and was knighted in 1967. His long service as a commissioner of the Geelong Harbour Trust (deputy chairman 1956-63; chairman 1963-77) was recognised in the launch of the motor tug *Sir Roy Fidge* in 1968. He was also a council member (1968-77) of the Association of Port and Marine Authorities of Australia. From 1971 to 1981 he was foundation chairman of the Capital Permanent Building Society. On 6 August 1949, at St Philip's Church of England, Church Hill, Sydney, he had married Nance Davidson (d.1979), a clerk. Still active in local affairs and a lifelong supporter of the Geelong Football Club, Sir Roy died suddenly on 13 January 1981 at Geelong, his death prompting columns of tributes in the *Geelong Advertiser* to one of the city's 'favourite sons'. Survived by the son—also a Geelong City councillor (1977-93) and mayor (1987-89)—and daughter of his first marriage, he was buried in Geelong Eastern cemetery.

R. S. Love and V. M. Branson, *Apex: The First Twenty-Five Years* (1980); G. Forth (ed), *The Biographical Dictionary of the Western District of Victoria* (1998); *Geelong Advertiser*, 2 Jan 1967, p 3, 14 Jan 1981, p 1, 15 Jan 1981, p 4; *Herald* (Melbourne), 24 Aug 1968, p 26; *Austn Municipal Jnl*, Feb 1981, p 220; private information.   JOHN LACK

FIELD, ALBERT PATRICK (1910-1990), French polisher, trade union official and politician, was born on 11 October 1910 at Durrington, Wiltshire, England, fourth of seven children of William Thomas Field, soldier, and his wife Mary Jane, née Kelly. His parents (d.1924) were often ill and Bertie spent much of his childhood in orphanages before attending the Gordon Boys' Home at Chobham, Surrey. He migrated to Australia in 1926 and worked in mines at Newcastle, New South Wales, and Mount Isa, Queensland, and on sheep stations. Enlisting in the Australian Imperial Force on 10 March 1943, he served in New Guinea in 1944-45 with the Australian Army Canteens Service, the 15th Mobile Laundry and Field Decontamination Unit, and the 13th Australian Mobile Ammunition Repair Shop. Discharged on 7 December 1945, he became a French polisher. On 28 October 1957 at the Church of Our Lady of the Assumption, Norman Park, Brisbane, he married with Catholic rites Jessie May Gorle, née Schabe (d.1971), a widow.

In 1937 Field had joined the Australian Labor Party. Having served as president of the Morningside branch of the party, he was elected president of the Queensland branch of the Federated Furnishing Trade Society of Australasia in the early 1970s. Concurrently, he began to feel disquiet over perceived economic mismanagement by the Federal Labor government of E. G. Whitlam. He was also motivated by his opposition to the government's Medibank, and to many symbolic issues of the day: socialism, homosexuality, abortion, an Australian republic and closer relations with China.

When the Queensland ALP senator Bert Milliner [q.v.15] died on 30 June 1975, the premier, (Sir) Joh Bjelke-Petersen, ordered the State Labor Party to nominate three potential senators from whom the government would select a replacement. Labor refused and chose Dr Mal Colston as their sole nominee. Field (now known as Pat) contacted the premier's office, offering his services as a 'Labor senator' and vowing never to vote for the Whitlam government. Bjelke-Petersen arranged to have Field's ALP membership card in his pocket when he personally nominated him for the vacancy. The parliamentary vote split the Queensland government but Field's nomination was carried by fifty votes to twenty-six. The Federal Opposition leader Malcolm Fraser asserted that the ALP's nominee should have been accepted; his deputy Doug Anthony maintained that Bjelke-Petersen had the right of nomination. The Opposition did not opt to 'pair' Field, which would have negated Bjelke-Petersen's tactics.

Expelled from the Labor Party, Field assumed his Senate seat as an Independent. Labor Senators absented themselves when he was sworn in on 9 September, except for the ALP Senate leader Ken Wriedt, who tried unsuccessfully to prevent the swearing in and then sat with his back deliberately turned to the newcomer. Field never delivered a maiden speech, and asked just one question, on superphosphate bounties. On 1 October he was served with a High Court writ challenging his right to occupy his position in the Senate, and was granted leave. Labor's loss of the position gave the coalition senators the numbers (thirty to twenty-nine) not only to block the budget but that month to move it be deferred unless Whitlam agreed to an election.

Assessments of Field and the breach of Senate convention became polarised. Contemporary Labor stalwarts considered him a turncoat or 'Labor rat'. Field responded: 'They are awful things to call someone ... [but] I suppose in a way, I am'. Editorial writers labelled his nomination a 'sick joke' and a 'shameful spectacle'. The Melbourne *Age* described the breach of convention as a 'political fraud' perpetuated by Bjelke-Petersen. Later Field was dubbed 'one of the loneliest figures in Australian politics'. Other interpretations present him as somewhat 'bewildered', and a pawn in the wider machinations of Bjelke-Petersen's feud with the Whitlam government.

Field stood for re-election in the Senate as an Independent in 1975 but was unsuccessful. He founded his own party in 1976, but it dissolved three years later. Living frugally on a pension at Norman Park, Brisbane, he volunteered his time at the Conservative Club bookshop and joined the National Party. He was a keen dancer; in his younger days he had been an enthusiastic soccer referee. Suffering from Parkinson's disease, he died of asphyxia by hanging on 1 July 1990 at Caboolture and was cremated with the forms of the Full Gospel Church. His daughter and stepdaughter survived him.

P. Kelly, *The Unmaking of Gough* (1976); H. Lunn, *Johannes Bjelke-Petersen* (1984); J. Bjelke-Petersen, *Don't You Worry About That!* (1990); *Courier-Mail* (Brisbane), 28 Aug 1975, p 4, 4 Sept 1975, pp 1 and

4, 5 Sept 1975, p 1; *Age* (Melbourne), 4 Sept 1975, p 9, 8 July 1990, p 8; *SMH*, 27 Feb 1979, p 7, 26 Oct 1985, 'Good Weekend', p 39; *Australian*, 3 July 1990, p 1; P. Shaw, interview with A. P. Field (ts, 1983, NLA).   JOHN WANNA

FIELD, FRANCIS (1904-1985), solicitor, politician and deputy-premier, was born on 23 December 1904 at North Carlton, Melbourne, son of Victorian-born William John Field, telegraphist, and his London-born wife Kate Emily, née Honeybone. Frank was educated at St Mary's Primary School, Dandenong, and won scholarships to St Kevin's Christian Brothers' College, Toorak, and the University of Melbourne (BA Hons, 1926; LL B, MA, 1928), also winning the Donovan Bursary to Newman College and gaining a tennis Blue. Admitted to practice on 1 May 1929, Field set up as a solicitor at Dandenong and then moved to the city in 1934. At St James' Catholic Church, Elsternwick, on 23 June 1934 he married Aileen Mary O'Brien.

In 1937 Field won the Victorian Legislative Assembly seat of Dandenong for the Australian Labor Party; he was returned in 1940, 1943 and 1945. On 13 April 1942 he enlisted in the Royal Australian Air Force. Commissioned next month, he controlled units of the Voluntary Air Observers Corps before transferring to the RAAF Reserve in November 1943. In John Cain's [q.v.13] short-lived government (14-18 September 1943), Field was minister of public instruction and a vice-president of the Board of Land and Works. When Cain formed another minority government in 1945, he resumed the portfolio of public instruction.

Given the economic privations of the immediate postwar years, Field was an innovative and productive minister. He launched a recruitment campaign for teachers, raised the school leaving age and abolished secondary and technical school fees. He also established a teachers' tribunal to regulate wages and, in 1946, launched the State Film Centre to promote the use of documentary and educational film in schools. His most enduring legacy was to act on the advice of the director of education, J. A. Seitz [q.v.11], in founding the Council of Adult Education in 1946. From World War II he was also a member of the Board of Business Administration, set up to advise on defence expenditure.

At a time of deep factionalism in the Labor Party, Field was (Kate White suggests) 'an independent-minded Catholic', taking care not to align himself with the remnants of the John Wren [q.v.12] 'machine' or an emergent Catholic Right led by Stan Keon [q.v.]. On the eve of assuming office in 1945, Cain outmanoeuvred the ambitions of the Wren-aligned Bill Barry to succeed the deputy-leader, Bert Cremean [qq.v.13], by installing Field in the position. Field, however, could not escape factionalism. He challenged Wren's interests by supporting the creation of an independent control board to replace the Victorian Racing and Trotting Association. Equally, he had no sympathy for the Catholic Social Studies Movement or the ALP Industrial Groups. When the government was forced to an election in October 1947, both Movement-aligned Catholics and the Wren faction worked against him. He lost his seat.

Field then returned to the law, and was a member (1954-72) of the Victorian Licensing Court (Liquor Control Commission after 1968) and the Liquor Reduction Board (1954-68). In 1957 he attempted a reconciliation between the ALP and the splinter Democratic Labor Party by convening a meeting between Cain and Frank McManus [q.v.]; Cain's death ended negotiations. Remaining active in many organisations including the management committees of Churchill National Park and the Dandenong and District Hospital, Field was vice-president of the Dandenong Football Club and a regular player at the Kingswood Golf Club. Predeceased by his wife (d.1980) and survived by their four daughters and son, Francis Field died on 4 June 1985 at Sandringham. Following a state funeral, he was buried in New Cheltenham cemetery.

K. White, *John Cain & Victorian Labor 1917-1957* (1982); J. Griffin, *John Wren* (2004); *PD* (LA, Vic), 2 July 1985; *Sandringham and Brighton Advertiser*, 4 Apr 1979, pp 3, 28.   B. J. COSTAR
                                        ALISTAIR HARKNESS

FINEY, GEORGE EDMOND (1895-1987), caricaturist and artist, was born on 16 March 1895 at Parnell, Auckland, New Zealand, son of English-born Solomon Finey, mariner, and his wife Rose Emily, née Newton, born in New Zealand. He studied (1912-14) at the Elam School of Art, Auckland, and sold his drawings to local newspapers. Enlisting in the New Zealand Expeditionary Force, he served as a driver in the Army Service Corps in Egypt (1915-16) and on the Western Front (1916-18), and rose to sergeant (1918). Given leave to study art at the Regent Street Polytechnic, London, he admired the political caricatures in the German magazines *Simplicissimus* and *Jugend*. He was repatriated and discharged in 1919.

Having moved to Sydney Finey worked on *Smith's Weekly* from 1921. He married Nellie ('Natalie') Phoebe Murray, a typist, at St Clement's Church of England, Mosman, on

25 March 1922. That year he started to draw 'the man of the week'. In fearless portraits he distorted people's features so that their characteristics and temperament were writ plain. He drew Archbishop Daniel Mannix [q.v.10] with recessed eyes and a drawn-in mouth, suggesting a severe and perhaps intolerant character, and portrayed (Sir) Thomas Bavin [q.v.7] as a whining orator. Finey's work appeared in *Art in Australia* in June 1924; remarkably, the entire June 1931 edition was devoted to his caricatures. (Sir) Lionel Lindsay [q.v.10] wrote that under Finey's hand 'the human countenance becomes elastic. Without truce or mercy he shapes it anew, yet preserves a curious memory of the original'.

After leaving *Smith's Weekly*, Finey worked (1931-33) for the *Labor Daily*, but his more political work had been increasingly rejected by both newspapers. His left-leaning political views were rarely evident in his caricatures, which could be either merciless or celebratory, but were almost always obvious in his cartoons and captions. During the Depression he targeted the New Guard and bloated capitalists, showing unemployed workers as their victims. Following a period with *Truth*, he was employed by the *Daily Telegraph* and by the *Sunday Telegraph* which, in 1940, published a book of war cartoons by Finey, Wep [q.v. W. E. Pidgeon] and Bill Mahony. Finey's war cartoons savaged Hitler and Mussolini. In 1944 he and Mahony were dismissed, allegedly for refusing to draw a political cartoon dictated by the editor, Brian Penton [q.v.15]. He was later reinstated for three years (1953-56). Finey also drew for communist publications including Len Fox's 1946 pamphlet *Wealthy Men*. Early in the 1940s he had left Sydney, which he called 'the garbage can', and moved to Springwood in the Blue Mountains.

A frequent exhibitor in Sydney, Finey also showed his art in Melbourne (1937), New York (1951, 1963), Japan (1952) and London (1963). Caricatures, including those of composers and screen favourites such as Fred Astaire, comprised only part of his work; he also painted and sculpted Australian flora and landscapes in a modernist style. In an interview with *People* (May 1950), Finey said that Australia had 'not been painted yet', with the exception of lucrative 'pretty harbor scenes', 'erosion paintings' in Vandyke brown and 'gum trees in thousands'. He wanted to see murals on business houses and factories, as in Mexico. The following year an exhibition of his flower pieces, musical caricatures and sculptural paintings—including Sturt's desert pea in a dilly-bag patterned with Aboriginal motifs—was shown in New York.

His self-published *Book of Finey: Poems and Drawings* (1976) revealed the eclectic range of his work, not all of which sold well. An exhi-bition of his art on musical themes, billing him as 'the last of the great Bohemians', opened at the Sydney Opera House in 1978. Most of the works were portraits or relief sculptures, using a wide variety of materials. The free-standing sculpture 'Corroboree' incorporated broken beer bottles with Aboriginal totems. He wrote *The Mangle Wheel: My Life* (1981), a chaotic autobiography, which reproduced some of his most significant work. The Blue Mountains Community Arts Council mounted a retrospective exhibition of his work in 1985, to mark his ninetieth birthday.

A small and impish man, Finey had paraded the streets of Sydney collarless, sockless and hatless. He had given up drinking in the early 1940s but continued to smoke for some years. His favourite subjects, from the world's economic ills to the food value of onions, were sprinkled through his conversation. Survived by his three daughters and three of his four sons, Finey died on 8 June 1987 in his home at Lawson and was cremated. His work is represented in the Art Gallery of New South Wales and the National Gallery of Australia.

G. Blaikie, *Remember Smith's Weekly?* (1966); V. Lindesay, *The Inked-in Image* (1979); G. Caban, *A Fine Line* (1983); *Art in Aust*, June 1924, p 21, June 1931, p 1; *People* (Sydney), 10 May 1950, p 3; *Australian*, 20 Jan 1978, p 8; G. Finey, service record (Archives NZ).   PETER SPEARRITT

FINGER, ALAN HENRY (1909-1985), medical practitioner and communist, was born on 6 December 1909 at Dandenong, Victoria, younger surviving child of Philip Charles Henry Finger, farmer, and his wife Minnie, née Freeman, both born in Victoria. Raised in poverty by his pious Wesleyan Methodist parents, Alan was educated at Maryborough and Melbourne High schools and, on a scholarship, at the University of Melbourne (MB, BS, 1934), where he lived at Queen's College. The harsh realities of the Depression—seen on visits with a local doctor to homes at Brunswick and while fruit-picking during university vacations—radicalised him. In 1933 he joined the Communist Party of Australia and next year was secretary of the Melbourne University Labor Club. On 8 December 1934 at Fitzroy he married with Pentecostal forms Joan Mary Hardiman, a journalist also active in Labor Club and Communist Party circles.

Dark haired and pleasant looking, Finger was disciplined and courteous but, as a resident medical officer at Royal Melbourne Hospital in 1935, he believed that his political associations were blocking his progress. Next year he moved to South Australia to take up a post as outpatients' registrar at (Royal) Adelaide Hospital. Within two months he transferred to the Metropolitan Infectious Diseases Hospital, Northfield, and later that year was promoted to superintendent. At Northfield for eleven years, he coped with diphtheria, scarlet fever and poliomyelitis outbreaks, and in 1941 acquired a diploma of public health at the University of Sydney. He initiated improvements in nurses' conditions, pay and training. On the medical board of the Mothers and Babies' Health Association, he campaigned successfully for earlier immunisation and council vaccination programs.

When they arrived in Adelaide, the Fingers had found the State CPA branch near collapse. They played leading roles in its revival, establishing study groups, strengthening the Left Book Club and the peace movement, and attracting a more middle-class element. Continuously for over forty years Alan held various executive positions on the State committee, including the presidency; in the early 1940s he was president of the local branches of the Australia-Soviet Friendship League and of the Russian Medical Aid and Comforts Committee. He stood as a communist in almost every State and Federal election between 1943 and 1967. His preferences allowed the Australian Labor Party to oust (Sir) Archibald Grenfell Price [q.v.16] from the Federal seat of Boothby in 1943, and to win Prospect in the 1944 State election. He was not a good public speaker, and once the Cold War set in he gained few votes. Although shocked by Nikita Krushchev's revelations about the Stalinist era in 1956, he remained in the party, visiting the Eastern Bloc in 1958, and campaigning for peace and social justice.

After a stint as a general practitioner in 1947-49 at Broken Hill, New South Wales, Finger practised at Pennington, Adelaide. He and his wife had divorced in 1947, and on 12 December 1949 at the office of the principal registrar, Adelaide, he married Jean Isobel Sams, née Marshall (d.1978), a divorcee, and an active party member. In 1969-75 he was a full-time medical officer with the Department of Public Health, gaining recognition for his work combating venereal diseases. After retiring he worked (1977) for a community health service at Kalgoorlie, Western Australia. On 11 March 1982 at the office of the principal registrar, Adelaide, he remarried his first wife, also widowed; they settled at Reservoir, Melbourne. Still fit and active, the brash, dogmatic communist had mellowed into a good-humoured family man. Survived by his wife, their two sons, and the daughter of his second marriage, he died on 24 January 1985 at Heidelberg and was cremated.

J. Sendy, *Comrades Come Rally* (1978); J. Moss, *Representatives of Discontent* (1983); *Advertiser* (Adelaide), 16 Dec 1975, p 4; *News* (Adelaide), 30 Jan 1985, p 14; A6119, items 3536-3547 (NAA); private information.   JENNY TILBY STOCK

FINGLETON, JOHN HENRY WEBB (1908-1981), journalist and cricketer, was born on 28 April 1908 at Waverley, Sydney, third of six children of Melbourne-born James Fingleton, tram conductor, and his wife Belinda May, née Webb, born in New South Wales. In 1913 his father was elected to the New South Wales Legislative Assembly as Labor member for Waverley. He was returned for Eastern Suburbs in 1920 but died that year of tuberculosis. Jack was educated at Christian Brothers' College, Waverley, where he developed a great love of literature. Aged 15 he began a career in journalism with the Sydney *Daily Guardian*, subsequently working for the *Daily Telegraph Pictorial*, the *Sun* and the *Sydney Morning Herald* (1928-42).

A member of the Waverley Cricket Club, Fingleton made his début for New South Wales in January 1929. He impressed when in November 1931 he resisted the opening onslaught of the Aboriginal fast bowler Eddie Gilbert [q.v.9], scoring 93. Following a century against the visiting South Africans, he was selected as twelfth man in three successive Tests against South Africa. His first game for Australia was the fifth Test, in February 1932, in which he achieved the second highest score (40) on a difficult pitch.

After Fingleton scored a courageous 119 not out as an opener for New South Wales against England, he was selected to play for Australia in the 1932-33 'bodyline' series. In the second Test he scored a stubborn 83 in almost four hours. Harold Larwood, the spearhead of the English attack, described him as the bravest of cricketers. Although Fingleton was battered by Larwood, he later helped him to migrate to Australia. After a 'pair' (consecutive ducks) at Adelaide Fingleton was dropped from the Test side and, despite a successful season in 1933-34, was omitted from the 1934 team to play in England. Hurt by his omission from this tour, he changed himself from a fluent stroke maker to a stodgy batsman who remorselessly accumulated runs. He later acknowledged that a possible reason for his non-selection was the persistent but erroneous belief that he had leaked 'bodyline' dressing-room comments to the press.

Fingleton had a successful 1935-36 tour to South Africa, scoring centuries in the last three Tests. When he made 100 in the Brisbane Test of the 1936-37 Ashes series, he became the first batsman to score four successive Test centuries. In the third Test of that series, he achieved another century. He failed to reach 50 in the Tests against England in 1938.

Fingleton was a right-hand opening batsman, whose 'doggedness, courage and perseverance' was noted by Johnny Moyes [q.v.15]. However, on occasions he was a fluent and attractive stroke maker. A dashing and athletic fielder, he excelled both in the covers and in the leg trap.

On 17 January 1942 Fingleton married Philippa Lillingston Whistler Street, second daughter of (Sir) Kenneth and Jessie Street [qq.v.16], at Mary Immaculate Catholic Church, Waverley. Serving in the Militia for twelve months from April 1942, Fingleton completed an intelligence course and, having been commissioned as a lieutenant in October, was posted to public relations duties. He spent three months as press secretary to W. M. Hughes [q.v.9] in 1943. A friend of another prime minister, (Sir) Robert Menzies [q.v.15], Fingleton persuaded him to initiate the annual prime minister's cricket match in Canberra. However, he avoided party politics and admired the Labor leaders John Curtin and Ben Chifley [qq.v.13].

Joining the Canberra press gallery in 1944, Fingleton worked as a political correspondent for Radio Australia and as Australian correspondent for a number of English (including the *Sunday Times*), Indian and South African newspapers. He published ten books, mostly on cricket, although his evocative autobiography, *Batting from Memory* (1981), includes some astute social and political observations. His cricket works included *Cricket Crisis* (1946) on the 'bodyline' series, a biography (1978) of Victor Trumper [q.v.12] and a book (1949) to mark the retirement of Sir Donald Bradman. In an era when Bradman was idolised, Fingleton was one of the few writers to temper praise with criticism. While he admired Bradman, he also cited examples of his aloofness, selfishness and ruthless determination to win. Menzies regarded Fingleton as 'the best of cricket writers'. Appointed OBE in 1976, 'Fingo' retired from the press gallery in 1978. On three occasions in 1979-80, he was a television guest of Michael Parkinson. The interviews manifested the flowering of a public personality: Fingleton as a raconteur with a keen sense of humour appeared a relaxed and gregarious public figure.

Survived by his wife and their two daughters and three sons, Fingleton died on 22 November 1981 at St Leonards, Sydney, and was buried in the Catholic section of Waverley cemetery. The scoreboard at Manuka Oval, Canberra, which had been moved from the Melbourne Cricket Ground in 1982, was named after him.

J. Pollard, *Australian Cricket* (1982); R. Cashman et al (eds), *The Oxford Companion to Australian Cricket* (1996); *Canberra Times*, 23 Nov 1981, p 4; *SMH*, 23 Nov 1981, pp 1, 27; *Wisden Cricketers'* *Almanac*, 1982, p 1198; B884, item N225443 (NAA); Fingleton papers (SLNSW).   R. I. CASHMAN

FINK, MIRIAM (MINA) (1913-1990), Jewish community leader, was born on 5 December 1913 at Bialystok, Poland, second of three children of Nathan Waks, merchant, and his wife Freda, née Kaplan. Mina, aged 8, and her brothers, Leo and Jack, were orphaned when their father died in a typhus epidemic and their mother committed suicide. Raised by her maternal grandparents in difficult financial circumstances, she attended the Druskin Gymnazium to matriculation. In 1932 she met Leo Fink [q.v.14], a locally born manufacturer who had migrated to Melbourne in 1928 and returned on a visit to Bialystok. They married there on 20 September that year and travelled to Melbourne. She gave birth to a daughter and a son, gradually acquired English, and assisted the immigration of her brothers and other relatives.

In 1938 the Finks visited Poland and were shocked by the deterioration in the fortunes of the Jewish community. The subsequent Holocaust fundamentally changed Mina's life: she continued to be haunted by the fate of her Polish family and friends. In 1943 she became a director of the United Jewish Overseas Relief Fund and then president (1945-47) of its Ladies' Group, co-ordinating fund-raising and the despatch overseas of money, clothing, medicines and foodstuffs. The fund also established seven hostels in Melbourne to provide initial settlement for postwar immigrants. Mina's responsibilities included meeting ships at Port Melbourne, the day-to-day running of hostels, and regular visits to the Bialystoker Centre, St Kilda.

Unlike some members of Anglo-Australian Jewry, Mina and Leo had a fiercely personal concern for the refugees, reflecting their direct Polish links. She 'adopted' a group of young war-orphans—many of them concentration camp survivors—who came to be known as the 'Buchenwald boys', meeting them on arrival ('with a big smile on her face', as one of them, Max Zilberman, recalled); finding them accommodation, employment and opportunities for further training; and offering them Sunday outings, and visits to her family's Frankston holiday home. An enduring friendship developed with many of them.

From 1947 to 1976 Fink was a board member of the UJORF's successor, the Australian Jewish Welfare and Relief Society. As professional social workers came to fill the roles she had performed so ably, she devoted herself to the National Council of Jewish Women. She was the first European-born woman to head (1957-60) the council's Victorian section. Increasingly, she saw the work of women's groups not merely as adjuncts to the tasks of men, but as a demonstration of women's independence. As national president (1967-73) she developed ambitious fund-raising programs to help both the Jewish and wider community, and to undertake projects in Israel. She attended (1954, 1963, 1966, 1969) conventions of the International Council of Jewish Women, and chaired the one held in Melbourne in 1975. She had been appointed MBE in 1974. In 1987 she was elected an honorary member of the ICJW executive. Both Mina and Leo were lifelong supporters of the Jewish homeland, their many visits including prolonged stays between 1960 and 1964.

Mina Fink assisted in the establishment of the Jewish Holocaust Museum and Research Centre, opened in Melbourne in 1984, and—at her request, and in recognition of her financial support—the museum building was named in honour of Leo, who had died in 1972. She insisted that the museum function as an educational institution, and worked to provide training for survivors who served as guides to visiting school groups; she also advocated seminars for teachers and encouraged the involvement of academics.

It was said of Fink that she read the current of the times before most others. Through force of personality she was able to recruit and inspire volunteers, persuade people to work together, foster talent, and place protégés in positions of leadership. Always forthright—overbearing in the view of some—she did not seek popularity but recognition and respect. It pleased Fink to be invited to grand occasions of state and to meet people of power and influence. Meticulous in grooming, dress, housekeeping and record-keeping, she was not too proud to scrub floors in hostels. Friends recalled her boundless energy, her passion for order, her zest for life and her warmth. Mrs Fink died on 2 May 1990 at Prahran and was buried in the Chevra Kadisha cemetery, Springvale. She was survived by her children. An NCJW leadership development fund was established in her memory.

M. L. Newton, *Making a Difference* (2000); *Sun News-Pictorial* (Melbourne), 15 May 1969, p 37; Mina Fink (ts, Talking History Project, Austn Centre for the Study of Jewish Civilisation, Monash Univ); L. and M. Fink papers (Univ of Melbourne Archives); private information.

ANDREW MARKUS

FITCHETT, IAN GLYNN (1908-1988), political journalist and war correspondent, was born on 11 September 1908 at Terang, Victoria, third of four children of Victorian-born parents Alfred Shaw Fitchett, solicitor, and his wife Nellie, née Delany. W. H. Fitchett [q.v.8] was his grandfather. Raised in the Catholic faith of his mother's Irish family, Ian was educated by governesses, at the local Convent of Mercy and at Xavier College, Melbourne. He was articled to his uncle, F. S. Fitchett, and admitted to practise as a barrister and solicitor on 1 March 1935. After a brief stint as associate to Justice (Sir) Hayden Starke [q.v.12], he forsook law for journalism.

In 1937 Sydney Deamer, the editor of the Sydney *Daily Telegraph*, with whom he had struck up a friendship, persuaded (Sir) Frank Packer [qq.v.13,15], the newspaper's proprietor, to let Fitchett join the paper as a fourth-year cadet. He was assigned to the federal round, which meant making contact with politicians at their Commonwealth offices in Sydney. This gave him a taste for political journalism, in which he was to excel in the postwar years. He enlisted in the Australian Imperial Force on 20 October 1939 and sailed for the Middle East as a sergeant with the 2/4th Battalion in January 1940.

On the way there Fitchett was made a war correspondent. He was then appointed acting official war correspondent, pending the arrival of Kenneth Slessor [q.v.16]. Discharged from the AIF on 27 February 1941, he became assistant official war correspondent, Middle East. He covered the Libyan campaign, spending eight weeks in Tobruk during the siege, filing some forty dispatches about the Australian garrison's activities, despite encountering difficulties with the 9th Division commander, Major General (Sir) Leslie Morshead [q.v.15], who, Fitchett said, 'claimed the right to vet everything'.

Appointed official war correspondent for the 8th Division in October 1941, Fitchett served in Malaya from December. According to Alan Reid [q.v.], his reporting from Malaya included 'some of the most distinguished writing that came out of World War II'. Five days before the surrender on 15 February 1942, he managed to get away from Singapore, travelling by sea to Java and then to Fremantle, Western Australia. He carried out assignments for the Department of Information in Australia, Papua and New Caledonia. In 1943 he became the *Daily Telegraph* and London *Daily Express* war correspondent with South-East Asia Command, covering operations in Burma, India and China until 1945.

After the war Fitchett went back briefly to the *Daily Telegraph*, then joined the Melbourne *Age*, which sent him to Canberra as political correspondent in 1947. He moved to the *Sydney Morning Herald* in 1960, spending the next ten years as its political correspondent and then three years writing on defence and diplomatic affairs. On leaving daily journalism, he was able to use his deep knowledge of Australian military history to undertake research for the Australian War Memorial, Canberra.

A massive Falstaffian figure, with disciplined gingerish hair and a thin, neatly trimmed moustache, and always immaculately turned out, 'Fitch' became a legend in the postwar Federal Parliamentary Press Gallery. He was respected by politicians and colleagues alike for his 'incisive pen', 'acid tongue' and 'quick wit'. With a range of contacts, from prime ministers down, unmatched by other journalists, he ranked as one of the outstanding political correspondents of the day, with Reid, Harold Cox and Don Whitington [q.v.16]. As head of the *Age* bureau, he initiated a succession of young journalists into the art of interpreting and reporting politics, among them Graham Perkin [q.v.15].

With 'a certain pomposity of manner, accentuated by a booming baritone voice', Fitchett was one of the few political correspondents prepared to match Prime Minister (Sir) Robert Menzies [q.v.15] in scathing repartee. Once, after he had written several critical stories about Menzies, Fitchett ran into him in Parliament House. 'I'll make you eat crow', Menzies said. Fitchett fired back, 'I will be happy to eat crow, Prime Minister, provided it is garnished with the sauce of your embarrassment'. On another occasion, soon after Fitchett had joined the *Sydney Morning Herald*, Menzies posed a question: 'What would Mr [R. A. G.] Henderson [q.v.] think of that, Fitch?' Fitchett shot back, 'Mr Henderson, like God, sir, has not yet been revealed to me'. Fitchett's clashes were not confined to politicians. At a campaign meeting in the Adelaide Town Hall in 1953, he traded punches with Menzies' usually restrained press secretary, Stewart Cockburn, much to the amazement of the thousand-strong audience.

Described as masking 'a genuine shyness with outbursts of bigotry and misogynism', the seemingly confirmed bachelor surprised everyone when he married Florence Myrtle Edlington, née Clutton (d.1974), a widow, on 24 January 1959 at St Aloysius' Catholic Church, Cronulla, Sydney. The epitome of the old-style Canberra journalist, Fitchett brought to his vigorous political reporting the lawyer's gift of getting to the heart of the matter and exposing the shams and half-truths that riddle politics. Survived by a stepson and a step-daughter, he died on 10 October 1988 in Canberra and was cremated.

G. Souter, *Company of Heralds* (1981); H. Myers, *The Whispering Gallery* (1999); *SMH*, 21 Oct 1941, p 9, 11 Oct 1988, p 8, 29 Jan 2003, p 13; John Fairfax Ltd, *Staff News*, May 1973, p 2; *Australian*, 21 Aug 1973, p 11; *Age* (Melbourne), 11 Oct 1988, p 23; *Canberra Times*, 14 Oct 1988, p 4; A. Martin, taped interview with I. G. Fitchett (1987, NLA); H. Rusden and M. MacCallum, interview with I. G. Fitchett (ts, 1987, NLA); J. Farquharson, interview with S. Cockburn (ts, 2002, NLA); B883, item NX4072, MP742/1, item 256/1/122, SP109/16, item Fitchett, SP112/1, item M97, SP312/1 (NAA); AWM54, item 773/4/76 (AWM); private information and personal knowledge.
JOHN FARQUHARSON

FITTON, DAME DORIS ALICE LUCY WALKDEN (1897-1985), theatrical producer, director and actor, was born on 3 November 1897 at Santa Ana, Manila, younger daughter of Walter Albert Fitton, an English-born broker, and his Victorian-born wife Janet Fraser, née Cameron. In 1902 the family moved to Australia but Walter returned to work in the Philippines, where he died two years later. His widow settled in Victoria and, although in straitened circumstances, sent her daughters to Loreto Convent, Portland, and Loreto Abbey, Mary's Mount, Ballarat. Doris then trained as a stenographer.

At the age of 17, Fitton was accepted as a student with Gregan McMahon's [q.v.10] Melbourne Repertory Theatre Company. She made her first stage appearance in *The Price of Thomas Scott* but, on the advice of her mother and McMahon, declined a professional engagement. On 22 April 1922 at St Patrick's Catholic Church, Sydney, she married Norbert Keck ('Tug') Mason, an articled clerk. She played Mary Fitton in G. B. Shaw's *The Dark Lady of the Sonnets* for McMahon's Sydney Repertory Theatre Society but otherwise made only occasional appearances until 1927, when she played a small role for J. C. Williamson [q.v.6] Ltd in a dramatic adaptation of Somerset Maugham's *Rain*, and then appeared in its Muriel Starr season. Fitton also worked for McMahon in his last Sydney productions in 1928. She joined Don Finley's newly formed Turret Theatre Ltd in 1929 as a performer, and in 1930 became its part-time secretary. When that theatre closed, Fitton organised twenty of its members to contribute ten shillings each as working capital for the establishment of her city-based Independent Theatre (Ltd).

As artistic director Fitton adhered to the precepts of the Russian director Konstantin Stanislavsky, as outlined in his book *My Life in Art* (c.1924). Seeing her foremost responsibility as being to attract an audience, she began the first season in 1930 with a Viennese comedy, *By Candlelight*; but productions of classics, including *Othello*, *The Merchant of Venice* and *The School for Scandal*, soon followed. The Independent Theatre also introduced Sydney audiences to contemporary writers such as Elmer Rice and S. N. Behrman. It offered about ten shows a year with Fitton —who had made her directorial début in 1931 with A. A. Milne's *Michael and Mary*— producing most of them. The company used a number of premises before Fitton decided to move to Miller Street, North Sydney, in 1939, where it opened with Terence Rattigan's *French without Tears*. Although the move from the city lost the Independent much of its established subscriber base, Fitton kept the theatre operating throughout World War II and built close links with the local community.

Because of a limited budget the stage settings in the early days were spare, the main feature being buff-coloured curtains, a style that was presented, and accepted, as creative and experimental. However, on occasion Fitton used the appeal of large casts and spectacular presentation to attract full houses for productions which, while critically acknowledged as innovative and stimulating, were perhaps beyond the company's technical capacity. These included Hugh McCrae's [q.v.10] Australian poetical and musical fantasy *The Ship of Heaven* and J. Elroy Flecker's Arabian Nights fantasy *Hassan*. But the policy also resulted in productions such as the successful *1066 and All That*, based on the book by W. C. Sellar and R. J. Yeatman.

During the golden years of the 1940s and 1950s, memorable shows included Friedrich Schiller's *Maria Stuart* and Eugene O'Neill's *Mourning Becomes Electra*, with Fitton appearing in both. Her production of Sumner Locke Elliott's *Rusty Bugles* proved both a censorship cause célèbre and a successful commercial venture. Fitton played the leading role in Lesley Storm's 'daring' love story *Black Chiffon* and produced the newly translated Polish play *Anna Lucasta*. In 1955 she toured for the Australian Elizabethan Trust in *Medea* and her last appearance was in 1974 in Stephen Sondheim's *A Little Night Music*. She made only one film, *The Stowaway* (1958). In the late 1950s and early 1960s Fitton embraced contemporary theatrical challenges, her choice of plays including those by Samuel Beckett and Eugène Ionesco. She maintained her policy of encouraging Australian writers even though their plays were often less successful commercially.

As an administrator Fitton had, through the Independent Theatre, a long association with the Council for the Encouragement of Music and the Arts (Arts Council of Australia). Her company presented *Red Oleanders* at the first arts festival held by the council, in 1944, and from 1946 to 1964 the Independent provided shows for the council's extensive country tours. In 1938-39 she had been secretary of the inaugural Playwrights' Advisory Board. In the postwar years she sat (1967-69) on the board of the National Institute of Dramatic Art and was a member (1961-69) of the Sydney Opera House Trust.

The Independent fostered a theatre for children, supported a school of dramatic art with, from 1954, a theatre workshop, and served as a major training ground for actors. It made a

significant contribution to the cultural life of Sydney. While the Independent often teetered on the edge of insolvency, 'the spirit that pervaded it' was, according to Sumner Locke Elliott, 'unconquerable, wilful, determined, exasperating, energetic, positive—Miss Fitton'. However, Fitton's 'free and unfettered' artistic control (enshrined in the company's code) was not conducive to successful adaptation to subsidised theatre: the Independent operated as a fully professional company only in 1967-68. Because of financial difficulty, it closed in 1977. Fitton's last production, a revival of Thornton Wilder's *Our Town*, was in her eightieth year.

Fitton's regimen had reflected the influence of her association with Gregan McMahon, and through him the tradition of the nineteenth-century actor-manager; her ways came to be seen as old-fashioned. According to John Kingsmill she was 'given to the grand manner, the old elaborate style' in performance and, by her own account, was an 'indecisive' actress, most effective when typecast. She was slow to learn her lines and her memory was unreliable. Being 'of the old school' and having come to acting when elocution was 'considered basic to the art', as a teacher she concentrated on stage delivery and technique. As a producer, she was skilled at casting, often against physical type.

A strong-willed woman with a finely chiselled face, a slightly aquiline nose, a jutting chin and penetrating brown eyes, Fitton could be demanding and impatient. Although she had a reputation as a formidable disciplinarian, her sense of humour often came to her own and her students' rescue. She had a flair for miming, a natural contralto voice, a distinctive and ready laugh and a tendency to 'get the giggles' on stage. In professional life she was encouraging to other actors, placing great emphasis on loyalty. Benita Brebach, who acted with the Independent, believed that she was 'the softest touch on earth, if you knew how to do it right'. Another actor, Allan Davis, saw in her 'the ability to persuade people to do things' for her.

Tug supported all Doris's activities and for many years the family lived at North Sydney in order to be near the theatre. She was an enthusiastic ballroom dancer and a dog lover. Fitton was appointed OBE (1955), CBE (1975) and DBE (1982). Her autobiography, *Not without Dust and Heat: My Life in Theatre*, was published in 1981. Predeceased by her husband (d.1972) and elder son (d.1968), and survived by her younger son, Dame Doris died on 2 April 1985 at St Leonards and was cremated.

A. McPherson, *A Dream of Passion* (1993); J. Kingsmill, *My Brief Strut upon the Stage* (2001);

Equity, June 1985, p 46; B. Coy, The Significance of the Little Theatre Movement in Sydney with Particular Reference to the Independent Theatre (BA Hons, UNSW, 1990); M. Park, interview with B. H. Brebach (ts, 1991, Stanton Lib, North Sydney).
AILSA MCPHERSON

FITTS, SIR CLIVE HAMILTON (1900-1984), physician, was born on 14 July 1900 at Carlton, Melbourne, third of five children of Victorian-born parents Hamilton Fitts, wool merchant, and his wife Catherine, née Pardey. Clive followed his two elder brothers to Scotch College, where he spent eight 'carefree' years. Strong-willed, he so resented a father-enforced transfer to Melbourne Church of England Grammar School that he refused to play in school teams and spent afternoons browsing in Cole's [q.v.3] Book Arcade, his literary interests quickened in classes shared with (Sir) Keith Hancock [q.v.] and 'Sandy' Boyce Gibson [q.v.14]. On his father's instructions, he enrolled in medicine at the University of Melbourne (MB, 1926; MD, 1929; BS, 1931), entering Trinity College in 1919. He played football for the university and tennis for Victoria, but his academic progress was fitful; he passed final year only at his third attempt: 'perhaps I was the first to demonstrate that the course needed lengthening', he remarked later.

Despite residencies at the Alfred and Children's hospitals, Fitts failed to gain further appointments before the Depression worsened his prospects. He was employed as a medical officer with the Commonwealth Department of Health, working successively at the School of Public Health and Tropical Medicine at the University of Sydney (DTM, 1930), the Commonwealth Serum Laboratories, Melbourne, and the Quarantine Service, where he so enjoyed the hazards of boarding ships that in 1931 he became surgeon in a tramp-steamer, bound eventually for Europe. In London he secured appointment as house physician, surgeon and assistant-superintendent at the Brompton Hospital for Consumption and Diseases of the Chest, and, after three months as acting-superintendent of the British Sanatorium in Switzerland, became medical superintendent (1933-34) at the National Heart Hospital, London, with (Sir) John Parkinson as mentor and later friend. In 1933 he was made a member of the Royal College of Physicians (fellow 1938). After returning to Switzerland to climb the Matterhorn, Fitts sailed for Australia via the United States of America with empty pockets but rich in experience.

In Melbourne Fitts persuaded the warden of Trinity College to create the post of resident medical tutor. He gained the appointments then essential for the higher reaches of his profession, as honorary physician to out-patients at St Vincent's Hospital (1935-40), to the thoracic department at the Austin Hospital (1939-66) and to out-patients (1939-47) and in-patients (1947-60) at the Royal Melbourne Hospital. At Trinity College Chapel on 14 October 1939 he married Yrsa Elizabeth Osborne, also a medical practitioner and daughter of William Alexander and Ethel Elizabeth Osborne [qq.v.11]. They settled at Hawthorn, with a seaside house at Shoreham, and entertained a remarkable range of friends.

Fitts had served with the Australian Army Medical Corps, Militia, from 1927 (major 1934), but was prevented by a stomach ulcer from joining the Australian Imperial Force. In June-November 1941 he carried out full-time service as staff officer to Major General Rupert Downes [q.v.8], accompanying him on his tour of inspection of medical facilities in North Africa, the Middle East and the Far East. A gifted clinician in the old, holistic tradition of Sir William Osler, whose *Principles and Practice of Medicine* he relished as 'a great work of literature' and read ten times, Fitts nevertheless championed cardiology as a separate discipline, guiding the creation of the Royal Melbourne's cardiac department. He also welcomed the establishment of clinical chairs in the faculty of medicine, although it ended the dominance of hospital honoraries over clinical training. In 1948 he held a Carnegie travelling fellowship in the USA, and in 1959 undertook a Colombo Plan assignment comparing medical conditions in Malaya, Thailand and Burma. He was also active in many medical organisations, including the Royal Australasian College of Physicians (foundation fellow 1938; councillor 1952-61; vice-president 1956-58) and the National Heart Foundation of Australia, which he helped to establish in 1961. On his retirement (1960) from the RMH he became an honorary consulting physician. He was knighted in 1963.

An eloquent speaker, Fitts gave many public addresses—including the Sir Richard Stawell, the (Joseph) Bancroft [qq.v.12,3] and the (Lord) Lister orations, and the Tudor Edwards memorial lecture at the Royal College of Physicians, London)—always arguing strongly for medicine as a humane discipline as well as a science. In manner courteous, but quizzical and blunt, he was a formidable witness when called in court actions, ready to correct foolishness, even in judges. He conducted his large private practice from rooms in leafy Parliament Place, a pleasant walk from the Melbourne Club, of which he was an assiduous member (president 1965), as he was of the Savage Club and the less formal Beefsteak and Wallaby clubs and the Boobooks. He was also a member of the councils of the University of Melbourne (1951-53, 1955-71), MCEGS (1960-69) and St Hilda's College, and became a fellow of Trinity College in 1980. Politically inactive (despite his reputation as a 'society doctor' with Sir Robert Menzies [q.v.15] among his patients), Fitts was a swinging voter, quietly but firmly opposed to the Vietnam War.

Fitts was also a passionate book lover, active on the board of Melbourne University Press and with the Friends of the Baillieu [q.v.7] Library. His encounter in 1946 with a young patient, Margaret Stones, prompted him to recruit his friends (Sir) Russell Grimwade and (Sir) Daryl Lindsay [qq.v.9,10] to help launch her career as a botanical artist. In turn, Lindsay recruited him as founding president (1947) of the National Gallery Society, and in 1955 he joined the Felton [q.v.4] Bequests Committee (chairman 1965-75), the functions of which he reformed by introducing selective grants for medical research and projects for social betterment, while defending its reliance on overseas advisers for art purchases for the gallery.

Always a keen tennis player, Fitts also shared with his wife a passion for fly-fishing: the sport took them as far afield as Norway. In 1978 he retired as a consultant physician. His last years were saddened by the illness of one of his daughters and the death in 1980 of his son David, a talented artist. Survived by his wife, their three daughters, and their other son, Sir Clive Fitts died on 7 February 1984 in East Melbourne and was cremated.

J. C. Wiseman and R. J. Mulhearn (eds), *Roll of the Royal Australasian College of Physicians*, vol 2, 1976-90 (1994); A. Gregory, *The Ever Open Door* (1998); J. Poynter, *Mr Felton's Bequests* (2003); *Australian*, 11-12 Feb 1984, p 5; *MJA*, 26 May 1984, p 674; Fitts papers (Univ of Melbourne Archives); private information and personal knowledge.

J. R. POYNTER

FITZGERALD, PATRICK CHARLES MITCHELL (1896-1984), businessman, was born on 21 June 1896 at Rockhampton, Queensland, eldest of seven children of Charles Borromeo Fitzgerald, a Queensland-born barrister, and his wife Joan Mary, née Cahill, who came from Ireland. Thomas Henry Fitzgerald [q.v.4] was 'Paddy's' grandfather. Educated by the Christian Brothers at Rockhampton, he left school at 14 to work as a shipping clerk with Walter Reid [q.v.6] & Co. Ltd. After his father's death in 1913 he helped to support his mother and siblings. On 6 April 1931 at St Joseph's Catholic Church, Rockhampton, he married Eugenie McDowall (d.1979).

In about 1933, after a failed business venture, Fitzgerald began work with Castlemaine Perkins [q.v.5] Ltd, Milton, Brisbane, where his paternal aunt's husband, J. N. Devoy, was managing director. The company, producer of XXXX Bitter Ale, then commanded 10 per cent of the Queensland beer market. At first a travelling sales representative on the Queensland

coast, Fitzgerald was promoted to sales manager in 1942 and joined the board in 1951. Becoming general manager in 1970, he oversaw the modernisation of the company's existing Brisbane city and suburban hotels and the construction of new ones in developing outer areas. When in March 1977 the firm decided to discontinue supplying beer in wooden casks, concerned patrons of Brisbane's historic Breakfast Creek Hotel asked Fitzgerald to intervene. After he announced at the hotel that the brewery would continue to supply Breakfast Creek with gravity-fed beer off the wood, thirty-six jubilant waterside workers hoisted their pint-sized hero on top of three 10-gallon (45 litre) kegs and the public bar became the 'Paddy Fitzgerald Bar'.

Fitzgerald was named managing director in 1977. Clever marketing encouraged the perception that XXXX was the State's brew of choice and, after decades representing the product, Fitzgerald came to be seen as synonymous with Little Mr Fourex, the diminutive, jaunty, suited figure with one thumb up, a wide smile and a wink, and a boater brandishing four big Xs, who appeared on Castlemaine's bottles and cans. Although they shared similar dimensions and demeanour, any resemblance was coincidental; the cartoonist Ian Gall [q.v.] had reputedly conceived Mr Fourex in 1924.

A conservative manager, Fitzgerald emphasised the importance of a good product and of staff loyalty. He regarded Castlemaine workers and long-term licensees as family, and recruited executives almost entirely from within the company. Only after he retired as managing director in February 1979 did the board announce (in November) a merger with Tooheys [q.v.6] Ltd. When he stepped down in 1981 as a director of Castlemaine Tooheys Ltd, it was Queensland's second largest publicly listed company and XXXX enjoyed a 75 per cent share of the State's beer market.

A keen Rugby League player, rower and swimmer in his youth, Fitzgerald was also a member and several times president of the Booroodabin Bowls Club. He was known for his impish sense of humour. On 10 September 1984 he died at his Bardon home; he was buried in Nudgee cemetery. Two sons and four daughters survived him; one daughter had died in infancy.

Courier-Mail (Brisbane), 14 Nov 1979, p 1, 12 Sept 1984, p 3; *Sunday Mail* (Brisbane), 24 July 1983, p 72, 16 Sept 1984, p 22; *Daily Sun* (Brisbane), 12 Sept 1984, p 4; *Fourex News*, Dec 1984, p 7; Lion Nathan Aust Pty Ltd archives, Brisbane; private information.

MARK MCGINNESS

FITZGERALD, ROBERT DAVID (1902-1987), surveyor and poet, was born on 22

February 1902 at Hunters Hill, Sydney, youngest of three children of Sydney-born parents Robert David FitzGerald, civil engineer, and his wife Ida Le Gay, née Brereton. His paternal grandfather was Robert David FitzGerald and his uncle was John Le Gay Brereton [qq.v.4,7]. Bob was educated at Sydney Grammar School and the University of Sydney, where he studied science for two years and wrote poetry for the literary journal *Hermes*. He decided to train as a surveyor and was licensed in 1925.

In 1926 FitzGerald began private practice in Sydney. He married Marjorie Claire Harris, an assistant-librarian, on 11 March 1931 at All Saints' Church of England, Hunters Hill. When his business foundered in the Depression, he obtained employment as a surveyor (1931-36) with the Native Lands Commission, Fiji. On his return to Sydney he worked at Katoomba and then with the Ryde and Manly municipal councils. In 1940 he joined the property and survey branch of the Commonwealth Department of Interior. He settled with his family at Hunters Hill. Elected a fellow (1959) of the Institution of Surveyors, Australia, he contributed mainly in the geodesic and cadastral fields. He retired as chief Commonwealth surveyor for New South Wales in 1966.

The Greater Apollo: Seven Metaphysical Songs (1927) was privately published by Fitz-Gerald, and thereafter he produced eight more volumes of poetry, four collections of selected verse, a book of literary criticism and another of essays. He attributed his productivity to the influence of Norman Lindsay's [q.v.10] attitude towards art as a conscious effort to produce. In 1938 FitzGerald came to wider notice when 'Essay on Memory' won the sesquicentenary poetry prize, judged by H. M. Green [q.v.14]. *Moonlight Acre* (1938) was awarded the gold medal of the Australian Literature Society for the best book by an Australian author published that year. He won the Grace Leven prize for poetry three times, for *Between Two Tides* (1952), *The Wind at Your Door* (1959) and *Southmost Twelve* (1962). In 1965 FitzGerald shared with A. D. Hope the Britannica Australia award for literature and in 1974 he won the Poetry Society of America's Frost medal.

FitzGerald had lectured on poetry at the universities of Melbourne and Queensland, and, in 1963 on a Fulbright scholarship, at the University of Texas. He saw the poet as the inheritor and preserver of a long tradition of craftsmanship, constantly evolving as its acknowledged masters adapted to change. Thus his own lean, metrical and rhymed verse conformed to the rhythm of everyday conversation. It also gave the impression of plain speech heightened to achieve moments of delight, surprise and emotional or imaginative impact. As FitzGerald expressed it in 'Diction

and the Time Lag' (*Southerly*, 1971): '[Poetry is] largely that extra vividness of imagination or extra emotional intensity given to thought or meaning by the subtlety and congruity of the choice of words'. Further, believing that poetry dealt with 'tangibles and actualities', he eschewed 'nouns abstract' for 'nouns concrete'—see *The Elements of Poetry* (1963) —and for his imagery drew on familiar everyday experience.

Yet FitzGerald's reputation had been established by a series of long, speculative, metaphysical explorations of big themes such as beauty ('The Hidden Bole'), creation ('The Face of the Waters'), time ('Essay on Memory'), history ('Heemskerck Shoals') and ancestry ('The Wind at Your Door'). According to Julian Croft the first two were 'among the most significant poems' written in twentieth-century Australia. Like W. B. Yeats, whom he admired, FitzGerald was to write some of his finer poems late in life: shorter, more direct and, occasionally, lyrical pieces, such as 'Tribute', 'Edge' and 'The Tempered Chill'.

Largish and gregarious, with a loud laugh, FitzGerald had a serious turn of mind but was an entertaining companion. Literary friends recall him as a forgiving, generous-minded man who enjoyed (and frequently spoke at) literary gatherings. He was forthright in expressing his opinions—for example, his opposition to the war in Vietnam, and to what he saw as fads in poetry, as in 'Just Once':

And, one final curse:
Hell take freak poetries; I like good verse.

He was appointed OBE in 1951 and AM in 1982. The University of Melbourne conferred on him an honorary Litt.D. in 1985. Survived by his wife and their son and three daughters, he died on 25 May 1987 at his son's home at Glen Innes, New South Wales, and was cremated. His portrait, painted by Norman Lindsay, is held in the National Library of Australia.

V. Buckley, *Essays in Poetry* (1957); A. Grove Day, *Robert D. FitzGerald* (1974); G. A. Wilkes, *R. D. FitzGerald* (1981); J. Croft (ed), *Robert D. FitzGerald* (1987); *Austn Surveyor*, vol 19, no 4, 1962, p 243, vol 33, no 7, 1987, p 663; *Southerly*, vol 26, no 1, 1966, p 3, vol 27, no 4, 1967, pp 233, 243, vol 29, no 4, 1969, p 288, vol 47, no 3, 1987, p 235.   STUART LEE*

FITZHARDINGE, HOPE VERITY (1908-1986), teacher and bookseller, was born on 12 December 1908 at Glen Innes, New South Wales, eldest of seven children of William Vigors Hewitt, a New South Wales-born farmer, and his wife Nina Marguerite Haast, née Sealy, from New Zealand. Verity attended Glen Innes Grammar School and the University of Sydney (BA, 1929), where she became engaged to Laurence Frederic Fitzhardinge. In 1930-33 she taught at Telopea Park Intermediate High School, Canberra. After visiting the United States of America in 1935, she taught in Wellington, New Zealand. On board ship she had fallen in love with George Lacey Lee, an English migrant. Planning marriage, they designed their future home but Fitzhardinge pursued her. Believing he needed her more, she hastily married him on 1 August 1936 at the registrar's office, Wellington, but instantly, permanently, regretted her 'folly of … compassion'. Verity and Lacey were to maintain an intense correspondence. She visited him in New Zealand in 1939 and was devastated when he died in January 1942 while serving as a lieutenant with the 2nd New Zealand Expeditionary Force in North Africa.

Laurie worked as a librarian in Canberra. Unhappy, loathing housework, his wife opened Verity Hewitt's Bookshop in East Row on 1 April 1938. From second-hand books, it expanded to sell new books, prints and artefacts, and to hold art exhibitions. Unsuccessful financially, it became a 'pool of light' for the book-starved community, reflecting the friendliness of its owner, who delivered library books by sulky. Her sister June took over when the Fitzhardinges returned to Sydney in 1945. The shop was to occupy seven locations, the last in Queanbeyan from 1968, when Verity resumed the management before selling up in 1974.

In Sydney Mrs Fitzhardinge studied Russian and taught part time at Abbotsleigh Church of England School for Girls and Bradfield Park migrant camp. Diverse cultures intrigued her. Secretary of the Russian Social Club, she hosted Pushkin Circle meetings at her Pymble home. Unworldly and generous, she took in the homeless; two such, migrants, informed the Australian Security Intelligence Organization that she was a communist. This rumour persisted but was not substantiated. She called herself a 'fellow traveller', a 'romantic'.

The Fitzhardinges spent 1947 at Oxford, England, Verity working on a farm. Next year she travelled to Russia. In 1951 they resettled in Canberra. Helped by Russian migrants, she ran an orchard at Narrabundah while tending her frail parents and retarded brother. ASIO kept both Fitzhardinges under surveillance. Undeterred, Verity learned Russian from, and taught English to, numerous officials, including Evdokia Petrov, at the Embassy of the Soviet Union. She also worked as a relief teacher. When her Canberra Grammar School pupils locked her in a cupboard, she was encouraged to resign. While respecting the military virtues, she was a passionate pacifist, a founder and secretary of the local Australia-USSR Society and a member of the Australian Labor Party. Her appearance grew weather-beaten and eccentric; some found her excessively ideological.

From 1959 the Fitzhardinges leased River View, near Queanbeyan, New South Wales; Verity raised Dorset cattle and held an executive position in the Primary Producers' Union. She leased more land near Captains Flat and was librarian at the local primary school. She continued teaching Soviet personnel and in 1963 revisited Russia. At the Australian National University (MA, 1965; Ph.D., 1968) she investigated Russian contacts with colonial Australia and, later, the Anglo-Russian construction in the 1880s of the border between Afghanistan and the Russian Empire. There, in 1966, she walked the entire border, alone.

In her seventies Fitzhardinge prepared Lacey's memoir: their letters, his diary jottings and war service, her recollection of despair and renunciation. She interviewed his wartime comrades in New Zealand. The moving, candid manuscript was complete when she died on 23 June 1986 in Canberra. An agnostic, she was cremated. Her husband and their two sons survived her. Laurie loyally shepherded *A Man's Man* through to publication in 1987.

Canberra Times, 29 Aug 1968, p 19, 17 Feb 1979, p 15, 5 July 1986, p B6, 31 Jan 1988, pp 1, 7; *Canberra Hist Jnl*, no 17, 1986, p 32; A6119, items 876-79 (NAA); private information.   SUZANNE EDGAR

FITZPATRICK, KATHLEEN ELIZABETH (1905-1990), historian, was born on 7 September 1905 at Omeo, Victoria, second of four children of Victorian-born parents Henry Arthur Pitt, civil servant, and his wife Gertrude Augusta, née Buxton. The family maintained social contact only with close relatives; Kathleen grew up shy and lacking self-confidence but resolutely feminist. She recalled that her education—at Loreto Convent (Albert Park and Portland), Presentation Convent (Windsor) and Lauriston Girls' School—largely lacked stimulus. At the University of Melbourne (BA Hons, 1926) she studied English and history. As taught by (Sir) Ernest Scott [q.v.11], history enlarged her imagination and academic ambitions. She also became an editor of the new student newspaper *Farrago*, and was active in student societies ranging from the Literature to the Melbourne University Labor clubs.

Pitt proceeded to the University of Oxford (BA, 1928; MA, 1934). Disaster followed: she felt her fellow-students were snobbish and contemptuous of women, and she miscalculated the effort involved in completing a second degree in two years instead of three. She emerged exhausted, the predicted first-class result reduced to a creditable second. She was forever convinced that this meant that she was no academic. Scott disagreed, and found her a stopgap lectureship at the University of Sydney

(1929). There followed a tutorship in English at Melbourne, from which she resigned to marry Brian Fitzpatrick [q.v.14] at St Patrick's Cathedral, Melbourne, on 27 August 1932. The marriage was over by 1935 and they were divorced in 1939. She began a business course at Melbourne Technical School and was soon teaching typing and commercial English there.

In 1938, Kathleen Fitzpatrick returned to tutor English at the university. Then Scott's successor, the young Professor R. M. Crawford, intervened: in 1939 she was appointed a lecturer in the department of history. As Max Crawford's close collaborator and trusted deputy, she was promoted to senior lecturer (1942) and associate professor (1948). Fitzpatrick was a watchful, sympathetic teacher with presence, elegance, wit and theatricality. She held her audience firmly, without apparent effort, and moved at a gentle pace suited to her packed audiences of first-year students.

Fitzpatrick undervalued the scholarship implicit in her teaching. For her, the study of seventeenth-century writings was much more than a literary exercise; it encouraged students to discover individual people, their concerns and values. She argued that history dealt with the human condition: any kind of evidence— clothes, manners, climate, land use—was potentially within its frame of reference. Literature was in itself historical evidence, and students should be aware of this. Her underlying theme was the perpetual tension between order and liberty. Passionately liberal, she was horrified by McCarthyism. She told her students that Milton's *Areopagitica* had been written to be read aloud. Forty years later, her reading of it was still remembered.

Fitzpatrick carried heavy and varied administrative responsibilities, particularly during Crawford's extended periods of ill health. In World War II she was president of the Council for Women in War Work. She supported the foundation of University Women's College (1937), University House (1952) and the university Staff Association (1944). A foundation member (1956) of the Australian Humanities Research Council, she also served (1960-67) on the interim council of the National Library of Australia.

Lack of time and accessible sources limited her publications, but she was also demoralised by a series of apparent false starts. A planned textbook was stillborn when another historian got in first, and her confidence in her generally well-received *Sir John Franklin in Tasmania* (1957) was ruined by one savage review. In the early 1950s Fitzpatrick was seen as a likely candidate for a second chair in history, but with low self-esteem and a 'black Irish pride', she would not apply.

In 1962, tired, frustrated, and distressed by the impact of an academic dispute on her department, she justified early retirement by her wish to complete a long-cherished study of Henry James. Sadly, this turned out patchy and long-winded. Its rejection by publishers devastated her. A commissioned history of Presbyterian Ladies' College, Melbourne (1975), gave her a new project, and her memoir, *Solid Bluestone Foundations* (1983)—which she thought lightweight—achieved sustained success. In 1964 she served on a committee to advise the State government on the site for La Trobe University and in 1971-75 she sat on the council of the University of Melbourne. She was awarded an honorary doctorate of laws (1983) by the university and in 1989 was appointed AO.

Kathleen Fitzpatrick died on 27 August 1990 at East Melbourne and was buried in Melbourne general cemetery with Catholic rites. From her estate, sworn for probate at $2 747 031, she left a large bequest to the Baillieu [q.v.7] Library, University of Melbourne, to buy books. Her greatest legacy was one she refused to recognise: the enduring influence of her lectures. Appropriately, an annual lecture is given in her name.

F. Anderson, *An Historian's Life* (2005); *Herald* (Melbourne), 3 Mar 1943, p 7; *Age* (Melbourne), 1 Sept 1990, p 20; K. Fitzpatrick papers and M. Crawford papers (Univ of Melbourne Archives); J. A. La Nauze papers (NLA); private information and personal knowledge.   ALISON PATRICK

FOLEY, HORACE JOHN (1900-1989), medical practitioner, mayor and alderman, was born on 23 November 1900 at Mudgee, New South Wales, fourth of five children of James Foley, schoolteacher, and his wife Margaret Mary, née English, both born in New South Wales. Educated at Mudgee High School, Horace studied medicine at the University of Sydney (MB, Ch.M., 1926). He began general practice at Strathfield but worked at Glebe from the early 1930s until his retirement in 1980. On 23 November 1932 he married Sarah Agnes May Farmer at St Joseph's Catholic Church, Rockdale.

A member of the local Australian Labor Party branch, Foley stood unsuccessfully for Burwood in the 1932 State election, representing J. T. Lang's [q.v.9] State Labor Party. In December 1934 he gained a seat on the Glebe Council. Soon the acknowledged ward boss of the district, he served as mayor in 1937 and 1938. He clashed with Lang's 'Inner Group' over control of inner-city branches of the ALP and, consolidating control of his branch and the council, led his 'Foley Labor Party' to victory against a Langite team in the municipal elections of December 1937. He contested, closely but unsuccessfully, the seat of Glebe in the 1938 State election for the anti-Lang

Industrial Labor Party led by R. J. Heffron [q.v.14].

In 1938 Foley was convicted of misusing council vehicles, fined £300 and hence disqualified to act as an alderman. Next year the Glebe Council was dismissed and an administrator was appointed. Foley was his own worst enemy in his frequent litigation, preferring bluster and attack of witnesses to answering questions directly.

Prompted by his anti-communism Foley returned to the Lang Labor Party, standing unsuccessfully for West Sydney in the Commonwealth elections of 1943 and 1949 and for King in the State polls of 1944, 1947 and 1950. In 1945 he won a by-election for the Phillip ward on the Sydney Municipal Council. At another by-election in 1947 he won a seat on the Glebe Council while still an alderman in the city. When Glebe was absorbed by Sydney City Council in 1948, Foley's Lang Labor ticket won both Glebe ward seats against the official ALP team. He resigned in 1950, but served again on the SCC in 1953-56.

In 1957 Foley was readmitted to the ALP. Within a short time he assumed control of his old branch, now called Glebe North. A councillor (1962-65) on the Hornsby Shire Council, he became an alderman for the Glebe ward when it was transferred to the Leichhardt municipality in 1968. He gave up his ambitions for public office in 1971. Bespectacled and podgy, he was prominent in ALP faction fights in inner suburban branches during the 1970s.

Dr Foley's significance is as a middle-class, socially conservative, Catholic political leader in a largely working-class Australian inner-city community. Although regarded as ruthless by his enemies, he commanded loyalty because of his supposed expert knowledge and contacts, and his reputation for generosity to the poor. From 1927 to 1944 he had been a captain in the Australian Army Medical Corps Reserve. A park in Glebe was named after him. He died on 3 July 1989 at Croydon and was buried in the Catholic section of Rookwood cemetery. Predeceased by two daughters, he was survived by his wife and their son and three daughters.

M. Hogan, *Local Labor* (2004); *Glebe Observer*, 30 June 1950, p 1; *Glebe and Western Weekly*, 12 July 1989, p 6.   MICHAEL HOGAN

FONG LIM, ALEXANDER (1931-1990), businessman and lord mayor, was born on 18 February 1931 at Katherine, Northern Territory, sixth of nine children of Fong Fook Lim (George Lim), storekeeper, and his wife Lau Suey Gee (Lorna Lim), both born in the Northern Territory. Alec's Chinese name was Fong Soong Lim. His grandparents had arrived in the Territory from China during the 1880s. In 1926 his parents were among the first inhabitants of the new town of Katherine, where they built a shop and residence of bush timber and corrugated iron, living in the rear and operating a bakery and general store at the front.

Alec was educated at primary schools at Katherine, Darwin and Alice Springs, and at Scotch College, Adelaide, where he obtained his Intermediate certificate. Returning to Darwin in 1946, he commenced a successful business career. He worked in the Victoria Hotel, which his father owned, until 1965. He had hoped, he later recalled, to attend university, but family ties obliged him to stay. On 19 November 1955 at St Andrew's Cathedral, Sydney, he married with Anglican rites Norma Elizabeth Chin, a packer. Between 1962 and 1977 he was a licensed bookmaker at the Fannie Bay racecourse, Darwin, and from 1967 to 1982 a wholesaler in wines, spirits and groceries. He was a director of Lim's Rapid Creek Hotel, later the Beachfront Hotel, between 1971 and 1983. Fong Lim also owned at various times a dress shop and a fruit-juice bar, and was a director of the Territory Building Society. A keen sportsman, he enjoyed Australian Rules football, baseball, basketball, cricket, darts, soccer and tennis. He loved all music, from classical to country-and-western.

Active in community affairs, Fong Lim was vice-president of the Northern Territory Spastics Association (1981-85), chairman of the St John Council (1975) and the Northern Territory Australia Day Council (1981-84), and a member of the Darwin Cyclone Tracy Relief Trust Fund (1975-80) and the Northern Territory council of the Australian Bicentennial Authority (from 1981). An admirer of Harry Chan [q.v.13], he was elected lord mayor of the city in a hotly contested poll on 26 May 1984. He held the position until ill health forced his resignation on 9 August 1990. His most notable achievements in office were the introduction of an innovative corporate plan that radically changed the style of council operations; the energetic oversight of Darwin's sister-city relationship with Ambon, Indonesia; and a highly successful operation to keep Darwin's beaches clear of rubbish. His daughter Tanya, later recalling his love of the job, observed: 'It wasn't uncommon for him to be going to five functions a day'. He was appointed AM in 1986 and made a freeman of the City of Darwin in 1990.

Fong Lim was remarkably popular. Articulate and intelligent, he had friends from a wide cross-section of the Darwin community and was respected as a hard worker. He was a proud Australian who believed that he lived in a community where Asians were generally well accepted. He did not, however, hesitate to point to the prejudice that his family and other Chinese in the Northern Territory had experienced before and during World War II. Applauding multiculturalism, he urged people to retain their cultural traditions, 'which enrich the community', but encouraged them to think of themselves 'first and foremost as Australians'. He liked to tease his Anglo-Saxon friends by saying, 'at least we were educated when you were still swinging from the trees'. The *Northern Territory News* commented at the time of his resignation that he 'always presented Darwinians with a jovial face and a solid confidence in the development potential of the city'. Of medium height, he was for a time very solidly built but, after being diagnosed with diabetes as a young man, he succeeded in losing a good deal of weight.

Survived by his wife and their six daughters, Fong Lim died of a cerebrovascular accident on 3 September 1990 in Darwin. Although baptised as a Presbyterian, he had a traditional Chinese funeral before being buried in Darwin general cemetery. He was widely mourned. The chief minister of the Northern Territory, Marshall Perron, captured the feelings of many when he said that Fong Lim was the embodiment of Australia's most successful multicultural community and a fine ambassador for Darwin during his many years of public life. The administrator of the Northern Territory, James Muirhead, reflected that, growing up in a multicultural society, Fong Lim 'understood the potential stresses involved, but there was nothing shallow or racial in his assessment of people'. He did not recognise social barriers; in him there was no humbug. He was 'both a strong and a gentle man'. The historian Diana Giese provided perhaps the most perceptive assessment. Fong Lim, she wrote in 1995, was 'a generous, outgoing, highly visible role model for those who took on an entire society, and won'.

D. Giese, *Beyond Chinatown* (1995); P. A. Rosenzweig, *For Service* (1995); *NT News*, 26 May 1984, p 7, 10 Aug 1990, p 8, 3 Sept 1990, pp 1, 8; S. Saunders, interview with A. Fong Lim (ts, 1981, NTA); private information.   DAVID CARMENT

FORD, SIR EDWARD (1902-1986), physician and professor of preventive medicine, was born on 15 April 1902 at Bethanga, Victoria, son of Australian-born parents Edward John Knight Ford, arsenic man, and his wife Mary Doxford, née Armstrong. Educated at Clunes Higher Elementary School, he joined the Postmaster-General's Department in April 1917 as a telegraph messenger. He was employed as an assistant in the accounts branch when he matriculated at the age of 24 and entered the medical faculty at the University of Melbourne (MB, BS, 1932; MD, 1946).

During the Depression he supported himself by coaching other students and continuing to work for the PMG.

After serving as a resident medical officer at the Melbourne Hospital, Ford was appointed Stewart lecturer in anatomy at the university in 1933. From 1934 to 1936 he was a senior lecturer in anatomy and histology. He came under the charismatic influence of Frederic Wood Jones [q.v.9], who fostered his love of books, and developed an interest in physical anthropology and then tropical medicine. In 1937 he moved to the University of Sydney, where he lectured at the School of Public Health and Tropical Medicine; he obtained its diploma in tropical medicine in 1938. For much of 1938-39 he was engaged on field studies for the Papuan administration. He then served as medical officer-in-charge of the Commonwealth Health Laboratory in Darwin.

On 1 June 1940 Ford was appointed major, Australian Army Medical Corps, Australian Imperial Force. Given command of the 1st Mobile Bacteriological Laboratory, he arrived in the Middle East in March 1941. He was attached to the 2/3rd Casualty Clearing Station in Syria from July to January 1942. Back in Australia in March, he was promoted to temporary lieutenant colonel in August (substantive in September) and made assistant-director of pathology, I Corps (and also New Guinea Force). In December he successfully appealed to General Sir Thomas Blamey [q.v.13] for anti-malarial work to be given a higher priority and for vigorous control measures to be introduced. Appointed as malariologist, Land Headquarters, Melbourne, in March 1943, Ford played an increasingly important part in the AIF's efforts to counter the inroads of mosquito-borne malaria in New Guinea and northern Australia. Among his best-known works was *Malaria in the South West Pacific* (1943). He became director of hygiene, pathology and entomology in March 1945, and was promoted to temporary colonel in May. On 25 June 1946 he transferred to the Reserve of Officers. He had been mentioned in despatches (1943) and appointed OBE (1945).

For his doctorate Ford wrote a thesis entitled 'Malaria Control in Australia and the Pacific Dependencies: With Special Reference to Antimosquito Methods'. Awarded a Rockefeller fellowship, he gained a diploma in public health at the London School of Hygiene and Tropical Medicine in 1947. That year he was appointed professor of preventive medicine and director of the School of Public Health and Tropical Medicine at the University of Sydney —positions which he retained until his retirement in 1968.

Among his many positions in academia, Ford was dean of the faculty of medicine and a fellow of the senate of the University of Sydney in 1952-57, and acting vice-chancellor in 1960-61. A member (1947-68) of the National Health and Medical Research Council, he accompanied the first Australian medical delegation to China in 1957. He sat on the inaugural council of Macquarie University, Sydney, helped to establish the medical school of the University of Western Australia and served on Sir Leslie Martin's [q.v.] committee on the future of tertiary education in Australia. He also found time to be a board member of Sydney University Press. Serving in the Citizen Military Forces, he was director of army health in 1953-64. He was knighted in 1960.

Ford's contributions to medicine, science, literature and history were recognised by many awards: he was a fellow of the Royal Australasian College of Physicians (1946), the Royal College of Physicians, London (1958), the (Royal) Australian College of Medical Administrators, the Zoological Society, London, and the Royal Sanitary Institute, London (later the Royal Society for the Promotion of Health), and an honorary fellow of the Royal College of Pathologists of Australia (1971) and the Royal Australian Historical Society (1957). In 1969 the RCP and the RACP (of which he was to be vice-president in 1970-72) awarded him the (Sir) Neil Hamilton Fairley [q.v.14] medal. He was granted an honorary D.Litt. by the University of Sydney in 1971.

Sir Edward's high-pitched voice and gentle manner concealed great single-mindedness, unfailing logic and a talent for using simple words beautifully chosen. He had little patience with red tape. Known as Ted to his friends and colleagues, he was not only hospitable but also something of a gourmet. His greatest passion, however, was collecting books and during his lifetime he donated thousands of valuable works, including early Australiana, to the libraries of the University of Sydney, Macquarie University and the RACP. From 1958 until his death he was an active curator of the RACP's library. He made a number of notable contributions to Australian medical history, including the important reference work *Bibliography of Australian Medicine 1790-1900* (1976). A member of the Australian and Sydney clubs, he also belonged to the Sydney group of the Round Table. He never married and spent his last years at Cahors, an art deco apartment building at Potts Point, where he mixed with an eclectic group of artists and professional people. Ford died on 27 August 1986 at his home and was cremated.

A. S. Walker, *Clinical Problems of War* (1952), *Middle East and Far East* (1953), and *The Island Campaigns* (1957); J. Hetherington, *Blamey* (1954); J. A. Young et al (eds), *Centenary Book of the University of Sydney Faculty of Medicine* (1984); *Lives of the Fellows of the Royal College of Physicians of London*, vol 8 (1989); J. C. Wiseman and R. J. Mulhearn (eds), *Roll of the Royal Australasian College of Physicians*, vol 2, 1976-1990 (1994); M. Tyquin, *Little by Little* (2003); T. Sweeney, *Malaria Frontline* (2003); Univ of Sydney, *Gazette*, Nov 1967, p 214; Ford papers (Royal A'asian College of Physicians Lib, Sydney); private information.   MICHAEL B. TYQUIN

FORDE, FRANCIS MICHAEL (1890-1983), prime minister and diplomat, was born on 18 July 1890 at Mitchell, Queensland, second of six children of Irish-born parents John Forde, railway ganger, and his wife Ellen, née Quirk. Educated initially at the local state school, Frank was sent to the Christian Brothers' College, Toowoomba, where he later worked as a junior teacher until he was 20. His bent was more practical, however, and he was more ambitious. As a clerk in the Queensland Railway Department at Toowoomba he studied telegraphy; as a telegraphist in the Commonwealth Postmaster-General's Department in Brisbane he studied to become an electrical engineer. In 1914 he was transferred to Rockhampton, where, with his good looks and friendly manner, he developed the social skills of debating, public speaking and dancing. With James Larcombe [q.v.9] as his mentor, he threw himself into public life, becoming a leading figure in numerous organisations, especially the Australian Natives' Association, the Australian Workers' Union and the Rockhampton Workers' Political Organisation.

The conscription plebiscite of 1916 and the ensuing split in the Australian Labor Party provided Forde with an opportunity to enter parliament. When the prominent conscriptionist John Adamson [q.v.7], member for the State seat of Rockhampton, was forced to resign from both T. J. Ryan's [q.v.11] ministry and the Labor Party itself, Forde nominated for the vacancy, won the preselection ballot, from a field of six, and the by-election in May 1917 with a comfortable majority. The youngest and possibly the most vigorous member in the Legislative Assembly, he espoused many causes, most notably the New State movement. After increasing his majority at the 1918 and 1920 elections, he took the opportunity afforded by William Higgs's [q.v.9] expulsion from the ALP in 1920 to gain the party's preselection for the Federal seat of Capricornia.

Winning that seat easily in December 1922, Forde steadily earned a reputation as a champion of sugar and cotton interests and a strong advocate of protective tariffs for all industries. As the only Labor member of the House of Representatives from Queensland in 1925-28, it fell to him not only to protect the State's economic interests, but also to defend its Ryan and Theodore [q.v.12] Labor governments against attacks by the conservative Federal government. Unfailingly attentive to his constituents, Forde was ubiquitous, leading the Queensland *Worker* to declare in 1928 that 'Frank is blessed with a wholesome superabundance of energy that makes his presence felt in any and every cause and question he takes up'. He served on the royal commission on the moving picture industry (1927-28) and on the Joint Committee of Public Accounts (1929). When Labor won the Federal election in October 1929, his energy, experience and representation of Queensland earned him a junior ministry in the Scullin [q.v.11] government.

Promotion was swift. As assistant-minister for trade and customs (1929-31), acting-minister for markets and transport (1930-31), and minister for trade and customs (1931-32), Forde was the principal architect of federal Labor's high-tariff policy, designed to mitigate the effects of the Depression on Australia's secondary industries. He was one of only fourteen of the forty-six Labor members who survived the Scullin government's defeat in December 1931. Early next year he was elected deputy-leader of the federal parliamentary Labor Party, a position he was to hold until 1946. But he had hopes of becoming prime minister. When Scullin resigned as party leader in 1935, Forde stood for the position. He lost to John Curtin [q.v.13] by ten votes to eleven; this was the first of three occasions when a single vote determined the course of his political career.

When Labor took office in October 1941, Forde became not only deputy prime minister but also—after Curtin and General Douglas MacArthur [q.v.15]—possibly the third most powerful public figure in Australia. During World War II he served on the Advisory War Council (from 1940) and in the War Cabinet (from 1941), for which contribution he was made a privy councillor in 1944. His principal roles, however, were as minister for the army between 1941 and 1946 and as acting prime minister for periods in 1944-45. The former was a difficult and thankless task, which he pursued with characteristic diligence and tact, envied by some for his remarkable ability to stay out of serious political trouble. He was also to serve as minister for defence in August-November 1946. But 1945-46 were for him difficult and disappointing years. He had led the Australian delegation to the United Nations Conference on International Organization, held at San Francisco, United States of America, in April-June 1945, but was completely overshadowed by the foreign affairs minister Dr H. V. Evatt [q.v.14]. Following Curtin's death in July 1945, Forde was prime minister from 6 to 13 July, but caucus soundly rejected him as a permanent leader in favour of the more charismatic J. B. Chifley [q.v.13].

Worse was to come. At the Federal election in September 1946 Forde lost Capricornia, the seat he had held for twenty-four years. Demobilisation, for which he had been ultimately responsible, was too slow for many local troops and their families; his Country Party opponent, Colonel (Sir) Charles Davidson [q.v.], was well respected in the region; and the Rockhampton *Morning Bulletin* had been particularly hostile towards him. Chifley's government rewarded his long and loyal service to the party by appointing him Australian high commissioner to Canada. He fulfilled his diplomatic duties with distinction; (Sir) Robert Menzies [q.v.15] extended his term. Forde later commented that his six years in Canada (1946-53) were the happiest of his life. Back in Australia, with the support of the powerful Queensland branch of the AWU, he became the Labor Party's State organiser.

A born politician who yearned to get back into parliament, Forde won preselection for the Federal seat of Wide Bay, centred on Bundaberg, but was defeated at the general election in May 1954. Although almost 65, he retained the faith and support of the Queensland branch of the party, which endorsed him for Flinders, a State seat that included the outback towns of Charters Towers, Hughenden and Julia Creek. Winning Flinders at a by-election in March 1955, he held the seat at the general election in May 1956 but lost it in August 1957—by one vote. Had he been returned he might—as several reports suggested—have become the leader of the State party, now suffering a dearth of experienced members. He successfully appealed against the result on technical grounds but lost the by-election in May 1958 by a convincing margin.

In 1959 Forde once more sought Labor preselection for Flinders, but the Queensland central executive decided against him by twenty-six to twenty-seven—the last time he was defeated by the narrowest of margins. Again he appealed and again he won the first stage of his political comeback. Although he lost the election in May 1960, he sought Labor preselection for a Senate seat in 1962, but was now in his seventies and largely a spent force. In 1964 Menzies, who had become a friend, asked him to represent Australia at MacArthur's funeral in Washington, a commission he was proud to accept. An inveterate 'joiner', in later life Forde was not one to decline invitations to the many functions he was asked to attend. He was awarded honorary doctorates from the universities of Laval, Montreal and Ottawa, Canada, and of Queensland.

Forde is typically remembered as the man who was prime minister for a week or, even more patronisingly, as 'always the bridesmaid, never the bride'. Such expressions obscure the fact that his parliamentary career was characterised much more by success than failure. Although not associated with any particular achievement—he was an administrator rather than a legislator or decision-maker—he not only won most of the electoral contests he fought but also spent most of his adult working life in State or Federal parliament. Moreover, while he was neither prime minister nor party leader for long, whether in government or Opposition he was a principal in the counsels of the Labor Party. In truth, he perhaps suffered less disappointment than most of his fellow parliamentarians, many of whom were far more ambitious. Most importantly, he was as loyal to his leader as he was to the party.

A short, stocky man, Forde was always concerned about his physical appearance and health; he was teetotal and a non-smoker. In his early years he liked shooting; in later life he enjoyed tennis and bowls. On 24 February 1925 at St Michael's Cathedral, Wagga Wagga, New South Wales, he had married Veronica Catherine O'Reilly (d.1967); they had three daughters and a son. Survived by his daughters, he died on 28 January 1983 in Brisbane; he was accorded a state funeral and was buried in Toowong cemetery. A portrait (1946) of Forde by Joshua Smith is held by Parliament House, Canberra. His daughter-in-law Leneen Forde was governor of Queensland in 1992-97.

N. Makin, *Federal Labour Leaders* (1961); L. Haylen, *Twenty Years' Hard Labor* (1969); C. A. Hughes, *Mr Prime Minister* (1976); M. Grattan (ed), *Australian Prime Ministers* (2000); *PD* (HR), 3 May 1983, p 65; *PD* (Senate), 3 May 1983, p 101; *Daily Standard* (Brisbane), 28 Apr 1917, p 9; *Worker* (Brisbane), 3 Oct 1928, p 6; *Table Talk*, 6 Feb 1930, p 13; *Australasian*, 4 Nov 1944, p 16; D. A. Gibson, The Right Hon. Francis M. Forde PC (BA Hons thesis, Univ of Qld, 1973); private information.

MALCOLM SAUNDERS
NEIL LLOYD

FORREST, SIR JAMES ALEXANDER (1905-1990), solicitor and company director, was born on 10 March 1905 at Kerang, Victoria, third of five children of Scottish-born parents John Forrest, draper, and his wife Mary, née Gray. Jim completed his secondary education at Caulfield Grammar School; he was keen to study medicine, but this was beyond his family's means. Instead, he gained a position as a filing clerk at one of Melbourne's leading law firms, Hedderwick Fookes & Alston. In 1925 he commenced an articled clerk's course at the University of Melbourne. Admitted to practise in 1930, Forrest was made a partner of the firm in 1933. At Christ Church, South Yarra, on 9 December 1935, he married Mary Christina Armit with Anglican rites.

Forrest soon became one of Melbourne's leading commercial lawyers, and was closely associated with the many interests of the Grimwade [q.v.9] family, including their involvement in Australian Glass Manufacturers Co. Ltd. He was made a director of their family company, Felton Grimwade & Duerdins Ltd.

Enlisting in the Royal Australian Air Force on 8 June 1942, Forrest was commissioned and employed on security duties, mainly at Townsville, Queensland, before being demobilised as an acting flight lieutenant in September 1943. He then worked for the Department of Aircraft Production, assisting with legal issues between the government and the suppliers of aircraft and parts.

Returning to practice at the end of the war, Forrest consolidated networks in industry and commerce that extended beyond his law firm and its clients: he was appointed to the Victorian board of the Australian Mutual Provident Society (1945-77) and in 1950 joined the board of AGM's successor, Australian Consolidated Industries Ltd (chairman 1953-77). The managing director of ACI at that time was the dominating and fiercely independent W. J. ('Gunboat') Smith [q.v.11], who had diversified the company's operations but treated its board as almost irrelevant. Forrest regarded Smith's conduct as impeding the board's responsibility to review the company's management and performance, and in 1957 dismissed him after a bitter confrontation. He then established a company policy (retained for over seventeen years) of not appointing company executives to its board. To reinforce the point, subsequent chief executives were titled 'general manager'.

In 1950 Forrest joined the board of the National Bank of Australasia Ltd. He was chairman in 1959-78. Under his direction both NBA and ACI embarked on significant programs of expansion. ACI developed technology partnerships with leading glass companies in Britain and the United States of America; established manufacturing plants in South-East Asia, New Zealand and the Territory of Papua and New Guinea; commenced fibreglass and tableware manufacture; and experienced sustained periods of financial success. The NBA, originally a trading bank, extended its activities into savings accounts and customer credit; formed joint ventures to attract international capital; expanded its representation throughout South-East Asia and in Papua and New Guinea; and rapidly increased its profits.

A senior partner in his law firm from 1967, Forrest retired to a consultancy in 1970. He held directorships in other companies including Drug Houses of Australia Ltd (1959-69), the AMP Society (1961-77) and Western Mining Corporation Ltd (1970-72). He was chairman of Chase-NBA Group Ltd (1971-80) and Alcoa of Australia Ltd (1970-78). In addresses and commentary regularly featured in the press, Forrest argued that Australia must expand the export of resources and build up industrial capacity; he looked to the Commonwealth government to lessen restrictions on the flow of capital and to manage the economy, particularly inflation and wage growth, in favour of business activity. A vigorous opponent of 'excessive economic nationalism', he criticised the Whitlam Labor government's 'failure to employ fiscal restraint'.

Knighted in 1967, Sir James was respected as a skilful, urbane chairman: modest and direct, and content to drive a Holden. His commitment to the training and education of youth was evident in service on the State and national councils of the Boy Scouts Association (1949-72), on the councils of Scotch College (1959-71) and Monash University (1961-71), on the Victorian Rhodes scholarship selection committee (1971-74) and as a founding member of the Royal Children's Hospital Research Foundation (1960-77). He was elected a fellow (1977) of the Australian Academy of Science and awarded an honorary doctorate of laws (1979) by Monash University.

In 1977, as Forrest began retiring from active business, the *Australian Financial Review* acknowledged him as 'one of the most dominant men among Australian company directors for a quarter of a century'. He died on 26 September 1990 at Malvern and was cremated. His wife and their three sons survived him.

G. Blainey and G. Hutton, *Gold and Paper* (1983); *Hist Records of Austn Science*, vol 8, no 4, 1991, p 245; *Herald* (Melbourne), 20 Dec 1973, p 20, 9 Mar 1977, p 22; *Austn Financial Review*, 9 Mar 1977, p 2.

TERRY GRIGG

FOSTER, ALLAN JOHN (1925-1987), medical practitioner and politician, was born on 4 September 1925 at Currie, King Island, Tasmania, second of five children of Reuben Jack Foster, a Tasmanian-born road overseer, and his wife Mary Veronica, née McCormick, from Scotland. Educated at Scottsdale High School, Allan left at 15 and became a junior clerk with the Department of Public Works in northern Tasmania. He enlisted in the Militia on 2 August 1944 and trained as a clerk. Transferring to the Australian Imperial Force in August 1945, he served with the 6th Prisoner of War Reception Camp in Singapore before being discharged on 19 November 1946 in Tasmania. Through the Commonwealth Reconstruction Training Scheme, he matriculated and studied science in 1948 at the University of Tasmania. Next year he was accepted into the medical faculty at the University of Melbourne (MB, BS, 1953). On 16 April 1949 at St Andrew's Presbyterian Church, Launceston, he married June Ada Watson, a salesgirl. They lived on the outskirts of Melbourne in a crude bungalow that they built with the help of friends, using timber from motorcar packing cases.

Returning to Tasmania in 1954, Foster became a resident medical officer at Launceston General Hospital and at Cosgrove Park Home for the Aged, where he developed an interest in geriatrics. Next year he set up in general practice at St Helens. Honorary geriatrician at LGH from 1960, he moved back to Launceston in 1962. On study tours in 1963 and 1966 he investigated developments in geriatric care in Britain and Europe. He was a founding member (1964), federal councillor (1965-74) and president (1971) of the Australian Association of Gerontology.

In 1965-68 Foster was director of geriatric services in the State Department of Health Services. He was appointed deputy director-general of health in January 1969, but he resigned and successfully contested the seat of Bass for the Australian Labor Party at the State election in May. In the House of Assembly he was immediately appointed shadow health minister. Seeing the need for integrated medical facilities and equality of access to curative and preventive care, he criticised the Commonwealth Grants Commission for equating health costs with the cost of hospital beds. He argued that aspects of community health care other than provision of hospitals, for example home care for the aged and the disabled, also needed financial help from the Commonwealth. In April 1972 he was re-elected to parliament and on 3 May was appointed minister for health, social welfare and road safety in E. E. Reece's new Labor government. He considered that his main achievement was negotiating with the Federal government a cost-sharing arrangement for the redevelopment of Launceston General Hospital.

Due to ill health caused by injuries sustained in a car accident, Foster resigned from parliament on 15 July 1974. Having been elected a fellow of the Royal College of Physicians, Edinburgh, in 1973, he returned to limited medical practice in Hobart, and worked extensively with cancer patients. In 1984 he chaired the joint Commonwealth and State review into the needs of intellectually disabled people in Tasmania. Survived by his wife and their two daughters and son, he died on 15 January 1987 at his Rose Bay home and was cremated.

PD (HA, Tas), 4 Mar 1987, p 20; *Examiner* (Launceston), 13 Apr 1972, p 7, 20 Jan 1987, p 9; *Mercury* (Hobart), 16 July 1974, p 1, 19 Jan 1987, p 5; B883, item TX17017 (NAA).   DOUG LOWE

FOSTER, DOROTHY ISABEL MAY (1908-1981), radio producer, scriptwriter and actress, was born on 14 February 1908 at Devonport, Tasmania, elder daughter of Victorian-born parents Charles Marshall Foster, engineer, and his wife Mary Isabel, née Collett. After leaving the Collegiate School, Hobart, Dorothy worked as a typist and organised the local children's session for the Australian Broadcasting Co. She married Alan Aubrey Salter, a draftsman, on 18 June 1930 at the Wesley manse, Hobart; they later divorced.

In 1934 Foster went to Melbourne, where she worked as a secretary for John Tait [q.v.12]. Next year she was employed as an announcer by radio-station 3UZ. Freelancing from 1937, she became well known on Victorian radio, especially as Dilly on radio 3AW's 'Shell Show'. She began her career as a radio producer with 'David Copperfield' and 'Bindle', while also performing in theatre with a Hal Percy [q.v.15] company. In 1939 she was appointed to the radio division of J. Walter Thompson Australia Pty Ltd in Sydney. On 5 May that year she married Robert Gray Nicolson, a wool buyer, at the Congregational manse, Woollahra; they divorced in 1947. By 1940 she had formed her own production company, Dorothy Foster Radio Features.

During World War II variety and comedy shows for radio were produced in Australia rather than coming from the United States of America. The most glamorous and costly of these productions was 'Calling the Stars', sponsored by Colgate-Palmolive Pty Ltd and presented on radio 2GB (2UE from 1946), and relayed interstate. Among its star-studded cast were the comedians Jack Davey, 'Mo' (Roy Rene) [qq.v.13,11] and Willie Fennell. Foster created 'Ada and Elsie' for this program, wrote almost all the scripts and played the role of Ada.

Introduced as 'those two old-fashioned girls', Ada and Elsie would flit to the microphone and gaze primly at their auditorium audience. They wore frilly-necked white blouses, round glasses and round flat straw hats. Although they spoke ingenuously, insinuations abounded in what they said, due largely to Foster's writing. Neither Ada nor Elsie was very bright. Playing the character was something of a triumph for Foster, who was a very intelligent woman. She was, according to Jacqueline Kent, 'small, dark-haired and birdlike'. Rita Pauncefort, who played Elsie, was tall and stately, with the hauteur and vowels of a 'grande dame'. Ada and Elsie made their last broadcast in 1954.

Through this period Foster was also a dress designer and owner of two 'frock salons'. Later she wrote and produced for radio-station 2CH. A woman of inexhaustible energy, she then opened a coffee shop. When the demand for radio writing and acting began to fall away with the coming of television, she became a real estate agent, continuing this job until her death. However, her heart was in show business. In 1980 she said: 'I still write a gag a day, just to keep in touch'. Survived by her adopted daughter, she died on 5 July 1981 at St Leonards and was cremated.

J. Kent, *Out of the Bakelite Box* (1983); *Listener In*, 20 Aug 1938, p 5, 7 Sept 1938, p 8, 10 Dec 1938, p 6, 18-24 Feb 1939, p 3; *ABC Weekly*, 20 July 1946, p 9, 24 Sept 1949, p 42; *People* (Sydney), 25 Feb 1953, p 10; *Daily Telegraph* (Sydney), 14 Feb 1978, p 7; private information.   RICHARD LANE

FOYSTER, JOHN ALEXANDER (1893-1988), mineral sands mining entrepreneur and horse-racing enthusiast, was born on 26 November 1893 at Mullamuddy, near Mudgee, New South Wales, fifth, and second surviving, of eight children of William Alfred Foyster, dairyman and former schoolteacher, and his wife Margaret, née McLeod, both born in New South Wales. In 1906 the Foyster family moved to Myrtle Creek, in the Richmond River district, and in 1913 to Crabbes Creek, in the Tweed River district. Jack later grew sugar cane and grazed cattle, and worked in Sydney for a time as a hairdresser. On 16 June 1928 at St John's Church of England, Darlinghurst, he married 17-year-old Olga May Easterbrook. They had four sons. Travelling periodically to Canadian Lead, near Gulgong, to mine for gold, he acquired a knowledge of mining techniques.

In the early 1940s when he was farming at Cudgen, Foyster observed the growing wartime interest in the 'black sands' of the local beaches. In 1944 he applied for leases over beachfront areas near Bogangar and Cudgen Headland. Development of the mineral sands business subsequently occupied the whole family. In 1947 they began stockpiling mineral sand, recovered from beach seams with a horse-drawn scoop. Despite postwar difficulties, plant and sheds were installed at Cudgen—some buildings were obtained from a former American army barracks at Grovely, Brisbane, and timber was cut on the site. The first sales of separated rutile and zircon concentrates were made in 1950. Business expanded rapidly, boosted during the Korean War by military demand for titanium.

In the mid-1950s the Foysters began prospecting the high dunes of North Stradbroke Island, Queensland, and in 1965 formed Consolidated Rutile Ltd to work their leases on the island. Cudgen R.Z. Ltd was floated in 1967. At this time the combined output of the two Foyster-controlled companies was 20 per cent of the total east coast rutile and zircon production. In 1969 all family members (apart from the eldest son, Clive, who had already left the industry) sold their shares in both companies for $13.1 million.

During the 1960s Foyster and his sons had begun to invest heavily in racehorses. Their bidding, particularly at Sydney and New Zealand yearling sales in 1967 and 1968, attracted much publicity. They bought and raced horses in varying co-ownerships within and outside the family, and three sons—Mark, Lloyd and John—established studs. Horses owned or co-owned by the Foysters included Just Ideal, Our Planet, Double Century, Stylish Century, John's Hope, Ming Dynasty and Mighty Kingdom.

A wiry and athletic man, Jack Foyster was full of vigour even in his late eighties. He lived at Tweed Heads and amassed considerable real estate holdings, especially on the southern Gold Coast. He died on 27 November 1988 at Southport, Queensland, and was buried in Allambe Garden of Memories, Nerang. His wife and their sons survived him.

I. W. Morley, *Black Sands* (1981); P. Pring, *The Star Kingdom Story* (1983); *Daily News* (Murwillumbah), 13 Dec 1963 'Supplement', 30 Nov 1988, p 2; *SMH*, 19 Jan 1968, p 12, 19 Apr 1968, p 1, 7 May 1969, p 24; *Austn Bloodhorse Review*, Jan 1989, p 5.

BRETT J. STUBBS

FRASER, SIR DOUGLAS WERE (1899-1988), public servant, was born on 24 October 1899 at Gympie, Queensland, eldest of three sons of Robert John Fraser, a Queensland-born clerk, and his wife Edith Harriet, née Shepherd, from New South Wales. Educated at Gympie State High School, in 1916 Douglas joined the Queensland Public Service Board in Brisbane as a junior clerk. In 1920 he transferred to the office of the newly appointed public service commissioner, J. D. Story [q.v.12]. He studied accountancy with the Federal Institute of Accountants and gained a certificate in accountancy from the University of Queensland. On 1 September 1927 at Albert Street Methodist Church he married Violet Pryke (d.1968), a public servant.

Influenced by Story's manner and style as an administrator, community leader and educator, Fraser became acting assistant-secretary to the public service commissioner in 1936 and secretary three years later. During World War II he took on the added roles of assistant-director of civil defence and secretary to the public safety advisory committee. He was promoted to senior public service inspector in 1947 and to deputy public service commissioner in 1952, and was appointed public service commissioner in 1956. When the Liberal-Country Party coalition came to power in 1957 after a long period of Labor government, he kept his position as titular head of the public service, testimony to his bipartisan support and apolitical stance. He served as an electoral commissioner in 1949-72 (chairman from 1959), and was a member of the University of Queensland senate in 1957-74. A fellow of the Australian Institute of Management, the (Royal) Australian Institute

of Public Administration (Queensland group), the Australian Society of Accountants and the Institute of Civil Defence, he was appointed ISO in 1962. He retired from the public service in December 1965 and was knighted next year.

President (1967-80) of the Queensland Ambulance Transport Brigade State council, Fraser visited the majority of branches and convened conferences, building the morale of the officers and their families. He emphasised the importance of training and oversaw establishment of a sound superannuation scheme. The Institute of Ambulance Officers made him an honorary fellow. In 1980 he was a member of the committee of review on ambulance services in Queensland, whose report resulted in a more efficient and centralised structure.

Fraser was a devotee of classical music. Vice-chairman (1955-71) and chairman (1971-79) of the Queensland Conservatorium of Music advisory council, he was made an honorary fellow in 1979. He was also chairman (1971-81) of the Queensland Light Opera Company. Interested in local history, he contributed articles on early settlement to the *Journal of the Royal Historical Society of Queensland* and presented papers to the Redcliffe Historical Society, of which he was patron from 1968. He wrote a seminal monograph, *The Public Service of Queensland, 1859-1959* (1981), and co-authored *Administrative History in Queensland* (1986), both published by the RAIPA. Former colleagues recalled him as a thorough gentleman, who always remembered names. His life was dedicated to public service. Survived by his three sons, Sir Douglas died on 2 January 1988 at Redcliffe and was cremated.

C. Lack (comp), *Three Decades of Queensland Political History 1929-1960* (1962); *Professional Officer*, Dec 1965, p 1; *Redcliffe Herald*, 18 Mar 1981, p 32; *Courier-Mail* (Brisbane), 6 Jan 1988, p 2.

KENNETH WILTSHIRE

FREEDMAN, HARRY MORDECAI (1901-1982), rabbi and Hebrew scholar, was born on 17 October 1901 at Vitebsk, Russia, son of Barnett (Dov) Freedman, tailor, and his wife Beila Henah. His family moved to England when he was a young child, settling in London, where he attended a government school, then studied at the Etz Chaim Yeshiva and the University of London (BA, 1923; Ph.D., 1930). Receiving his rabbinical ordination from Jews' College in 1924, he was appointed as minister of the North Manchester Synagogue. He married Rebecca (Bea) Ginsberg on 17 March 1925 at Philpot Street Synagogue, Mile End, London. While undertaking his pastoral duties, he completed his doctorate as an external student at the University of London. He was naturalised as a British citizen on 22 October 1931.

In 1938 Freedman moved to Australia as rabbi of the Melbourne Hebrew Congregation at South Yarra, being inducted on 16 August 1938. He also served as the Av Beth Din (head of the Jewish rabbinical court) in Melbourne. In 1947 he was appointed rabbi of the Elwood Talmud Torah Congregation. On accepting a position as rabbi at the Yeshiva Ketana of Bensonhurst at Brooklyn, New York, in 1950, Freedman moved to the United States of America. He taught Jewish philosophy at the Yavneh Seminary and at the Teachers' Institute at Yeshiva University. Returning to Australia in 1956, he became the senior rabbi at the Central Synagogue, Bondi Junction, Sydney. He was invited to serve on the Sydney Beth Din and continued to do so until his retirement in 1965, when he and his wife moved back to Melbourne to be nearer their family.

A world-renowned Hebrew scholar, Freedman translated into English eight of the thirty-four volumes of *The Babylonian Talmud* (1935-48). He also translated *Midrash Rabbah* with Maurice Simon (ten volumes, 1939) and five volumes of Menahem Kasher's *Torah Shelemah* (complete Bible) under the title *Encyclopedia of Biblical Interpretation* (1953-79), and translated and co-edited several of the volumes of the *Encyclopedia Talmudica*. With A. Newton Super he compiled *One Hundred Years: The Story of the Melbourne Hebrew Congregation 1841-1941* (1941). He published commentaries on Genesis, Joshua and Jeremiah in *The Soncino Books of the Bible* and served as a member of the advisory committee for the new English translation of the Bible for the Jewish Publication Society of America. In 2001 his children published posthumously his *Chumash* (five books of Moses) with commentaries, based on the JPS translation.

Rabbi Freedman was an active Zionist when Zionism was still a fringe movement in the Anglo-Jewish world, and a strong supporter of the Mizrachi religious Zionist movement. In addition to helping to establish the department of Semitic studies at the University of Melbourne in 1944, he campaigned for the creation of Mount Scopus Memorial College, a Melbourne Jewish day school, in 1949. He was active in interfaith dialogue in Melbourne. Survived by his wife and their son and two daughters, he died on 4 December 1982 at North Caulfield, Melbourne, and was buried at the Chevra Kadisha cemetery, Springvale.

H. L. and W. D. Rubinstein, *The Jews in Australia* (1991); J. Aron and J. Arndt, *The Enduring Remnant* (1992); M. Jones and I. Lutman, *Orach Chaim* (2000); *Jnl of Procs* (Austn Jewish Hist Soc), vol 9, pt 4, 1982, p 307; *Austn Jewish News*, 10 Dec 1982, p 35; private information.

SUZANNE D. RUTLAND

FREELAND, JOHN MAXWELL (1920-1983), air force officer and professor of architecture, was born on 11 July 1920 at Trevallyn, Launceston, Tasmania, eldest of three sons of Tasmanian-born parents John Douglas Freeland, bank clerk, and his wife Mary Grant, née Waterhouse. In 1922 the family settled at Surrey Hills, Melbourne. After education at Surrey Hills State and Mont Albert Central schools, and at Scotch College, Max worked for the Commonwealth Bank of Australia in Melbourne.

Enlisting in the Royal Australian Air Force on 1 March 1941, Freeland trained as a pilot in Australia and Canada and was commissioned in November. By June 1942 he was serving in No.6 Squadron, Royal Air Force, flying Hurricanes on low-level, tank-destroying operations in North Africa. After four weeks of this hazardous work, only six of the original twenty-four pilots were alive. On 8 April 1943 Freeland made a forced landing behind German lines, took cover from enemy fire in a wadi and walked for eight hours before a scouting British armoured car picked him up. He was awarded the Distinguished Flying Cross. In August he was transferred to No.1 Aircraft Delivery Unit and in November was promoted to flight lieutenant.

On 10 September 1944 Freeland returned to Australia. Fifteen days later, he married with Methodist forms Kathleen Elizabeth Horton, a bank officer, at his parents' home at Essendon. Posted to No.8 Operational Training Unit, Parkes, New South Wales, he spent two weeks on Morotai in June-July 1945. On 1 September he led a fly-past at the celebrations in Melbourne to mark the end of the war. His RAAF appointment was terminated on 21 December. For six months in 1950-51 he served in the Active Citizen Air Force and from June 1952 to April 1953 in the Permanent Air Force.

When in hospital recovering from a bout of malaria, Freeland read by chance some architectural magazines and decided to become an architect. With the help of the Commonwealth Reconstruction Training Scheme he matriculated and entered the school of architecture at the University of Melbourne (B.Arch., 1952; Diploma of Town & Regional Planning, 1957; M.Arch., 1957). In 1954 he was awarded the Australian Planning Institute prize. While he was studying, his jobs ranged from hawking babies' blankets embroidered by his wife to working for the Victorian Railways. After graduation Freeland entered the office of Godfrey & Spowers, Hughes Mewton & Lobb. In March 1955 he joined the firm of Stephenson & Turner and in May a friend asked him to take over his teaching position at Royal Melbourne Technical College. He became a senior lecturer (1955-57) in the school of architecture and building.

Appointed an associate-professor in the school of architecture and building at the New South Wales University of Technology (University of New South Wales) in 1957, Freeland moved his family to Roseville, Sydney. In 1961 he was appointed to the second chair of architecture. As chairman of the faculty he advocated three teaching guidelines: integration of separate strands of the course with design as the amalgam; a measured progression through the course; and a causal philosophy based on the primary need to provide shelter from the elements with the proviso that the interests of art be not neglected. He involved the profession in implementing the guidelines by building up a group of part-time teachers who were practising architects. Determined in the pursuit of his goals, he nevertheless greeted his colleagues with a ready smile.

Freeland was a member of the New South Wales Board of Architectural Education (1957-70) and the Board of Architects of New South Wales (1961-64); chairman (1970-73) of the historic buildings committee of the National Trust of Australia (New South Wales); life fellow (1970) of the Royal Australian Institute of Architects; fellow of the Royal Society of Arts; member of the societies of Architectural Historians of Great Britain, and of the United States of America; foundation vice-chairman (1976) of the Australia branch of the International Council on Monuments and Sites; councillor (1976-80) of the Royal Australian Historical Society; and from 1978 a member of the technical advisory committee of the Australian Heritage Commission. The University of New South Wales conferred on him the degrees of master of architecture (*ad eundem gradum*) in 1971 and doctor of letters for his published work in 1972.

In 1974 on completion of a course of lectures at the Rensselaer Polytechnic Institute at Troy, New York, Freeland, a heavy smoker, suffered a heart attack which necessitated surgery. Awarded a Fulbright travel scholarship in 1977, he lectured at the University of Wisconsin, Milwaukee. After his return to UNSW in 1978 he brought to life and headed a multi-disciplinary graduate school of the built environment. He retired in 1981.

Teaching the history of architecture and expounding its meaning for our time was Freeland's abiding passion. He said that design must be founded on understanding of the past, but without the trammel of precedent. His publications contained the essence of this philosophy: they included *Melbourne Churches, 1836-1851: An Architectural Record* (1963), *The Australian Pub* (1966), *Architecture in Australia: A History* (1968), *Rude Timber Buildings in Australia* (1969, with Philip Cox and Wesley Stacey) and *Architect Extraordinary: The Life and Work of John Horbury Hunt, 1838-1904* (1970). *The Making of a Pro-*

fession: A History of the Growth and Work of the Architectural Institutes in Australia (1971) was written at the request of the Royal Australian Institute of Architects. In 1982 the Australian Broadcasting Commission produced 'Architects of Australia', biographical scripts for radio written by Freeland on John Horbury Hunt, Florence Taylor, William Hardy Wilson and Robin Boyd [qq.v.4,12,13].

Freeland had become a Freemason in 1954, joining the Erskine Murray Lodge at Kew, Melbourne. When a lodge was formed at the University of New South Wales in 1961, he was installed as senior warden. Two years later he became master. He was appointed AM in 1983. Survived by his wife and their two sons and daughter, he died of myocardial infarction on 7 September 1983 at his Roseville home and was cremated after a Presbyterian service.

Architecture Aust, vol 73, no 1, 1984, p 26; *SMH*, 9 Sept 1983, p 6; *Architecture Bulletin*, Nov 1983, p 13; J. M. Freeland, RAAF statement of service (Dept of Defence, Canberra); H. de Berg, interview with J. M. Freeland (ts, 1971, NLA); private information.

PETER REYNOLDS

FREEMAN, ADA ELIZABETH; *see* CORDER

FREEMAN, GEORGE DAVID (1935-1990), criminal, gambler and racing commission agent, was born on 22 January 1935 at Annandale, Sydney, third child of William David Freeman, builders' assistant, and his wife Rita Eileen, née Cook. George had a disturbed and hard upbringing. After his father deserted his young family George's mother—remarried, to a man with a criminal record who died soon after—struggled to bring up her three children in a tiny two-bedroomed slum: 'Food was bread and dripping, chips, treacle, stuff like that'. Expelled from two schools, at 12 he was arrested for stealing and put on two years' probation. Leaving Glebe Junior Technical School at 14 he worked for about two years as a stableboy, frequented poolrooms hustling for money, and drifted into crime.

Convictions for breaking and entering, car stealing and a smash-and-grab raid resulted in a sentence of two years in Mount Penang Training School, Gosford, in 1951. Transferred for continual misbehaviour to the notorious Tamworth Boys' Home, he swallowed soap to make himself sick in the hope of a transfer. When the prison doctor diagnosed his condition as acute appendicitis, he was forced to have an unnecessary operation. To tell the truth would have meant a severe beating from the guards.

'With a new suit, five bob and a train pass to Sydney', Freeman was released in January

1953. Next year he was sentenced for stealing and in Parramatta gaol met his boyhood hero, the prison escapee Darcy Dugan. On release he worked at the State Abattoirs at Homebush, but further gaol terms, usually for petty theft, followed. He married Marcia Bedford, née McDonald, a divorcee, on 5 February 1963 at the registrar general's office, Sydney. In 1968 he served his last gaol term, in Fremantle, Western Australia. With his boyhood friend Stanley ('The Man') Smith, he went on a false passport to visit the United States of America as a guest of an acquaintance, Joe Testa, an alleged member of a crime syndicate interested in infiltrating Australia. When Testa visited Sydney in 1969 and 1971 Freeman renewed his association with him.

For the next twenty years Freeman concentrated on the racing industry, working as a commission agent and illegal off-course betting operator and becoming one of the most talked-about alleged leaders of organised crime in the State during a time of corrupt police and politicians. In June 1971 he was said to have been part of a syndicate that broke the Canberra Totalisator Agency Board jackpot with a win of $500 000. In 1973, examined before the royal commission into organised crime in clubs in New South Wales (chaired by Athol Moffitt), Freeman denied on oath that he was involved. It was alleged that in June 1976 he was part of, or supportive of, the 'Taiping conspiracy'—a plan, hatched in a Chinese restaurant, to bribe politicians in order to gain control of a proposed casino board.

In 1978 Freeman was detained in the USA as an 'excludable person' and named in the New South Wales parliament as an organised-crime figure. That same year he bought a palatial waterfront mansion at Yowie Bay, Port Hacking, protected by high walls, security cameras and guard dogs. In 1979 a police intelligence report on him, tabled in parliament, alleged that he was heavily implicated in illegal off-course betting. On 25 April Freeman was shot in the neck by an unknown assailant, but survived. He was also named as a 'crime boss' in P. M. Woodward's royal commission on drug-trafficking. Divorced in 1977, on 6 August 1981 Freeman married 24-year-old Georgina Catherine McLoughlin, an orthoptist and a former actress and model, at St Stephen's Uniting Church, Sydney.

Accused of murder, assault, fixing horse races (as in the 'Mr Digby' affair), running illegal casinos, bribing police and dealing with American crime figures, Freeman featured in Sir Laurence Street's royal commission into committal proceedings against K. E. Humphreys (1983) and in D. G. Stewart's royal commission into alleged telephone interceptions (1985). But Freeman's only convictions, in 1983 and 1986, were for illegal betting, for which he was fined $500 and $5000 respec-

tively. ('On reflection', a friend remarked, 'the only thing George never got the blame for was the [Newcastle] earthquake'.) Because of his record he and his wife were barred from entering Britain in 1985.

Freeman, 5 ft 8½ ins (174 cm) tall, handsome, white-haired and tattooed, was a smart dresser. Described by a police source as 'hard, smart and charming', he had a certain degree of social acceptability despite his reputation. In 1988, admitting that he had been 'right in the guts of Sydney's underworld, in tough and controversial times', he took the unusual step of publishing *George Freeman: An Autobiography*. An apologia for his life, it relates frankly and movingly his youthful drift into crime, but is somewhat less satisfying on his later life.

In poor health for some years with asthma and kidney disease, and addicted to the painkiller pethidine, Freeman died of asthma in Sutherland Hospital, Caringbah, on 20 March 1990 and was buried in Waverley cemetery. He was survived by his wife, two sons of his first marriage and three sons and a daughter of his second.

D. Hickie, *The Prince and the Premier* (1985); E. Whitton, *Can of Worms II* (1987); B. Bottom, *The Godfather in Australia* (1988); *SMH*, 26 Apr 1979, p 1, 27 Apr 1979, p 1, 20 June 1983, p 3, 25 June 1983, p 4, 27 June 1983, p 3, 27 Aug 1983, p 1, 9 Aug 1985, p 3, 1 Mar 1988, p 5, 21 Mar 1990, p 2, 24 Mar 1990, p 4, 15 Apr 1991, p 3, 3 Aug 1991, p 41; *Bulletin*, 21 June 1983, p 20; *Australian*, 5 Nov 1984, p 3, 21 Mar 1990, p 6, 24-25 Mar 1990, p 5; *Sun-Herald* (Sydney), 4 Aug 1985, p 2, *Age* (Melbourne), 21 Mar 1990, p 1.

G. P. WALSH

FREEMAN, SIR NATHANIEL BERNARD (1896-1982), film distributor, was born on 1 September 1896 in Sydney, third child of Russian parents Adolph Freimann, jeweller, and his wife Malvina, née Marks, and named Nathan Bernard. Educated at Xavier College, Melbourne, Bernard left school at 16 to work for a firm of cider makers, and later became a sales representative for a manufacturer of ladies' clothing. Enlisting in the Australian Imperial Force on 2 February 1916, he sailed for Britain, where he was commissioned in the Australian Flying Corps and promoted to lieutenant. He joined No.3 Squadron in Belgium in December 1918. His AIF appointment terminated in Melbourne in July 1919. In a statutory declaration in November 1919 he declared his name to be Nathaniel Bernard Freeman. He briefly resumed his former occupation as a salesman before travelling to the United States of America with a friend.

Adolph Zukor, head of Paramount Pictures Corporation, engaged Freeman and in 1920 sent him to represent the firm at Albany, New

York, where he obtained a grounding in film publicity, distribution and sales. In 1924 Marcus and Arthur Loew of the newly formed Metro-Goldwyn-Mayer company persuaded Freeman to leave Paramount and become their firm's first managing director for Australia and New Zealand. After his return to Australia in January 1925, he took an office in Sydney, the precursor of offices in all Australian capitals, and employed three staff. In October 1925 Metro-Goldwyn Films Co. mounted its first season, a successful one, with *The White Sister*, starring Lillian Gish and Ronald Colman, at Queanbeyan, New South Wales. Freeman married Marjorie Arabel Bloom on 16 February 1926 at the Great Synagogue, Sydney.

Embarking on an energetic building program, Freeman constructed cinemas to show exclusively Metro-Goldwyn-Mayer (Pty) Ltd products throughout Australia. He ensured that M-G-M theatres maintained high standards of presentation, upkeep and cleanliness, and that house managers, particularly those in suburban and country centres, gave patrons personal attention. Freeman also built in Chalmers Street, Sydney, a three-storey building which housed the firm's national and State headquarters from the end of 1933. Under his direction M-G-M led the local industry from the 1930s to the 1960s, presenting such landmark attractions as *Ben-Hur* (1927), *Gone with the Wind* (1940) and *Dr Zhivago* (1965). With the construction of twin drive-in cinemas at Chullora, Sydney, and Clayton, Melbourne, in the 1950s, his company was among the pioneers of this form of entertainment outside the USA. M-G-M later diversified into indoor bowling alleys.

When Freeman retired on 31 December 1966, M-G-M had about one thousand employees, many having served since the 1930s. Retirement was not entirely his choice but rather the result of overseas-driven company politics; his retention in an honorary capacity did little to assuage his bitterness. He devoted the rest of his life to charitable activities and to his favourite recreation, lawn bowls. A life member of the State branch of the Returned Sailors', Soldiers' and Airmen's Imperial League of Australia from 1945, and of the federal organisation from 1948, he was also chairman of the Anzac House Trust from 1947, the Miss Australia Quest, the New South Wales Committee for World Refugee Year and the United Nations Appeal for Children; president of the Rotary Club of Sydney; a member (1962-69) of the Sydney Opera House Trust and its music and drama panel; chairman (1962-67) of the Universities' International House appeal and a member of the board of management of the International houses of the universities of Sydney and New South Wales; and a life governor (1961) of the Royal New South Wales Institution (Institute) for Deaf and Blind Children and of the Royal Victorian Eye & Ear Hospital. Having been appointed CBE in 1956, he was knighted in 1967.

Freeman was energetic and tough, but fair; he expected loyalty from his employees but was always prepared to accept advice. With drive, acumen and vision he created a major Australian business entity from almost nothing and successfully guided its operations for forty-six years. Although short and stocky, he was in youth a skilful footballer, cricketer and rower. He never lost the common touch. One of his least known but most characteristic activities was to arrange Saturday morning film showings for disadvantaged children. His nickname, 'Sonny', dated from World War I when he signed letters to his family that way. Survived by his wife, and their son and daughter, Sir Bernard died on 26 November 1982 at his Darling Point home. He was Jewish but not Orthodox: his funeral took place at the Chevra Kadisha, Woollahra, and he was buried in the Jewish section of Rookwood cemetery.

Royal Commission on the Moving Picture Industry in Australia, *Minutes of Evidence* (1927); R. Brasch, *Australian Jews of Today* (1977); *A'asian Cinema*, 22 June 1984, p 6; *SMH*, 29 Nov 1982, p 9; B2455, item Nathaniel Freeman (NAA); private information.   JOEL GREENBERG

FREILICH, MEILECH (MAX MELECH) (1893-1986), manufacturer and Zionist, was born on 8 June 1893 at Lesko, Galicia, Austro-Hungarian Empire (Poland), fourth of eight children of Aron Freilich, wholesale grocer, and his wife Jueta (Yetta), née Dym, both from Orthodox Jewish families. Aged 13 he was sent to study with Rabbi Halberstam in eastern Galicia; he was the youngest student, known as an *ilui*, a Talmudic prodigy. His parents presumed that he would become a rabbi, but he returned home and worked in his father's business while secretly beginning secular studies. In 1913 Max moved to Vienna to prepare for his matriculation but next year enlisted in the Austro-Hungarian army, serving on the Russian front. Late in 1917 he received extended leave to complete his matriculation in Vienna. He enrolled in chemistry at the University of Vienna but experienced anti-Semitism and did not graduate. On 5 September 1920 he married Cypora (Sasha) Landau in Vienna.

As a businessman, aware of the depressed Austrian economy, Freilich decided to join a relative in New Zealand and work as a diamond merchant's agent. Arriving with his family in 1926, next year he investigated business prospects in Sydney and subsequently moved his family there. He planned to manufacture cigarette paper but, because of competition, soon resolved instead to produce toilet paper, naming the company Safre Australasian Paper Industry Co.; Safre was an abbreviation of Sasha Freilich. In 1934 he was naturalised. Believing that war was inevitable and that importing would become difficult, Freilich borrowed £100 000 to import bulk paper from Scandinavia. Almost all of it arrived, enabling continued production throughout the war both for Safre and its manufacturing competitor to whom he agreed to supply paper. Freilich's elder son, Theodore, joined Safre after the war. In 1961 they sold the business to Kimberly Clark of Australia Pty Ltd. Max retired in 1963; Theodore left a couple of years later.

From childhood Freilich was committed to the Zionist movement: when only 11 he had made a donation and in 1913 had attended the Eleventh Zionist Congress, in Vienna, as an observer. In 1930 he was elected to the executive of the Union of Sydney Zionists, later introducing two friends, Horace Bohmer Newman [q.v.15] and Norman Schureck. He helped to establish the State Zionist Council of New South Wales in 1939 and served (1942-45, 1948-52) as its president. Commissioner (1937-67) for the State Keren Hayesod (Palestine Foundation Fund, later United Israel Appeal), he published 25 Years of Keren Hayesod (1945). From 1953 to 1958 he was president of the Zionist Federation of Australia and New Zealand. He supported every aspect of Zionism, including the Hebrew University of Jerusalem, Youth Aliyah, and trade through the Australia-Israel Chamber of Commerce and Industry.

The murder of most of Freilich's family in Europe during the Holocaust spurred him on. Through Abram Landa [q.v.] and Sydney Einfeld, he became friendly with H. V. Evatt [q.v.14], minister for external affairs, who played a central role in the partition of Palestine. Freilich also encouraged Peter Fraser, the New Zealand prime minister, to support the United Nations General Assembly Resolution 181 of November 1947.

Freilich believed that Israel and diaspora Jewry were a partnership for Jewish survival. He insisted that the State Zionist Council affiliate with the New South Wales Jewish Board of Deputies, for which he served as chair of its overseas Jewry committee, as honorary treasurer and later as vice-president. In 1966 he was appointed an honorary life member. Freilich worked hard for Jewish education: he chaired the New South Wales Day School Council and the King David School, and became a trustee (1972-86) of, and a major donor to, Moriah College. He was a member of both the Great and Central synagogues. In 1964 a watchtower was established in his honour in Kerem Maharal, a Jewish National Fund project centre in the Carmel, and in 1968 he became the first Australian life member of the World Zionist Organization. He was given the 1973 M. Ashkanasy [q.v.13] award for Australian Jew of the Year and was appointed OBE in 1982.

Five ft 6 ins (168 cm) tall, and of slim build with brown eyes and dark hair, Freilich was diminutive in stature but not personality. A laryngectomy in 1956 did not lessen his commitment. He published his memoirs, Zion in Our Time, in 1968. Survived by his wife and their two sons, he died on 19 October 1986 in his home at Bellevue Hill and was buried in the Jewish section of Rookwood cemetery. The Australian Jewish Times described him as 'an initiator, a doer, a fighter with courage and determination'. Judy Cassab painted two portraits of him: one (1955) is held privately, and the other (1963) is in the United Israel Appeal office, Darlinghurst.

W. D. Rubinstein, The Jews in Australia, vol 2 (1991); G. H. Gordon, Guardians of Zion (1996); S. D. Rutland and S. Caplan, With One Voice (1998); S. D. Rutland, Edge of the Diaspora (2001); Sydney Jewish News, 8 Mar 1968, p 13; Austn Jewish Times, 21 June 1973, p 15, 23 Oct 1986, p 25; Great Synagogue Jnl, Feb 1987, p 7; A659, item 1943/1/2845, A6126, item 79 (NAA); private information and personal knowledge.   SUZANNE D. RUTLAND

FREW, SIR JOHN LEWTAS (1912-1985), physician, was born on 10 September 1912 at Carlton, Melbourne, son of Melbourne born parents Joseph Davidson Frew, master mariner, and his wife Charlotte Lewtas, née Neale. Educated at Camberwell Grammar School and Scotch College, Jock (as he was known) studied medicine at the University of Melbourne (MB, BS, 1935; MD, 1938) and gained Melbourne and Australian university Blues for Rugby. In 1932, as a student, he began a lifetime association with the (Royal) Melbourne Hospital, becoming a resident medical officer (1936), senior resident medical officer (1937) and medical superintendent (1938-41). On 24 July 1940 at Littlejohn [q.v.10] Memorial Chapel, Scotch College, he married Joyce Margaret Euphan Bell, also a medical practitioner.

On 1 March 1941 Frew was appointed a captain in the Australian Army Medical Corps, Australian Imperial Force. He was sent to Malaya with the 2/13th Australian General Hospital. While a prisoner of war (from 1942), he treated soldiers and civilian labourers working on the Burma-Thailand Railway. His own health suffered. Repatriated in 1945, he was transferred to the Reserve of Officers on 5 December.

Establishing a private practice in Melbourne, Frew also resumed work at the RMH. Over coming years he held every post available to him at the hospital: honorary physician to out-patients (1946-57) and in-patients (1958-72), subdean of the clinical school (1947-55) and consultant physician (1972-85). He was also visiting specialist (1948-79) to the Repatriation General Hospital, Heidelberg. With a Red Cross fellowship (1947) he worked on hypertension with Max (Lord) Rosenheim at University College Hospital, London; renal disease was another special interest. But it was as a general physician—'one of the last giants in general medicine' (in Stanley Goulson's words)—that his reputation grew.

A gifted teacher, Frew was a clinical instructor (1948-72) at the University of Melbourne's faculty of medicine; his insistence on high standards was combined with sometimes teasing encouragement in preparing doctors for examination. Through the Colombo Plan and the Royal Australasian College of Physicians (member 1938; fellow 1951), he advised on the development of medicine in India and South-East Asia. Powerful in medical circles, he was a natural leader and an outstanding administrator. He served as a member (1954-79), vice-president (1968-73) and president (1973-79) of the RMH committee of management, as well as chairman (1967) of the hospital's medical staff. For the RACP he was censor (1956-66), censor-in-chief (1966-70), vice-president (1970-72) and president (1972-74). He was a member of the Medical Salaries Committee (1959-62), the Victorian Nursing Council (1963-74), the Australian Hospital Association (1977-79), the Victorian Hospitals Association (1974-79) and the National Health and Medical Research Council's first medical research ethics committee (1982-84); a commissioner (1967-69) of the Commonwealth Serum Laboratories; and chairman of the Australian Drug Evaluation Committee (1982-85) and the Freemasons Hospital board of management (1983-85).

Six ft 2 ins (188 cm) tall, and of distinguished appearance, a heavy smoker and an indefatigable worker, Frew could be difficult or charming, with an impish sense of humour. Appointed OBE in 1976 and knighted in 1980, he was a fellow (1960) of the Royal College of Physicians, London, and an honorary fellow of the Academy of Medicine of Singapore, the Australian Medical Association and the American College of Physicians. Increasingly, he regretted the loss of collegiality that accompanied specialisation in medicine, and in 1980 described himself as 'one of the last relics of the old honorary system'. Away from work, he had a passion for watching cricket. Sir John died suddenly on 8 May 1985 at Tullamarine Airport and was cremated. His wife and son survived him. The Royal Melbourne Hospital established a scholarship in his name. It holds a portrait of Frew by Paul Fitzgerald, as does the RACP, Sydney.

J. C. Wiseman and R. J. Mulhearn (eds), *Roll of the Royal Australasian College of Physicians*, vol 2, 1976-90 (1994); D. McCaughey, *Tradition and Dissent* (1997); A. Gregory, *The Ever Open Door* (1998); Royal Melbourne Hospital, *Annual Report*, 1984-85, p 37; *Age* (Melbourne), 14 Jan 1960, p 8; 31 Dec 1980, p 15; *MJA*, 11 Nov 1985, p 467; private information.   ALAN GREGORY

FRIEND, DONALD STUART LESLIE (1915-1989), artist and writer, was born on 6 February 1915 at Cremorne, Sydney, second of four children of Sydney-born parents Leslie William Moses, grazier, and his wife Gwendolyn Emily, née Lawson. His maternal grandfather was James R. Lawson [q.v.10]. After a family quarrel in about 1920, Leslie Moses, with his brother Henry and their families, reverted to their mother's maiden name of Friend. Donald attended Tudor House, Moss Vale, Cranbrook School, Sydney, and Sydney Grammar School, studied art with Sydney Long [q.v.10], and learned etching. On leaving school in 1931, he worked on the family property Glendon, near Warialda. With his mother's clandestine support he ran away from home in 1932 and travelled north to Queensland and Torres Strait. When he returned to Sydney in 1934, he attended Antonio Dattilo-Rubbo's [q.v.11 Rubbo] classes.

In 1936 Friend went to London and enrolled at the Westminster School of Art under Mark Gertler and Bernard Meninsky. His drawings were shown in a group (1937) and a one-man (1938) exhibition at R. E. A. Wilson's Gallery. In London Friend was impressed by the paintings of Paul Gauguin, Pablo Picasso, Georges Braque, El Greco and Hieronymus Bosch. Enjoying the African nightclubs, he fell in love with Ladipo, a Nigerian man from Ikerre, and in 1938 travelled to Nigeria, where, next year, he became an adviser to the *Ogoga* (leader) in Ikerre. Friend sought to understand Nigerian life and attempted to make sculpture with the casters' guild, using their methods of 'lost wax' bronze casting.

On his return to Sydney in 1940 Friend mixed with the artists (Sir) Russell Drysdale [q.v.] and (Sir) William Dobell [q.v.14], and exhibited at the Macquarie Galleries and with the Society of Artists, Sydney. Enlisting in the Australian Imperial Force on 29 June 1942 as a gunner, he volunteered to be a guinea pig in experiments carried out in North Queensland in 1943 to test the efficacy of anti-malarial drugs. In March 1945 he was commissioned as a lieutenant and appointed a war artist. From May to September he served on Morotai and in Borneo. Back in Australia, he relinquished his appointment in March 1946. Many dramatic works—including evocative depictions of the Japanese dead—resulted from his official commission. His war diaries were published as *Gunner's Diary* (1943) and *Painter's Journal* (1946). He had painted his first important works in Brisbane—dark, powerful images of human figures in the landscape.

In 1946 Friend moved into Merioola, a boarding house at Woollahra that was a Bohemian enclave. When he tired of that life he visited North Queensland and western New South Wales. In 1947 he purchased a wattle and daub miner's cottage at Hill End, in which he lived with Donald Murray. Friend produced many images of Hill End and wrote a social history, *Hillendiana* (1956).

Ever restless, from 1949 Friend moved between Italy, Greece and England. In 1951 he was awarded the Flotta Lauro travelling art prize for his mural design *Australiana*. In Italy he met Attilio Guarracino, who became an enduring friend. Impressed by the Italian masters, Friend created a number of works in the Byzantine manner based on the icons that he collected. On his return to Australia in 1953 he painted at Hill End, in North Queensland, and at Drysdale's studio in Sydney, with an occasional visit to Melbourne; he was often running away from unhappy love affairs.

In 1955 Friend won the Blake prize for religious art with 'St John the Divine and Scenes from the Apocalypse'. From 1957 to 1962 he lived in Ceylon (Sri Lanka), and between 1967 and 1979 in Bali, Indonesia, where he became known for a luxurious life in his house at Batujimbar, Sanur, surrounded by his collection of Balinese bronzes, carvings and porcelain. There he lived like a feudal lord, attended by houseboys and gardeners, and entertained by his own gamelan orchestra. He wrote *Donald Friend in Bali* (1972); a picaresque novel, *Save Me from the Shark* (1973); a celebration of Balinese life and culture, *The Cosmic Turtle* (1976); and an account of factual and fictional birds of Indonesia, *Birds from the Magic Mountain* (1977). An English film crew made a documentary, *Tamu (The Guest)* (1972), about him.

Suffering health problems and difficulties with Balinese authorities, in 1979 Friend returned to Australia, living first in Melbourne with Attilio and Ailsa Guarracino and from 1981 in Sydney. He published *Coogan's Gully* (1979), *Bumbooziana* (1979), *The Farce of Sodom* (1980), *An Alphabet of Owls Et Cetera* (1981) and *Songs of the Vagabond Scholars* (1982). His last book, *Art in a Classless Society & Viceversa* (1985), was a satire of the Australian art world. In 1987 he suffered the first of several strokes. Previously left handed, he taught himself to paint with his right hand.

Friend's drawings have a decorative, flowing quality, with a remarkable facility of line. His figure drawings reveal a sensuality that reflects his attraction to young men. The humorous vein in his work had a serious purpose, in the tradition of English illustrators such as William Hogarth and Thomas Rowlandson, and Shakespearean clowns. He made appealing drawings in Bali—exotic watercolours with oriental patterns and motifs—but many lacked the perception and vigour of his European and Australian work. Following his return from Bali he concentrated on still lifes, interiors and window views, in which he used sumptuous colour and dramatic compositions.

Despite his strong sense of self, Friend experienced considerable inner doubt. At 16 he had believed that he was 'blessed with a genius for art and a talent for writing'. Coming from a privileged background he endorsed upper-middle-class values, yet he delighted in a creative rebelliousness. His assertive presence gave the impression of arrogance. A good conversationalist, he enjoyed playing practical jokes—in his life and art. Although he was noted for his biting wit and prickly nature, he also had qualities that enabled him to make strong friendships. He was flamboyantly homosexual but an affair in London in 1938, with the mistress of his dealer R. E. A. Wilson, had resulted in the birth of a daughter.

Friend painted many self-portraits including 'Donald Friend Starring in "Hamlet the Broken Hearted Clown"' (1966, National Gallery of Australia), in which he showed himself with many heads, like Cerberus, and cast himself as Hamlet, the thinker, who feigned madness. Drysdale twice (1943 and 1948) painted Friend's portrait: the former is held privately, the latter by the Art Gallery of New South Wales. The University of Sydney Union awarded Friend a university medal for his art in 1988. He died on 17 August 1989 in his home at Woollahra and was cremated. A retrospective exhibition was held at the Art Gallery of New South Wales in 1990. The National Library of Australia has published his diaries.

R. Hughes, *Donald Friend* (1965); G. and C. Fry, *Donald Friend: Australian War Artist 1945* (1982); B. Pearce, *Donald Friend 1915-1989* (1990); L. Klepac (ed), *The Genius of Donald Friend* (2000); *The Diaries of Donald Friend*, vol 1, A. Gray ed. (2001), vols 2 and 3, P. Hetherington ed. (2003, 2005); B883, item NX96987 (NAA).

ANNE GRAY

FRITH, HAROLD JAMES (1921-1982), wildlife biologist and conservationist, was born on 16 April 1921 at Kyogle, New South Wales, younger son of Richard Frith, butcher, and his wife Elizabeth, née Marshall, both born in New South Wales. Harry was a keen pigeon-shooter from the age of 8 and an excellent naturalist. Educated at Lismore High School and Scots College, Sydney, he proceeded to the University of Sydney (B.Sc.Agr., 1941; D.Sc.Agr., 1964). Despite strong results, he enlisted in the Australian Imperial Force on 5 September 1941 instead of completing the honours course.

Arriving in the Middle East in November, Frith was allotted to the 2/6th Field Regiment in January 1942. Back in Australia in March, he sailed for Papua in September and was posted to the 2/1st Tank-Attack Regiment in December. He took part in the Buna campaign and became interested in the rich wildlife of the area. Promoted to sergeant in April 1943, he returned to Australia in October. On 20 November at St Philip's Church of England, Sydney, he married Dorothy Marion Francis Killeen, a research assistant. Commissioned as a lieutenant in September 1944, he was made inspector, food supplies, at Land Headquarters, Melbourne. His AIF appointment terminated on 19 October 1945.

Frith and his wife moved to Griffith, New South Wales, where his first job was as assistant works manager and technologist at Griffith Cannery Pty Ltd. In 1946 he joined the nearby irrigation research station of the Council for Scientific and Industrial Research (Commonwealth Scientific and Industrial Research Organization from 1949). Under the guidance of Eric West, his first projects concerned the cultivation of citrus trees. Experiments in frost protection using wind fans were the subject of many early publications, but he found himself increasingly drawn to the zebra finches nesting in the trees, rather than to horticultural experimentation. In 1951 the officer-in-charge of the wildlife survey section of CSIRO, Francis Ratcliffe [q.v.16], sought Frith's help with monitoring the spread of the newly released myxoma virus among rabbit populations. Frith seized the opportunity to make wildlife biology the centre of his research, transferring formally to the section in July 1952.

Fascinated by birds, Frith studied their ecology and behaviour, both at work and after hours. His 'unofficial' work on the mallee-fowl, *Leipoa ocellata*, which incubates its eggs by controlling the temperature of its mound, attracted international attention. As well as nine scientific papers on the species, he wrote an important popular book, *The Mallee-Fowl* (1962), which suggested guidelines for its conservation. His 'official' work built on his long interest in wild ducks and geese. In 1955 the CSIRO asked him to go to the Northern Territory to establish a scientific project on the magpie goose, perceived by the nascent rice-growing industry as vermin. He followed the geese well beyond the experimental rice-farming areas and became familiar with the monsoonal swamps ranging from 'Goose camp', near the Alligator rivers, to the southern Daly River.

Frith found himself increasingly responsible for overseeing the scientific work of others. His leadership style drew on practical 'bush ecology'—getting things done despite obstacles. A naturalist by inclination, he liked to work closely with animals in the wild. His down-to-earth qualities endeared him to 'people in the out-country', but sometimes alienated leading theoreticians. His biological theory was largely self-taught, learned as required. He naturally linked 'basic' and 'applied' science, and was intolerant of well-educated 'fools' who could not make necessary practical connections.

Best known as a bird specialist, Frith was interested in other animals too. He expanded the Australian Bird-Banding Scheme to include bats. In 1959 he started a major project on the ecology of the red kangaroo, which required an understanding of embryology and endocrinology. According to the Harvard biologist Ernst Mayr, Frith 'acquired the necessary know-how without hesitation'. He co-authored *Kangaroos* (1969) with John Calaby.

In 1956 Frith had moved with his family to Yarralumla, Canberra. By April 1961, when he was appointed Ratcliffe's successor, he had spent 'significant periods in all ecological regions' of the continent and also in New Guinea. In 1962 the wildlife section became a division of CSIRO, with Frith as its chief. From major centres in Canberra, Perth and Darwin, his division reviewed and planned many national strategies for conservation, always beginning by understanding the ecology of the animals concerned. Numerous small remote stations were established to pursue particular projects, especially in northern Australia. Under Frith's guidance, conservation concerns moved beyond reserves to include production landscapes: 'many important species can be adequately conserved only on sheep stations, irrigation areas and in wheatfields'. He also opened discussion with water conservation engineers, recognising the links between irrigation, salinity and land degradation, and the plight of wild ducks. In 1965 he declared unfashionably: 'we must ensure flooding of the rivers—even if this does damage the nation's economy'.

Frith was proud of his success, in monsoonal Australia, in having the Kakadu area (which included his beloved 'Goose camp') declared a national park. The rich birdlife continued to enthuse him throughout the 1960s and 1970s, and he managed, despite his commitments as a manager, to undertake parts of the fauna surveys critical to its status as a World Heritage listed area.

A driven leader, Frith felt competitive with Ratcliffe. But CSIRO's executive appreciated his 'rough diamond' style, and valued his practical management skills and excellent publications. His fluent writing style translated easily to a general audience and his natural history books included *Waterfowl in Australia* (1967), *Birds in the Australian High Country* (edited in 1969), *Conservation* (co-edited in 1971 with Alec Costin) and *Wildlife Conservation* (1973). In 1976 he edited the first *Reader's Digest Complete Book of Australian Birds*, writing the accounts of fifty-six species himself. Elected a fellow of the Australian Academy of Science (1975) and the Australian Academy of Technological Sciences (1976), he was a fellow of the ornithological unions of Australasia, Britain, Germany, France and the United States of America. In 1979 and 1982 he was awarded the (G. P.) Whitley [q.v.16] medal by the Royal Zoological Society of New South Wales. He was appointed AO in 1980.

In 1974 Frith persuaded the International Ornithological Congress to come south of the Equator for the first time since its establishment in 1884. Despite logistical difficulties, he organised in Canberra an exemplary meeting that greatly excited the distinguished visitors. He refused to admit to the personal discomfort he felt throughout the year leading up to the congress, following a serious motorcar accident. A second blow struck him four months later, when Cyclone Tracy flattened the homes of the scientists he had located in Darwin. He became increasingly depressed about the division and retreated to his own work, focusing on the aviary of pigeons he had built adjoining his office at Gungahlin. His failing health led him to announce that he would retire on his sixtieth birthday. He purchased land near his boyhood home, where he started to re-create a piece of rainforest. His last year at CSIRO was anxious, and he suffered a heart attack. Survived by his wife, and their two daughters and son, he died of another myocardial infarction on 28 June 1982 at Lismore and was buried in the local lawn cemetery.

CSIRO Division of Wildlife Research, *Report*, 1962-82; *Hist Records of Austn Science*, vol 10, no 3, 1995, p 247, and for publications; L. Robin, 'International Ornithology Comes to Australia', *Hist Records of Austn Science*, vol 13, no 3, 2001, p 233; *Canberra Times*, 30 Apr 1966, p 2, 26 Jan 1980, p 11, 1 July 1982, p 9; *CoResearch*, Aug 1982, p 2; A8520, item PH/FRI/1, A9697, items C2/25 and C2/25B, K1348 (NAA); International Ornithological Congress papers (AAS 1225, Basser Lib, and MS 11437, Box 19A, SLV).   LIBBY ROBIN

FURLEY, MABEL EILEEN (1900-1985), Liberal politician, was born on 13 March 1900 at Mosman, Sydney, only child of Frederick John Griffith Llewelyn, a Victorian-born accountant, and his wife Alice, née Thompson, of Sydney. Educated at St Hilda's Grammar School, Mosman, and St Scholastica's College, Glebe Point, Eileen worked as a secretary for an engineering firm and then as a private secretary to a structural engineer. On 14 February 1931 she married Norman William Furley, a salesman, at St Andrew's Church of England, Roseville. Remaining childless, she threw herself into charitable and civic works. She was officer-in-charge (1942-45) of sugar rationing in New South Wales; secretary of the Council for Women in War Work; a member of the National Council of Women and of the Food for Britain Fund; and superintendent of the Mosman National Emergency Services.

In 1943 Eileen Furley became a member of the Liberal Democratic Party of Australia, which its creator, (Sir) Ernest White [q.v.], hoped would form the nucleus of a new non-Labor party. In 1945 she left the quarrelsome White to devote herself to the new Liberal Party of Australia. She served on the State executive, chaired the women's group of the party's New South Wales division and the federal women's committee, and was a State delegate to the federal council and a State vice-president. In 1949, elected female vice-president of the federal organisation, she wondered why the Liberals did not advertise the fact that no position in the party was beyond a woman's reach. A zealot for female participation and advancement, Furley none the less opposed what she called 'a certain militantly feminist section of women' who wanted complete autonomy within the Liberal Party and who were taking up separatist causes.

Furley was appointed OBE in 1954 for her contributions to social welfare. Active in the New Settlers' League of New South Wales and the Good Neighbour Council of New South Wales, in 1956 she assumed the chairmanship (which she retained for two decades) of the Migrant Advisory Council. The Liberals in New South Wales formed the council to enable the delegates of twenty-seven national groups to bring their concerns to the attention of government departments, and to establish direct contact between Liberal parliamentarians and migrant communities. An additional objective was to counter Labor's perceived advantage of contacts with migrants through the workplace.

After several attempts to win Liberal Party endorsement Furley surprisingly defeated Senator J. A. McCallum for third place on the coalition's ticket for the 1961 Senate election. She was the first woman from New South Wales to gain Liberal selection for the Senate but the post-credit-squeeze swing against the Menzies [q.v.15] government rendered the third spot unwinnable. Next year she won the Liberal Party's nomination to fill a casual vacancy in the New South Wales Legislative Council. Her presence, as the first Liberal woman to sit in the council chamber, was initially resented by her Upper House colleagues, who felt that the Liberals in the Legislative Assembly, embarrassed by the paucity of female representation, had foisted her upon them. Re-elected in 1964, she retained the seat until retiring voluntarily in 1976.

Later described by a former clerk of the Legislative Council as 'a lady from an earlier generation', Furley, who made many of her own clothes, was always well groomed in public. She looked like the conservative she had become. Having initially opposed a complete ban on the Communist Party of Australia in 1948, Furley chaired in the early 1960s the State division's committee of headstrong anti-communists who wanted to expose the New South Wales Teachers' Federation. She was also an active patron of the anti-Soviet Captive Nations Council of New South Wales.

Her principal crusades, however, were moral. Long concerned about 'the deterioration of the morals and behaviour of young people', Furley chaired in 1968-69 a Legislative Council select committee that inquired into violent sex crimes in the State. The committee's report reflected her view that instability in the home underlay many of society's moral evils and her belief that sex education in schools should be integrated 'into the training of the whole personality'. Although the report was generally applauded the *Sydney Morning Herald* rightly argued that 'Mrs Furley's mop' could not halt the rise of the permissive society.

Furley served on several bodies outside politics: the convocation of Macquarie University, the Children's Film and Television Council, the Australian Council of Social Service and the Mothers' Union of the Church of England. Predeceased (1966) by her husband, Eileen Furley died on 20 September 1985 at Mosman and was cremated. The grandfather clock that she donated stands in the Legislative Council vestibule. Within the Liberal Party, where one of her greatest contributions was to press for the promotion of women in the face of female apathy and male resistance, she is hardly remembered at all.

Austn Liberal, Aug 1960, p 4; *SMH*, 9 Aug 1969, p 2; *Daily Telegraph* (Sydney), 14 Nov 1969, p 18; Furley papers (Soc of Austn Genealogists, Sydney); Liberal Party of Aust (Federal) records (NLA); Liberal Party of Aust (NSW) records (SLNSW); private information.   I. R. HANCOCK

FYFE, WALLACE VERNON (1894-1982), surveyor-general, was born on 7 April 1894 in South Melbourne, second of four children of Victorian-born parents Alexander Parker Fyfe, clerk, and his wife Marion, née Howard. In 1897 Vernon moved with his family to Western Australia, first to Coolgardie, then in 1900 to Kalgoorlie, and later to Nannup in the south-west, where he completed his schooling. At 14 he started work in a local store. In 1909 he joined a party surveying a timber-mill railway line and next year was apprenticed to the surveyor Marmaduke Terry, studying for his preliminary examinations by correspondence.

On 18 July 1916 Fyfe enlisted in the Australian Imperial Force. He attended the Engineer Officers' Training School, Roseville, Sydney. At St Mary's Church of England, Busselton, Western Australia, on 19 December 1917 he married Venetia Thompson (d.1977). He sailed for Britain in May 1918, served briefly in France after the Armistice and completed a course at the AIF Survey School, Southampton, England, before being discharged in Perth on 5 September 1919. On 21 October he was registered as a licensed surveyor. Following a brief period of contract surveying in the agricultural districts, in 1921 he joined the Commonwealth Department of the Treasury as a junior land valuer in the Commonwealth-State taxation branch, Perth. In 1926 he was promoted to senior valuer. He studied accountancy, becoming an associate in 1934 and later a fellow of the Commonwealth Institute of Accountants.

In 1938 Fyfe transferred briefly to the Treasury, Canberra, as secretary of the new national insurance branch. Appointed surveyor-general of Western Australia on 24 October, he returned to Perth. In 1940, as royal commissioner, he investigated the financial and economic position of the pastoral industry in the leasehold areas of the State. He conducted an Australia-wide survey of land laws, tenures and valuation systems for the Commonwealth Rural Reconstruction Commission in 1944, and updated it with a supplementary report in 1948.

Fyfe had become director of land settlement in Western Australia in 1945. His administration of the War Service Land Settlement Scheme was criticised by a 1948 committee of inquiry; he was removed from his post but was immediately reappointed surveyor-general. Over the next eleven years he encouraged the development of aerial mapping and geodetic surveying, and oversaw a comprehensive survey of the northern Kimberley area and an assessment of land potential in the low-rainfall lands to the south-east. Meticulous and practical, he earned a reputation for completing tasks on time. His staff found him approachable; he often greeted new surveying cadets with an outstretched hand, saying, 'My name's Fyfe—what's yours?' He joined in staff socials, nursing a soft drink as he was a lifelong teetotaller.

During the course of his career, Fyfe was chairman of numerous State bodies including the Select Committee of Advice on Manpower (1939-45); Soil Conservation Committee (1939-45); Land Purchase Board (1938-48); Land Settlement Board (1948-56); and Pastoral

Industry Debt Adjustment Committee (1941-48). Active in the Institution of Surveyors, Australia, Western Australian Division (fellow 1932; life fellow 1975), he served as president in 1935-38 and helped to establish a memorial to the explorer A. W. Canning [q.v.7]. He was a founding board-member (1931) and president (1937-38) of the Western Australian division of the Commonwealth Institute of Valuers. State representative on the National Mapping Council (1945-46, 1948-59), in 1951 he became the first patron of the newly formed Australian Institute of Cartographers (Western Australia).

Fyfe retired on 7 April 1959. Next day his successor commissioned him to conduct a topographical survey and classification of a vast area of country between the Trans-Australian railway and the coast from Balladonia to the South Australian border. He then established himself in a surveying practice. His services to the surveying profession were recognised in 1969 with the naming of Fyfe Hills in Antarctica. Within the community Fyfe held responsibilities in many organisations. He was chairman (1961-66) of the Metropolitan Valuation Appeal Court; a director (1961-73) of the Perth real estate firm Peet & Co. Ltd; president (1967-69) of the Royal Automobile Club of Western Australia; chairman (1972-74) of RAC Insurance Pty Ltd; a State vice-president (1969-70) of the Girl Guides Association of Western Australia; consultant surveyor to the Western Australian Trotting Association; patron (1974-77) of the Trigg Island Surf Life Saving Club; and chairman of the King's Park Honour Avenue maintenance committee.

Five ft 11 ins (180 cm) tall, with a ramrod-straight back, Fyfe had a commanding stature, a pronounced jaw and an unflinching gaze. He had been a keen rower and, in the 1920s, club champion, captain and president of the Mount Lawley Tennis Club. Forthright, loyal and trustworthy, Fyfe rarely displayed any emotion either in his professional life or at home. He had a remarkable memory for names and details but never voiced an opinion on politics. Survived by his two daughters, he died on 17 January 1982 at Nedlands and was cremated. His unpublished memoir, 'Reminiscences of a Surveyor', edited by Christopher Fyfe, is held by the State Library of Western Australia.

Road Patrol, June 1974, p 19; *West Australian*, 23 Jan 1982, p 33; *Eyepiece*, Apr 1982, p 1; *Austn Surveyor*, Dec 1982, p 284; C. Jeffery, interview with W. V. Fyfe (ts, 1978-79, SLWA); Fyfe papers (SLWA); private information.   CHRISTOPHER FYFE

G

GADEN, JOHN ROBERT (1938-1990), Anglican priest and theologian, was born on 3 June 1938 at Leicester, England, the son of Stanley Simeon Victor Gaden, Church Army captain, and his wife Frances Hughes, née Mullins. The family migrated to Australia after World War II and John was educated on a scholarship at Geelong Church of England Grammar School before studying classics at the University of Melbourne (BA Hons, 1961; MA, 1964). An active member of the Australian Student Christian Movement, he was also profoundly influenced by Dr Barry Marshall [q.v.15], chaplain at Trinity College. Appointed a tutor (1962) in classics at the university and at Trinity, Gaden commenced studies at the Australian College of Theology (Th.L. Hons, 1964; Th.Schol., 1966). On 8 December 1962 at Trinity College chapel he married Janet Eade Agar, also a university teacher.

Made deacon (1963) and ordained priest (1964) in the Church of England, Gaden served in the parish of Mudgee, New South Wales (1965-68), until winning a Mercer scholarship to the General Theological Seminary, New York (Th.D., 1972). He returned to Melbourne and served as assistant-chaplain at Melbourne Church of England Grammar School (1972-73), chaplain at Monash University (1974-76), and chaplain also to the national church's commission on doctrine (1973-89), for which he was a highly influential secretary (1975-89). In 1977 he became director of theological studies at Trinity College and consultant theologian to the archbishop of Melbourne.

An 'innovative and courageous' theologian (as Archbishop Keith Rayner later recalled), Gaden first gained public prominence in 1976 for leading the campaign for the ordination of women as priests. In 1981-84 he was president of the Australian and New Zealand Association of Theological Schools, and in 1982-90 a member of the International Anglican/Orthodox Joint Doctrinal Discussions. Anglo-Catholic in sympathies and lucid in conveying complex issues, Gaden encouraged free, theologically informed debate. He was criticised for his refusal to have his children baptised as infants, for referring to the Holy Spirit as 'she' in a 1985 sermon, and for challenging the church's negative attitude to sexuality.

After years of intense work in Melbourne, in 1986 Gaden was appointed warden of St Barnabas' Theological College, Adelaide. Controversy followed him: the failure of the 1987 Anglican General Synod to permit the ordination of women prompted him to renounce his priestly duties for more than a year. Bearded and nuggety in later life, Gaden could defuse confrontation with his infectious laugh. If not well published as an academic, he produced many reports and addresses that provoked wide-ranging debate in church and society. Some of his theological papers were gathered in D. Reid (ed), *A Vision of Wholeness* (1994). His most lasting influence was personal, and exercised through hospitality and conversation, whether as teacher, preacher, mentor or friend.

On 27 January 1990 John Gaden died suddenly of coronary artery disease while on study leave at St Paul's College, Camperdown, Sydney. He was survived by his wife, a theologian and leader of the Movement for the Ordination of Women, who had been made deacon in 1988 (ordained priest, 1992), and by their three sons and their adopted daughter. Only two weeks before his death Gaden had been interviewed as a potential archbishop of Melbourne. He was cremated and his ashes were buried in the grounds of Trinity College.

M. Porter, *Women in the Church* (1989); K. Rayner, 'Foreword' in D. Reid (ed), *A Vision of Wholeness* (1994); *Age* (Melbourne), 8 Aug 1978, p 12; *Advertiser* (Adelaide), 9 Oct 1987, p 1; *See* (Melbourne), Mar 1990, p 16; *Corian*, June 1991, p 106.

PETER SHERLOCK

GAINFORT, RUBINA HOPE (1890-1985), headmistress, was born on 7 April 1890 at Clifton Hill, Melbourne, second daughter of Dublin-born Edward Gainfort, gentleman, and his Victorian-born second wife Sarah, née Cordy. Following her father's death (1901), Rubina, her sister, Winifred, and their mother became a tight-knit family. Both sisters began their education at Clifton Hill (Gold Street) State School; in 1905 Rubina enrolled in the newly established Melbourne Continuation School, and in 1909 entered the Melbourne Teachers' College. She showed particular flair in mathematics, and—after gaining her trained teacher's certificate (1912)—combined full-time work with further academic studies at the University of Melbourne (BA, Dip.Ed., 1950). In her first year she taught at Goorambat, Merino, Ferntree Gully, Toolern Vale and Chilwell.

Noted as an earnest and methodical teacher, Miss Gainfort found placements in higher elementary and secondary schools in country districts. She became a temporary assistant at Kyabram (1912), third mistress at Echuca (1914) and second mistress at Bairnsdale (1918). An effective organiser, capable of exerting 'a good influence', in 1921 Gainfort became senior mistress at Shepparton High School. Keen to return to her mother and sister, then living at Northcote, Melbourne, she transferred to Williamstown (1926) and then Geelong (1928) High schools. In 1929 she was appointed assistant-in-charge at her alma mater, by that time Melbourne Girls' High School, which soon left dilapidated premises to occupy the vacant Government House until an endowment from Sir Macpherson Robertson [q.v.11] enabled the building of the renamed MacRoberston Girls' High School (1934). Gainfort flourished through these transitions. Ennis Honey, a student of those years, recalled her as 'assured and dignified': a passionate teacher of mathematics, direct in manner, dry in humour, but often kind in gesture.

In 1940-41 Gainfort taught at University High School before being appointed acting principal of the Emily McPherson College of Domestic Economy. There, amid wartime strain, she brought a sympathetic approach to staff and students and became a forceful advocate for the professional training offered by the college. In 1946 she returned to MacRobertson as vice-principal, and in 1949 succeeded Mary Hutton [q.v.14] as principal. An excellent role model for adolescent girls, Gainfort increasingly welcomed the 'more friendly attitude between teacher and pupil' that had developed over the years of her teaching, the greater use of scientific equipment, the fuller participation of students in class, and the shaping of a curriculum that better reflected their future lives. She was reputed to have known all seven hundred by name.

'A quiet but strong personality', as her Department of Education records noted, Gainfort was proud of the academic standing achieved by MacRobertson, and of her long association with the school. Over twenty-three years, as student, teacher and principal, she wielded a great influence. After retirement in 1955, she maintained an active involvement through the ex-student Palladian Association. She enjoyed contract bridge, gardening and motoring, and drew much support from her sister, with whom she lived until Win's death in 1968. Rubina Gainfort (Ruby to her friends) died on 22 November 1985 at Camberwell and was cremated.

J. Docherty, *The Emily Mac* (1981); E. Honey, *Nymphs and Goddesses* (1994); *Herald* (Melbourne), 26 Mar 1955, p 29; MacRobertson Girls' High School Archives; private information and personal knowledge.
                                      SUSAN SHERSON
                                      PAULINE F. PARKER

GAIRDNER, SIR CHARLES HENRY (1898-1983), governor, was born on 20 March 1898 in Batavia, Netherlands East Indies (Jakarta, Indonesia), son of Charles Arthur Gairdner, an Anglo-Irish merchant, and his wife Johanna Theodora, née Bergsma. Brought up in County Galway, Ireland, Charles junior received his secondary education at Repton, Derbyshire, England, where he was once thrashed by the headmaster and future archbishop of Canterbury William Temple for submitting a poem by Henry Longfellow as his own composition. Graduating from the Royal Military Academy at Woolwich in World War I, he was commissioned in the artillery in May 1916 and sent to the Western Front. He sustained a serious wound to his right leg that was to cause him pain through most of his life and necessitate twenty-seven operations.

After the war Gairdner transferred to the cavalry. A versatile sportsman, he played tennis, hockey, polo and golf. On 19 May 1925 at the parish church, Wimbledon, Surrey, he married the Honourable Evelyn Constance Handcock, daughter of the 5th Baron Castlemaine. He attended the Staff College, Camberley, and by 1937 was a lieutenant colonel, commanding the 10th Royal Hussars. In World War II he won rapid promotion in a succession of staff posts and two brief commands of armoured divisions in the Middle East, North Africa and India. Appointed chief of staff of Force 141 in Algiers in 1943, he was, in the opinion of the historian Carlo D'Este, 'woefully ill-equipped' for the role and sought release from it within a few months. His next employment, as director of armoured fighting vehicles in India, was safer but less glamorous.

In March 1945 Gairdner was promoted to acting (later substantive) lieutenant general and sent to the headquarters of General Douglas MacArthur [q.v.15] as Prime Minister (Sir) Winston Churchill's personal representative. Following the Japanese surrender he was Prime Minister Clement (Earl) Attlee's representative in Tokyo, in which role he clashed with the commander of the British Commonwealth Occupation Force, (Sir) Horace Robertson [q.v.16], over their personal status and the relative priorities of British and broader Commonwealth interests. Recalled in 1948, Gairdner retired from the army next year. He had been appointed CBE (1941), CB (1946) and KCMG (1948), awarded the American Medal of Freedom and mentioned in despatches. He purchased a property in County Westmeath, Ireland, not far from the Castlemaine seat Moydrum Castle, where he hunted two days a week.

On 6 November 1951 Gairdner succeeded Sir James Mitchell [q.v.10] as governor of Western Australia. He brought with him some ten servants whom he had personally recruited in London for Government House. Very popular with the Western Australian public, he had a lightness of touch in engaging with 'the people', a sound memory for names and faces, a love of sport, and an eagerness to visit the most remote parts of the State. Resolving early in his term that there would be no 'Government House set' in Perth, he invited a range of improbable guests to vice-regal functions. Nevertheless he was capable of aloofness, and his administrative style was regarded as 'austere' by some observers. Not an inspired public speaker, he confessed in retirement that speech-making had been 'absolute purgatory'. His imperialist outlook was quite acceptable to most Western Australians of that era.

The eleven years of Gairdner's tenure were relatively free of political or constitutional crisis although, when the Bunbury by-election of October 1955 deprived A. R. G. Hawke's [q.v.] Labor government of its parliamentary majority, the possibility was raised that the governor might have to exercise his reserve powers. In the event the parliament went into recess and Labor won the ensuing 1956 election. Gairdner was appointed KCVO (1954) and KBE (1960). In 1956 the University of Western Australia conferred on him an honorary D.Litt. The Sir Charles Gairdner Hospital was named in his honour in May 1963. He stepped down from his post on 26 June.

On 23 September Gairdner, having lobbied vigorously for the position, replaced Lord Rowallan [q.v.16] as governor of Tasmania. His five-year term was devoid of drama, but he did not receive the same public acclaim as in Western Australia. He was awarded (1967) an honorary LL D by the University of Tasmania. In January 1969 he was appointed GBE, and in February the Gairdners returned to Perth and settled at Peppermint Grove. Still an active sportsman, he sailed his dragon class yacht *Barbara* on the Swan River. He enjoyed knitting, a pastime he had first taken up while in hospital in World War I. In 1976 his bad leg was amputated. Survived by his wife, Sir Charles died on 22 February 1983 at Nedlands and was cremated after a state funeral. Sir Ivor Hele's portrait of him hangs in Parliament House, Perth.

C. D'Este, *Bitter Victory* (1988); J. Grey, *Australian Brass* (1992); *West Australian*, 26 June 1963, p 7, 27 June 1963, p 2, 23 Feb 1983, pp 1, 54, 24 Feb 1983, p 27; *Sunday Times* (Perth), 16 June 1963, p 30; WA State files, items 1351 and 1392 (SRWA); item GO79/1/61 (TSA); C. Gairdner, The Other Side of the Coin (ts, SLWA).   PETER BOYCE

GALBALLY, JOHN WILLIAM (1910-1990), politician and lawyer, was born on 2 August 1910 at Port Melbourne, the second of nine children of Victorian-born parents William Stanton Galbally, draper's salesman, and his wife Eileen, née Cummins. Educated at St Patrick's College, East Melbourne, and Melbourne High School, Jack won a scholarship to Newman College and supported his studies

at the University of Melbourne (LL B, 1931) by working as a car salesman, shop assistant, primary school teacher and fruit picker. Admitted as a barrister and solicitor on 1 March 1933, he practised in Collingwood, and was later joined by his brother Frank (1922-2005). In 1933 Jack also became a member of the Australian Labor Party; began two seasons playing for Collingwood Football Club, of which he was later a life member (1943) and vice-president (1951-62); and won the Murray Valley tennis championship, which he won again in 1946 and 1947. On 14 October 1937 at Newman College chapel he married Sheila Marie Kenny.

In June 1949 Galbally was elected as member of the Legislative Council for Melbourne North, defeating an Independent, Likely Herman McBrien [q.v.15]. His program included the abolition of the undemocratic Upper House, but he was to say in his farewell speech to the House: 'I had not been here for more than a few weeks when I fell in love with it and I am still in love with it'. He held the seat (under a reformed franchise after 1950) until his retirement in July 1979. He was well acquainted with members of John Wren's [q.v.12] political machine (even if not part of it) and in November 1950 he acted for the Wrens in committal proceedings for criminal libel against Frank Hardy for publishing *Power without Glory*. Galbally's commitment as an independent legislative reformer was soon evident when, in 1951, his private member's bill allowing road accident victims to claim compensation despite contributory negligence was adopted by the McDonald [q.v.15] minority Country Party government.

After John Cain [q.v.13] swept Labor to power in December 1952, Galbally became minister for electrical undertakings (1952-55), for forests (1952-54) and for labour and industry (1954-55). The Victorian ALP split in March 1955 following attacks by the federal leader, H. V. Evatt [q.v.14], on 'disloyal' elements—linked to B. A. Santamaria's Catholic Social Studies Movement and backed by Archbishop Daniel Mannix [q.v.10]—that dominated the State conference and central executive. Like some other practising Catholics in the party, among them Arthur Calwell [q.v.13] and Pat Kennelly [q.v.], Galbally was deeply troubled by this division, but remained a supporter of Cain and the pro-Evatt position. In April the breakaway members defeated the premier in a no-confidence motion; in May the government was overwhelmingly beaten at the polls.

Galbally then became leader of the Opposition in the Legislative Council, a position that he retained until 1979 apart from two months in 1970 when he was suspended from party and caucus membership for supporting the federal ALP's policy on state aid for independent schools. Through these years he introduced forty-one private members' bills. They covered causes including equal pay, prohibiting corporal punishment in prisons, decriminalising vagrancy, preventing cruelty to animals and preserving natural reserves. His bill to ban live trap bird shooting—a favoured sport of the premier, (Sir) Henry Bolte [q.v.]—was carried in 1958.

Chief among Galbally's concerns was the abolition of capital punishment. He introduced his bill on this matter on fifteen occasions between 1956 and 1974. While always defeated on party lines, the bill provoked extended debates. In 1975, when Rupert Hamer, the Liberal premier, successfully moved to abolish the death penalty, Galbally seemed aggrieved that his own bill had not been adopted: his second reading speech was short and grudging.

Galbally revived the role of council committees, initiating inquiries into proposed development in the Royal Botanic Gardens (1968-69) and settlement in the Little Desert (1969-70). Concerned at the increasing power of central government, in September 1969 he moved a motion calling for a constitutional convention that was adopted by the Victorian Parliament and accepted in principle by all governments; he was a delegate to the first Australian Constitutional Convention, which met in September 1973. He also served on the councils of the University of Melbourne (1954-55) and La Trobe University (1965-76). Having signed the roll of counsel on 2 February 1959, he took silk in 1968. In 1979 he was appointed CBE.

A passionate debater, disciplined, witty and widely read, often drawing on classical and biblical allusions, Galbally exerted great influence over the Victorian parliament. He remained vigorous, jogging and playing golf until increasingly afflicted with Alzheimer's disease. Predeceased by his wife (1977), Jack Galbally died on 8 July 1990 at Camberwell and was buried in Melbourne general cemetery with his well-worn copy of the *Complete Works of William Shakespeare*. His two sons and three daughters survived him: Peter was appointed QC in 1989 and Ann became an art historian.

PD (LC, Vic), 28 Aug 1990, p 1; *Herald* (Melbourne), 19 Apr 1979, p 7; *Age* (Melbourne), 28 July 1979, p 21, 17 July 1990, p 13; personal knowledge.
BARRY O. JONES

GALBRAITH, JAMES BIGGAM DOUGLAS (1894-1984), physician, was born on 11 July 1894 at Liverpool, England, son of Andrew Biggam Galbraith, marine engineer, and his wife Grace, née McWilliam. Douglas was educated at Stranraer High School in south-west Scotland and at the University of Glasgow (MB, Ch.B., 1917; MD, 1923). In 1915 he was a surgeon probationer in the Royal Navy Volunteer Reserve, serving in destroyers. Joining the Royal Army Medical Corps in 1917, he was posted to Mesopotamia and Kurdistan before being demobilised in 1920 as a captain. He then worked in Glasgow hospitals until migrating to Australia in 1923.

Establishing a private practice in Melbourne, Galbraith, as honorary physician to out-patients (1925-35), began an enduring relationship with the (Royal) Children's Hospital. On 22 March 1926 at Scots Church, he married Esther Struthers Marshall. After convalescing from pulmonary tuberculosis, he was appointed medical superintendent (1935-40) of the Frankston orthopaedic section of the hospital, where he introduced Australia's first comprehensive regime of paediatric rehabilitation. He developed a cohesive plan that treated the children in the context of family and community, emphasised their social and psychological adjustment, and identified the social, educational and vocational services essential to their integration into society. In 1935 he was a foundation council member (vice-president 1937-67; honorary member and patron from 1967) of the Victorian Society for Crippled Children (Yooralla Society of Victoria after 1977). He was elected a foundation fellow of the Royal Australasian College of Physicians in 1938.

Commissioned in the Militia (May 1940) then in the Australian Imperial Force (May 1941), Galbraith joined the staff of the director-general of medical services in Melbourne. In 1941 he oversaw the conversion of the Dutch liner *Oranje* into a hospital ship and made two trips to the Middle East in her as officer commanding Australian troops. He was appointed a commander of the Netherlands Order of the Oranje-Nassau (1944) for this work. In September 1942 he was promoted to lieutenant colonel and in July 1944 was appointed the army's medical rehabilitation officer. His service ended in May 1946.

On secondment to the Department of Post-War Reconstruction as co-ordinator of rehabilitation (1946-47), Galbraith prepared a *Report on the Provision in Australia of a National Scheme for the Rehabilitation of Physically Handicapped Persons* (1947), which led to the establishment of the Commonwealth Rehabilitation Service in 1948. With Kathleen Best [q.v.13], he founded the Occupational Therapy School of Victoria, and served (1948-54) on its board of management. Returning to the Children's Hospital in 1948 as honorary physician to in-patients, he resumed his work in paediatric rehabilitation and chaired the interim planning committee for the hospital's new premises in Parkville. He retired in 1960.

Galbraith's outstanding professional qualities were his ability to see the wider perspectives of medicine, and his vision for the full social integration of disabled people into the community. In retirement, interested in the health of Indigenous children, he spent two months at Cape York as a locum with the Royal Flying Doctor Service. He served on the medical services committee of the Australian Red Cross Society (1948-55), several committees of the Australian Council for Rehabilitation of the Disabled (life member, 1968) and the National Rehabilitation Advisory Committee, and was an active member of the Australian Council for the Physically Handicapped (after 1963, the Australian Council for Rehabilitation of the Disabled). In 1965 he was appointed OBE. Proud of his Scottish origins, Douglas Galbraith had a noticeable accent and a dry sense of humour. He was an excellent raconteur, a keen sailor and an expert in Scottish dancing. Survived by his wife and their daughter, he died on 25 August 1984 at Mount Eliza, Victoria, and was cremated.

A. M. Norris (ed), *The Society* (1974); J. Tipping, *Back on Their Feet* (1992); P. Yule, *The Royal Children's Hospital* (1999); *Austn Paediatric Jnl*, vol 21, no 5, 1985, p 5; personal knowledge.

GORDON KEYS SMITH

GALL, IAN STUART (1904-1981), illustrator and cartoonist, was born on 23 November 1904 at Wooloowin, Brisbane, youngest of four children of William Gall [q.v.8], a Queensland-born public servant, and his wife Louise, née Wohlgemuth, from Germany. Ian was educated at the Normal School and at Brisbane Boys' College, where he was cox of the rowing eight in 1918, senior 100 yards champion in 1920, and captain of the Australian Rules football and swimming teams in 1921. School-time doodling led to art classes at the Brisbane Technical College and he abandoned the idea of dentistry as a career.

The *Brisbane Courier* published occasional cartoons by Gall in the 1920s, covering political issues such as the Queensland government surplus (1923) and the strike by members of the Waterside Workers' Federation of Australia (1928). In October 1924 the enduring 'Mr Fourex' character, thought to be one of Gall's whimsical inventions, made his first appearance in an advertisement for Castlemaine Brewery and Quinlan Gray [q.v.9 G. W. Gray] Co. (Brisbane) Ltd's XXXX Bitter Ale. Gall spent some time in Melbourne and Sydney drawing for the *Bulletin* (illustrating the joke page) and *Smith's Weekly*. Returning to Brisbane, he illustrated the covers of pictorial supplements for two newspapers. On 23 September 1932 at St Andrew's Presbyterian Church he married Agnes Annie Stuart Stitt, a stenographer. He was employed at the *Telegraph* for six years before joining the *Courier-*

Mail, where his initial three-a-week output quickly increased to daily cartoons. His ability to engage readers of all ages in serious topics was demonstrated by a Toowoomba school student's tribute in the 1939 *Glennie* [q.v.4] *Gazette*. Although the bulk of his work concerned political events, he had difficulty in treating politicians harshly.

Renowned for his wartime depictions, in 1946-48 Gall was chief cartoonist for *News of the World*, London. He produced a weekly cartoon and, while in Britain with his family, enjoyed his hobbies of hunting and fishing. At the urging of his wife and children he returned to Brisbane and the *Courier-Mail* in 1948. After Nils Josef Jonsson's [q.v.9] death in 1963 Gall took over his comic strip featuring Radish the horse, and for some time also produced an adventure strip, 'Dare Dalton'.

To emphasise salient points Gall labelled his characters, whether people, animals or birds. Cartoons featured the flying pigs 'Rhyme' and 'Reason'; Premier William Forgan Smith's [q.v.11] Scottish terrier named Logan, who wore a placard saying 'fares please' attached to his tail (part of a campaign to have the Logan Bridge toll removed); and Dim Sim, a dragon symbolising cheap Asian petrol which Premier Vince Gair [q.v.14] was threatening to import. Gair himself was portrayed as a bespectacled bullfighter. Later Gall used captions and 'talk bubbles' to carry messages. Rarely subject to editorial control, he ranged over local issues such as mosquito plagues, sporting tussles and country life as well as world events. He retired as the paper's cartoonist in 1969, but contributed a Saturday strip until 1972.

Gall had become well known as a fisherman, naturalist and conservationist. In 1961-71 he wrote a regular column, 'Going Bush', for the *Courier-Mail*. He published *Fishing for the Fun of It* (1970), stories of angling in Queensland in which he urged respect and caution when using local waterways. In *Going Bush with Ian Gall* (1971), a collection of articles that had appeared in his column, he used pen and ink 'scraper board' drawings of wildlife, accompanied by wry descriptions of fauna such as spangled drongo and spine-tailed log-runner birds, crocodiles, dugongs and *bêche-de-mer*.

A large, gentle man, with blue eyes twinkling as he laughed, Gall was never happier than when dressed in comfortable fishing gear and his favourite floppy hat. His wife died in 1971 and on 8 June 1974 at St Augustine's Church of England, Hamilton, he married Sydis May Best, née Keily, a widow. In 1978 the Philip Bacon Galleries featured an exhibition of Gall's drawings, paintings and cartoons. Survived by his wife and the son and daughter of his first marriage, he died on 25 June 1981 in Royal Brisbane Hospital and was cremated; a stroke eighteen months earlier had confined him to a wheelchair. Stewart McCrae, his successor as the *Courier-Mail*'s cartoonist, described him as 'Mr Queensland as far as cartoons were concerned'.

T. M. Hawkins, *The Queensland Great Public Schools* (1965); F. McBride and H. Taylor, *Brisbane: 100 Stories* (1997); *Courier-Mail* (Brisbane), 26 Dec 1945, p 2, 15 Oct 1963, p 27, 24 June 1978, p 11, 27 June 1981, p 3; private information and personal knowledge.
JENNIFER HARRISON
PATRICIA ANDERSON

GATACRE, GALFRY GEORGE ORMOND (1907-1983), naval officer and company director, was born on 11 June 1907 at Wooroolin, Queensland, second son of Reginald Henry Winchcombe Gataker, an English-born farmer, and his wife Christian Esson, née Gordon, from Scotland. In 1930 he was to change the spelling of his surname to Gatacre by deed poll. He was educated at home, then as a boarder at the Church of England Grammar School, Brisbane, and subsequently at Brisbane Boys' College after his family moved to the city. Inspired by his godfather, Admiral Sir Reginald Tupper, RN, he developed an interest in the sea. In 1921 he entered the Royal Australian Naval College, Jervis Bay, Federal Capital Territory. One of two chief cadet captains in his final year (1924), he graduated with colours for cricket, Rugby Union football and tennis.

Appointed midshipman on 15 May 1925, Gatacre served in a variety of RAN and Royal Navy ships in the Far East and Mediterranean. He was promoted to sub-lieutenant in April 1928 and, after further training in Britain, was posted to HMAS *Canberra* in November as a watch-keeping officer. Made lieutenant in January 1930, he became flag lieutenant to the commodore commanding the Australian Squadron in May 1931. He continued to play sport and had notable success at cricket as a spin bowler; he had played for the Royal Navy in 1928 and came to the notice of some Australian State cricket coaches, but shied away from higher grade cricket.

On 16 January 1933 at the Presbyterian Church, Mosman, Sydney, Gatacre married Winifred ('Wendy') May Palmer (d.1978); they were to have a son and a daughter. The Gatacres soon sailed for Britain, for 'Gat', as he was known in naval service, to undertake specialist navigation training. Following postings to the small sloop HMS *Harebell* and the destroyer HMAS *Stuart*, he completed an advanced navigation course in Britain in 1937. He joined HMS *Devonshire* late that year. In January 1938 he was promoted to lieutenant commander. He was in HMS *Edinburgh* when World War II broke out and afterwards served in the battle cruiser *Renown* and in the battleships *Nelson* and *Rodney*, revealing a capacity for long hours and hard work. As navigator of *Rodney* he was involved in the hunt for and sinking of the German battleship *Bismarck* in May 1941. For his 'accurate navigation and judicious selection of courses' during the action, he was awarded the Distinguished Service Cross. He had been mentioned in despatches.

Promoted to commander in December 1941, Gatacre returned to Australia in April 1942 and next month was appointed to HMAS *Australia* as staff officer (operations and intelligence) to the commander of the Australian Squadron. He served with distinction in this demanding role under three different commanders for more than two years, participating in many operations in the South-West Pacific theatre, including the battles of Savo Island and the Eastern Solomons, and most of the amphibious landings along the New Guinea coastline. For his 'skill, resolution and coolness' in the Solomon Islands in July-August 1942 he was awarded a Bar to his DSC. In August 1944 he was given his first shore job after eleven years of marriage and over twenty years in the RAN. He was the staff officer for post-hostilities planning at Navy Office, Melbourne, for a year before being placed in command of the destroyer HMAS *Arunta* in August 1945. *Arunta* operated throughout the Asian region assisting with demobilisation and the British Commonwealth Occupation Force in Japan.

Gatacre was posted to Flinders Naval Depot, Westernport, Victoria, in October 1947. Promoted to captain in June 1948, he became deputy chief of Naval Staff at Navy Office in October. After attending the 1951 course at the Imperial Defence College, London, he was appointed commander of HMAS *Anzac* and the 10th Destroyer Squadron in February 1952. From September *Anzac* patrolled off the east and west coasts of Korea and spent more time in the combat area than any other Commonwealth ship. Gatacre, as a senior captain, also commanded a number of task units and forces at various times. For his service in the Korean War he was awarded the Distinguished Service Order (1953). In July 1953 he was posted to the United States of America as the Australian naval attaché in Washington, a position he held for two years before being appointed commanding officer of the aircraft-carrier HMAS *Melbourne*, commissioned in October 1955.

In January 1957 Gatacre was again made DCNS, his appointment reflecting the small number of experienced senior officers in the RAN at the time. Eighteen months later he was promoted to rear admiral and in January 1959 named flag officer commanding HM Australian Fleet, the most senior seagoing post in the navy. He was appointed CBE in 1960. In January that year he was sent to Washington, this time as head of the Australian Joint Services Staff, where he remained for two years. He became second naval member of the Naval Board (chief of naval personnel) in January 1962 and flag officer-in-charge, East Australia Area, based in Sydney, in July. In February 1964 units under his command were involved in rescuing survivors of the collision between HMA ships *Melbourne* and *Voyager*.

Gatacre retired from the RAN on 10 June 1964 and began a career in business. He was a director of the RSL Permanent Building Society Ltd and of Elliott-Automation (Pty) Ltd (later the General Electric Co. of Australia Ltd), for which he was also a representative of the defence and aerospace arm. A keen golfer, he played mostly at the Royal Sydney Golf Club. His memoirs, *Reports of Proceedings*, were published in 1982. Survived by his son, he died on 11 August 1983 at Eastwood and was cremated.

F. B. Eldridge, *A History of the Royal Australian Naval College* (1949); G. H. Gill, *Royal Australian Navy 1942-1945* (1968); R. O'Neill, *Australia in the Korean War 1950-53*, vol 2 (1985); A6769, item Gatacre G G O (NAA); private information.

ALASTAIR COOPER

GAULT, EDWARD WOODALL (1903-1982), medical practitioner and medical missionary, was born on 15 March 1903 at Carlton, Melbourne, second of three children of Edward Leslie Gault, a medical practitioner from Manchester, England, and his Victorian-born wife Gertrude, née Woodall. Ted was raised in a devout Methodist home: his father was a founding member of the Laymen's Missionary Movement (1909) as well as the Royal Australasian College of Surgeons (1926). After his mother's death in 1906, Gault and his sisters were cared for by her cousin, Dora Swanton, who later married their father. Educated at Wesley College, Ted enrolled at the University of Melbourne (B.Sc., 1925; MB, BS, 1928; MD, 1931, MS, 1934), gaining a rowing Blue, living for several years in Queen's College and becoming an active member (president, 1926) of the Australian Student Christian Movement. He completed his internship at the (Royal) Melbourne Hospital, where he was appointed house surgeon, registrar and, in 1929, resident medical officer.

At the Congregational Church, Killara, Sydney, on 22 February 1932 Gault married Edna Isabel Baylis (1904-1992), also a medical practitioner, whom he had met through the ASCM while she was a student at the University of Sydney (MB, BS, 1929). They were both committed to medical missionary work in India but a downturn in family finances delayed their planned departure; in the meantime, they established a general practice at Surrey Hills, Melbourne, and pursued specialist training; he also taught at the university to supplement their savings and in 1935 was admitted a fellow of the RACS. In October 1937 they sailed with their two children for Azamgarh, northern India, where Gault was to work as medical superintendent for the Methodist Missionary Society of Australasia's Christian Hospital for Women. His elder sister, Adelaide Gertrude Gault (1899-1977), had founded this hospital in 1923 and had been its first doctor; the strain of work there had forced her back to Melbourne in 1924.

Gault's appointment broke the practice of using only women doctors and gradually the hospital was expanded to include male patients. He created a laboratory, greatly improved the hospital's surgical department, supervised a building program that extended bed capacity, and routinely visited outlying villages to preach and provide medical care. In the process, he learnt Urdu—the first of several Indian languages in which he became fluent—and developed a keen awareness of the challenges of taking 'the healing ministry' across religious and traditional boundaries.

In 1943 Gault became eligible for furlough: the family travelled first to Britain, where he sought treatment for a recurrent depressive illness, and then to Melbourne, where he advocated changes to the White Australia policy to allow limited migration from India and began preparing for his next appointment. He had been named foundation professor of pathology at the Christian Medical College, Vellore, southern India, which was being converted from a women's to a co-educational medical training college. Under Gault's leadership from 1944 to 1962, the pathology department was recognised as a training institution for doctors completing postgraduate studies at the University of Madras. He was largely responsible for raising funds to support this development, partly through the Friends of Vellore groups that he had set up throughout Australia. Staff and students valued not only the extensive medical knowledge but the warmth and understanding of their high-principled, compassionate professor. In 1960-61 he served as president of the Indian Association of Pathologists; in 1973 the chair in pathology at Vellore was named in his honour.

Returning to Australia, Gault and his wife established a home and garden at Warrandyte. He began work (1962-68) for the RACS, providing courses and advice (particularly in pathology) to postgraduate students, initiated a registry of soft tissue tumours, and curated a museum for the college. In 1969-73 he held a part-time appointment as senior demonstrator in pathology at the Austin Hospital, Heidelberg; he was later commissioned with Alan Lucas to write its centennial history—*A Century of Compassion* (1982). Tall, fair and lightly built, with an enduring enthusiasm for athletics and sport, Gault was zealous and yet often whimsical in temperament; he continued, however, to wrestle with worsening depressive episodes. Ted Gault died on 13 October 1982 at Heidelberg and was cremated. He was survived by his wife and their son and daughter.

R. Winton, *An Amazing Man* (1987); B. McLaughlin, *A Very Amazing Life* (1993); *Sun News-Pictorial* (Melbourne), 18 Oct 1937, p 11, 13 Nov 1943, p 25; *MJA*, 5 Feb 1983, p 144, 6 Sept 1993, p 343.
SUZANNE PARRY

GAWITH, CHARLES SHERWIN (1910-1982), bread manufacturer, politician and racehorse owner, was born on 3 June 1910 at Wallasey, Chester, England, son of Thomas George Gawith, baker, and his wife Elizabeth, née Roberts. Charlie was educated at St Augustine's school, Liverpool, and in 1927—following the failure of his father's business—migrated to Australia with an older brother, George. They took whatever work they could find until, in 1930, in the depths of the Depression, they determined to return to their father's trade.

Purchasing a shop at Brunswick, Melbourne, for £50, the brothers began baking pies and pastries, initially buying a bag of flour each day. Gradually they expanded into bread production and in the mid-1930s moved to premises at Elsternwick and then Prahran. The firm of Gawith Brothers was ideally located to expand with the postwar growth of Melbourne's south-eastern suburbs. They pioneered the packaging of sliced loaves and by 1953 sixty distinctive red, white and blue delivery vans were distributing their bread from the Dandenongs to Mornington. In 1960 their South Yarra bakery was celebrated as the first fully automatic bread-making plant in the world.

This success enabled Charlie, the firm's 'outside man', to pursue other interests. He established a Hereford cattle stud at Officer, and became chairman of the engineering company Milgate Jones & Gawith Pty Ltd, and a director of Willetts Pty Ltd, Consolidated Insurance of Australia and Gawith Biscuits. In 1968 Gawith Brothers was sold to Sunicrust Bakeries. From 1949 to 1964 Charles was a conscientious Prahran City councillor (mayor, 1953-54, 1960-61). He launched the Gawith Villa Trust in 1954 to establish a training centre for children with intellectual disabilities,

and served on the councils of Melbourne High School and Prahran Technical School (chairman, 1955). Having unsuccessfully contested the Legislative Assembly seat of Prahran for the Liberal Party in 1952, in a 1955 by-election he became the member for Monash province in the Legislative Council. As a parliamentarian, however, he made little impact beyond bitter exchanges with the outspoken Labor member Jack Galbally [q.v.]. He failed to gain preselection for the 1967 election.

Both brothers were keen racehorse owners, although Charlie—a 'dapper man', smart in dress and proud in demeanour—became the more public figure through a series of controversies surrounding their most successful horse, Big Philou. The winner on appeal of the 1969 Caulfield Cup, Big Philou was 'nobbled' for the Melbourne Cup later that year (Gawith offered $5000 for information leading to a conviction for this offence) and scratched from the same event in 1970 following Gawith's open break with his trainer, Bart Cumings.

On 31 January 1942 at All Saint's Church of England, St Kilda, Gawith had married Beryl Constance Holden, a dental nurse; they divorced in 1965. On 27 August that year he married Margot Frieda Irmgard Schwisow, a nurse, at the office of the government statist, Melbourne. Charlie Gawith retired to Queensland and died on 16 September 1982 at Buderim. Survived by two sons and a daughter from his first marriage, and by his wife and their daughter, he was cremated.

A. Watson, *Breaking Wishbones* (2003); *PD* (LC, Vic), 21 Sept 1982, p 142; *Herald* (Melbourne), 13 July 1960, p 27, 18 Nov 1969, p 2, 7 Oct 1970, p 7, 13 Oct 1984, p 4; *Sun News-Pictorial* (Melbourne), 27 Sept 1964, p 7, 8 Oct 1970, p 35.
CHARLES FAHEY

GEDDES, WILLIAM ROBERT (1916-1989), anthropologist, was born on 29 April 1916 at New Plymouth, New Zealand, youngest of five children of Scottish parents Joseph Geddes, farmer, and his wife Edith, née Urquhart. After attending New Plymouth Boys' High School Bill went to the University of Otago (BA, 1938; MA, 1939), Dunedin, where he majored in philosophy. In 1939-40 he was a demonstrator in the university's department of psychology. He put H. D. Skinner's one-year anthropology course to good use during his service (1941-45) in the 2nd New Zealand Expeditionary Force. Rising to staff sergeant, he spent most of his time in Fiji. This experience was the basis for his Polynesian Society memoir, *Deuba: A Study of a Fijian Village* (1945), written during the Bougainville campaign, and his University of London (Ph.D.,

1948) thesis, 'An Analysis of Cultural Change in Fiji', written at the London School of Economics and Political Science. In 1947-48 he lectured in psychology at Birkbeck College, University of London.

On 27 March 1948 Geddes married a New Zealander, Maud Seymour Eaton, at St Alban's parish church, Golders Green, Middlesex; she died in 1956. Selected to work with the Land Dayaks of Sarawak under a scheme sponsored by the Colonial Social Science Research Council, he published his work: first as a report to the council, *The Land Dayaks of Sarawak* (1954); and then as a well received book, *Nine Dayak Nights* (1957). In 1951 he took a lectureship at the Auckland University College (senior lecturer 1954; associate professor 1957).

While visiting Peking (Beijing) in 1956, Geddes contacted Fei Hsiao-tung, a Chinese anthropologist who had written *Peasant Life in China* (1939), a study of a village on the Yangtze plain west of Shanghai. Fei Hsiao-tung helped to negotiate an arrangement whereby Geddes was able to write a sequel, *Peasant Life in Communist China* (1963), based on an intensive four-day re-investigation. It was, according to the sinologist Dr Jonathan Unger, 'a special window' on a period when most sources were either governmental or partisan.

For Geddes, anthropology was important as a force for cross-cultural understanding, tolerance and appropriate action. When he took up the chair in social anthropology at the University of Sydney in 1959, he made the subject available from first year, rather than only from second year as it had been previously. In 1964-70 he chaired the Foundation for Aboriginal Affairs, Sydney. On 24 May 1963 he had married Ngaere Adele Te Punga, a Maori schoolteacher, at the registrar general's office, Sydney.

Geddes believed that anthropologists should play a role in practical affairs in their areas of expertise. Between 1957 and 1962 he had undertaken three spells of field-work among one of the ethnic minorities of northern Thailand—hill tribesmen in and at the margins of the Golden Triangle. In 1964-65 he was adviser to the Tribal Research Centre set up in Chiang Mai by the Thai government. His major monograph, *Migrants of the Mountains: The Cultural Ecology of the Blue Miao (Hmong Njua) of Thailand* (1976), discussed the economic and cultural role of opium among the Miao (Hmong) in particular and the hill tribes in general. He was a member of United Nations study missions on opium in 1966-67 and 1970; for the latter he drew up a plan for alternative crops. In the *New York Review of Books* of 19 November 1970 two anthropologists alleged that data collected by the TRC was being used by the Thai and American governments for counter-insurgency purposes in South-East Asia. Australian activists opposed to the Vietnam War accused Geddes of complicity, leading him to take legal action that resulted in an out-of-court settlement in his favour and a public retraction. Some anthropologists asked, more generally, whether accepting any government or private contracts threatened academic autonomy and free inquiry. The 'Thailand controversy' added to existing tensions in the anthropology department in Sydney.

Increasingly Geddes turned his attention to other interests, including ethnographic film. He was a skilled and sensitive still photographer, who had taught himself filming. His first effort was with the Miao in the late 1950s, and the British Broadcasting Corporation produced a thirty-minute version of it, *The Opium People*, with commentary by David Attenborough. In 1961 he filmed *The Land Dayaks of Borneo* (produced in 1966), and in the mid-1960s, *Miao Year* (produced in 1968). Both were examples of the descriptive documentary used in education to complement written accounts. He was quick to appreciate the importance of film as a record of fast-disappearing ways of life. A foundation (1962) councillor of the Australian Institute of Aboriginal Studies, he convened its film committee for almost a decade from 1963 and played a significant role in the development of ethnographic filming. During the 1970s and 1980s, in Fiji and Sarawak, he filmed ceremonies which were unlikely to be performed much longer.

Following his retirement in 1981, Geddes travelled widely to represent the Academy of the Social Sciences in Australia (of which he was a fellow) at meetings of the Association of Asian Social Science Research Councils. He chaired the planning committee of the association's fifth biennial conference, held in Sydney in 1983, and edited the proceedings of one of its symposia, *Asian Perspectives in Social Science* (1985).

Bill Geddes displayed a stubborn fixity of purpose that went well with his stocky build. He mixed tenacity with shrewdness and tempered both with a deep humanity and a self-deprecating sense of humour. Quiet and unassertive, he enjoyed the pleasures of gardening, fishing and the company of friends. Survived by his wife, he died on 27 April 1989 at Wahroonga and was cremated.

P. Flanagan, *Imperial Anthropology* (1971?); P. Read, *Charles Perkins* (1990); *American Anthropologist*, vol 61, no 2, 1959, p 322, vol 66, no 3, 1964, p 688, vol 69, no 1, 1967, p 127; *Anthropology Newsletter* (American Anthropological Association), Feb 1976, p 3; J. Golson, 'Professor W. R. Geddes', *Austn Aboriginal Studies*, no 2, 1989, p 98; *Oceania*, vol 60, no 1, 1989, p 60; *Anthropology Today*, vol 8, no 2, 1992, p 22; *Austn Jnl of Anthropology*, vol 13, no 2, 2002, p 155; W. Geddes, service record (Archives NZ).

JACK GOLSON

GEEVES, PHILIP LESLIE (1917-1983), radio broadcaster and historian, was born on 26 April 1917 at Bexley, Sydney, fourth child of Sydney-born parents Albert Geeves, postal sorter, and his wife Margaret May, née Canavan. Philip attended Rockdale Public and Canterbury Boys' High schools, where he excelled in languages, especially German. In 1936 he joined Amalgamated Wireless (Australasia) Ltd as a junior announcer at radio station 2CH; he became involved in short-wave broadcasting at VK2ME, known as the 'Voice of Australia'.

When World War II broke out in 1939, Geeves enlisted in the Militia. Commissioned next year, he transferred to the Australian Imperial Force in March 1941. He served in the Middle East in 1941-42 with the 2/5th Field Regiment, Royal Australian Artillery, before returning to Australia. For his technical intelligence work as a staff captain (1943-45) at headquarters, New Guinea Force, he was mentioned in despatches. In September 1945 he was posted to the United States Army's School of Military Government at the University of Virginia, Charlottesville. Back in Australia in February 1946, he was attached to the British-Australian Long Range Weapons Project, setting up the range at Woomera, South Australia. He transferred to the Reserve of Officers on 17 December.

Geeves returned to 2CH as a senior announcer, later becoming program director. Recognising the changing nature of postwar Australia, he introduced foreign-language music programs for European immigrants, working closely with the Department of Immigration and sponsors seeking new customers. Impressed by the passion for history in the USA, Geeves contacted his former science teacher, James Jervis, who was a keen local historian. Together they wrote *Rockdale* (1954), a history of the suburb where Geeves's forebears had settled. In response to a request from the Royal Australian Historical Society, Geeves published *Local History in Australia* (1967) on methods of research. A history of Ryde municipality, *A Place of Pioneers* (1970), followed. At AWA he started work on a history of the company and radio broadcasting, posthumously published as *The Dawn of Australia's Radio Broadcasting* (1993). He wrote 137 historical radio and television features produced by the Australian Broadcasting Commission for school children and adults. On 2CH his 'Streets of Sydney' ran for fifteen years and 'Moments in History' daily for two years.

Because of ill health Geeves retired from AWA in the 1970s, but continued to work on historical commissions, including casual segments for ABC Radio. As the ABC's 'resident historian' he broadcast, with Caroline Jones, a regular radio program from 1978, answering queries from the scores of letters he received each week, especially about family history. From 1980 he also responded to them through his weekly column in the *Sydney Morning Herald*.

Geeves had married with Methodist forms Leona Phyllis Deane, a radio executive, on 10 July 1942 at Wesley Church, Melbourne. An imposing figure, he was six feet (183 cm) tall with bright, hazel eyes and a well-modulated voice. He was a man of disciplined routine, rising early for a Spartan breakfast, reading the newspapers and completing the crossword before settling to work in his book-lined study. He was a councillor (1954, 1963-71) and fellow (1972) of the Royal Australian Historical Society. In 1980 he was awarded an OAM. Survived by his wife and their two daughters, he died of a stroke on 16 August 1983 at Kogarah and was cremated.

Sun-Herald (Sydney), 19 Nov 1978, p 27; *SMH*, 8 May 1980, p 19, 18 Aug 1983, p 13; *Newsletter of the Royal Austn Hist Soc*, Oct 1983, p 7; Geeves papers (SLNSW); B883, item NX70702 (NAA).

CAROL LISTON

GELL, HEATHER DORIS (1896-1988), kindergarten teacher, eurhythmics pioneer and broadcaster, was born on 19 May 1896 at Glenelg, Adelaide, eldest of three children of English-born parents Harry Dickson Gell, accountant, and his second wife Annie Elizabeth, née Webster. From early childhood Heather swam, she said, 'like a fish' and delighted in physical movement. Educated at Caroline Jacob's [q.v.9] Tormore House School, she played cricket and in 1914 was selected for the State women's hockey team. As a student at Adelaide Kindergarten Training College in 1915-16, she was inspired by the short eurhythmics course conducted by Agnes Sterry. This new branch of music education— devised by a Swiss, Emile Jaques-Dalcroze— involved listening and moving, and was little known in Australia. Having graduated with the kindergarten teaching certificate, in 1918 Gell was appointed director of Clayton Congregational Kindergarten, Norwood. Although not officially qualified, she also taught eurhythmics at the training college. She had piano lessons from Miss Sterry and studiously observed her Saturday children's lessons in aural training and eurhythmics.

Deciding to make eurhythmics her career, Gell undertook the three-year certificate course (1921-23) at the London School of Dalcroze Eurhythmics. In Geneva, Switzerland, she saw a spectacular Dalcroze eurhythmics display; it was to be a model for her many presentations. Back in Adelaide in 1924 as a qualified instructor, she popularised eurhythmics, teaching in her own city studio, in private schools and at the kindergarten training college. Young women and children of all ages, barefoot and simply clad (the children in blue bathing costumes), responded to her skilful piano improvisation with rhythmic, creative body movements designed to develop aural awareness and musical understanding. She was definite, critical and sometimes peremptory, stretching older students to the limit, but was remembered as 'wonderful with children'. Although some adults found her formidable, many warmed to her dedication and sense of humour. Although unprepossessing in appearance, being plump and somewhat ungainly looking, she was remarkably light on her feet.

The Dalcroze Society of South Australia, founded by Gell in 1924 and presided over by E. Harold Davies [q.v.8], arranged and presented eurhythmics performances. Gell confidently joined Adelaide's theatre scene and her productions, often in aid of children's causes, captivated audiences. In 1936, sponsored by the Women's Centenary Council of South Australia, she staged *Heritage: A Pageant of South Australia*, written by Ellinor Walker [q.v.]. Performed for ten nights at the Tivoli Theatre, it combined the talents of South Australian composers, musicians, singers, actors and eurhythmics students. Gell's youngest pupils appeared as gumnuts.

In 1931 Gell gained the licentiate in aural training from the Royal Academy of Music, London. Appointed a part-time teacher at the Elder [q.v.4] Conservatorium of Music in December 1934, she prepared the musical perception syllabus for the teachers' licentiate of the Australian Music Examinations Board; it was adopted in 1935. Returning to London in 1937, she studied stage direction and prepared Dalcroze eurhythmics students for examination. She was impressed by the British Broadcasting Corporation's program 'Music and Movement' and received some training in radio broadcasting. In Adelaide from mid-1938 she created and conducted Australia's first music for schools program, 'Music through Movement', an adapted form of Dalcroze eurhythmics, for the Australian Broadcasting Commission. From the start children responded eagerly. When it became national in February 1939, she moved to Sydney. Besides starting eurhythmics classes, for twenty years she created and presented two 20-minute programs per week, each for different ages. Clement Semmler, an ABC manager, regarded 'Music through Movement' as 'a gem in the crown of ABC educational broadcasting'.

Early in the 1940s Gell also broadcast a music appreciation program for older children, 'Let's All Listen'. Appointed in 1943 to the first advisory committee for the ABC's 'Kindergarten of the Air', she trained the program's presenter and was its first pianist. Each Christmas she presented a dramatic produc-

tion; in 1945 it was *The Pied Piper of Hamelin* at Sydney's Theatre Royal, with (Sir) Charles Mackerras as conductor of the orchestra. Her interpretive book *Music, Movement, and the Young Child* (1949) encouraged teachers to 'look for a delight in discovering originality' instead of turning children into 'little metronomes'. Reissued five times until 1978, it was translated into Japanese in 1958.

In 1951-53 Gell took a three-year course in England, which, with visits to Geneva, qualified her to train Dalcroze eurhythmics teachers. She produced *The Pied Piper* in London in 1953, again with Mackerras conducting. In Sydney her assistants maintained her thriving city and suburban eurhythmics classes until her return and her radio programs, recorded at the BBC, continued. Back in Sydney, armed with the diploma of L'Institut Jaques-Dalcroze and using her own funds, she founded and directed the Australian Dalcroze School of Music and Movement; the first teachers graduated in 1957. She taught at the Nursery School Teachers' College, Sydney, for some years, and briefly at the New South Wales State Conservatorium of Music.

Gell tried with little success to have Dalcroze methods accepted in music education courses. Turning to the new world of children's television, in 1960 she devised and presented the popular pre-school program 'Playroom' on ADS-7, Adelaide, using bush animal puppets. With habitual thoroughness she planned every detail of her scripts and scores and sent them to her Adelaide colleagues, then every three weeks arrived for one day's production of three programs. From 1963 videotaping enabled the program to be transmitted to Sydney and Melbourne. Later she presented it for seven years from TCN-9, Sydney.

In 1965 Gell joined centenary celebrations of Jaques-Dalcroze's birth in Geneva, where a film of her work with children was acclaimed. In London she investigated children's television, and while in Tokyo for a music education conference taught eurhythmics to children for a week. The foremost Dalcroze authority in Australia, in 1970 Gell founded the Dalcroze Society of Australia and the Dalcroze Teachers' Society. In 1977 she was appointed MBE. She moved back to Adelaide in 1982 for 'semi-retirement'. Never married, she died on 23 October 1988 at Christies Beach and was cremated. The Heather Gell Dalcroze Foundation was established in 1993 to develop teacher-training courses in Australia.

L. Cox, P. Holmes and J. Pope (comps), *Recollections: A Tribute to Heather Gell* (1995); J. Pope (ed), *Heather Gell's Thoughts on Dalcroze Eurhythmics and Music through Movement* (1996); *ABC Weekly*, 4 Feb 1950, p 19; Gell papers (SLSA); private information and personal knowledge.   HELEN JONES

GENTLE, STANLEY WALLACE (1932-1989), forester and public servant, was born on 19 July 1932 at Tamworth, New South Wales, son of Frank Watson Gentle, a farmer from Armidale, and his wife Dulcie Melba Kathleen, née Webb, born at Tarana. Dux of Tamworth High School, Wal graduated from the University of Sydney (B.Sc.(For.), 1954) and received the Commonwealth Diploma of Forestry from the Australian Forestry School, Canberra. In 1949 he had entered the New South Wales public service as a cadet. He worked for the Forestry Commission of New South Wales at Batlow from 1954.

In 1957 Gentle was awarded a Fulbright travel grant and an Agnes H. Anderson fellowship to the University of Washington College of Forest Resources (Ph.D., 1963), United States of America, where he researched tree physiology. At the university's Laboratory of Radiation Biology (associated with the United States Atomic Energy Commission), he undertook post-doctoral research on the Marshall Islands testing program. He married Janice Marlene Larson, a dietitian from Glasgow, Montana, on 17 October 1958 at the University Methodist Temple, Seattle.

Back in Australia in the 1960s, Gentle studied pine plantations grown in poor soils. His development of assessment techniques to determine the available nutrient levels led to considerations of soil/fertiliser reactions that laid a scientific basis for the use of phosphate fertilisers in forestry. He also designed and installed the first forest hydrological experiments on a complete-catchment scale in Australia. While working for the Forestry Commission at Bathurst, he conceived a new method of calculating returns from pine plantations, which introduced some predictability in forest yield estimation.

In 1971 Gentle was appointed to the newly formed State Department of Environment; he became deputy director jointly of the department and of the State Pollution Control Commission. Credited with introducing environmental assessment to Australia, he advised State ministers from three political parties on forest and land use issues. In 1976-77 he served as one of two commissioners on the board of inquiry into private forestry development in Tasmania. He was a member (1977-78) of the Wran government's land conservation study group.

Named an assistant-commissioner of the Forestry Commission of New South Wales in 1979, Gentle became commissioner in 1981. He was committed to a balance between the commercial and the environmental bases of forestry. Through research he sought to mitigate the impact of forest operations while improving their efficiency and productivity. He served on a range of specialist bodies, including the Australian Forestry Council's standing committee on forestry and the New South Wales Science and Technology Council. A thoughtful and challenging public speaker with a lively sense of humour, Gentle represented Australia at numerous international congresses. In 1989 the Institute of Foresters of Australia awarded him the N. W. Jolly [q.v.9] medal.

In rare moments away from forestry, Gentle farmed lucerne and raised cattle on his family's property near Tarana. Other interests included opera, classical music, history, wine and politics. Survived by his wife and their son and two daughters, he died of a cerebral tumour on 25 October 1989 at Greenwich and was buried in St Paul's Anglican Churchyard cemetery, Muttons Falls, via Tarana. In 1990 the Australian Academy of Science, with the Institute of Foresters of Australia and the University of Washington Foresters Alumni Association, established the Wal Gentle scholarship fund for postgraduate study.

Forestry Commission of NSW, Annual Report, *PP* (NSW), 1990-91, vol 9, paper no 120, p 6; *SMII*, 6 Sept 1971, p 7, 24 Oct 1973, p 3, 21 Sept 1979, p 11, 12 June 1981, p 15, 16 Sept 1981, p 3, 27 Oct 1989, p 5; NSW Forest Products Assn, *Prologue Notes*, Feb-Mar 1990, p 3; Wal Gentle Scholarship Fund file (Basser Lib, Canberra); private information.

ANTHEA KERR

GIBBS, PEARL MARY (GAMBANYI) (1901-1983), Aboriginal leader, was born in 1901 at La Perouse, Sydney, younger daughter of Mary Margaret Brown, who was born in Brewarrina to Maria, an Aboriginal woman of the Ngemba or Muruwari language, and a white station worker, George Brown. Pearl's father, David Barry, was estranged from the family. After Pearl's birth, her mother returned to her employment in Yass, where Pearl and her sister, Olga, later attended Mount Carmel School. Although Pearl's skin was fair, racial discrimination in her schooling caused her to identify strongly as Aboriginal.

By 1910 the family had settled near Bourke, where Margaret married an Aboriginal widower, Richard Murray. They worked on a sheep station near Byrock; Olga and later Pearl were maids. In 1917 the sisters left for Sydney to take jobs as domestic servants. Pearl found steady employment in the Potts Point area, but she met Aboriginal girls who had been removed from their country homes unwillingly and had been 'apprenticed' or indentured by the Aborigines Protection Board as domestic servants. Disturbed by their position, she tried to help them by acting as advocate with the board.

Pearl married Robert James Gibbs, an English-born naval steward, on 14 April 1923 at the registrar's office, Paddington, Sydney; they had two sons and a daughter. One son, Charles Reginald, served (1937-50) in the Royal Australian Navy. When the marriage broke down late in the 1920s, she lived in an unemployment camp at Happy Valley near La Perouse. She became more acutely aware of the protection board, as police tried to reduce contact between the unemployed workers and the nearby reserve community. With her mother and stepfather she picked peas at Nowra to eke out a living away from the board's control. She encouraged residents at the Wallaga Lake Aboriginal reserve to defy the board manager's control over their income, and helped pea pickers to seek better conditions.

New legislation in 1936 widened the board's powers to allow the confinement of anyone 'apparently having an admixture of aboriginal blood' at one of its managed stations; this change meant that Pearl was now covered by the legislation. In 1937 she travelled to Sydney and began work for the fledgling Aborigines Progressive Association with Bill Ferguson and Jack Patten [qq.v.8,11]. She collected information at Brewarrina that assisted the association to publicise the deteriorating conditions on overcrowded reserves, and to obtain an inquiry into the protection board; a select committee sat during 1937 and 1938.

As secretary (1938-39) of the Aborigines Progressive Association, Pearl focused her public speaking on the issues of women's and children's rights, exposing the appalling nutritional and health conditions mothers and children faced on government-managed reserves. She renewed her contact with Aboriginal 'apprenticed' girls, and worked with the middle-class white activist Joan Kingsley-Strack to publicise the labour and sexual exploitation these girls faced as isolated domestic servants far from home. Pearl was one of the few women, white or black, who spoke in public political forums such as the Domain. She became a link between the white women's and Aboriginals' movements, serving, for example, on the management committee of the Union of Australian Women. The Committee for Aboriginal Citizenship, of which she was a member, drew many white sympathisers, from militant left-wing unionists to more diversely motivated people such as Michael Sawtell [q.v.Supp.], into the campaign. Pearl had a strong association with the activists Jessie Street [q.v.16] and Faith Bandler.

Conscious of the importance of media coverage, Pearl ensured that journalists were kept informed. Although often outspoken and abrasive, she could also be charming and persuasive. She reached a wide audience in Sydney and Wollongong when she spoke about women's and general Aboriginal issues on radio station 2GB in 1941. Her writing appeared in the women's, local and Sydney press.

A good organiser, Gibbs helped to plan the Day of Mourning protest on Australia Day 1938. She became secretary of the Dubbo branch of the Australian Aborigines' League in 1950. After a State branch of the Council for Aboriginal Rights was established in 1952, Pearl became organising secretary. However, her greatest impact was in her behind-the-scenes role of bringing people together to undertake new campaigns. She was a loyal friend to many Aboriginal activists over the years, from Ferguson and Bert Groves [q.v.14] in the 1950s to Kevin Gilbert in the 1970s.

After World War II Gibbs had settled in Dubbo with her widowed mother, actively supporting attempts by Aboriginal people in the region to get better conditions under the Aborigines Welfare Board. Her understanding of the broad questions of social reform and her determination, integrity and forthright nature were admired. A railway worker, Jack Booth, commented: 'She could adapt herself to any audience—be fiery or softspoken—she wouldn't pull her punches'.

As the Aborigines Welfare Board's policies hardened into aggressive assimilation, in 1954 Gibbs was elected to the seat on the board that was assigned to mixed-race Aborigines. She found that there was no real power for an Aboriginal member of the board; she could not inspect reserves unless on an official tour. As both an Aboriginal and a woman, she believed she was excluded from key decision-making, some of which took place over drinks in hotel bars.

In 1956 Gibbs drew together significant people and sparked the formation of the Aboriginal-Australian Fellowship, which was an energetic and stimulating advocate for Aboriginal rights and a fertile meeting place for black and white activists until the late 1960s. Vice-president in its first year, Pearl found it a more effective and satisfying forum than the welfare board. She campaigned against the continuing limits to Aboriginal civil rights, including restrictions on access to alcohol. In 1957 she worked for the petition launched by the AAF to change the Australian Constitution.

Later in 1957 Gibbs resigned from the welfare board and her official role in the fellowship, although she continued to be an active member of the latter and was elected a life member in 1962. She established a hostel for Aboriginal people who came to Dubbo for medical treatment, convincing the Waterside Workers' Federation of Australia to fund the hostel—a small weatherboard cottage—and the Aborigines Welfare Board to provide her modest allowance as warden. On 28 April 1983 she died at Dubbo and was buried in the new Catholic cemetery.

J. Horner, *Vote Ferguson for Aboriginal Freedom* (1974) and *Seeking Racial Justice* (2004); A. Cole et al (eds), *Uncommon Ground* (2005); H. Goodall, 'Pearl Gibbs: Some Memories', *Aboriginal History*, vol 7, no 1, 1983, p 20, see also pp 4, 10; *Weekend Liberal and Macquarie Advocate*, 29-30 Jan 1983, p 6; H. Goodall, A History of Aboriginal Communities in New South Wales, 1909-1939 (PhD thesis, Univ of Sydney, 1984); Gibbs papers (SLNSW); private information.   HEATHER GOODALL

GIBSON, GRACE ISABEL (1905-1989), radio executive producer, was born on 17 June 1905 at El Paso, Texas, United States of America, daughter of Calvin Newton Gibson, rancher, and his wife Margaret Escobara, née Schultz, born in Mexico City. After graduating from high school at Hollywood, California, Grace began working for the Radio Transcription Co. of America. Previously married and divorced, on 29 November 1930 she married Thomas Atchison at Hollywood with Methodist forms; they were later divorced. Clever and ambitious, with a brash, cheerful personality, by her late twenties she was the company's leading saleswoman. She so impressed A. E. Bennett [q.v.7]—Sydney radio-station 2GB's general manager, who was visiting the USA—that he invited her to help him set up and manage a company, American Radio Transcription Agencies (later Artransa Pty Ltd), which sold American recorded radio programs throughout Australia. Gibson agreed to go to Sydney for six months, but stayed on. In 1933 2GB was the first radio-station in Australia to broadcast 16-inch (41 cm) quarter-hour recordings of drama and music. Two of these, 'Tarzan of the Apes' and 'Pinto Pete and his Ranch Boys', sold to the sponsors Pepsodent Co. (Aust.) Pty Ltd and Lever Bros Ltd respectively, gained immense popularity.

In 1941 Gibson, in the USA to buy more programs, was stranded when that country entered World War II. Three years later she was managing her old firm, the Radio Transcription Co. of America. She returned to Australia in 1944 and on 18 August at the registrar general's office, Sydney, married Randal Robert McDonnell Parr, an Irishman serving in the Australian Imperial Force.

The ban on the importation of non-essential goods during the war was a boon for Australian-made products including radio programs, which were now locally produced and increasingly locally written. Gibson set up her own company, Grace Gibson Radio Productions Pty Ltd, in Sydney, using American scripts with local actors as compères or narrators. Among them were Ron Randell in 'These Are the Facts' and 'The Drama of Medicine', and Reg Johnston in 'The History of Flight'. With her customary flair, Gibson sold these and other programs to various Sydney and interstate radio stations. 2CH, 2UE and 2UW competed against each other to broadcast the 'Nyal Radio Playhouse', which featured locally produced half-hour plays. Her first serial, in half-hour episodes, was 'Mr and Mrs North'.

Gibson was astute in her choice of drama directors who, in turn, cast good actors, resulting in high-quality, successful productions. Talented writers adapted the American scripts to local conditions and created original material when the American scripts ran out. They were encouraged to write their own serials—with some outstanding results such as Lindsay Hardy's spy thrillers 'Dossier on Dumetrius', 'Deadly Nightshade' and 'Twenty Six Hours'.

By 1954 Grace Gibson Productions was putting out thirty-two programs per week. They went to air in Australia, New Zealand, South Africa, Hong Kong and Canada. Most were for evening listening ('Night Beat' being an enduring favourite), but her two flagship productions, 'Dr Paul' and 'Portia Faces Life', were marathon runners among the morning soap operas. 'Dr Paul' (originally written by an American, Virginia Crosby) ran for 4634 quarter-hour episodes from 1949 to 1971. Sponsored by the soap manufacturer Lever Bros, it was heard on forty-eight stations throughout Australia four mornings a week, and was also sold overseas. 'Portia Faces Life', with Lyndall Barbour [q.v.] in the leading role of the lawyer Portia Manning, ran for 3544 episodes from 1954 to 1970. By then television ruled the air waves and Gibson, who claimed to be the sole survivor among operators of commercial studios, scaled down her production to serials of four-minute episodes, one of which was 'I Killed Grace Random'.

Dark eyed, dark haired, and generously proportioned, Grace Gibson was always well groomed. Stories of her tight-fistedness abound, yet her staff were fiercely loyal to her, and after her retirement she made a large donation to the Actors' Benevolent Fund. With her toughness she had a self-mocking humour. She retained her Texan drawl and an American, feminine, almost girlish quality, evident when she spoke of her first meeting with her Parr: 'He made my little heart go pit-i-pat'. Typical of Grace was her quip when told of a fire in a rival production studio: 'Nothing trivial, I hope'. In 1978 Gibson retired and sold the business. Her beloved husband Ronnie died in 1985 and she lived alone for the rest of her life in the large stylish apartment at Potts Point that had been the scene of great social life in their heyday. She died there on 10 July 1989 and was cremated.

N. Bridges, *Wonderful Wireless* (1983); J. Kent, *Out of the Bakelite Box* (1983); R. Lane, *The Golden Age of Australian Radio Drama 1923-1960* (1994); *ABC Weekly*, 30 Jan 1954, p 20; *Broadcasting and Television*, 18 June 1954, p 17; *Mercury* (Hobart), 25 Nov 1987, p 20; personal knowledge.

LYNNE MURPHY

GIBSON, RALPH SIWARD (1906-1989), communist organiser and writer, was born on 19 February 1906 at Hampstead, London, third of five sons of William Ralph Boyce Gibson [q.v.8], philosopher, and his wife Lucy Judge, née Peacock. Alexander Boyce [q.v.14] was his brother. After Ralph's father was appointed (1911) to the chair of philosophy at the University of Melbourne, the family lived at Toorak, moving to Mont Albert in 1918. Ralph was educated at Glamorgan Preparatory and Melbourne Church of England Grammar schools, and at the University of Melbourne (BA Hons, 1927), where he studied history and politics.

In 1925 Gibson joined Brian Fitzpatrick [q.v.14], W. Macmahon Ball, Kathleen Fitzpatrick (née Pitt) [qq.v.] and Lloyd Ross in founding the university Labor Club; he also became active in the Labor Guild of Youth. In 1927 he sailed for England. At the University of Manchester (MA, 1930), he wrote a thesis on unemployment insurance. Gibson represented the university's Socialist Society at a University Labour Federation conference and served as an organiser for the Labour Party in the 1929 British general election. While inheriting the family's high-minded philosophical idealism, and sharing his mother's interest in the Indian poet Rabindranath Tagore, Gibson inclined to secular schemes of socialist fellowship. His encounter with poverty in Britain's industrial heartlands was formative; he expected much of the working-class governments elected on the eve of the Depression in Britain and Australia.

Returning to Australia, Gibson took a job in 1931 as an extension lecturer for the Workers' Educational Association on the north coast of Tasmania. His lectures were increasingly critical of the Scullin [q.v.11] government's failure to stem mass unemployment. At the end of the year he rejected the offer of a lectureship at the University of Western Australia. In January 1932 he joined the Communist Party of Australia.

For nearly forty years (apart from three years working for the Forests Commission of Victoria during World War II) Gibson was a full-time party organiser. He never complained about meagre payment, readily accepted long hours, ran between meetings and bounded up stairs. Notoriously careless of his appearance, he looked the part: below medium height, spare in build, fair in appearance,

untidy, urgent. His writing and speech betrayed his class origins: although he adopted the Comintern lexicon and his voice became roughened by constant open-air speaking, his syntax and accent remained those of a bourgeois intellectual.

In 1933 Gibson was jailed for three weeks for addressing an illegal street meeting—one of several such convictions; later that year he made the first of many attempts to enter State and Federal parliament as a CPA candidate. He married Dorothy Alexander [q.v.14 Gibson], a divorcee, at the office of the government statist, Melbourne, on 16 March 1937, after he returned from the World Peace Congress in Brussels. They had met through the peace movement. Her warmth complemented his intensity; with common interests in literature, art and music, and without children, they dedicated themselves to the same cause. Living in Oakleigh, Melbourne, they also spent much time at his mother's cottage at Olinda, in the Dandenong Ranges.

Celebrated for his fidelity to the party, Gibson went wherever he was sent, carrying out all tasks with a brisk efficiency. He served as State secretary, as State president, as a long-standing member of the central (national from 1967) committee, and as editor (1943-48) of the *Guardian*. Yet he would never exercise leadership of an insistently proletarian movement. He saw his role as justifying and propagating communist policy with a single-minded loyalty. As the principal witness before the Lowe [q.v.15] royal commission (1949-50) into communism in Victoria, he gave a sustained and cogent justification of its activity while also offering a chilling definition of communist morality: whatever advanced the cause was good; whatever hindered it was bad. Khrushchev's 1956 revelations of Stalin's crimes made little impression on him. In the early 1960s he tried to avert the split with the pro-Chinese faction of the CPA; a decade later he sympathised with a breakaway pro-Soviet faction, but still stood firm with the party.

Following Dorothy's death in 1978, Gibson travelled and embarked on literary projects. He had written many pamphlets, among them an anticipation of *Socialist Melbourne* (1937) that was repeatedly reissued. In 1966 he published *My Years in the Communist Party*; a memoir of Dorothy, *One Woman's Life*, appeared in 1980; then came two massive, detailed accounts of communist activity in Australia and the world, *The People Stand Up* (1983) and *The Fight Goes On* (1987). These studies combined autobiography, almost impersonal in its modesty, with generous reminiscences of contemporaries and historical analysis that was trapped within the political faith he had never abandoned. Ralph Gibson died on 16 May 1989 at East Malvern, Melbourne, and was cremated.

J. Sendy, *Ralph Gibson* (1988); S. Macintyre, *The Reds* (1998); R. and D. Gibson papers (NLA); Gibson papers (Univ of Melbourne Archives).

STUART MACINTYRE

GIBSON, WILLIAM NORMAN (1915-1982), air force officer, was born on 28 April 1915 at Petersham, Sydney, third child of London-born parents Hamilton Ross Gibson, packer, and his wife Lily Georgina, née Nesbit. His father was killed in action in World War I. Educated at Parramatta High School, where he excelled in sport, led the debating team and obtained the Intermediate certificate, Bill also gained distinction as a Boy Scout. He joined the New South Wales Government Railways and Tramways as an apprentice fitter and turner, and served for two years as a sapper in the Militia.

Enlisting in the Royal Australian Air Force as a cadet on 16 July 1934, Gibson graduated as a pilot and was commissioned on 1 July 1935. Posted to Richmond, New South Wales, he spent the early years of his service on seaplane flying duties, co-operating with the Royal Australian Navy. He was promoted to flight lieutenant in 1938. On 12 March that year at St Philip's Church of England, Sydney, he married Grace Doreen Downton. At the outbreak of World War II he was in Britain taking delivery of the RAAF's new Sunderland flying boats as part of No.10 Squadron. The unit remained in Britain and in June 1940 Gibson was promoted to temporary squadron leader. On 1 July his aircraft sank the RAAF's first U-boat and then directed the rescue of its crew. He was awarded the Distinguished Flying Cross.

Gibson, better known by his nickname 'Hoot', returned to Australia in June 1941 and converted to Catalinas, assuming command of No.20 Squadron in Port Moresby in August. A temporary wing commander from January 1942, he took command of RAAF Station, Port Moresby, next month. From July he served as a staff officer at Allied Air Forces Headquarters, South-West Pacific Area, and then RAAF Command Headquarters under Air Vice-Marshal W. D. Bostock [q.v.13]. He had risen to acting group captain in December. In July 1944 he was appointed senior air staff officer, No.10 (Operational) Group (First Tactical Air Force from October), at Noemfoor and later Morotai, Netherlands East Indies, under Air Commodore A. H. Cobby [q.v.8].

In April 1945 eight senior officers, dissatisfied with what they considered to be an operational policy that was wasteful of men and materiel, tendered their resignations. At Bostock's request, the chief of the Air Staff, Air Vice-Marshal (Sir) George Jones, removed Gibson (and another officer) whom Bostock believed to have contributed to poor morale.

An inquiry by (Sir) John Barry [q.v.13] found that Gibson's attitude to operational commanders was 'indifferent and on occasions high handed'. This conclusion led the Air Board to determine that as Gibson's conduct was 'a primary cause of the widespread condition of discontent and dissatisfaction' within First Tactical Air Force, his commission was to be terminated. Postwar reviews of the Morotai affair showed that this treatment of Gibson was fair and just. He fought his dismissal, however, and the Air Board later rescinded its decision. With the concurrence of the minister for air A. S. Drakeford [q.v.14], it censured him while permitting him to retain his commission at temporary wing commander rank. He had been appointed to the United States Legion of Merit (1945).

Gibson then embarked on a successful postwar career in the RAAF. He commanded bases at East Sale, Victoria (1953-54), and Amberley, Queensland (1959-63), and completed staff training in Britain at the Joint Services Staff College (1951) and the Imperial Defence College (1958). In 1956 he was appointed CBE. Having been promoted to group captain in July 1951 and air commodore in July 1958, he was made acting air vice-marshal in August 1964 and appointed SASO at headquarters, Far East Air Force, Singapore, during 'Confrontation'. Illness led to his early repatriation. He retired from the air force on 14 July 1967 on medical grounds with the honorary rank of air vice-marshal and settled at Newport, Sydney. His recreations included golf, swimming and boating. Survived by his wife and their daughter, he died of myocardial infarction on 31 July 1982 at Mona Vale and was cremated.

J. Herington, *Air War against Germany and Italy 1939-1943* (1954); G. Odgers, *Air War against Japan 1943-1945* (1957); D. Gillison, *Royal Australian Air Force 1939-1942* (1962); A. Stephens, *Power Plus Attitude* (1992); AWM65, item 2290 (AWM); W. N. Gibson RAAF service record (Office of Air Force History, Dept of Defence, Canberra).

DAVID N. ROGERS

GILBERT, ROLLY (c.1901-1990), Aboriginal elder, was born near Macaroni station, Normanton, Queensland, son of George Gilbert and his wife Polly. The date of Rolly's birth is not known but is assumed to be about 1901, as he recalled hearing about World War I as a young man. He took his birthplace to be at a site called Manakorr, close to the mouth of the Gilbert River. Of Kurtjar descent, he was called Mpunywithal, a name that related him to the pelican (*mpunyngkuath*), one of his 'dreamings', or totems. In the early 1900s the Kurtjar people were coming in from the bush to live and work on cattle stations in the area, and Rolly became a stockman on Macaroni. He was treated harshly by his employer, once being beaten with a chain and on another occasion receiving only a drink of rum as payment for a day's labour. He spent some time as a police tracker and in the 1970s he was still employed, looking after public grounds at Normanton.

By the 1960s most Indigenous people had moved into the town, with some going out seasonally to work on cattle stations in the district. As a Kurtjar elder, Gilbert spoke out on such issues as Aboriginal housing in Normanton. In the 1970s he was intent on finding some way to help his people return to their own land. Soft-spoken and patient, he relied less on rhetoric than on the truth and justice of his position. In the information he provided for the pamphlet 'About Kurtjar Land' (1980) he described the problems encountered since white settlement in the 1860s. He helped to determine the boundaries of his tribal territory and documented the location of sacred sites, including bora rings and other ceremonial grounds. His efforts paid off when, in December 1982, the Aboriginal Development Commission bought all the shares in Delta Downs Pastoral Co., thereby acquiring the pastoral lease. This provided the Kurtjar people with 4002 km² of land, enabling them to maintain protection of sacred sites and to operate a viable cattle enterprise.

Although barely literate, Gilbert was a natural scholar who had a talent for drawing perceptive conclusions from keen observations. He helped to preserve knowledge of his people's traditional language and culture and co-operated with linguists and other researchers doing the same. A draft Kurtjar dictionary and an (unpublished) book of Kurtjar stories could not have been completed without his support. Gilbert also provided cultural information in a long interview recorded by the Australian Broadcasting Corporation. In recognition of his various contributions, he was made an associate-member (1977) and a full member (1989) of the Australian Institute of Aboriginal Studies (since 1990 the Australian Institute of Aboriginal and Torres Strait Islander Studies).

Gilbert had married Ruby about 1940 at Delta Downs station. Predeceased by his wife, and survived by his three sons, he died on 30 June 1990 at Normanton and was buried with Anglican rites on Delta Downs.

Aboriginal Development Commission, *Annual Report*, 1982-83, p 19; *Identity*, vol 4, no 4, 1981, p 16; P. Black, 'Rolly Gilbert', *Austn Aboriginal Studies*, no 2, 1990, p 99; personal knowledge.

PAUL D. BLACK

GILL, EDMUND DWEN (1908-1986), palaeontologist, geomorphologist and museum administrator, was born on 11 December 1908 at Mount Eden, Auckland, New Zealand, son of New Zealand-born Arthur Gill, postman, and his Irish-born wife Mary Ann, née Dwen. Inspired by his rector and his science master at Gisborne High School, Ed enrolled at the University of Melbourne (BA, 1935) and the Melbourne College of Divinity (L.Th., 1933; BD, 1938). On 10 December 1935 at Warrnambool, Victoria, he married with Baptist forms Kathleen Winnifred Brebner, a music teacher.

Ministering in Essendon, Gill showed particular interest in youth work: he served as director of the Baptist Union of Victoria's youth and religious education departments, and as a foundation member of the associated youth committee of the National Fitness Council of Victoria. Science, however, increasingly claimed him. In 1938 he published his first paper (on Yeringian trilobites) in the *Victorian Naturalist*, and for several years he studied zoology part time at the university. His ideas on evolution brought him into conflict with his Church. Already appointed (1944) honorary associate in palaeontology at the National Museum of Victoria, in 1948 he resigned from the ministry and became the museum's curator of fossils, succeeding Robert Keble [q.v.14]. He was appointed assistant-director in 1964 and deputy-director in 1969.

Gill's work on Victorian and Tasmanian Siluro-Devonian stratigraphy and palaeontology expanded to include New Zealand, the Cretaceous and Tertiary periods, and overlapping fields of geomorphology, Quaternary environments and archaeology. His interests encompassed vulcanology, lakes and lunettes, megafauna, past floras and Quaternary palaeoclimate, Quaternary vertebrates and Aboriginal prehistory. The first to apply radiocarbon dating in Australian archaeology, he also used fluorine testing, oxygen isotope determinations of palaeotemperatures, archaeological excavation techniques in investigating the age of tektites, and maghemite readings in dating soils. In 1966 he suggested a date of fifteen thousand years for the human cranium found at Keilor, making it then the oldest known human remains in Australia; he also worked on the provenance of the Talgai skull.

An all-rounder in understanding the landscape of Victoria (recording his field-work in some sixty notebooks—together with religious and philosophical musings), Gill developed a detailed knowledge of the Melbourne area, including the built-over landscape, the River Yarra and the coastline of Port Phillip Bay. Studying the terraces of the Maribyrnong River, he evaluated the influence of sea level and climate change. From 1967 he directed a large research project on the Murray River at a time when a proposed dam at Chowilla would have flooded 529 square miles (1370 km²). The resulting Chowilla-Lake Victoria survey, published (1973) as a special volume of the museum's memoirs, was an early example of a modern environmental study.

As the public face of the museum, Gill contributed lectures, articles, and newspaper and radio items to the community. In several instances, his research provoked dispute. He was criticised for his field mapping, and his dating of certain Siluro-Devonian units (later accepted) brought him into conflict with other workers, including David Thomas [q.v.16]. His studies of shorelines and changes in sea levels were challenged by Professor E. S. Hills [q.v.]; although Gill was vindicated by later scholarship, his relationship with the university was strained for some years.

Gill had difficulty in accepting criticism, but his activity was undiminished. He was organiser of an international symposium on the Silurian and Devonian in Melbourne in March 1965; a highly productive secretary (1952-73) of the Australian and New Zealand Association for the Advancement of Science's Quaternary Shorelines Committee; president of the International Union of Quaternary Research Shorelines subcommittee on the Pacific and Indian oceans; and co-editor for *Palaeogeography, Palaeoclimatology, Palaeoecology* (1965-86) and *Pacific Geology* (1971-81). In 1966 he was visiting professor at the California Institute of Technology; he also lectured widely elsewhere in the United States of America, and in New Zealand, Hong Kong, the United Kingdom and South Africa. He was a fellow of the Royal Geographical Society, the Geological Society, London, and the Geological Society of America; a member of the Palaeontological Society; a foundation member of the Geological Society of Australia (1952) and of the Australian Institute of Aboriginal Studies (1964); and vice-president (1965-75) of the Anthropological Society of Victoria.

As honorary secretary (1956-65), research secretary (1966-68), president (1969-70) and honorary treasurer (1973-79), Gill revived a moribund Royal Society of Victoria. He organised a symposium on the basalt plains of Western Victoria that resulted in one of the first scientific regional studies published (1964) by the society. Awarded the RSV research medal (1967), he was made a life member (1972), and was honoured by a symposium on Victoria's coasts (1979) and an annual research grant established in his name (1987). He was also a devoted speaker and excursion leader for the Field Naturalists Club of Victoria, publishing more than seventy papers in the *Victorian Naturalist* and receiving the Australian Natural History medallion (1973).

Retiring from the museum as an honorary associate in palaeontology in 1973, Gill became a research fellow (1974-79) in the Commonwealth Scientific and Industrial Research Organisation's division of applied geomechanics, Melbourne, continuing work on coastal processes. Known for his 'rapid-fire pen', Gill published approximately four hundred papers. A member of the Wallaby Club from 1959 (president, 1967), he was sketched by Professor John Turner in the field in 1980: with his neatly trimmed moustache, spectacles, coat, tie and tweed hat, he appeared to some an antipodean James Joyce. Gregarious and generous, especially to young workers, Gill possessed great charm, combined with a meticulous, formal style. Early in 1986, in declining health, he demonstrated the nature of shell middens at Hopkins River, Warrnambool, perhaps among the earliest evidence of human activity in Australia. Survived by his wife, two sons and a daughter, Edmund Gill died on 13 July 1986 and was cremated. Their eldest child, Adrian, a leading meteorologist and oceanographer, had predeceased him in April.

H. Attwood (ed), *The History of the Wallaby Club 1894-1994* (1993); *Procs of the Royal Soc of Vic*, vol 92, no 1, 1981, p 1; *Austn Archaeology*, no 24, 1987, p 48; *Jnl of Paleontology*, vol 61, no 4, 1987, p 855; *Quaternary A'asia*, Oct 1986, p 62; E. Gill papers (Deakin University and SLV).

E. B. JOYCE

GILL, EUNICE ELIZABETH PERROTT (1918-1987), sportswoman, administrator, coach and academic, was born on 5 January 1918 at Armadale, Melbourne, second child of Victorian-born parents Alexander Joseph Gill, government dairy supervisor, and his wife Emily Felicia, née Perrott. Educated at St Michael's Church of England Girls' Grammar School, Eunice studied at the University of Melbourne (BA, 1941; Dip.Phys.Ed., 1945; Dip.Ed., 1957) and became a player of women's basketball, the name of which was changed to netball in 1970. A member of the State team (1945-46), and captain of the All Australia carnival team (1946 and 1947), she toured New Zealand with the national team in 1948.

In 1949 Gill was appointed acting-lecturer in the university's department of physical education, becoming temporary lecturer the following year and gaining permanency in 1953. Her teaching interests, which included human movement and sports practice, reflected the influence of Rudolf Laban, whose work in dance analysis and therapy had impressed her during her study leave in Britain in 1952. While formal and 'perhaps a little aloof' (so her students recall), Gill was also encouraging, inspirational and challenging in developing her subject. She was promoted to senior lecturer in 1960 and used study leave in 1972-73 to complete an MA (1973) at the University of Leeds.

Beyond the university Gill had an extensive influence on the development of her sport. Elected president (1954) and honorary secretary-treasurer (1958-60, 1966-68) of the All Australia Women's Basketball Association, she also coached the Victorian (1954) and Australian (1960) teams and was delegate to three world tournaments (1967, 1970-71, 1979). Through the International Federation of Netball Associations (vice-president 1959-67, 1983-87; senior vice-president 1975-83) she helped to establish an international code for the game in 1960. The previous year she had become a life member of the Victorian association and received a service award from both the AAWBA (1966) and the IFNA (1983).

A long-standing Victorian representative on the council of the Australian Physical Education Association, Gill organised its 1968 biennial conference in Melbourne. She was also an active member of the Australian Council of Health, Physical Education and Recreation, president of the Victorian Women's Amateur Sports Council, and Australian representative on the council of the International Association of Physical Education and Sport for Women and Girls. In 1976 she was a foundation member of the board of the Confederation of Australian Sport (vice-president, 1982-86), and next year became the only woman on the Federal government's Sports Advisory Council. A forceful advocate for improving standards in school curricula and examinations, and for the role of team sports in upholding 'an Australian way of life', Gill presided over the ACHPER and chaired its Sport in Schools Committee and the Australian Sport Coaches Assembly (1982-86), overseeing the accreditation of thirty-three thousand registered coaches. She was appointed MBE in 1975.

Following her retirement from the university in 1983, Gill continued to work in sports policy and administration; in 1986 the CAS made her a fellow and presented her with its gold award. She was a 'quiet leader' in Soroptimist International of Victoria and patroness (1985) of the Victorian Lawn Bowls Association. Falling ill in 1986 she stepped down from most of her responsibilities. She died of cancer on 4 December 1987 at Canterbury, Melbourne, and was cremated. Tributes recalled her 'wisdom', 'analytical mind' and 'innate dignity', and her success in raising the profile of women in the community. The Eunice Gill memorial award for coach development honours her work. In 1995 she was inducted into the Sport Australia Hall of Fame as an associate member—administration.

Herald (Melbourne), 14 Aug 1980, p 41; *Sport Report*, June 1986, p 3; *Austn Netball News*, 7 Mar 1988, p 6; Board of Studies in Physical Education, Minutes of Meetings, 1941-53 (Univ of Melbourne Archives); biog file (Netball Victoria, Melbourne); private information.   JUDITH SMART

GILLILAND, MARGARET SYLVIA (1917-1990), biochemist, was born on 8 September 1917 at Grenfell, New South Wales, second child of Robert Dugald Bertie, a Sydney solicitor, and his wife Kathleen, née Crommelin, both born in New South Wales. C. H. Bertie [q.v.7] was her uncle. Margaret's mother died early; her father spent some years as a planter in the Mandated Territory of New Guinea and she lived for much of her girlhood with two unmarried aunts in Sydney. While studying biochemistry at the University of Melbourne (B.Sc., 1939), she developed a lifelong interest in fast cars and at 20 drove a super-charged MG Magnette in a Sydney-to-Melbourne sports car rally. She was engaged briefly to a racing-car driver, but on 24 October 1942 at St Mark's Church of England, Darling Point, Sydney, she married Alexander Forbes Gilliland, a 'Tobruk rat' recently returned from North Africa. They had two daughters and a son.

Alexander was discharged from the army in 1946 and the family settled at Sherwood, Brisbane. After his death in 1958 Gilliland moved to Taringa, close to the University of Queensland, where she had taken a job as a demonstrator in biochemistry. Senior demonstrator from 1957, for the next six years she organised the large second-year practical classes. In 1962 she was awarded an M.Sc. for a thesis on aspects of bacterial metabolism, and next year was promoted to lecturer. Suffering from severe bronchial asthma, possibly triggered by contact with solvents used in her research, she spent most of 1964 on extended sick leave.

Known as 'Mrs G' to her students, Gilliland was a tall (5 ft 8 ins or 173 cm), slim, angular woman with a sharp, intelligent face, twinkling eyes and a wry smile. In 1965 she resumed her administrative and teaching responsibilities, but allowed her laboratory-based research to languish, partly through fear of a physical relapse. None the less, she won an American Association of University Women graduate fellowship, sufficient to fund a year's study leave in 1969 at the University of California, San Diego (La Jolla), United States of America. There she pursued her work on bacterial metabolism and pigmentation, experiencing only a brief recurrence of asthma. With a growing interest in science communication, she also studied large-class teaching strategies at several institutions in California.

Gilliland was an active member of the Queensland Association of University Women. Early in the 1970s she became something of a radical. She was outraged by the French nuclear-testing program in the Pacific and in 1973 helped to plan the *Yooringa* protest group's expedition to Muroroa Atoll. In a letter to the vice-chancellor, (Sir) Zelman Cowen, she wrote that she had 'verbally deplored such happenings long enough', and that 'women should be represented on this boat'. However, the proposed trip into the testing zone was cancelled because of problems with insurance cover. As the QAUW representative on the council of the University of Queensland Union (which she chaired in 1975 and 1977), she prosecuted students' concerns vigorously, mounting campaigns for the appointment of a university ombudsman, for part-time student jobs on campus, and for free on-site buses.

In 1976 Gilliland's second period of study leave initiated the most important phase of her career. Passionate about social justice and the need to address global poverty, in the Philippines, at the East-West Center, Hawaii, and at the University of California, Berkeley, she investigated nutritional education and schemes of intervention. In 1978, supported by the Australian Development Assistance Bureau, she set up a master's degree in community health (nutrition) at the University of Queensland and was seconded to act as director of the course. The ambitious, multi-disciplinary program, originally designed for community health workers in the Philippines and Australia, later extended its reach to Thailand, Malaysia, Fiji and parts of Africa, and graduated some two hundred students from around the world. Gilliland was the organising genius and tireless servant of the program but her contribution was not deemed sufficient for promotion until 1982, when ADAB paid her full salary (as senior lecturer and then associate professor). Her university appointment was renewed annually until she retired in 1988.

Optimistic, energetic and determined, with a capacity for helpless laughter, Gilliland loved parties and practical jokes. She was devoted to her grandchildren, enjoyed books, the ballet and the opera, and had a strong if informal belief in a spiritual dimension. Survived by her three children, she died on 18 May 1990 at Karana Downs, near Ipswich, and was cremated.

Austn Federation of Univ Women (Queensland), *Newsletter*, June 1990, p 8; Gilliland staff file (Univ of Qld Archives); Gilliland papers (Univ of Qld Lib); private information and personal knowledge.

PATRICK BUCKRIDGE

GILLON, LESLIE MILES (1916-1981), army officer and stockbroker, was born on 17 May 1916 at Aspendale, Melbourne, third child of Joseph Leslie Gillon, builder and contractor, and his wife Annie May, née I'Anson, both Melbourne born. Educated at Melbourne Church of England Grammar School, Miles worked with the stockbroking firm of J. B. Were [q.v.2] & Son. After serving as a gunner in the 2nd Field Brigade, Militia, he enlisted in the Australian Imperial Force on 20 June 1940.

Commissioned as a lieutenant on 1 January 1941, Gillon was posted to the 2/10th Field Regiment. His regiment arrived in Singapore next month and, with other units of the 8th Division, was engaged in a series of training exercises in Malaya. In December Japanese forces landed on the beaches of northern Malaya and began their push to the south. Allied forces were unable to offer effective resistance, the last Australian troops crossing the causeway to Singapore on 31 January 1942, with the entire garrison surrendering on 15 February.

In March 1943 Gillon was part of the 1000-strong 'E' Force that was shipped by the Japanese to Berhala Island, off Sandakan, British North Borneo. He made contact with a number of fellow Australians who were determined to escape, among them R. K. McLaren and C. A. Wagner [qq.v.15,16]. They befriended a guard, who helped them to get away, arranging for a boat to take them to the island of Tawitawi. There Gillon and his seven compatriots were formally commissioned into the United States Forces in the Philippines on 30 June, Gillon becoming second-in-command of the 1st Battalion, 125th Regiment. After engaging the Japanese in several operations, the Australians were ordered in late October to report to the guerrilla headquarters at Liangan on Mindanao, a dangerous journey of some 500 miles (805 km) that took them until December to complete.

Promoted to temporary captain in January 1944 and temporary major in December that year, Gillon served as deputy chief of staff, 108th Division, Tenth Military District, directing operations in the Liangan area of Lanao province and personally leading combat patrols. On 14 and 15 December he commanded a motor whaleboat as part of a larger force that attacked Polloc Harbour and Malabang respectively. For these actions, and for his leadership of the guerrilla forces, he was awarded the Distinguished Service Order and mentioned in despatches. He arrived back in Australia in April 1945 and his AIF appointment was terminated on 23 July.

Gillon bought a seat on the Stock Exchange of Melbourne on 29 August 1945 and formed L. M. Gillon & Co., a private-client broking house which became Gillon Derham & Co. in 1960. He served as the stock exchange's odd-lot specialist from 1954 and on its committee in 1958-64. On 8 November 1945 he had married Gweneth Alice Dadswell in the chapel of his old school. A champion athlete in his youth, he was a member of the Royal Melbourne Golf Club and the Royal South Yarra Lawn Tennis Club. He died of hypertensive heart failure on

19 November 1981 at Richmond and was cremated; his wife and their son and two daughters survived him.

S. Ross, *And Tomorrow Freedom* (1989); B883, item VX34838 (NAA); private information.

PETER DENNIS

GIORDANO, ANTONIO (1907-1984), journalist, author and community leader, was born on 12 May 1907 at Naples, Italy, only child of Salvatore Giordano, a landowner and operatic tenor from Caronia, Sicily, and his wife Eucharis, née Bagli, from Rimini. Having trained as a cadet in the merchant navy, Antonio worked his passage in a French steamer and disembarked at Fremantle, Western Australia, in September 1924. He travelled through all the mainland States for ten years with a swag on his back, stopping for a month or two at a time to accept any employment that he could find. A big man, he took on various labouring jobs and worked as a shop assistant, waiter, cook, ice-cream vendor, and tent hand with Wirth [q.v.12] Bros Ltd's circus. Along the way he had minor brushes with the law.

While unemployed in 1930 Giordano joined the Communist Party of Australia; the Italian consul-general in Sydney sent his name to Rome for inclusion in the Mussolini government's files of anti-fascist subversives. In 1932 Giordano quit the party, sent a retraction to the consul-general and embraced fascism, possibly hoping for assistance with repatriation. Towards the end of the decade he settled in Sydney and in 1938-40 was a journalist on the pro-fascist *Italo-Australian* newspaper. He joined the local fascist party and took on clerical duties at the Italian Club. Interned on 15 June 1940, he was sent to Loveday camp, South Australia. He was released in February 1944 when the Commonwealth Crown Solicitor's Office sought his services as a court interpreter and translator.

On 18 August 1945 at the Unitarian Christian Church, Adelaide, Giordano married Lucy Gwenda Beatrice Trueman, a stenographer. After the war he returned to Sydney; he was naturalised on 6 November 1946 and in 1952 moved to Adelaide. An advocate for newly arrived Italians, he promoted the establishment of an Italian cultural and social centre. In 1955 he helped to set up the Roma Amateur Sports Club for young single Italians and edited its magazine, *Roma*. He opened the Italian Information Service in January 1956. From 1959 he was South Australian delegate to the Italian Chamber of Commerce in Victoria, South Australia and Tasmania and was founding secretary (1970-83) of the South Australian branch. In 1961 he set up the National Association of Emigrant Families.

He was chairman (1960-62) of the Adelaide Juventus Sports and Social Club, a founding council-member (1962) of the South Australian Soccer Federation and an active member of the Good Neighbour Council. In the 1970s he was contracted to the Telephone and State Interpreter services.

As a journalist Giordano wrote for *La Fiamma*, *Il Corriere d'Australia*, *Settegiorni* and *Soccer News*, edited *King Soccer* and broadcast over an ethnic radio station. His many letters to the Australian press over the years gained him a reputation as a champion of minority groups. Outspoken and blunt, he was never afraid to speak his mind in defence of a cause. He wrote several pamphlets and books dealing with the Italian influence on Australian history, including *Alessandro Malaspina* (1973), *A Dream of the Southern Seas: The Life Story of James Mario Matra* [q.v.Supp.] (1984), and *Marco Polo and After: A Brief Survey of Italian Travel and Exploration in South East Asia, New Guinea and Australia* (1974).

Giordano was appointed AM in 1979. Survived by his wife, he died on 16 December 1984 at his Mile End home and was buried in Centennial Park cemetery. There were no children. In 1985 he was made posthumously an officer of the Order of Merit of the Italian Republic.

D. O'Connor, *No Need to Be Afraid* (1996); *Advertiser* (Adelaide), 27 Aug 1955, p 4, 26 Jan 1956, p 4; *La Fiamma* (Sydney), Oct 1963, 'supp', p 55; A367, item C18000/92, ST1233/1, item N36845, MP14/1, item NN (NAA); Giordano papers (SLSA).

DESMOND O'CONNOR

GIOVANELLI, RONALD GORDON (1915-1984), physicist and solar researcher, was born on 30 April 1915 at Grafton, New South Wales, only child of Irwin Wilfred Giovanelli, schoolteacher, and his wife Gertrude May, née Gordon, both born in New South Wales. Ronald attended Fort Street Boys' High School in Sydney and the University of Sydney (B.Sc., 1937; M.Sc., 1939; D.Sc., 1950), graduating with first-class honours in physics. His earliest appointments were as a research fellow (1937-39) at the Commonwealth Solar Observatory at Mount Stromlo, Canberra, and as a physics teacher (1939-40) at Sydney Technical College.

In 1938 the Commonwealth government had decided to create within the Council for Scientific and Industrial Research (Commonwealth Scientific and Industrial Research Organization) a National Standards Laboratory with responsibility for establishing Australia's national standards of measurement. Giovanelli was one of nine scientists recruited to develop the NSL, their first assignment being to work at the British National Physical Laboratory to gain experience in standards. He sailed in

February 1940 for London, where he specialised in optics, light and photometry.

On his return in April 1941 to the newly constructed NSL building at the University of Sydney, Giovanelli was at first engaged in commissioning equipment purchased while abroad and in training staff. World War II soon diverted NSL to urgent defence projects. Giovanelli welcomed this opportunity to provide direct support to the war effort. His contributions included developing special goggles to protect anti-aircraft spotters from eye damage by the sun; designing an illumination system for aircraft instrument panels that did not impair the 'dark adaptation' of pilots and gunners; and helping to establish an Australian capability to manufacture high-grade optical glass. In 1945 the NSL sections became full divisions of CSIR. Giovanelli married Katherine Hazel Gordon, one of his laboratory assistants and a talented painter, on 8 February 1947 at St Michael's Church of England, Vaucluse.

After the war Giovanelli returned to his standards work and in addition undertook applied projects on diverse topics such as retroreflectors for road signs and vehicles, colorimetric measurement of haemoglobin, and the reflective properties of diffusing media. With the encouragement of the chief of the physics division, G. H. Briggs, he also started a program of solar physics research, initially theoretical and mainly concerned with solar flares and radiative transfer of energy in the solar atmosphere. The excellence of his solar research was soon widely recognised. The Royal Society of New South Wales awarded him the 1948 Edgeworth David [q.v.8] medal and the Australian Academy of Science elected him a fellow in 1962.

In 1958 Giovanelli had become chief of the CSIRO division of physics. This job brought a heavy administrative load and an obligation to serve on external bodies including the National Standards Commission (1959-76). He was a stern yet likeable leader, encouraging his staff to attain world standards throughout their wide range of scientific programs. In solar physics research Giovanelli developed a strong support team but also continued to make important personal contributions. He published widely and gained further international acclaim for his advances in such fields as radiative transfer in the absence of thermodynamic equilibrium, the origin and effects of solar magnetic fields, and the solar magnetic cycle. To underpin their theoretical work, he and his colleagues established three solar observatories in succession, equipping them with novel and sophisticated optical instruments that enabled previously inaccessible parameters of the sun to be measured. Despite his workload Giovanelli made time to provide university lecture courses in physics and astronomy, and to work with postgraduate students in astronomy. A foundation councillor of the Astronomical Society of Australia in 1966 (president 1968-69), he was also active in the International Astronomical Union and a fellow (1940) of the Royal Astronomical Society. He received and accepted many invitations from solar observatories in North America, Europe and Asia to give lectures and serve as a visiting scientist.

Unwell and increasingly frustrated by the inroads that his administrative duties made on his time, Giovanelli resigned from his position as chief in 1974 to become a full-time solar researcher, as a CSIRO senior research fellow until 1976 and then as an honorary research fellow. Despite his illness, he continued to travel and work overseas and wrote a monograph, *Secrets of the Sun* (1984), which was published posthumously. Survived by his wife and their daughter and son, he died of fibrosis of the lung on 27 January 1984 at Camperdown and was cremated. Commemorative workshops and colloquia were held in Brisbane, Sydney and Tucson, Arizona.

D. P. Mellor, *The Role of Science and Industry* (1958); J. F. H. Wright, *Measurement in Australia 1938-1988* (1988); R. Bhathal, *Australian Astronomers* (1996); *Hist Records of Austn Science*, vol 6, no 2, 1985, p 223; Giovanelli papers (Basser Lib, Canberra).   W. R. BLEVIN

GLAESSNER, MARTIN FRITZ (1906-1989), geologist and palaeontologist, was born on 25 December 1906 at Aussig an der Elbe, Bohemia, Austro-Hungarian Empire (Ústí nad Labem, Czech Republic), only child of Arthur Glaessner, chemist, and his wife Luise, née Feigl. As a child in Vienna Martin became interested in geology and palaeontology; by the age of 16 he was a research associate at the Museum of Natural History and by 20 had published three papers on fossil crabs. Having matriculated from Währing secondary school, in 1925 he entered the University of Vienna, where he obtained doctorates in law (1929) and philosophy (1931). In 1930 and 1931 he was a visiting research associate at the British Museum (Natural History).

Recognising the importance of micropalaeontology and especially fossil foraminifera in petroleum exploration and development, in 1932 Glaessner moved to Moscow to work for the State Petroleum Research Institute of the Soviet Union. In 1934 he transferred to the Institute of Mineral Fuels, to establish its micropalaeontological laboratory. His research focused on fossil-bearing strata in the Bol'shoy Kavkas (Caucasus) mountains. On 29 June 1936 at a registry office in Moscow, he married Christina Tupikina. Having declined to take out Soviet citizenship, he was obliged to leave the country by the end of 1937. He returned to Vienna but, part-Jewish, soon left for London because of the *anschluss* (1938). Employed by the Anglo-Iranian Oil Co., he was sent to Port Moresby, Papua, to establish a micropalaeontological laboratory for the Australasian Petroleum Co. Pty Ltd.

Evacuated from Papua in 1942, Glaessner worked in Melbourne. In the next three years he prepared a geological map of Papua and New Guinea for the Australian Military Forces and was a consultant to the Iraq Petroleum Co. Ltd. In 1945 he was naturalised. That year he published *Principles of Micropalaeontology*, which was to become a standard textbook for thirty-three years. In 1948 he gained a D.Sc. from the University of Melbourne. Back in Port Moresby after the war, he resumed the research that was to culminate in a series of reviews on the stratigraphy and tectonics of Australia, New Zealand, New Guinea and the South Pacific.

At the invitation of Sir Douglas Mawson [q.v.10], in 1950 Glaessner joined the department of geology at the University of Adelaide as senior lecturer. He was promoted to reader (1953) and professor (1964). His academic career focused first on micropalaeontology and associated stratigraphy, and included consulting work on oil- and gas-drilling projects on Australia's continental margins and in Timor, Papua and New Guinea, and New Caledonia. An outstanding lecturer, he provided an intellectually challenging overview ranging across stratigraphy, ancient climates, tectonics and palaeogeography, and attracted several highly talented postgraduate students. Continuing his work on fossil crabs, he established an international reputation in the field with his contribution to *Treatise on Invertebrate Paleontology* (1969), edited by R. C. Moore and published under the auspices of the Geological Society of America.

By the mid-1950s Glaessner had begun investigating the taxonomy, palaeobiology and stratigraphy of the well-preserved early fauna remains at Ediacara in South Australia's Flinders Ranges, research that resulted in *The Dawn of Animal Life* (1984). Author of more than 150 papers and four books or treatises, and involved in editing several others, he was highly regarded as the foundation editor (1953-58) of the *Journal of the Geological Society of Australia*. Retiring in 1971, he was appointed emeritus professor. He was an honorary research fellow at the University of Adelaide until 1989.

The Royal Society of New South Wales's (W. B.) Clarke [q.v.3] memorial lecturer (1953) and Walter Burfitt [q.v.7] prizeman (1962), Glaessner was elected (1957) a fellow of the Australian Academy of Science and was chairman (1962-77) of its national committee of geological sciences. He received the Sir Joseph

Verco [q.v.12] medal from the Royal Society of South Australia (1970) and the Lyell medal from the Geological Society of London (1974), and became a fellow of the German Academy of Scientists Leopoldina (1971) and an honorary member of the Geological Society of Australia (1976). The United States of America's National Academy of Sciences awarded him its Charles Doolittle Walcott medal in 1982. In 1985 he was appointed AM.

Glaessner's relationships with his colleagues were mainly friendly but not close: Professor Brian McGowran described him as a 'somewhat shy man' who, although kindly, could be abrupt. Former students remember him with affection. Survived by his wife and their daughter, he died on 22 November 1989 in Adelaide and was cremated.

J. B. Jones and B. McGowran (eds), *Stratigraphic Problems of the Later Precambrian and Early Cambrian* (1972); B. P. Radhakrishna (ed), *The World of Martin F. Glaessner* (1991); *Austn Geologist*, no 75, June 1990, p 39; *Hist Records of Austn Science*, vol 10, no 1, 1994, p 61; A435, item 1944/4/6138 (NAA); private information. BERNARD O'NEIL

GLANVILLE-HICKS, PEGGY WINSOME (1912-1990), composer and music critic, was born on 29 December 1912 at St Kilda, Melbourne, eldest child of English-born Ernest Glanville Hicks, journalist, and his New Zealand-born wife Myrtle, née Barley. Peggy began composing at the age of 7, encouraged by her mother, an amateur singer and artist, and her father, author of *The Turn of the Tide and Other Poems* (1932). Educated at Milverton, Methodist Ladies' College and Clyde School, Woodend, she studied composition with Fritz Hart [q.v.9] at the Albert Street Conservatorium, East Melbourne. In 1932, following a farewell concert in the Melbourne Town Hall, she left Australia and, over four years at the Royal College of Music, London, supported by scholarships, studied composition with Ralph Vaughan Williams, conducting with (Sir) Malcolm Sargent and piano with Arthur Benjamin [q.v.7]. Her early works included the opera *Caedmon* (c.1936), music for film, and the *Spanish Suite* (c.1935). The Octavia travelling scholarship enabled her to study with Egon Wellesz in Vienna (1936) and Nadia Boulanger in Paris (1937).

After a brief visit to Melbourne in 1938, Glanville-Hicks (she later hyphenated her name) returned to London for the performance of two movements from her suite for female voices, oboe and strings (*Choral Suite*, 1937) at a concert of the International Society for Contemporary Music. She was the first Australian whose work was performed for the ISCM, and one of the youngest composers represented. Several of her songs were published that year by Louise Dyer's [q.v.8] Editions de l'Oiseau-Lyre in Paris. Dyer's recording company released the *Choral Suite* in 1940. On 9 November 1938 at the Kensington register office Glanville-Hicks had married Stanley Richard Henry Bate, an English composer. In 1940 a British Council grant allowed them to travel to Australia; in 1941 they sailed for the United States of America and settled in New York.

When in 1947 Glanville-Hicks reviewed an ISCM festival in Copenhagen for the *Musical Courier*, she embarked on a career as a respected critic and commentator on modern music. The composer Virgil Thomson, chief critic of the *New York Herald Tribune*, employed her as a 'stringer'; the first of five hundred reviews appeared on 27 October 1947. Through the 1940s she also contributed major pieces to *Music & Letters* (on Paul Bowles), *Musical America* (on John Cage) and *Musical Quarterly* (on Thomson). In 1948 she travelled to the ISCM festival in Amsterdam to hear a performance of her *Concertino da Camera* and in 1950 she embarked on a lecture tour of universities in America's mid-west. She became an American citizen in 1949, and in the same year obtained a divorce from Bate. On 4 January 1952 she married Rafael da Costa, a journalist, in a civil ceremony in New York; they divorced next year.

The 1950s brought Glanville-Hicks to prominence as a composer of 'exotic' music and as a catalyst for the performance of new music. Her most performed work, a sonata for harp, was premièred by Nicanor Zabaleta in Caracas (1951) and New York (1952); in 1953 her *Letters from Morocco* (1952), conducted by Leopold Stokowski, featured in one of the concerts she initiated as a member of the junior council of the Museum of Modern Art. Among the works that followed were the *Etruscan Concerto* (1954, written for the pianist Carlo Bussotti), *Concertino Antico* (1955, for the harpist Edna Phillips), *Concerto Romantico* (1956, for the violist Walter Trampler) and *The Glittering Gate* (1956), based on a story by Lord Dunsany.

In 1951-60 (except the 1955-56 season) Glanville-Hicks was director of the Composers' Forum, an enterprise overseen by the most eminent New York composers. She contributed 106 articles on American and Danish composers to the fifth edition of *Grove's Dictionary of Music and Musicians* (1954). Until 1955 she worked for the *Tribune* from October to April each year and spent her summers composing and attending festivals in Europe, Jamaica and Australia.

In 1953 Glanville-Hicks won an American Academy of Arts and Letters award, and was offered a commission by the Louisville Philharmonic Society, through the Rockefeller Foundation, to write an opera—the first such offer, she claimed, made to a woman. This opera, *The Transposed Heads*, based on a story by Thomas Mann, had its première in Louisville (1954) and was staged in New York in 1958. It demonstrated her interest in Indian music and increasing desire to promote a fusion of Eastern and Western compositional methods. In 1956-58 she was supported by Guggenheim Foundation awards for composition.

After major surgery in 1956, and again in 1959, Glanville-Hicks moved to Athens. In 1960 she was awarded a Rockefeller Foundation grant to 'study the relationships among musical forms in the West, the Middle East and Asia'; a Fulbright award (1961) was devoted to research into the traditional music of Greece. Her opera *Nausicaa* (1960)—with a libretto drawn from Robert Graves's novel *Homer's Daughter* and set in the ninth century BC—was performed at the Athens Festival in August 1961, after heroic efforts to arrange funding and import a company of Greek-American singers, a choreographer and conductor, as well as a marimba. It was recorded and broadcast in the USA, reviewed in major publications in several languages, and praised for its lyricism and ingenious orchestration.

Commissioned by the San Francisco Opera (and supported by a Ford Foundation grant), Glanville-Hicks's next opera, *Sappho* (1963), derived from a play by Lawrence Durrell, was written to a punishing schedule; it was not produced and the composer remained unhappy with it. Her major works of the 1960s were ballets, devised in conjunction with the New York choreographer John Butler, including *Saul and the Witch of Endor* (1959) and *Jephthah's Daughter* (1966) for CBS TV, and *A Season in Hell* (1967) for the Harkness Ballet. After years of failing eyesight, in June 1966 she underwent surgery in New York for a pituitary tumour; further surgery was required in April 1969. As well as robbing her of the ability to compose, the effects of surgery and radiotherapy undermined her health for the rest of her life.

In 1970 Glanville-Hicks travelled to Australia for a performance of *The Transposed Heads* in Sydney. In 1972 *The Glittering Gate* was performed at the Adelaide Festival. The works were heard jointly at the 1986 festival. She returned permanently in 1975, her affinity with the Asian inspirations of younger composers leading to a position as consultant for Asian Music Studies at the Australian Music Centre, Sydney. In 1987 she was awarded an honorary doctorate of music by the University of Sydney. On 25 June 1990 she died at Darlinghurst, Sydney, and was buried in the Field of Mars cemetery, Ryde. She bequeathed her house at Paddington as a residence for young composers.

Glanville-Hicks was delicate and slight in appearance, but in character brilliant and articulate. Her works were often modal (demonstrating her interest in folk song), transparent in texture and colourful in instrumentation. She was a major figure in mid-twentieth century music, her profile formed as much by prodigious organisational skills and wit as by her elegant music.

D. Hayes, *Peggy Glanville-Hicks* (1990); W. Beckett, *Peggy Glanville-Hicks* (1992); J. Murdoch, *Peggy Glanville-Hicks* (2002); Glanville-Hicks papers (NLA, SLNSW and SLV); Methodist Ladies' College Archives, Melbourne.

SUZANNE ROBINSON

GLASS, DUDLEY JACK (1899-1981), composer, pianist and author, was born on 24 September 1899 in North Adelaide, only child of Philip Joseph Glass, waterproof-garment manufacturer, and his wife Jeannie Golda, née Glass. Barnet Glass [q.v.9] was his grandfather. Dudley attended Melbourne Church of England Grammar School, studied composition with Fritz Hart [q.v.9] at the Albert Street Conservatorium, East Melbourne, for two terms in 1918, and graduated (BA, 1920) from the University of Melbourne. Already a prolific composer and lyricist, in July 1925 Glass secured the performance of his *Australia, Land of Ours* in a pageant marking the visit of the United States Pacific Fleet; this anthem was adopted by the New South Wales and Victorian Education departments for use in schools. Later that year he travelled to London, via New York, as the Melbourne *Herald*'s musical and dramatic correspondent, and settled there.

Developing extensive networks, Glass was soon composing musical plays and light operas. The most successful, *The Beloved Vagabond*, opened in London in 1927; its Australian première at the Princess Theatre, Melbourne, in 1934, starred Gladys Moncrieff and George Wallace [qq.v.10,12]. Other works included *The Toymaker of Nuremberg* (1930); an adaptation of Beatrix Potter's *The Tale of Peter Rabbit* (1951), produced in New York in 1961; and *Drake of England* (1953)—for which he provided the music and lyrics— broadcast by the Australian Broadcasting Commission to coincide with the coronation of Queen Elizabeth II. He also wrote English lyrics for *A Night in Venice* by Johann Strauss. Other compositions included musical revues, an unperformed opera, over a hundred songs (including settings of nonsense poems by Edward Lear and Hilaire Belloc, and, in 1940, the patriotic *The Empire is Marching*) and an orchestral piece, *Will-o'-the-Wisp* (1928).

Glass often returned to Australia to attend performances of his work and to undertake the broadcasting and lecturing commitments that became an integral part of his career. With an engaging manner and 'business-like air' (so the *Sydney Morning Herald* noted in 1934), he had a keen sense of what would entertain. Always versatile, in 1933 he had published the first of two children's books, *Round the World with the Redhead Twins*. In 1937 he published two works reflecting his extensive travel: *The Book about the British Empire* and *Australian Fantasy*. During World War II he gave more than a thousand performances in Britain as a pianist and speaker for the Army Education Corps. After the war he increasingly devoted his time to similar activities, making lecture tours of the United States of America and lecturing in Britain for the London County Council, the Imperial Institute, the Royal Empire Society, the Royal Academy of Music and the Royal Society of Arts. He also gave regular talks for the British Broadcasting Corporation and the ABC.

'Still an Australian', as Glass insisted in 1960, he was an untiring ambassador and educator for his country. He was a widely published theatre and arts critic, writing for *Everybody's Weekly* and, from 1964, the *Irish Times*. A member of the Savage Club, PEN International and the Royal Commonwealth Society, Dudley Glass never married. He died at Lambeth, London, on 29 November 1981 after being struck by a bus near the British Library, which he visited almost daily.

Jnl (Austn Jewish Hist Soc), vol 10, no 5, 1989, p 399; *SMH*, 22 Aug 1934, p 12; *Herald* (Melbourne), 3 Oct 1956, p 18; *Sun News-Pictorial* (Melbourne), 9 July 1960, p 13; Glass papers (NLA).

PETER CAMPBELL

GOBLE, DOROTHY ADA (1910-1990), politician, was born on 11 March 1910 at Richmond, Melbourne, daughter of Arthur Robert Taylor, a clerk from London, and his locally born wife Ada Elizabeth, née Deumer. Educated at North Richmond and Canterbury state schools, Dorothy completed secondary studies at University High School, where she then worked as secretary (1928-34). On 4 October 1934 at the Congregational Church, Canterbury, she married Kenneth George Goble, a stationery manufacturer.

Through the 1940s Mrs Goble became active within the Victorian division of the Liberal Party of Australia, later holding offices in the Hartwell and Blackburn branches, and becoming vice-chairman of the Victorian women's section (1962-67) and a member of the State executive (1965-67). In April 1967 she won the Legislative Assembly seat of Mitcham, having defeated thirteen men to gain pre-selection. Her election drew considerable attention, given that she was female, 56 years old and a grandmother. She was also the first woman to be elected to the Victorian parliament in nineteen years, and the first from the Liberal Party.

Holding Mitcham until her retirement (1976), Goble was an effective local member and a gracious, if sometimes tenacious, parliamentarian. Her social conscience was unconstrained by party ideology. She believed that women should receive equal pay despite this being a policy of the Australian Labor Party. While resisting any suggestion that she was a feminist (stressing instead that she was a Liberal and woman first), she argued for women's rights.

In 1967 Goble challenged the entitlement of women to remove their names from the jury list, insisting that with expectations of equality came acceptance of responsibility. The provision was removed in 1975. In 1971 she urged that women be admitted to the Victorian Public Service at the same level as men, objecting to an advertisement inviting 'young men' to sit an entrance examination. She returned to the issue in 1972, in response to a complaint that a woman had faced prejudice in applying for a public service cadetship. The Victorian Public Service Board lifted the bar on recruitment of women to the administrative division later that year.

Goble's interests embraced social welfare, health and consumer affairs, with a particular commitment to improving standards of education for children, especially those with intellectual disabilities. Her concern extended to the needs of Indigenous Australians. She served on the Library (1970-76) and Subordinate Legalisation (1973-76) parliamentary committees. Unperturbed at being the only woman in the assembly, in 1971 she attended the men-only Queen's Birthday levee at Parliament House. The last woman to confront this custom had been Fanny Brownbill [q.v.13] over twenty years before, but she had been announced as a 'gentleman'.

Outside parliament, Mrs Goble was involved in many community organisations, including the councils of Mitcham High and Technical schools, the Asthma and Alcoholism foundations of Victoria, the Nunawading Historical Society and the Mitcham Repertory Group. She was a member of the planning committee of the Maroondah Hospital and a life member of the Blackburn and District Tree Preservation Society. Predeceased by her husband (1982), and survived by their son and daughter, Dorothy Goble died on 22 October 1990 at East Malvern and was cremated.

PD (LA, Vic), 30 Oct 1990, p 1551; Sun News-Pictorial (Melbourne), 24 Sept 1966, p 43; Age (Melbourne), 9 May 1967, p 31; Herald (Melbourne), 12 June 1971, p 2, 19 May 1975, p 15.

JUDITH STARCEVICH

GODFREY, GEORGE FULLER (1904-1989), journalist and union official, was born on 5 November 1904 at Battersea, London, third of five children of Francis George Godfrey, schoolteacher, and his wife Millie, née Fuller. George attended the Strand School, London, where he won a mathematics scholarship to Queens' College, Cambridge (BA, 1926; MA, 1972). During Britain's general strike in May 1926 he enlisted as a special constable in the emergency force to maintain order and essential services. He decided to migrate to Australia and landed in Melbourne in 1927 with £5 in his pocket.

After teaching mathematics for one term at Essendon High School, Godfrey was appointed a cadet reporter on the Melbourne *Argus* in May 1927. He moved to Sydney in 1930 to join the *Sun*, an afternoon broadsheet, where he revelled in the challenge of police, civic and parliamentary rounds; he was to become a sub-editor in 1943 and later relieving editor. On 21 June 1932 he married Phyllis Berenice Alethia Carling, a clerk, at St Augustine's Church of England, Neutral Bay.

A member of the Australian Journalists' Association from 1927, Godfrey was elected to the New South Wales district committee in 1934, and again in 1940; he served as president in 1941-44 and 1953-63. In 1943 he became a trustee of the State AJA benevolent fund and next year he was awarded the AJA's gold honour badge. He held the federal presidency in 1963-74 and in 1971 he was made a life member. One of his legacies was the adoption of an AJA code of ethics federally in 1943. In a letter to the *Sydney Morning Herald* on 3 October 1942 he explained that the eight-point code was designed to 'raise the Press and its members in public esteem', to 'eliminate criticism of Press standards', to 'protect the public against misrepresentation' and to 'justify confidence in the virtue of Press freedom'. He campaigned for twenty-five years for the establishment of the Australian Press Council; this occurred in 1976.

Godfrey's prominence in the New South Wales branch of the Australian Labor Party began in 1944 when he became president of the decidedly unproletarian Mosman branch. Editor (1945-46) of the *Labor Digest*, he attended his first party conference as a delegate in 1946 and served (1959-71) on the State executive. Abhorring the political extremes of left and right, he was an ardent member of the Fabian Society and in a letter to the *Sydney Morning Herald* on 2 April 1957 described democratic socialism as 'mankind's nearest approach in the Western world to practical Christianity'. He captured a footnote in ALP history when in 1955 he provided the federal Labor leader Dr H. V. Evatt [q.v.14] with a valid party ticket from the Mosman branch, following a staff member's failure to renew 'the Doc's' party membership.

Early in the 1960s Godfrey wrote a pithy column, 'Gloves Off', for the *A.L.P. News*, the official paper of the New South Wales branch, and from 1960 to 1968 he published in the *A.L.P. Journal* a series of sixty-seven articles on 'Paths to Democratic Socialism' which the journalist-historian Clem Lloyd described as possibly 'the longest sequence of articles ever written by a journalist anywhere on anything'. Opposed to censorship, Godfrey had campaigned, as president of the Australian Book Society, against the gaoling in 1948 of the author Robert Close for obscene libel over his bawdy novel *Love Me Sailor* (1945). Godfrey objected to Prime Minister (Sir) Robert Menzies' [q.v.15] 1950 Communist Party dissolution bill and to the ban on the Russian journalist Vadim Nekrasov imposed by (Sir) Alexander Downer [q.v.], minister for immigration, in 1963.

By the early 1970s Godfrey was out of step with the new wave of more militant journalists who opposed the clubby relationship between the union hierarchy and the media proprietors. In his 1972 presidential report he railed against the 'illogical discontent' and 'organised spite against the A.J.A. administration' that had 'spread its tentacles virtually throughout Australia'. He claimed that outside forces were trying to 'create dissension within the Australian community and to undermine unions that are making a success of the process of conciliation'. Although he retired from the *Sun* in 1971, he continued there on a casual basis and from 1976 worked for the *North Shore Times* for ten years. In 1972 he had been appointed CBE. A keen Freemason, he belonged to the Lodge Literature and the Mosman Lodge. Survived by his son and daughter, he died on 16 September 1989 at Mosman and was cremated; his wife had died in May. An obituary in the *Journalist* concluded: 'He never did return to England and although proud to be an Englishman was prouder still to be a part of Australia and its history'.

C. Lloyd, *Profession: Journalist* (1985); K. Buckley et al, *Doc Evatt* (1994); *Journalist*, Oct 1989, p 1; M. Pratt, interview with G. Godfrey (ts, 1975, NLA); G. Godfrey papers (SLNSW).   ALEX MITCHELL

GOLDING, WILLIAM ROBERT (1890-1985), alderman and harbour board chairman, was born on 24 November 1890 at Gladstone, Queensland, second of four children of locally born parents William Robert Golding, carpenter, and his wife Fanny, née Fry. Educated at Gladstone State School, Bill was apprenticed to his father and became a builder. He later studied at Brisbane Technical College. On 11 March 1914 at Holy Trinity Church of England, Mackay, he married Lillian Annie Reidy, a nurse.

Active in local government from the age of 26, Golding was an alderman (1917-21 and 1930-76) and mayor (1967-73) of the Gladstone Town Council. He served on the Gladstone Harbour Board for thirty-seven years from 1942. As chairman in 1946-48 and 1959-79, he worked to achieve recognition for the port—which was under-used because of its proximity to Rockhampton—planning each step and negotiating overseas loans for the expansion of infrastructure. His role in what came to be known as 'the battle of the ports' was crucial after Comalco Industries Pty Ltd purchased land in 1963 for a harbourside alumina refinery. Commencing operations in 1967, the refinery was the catalyst for further development; new facilities for the export of Central Queensland coal and grain were progressively built, Lake Awoonga was constructed on the Boyne River and the State's biggest power station was built in stages. In 1982 Queensland Cement & Lime Co. Ltd's clinker cement plant and Comalco Ltd's alumina smelter on Boyne Island were officially opened. As a result Gladstone's population quadrupled and its port became one of the busiest in Australia.

During the latter half of his life Golding wrote and self-published six books on Central Queensland history: *'The Pearl of the Pacific': Gladstone and Its District* (1966?); *The Birth of Central Queensland, 1802-1859* (1966); *Pathway to Progress, 1860-1973* (1973); *The Students Friend: The Gladstone Story, 1770-1975* (1975); *Shanties, Pubs, Hotels, 1854-1977* (1977); and *Beyond Horizons* (1979). In 1984 he completed an unpublished family history, 'From an English Acorn'. Made an honorary life member of the (Royal) Historical Society of Queensland in 1948, he was also a fellow of the Royal Geographical Society of Australasia.

Known as 'Mr Gladstone', Golding was involved with many community organisations. He served on the Gladstone hospitals board for twenty-five years, chaired the Gladstone-Calliope aerodrome committee, and was patron of the Little Theatre, the Municipal and Thistle Pipe bands, the Port Curtis Tennis Association, and the Gladstone Bowls and Turf clubs. He was appointed MBE (1957) and CMG (1971). His wife died on 6 April 1979, and on 28 April at Queen of the Apostles Catholic Church, Stafford, Brisbane, he married Margaret Jean Smith, a 50-year-old deputy school principal. Retiring from public life in May, at the age of 88, he remarked that he had seen 'Gladstone rise from a doom town to a boom town'. A colleague, L. J. Hyne, wrote to him: 'When I think of what you have contributed to Gladstone, I think of [Christopher] Wren's memorial in St Paul's Cathedral [London]—"If you seek his monument, look around"'.

Golding and his wife lived at Margate, near Brisbane, and enjoyed travelling overseas. He died on 16 September 1985 at Margate and was buried with Anglican rites in Gladstone cemetery. His wife, and two sons and a daughter of his first marriage survived him; one son had predeceased him.

J. Kerr, *Going in Deep* (1988); L. McDonald, *Gladstone, City that Waited* (1988); *Gladstone Observer*, 17 Sept 1985, p 1; private information and personal knowledge.   LORNA MCDONALD

GOLDSMITH, ROBERT BERNARD (1946-1984), symbol for the gay community, was born on 8 March 1946 at Hurstville, Sydney, second child of Alan Goldsmith, fitter, and his wife Nancy Gunn, née Hodgman, both born in New South Wales. Robert began his education at Burcher Provisional School (between Condobolin and West Wyalong). From the age of 6 he boarded with his elder sister at St John's Anglican Hostel, Forbes, while a pupil at the local public and high schools. On a scholarship he attended (1964-65) Teachers' College, Sydney, and in 1966 was posted to Captain's Flat Public School. After a few months he forfeited his bond and entered the Commonwealth Public Service in the National Library of Australia, Canberra, studying part time at the Australian National University. Two years later he moved to Sydney, where he worked in the Commonwealth Repatriation Department (later Department of Veterans' Affairs).

Known as Robert to his family and Bob or Bobby to his colleagues and friends, Goldsmith was a charming and open person with an excellent sense of humour. He was particularly fond of opera and of social activities, especially 'nightclubbing' and dancing, and he regularly travelled overseas. A surfer in his early days, Goldsmith always maintained a trim physique and suntan. He was a keen recreational swimmer who, at the inaugural Gay Games in San Francisco in 1982, won 17 of the Australian team's 21 medals: 4 gold, 11 silver and 2 bronze. A participant in all four strokes plus the individual medley, he swam distances from 50 to 800 yards. His gold medals were for the 100- and 200-yards butterfly and 400- and 800-yards freestyle events, all in the 36-45 age category.

It is likely that Goldsmith contracted the human immunodeficiency virus that causes acquired immune deficiency syndrome during one of his visits overseas. By 1983 he was terminally ill. His many friends rallied round to care for him and to organise a fundraising event, held under the auspices of the Gays Counselling Service on Mother's Day, 13 May 1984, at a gay venue, the Midnight Shift, Oxford Street, Sydney. Some of the money raised was used to buy a commode, a video player to enable him to watch opera, and a support mattress to enable him to remain at home rather than in hospital. He died of acquired immune deficiency syndrome at his home in Surry Hills on 18 June 1984. His was the first publicly acknowledged HIV-AIDS death in New South Wales. After a funeral with high Anglican rites at Christ Church St Laurence, Sydney, he was cremated and his ashes were scattered in the sea between Bondi and Tamarama. His estate was divided between his partner, Kenneth Raymond Bryan, his father and his sister.

The initial benefit function had raised over $6000; following his death a trust was set up in his memory to assist other AIDS patients. The Bobby Goldsmith Foundation was formed in July 1984 to provide community-based care and financial and practical support for people living with HIV-AIDS.

Star (Sydney), 10 Sept 1982, p 1, 18 May 1984, p 1, 28 June 1984, p 4, 26 July 1984, p 7; *MJA*, 27 Oct 1984, p 573; Bobby Goldsmith Foundation archives, Sydney.   ANNE-MAREE WHITAKER

GOOD(E), CYRIL HARRY EVERARD (1907-1982), poet and short-story writer, was born on 5 October 1907 at Grenfell, New South Wales, third child of Victorian-born parents Henry Francis Good, farmer and grazier, and his wife Mary, née Gibson (d.1915). Cyril was educated at home by a tutor and then at bush schools as drought drove the family from a succession of properties. In 1920 they settled at Brighton, Melbourne, and he completed two years at a local school. An avid reader inspired by the poetry of Adam Lindsay Gordon [q.v.4], he joined pilgrimages to Gordon's grave at Brighton cemetery—only to be reprimanded at church for honouring a notorious drinker, horse-racing enthusiast and suicide. After working in a warehouse, in 1925 he left with his father for Western Australia, where they purchased settlement blocks near Southern Cross.

Living alone in a tent, Good began writing (as Cyril E. Goode) sketches and bush ballads, which appeared in Western Australian newspapers and journals and in the Sydney *Bulletin* and *Smith's Weekly*. He also started a diary, introspective and frank, which he kept all his life. After seven years of clearing, fencing and cropping, he was driven from the land by the collapse of wheat prices. Returning to Victoria, he published a selection of poems, *The Grower of Golden Grain* (1932), and worked as a shearer, tractor driver and teamster. In 1935 he went to the Western Australian goldfields and at Wiluna met Jessie Morrison, a Scottish-born nurse; they married on 22 June 1940 at

St Andrew's Presbyterian Church, Caulfield, Melbourne. Rejected for military service, Good was drafted into munitions work (where he befriended the balladist Edward Harrington [q.v.14]) and was then employed on the construction of Melbourne City Council's Spencer Street power plant. Having qualified as an engine and turbine driver, he remained at the station until 1972.

Good had been radicalised by the Depression: its imagery recurred in the thirteen books he published between 1932 and 1973. Repudiating organised Christianity, he turned to rationalism and found his political faith in communism. While his books were mostly self-published in small numbers, some works —notably the ballad 'The Bridge Party at Boyanup'—won a wider audience; he also gained recognition for innovative and striking sonnets, and had poems translated into Russian and Italian. He won the Henry Lawson Festival of Arts short-story award (1960) and the Litchfield prize for poetry (1965).

An enthusiastic participant in Melbourne literary circles, Good frequented the soirées of J. K. Moir [q.v.15] and meetings of the Adam Lindsay Gordon, Henry Lawson [q.v.10], Australian Literature, and Australian Poetry Lovers' societies, the Bread and Cheese Club (president 1979), the Fellowship of Australian Writers, PEN, and the World Congress of Poets. He wrote and demonstrated against the Vietnam War, and, with Jessie, travelled abroad during the 1960s and after retirement.

In 1945 the threatened demolition of Gordon's last home had prompted Good to appeal, unsuccessfully, to the Brighton City Council for its preservation. He then bought the cottage and spent two years dismantling it and carting 25 000 bricks to his Newport backyard. An attempt in 1968 by the Brighton Historical Society to re-erect the building was abandoned. Humble, eccentric and dedicated, Cyril Good died on 25 December 1982 at Newport and was cremated. His wife and their daughter survived him. He had entrusted the Gordon cottage materials to a sympathetic Dandenong businessman, whose family retains them.

Age (Melbourne), 18 Nov 1969, p 2; *Melbourne Observer*, 27 Feb 1972, p 12; *Herald* (Melbourne), 2 May 1979, p 7; *Sunday Press* (Melbourne), 4 July 1982, p 13; *Lawsonian*, June 1983, p 2; P. Adam-Smith, taped interview with C. E. Goode (SLV); Goode papers (SLV).   JOHN LACK

GOODMAN, MOSES ISIDORE (ISADOR) (1909-1982), pianist, composer and conductor, was born on 27 May 1909 at Cape Town, South Africa, elder child of Nathan Goodman, mercer, and his wife Sarah, née Crown. Isidore (later Isador) made his first public appearance at the age of 7, playing Mozart's *Piano Concerto No.20 in D minor* with the Cape Town Symphony Orchestra. At age 13 he went to London to study at the Royal College of Music, making his début there in 1926. He won an open scholarship and the Chappell and Challen gold medals, and was appointed to the staff.

Arriving in Australia at the end of 1929, Goodman joined the New South Wales State Conservatorium of Music in Sydney. The appointment of a young pianoforte teacher from abroad caused some resentment. He gave his first performance in February 1930 at the conservatorium and played in the ceremony for the inauguration of the Australian Broadcasting Commission in 1932. In order to supplement his income he crossed the barrier between the worlds of classical and popular music, playing jazz and lighter music for clubs and cinemas. He married Pattie Evelyn Nathan on 29 January 1933 at the Great Synagogue, Sydney; they were divorced in 1936. In 1942-44 Goodman served in the Militia and the Australian Imperial Force, rising to temporary captain in the Australian Army Education Service. While attached to headquarters, New Guinea Force, in April-May 1944, he gave concerts and wrote, by lamplight, *New Guinea Fantasy*, which was recorded by the Melbourne Symphony Orchestra.

Between 1946 and 1948 Goodman toured England, appearing with the Hallé, British Broadcasting Corporation Theatre, Philharmonia and London Symphony orchestras. He also played for radio and television and recorded for Decca Records Ltd. In 1949 he married Sadie Seltzer at Cape Town; the marriage was brief. That year he resumed his concert appearances in Sydney. He married Hope Tillett, née Rodgers, a 29-year-old widow, on 5 July 1952 at the registrar general's office, Sydney. Divorcing her in November 1959, he married 23-year-old Virginia McGregor on 12 December at the registrar general's office, Sydney.

Although remembered best as a concert pianist who toured Australia extensively, Goodman also broadcast for radio and television and performed in stage productions. He recorded many works including Richard Addinsell's *Warsaw Concerto*, Henry Litolff's *Scherzo* from *Concerto Symphonique No.2*, George Gershwin's *Rhapsody in Blue*, Franz Liszt's *Piano Concerto No.1* and Sergei Rachmaninov's *Piano Concerto No.2*, as well as the romantic work *Idyll* by Lindley Evans [q.v.], an Australian composer and a friend. In 1968 he returned to the conservatorium and taught there until 1980. The Australian composer Margaret Brandman thought he was 'encouraging and effective' as a teacher; he introduced her to an eclectic range of music and instilled a love of the chords that feature strongly in

Romantic music. His playing suffered a set-back when his left hand was injured in a car accident in 1969 but he made a successful comeback to the concert stage in 1973 and continued to perform until 1982. His activities as a conductor included forming theatre orchestras in Melbourne and Sydney. He was the composer and musical director for the films *The Burgomeister* (1935) and *Jedda* (1955).

Tall and thin with aquiline features, Goodman had long fingers. When playing the piano, his hand position was fairly flat, but this unconventional technique did not hinder his command of the keyboard; Brandman described his playing as 'effortless and with subtle nuances'. Sir Neville Cardus [q.v.13] said it was as 'natural as spring air' and wrote of his 'light-fingered iridescence' and the 'brilliant and lovely technique' he placed at the service of the composers. He was appointed AM in 1981. Survived by his wife and their daughter, he died on 2 December 1982 at Concord and was cremated. His recorded works have enjoyed multiple re-releases, as well as regular broadcasts, many years after his death.

R. Brasch, *Australian Jews of Today* (1977); V. Goodman, *Isador Goodman* (1983); D. Collins, *Sounds from the Stables* (2001); *SMH*, 26 May 1973, p 2, 3 Dec 1982, p 12; *Canberra Times*, 3 Dec 1982, p 9; B883, item VX117152 (NAA).

ANN CARR-BOYD

GOODSELL, SIR JOHN WILLIAM (1906-1981), public servant, was born on 6 July 1906 at Marrickville, Sydney, third of four surviving children of Sydney-born parents Sidney Percival Goodsell, salesman, and his wife Lillian Adelaide, née Ragan. At age 15 Jack left Canterbury Boys' High School, where he had been champion athlete of his year, and worked as a grocer's assistant until his appointment to the New South Wales Public Service on 18 April 1922 as a junior clerk in the accounts branch of the Department of Public Works. A transfer to the district office of the Avon and Nepean dams three years later broadened his education; associating with construction workers exposed him to both technical issues and colourful language. On his return to Sydney in 1928 he worked as a clerk on various projects including the Sydney Harbour Bridge and, after a promotion, on the administration of the department's water supply and electricity undertakings and district and construction offices.

Eager for advancement, Goodsell qualified as an accountant and as a town and shire clerk, and passed the public service promotion examinations. He married Myrtle Thelma Austin on 6 February 1932 at Leigh Memorial Methodist Church, Parramatta; they purchased a house in Ashbury. After three years as a local government inspector, in March 1938 he obtained the position of sub-accountant in the Chief Secretary's Department, where he set about reforming the system of accounts. Impressed by his zeal and common sense, the Public Service Board chairman Wallace Wurth [q.v.16] appointed him a member of his inner circle, known jocularly to senior public servants as the 'palace guard', first as an inspector and in 1943 as a senior inspector. During World War II, as second-in-charge of the Department of National Emergency Services, Goodsell worked closely with his minister, R. J. Heffron [q.v.14], who found him a capable and congenial administrator. He was involved in the establishment of the Housing Commission of New South Wales and the re-establishment of the State Dockyard.

Goodsell's performance at the PSB earned him in March 1946 appointment as head of the elite budget branch of the New South Wales Treasury. A year later he was assistant under-secretary; after a further fifteen months the 'crown prince' had his own domain as under-secretary and permanent head of Treasury and of eight other organisations including the Government Printing Office and Government Insurance Office. As vice-president of the Metropolitan Water Sewerage and Drainage Board from 1949, and chairman or member of many other bodies, such as the Sydney Harbour Transport Board, he had a sphere of influence that extended well beyond balancing the State's books. His achievements in reorganising the Treasury to emphasise its role in the determination of policy, mainly through the budget process, were well regarded by the premiers of the day, J. McGirr and J. J. Cahill [qq.v.15,13]. Likewise Treasury staff appreciated his management reforms: he established a corporate management group, encouraged delegation, and involved subordinates in discussions with the treasurer. The New South Wales Treasury became a model for other States.

In 1954 Goodsell was appointed CMG. Next year he became president of the Metropolitan Water Sewerage and Drainage Board. Completion of the Warragamba dam to ensure Sydney's water supply was vital, as was extension of the sewerage system. With the board's expenditure in the order of £20 million, Goodsell put his financial knowledge and early experience to good use, as well as controlling a sometimes fractious board by dint of his diplomacy and acumen.

On Wurth's sudden death in September 1960 Goodsell—his named successor—was appointed chairman of the PSB. He rapidly set about establishing a very different style and culture in the New South Wales Public Service; essentially 'management' was to replace 'legalism'. Indicative of this approach was his refusal to sit on any disciplinary hearing. 'Efficiency' was to replace 'economy', and constantly he stressed the communality of management and the similarity between the public and private sectors. Air travel, modest entertainment allowances, and provision of cars and drivers for departmental heads were symbolic of the change, but of greater significance were delegation of the board's authority, computerisation of the service and the construction of modern office accommodation.

The PSB became the policy-making body for the public service as a whole, rather than the detailed regulator, with its chairman now more *primus inter pares* among department heads, who were in turn encouraged to delegate their authority as far as possible and to adopt the modified culture. This apparent weakening of the board's control was offset by the Treasury's agreeing to fund automatically any additional staff approved by the board. A visit to the United States of America, Great Britain and Europe confirmed Goodsell's view that automatic data processing was the 'greatest management-tool ever devised'. He created a unit within the board to speed its adoption throughout the service, thus placing New South Wales a decade ahead of other States in this area. A government information and sales centre was created. Goodsell was not successful in reforming the Byzantine system of public service seniority—the Achilles heel of his claim of public and private universality. This was rectified after his retirement, when, as a member of Sir Philip Baxter's [q.v.] panel appointed to inquire into promotion and seniority, he voted with its chairman to recommend that efficiency should be the primary criterion in promotions.

Although Goodsell initially played less of a political role than had his predecessor, his relations with the premiers R. J. Heffron and J. B. Renshaw [q.v.] were cordial and the practice of sending all draft cabinet minutes to the chairman for comment continued until his retirement. The incoming Askin [q.v.] government was also dependent on Goodsell's advice. The premier, for instance, was persuaded to postpone a decision on renewed demands of the New South Wales Teachers' Federation for an education commission. Although generally conciliatory to unions, Goodsell was alarmed at the potential cost of the education sector.

To promote further his ideology of public and private equivalence, Goodsell persuaded the Askin government that the State's managers were as deserving of knighthoods as captains of industry. He was knighted in 1968. Before his retirement in July 1971, he belonged to at least thirty-five educational, health, service, cultural and sporting bodies. He was a member of the council of the University of New South Wales and of several of its committees;

a director of Unisearch Ltd and the Medical Foundation; a member of the New South Wales State Cancer Council and of the board overseeing Prince Henry, Prince of Wales and Eastern Suburbs hospitals; a member of the Captain Cook [q.v.1] Bi-centenary Celebrations executive committee; president of the New South Wales group of the Royal Institute of Public Administration; and director of the Winston Churchill Memorial Trust. He was also an active Rotarian. In 1967 the University of New South Wales named the new School of Commerce building after him, and the State government followed suit in 1970 with a new office block in Sydney—testimony to his achievements in administrative reform, which placed him in the top rank of twentieth-century public servants.

Throughout his career Goodsell remained a devoted family man. He was short, with a round face and an avuncular appearance. Despite his reserve as a young man, the later sobriquet of 'jovial Jack' was bestowed with good reason, although he could be serious and formal. He genuinely liked to talk to those on the 'shop floor'. On his retirement in July 1971, he claimed that his greatest satisfaction was being thanked by public servants for having given them back their souls. His four articles published (1950, 1957, 1962, 1970) in *Public Administration*, while predominantly factual, contained some astute observations. Survived by his wife and their three daughters, he died on 3 July 1981 at Ashfield and was cremated.

Report of the Public Service Board (NSW), 1960-71; *SMH*, 8 Mar 1969, p 2, 5 July 1971, p 7, 8 July 1981, p 8; B. N. Moore, Administrative Style: Its Effect on the Functioning of an Organisation (PhD thesis, Univ of Sydney, 1986); Public Service Board, Records of the Chairman and Board Members (SRNSW).   ROSS CURNOW

GORDON, JAMES HANNAH (HEATHER) (1907-1986), soldier, was born on 7 March 1907 at Rockingham, Western Australia, fifth of eight surviving children of Australian-born parents William Beattie Gordon, member (1901-11) of the Legislative Assembly and later farmer, and his wife Harriett Ann, née Scott. (Sir) John Hannah Gordon [q.v.9] was his uncle. Jim grew up on his parents' properties at Namban, near Moora, and (from 1917) at Gingin. Educated at local state schools, he worked as a drover, rouseabout and farmer. He was employed on the goldfields as a battery worker when World War II broke out.

On 26 April 1940 Gordon understated his age and enlisted in the Australian Imperial Force, giving his middle name as Heather. He was 5 ft 9 ins (175 cm) tall and of medium build, with brown eyes and dark hair. At St

Edmund's Church of England, Wembley Park, Perth, on 14 June that year he married Myrtle Anzac Troy. He embarked for the Middle East in September and joined the 2/31st Battalion in February 1941. In June-July the unit was engaged in the Syrian campaign against the Vichy French. On the night of 9–10 July Gordon's depleted company was ordered to seize the high ground overlooking the villages of Amatour and Badarane, north of Jezzine. An enemy machine-gun post held up the advance. On his own initiative, Gordon crept forward through a hail of bullets and grenades until he was near the post. He leapt to his feet and charged it from the front, killing its four crew members with his bayonet. His action demoralised the enemy in the area and inspired his comrades to continue the attack. He was awarded the Victoria Cross.

Corporal Gordon arrived back in Australia with his unit in March 1942. Having recovered from a bout of malaria, he reached Papua late in November, by which time the 2/31st was fighting the Japanese around Gona. In January 1943 he returned to Australia and was made acting sergeant. He was confirmed in the rank en route to Port Moresby in July. During the advance towards Lae, New Guinea, in September, he led a charge against a machine-gun nest. It is likely that he was considered for a further decoration, perhaps another VC, but no award was forthcoming. 'Just as well, too', he later said. 'Imagine what my cobbers would have called me then'. After taking part in the subsequent operations in the Markham and Ramu valleys, he came home to Australia in January 1944. He spent more time in hospital with malaria and performed administrative duties before being discharged on 17 February 1947. His brothers Talbot and Ken also served in the AIF; Talbot was killed at El Alamein, Egypt, in 1942.

Finding that a job with the State Electricity Commission of Western Australia did not suit him, and missing army life, Gordon joined the Australian Regular Army on 2 December 1947. Employed as an instructor of cadets in Western Australia, he was promoted to temporary warrant officer, class two, in October 1949 (confirmed 1 February 1950). He retired from the army on 1 August 1968, then worked as a groundsman at Campbell Barracks, Swanbourne, until 1975.

A quiet, unassuming man, Gordon often hid his VC ribbon in his pocket after ceremonial occasions. He enjoyed fishing and gardening, liked cricket and avidly followed Australian Rules football. Survived by his wife and their son, he died on 19 July 1986 at the Repatriation General Hospital, Nedlands, and was cremated with full military honours. (Sir) William Dargie's portrait (1941) of Gordon, which won the 1942 Archibald [q.v.3] prize, is held by the Australian War Memorial, Canberra.

L. Wigmore (ed), *They Dared Mightily* (1963); J. Laffin, *Forever Forward* (1994); *People* (Sydney), 2 Aug 1950, p 7; *Stand-To* (Canberra), Nov 1958-Jan 1959, p 1; private information.   JOLYON HORNER

GORHAM, KATHLEEN ANN (1928-1983), dancer, was born on 7 September 1928 at Narrandera, New South Wales, second of four children of Marcus Gorham, an Irish-born railway employee, and his wife Hilda Muriel Florence, née Somers, from England. Kathy grew up at Bankstown, Sydney, and was educated at Bethlehem College, Ashfield. She began learning ballet aged 7 but, severely injured in a motor accident, had to begin again a year later. From the Kathleen Danetree School of Dance she went to Leon Kellaway's [q.v.] George Street studio to strengthen her pirouettes. Soon, under his tuition, multiple turns of every kind were her specialty.

When she was only 15, Gorham caught the attention of Edouard Borovansky [q.v.13], whose young company had recently completed its first tour of Australia and New Zealand. In 1946 she was taken to Melbourne and given a small part in his production of *Schéhérazade*, but by an oversight was not signed up on a contract, so that for two weeks she existed on broken biscuits. The following year she was made a junior ballerina with the Borovansky Ballet. When the English Ballet Rambert was making its successful Australian tour (1947-49), Gorham was invited to join the company, which she did under an adapted family name, Ann Somers. She returned with Rambert to London, took lessons with the celebrated Russian teacher Vera Volkova, and gained a scholarship to the Sadlers Wells School. On leaving she toured Britain with Roland Petit's Ballet de Paris, and performed with the Sadler's Wells Theatre Ballet.

In 1951 Gorham returned briefly to Australia for a Borovansky season, in which she first danced her most famous role, Giselle. By 1953, as a leading dancer with the Grand Ballet du Marquis de Cuevas in Paris, she was, *Le Figaro* reported, 'a revelation' but, although she was to dance with de Cuevas again, she returned to head the Borovansky company, joining them in *Pineapple Poll* for their 1954 season. She remained with the company until its demise early in 1961.

After another year abroad dancing with various companies, Gorham joined the new Australian Ballet in 1962 as its first prima ballerina. She played a significant part in its artistic development. Working in close association with (Sir) Robert Helpmann [q.v.], who declared her his favourite dancer, she created the female lead roles in his ballets *The Display* (1964) and *Yugen* (1965) and danced the lead in the Australian première of his *Elektra*

(1966). She travelled to Britain and Europe with the young company in 1965. Retiring next year, she was appointed OBE in 1968.

Gorham was small—five feet (152 cm) in height—but in movement her intensity inscribed every gesture on the mind. To speed and brio she added an exactitude that gave her dancing its compact, faceted brilliance. Her large, dark, expressive eyes and her capacity for mime inspired her popularity in tragic roles such as Giselle. The critic Geoffrey Hutton [q.v.] praised her 'beautifully articulated and intensely moving' performance in 1960. It was 'a complete Giselle, ranging from innocent gaiety to terrifying madness and resolved in pure dancing'. With 'Boro', and later with the Australian Ballet, her repertoire also included *Swan Lake, The Sleeping Princess, The Nutcracker* and *Coppélia*.

On 18 November 1958 Gorham had married Robert Michel Pomie, a French choreographer and dancer, at the district registrar's office, Parramatta, Sydney; they had one son. Divorced in 1964, she married Barney Frank Marrows, an engineer, on 6 September 1967 at the office of the government statist, Melbourne. In retirement she appeared in plays and television drama, and became a co-director of the Kathleen Gorham-Rex Reid Ballet Academy and then of the National Theatre Ballet School, Melbourne. After a stroke in 1979, perhaps brought on by years of overwork and heavy smoking, she settled in 1981 at Southport, Queensland, and continued to teach. She died there of myocardial infarction on 30 April 1983 and was cremated with Catholic rites. Her husband and son survived her. For two decades she was the best loved of Australian classical dancers.

E. H. Pask, *Ballet in Australia* (1982); *Dance Aust*, no 13, 1983, p 8; *Sunday-Herald* (Sydney), 8 Apr 1951, p 12; *SMH*, 15 Dec 1959, p 25, 3 May 1983, p 13; *People* (Sydney), 28 July 1954, p 28; *Bulletin*, 10 Oct 1964, p 35; *Aust Women's Weekly*, 29 Apr 1981, p 22; *Age* (Melbourne), 2 May 1983, p 12.

ROBIN GROVE

GRAHAM, GORDON DONALD (1910-1990), bank clerk, air force officer and builder, was born on 18 January 1910 at Beaudesert, Queensland, ninth child of Thomas Graham, dairy farmer, and his wife Margaret Jane, née Mullen, both Queensland born. Educated at Beaudesert State, The Southport and Brisbane High schools, Gordon joined the Commercial Bank of Australia Ltd and worked as a clerk, first in Brisbane and then at Coolangatta and Cairns. He completed two years' compulsory military training. A member of the Tweed Heads and Coolangatta Surf Life Saving Club in the 1930s, he saved a swimmer from a shark attack and in 1934-35 represented Queensland in surf lifesaving competitions. He was also a member of the Queensland lacrosse team in the mid-1930s. In June 1940 he joined the Royal Australian Air Force Reserve. At St John's Church of England, Cairns, on 3 August that year he married Portia Downes, a clerk.

On 6 December 1940 Graham was called up for full-time service in the RAAF. Five ft 9½ ins (177 cm) tall and 11 st. 9 lb. (74 kg) in weight, he had a fair complexion, brown eyes and auburn hair. He trained in Australia and Canada under the Empire Air Training Scheme. In September 1941 he arrived in Britain as a sergeant pilot, and was posted in April 1942 to No.460 Squadron, RAAF, a bomber unit flying Wellington aircraft. During a raid on the city of Saarbrücken, Germany, while under heavy anti-aircraft fire, he made three runs over the target before releasing his bombs. Commissioned on 29 July, 'Bluey' Graham flew twenty-seven sorties before completing his first operational tour in August. He trained in four-engined bombers and was selected as a flying instructor to convert No.12 Squadron, RAF, from Wellingtons to Lancasters, a task that was completed in just five weeks. Made an acting flight lieutenant in January 1943, he was posted to No.1656 Conversion Unit.

In November Graham was transferred to No.550 Squadron, RAF, as an acting squadron leader. Between December and May 1944 he flew twenty operational sorties, including a raid on Nuremberg on the night of 30–31 March. In June-September he attended the RAF Staff College, Andover, where he was assessed as 'a strong and sound character' who demonstrated self-confidence, judgment and initiative in practical issues. Having been mentioned in despatches, he was awarded the Air Force Cross (1944) and, for displaying 'high skill, fortitude and devotion to duty' in completing 'many successful operations against the enemy', the Distinguished Flying Cross (1944). He returned to Australia in December. In January 1945 he was posted to headquarters, North-Eastern Area, at Townsville, Queensland, where he remained for the rest of the war.

Demobilised on 24 January 1946, Graham declined offers to remain with the Interim Air Force or to take up a career as a commercial pilot, and embarked on a new enterprise. Predicting the postwar demand for housing, he established a building company and remained in the industry until his retirement. In his spare time he enjoyed fishing. He died on 13 January 1990 at Kangaroo Point, Brisbane, and was cremated with Uniting Church forms. His wife and their two sons and two daughters survived him.

J. Herington, *Air War against Germany and Italy 1939-1943* (1954); M. Middlebrook, *The Nuremberg Raid* (1986); P. Firkins, *Strike and Return* (2000);

AWM65, item 2387 (AWM); A9300, item Graham G D (NAA); private information.

PETER HELSON

GRAHAM, HERBERT ERNST (1911-1982), draftsman and politician, was born on 6 April 1911 at Narrogin, in the Western Australian wheat-belt, second child of South Australian-born parents William Le Fevre Graham, farmer, and his wife Thekla Emma, née Pustkutchen. Educated at Narrogin State and Northam High schools, Herbert was employed by the Department of Lands and Surveys as a cadet draftsman (1928-34) and by the Department of Forests as a draftsman (1934-43). He was promoted to first-class draftsman in 1941. On 15 January 1936 at St Mary's Catholic Cathedral, Perth, he married Norma Eileen Wilson.

Having joined the Australian Labor Party in 1929, Graham had been a member of the party's State executive from 1933. Twice he attempted to enter Federal politics: in 1934 he stood as the ALP candidate for the House of Representatives seat of Perth and in 1940 for the Senate. In 1942 he was elected president of the Perth Trades Hall and of the metropolitan district council of the ALP. On 14 August 1943 he won the Legislative Assembly seat of East Perth in the by-election that followed the resignation of T. J. Hughes [q.v.14]. He was to represent East Perth until 1962 and then, after the electorate disappeared in a re-distribution, Balcatta. After Labor's defeat in the 1947 State election Herb Graham played an active parliamentary and public role in the Opposition ranks, especially in the campaign against capital punishment. A big, amiable man, he was nevertheless known for his bellicose oratorical style. He served on the Joint House Committee in 1947-53. Divorced in 1951, on 5 January 1952 at the district registrar's office, Cannington, he married Beryl Grace Kirkby, a clerk.

When the A. R. G. Hawke [q.v.] Labor government came to power in February 1953 Graham was appointed minister for both housing and forests. A somewhat contentious minister for forests, he soon ousted T. N. Stoate [q.v.16] as conservator of forests. As minister for housing he relieved the postwar housing shortage by rapidly increasing the number of State Housing Commission homes. He also took over the transport portfolio in April 1956. In 1957 he chaired the joint select committee inquiring into the provisions of the Metropolitan (Perth) Passenger Transport Trust Bill; the subsequent Act introduced a modern co-ordinated bus system to Perth. Back in Opposition after 1959, he became steadily more prominent in Labor's parliamentary party and on 13 December 1966, when J. T. Tonkin replaced Hawke as leader, was chosen as deputy-leader. Labor regained power with a one-seat majority on 20 February 1971 and Graham became deputy-premier and minister for industrial development (development from 12 October 1971) and decentralisation. He was also minister for town planning until 7 February 1973 and for the North-West (from 12 October 1971).

As problems mounted for the government, including threats to supply, Graham became increasingly frustrated and at odds with Tonkin. On 30 May 1973 he resigned from parliament, coincidentally during the celebration of the first Western Australia Week, a concept that he had conceived and inaugurated. Having campaigned strongly for reform of the State's liquor laws, he was appointed to a three-year term as chairman of the Licensing Court of Western Australia. As chairman he encouraged a diversification of drinking outlets, favouring taverns over hotels, and extended drinking hours. His departure from politics almost brought down the government; in the by-election that followed, the future premier Brian Burke won his seat by thirty votes thus preserving Labor's slender parliamentary majority. A man of compassion but a tough politician, Graham had fallen just short of leading the party to which he had devoted his political life.

Graham was a board-member (1930-53) of the Australian Natives' Association of Western Australia. Developing close connections with the Italian community, he learnt to speak the language fluently, became a life member of the Western Australia Italian Club and in 1968 was appointed an officer of the Order of Merit of the Italian Republic. In later years he was patron or life member of several sporting clubs—including East Perth Football Club (1957-76), and Osborne Park and Forrest Park bowling clubs—the Western Australian Debating League and the Tree Society of Western Australia. He died of cancer on 17 March 1982 at Stirling and was cremated with Uniting Church forms. His wife, their daughter and son, and the daughter and two sons of his first marriage, survived him.

West Australian, 3 May 1968, p 8, 3 Mar 1971, p 1, 24 May 1973, p 5, 18 Mar 1982, p 9; *Daily News* (Perth), 2 May 1973, p 5; *Labor Voice*, Apr 1982, p 13; Graham papers (SLWA); private information.

DAVID BLACK

GRAINER, RONALD ERLE (1922-1981), composer, was born on 11 August 1922 at Atherton, Queensland, son of Ronald Albert Grainer, storekeeper, and his wife Margaret, née Clark, both born in Queensland. Educated at Mount Mulligan and Cairns state schools and at St Joseph's College, Nudgee, Brisbane,

Ron learned to play the violin, achieving success in regional eisteddfods and music examinations. In 1939 while enrolled (for one term) in the faculty of science, University of Queensland, he took piano lessons with Percy Brier [q.v.7]. His initial forays into composition began at this time and included a rhapsody written for performance at Brier's piano master-class.

Enlisting in the Royal Australian Air Force on 30 December 1940, Grainer served in Australia as a wireless operator mechanic. He played in unit concerts and with American musicians who exposed him to contemporary trends in jazz and blues. On 3 September 1945 he was discharged from the RAAF as a sergeant.

After the war Grainer studied under Frank Hutchens and (Sir) Eugene Goossens [qq.v.9, 14] at the New South Wales State Conservatorium of Music, Sydney, graduating in 1949 with a diploma in performance. As a mature student, Grainer revealed his warm and generous personality as mentor to fellow students, particularly those from North Queensland. Back in Brisbane, he worked as a freelance musician. On 17 September 1952 at the Presbyterian manse, Norman Park, he married 41-year-old Marjorie Boyce Adolphus, née White, a divorced businesswoman.

Moving to London, and again freelancing, Grainer found regular employment in a variety act. Work as a rehearsal pianist for television led to the opportunity to compose the theme for the 1960 series 'Maigret'. Cleverly capturing the Gallic flavour of the series through unusual and evocative instrumentation that included banjo, harpsichord and clavichord, the composition won an Ivor Novello award in 1961. A second 'Ivor' next year for his 'Steptoe and Son' theme ensured regular commissions from production houses such as the British Broadcasting Corporation, Independent Television and Thames Television. At the BBC radiophonic workshop in 1963 he composed his most striking work, the enduring theme for the series 'Dr Who'.

Grainer's heavy work commitments began to affect his health. A bout of temporary blindness attributed to working in poor light prompted him to move to southern Portugal in 1963 in search of sunlight. In 1964 he won a third 'Ivor', for 'outstanding score for a stage musical', with *Robert and Elizabeth*. The cast, which included June Bronhill and Keith Michell, gave over nine hundred performances in London's West End. Later works for theatre were less successful, but Grainer continued to write music for television and for films, including *A Kind of Loving* (1962), *To Sir with Love* (1967) and *The Bawdy Adventures of Tom Jones* (1976).

Divorced in 1966, on 19 August that year at the Marylebone register office, London, Grainer married 21-year-old Jennifer Marilyn Dodd, a singer. After their divorce in 1976 he settled near Brighton, England. Survived by his son, he died of cancer on 22 February 1981 at Cuckfield Hospital, West Sussex, and was cremated. Despite early recognition and support, he had felt neglected by the Australian music fraternity. Early in the twenty-first century there was renewed interest in his 'sci-fi' music, composed for television series such as 'The Prisoner' (1967) and films such as *The Omega Man* (1971).

Australian, 20 Dec 1975, p 20; *Times* (London), 23 Feb 1981, p 14; *Courier-Mail* (Brisbane), 24 Feb 1981, p 2; private information.

STEPHEN CRONIN

GRANT, ALFRED FRANK GALLARD (1917-1983), land developer, pastoralist and racehorse-breeder, was born on 20 March 1917 at Murwillumbah, New South Wales, son of Walter Alfred Grant, farmer, and his wife Elsie, née Gallard, both born in New South Wales. Alfred started dealing in cattle aged 17, and by 21 had acquired seventy dairy cows, leased a property on the Tweed River and hired a manager for his farming enterprise. He used the profits to put himself through an accounting course and then moved to Melbourne, where he worked as a clerk in an accounting firm and a stock and station agency.

Enlisting in the Australian Imperial Force on 3 November 1939, Grant served in the Middle East (1940-42) with the Army Canteens Service and in the Solomon Islands (1944-45) with the 2/1st Movement and Transportation Group. He was discharged in Australia on 3 November 1945 as a sergeant. On 27 October 1943 at Scots Presbyterian Church, Melbourne, he had married Olive Patricia O'Leary (d.1981). Resuming civilian work as a travelling salesman, in 1949 he turned to selling real estate for a firm that soon appointed him manager of a new branch office in Toowoomba, Queensland, and then promoted him State manager. In 1955 he started out on his own to develop coastal properties in Queensland and northern New South Wales.

Visits to Florida, United States of America, and Hawaii convinced Grant that the Gold Coast offered excellent opportunities for canal and country club developments, and that it was possible to convert flood-prone swamps into prime building blocks by pumping water out of sand along the Nerang River. With the architect Karl Langer [q.v.15], he pioneered 'man-made waterway estates' in south-east Queensland; using sophisticated town planning principles they created Miami Keys and Rio Vista in 1957. (Sir) Bruce Small's [q.v.16] and Stanley Korman's [q.v.] canal estates soon followed. In 1961 Grant began work on an estate at Kawana Waters, on low-lying coastal land between Caloundra and Mooloolaba. However, he faced a number of problems, including poor drainage and apparent buyer resistance to the flat terrain and inadequate services. He later developed further waterfront and country club estates, and built restaurants and bowling clubs.

Continuing to pursue his farming interests, Grant planned an innovative scheme combining intensive agriculture with fattening cattle. His pastoral company cleared coastal scrub at Beerwah and Sippy Downs and planted tropical legumes and grasses, intending to bring cattle from inland Queensland, fatten them on the improved pastures and send them by train to southern markets. The project was to meet with mixed success.

Having accumulated a substantial fortune from his various agricultural endeavours and property development, Grant concentrated on horse-racing and breeding. His horse Intrepid Clipper won the Queensland Derby in 1969. Early in the 1970s Grant built up Gainsborough Lodge, near Toowoomba, into an elaborate breeding property, importing the expensive stallions Beau Brummel, Charlton and Rock Roi. By 1974 it was the largest and possibly best-equipped stud in the Southern Hemisphere, with an airstrip, a horse hospital and an all-weather training track alongside architect-designed breeding barns and training stable. Now the dominant figure in Australian stud-breeding, Grant set out ambitiously to create a second stud, Wellcamp, on 3000 acres (1214 ha) adjacent to Gainsborough. In 1976 he sold more than one hundred yearlings.

By the 1970s Alfred Grant Pty Ltd was probably the biggest family-owned real estate company in Queensland. Grant divided his interests between Alfred Grant Holdings Ltd, a publicly listed property development company (in which he held three-quarters of the stock) and Alfred Grant Pastoral Properties Pty Ltd. Capitalised in 1974 at over $12 million, Alfred Grant Holdings soon ran into severe financial difficulties. In 1975 the development rights for the troubled Kawana Waters estate were sold. In March 1977 three subsidiaries collapsed and Grant declared himself bankrupt. The stud was liquidated and a dispersal sale of the thoroughbred stock was held in July. Next year Grant abandoned his last remaining agricultural enterprise, at Sippy Downs. He returned to the family farm in the Tweed Valley.

Known as the 'shy man of real estate', Grant did not mix in the rambunctious political circles of the Gold Coast in the 1960s and 1970s. However, he had helped to transform the coast of south-east Queensland, creating a distinctive urban form. Survived by his three daughters, he died of pneumonia on 11 Nov-

ember 1983 at Auchenflower, Brisbane, and was buried in Pinnaroo lawn cemetery, Aspley.

M. Jones, *A Sunny Place for Shady People* (1986); *South Coast Bulletin*, 17 Sept 1958, p 29; *Nambour Chronicle*, 2 Feb 1967, p 1; *Herald* (Melbourne), 22 Mar 1974, p 2, 11 July 1977, p 1; *Courier-Mail* (Brisbane), 12 Nov 1983, p 5.
                                          CHRIS MCCONVILLE

GREEN, HENRY WILLIAM (1908-1989), music college principal, was born on 15 September 1908 at Birkenhead, Port Adelaide, son of Henry James Green, railway engineman, and his wife Ada Catherine, née Burgess, both 'Portonians' by birth. Young Harry obtained free Catholic secondary schooling at the St Enda's juniorate of the Irish Christian Brothers, Strathfield, Sydney. After transferring to the adjacent Mount St Mary's novitiate in September 1924 he gained some tertiary education and chose the religious name 'Brother Jerome'. From January 1926 he taught in the Brothers' schools at Lewisham, in East Melbourne and then at Wagga Wagga, New South Wales, where he made his final profession in 1933 and won local renown as an art teacher. He was granted leave in 1935 to teach for a term in a London art school. Next year, soon after his return to Australia, for unrecorded reasons he was dispensed from his vows. The break was amicable and for the rest of his life he called and signed himself 'Harry J. Green'.

Moving to Adelaide, Green found work as a shop assistant at the Myer [q.v.10] Emporium (SA) Ltd store, and for relaxation painted, played the piano and acted in amateur theatricals. He supplemented his income by conducting art classes, again with success, at the Marist Brothers' Sacred Heart College, Somerton. On 7 January 1939 at St Francis Xavier's Cathedral he married Jean Colbey (d.1988), a secretary and a convert from Anglicanism. They lived at Glen Osmond and had a son and a daughter. In November 1939 he was appointed a justice of the peace.

That year Green helped (Sir) Ellerton Becker [q.v.13] to stage his extravaganza *On Parade* in the Theatre Royal. Green transformed the production by creating stunning sets and introducing Hollywood-style costuming and movement. He then quit his other employment to become vice-principal of Becker's Adelaide College of Music. In 1941 Becker appointed Green principal and next year he sold the college and the Stradivarius Instrument Co. Pty Ltd to the impecunious ex-Brother for a deposit of £1, expecting Green soon to make enough to pay the balance.

The confidence was justified. Under the college's new ownership and direction, in the next twenty years its enrolments rose from fewer than 1200 to over 9900 and its teaching staff from thirty-seven to almost four hundred. The already large brass, woodwind, drum and banjo-mandolin classes continued growing. Green added tuition in jazz, choral singing, recorders, piano accordions, fiddles and acoustic and Hawaiian guitars. Thousands more studied piano by the 'rhythm method', learning to play simple melodies accompanied by chords. The system avoided the need for mastering scales and arpeggios but limited most pupils' capacity for advancing beyond a perfunctory rendition of foxtrots, quicksteps and waltzes. Many students or their parents bought their instruments at Green's shop.

Until 1969, and then in 1972, 1973 and 1975, the students' talents were showcased in the annual production *On Parade*. It ran for nine nights, always sold out in advance and was excellent publicity for the college. Most of the revenue went to meet expenses and the Federal government's entertainment tax, but in the last years of World War II the show yielded £2000 for the Young Men's Christian Association's military services appeal, and subsequently £11 000 for the Adelaide Children's Hospital, which in 1959 made Green a life governor.

Several of the college's brass, clarinet and percussion students gained celebrity. Bruce Gray, Bill Munro and Bob Wright became central to the development of traditional jazz in Australia. Syd Beckwith became a well-known band leader in Canada. Errol Buddle and Jack Brokensha formed the Australian Jazz Quartet/Quintet which, according to the jazz historian Andrew Bisset, won 'widespread critical and popular approval' while touring the United States of America in 1954-58. In a branch of the college called the Radio Institute of Australia, Green developed training in announcing, play-reading, script-writing, radio production and advertising and, later, television work. One of his students, Bobby Limb, became a renowned radio and television personality. Green further capitalised on the craze for popular music by founding other colleges of music, in South Australia at Port Adelaide and Berri, in New South Wales at Broken Hill, and in Brisbane and Perth. By 1963 he had persuaded the independently owned Sydney and Melbourne colleges of Music to join his own in a body called the Associated Music Colleges of Australia Pty Ltd. He became its governing director.

Green had entered into competition with the Elder [q.v.4] Conservatorium of Music from 1944, undercutting its charges for those seeking individual tuition in concert music. Enlisting the services of private teachers and most members of the South Australian Symphony Orchestra, he formed a division that in 1953 was renamed the Adelaide Conservatorium of Music. By 1960 it was preparing 2100 pupils per year for examinations conducted by the Australian Music Examinations Board or the Royal College of Music, London. Two students of singing became principal tenors: Kevin Miller with the English National Opera, and Lance Ingram (stage name Albert Lance) with the Paris Opéra.

From the 1960s enrolments declined. In 1975 Green sold the business to Music Houses of Australia Ltd, which retained him as principal and manager of the instrument shop. A few months later Music Houses was taken over by EMI Ltd, whose main focus was selling records, audiotapes and electrical goods. On 11 November 1975 Green and his staff were told that teaching was to cease immediately. Offered assistance if he wished to find new premises and relaunch the Adelaide College as an independent entity, he chose to become a travel consultant.

Plain and bespectacled, but impressive in height, speech and manner, Green loved the limelight. He was president of the Gilbert and Sullivan Society of South Australia (1949-66), the Music Teachers' Federation of Australia (1956-68), the State division of the Australian-American Association (1956-65) and the South Australian Italian Association (1958-63), and vice-president of the Australian-Asian Association of South Australia (1962-64). He was a member of the Knights of the Southern Cross (1938-67). As president (1971-72) of the Lions Club of the City of Adelaide he promoted its interest in assisting the vision-impaired; as president (1955-77) and vice-president (1977-86) of the Catholic Blind Association of South Australia, he helped to found (1961) St Raphael's Home for the Aged Blind at Fullarton. Survived by his daughter, Green died on 2 February 1989 in North Adelaide and was cremated.

A. D. McCredie (ed), *From Colonel Light into the Footlights* (1988); P. A. Howell, 'The Adelaide College of Music and Its Founder', *Jnl of the Hist Soc of SA*, no 20, 1992, p 5; *Advertiser* (Adelaide), 11 Dec 1999, p 52, 18 Dec 1999, p 52; J. Peoples, taped interview with H. W. Green (1982), and Associated Music Colleges of Aust Pty Ltd records (Performing Arts Collection of SA); private information.

P. A. HOWELL

GREEN, ISABEL ALICE (1893-1984), manager, was born on 9 May 1893 at Ballarat, Victoria, only daughter and third of five children of Victorian-born parents James Menzies, coach-painter, and his wife Kate, née Sampson. The family moved to Jeparit that year. Belle went to the local state school then boarded with her paternal grandmother at Ballarat while attending the Humffray Street State School and Ellerslie College. From 1910 the family, including her brothers (Sir) Robert and

Frank Menzies [qq.v.15], lived in Melbourne. A 'beautiful and vivacious young woman of outstanding ability', according to a visitor, she was sent to the Emily McPherson College of Domestic Economy. Against the wishes of her family she eloped with George Claridge Green, a soldier; they married with Anglican rites on 2 December 1916 at Maribyrnong camp, a few days before he embarked with the 4th Field Artillery Brigade, Australian Imperial Force.

Following his return to Australia in June 1919 and demobilisation, Isabel Green accompanied him to the soldier settlements at Red Cliffs, where she lived in primitive conditions. Having borne three children in just over two years, she became secretary (later president) of the women's club and baby health centre. After Green's stock and station agency failed in 1929, they moved to Melbourne. Desperate, Isabel persuaded Sidney Myer [q.v.10] to allow her to run a service bureau at the Myer Emporium Ltd. In 1933-36 she was honorary secretary of the auxiliary of the (Royal) Melbourne Hospital, and in 1936-38 she worked in public relations for the *Argus*.

George was a sustenance worker until appointed secretary to the trustees of the Exhibition Building in 1931. Provided with a cottage in the grounds, the Greens created an old-world garden with herbaceous borders, roses, paved pathways and tall leafy trees. Following her husband's death in 1938, Mrs Green succeeded him as secretary at a salary of £400, with fuel, light and quarters. Businesslike and capable, with the common sense of a practical woman, she soon silenced her critics. Her many and varied duties included management of the Great Hall, the Palais Royale and the Aquarium, and responsibility for the exhibitions, concerts, pageants, balls and other public events held there. Fascinated by the Aquarium, Isabel Green corresponded with experts and curators, and collected live specimens from South-East Asia, the Pacific, and Australian waters. When the Royal Australian Air Force requisitioned the Exhibition Building in October 1940 she concentrated on promoting the Aquarium. Her sons and daughter served in World War II. After the war she had to contend with rent losses and damage to the building.

Promoted to secretary-manager, in March 1946 Mrs Green, who adored fancy dress parties, organised an '1890 night' to aid the Food for Britain fund; she appeared as the 'Countess of Carlton' in 'a magnificent frock of blue moire with draped panniers', carrying her lorgnette. In 1953 she attended the coronation of Queen Elizabeth II in London. Her dream of using the Exhibition Building to entertain royalty became reality when state functions for the Queen and the Duke of Edinburgh were held there in 1954. On her retirement in December 1955, Isabel Green was honoured with a party hosted by the Victorian Chamber of Manufactures and attended by fifty-five businessmen.

Mrs Green moved to an apartment at Kew and visited Britain, the United States of America and the Territory of Papua and New Guinea. Vigorous and forthright, with a firm tread, she was secretary of the Kew branch of the Liberal Party and of the Australian-American Association. She was a long-standing barracker for the Carlton football team, and a good storyteller who could create a saga even out of encountering a cockroach. Plump, with silver hair and vivid blue eyes, she had an 'enviably fresh complexion'. On three occasions she acted as official hostess for her brother Robert at the Lodge in Canberra (while Dame Pattie was overseas) and thoroughly enjoyed the international atmosphere and interesting guests. Isabel Green was appointed OBE in 1970. She died on 20 December 1984 at Camberwell and was cremated with the forms of the Uniting Church. Her elder son and her daughter survived her. The family holds her portrait by Alice Stone.

J. C. Elden, *The Exhibition Trustees, Royal Exhibition Building Melbourne* (1984); D. Dunstan, *Victorian Icon* (1996); *Argus*, 22 Aug 1936, p 14, 22 Dec 1955, p 8; *Sun News-Pictorial*, 7 Jan 1939, p 33, 19 Dec 1945, p 14; *Age*, 9 Mar 1946, p 6, 10 Sept 1955, p 7, 8 Mar 1960, p 11, 13 June 1970, p 4; Isabel Green, notes (1979), held by ADB; private information.

MARTHA RUTLEDGE

GREEN, KENNETH DAVID (1917-1987), engineer, public servant and soldier, was born on 20 November 1917 at Footscray, Melbourne, only child of Victorian-born parents, David William Green, timber merchant, and his wife Helena Harriet Segler, née Bruce. Ken attended Williamstown and Melbourne High schools and graduated from the University of Melbourne (BCE, 1937) with honours and the Argus research scholarship. After a year as a demonstrator in civil engineering at the university, he joined the State Rivers and Water Supply Commission in 1939 as assistant-engineer.

Mobilised in the Citizen Military Forces on 31 October 1941 as a lieutenant, Royal Australian Engineers, Green transferred to the Australian Imperial Force in August 1942 and served in mainland New Guinea (1943-44) and on Bougainville (1945) as a captain with the 15th Field Company. He rose to second-in-command of the unit and was mentioned in despatches. On 23 June 1945 at St John's Church of England, Milsons Point, Sydney, he married Phyllis May Roohan, who was then serving in the Australian Women's Army Service. In 1946 he transferred to the Reserve of Officers.

Returning to the SRWSC, as hydrographic then senior designing engineer, Green was involved in planning Eildon Dam, overseeing large-scale irrigation and town-water services and, as senior executive engineer, designing drainage schemes for irrigation areas. 'Our ultimate aim', he declared in 1951, was 'the production of food for a hungry world'. He also became active in the affairs of professional associations, as a member (later fellow) of the Institution of Engineers (Australia), the Institution of Civil Engineers, London, and the American Society of Civil Engineers. As divisional engineer for Loddon (1958-65), he managed a staff of 400 and a budget of £900 000, and as a commissioner (1965-71), he represented Victoria on the River Murray Commission and the Snowy Mountains Council. He continued to publish technical papers and travelled to conferences in, and on missions to, India, Europe, the United States of America, Taiwan, Thailand and Malaysia.

Alongside his service to the SRWSC, in 1948 Green rejoined the CMF and, as deputy chief engineer, Southern Command, was appointed OBE (1959). He commanded the 4th Task Group (1966-69) and Southern Command Training Group (1969-70) as a brigadier and the 3rd Division (1970-73) as a major general. Welcoming the end of national military service in 1973, Green was a member of the committee of inquiry into the CMF that in 1974 recommended the formation of the Australian Army Reserve. In 1976-82 he was representative colonel commandant of the RAE.

In December 1971 Sir Henry Bolte [q.v.] had appointed Green secretary to the Department of the Premier, making him the last incumbent to be chosen by the premier's fiat. As the State's senior public servant he was principal adviser, and a conduit for information from across the service to the premier. His job, as he later confided, was 'to assist the boss to be the boss'. He served Bolte's successors (Sir Rupert) Hamer and Lindsay Thompson as an astute administrator and, in Hamer's words, 'a faithful servant'. He was also a commissioner (1973-76) on the Whitlam Federal government's Cities Commission. Appointed CB in 1981, Green expected the defeat of the Victorian Liberal government in April 1982, and knew of John Cain's plans to reduce the influence of permanent and statutory heads. When Labor assumed office, he advised the new premier that he wished to retire early, despite Cain's encouragement to stay; leaving in July, he commented that bureaucracy needed a regular change of government to operate efficiently, and regretted the media's increasing influence on policy.

An impression of severity, intensified by a heavy moustache, was quickly dispelled by Green's ready smile, natural charm and generosity. Always proud of his trim, six-foot (183 cm) frame and military bearing, from 1971 to 1981 he chaired both the National Fitness Council of Victoria and the Victorian State committee of the Duke of Edinburgh's award in Australia. Having joined Melbourne Legacy in 1959, he served on the federal co-ordinating council and board of management and as president (1981); he was also a long-standing member of the Rotary Club of Melbourne. His long involvement with the Scout Association of Australia, Victoria branch, culminated in his vice-presidency (1984-87). In 1982 he became foundation president of the council of Chisholm Institute of Technology; he remained a member until 1987. He enjoyed golf, swimming and watching cricket, and was a member of the Athenaeum, Melbourne, Naval and Military, Melbourne Cricket and Huntingdale Golf clubs. Survived by his wife and their son, Green died of cerebral thrombosis on 2 October 1987 at Fitzroy and was cremated.

Herald (Melbourne), 20 Dec 1969, p 24; *Sun News-Pictorial* (Melbourne), 28 Mar 1973, p 7; *Age* (Melbourne), 14 Oct 1981, p 3, 10 July 1982, p 13; *Melbourne Legacy Bulletin*, 15 Oct 1987, pp 16, 18; private information.   F. J. KENDALL

GREENWOOD, GORDON (1913-1986), historian, was born on 17 September 1913 at Terowie, South Australia, son of Rudolph Oertel Nadebaum, Congregational minister, and his wife Lizzie Ann, née Hales, both born in South Australia. About 1915 the family adopted Greenwood as its surname and moved to Sydney, where Gordon's father taught at Knox Grammar School, Wahroonga, and his mother at nearby Abbotsleigh girls' school. After attending Turramurra College and Knox, Gordon excelled at the University of Sydney (BA, 1935; MA, 1937, both with first-class honours in history and the university medal). (Sir) Stephen Roberts [q.v.16] was a great influence. While completing his master's thesis—pioneering work on early Australian-American relations—Greenwood undertook a research project on current affairs commissioned by the State government.

Awarded a Woolley [q.v.6] travelling scholarship, Greenwood investigated Australian federalism at the London School of Economics and Political Science (Ph.D., 1939), supervised by Harold Laski. On 16 February 1939 at the Kensington Chapel, he married with Congregational forms Thora Jean Smeal. That year he took up a lecturing post at the New England University College, Armidale, New South Wales. His master's and doctoral theses were published in revised form in 1944 and 1946. He moved to the University of Sydney as a lecturer in 1942 and was acting-professor in 1947-48.

Appointed (Sir Samuel) McCaughey [q.v.5] professor of history at the University of Queensland in 1949, Greenwood threw himself into expanding the scope of his department, which, in 1952-65, also embraced political science. In 1949 Greenwood had three lecturers on his staff; in the mid-1970s he presided over twenty-five lecturers and twelve tutors. He emphasised good teaching, promoted new ideas and encouraged innovation in research topics: apart from political science he fostered work on contemporary international relations, Australian foreign policy and relations with Asia, Britain, the Commonwealth and the United States of America.

Greenwood's published work, and that of his staff, increased substantially the status and reputation of the department. The synoptic general history *Australia: A Social and Political History* (1955), edited by Greenwood, was widely used as a text. He founded the *Australian Journal of Politics and History* in 1955 and edited it until 1982. With John Laverty he produced a history of Brisbane for its centenary in 1959. Greenwood's broad interpretive approach was evident in *The Modern World* (1964). His interest in Australian foreign policy resulted in four volumes of *Australia in World Affairs* (1950 to 1970), co-edited with Norman Harper [q.v.]; *Approaches to Asia: Australian Postwar Policies and Attitudes* (1974); and *Documents on Australian International Affairs 1901-1918* (1977), co-edited with Charles Grimshaw. He promoted international studies, especially through the Australian Institute of International Affairs, of which he was federal president in 1961-65. His articles in journals such as *Australian Outlook*, *World Review* and *Pacific Affairs* explored Australia's role in the world. Internationally recognised, he represented Australia at Commonwealth and United Nations conferences, and won grants (including a Carnegie fellowship) for study in the USA.

Within the university Greenwood was an influential member of the senate in 1953-83. As chairman (1964-76) of the library committee he strove to strengthen the university's research capacity by developing its library holdings. He also chaired the library sub-committee of the Commonwealth Advisory Committee on Advanced Education, helping to secure increased funding for libraries at colleges of advanced education. With Harrison Bryan he edited *Design for Diversity: Library Services for Higher Education and Research in Australia* (1977). In 1984 he received the (Sir) Redmond Barry [q.v.3] award from the Library Association of Australia.

A member (1950) of the Social Science Research Council of Australia and then fellow (1971) of the Academy of the Social Sciences in Australia, Greenwood was also a member of the Australian Humanities Research Council (1956) and fellow (1969) of the Australian Academy of the Humanities. He served on the national committee of the *Australian Dictionary of Biography* (1960-74) and on the interim council (1967) of the University of Papua New Guinea.

Despite his critical and inquiring disposition, in the 1970s Greenwood had trouble reading the tenor of the time and did not adjust to the radical and democratising pressures sweeping through universities. Operating in the tradition of the god-professor, his liberal-conservative nature asking for rational discussion and gradual change, he was buffeted in the last years before standing down as head of department in 1978. Appointed CMG in 1982, he retired that year. The university bestowed on him an honorary D.Litt. (1983).

Greenwood enjoyed conviviality. Colleagues, friends, students and visitors remember him singing 'Onward Christian Soldiers'—in the words of Jane Greenwood: 'tone-deaf, but loving sound and feeling, conducting, cigarette in hand, the patriarch'. He was passionate about Rugby Union football and cricket. Survived by his wife and their daughter and three sons, he died on 4 November 1986 in South Brisbane and was cremated. In 1989 a building at the university was named after him.

D. P. Crook (ed), *Questioning the Past* (1972); M. I. Thomis, *A Place of Light & Learning* (1985); *Austn Jnl of Politics and History*, vol 29, no 2, 1983; Academy of the Social Sciences in Aust, *Annual Report*, 1986-87, p 47; *InCite*, 6 Mar 1987, p 7; *Words'Worth*, July 1992, p 17; N. Meaney, interview with G. Greenwood (ts, 1986, NLA); private information and personal knowledge.

W. ROSS JOHNSTON

GREENWOOD, JOHN NEILL (1894-1981), professor of metallurgy, was born on 12 December 1894 at St Helens, Lancashire, England, youngest of six children of Walter Greenwood, grocer, and his wife Ellen, née Neill. Leaving school at 13, Neill studied at night at St Helens Technical College while working as a laboratory assistant in a lead-smelting works. In 1913 he won a scholarship to the University of Manchester (B.Sc., 1916; M.Sc., 1917; D.Sc., 1922) and graduated with first-class honours in metallurgy. Although attracted by research, he sought further experience in industry. Appointed chief of the research department (1919) at Samuel Fox & Co. Ltd, Stocksbridge, Yorkshire, Greenwood carried out, under a Carnegie scholarship, work on optical pyrometry. His marriage to Gladys Uhland, a scientific chemist, on 3 May 1920 at the Prestwich register office, was followed by a ceremony conducted under Theosophical auspices.

In 1924 Greenwood was appointed to the chair of metallurgy in the faculty of engineering, University of Melbourne—the first such chair in Australia. He quickly set about devising courses that would provide an educational bridge from primary to secondary industry, from ore-extraction to metal manufacturing and processing. He designed and equipped a new laboratory; established evening lectures for working students; oversaw the introduction of courses in physical metallurgy in technical schools; and upgraded the university's course in dental metallurgy. From the mid-1920s he toured the major mining and metallurgical centres to learn their needs and—with a 'terrier-like determination in fund-raising'—solicit support to develop a research program. Made a doctor of science at Melbourne in 1927, Greenwood was also awarded a master's degree in metallurgical engineering (1931) in recognition of his investigations into the failure of boilers at Yallourn.

A dedicated and inspiring teacher, Greenwood sought to create an inclusive department; his generous leadership attracted outstanding students, many of whom went on to prominent positions in industry, research and teaching. With their assistance and in collaboration with the Council for Scientific and Industrial Research (the Commonwealth Scientific and Industrial Research Organization after 1949), he developed an internationally recognised program of research into phenomena such as metal creep. With the outbreak of World War II, he and his team turned to producing much-needed tungsten carbide cutting tools, rods and wires. In 1946 he was appointed to a chair of metallurgical research largely financed by the Broken Hill group of mining companies, and with laboratories supported by the Baillieu [q.v.7] family.

For all his academic success, Greenwood felt himself an outsider at the university—a situation exacerbated by his sympathetic interest in the Soviet Union, which he had visited in 1932. In 1935 he had founded the Society for Cultural Relations with the Soviet Union. His divorce, in 1932, had caused further stress. On 19 January 1934 he married Mabel Winifred Borrie (d.1977) in a civil ceremony in Melbourne. Greenwood's 5-acre (2 ha) bush block in Kinglake National Park was a solace in a dark period. He was a committed member (1926-48) and chairman (1940-48) of the park's committee of management. In the Cold War atmosphere of the early 1950s he felt so isolated at the university that he spent lunchtimes writing a novel rather than enduring 'distracting silences when there should have been conversation'.

As the political climate in the university thawed, Greenwood's quest to 'blend the cultural with the technological' bore fruit. After a term as dean (1957-59) of the faculty of science,

he persuaded the university to establish a new faculty of applied science, in which he accepted a personal chair (1960-64) and served as dean. There he applied his talents to creating an innovative program but, five years after his retirement as professor emeritus in 1964, the faculty was dissolved.

Beyond the university Greenwood's expertise was widely recognised. He was an early member of committees of the Australian Commonwealth Engineering Standards Association (Standards Association of Australia after 1929), an active council member of the Australasian Institute of Mining and Metallurgy (president 1936; medallist 1961) and a recipient of the Australasian Institute of Metals' silver medal (1958). In 1962, as a royal commissioner inquiring into the failure of Kings Bridge, Melbourne, he was the principal author of an outstanding example of a report into such an event. Awarded an honorary doctorate in applied science (1968) by the University of Melbourne, Greenwood was also made an honorary doctor of engineering by Monash University (1974) and an honorary fellow of the Institution of Metallurgists (1979).

Small, compact and dark-haired, Greenwood never lost his pleasure in detailed research nor his capacity for long hours of sustained work. His greatest friendships remained with his students, many of whom acknowledged their debt to 'the little man' by raising funds to support a medal in his name for the university's best metallurgical student; in 1968 former colleagues and students also presented to the university a portrait of Greenwood by Noel Counihan [q.v.]. Survived by a daughter and two sons from his first marriage, Neill Greenwood died on 30 August 1981 at Mornington and was cremated.

Presentation of the Medal of the Australasian Institute of Mining and Metallurgy to J. Neill Greenwood, on May 25th, 1962 (1962); C. Rasmussen, *The Lesser Evil* (1992); J. Poynter and C. Rasmussen, *A Place Apart* (1996); Paper Clip Collective, *Melbourne University Portraits* (1996); *Procs* (A'sian Inst of Mining and Metallurgy), no 280, 1981, p 4; J. N. Greenwood papers (Univ of Melbourne Archives).   CAROLYN RASMUSSEN

GRENNING, VICTOR (1899-1984), forester, was born on 17 January 1899 at Zillmere, Brisbane, elder child of Jens Peter Grenning, a Queensland-born labourer, and his wife Emma Christine, née Alfredson, from Denmark. Like his father and grandfather, Victor was generally called Peter. At Zillmere and Brisbane Normal state schools, and at Brisbane Grammar School, he excelled both in the classroom and on the sporting field. He gained first place in the state school scholarship examination (receiving the Lilley [q.v.5] medal) in 1912, and in the junior public (1915) and senior public (1917) examinations. Dux of Brisbane Grammar in 1917, he won numerous prizes and awards. He represented the school in cricket, Rugby Union football, athletics and rifle-shooting. Winner of an open scholarship to the University of Queensland, he enrolled in 1918 in an applied science course. In 1918-19 he played Rugby Union for Queensland against New South Wales.

Awarded a Rhodes scholarship in 1919, Grenning left university without sitting the end-of-year examinations, to earn money as a tutor to pay for the trip to England. In October 1920 he entered Balliol College, Oxford. He studied forestry for three years, spending several months in the forests of Germany, France, Austria and Switzerland, and also visited Denmark. Grenning was a Rugby Union forward for his college and for the university. Too ill to sit the finals, he did not take his degree. On the way home he visited Burma (Myanmar), India, Federated Malay States (Malaysia) and the Philippines.

Back in Brisbane in 1924, Grenning took up a post in the Queensland Forest Service, Department of Public Lands, as research officer and instructor in silviculture and working plans. In 1925 he played hockey for Queensland against New South Wales. On 12 October 1926 at St Andrew's Presbyterian Church, Brisbane, he married Helen McMillan Gaffney, a commercial artist. He served on the Provisional Forestry (1929-32) and Land Administration (1932-57) boards, and on the Rural Fires Board for some years from 1930. On 18 May 1933 he succeeded E. H. F. Swain [q.v.12] as director of forests. For six months in 1936-37 he studied forestry practices in the United States of America, Canada and New Zealand.

Under Grenning's direction the area of reserved forested land and of softwood plantations in Queensland increased significantly and research was undertaken in timber use and seasoning, plantation tending, fire detection and control, and other forestry matters. During World War II, despite manpower shortages, the forest service assisted the timber industry in supplying vast quantities of timber for the war effort. In the postwar period it concentrated on forestry reconstruction, relying on migrants for labour and aided by increased mechanisation. Grenning's technical papers included *Production of Quality Wood in Coniferous Plantations in Queensland* (1957). His organisation also administered national parks; in his 1958-59 report he asserted that the parks 'must be preserved as far as possible in that simplicity and unspoiled beauty which makes them unique'. During his tenure, many of the islands within the Great Barrier Reef were added to the national park estate.

In 1952 the University of Queensland had conferred on Grenning an honorary M.Sc.

degree. The Institute of Foresters of Australia awarded him the inaugural N. W. Jolly [q.v.9] memorial medal in 1959. In December 1957 the Department of Forestry had come into being, and in 1960 he was given the title conservator of forests. That year Grenning reported on national park policy and administration in North America. Described as kindly, genial, firm, trustworthy, quiet and modest, he retired in 1964, having steered the organisation through the turbulent times of war and reconstruction into the relatively stable 1960s.

Grenning was a champion bowls player; he was president (1940-41) and later patron of the Graceville Bowling Club. A trustee (1942-68) of Brisbane Grammar School, he was chairman in 1948-52. He was also a member of Brisbane Rotary Club. Survived by his wife and their son and two daughters, he died on 1 September 1984 at Sinnamon Retirement Village, Oxley, and was cremated. In March 2001 the Brisbane City Council named a park at Zillmere after him. Grenning's granddaughter Kate Carnell was chief minister of the Australian Capital Territory in 1995-2000.

P. Taylor, *Growing Up* (1994); Dept of Forestry (Qld), *Annual Report*, 1958-59, p 33, 1963-64, p 20; *Austn Forestry*, vol 47, no 3, 1984, p 137; *Daily Standard* (Brisbane), 1 May 1933, p 1; *Bayside and Northern Suburbs Star*, 28 Mar 2001, p 14; V. Greening personal file, Public Service Board (QSA); private information.					PETER HOLZWORTH

GREY-SMITH, GUY EDWARD (1916-1981), artist, was born on 7 January 1916 at East Wagin, Western Australia, second child of Victorian-born parents Francis Edward Grey-Smith, station manager, and his wife Ada Janet, née King. Francis Grey Smith [q.v.6] was his great-grandfather. Educated at Boyup Brook State and Bunbury High schools, Guy joined the Royal Australian Air Force on 20 January 1936 and trained as a pilot. Next year he took a short-service commission in the Royal Air Force and moved to England. On 19 October 1939 at the parish church, Godmanchester, Huntingdonshire, he married Helen Dorothy Stanes. Following the outbreak of World War II he went to France with No.139 Squadron. In May 1940 his Blenheim bomber was shot down over enemy territory. Baling out, he was hit on the head by the tailplane and severely wounded. While he was in a German prisoner-of-war camp, he began to sketch, using materials supplied by his wife. He developed tuberculosis of the lungs; sent to Britain on a prisoner exchange in 1944, he was admitted to the sanatorium at Midhurst, Sussex, where his interest in painting was further stimulated by an art therapy program.

In 1945-47 Grey-Smith studied at the Chelsea School of Art under Ceri Richards, Henry

Moore and Robert Medley. He also took a part-time pottery course with Heber Mathews at Woolwich Art School. Pronounced medically unfit, he relinquished his RAF commission on 22 April 1947. Next year he returned to Western Australia. In 1950 he renovated a house and built a studio at Darlington in the hills above Perth. Setting up a home pottery and digging clay from a nearby road, he made slip-decorated earthenware. The family became self-sufficient, keeping chickens, pigeons, and a goat for milking, growing vegetables and fruit, and eating from his home-made earthenware.

In 1952 Laurie Thomas [q.v.16], then director of the Art Gallery of Western Australia, promoted Grey-Smith's work and that of his wife, also an artist and a printmaker, and acquired a Grey-Smith painting for the gallery. After recovering from a recurrence of tuberculosis, Grey-Smith took his family back to England in 1953. He studied fresco painting with Louis le Brocquy and Hans Tisdall at the Central School of Art and Design, London, and was impressed by an exhibition in Paris of Fauve painters. Back in Perth in 1954, he was employed part time at Perth Technical College and at the AGWA. He initiated art therapy classes at Wooroloo Sanatorium and Perth Chest (Sir Charles Gairdner [q.v.]) Hospital.

Grey-Smith was strongly influenced by the worker of Paul Cézanne; his paintings of the Western Australian landscape were emotive, with strong, demanding colour. In the 1950s he held successful exhibitions in Perth, Sydney, Melbourne and Adelaide, gaining a national reputation. He was represented in several international exhibitions of contemporary Australian painting: in Canada (1957), in London (1961), and in London and Ottawa (1963-1964). Between 1955 and 1978 he won eleven important Australian art prizes. In this period annual trips to the State's North-West and, increasingly, the work of the French painters Nicholas de Staël and Georges Rouault influenced his art, which became more abstract.

A part-time teacher (1969-76) at the Western Australian Institute of Technology, in 1971, under the auspices of the Department of Foreign Affairs, Grey-Smith lectured in painting, drawing and ceramics at the Royal University of Fine Arts, Phnom Penh. He was founding president (1966) and patron of the Western Australian branch of the Contemporary Art Society of Australia. Awarded a $10 000 grant by the Australia Council's visual arts board in 1973, he gave most of the money away to help students. In 1977-80 he was a member of the board. A retrospective of his work was held at the AGWA in 1976.

Grey-Smith welcomed fellow painters, friends and young students to his Darlington home. His passion for 'burning off' sometimes caused fires that required visits from the local bush-fire brigade. To raise money for the brigade he inaugurated the Darlington Arts Festival, encouraging artists and craftspeople in the neighbourhood to exhibit. He spent the last seven years of his life at Pemberton amid the karri forests. Having regained his pilot's licence he bought a small Cessna aircraft, using it to fly to Perth, sometimes landing in paddocks en route and asking their owners for a cup of tea. In 1981 he was appointed AM. Survived by his wife and their daughter and son, he died of tuberculosis on 11 August 1981 at Pemberton and was buried in the local cemetery. His work is represented in all State galleries, the National Gallery of Australia, Canberra, and other public and private collections in Australia, Britain and the United States of America.

L. Klepac, *Guy Grey-Smith Retrospective* (1976); L. Thomas, *The Most Noble Art of Them All* (1976); B. Hawthorn, *Some Contemporary Western Painters and Sculptors* (1982); A. Davis, *Guy Grey-Smith* (1996); H. de Berg, interview with G. Grey-Smith (ts, 1965, NLA).   JENNY MILLS

GRIEVE, SIR HERBERT RONALD ROBINSON (1896-1982), medical practitioner, was born on 6 June 1896 at Vaucluse, Sydney, third child of Gideon James Grieve, a Scottish clerk who was later a lieutenant of the Black Watch, and his Queensland-born wife Julia Australia, née Robinson. Gideon was killed in 1900 at Paardeberg during the South African War. Ronald attended Sydney Grammar School and later served as president (1958-60) of the Old Sydneians' Union. Although he enlisted in the Australian Imperial Force on 27 June 1918 he was not called up before the war ended. He studied medicine at the University of Sydney (MB, Ch.M., 1920). After a year at Newcastle Hospital he worked as a resident at Manchester Royal Infirmary, England, in 1922. Returning to Australia the following year, he set up in general practice at Undercliffe (Earlwood), Sydney.

Interested in conservative politics, Grieve belonged to the National Association of New South Wales and then became a member of the interim management committee of the United Australia Party. He was appointed to the Legislative Council in 1932 by the Stevens [q.v.12] government but lost his seat in the (indirect) election of 1934. A photograph from the early 1930s shows a serious man, with his hair already greying. He served on the UAP council from 1932 to 1942.

Grieve was hostile to government health benefits schemes that appeared to threaten medical autonomy. Elected to the State council of the British Medical Association in 1937, he opposed the Lyons [q.v.10] government's scheme of national health insurance. In June 1938 he represented New South Wales general practitioners, conveying their intransigence to the federal council and the more moderate Victorian branch. After the failure of Lyons to implement his scheme, Grieve remained a member of the State council until 1956 and served on the BMA's medical assurance committee from 1938 to 1945. He was branch president (1947-48) at the height of the profession's battle against the Chifley [q.v.13] government's plans for pharmaceutical and national medical benefits schemes. In 1947-56 he represented New South Wales on the federal council.

Although Grieve was an architect of the State branch's hostility towards national medical benefit schemes, he recognised that the profession would have to craft an alternative. In 1943 he persuaded the New South Wales branch to establish a fund that reimbursed its subscribers' medical bills on a fee-for-service basis. The Medical Benefits Fund of New South Wales (later, of Australia Ltd), with Grieve as president (1946-75), met with derision from other branches of the BMA, especially Victoria, which saw it as a quixotic dream. On Grieve's urging, the New South Wales branch persisted, although the MBF lost large amounts and had a low subscriber base. The BMA in New South Wales provided capital to keep it afloat. When the minister for health, Sir Earle Page [q.v.11], proposed to use friendly societies as the agents for a capitation-based health scheme, the BMA, again led by New South Wales, launched boycotts until the friendly societies shifted to a fee-for-service model. The government acquiesced. Grieve helped to shape other aspects of Page's national health scheme, serving on the Federal pensioner medical services committee of inquiry.

Government subsidies ended the financial travails of the MBF and Grieve led its consolidation as Australia's largest private health fund. He helped to foster private health funds elsewhere in Australia, serving as president of the Blue Cross Association of Australia and chairman of the Voluntary Health Insurance Council of Australia. After assisting in drafting the constitution for the International Federation of Voluntary Health Service Funds, he was elected its first president (1968-70). He had been a member (1941-63) of the Medical Board of New South Wales. He retired from his Earlwood practice in 1981.

Grieve had married Helen Graham MacKenzie, a Scottish nurse, on 14 November 1924 at St Stephen's Presbyterian Church, Sydney; they divorced in 1945. On 7 December that year at Scots Presbyterian Church, Sydney, he married Florence Ross Timpson, an army nurse who was born in England; she died in 1969. He married Margaret Du-Vé, a

52-year-old secretary, on 12 February 1972 at Our Lady of Lourdes Catholic Church, Earlwood. A complex character, he leavened his high-minded principles and determination with a passion for horse-racing, owning horses with his friend Sid Webb, QC, and belonging to the Australian Jockey Club. He was knighted in 1958 and elected a fellow of the Australian Medical Association in 1968. Survived by his wife and a son and the younger daughter of his first marriage, Sir Ronald died on 1 July 1982 at Long Jetty and was buried in the Catholic section of South Head cemetery. He had supported the Little Sisters of the Poor, Randwick, for many years.

J. A. Gillespie, *The Price of Health* (1991); J. Murray, *Lifework* (1997); *United Aust Review*, 21 Oct 1932, p 16; *MJA*, 8 Jan 1983, p 48; obituary notes (MBF archives, Sydney). JAMES GILLESPIE

GRIMES, LOUISE CATHERINE (1907-1990), musician and schoolteacher, was born on 6 September 1907 at Lutwyche, Brisbane, third of five children of Queensland-born parents Alfred Kingsford Grimes, clerk, and his wife Lilian Elizabeth, née Maynard. Louise attended Windsor State and Brisbane Girls' Grammar (1921-23) schools. Appointed to the Department of Public Instruction on 1 January 1924, she was a student (1924-25) at the Queensland Teachers' Training College. Learning piano from George Sampson [q.v.11], she passed the examinations of Trinity College, London (ATCL, 1926; LTCL, 1928; L.Mus.T.C.L., 1930; FTCL, 1930). She studied music at the University of Adelaide (Mus.Bac., 1937) and arts part time at the University of Queensland (BA, 1942).

In the 1930s Grimes taught music full time at Windsor State School. Later she was a peripatetic singing and music specialist at Brisbane primary schools. As the department's supervisor of music in 1941-47, she oversaw the development of music education in Queensland. In 1938-52 she also broadcast educational programs for the Australian Broadcasting Commission.

On 1 June 1947 Grimes succeeded Sampson as organist and choir director at St John's Anglican Cathedral, Brisbane. She transformed the predominantly Victorian music library to one that was more comprehensive by including previously ignored music from the Tudor period and promoting the twentieth-century liturgical repertoire. Her sister Lilian helped her to raise funds to buy not only additional scores and new choir robes, but also a fine high-fidelity sound system and recordings that were used as educational aids for the boys. Perhaps because she suffered from arthritis, Grimes had no particular reputation as a virtuoso organist. Her conducting style has been described as that of a somewhat limited primary-school teacher. Nevertheless, at the cathedral she organised the first performances in Brisbane of works such as Benjamin (Lord) Britten's cantatas *Saint Nicolas* and *Noye's Fludde*. She resigned as organist in 1960.

In 1957 Grimes had joined the lecturing staff at QTTC (from 1961 Kelvin Grove Teachers' College). Transferring to the new Kedron Park Teachers' College in 1960, she established its music department with H. R. Millett. In 1963-73 she was dean of women. Miss Grimes was remembered with affection, respect and gratitude as a gracious and compassionate lady. After her retirement in 1973 she bought a five-acre (2 ha) property at Jimboomba, where she enjoyed life as a part-time hobby-farmer, thus fulfilling a childhood ambition. Never married, she died on 5 September 1990 at Chermside and was cremated with Anglican rites.

A. Yarrow and J. Millwater (eds), *History and Hearsay* (1994); *Courier-Mail* (Brisbane), 30 Nov 1973, p 10, 21 Sept 1990, p 21; private information.
ROBERT K. BOUGHEN

GROOM, SIR THOMAS REGINALD (1906-1987), accountant, businessman and lord mayor, was born on 30 December 1906 at Teneriffe, Brisbane, second child of Victorian-born Roy Graeme Groom, accountant and auditor, and his Brisbane-born wife May Augusta, née Bourne. Reginald was educated at Brisbane Grammar School and the University of Queensland (BA, 1928; B.Com., 1932). An outstanding oarsman, he won a university Blue in 1925. He was president of the University of Queensland Union in 1928. Excelling at his accountancy studies, he won the Murphy memorial prize for the best pass in Queensland in both the intermediate and final examinations in accountancy and auditing. Admitted as an associate-member of the Institute of Chartered Accountants in Australia in 1931, he became a fellow in 1939. On 7 January 1932 at Ann Street Presbyterian Church, Brisbane, he married Jessie Mary Grace Butcher. That year he joined his father's accountancy firm, R. G. Groom & Co., and was soon a senior partner. He was managing director (1938-58) of Unit Trusts Ltd and a board-member (1948-56) of General Rubber Co. Ltd.

An interest in community affairs, and knowledge of the operations of the Brisbane City Council gained while auditing its accounts, prompted Groom to contest the Ithaca ward, representing the Citizens' Municipal Organization, in the municipal elections of 1943. He won what had been an Australian Labor Party stronghold; however, when he stood in the 1944 State election, in the same constituency, as the candidate for (Sir) John Chandler's [q.v.13] newly formed Queensland People's Party, he failed to unseat Labor's E. M. Hanlon [q.v.14]. After his father died, in 1946, he temporarily retired from municipal politics to concentrate on his business activities. He won the Sherwood ward for the CMO in 1952; elected Opposition leader in council, he was subsequently selected as the CMO's candidate for the lord mayoralty. In 1955 the organisation won fourteen of the twenty-four seats, partly due to the 'training school' for CMO candidates that he had set up in 1953 and partly because of a split in the municipal Labor ranks.

Groom was elected lord mayor. In his campaign he had promised to bring efficiency and business management to the city administration and to implement a program of 'balanced development'. In a city where the population was expanding rapidly and sub-division of land on its fringes was continuing unabated, this was a tall order, especially as experience since World War II had shown that the council lacked the financial resources to meet the challenges such growth presented. The administration was hamstrung from the beginning by a Commonwealth credit 'squeeze' that severely restricted the availability of loan funds. The bulk of the capital raised was used to continue construction of the Tennyson powerhouse; to develop water supply facilities at Mount Crosby, ring-water-mains and service reservoirs; and to duplicate and extend sewerage mains. Mounting public transport losses also continued to eat into council revenues, despite the implementation of cost-saving measures.

During Groom's second term (1958-61) the imposition of more stringent requirements on land developers released funds for electricity, water supply and sewerage purposes, but a serious backlog in road development occurred. He took steps to develop a new town plan. The council's continued financial impotence provided the State government with the opportunity to take over the council's electricity undertaking and to create a regional water authority. Although Groom was a careful and astute businessman, as lord mayor he was unable to deal effectively with the city's financial and developmental problems. Influenced by his wife and dominated by the town clerk, J. C. Slaughter [q.v.], he sometimes ignored the sound advice of his fellow aldermen and departmental officers. At the 1961 election Clem Jones and his Labor team comprehensively defeated him and the CMO. Jones's subsequent success as lord mayor, however, was partly based on completing civic works initiated during Groom's term.

Knighted in 1961, Groom became the senior partner in the chartered accounting firm

Groom Sanderson & Co. and later, on amalgamation in the mid-1970s, a partner in Peat, Marwick, Mitchell & Co. His six years as lord mayor had given him a public profile and managerial experience that were to stand him in good stead for his future career: he was a member (1961-75) of the Australian National Airlines Commission (operating as Trans-Australia Airlines) and a councillor (1963-79) of the Australian Administrative Staff College, Mount Eliza, Victoria. He was chairman of Brolite Industries Ltd (1959-72), a director of Fire Fighting Enterprises Ltd (1961-71), Mount Isa Mines Ltd (from 1970 M.I.M. Holdings Ltd) in 1962-77, Besser Vibrapac Masonry (Qld) Ltd (1963-71), the Commonwealth Banking Corporation (1964-74), Consolidated Rutile Ltd (1966-77) and P & O Australia Ltd (1973-77). He was also on the boards of several unlisted companies.

Groom was president (1943) of the local Rostrum club, a member of the Brisbane and South Coast Hospitals Board, a councillor of the Presbyterian and Methodist Schools Association, a governor (1977-78) of the Australian Elizabethan Theatre Trust, a member (1977-79) of the Queensland Local Government Grants Commission, and chairman (1978) of the golden jubilee committee of the Royal Flying Doctor Service of Australia (Queensland section). He was also a member of the Johnsonian (Brisbane), Athenaeum (Melbourne) and Union (Sydney) clubs.

Standing just over six feet (183 cm) tall and weighing fifteen stone (95 kg), Sir Reginald was an imposing, courteous and dignified man, not given to indulging in personalities or aggrandisement. Both associates and opponents considered him a gentleman. He retired from his accountancy practice in 1978 and from professional life altogether after he suffered a stroke the following year. A tennis player in his younger days, he later preferred surfing, fishing and golf. Survived by his wife and their two sons and two adopted daughters, he died on 28 June 1987 at the property of his elder son at Guyra, New South Wales, and was cremated.

G. Greenwood and J. Laverty, *Brisbane 1859-1959* (1959); J. R. Laverty, 'Greater Brisbane in Retrospect', *Brisbane Retrospect* (1978); J. R. Cole, *Shaping a City* (1984); *Courier-Mail* (Brisbane), 23 Feb 1944, p 3, 18 Apr 1961, p 2, 30 June 1987, p 9; *Sunday Mail* (Brisbane), 29 July 1973, p 20; Brisbane City Council minutes, 1955-61 (Brisbane City Council Archives).

JOHN LAVERTY

GROOM, WILLIAM HENRY GEORGE (1900-1984), journalist and newspaper proprietor, was born on 1 September 1900 at Toowoomba, Queensland, second of four children of locally born parents Henry Littleton Groom [q.v.9], journalist, and his wife Marion Flora, née Black. W. H. Groom [q.v.4] was his grandfather; Sir Littleton Groom [q.v.9] was his uncle. Always known as George, he was educated at state and private schools. Growing up in a newspaper environment, he began his working life as a cadet journalist in January 1918 at the *Toowoomba Chronicle*, where his father was managing director. After stints on the *Maryborough Chronicle* and the Brisbane *Daily Mail*, he managed the Longreach *Leader* (formerly *News*) and its printing interests from September 1922 for a few months. In May 1923 he joined the staff of the Melbourne *Herald*.

Returning to Queensland in 1926 Groom worked 'bloody long hours' to establish the *Bundaberg Daily Times*, launched on 16 August that year by a syndicate of businessmen. Because of ill health he resigned in October. In March 1927 he became executive secretary to (Sir) Keith Murdoch [q.v.10], managing director of the Herald & Weekly Times Ltd, Melbourne. He found Murdoch 'a tremendous man to work with' but hated the Melbourne climate. On 28 August 1928 his mother, now widowed, bought the *Johnstone River Advocate* and the *Northern Sportsman*. Taking charge, Groom immediately shut down the loss-making, year-old *Sportsman*, upgraded the plant, and made the weekly *Advocate* a bi-weekly from 1 January 1929.

Innisfail struck Groom as 'back-block America, all except the revolvers'; he found that 'sugar was a god, and you mustn't touch it'. Determined to build up the *Advocate* into a viable newspaper, he kept reminding his readers that it had been established with the motto, 'fair, fearless and free'. His brother Spencer David (1904-1983) and sister Marion Flora (1907-1988), known as 'Dolly', were soon working on the paper as journalists. He developed a small chain of newspapers, starting with the acquisition of the Atherton *Tableland Examiner*, into which he incorporated (1931) the *Atherton News & Barron Valley Advocate*.

Attempting to find suitable industries other than sugar for the region, he helped to establish the Palmerston Province Development League and operated it at his own expense. The group advocated building a new road from Innisfail to Millaa Millaa on the Atherton Tableland to 'open lands' and to allow transport of timber. His editorials helped to initiate the royal commission on the development of North Queensland, established in 1931 by the A. E. Moore [q.v.10] government. He encouraged local business; in 1936-37 he was president of the Federated Chambers of Commerce of Far North Queensland and in 1937-38 of the Queensland body. In 1941 he was elected a life member of the Innisfail Chamber of Commerce. Active in other community organisations, he was also president of both the local Rotary club and the show society.

A *Johnstone River Advocate* report won national attention in 1934 when Groom investigated rumours that a Japanese sailing ship was seeking trochus shell in Australian waters near Dunk Island. After an unsuccessful aerial search over the Great Barrier Reef he chartered a speedboat, found the vessel and through an interpreter interviewed its captain. He and the crew of the speedboat were later threatened with prosecution because they had boarded an overseas vessel and returned to port without undergoing quarantine examination.

In 1935 Groom was a delegate to the Imperial Press Conference held in South Africa. He launched the *Sunday Australian* at Cairns in February 1939 and published it, on pink paper, until 4 April 1952. The *Johnstone River Advocate* became a daily on 25 November 1940, and on 19 May 1941 changed its name to the *Evening Advocate*; circulation was little more than 1500 and during the late 1940s and the 1950s it competed with the *Cootamundra Herald*, New South Wales, for the title of the smallest-circulation daily in Australia. In 1973 Groom protested effusively in print when the abolition of postal and telecommunications concessions to newspapers resulted in a 1000 per cent increase in charges for receiving telex news from within Australia and overseas. He announced plans to close the paper on 28 September but was persuaded to continue publication from 1 October as a tri-weekly, without news received by telex. In January 1978 he sold the *Evening Advocate*. Spencer retired at the same time; Dolly had returned to Toowoomba after her marriage to V. G. Bancroft in 1939. Never married, George Groom died on 2 July 1984 at Cairns and was cremated after a funeral service in St Alban's Church of England, Innisfail.

R. Kirkpatrick, *Sworn to No Master* (1984); *Toowoomba Chronicle and Darling Downs Gazette*, 3 Oct 1922, p 2; *Queenslander*, 26 Jan 1933, p 33; *Johnstone River Advocate and Innisfail News*, 10 Apr 1934, p 1, 'special souvenir issue', July 1936, p 10; *Evening Advocate* (Innisfail), 1 Oct 1973, p 1; *Innisfail Advocate*, 4 July 1984, p 1; R. Kirkpatrick, 'The Groom Family Dynasty Implodes and a New Chain Emerges in the North', *PANPA. Bulletin*, Sept 2002, p 59; private information and personal knowledge.

ROD KIRKPATRICK

GROUNDS, SIR ROY BURMAN (1905-1981), architect, was born on 18 December 1905 at St Kilda, Melbourne, fourth son of Victorian-born parents Herbert Algernon Haslett Grounds, chemist, and his wife Maud Hawkesworth, née Hughes. Roy attended several schools before completing his secondary education at Melbourne Church of England Grammar School. Unsettled in his search for employment, he eventually joined his brother, Haslett, as an articled pupil in the practice of Blackett [q.v.7] & Forster. He attended the Melbourne University Architectural Atelier (1927-28) and took night classes at Brighton Technical School, developing an interest in the Bauhaus and architectural modernism.

With Geoffrey Mewton, also at Blackett & Forster, Grounds began experimenting with house plans that fused living and dining areas and minimised passage ways. In 1928 their winning entry in a Royal Victorian Institute of Architects competition for a house to cost £1000 was praised for its fresh 'Australian style'; that year Grounds also won the RVIA's annual war memorial scholarship, and travelled to Britain with Mewton and Oscar Bayne, a colleague at the university atelier.

After working for a variety of employers in Britain and Europe, Grounds sailed for the United States of America. He settled at Santa Monica, California, and began designing studio sets for Radio-Keith-Orpheum Pictures and Metro-Goldwyn-Mayer Inc., and accepting architectural commissions. On 9 August 1932 at the office of the Los Angeles registrar, he married Virginia Lammers, née Marr, an American divorcee whom he had met aboard the ship to Britain. Grounds returned to Melbourne that year and established a partnership with Mewton. As the Depression passed, they became known as the leading Australian exponents of modernism in house design.

Mewton & Grounds's industrially grained aesthetic was evident in their prize-winning entry for the Centenary Homes exhibition of 1934. Increasingly, however, Grounds was moving away from an 'International Style' to a more regionally attuned architecture. His Lyncroft at Shoreham (1934) and Chateau Tahbilk homestead (1935-37) adopted a weathered, later limed and pastelled colouration, and softly textured walls; using materials drawn from each site, these houses had overtones of rural vernacular. In 1938 poor health prompted a temporary retirement to Provence, France, and another period in Britain but by 1939 he was back, resuming practice from a flat in Toorak. On 24 October 1941—the day of his divorce from Virginia—at the office of the government statist, Melbourne, Grounds married Alice Bettine Ramsay, née James, a secretary and also a divorcee (for whom he had designed a house in 1933).

Four apartment buildings in Toorak, designed by Grounds in 1939-41, attracted attention in Australia and overseas. Clendon and Clendon Corner were elegant in a stripped neo-Georgian mode, with flat roofs, mews paving and open plans. Moonbria and Quamby showed Californian references in their lanai terraces and sundecks. All, however, were distinctive Grounds syntheses in their explicit urban form and adaptation to often challenging sites. Robin Boyd [q.v.13] assisted with these projects, and—seeing Grounds as the pivotal figure in the arrival of the 'modern house' in Australia—admired their honesty and ingenuity. In 1940 Grounds was registered as an architect.

From 21 February 1942 Grounds served in the Royal Australian Air Force, performing works and camouflage duties in the South-West Pacific Area and finishing as a temporary flight lieutenant. His appointment terminated in May 1945, and—suffering nervous strain—he took to orcharding at Mount Eliza, then dairy farming at Buxton, north of Melbourne. Following the death of their infant daughter, Roy and his wife returned to the city. At the University of Melbourne (B.Arch., 1951) Grounds became a senior lecturer (1951-53) in the faculty of architecture. He retained a right of private practice, became an associate (1947) of the RVIA (fellow 1951) and undertook thirty-five projects over the next six years. Styling himself both a modernist and traditionalist, he also gained a reputation for radicalism in handling geometric forms, notably in the triangular Leyser house at Kew (1950-51) and the circular Henty house at Frankston (1951-52). His own house in Hill Street, Toorak, won the Victorian Architectural medal (1954): its circular courtyard divided a set of rooms within a square perimeter; three adjoining flats adopted the double height subdivision synonymous with Le Corbusier. Other projects from this period included prefabricated classrooms—'Bristol portables'—which appeared in schools all over Victoria without the sun protection Grounds had specified.

In 1953 Grounds formed a partnership with his university colleagues Boyd and Frederick Romberg. Over the next eight years the firm designed some of the leading modern buildings in Australia. While working on several houses, at Brighton, Toorak and Mount Eliza, Grounds now concentrated mainly on large projects. In 1957-58 he designed a workers' village at Glenorchy, Tasmania, for Claudio Alcorso's Silk and Textile Printers Ltd, Alcorso's first, circular house (1955) and a second house in 1965. With Romberg he oversaw a fanning sound shell in 1956 for the Sidney Myer [q.v.10] Music Bowl (a project completed by Yuncken Freeman Griffiths & Simpson). Through Oscar Bayne he gained the Australian Academy of Science building (Canberra, 1957-59): a remarkable dome in shell concrete drawing on Saarinen's sculptural architecture, which won the RAIA Canberra chapter's award (1957) and the Sulman [q.v.12] award (1959) and which, in 1984, was nominated for the international register of significant twentieth-century architecture. Other projects in Canberra followed, including the Phytotron (1962) for the Commonwealth

Scientific and Industrial Research Organization, and the Botany building (1968) at the Australian National University.

In 1958 Grounds and his assistants prepared a master plan for the extension of Ormond [q.v.5] College, University of Melbourne; by 1962 he had designed the master's and vice-master's lodges. Reflecting an interest in the Italian Neo-Liberty movement, Grounds drew on palazzo forms and medieval references for the university's John Medley Building (1971). Such evocations of hybrid historical detail were seen by some critics as a betrayal of modernism; it was an approach, however, already evident in the design Grounds prepared for Melbourne's National Art Gallery and Cultural Centre in the late 1950s.

The public astonishment that met the unveiling of the plans for the gallery and cultural centre in late 1961 had been more than matched by that of Grounds's partners when, in 1959, he was selected as the sole commissioned architect for the project. Boyd had misgivings over Grounds's highly sculpted and monumentalising bronze tower; Romberg—the most experienced of the partners on larger buildings and concrete construction—felt overlooked; the profession in general was unhappy that there had been no open competition. Earlier tensions among the partners over financial management and over Grounds's desire to run for the city council were exacerbated by his new prominence. Amid the dismay and anger of colleagues and friends, in July 1962 Grounds left the partnership, having already established his own design team.

Completed in 1968, the project's first section, the National Gallery of Victoria, received a mixed reception from architects, who were still not persuaded by elements such as the severe bluestone exterior redolent of the nearby barracks and an assortment of warehouses, 'pubs' and gaols, or the perceived theatricality of the quasi-medieval Great Hall. Gallery staff soon complained about the general functioning and spatial gradation of the building. Grounds soldiered on, encouraged by the Royal Australian Institute of Architects' gold medal (1968) and a knighthood (1969). The neighbouring Concert Hall was developed between 1977 and 1981; the State Theatre was finished posthumously in 1982. The proposed tower—still among the most controversial of the centre's aspects—was completed as a rather timid space frame, given remedial height by Peter McIntyre.

Grounds continued to gain commissions for houses and larger projects: his George Street Cinema Complex in Sydney (1976) was appropriately festive; the imposing Blackwood Hall at Monash University (1971) was a more serious undertaking, emulating a great cathedral in its west front and rose window; and the Wrest Point Casino and hotel complex,

Hobart (1973), was the first large building of its type in Australia. Through his later years his environmental commitment was reflected in a group of improvised buildings at Penders, near Tathra on the New South Wales south coast, which he would visit regularly. Next to them was a house he had designed for Ken Myer, whose patronage of the Arts Centre reshaped Grounds's later career.

Handsome, of medium height, with thick dark hair, often unruly over a quizzical glare and a sharply trimmed moustache, Grounds was declamatory and sometimes abrasive in manner, with a flair for the dramatic in timing and demeanour. He was direct and often blunt—although it was his practice to rehearse a professional interview for a week. Enjoying a dual reputation as a leader in reshaping Australian architecture under modernist influence and as a traditionalist, he came to suspect that modernism was a scientific delusion. Sociable himself in clubs and discussion groups, including the Melbourne Club, the Boobooks and the Chevaliers du Tastevin, he also encouraged the Halftime Club, a forum for Melbourne's emerging architects and students. He was more accomplished as a house designer than a shaper of large buildings, although he came to see the latter as 'the only real architecture' and attempted so much in institutional architecture that his reputation in that field was also assured. Sir Roy died on 2 March 1981 at Parkville, Melbourne, and was cremated; he was survived by his wife, their younger daughter, and a son from his first marriage.

R. Boyd, *Victorian Modern* (1947); J. Hetherington, *Uncommon Men* (1965); C. Hamann, 'Roy Grounds 1905-', Frederick Romberg 1913- and Robin Boyd 1919-1971', in H. Tanner (ed), *Architects of Australia* (1981), and C. Hamann, 'Arenas of the Public Good', *Backlogue*, vol 3, 1999, p 119; *Architecture*, vol 44, no 1, 1955, p 22; *Backlogue*, vol 3, 1999, p 73; *Argus* (Melbourne), 1 May 1928, p 17; *People* (Sydney), 6 May 1953, p 12; Grounds, Romberg and Boyd papers (SLV).   CONRAD HAMANN

GROVE, RUPERT HOWARD (1906-1982), solicitor and Methodist (Uniting Church) layman, was born on 27 March 1906 at Dulwich Hill, Sydney, son of Victorian-born Howard Thomas Grove, architect, and his Sydney-born wife Aphra Marian, née McCoy. Educated at North Sydney Boys' High School, Rupert graduated from the University of Sydney (LL B, 1928). He was admitted as a solicitor on 9 May 1929 and that year became a partner in the busy city law firm of McCoy, Grove & Atkinson. On 17 October 1935 he married Ina Margaret Hulme at the Methodist Church, Gordon.

A member of that church for more than forty years, Grove served as a local preacher and lay leader. As a young man he was prominent in Christian Endeavour and in the local branch of the highly popular Order of Knights, in which he became a knight grand commander. Youth leadership took him to circuit quarterly meetings, thence to the New South Wales Conference (1936-77) and the General Conference (1947-77) of the Methodist Church of Australasia. At conference level he bore a heavy load of committee work, spread over a broad range of responsibilities but unified by three principal concerns: sound governance of the church at all its levels; its mission to evangelise and to strengthen its influence in the community; and church union, which he believed would create a renewed and influential church.

In the progression towards the union of the Congregational, Methodist and Presbyterian churches in Australia, Grove made a decisive impact. The Methodist General Conference of 1954 was on the point of voting to join only with the Congregationalists, negotiations with the Presbyterians having stalled. Grove moved an amendment that action be deferred pending further approaches to the Presbyterians. His strategy was successful and he was involved in the continued negotiations as a member of the Methodist General Conference committee on church union and as the only Methodist lay representative on the Joint Commission on Church Union and the Joint Constitution Commission. The Uniting Church in Australia came into existence in 1977.

Concern for the Church's mission was expressed in Grove's membership (from 1936) of the Department of Home Missions in the Methodist Church and his chairmanship of the board of the United Church in North Australia (1972-77) and of the Uniting Church's Commission for National Mission (1977-82). He was a member of the Newington College council for forty-one years. Colleagues emphasised Grove's ability to identify and clarify issues and hasten business. Clear and authoritative in reasoning, he was noted in debate for his vigorous, emphatic, even passionate, delivery, tempered by charity, understanding and a dry humour. He was generous in sharing his legal knowledge. A man of great strength of character, he was seen as unspoiled, modest and humble. Survived by his wife and one of their two daughters, he died on 8 August 1982 at his Killara home and was cremated.

A. H. Wood, *'Not Lost but Gone Before'* (1987); Methodist Church of A'asia, *Minutes of the General Conference*, 1954, 1957; Uniting Church in Aust (NSW Synod), *Year Book*, 1981, p 15, 1983, p 6; Uniting Church in Aust, *Minutes of the Third Assembly*, 1982; J. S. Udy, Church Union in Australia (MA thesis, Univ of Sydney, 1985); Church records (Uniting Church archives, North Parramatta, Sydney).   JOAN MANSFIELD

GUERTNER, BERYL ANNIE BLANCHE (1917-1981), magazine editor and author, was born on 22 October 1917 at Paddington, Sydney, daughter of Eugene Henry Gürtner, a German-born pastry-cook and sports masseur, and his Sydney born wife Maude, née Ireland. Beryl was educated (1931-33) by the Presentation Sisters at Mount Erin, Wagga Wagga, before training as a secretary. Drawn to the written and spoken word, the natural actress in her saw the writing of elegant and informed prose and the ability to hold an audience as skills that might lead her into a more creative world. Metropolitan life beckoned; she went to Sydney aged 21, and lived in the Mosman Bay area until 1949. She worked in the publicity department of Paramount Pictures and as a journalist on the *Daily Telegraph*. An active member of the Society of Women Writers of New South Wales, she was its president in 1960.

During the late 1940s, after years of economic recession, wartime shortages and frugal living, there was a surging demand for new homes, household equipment and fresh interior decoration. Ken Murray, an enterprising young magazine publisher, sensed the opportunity and found a suitable editor in Guertner to tap the market. With only sixteen weeks and limited resources, Guertner, buoyed by her natural drive and sharp eye, produced the first issue of *Australian House and Garden* in December 1948. Almost alone in its field, this magazine opened up the possibilities of living with style on modest means, and of pushing aside staid 'cream and mushroom pink' residential conformity. It was an era of self-help, and the magazine provided ingenious small-home plans by the architect W. Watson-Sharp, conveyed the excitement of good design, and promoted innovative paint colours and decorative schemes. From the start Guertner introduced the public to important designers such as Robin Boyd, Syd Ancher [qq.v.13], Harry Seidler, Grant Featherston and Marion Hall Best [q.v.]. Gardening advice was influenced by her friend Margaret Davis, founder of the Garden Club of New South Wales (Garden Club of Australia).

As an editor for the K. G. Murray Publishing Co. Pty Ltd (which came to include Gregory's guides and maps), Guertner was responsible for *Australian House and Garden* until 1973 and *Good Gardening* in 1970-77. She wrote many books including *The Australian Book of Flower Arrangement* (1964) and the *Australian Book of Furnishing and Decorating* (1967); her *Gregory's Guide to Better Gardens* (1964?) ran to six editions; and she produced over thirty homemaker and gardening guides.

At Warrimoo in the Blue Mountains Guertner and Catherine (Kate) Warmoll created from 1949 a sophisticated country retreat for themselves. Moving to Macmasters Beach, they retired from full-time careers in 1973, and made a subtropical garden beside Lake Cockrone. Guertner was of medium height, with an expressive face, brown eyes, and blonded hair, and was always smartly dressed. Recalled as a strong and engaging personality—of great warmth, generosity and quick wit—she was a persuasive advocate for the new ideas and designs that helped transform domestic life in postwar Australia. She died of cancer on 25 November 1981 at Gosford and was cremated.

R. Aitken and M. Looker (eds), *The Oxford Companion to Australian Gardens* (2002); *Austn House and Garden*, Dec 1973, p 35, Dec 1988, p 8, Dec 1998, p 18; private information.   HOWARD TANNER

GUNTHER, SIR JOHN THOMSON (1910-1984), medical practitioner, public servant and vice-chancellor, was born on 2 October 1910 in Sydney, eldest of three children of New South Wales-born Cyril Maynard Gunther, sugar analyst, and his wife Jean Graeme, née Thomson, who came from Brisbane. Cyril, an industrial chemist with the Colonial Sugar Refining Co. Ltd, moved north to the Tweed River when John was still an infant but returned to Sydney in 1917 on being appointed manager with the importing firm of R. W. Cameron & Co. John grew up in a family well connected in business and the professions but possessing little capital.

After attending Cranbrook School, John was educated (1924-28) as a boarder at The King's School, Parramatta, on an old boys' scholarship. Lacking sufficient funds to go on the land, he chose to study medicine at the University of Sydney (MB, 1935), where his mother had been one of the early women medical graduates. Gunther represented Sydney in inter-university boxing and Rugby. After a year's residency at Sydney Hospital, in 1935 he applied to be medical officer with Lever's Pacific Plantations Ltd, which ran coconut plantations.

Working out of Gavutu and Tulagi in the British Solomon Islands Protectorate, Gunther travelled widely to over thirty of Lever's properties and made his first visit to Papua on a trip to Lever's Giligili plantation at Milne Bay. On 1 March 1938, while on leave and working as a locum, he married Grace Rickard-Bell, née Blythe, a widow, in a civil ceremony at Bourke, New South Wales. Believing that his wife would not like the tropics, he took the position of chairman of the medical board at Mount Isa, Queensland, and investigated plumbism.

On 30 June 1941 Gunther was commissioned as a flight lieutenant in the Royal Australian Air Force's Medical Branch. His early postings were to Laverton, Victoria, and Sandgate, Brisbane. The RAAF sent him to

Papua in September 1942 to help combat malaria. Next month he was promoted to temporary squadron leader. By ensuring the use of anti-malarials and protective clothing, reducing the numbers of mosquitoes and arguing for a quicker return to duty, Gunther lessened the impact of malaria on service personnel in Port Moresby and at Milne Bay. From July 1943 he was based in Australia but spent much time visiting RAAF bases in Papua and New Guinea. He also obtained diplomas of tropical medicine and public health (1944) from the University of Sydney. In December 1944 he took command of the Tropical Research Field Unit in New Guinea; after conducting research on Bat Island, near Manus, he wrote a sixty-page report on scrub typhus. Demobilised in June 1946, he had had, he said, a 'very interesting war'.

In 1942 Gunther's wife had been killed in a motorcar accident. On 17 July 1943 he married Elvie Phyllis Hodge, a nurse with the RAAF, at St Mark's Church of England, Darling Point, Sydney. 'Dot', as she was known, cared for his two young daughters; together they had a son and a daughter. Offered the position of director of public health in the Territory of Papua-New Guinea in 1946, Gunther agreed to go to Port Moresby before deciding. Not the first choice for director, he arrived 'unsung and unwanted', worked from a tin-roofed office with a mud floor, had few resources and faced the problems of a population devastated and neglected by war. But he took the post. He was then 35 years old, of medium height, strongly built, and aggressive in speech and movement: he worked hard and played hard.

Gunther's main problems were recruiting trained personnel, carrying services to remote communities and protecting the many recently contacted communities from new diseases. By employing refugee doctors from Europe and by training expatriate and indigenous medical assistants, Gunther built up the staff. He arranged for those few Papua New Guineans with sufficient education to go to the Central Medical School in Suva before the Papuan Medical College was established in 1958. A system of aid posts, sub-district hospitals and district hospitals supported by medical patrols brought most people within a day's walk of medical care. The department concentrated on readily diagnosed diseases with known cures, vaccinated widely, and introduced maternity and child health clinics and mobile units, and a malaria control policy (including controversial insecticide spraying). Permitting briefly trained staff to treat patients, and by-passing other safeguards observed in advanced countries, involved risks but Gunther argued that overall the policies had saved thousands.

As director of public health, Gunther approved the start of the Highlands Labour Scheme in 1950, organised the medical ser-

vices after the disastrous Mount Lamington eruption of 1951 and directed the initial response to the degenerative disease kuru. He had inherited a system of racially segregated hospitals; in the face of white opposition new hospitals were designed as single buildings with separate paying and non-paying wings. The health service was a major achievement of the Australian postwar administration of Papua and New Guinea.

Appointed assistant-administrator in 1957, although again not the first choice, Gunther gradually won the confidence and friendship of both (Sir) Paul Hasluck and (Sir) Donald Cleland [q.v.13]. The three men dominated the making and implementing of Australian policy in the Territory for the next seven years. Gunther was government leader in the Legislative Council, chairman of the select committee on constitutional development that recommended the establishment of the first House of Assembly with universal suffrage, and a member of the Currie [q.v.] commission on higher education in Papua and New Guinea that led to the creation of the University of Papua and New Guinea. He directed the government response to the disruptive Hahalis movement on Buka Island, and he argued the case for separate salaries for Papua and New Guinean public servants although, disturbed by the anomalies in the two scales, he secured Robert Hawke to represent Papua New Guineans in arbitration. From 1948 he served on the research council of the South Pacific Commission. He acted as administrator in Cleland's absence.

As a member of the Administrator's Advisory Council and, from 1964, senior government member in the new House of Assembly, Gunther continued to be responsible for getting government business through the House. A fair speaker, well briefed, respected and combative, he was a dominant member, who objected to increased interference from Canberra: 'any influence I'd had with Cleland and Hasluck I lost entirely 1964-1965'. He was a special representative at the United Nations in 1965 when Australia was under pressure to give Papua New Guinea independence.

Gunther was looking for a new challenge when he was appointed foundation vice-chancellor of the University of Papua and New Guinea in 1966. Although inexperienced in university administration he brought to it a determination to get things done, a shrewd assessment of staff, a tolerance of beliefs, and an office and house open to all ranks and races. He lost arguments to bring medicine, engineering and agricultural science into the university from the start, but he was a strong advocate for the autonomy and standards, of the new institution. By the first graduation, in 1970, UPNG had the finest buildings and grounds then built by the Australians in their colony, and the campus was a centre of creativity and scholarship.

On his retirement in 1972 Gunther spoke of his hope of leaving a 'lively enquiring' university that served both national and individual needs. At first at Buderim, Queensland, and then in Melbourne, he maintained his long-standing interest in gardening and served as a director of Bougainville Copper Pty Ltd. Appointed OBE in 1954, he was elevated to CMG in 1965, and knighted in 1975. The Cilento [q.v.] medal (1965) and honorary doctorates from UPNG, the University of Sydney and Monash University also recognised his contribution. Long debilitated by emphysema, Sir John Gunther died on 27 April 1984 at West Heidelberg and was cremated. His wife and four children survived him. There is a bronze bust by John Dowie and a Gunther building at UPNG. Hasluck said that in postwar Papua New Guinea Gunther 'was easily the strongest single driving force in the Administration'.

P. Hasluck, *A Time for Building* (1976); I. Downs, *The Australian Trusteeship* (1980); I. Howie-Willis, *A Thousand Graduates* (1980); D. Denoon, *Public Health in Papua New Guinea* (1989); B. G. Burton-Bradley (ed), *A History of Medicine in Papua New Guinea* (1990); *New Guinea and Australia, the Pacific and South-East Asia*, vol 1, no 5, 1966, p 29; *SMH*, 9 Feb 1966, p 2, 7 Jan 1971, p 4, 28 Apr 1984, p 6; *MJA*, 21 Jan 1985, p 153; Gunther papers, and interviews with D. Denoon, H. Nelson and I. Willis (NLA); personal knowledge.   H. N. NELSON

GUNZ, FREDERICK (FRIEDRICH) WALTER (1914-1990), haematologist, was born on 17 November 1914 at Munich, Germany, son of Hugo Gunz, lawyer, and his wife Johanna, née Loewenfeld. His secondary education was at the Herder Oberschule in Berlin. In 1933 his family, of Jewish extraction, moved to London to avoid Nazi persecution. Although he had only limited English on arrival in England, after attending a cramming course he matriculated and gained an entrance scholarship to St Bartholomew's Hospital medical school, University of London (MB, BS, 1939; MD, 1942), where he won the gold medal for medicine. There was no trace of an accent in his adopted language for the rest of his life.

An internee, Gunz was sent to Canada for eighteen months in 1940-41. He had wished to join the British Army. In 1942 after his return to England, he became a member of the Royal College of Physicians (fellow 1969). He was an assistant clinical pathologist (1943-46) at Addenbrooke's Hospital, Cambridge, and then held (1946-50) a Saltwell research studentship at the University of Cambridge (Ph.D., 1949). The research he conducted there in the department of radiotherapeutics started his career

in leukaemia research. He had married Joan Phelps Tuckey on 23 September 1944 at Holy Trinity parish church, Cambridge, and was naturalised in 1946.

At the end of the 1940s the North Canterbury Hospital Board in New Zealand was seeking to update and expand pathology services. In 1950 Gunz went to Christchurch to take up the position of haematologist at the hospital. He expanded the blood transfusion service, introducing a mobile donor unit for which he drove the bus to each township in the area, and set up a tumour research unit, later to become a cytogenetics unit of which he was the director (1962-67). With Peter Fitzgerald and Angela Adams he achieved international recognition in 1962 for describing the role of the abnormal Christchurch chromosome in lymphocytic leukaemia. In 1954-66 he served part time in the Royal New Zealand Army Medical Corps, Territorial Force, rising to temporary major.

During his career Gunz published more than sixty papers on clinical research, treatment and palliative care but his international fame rested largely on the book *Leukemia* (1958), written with William Dameshek. During sabbatical leave in 1956 at Dameshek's laboratory in Boston, United States of America, he had pursued his interest in this disease, particularly its aetiology and chromosome abnormalities. Dameshek invited him to collaborate on the work. It was a pioneering account by two pre-eminent haematologists of the origins of leukaemia, the manifestations of its various forms, and its treatment. Several editions have been produced. In his lucid style, Gunz also contributed chapters to works on haematology and cancer research.

In 1967 Gunz moved to Australia to become director of medical research at the Kanematsu Memorial Institute at Sydney Hospital. As well as establishing a haematology unit, he was involved with renal medicine, transplantation, blood-pressure research, haemorheology and cancer immunology, showing his talent for guiding and integrating research over apparently diverse fields. He also managed, in an inner-city hospital chronically short of space, to double the size of the department and to oversee the construction of a five-storey extension for the institute. His wife worked with him at the Kanematsu on a study of the familial incidence of leukaemia. He was elected a fellow of the Royal Australasian College of Physicians in 1967.

After retirement in 1980 Gunz devoted his energies to support groups and palliative care services for cancer patients. He established a pioneer support service for the northern metropolitan health region of Sydney at the Royal North Shore Hospital. President (1981-86) of the New South Wales Palliative Care Association, in 1985 he became chairman of the patient care committee of the New South Wales State Cancer Council. That year the Australian Cancer Society awarded him its gold medal. In 1981-90 he edited *Cancer Forum*. His humanity was also evident in his support of the Wayside Chapel.

Gunz was active in the New Zealand Society of Pathologists, and in the (Royal) College of Pathologists of Australia (from 1979, Royal College of Pathologists of Australasia). He served the college as chief examiner in haematology from 1967, as chairman (1973-77) of the board of censors, and as editor (1978-85) of the college's journal, *Pathology*, with which Joan ably assisted him. In 1986 the college gave him its distinguished fellows' award. He was a friendly, distinguished and courteous man, who had a keen interest in music. Survived by his wife (d.2002), their two daughters and a son, he died on 30 October 1990 at St Leonards and was cremated.

J. C. Wiseman and R. J. Mulhearn (eds), *Roll of the Royal Australasian College of Physicians*, vol 2 (1994); *Lives of the Fellows of the Royal College of Physicians of London* (2000); *Pathology* (Sydney), vol 23, no 1, 1991, p 80; *NZ Medical Jnl*, 27 Feb 1991, p 82.   BRENDA HEAGNEY

GUTHRIE, SIR RUTHERFORD CAMPBELL (1899-1990), politician and grazier, was born on 28 November 1899 at Donald, Victoria, son of Australian-born Thomas Oliver Guthrie, station manager, and his Scottishborn wife Jessie Blackwood, née Hannah. Ford—as he became known—was raised at the family property Rich Avon, near Donald, and educated at Melbourne Church of England Grammar School. In 1918 he interrupted studies at Jesus College, Cambridge (BA, 1921), to serve in the Royal Field Artillery, in which he was commissioned in April 1919. His height of 6 ft 2½ ins (189 cm) and strong build helped him to become a fine sportsman; he rowed for Cambridge.

In 1922 Guthrie returned to Australia. He followed in the steps of his uncle, James Guthrie [q.v.9], in establishing a Poll Hereford cattle and Corriedale sheep stud at his property Warrawidgee, near Linton, Victoria. On 29 November 1927 at Noorat he married Rhona Mary McKellar with Presbyterian forms. He became a batsman of some repute in the Western Plains District.

Enlisting in the Citizen Military Forces in 1935, Guthrie was commissioned in the 4/19th Light Horse Regiment two years later. On 27 June 1940 he transferred to the Australian Imperial Force as a captain, and in May 1941 joined the 9th Divisional Cavalry in the Middle East. At El Alamein, Egypt, in July 1942 he suffered a gunshot wound to the right arm. He was promoted to major that month and repatriated in March 1943. For gallantry in North Africa he was mentioned in despatches. After serving in northern Australia, he transferred to the Reserve of Officers on 18 April 1944.

A member (1946-74) of the Ripon Shire Council, Guthrie served three terms as president (1951-52, 1954-55, 1963-64). In 1947 he won the Victorian Legislative Assembly seat of Ripon for the Liberal Party, and in December 1948 was appointed minister of soldier settlement in the Hollway [q.v.14] government; he also became commissioner of crown lands and survey and president of the Board of Land and Works. 'Not particularly suited to the hurly-burly of politics' (according to Thomas Austin, a later Liberal member for the seat), Guthrie lost Ripon to the Australian Labor Party in 1950. He remained active in the Liberal and Country Party as president (1956-60) and treasurer (1960-63).

Committed to serving primary industry and his community, Guthrie was an active member of numerous local organisations including the Central Highlands Regional Development Committee, Ballarat Legacy, the Ballarat Agricultural Society and the Australian Corriedale Association. He also served as a director of the Phosphate Co-operative Co. of Australia Ltd (chairman 1971-72), Federal Woollen Mills Ltd (chairman 1966-67) and Perpetual Executors and Trustees Association of Australia Ltd (1958-63). He was president in 1960 of the Melbourne Club. Appointed CMG in 1960, he was knighted in 1968.

Guthrie was a gregarious man. His private life was tinged with sadness due to the death of his younger son in 1973. His health deteriorated in his later years, following retirement to Gisborne. Lady Guthrie was killed in a car accident in 1989. Survived by his elder son, Sir Rutherford died on 20 February 1990 at Gisborne and was buried in Macedon cemetery. His estate was sworn for probate at $2 221 471.

PD (LA, Vic), 1990, p 43; *Telegraph* (Gisborne, Vic), 27 Feb 1990, p 4.   SARAH TYRELL

GUY, MARGARET FRANCES; *see* LOOKER, M.

H

HAAG, STEFAN HERMANN (1925-1986), singer, director, designer and arts administrator, was born on 26 March 1925 in Vienna, only child of Stefan Haag, bank official, and his wife Anna, née Dittenbacher. A student at the Rudolfsheim State School, Stefan trained with the Vienna Boys' Choir and joined the Boys' Choir of the Vienna State Opera in 1935. Next year he entered the Vienna Mozart Boys' Choir and in 1937-39 toured internationally with it. Stranded in Perth when World War II started, the choir was re-settled as the St Patrick's Cathedral Choir, Melbourne. Although he had little English, Stefan was enrolled at St Joseph's Christian Brothers Technical College, Abbotsford, and fostered with Australian families. He accepted his circumstances philosophically. From 1943 he served in the Civil Aliens Corps at Alice Springs, where, while still learning English, he began directing plays.

In 1945 Haag resumed musical studies with Adolph Spivakovsky. He gave recitals as a lieder singer (earlier using the name Louis Waters), conducted choirs, worked as a music copyist and taught in schools. In 1947 he joined Gertrude Johnson's [q.v.14] pioneering National Theatre Opera Company as a singer and assistant chorus master, and in 1949, at the age of 24, became the company's producer, directing six operas, including *The Magic Flute* and *Don Giovanni*, in which he also sang. Naturalised in 1950, he won a Victorian government scholarship to study overseas, worked as assistant producer at the Royal Opera House, Covent Garden, London, and had his first reunion with his mother. In 1952 he was appointed production director for the National Theatre Opera Company in Melbourne. He directed the Australian première of Gian Carlo Menotti's *The Consul* with Marie Collier [q.v.13] and John Shaw in 1953, and *The Tales of Hoffmann* for a royal performance in 1954. Louis Kahan, an artist friend, designed the sets and costumes for many operas including *The Consul*. Haag married Sapientia Coco, a student born in Austria, on 4 April 1952 at Holy Cross Catholic Church, South Caulfield; they divorced in 1957. From 1954 to 1956 he was overseas.

After working as production manager for Garnet H. Carroll [q.v.13] on musicals including *West Side Story*, Haag was production director (1956-60) and artistic director (1960-62) with the Australian (from 1957 Elizabethan Theatre Trust) Opera Company. Between 1956 and 1975 he directed more than twenty operas for the trust's opera company (known as the Australian Opera from 1970) and was guest producer for the New Zealand Opera Company and for the Perth Festival. He directed *Salome* (1960) and *Tosca* (1968) for the Adelaide Festival of the Arts. A patient and practical opera director, he knew the repertoire, encouraged singers to develop their roles and frequently worked all night on the technical effects.

Haag was executive director (1962-68) and artistic adviser (1968-69) of the Australian Elizabethan Theatre Trust. He advocated subsidised theatre in Australia, negotiated tours by overseas companies and staged performances by Aboriginal tribal dancers in 1963 and the Asian pageant at Sydney Showground in 1964. Working with the entrepreneur Harry M. Miller and supported by Dr H. C. Coombs, chairman of the trust, Haag introduced subscription-booking procedures for the opera, ballet and State theatre companies, while continuing to direct productions such as *The Fantasticks* for the Union Theatre Repertory Company in Melbourne. His work, described by colleagues as 'inventive' and 'extraordinarily versatile', was often done on shoestring budgets and was dependent on his exceptional musical and technical skills.

In 1968 Haag was appointed OBE, and awarded a leadership grant by the State Department of the United States of America, where he examined developments in theatrical entertainment and encountered the musical *Hair*, which he encouraged Harry M. Miller to produce in Australia. Resigning next year from the trust, where management duties had increasingly encroached on his creative time, he was executive producer for *Hair* in 1969 and production co-ordinator for *Jesus Christ Superstar* in 1973, also directing a revival of the latter when it toured Australia in 1976. He produced the Australian entertainment at Expo 70 in Japan and spent two years in television, producing Barry Crocker's 'Sound of Music' and other programs, for which he received two Logie awards. Inspired by the Australian outback since his time at Alice Springs, Haag staged appearances by Aboriginal performers at the South Pacific Arts Festival (1972) in Fiji and at the World Black and African Festival of the Arts (1977) in Nigeria.

During the 1970s Haag ran his own company, the Scenery Centre Pty Ltd, and continued to design and direct musicals. While working in New York in 1976 he wrote *Beatlemania*. He was artistic director for Australia 75 (a festival of creative arts and sciences staged in Canberra) and the inaugural Indian Ocean Arts Festival, in Perth in 1979, and consultant to the 3rd South Pacific Festival of Arts, in Papua New Guinea in 1980. In 1983-84 he was director of opera at the Queensland Conservatorium of Music. He also lectured and tutored at the New South Wales State Conservatorium of Music and at the National Institute of Dramatic Art in Sydney, of which he was a foundation member.

Haag was active as a trustee, board member or adviser in many arts organisations including the Sydney Opera House Trust, the Canberra Theatre Trust, the Adelaide Festival, the Marionette Theatre of Australia, the Australian Ballet School, the Producers and Directors' Guild, the Aboriginal Theatre Foundation and the advisory committee on cultural grants of the New South Wales Ministry of Cultural Activities (Department of Culture, Sport and Recreation). Although imbued with a European sensibility and awareness of overseas traditions and practices, he was adamant that Australia should seek artistic expression that 'emanates from its own society' rather than 'pursue the artistic expression of societies far removed from it in time and distance'.

On 30 August 1958 at the registrar general's office, Sydney, Haag had married Helen Mitchell McAra, a secretary from New Zealand with whom he worked at the trust. For recreation, he enjoyed sailing his 24-foot (7.3 m) yacht on Sydney Harbour. Survived by his wife and their daughter and son, he died of cancer on 25 December 1986 at his Double Bay home and was cremated. His portrait (1988) by Kahan is held by the State Library of New South Wales.

H. M. Miller, *My Story* (1983); J. Sumner, *Recollections at Play* (1993); F. Van Straten, *National Treasure* (1994); *Masque*, Dec 1968, p 8; *Elizabethan Trust News*, Mar 1975, p 22; H. de Berg, interview with S. Haag (ts, 1965, NLA); private information.

MARGARET LEASK

HADGRAFT, CECIL HARRY HUDDLESTONE HAY (1904-1987), university lecturer and literary critic, was born on 8 June 1904 at Moonee Ponds, Melbourne, eldest of three children of English-born Henry Benjamin Hadgraft, storeman, and his wife Fanny Huddlestone, née Slater, from Rockhampton, Queensland. Brought up at Rockhampton, Cecil attended the local grammar school and at 16 won an open scholarship to the University of Queensland. Advised by his headmaster and mentor H. A. Kellow [q.v.9], he repeated his senior year before entering the science faculty in 1922. He was associate-editor (1922-23) and editor (1924) of the university magazine, *Galmahra*. After failing his final year he taught (1925-30) at Rockhampton Grammar School and studied English and philosophy as an external student at his university (BA, 1929). Back in Brisbane in 1931, he gained first-class honours in English with a thesis on aspects of the mock-heroic in English verse and drama to 1781.

In 1932-33 Hadgraft was an English teacher and housemaster at Wolaroi College, Orange, New South Wales. On 9 September 1933 at St Hilda's Church of England, Katoomba, he married Jessie Hartley, a teacher. Returning to Queensland, he became English master at Ipswich Grammar School in 1934. He continued his studies at the university (MA, 1937; Dip.Ed., 1942) and wrote a series of high school textbooks, including *Exercises in Sub-Junior English* (1942) and *An Approach to English Literature* (1945). Enlisting in the Royal Australian Air Force in September 1942, he served as an education officer at bases in Australia before being demobolised as a temporary flight lieutenant in 1946. That year the University of Melbourne awarded him a B.Ed. for a thesis based on his adult education work in the RAAF.

Hadgraft resumed teaching at Ipswich Grammar. By 1947 he was also publishing critical articles on Australian literature and reviewing books for the Australian Broadcasting Commission. In 1948 he lectured in the evenings in the department of English at the University of Queensland. Next year he travelled to England and started a Ph.D. in medieval phonology at the Victoria University of Manchester, but abandoned it after a year to return to Queensland as assistant-lecturer in English at the university. In 1951 he delivered the Commonwealth Literary Fund lectures in Queensland and next year was chief examiner for the State's public examinations in English. He was promoted to lecturer in 1955 and senior lecturer in 1958. In 1956-57 he travelled on a John Hay Whitney fellowship to the United States of America, where he gained expertise in American literature and literary theory at the University of Nebraska at Omaha and Louisiana State University, Baton Rouge.

Committed to the study of Australian literature, in the 1950s Hadgraft spent most university vacations in Sydney, reading in the Mitchell Library and preparing his books *Queensland and Its Writers* (1959) and *Australian Literature: A Critical Account to 1955* (1960). Douglas Stewart [q.v.] invited him to select Australian short stories for Angus & Robertson's [qq.v.7,11] Ltd's anthology *Coast to Coast* (1961). In 1962, the year he became reader, he introduced courses in Australian literature. He edited a series of nineteenth-century Australian texts: Henry Savery's [q.v.2] *Quintus Servinton* (1962) and *The Hermit in Van Diemen's Land* (1964), Frederick Sinnett's [q.v.6] *The Fiction Fields of Australia* (1966) and, with Raymond Beilby, *Uncle Piper of Piper's Hill* (1969) by Tasma (Jessie Couvreur [q.v.3]). In 1967 he won the Xavier Society's literary award for his biography,

James Brunton Stephens [q.v.6], published in 1969.

Hadgraft's criticism, which showed the influence of his early reading in eighteenth-century literature, was pre-eminently cautious and judicial. He described, weighed and balanced. Occasionally waspish—he once described a brother critic's work as 'flitting from hyperbole to cliché'—he enjoyed the cut and thrust of academic debate and playing devil's advocate. His favourite teaching format was a dialogue lecture with Val Vallis, in which he would challenge the latter's enthusiastic Romanticism with sceptical materialism.

A keen bibliophile, Hadgraft was on familiar terms with antiquarian booksellers in Brisbane and Sydney. For many years he devoted his Saturday mornings to scouting the second-hand bookshops in Brisbane. A strong supporter of his university's Fryer Memorial Library, in 1967 he helped it to secure Edward Leo Hayes's [q.v.14] wide-ranging collection. He formally retired in 1974 but continued to teach and research as an honorary reader. James Cook University of North Queensland, Townsville, acquired his personal library, and he then accumulated another small but valuable collection of books. In 1986 he published an anthology, *The Australian Short Story Before Lawson* [q.v.10]. Survived by his wife and their son and daughter, he died on 19 February 1987 in Brisbane and was cremated.

J. H. Allsopp, *A Centenary History of the Ipswich Grammar School 1863-1963* (1963); L. Cantrell (ed), *Bards, Bohemians, and Bookmen* (1976); T. A. Clinch, *The History of the Rockhampton Grammar School, Centenary 1881-1980* (1982); *Friends of the Fryer Library Newsletter*, May 1987, p 4; Hadgraft papers (Univ of Qld Lib); private information and personal knowledge.   CHRIS TIFFIN

HAILES, DOROTHY JEAN (1926-1988), medical practitioner, was born on 22 June 1926, at Ascot Vale, Melbourne, second of three daughters of Victorian-born parents William Allan Hailes [q.v.9], surgeon, and his wife Mary Maud, née Whitfield. Jean was educated at Melbourne Church of England Girls Grammar School, where she was head prefect in 1943, and then at the University of Melbourne (MB, BS, 1949). She completed her medical training as a resident medical officer (1950) at the Royal Melbourne Hospital. On 21 November 1951 at Christ Church, South Yarra, she married with Anglican rites Henry Buckhurst Kay, also a medical practitioner.

Hailes's interest in women's health was stimulated early in her career. As a medical officer at Travancore Developmental Centre, a Mental Hygiene Authority facility for intellectually disabled children, she realised the importance of a mother's good health for the well-being of her family. Later, in general practice, her sense of fairness was affronted by fellow doctors' neglect of the 'minor' symptoms brought to them by ageing women. These concerns were focused when, during a visit to the United States of America in the late 1960s, she met Robert Greenblatt, a physician and early advocate of the use of hormone therapy to address the health needs of menopausal women.

Returning to Melbourne, Hailes confronted the reluctance of Australian medical practitioners to promote this treatment, because of their concerns about side-effects. She gained the support of Professor Bryan Hudson, honorary director, and Dr Henry Burger, executive director, of the Medical Research Centre, Prince Henry's Hospital. As honorary clinical assistant (1971-80) she began seeing women with menopausal symptoms in the hospital's department of endocrinology and diabetes and established a weekly half-day clinic, staffed by sympathetic women doctors, and accepting patients without medical referral. An overwhelming response vindicated Hailes's enterprise. In 1976 a second clinic was established at the Royal Women's Hospital. Hailes, who was working there as a clinical assistant in the family planning clinic, became a menopause counsellor (1978-86).

Through well-balanced advocacy, Hailes won support in mainstream medicine for the development of clinical and research expertise relating to the health of older women. At Prince Henry's she developed a research program in hormone replacement therapy; the first of her several papers on this subject, 'Oestrogens and Menopausal and Post-menopausal Women', was written with Burger and published in the *Medical Journal of Australia* in 1977. In 1982 she was one of a group of doctors who established a national conference on menopause, the forerunner of the Australasian Menopause Society; she funded an annual prize for the best paper given at society meetings.

Direct in confronting 'myths', Hailes was also skilled in raising public awareness, and ready to speak on talkback radio and to community groups. Her popular booklet *The Middle Years* (1980) had run to three editions by 1986. She sought to extend the control that women already had of their fertility to their management of menopause, to encourage healthy, productive lives. Her emphasis on autonomy was shared with the feminist movement's concurrent campaign to establish women's health services; her work, however, was distinguished by its confidence in the treatment of menopause as a hormone deficiency condition.

With highly developed self-discipline, reflecting her experience in a professional environment dominated by masculine values,

Hailes maintained an extensive commitment to health care, including service as medical officer to the Australian Red Cross Society (Victorian division) blood transfusion service (1962-72) and to the student health services of Monash University (1972) and the University of Melbourne (1972-75). In 1986 she was appointed AM. She died of cancer on 27 November 1988 at South Yarra and was cremated. Her husband, their two daughters and their son survived her. The Jean Hailes Foundation for Women's Health, established in 1992, has ensured the continuation of her work in its clinical, research and educative dimensions.

Age (Melbourne), 30 Sept 1977, p 13, 3 Sept 1980, p 16; *MJA*, 16 Oct 1989, p 482; M. Guillemin, Unravelling the Account of Menopause as Hormone Deficiency: Working Practices of the Menopause Clinic (PhD thesis, Univ of Melbourne, 1996); private information.   CECILY HUNTER

HALBERSTATER, LESLIE (1901-1988), medical practitioner, was born on 9 August 1901 at Mount Morgan, Queensland, eldest of four children of Louis Halberstater, grazier, and his wife Mary, née Sheehan, both born at Rockhampton. After completing his schooling at Mount Morgan and at St Joseph's College, Nudgee, Brisbane, in 1919 Les won an open scholarship to the University of Queensland and next year enrolled in the faculty of science. In 1921 he transferred to the medical faculty at the University of Sydney (MB, Ch.M., 1925). He represented the university in Rugby League football and toured New Zealand with the team in 1924. Following a residency at Brisbane Hospital in 1927, he commenced general practice at Hermit Park, Townsville, in 1928, but was soon appointed medical superintendent of the city's general hospital. On 19 December 1929 at St Brigid's Catholic Church, Marrickville, Sydney, he married Mary Angela Walsh (d.1984).

'Halby' found his post challenging: a new maternity wing opened a few days after he started, and in the next seven years he oversaw sweeping changes that modernised and improved the hospital, particularly the radiology and surgery departments. In 1932 he became chairman of the first cancer clinic in the city. Resigning as medical superintendent in 1935, he bought a general practice and the Lister Private Hospital. He was government medical officer and visiting medical officer at the local prison in 1937-80. In World War II he was an honorary captain in the Australian Army Medical Corps and was attached to the 31st Battalion, Citizen Military Forces. He was also involved in organising Townsville's air raid precautions.

In 1945 the Sisters of Mercy took over 'the Lister' and it became Townsville's first Mater Misericordiae Hospital. Halberstater remained medical superintendent and from 1946, when the Mater was accredited as a training school for nurses, lectured to the students. In 1954 he became president of the New Mater Hospital Appeal Committee, which raised funds for a building in Fulham Road; the new hospital opened in 1962. Dr K. L. King, who followed him as chairman of the committee in 1970, considered that the success of the appeal was due mainly to Halberstater's 'initiative, drive and enthusiastic perseverance'. Halberstater served on the Mater's medical advisory board from 1960.

A knowledgeable racing devotee, Halberstater had been elected in 1934 to the committee of the Townsville Turf Club; he later served (1953-77) as president. A number of his gallopers were successful not only in North Queensland but also in Brisbane: among them were Tralee Rose, Philemon (which won the Brisbane Handicap in 1951), Roseglade, New Romance and True Rose. President of Past Brothers Rugby League Football Club (1940-49), he coached a team for two seasons. He was made a life member of Past Brothers, Townsville Rugby League Football and Townsville Turf clubs. In 1971 he was appointed OBE.

Failing eyesight forced Halberstater to retire in 1980. Throughout his life he was a devout Catholic, supporting the Society of St Vincent de Paul and the Church's educational initiatives. Foundation president and a life member of the local Christian Brothers Old Boys' Association, he had helped to establish (1969) St Paul's College in James Cook University of North Queensland. In 1983 he published an autobiography, *The Name of the Game*. On 28 August 1988 he died at Townsville and was buried in Belgian Gardens cemetery. He had no children. His portrait by Sister Mary Leonard hangs in the Mater Hospital.

J. Maguire, *Prologue: A History of the Catholic Church as Seen from Townsville 1863-1983* (1990); K. Jaumees (comp), *History of Townsville General Hospital 1866-2001* (2001); *Townsville Bulletin*, 2 Sept 1988, p 5; *MJA*, 2 Oct 1989, p 416.
                              DOROTHY M. GIBSON-WILDE

HALDANE, WILLIAM HAMILTON (1912-1983), commercial fisherman, was born on 28 November 1912 at Newport, Melbourne, eldest of five children of a Scottish-born shipwright Hugh Ross Haldane, and his wife Rebecca, née Hamilton, from Queensland. Hugh later became a lighthouse-keeper and harbour-master at Port Fairy. Completing his schooling at Footscray Technical School, Bill was apprenticed to a builder and cabinet-maker. He attended night classes at Footscray

Technical College and qualified as a boat builder. With help from his two brothers he built a 40-ft (12 m) fishing cutter, the *Amaryllis*. Launched in 1935, it was used next year by members of the University of Melbourne's (Sir Frederick) McCoy [q.v.5] Society to visit Lady Julia Percy Island, 23 miles (37 km) off Portland. In 1939 the Haldanes built another 40-ft boat, the *Dolphin*. On 12 September 1942 at St John's Church of England, Port Fairy, Bill married Christina Dorothy Elizabeth Porter. He joined the Royal Australian Naval Volunteer Reserve in March 1943.

In 1944 the brothers decided to construct a larger vessel so that they could fish in deeper waters. Acquiring plans from the United States of America, they selected for felling blue-gum trees in the Otway State Forest and processed the logs by hand in their backyard by the Moyne River. The South Australian government, keen to establish a viable fishing industry in South Australian waters, provided a loan to help finance construction. The Haldanes launched the *Tacoma*, an 84 ft (26 m) tuna clipper, on 5 November 1951 and arrived at Port Lincoln, South Australia, the following January. They had problems with their purse-seine-nets and in 1956 the government brought out the Jangaard brothers from California to demonstrate the pole and live-bait fishing method for catching tuna. The *Tacoma* was then refitted for poling. Once the Haldanes had demonstrated the profitability of tuna fishing in the Great Australian Bight, others entered the industry, using the same method.

Bill Haldane helped to persuade the government to erect navigation lights at the end of Eyre Peninsula and a government slipway at Port Lincoln. In 1967 tuna numbers showed signs of declining, possibly because of over-fishing, and the *Tacoma* was converted to accommodate prawn fishing. The Haldanes designed and patented a prawn-grading machine and sorting table, widely used throughout Australia. By 1977 they were catching, freezing and processing prawns on board the *Tacoma*, ready for export. In the 1970s Haldane chaired the Australian Bight Fishermens Society Ltd, which he had helped to establish in 1969.

Haldane was 5 ft 11 ins (180 cm) tall and of medium build, with dark hair. A keen yachtsman in his youth, in later years he owned and raced a Soling. In 1983 he received an Australian Fishing Industry Council award for service to the industry. Survived by his wife and three of their four sons, he died of cancer on 16 November 1983 at Port Lincoln and was buried with Uniting Church forms in North Shields cemetery.

E. Wallace-Carter, *For They Were Fishers* (1987); J. E. Plevin, *The Haldane Family & MFV Tacoma* (2000); *Port Fairy Gazette*, 26 Aug 1935, p 3; *Herald* (Melbourne), 11 Jan 1936, p 4, 7 Sept 1948, p 3; *Port Lincoln Times*, 18 Nov 1983, p 3; private information.
JOHN E. PLEVIN

HALL, ROBERT LOWE, BARON ROBERT-HALL OF SILVERSPUR, QUEENSLAND, AND TRENANCE, CORNWALL (1901-1988), economist, was born on 6 March 1901 at Tenterfield, New South Wales, third of five surviving children of Edgar Hall, an English-born metallurgist, and his Australian-born wife Rose Helen, née Cullen. Robert grew up at Silverspur, near Texas, Queensland, where his father was mine-manager, attending the local state school and enjoying the adventures of a bush boyhood. After the mine failed in 1912 the family experienced financial hardship. A scholarship enabled Robert to board at Ipswich Grammar School and in 1916 he was awarded the T. J. Byrnes [q.v.7] medal for the best pass in the State in the junior public examination. He was a prefect and head boy, a member of the magazine committee and a champion runner. At IGS he formed his closest and longest friendship, with Herbert ('Joe') Burton [q.v.], then known as 'Jersey'. His own nickname was 'Hoss'. In the senior public examination in 1918 he was ranked seventh in the State, earning an open scholarship that enabled him to study engineering at the University of Queensland (BE, 1923).

At university Hall won half-Blues in the mile and half-mile events, played Rugby Union football and took up rowing. Secretary of the University of Queensland Union in 1920-22, he helped to draw up a new constitution. He was also active in the dramatic and debating societies. A resident at St John's College, he worked on the college magazine and became friends with the mercurial P. R. 'Inky' Stephensen [q.v.12], who encouraged him to apply for a Rhodes scholarship. Successful in 1923, he gained a first in 'modern greats'— philosophy, politics and economics—at Magdalen College, Oxford (BA, 1926; MA, 1929).

Hall hoped ultimately to enter public life in Australia but instead made his career in Britain. A fellow (1927-50) of Trinity College, Oxford, he lectured in economics. He was college dean in 1927-38 and estates bursar (1938-39). On 7 December 1932 at the register office, Oxford, he married Laura Margaret Linfoot, an Oxford graduate and later a fellow at Somerville College. Applied economics and political economy became his specialty and, after 1930, J. M. (Lord) Keynes's work (notably *A Treatise on Money*) formed the core of his teaching. In 1935 he was a founder of the Oxford Economists' Research Group and in 1937 he published *The Economic System in a*

Socialist State. He was also a fellow of Nuffield College in 1939-47.

Although Hall classed himself as a socialist, he was not a political activist. In 1939-45 he was seconded to the raw materials department of the new Ministry of Supply, at Whitehall. His wife and their two daughters spent the early war years with his relations at Toowoomba, Queensland. In 1942-44 he was based in Washington; his wife joined him there but he was not to see his daughters again until 1945. From 1943 his work largely involved postwar economic planning.

Resuming teaching at Oxford in September 1945, Hall commuted to London to work part time as an adviser to the Board of Trade. In 1947-61 he was director of the economic section, first with the Cabinet Office and then with the Treasury, advising a succession of governments and eight chancellors of the exchequer. He was appointed CB in 1950 and KCMG in 1954. The University of Queensland conferred an honorary D.Sc. on him in 1960. He was president (1958-60) of the Royal Economic Society, chairman (1962-70) of the National Institute of Economic and Social Research, and president (1968-73) of the Society of Business Economists. In 1964-67 he was principal of Hertford College, Oxford.

Divorced in 1968, on 16 August that year at the register office, Westminster, he married Perilla Thyme Nowell-Smith, née Southwell, a divorcee. In 1969, on being made a life peer, he changed his name by deed poll to Robert Lowe Roberthall. He then divided his time between his wife's cottage at Trenance, Cornwall, where he developed an extensive garden, and a 'bedsit' in London. He spoke in most of the economics debates in the House of Lords. In 1981 he joined the new Social Democratic Party, and in 1986 made his last contribution to the Lords.

A good-looking and rather dapper man, Hall was widely admired, not only for his integrity and intelligent grasp of complex economic issues, but also for his good humour and modesty. As an outsider with a 'faint Australian accent' he was trusted and valued by those with the difficult task of rebuilding Britain after the war. Survived by his wife and daughters, Lord Roberthall died on 17 September 1988 at Trenance.

C. Munro, *Wild Man of Letters* (1984); A. Cairncross (ed), *The Robert Hall Diaries 1947-1953* (1989); K. Jones, *An Economist among Mandarins* (1994); *ODNB* (2004); *Times* (London), 19 Sept 1988, p 18.   CRAIG MUNRO

HALLIDAY, JOHN HOWELL (1899-1990), cardiologist, and SIR GEORGE CLIFTON (1901-1987), ear, nose and throat surgeon,

were born on 17 September 1899 and 22 April 1901 at Cooma, New South Wales, eighth and ninth of thirteen children of Edward James Halliday, staff surveyor, and his wife Isabel Wild, née Howell, both born in New South Wales. Despite early fears that John would not survive to adulthood, he attended King's College, Goulburn, and matriculated in 1916 with first-class honours in mathematics. He studied medicine at the University of Sydney (MB, Ch.M., 1923), residing at St Andrew's College. After graduation he was a resident medical officer at Royal Prince Alfred Hospital (1923-24), and at the Coast Hospital (1924-25). He married Muriel Margaret Burkitt on 9 June 1925 at Holy Trinity Church of England, Dubbo, and then practised medicine at Muswellbrook.

In 1931 John Halliday went to Britain, where he studied for two years at the London Hospital, the Hospital for Consumption and Diseases of the Chest, Brompton, and the National Hospital for the Relief and Cure of Diseases of the Nervous System, Queen Square. On his return to Australia he was appointed to Lewisham and Callan Park Mental hospitals and in 1934 became an honorary assistant physician at Royal Prince Alfred Hospital. His interest in electrocardiography began with his early association with Dr Sinclair Gillies and developed in London. In 1938 he became a foundation fellow of the Royal Australasian College of Physicians, of which he was later councillor (1958-64), vice-president (1964-66) and chairman of the finance committee (1966-71).

On 21 May 1940 Halliday was commissioned in the Australian Army Medical Corps, Australian Imperial Force, and next day was promoted to major. When he embarked for the Middle East in October to join the 2/5th Australian General Hospital, he took a portable electrocardiograph with him and, after his arrival, did cardiac assessment for the British and Australian armies. In 1942 he was repatriated and promoted to lieutenant colonel. He served in Australia until he transferred to the Reserve of Officers on 7 May 1944.

Continuing at Royal Prince Alfred Hospital, Halliday joined (Sir) J. Kempson Maddox [q.v.] and others in establishing (1949) the Hallstrom [q.v.14] Institute of Cardiology. He was a medical officer (from 1946) and chief medical officer (1952-64) at the Australian Mutual Provident Society. There he helped to revise the rating system for 'substandard lives', and played a key part in establishing the Life Insurance Medical Research Fund of Australia and New Zealand serving as its first medical director (1953-59). He was a founder (1952) and president (1962-64) of the Australasian Cardiac Society (Cardiac Society of Australia and New Zealand) and one of the committee (1958) that established the National Heart Foundation of Australia. In 1955 he was elected a fellow of the Royal College of Physicians, London. A fine teacher and excellent clinician, he maintained a busy private practice, encouraged the development of younger cardiologists and wrote many papers.

John Halliday was a member of the Union and Royal Sydney Golf clubs. In his younger days he had played good tennis; later he enjoyed golf, bowls and bridge, and was an expert fly fisher. He retired to Moss Vale in the late 1960s but found he was in demand there as a consultant until illness in the mid-1970s caused him to give up practice. With his wife, who had become blind, he later returned to Sydney. Survived by his daughter and two sons, one of whom, Peter, was a surgeon, he died on 27 December 1990 at Elizabeth Bay and was cremated.

George Halliday, also educated at King's College, Goulburn, took his final year at The King's School, Parramatta, where he was dux. Winner of the State under-16 lawn tennis singles championship, he was also in the Great Public Schools first XI (cricket) and a State country hockey representative. His application to the Royal Military College, Duntroon, was rejected on the grounds that his body was asymmetrical; the right side was hypertrophied because of his sporting activities. After teaching mathematics at The King's School for a term, he studied medicine at the University of Sydney (MB, Ch.M., 1925) residing at St Paul's College.

On 2 June 1927 at St James's Church of England, Sydney, Halliday married Hester Judith Macansh. A general practitioner at Tamworth for several years, he then went to Edinburgh (FRCS, 1934) to train in otolaryngology. He returned to Sydney and was appointed to the otolaryngology staff at Royal Prince Alfred Hospital, where he served until 1961; he also practised as senior surgeon (1936-47) in that specialty at St George Hospital.

Appointed as a captain in the AAMC, AIF, on 1 July 1940 and promoted to major in November, Halliday joined his brother in the Middle East. In April-May 1941, with the 2/6th AGH, he took part in the disastrous campaigns in Greece and Crete. Back in Australia in 1943, he served in North Queensland before transferring to the Reserve of Officers on 23 August 1943.

In 1946 George Halliday went to New York for further study. He combined his busy private practice with lecturing (1948-60) on diseases of the ear, nose and throat at the University of Sydney, and further study visits abroad. His service (councillor 1945-56; president 1950-51) on the State branch of the British Medical Association included the period in the late 1940s when it was resisting the Federal Labor government's attempts to nationalise the profession. In 1950 he was the prime mover in the formation of the Oto-Laryngological Society of Australia, of which he became president in 1962. An honorary member (1970) of the otology section of the Royal Society of Medicine, London, he was an invited speaker at international congresses. He introduced to Australia the fenestration operation to cure deafness caused by otosclerosis. Knighted in 1967, he was a fellow of the Australasian College of Surgeons and an honorary fellow (1985) of the University of Sydney.

Halliday was governor (1954-77) and honorary secretary (1975-77) of The King's School council. He remained a keen competition tennis player. A sociable man, he belonged to the Union, Elanora Country and Royal Sydney Golf clubs. Sir George died on 25 July 1987 at his home at Rose Bay and was cremated. His wife and their daughter and two sons, one of whom, George ('Mac'), was also an ear, nose and throat specialist, survived him.

J. B. and K. P. Hickie (eds), *Cardiology in Australia and New Zealand* (1990); J. C. Wiseman and R. J. Mulhearn (eds), *Roll of the Royal Australasian College of Physicians*, vol 2 (1994); *Archives of Otolaryngology*, vol 86, Aug 1967, p 127; B883, items NX34865 and NX70333 (NAA); private information.

ROBERT A. B. HOLLAND

HALLIWELL, KEITH (1916-1983), mechanical engineer and inventor, was born on 3 September 1916 at Sunbury, Melbourne, second of four children of Eric Halliwell, an English-born electrical engineer, and his Victorian-born wife Olive Muriel, née Baulch. Keith grew up at Maroubra, Sydney, attending Randwick Boys' Intermediate and Sydney Technical High schools. After taking a mechanical engineering trade course on refrigeration and electric motors, in 1933 he joined F. C. Lovelock Pty Ltd in the expanding refrigeration and air conditioning industry. He was a foundation member and honorary secretary of the Society of Refrigerating Engineers (New South Wales).

Having served (1935-38) in the Australian Tank Corps, Militia, Halliwell enlisted in the Royal Australian Air Force on 9 September 1940. He was employed as an instrument maker in No.24 Squadron (1941-42) and No.32 Squadron (1942) and as a refrigerator mechanic at RAAF Headquarters, Melbourne, and rose to acting warrant officer before being discharged on 28 November 1945. He had married Elizabeth Bird Reid McMechan, a paper finisher, on 3 May 1943 at Fullerton Memorial Presbyterian Church, Sydney. They moved to a new Hudson fibro-cement home on one of four blocks of land he had bought at Manly Vale.

In 1948 Halliwell designed a garage door that helped to change the face of Australian suburbia. In the postwar context of do-it-yourself heroes battling bureaucratic red tape, the story would be told that the Warringah council objected to conventional swing doors blocking the footpath, and in response Halliwell's ingenuity produced the innovative lift-up 'tilt-a-dor'. In reality he simply designed a space-saving door for a tricky block of land. His original wooden door, complete with a fashionable porthole window framed by an old bicycle wheel rim, opened inwards along curved tracks made from disposal aircraft parts, and was fully contained within the roof space. He later refined the design: springs replaced heavy concrete weights and the door swung up and outwards to provide more usable space inside. The original garage became a small factory, and the Tilt-a-dor joined the Hills [q.v. L. Hill] Hoist and Mervyn Richardson's [q.v.16] Victa lawnmower in tapping the growing consumer market based on postwar suburbanisation.

Bypassed for promotion in the Frigidaire division of General Motors-Holden's [q.v.9] Ltd in 1950, Halliwell was sufficiently confident to resign and set up his own business. He bought American patents for other tilt-door systems, built a factory in 1955, outgrew it and built another in 1962. His brother Ian introduced the 'magic button' garage opener in 1956. Ultimately employing over one hundred staff directly, Tilt-a-Dor Pty Ltd manufactured the fittings but Halliwell's innovation was to set up a network of independently owned sales and installation businesses, supported by extensive advertising.

A keen game fisherman and boat owner, Halliwell was also a foundation member of the Manly Civic Club and chairman of Seaforth Technical College. He died of myocardial infarction on 29 September 1983 at his Collaroy home and was cremated. His wife, their four daughters and two sons survived him. The business was sold in 1986 to B & D Doors (New South Wales), manufacturers of the 'Roll-A-Door', with whom he had maintained gentlemanly competition since 1956.

Manly Daily, 11 Mar 1978, p 11, 5 Oct 1983, p 5; *SMH*, 4 Oct 1983, p 11; A9301, item 33711 (NAA); Warringah Council records; private information.

RICHARD WHITE

HAMILTON, KEITH REGINALD (1928-1984), airline administrator, was born on 4 June 1928 in North Sydney, son of Australian-born parents Clarence Reginald Hamilton, police constable, and his wife Eileen Dorothy, née Kyle-Little. Educated at North Sydney Boys' High School, Keith joined Qantas Empire Airways Ltd in 1948 as a traffic officer. He soon began to make his mark through a series of overseas postings. Sent to Jakarta in 1952, he was promoted to chief traffic officer and then to assistant-manager for Indonesia. He was made manager in South Africa in 1957 and in Indonesia in 1958. There he kept Qantas flights landing despite strained relations between Australia and Indonesia. He was seconded to Malayan Airways Ltd in 1960 as deputy general manager and in 1963 appointed general manager of the renamed Malaysian Airlines Ltd, which became Malaysia-Singapore Airlines Ltd in 1967. In 1968 he was caught up in a dispute between Singapore and Malaysia, and he resigned from MSA.

Returning to Qantas Airways Ltd in 1969, Hamilton was appointed director of airline operations in 1971. When the governments of Malaysia and Singapore decided to establish separate national airlines, he led the Qantas team that assisted in establishing Malaysian Airline System, which became operational in 1972. He was made deputy general manager of Qantas in July 1973 and general manager in July 1976. In June 1980 he joined the board of directors and became the airline's chief executive. He was appointed CBE in 1981.

Hamilton saw significant changes at Qantas from the days of piston-engined airliners carrying relatively small passenger loads from Sydney to London in five days, to those of Boeing 747s capable of the same flight in less than a day carrying almost four hundred passengers. In the 1970s he played an important role in developing air transport for a mass market with cut-price fares, charter flights and package tours. As general manager and chief executive, he successfully steered Qantas through a difficult period during which most international airlines made substantial losses. He oversaw major initiatives that kept Qantas at the forefront of international air travel, including strategies to attract business passengers; new airliners; direct services between Australia and Beijing; promotion of the air-cargo market; and strenuous cost cutting to bring the airline to profitability in 1983.

Having risen to the top by 'sheer ability', Hamilton was regarded in the aviation industry as one of the world's most energetic and innovative airline executives. Nevertheless, he was not a flamboyant personality; he studiously avoided publicity and rarely gave interviews. He listed his recreation as gardening. On 7 March 1957 in Bern he had married Sonja Enenkel; they had no children. Survived by his wife, he died of coronary artery disease on 15 December 1984 in his home at Pymble, Sydney, and was cremated with Anglican rites.

J. Gunn, *High Corridors* (1988); *SMH*, 6 Apr 1976, p 7, 17 Dec 1984, p 2; *Austn Financial Review*, 4 June 1979, p 18; *Austn Aviation*, June 1982, p 64; *Age*

(Melbourne), 17 Dec 1984, p 10; *Australian*, 17 Dec 1984, p 2; *Qantas News*, Jan 1985, pp 1, 2.

LEIGH EDMONDS

HAMILTON, LESLIE BRUCE (1911-1989), public servant, was born on 4 July 1911 at Nook, Tasmania, second son of George Hamilton, farmer, and his wife Margaret Ann, née Peters, both Tasmanian born. Bruce attended Launceston Junior Technical School and the University of Tasmania. He joined the Commonwealth Public Service as a junior mechanic (in training) in the Postmaster-General's Department in 1928 but, when this post was cancelled in 1931 due to the Depression, he worked as a telegraph messenger. Hamilton successfully sat the examination for the third division of the public service in 1933, following which he became a clerk in the Postmaster-General's Department. He was appointed to the Department of Commerce in Victoria in 1934, and subsequently to the accounts branch of the Postmaster-General's Department in Tasmania and the finance branch in Melbourne. In 1937 he transferred to the Department of the Treasury in Hobart. At Swan Street Methodist Church, Hobart, on 19 December 1936 he had married Amy Mary Adams, a public servant; they were to have two daughters and a son.

On his promotion to the finance branch of the Treasury in 1940, Hamilton moved to Canberra, where he lived for the rest of his life. During World War II he served (1942-44) part time in the Volunteer Defence Corps. Rising through the ranks of the Treasury, he worked in the banking, trade and industry branch and the social services branch, becoming assistant-secretary (1957-59) and first assistant-secretary (1959-65). The culmination of his career was his term as director-general of the Department of Social Services (1966-73). Among his achievements were Commonwealth provision of subsidies to the States to enable them to help mothers who had to raise children alone and who were not eligible for the normal Commonwealth payments (1968), and the development of community-based home-care services for the aged or invalids (1969). Even when responsible for more than four thousand people in the department, Hamilton still tried to know many of the staff personally. Colleagues regarded him as an 'old-style public servant', intending this as a compliment. He was appointed OBE in 1966 and CBE in 1972.

A staunch Methodist, and from 1977 member of the Uniting Church, Hamilton filled many roles in his church communities, from steward to treasurer to bricklayer. Initiated in 1949 into Lodge Canberra, he was worshipful master in 1957-58. His dedication extended into civic activities: he was treasurer (1961-65) of the Goodwin Centre Development Association, secretary (1975-78) of the board of the Australian Capital Territory division of the National Heart Foundation of Australia, and member of the council (1973-79) and treasurer (1977-79) of Burgmann [q.v.13] College, Australian National University. A keen sportsman, he had been a good cricketer in his younger days and was an excellent croquet player in retirement.

Bruce Hamilton's wife died in 1975. On 11 September 1976 he married Isobel Elizabeth Dahl, a public servant, at the Methodist Church, Reid. Survived by his wife and the two daughters of his first marriage, he died on 12 June 1989 at Royal Canberra Hospital and was cremated. Clive Gesling's eulogy portrayed a humane, down-to-earth and much-loved man.

Dept of Social Services (Cwlth), *Annual Report*, 1966-72; *Canberra News*, 9 Jan 1973, p 8; *Mercury* (Hobart), 9 Jan 1973, p 6; *Canberra Times*, 12 July 1989, p 23; Canberra & District Hist Soc, *Newsletter*, Aug-Sept 1989, p 11; C. Gesling, A Tribute to Bruce Hamilton (ms, 1989, copy on ADB file); private information.
PAM CRICHTON

HAMMERMAN, BERNHARD (1913-1983), furrier and arts patron, was born on 6 April 1913 in Berlin, Germany, eldest son of Samuel Hammermann, furrier, and his wife Basia (Betty), née Bernfeld, both from the small Jewish settlement of Kalush, Austria (Poland, Ukraine). On leaving school Bernhard became an apprentice furrier. Interested in the arts and in film-making, he worked during the Depression for the German film company Universum-Film A.G., known as UFA, as a cameraman. His hopes of eventually producing his own film were cut short in 1933 with the Nazis' seizure of power and the subsequent discrimination against Jews. After he intervened to help an elderly Jewish milkman who was being tormented by a group of young Nazi thugs, he knew he should leave Germany.

On arriving in London in August 1933, Hammerman found employment with a British fur company, Revellion Feres, and learned English. In 1937 the Home Office refused to renew his residence permit unless he established a business that would employ British labour. The British Jewish Refugee Committee obtained a passage to New Zealand for him. When his ship docked at Sydney in April 1937 he decided to stay; he worked as a furrier for David Jones [q.v.2] Ltd. Naturalised in October 1938, he helped his parents and siblings to travel to Australia before World War II. In 1939 he set up his own fur business, Bernhard Hammerman Pty Ltd, which grew to have nine retail outlets around Australia, some of them franchises in David Jones. Forty-two people were employed in his Sydney workroom alone. Hammerman was president of the Fur Traders' Association of New South Wales. On 4 March 1941 he married Ida Moses, a stenographer, at the Great Synagogue, Sydney. She was the daughter of a Sydney dentist, Phillip Moses, and granddaughter of Rabbi Abraham Tobias Boas [q.v.7].

Hammerman was a man of culture and a patron of the arts. From the time of his arrival he frequented the world of Sydney artists, whose paintings he bought, and intellectuals, who gathered in cafés and restaurants in eastern Sydney and Kings Cross; he mixed with writers, including Frank Dalby Davison [q.v.13], Xavier Herbert and Dymphna Cusack [qq.v.], the poet Peter Hopegood, and the painters Elaine Haxton, James Cant and Sali Herman, and participated in amateur theatre at Circular Quay with Thea Rowe. He was keen to improve his English through acting but his German accent marked him for roles of a foreigner, such as that of a German scientist in Robert Sherwood's play *Idiot's Delight*. His accent was also helpful for his role in the Australian Broadcasting Commission radio program 'English for New Australians'. He played the character of Paul, a new arrival prone to language mistakes; his career ended when his pronunciation was not deemed to be sufficiently foreign.

In 1952 Hammerman was a co-founder of the All Nations Club, an organisation that at its peak had more than 1300 members, and whose aim was to build a bridge between 'old' and 'new' Australians. According to Hammerman, many 'New Australians' could find their way in business or religion in their adopted country but found it hard to make cultural contacts. The All Nations Club attempted to address this problem. By the 1970s it had outlived its purpose, as the integration of the post-World War II immigrants had largely been achieved. Hammerman was also very active in the production of the *Bridge*, a magazine for the Australian Jewish community.

In 1972 Hammerman was appointed an inaugural governor of the John Power [q.v.11] Foundation for Fine Arts because of his 'unique contribution' to Sydney's cultural life. He was awarded the OAM in 1982. Survived by his wife (d.1991) and their daughter and two sons, he died on 21 April 1983 at The Hague after attending the Frankfurt Fur Fair. He was buried in the Jewish section of Rookwood cemetery following a service at the Chevra Kadisha, Woollahra. Rotund, with twinkling eyes and a ready smile, he celebrated the human capacity for creativity and adaptation.

People (Sydney), 3 June 1953, p 42; *Wentworth Courier*, 27 Apr 1983, p 11; A12217, item L11536 (NAA); H. de Berg, interview with B. Hammerman (ts, 1981, NLA); private information.

JÜRGEN TAMPKE

HAMPSHIRE, KEITH MACDERMOTT (1914-1982), air force officer, was born on 10 September 1914 at Port Macquarie, New South Wales, second son of Percy George Hampshire, dairy inspector, and his wife Gladys May, née Macdermott, both born in New South Wales. After the family moved to Perth, Keith attended Scotch College, where he obtained his junior certificate. He called himself a grazier when he joined the Royal Australian Air Force as a cadet on 18 January 1937 and entered No.1 Flying Training School, Point Cook, Victoria. Six feet (183 cm) tall and strongly built, he had represented Western Australia in surfing. Graduating with the highest flying marks, he was commissioned in December and posted to No.2 Squadron. In June 1938 he was promoted to flying officer. He attended navigation courses and in 1939 completed a specialist signals course at Cranwell, England.

Before Hampshire left England World War II had broken out, and on his return to Australia he held appointments with No.12 Squadron, and as signals officer at RAAF Station, Darwin, and Northern Command Headquarters, Townsville, Queensland. Promoted to temporary squadron leader in January 1941, he commanded No.6 Squadron at Richmond, New South Wales, from September and No.23 Squadron at Archerfield, Amberley and Lowood, Queensland, from March 1942. Much of the flying was patrolling and escorting convoys, and it was not until December, when he took over No.22 Squadron in Port Moresby, that he served in a front-line unit. He had been made temporary wing commander in October. Aggressively competitive, he was soon in action in the squadron's twin-engined Bostons, supporting the Australian and American ground forces in their final battles in Papua. On 14 December, separated by bad weather from the rest of the formation, he sighted Japanese destroyers unloading troops and equipment and 'wrought havoc' by bombing and strafing.

In spite of often having just six or seven serviceable aircraft, Hampshire led No.22 Squadron in frequent attacks against the strongly defended Japanese airfields at Lae and Salamaua, New Guinea. A dawn strike on 2 March 1943 helped to prevent the Japanese from protecting their convoy in the battle of the Bismarck Sea. On 5 March shrapnel lodged in his leg when his aeroplane was hit as he approached Lae, but he bombed the target and led the formation back. After a brief spell in hospital, on 16 March he led seven

Bostons in a successful raid on Salamaua, one of the raids on which William Newton [q.v.15] distinguished himself. Through the following months Hampshire flew many sorties in support of the Australians advancing from Wau. Mountainous terrain, unpredictable weather and the need for precision in attack made flying difficult and dangerous. To ease the primitive living conditions of the crews, he organised better facilities and he promoted sport to lift morale, including open-air boxing tournaments between Australians and Americans that attracted crowds of thousands. He was awarded the Distinguished Service Order (1943) for his leadership and bravery.

Transferred to England in July 1943, Hampshire completed a fighter conversion course and in December took command of No.456 Squadron, RAAF, then stationed at Fairwood Common, Wales, and being equipped with new Mosquitoes carrying improved radar. A demanding leader who enforced the division between the officers and non-commissioned aircrew, he drove the squadron hard, and it was well prepared when shifted to Ford, Sussex, in March 1944. In the path of German intruders, the squadron, operating as night fighters, was soon in action.

Over the next months No.456 flew in support of the D-Day (6 June) invasion, attacked trains and other targets in Europe, diverted German defences from the main bomber stream and destroyed over twenty flying bombs. The squadron, which had shot down six enemy aircraft before Hampshire arrived, was credited with thirty-eight when he left. His own score was seven. The citation for his Distinguished Flying Cross (1944) noted that twice he was so close to an enemy aircraft that its disintegration damaged his Mosquito. He was promoted to temporary group captain in July and awarded a Bar to his DSO (1945) for his 'iron determination' and the success of his squadron.

His younger brother JOHN MACLEAN HAMPSHIRE (1916-1990) was born on 27 February 1916 at Port Macquarie. John followed Keith to Scotch College and then in January 1938 to Point Cook; he was commissioned in the RAAF in December. Posted to No.11 Squadron in September 1939, he piloted flying boats in the South-West Pacific Area. On 11 August 1941 at St John's Church of England, Glebe, Sydney, he married Margaret Irene Constance Taylor (d.1969), a nurse. He was awarded the Distinguished Flying Cross for evacuating some ninety RAAF personnel from the Netherlands East Indies in January-February 1942. After commanding No.33 and No.41 squadrons and having been promoted to temporary wing commander in December 1943, he was transferred to England. There he assumed command of No.461 Squadron, RAAF, flying Sunderlands, in February 1944.

Both commanding squadrons on the south coast of England, the brothers attracted publicity, especially when selected to take part in what was said to be England's first surf carnival. Mentioned in despatches, John returned to Australia in June 1945. After his RAAF appointment terminated in August, he worked as a pilot for Qantas Empire Airways Ltd. Survived by his three sons and daughter, he died on 21 March 1990 at Point Piper, Sydney, and was cremated.

Keith was posted to Transport Command in November 1944 and ceased combat flying. His RAAF appointment terminated in Australia on 29 April 1946. He worked in the Far East and Australia for the British Aviation Insurance Group, and tried oil prospecting, aircraft sales and importing. At Trinity College, Cambridge (BA, 1963; MA, 1970), he studied economics. His confidence, even arrogance, in decision-making, his courage, skill, competitiveness and acceptance of the loneliness of command that had served him well in the air war did not transfer easily into business. In the end, he may also have lacked mental stability. He never married. On or about 17 November 1982 he died from injuries sustained when he fell from a beach cliff at Palos Verdes, California, United States of America; he was cremated. The coroner recorded that his death was accidental. His portrait (1957), by (Sir) William Dargie, is held by the Australian War Memorial, Canberra.

G. Odgers, *Air War against Japan 1943-1945* (1957); D. Gillison, *Royal Australian Air Force 1939-1942* (1962); J. Herington, *Air Power over Europe 1944-1945* (1963); D. Vincent, *Mosquito Monograph* (1982); B. Rice, *22 Squadron R.A.A.F.* (1987); J. Bennett, *Fighter Nights* (1995); A. D. Garrisson, *Australian Fighter Aces 1914-1953* (1999); A9300, items Hampshire K M and Hampshire J M, A705, item 166/17/67, A9186, items 45, 48 and 142 (NAA); AWM65, items 2480 and 2481 (AWM); private information.   II. N. NELSON

HAMPTON, KENNETH VALENTINE (1935-1987), Aboriginal community leader and Anglican deacon, was born on 3 December 1935 in Darwin, one of eleven sons of Timothy Hampton, miner, and his wife Sarah, née Johnson, both Alawa people from the Roper River district. Removed from his family aged 3, Ken lived in Church of England children's homes at Mulgoa and Mount Wilson, New South Wales, and, with his parents' support, at St Francis House, Semaphore, Adelaide. There he was nurtured in Christianity and taught to be proud of his Indigenous heritage. After attending Le Fevre Boys' Technical High School he became an apprentice fitter and turner, qualifying in 1956. Rejected by the

Royal Australian Navy because of his Aboriginality, he worked for Commonwealth Railways at Port Augusta and for Broken Hill Proprietary Co. Ltd at Whyalla. On 12 November 1956 at the office of the principal registrar, Adelaide, he married Daphne Lorraine Sultan.

Previously a schoolboy athletics champion, in 1961 Hampton won Adelaide's Bay Sheffield sprint race. Developing a commitment to Indigenous issues, he joined the South Australian Department of Aboriginal Affairs, working at Port Augusta and Koonibba. He overcame a dependence on alcohol and a consequent propensity to act violently. In 1972 he was appointed a vocational officer with the Commonwealth Employment Service and was subsequently seconded back to the State DAA. A founding committee-member (1971) of the Aboriginal Publications Foundation, he helped to establish (1973) the Aboriginal Task Force at the South Australian Institute of Technology. In 1974-81 he was on the management committee of the Aboriginal Community College, Largs Bay. He was appointed (1976) the first Aboriginal justice of the peace in South Australia. Divorced in 1976, on 10 August 1979 at the office of the principal registrar, Adelaide, he married Margaret Lorraine Smits, née Nayda, an Aboriginal health worker and a divorcee.

In the 1980s Hampton became increasingly involved with the Anglican Church, which had resolved to offer greater support to Indigenous aspirations. Appointed archbishop's lay chaplain to Aboriginal people in December 1982, he worked with alcoholics and prisoners, and offered pastoral care to Indigenous country people undergoing medical treatment in Adelaide. In 1985 he was awarded the OAM. He was made deacon on 20 December 1986 in St Peter's Cathedral, Adelaide, despite having had no formal training. Archbishop Keith Rayner, acknowledging that this was not 'the normal course of action', declared that Hampton was 'the person whom God has raised up' for ministry among Aboriginal people. He was the first remarried divorced person with a former spouse still living to be ordained in the Anglican Church in South Australia. Hampton's vision of a centre where Aborigines could gather, in an environment that affirmed Indigenous spirituality and culture, was partly realised in the Nunga Anglican ministry, inaugurated on 30 August 1987.

On the 'Aboriginal' executive committee of the Jubilee 150, Hampton co-edited *Survival in Our Own Land* (1988), a history of Indigenous South Australians. When the State government sold the publishing company Wakefield Press, he and his co-editor Christobel Mattingley, believing Indigenous rights to the royalties to be jeopardised, fought to retain them for an Aboriginal trust fund.

Having struggled with illness for many years, Hampton had had a kidney transplant in 1974 and a coronary bypass in 1979. Survived by his wife, two sons and five daughters, Hampton died of coronary artery disease on 11 September 1987 at Woodville South, Adelaide, and was buried in Enfield cemetery. He was described as wise, gentle, caring, passionate and determined, and capable of transcending factions.

J. P. McD. Smith, *The Flower in the Desert* (1999); *Year Book: Anglican Church in Australia, Province of SA*, 1983-84, 1987-88; *Advertiser* (Adelaide), 18 June 1985, p 2, 19 Dec 1986, p 3, 12 Sept 1987, p 4, 17 Sept 1987, p 17; *Church Scene*, 24 Oct 1997, p 9.

JUDITH RAFTERY

HANCOCK, SIR WILLIAM KEITH (1898-1988), historian, was born on 26 June 1898 at Fitzroy, Melbourne, youngest of five children of Victorian-born parents William Hancock [q.v.9], clergyman, and his wife Elizabeth Katharine, née McCrae. When Keith was not yet 2 years old the family moved to Bairnsdale, on account of his mother's poor health. The town, and rural Australia, were to make an enduring impression on him, even though the family returned to Melbourne when he was 10. Entering Melbourne Church of England Grammar School on a scholarship, he was acutely conscious of his relative poverty compared with his classmates, but high intelligence and a quirky personality enabled him to make friends; holding the bronze medal of the Royal Humane Society of Australasia for having rescued a child from drowning in 1908 may also have helped.

In 1917 Hancock began studying classics at the University of Melbourne (BA Hons, 1920) but, impressed by the teaching of (Sir) Ernest Scott [q.v.11], switched to history. A keen student, he none the less took an active part in extracurricular activities. At Trinity College he was an eager debater; he also edited *Melbourne University Magazine*, and soon emerged as a leader in the university's Public Questions Society. His tact in his role as secretary of the society and his evident serious-mindedness helped allay the suspicions of the professoriate when speakers were brought in from the wider community. He graduated with first-class honours in history, and almost immediately took up a temporary lectureship at the University of Western Australia, Perth. There he provided the only assistance to E. O. G. Shann [q.v.11], who helped to develop his interest in economic history. Gaining immensely in academic and personal confidence, he would look back on his eighteen months in Perth as a golden period.

Having won (1920) a Rhodes scholarship, in 1922 Hancock sailed to England and entered

Balliol College, Oxford (BA, 1923; MA, 1930), where he was influenced by the master, A. L. Smith, and more particularly by two other historians, the austere Humphrey Sumner and the affable Kenneth Bell. At Oxford, Hancock kept his nose to the grindstone, for initially he was intent on returning to Australia as soon as possible. Gaining a first in modern history, he was persuaded to sit for examinations at All Souls College, and secured a coveted prize fellowship (1923). To Hancock, already institutionalised by Trinity and Balliol, All Souls gradually became an English home, one to which he would return periodically for the rest of his life.

A keen traveller in university vacations, Hancock went to Tuscany on a walking tour in 1923. Entranced by the landscape, and in particular by the way it had come to absorb a human imprint over many centuries, he chose Italian history for the subject of his first book. *Ricasoli and the Risorgimento in Tuscany* (1926) resulted from pondering the authoritarian antecedents to Mussolini. The book was held in high regard when it appeared, but a proposal to translate it into Italian to give it wider currency was stillborn.

On 6 March 1925 Hancock married with Anglican rites Theaden Nancie Brocklebank (d.1960) at the Eccleston Square Congregational Church, London. Although his desire to return to Australia had weakened, in 1924 he had accepted the chair of modern history at the University of Adelaide. When he arrived in 1926, he was widely hailed as the youngest professor in the British Commonwealth. Having held no previous teaching post, he was a little overwhelmed at first. But soon he was reconfiguring the history course, making it more Imperial and European, and more concerned with international affairs. Australian students, he believed, needed to be exposed to the big books and the general sweep of history, since Australia's 'past was no more than the world's present'.

Nevertheless, Hancock became more engrossed with the country, contributing a series of articles for the *New Statesman* and then writing *Australia* (1930). In this book he attacked the three pillars of the Australian settlement—protection, state socialism and the White Australia policy—which he saw as together working for stagnation. Protection should be abolished, he argued; it featherbedded Australian industry and work practices, and had led to the situation where the government drew half of its revenue from customs duties. The Australian tendency had been to regard government as a huge commissariat, and state socialism needed to be rolled back, with business made more competitive. Ultimately the existing situation rested on White Australia, which in turn rested on British power; the time might come when

immigration policy—however well it served at the moment—might have to be changed too. Although *Australia* was cautiously optimistic about the nation's prospects, it bristled with aphorisms about the country's shortcomings. This quality helped the book to become one of the most influential accounts of Australia written in the twentieth century.

Hancock was aware of his position as both an outsider and insider; as he saw it, this condition provided the necessary balance between analysis and affection. But once *Australia* was completed, he concluded that he was marking time in Adelaide. In 1934 he returned to England to take up the chair of modern history at the University of Birmingham. He hoped that this would enable him to resume work in European history—either on the big book he was planning on the origins of the nation state, or perhaps in Italian history. Almost immediately, however, he was approached by Arnold Toynbee on behalf of the Royal Institute of International Affairs, and asked to write a study of the British Commonwealth. Hancock's earlier links with the Round Table now bore fruit; to be a Commonwealth expert in Britain might be an acceptable resolution of the tensions he felt between country and calling.

Insisting on authorial independence, Hancock threw himself into the task, travelling extensively throughout the Empire and Commonwealth, and focusing particularly on flashpoints such as South Africa, Ireland and Palestine. The two volumes of his *Survey of British Commonwealth Affairs* appeared in 1937-42, the second so large that it was published in two parts. The view that Hancock remains the greatest of the historians of the Commonwealth rests substantially on the *Survey*. His illumination of contemporary problems arose from an Olympian treatment of historical forces—sometimes, as in the case of Palestine, with an implicit sense of tragedy.

When World War II broke out in 1939 Hancock was still at Birmingham, and was soon active in the Home Guard. In 1941 he became supervisor of a unit of professional historians attached to the Cabinet Office, charged with producing twenty-seven of the twenty-eight volumes of the civil series of the official history of Britain in World War II. At its greatest extent, in 1946, the historical section employed twenty-five people supplemented by a dozen part-timers. Hancock largely determined the scope of individual volumes, which he shaped according to subject or theme rather than departmentally, closely editing and even rewriting some of them. Although the volumes on wartime production were delegated to (Sir) Michael Postan, Hancock's workload was extremely heavy. It was not helped by his insistence on fire-watching at St Paul's Cathedral once a week, or by the new duties he took on when appointed Chichele professor of economic history at Oxford in 1944. His own projected central volume, which metamorphosed into *British War Economy* (1949), involved and developed the skills of his assistant, Margaret Gowing, to such an extent that he felt honour-bound to acknowledge her as co-author. Characteristically, he had insisted on authorial independence, but the manuscripts were circulated widely for official comment and could be the subject of intense negotiation. The one by Richard Titmuss on social policy was seen by sixty civil servants in eight different departments yet, despite this scrutiny, on reaching the printers it had been recalled: Hancock prepared himself to resign over this interference.

During the war Hancock had looked forward to the possibility of an appointment in Australia, but his strong wish to return did not preclude his contesting, unsuccessfully, the wardenship of All Souls in the election of 1945. Next year he became one of the four academic advisers charged with helping to shape the new, entirely postgraduate Australian National University in Canberra. It was envisaged that the four would become directors of research schools, and it was assumed that Hancock would head a school of social sciences, but he backed away from such a concept, describing himself as 'more of a social artist than a social scientist'. Influential figures in Canberra pressed for a school that would engage pragmatically with the nation and the region, by departments or teams; Hancock spoke of 'chaps', and had in mind independent research. With the resignation of (Sir) Raymond Firth, the intended director of a school of Pacific studies, Hancock proposed temporarily to extend his intended fiefdom. Because his existing commitment to the new institution was felt to be incomplete, and there were doubts about his highly personalised mode of recruiting, this suggestion caused alarm. In 1949 he was told that he would not be appointed.

Hancock was shaken by this turn of events, but the recent upsurge of academic interest in colonial development, which he had helped to foster, now came to his rescue. Later in 1949 he was appointed director of the Institute of Commonwealth Studies, a new research institute within the University of London. He spent much energy supervising the refurbishment of an eighteenth-century house on Russell Square, to which various Commonwealth governments and universities contributed furnishings and publications. The institute conducted high-powered seminars attended by academics, postgraduate students, and personnel from the Colonial Office; not only papers but also summaries of the subsequent discussion were circulated. Hancock was knighted in 1953.

Next year the governor of Uganda, Sir Andrew Cohen, asked Hancock to conduct a mission to Buganda, the core kingdom of the protectorate. The governor had deposed the *kabaka*, or ruler, in 1953 and had immediately exiled him to England. The situation was now one of sullen stalemate. Arriving in Uganda, Hancock insisted on the independence of his investigation, and then sat down with a committee from the *lukiiko*, or parliament, to discuss various constitutional changes. The most important of these amendments involved turning the *kabaka* into a constitutional monarch, and persuading the people of Buganda to participate—as they had previously declined to do—in the Legislative Council for the whole of Uganda. Negotiations then proceeded with the governor, who wisely, and unprecedentedly, abdicated the chairmanship of the conference at Namirembe to Hancock. A favourable outcome was achieved, but Hancock's recommendations were first modified and then eclipsed by Uganda's rapid progress towards independence.

Africa remained a major preoccupation for Hancock. In 1951, after a reconnaissance visit to South Africa, he had accepted a commission from Cambridge University Press to write a biography of the statesman Jan Christiaan Smuts. The war histories dragged on for sixteen years, and this project would engage him for just as long. He had a number of affinities with his subject: Smuts's originality as a botanist now sharpened Hancock's interest in the environment, while his importance as an international figure enabled Hancock to revisit issues of war and peace and the maintenance of a world order that had concerned him since he was an undergraduate.

Moreover, just as Hancock's Australianness was proclaimed in Uganda as a guarantee of his independence, so too in South Africa it provided a neutral position: despite his knighthood, he was neither British nor English South African, but came from another Southern-hemisphere country whose Europeans, like the Afrikaners, identified themselves with the land. He was therefore able to enter Afrikaner ruling circles with relative ease. Hancock spent extended periods in South Africa in 1955 and 1966. He produced a massive two-volume biography, *Smuts* (1962-68), as well as four volumes of *Selections from the Smuts Papers* (1966), co-edited with his research assistant and collaborator Jean van der Poel. At the time *Smuts* was ground-breaking in its attention to many areas of South African history, but it is less highly regarded today. Hancock's opposition to fascism may have led him to cast the Nationalists in a similar role, for he more easily sympathised with the liberalism of South African Whites than with the liberation struggle of the Blacks.

Despite his earlier rebuff, Hancock had maintained connections with the ANU. Eventually he was invited to take up the positions of director of the Research School of Social Sciences (1957-61) and professor of history (1957-65). Although preoccupied with *Smuts*, he nevertheless saw his role as a national one, and was active in founding the *Australian Dictionary of Biography* (chairman 1959-65) and the Australian Academy of the Humanities (president 1969-71). Concerned to broaden historical studies, he made appointments in European medieval history and in Indian history, and also convened the Wool Seminar (1957-59), which is still admired for its interdisciplinarity.

When Hancock retired in 1965, it was only his administrative role that fell away. He continued to attend seminars—a diminutive figure with his sweep of white hair, and his pipe in hand—delivering an occasional incisive comment almost hesitantly. Once the second volume of *Smuts* was completed, he handed over the remaining half of the associated document project to van der Poel, and settled down to write *Discovering Monaro* (1972). Quite deliberately Hancock was opting for the 'parish pump', a consummation of his involvement with the Canberra region as resident and bushwalker. The book also marked a return to the environmental issues foreshadowed in *Australia*, and these were to dominate the last years of his life. He actively supported the Botany Bay Project, a study of environmental impact in the Sydney region, and in 1973-75 was a tireless publicist for an unsuccessful campaign to prevent the Postmaster-General's Department from building a telecommunications tower on Black Mountain, Canberra. His radicalism went further. In 1972 he joined fifteen other notables in signing a letter to the newspapers pointing out the absolute necessity of a change of government for the health of democracy in Australia. Later, alarmed by the continuing arms race, he advocated a non-nuclear Australia and, towards the end of his life, spoke of the desirability of neutrality.

Unusually, Hancock wrote both an autobiography, *Country and Calling* (1954), and a set of autobiographical essays, *Professing History* (1976). A good deal of the latter was taken up with his views on his craft, which—apart from his well-known watchwords of attachment, justice and span—were rather less original than he imagined. Distrusting theory, he put his faith in reason; Christianity remained a primal influence, and he gradually returned to it. Although dutiful and drawn to the (British) Establishment, he none the less insisted on his independence and remained a democrat by instinct. His writings, impressive in range, quality and volume, make him a serious contender for the title of Australia's greatest historian. Certainly he was the most distinguished. Nine universities awarded him honorary doctorates. At the instigation of the Australian government, he was appointed

KBE (1965). He was also appointed to the Order of Merit of the Republic of Italy (1961).

On 22 May 1961 at the Church of St John the Baptist, Reid, Canberra, Sir Keith married Marjorie Eyre, who had worked with him as secretary and research assistant since World War II. She survived him when he died on 13 August 1988 in Canberra; there were no children of either marriage. He was buried in Woden cemetery. A library at the ANU was named after him. Portraits by June Mendoza (1971) and Frances Philip (1972) are held by the ANU; a bust (1952) by Alan Jarvis is at the Institute of Commonwealth Studies, London.

W. G. Osmond, *Frederic Eggleston* (1985); S. G. Foster and M. M. Varghese, *The Making of the Australian National University 1946-1996* (1996); D. A. Low (ed), *Keith Hancock* (2001); *ODNB*, vol 25 (2004), p 18; Hancock papers (NLA and Noel Butlin Archives Centre, ANU, Canberra); information collected in preparation for a biography.

JIM DAVIDSON

HANRAHAN, ETHEL FRANCES (1909-1981), army and repatriation hospital matron, was born on 6 May 1909 at Longreach, Queensland, eldest child of John Joseph Hanrahan, police constable, and his wife Ethel Frances, née Baker, both Queensland born. Young Ethel trained in nursing at Brisbane General Hospital in 1930-34 and worked at Rosemount Repatriation Hospital from 1935. On 15 December 1939 she joined the Australian Army Nursing Service, Australian Imperial Force, as a sister. She was 5 ft 6 ins (168 cm) tall, with an olive complexion, grey eyes and black hair. Posted to the 2/3rd Field Ambulance, she arrived in Britain in June 1940 and was sent to the 2/3rd Australian General Hospital at Godalming, Surrey, in August. Five months later she proceeded to the Middle East for duty with the 2/2nd AGH at Kantara, Egypt. For her service there she was twice mentioned in despatches.

Returning to Australia in March 1942, Hanrahan was appointed matron of, successively, the 117th AGH at Toowoomba, Queensland (June), the 2nd Australian Women's Hospital at Redbank (December 1943), and the 116th AGH at Charters Towers and Cairns (April 1944). From January 1945 she was matron of the 107th AGH in Darwin and principal matron, headquarters, Northern Territory Force. Appointed major in March 1943, she was promoted to temporary lieutenant colonel in May 1945 (substantive in September). Most of her patients were Australian veterans of the New Guinea campaigns. At the end of the war she received and cared for recently liberated Australian prisoners of war of the Japanese. Matron of the 112th Military

Hospital, Greenslopes, Brisbane, from October 1945, she also held the position of principal matron, headquarters, Northern Command, from June 1946. She transferred to the Reserve of Officers on 23 January 1947.

In February 1947 Hanrahan was appointed the first matron at the Repatriation General Hospital, Heidelberg, Melbourne. For the next twenty-two years Matron 'Billie' Hanrahan helped to nurse many ex-servicemen and women and care for their families. Her own war experience gave her a deep and personal insight into the sacrifices that Australian servicemen and women had made during the war, and she knew that their suffering did not necessarily end with the cessation of hostilities.

Hanrahan's philosophy of nursing was simple: 'A nurse has to give a lot to her patients. And a kind nurse is a good nurse—she doesn't become hardened by her experiences'. Committed to keeping alive the memory of AANS nurses who had died during the war, she was often seen walking in the hospital's memorial rose garden, which was dedicated to them. On special occasions she picked the roses and gave them to staff members to remind them that they were 'part of a venerable profession'. When she retired in May 1969, she stressed the continuing need 'for nurses at the Repat to care for the "boys"'. In 1963 she had been appointed OBE. She died on 17 August 1981 at Southport, Queensland, and was buried with Catholic rites in its lawn cemetery. One of many published tributes to her observed: 'She was loved and respected by patients and staff alike'.

R. Goodman, *Queensland Nurses* (1985) and *Our War Nurses* (1988); G. Hunter-Payne, *Proper Care* (1994); *Age* (Melbourne), 5 May 1969, p 18; *UNA*, Aug 1969, p 2; B883, item QX6107 (NAA).

ROSALIND HEARDER

HARDMAN, SIR JAMES DONALD INNES (1899-1982), air force officer, was born on 21 February 1899 at Oldham, Lancashire, England, son of James Hardman, master cotton-spinner, and his wife Wilhelmina Innes, née Gibson. Educated at Malvern College, he enlisted in the Artists' Rifles in 1916 and next year joined the Royal Flying Corps. He was commissioned on 10 May 1917 and after pilot training was posted to No.19 Squadron in February 1918. Flying the unpopular Sopwith Dolphin, he destroyed his first German aircraft in May and was made a flight commander as an acting captain in September. He finished the war with seven confirmed victories and a Distinguished Flying Cross (1919), and was transferred to the Unemployed List in March 1919.

In 1920 Hardman entered Hertford College, Oxford, to study economics, but on 18 October 1921 he rejoined the Royal Air Force on a short-service commission which was later converted to a permanent appointment. After serving in India, Britain and the Middle East, he attended the RAF Staff College, Andover, in 1935 and the British Army Staff College, Camberley, in 1938. He was promoted to squadron leader in February 1936 and wing commander in January 1939.

On the outbreak of World War II Hardman went to France with the air component of the British Expeditionary Force. Serving as head of the Directorate of Military Co-operation—Directorate of Operations (Tactical) from November 1940—he was promoted to temporary group captain in March 1941 and acting air commodore in September. He ended the war as air officer commanding No.232 (Transport) Group at Comilla, India, and was made acting air vice-marshal in October 1945. Appointed OBE (1940) and CB (1945), he was mentioned in despatches (1941) and awarded the United States of America's Bronze Star Medal (1946).

Hardman was air officer in charge of administration, Air Command, South-East Asia (later Far East), in 1946-47; assistant chief of the Air Staff (operations) in 1947-48; and commandant, RAF Staff College, Bracknell, in 1949-51. From 1951 he was air officer commanding-in-chief, Home Command. He was made acting air marshal in October (substantive July 1952). In 1950 (Sir) Robert Menzies [q.v.15] had asked the British chief of the Air Staff, Sir John Slessor, for the services of an RAF officer to replace (Sir) George Jones as chief of the Air Staff, Royal Australian Air Force. Hardman was appointed to the post on 14 January 1952. An accomplished and experienced officer, he had a tactful, urbane and easy yet forceful personality. These attributes were necessary as the air force he arrived to command was a divided service, a legacy of the personal and professional antagonism that had been endemic in its senior ranks since its inception.

Hardman's main task was to improve RAAF morale. To this end he carried out a thorough reorganisation of the Air Board. In the process he forged an excellent working partnership with the newly appointed secretary of the Department of Air, (Sir) Edwin Hicks [q.v.]. The relationship with the civilian element in the department, which had been damaged during the long tenure of M. C. Langslow [q.v.15], was consequently greatly improved. Hardman also oversaw and implemented a major shift in RAAF organisation, with a move from area to functional commands. This rearrangement was designed to decentralise control away from the Air Board and to increase wartime efficiency. Hardman argued that the spread of the Cold War imposed a need for operational flexibility, as the air force could be operating anywhere in the world and possibly under foreign control. The area organisation was replaced by three commands: Home, Training and Maintenance. Within each command, units might be formed or disbanded, aircraft allotted to sub-formations and major items of equipment bought, all without reference to the Air Board, which now was expected to issue only broad directives.

An energetic and persuasive proponent of the role of air power, Hardman set out to make the air force the first line of defence. His argument was as follows: aircraft should take over the protection of sea lanes; the maritime Neptune squadrons could carry out any task the navy could, and do it better; and the army was engaged in training a force that would be of little use in the Cold War. If the air force, he contended, were equipped with the then emerging V-bomber (the Victor, Valiant or Vulcan), it could be employed in a most offensive capacity, a source of striking power that could be used by the Commonwealth as a whole if deterrence failed.

An RAAF operating a nuclear-equipped V-bomber strike force would coincide neatly with current British defence policy thinking and also fit well with the American doctrine of 'massive retaliation'. In 1954 the Menzies government followed British and American policies in stipulating that air power would become the first line of Australian defence. Yet Hardman's suggested strike force of V-bombers never came to fruition. His term as CAS ended on 17 January 1954 and when he returned to Britain Menzies remarked that he would be remembered for his influence on the development of the postwar air force and 'particularly for the complete reorganization of the structure of the RAAF itself'. Within two years Hardman had contributed greatly to replacing the previous ill feeling within the service with a new sense of purpose.

Back in Britain, Hardman became air member for supply and organisation in May 1954. He was promoted to air chief marshal on 1 April 1955. Having been elevated to KCB in June 1952, he was raised to GBE in January 1958. On 29 January that year he retired from the RAF. He had married Dorothy Ursula Ashcroft Thompson on 8 July 1930 at the parish church of St George, Hanover Square, London. Survived by his wife, and their daughter and two sons, Sir Donald died on 2 March 1982 at Estoril, Portugal.

J. McCarthy, *Defence in Transition* (1991); A. Stephens (ed), *Australia's Air Chiefs* (1992); A. Stephens, *Going Solo* (1995) and *The Royal Australian Air Force* (2001); P. Dennis et al, *The Oxford Companion to Australian Military History* (1995); A. Stephens and J. Isaacs, *High Fliers* (1996); *Aircraft*, Dec 1951, p 34; *Times* (London), 9 Mar 1982, p 14, 15 Mar 1982, p 10.

JOHN MCCARTHY

HARDY, MARY VERONICA (1931-1985), entertainer, was born on 14 October 1931 at Warrnambool, Victoria, youngest of eight children of locally born parents Thomas John Hardy, farm inspector, and his wife Winifred Mary, née Bourke. Mary's childhood was spent at Bacchus Marsh, where she was educated at a convent. She made her first stage appearance at the Mechanics Hall. Following her father's death (1943), she moved with her mother to Gardenvale, Melbourne, and cared for her until, at 14, she was orphaned. She sought auditions while taking a range of work, and gained roles with the National Theatre and the Council of Adult Education's touring company. She played Peter Pan in a J. C. Williamson [q.v.6] Ltd pantomime at the Princess Theatre in 1957-58, once outraging parents in the audience with a burst of profanity after the 'flying' mechanism jammed, leaving her in mid-air.

In the late 1950s Hardy won critical acclaim as a 'straight' actress with the Union Theatre Repertory Company: her roles included the cabin boy in *Moby Dick—Rehearsed* (1959) and the rebellious Beatie in Arnold Wesker's *Roots* (1960). Yet, despite her striking talent, as Joy Westmore noted, Hardy really 'wanted to be a personality'. She starred in revues in Sydney and Melbourne and later returned to the stage as Agnes Gooch in *Mame* (1968), winning the Dolia Ribush [q.v.11] award for best supporting actress (1969).

Hardy's fast-talking, uninhibited approach, her gifts for ad-libbing and rapport with ordinary people, made her a greatly loved figure on long-running radio programs with Noel Ferrier on 3UZ (1965-68) and, from 1972, on 3AW's 'Mary Hardy Show', a daily talkback program. On television she proved more than equal to such skilled improvisers as Graham Kennedy, and became co-host of 'The Penthouse Club' (Channel 7) in 1970. Five times between 1966 and 1979 she was voted Victoria's most popular female entertainer in the *TV Week* Logie awards. In 1978, however, she 'stormed out' of both programs, amid clashes with management and colleagues. While soon returning to 3AW, she did not again secure sustained work.

Success took its toll. Her friend Bob Hornery described her as a 'true eccentric' who was, in later years, very fragile. An insomniac, she also suffered from depression. Elfin and flamboyant, she mourned her lack of beauty. She had married Ian Gordon Pearce, a musician, on 5 April 1962 at St Mary's Catholic Church, East St Kilda. The failure of their marriage (leading to divorce on 19 September 1975), her longing for children and her lapsed Catholicism contributed to her unhappiness. Her casting in *Shut Your Eyes and Think of England* (1980) gave hope of a 'comeback' but she was dismissed, allegedly because she was too outrageous for the mousy role of Joyce Pullen.

Hardy was never far from public attention: in April 1983 charges against her were dropped following her arrest for heckling the former prime minister, Malcolm Fraser; in June the press reported another 'nervous breakdown'. Between 4 and 7 January 1985 she shot herself in her Middle Park apartment; she was buried in New Cheltemham cemetery. Her last days were interpreted in a short film, *The Mary Hardy Show* (1987), directed by Barbara Karpinski; *Mary Lives!*, a biographical play by her brother Frank Hardy was first performed in 1992.

J. Sumner, *Recollections at Play* (1993); J. Hocking, *Frank Hardy* (2005); *Herald* (Melbourne), 9 July 1976, p 19; *Sun News-Pictorial* (Melbourne), 27 May 1977, p 37, 11 Feb 1978, p 25; *National Times*, 12 Apr 1985, p 16; *Age* (Melbourne), 14 Oct 1987, p 22; *Australian*, 23 May 1992, 'Mag', p 8; private information.   BRIAN MCFARLANE

HARDY, WILLIAM DICK (1914-1985), agronomist, public servant and grazier, was born on 20 July 1914 at Port Macquarie, New South Wales, eldest child of John Henry Hardy, machinist, and his wife Bella, née Dick, both born in New South Wales. Dick was educated at Ryde Public School, Carlingford District Rural School, and Hawkesbury Agricultural College, where he was dux in 1933 and an excellent sportsman. He then worked on a mixed farm at Crookwell and as assistant orchardist at Bathurst Experiment Farm. In 1935-38, on a scholarship from the Royal Agricultural Society of New South Wales, he studied agriculture at the University of Sydney (B.Sc.Agr., 1939). He was a member of the South Curl Curl Surf Life Saving Club in his undergraduate days.

In 1939-47 Hardy worked as a district agronomist with the New South Wales Department of Agriculture, based first at Goulburn and then at Moss Vale. During this time he advised the writer Gwen Meredith on technical matters for her radio serials 'The Lawsons' and 'Blue Hills', both of which had a rural background. During World War II he tried to enlist in the Royal Australian Air Force but was refused leave to do so, as his work, especially in advising and encouraging vegetable growers, was thought by the authorities to be more important to the war effort. On 15 June 1940 at St Giles's Church of England, Greenwich, Sydney, he married Dorothy Beatrice Barbour, a stenographer.

Hardy joined the Commonwealth Department of Commerce and Agriculture in 1948. He was principal investigation officer of the Bureau of Agricultural Economics (1949-50)

in Canberra, then supervisor of fresh fruit and vegetable exports (1950-53) and assistant-director of the division of agricultural production (1953-54) in Melbourne. In 1954-57 he was the Australian government trade commissioner in San Francisco, United States of America, charged with increasing Australian exports to western USA and obtaining information on production techniques that might be applicable to Australian conditions. He so excelled in this office that he was offered further overseas trade postings, but for the sake of his children's education he declined them.

Back in Australia, Hardy occupied senior positions in the Department of Primary Industry, where he was deputy assistant secretary (1958-64), secretary of the Australian Agricultural Council (1964-73) and principal executive officer (livestock) (1974-75). He was secretary-general of the XIIth World's Poultry Congress in 1962 and a councillor of the World's Poultry Science Association from 1962 to 1968. In 1959-64 he was a member of the Australian National Film Board.

At 48 Mugga Way, Red Hill, Canberra, Dick and his wife won the *Sydney Morning Herald* State-wide country garden competition several times in the 1960s; he was president (1964-66) and a life member of the Horticultural Society of Canberra, and his wife founded Canberra's first garden club. He also took pride in building up a Murray Grey cattle stud on his 1977-acre (800 ha) property, Malumba, at Tharwa. He exhibited successfully at shows in New South Wales and Victoria, held office in the Murray Grey Beef Cattle Society and the Royal National Capital Agricultural Society, and organised the first sale of Murray Greys in the USA.

A genial and gregarious six-footer (183 cm) with a good sense of humour, Dick Hardy remained fit and active until his death. He died on 22 July 1985 at St Leonards, Sydney, and was cremated. His wife and their two sons survived him.

Canberra Times, 7 Aug 1985, p 10; private information.   G. P. WALSH

HARPER, NORMAN DENHOLM (1906-1986), historian and educator, was born on 27 April 1906 at Subiaco, Perth, son of Victorian-born parents Edward Denholm Harper, warehouseman, and his wife Jessie, née Finlay. After the family's return to Victoria, Norman was educated at Melbourne High School and, following his graduation from the University of Melbourne (BA Hons, 1927; Dip.Ed., 1928; MA, 1929; B.Ed., 1938) with the Dwight [q.v.4] prize in history and political science, and a Wyselaskie scholarship, he returned to the school as senior history master (1927-39). He combined this teaching with part-time appointments in the university's history department until 1939, when he secured a full-time lectureship. On 17 January 1934 at St John's Presbyterian Church, Elsternwick, he married Gladys Agnes Mills, a teacher.

Harper was a demanding but supportive lecturer, teaching most subjects offered in the department. Promoted to senior lecturer in 1943 and associate professor in 1955, he established the first continuing course in American history at an Australian university in 1948. He was a self-taught Americanist, his approach informed by undergraduate training in sociology as well as history, and encompassing the spread of settlement, labour and race relations, and culture conflict. Internationally known for his essays on Frederick Jackson Turner's frontier thesis, Harper sought in America's westward expansion themes that offered some analogy with Australia's past. In 1966 he was appointed to a personal chair in American history; his major work, *Great and Powerful Friend: A Study of Australian-American Relations between 1900 and 1975*, was published posthumously in 1987.

Dedicated to advancing the teaching of history at all levels, Harper fostered links between teachers and universities throughout his career. He chaired matriculation syllabus and examining committees. Several of his books were written for a school readership, and generations of Australian children were introduced to Asia and the Americas through *Our Pacific Neighbours* (1953), written with G. S. Browne [q.v.13]. A president (1953-59) of the Historical Association of Victoria, he was the driving force behind an annual 'safari' that brought university lecturers to senior secondary school audiences throughout rural Victoria. In 1974-81 an annual lecture in his name was given at Swan Hill High School. He maintained a close association with Melbourne High School as a member (1941-71) of the advisory council and as president (1936-51) of the Old Boys' Association. Admitted a fellow (1968) of the Australian College of Education, he was appointed OBE in 1977.

Harper also pioneered the study of international affairs, through scholarship and public commentary, over more than forty years. A tireless advocate for greater understanding of Australia's Asian neighbours, he promoted educational programs such as the Colombo Plan and Fulbright scheme. With Gordon Greenwood [q.v.], he edited four volumes of *Australia in World Affairs*, covering the period 1950-70, and from 1954 was a member of the Melbourne Round Table group. A regular adviser to the Department of External Affairs, he frequently interrupted classes with a polite request that students leave his study because 'the Minister' or 'the Department' was on the telephone. In addition to representing

Australia at many international conferences, he held several visiting fellowships and professorships. As president (1955-65) of the Victorian branch of the United Nations Association, he supported an expanded role for the UN. He was a member of the Australian delegation to its Twenty-Third General Session in 1968.

The extent of Harper's extramural activity intrigued some colleagues: it included the posts of Victorian branch president (1954-55), Commonwealth research chairman (1961-65) and president (1965-70) of the Australian Institute of International Affairs; service on many committees of the Social Science Research Council of Australia (Academy of the Social Sciences in Australia after 1971), to which he had been elected in 1959; and membership of the council of the University of Melbourne (1955-66). Founding president (1964-68) of the Australian and New Zealand American Studies Association, he convened seven of its biennial conferences and edited their proceedings. A stickler for rules as a means to ensure balance and consistency, Harper was not beyond using them to extract the result he wanted on a matter of policy or the election of his preferred candidates. He derived great satisfaction from his responsibilities, and from the prominence that came with them.

An avid baseball player and athlete in his youth (awarded a university Blue in 1927), Harper was, in later years, stout and florid but distinguished in appearance—an image complementing the avuncular role he adopted with junior colleagues and favoured students. Childless, he delighted in the careers of those he published first in conference proceedings or assisted to undertake postgraduate study in the United States. Norman Harper became emeritus professor on his retirement in 1972. Survived by his wife, he died on 14 October 1986 at Kew, Melbourne, and was cremated.

A'asian Jnl of American Studies, vol 5, no 2, 1986, p 1; *Hist Studies*, vol 22, no 88, 1987, p 494; Academy of the Social Sciences in Aust, *Annual Report*, 1986-87, p 52; Harper papers (Univ of Melbourne Archives).   ALLAN JOHNSTON

HARRISON, ARTHUR MANDER (1912-1986), civil engineer and air force officer, was born on 30 June 1912 in South Brisbane, second of four sons of Reginald Ainsworth Harrison, a Victorian-born warehouse manager, and his English-born wife Winifred Nellie, née Jones. Peter Firman Harrison [q.v.] was his younger brother. Educated in Sydney, Arthur studied civil engineering at Sydney Technical College and town planning at the University of Sydney. In 1928 he was employed as a draughtsman. Next year he was appointed assistant-engineer with Petersham Municipal Council. He became engineer manager of Australian Roads Ltd in 1935 and of C. R. McKenzie Pty Ltd in 1939. On 4 September 1941 at All Saints Church of England, Woollahra, he married Dorothy Lorraine Foster.

Having served in the Militia for four years, Harrison was commissioned in the Royal Australian Air Force on 20 October 1941; for reasons unknown he gave his year of birth as 1906. He was posted to the Directorate of Works and Buildings, RAAF Headquarters, Melbourne. In January 1942 he was sent to the North-Western Area, where he selected sites for airfields. He was promoted to flying officer in April. From October he was engaged in designing, and supervising the construction of, airfields and other works in Queensland. Appointed commanding officer of No.9 Works Maintenance Unit (later Airfield Construction Squadron) in February 1943, he was responsible for establishing airfields and facilities in the Northern Territory, most notably airstrips for fighters on Melville Island. Made temporary flight lieutenant in August and acting squadron leader in March 1944 (temporary in January 1945), he was mentioned in despatches (1945). In May 1945 he took part in the invasion of Tarakan Island, Borneo, while attached to No.61 Airfield Construction Wing. He took No.9 ACS from Australia to Balikpapan, Borneo, in September.

Posted to No.5 ACS at Labuan in November, Harrison assumed command in December. The squadron was deployed to Japan in February 1946 as part of the British Commonwealth Occupation Force; it played a vital role in the rebuilding of airfields and facilities at Bofu, Miho and Iwakuni. Harrison was promoted to acting wing commander in December (substantive in March 1950). He impressed the air officer commanding the British Commonwealth Air Group, Air Vice-Marshal (Sir) Cecil Bouchier, as a 'man of integrity' who had 'great personal charm' and who was 'a born leader of men'. After returning to Australia in October 1948, he commanded No.2 ACS in February-September 1949 and performed staff duties. From July 1951 he again commanded No.5 ACS. He was appointed OBE in 1953. In May 1955 his squadron moved to Darwin, where it extended the runway and built domestic and operational facilities.

Harrison was promoted to acting group captain in October 1957. On 1 July 1960 he was placed on the Retired List and granted the honorary rank of group captain. He set up as a consulting engineer. Divorced in February 1971, he married Judith Mary Rogers (d.1984), a typist, on 11 May that year at the district registrar's office, St Leonards, Sydney. He died on 15 July 1986 at Mosman and was cremated; the daughter of his first marriage survived him.

A. Stephens, *Going Solo* (1995); D. Wilson, *Always First* (1998); A. M. Harrison RAAF service record (Dept of Defence, Canberra).   DAVID WILSON

HARRISON, PETER FIRMAN (1918-1990), architect and town planner, was born on 21 October 1918 at Annerley, Brisbane, third of four sons of Reginald Ainsworth Harrison, a Victorian-born warehouse manager, and his English-born wife Winifred Nellie, née Jones. Arthur Mander Harrison [q.v.] was his elder brother. Growing up in Sydney during the Depression, Peter was educated at Rose Bay and Darlinghurst Superior public schools and at the Central Technical School, Ultimo, where he completed his Intermediate certificate in 1933. His first job was in a factory at Woolloomooloo, polishing pick handles.

In 1934 Harrison obtained a position in the drawing office of the Australian Gas Light Co. Two years later he commenced a civil engineering night-school course at the Sydney Technical College. He became a draughtsman in the works and services branch of the Commonwealth Department of the Interior in 1939. In the same year he switched to the architecture course, gaining his diploma in 1942. Through his studies he developed an enduring interest in the work of Walter Burley Griffin [q.v.9]. His own experience and acute observations of the realities of commercial life for 'ordinary people' left him with an abiding appreciation of their aspirations and sensibilities.

At St John's Church of England, Georges Plains, on 22 June 1942 Harrison married Joyce Paddison, a trained nurse. On 23 October that year he enlisted in the Royal Australian Air Force. He served as an architectural draughtsman at No.1 Divisional Works Office, Sydney, and was promoted to temporary sergeant in January 1945. Discharged on 8 October, he joined the Commonwealth Department of Works and Housing. He was a draughtsman and planning officer for the Cumberland County Council in 1946-50, while studying part time at the University of Sydney for a diploma in town and country planning (1951). On completion he was appointed senior lecturer in Denis Winston's [q.v.16] department of town and country planning at the university. Divorced on 30 May 1957, he married Sheila Winifred Booth, a planning officer, on 22 June at St Andrew's Scots Church, Rose Bay.

In 1955 Harrison was a member of the committee of the (Royal) Australian Planning

Institute that made a submission to the Senate Select Committee on the Development of Canberra, arguing that the Griffin plan should be implemented. The National Capital Development Commission, established in 1958, appointed Harrison as its first chief planner early in 1959. He made a strong case for the expansion of Canberra, mounted a vigorous defence of Griffin's approach and developed the case for the 'Y-Plan' for the layout of the city, which was adopted in 1967. One of his critical responses to some of the more adventurous planning proposals he dealt with was to apply the 'mother test', as in 'Would my mother live in it?' A man of high principle, he was impatient with humbug, and he dismissed cant and hypocrisy in colourful terms.

Harrison left the NCDC as first assistant commissioner to take up a fellowship (1967-79) in the urban research unit, Research School of Social Sciences, Australian National University. In 1971 the University of New South Wales conferred on him a master's degree in architecture for his thesis on Griffin, published posthumously by the National Library of Australia in 1995. He was awarded life fellowship of the Royal Australian Institute of Architects (1971) and the RAPI (1978). In 1972 the Sydney division of the RAPI awarded him its Sidney Luker [q.v.15] memorial medal in recognition of his contribution to town and regional planning.

Although his published output was prodigious, Harrison made few contributions to academic journals, preferring to exert his profound influence on his colleagues through professional journals, conference presentations and the popular press. His strong defence of the public interest in urban planning often saw him take issue with political leaders, senior bureaucrats and private entrepreneurs alike. This aspect of his independent character was not always welcomed although he did earn respect for his courage and independence.

In 1980 Harrison was appointed AM. His distress at proposals for Canberra's development led him, in 1985, to resign from the Order. He also resigned his life fellowship of the RAIA in 1990 in protest at the policies of the institute's Australian Capital Territory chapter on the Metropolitan Canberra Policy and Development Plan. Harrison lived modestly but was generous to students and colleagues. Survived by his wife, he died on 30 October 1990 in Royal Canberra Hospital and was cremated. He had no children. His most enduring legacy lies in his adaptation of the Griffin plan to accommodate the growth of Canberra.

E. Sparke, *Canberra 1954-1980* (1988); *Austn Planner*, vol 28, no 4, 1990, p 47; *Canberra Times*, 6 Nov 1968, p 19, 4 Nov 1990, p 21; *Austn Business*, 28 Nov 1990, p 43; P. Spearritt, interview with P. F. Harrison (ts, 1983, NLA); J. Weirick, interview with P. F. Harrison (ts, 1990, NLA); A9301, item 72027 (NAA); Harrison papers (NLA); personal knowledge.   P. N. TROY

HART, SIR BYRNE (1895-1989), soldier, accountant and company director, was born on 6 October 1895 in Brisbane, second of identical twins and youngest of three surviving sons of Queensland-born parents Frederick MacDonnell Hart, accountant, and his wife Isabella, née Byrne. The twins attended Bowen Bridge Road State and Brisbane Grammar schools before becoming boarders at The Southport School. In 1913 Byrne was apprenticed to an architect. He was commissioned in the Australian Imperial Force on 25 July 1915 and by April 1917 was serving on the Western Front with the 49th Battalion. Following an attack at Messines, Belgium, on 7 June, he was one of only two officers left standing. For rallying the men, consolidating the line and holding out during three days of intensive bombardment, he was awarded the Military Cross. He was promoted to lieutenant and in September was severely wounded at Zonnebeke. His twin, Morris, had also joined the AIF and was killed in action in October. Byrne was invalided to Brisbane, where his AIF appointment terminated on 16 October 1918.

On 20 March 1922 at St Stephen's Presbyterian Church, Toowoomba, Hart married Margaret Hannah Cramond; they had three sons. He had decided to take up accountancy and to fill his brother's place in their father's firm, F. M. Hart & Co. Becoming a partner, he was a fellow of the Institute of Chartered Accountants in Australia from 1933. He also helped to manage Her Majesty's Theatre, long held by the Byrne family, and an adjoining hotel in Queen Street, Brisbane.

Called up for full-time duty in September 1941 as a temporary major with the 61st Battalion, Militia, he was bitterly disappointed to be given a supporting role at Northern Command headquarters as deputy assistant quartermaster general. One of his roles was to arrange for the reception of the first American troops to arrive in Brisbane. In October 1942 he joined the AIF and from January 1943 commanded the 2nd Australian Water Transport Group, based on Thursday Island. He was promoted to temporary lieutenant colonel in November and transferred to the Reserve of Officers in August 1944. His son Morris was accidentally killed in December 1945 while serving with the AIF.

Back in Brisbane, Hart became senior partner in F. M. Hart & Co. Over many years a director of some nineteen companies, mostly Queensland based, he was chairman of several, including Hornibrook Highway Ltd (1948-76); National Bank of Australasia Ltd, Queensland board of advice (1966-70); Mactaggarts Primary Producers' Co-operative Association Ltd (1954-74); Amagraze Ltd (1960-73); Utah Mining Australia Ltd (1970-76); and Castlemaine Perkins Ltd (1973-77). He had a grazing property at Kandanga, Central Queensland.

Hart was president of the Brisbane Gun (1939) and of the Queensland (1954-56) clubs, and a member of the Union Club (Sydney). As a trustee of the United Service Club for some thirty-four years he assisted war widows and Legacy. He was a Freemason. Honorary treasurer (1949-66) and chairman (1966-74) of the Queensland Turf Club, he was a modestly successful horse-breeder and owner. He was appointed CBE in 1968 and knighted in 1974.

Sir Byrne was 5 ft 10 ins (178 cm), of slight build, with short dark hair when young, bespectacled blue eyes, and fair to olive complexion. Despite the wounds he had received in World War I, he was fit enough to enjoy horse-riding into his late seventies. His interests included fishing and sailing; he was a member of the Royal Queensland Yacht Club. Survived by his wife and two younger sons, he died on 19 March 1989 at his Ascot home and was cremated with Anglican rites. Since 1990 the Sir Byrne Hart Stakes has been a major event in the Queensland racing calendar. A portrait of him by Sir William Dargie is held by the QTC.

P. Edgar, *To Villers-Bretonneux with Brigadier-General William Glasgow DSO and the 13th Australian Infantry Brigade* (1998); *Bulletin*, 13 July 1968, p 42; *Australian*, 21 Mar 1970, p 14; *Telegraph* (Brisbane), 10 June 1971, p 2, 19 Nov 1973, p 27; *Sunday Mail* (Brisbane), 8 July 1973, p 24; *Courier-Mail* (Brisbane), 2 Jan 1974, p 1; private information.

MARK McGINNESS

HART, IRIS CORRELL (1910-1983), singer, actor and director, was born on 9 August 1910 at Yorketown, South Australia, eldest of three children of Wilfred Jacob Hart, agent, and his wife Eleanor Jane, née Correll, both South Australian born. Educated at Edithburgh Public School and Presbyterian Girls' College, Adelaide, Iris studied singing with Frederick Bevan at the Elder [q.v.4] Conservatorium of Music, University of Adelaide. In 1930 an anonymous reviewer of a lunch-time concert wrote of her 'promising voice, free from the prevalent vice of vibrato', and reported that her enunciation was so good that 'it triumphed over the bad acoustics of the Elder Hall'.

In 1933, while still a student, Hart took the lead in Louis Hirsch's musical comedy *The O'Brien Girl* for the South Australian Operatic Society. She acted in several Adelaide Repertory Theatre plays including Goethe's *Faust*, as Margaret (1934), and Max Afford's [q.v.13] *Colonel Light—the Founder*, as Sieglinda Mannheim (1936). Also in 1936 she had the lead in J. C. Williamson [q.v.6] Ltd's production of *Anything Goes* by Cole Porter. Later that year she contracted spontaneous pneumothorax which ended her singing career; thereafter she took only speaking parts. On 6 February 1937 at St Saviour's Church of England, Glen Osmond, she married Maurice Dale Chapman, a manager; they were divorced in 1946. Very beautiful, and known as 'the duchess', she lived in 'performance mode'. She had a wide circle of friends, loved parties and was renowned for her tapestry.

Among many roles at the Tivoli Theatre, Hart played Elizabeth Barrett in *The Barretts of Wimpole Street* by Rudolf Besier. For the Adelaide University Theatre Guild she acted in Molière's *The Miser* (1950) and other plays. In 1952 she toured with the John Alden [q.v.13] Company, as Hippolyta in *A Midsummer Night's Dream* and as Emilia in *The Winter's Tale*. Two years later she directed and acted in four plays for the Adelaide Theatre Group, including *Tartuffe* by Molière. Among her final stage performances were a role in Lillian Hellman's *The Children's Hour* (1962) for Theatre '62, and parts in plays produced (1962, 1966) for the Adelaide Festival of Arts.

Remuneration for work in amateur theatre was minimal and in 1945-66 Hart acted in many radio serials and dramas, including live productions on 5AD. She taught acting and stagecraft to amateur groups in Adelaide. For the Australian Broadcasting Commission she was a performer in about four hundred plays, a freelance interviewer, and a producer of 'Kindergarten of the Air'. She retired in 1966, and on 15 October that year married at St Andrew's Presbyterian Church, Mount Gambier, Thomas Romer Paltridge, a grazier and a divorcee. Moving to the district, she assisted local theatre enterprises, particularly the Lucindale Drama Group, which won two Arts Council awards at South-East drama festivals. Survived by her husband and the daughter of her first marriage, Iris Paltridge died on 27 October 1983 at Mount Gambier and was buried with Anglican rites in the Carinya Gardens cemetery.

Advertiser (Adelaide), 24 Apr 1952, p 3, 31 Oct 1983, p 16; I. Hart, newsclippings (Performing Arts Collection of SA); private information.

JOYCE GIBBERD

HARTIGAN, TREVOR RUSSELL (1940-1990), barrister and judge, was born on 20 February 1940 at Greenslopes, Brisbane, son of Queensland-born parents Reginald Russel Hartigan, electrician, and his wife Enone Elizabeth, née Short. Educated at St Laurence's (Christian Brothers') College, South Brisbane, and at the University of Queensland (LL B, 1965), Trevor was admitted to the Bar on 15 December 1965. At the Catholic Church of St Peter and St Paul, Bulimba, on 23 August 1967 he married Marie Theresa Conlon, a bank officer.

In 1966 Hartigan had set up a private practice in Brisbane that developed to include trial and appellate work in criminal, civil, industrial and administrative law. He took silk on 23 November 1981. Active in the Bar Association of Queensland, he served as a member of its committee (1979-84) and as vice-president (1984-87) before being elected president in 1987. He had considerable skills in Bar politics: a more prominent silk had quickly abandoned his challenge to Hartigan for the presidency and stood as vice-president, on a joint ticket with him. Hartigan was also chairman (1985-87) of the Barristers' Board of Queensland. With (Sir) Gerard Brennan and then F. N. Albietz, he co-authored three editions of *An Outline of the Powers and Duties of Justices of the Peace in Queensland* (1967-87).

On 13 August 1987 Hartigan was appointed president of the Administrative Appeals Tribunal and a judge of the Federal Court. He oversaw the relocation in 1989 of the tribunal's principal registry from Canberra to Brisbane. This decentralisation of Commonwealth administrative power beyond Canberra, Sydney and Melbourne provoked controversy—generated in part by Hartigan's residence in Brisbane and, in part, by Sydney, a busier registry, being passed over—but the attorney-general Lionel Bowen insisted that administrative efficiency required the move from Canberra and that cheaper accommodation costs justified choosing Brisbane over Sydney. At the time of Hartigan's appointment a large expansion in the tribunal's workload had occurred, due, in part, to the transfer to it of some seventy-five thousand tax cases following the abolition of the taxation boards of review in mid-1986. Working with a reduced staff, he supervised a system that, by early 1989, had halved this tax backlog while dealing efficiently with the general work of the tribunal.

Dignified in dress and manner, and precise in his enunciation, Hartigan was solidly built but not tall. He was a practising Catholic and an Australian Labor Party supporter. A good citizen, he gave conscientious service to a number of Queensland organisations, not all of which, in the Bjelke-Petersen era, attracted ambitious barristers. He served on various professional, church and other bodies, including two involved with homeless and unemployed youth, and on the committee of the Queensland Council for Civil Liberties, of which he was a founding member and, later, secretary for five years.

His career cut short by cancer, Hartigan was unable to show the full extent of his leadership and administrative skills. He died of a melanoma on 24 April 1990 in Royal Brisbane Hospital and was buried in Nudgee cemetery. His wife and their two daughters survived him.

PD (Senate), 4 Apr 1989, p 907; Administrative Appeals Tribunal, *Annual Report*, 1989-90; *Austn Law Jnl*, vol 64, no 7, 1990, p 446; *Qld Bar News*, June 1990, p 9; Bar Assn of Qld records; private information.   DOUG DRUMMOND

HARTIGAN, WILLIAM ANTHONY GERARD (1908-1989), telegraphist and Australian Labor Party official, was born on 23 June 1908 at Lithgow, New South Wales, younger child of Edward Andrew Hartigan, railway fettler, and his second wife Ann, née Shallvy, both born in New South Wales. Bill was educated at Springwood Public School, a convent school at Penrith, and Marist Brothers' High School, Darlinghurst, Sydney. At the age of 15 he started work as a telegraph messenger in the Postmaster-General's Department at Springwood. He became a telegraphist and worked at Mount Victoria, Dubbo, Wagga Wagga, Adelaide, Sydney and Rockhampton, Queensland. On 27 January 1934 at St Brigid's Catholic Church, Marrickville, Sydney, he married Muriel Rita Barnsley. The couple and their three children moved to Canberra in 1937.

After leaving the Postmaster-General's Department in 1952, Hartigan operated a communications system at Federal parliament for Australian United Press Ltd and the Melbourne *Age*. In addition, he worked for Dobell Pty Ltd as an office furniture salesman from 1955 to 1963. He was a newspaper and magazine distributor for John Fairfax [qq.v.4,8] & Sons Ltd from 1963 until his retirement in 1971. A colleague at Parliament House described him as congenial and dapper, and a very fast, efficient and hard worker, with a mane of hair earning him the nickname 'Old Silver'. In 1965 in a traffic collision he had sustained injuries that included the loss of his left eye.

At the urging of J. B. Chifley [q.v.13] Hartigan had joined the ALP in 1926; he was to remain a lifelong member. He was active in the Fourth Division Postmasters, Postal Clerks and Telegraphists' Union and later the Australian Journalists' Association. As president (1973-74) of the Canberra South branch of the ALP, he was a stickler for the party rule book. He admired Chifley and disliked H. V. Evatt [q.v.14]. A fellow member described him as more inclined to see himself as 'non-factional' than was justified by the strong stands he took on some issues. Scathing about moves towards self-government for the Australian Capital Territory, he also had a low opinion of job-grabbing and opportunistic Labor careerists.

The large Hartigan family lived at Reid, and then at Griffith. From the mid-1940s to the early 1960s Muriel, vivacious, active and an accomplished pianist, conducted the popular Hartigan's Orchestra and Hartigan's Band at many social functions. Bill was president (1952-53) of the Canberra Workmen's (later Workers') Club and publicity officer (1972-83) of the Canberra South Bowling Club. In 1946 he had helped to set up the Canberra branch of the New South Wales Postal Institute. Settling finally at Narrabundah with Muriel, Bill enjoyed dancing and the theatre, and was fond of social drinking and congenial company. Of medium build, well dressed, affable and assertive, with a dry and original sense of humour, he was one of the ALP's elder statesmen and stern critics. He died on 23 August 1989 at Garran and was cremated. His wife and their four sons and two daughters survived him.

A. J. Phillips et al, *From Workmen to Workers* (1980); *Canberra Times*, 22 Mar 1967, p 8, 14 Feb 1973, p 8, 30 Jan 1974, p 2, 25 June 1988, p B2, 24 Aug 1989, p 4; ALP (ACT), *Lobby*, Nov 1989, p 48; Supreme Court of the ACT, Transcripts of Proceedings, 1966-67 (Supreme Court, ACT); R. Aitchison, interview with W. A. G. Hartigan (ts, 1975, NLA); J. Cocker, taped interview with W. A. G. Hartigan (1983, NLA); private information.

BILL TULLY

HARTNELL, GEOFFREY CLARK (1916-1981), air force officer, was born on 15 April 1916 at East Malvern, Melbourne, third child of Victorian-born parents Frederick Bernard Hartnell, soft-goods manufacturer, and his wife Ada Gertrude, née Emery. Geoff was educated at Wesley College (1925-34). Solidly built, he captained the first XVIII, rowed in the first VIII and excelled in gymnastics. In 1935 he began to study chemistry and engineering at the University of Melbourne, but he left after the first term because of financial difficulties and found employment as a salesman for G. J. Coles [q.v.13] & Co. Ltd.

On 20 January 1936 Hartnell joined the Royal Australian Air Force as a cadet. He completed flying training at Point Cook and was commissioned on 1 January 1937. Promoted to flying officer in July, he qualified as a specialist air navigator in 1938-39. He was posted to No.6 Squadron in January 1939 and promoted to flight lieutenant in September. Serving at station headquarters, Richmond, New South Wales, from January 1940 and at RAAF Head-

quarters, Melbourne, from April, he was made acting squadron leader in July. On 7 June 1941 at Christ Church, South Yarra, he married with Anglican rites Joyce Margaret Webster, a cookery demonstrator.

Promoted to temporary wing commander in April 1942, Hartnell commanded No.20 (Catalina) Squadron, based at Bowen then Cairns, Queensland, from September to January 1943, undertaking night-bombing and supply-dropping missions in New Guinea. He was then posted to the European theatre to command (from March) No.10 Squadron, RAAF, which, based at Mount Batten, Devon, carried out anti-submarine patrols in the Atlantic and the Bay of Biscay. One of Hartnell's many diverse qualities was a technical turn of mind; he contributed directly to improvements in the power plants and the armament of the squadron's Sunderland aircraft. In December he was promoted to temporary group captain and appointed senior air staff officer at RAAF Overseas Headquarters, London. From December 1944 he commanded Royal Air Force Station, Driffield, Yorkshire, where two RAAF squadrons, No.462 and No.466, were based.

Back in Australia in March 1945, Hartnell was appointed commanding officer of No.1 Operational Training Unit, East Sale, Victoria. He became director of Allied air intelligence, RAAF Command, in July and commanding officer of RAAF Station, Pearce, Western Australia, in September. Director of intelligence at RAAF Headquarters from July 1946, he attended the RAF Staff College, Andover, England, in 1949. He commanded the Base Squadron, Point Cook, in 1950-51 and RAAF Station, Amberley, Queensland, in 1951-53. In 1952 he operated a special force of eight Lincoln bombers from a temporary base at Broome, Western Australia, in support of British nuclear tests at the Monte Bello Islands, for which he was appointed CBE in 1955.

Hartnell was director of air staff plans and policy, RAAF Headquarters, in 1953-56. Promoted to air commodore in January 1956, he was SASO at headquarters, Home Command, in 1956-58. After completing the 1959 course at the Imperial Defence College, London, he commanded RAAF Base, Butterworth, Malaya, in 1960-62. He was director-general of plans and policy, Department of Air, Canberra, in 1962-63. In December 1963 he was made head of the Australian Joint Services Staff, London, as an acting air vice-marshal (substantive 3 February 1966). In March 1966 he became director of joint service plans, Department of Defence, Canberra. He was considered successful in every appointment, without ever being spectacular in a service that provided opportunities for extrovert behaviour. His manner in command displayed a concern for all members of the team, at times bordering on the avuncular. In staff appointments his application, patience and depth of perception made him a welcome addition to the various headquarters in which he served.

Following his retirement from the RAAF on medical grounds on 18 April 1968, Hartnell took up an appointment as the Canberra representative of Racal Electronics Pty Ltd. He had a deep sense of history. A trustee of the Australian War Memorial, he was the author of the air force entry in *The Australian Encyclopaedia* (1977). He wrote several important papers on aspects of defence philosophy, including problems of command. A kind and gentle man, he enjoyed woodwork, photography and gardening. He died of myocardial infarction on 16 May 1981 at Greenwich, Sydney, and was cremated with full air force honours; his wife and their two sons and daughter survived him.

J. Hetherington, *Air War against Germany and Italy 1939-1943* (1954); K. C. Baff (comp), *Maritime Is Number Ten* (1983); C. D. Coulthard-Clark, *The Third Brother* (1991); A. Stephens, *Going Solo* (1995); *Canberra Times*, 8 June 1981, p 6; A12372, item O343 (NAA); private information and personal knowledge.   RICHARD KINGSLAND

HARTNETT, SIR LAURENCE JOHN (1898-1986), businessman, was born on 26 May 1898 at Woking, Surrey, England, only child of John Joseph Hartnett, physician and surgeon, and his wife Katherine Jane, née Taplin. When his father died seven months later, Katherine took her son to live with her sister and brother-in-law, first in Southsea and then in Kingston-upon-Thames. There he was imbued with a wide-ranging curiosity, a strong sense of duty and a lofty disdain for hidebound bureaucracy. He also acquired an underlying sense of not really belonging that developed into a lifelong craving for recognition.

Educated at Kingston Grammar School and Epsom College, which specialised in preparing boys for medical studies, Hartnett felt a driving urge to emulate his father. He became apprehensive, however, of being at the beck and call of patients and was increasingly fascinated by contemporary technological developments, particularly those connected with internal combustion and mass production. In 1915 he disappointed family expectations by joining the armaments firm Vickers Ltd, as a management apprentice. Initiated into the latest production techniques, he admired the firm's readiness to improvise under hectic wartime pressures. Contact with political radicals on the shop floor tempered the rigid conservatism he had absorbed in childhood.

In 1918 Hartnett trained as a pilot with the Royal Naval Air Service and the Royal Air Force, but the war ended before he saw action. He had liked the 'dash' and 'sporting aspect' of flying. Restless for a new challenge, he developed a used-car business in Wallington that failed in 1921 with the collapse of the post-war boom; he then tried his luck as a freelance automobile consultant. In 1923 he accepted a position in Singapore, importing and marketing motor vehicles for the trading firm Guthrie & Co. Immensely energetic (and helped initially by a fortuitous rise in rubber prices), he greatly enlarged the business while revelling in expatriate social life, exploring local indigenous culture, purchasing rubber plantations on commission for an English firm and briefly establishing the island's first radio station—which broadcast for about fifteen minutes a day before the irate authorities closed it down. At St Andrew's Cathedral, Singapore, on 26 February 1925 he married with Anglican rites his childhood sweetheart, Gladys Winifred Tyler.

Believing himself insufficiently appreciated by Guthrie, in 1926 Hartnett took the post of southern Indian field representative for General Motors Corporation, whose international operations were expanding to meet mounting demand. His reorganisation of dealer and distributor networks made such a favourable impression that in 1927 he was summoned to the United States of America to familiarise himself with GMC operations there, visiting factories, participating in feasibility studies for overseas assembly plants, and absorbing corporate principles of scientific management. After a stint as sales manager (1928-29) of General Motors Nordiska in Sweden—where he enthusiastically applied the strategy of using styling and prestige to sell automobiles —he took charge of exports for General Motors' British subsidiary, Vauxhall Motors Ltd. His maturing entrepreneurial skills, aided by a timely currency devaluation, made this one of the few automotive undertakings anywhere to thrive during the Depression. He was appointed to Vauxhall's board of directors (1933-41) in recognition of this success.

In 1934 Hartnett became managing director of General Motors-Holden's [q.v.9] Ltd in Australia, an organisation rent by internal bickering, impeded by a cumbersome administrative structure and widely resented as a rapacious foreign profiteer. With tact, he restored internal harmony, overhauled management procedures and tirelessly publicised the company's contribution to local employment and industrial development, while reducing its perceived profitability by means of adroit book-keeping. As the economy revived, he built two new assembly plants, reopened four others, and selected Fishermen's Bend, Melbourne, as GMH's headquarters, thereby significantly influencing Australian industrial geography. In 1935 he was appointed GMC's regional director for Australia and New Zealand, and in 1936 became a vice-president of the corporation's export company.

Constantly seeking fresh opportunities, Hartnett also interested himself in various non-automotive enterprises, including aluminium production. He played a decisive role in establishing aeronautical research and, with Essington Lewis [q.v.10], in founding the Commonwealth Aircraft Corporation (director 1936-47), jointly owned by GMH and five British and Australian concerns. Inclusion of his American-controlled firm caused a diplomatic row with Britain, especially when CAC began by manufacturing a monoplane (later known as the Wirraway) designed by an American company partly owned by GMC.

Short, stocky, with a moustache and a perennially eager expression, Hartnett was an indefatigable industrial lobbyist, active in organisations such as the Victorian Chamber of Manufactures, of which he was a council member in 1935-37. By 1938 his contacts and overseas travel had left him troubled by the imminence of war and convinced that complacency prevailed in Australia's defence planning. Following the outbreak of World War II, continuing to prize public service, he was appointed director (1940-45) of ordnance production, Department of Munitions, and chairman (1942-46) of the Army Inventions Directorate. He found the frenetic pace of this work 'wonderfully exhilarating' and in January 1942 volunteered to fly to Singapore in a perilous last-ditch effort to salvage manufacturing equipment—a mission aborted when Japanese forces got there first.

The industrial capacity developed during wartime strengthened Hartnett's conviction—shared with (Sir) John Storey and (Sir) John Jensen [qq.v.16,14]—that Australia must develop its own automobile manufacturing industry. Already in the 1930s he had covertly lobbied the government to exert pressure on GMC to that end. In January 1945 he announced GMH's intention to produce an Australian car, but at this point relations with his American head office turned sour. Though generally an effective team player, Hartnett also took pride in a maverick streak. Fervently believing that the vehicle should be 'designed within Australia' by Australians 'to suit Australian conditions', he was bitterly disappointed when a design by his local team, drafted without authorisation, was dismissed as 'crazy' and 'a waste of time'. His tendency to take such unsanctioned initiatives resulted in his removal as head of GMH in December 1946; his successor promised that 'the old regime under which there was insufficient consideration given to company policy is ended'.

Hartnett was devastated by this decision, which deprived him of the prestige of launching the Holden car. Despite being offered an executive post with GMC in America, in April 1947 he resigned, preferring to live in Australia. But without powerful corporate backing, his ventures were now more prone to frustration and this, together with his propensity for wishful thinking and unbridled enthusiasm, often clouded his judgment. He wrathfully berated the government for declining to rescue his attempt to manufacture a passenger vehicle, called the Hartnett, which, being severely undercapitalised, failed to survive a 1950s steel shortage. One of the seventy-odd cars produced is in the collection of the National Museum of Victoria; another is in the National Motor Museum, Birdwood, South Australia. In 1960 he became Australia's first large-scale importer of Japanese vehicles, under licence from the Nissan Motor Co. At first this partnership prospered; in 1966, however, it broke up acrimoniously when Hartnett was enraged by criticism from Tokyo. He was particularly embittered as the row ended his hopes of creating a jointly owned local automobile manufacturing operation with Nissan.

Nevertheless Hartnett retained diverse interests including a very remunerative machine tool importing business. In 1961 he became industrial consultant to the Singapore government—although this association was also marked by petulant bickering when it was learned that he had accepted commissions from a company whose equipment he recommended for use in Singapore's small-arms factories. A trustee (1945-77) of the Museum (later Institute) of Applied Science, Victoria, Hartnett claimed a central role in establishing its planetarium in 1965. As president (1975-76) of the Victorian Civil Ambulance Service, he chaired a committee investigating ambulance design. A fellow (1952) of the Royal Society of Arts, in 1970 he took particular pleasure in establishing a Victorian chapter of the society, which instituted (1985) a biennial medal in his name.

Although justly proud of his many contributions, Hartnett felt increasingly undervalued. To compensate, he often exaggerated his achievements, as in his lively but unreliable autobiography, *Big Wheels and Little Wheels* (1964). The gratuitous advice he was forever offering politicians on subjects ranging from public transport to refugee policy became increasingly erratic in later years, and he grew nostalgic for the time when prime ministers 'not only called upon me to discuss matters but invited me to dine'. He complained that the views of 'economists and financial experts' were now prized above those of 'men who have … practical technical knowledge'. Australians, he said, seemed 'ashamed of manufacturing industry' and did not want 'the likes of me'. Yet he was overjoyed to be knighted in 1967 and proud to be awarded Singapore's Public Service Star (1974) and an honorary doctorate of laws from the University of Melbourne (1983).

With increasing infirmity, by the late 1970s Hartnett found it harder to travel between his city residence and his much-loved mansion Rubra, at Mount Eliza, which provided the centre for his treasured extended family. Survived by his wife and their three daughters, Sir Laurence died on 4 April 1986 at Frankston and was cremated. His estate was sworn for probate at $1 823 335.

S. J. Butlin and C. B. Schedvin, *War Economy 1942-1945* (1977); J. Rich, *Hartnett* (1996); R. Conlon and J. Perkins, *Wheels and Deals* (2001); P. L. Swan, *General-Motors Holden's and the Australian Automobile Industry in Economic Perspective* (PhD thesis, Monash Univ, 1972); Essington Lewis papers, Laurence Hartnett papers, and J. Rich and A. Warden taped interviews with L. J. Hartnett (Univ of Melbourne Archives); John Storey papers (NLA).

JOE RICH

HART-SMITH, WILLIAM (1911-1990), poet, was born on 23 November 1911 at Tunbridge Wells, Kent, England, eldest of three children of George May Coleridge Hart-Smith, assistant bank manager, and his wife Florence Amelia Gomer, a household servant known as 'Gypsy' and said to be of Spanish descent. He had a difficult childhood and received a modest education; in 1924 the family was 'sent out' to Auckland, New Zealand, his father's syphilis-induced erratic behaviour having caused embarrassment. Bill began work as a radio mechanic. Inspired in his twenties by H. G. Wells's *First and Last Things* (1908) and D. H. Lawrence's *Birds, Beasts, Flowers* (1923) to write poetry, he was given direction by imagist poets represented in Louis Untermeyer's *Modern American Poetry* (1921). In 1936 he left for Australia; after nearly two years in Tasmania, he settled in Sydney and found employment as a radio copywriter. On 7 October 1939 at St Jude's Church of England, Randwick, he married Mary Lola Wynn, a library assistant. He developed a strong sympathy for Aboriginal culture and from 1940 published as a Jindyworobak. Enlisting in the Australian Imperial Force in January 1942, he did not go overseas and was discharged in August 1943 as a sergeant in the Australian Army Education Service.

Although a communist sympathiser in the 1940s and 1950s, Hart-Smith was apolitical in his poetics: the *Bulletin* published a hundred of his early poems and *Quadrant* a hundred later ones. An element of mysticism in his work was derived from his reading of Gurdjieff, Ouspenski and the sufis. Poetry, he said, was his 'prime obsession'. His 'free' verse resulted from firm control; his poems were lapidary, acutely observed, sharply rendered, and wry rather than ironic. He edited the *Jindyworobak Anthology* in 1944 and in 1948 published what several critics considered his masterpiece, *Christopher Columbus: A Sequence of Poems*. Douglas Stewart [q.v.] called it 'a rare and beautiful achievement'; Bruce Beaver described it as 'probably one of the best verse sequences in modern Australian poetry'; H. M. Green said that if his development continued in range and quality he would be 'among the leaders in the poetic world on this side or the other of the Tasman'.

In 1946 Hart-Smith returned to New Zealand and became an adult education tutor and organiser in South Canterbury. Divorced next year, on 8 January 1949 at Chalmers Presbyterian Church, Timaru, he married 19-year-old Patricia Anne McBeath. They had two sons and a daughter. In 1960 he was awarded the Australian Literature Society's R. A. Crouch [q.v.8] gold medal for *Poems of Discovery* (1959) and in 1966 the Grace Leven prize for *The Talking Clothes*, published that year. He had moved back to Sydney in 1962 and in 1963-64 was president of the Poetry Society of Australia. Separating from his wife, he moved to Perth in 1970 with Dorothy Donnelly; they had had a son in 1968. A handsome, well-groomed and well-spoken man, Hart-Smith attracted women ever younger than he into relationships that never lasted.

For some years Hart-Smith was a senior tutor in creative writing at the Western Australian Institute of Technology and in 1976 was briefly writer in residence at the University of Western Australia. In 1973 and 1977 he won Commonwealth Literature Board fellowships. From 1978 he lived in Auckland with Joan Dale, a friend from childhood. Over the course of his career he had written thousands of poems and published some 650. He called himself 'the first Australasian poet', but he often seemed a poetic expatriate from both New Zealand and Australia. In 1985 he won the Christopher Brennán [q.v.7] prize for *Selected Poems 1936-1984* (edited by Brian Dibble), and in 1987 the Patrick White [q.v.] award for authors who 'have not received due recognition for their contribution to Australian literature'.

Hart-Smith's interests included philately and conchology; a species of cowrie, *Notadusta* (now *Notocypraea*) *hartsmithi*, was named after him in 1967. Survived by his wife and Joan Dale, and by his four children, he died on 15 April 1990 at Whangaparaoa and was cremated.

B. Petrie (ed), *William Hart-Smith, Hand to Hand* (1991); B. Dibble, '"He Will Be Lonely in Heaven": Australasian Poet', *Southern Review*, Nov 1990, p 191;

SMH, 20 Apr 1990, p 4; *ArtsWest*, Nov-Dec 1992, p 4; Hart-Smith papers (NLA and Univ of Sydney Lib); personal knowledge.   BRIAN DIBBLE

HARVEY, WILLIAM COTTER BURNELL (1897-1981), thoracic physician and anti-smoking crusader, was born on 24 September 1897 at Grenfell, New South Wales, eldest of three children of Irish-born Lucius Watson Harvey, medical practitioner, and his Sydney-born wife Hilda Gray, née Leibius. Lucius Harvey later established a practice at Manly. While Cotter was at Sydney Grammar School, Lucius was diagnosed with pulmonary tuberculosis, which had also affected some of his family in Ireland. He went into semi-retirement at Leura. At the University of Sydney (MB, Ch.M., 1920), Harvey lived in St Paul's College. He became a resident medical officer at Royal Prince Alfred Hospital, Sydney. His father travelled to Geneva in 1921 for tuberculin treatment but, following a lung haemorrhage, died in his hotel. Harvey later said that family experience had caused him to direct his professional life to the treatment of tuberculosis.

After his residency Harvey went to Britain and Europe, where he worked at the Hospital for Consumption and Chest Diseases, Brompton, London, and at a sanatorium in Switzerland. In 1923 he gained a diploma in tuberculosis diseases from the University College of South Wales and Monmouthshire, University of Wales, a rare qualification for an Australian. Returning to Sydney he married Laura Hingst (d.1977) on 2 February 1924 at St James's Church of England, Sydney. He was appointed in 1924 as a physician for pulmonary diseases at Royal North Shore Hospital and next year as an honorary assistant physician at Royal Prince Alfred Hospital. At the North Shore he took over the tuberculosis out-patients' clinic and fought hard for a separate chest unit with its own building. This came in 1941, with a larger one in 1949. Surgical colleagues were appointed and a postgraduate course in thoracic nursing was introduced.

Harvey had enlisted in the Australian Imperial Force on 27 June 1918 but was not called up for service. In January 1941 he was appointed as a lieutenant colonel in the Australian Army Medical Corps, AIF. Next month he sailed for Malaya as senior physician with the 2/10th Australian General Hospital. Captured when the Japanese took Singapore in February 1942, he treated patients, including some with tuberculosis, at Changi and Kranji, strove to improve the prisoners' diet and presided over the Changi Medical Society. For his work he was mentioned in despatches. He developed beriberi and diphtheritic polyneuropathy, which threatened his life. After his release in August 1945, he returned to Sydney, where he was transferred to the Reserve of Officers in December.

Moving away from general medicine, Harvey became head of the thoracic unit at Royal Prince Alfred Hospital, which from 1957 was housed in the Page [q.v.11] Chest Pavilion. His work in tuberculosis management was helped by the appointment of his friend (Sir) Harry Wunderly [q.v.16] as the first Commonwealth director of tuberculosis in 1947; they corresponded frequently. Harvey worked long hours at the RPAH and the North Shore and at his consulting rooms in Macquarie Street, and regularly visited sanatoriums in Sydney, Picton and the Blue Mountains. He was highly regarded by the nursing staff and by his patients, most of whom were necessarily long-term. Although he retired from the honorary staff of both hospitals in 1957 aged 60, he continued in private practice until 1975. With improved tuberculosis detection and the advent of chemotherapy, he saw a significant reduction in the incidence and severity of this disease.

Harvey published a number of papers on tuberculosis and participated with colleagues on surveys in Sydney and Singapore relating to the incidence of the disease. He was a member of the National Health and Medical Research Council's tuberculosis committee (1945-50) and the National Tuberculosis Advisory Council (1949-70), and was president of the National Association for the Prevention of Tuberculosis and Other Chest Diseases (later National Tuberculosis and Chest Association) (1961-66). With colleagues he founded the eastern regional committee of the International Union Against Tuberculosis (of whose parent body he had been a member since the early 1920s) and served as president. In 1952 he was a founder of the Australian Laennec Society, the forerunner of the Thoracic Society of Australia and New Zealand. A member (1940-67) and president (1955-67) of the Medical Board of New South Wales, he was the first president of the General Medical Council of Australia from 1963.

Concerned by the growing incidence of carcinoma of the lung, Harvey led the campaign against tobacco smoking. In 1965 he urged the founding of the Australian Council on Smoking and Health. He incurred some unpopularity, particularly with the tobacco companies, who continued to deny that there was a causal link between smoking and disease. He visited schools and sporting bodies, regularly wrote to the press, and persuaded other medical organisations and colleagues to join the campaign. One specific achievement was the banning of cigarette vending machines in hospitals. When progress seemed slow, he persisted, saying that he had great faith in 'the inevitability of gradualness'. Much of the change in the attitudes of Australians to smoking can be attributed to Harvey and those whom he mobilised.

A foundation fellow (1938) of the Royal Australasian College of Physicians, Harvey served (1954-58) on its State committee. He was appointed CBE in 1965 and awarded the Sir Robert Philip medal of the Chest and Heart Association (England) in 1967. Tall, lean, of patrician appearance, and proud of his Irish Protestant heritage, he moved and talked quickly with an air of energy and authority. He belonged to the Union, University and Royal Sydney Golf clubs. A keen gardener and surfer, he played tennis and golf, and bowls in later years. He died on 17 October 1981 at his home at Bellevue Hill and, after a funeral service in St Paul's College chapel, was cremated. His three sons and two daughters survived him. The Australian War Memorial holds a pencil drawing (1943) of Harvey by Murray Griffin.

A. S. Walker, *Middle East and Far East* (1953); A. J. Proust (ed), *History of Tuberculosis in Australia, New Zealand and Papua New Guinea* (1991); J. C. Wiseman and R. J. Mulhearn (eds), *Roll of the Royal Australasian College of Physicians*, vol 2 (1994); *MJA*, 21 Aug 1965, p 338; *SMH*, 18 June 1969, p 4, 19 Oct 1981, p 8, 5 Nov 1981, p 6; B2455, Harvey, W C B, B883, item NX70668 (NAA); Harvey war diary (AWM); Harvey papers (Royal A'asian College of Physicians Lib, Sydney); private information.
ROBERT A. B. HOLLAND

HARVIE, EDYTHE ELLISON (1902-1984), architect, was born on 18 May 1902 at Prahran, Melbourne, daughter of Victorian-born parents Robert William Harvie, photographer, and his wife Alice Edington, née Marshall. Wanting to be an architect from an early age, Ellison was educated at Warwick, a girls' school at East Malvern. In 1920-23 she took courses at Swinburne Technical College. One of her lecturers, (Sir) Arthur Stephenson [q.v.12], invited her to serve her articles in the partnership he had recently established. She joined the firm in 1921 and remained there throughout her professional life.

In 1925-28 Harvie attended the Melbourne University Architectural Atelier (1925-28), where she excelled, her work being later recognised in the award of a diploma of architectural design (1938)—the first received by a woman. Registered as an architect and elected an associate (1928) of the Royal Victorian Institute of Architects, Harvie specialised in hospital architecture, a field in which Stephenson & Meldrum gained an international reputation. She led work on the Jessie Macpherson wing of the Queen Victoria Hospital (1928), and on designs for the St Vincent's (1933), Mercy (1934, 1937-39) and Freemasons (1935) hospitals. Hers was, she insisted, a 'co-operative profession'. Stephenson dubbed her his 'right hand' and the journalist Nora Cooper called her in 1936 'an architect of brilliant achievement and great promise'.

Harvie was made an associate of the new partnership Stephenson & Turner in 1938 and soon placed in charge of work on the Royal Melbourne Hospital. The demands of World War II meant she effectively ran both the practice and project, extending her interests in office management, qualifying as an accountant and developing a form of building contract that could adjust to economic instability. In 1946 she was made a partner of the firm and elected a fellow of the RVIA—the first woman to gain this status. She was also a member of the Royal Institute of British Architects and, later, a life fellow of the Royal Australian Institute of Architects.

A committed modernist, Harvie drew much of her inspiration from the innovative institutional work she observed during travels through the United States of America and Europe. Deploring the lack of architectural appreciation in Australia, she served on the RVIA's Board of Architectural Education (1946-56) and on the board of the University of Melbourne's faculty of architecture (1945-73).

Harvie also became an advocate for the professional development of women, urging their full participation in public life and an end to discrimination against them in employment. She continued to work on hospitals until her retirement from full-time practice in 1968, but also designed two buildings specifically serving women: the Lyceum Club (1959) and St Hilda's College (1963), University of Melbourne. The former has an elegance typical of late 1950s modernism; the latter, in spare, pale brick, is tempered with modest references to the traditions of collegial gothic.

Quietly charming, if austerely groomed—and to some younger colleagues daunting in her dedication—Ellison Harvie was president (1963-65) of the Lyceum Club and a foundation member (1948) and honorary treasurer of the Melbourne Soroptomist Club. A member of the Royal Society of Arts, London, and the Victorian Artists Society, she enjoyed landscape painting. Chess and golf were other interests. She had a working knowledge of Japanese, Chinese and Greek, and some Danish and Swedish. She died at East Melbourne on 27 September 1984 and was buried in Boroondara cemetery, Kew.

J. Willis and B. Hanna, *Women Architects in Australia 1900-1950* (2001); *Austn Home Beautiful*, 1 Aug 1936, p 13; *Sun News-Pictorial* (Melbourne), 21 Feb 1948, p 9; *Melbourne Univ Gazette*, Dec 1984, p 14.
HARRIET EDQUIST

HASELGROVE, COLIN POWELL (1904-1982), winemaker, was born on 30 April 1904 at Unley, Adelaide, youngest of six sons of Charles Frederick Haselgrove, ironmonger, and his wife Emilie Martha, née Powell. He was educated at Kingswood and Adelaide High schools and at Roseworthy Agricultural College (RDA, 1924). In his final year, as dux of Roseworthy, he was awarded its gold medal. As part of his course he studied oenology and viticulture. He worked the 1924 wine vintage at Angove's Pty Ltd's cellars, Renmark, and then joined Thomas Hardy [q.v.4] & Sons Ltd at McLaren Vale. In 1926 he studied wine-making at the Ecole Nationale d'Agriculture at Montpellier, France. Next year he studied distillation in the Cognac region and, at a winery at Tipasa, Algeria, learnt valuable lessons about making red wines in hot climates. Returning to work with Thomas Hardy, McLaren Vale, he transferred to the company's head office in Adelaide as chief winemaker in 1929. On 25 November that year at St Bartholomew's Church of England, Norwood, he married Joan Lashbrooke Austin.

After experimentation, Haselgrove (with Roger Warren [q.v.16]) produced Hardy's cabernet claret, released in 1936 and a top-selling wine for the next forty years. He took on an additional responsibility in 1930, as technical director at the London-based Emu Wine Co. Pty Ltd's winery at Morphett Vale. In 1938 he was appointed technical director of Hardys and also managing director of Emu Wines; he oversaw Emu's expansion in Western Australia. He was with Hardys for twenty-eight years; according to Rosemary Burden he had a 'phenomenal palate' and his contribution to the company was 'incalculable'. Divorced in 1946, on 4 July that year at the office of the principal registrar, Adelaide, he married Sybil ('Peg') McIntyre; they lived on the waterfront at Seacliff.

In May 1953 Haselgrove was appointed managing director and chief winemaker of Walter Reynell [q.v.6] & Sons Ltd, Reynella. There he developed premium table wines, including Reynella's Reserve cabernet sauvignon, and its popular Alicante sherry (dry flor). He retired in 1970. A founding council-member (1954-71) and chairman (1959-62, 1968-71) of the Australian Wine Research Institute, and member (1966-69) of the Australian Wine Board, he represented South Australia (1944-61, 1967-69) on the executive committee of the Federal Viticultural Council of Australia (from 1961 Federal Wine and Brandy Producers' Council of Australia). He was appointed OBE in 1971. In 1974 he helped to establish a new vineyard and winery, Heemskirk, at Pipers Brook, Tasmania. The wine writer John Stanford described him in 1983 as 'trim, tanned, handsome and apparently ageless'. He was 'a continuing senior authority, industry stirrer and consultant on technical matters'.

Well known as an ocean-racing yachtsman, Haselgrove won the Sydney to Hobart yacht race in 1950 with his yawl *Nerida* and came second in 1955 with his sloop *Cooroyba*. He was a vice-commodore (1937-52) of the Royal South Australian Yacht Squadron. Point Haselgrove, near Port Lincoln, was named for him. On 10 December 1982 he died at Brighton, Adelaide, and was cremated. He was survived by his wife and their three daughters, and by a son and one of two daughters of his first marriage.

His brother HARRY RONALD (1900-1978), also a winemaker, was born on 23 April 1900 at Unley. Educated at Kingswood High School and Roseworthy Agricultural College (RDA, 1919), Ron completed a wool-classing course before returning to Roseworthy in 1920 as a temporary analytical chemist. Next year he did his first vintage, at Renmark Growers' Distillery Ltd under the direction of Leo Buring [q.v.3]. In 1922-24 he studied at L'Ecole Nationale d'Agriculture, Montpellier. Back in Australia, working at Angove's Pty Ltd, Renmark and Tea Tree Gully, he helped to develop St Agnes brandy. In 1934 he became technical adviser for Mildura Winery Pty Ltd (from 1961 Mildara Wines Ltd) at Merbein, Victoria, as well. He left Angove's after becoming a director of Mildara in 1935. By improving the quality of their wines and introducing Mildara Supreme sherry, he effectively turned around the fortunes of the struggling winemaker; he was appointed managing director in 1949. Early in the 1950s he began to produce claret-style wines, purchasing grapes from the then little known Coonawarra district of South Australia. In 1955 Mildara bought land at Coonawarra, eventually developing 914 acres (370 ha) of vineyards. Haselgrove was chairman of the company in 1957-74.

Representing (1947-59) the Victorian Wine and Brandy Producers' Association on the Federal Viticulture Council, Ron Haselgrove served as its president in 1954-57. He was a member of the Australian Wine Board (1949-67) and a founding council-member (1954-72) and chairman (1958-59) of the Australian Wine Research Institute. In 1964 he was appointed OBE. Retiring as managing director in 1971, he devoted more time to his other interests: Australian Rules football, shooting, fishing and sailing. On 23 November 1926 he had married Elsie Janet Wigan at St Augustine's Church of England, Unley. Survived by his wife and their two sons and three daughters, he died on 2 April 1978 at his St Georges home and was cremated. His *Recollections of a Lifetime in the Australian Wine Industry* was published in 1985.

R. Burden, *A Family Tradition in Fine Wine-making* (1978); G. C. Bishop, *Australian Wine-making, the Roseworthy Influence* (1980); S. Wells (comp), *Fine Wines from the Desert* (1980); *Australian*, 22-23 Apr 1978, 'Mag', p 11, 15-16 Jan 1983, 'Mag', p 15; private information.

GEOFFREY C. BISHOP

HASTINGS, PETER DUNSTAN (1920-1990), journalist and editor, was born on 1 October 1920 at Wahroonga, Sydney, only child of Roland Hastings, Melbourne-born secretary and later barrister, and his wife Olive Mabel, née Waters, born in Tasmania. From the age of 7 Peter grew up at Manly, the beach suburb to whose sultry ambience he partly attributed his fascination with Melanesian and Indonesian regions. Another formative influence was a geography honours course at Sydney Grammar School that concentrated on the economic and human geography of the Pacific basin, including the Netherlands East Indies. He matriculated in 1941, and attended the University of Sydney without graduating.

In May 1941 Hastings enlisted in the Citizen Military Forces and on 26 January 1942 transferred to the Australian Imperial Force. As an acting sergeant in intelligence, he served in Brisbane and Melbourne with the Central Bureau, a code-breaking signals unit, and with the Far Eastern Liaison Office, which disseminated propaganda in enemy-occupied territory. In the course of his work he heard for the first time such resounding Indonesian nationalist names as Sukarno and Hatta. On 3 July 1944 he was discharged from the AIF as medically unfit.

Hastings was, however, singularly fit for journalism, already surprisingly well read and a natural writer. After the war ended he joined Consolidated Press Ltd and in 1948 was posted to New York. His Scottish-born wife Jeanette (Jan) Duncan England, whom he had married on 7 March 1946 at Harbord Presbyterian Church, accompanied him. In his dispatches to the *Daily Telegraph* during the next six years, Hastings paid particular attention to the United Nations. His main contact there was Gordon Jockel, a member of Australia's UN delegation.

Back in Sydney, Hastings held some uncongenial editorial posts on the *Sunday Telegraph*. But he also kept abreast of Australia's changing relations with colonial neighbours such as the Territory of Papua and New Guinea, and the newly independent Indonesia. That interest was deepened by his visit to the latter during a lengthy tour of South-East Asia in 1961. After the colonial order of Malaya and Singapore, he wrote, Jakarta was like 'a blow in the face'. But he was soon intrigued by Indonesia, especially by what he came to see as the new 'clash of civilisations' between Indonesian and Papuan ways of life in Irian Jaya (West Papua). From 1961 his attitude towards Indonesia changed from instinctive suspicion to pragmatic acceptance of Indonesia's claim to West New Guinea as advocated in Australia's diplomatic and academic communities. To an extent unrivalled by any of his journalistic peers, Hastings became a respected figure in both those communities.

As editor of Consolidated Press's *Bulletin* (1962-64), and foreign affairs writer for News Ltd's *Australian* (1966-70) and John Fairfax & Sons [qq.v.4,8] Ltd's *Sydney Morning Herald* (1970-74, 1976-90), Hastings enjoyed convivial access to Asian government officials, and to friends at various Australian embassies and in Canberra. He played 'the telephone like a virtuoso', and charmed his Indonesian contacts with such exotic vernacular as 'mate' and 'hooroo'. Although regarded by some as too tolerant of Indonesian aggrandisement, and sometimes rumoured to be an intelligence operative, Hastings was in fact always his own man. Banned from Indonesia for exposing its military preparation for the 1975 invasion of Portuguese Timor and again in 1984 for reporting the murder of the anthropologist Arnold Ap in Irian Jaya, on both occasions he was soon readmitted.

To the Joint Intelligence Organization Hastings was a valued but never contracted source of information and opinion. Nor was he immune from surveillance. His telephone was tapped and his Australian Security Intelligence Organization file, while containing 'nothing to his detriment', noted a talk by him on 'Colonialism—White or Brown', and his 'slight speech impediment'. The latter, a residual consequence of a cleft palate and lip, had been largely overcome by juvenile surgery and an adult moustache which gave him the appearance of a lean, safari-suited kaiser.

Between 1964 and 1977 Hastings combined journalism with other activities: he was the executive officer of the Council on New Guinea Affairs, a 'think tank' which he and (Sir) John Kerr had helped to found, editor of the council's influential journal, *New Guinea and Australia, the Pacific and South-East Asia*, and author of *New Guinea: Problems & Prospects* (1969). Joshing his way into the confidence of people like (Sir) Michael Somare, the first prime minister of Papua New Guinea, he devoted as many of his newspaper columns to that evolving state as he did to Indonesia.

From 1974 to 1976, during which time East Timor was invaded by Indonesia, Hastings was senior research fellow at the strategic and defence studies centre, Australian National University, in Canberra. Rejoining the *Sydney Morning Herald*, he was in 1979 appointed associate editor with responsibility for foreign affairs. His first marriage ended in divorce in 1980; he married Jolika Barbara Tie, née Bartsch, a Czechoslovakian-born public servant and divorcee, on 28 March 1981 at the registry of births, deaths and marriages, Sydney.

One of Hastings's best-remembered articles, published by the *SMH* on 13 February 1985 under the heading 'Corruption as an Art Form', left him harassed, though not subdued, for the rest of his life. It alleged the squandering of the equivalent of $US 9 billion of public money by the Filipino president, Ferdinand Marcos, and such 'cronies' as the coconut tycoon Eduardo Cojuangco. The latter tried, through legal process in Australia, to make the Fairfax company and Hastings reveal his sources and notes. Both refused. In court after court the case ran for five years, an inconclusive landmark in the history of Australian press freedom. Hastings died, after years of emphysema and ischaemic heart disease, on 7 August 1990 at his home at Manly shortly before the case was resolved. Survived by his wife and the two sons of his first marriage, he was cremated and his ashes were scattered in Manly's part of the Pacific basin. Earlier that year Hastings had been appointed AO and Griffith University, Queensland, had published his Indonesian memoir, *The Road to Lembang*.

Inside Indonesia, no 24, Oct 1990, p 11; *Asian Studies Review*, vol 14, no 2, 1990, p 185; *SMH*, 29 Nov 1984, p 3, 9 Aug 1990, pp 2, 11; B883, item NX85718, B884, item N109887 (NAA); private information.   GAVIN SOUTER

HAWKE, ALBERT REDVERS GEORGE (1900-1986), premier, was born on 3 December 1900 at Kapunda, South Australia, sixth of seven children of James Hawke, miner, and his wife Elizabeth Ann Blinman, née Pascoe, both born in South Australia. Albert's uncle, Richard Hawke, a prominent Australian Labor Party figure at Kapunda, was an early influence. Educated at Kapunda State School, 'Bert' left at 13; a serious boy with a keen sense of social justice, he was soon drawn towards politics. In 1916, aged 15, he joined the Kapunda branch of the ALP and became active in anti-conscription activities, forming views that he was to hold throughout his life. He had a series of jobs at Kapunda, Peterborough and Terowie, before becoming a non-articled clerk to a solicitor at Peterborough. On 25 September 1923 at Holder Memorial Methodist Church, West Adelaide, he married Mabel Evelyn Crafter (d.1967), a clerk. Securing Labor endorsement for the State seat of Burra Burra in 1923, he won it next year at a general election. His success was short-lived and he lost the seat in 1927.

Employed briefly by the South Australian Harbors Board, Hawke was appointed in October 1928 by the Western Australian ALP as country political organiser. For four years he worked on State and federal campaigns, travelling throughout Western Australia and gaining a reputation as an exceptional speechmaker. An accomplished writer, early in the 1930s he contributed a column, 'Labour Notes', to the *West Australian*. In April 1933 Hawke was elected to the Western Australian parliament defeating the sitting member, the Nationalist premier Sir James Mitchell [q.v.10], in Northam. His progress was rapid and in May 1936 he became minister for employment and labour in Philip Collier's [q.v.8] government. Serving (1936-47) in the cabinets of J. C. Willcock [q.v.12] and F. J. S. Wise [q.v.], he was variously minister for labour, employment, industrial development, works and water supplies.

Hawke was a reformist; for example, in 1937 when minister in charge of child welfare, he sponsored reforms of the Western Australia Children's Court, abolishing the requirement for the presiding magistrate to be a lawyer. He subsequently gave the post to a Methodist minister whose church he had attended at Northam. A self-described Christian socialist, he was always comfortable in the presence of clerics: his brother A. C. Hawke (father of the future prime minister R. J. L. Hawke) and an uncle were both ordained ministers. His social justice agenda was evident in 1946 when he took responsibility for an ambitious scheme to bring water to 12 million acres (4.9 million ha) of rural Western Australia. He saw the plan as revolutionising living and social conditions on farms and in country towns but it was opposed vigorously in the conservative-dominated Upper House, mainly on economic grounds, and shelved. In 1947 a new Liberal-Country Party government implemented a large part of the scheme, generously acknowledging Hawke's initiative.

In July 1951 Hawke succeeded Wise as Opposition leader. Tall, athletic, and ascetic-looking, he had a forceful and charismatic personality. His oratory and early exposure to working-class attitudes made him a powerful Labor figure in Western Australia. He revelled in the cut and thrust of parliamentary debates, and was masterful with interjections. At the same time he lacked the rigid, doctrinaire approach of other, less successful, Labor leaders. Many on the non-Labor side of politics admired him, pointing to his fair play and sense of humour. On 14 February 1953 he led the ALP to victory and became Western Australia's eighteenth premier.

As premier, treasurer, minister for child welfare and minister for industrial development, Hawke was to the forefront of significant social reform. In 1953 his government moved to give

Western Australian Aborigines citizenship rights; the bill passed the Lower House with considerable bipartisan support, but foundered in the Upper House. A fresh but watered-down version passed in 1954 in what was later described as a landmark for the State's Aborigines. The government also presided over a public housing boom aimed at reducing wartime waiting lists and building-material restrictions.

However, Hawke was seen to nurse strong suspicions, even animosity, towards business interests. While many saw him as moderate, others saw in him a deeply committed social-ist. He was quick to defend state-run enter-prises, many of which he had helped to expand, and was bitter in his denunciation of what he saw as the plundering of the railway system by the 'high priests of private enter-prise'. When under attack for failing to deal with communists in Western Australian unions, he branded as menaces to society both unscrupulous businessmen and communists. In August 1956 he announced plans for anti-profiteering legislation, a move denounced by business. Critics in the eastern States and overseas also strongly condemned it, claiming that the proposals would scare off much needed overseas investment. After protracted debate, and considerable amendment, the bill was passed with Country Party support. It was to be a hollow victory since the legislation dogged Hawke in the years ahead. In 1958 the London *Financial Times* reported remarks from a leading British industrialist, Sir Halford Reddish, describing Hawke's government as 'socialist'.

Other observers, for example Rohan Rivett [q.v.16], argued that Hawke exhibited strong and wise leadership, at the time lacking in Labor federally. John Graham, writing in the Sydney *Observer*, described him as 'the only Labour [*sic*] politician who might have carried on the Chifley [q.v.13] tradition of balanced and effective leadership'. Later, Arthur Calwell [q.v.13], not unreasonably, disputed these and other similar assessments. In any event Hawke saw no value in trading the premiership for the prospect of uncertain federal leadership.

There can be little doubt that the bruising public debate over Hawke's attitude to busi-ness contributed to his loss at the polls in 1959. His next six years in Opposition climaxed, virtually on the eve of the February 1965 gen-eral election, in a bitter public feud between himself and the powerful Western Australian and federal ALP secretary, F. E. (Joe) Chamberlain [q.v.], over Hawke's public advo-cacy of talks between the ALP and the Demo-cratic Labor Party. Chamberlain, rigid and doctrinaire, trenchantly opposed such rapport and blamed Hawke for Labor's defeat in Western Australia in 1965; none the less, within days of the poll Hawke was re-elected unopposed to the leadership. A Chamberlain-inspired censure of Hawke by the federal exec-utive followed in May.

Realising that his public life was nearing its end, Hawke resigned the leadership in De-cember 1966. Next year he publicly opposed 'Australia's ghastly policy of conscripting twenty-year-olds to the Vietnam War'. He retired from parliament in 1968 and in 1974 returned to his native South Australia. In his spare time he enjoyed tennis, billiards and reading. Survived by his daughter, he died on 14 February 1986 in Adelaide and was cremated.

F. K. Crowley, *State Election: The Fall of the Hawke Government* (1959); P. Biskup, *Not Slaves, Not Citizens* (1973); D. Black (ed), *The House on the Hill* (1991); *News* (Adelaide), 24 July 1956, p 19; *Financial Times* (London), 28 Apr 1958, p 2; *Observer* (Sydney), 13 Dec 1958, p 679; *Independent* (Perth), 28 Dec 1969, p 9, 4 Jan 1970, p 14, 11 Jan 1970, p 16, 18 Jan 1970, p 22, 25 Jan 1970, p 20; P. Pendal, interview with A. R. G. Hawke (ts, 1971-73, SLWA); personal knowledge.

PHILLIP PENDAL

HAWTHORNE, FIFI OLIVE ANNETTE (1899-1986), headmistress, was born on 16 July 1899 at North Sydney, only child of Frank Hawthorne Anthony Wilson, an actor born at Dunedin, New Zealand, and his locally born wife Eliza (Biddie), née Nitzschmann. Fifi later used Hawthorne as her surname. As her parents were both theatre professionals, in early childhood she toured with them in South and Western Australia and New Zealand. After attending Miss Layton's school, North Sydney, she boarded at the Collegiate High School for Girls, Paddington, which became St Gabriel's College and Kindergarten for Girls, Waverley. The Sisters of the Church, an Anglican order who ran the school, inspired her to take up a teaching career. Her attachment to the Anglo-Catholic branch of the Anglican Church remained an enduring feature of her life. It was an attachment shared by her friend Hilda Epstein, who taught with her at St Gabriel's and later at Kambala Church of England School for Girls. While attending the Univer-sity of Sydney (BA, 1922), Fifi lived at St Gabriel's and, from 1920, taught there with responsibility for sport. She became secretary of the Secondary Schools' Tennis Association in 1921. In 1932 she taught at Methodist Ladies' College, Burwood.

As principal of Kambala at Rose Bay from 1933, Miss Hawthorne was organised, meti-culous and compassionate. Her priorities were firmly academic, and some of those to whom she taught Latin declensions never forgot them. She placed importance on the study of languages, but later accepted the need for more science, and in 1958 chemistry was introduced to the senior school. Taking responsibility for the daily hymns and prayers in assembly, she also taught scripture in the junior high school and prepared the girls for confirmation. She believed that pupils were leaving school too young. Before the Wyndham [q.v.] scheme introduced an additional year's schooling in New South Wales in 1962, Kambala girls on leaving were usually a year older than the norm. Living at the school —in small quarters until given a flat in 1958— she was always in evidence, her hair in a neat bun, her black gown flapping, as she walked around inspecting everything from the blinds to the gardens. 'Her' girls were in awe of her but they sensed the sympathetic and motherly concern behind her meticulous checks on their behaviour and uniforms. All the milestones in their later lives were marked by a letter in her distinctive handwriting.

A member (1940-65) of the council of the Teachers' Guild of New South Wales, Hawthorne was later made an honorary life member. She also served (1941-64) on the committee of the Teachers' Central Registry. Honorary secretary (1950-52) of the Headmistresses' Association of Australia, she was also president (1939 and 1956) of the Association of Headmistresses of the Independent Schools of New South Wales. After her retirement in 1966 she moved to her house at Northbridge, from which she entertained former staff and pupils. In 1972 she was appointed MBE. The history of Kambala that she compiled for the Old Girls' Union was published that year. Never married, she died on 9 July 1986 at Greenwich and was cremated.

A. Nobbs, *Kambala* (1987).

ALANNA M. NOBBS

HAY, ALICE IVY; see WIGMORE, A.

HAYES, VINA EVELYN (EVIE) (1912-1988), entertainer, was born on 1 June 1912 in Seattle, Washington, United States of America, daughter of George Hayes, stage mechanist, and his wife Eva, a soubrette. Evelyn's childhood was spent on the theatre circuit; her stage début, aged 4, was singing and dancing in a Christmas show. She took acting classes, toured the West Coast vaudeville summer circuits under the care of her mother, and appeared as an extra in Hollywood films, gaining a small role in Warner Brothers' *Hold Everything* (1930) and making several musical shorts.

After touring with Georges Carpentier's revue company, Hayes moved in 1934 to New York, where she worked as a 'song plugger' at Irving Berlin's music publishing house and sang on radio and in nightclubs. Will Mahoney [q.v.15] soon engaged her as his leading lady for a variety tour of the United Kingdom and Europe and, now known as Evie, she sang for the British Broadcasting Corporation, appeared in cabaret and cut her first records. On 26 March 1938 at the register office, Westminster, London, Evie and Will were married. It was Mahoney's third marriage; he was 44 years old and she was 25.

While on their honeymoon, Mahoney and Hayes travelled to Australia to appear on the Tivoli variety circuit. The Melbourne première of their revue, *Why Be Serious?*, on 22 August was (the *Age* declared) a 'triumph'. They toured Australasia for several years. In 1943-48 Mahoney managed the Cremorne Theatre, Brisbane, and with Hayes presented revues, pantomimes and musicals that proved immensely popular with Australian and American troops. They raised £500 000 for war charities.

Though not a conventional beauty, Hayes possessed a vivacious charm, an affable American accent and a singing style that ranged from sultry to strident. In 1947 she won the coveted lead role, originally played by Ethel Merman, in *Annie Get Your Gun*, which opened at His Majesty's Theatre, Melbourne. This was the first large-scale new musical staged in Australia after the war; at the end of its marathon three-and-a-half-year tour, Hayes visited the USA and underwent plastic surgery to reshape her nose. She returned to Melbourne in 1952 for a brief revival of *Annie*, then starred in *Kiss Me, Kate*, a revival of *Oklahoma!* and, in 1953, another Merman show, *Call Me Madam*.

From 1958 Hayes appeared regularly on television; she worked as a compère, singer, comedian and commercial presenter on Graham Kennedy's 'In Melbourne Tonight'. In 1963 she took the title role in the Australian musical *Mata Hari, the Flame of Istanbul*, at the Bowl Music Hall, and three years later toured as Mrs Brice in *Funny Girl*. After Mahoney's death in 1967, she established a talent school for children, which led in 1971 to new prominence as a judge on Channel 10's 'Young Talent Time'. Her warmth and gentle encouragement endeared her to a rising generation of performers.

In 1969 Hayes was diagnosed with multiple sclerosis, but she persisted with teaching, television and speaking engagements. On 26-27 October 1988 she sang in a World Expo '88 variety concert at the Lyric Theatre, Brisbane. Eight weeks later, on 26 December 1988, Evie Hayes died at South Caulfield, Melbourne; she was buried in Melbourne general cemetery.

J. Crampton, *Evie Hayes* (1992); P. Parsons (ed), *Companion to Theatre in Australia* (1995); *People* (Sydney), 24 Mar 1954, p 17.   F. VAN STRATEN

HAYTER, LORNA; *see* BYRNE

HAYWARD, SIR EDWARD WATERFIELD (1903-1983), businessman and philanthropist, was born on 10 November 1903 at Kent Town, Adelaide, younger son of South Australian-born Arthur Dudley Hayward, draper, and his wife Mary Anne, née Pagan, from Scotland. Arthur was later chairman and managing director of John Martin & Co. Ltd, Adelaide. Educated at Westminster School, London, and the Collegiate School of St Peter, Adelaide, Edward, known as 'Bill', spent three years in New South Wales as a jackeroo on sheep stations, including F. B. S. Falkiner's [q.v.8] Haddon Rig, Warren, and bought a pastoral property at Narrabri. To gain experience in retailing, he worked in 1930 for (Sir) Sydney Snow [q.v.12] Ltd, Sydney. At his father's request, he joined John Martin's next year and soon became a director. In 1933 he initiated the store's annual Christmas pageant, to give pleasure to children suffering from the effects of the Depression. The floats and costumes, and the 'magic cave', were designed and produced with the resources of John Martin's.

On 12 February 1935 at St Peter's College chapel, Hayward married with Anglican rites Ursula Barr Smith, daughter of Tom Elder Barr Smith [q.v.11]. As a wedding gift Barr Smith gave the couple 100 acres (40 ha) of land at Springfield, on which they built a large 'Jacobethan'-style house, designed by (Sir) James Irwin [q.v.]. They named it Carrick Hill. It incorporated oak doors, windows and panelling, and the 'Waterloo' staircase, all purchased at the demolition sale of a 1546 mansion, Beaudesert, in Staffordshire, England. Eventually they developed extensive landscaped grounds around the house.

Commissioned in the Militia on 4 September 1939, Hayward performed intelligence duties at Keswick Barracks, Adelaide, before joining the Australian Imperial Force in July 1940. He arrived in the Middle East in February 1941 and served at Tobruk, Libya, with the 2/43rd Battalion. In August he transferred to the Australian Army Canteens Service as a major. Back in Australia, in June 1943 he was promoted to lieutenant colonel and appointed a deputy director in the AACS. His duties took him to Papua, New Guinea, Morotai and Labuan. He was twice mentioned in despatches and was awarded the American Bronze Star Medal for his work. On 20 November 1945 he transferred to the Reserve of Officers.

Hayward returned to Adelaide and in 1946 became joint managing director (with his brother) of John Martin's. During the war he had noticed that American soldiers were willing to swap a bottle of whisky for three bottles of Coca-Cola; recognising that it was a profitable product, he acquired the franchise and in 1950 founded Coca-Cola Bottlers (Adelaide) Pty Ltd with the help of other local businessmen. He was to remain chairman of this company until 1983.

In 1947 Hayward had joined the South Australian Centre of the St John Ambulance Association committee; he served as inaugural chairman of the St John Council for South Australia in 1950-76 and as president in 1976-83. In 1951 he arranged for the council to take over the State's ambulance services. He was appointed K.St.J. in 1959.

Knighted in 1961, Sir Edward was made chairman of John Martin's in 1964; he oversaw the expansion of the business into the suburbs. He was also chairman of South Australian Telecasters Ltd (1966-70) and of South Australian Insurance Holdings Ltd (1972-75), deputy-chairman of the Finance Corporation of Australia Ltd (1963-78), and a board-member of the Bank of Adelaide (1970-78), and Bennett & Fisher Ltd (1962-83). Continuing to pursue his pastoral interests, he and his wife bred prize-winning Hereford cattle at their Silverton Park stud at Cape Jervis. He also bred and owned racehorses.

Keen on sport, Hayward played in the State polo team until middle-aged and was president of the South Australian Polo Association (1956-60) and the Adelaide Polo Club (1958-60). He also enjoyed swimming, golf and tennis. A founding governor (1960-66) of the Adelaide Festival of Arts, he loved music, especially jazz. He and his wife enjoyed travel. They filled their home with valuable collections of sculpture, antique furniture, objets d'art and paintings, mainly Australian, French and English. At John Martin's main store there was a fine art gallery. Hayward was an ardent monarchist and from 1928 a member of the Adelaide Club.

Widowed in 1970, Sir Edward married Jean Katherine Bridges, née Folder, a widow, on 30 June 1972 at the register office, Westminster, London. In 1973, although he had no children, he was named South Australian Father of the Year in acknowledgment of his continuing commitment to the children's Christmas pageant. Genial and, by then, silver-haired, 'Mr Bill', as he was always known at the store, blew a special gold whistle to start off the pageant. He retired as chairman of John Martin's in 1980. Survived by his wife, he died suddenly on 13 August 1983 at Carrick Hill and was cremated. In 1970 he and his first wife had decided to bequeath the property and its contents, including their extensive art collection, to the South Australian government; it is now open to the public.

I. Howie-Willis, *South Australians and St. John Ambulance, 1885-1985* (1985); J. Henley (ed), *S.A.'s Greats* (2001); *News* (Adelaide), 8 Dec 1970, p 42; *Advertiser* (Adelaide), 15 July 1983, p 6, 15 Aug 1983, p 14; B883, item SX8887 (NAA).   ROSE WILSON

HEALY, GEORGE (1905-1982), fireman and public servant, was born on 1 July 1905 at Mangalore, Victoria, third of eight children of Victorian-born parents John Healy, railway porter, and his wife Charlotte, née Walmsley. Leaving school at 14, George was employed in various clerical positions before joining the Melbourne Metropolitan Fire Brigade in June 1927. On 19 June 1928 at the Sacred Heart Catholic Church, Kew, he married Mary Berenice Bond. Advancing through the ranks to station officer, he was a member of the Institute of Fire Engineers and of the United Fire-fighters' Union of Australia. In August 1942 he became deputy chief officer of the Brisbane Metropolitan Fire Brigades and on 17 July 1946 was appointed chief officer. He was an inaugural member (1948) of the Queensland Rural Fires Board, serving as chairman in 1964-82.

Highly regarded as a fire-fighter, Healy insisted that firemen undertook rigorous training, especially in the use of breathing apparatus. This paid dividends many times, particularly at fires inside ships on the Brisbane River. He made a point of knowing the names of all the men under his command and personally supported them on the fire-ground; he would not send his men where he himself was not prepared to go. Injured in a fuel-depot fire in 1969, he subsequently received a commendation from the governor Sir Alan Mansfield [q.v.15]. He liked publicity and encouraged the press to cover fires and to issue regular warnings on fire risk.

Interested in politics and history, Healy was a long-time member of the Australian Labor Party. He published *A.L.P.: The Story of the Labor Party* (1955); his name was spelt Healey on the title page. In 1960 he supported the Metropolitan Fire Brigades Board and the Australian Workers' Union, which had represented Queensland firemen since 1917, when firemen were struggling to form a local branch of the United Firefighters' Union. Their application was rejected in a decision upheld by the Industrial Court. Healy's life member-ship of the UFU in Victoria was subsequently revoked, partly because he resigned from the ALP and joined the Democratic Labor Party. In 1967 he graduated BA from the University of Queensland. He retired in 1970 after a record twenty-four years as chief officer.

In the late 1940s and early 1950s Healy had been president of the Queensland Australian National Football League. He was a member from 1948 of the Queensland Health Education Council, serving as chairman in 1955. President of the Returned Services League of Australia's Anzac House appeal, he was also inaugural chairman (1971-75) of the Salvation Army's Red Shield appeal in Brisbane. He was a member of the Brisbane North Rotary Club. As chairman of the Queensland Rostrum Council of Freemen, Brisbane, he was admired for his ability to summarise accurately, without taking notes, the arguments of debating teams. He was appointed OBE in 1976. Survived by his wife and their son and daughter, he died on 23 March 1982 at Auchenflower and was cremated. His son, Anthony, was a judge of the District Court of Queensland in 1987-2005.

K. D. Calthorpe and K. Capell, *Brisbane Ablaze* (2000) and for sources; *Courier-Mail* (Brisbane), 10 June 1950, p 5, 22 Apr 1958, p 7, 29 Jan 1963, p 5, 24 Mar 1982, p 3; *Telegraph* (Brisbane), 29 Aug 1960, p 13, 24 July 1965, p 1; *Sunday Mail* (Brisbane), 16 Feb 1969, p 1; private information.
                                                K. CAPELL

HEALY, GERTRUDE (1894-1984), musician and Sister of Mercy, was born on 18 March 1894 at Ballarat East, Victoria, third surviving child of Victorian-born parents, Michael John Healy, railway engine driver, and his wife Mary Helena, née Costello. Educated locally at Sacred Heart College, Gertrude demonstrated prodigious gifts as a violinist, first coming to prominence in the Royal South Street Society competitions, where she competed against (Sir) Bernard Heinze [q.v.] in 1906, 1907 and 1908, winning many awards for violin. In 1907 she gained first prize for solo violin at the First Australian Exhibition of Women's Work, and came to the attention of G. W. L. Marshall-Hall [q.v.10], who awarded her a scholarship to his Albert Street Conservatorium of Music, East Melbourne. She studied violin with Franz Dierich and cello with Louis Hattenbach and in November 1908 made her Melbourne Town Hall début, performing Beethoven's *Romance in F* with the conservatorium orchestra.

Having endured twice-weekly trips from Ballarat to Melbourne for more than a year, in 1909 Gertrude moved with her family to North Melbourne. Marshall-Hall, supporting her registration as a teacher of violin, noted that Healy's 'musical intelligence' was 'quite exceptional'. After coming second to Heinze in contesting the Clarke scholarship to the Royal College of Music in 1912, she determined to make her own way to Europe. As one critic noted of her fund-raising concert, held at the Melbourne Town Hall in April 1913, she was 'easily first' among 'all the violinists who have come forward in recent years': her tone was 'pure and rich', and her intonation 'almost beyond reproach'. In February 1914 she sailed from Melbourne with her sister Kathleen.

Healy studied with Siegfried Eberhardt in Berlin until the outbreak of war, and then in London with Albert Sammons, to whom she owed her affinity with the works of Bax, Delius and Elgar. While in England she undertook patriotic work, playing in hospitals and for charities. She also performed in Ireland and would later play Irish airs with conviction. The sisters returned to Melbourne via New York in 1920.

A highly respected teacher of violin at Albert Street from 1923, and later conductor of its chamber orchestra, Healy exposed Australian or Melbourne audiences to works by Bax, Bloch, Delius, Dohnanyi, Elgar, Roussel, Goossens [q.v.14] and Glanville-Hicks [q.v.]. The often provocative modernity of her programs also encompassed Franck, Stravinsky, Hindemith and Nielson. In 1925 she impressed the visiting Austrian violinist and composer Fritz Kriesler, who invited her to return to Europe and continue her studies with him— an offer she declined. As a soloist, and in ensembles including the Melbourne Trio with Rita Hope and Dallas Fraser, she appeared on many concert stages, performing for the Australian Musical News Chamber Music Club, the British Music Society, the Melbourne Music Club and the Australian Broadcasting Commission, and with the Melbourne Symphony Orchestra.

Following Kathleen's death in 1947, Healy resigned from the conservatorium and in January 1948 entered the Convent of Mercy, Ballarat East, joining her sister Eileen (Mother Bonaventure) [q.v.14 Healy] and taking as her name in religion Sr Catherine of Siena. She taught music at Sacred Heart College, tutored the college orchestra and in 1950 established its annual Music for Strings concerts, through which she continued to introduce new works, including those of Britten and her own compositions. These activities, and her teaching, enhanced the college's reputation for excellence in music education. Remembered for possessing a profound spirituality, she died on 6 October 1984 at Ballarat and was buried in its new cemetery.

Austn Musical News, 1 Sept 1920, p 47, 1 Feb 1923, p iii; *Herald* (Melbourne), 31 Jan 1977, p 13; P. J. Lynch, Gertrude Healy (MA thesis, Monash Univ, 1996); Marshall-Hall Conservatorium diary (Melba Memorial Conservatorium of Music Archives); teacher registration file, VPRS 10061 (PRO, Vic).   PETER LYNCH

HEBART, SIEGFRIED PAUL (1909-1990), Lutheran theologian, was born on 14 September 1909 at Tanunda, South Australia, second child of German-born Theodor Jacob Hermann Gottlob Hebart, Lutheran minister, and his wife Anna Charlotte, née Lademann, who was born at Hermannsburg mission station, Northern Territory. Siegfried grew up in the manse at Tanunda; he attended the Langmeil Church and Tanunda Public schools, and Immanuel College at Point Pass and North Adelaide. A gifted and hard-working student, he gained a government scholarship and entered the University of Adelaide (BA, 1930; MA, 1932), where he concentrated on classics, history, philosophy and German. He was strongly involved in the Australian Student Christian Movement.

After studying in 1932-33 at Immanuel Theological Seminary, Adelaide, Hebart continued his training at Friedrich-Alexander University of Erlangen (Th.D., 1939), north of Nuremberg, Germany, where he was influenced by Werner Elert, Paul Althaus, Hermann Sasse and Otto Procksch. His doctoral dissertation on the nineteenth-century Lutheran churchman, Wilhelm Löhe, was published in German in 1939. On 30 January that year he married Anny Dietz of Nuremberg. Back in South Australia, on 11 June he was ordained into the ministry of the United Evangelical Lutheran Church in Australia by Rev. J. H. S. Heidenreich [q.v.4]. He taught at Immanuel College until 1942, when he became the first Australian-born lecturer at Immanuel Theological Seminary; in 1945 he was appointed principal. Besides teaching systematic theology and other subjects, in 1948-53 he also edited and contributed papers and book reviews to the *Lutheran Quarterly*. From 1954 he was active in the Lutheran Student Fellowship at the University of Adelaide, where for a number of years he taught German. In 1955-59 he was chairman of the ASCM State council.

Secretary of the intersynodical committee that planned the amalgamation of the two Lutheran churches in Australia, Hebart was a skilful communicator and negotiator. After union in 1966, Immanuel and Concordia seminaries merged the following year, and in 1968 Hebart became principal of the newly named Luther Seminary. At synods, pastors' conferences, retreats, and in-service training schools he was always heard with attention and respect, especially for his positive and progressive thinking. He was an early member of the Adelaide Theological Circle. An ecumenist, he promoted inter-church co-operation in theological education, co-chaired the Roman Catholic-Lutheran dialogue and formulated a number of common theological statements. He was a popular presenter of talks and devotions on radio and television. In the pulpit he presented Christocentric sermons that his listeners could relate to their daily lives.

Invited to lecture on the Continent and in the United States of America, Hebart had served (1964-67) as chairman of the Lutheran World Federation's Commission on Education. In the 1970s his international reputation took him to South-East Asia for conferences and meetings to build up relationships between Australian and Asian theological schools. He retired in 1979 and next year was appointed AM. His interests included music, walking and the theatre. Survived by his wife and their two daughters and two sons, he died on 12 November 1990 in North Adelaide and was buried in Langmeil cemetery, Tanunda.

D. E. and I. V. Hansen, *With Wings* (1995); J. T. E. Renner, 'Siegfried Paul Hebart: A Tribute', *Lutheran Theological Journal*, vol 13, nos 2 & 3, Nov 1979, p 6; M. E. Schild, eulogy given at S. Hebart's funeral (ts, 1990, copy in ADB file); private information and personal knowledge.

J. T. E. RENNER

HEDDERMAN, JOHN WILLIAM (1916-1986), army officer and builder, was born on 25 June 1916 at Rocky River, near Uralla, New South Wales, fourth of six children of William Maurice Hedderman (d.1933), maintenance man, and his wife Grace, née Dowling, both born in New South Wales. Being the eldest son, John left school early to work on the family farm. His mother relied heavily on his labour and the income he received from working with his uncle on fence-building jobs. When his eldest sister, Daisy, married in 1936, she and her husband assumed the running of the family property and John left to seek work.

Having moved to Melbourne, on 22 April 1940 Hedderman enlisted in the Australian Imperial Force. He was 5 ft 11 ins (180 cm) tall, with a fair complexion, blue eyes and brown hair. In September he embarked for the Middle East, where he joined the 2/6th Battalion in February 1941. He fought in the Greek campaign in April. His battalion then underwent a period of refitting and training in Palestine and performed garrison duties in Syria before sailing to Ceylon (Sri Lanka) in March 1942 to counter a possible Japanese invasion. When this failed to materialise, the unit returned to Australia in August. Hedderman had been promoted to corporal in May.

The 2/6th arrived at Milne Bay, Papua, in October and flew to Wau, New Guinea, in January 1943. Hedderman was made lance sergeant in February. In June he led a patrol during a period of fierce fighting in the Mubo area. Over four days he repeatedly risked his life, directing mortar fire from positions dangerously close to the enemy, rescuing wounded men while under heavy fire and attacking Japanese positions, sometimes single-handedly. He was awarded the Military Medal for his 'great personal courage, initiative and leadership'. In August he was promoted to sergeant.

The battalion returned to Australia in September and next month Hedderman was sent to an officer cadet training unit. On 12 February 1944 he married Monica Bernadette Fitzpatrick, a typist, at St James's Catholic Church, Gardenvale, Melbourne. Rejoining his unit in March, he sailed for Aitape, New Guinea, in December. Late in March 1945 he led a series of reconnaissance and fighting patrols in the Maprik area. For his selfless bravery over several days of heavy fighting, during which he once again carried out the daring rescue of a wounded man, he was awarded the Distinguished Conduct Medal.

On 9 August 1945 'Smoky' Hedderman was commissioned lieutenant, but the war was soon over and he transferred to the Reserve of Officers on 5 December. He rejoined his family at Brighton, Melbourne. Having survived the war unscathed, he was wounded by an explosion at a brick-factory kiln in 1949. Next year they moved to Box Hill, where Hedderman planted a wide variety of fruit trees. Beginning work in the building industry with an ex-army mate in 1954, he became a works supervisor with the Craig Davis company in 1955. He also volunteered his time to help to build local schools. In retirement he enjoyed cooking and indulged his lifelong love of reading. Widowed in 1980, he died of chronic alcoholism on 22 December 1986 at Hawthorn and was cremated. His four sons and daughter survived him.

D. Dexter, *The New Guinea Offensives* (1961); G. Long, *The Final Campaigns* (1963); D. Hay, *Nothing over Us* (1984); B883, item VX12728 (NAA); private information.   IAN HODGES

HEFFERNAN, JAMES PATRICK (1926-1981), farmer and lobbyist, was born on 17 March 1926 at Naracoorte, South Australia, fourth surviving child of John Heffernan, farmer, and his wife Mary Mabel, née Knight, both Victorian-born. Jim was educated at Kybybolite State School and the Christian Brothers' Rostrevor College, Adelaide. He trained briefly as an electrical engineer with Broken Hill Proprietary Ltd, Whyalla, until 1947 when, attracted by the postwar boom in agriculture, he joined his father in farming at Kybybolite. In 1965 he moved to Apsley, Victoria, purchasing a 2150-acre (870 ha) property, Bringalbert, where he raised merino sheep and Murray Grey-cross beef cattle. On 8 December 1951 at Rostrevor College chapel, he had married Joyce Leslie Dickenson, a telephonist.

Dismayed by the lack of organisation among farmers and graziers, in 1959 Heffernan joined the South Australian branch of the Australian Primary Producers' Union. As State (1961) and federal (1962-67) president, he lobbied for the merger of farmer organisations. He took a particular interest in the marketing of rural produce, serving as chairman of the Co-operative Farmers and Graziers Direct Meat Supply Company (1970-74) and of the Wool Committee of the Victorian Farmers' Union (1971-72), and as a member of the Australian Wool Industry Conference.

In 1973-79 Heffernan was president of the VFU. Described by a journalist as 'well-spoken, tall, with well-groomed greying hair and taste-ful tailor-made suits', he was prepared to work with both Labor and coalition governments while sparing neither in his criticism. During his presidency farmers suffered severe declines in wool and wheat prices. Forcefully advancing their interests, he condemned the decision of the Whitlam government to end the superphosphate bounty while also accept-ing appointment as chairman (1974-75) of its National Rural Advisory Council. In 1977 he rejected the defence of the coalition treasurer, (Sir) Phillip Lynch [q.v.], that the government had limited powers to stem falling prices for farm products. The provision of a floor price for wool and a stabilisation scheme for wheat were, he argued, examples of the 'orderly mar-keting' through which statutory bodies could save farmers from the 'rapacious onslaughts of laissez-faire capitalists'.

Heffernan travelled constantly throughout rural Victoria, often flying himself in a hired aircraft, listening closely to farmers and speak-ing on rural issues. He opposed death duties, called for council amalgamation to reduce farmers' costs, proposed cheaper telephone connection fees, and was alarmed by the age-ing of farmers and the drift of population to the cities. A critic of trade unions and the Common-wealth Arbitration Court, he opposed tariffs for local manufacturing industries and had little sympathy with the environmental move-ment. Championing the export of uranium, he also favoured the use of herbicides, the export of kangaroo meat and the culling of corellas.

In 1979 Heffernan became the first treasurer of the National Farmers' Federation. He remained a prominent rural lobbyist. On 23 March 1981 at Bringalbert he died suddenly of myocardial infarction, survived by his wife, their four daughters and two of their three sons. He was buried in Naracoorte cemetery.

T. Connors, *To Speak with One Voice* (1996); *Sun News-Pictorial* (Melbourne), 6 July 1973, p 19; *Herald* (Melbourne), 16 Feb 1974, p 3; *Weekly Times* (Melbourne), 7 Dec 1977, p 5.   CHARLES FAHEY

HEINZE, SIR BERNARD THOMAS (1894-1982), musician and conductor, was born on 1 July 1894 at Shepparton, Victoria, fourth child of Victorian-born parents Benjamin Heinze, jeweller, and his wife Minnie Frederica, née Greenwell. Both parents were amateur musi-cians who encouraged their children to follow their example. Educated at St Patrick's Col-lege, Ballarat, Bernard became a pupil of Walter Gude, the founder of the local Lyric Orchestra. At 16 he won an Australian Music Examinations Board scholarship to the Mel-bourne University Conservatorium (MA, 1948). He was awarded the (Sir William) Clarke [q.v.3] scholarship at the end of his first year, enabling him to study at the Royal Col-lege of Music, London, where his teachers included the violinist Achille Rivarda, the pianist Herbert Sharpe, and the composers Frank Bridge and Sir Charles Stanford.

World War I interrupted Heinze's studies. Commissioned on 23 September 1915 in the Royal Garrison Artillery, he served on the Western Front and as an aide-de-camp to Major General Sir Herbert Guthrie Smith, the director of artillery. After being demobilised in 1920 he wrote music criticism for the London *Saturday Review* while completing his term as Clarke scholar. In 1920 the Gowland Harrison scholarship took him to the Schola Cantorum, Paris: he studied history and com-position under its founder, Vincent d'Indy, violin with Nestor Lejeune, and *solfège* with G. De Lioncourt. Having a particular interest in orchestral techniques, he attended re-hearsals of the Concert Coloune under Gabriel Pierné. In 1922 he toured southern Europe as a member of the Lejeune String Quartet, but left it after only a few months to study violin with Willy Hess in Berlin.

In 1923 Heinze returned to Australia, in part to adjudicate the South Street eisteddfod, Ballarat. The following year he joined the Mel-bourne University Conservatorium as teacher of violin. He rapidly gained prominence and supporters as conductor of the Melbourne University Symphony Orchestra and founder of the Melbourne String Quartet. In 1925 he succeeded William Laver as Ormond [qq.v.10, 5] professor of music: 'his energy is bound-less', *Table Talk* noted, 'his ambition, the same'.

Heinze was committed to increasing the public performance of music, and to securing the professionalism of players. In 1925 he in-augurated free concerts for schools at which he lectured and conducted; he also introduced subscription series and, after a short visit to Europe in 1928, launched celebrity concerts, featuring many outstanding overseas per-formers. Already the conductor of the Royal Melbourne Philharmonic Society (1927-53), after a period of competition with Fritz Hart's [q.v.9] Melbourne Symphony Orchestra, in

1933 he amalgamated the USO with the effectively bankrupt MSO (Victorian Symphony Orchestra after 1949), remaining with it until 1956.

As a conductor, Heinze revealed his strength in the interpretation of the Romantics, from Beethoven to Tchaikovsky and Elgar; Richard Strauss, Mahler and Sibelius were also high on his preferred list. New music featured regularly in his programs: in 1929 he gave the first Melbourne performances of works by Grainger [q.v.9], Rimsky-Korsakov and Borodin, and in 1933 the first Australian performance of Bruckner's symphony in C minor. In 1931 he was made a fellow of the Royal College of Music. At Newman College chapel, University of Melbourne, on 6 July 1932, he married Valerie Antonia, daughter of Sir David Hennessy [q.v.9].

Heinze's influence was greatly enhanced by his appointment in 1929 as part-time director-general of music to the Australian Broadcasting Co., and consolidated by his role from 1934 as part-time music adviser to its successor, the Australian Broadcasting Commission. In these positions he supervised performance of music for broadcast, co-ordinated educational concerts, and championed the ABC's policy, adopted in 1936, of establishing professional symphony orchestras in each State. In 1938 he toured Europe and the United States of America to investigate the role of radio in promoting music, also conducting in Paris, Berlin, Budapest and Helsinki, and serving as a juror for the Concours Ysaÿe in Brussels (for which he was appointed to the Ordre de la Couronne).

Amid the stringencies of war, in 1941-45 the university agreed to release Heinze to act as chief resident conductor for the ABC's celebrity concert seasons. In part through wartime necessity, he included Australian artists as soloists. Music could easily have stagnated in such a climate, but instead it flourished. While staging popular festivals featuring Beethoven's and Russian music (in Melbourne and Sydney respectively, in 1944) and challenging audiences with a radical series of symphonies by Honegger, Heinze also featured works by Australian composers of 'great promise', Roy Agnew, (H. J.) Brewster Jones, Clive Douglas [qq.v.7,9,14], Miriam Hyde and Robert Hughes among them.

Resuming his duties as Ormond professor early in 1945, Heinze remained a pervasive force at the ABC. In 1947, after a tour as guest conductor for the Canadian Broadcasting Commission (which was to lead to an honorary doctorate of laws from the University of British Columbia, 1947), he introduced to Australia the youth concert series that would shape the musical taste of a generation. He welcomed steady increases in subscriptions to orchestral series, devising innovative pro-

grams offering works by Shostakovich, Britten and Bartōk. Critics were sometimes uneasy with the dominance of his personality and occasional lapses in direction, but none the less welcomed the freshness he brought to both the podium and the audience. Some concerts, Kenneth Hince later recalled, were 'careless' but 'none was dull'. If Heinze's frequent absences from the university provoked questions, the conservatorium still benefited from his prestige and energy. During what he called his 'golden years' as director, it produced composers of the calibre of Donald Banks [q.v.13], James Penberthy and Peter Sculthorpe. Heinze was knighted in 1949; later that year he received an honorary doctorate of music from the University of Western Australia.

Tall, urbane, impeccably groomed and a noted raconteur with a carefully cultivated, mellifluous voice, Sir Bernard had, at least in public, a contagious enthusiasm and cheerfulness. In 1956 he resigned from the conservatorium and succeeded (1957-67) Sir Eugene Goossens [q.v.14] as director of the New South Wales State Conservatorium of Music. With legendary restlessness he continued to travel extensively, promoting music. In a daring initiative given the political climate of the times, he undertook a conducting tour of the Soviet Union and Eastern Europe in 1958. Across Australia audiences continued to adore him; his players, however, generally considered him dictatorial, anti-female, and someone to be feared. His extensive influence ensured that a word in the right quarter could make or break a career.

Heinze had always drawn much power from his control of strategic committees, through chairmanship or sheer gamesmanship. Beyond the ABC, these included service as a representative of education in music on the Victorian Council of Public Education (1936-57), as a close associate of the AMEB, as vice-patron of the Arts Council of Australia, Victorian division, and as an active member and international representative (Belgium, 1953) of the Australian National Advisory Committee for the United NationsEducational, Scientific and Cultural Organization. In Sydney, and with expanding public support for the arts, new opportunities arose. He served as vice-patron (1955-65) of the Arts Council of Australia, New South Wales division; on the executive committee (1957-66) and later as a trustee of the Sydney Opera House; and as foundation chairman of the advisory board of Commonwealth Assistance to Australian Composers (1967), and the music advisory committee of the Australian Council for the Arts (1968).

Without doubt the dominant musical figure of twentieth-century Australia, Heinze raised and maintained national musical standards, providing an unparalleled example of leadership to the profession. He thought of music in nineteenth-century 'high art' terms, seeing it as a moral good to which the community should aspire while using contemporary means to ensure that outcome. He also gained recognition for music teaching as an accredited profession in schools. As Felix Werder noted, Heinze 'was not simply another curator-conductor, he was godfather to the Australian composer'. The fiftieth anniversary of his first public appearance as conductor was celebrated at the Melbourne Town Hall in 1974. He was named Australian of the Year in 1975, appointed AC in 1976 and in 1979 became the first Australian to receive UNESCO's International Music Council award.

Fit and active well into his eighties, Sir Bernard Heinze remained a keen gardener and collector. He died at Bellevue Hill, Sydney, on 10 June 1982, survived by his wife and their three sons. Following a requiem Mass at St Peter's Catholic Church, Toorak, at which Fauré's *Requiem* was sung, he was buried in Brighton cemetery, Melbourne. He left behind an immense legacy, securing for serious music a permanent place in Australia, not as a remote European inheritance but as the ancestral house in which Australians could live and grow. In 1957 a portrait by Paul Fitzgerald was presented to the university conservatorium, and in 1975 the ABC televised a biographical feature, 'The Bernard Heinze Story'. An annual award in his name, established in 1985, is given in recognition of an outstanding contribution to music in Australia.

K. S. Inglis, *This Is the ABC* (1983); T. Radic, *Bernard Heinze* (1986); P. J. Tregear, *The Conservatorium of Music, University of Melbourne* (1997); *Table Talk*, 26 Aug 1926, p 17; *Australian*, 19 Oct 1974, p 21; Heinze papers (SLV).

THÉRÈSE RADIC

HELE, GEORGE ALFRED (1892-1982), cricket umpire, was born on 16 July 1892 at Hindmarsh, Adelaide, second of six surviving children of Andrew William Hele (1868-1938), storeman, and his wife Elizabeth Ann, née Patterson. An enthusiastic sportsman, Andrew played for the Bowden Cricket Club in the Adelaide and Suburban Cricket Association and was, according to George, 'an excellent wicketkeeper'. He encouraged his sons to play cricket and Australian Rules football. George left school at 13 and began work as a labourer in a soft-drink factory. Like his father, he kept wickets for the Brompton Methodists and eventually played for the West Torrens Cricket Club.

Having turned to umpiring, again like his father, Hele stood for his first district cricket game at the Adelaide Oval in 1918 and made his first-class début at the same ground in 1921. He had been umpiring for ten seasons in Adelaide club cricket and for seven in first-class games when he was named for his first Test match in Brisbane in 1928. Hele umpired all ten Tests during the Marylebone Cricket Club's (England) tours led by Percy Chapman in 1928-29 and Douglas Jardine in the 'body-line' series of 1932-33. He also stood in the five Tests against South Africa in 1931-32 and in one against the West Indies in 1930. In all, he umpired fifty-six first-class matches between 1921 and 1935.

Best remembered as 'the bodyline umpire', Hele wrote a 'behind-the-wicket eyewitness account' of the games, *Bodyline Umpire* (1974), with R. S. Whitington. He condemned the tactics of the English captain Jardine 'unequivocally' and suggested that he had 'never seen more vicious bowling' than that of Harold Larwood to a packed leg-side field. As in all his matches he had adhered resolutely to the rules of the game, but he admitted that he had been 'horrified' and had wondered about the outcome for Anglo-Australian cricket.

Despite the controversy, Jardine rated Hele the equal of England's umpire Frank Chester. In a letter to the Australian cricket official Bill Kelly in 1932 he wrote: 'As you know, we in England bracket Hele and Chester as the two best umpires in the world'. In his book *Farewell to Cricket* (1950), Sir Donald Bradman agreed with Jardine: 'I think the Englishmen who played under Hele would agree that he was the best Australian umpire between the two wars'. Writing in 1959, A. G. ('Johnny') Moyes [q.v.15] contended that Hele 'was perhaps the finest umpire Australia has produced' and that players held him in high esteem. He was 'a great communicator' with players on the field. In 1970 a journalist described him as a 'gentle' man, still tall and erect with a 'keen eye'.

Hele had married Matilda Jane Hann (d.1969), a telephonist, on 12 March 1918 at the Baptist Church, Flinders Street, Adelaide. In 1933 they moved to Melbourne, where Hele worked as a salesman and mains recorder. They had one son, Raymond George Hele (1920-1983), who followed his father as a player and umpire, thus creating a cricketing record of three generations umpiring the game. Ray stood for thirty-one first-class matches but, unlike his father, was not named for any Tests. George Hele died on 28 August 1982 at Preston, Melbourne, and was cremated.

D. Bradman, *Farewell to Cricket* (1950); A. G. Moyes, *Australian Cricket* (1959); S. Downer, *100 Not Out* (1972); R. Cashman et al (eds), *The Oxford Companion to Australian Cricket* (1996); *Advertiser* (Adelaide), 10 Feb 1970, p 14.

JOHN A. DALY

HELMRICH, DOROTHY JANE ADELE (1889-1984), singer and arts administrator, was born on 25 July 1889 at Woollahra, Sydney, youngest of six surviving children of John Hellmrich, civil servant, and his wife Esther Isabel, née Pepper, both born in New South Wales. Dorothy enjoyed a carefree childhood; her education at Mosman Academy and Mosman Public School was followed by a year's commercial training. She dropped the second 'l' in the family name.

Raised in a musical family, to whom she was known as Jane, she began piano lessons at 7, saw her first musical at 8, and started singing with Mosman Musical Society. She decided to have voice instruction with its lead singer, William Beattie. At society musicales her voice attracted attention, and Alice, Lady Cooper, an Australian expatriate revisiting Sydney from London, became her patron, arranging for singing lessons at the New South Wales State Conservatorium of Music with Stefan Mavrogordato, and then at the Royal College of Music, London (1919-22) and the London School of Opera. Dorothy thought of Cooper as 'a real fairy godmother'.

Impressed by her talent, her teacher Sir George Henschel arranged Helmrich's début at the Wigmore Hall, London. Provincial engagements followed. Her career coincided with the beginnings of broadcasting and the renaissance of English music; she was a regular soloist at Sir Henry Wood's Promenade Concerts. She toured widely in Britain and Europe, as well as America, and performed at the Salzburg Festival. A mezzo-soprano who made her name as a German lieder singer, Helmrich built her international reputation on sincerity, professionalism and an extensive repertoire. A Polish reviewer wrote: 'The voice is clear and voluminous, the quality is velvet and the colour very warm'.

In 1936 Helmrich toured Australia for the Australian Broadcasting Commission; she also performed in New Zealand. Stranded in Sydney in 1941 after another tour which included Java, Singapore and New Zealand, Helmrich accepted a post at the conservatorium. In 1944 she sang in its production of *The Pearl Tree*, an opera composed by its director, Edgar Bainton [q.v.7]. Helmrich remained on the staff, a respected vocal coach specialising in lieder, until 1974.

In 1943, on the basis of earlier war work in England, Helmrich founded the Australian Council for the Encouragement of Music and the Arts 'to bring art, in all its forms, to the people'. She made a study tour of Britain in 1946. The CEMA was next year renamed the Arts Council of Australia; Helmrich was president (1943-63) of the New South Wales division. With negligible resources, she built a broad-based organisation sponsoring art, drama, music and arts education nationwide,

particularly in schools and rural areas. The première in 1950 of the ballet *Corroboree*, by the Australian composer John Antill [q.v.], and a royal gala performance in 1954 were great successes. Other early movements aided by the Arts Council with Helmrich's personal attention included the Bodenwieser [q.v.13] Ballet, and (Dame) Doris Fitton's [q.v.] Independent Theatre.

In 1947 Helmrich secured a grant of £600 for the Arts Council from the Advisory Board of Adult Education, of which she was a member. In 1950 she persuaded the Joint Coal Board to give a pantechnicon to transport the first mobile theatre unit; by 1965 there were four. While the State divisions attracted funds from their respective governments, Commonwealth funding did not appear until later. She published *The First Twenty-Five Years: A Study of the Arts Council of Australia* in 1968.

In the wider cultural community Helmrich served on the Australian United Nations Educational, Scientific and Cultural Organization's committee for music, the ABC's State broadcasting advisory committee and the Sydney Opera House's advisory committee for music and drama. Awarded the Society of Artists' medal in 1955, she was appointed OBE in 1959. Helmrich's associates described her as persuasive, determined, charismatic and charming, and commented on her vision and pioneering achievement in making the arts widely available. She elicited support for Arts Council projects, according to her colleague Colin Ballantyne, by handling people in person 'with a mixture of quiet authority and twinkling good humour'. Twice engaged, she never married. Although raised an Anglican, from the age of 19 she had espoused theosophy, which, she said, provided her with 'a philosophical basis for living'. In London she had joined the United Lodge of Theosophists, and her theosophical contacts in Australia were invaluable throughout her career. She died on 1 September 1984 at Strathfield and was cremated. At her request excerpts from *The Light of Asia* and the *Bhagavad Gita* were read at the funeral.

Arts Council of Aust (NSW), *A Five Years' Record, 1943-1947* (1947); B. and F. Mackenzie, *Singers of Australia* (1967); V. Carell and B. Dean, *On Wings of Song* (1982); H. de Berg, interview with D. Helmrich (ts, 1975, NLA); Helmrich papers (SLNSW); Sydney Conservatorium of Music Archives.   JILL ROE
                                    JANE E. HUNT

HELPMANN, SIR ROBERT MURRAY (1909-1986), ballet dancer, actor, producer, director and choreographer, was born on 9 April 1909 at Mount Gambier, South

Australia, eldest of three children of James Murray Helpman, a Victorian-born stock and station agent, and his wife Mary, née Gardiner, born in South Australia. Benjamin Helpman [q.v.1] was his great-grandfather. Robert was educated at Prince Alfred College, Adelaide, but left school at 14. His mother—herself stage-struck from an early age—was to be a driving force in his career. Taught ballet by 'Nora' Stewart [q.v.12], he first appeared on stage at the Theatre Royal, Adelaide, in 1922 as a solo dancer in *The Ugly Duckling*. As a student he toured Australia and New Zealand in 1926 with Anna Pavlova's company. His professional career began in 1927 when he joined J. C. Williamson [q.v.6] Ltd as the principal dancer in *Frasquita* for its Australasian tour.

For the next five years Helpman featured as the principal dancer in a range of J. C. Williamson productions. His break came in December 1931 when he was seen performing in a Christmas pantomime in Melbourne by the English actress Margaret Rawlings, who was in Australia to play the lead in *The Barretts of Wimpole Street*. Impressed by this 'most rare and imperative original talent', Rawlings engaged him for the minor role of Septimus Barrett. The play toured Australia and New Zealand until late 1932, then Rawlings persuaded him to travel to London. She found him work at the Gate Theatre and, more significantly, introduced him to (Dame) Ninette de Valois, who employed him in 1933 as a member of the *corps de ballet* in her Vic-Wells Ballet. De Valois recorded her assessment of him in her logbook. On the credit side she found him 'talented, enthusiastic, extremely intelligent, [with] great facility, witty, cute as a monkey, quick as a squirrel, a sense of theatre and his own possible achievements therein'. On the debit side he was 'academically technically weak, lacking in concentration, too fond of a good time and too busy having it'.

Helpman was ambitious, flamboyant, and out to make an impression. Lilian Baylis, the owner-manager of the Sadler's Wells Theatre, remarked to de Valois, 'I like the boy, dear, who puts too much brilliantine on his hair; do stop him, his head's rather large anyway, and it makes one keep looking at him'. To this, de Valois replied, 'Perhaps that is what he means you to do'. In 1934, at Rawlings' suggestion, he added a second 'n' to his surname to give it a more exotic, European appeal. His theatre colleagues knew him more familiarly as 'Bobby'.

Having formed what was to be a brief partnership with Vic-Wells's prima ballerina (Dame) Alicia Markova, Helpmann was promoted in 1935 to principal male dancer, a position he retained with increasing authority until he resigned in 1950. In 1937 he created an enduring partnership with (Dame) Margot Fonteyn. Not a great classical virtuoso dancer, nor especially athletic, he had, however, a technique that, according to Leo Kersley, 'allowed him to do what he wanted with sureness, precision and smoothness'. Moreover, he had enormous power of projection and dramatic presence, described by Rawlings as an 'unrivalled quality of moving an audience'. De Valois wrote that there was also, at times, a 'wild poetry about his dancing'. Helpmann's innate theatricality enabled him to create important roles in the company's repertoire, including the lead in de Valois's *The Haunted Ballroom* (1934), *The Prospect before Us* (1940) and *Don Quixote* (1950), and the Red King in *Checkmate* (1937), a role created for him by de Valois. The company's resident choreographer, (Sir) Frederick Ashton, also used Helpmann's talents in his ballets, including *Apparitions* and *Nocturne* (both 1936), *A Wedding Bouquet* (1937), *Dante Sonata* (1940), *The Wanderer* (1941) and *Don Juan* and *Cinderella* (both 1948).

During World War II Helpmann toured with the Sadler's Wells Ballet on behalf of the armed services and, through his humour and grit, emerged, according to Fonteyn, as 'the person who more than any other kept the company going'. Back in London, and in the absence of Ashton, who had enlisted for war service, he turned to choreography. In 1942 he created three professional ballets for the company— *Comus*, *Hamlet* and *The Birds*—followed by two noteworthy later ones: *Miracle in the Gorbals* (1944) and *Adam Zero* (1946). Though each of these works received critical acclaim in varying degrees, Helpmann was never a choreographer in the purist tradition. His choreographic inventions were essentially narrative, often based on some literary or psychological theme, and invariably strongly dramatic.

In the 1930s, in parallel with his dancing career, Helpmann had performed small parts in the dramatic theatre, most notably in 1937 when he played Oberon to Vivien Leigh's Titania in (Sir) Tyrone Guthrie's production of *A Midsummer Night's Dream*. In the 1940s he appeared in *Hamlet* with the Old Vic company (1944) and, under the direction of Michael Benthall, took the role of Flamineo in John Webster's *The White Devil* (1947), next to Margaret Rawlings. Again under Benthall's direction he featured at the Stratford-upon-Avon Festival in 1948, in the name roles of *Hamlet* and *King John*, and as Shylock in *The Merchant of Venice*. Sir John Gielgud recalled in 1987 that, in moving into straight acting, Helpmann 'took endless pains with his diction and phrasing'; his miming was always brilliant, but one fellow actor felt 'his handling of the text, however carefully studied, did not completely synchronise with his pictorial handling of his performances'.

Having previously appeared in the films *One of Our Aircraft is Missing* (1941) and (Sir) Laurence (Lord) Olivier's *Henry V* (1944), Helpmann again turned to the screen in 1948, playing the principal dancer role of Ivan Boleslawsky in the first British ballet film *The Red Shoes*, for which he was also choreographer. Later that year, he resumed dancing with the Sadler's Wells Ballet, touring with the company to the United States of America in 1949 and again in November 1950; he gave his final performance as a regular company member in San Francisco. Earlier that year he had produced his first opera, *Madama Butterfly*, at Covent Garden.

In the 1950s Helpmann concentrated increasingly on directing for the dramatic stage and opera. His output at the Old Vic was prolific, and included T. S. Eliot's *Murder in the Cathedral* (1953), and a succession of Shakespearean plays: *The Tempest* (1954), *As You Like It* (1955), *Romeo and Juliet* (1956) and *Antony and Cleopatra* (1957). At the same time he maintained a demanding acting schedule: roles included the Egyptian doctor (opposite Katharine Hepburn) in G. B. Shaw's *The Millionairess* (1952), the Devil in Stravinsky's *The Soldier's Tale* (1954), Oberon in *A Midsummer Night's Dream* (1954) and, for the 1956-57 season at the Old Vic, Shylock in *The Merchant of Venice*, Launce in *The Two Gentlemen of Verona*, Saturninus in *Titus Andronicus*, Dr Pinch in *The Comedy of Errors* and Richard, duke of Gloucester, in *Richard III*.

After an absence of twenty-two years Helpmann returned to Australia in 1955 to lead, with Katharine Hepburn, a Shakespearean company sent out by the Old Vic company with a repertoire of three plays. He performed the roles of Shylock in *The Merchant of Venice*, Petruchio in *The Taming of the Shrew* and Angelo in *Measure for Measure*. Back in Australia three years later, he toured in (Sir) Noël Coward's *Nude with Violin*, and also danced with his old ballet company (renamed The Royal Ballet) in *The Rake's Progress*, *Coppélia*, *Façade* and *Hamlet*. In 1962 he performed again for Australian audiences in another Old Vic company, this time headed by Vivien Leigh, and played the role of Prince Tuan in the film *55 Days at Peking*.

In 1963 Helpmann choreographed his sixth work for The Royal Ballet, the short-lived and critically damned *Elektra*, and produced a new version of *Swan Lake*. He choreographed and produced *The Display* (1964) for the fledgling Australian Ballet. In 1965 he was appointed co-artistic director of the company, with (Dame) Peggy van Praagh [q.v.]. He used the company as a vehicle for his choreography—*Yugen* (1965) and an expanded version of *Elektra* (1966), followed in 1968 by *Sun Music*, which received mixed reactions from Australian critics and the public. In 1970, in collaboration

with Rudolf Nureyev, he staged and danced in *Don Quixote*. He mounted a popular production of *The Merry Widow* (1975). That year he was appointed sole artistic director of the Australian Ballet but in 1976 was ousted by the board. He had served in 1968 as consultant and in 1970 as artistic director for the Adelaide Festival of Arts.

Helpmann's legacy to Australian ballet was significant. His co-artistic directorship with van Praagh was, for the most part, productive. They complemented each other with their different personalities and skills: she the pedagogue, teacher and administrator; he the restless 'jet-setting' star who spent six months of the year overseas and attracted international names to perform with the company.

In his later years Helpmann steadfastly refused to retire. He made various guest appearances in ballets in Australia and abroad, and continued to act and produce. In 1978 he directed *Stars of World Ballet*, a collection of international solo dancers, which toured the major Australian capital cities. For the Australian Opera he directed Handel's *Alcina* in 1981 and the same opera and Gounod's *Romeo and Juliet* in the 1982-83 season. He returned to acting during the Sydney Theatre Company's 1983 season to portray Lord Alfred Douglas in Justin Fleming's play *The Cobra*. His last appearance on stage, poignantly, was in July 1986 as the Red King in the Australian Ballet's production of *Checkmate*.

Helpmann was the complete man of the theatre. Some thought he spread his talents too thinly, denying him mastery over any one area. Opinions vary: Malcolm Williamson, Master of the Queen's Musick, argued that 'he never became a Gielgud, Olivier or Redgrave, or an Ashton, Balanchine or Petit because he was the most pluralistic of the lot'; Moira Shearer thought that 'he wasn't a great dancer —he wasn't a great actor—but he was most certainly a great mime, the perfect bridge between the two'. He had a wicked wit, its impact aided by his bulbous eyes and a sometimes Mephistophelean expression; he could be abrasive and did not allow the warmth below the surface to show often. The actor John McCallum observed that he 'inspired affection from those who knew him well, but gave little back. He inspired animosity in many people, and delighted in giving it back'. Seeing people and things, including himself, with piercing accuracy, he was amusing and irreverent, and no one was spared: when asked, 'Does your mother resemble you?', he replied, 'She looks like me as Dr Coppelius'.

Despite his showmanship, Helpmann was a private man. The great love of his life, with whom he shared a flat in London, was Michael Benthall (d.1974). The only family he knew were his younger siblings Max and Sheila, both actors. Many women, including Rawlings,

Hepburn, Leigh, and Claire Bloom, who remembered his 'extraordinary magnetism and magic, on and off stage', adored him. Although he disdained ostentation and despised sycophancy, he had a strong streak of vanity and a sense of his own worth. In 1953 he received a Queen Elizabeth II coronation award; in 1954 he was appointed to the Royal Order of the Polar Star (Sweden) and in 1957 made a knight of the cedar (Lebanon). Appointed CBE in 1964 and knighted in 1968, he was named Australian of the Year for 1965.

Sir Robert died on 28 September 1986 in Sydney and was cremated after a state funeral in St Andrew's Anglican Cathedral. On 7 October Prime Minister R. J. Hawke moved a condolence motion in the House of Representatives —a rare tribute for a non-politician. On 25 November a memorial service was held at St Paul's Church, Covent Garden, London. His portrait by Judy Cassab hangs in the Sydney Opera House. The Helpmann awards, recognising artistic achievement and excellence in the performing arts in Australia, were established by the Australian Entertainment Industry Association in 2001.

C. Brahms, *Robert Helpmann: Choreographer* (1943); G. Anthony, *Robert Helpmann* (1946); K. S. Walker, *Robert Helpmann* (1957); N. de Valois, *Come Dance with Me* (1957); M. Helpman, *The Helpman Family Story, 1796-1964* (1967); M. Fonteyn, *Margot Fonteyn* (1975); E. Salter, *Helpmann* (1978); *ODNB* (2004); *PD* (HR), 7 Oct 1986, p 1515; *Equity* (Actors' and Announcers' Equity Assn), Dec 1986, p 27; Helpmann papers (NLA); private information.
                                      CHRISTOPHER SEXTON

HENDERSON, RUPERT ALBERT GEARY (1896-1986), newspaperman, was born on 26 February 1896 at Camperdown, Sydney, eldest of five sons of Sydney-born Robert Francis Geary Henderson, a gentleman of independent means, and his second wife Isabel Jane McLymont, née Caldwell, from Victoria. Rupert was educated at Glebe Superior Public School. After leaving school and an unhappy home at age 13, he went to sea in coastal ships briefly, and then worked as a solicitor's clerk in Sydney. He was a top sprinter with the South Sydney Harriers' Amateur Athletic Club. On 5 December 1914 he married Helene Mason at St James's Church of England, Sydney. Encouraged into journalism by the club's secretary, he was appointed a cadet reporter on the *Sydney Morning Herald* in June 1915.

Over the next seven years Henderson became chief shipping reporter, Newcastle representative and chief political reporter in Sydney. In 1923 he was appointed to take charge of the *Herald*'s business and journalism in London. Before he left, he was introduced to (Sir) Warwick Fairfax [q.v.]. Henderson returned to Sydney in 1926, straining at the leash in various editorial and administrative jobs until he became secretary to the general manager, Athol Stuart [q.v.12].

When Stuart left in 1938 Henderson became general manager. At 42, he was dynamic, urgent and immediately in charge, setting up a major re-equipment program for the printing plant in Hunter Street. Divorced in 1937, he married Hazel Harris on 27 September 1939 in New York. Back in Sydney Henderson threw himself into the newspaper industry's affairs, succeeding Sir Keith Murdoch [q.v.10] as chairman (1940-49) of Australian Associated Press Pty Ltd. With Murdoch, he organised a partnership between AAP, Reuters and the New Zealand Press Association, becoming a director (1947-50), Australian trustee (1952-61) and chairman of trustees (1961-78) of Reuters Ltd. As president (1942-46) of the Australian Newspaper Proprietors' Association, he handled the clashes with the Commonwealth government over newsprint rationing and censorship which culminated in a famous confrontation in 1944 with the minister for information, Arthur Calwell [q.v.13], and resulted in a victory for the ANPA. Calwell never forgave the proprietors and, in another clash in 1946, he referred, in parliament, to Henderson as 'that Quilp-like creature', a reference to the repulsive dwarf and moneylender in *The Old Curiosity Shop*.

'Rags', as Henderson was known behind his back, became managing director in 1949, shortly after the *Sunday Herald* was launched. In mid-1951 he reacted to the threatened publication of a new financial newspaper by bringing out a weekly, the *Australian Financial Review*. This was the start of the basic strategy he called 'protecting the crown jewels'— that is, the advertising revenues generated by the *Sydney Morning Herald*. The strategy entailed keeping other large publishers out of New South Wales, limiting the growth of the Fairfax company's great Sydney rival, (Sir) Frank Packer's [q.v.15] Consolidated Press Holdings Ltd, and acquiring ownership of radio and television.

Henderson bested Packer and the bigger Herald & Weekly Times Ltd group of Melbourne in takeover contests for Associated Newspapers Ltd (the Sydney *Sun*, the *Sunday Sun* and the Sungravure magazine group) in 1953, and Truth & Sportsman Ltd (the *Daily Mirror* and *Truth*) in 1958. O'Connell Pty Ltd, a company financed and ultimately controlled by Fairfax, bought Truth & Sportsman Ltd from Henderson's occasional lunch companion Ezra Norton [q.v.15]. Two years later, against Warwick Fairfax's wishes, Henderson sold the company, renamed Mirror Newspapers Ltd, to Rupert Murdoch. In December 1955 the John Fairfax [q.v.4]-Associated Newspapers newspaper operations had moved from the city to a vast new building at Broadway.

The rapid expansion of the firm strained the private company's finances and John Fairfax Ltd was floated as a public company in 1956, raising £2 million with a public share issue. The family retained a controlling interest of slightly over 50 per cent. Henderson's goal was to protect not only the 'crown jewels' but also the family's interest. He encouraged family members with small holdings to sell their shares to larger holders, particularly to W. O. Fairfax and his son James. In this way the family interest was not dispersed and control weakened, as was the case with the Syme [q.v.6] family's holding in the company publishing the *Age* in Melbourne—a circumstance that ultimately led to John Fairfax Ltd's buying control of the *Age*.

Henderson took the company into television (ATN-7, Sydney, which started transmission in 1956, and QTQ, Brisbane, three years later). He again beat Packer by acquiring a controlling interest in Newcastle Newspapers Pty Ltd (1961) and by converting the *Australian Financial Review* to a daily (1963) after Packer had briefly challenged with a business paper of his own, the *Australian Financial Times* (1961-62). In 1964 Henderson and Arthur Shakespeare [q.v.11], chairman and managing editor of Federal Capital Press of Australia Pty Ltd, implemented a long-standing agreement when Fairfax bought the *Canberra Times*. Later that year he outbid Packer to buy the Australian assets of the Associated Television Corporation Ltd, London, in a frenzied day of negotiations with (Lord) Lew Grade and his lawyers. This purchase gave John Fairfax Ltd broadcasting assets which became Macquarie Broadcasting Holdings Ltd, the Australian franchise for Muzak and greatly enlarged television investments. As a takeover deal it was the greatest 'bonzana' (a favourite Henderson malapropism) of them all.

In 1961 Henderson and Calwell had met again. W. O. Fairfax concluded that the Menzies [q.v.15] government had lost its way, and the *Herald* backed the Australian Labor Party, led by Calwell, in the 1961 Federal election. Henderson told Calwell that he did not agree with this policy but, with typical energy, threw the company's resources behind Calwell's campaign. Menzies won by two seats. When Menzies called an early election in 1963 W. O. Fairfax decided that the government was back on the right track and the *Herald* swung behind Menzies. Henderson was not consulted. This time Menzies won handsomely. Fairfax ran the politics; Henderson ran the business, the success of which added to Fairfax's political weight.

After his retirement as managing director of John Fairfax Ltd in 1964, Henderson remained a director until 1978. He continued as chairman of Amalgamated Television Services Pty Ltd until 1974, and of Australian Newsprint Mills Holdings Ltd and Macquarie Broadcasting Holdings Ltd until 1978. Still interested in every aspect of the company's affairs, he threw up ideas for television programs, and for turning the *Newcastle Morning Herald and Miner's Advocate* into an Australian *Manchester Guardian* and the *Canberra Times* into an Australian *Washington Post*. He was an outstanding example of the last generation of big business leaders who grew up in the companies they ultimately led, who knew and lived their operations, and who could act quickly and decisively, without a retinue of investment advisers but with the close counsel of the company's solicitors. At a time when newspaper industry leaders traditionally received knighthoods, he gained no official honours.

Although small and bony, Henderson was a formidable, potentially volcanic, presence. He used language and gestures with explosive force. Even his silences were intense. Events tended to be either 'bonzanas' or 'disasters'. To the few people close to him he was brilliant, attractive and difficult. In the company he was on Christian name terms only with the other directors. Working long hours in his panelled fourteenth-floor Broadway office, he rarely took holidays although he spent most weekends at his property near Exeter on the Southern Highlands of New South Wales. He often travelled on business to New York and London, where he was an avid theatre-goer.

When Packer rang Henderson's office he would ask for 'Ebenezer', a reference to another Dickens character, Scrooge. Henderson was as careful with his own money as he was with that of the company. Although he had been left five houses when his father died, he liked to reflect on his humble beginnings. In 1945 he had formed a business partnership with Hanne Anderson, who was soon to become W. O. Fairfax's second wife. The partnership acquired control of the Wagga Wagga *Daily Advertiser* and, later, the *Illawarra Mercury*. In 1959 Henderson bought Hanne Fairfax's share at the time of her divorce. These Henderson family interests were expanded by the purchase of newspapers in the Riverina and at Goulburn and a substantial shareholding in Riverina & North East Victoria TV Ltd, which owned broadcasting licences in Albury and Wagga Wagga. In 1969 John Fairfax Ltd bought the *Illawarra Mercury* for $2.4 million, thus completing the geographical defensive perimeter—Wollongong, Canberra and Newcastle—around Sydney. The Riverina television interests were sold to Prime Television (Victoria) Pty Ltd for $14.4 million. Henderson's family companies still owned the Wagga Wagga *Daily Advertiser*, some smaller country newspapers and substantial investments, including property, when he died on 9 September 1986 at Potts Point, Sydney. Predeceased by the son of his first marriage, he was survived by his wife and their daughter and was buried in Northern Suburbs cemetery.

G. Souter, *Company of Heralds* (1981); J. Fairfax, *My Regards to Broadway* (1991); *SMH*, 12 Sept 1986, p 2; R. A. Henderson and W. O. Fairfax files (John Fairfax Holdings Ltd archives, Sydney).

V. J. CARROLL

HENDERSON, WALTER (1887-1986), public servant and lawyer, was born on 29 November 1887 at Enfield, South Australia, fourth of five children of Thomas Henderson, an Ulster-born farmer, and his wife Maria Shapland, née Ford. Diminutive in stature, Walter was bullied at school and from about the age of 12 was privately tutored, largely by his father. To counter the humiliations associated with his lack of height, he developed two defences that were to shape the rest of his life: a devotion to scholarship, especially the study of European history, philosophy and law; and a combative, often aggressive personality.

Joining the South Australian Public Service in 1904, Henderson was by 1914 a reporter in the government reporting department. On 23 June 1913 at the Methodist manse, South Terrace, Adelaide, he married French-born Gertrude Ellen Jaunay. He enlisted in the Australian Imperial Force on 26 November 1914 and served in Egypt and France with the 1st Australian General Hospital, becoming a staff sergeant and company sergeant major. Discharged on 9 July 1919 in England, he moved to Paris to study law and history at l'Ecole Libre des Sciences Politiques. He graduated first in his class with a diploma 'en section generale' on 5 July 1921. His qualifications were those of a European administrator or diplomat, and through his marriage he claimed links with France's Protestant elite.

Prime Minister S. M. (Viscount) Bruce [q.v.7] returned to Australia from the 1923 Imperial Conference dissatisfied with existing arrangements for information and advice on Imperial and foreign affairs. Advised by A. W. A. Leeper [q.v.10] of the British Foreign Office, he initiated the creation of two new public service positions: director of an external affairs branch in the Prime Minister's Department in Melbourne and a liaison officer in London to be the principal channel of confidential information and views between the Australian prime minister and the British government. In 1924 Henderson and R. G. (Lord) Casey [q.v.13] respectively were appointed to these posts. After exchanging places with Casey for six months in 1927, Henderson spent much of 1928 and 1929 in a strenuous bureaucratic battle aimed at establishing a separate department of external affairs and diplomatic service. The Prime Minister's Department was opposed and the Public Service Board approved only a highly diluted version of his proposals. Bruce, who was initially pleased with Henderson's work, became critical of his abrasive style.

The Australian Labor Party's victory at the 1929 election proved disastrous for Henderson's prospects. He later claimed that when, at their first meeting, the new prime minister, James Scullin [q.v.11], said breezily: 'Call me Jim', he could only stutter in reply: 'I am sometimes called Lord H.', a nickname earned by his superior manner. Scullin commissioned a report by two senior public servants, (Sir) John McLaren [q.v.10] and H. C. Elvins, on the organisation of the external affairs office. They saw little need for independent Australian diplomacy. Personal antagonism from Henderson's subordinates helped to ensure the demise of his plans. He resigned, denouncing a Catholic-dominated Labor government for ejecting a conservative, highly educated Protestant, seemingly unaware that his manner, more than his social and religious identification, had caused his downfall.

Henderson settled in London; called to the Bar at Gray's Inn on 26 January 1933, he practised international law for the rest of his career. He retired to Adelaide in the 1950s. In 1965 he led opposition to the mayor of Burnside's proposal for a new swimming centre in Hazelwood Park. Eventually a pool was built, but without facilities that would have created unwelcome noise in the suburban neighbourhood. In the late 1960s and early 1970s he wrote pungent pieces for the Australian League of Rights and its offshoots. In particular he supported Ian Smith's regime in Southern Rhodesia (Zimbabwe) following the unilateral declaration of independence in 1965. His tracts for the South Australia-Rhodesia Association and the Federal Council of Australia Rhodesia Associations (of which he was president) drew on his legal training and conservative values. They argued that the United Nations sanctions on the Smith regime were illegal and that the latter was justified in its constitutional position and political actions. He was widowed about 1972. On 21 June 1980 at his Glenunga home he married in a civil ceremony Marion Eileen Parish, née Gibbs-Jones, a widow. Childless, he died on 9 August 1986 at Kingswood and was cremated. His wife survived him.

P. G. Edwards, 'Dr Walter Henderson—A South Australian in Charge of an Australian Foreign Office', *Jnl of the Hist Soc of SA*, no 11, 1983, p 3; *Advertiser* (Adelaide), 22 Feb 1982, p 5, 12 Aug 1986, p 16; *News* (Adelaide), 13 Aug 1986, p 9; J. Cumpston, interview with W. Henderson (ts, 1967, NLA); W. Henderson diary, 1927 (NLA); private information.

PETER EDWARDS

HERBERT, ALFRED FRANCIS XAVIER (1901-1984), author and pharmacist, was born on 15 May 1901 at Geraldton, Western Australia, illegitimate son of Victorian-born Amy Victoria Scammell. He was registered at birth as Alfred Jackson, son of John Jackson, auctioneer, with whom his mother had already had two children, but his father was almost certainly Benjamin Francis Herbert, a Welsh-born engine driver. Amy and Ben had three more children before marrying in 1917. Herbert's novels *Capricornia* (1938) and *Poor Fellow My Country* (1975) would later explore the theme of illegitimacy, based on personal experience, in the larger context of Australia's colonial origins, its historical relationship to Britain and its mistreatment of Aborigines.

Educated at Midland Junction and Fremantle Boys' State schools and at Christian Brothers College, Fremantle, at 14 Alfred found employment in a chemist's shop and began studying pharmacy at Perth Technical College. He was registered on 21 May 1923 in the name of Alfred Xavier Herbert (he added the name Francis and later adopted Xavier as his preferred name), and was to work sporadically as a pharmacist throughout his life. He moved to Melbourne, enrolled (1925) at the University of Melbourne to study medicine, and began to consider writing as a career. Once the *Australian Journal* had accepted some of his short stories for publication he withdrew from the course. Generally written to a formula of colonial romance and adventure, or crime and mystery, for the popular magazine and newspaper market, they were published under a range of pseudonyms, the most common being Herbert Astor.

Leaving for Sydney in 1926, Herbert briefly freelanced as a journalist. That year he was influenced by Leon Gordon's controversial *White Cargo: A Play of the Primitive*, a portrayal of sexual relations between white men and black women in West Africa. He realised that urban Australia was largely ignorant of frontier realities, especially the continuing sexual exploitation of Aboriginal women, and decided to write about the subject. Lacking experience to do so immediately, he travelled in 1927 to the Northern Territory, where he worked as a drover, railway fettler, pearl diver and pharmacist. He was a dispenser in the Solomon Islands for a few months.

In 1930 Herbert departed for England, hoping to make his literary name and fortune. In this he failed, but found on the voyage his life's companion, Sarah ('Sadie') Cohen, née Norden (1899-1979), who was returning to England after a failed marriage. In London she looked after and encouraged Herbert while he wrote *Capricornia*. Back in Australia in 1932, Herbert took up the struggle to publish the book. He worked first in Sydney as a garage attendant, then at Darwin as a pharmacist, superintendent of the Aboriginal Compound, organiser for the North Australian Workers' Union, and miner.

Capricornia was finally published in 1938 by the Publicist Publishing Co. and promptly won the Commonwealth sesquicentenary literary competition and the Australian Literary Society's gold medal for 1939. Herbert, however, was ill-prepared for fame. His creativity stalled and he was unable to complete his next novel, instead enduring twenty years of self-imposed isolation, self-analysis and dormant creativity, during which he abandoned one project after another in a continuing crisis of confidence. Through his publisher W. J. Miles and his editor P. R. Stephensen [qq.v.10,12], he became involved with the radical nationalist Australia-First Movement, for which he narrowly avoided internment in World War II. He enlisted in the Australian Imperial Force on 29 May 1942 and served as a sergeant in the North Australian Observer Unit before being discharged in August 1944.

In 1951 Herbert and Sadie settled at Redlynch, near Cairns. On 26 June 1953, giving their ages as 47, they married at the Cairns Court House. He was awarded several Commonwealth Literary Fund fellowships and in 1959 published *Seven Emus*. It had been completed during the war but, initially serialised in the lowbrow *Australian Journal*, had previously escaped serious notice. A slim novella with quirky punctuation, developed (according to Herbert) to discover and liberate his 'style', *Seven Emus* offered a satirical critique of the anthropological exploration and exploitation of Aboriginal sacred sites in northern Australia. His next novel, *Soldiers' Women* (1961), purported to be a study of women liberated by the absence or relative scarcity of men during World War II. The least critically popular of his works, it expounded a highly idiosyncratic theory of sexuality. It is none the less a fascinating companion to the classic novel written by Dymphna Cusack [q.v.] (with whom Herbert had a brief but passionate wartime affair) and Florence James on the same subject, *Come In Spinner* (1951).

During the periods of self-promotion that accompanied release of these works Herbert made carefully orchestrated and often controversial forays from the isolation of his North Queensland home into what he regarded as the more 'civilised' and easily shocked cities of the south, Sydney and Melbourne. Increasingly aware of his own mythology, in 1963 he published an unreliable autobiography of his youth, the rake's progress *Disturbing Element*. It contains a series of self-consciously psychologised revelations of the self that he chose to bring forward from behind his fiction.

Poor Fellow My Country, Herbert's *magnum opus*, marked a return to the thematic concerns of *Capricornia*, extending the chronology from 1936 to 1942. Satirising his old enemies, he exposed social absurdity and injustice and dramatised what he regarded as the tragedy of Australia: its failure to uphold the ideals of the 'True Commonwealth', or to connect with the spiritualised land and its original inhabitants. *Poor Fellow My Country* famously decries Australia as a land 'Despoiled by White Bullies, Thieves, and Hypocrites'. It won him the Miles Franklin [q.v.8] literary award in 1975. The universities of Queensland and Newcastle each conferred on him an honorary D.Litt. in 1976.

Herbert claimed to be a social revolutionary by national necessity rather than an artist by individual destiny, and although this contention brought him into conflict with the foremost writer of his day, Patrick White [q.v.], it nevertheless contains some truth. Herbert's importance to Australian literature is undoubtedly his contribution to debates on race and nation. However, the complexity of his writing is as much psychological as social and cultural. He was a profoundly contradictory and volatile personality who, despite his verbal facility, believed that physical fights were the only way to settle disputes among men. Outrageously pugnacious, deeply fascinated by his own masculinity, obsessed by his own sexuality, he was passionate in his devotion to Australia and fiercely republican. Early in 1984 he moved to the Northern Territory. He died on 10 November that year at Alice Springs and was buried in the local cemetery after a funeral ceremony at which Kungarakany elders and Patrick Dodson, an Aboriginal former Catholic priest, officiated.

R. McDougall, *South of Capricornia* (1990); D. Carment et al (eds), *Northern Territory Dictionary of Biography*, vol 1 (1990); F. de Groen, *Xavier Herbert* (1998), and *Xavier Herbert's Birth* (1998); *Australian*, 12 Nov 1984, p 1; Herbert papers (NLA and Univ of Qld Lib)   RUSSELL MCDOUGALL

HERFORD, SEYMOUR VIVIAN ('SAM') (1912-1983), swimmer, surf lifesaver and swimming coach, was born on 28 December 1912 at Manly, Sydney, son of David Herford, a Sydney-born accountant, and his Victorian-born wife Gladys Emilie Filemore, née Eaton. Sam attended Manly Public School and Blue Mountains Grammar School. A keen surfer at Manly, he came second in the Australian under-18 surf lifesaving title in the 1930-31 season and won the open teams title with Manly in 1931-32 and the open individual surf title in 1932-33.

Athletically built with broad shoulders, Herford was also a talented distance swimmer with the Manly Amateur Swimming Club. He was a member of the Manly team that won the 880-yards freestyle relay at the State swimming championships from 1932 to 1935. His best individual distance at State level was 1 mile; in this event he secured a place from 1932 to 1935; he won in 1933. He competed in the national championships from 1934 to 1936, most successfully in the 1935 season, when he won the national freestyle titles over 440 and 880 yards and 1 mile. His swimming career was partially eclipsed by Andrew 'Boy' Charlton [q.v.7] and Noel Ryan. Herford forfeited his amateur status by becoming a professional coach in 1937.

On 14 October 1939 at St Matthew's Church of England, Manly, Herford married Thora Miller Dennis, a salesgirl, who was a swimmer and a sister of Clare Dennis [q.v.13]. He served in the Militia from 1940 and was a corporal in the New South Wales Lines of Communication Area Records Office when discharged in 1943. Having taught and coached at many Sydney pools—North Sydney, Granville, Balmain, Lane Cove, Double Bay and the Spit Baths at Manly—he started a swimming club at Mosman in the late 1960s. His children were involved in this business.

Herford was an accredited Australian coach for the 1956 (Melbourne) and 1960 (Rome) Olympic Games, at which two of his charges, Murray Rose and John Devitt, were extremely successful. He was also a coach for the Australian Commonwealth Games swimming team in 1958 and 1962. His swimmers participated over distances from 100 to 1500 metres. Rose, who won three Olympic gold medals in 1956 and one gold, one silver and one bronze in 1960, described Herford as an emotional, clever trainer who could bring out the best in him. He saw him as a 'nonscientific coach' who 'worked from his gut instincts'.

Herford's son and daughter, Gary and Kim, represented Australia at the 1964 Tokyo Olympics in rowing and swimming respectively. Herford was a choral singer with a deep baritone, whose 'signature tune', *Old Man River*, became a nickname. Survived by his wife and their children, he died of a stroke on 15 May 1983 at his Manly home and was cremated. His contribution to swimming was recognised in 1992 by the International Swimming Hall of Fame, which inducted him as an 'honor coach'.

J. Wilson, *Australian Surfing and Surf Life Saving* (1979); A. Clarkson, *Lanes of Gold* (1990); H. Gordon, *Australia and the Olympic Games* (1994); *Sun-Herald* (Sydney), 5 Feb 1967, p 64; *Manly Daily*, 17 May 1983, p 2; *SMH*, 18 May 1983, p 15; private information.
                                         MURRAY G. PHILLIPS
                                         GARY OSMOND

HERMAN, MORTON EARLE (1907-1983), architect, historian and author, was born on

29 September 1907 at Woollahra, Sydney, and named Erskine Morton, second of three children of Joseph Earle Hermann, an English-born company promoter, and his wife Lily May, née Burghardy, born in New South Wales. After attending Randwick Public and Sydney Technical High schools, Morton won a scholarship to the University of Sydney (B.Arch., 1930), where he studied under Leslie Wilkinson [q.v.12]. On graduating with first-class honours, he won the Australian medallion and the travelling scholarship of the New South Wales Board of Architects, and a steamship scholarship.

Six years of practice and study in England and Europe included working for the English architect and historian H. S. Goodhart-Rendel and for Robert Atkinson, with whom he established the Building Centre in London. As its first resident architect he was a pivotal figure in the Ideal Home Exhibition held in London in 1933.

Returning to Australia in 1937, Herman joined the architects Louis S. Robertson & Son, and remained with them until 1942. He married Laura (Barbara) McPhail, a stenographer, on 1 January 1938 at St James's Church of England, Sydney. During World War II, working with the Allied Works Council, he designed prefabricated hospitals and warehouses for transportation in Liberty ships for the United States Army. After release from wartime duties, he entered sole private practice. In 1946 he joined the part-time staff of the Sydney Technical College at the invitation of Henry Pynor, head of the school of architecture. Known as 'Mick', Herman taught history, design and mechanics, and continued to do so when the school was absorbed by the University of Technology (later University of New South Wales) in 1949. For many years the college had conducted an architecture course at the Newcastle Technical College. In 1948, travelling regularly from Sydney, Herman revitalised what had become a professionally disregarded course. His work allowed a smooth takeover when the first permanent head was appointed in 1957.

During his student days, although a modernist, he had been inspired by the work of W. Hardy Wilson [q.v.12] to spend his spare time drawing colonial buildings around Sydney. Where Hardy Wilson had glossed over blemishes in the buildings, Herman recorded their extant state by executing accurate measured studies. His work had become the basis of his graduation thesis from the University of Sydney and had ultimately led to his first book, *The Early Australian Architects and Their Work* (1954). This seminal publication gave a foundation to the study of Australian architectural history. Fearing the destruction of postwar Sydney by development, he pub-

lished *The Architecture of Victorian Sydney* (1956). *The Blackets* (1963) established the significance of Edmund Thomas Blacket [q.v.3] in Australian architecture. A projected book on John Horbury Hunt [q.v.4], for which he had executed drawings, never eventuated. Many articles featuring modernist-style buildings and urging retention of significant structures appeared in 1937-75.

Herman was chairman of the Sir John Sulman [q.v.12] architectural award jury (1937-40, 1953); president of the Modern Architectural Research Society (1939-40); fellow (1951) and federal councillor (1955-59) of the Royal Australian Institute of Architects; councillor of the Royal Australian Historical Society (1954-58, 1963-66); and a member of the building advisory committee of the City of Sydney (1937-48), the historic buildings committee of the Cumberland County Council, and the Society of Architectural Historians (US).

In 1958 Herman was appointed visiting lecturer in the history of architecture and examiner in design for the extension board at the University of Melbourne, which conferred on him the degree of master of architecture in 1960. The University of Newcastle, where he had been a part-time lecturer, awarded him an honorary D.Litt. in 1966. The 'father of architectural history and conservation in this country' was appointed AM in 1979.

Divorced in 1970, from about 1975 Herman went into a serious decline while living at Kings Cross. One consequence was the dispersal of most of his papers and architectural drawings. About 1979, Philip Cox, a Sydney architect, moved him to the A. C. Mackie Nursing Home at Paddington and contributed to his maintenance. Herman died there on 25 March 1983 and, survived by his daughter, was buried in Botany cemetery. The Morton Herman prize in architecture at the University of New South Wales recognises the best performance in studies of historic structures.

B. Donaldson and D. Morris, *Architecture Newcastle* (2001); *Architecture in Aust*, vol 56, no 1, 1967, p 77, vol 73, no 3, 1984, p 31; *SMH*, 24 Aug 1937, p 8; 31 Mar 1983, p 8; H. de Berg, interview with M. Herman (ts, 1972, NLA); private information.

PETER REYNOLDS

HERRING, SIR EDMUND FRANCIS (1892-1982), chief justice and soldier, was born on 2 September 1892 at Maryborough, Victoria, third child of New Zealand-born Edmund Selwyn Herring, solicitor, and his Irish-born wife Gertrude Stella, née Fetherstonhaugh. Educated at Maryborough High School, Ned won scholarships to Melbourne Church of England Grammar School, where he excelled in classics and was dux of the school, and then to Trinity College, University of Melbourne. An outstanding schoolboy batsman, he represented the university in cricket and also in tennis. In 1912, selected as Victoria's Rhodes scholar, he proceeded to New College, Oxford.

The outbreak of World War I interrupted Herring's studies. Having enlisted in the King Edward's Horse in 1913, he transferred to the Royal Field Artillery in December 1914 and was commissioned as a second lieutenant. He was posted to the 99th Brigade, serving in France and then in Macedonia, where he captained a battery and won the Military Cross in 1917 for gallantry on the Doiran front. Energetic, eager and capable, by the end of the war he was commanding officer of the brigade as a temporary major. He was awarded the Distinguished Service Order in 1919 and mentioned in despatches.

Intending to practise law, Herring returned to Oxford (BA, 1919; MA, BCL, 1920) and was called to the Bar at the Inner Temple. He returned to Melbourne in November 1920 and, on a motion by Sir Edward Mitchell [q.v.10], was admitted to practise as a barrister and solicitor on 1 March 1921. On 6 April 1922 at Toorak Presbyterian Church, Herring married (Dame) Mary Ranken Lyle [q.v. Herring].

Clarity of mind, attention to detail and capacity for hard work brought Herring rapid success as an Equity barrister; he also lectured in Equity at the University of Melbourne (1927-30). Appointed KC in 1936, he sat on a committee inquiring into the crash of the *Kyeema* on Mount Dandenong, Victoria, in October 1938, which claimed eighteen lives. The committee's report made many recommendations for reform of national civil aviation standards.

Herring's flourishing legal career did not deter him from numerous outside interests. For more than a decade he was active in conservative politics. A founding member (1925) of the Constitutional Club, he joined the Young Nationalists in 1932 and, in the same year—having unsuccessfully sought preselection for the United Australia Party—assisted in its State election campaign. In 1935 he stood as an unendorsed UAP candidate for the Legislative Assembly seat of Brighton against the sitting UAP member, Ian Macfarlan [q.v.15]; after a rugged campaign he lost by only five hundred votes.

Troubled by the rise of communism and international disorder, Herring believed that the regular army should be supported by citizen forces capable of mounting resistance in case of an invasion. In 1922 he accepted a commission as legal staff officer with the 3rd Cavalry Division, Militia. Within a year he was offered command of the 44th Battery, 22nd Brigade, Australian Field Artillery. From 1929 he was to command a succession of field artillery brigades as a lieutenant colonel. His superiors regarded him as 'the best type of officer and one who should be employed to the utmost'.

The police strike of 1923, during which Herring worked as a special constable, saw the formation of the White Guard, a secret organisation consisting of former soldiers ready to act swiftly and suddenly against communist subversion. 'Vigilance' was a watchword for the White Guard, and always remained so for Herring. Organised in small cells, and with a strong presence in Militia units, the White Guard was most active during the early years of the Depression, and was largely effective in preserving its secrecy. Herring served as a regional commander, with responsibility for the Mornington Peninsula. (Sir) Thomas Blamey [q.v.13] was a central figure in the organisation and, despite their very different temperaments, he and Herring maintained a strong mutual regard.

At the outbreak of World War II in 1939, Herring accepted Blamey's invitation to join the AIF as a temporary brigadier and commander of the 6th Division's artillery. In North Africa in January 1941 Herring's gunners played a significant part in the decisive victories over the Italians at Bardia and Tobruk; for his leadership he was appointed CBE (1941). Three months later, during the ill-fated Greek campaign, his highly effective use of artillery was vital in delaying advancing German forces and enabling orderly retreats. He was awarded the Greek Military Cross (1942). In August 1941, as a temporary major general (substantive February 1944) he assumed command of the 6th Division, reforming in Palestine, after its heavy casualties in Greece and Crete. From October the 6th became part of the occupying force in Syria until ordered to return to Australia to face the impending Japanese threat. Herring anticipated that his troops would have to fight 'a damn sight harder than we have been asked to fight yet'.

Appointed commander of forces in the Northern Territory in March 1942, one month after the devastating air raid on Darwin, Herring was ruthless in dismissing officers of the former command or replacing them with experienced AIF officers. During the next five months he worked ceaselessly to improve and reorganise the Territory's defences. After briefly commanding II Corps at Esk, Queensland, he succeeded (Sir) Sydney Rowell [q.v.16] in command of New Guinea Force and I Corps in October 1942, with the rank of temporary lieutenant general. Blamey wanted a 'commander of cheerful temperament' who was 'prepared to co-operate to the limit'. The close professional partnership of Herring and Blamey has been described by Herring's biographer, Stuart Sayers, as 'rare, perhaps unique at such a level of command in the Second AIF'. Some wondered if 'co-operation' disguised the reality that Blamey, operating through Herring, was effective commander in Papua and New Guinea. Herring claimed that Blamey never interfered, expecting him 'to get on with the job, and really command one's show'. He held the New Guinea command until August 1943, continuing as I Corps commander until February 1944.

Herring regarded his principal task as ensuring a good working relationship between the Australians and their American allies in the battle for the Papuan beachheads of Buna, Gona and Sanananda between September 1942 and January 1943. At the higher command level, the nature of the campaign in difficult terrain did not allow for sweeping military initiatives, and was a severe test of administrative capacity. In January 1943 Herring was awarded the American Distinguished Service Cross and in May he was appointed KBE for his service in Papua.

Over the next six months the Allied forces conducted successful assaults in New Guinea on Lae, Salamaua and Finschhafen. The Finschhafen campaign, in September, was probably the most difficult month of the war for Herring. Unable to secure adequate transport support from the United States Navy, he was further frustrated by initial indifference from the New Guinea Force Headquarters, under the newly appointed New Guinea Force commander, Sir Iven Mackay [q.v.15]. The military historian David Horner considers that Herring failed to approach 'the problem as tactfully as he might', but endorses Herring's claim that 'we damn nearly lost Finschhafen'. On 28 September Herring's aeroplane crashed when taking off for Milne Bay: he was uninjured, although a close friend and colleague, Brigadier R. K. Sutherland, died in the seat next to him.

One of Herring's duties was to confirm the death sentences of twenty-two Papuans, hanged publicly in September 1943, after being found guilty of various charges of murder and treason. In 1978, when his role in the executions was made public, he said that the men had been fairly tried and that his conscience was clear.

Described by the official war historian Dudley McCarthy as a 'small and quiet' man with great depth of character, Herring possessed a natural capacity to get on with people and look for the best in them. While courteous, he was also—according to Sayers—'implacably competitive', and capable, with his 'blue-glacier stare', of delivering 'paralysing rebukes without lifting his voice'. He was not flamboyant, earned no nicknames and did not court popularity, but gained respect from most who served with him. His chief staff officer saw in his method of command—working 'carefully round any problem, discussing factors and courses'—the habits of a barrister: he took his time, but was thorough.

Sir Edmund's active service ended with his swearing in as chief justice of Victoria on 10 February 1944; he soon made a particular mark on the court through his administrative ability. By August he had established a Law Reform Committee, which he chaired until 1957, and which ranged across all areas of Victorian statute law. Aware that antiquated accommodation and greatly increased litigation were threatening the effectiveness of the court, he worked to strengthen the bench and to increase space for both Supreme and County courts. Herring attached considerable importance to the symbolism and dignity surrounding the judicial arm of government, initiating the formal opening of the legal year and replacing the informal swearing-in of justices of the peace with a Full Court ceremony. He revived the practice of judges reporting annually to the government on the state of the courts. When in 1954 the premier, John Cain [q.v.13], ignored a resolution in which judges protested at the inadequacy of their new salary scales, Herring publicly criticised the government's violation of a vital constitutional principle—the judges' right to be heard.

From 1945 to 1972 Herring also held the post of lieutenant-governor. He was appointed KCMG in 1949. Given his high judicial and executive offices, he was unusually outspoken on public issues. His frequent public utterances reflected his commitment to the British Empire and the American alliance, and his deep concern that the nation was in danger both from the external threat of communism and from internal subversion. Widespread selfishness, apathy and a lack of community spirit were equally deplored. His views could be—and sometimes were—too easily criticised as nothing more than unreflecting, rigid conservatism. The basis of his beliefs was a firm Christianity, and a conviction that problems of economics and politics could only be solved 'where attention was paid to ethical values as well'. In 1950-51, during the Korean War, his fears over the inadequacy of Australia's defences led him to step aside temporarily from the chief justiceship and serve as director-general of recruiting.

Herring's most notable attempt to arouse public spirit was the 'Call to the People of Australia'; he was the driving force behind its promotion. The Call was broadcast across the nation on the evening of Remembrance Day, 11 November 1951. Signed by Herring and four of his fellow chief justices, and by religious leaders—Catholic, Protestant and Jewish—the Call told Australians that they were 'in danger'. Threatened by external forces and 'moral and intellectual apathy', citizens had 'a duty' to 'defend the community against evil designs' and take an 'active concern in public affairs'. Ending with 'Fear God, Honour the King', the Call evoked vehement reactions of praise and censure; while campaigns in its name continued until 1957, its initial impact did not endure.

Among his many public activities, Herring served as chancellor of the Church of England Diocese of Melbourne (1941-80) and as State (1945-68) and national (1958-77) president of the Australian Boy Scout Association (from 1958 the Scouts Association of Australia). President of Toc H Australia (1947-82), he was chairman of the trustees of the Melbourne Shrine of Remembrance (1945-79) and the Australian War Memorial (1959-74), and a member of the councils of Trinity College (1919-79), Melbourne Grammar (1939-40, 1941-82), the University of Melbourne (1945-57), and the Victorian Rhodes scholarship selection committee (1923-32). From 1961 a vice-president of the British and Foreign Bible Society, Herring was also chairman of the advisory board of the Council of Christian Education in Schools (1952-82). In 1953 he had led the Australian contingent to the coronation of Queen Elizabeth II.

In supporting his application for a Rhodes scholarship, Dr Alexander Leeper [q.v.10] had described Herring as 'strong, alert and efficient alike in mind and body', 'straightforward, resolute and self-controlled and of the firmest moral principles'. Those qualities remained in evidence throughout his life. An honorary fellow of New College, Oxford (1949), he was awarded honorary degrees by the University of Oxford (DCL, 1953) and Monash University (LL D, 1973). Predeceased by his wife and survived by his three daughters, Sir Edmund Herring died at Camberwell, Melbourne, on 5 January 1982. He was cremated after a state funeral at St Paul's Cathedral. Portraits by Sir William Dargie are held by the Australian War Memorial and the Supreme Court of Victoria Library; the Australian War Memorial also holds a portrait by Sir Ivor Hele. Herring Island, in the River Yarra at South Yarra, is named after him.

D. McCarthy, *South-West Pacific Area—First Year* (1959); S. Sayers, *Ned Herring* (1980); D. M. Horner, *High Command* (1982), and (ed), *The Commanders* (1984); *Herald* (Melbourne), 14 Aug 1944, p 6; *Bulletin*, 22 May 1978, p 17; *Age* (Melbourne), 6 Jan 1982, p 5; Herring papers (SLV).

GEOFF BROWNE

HERRING, DAME MARY RANKEN (1895-1981), medical practitioner, was born on 31 March 1895 at Carlton, Melbourne, eldest child of Irish-born (Sir) Thomas Ranken Lyle [q.v.10], professor of natural philosophy at the University of Melbourne, and his Victorian-born wife Clare, nee Millear. Mary was educated at Toorak College, where she excelled both scholastically and in sport, and was head of school (1911-12). She studied at the University of Melbourne (MB, BS, 1921), graduating with first-class honours and several prizes in medicine, winning Blues in hockey and tennis and serving on the Students' Representative Council. Her internship at the (Royal) Women's Hospital shaped a commitment to advance women's and children's welfare.

On 6 April 1922 at Toorak Presbyterian Church, Melbourne, Mary married (Sir) Edmund Francis Herring [q.v.], a barrister whom she had met on his leave from military service in 1918. A devoted mother of three daughters, she maintained contact with medical colleagues, including R. H. Fetherston and Vera Scantlebury Brown [qq.v.8,11] who sought to improve ante-natal care. At Fetherston's invitation, in 1926 she established a clinic providing such services at the Prahran Health Centre. One day each week until 1945 she treated impoverished women, many with debilitating illnesses, who struggled to survive in sub-standard conditions, often worked throughout their pregnancy to provide for their families, and experienced high rates of maternal mortality.

Galvanised by this exposure, and her long association with the Melbourne District Nursing Society (vice-president, 1943-53), in 1934 Dr Herring joined George Simpson and Victor Wallace [qq.v.16] in opening the Women's Welfare Clinic. Against opposition from some in the medical fraternity and conservative sections of society, she pioneered family planning services. While in her later years concerned that access to birth control had resulted in promiscuity, she maintained that, in the straitened circumstances of the 1930s, this assistance was vital for women who had no other access to medical care.

With the outbreak of World War II, Mary Herring was active in the formation of the AIF Women's Association (foundation chairman, 1940; president, 1943-46) to assist women while their husbands, sons and brothers fought overseas. When her husband became chief justice (1944) and lieutenant-governor (1945) of Victoria, Lady Herring put aside medical practice and assumed a wide range of official posts including those of founding president of the Victorian Council of Social Service (1946-50), chairman of the Scantlebury Brown Memorial Trust (1946-79), and deputy-president of the Victorian division of the Australian Red Cross Society (1944-63) and of the Victoria League (1945-72). President of Toorak College council (1947-48 and 1960-70) and of the Australian council of the Save the Children Fund (1962-67), she was a tireless worker and patron for many charities, with particular interests in spastic and handicapped children, child-care organisations and amateur sporting organisations for girls and women. She was a member of the Lyceum and Alexandra clubs.

The *Argus* in 1949 described Lady Herring as an outstanding example of 'selfless devotion to the service of others': 'calm, kindly, clear-minded, and intensely logical'. She was appointed a Commander of the Order of St John in 1953 and DBE in 1960. Dame Mary died on 26 October 1981 at Camberwell, Melbourne, predeceasing her husband by ten weeks, and survived by their daughters. She was cremated. The Mary Herring hall and scholarship at Toorak College commemorate her service.

N. Rosenthal, *People—Not Cases* (1974); J. Robinson, *The Echoes Fade Not* (1987); D. Hilton, *Dr Mary* (1989); J. McCalman, *Sex and Suffering* (1998); *Argus* (Melbourne), 'Women's Mag', 6 Sept 1949, p 3.

CHERYL CROCKETT

HEWITT, JOSEPH ERIC (1901-1985), air force and naval officer, was born on 13 April 1901 at Tylden, Victoria, younger son of Joseph Henry Hewitt, Presbyterian clergyman, and his wife Rose Alice, née Harkness, both Victorian born. Eric spent his early life at Murchison. After the family moved to Melbourne in 1908, he attended Mentone High School and then Scotch College. In 1915 he entered the Royal Australian Naval College, Jervis Bay, Federal Capital Territory. Graduating in 1918, he was appointed midshipman on 1 January 1919 and sent to Britain to serve with the Royal Navy.

While on board the battleship HMS *Ramillies*, Hewitt witnessed the scuttling of the German fleet at Scapa Flow, Orkney Islands, in June 1919 and took part in the salving of some of those ships. He then participated in postwar operations in the Mediterranean and Black seas. Back in England, he was promoted to sub-lieutenant in February 1921 and from April he served in the destroyer HMS *Whitley*. In September he moved to the RN College, Greenwich, and then to Portsmouth for a series of professional courses before returning to Australia in September 1922. He was made lieutenant in November.

After leave and service in HMAS *Anzac*, Hewitt was seconded to the Royal Australian Air Force in January 1923. That year he undertook pilot training at No.1 Flying Training School, Point Cook, Victoria. Over the next decade he moved between the RAAF, the RAN and the RN, most of his postings being associated with seaplane training and operations. On 10 November 1925 at Christ Church, Paddington, London, he married with Anglican rites Lorna Pretoria Bishop (d.1976). In

April 1928 he transferred permanently to the RAAF. He was posted to No.101 (Fleet Co-operation) Flight, Point Cook, in October 1929 and elevated to commanding officer in February 1931 as a squadron leader.

Hewitt attended the RAF Staff College, Andover, England, in 1934, then served as assistant liaison officer in London and performed staff duties. In April 1936 he was appointed commanding officer of No.104 (Bomber) Squadron, RAF, at Abingdon, Berkshire, and later Hucknall, Nottinghamshire, flying Hawker Hind aircraft. The two-year posting indicated the esteem in which he was held by both the RAAF and the RAF, and in January 1938 he was promoted to wing commander. After his return to Australia, he was appointed in June to be senior air staff officer at RAAF Station, Richmond, New South Wales. For his work there he was appointed OBE (1940).

At the outbreak of World War II, Hewitt was the commanding officer of RAAF Station, Rathmines. In December 1939 he was appointed senior administrative staff officer, Southern Area headquarters, Melbourne, and made temporary group captain. He became director of personal services, Air Force Headquarters, in July 1940, deputy-chief of the Air Staff in October 1941 as an acting air commodore, director of plans and air operations at Australian-British-Dutch-American Command, Netherlands East Indies, in January 1942 and assistant-chief of the Air Staff in March.

A small, dark-haired, dapper man, Joe Hewitt, as he was known in the RAAF, had many supporters and many detractors. He was assertive, aggressive and often abrasive. However, he was also intelligent, quick-witted, determined and very hard working. In May 1942 he was appointed director of intelligence, Allied Air Forces Headquarters, South-West Pacific Area. He became air officer commanding No.9 (Operational) Group in the New Guinea area in February 1943. This was the largest and most important operational command in the RAAF. Hewitt was an active and vigorous commander. He worked hard and expected those under his command to do likewise. In March No.9 Group played an important part in the battle of the Bismarck Sea, in which a large Japanese convoy was intercepted and its plans to land troops in New Guinea thwarted by the efforts of Allied aircraft.

Air and maritime operations in the South-West Pacific Area at this time were dominated by the large Japanese base at Rabaul, New Britain. The commanding officer of No.8 Squadron, Wing Commander G. D. Nicoll, developed a plan to attack shipping in Rabaul harbour using twelve Beaufort torpedo bombers. The plan, supported by Hewitt, was scheduled for 8 November but Nicoll lost confidence in it. After a late-night confrontation on the airfield between the two, an attack using only three aircraft was made with the loss of one aircraft and its crew and little damage to the Japanese ships.

Two days later Hewitt removed Nicoll from his post and sent him back to Australia. This action was countermanded by the chief of the Air Staff, Air Vice-Marshal (Sir) George Jones, who in December removed Hewitt from his command and returned him to his previous position of director of intelligence. None of the significant players in this drama performed well, but Hewitt suffered most damage to his reputation and that was out of proportion to his mistakes. Subsequent events suggest that Jones came to a similar view for, in the citation to his appointment as CBE in 1951, Hewitt was commended for his work in the very post from which he had been relieved.

However, Hewitt's most important work was yet to come. From 1945 to 1948, as the air member for personnel, he was responsible for the demobilisation of the wartime RAAF and the development of a postwar professional air force. With considerable skill and keen judgment, he oversaw the reduction of service personnel from more than 160 000 to fewer than 10 000. His restructuring of education and training resulted in an air force that was properly prepared for the new era. Under his leadership, the first steps were taken to establish the Apprentice Training Scheme, the RAAF College and the RAAF Staff College. Promoted to temporary air vice-marshal in January 1947 (substantive 1 October 1948), he became Australian defence representative in London (1949-51) and air member for supply and equipment (1951-56), and attended to both positions with characteristic determination and vigour.

Retiring from the RAAF on 13 April 1956, Hewitt was manager, education and training, with the International Harvester Co. of Australia Pty Ltd, for ten years. He refused to allow a diagnosis of cancer in 1973 to affect his activities. Throughout his life he had been meticulous in keeping a diary. From his records, he developed two volumes of autobiography, *Adversity in Success* (1980) and *The Black One* (1984). It was typical of the man that he founded his own publishing company to ensure that they were properly produced. Survived by his three daughters, he died on 1 November 1985 at Windsor, Melbourne, and was cremated with full air force honours.

G. Odgers, *Air War against Japan 1943-1945* (1957); D. Gillison, *Royal Australian Air Force 1939-1942* (1962); C. D. Coulthard-Clark, *The Third Brother* (1991); A. Stephens, *Power Plus Attitude* (1992), *Going Solo* (1995) and *The Royal Australian Air Force* (2001); A6769, item Hewitt J E, A12372, item O32 (NAA); Hewitt papers (AWM); private information.   RAY FUNNELL

HEWITT, VERITY; *see* FITZHARDINGE

HEYMANSON, SIR SYDNEY HENRY (RANDAL) (1903-1984), journalist, was born on 18 April 1903 at South Yarra, Melbourne, son of Frederick Leopold Heymanson, commercial traveller, and his wife Bertha, née McDonnell. Sydney was educated at All Saints' Grammar School, East St Kilda (where he was editor of the *Grammarian*), and at Melbourne Church of England Grammar School. A brilliant student, he won a scholarship to the University of Melbourne (BA Hons, 1924; MA, 1947), gaining first-class honours and the Dwight [q.v.4] prize in history and political science, and the Wyselaskie scholarship in political economy. In 1924 he was elected editor of the *Melbourne University Magazine* and in 1925 he founded and became the first editor of the university student newspaper *Farrago*.

While working on *Farrago* Heymanson was also a history master (1924-25) at Melbourne Grammar; he taught with enthusiasm and by 1926 had saved enough money to fulfil his ambition to travel to England. He carried out doctoral studies (1927-28) with Arnold Toynbee at the London School of Economics and Political Science and, to help meet expenses, lectured (1928-30) in the University of London's extension program. Finding the academic world narrow and restricting, he turned to journalism.

In 1927 Heymanson accepted an invitation from (Sir) Lloyd Dumas [q.v.14] to join the London staff of the Melbourne *Herald*. As European correspondent for the Herald and Weekly Times Ltd's Australian Newspaper Service, Heymanson specialised in covering international affairs, and also began contributing to British papers. He was an early commentator on Hitler's rise to power, noting that the energy and resentment of the German people could lead to militarism and war. With Roy Lewis he launched *Vital News* (1939-41), which had a confidential circulation among policy-makers in England and the United States of America.

Heymanson became closely associated with Sir Keith Murdoch [q.v.10], and when it became apparent that the entry of the United States into World War II was essential for Allied victory, Murdoch invited him to open a New York bureau for the *Herald*'s Australian Newspaper Service. From 1940, as manager and editor, Heymanson (his first name now changed to Randal) cabled authoritative reports back to Australia. He also developed extensive professional and personal networks. In 1942-43 he was president of the Foreign Press Association, and in 1948—sharing Murdoch's conviction that Australia must look to the United States for protection and development—he became one of the founders of the American-Australian Association. Serving as director (1948-84), vice-president (1949-65), president (1966-67) and chairman (1967-84), Heymanson developed it into a forum in which visiting Australian businessmen, politicians and diplomats conferred with prominent, influential Americans.

Lean, gentle, urbane and sagacious, Heymanson was admired by Sir Robert Menzies [q.v.15], who described him as 'the best informed Australian living in America'. He was appointed OBE (1955) and CBE (1965), and knighted in 1972. Sir Randal retired from the *Herald*'s New York bureau in 1969, but continued to write for the Australian press and to maintain a keen interest in travel, art and literature. He never married. Following his death on 27 August 1984 in New York, Australia's ambassador to the United States, Sir Robert Cotton, lamented that 'Australia has lost a great citizen and the US a great friend'. Heymanson was cremated and his ashes returned to Australia.

Herald (Melbourne), 7 Sept 1984, p 10; M. Humphries, A School That Has Passed (MEd thesis, Univ of Melbourne, 1986); Heymanson papers (NLA); private information.

MICHAEL E. HUMPHRIES

HIBBERD, Sir DONALD JAMES (1916-1982), businessman, was born on 26 June 1916 at Mosman, Sydney, son of London-born William James Hibberd, commercial traveller, and his New South Wales-born wife Laura Isabel, née Abernethy. Educated at Fort Street Boys' High School, Donald won a bursary to study part time at the University of Sydney (B.Ec., 1939), while working in the State Auditor-General's Office, and in 1939 joined the Commonwealth Department of Trade and Customs. On 4 April 1942 at Deepdene, Melbourne, he married Florence Alice Kennedy Macandie.

In 1946 Hibberd transferred to the Commonwealth Treasury: he was involved in preparing Prime Minister Chifley's [q.v.13] bank nationalisation plans in 1947 and—when the legislation was found in the High Court of Australia and Privy Council to be unconstitutional—in setting up the Commonwealth Trading Bank. Promoted to first assistant secretary of the banking, trade and industry branch (1953), he also served as a member of the Australian

Aluminium Production Commission (1953-57), established in recognition of the strategic importance of such a processing capacity.

In 1957 Hibberd accepted (Sir) Maurice Mawby's [q.v.15] invitation to become executive director of the Commonwealth Aluminium Corporation Pty Ltd (Comalco), a company formed to exploit new opportunities to develop an integrated aluminium industry in Australia following the discovery of bauxite at Weipa, Queensland. As Comalco's managing director (1960-69), chairman and chief executive (1969-78), and non-executive chairman (1978-80), Hibberd sought to raise finance and secure expert partners. Following the failure in 1960 of the partnership with British interests, Hibberd persuaded the California-based Kaiser Aluminium & Chemical Corporation to join Comalco and Consolidated Zinc Pty Ltd (later Conzinc Riotinto Australia) in developing the Weipa mine. He was made a director (1962-71) of CRA. In 1960 he also became a director of the Aluminium Production Corporation Ltd, formed to purchase and expand the AAPC smelter at Bell Bay, Tasmania. He later drew together an international consortium to build the Queensland Alumina Ltd refinery at Gladstone; he was vice-chairman in 1964-80.

Hibberd's successes not only benefited Comalco but improved the Australian resource sector's international standing. To underpin Weipa's development, Comalco secured long-term Japanese bauxite contracts and convinced European aluminium companies that Australia was a viable source of raw materials. Through the 1970s, despite economic fluctuations, Comalco became the world's largest bauxite exporter. Its operations included smelting and refining works in Italy and New Zealand. Hibberd was chairman of New Zealand Aluminium Smelters Ltd in 1977-80. He took particular pride in the development of several residential communities for workers.

A large-framed, disciplined, modest and softly spoken 'man of vision' (according to the *Australian*), with 'an infectious smile', Hibberd was a member of the board of the Reserve Bank of Australia (1966-80), the council of the University of Melbourne (for which he chaired the finance committee in 1966-82) and the Australian Mining Industry Council (president 1972-73). He was a long-serving member of the Australia-Japan Business Co-operation Committee and a delegate with the first Australian trade mission to China in 1973. In 1956-81 he sat on the Royal Victorian Eye and Ear Hospital's committee of management. Appointed OBE in 1957, he was knighted in 1977. Survived by his wife and their son and daughter, Sir Donald died of cancer at Richmond, Melbourne, on 31 December 1982; he was cremated. A visiting lectureship at the University of Melbourne's Graduate School of Management was established in his memory.

B. Carroll, *Potlines and People* (1980); *Australian*, 5 June 1976, p 12, 13 May 1967, p 14; *CRA Gazette*, 14 July 1978, p 4; Hibberd papers (Univ of Melbourne Archives); private information.

MICHAEL BELL

HICKMAN, VERNON VICTOR (1894-1984), zoologist, was born on 28 August 1894 at Glenorchy, Hobart, elder son of Tasmanian-born George Milford Hickman, storekeeper, and his wife Pauline, née Patterson. Vernon was educated at the Friends' High School and the University of Tasmania (B.Sc., 1915; BA, 1927; D.Sc., 1937). Briefly a visiting master in mathematics at the Collegiate School, Hobart, in 1915-16 he lectured in chemistry and mineralogy at Zeehan School of Mines and Metallurgy. During World War I he relinquished a commission in the Militia to enlist on 28 August 1917 in the Australian Imperial Force. From April 1918 he served on the Western Front with the 40th Battalion. Promoted to corporal in August, he returned to Tasmania in April 1919 and was discharged from the AIF on 23 May. His wartime experiences left him with nightmares for many years. On 10 April 1920 at Burnie he married with Methodist forms Elvie Frances Eddy.

Appointed head of chemistry at Launceston Technical College in 1920, Hickman pursued an interest in invertebrates, in particular the mountain shrimp, *Anaspides tasmaniae* (a crustacean), and by 1932 had published eight papers. That year he succeeded T. T. Flynn [q.v.8] as Ralston lecturer in biology at the University of Tasmania. The terms of the Ralston bequest required him to devote one term a year to research; because teaching responsibilities made this impossible he fitted out a laboratory at home so that he could fulfil his contract.

Hickman became internationally recognised for his research on arachnids and was promoted to a chair in 1943. A well-built man of about 5 ft 8 ins (173 cm), he always came to work in a suit and hat, carrying a Gladstone bag containing his lunch. He rarely missed a day due to illness. Very reserved, he disliked committee work, spoke little in meetings and had difficulty dealing with the more rambunctious members of the professorial board. Expecting people to listen to his point of view, he could be stubborn and he ignored matters not in the interests of his department. He encouraged his staff to pursue research interests and provided students with helpful advice and practical assistance. On his retirement in 1959 he was appointed emeritus professor.

A zealous field-collector, he discovered a species of spider named *Hickmania troglodytes*. It was later placed in a new family, Hick-

maniidae. He developed an encyclopaedic knowledge of invertebrates and their relationships, and occasionally studied other animal groups, including mammals. In his regular contributions to scientific journals, he skilfully illustrated his papers and provided his own innovative photographs. The Royal Society of Tasmania awarded him its medal in 1940 and the Clive Lord [q.v.10] medal in 1960, and made him a life member in 1967. Elected a fellow of the Australian and New Zealand Association for the Advancement of Science in 1940 and of the Royal Entomological Society of London in 1947, he won the Anders Retzius medal of the Royal Physiographical Society of Lund, Sweden, in 1951. In 1977 he was made an honorary life member of the Entomological Society of New South Wales. He had been a corresponding member of the Zoological Society of London since 1934, but never travelled overseas to meet other scientists. A modest man, he rarely talked of his work or achievements, but was proud of his Swedish award.

Hickman loved music; he played the piano and organ and, a staunch Methodist, sang in his church choir. He played grade cricket and enjoyed chess. In 1979 he was appointed OBE. He died on 20 November 1984 at his New Town home and was cremated. Predeceased by his wife, he was survived by two sons and a daughter.

General and Applied Entomology, vol 17, 1985, p 3; *Mercury* (Hobart), 1 Dec 1984, p 13; private information and personal knowledge.   ERIC GUILER

HICKS, SIR EDWIN WILLIAM (1910-1984), public servant and diplomat, was born on 9 June 1910 at Elsternwick, Melbourne, son of William Banks Hicks, draftsman, and his wife Elsie May, née Kitching, both Melbourne born. Educated at Haileybury College and Melbourne Church of England Grammar School, Ted moved with his parents to Canberra in 1927. Next year he became a temporary officer with the Federal Capital Commission. Appointed a permanent officer in the Commonwealth Public Service in 1929, he had postings to the Public Service Board and the Bureau of Census and Statistics. At St Andrew's Church of England, Brighton, Melbourne, on 22 December 1937 he married Jean MacPherson, who worked in her family's business. Next year he joined the Department of Trade and Customs.

On 18 July 1942 Hicks enlisted in the Royal Australian Air Force. Commissioned on 9 October 1943, he held various administrative positions and was promoted to flying officer in April 1944. His RAAF appointment terminated on 2 October 1945. Back in Trade and Customs, he became principal research officer in the commercial policies branch in 1947. Another stint at the Public Service Board followed, first as an inspector (from 1948) and then as senior inspector investigating the organisation and methods of government departments (from 1950). He had qualified as an accountant and studied at Canberra University College (B.Com., 1948), later becoming a fellow (1972) of the Australian Society of Accountants; he saw accountancy qualifications as a prerequisite for an administrative career.

Hicks was appointed secretary of the Department of Air on 22 December 1951. His effectiveness there led to his being selected to succeed the long-serving and formidable Sir Frederick Shedden [q.v.16] as secretary of the Department of Defence on 29 October 1956. He made his strongest mark in higher administration and policy at Defence. An adviser and confidant to ministers and prime ministers, he was respected and valued by his peers. However, his last few years in office were clouded by a communication breakdown between himself and his minister, (Sir) Allen Fairhall, who had succeeded Sir Shane Paltridge [q.v.15] in 1966. More thoughtful and intellectual in his approach to problems, Hicks could not find a meeting of minds with the technically inclined Fairhall.

Within the department, though, and in relation to the armed services, Hicks had a gift of communication and understanding. Soon after he took over, he gave the first staff Christmas party held at Defence, with a bar set up in his own office. Throughout his term he was chairman of the Defence Committee; he was also a member of the Morshead [q.v.15] committee, which in 1957 reported to the government on future defence administration. Having organised the transfer (from 1959) of the Defence group of departments from Melbourne to Canberra, he presided over what until then was one of the greatest expansions in Australia's defence program. He strongly defended the purchase of the controversial F-111 strike bomber from the United States of America.

After his wife died in 1959, Hicks married Lois Una Swindon, a trained nurse, on 14 January 1961 at the Church of St John the Baptist, Reid. He was appointed CBE in 1956 and knighted in 1965. In January 1968 he retired from Defence and became high commissioner to New Zealand. He returned to Canberra in 1971. His contribution to Canberra's community life had begun in sporting circles, where he made his mark in cricket, Australian Rules football and tennis. Later he was an active golfer, serving as honorary treasurer (1971-73) and vice-president (1973-74) of the Royal Canberra Golf Club. He was a member (1972-73) of the board of Canberra Church of England Girls' Grammar School; chairman (1974-82) of the council of Burgmann [q.v.13]

College, Australian National University; honorary treasurer (1972-75) of the Winston Churchill Memorial Trust; and a member (1978-84) of the interim council of the Royal Military College, Duntroon. He supported St John's, Reid, and the establishment (1972) of St David's Church, Red Hill, and served on the advisory board of the Salvation Army.

Hicks played a part in Canberra's commercial life through his appointment as chairman of the board of Capital City Broadcasters Pty Ltd, the licensee of radio station 2CC. He was also a consultant to the Boeing International Corporation. His genial, chubby-faced appearance belied the big, capable mind he brought to bear on all he undertook. Among colleagues he commanded respect as a 'straight-down-the-centre man of innate honesty, never swayed by friendship or a useful argument that might not be valid'. Survived by his wife and their son and daughter, and by the two sons and daughter of his first marriage, Sir Edwin died on 14 May 1984 in Canberra and was buried in Gungahlin cemetery.

P. Dennis et al, *The Oxford Companion to Australian Military History* (1995); P. Hasluck, *The Chance of Politics* (1997); E. Andrews, *The Department of Defence* (2001); *Canberra Times*, 7 Dec 1967, p 1, 17 Jan 1968, p 18, 19 May 1984, p 6; *Australian*, 5 Jan 1968, p 3; *Austn Accountant*, Dec 1972, p 443, June 1984, p 342; A9300, item Hicks E W (NAA); private information.   JOHN FARQUHARSON

HIGGINS, CHRISTOPHER IAN (1943-1990), public servant and economist, was born on 3 April 1943 at Murwillumbah, New South Wales, eldest of four sons of Australian-born parents George Patrick Higgins, sawmill employee, and his wife Muriel Adelaide, née McEwan. The family struggled financially—Chris did not wear shoes until sixth grade—and an academic secondary school program was out of his reach until the local headmaster and business community provided financial assistance. In his final year at Ballina High School he won a cadetship from the Commonwealth Bureau of Census and Statistics to study economics at the Australian National University (B.Ec., 1964), Canberra. An outstanding student, he graduated with first-class honours and the Tillyard [qq.v.12] prize before beginning work with the statistics bureau.

In September 1964 Higgins commenced research at the University of Pennsylvania (Ph.D., 1968), United States of America, under Professor Lawrence Klein, who rated him one of the best students he ever had. On 22 December 1966 at Wynnewood, Pennsylvania, Higgins married Paula Abigail Gomberg, a fellow student. On his return to Australia in January 1968, he rejoined the statistics bureau. Using his newly acquired skills in econometrics and economic modelling, he pioneered the first official national-income forecasting model. His work in this field led him to move to the Treasury in 1969. There he was an influential adviser from an early stage, particularly on economic conditions and macroeconomic policy.

Higgins's career was distinguished by his enduring determination to combine his interest in academic economics with his professional work as a public servant. He spent 1973-74 as an academic at the University of Pennsylvania and the University of British Columbia, Canada. After serving as minister (economic and financial affairs) in the Australian delegation to the Organisation for Economic Co-operation and Development, Paris, in 1980-81, he took leave from the Treasury to become director of the general economics branch of the economics and statistics department of the OECD, in 1981-84. Back in Australia, he was appointed deputy-secretary (economic) in February 1985. In 1987 he was elected a fellow of the Academy of the Social Sciences in Australia. He took up his final position as secretary of the Treasury on 18 September 1989.

In a Treasury department proud of its intellectual foundations, Higgins provided leadership. His influence stemmed from a rare combination of strong convictions about the direction of policy and an open and enquiring mind. He proposed policies to reduce inflation in the 1980s, and to effect microeconomic reform. Both treasurers in the 1980s—John Howard and especially Paul Keating—held Higgins in high regard. Unusually for a senior public servant, he maintained his membership of the Australian Labor Party, and this was symptomatic of his unfailing commitment to social justice. At the same time he appreciated early on that society's well-being and low unemployment depend on maintaining national competitiveness and low inflation. The improved performance of the Australian economy since the 1980s owed much to his foresight and the power of his advocacy.

Higgins enjoyed to the full his short life, which was marked by his sense of fun and his enthusiasm for whatever he tackled. Family and friends, food and wine, and sport all provided a balance to his considerable commitment to work. He collapsed and died of myocardial infarction on 6 December 1990 at Bruce, Canberra, after competing at an athletics meeting. He had undergone a coronary angioplasty in 1989 and knew the risks that he was taking, but nothing would ever hold him back. Survived by his wife and their two sons, he was cremated with Presbyterian forms.

Treasury (Cwlth), *Annual Report*, 1970-91; *SMH*, 13 Aug 1984, p 17; *Canberra Times*, 9 July 1989, p 28, 8 Dec 1990, p 15, 12 Dec 1990, p 3; *Age* (Melbourne), 4 Mar 1990, 'Money', p 1; *Australian*, 8-9 Dec 1990, p 4; *Austn Financial Review*, 10 Dec 1990, p 8; private information.					MICHAEL KEATING

HILEY, SIR THOMAS ALFRED (1905-1990), accountant and politician, was born on 25 November 1905 in Brisbane, fourth of six children of William Hiley, an English-born Commonwealth public servant, and his wife Maria, née Savage, from Brisbane. Educated at Brisbane Central State and Brisbane Grammar schools, in 1921 Tom joined the State public service; he worked in the Public Service Commissioner's Department and the State Audit Office while studying accountancy. He entered private practice as a public accountant in 1926, becoming a partner next year with C. A. Le Maistre Walker, Brisbane. On 11 October 1929 at the Methodist Church, West End, he married Marjory Joyce Jarrott (d.1972), a schoolteacher.

Admitted to membership (1933) of the Institute of Chartered Accountants in Australia, Hiley was Queensland chairman (1942-44) and federal president (1946-48). In 1935-75 he was on the board of the faculty of commerce, University of Queensland; he wrote *Solicitors' Trust Accounts* (1941). During World War II he developed a significant practice while serving as honorary treasurer of the Queensland Patriotic Fund and the State division of the Australian Comforts Fund. His practice was to become T. A. Hiley, Jarrott & Doggett in 1957.

Disillusioned with the United Australia Party, in 1943 Hiley joined a group of businessmen led by (Sir) John Chandler [q.v.13] that formed the Queensland People's Party. In April 1944 he was elected to the Legislative Assembly as the member for Logan. He was later to represent Coorparoo (1950-60) and Chatsworth (1960-66). Chandler, as leader of the parliamentary party, failed to make an impact on the Labor government, and was replaced by Bruce Pie [q.v.15] in May 1947 and by Hiley in February 1948. Hiley soon proved to be an effective, hard-working and respected leader; he was later described by Clem Lack [q.v.15] as the most polished debater in the Queensland parliament since T. J. Ryan [q.v.11]. In July 1949 the QPP became the Liberal Party of Australia, Queensland division; at the 1950 election its primary vote was 29.91 per cent. Hiley resigned as leader in August 1954, claiming that his salary was inadequate, and the energetic but less capable (Sir) Kenneth Morris [q.v.15] was elected in his place.

On 12 August 1957 the Country Party-Liberal Party coalition took office, with (Sir) Frank Nicklin [q.v.15] as premier. Appointed treasurer and minister for housing, Hiley resigned his business interests as an accountant and as a director of companies that had included Appleton Industries Ltd, Burley Industries Ltd, Cribb & Foote Ltd and Keith Morris [q.v.] Construction Ltd. He was a competent administrator who helped to develop an effective cabinet, the members of which had no previous experience in government. His first achievement was to establish a cabinet secretariat to formalise the decision-making process. A firm coalitionist, he supported the Electoral Districts Act (1958), which continued the zonal system of redistribution.

As treasurer Hiley soon set up a system of transferring unused loan entitlements between local authorities so that Queensland's allocation from the Australian Loan Council could be raised and spent. In 1958 he introduced a new format for the budget papers that made the State's financial affairs easier to understand. The Treasury Funds Investment Act Amendment Act (1960) enabled Treasury to obtain a better return by investing in the short-term money market. Computers were introduced and more economists employed. Hiley negotiated finance for economic development, including the rebuilding of the railway line between Mount Isa, Townsville and Collinsville. He provided funds for the construction of more high schools and for improvements to education generally. Working to increase the financial reimbursement from the Commonwealth, he also introduced legislation to reform succession and probate duties, gift duties and land tax. In 1960 legislation widened the powers of the State Government Insurance Office as to its investments. Benefits relating to workers' compensation were boosted. Hiley sponsored the introduction in 1962 of the Totalisator Administration Board of Queensland. A boating enthusiast, he ensured that more jetties and boat ramps were built. Fisheries inspectors were provided with modern vessels and fish sanctuaries were gazetted.

Hiley developed sound relationships with senior public servants such as Sir James Holt [q.v.] and advanced the careers of capable and energetic officers, including (Sir) Allan Sewell, under-treasurer (1961-69), B. E. Riding, general manager of the SGIO (1963-71), and (Sir) Leo Hielscher, assistant under-treasurer (1964-69). As minister for housing, he introduced legislation enabling the Queensland Housing Commission to sell houses to reliable tenants and to build flats; and permitting developers to construct canal estates. In January 1965 Hiley was again elected leader of the party; he resigned as both leader and treasurer on 23 December and retired from parliament at the election in 1966. He was knighted that year; the University of Queensland had con-

ferred on him an honorary M.Com. in 1959. In 1974 he was made a life member of the ICA.

Hiley settled at Tewantin, where he participated in community affairs. He took on directorships of several companies from 1967, including Appleton Industries Ltd, Evans [q.v.8 D. Evans] Deakin Industries Ltd, Austral Motors Holding Ltd and Keith Morris Construction Ltd. In 1973-80 he was also a board-member of R.T.Z. Pillar Pacific Pty Ltd (later Pillar Industries Pty Ltd) and in 1973-77 of Alfred Grant [q.v.] Holdings Ltd. A keen sportsman, he enjoyed duck-shooting and fishing; when young he had played tennis and golf and in later years he took up lawn bowls, winning several club championships. He was president (1965-70) of the Queensland Cricket Association, Queensland chairman from 1966 of the Duke of Edinburgh's award scheme in Australia, and chairman of trustees (1968-74) of Brisbane Grammar School.

Well dressed and known for his red carnation and cigar, Sir Thomas was intelligent, warm and friendly. A man of integrity, he set himself high standards and demanded the same from others. In 1982 he alleged corruption in the Hanlon Labor government and revealed that Frank Bischof [qq.v.14,13], a former police commissioner, had received graft payments. Survived by his two sons, he died on 6 November 1990 at Cooroy and was cremated.

C. Lack, *Three Decades of Queensland Political History, 1929-1960* (1962); M. I. Thomas and M. Wales, *From SGIO to Suncorp* (1986); *PD* (Qld), 9 Nov 1990, p 4754; *Courier-Mail* (Brisbane), 27 Oct 1943, p 3, 17 Apr 1944, p 1, 16 Aug 1954, p 9, 18 Sept 1982, p 1, 7 Nov 1990, p 9; *Telegraph* (Brisbane), 30 Sept 1950, p 5; S. Lunney, interview with T. Hiley (ts, 1974, NLA).   MANFRED CROSS

HILL, EDWARD FOWLER (1915-1988), barrister and communist activist, was born on 23 April 1915 at Mildura, Victoria, third surviving child of Victorian-born parents James Frederick Hill, principal of Mildura Agricultural High School, and his wife Alice Steele, née Fowler. Educated at Hamilton High School, where his father had become head teacher, Ted then worked as a clerk for Bill Slater [q.v.16] and in 1933 began to study law at the University of Melbourne. He won the Bowen (1936) and Supreme Court (1937) prizes, but did not graduate LL B until 1981; instead, inspired by Marxism and angered by the injustice exposed by the Depression, he had joined the Communist Party of Australia in 1936 and embraced political activism. He was admitted to practise as a barrister and a solicitor on 1 September 1938. On 5 April 1940 at the office of the government statist, Melbourne, he married Joyce Alison Wood, a clerk.

After a brief partnership with Jack Lazarus, in 1943 Hill was made a partner in the firm of Slater & Gordon; he developed redoubtable expertise in workers' compensation. He also tutored (1944-48) in law at the university, built strong networks as a legal adviser to trade unions and to the Victorian Trades' Hall Council, and later co-authored (with J. B. Bingeman, 1981) a leading textbook in compensation law. Yet, while held in high professional regard throughout his career, Hill became particularly associated with the doctrinal 'leftism' of the Communist Party in Victoria, of which he was State secretary in 1945-62. A tutor in industrial history at the Victorian Labor College from 1937 and a regular lecturer at Marx School, he made a major contribution to the party's public educational mission: he was a prolific author of pamphlets and booklets and a prominent public speaker. In 1944 he was denounced in the Victorian Legislative Assembly by Bert Cremean [q.v.13] as a 'blackguard of the very worst type' following his appointment as acting registrar of the Opticians Registration Board.

In 1948 Hill established his own practice as a barrister and was elected State secretary of the CPA. He appeared as a witness before the Lowe [q.v.15] royal commission (1949-50) into communism in Victoria, and as a witness and counsel at the royal commission on espionage (1954-55); he was a vigorous opponent of the Communist Party Dissolution Act (1951). A staunch defender of civil liberties, he advised Frank Hardy in the criminal libel action against him in 1951 while himself becoming the subject of frequent press vilification and close surveillance by the Australian Security Intelligence Organization. Throughout the 1950s he travelled extensively to the Soviet Union and Czechoslovakia, his visits including party congresses in Moscow in 1956 and 1959. As Australian delegate to the former, he heard Khrushchev's denunciation of Stalin but suppressed discussion of that speech on his return, dismissing as 'revisionism' any such challenge to party unity.

Hill's growing alignment with the Chinese Communist Party in its dispute with Soviet models of 'peaceful transition' to socialism led to his resignation as State secretary and, in August 1963, his expulsion from the CPA. He then formed and chaired (1964-84) the Communist Party of Australia (Marxist-Leninist), espousing the need for 'all forms of struggle— peaceful and armed, open and secret, legal and illegal'. Over the next two decades his frequent trips to China, where he was fêted by Premier Chou En-lai and Chairman Mao Tse-tung, and his meeting with the Khmer Rouge leader Pol Pot in 1978 reflected his international standing while also underscoring enduring divisions in Australian communism.

Regarded as one of the most rigid and single-minded of Australian communists, Hill possessed—Bernie Taft recalled—a 'commanding personality', a 'cold, penetrating stare', and a 'compelling logic' which reduced issues to simplicity. His commitment extended to assisting conscientious objectors to national service in the 1960s and supporting unionists including Clarrie O'Shea [q.v.], and Norm Gallagher (1931-1999), State secretary (1970-91) of the Builders' Labourers' Federation. For the last fifteen years of his life Hill suffered from Hodgkin's disease but maintained a daily routine of office work after an early morning swim at the Brunswick baths. Survived by his wife and their son and daughter, he died on 1 February 1988 at East Melbourne, and was cremated. 'Ted Hill never forgot why he became a socialist', one of many tributes reflected: he sought to practise solidarity with, according to Ralph Gibson [q.v.], 'self-sacrifice', 'determination' and an 'unswerving loyalty to the working people'.

JAMES FREDERICK HILL (1918-1973), public servant and Ted's younger brother, was born on 1 April 1918 at Hamilton and educated at Essendon High School (where his father was principal) and the University of Melbourne (LL B, 1940; BA, 1947). Serving full time in the Militia from March 1942 and the Australian Imperial Force from June, Jim was a driver in the Northern Territory, where he was wounded by a bomb blast. He transferred to the Australian Army Education Service and served in Queensland and briefly in Netherlands New Guinea before being discharged on 22 May 1945 as a warrant officer, class two. On 10 January 1942 at St Paul's Church of England, Ascot Vale, Melbourne, he had married Marjorie Irene Royle, a typist.

Thickset like Ted, and gregarious, Hill worked as a temporary research officer in the Department of External Affairs until gaining permanent appointment in 1947 and travelling to New York to assist H. V. Evatt [q.v.14] at the United Nations General Assembly. By 1950, having risen rapidly to acting first secretary in London, he was placed under close surveillance and interrogated by Military Intelligence 5 over alleged involvement in Soviet spying. He returned to Canberra and— still under investigation—was eventually transferred to the Attorney General's Department's legal service bureau in Melbourne. No charges were laid against him. In 1953 he joined Slater & Gordon and became a junior partner. He died suddenly of myocardial infarction at Oxley, Victoria, on 22 April 1973, and was buried in Wangaratta cemetery. His wife and their two daughters survived him.

R. Gibson, *My Years in the Communist Party* (1966); A. Davidson, *The Communist Party of*

Australia (1969); B. Taft, *Crossing the Party Line* (1994); M. Cannon, *That Disreputable Firm* (1998); *PD* (Vic), 7 Dec 1944, p 2846; *Arena*, no 82, 1988, p 99; *Herald* (Melbourne), 3 July 1986, p 6; *Age* (Melbourne), 2 Feb 1988, p 14; *Australian*, 2 Feb 1988, p 4; A6119, items 209-15, 344-46, 778-84 and A6980, item S201308 (NAA); Communist Party of Aust records (SLNSW).   HUGH ANDERSON

HILL, LANCELOT LEONARD (1902-1986), manufacturer, was born on 15 December 1902 at Knoxville, Adelaide, second of four children of Alfred William Hill, slaughterman, and his wife Lillian Ethel, née Mott. Educated at Glen Osmond Public School, at 14 Lance joined the staff of the Hill family's long-established bacon factory and meat cannery. He gained a steam engineer's certificate and was put in charge of the boilers. More interested in petrol engines, in the 1930s he opened a motor garage at Prospect. He earned extra money at weekends by riding Indian and AJS motorcycles in dirt-track speedway races and by giving joy-rides in speedboats from the Glenelg jetty. Gregarious, witty and liked by all who met him, he wore spectacles and was only 5 ft 7 ins (170 cm) in height. On 4 October 1939 at Payneham Methodist Church he married Cynthia Harriett Mary ('Sherry') Langman, née Carpenter, a saleswoman and a divorcee. They settled in Bevington Road, Glenunga, near his parents and other relations.

Closing his garage and enlisting in the Militia on 7 January 1942, Hill rose to acting warrant officer, class two, in September and transferred to the Australian Imperial Force in October. He remained in South Australia, instructing motor mechanics and motorbike despatch-riders. After his discharge from the army in August 1945 his wife complained that citrus trees in their backyard had grown so much that there was no room to hang out the washing on their single-wire clothes-line. To solve the problem he built a rotary hoist, using scrap metal and oxyacetylene equipment. After family and neighbours admired the result and placed orders he decided to earn his living making hoists.

Since 1905 several Australian firms had been manufacturing rotary clothes-lines. Many could not be raised or lowered and users pegged out washing by standing on a platform. Others were lifted hydraulically. From 1925 Gilbert Toyne produced hoists with a wind-up mechanism in Adelaide but they were too expensive to become popular. In 1928 he licensed his South Australian and Western Australian rights to the Lambert brothers at Fullarton. Their hoists were made of wood, which limited size and durability, and they sold few; Hill used only steel. His first small classified advertisement in the *Advertiser* in November 1945 drew six orders. Its suc-

cessors brought an increasing flow. Most of the early customers were women. The price was ten guineas, plus £1 for delivery and installation, and five shillings extra if the hoist was set in concrete.

Postwar shortages posed a challenge. Damaged military aeroplanes became the main source of wire and anti-submarine mesh salvaged from Sydney Harbour furnished the stay rods. Hill's father, Alf, straightened, cleaned and cut old pipes scrounged from many sources, and built a handcart to transport the hoists. Sherry Hill painted the finished product. By February 1946, struggling to meet demand, the Hills were working sixteen-hour days. Lance's brother-in-law Harold Ling [q.v.15] joined the business and took charge of accounts and marketing. Additional staff were recruited and production moved from the Hills's backyard to leased land on Glen Osmond Road, Fullarton. Old army trucks were bought for deliveries. The first models were dubbed 'chinwackers', as they were raised by a lever that could fly from the operator's grasp. Ling failed in attempts to buy a right to use Toyne's patented winding mechanism and in late 1946 Hill designed and produced his own.

The first interstate branch was established in Sydney in 1947. To raise money for further growth, a company, initially called Hills Hoists Ltd, was formed in January 1948, with Hill as chairman. Its purchase of pipe-making and galvanising plants eliminated the need for painting. Modest prices and the 'lifetime guarantee' offered by Hill from the beginning enabled the Hills hoist to outclass competitors. By 1954, when most operations had moved to a 10-acre (4 ha) site at Edwardstown, sales had reached six hundred hoists a week and there were branches throughout Australia. The hoist became a national symbol. Hill developed additional products, including laundry trolleys, ironing boards and children's playground equipment.

While on a trade mission in New Zealand in 1956 Hill suffered a major cardiac incident. On doctors' advice, he resigned from the company. He sold his shares to Ling but stayed on as a consultant, assisting in crises at the factory and working on innovations. In retirement he became a keen angler and water-skier and, with his wife, enjoyed many caravan holidays to Queensland and Central Australia. Survived by his wife and their daughter and son, he died on 7 March 1986 at Largs Bay and was cremated. By then over one million Hills hoists had been sold.

D. Harris, *What a Line* (1996); *Sunday Mail* (Adelaide), 30 Sept 1979, p 28; *Advertiser* (Adelaide), 10 Mar 1986, p 16; L. Hill, order book, 1945-46 (SLSA); private information.   P. A. HOWELL

HILL, MIRRIE IRMA JAFFA (1889-1986), composer, was born on 1 December 1889 at Randwick, Sydney, third child of Jewish parents Levien Jaffa Solomon, merchant, and his wife Kate Caroline, née Marks, both born at Goulburn, New South Wales. Mirrie attended Shirley school, Edgecliff, and studied piano with Josef Kretschmann and Laurence Godfrey Smith, harmony with Ernest Truman [q.v.12] and composition with Alfred Francis Hill [q.v.9]. In 1914 her first orchestral work, *Rhapsody for Piano and Orchestra*, was performed at the Sydney Town Hall by Godfrey Smith with the Sydney Amateur Orchestral Society conducted by Alfred Hill. World War I forced her to cancel plans to study in Germany. Instead, she enrolled at the newly opened New South Wales State Conservatorium of Music, receiving a composition scholarship for 1916-18 awarded by its first director, Henri Verbrugghen [q.v.12]. She married Hill on 1 October 1921 at Mosman registry office. They built a home at Mosman where they resided for the rest of their lives. Mirrie had no children, but Alfred had three from his first marriage.

Immediately after completing her studies, Mirrie had been appointed to the conservatorium staff as assistant-professor of harmony, counterpoint and composition. Also teaching aural training from 1935, she wrote a textbook, *Aural and Rhythmic Training* (1935). She retired from the conservatorium in 1944. From 1959 to 1966 she was an examiner for the Australian Music Examinations Board.

Creating over five hundred works, with almost half of them published, Hill was one of the most prolific Australian composers of her time. A few of her compositions were published under male pseudonyms. She gained a reputation as a miniaturist, because most of her published or broadcast compositions were for voice and piano or short piano works for educational purposes, but she also wrote many larger pieces for orchestra, chamber ensembles, solo instruments, choir and film. The conductor Henry Krips [q.v.] performed and recorded some of her orchestral works for the Australian Broadcasting Commission.

Mirrie accurately described her music as 'not [in] the very modern idiom but entirely individual as to style and content'. She drew inspiration from recordings of Aboriginal music made by the anthropologist C. P. Mountford [q.v.15] for *Three Aboriginal Dances* (1950), *Aborigines of the Sea Coast* (1951) and *Symphony in A: Arnhem Land* (1954); from traditional Hebrew melodies for *Abinu Malkenu* (1971); and from verses by Australian poets such as Dame Mary Gilmore, John Wheeler and Hugh McCrae [qq.v.9,12,10].

The composer Dorothy Dodd observed: 'With her innate sense of humour and serenity, she radiated such quiet happiness to those around her'. Shy and self-effacing, Hill found it difficult to promote her own work and willingly allowed Alfred's composing career to come before her own. It was not until several years after her husband's death in 1960 that she began to receive appropriate recognition: she was appointed an honorary life member of the Fellowship of Australian Composers in 1975 and OBE in 1980. Mirrie Hill died on 1 May 1986 at St Leonards and was cremated.

Canon (Sydney), July 1960, p 277; *Quarterly Mag* (Federation of Austn Music Teachers' Assns), May 1980, p 27; *APRA: Mag of the A'asian Performing Right Assn*, Dec 1986, p 41; H. de Berg, interview with M. Hill (ts, 1975, NLA); Mirrie Hill (video, 1982, Aust Council); R. Pearce, Rediscovering Mirrie Hill (1889-1986) (MMus thesis, Univ of Melbourne, 2003); SP827/2, Mirrie Hill (NAA); Hill family papers and Olive Lawson papers (SLNSW).

MEREDITH LAWN

HILLS, EDWIN SHERBON (1906-1986), geologist, was born on 31 August 1906 at Carlton, Melbourne, son of Melbourne-born parents Edwin Sherbon Hills, hatter, and his wife Blanche Eva, née Toe. Edwin was dux of Lee Street State School, Carlton, and won scholarships to University High School, Parkville, where he played cricket and football and became senior athletics champion. He also co-edited (1923-24) the *University High School Record*, to which he contributed two poems. In 1925 he entered the University of Melbourne (B.Sc., 1928; M.Sc., 1929; D.Sc., 1938) with a metallurgy bursary and a senior government scholarship, intending to become a chemist. Soon, however, he was drawn to geology, in part through field excursions and also through the discovery of his colour blindness, which did not impede his accuracy in petrology. An outstanding student, he won several exhibitions, and with the Howitt [q.v.4] natural history scholarship (1928) commenced work in the Cerberean Ranges on fossil fish, cauldron subsidence and acid vulcanism and physiology that won him the Kernot [q.v.5] research scholarship. These became lifelong interests.

In 1929, assisted by an 1851 Exhibition scholarship, Hills undertook research at the Imperial College of Science and Technology, University of London (Ph.D., 1931). Elected a fellow of the Geological Society of London (1930), he declined possible appointments in the United Kingdom to return to Melbourne in 1932 as lecturer in geology—a position created for him by Professor E. W. Skeats [q.v.11]. On 26 August at the registrar-general's office, Melbourne, he married Claire Doris Fox, who had joined him from London.

Hills carried a heavy teaching load, including palaeontology, stratigraphy, engineering geology, petrology, economic geology and physical geography. Awarded the David Syme [q.v.6] prize for scientific research in 1940, that year he became senior lecturer and published the first editions of his classic books *Outlines of Structural Geology* and *The Physiography of Victoria: An Introduction to Geomorphology*. Students recalled him as 'an excellent lecturer', particularly to large first-year classes. Well organised and intellectually thorough, he favoured fact over theory; his lectures also 'brought out the actor in him', revealing a dry, keen sense of humour and timing.

Made an associate professor in 1942, Hills was released by the university in 1943 and, holding the rank of captain in the Australian Military Forces, was attached to the North Australia Observer Unit by the Directorate of Research. He travelled through central and northern Australia, acquiring geological data for the construction of a detailed relief model. After the war this project was completed for the whole of Australia. The south-eastern portion of the model was mounted on the east wall of the lecture theatre of the School of Earth Sciences, University of Melbourne.

In 1944 Hills was appointed to the chair of geology and mineralogy at Melbourne. He immediately sought to improve facilities in his department amid the university's postwar expansion. A library and workshop were built, the mineragraphic section of the Council for Scientific and Industrial Research was rehoused in a new extension, and research capacity was enhanced by the acquisition of equipment including an X-ray diffraction unit, a direct-current arc-emission ultraviolet spectrograph and one of the first thermogravimetric units for quantitative clay mineral analysis. He recruited new staff and later introduced courses in geophysics, geochemistry and geomorphology. Committed to encouraging original work from staff and students, he valued independence and individual enquiry; he had little time for research groups.

An innovative, eclectic and multidisciplinary scientist, Hills was, according to his colleague Dorothy Hill, capable of evaluating all aspects of an issue and seeing decisively 'to the heart of any problem'. His own work—amounting to 130 scholarly publications—developed across four broad fields: fossil fish, acid igneous volcanism, physiography and structural geology. His study of fossil fish spanned the Palaeozoic and Cenozoic periods and the biological and biostratigraphical aspects of the faunas. He was intrigued by the evolution of landscapes. His physiographical studies explored diverse topics such as Cenozoic basalts, the Murray Basin and coastal geomorphology. Increasing pressures of administration kept him from completing his major work on acid volcanic cauldron subsidences, but his contributions to petrology and mineralogy demonstrated acute powers of observation. While dubious about theories of continental drift (conceding that he 'couldn't imagine the mechanism' required to move huge tectonic plates), he made substantial contributions in structural geology, particularly his studies of lineaments and their relevance to the location of economic ore deposits and resurgent tectonics. Hills's *Elements of Structural Geology* (1965), like his *Outlines*, went into several editions; between them, they were translated into Bulgarian, Spanish, Russian, Chinese, Japanese and Hindi.

The applications of Hills's research were extensive, particularly in economic geology and arid zone research. In the former, the mapping and survey work he began in the 1940s established interpretations that influenced subsequent mineral exploration. Representing Australia at the Royal Society Empire Scientific Conference, held in England in 1946, he called for greater Australian investment in developing 'applied' geology. In the latter field, his appointment in 1951 as Australian representative on the United Nations Educational, Scientific and Cultural Organization's advisory panel on arid zone hydrology and hydrogeology (from 1957 member, sometime chairman, of the UNESCO International advisory committee on arid zone research) led to work on issues in Australia, Egypt, Syria, Lebanon, Israel, North Africa, Pakistan and India. Editor of *Arid Lands: A Geographical Appraisal* (1968), Hills made far-reaching observations on questions such as salinisation and contributed to the conservation and use of arid and semi-arid lands.

As a founding fellow (1954), member of council (1961-63), and vice-president (1963) of the Australian Academy of Science, Hills urged the establishment of the academy's sub-committee (later national committee) on hydrology (chairman, 1959-68), and did much to advance the national and—again in association with UNESCO—international study of scarce water resources and their management. From 1946 he fostered strong links between his department and the Geological Survey of Victoria, working closely with David Thomas [q.v.16] in encouraging young graduates to join the survey and undertake projects that were submitted for higher degrees at Melbourne and often published in the survey's *Memoirs*. He also played a fundamental role in the establishment of the Geological Society of Australia and became its foundation president (1952-55).

Fostering science more generally, Hills was active in the organisational structure of the Australian and New Zealand Association for the Advancement of Science, serving as president of its geography (1947) and geology (1959) sections and joining its advisory committee in

1958. He was a prominent trustee (1946-70) of the National Museum of Victoria (deputy chairman, 1959-61; chairman, 1962-68; councillor, 1971-78). President (1955-56) of the Royal Society of Victoria, and chairman (1947-55) of its editorial committee, he exerted great influence on the standards of publication in its *Proceedings*.

Alongside such diverse academic and public work, Hills became a respected university administrator. He served as dean of science (1947-48), chairman of the professorial board (1959-61) and pro-vice-chancellor (1962, 1967) before being appointed Melbourne's first deputy vice-chancellor (1962-71) at the beginning of a long period of mounting administrative crisis in the university. In this role, and particularly on staff and appointment matters, Hills was an innovator who struggled against ingrained institutional conservatism in overseeing, and consulting on, a 'complete review of the university' to meet new stringencies. These demands led him to relinquish his chair in 1962, but he retained the title of research professor in geology until his retirement in 1971, when the university council elected him professor emeritus.

For over four decades Hills was perhaps Australia's most widely known and influential geologist. His work was recognised by the Geological Society of London's Wollaston Fund award (1942) and Bigsby medal (1951), by an invitation to give its William Smith lecture (1960), and by an honorary fellowship (1967). He was elected a fellow (1954) of the Royal Society of London. The University of Durham awarded him an honorary D.Sc. in 1960. In 1971 he was appointed CBE. He attended many international conferences and visited universities and scientific institutions in Eastern and Western Europe, North and South America, South and South-East Asia, and China.

In retirement, Hills continued to serve on many committees of the AAS. In 1979 he was awarded the W. R. Browne [q.v.13] medal of the Geological Society of Australia. Of average height, sandy-haired, always neat and energetic, he retained orderly thinking as his hallmark—although a lighter side could sometimes erupt (according to his successor as professor of geology, C. M. Tattam) with 'almost alarming ebullience'. He treasured his family, often placing its needs over personal ambition. On 2 May 1986 Edwin Hills died at Kew, Melbourne, survived by his wife, and their daughter and two sons. He was cremated.

Austn Academy of Science, *The First Twenty-Five Years* (1980); R. W. Le Maitre (ed), *Pathways in Geology* (1989); *Austn Geologist*, no 59, 1986, p 32; *Hist Records of Austn Science*, vol 7, no 1, 1987, p 79; Univ of Melbourne, *Gazette*, Oct 1972, p 8; H. de Berg, interview with E. S. Hills (ts, 1973, NLA); Hills papers (NLA); private information.   N. W. ARCHBOLD*

HILTON, CHARLES RHOADS (1889-1982), mining engineer, was born on 16 September 1889 at Tama, Iowa, United States of America, son of Charles A. Hilton, merchant, and his wife Ida, née Rhoads. After attending primary school at Tama, he completed his secondary education at Modesto, California, and studied organic chemistry at the University of Nevada (BA, 1914). His mining career commenced at Goldfield, Nevada. Hilton enlisted in the United States Army in August 1917 and served as a lieutenant in the Corps of Engineers in France. Discharged on 8 May 1919, he joined the American Smelting & Refining Co.'s lead plant at Selby, California. After seven years' metallurgical experience, he transferred to Leadville, Colorado, and in 1927 to East Helena, Montana. In January 1933 he was promoted as smelter superintendent to ASARCO's operation at Mount Isa, Queensland, teaming up with Julius Kruttschnitt [q.v.9].

Having solved problems with the mill and lead smelter, Hilton became manager of Mount Isa Mines Ltd in 1937, his appointment coinciding with its first profit. Next year he was promoted to general manager. Two significant, related issues that he handled with quiet authority were workforce attrition rates and community housing. By 1939 the workforce was turning over by half annually; by 1946 the rate reached 113 per cent. Hilton subsidised cultural, social and sporting organisations, and undertook a revised company housing program. Between 1938 and 1940 forty-two new family homes were built. In 1946 alone three dormitories for a hundred single men were completed. The company subsequently provided a swimming pool, tennis courts, children's playgrounds, library and improved roadways. Its store continued to subsidise foodstuffs and domestic requirements.

Another issue for Hilton was the lead bonus, believed by many to be a trade-off for plumbism within the workforce. Introduced in 1937, the bonus initially lasted for only a few months, but was reinstated in 1946 and linked to world metal prices. By early 1951, when the basic wage for miners stood at £9 6s. 5d. per week, the lead bonus gave an additional £15 10s. in the pay packet. Hilton wryly noted its effect on industrial harmony.

Hilton was a director of the company in 1948-53. However, his major contribution to Mount Isa's prosperity was his far-sighted interest from the 1930s in leases to the north. They were pegged but remained idle for decades until developed from 1970 and known as the Hilton Mine; its lead reserves were projected to be larger than Mount Isa's big lode.

Preferring his mineralogical texts and technical journals in the evening to social functions, Hilton led a quiet life. His broad physique contrasted with a gentle, courteous nature. His wife, a hypochondriac, loathed her time in

Australia and returned permanently to the USA in the mid-1940s, leaving Hilton to serve out his contract, which he terminated in March 1953. He was affectionately known as 'Uncle Charlie' by staff and workers; his farewell, according to Geoffrey Blainey, 'created one of the densest traffic jams seen in Mount Isa' and was attended by two thousand people. Accompanied by his daughter Sally, he toured Australia, England and France before retiring to California. He later lived with his other daughter, Marybelle, at San Carlos. Predeceased by his wife, he died on 19 December 1982 at Belmont and was cremated.

G. Blainey, *Mines in the Spinifex* (1960); D. Chaput and K. Kennedy, *The Man from ASARCO* (1992); K. Kennedy and N. Kirkman, 'The Evolution of Company Welfare Practices at Mount Isa, Queensland', in K. Tenfelde (ed), *Sozialgeschichte des Bergbaus im 19. und 20. Jahrhundert* (1992); N. Kirkman, *Mount Isa* (1998); Mount Isa Mines Ltd, *Report and Accounts*, 1937-53; *Mimag*, Aug 1952, p 13, Apr 1953, p 2; *M.I.M. News*, 13 Mar 1980.

K. H. KENNEDY

HINE, CLYTIE MAY (1887-1983), soprano and vocal teacher, was born on 8 May 1887 in Adelaide, only child of William Henry Hine, South Australian-born jeweller, and his wife Mary, née McDonald. At 7 Clytie began piano lessons with W. R. Pybus, and at 16 entered the Elder [q.v.4] Conservatorium of Music, University of Adelaide, to study with Bryceson Treharne. She later learnt singing from Professor Frederick Bevan, and in 1906 was awarded an Elder singing scholarship. As a lyric soprano she rapidly became a popular figure on Adelaide concert platforms. She graduated as an associate in music in 1908, and in April next year travelled to London to study voice at the Royal College of Music under Medora Henson. Her striking beauty rendered her particularly effective in opera and she made a successful début in 1911 at Covent Garden as Freia in Wagner's *Das Rheingold*. In 1913 she was a member of the Denhof Opera Company.

On 18 March 1914 at the parish church of St John the Evangelist, Kilburn, London, Hine married John Mundy (d.1971), a cellist. During the war years she sang with the (Sir Thomas) Beecham Opera Company: her roles included Nedda in *Pagliacci*, Santuzza in *Cavalleria Rusticana*, Musetta in *La Bohème*, Elsa in *Lohengrin*, Desdemona in *Otello*, and the countess in *The Marriage of Figaro*. She also appeared in concert and in oratorio. In 1915 she was the soprano soloist in the first production of Algernon Blackwood's *The Starlight Express*, with incidental music by Sir Edward Elgar, an important engagement of her early career.

The Mundys left Britain for the United States of America late in 1920. They settled in New York, and established a reputation for their innovative joint recitals featuring early English music. In 1924 Hine toured extensively throughout the USA and beyond with William Wade Hinshaw's Mozart Opera Company. Retiring from performing in the late 1920s, she became a renowned singing teacher. Her students included Arthur Kent, Irene Jordan, Alfred Drake, Nanette Fabray, Celeste Holm and, when they visited New York, (Sir) Peter Pears and Kathleen Ferrier.

As part of the training for her students, Hine directed scenes from opera, sometimes with Benjamin (Lord) Britten at the piano; and occasionally with (Sir) John Barbirolli or Giorgio Polacco conducting. She was closely associated with Britten and Pears, both professionally and personally, for many years. Pears found her 'a wonderful woman to work with, very sympathetic and forthright'. Before the American première of Britten's *Peter Grimes* in 1946, she supervised a reading at her studio for Serge Koussevitzky (who had commissioned the opera) and Leonard Bernstein.

Hine also taught at the Academy of Vocal Art, Philadelphia, Pennsylvania, and was musical adviser to the American Theatre Wing. Actors such as Kirk Douglas and John Forsythe studied speech with her. She retired in the late 1950s; in 1970 the Royal College of Music established an annual scholarship in her name. Survived by her son, John Hine Mundy, a medieval historian, and her daughter, Meg Mundy, an actress, she died on 27 June 1983 in New York.

C. Headington, *Peter Pears* (1992); *Register* (Adelaide), 11 Sept 1909, p 5, 22 Jan 1910, p 5, 31 Dec 1910, p 8, 28 Oct 1911, p 8; *Times* (London), 20 Oct 1911, p 9, 12 Aug 1983, p 10; *Austn Musical News*, 1 Aug 1934, p 2; *Opera News* (New York), 14 Dec 1974, p 28; W. Hancock, 'Clytie Hine Mundy', *Music Stand*, Oct 1996, p 6, and Nov-Dec 1996, p 8; W. Hancock and M. Elphinstone, Clytie Hine: The Student Years (ts, 1995, copy on ADB file).

WAYNE HANCOCK

HOBAN, MARY ELIZABETH ('MAIE') (1887-1984), speech and drama teacher, was born on 29 September 1887 at Spring Mount, near Creswick, Victoria, daughter of Victorian-born parents Edmond Butler, farmer, and his wife Rosina, née McCormack. Maie was educated at Mary's Mount convent, Ballarat, and, encouraged by the eisteddfod culture of that city, attained licentiates of the Royal School of Music and Trinity College of Music, London. She played the piano and organ, and appeared in concerts. Her true *métier*, however, was discovered in preparing Ballarat children and adults for speech and drama examinations and for the South Street eisteddfod.

On 18 November 1915 at St Patrick's Cathedral, Melbourne, Maie married Daniel James Hoban, an auctioneer who had enlisted in the Australian Imperial Force. In March 1916 he embarked for the Western Front, where he lost a leg. Invalided back to Australia, he established a real estate agency in Melbourne and became particularly associated with the development of Springvale. His death in 1931 left Maie with five children to support.

In the depths of the Depression, Maie Hoban returned to teaching, renting a studio and soon acquiring a loyal following of students, many of whom joined the amateur theatre company she established, known as the Unnamed Players (later, the Australian Repertory Players). Using venues such as suburban town halls, she drew mostly on such English dramatists as John Galsworthy, Sir James Barrie and (Sir) Noël Coward. A more unusual recurring favourite (because of its all-female cast) was Christa Winsloe's *Children in Uniform*. Other adventurous choices included T. S. Eliot's *The Cocktail Party* and Jean Cocteau's *The Eagle Has Two Heads*. She encouraged Australian playwrights by various means, including competitions for new work, but she regretted their general lack of stagecraft.

In 1939, after brief sojourns in rooms at Her Majesty's and the Garrick theatres, Hoban moved her school, now known as the Australian School of Speechcraft and Drama, to a workroom in the grounds of St Peter's Church of England, Eastern Hill, which she converted into a small theatre—the Pilgrim Theatre. Already a public figure, she was a frequent commentator on controversies concerning Australian speech. Australians, she maintained, spoke more correctly than other English-speaking nations, but their voice production was poor. In 1948 Hoban travelled to the United States of America, where she lectured under the auspices of the English Speaking Union and studied remedial speech technique. She toured the USA again in 1954, partly investigating television production, and also visited England, attending a course sponsored by the British Drama League.

A woman of considerable presence, Hoban had the entrepreneurial drive needed to make a career in a marginal field. While her own vocal delivery has been described by Patricia Kennedy as mannered, no one doubted her gifts as a teacher. Several of her students later became professional actors, Kennedy, Coral Browne, Frederick Parslow and Terry Norris among them. Others were coached in public speaking; the swimmer Dawn Fraser was 'fascinated by her poise' and inspired by her capacity to stimulate awareness of 'an inner life'. Brought up a Catholic, Hoban remained loyal to the Church, often organising entertainments in support of its charities. She closed her school in 1968. Maie Hoban died on 10 September 1984 at Kew, Melbourne, survived by her four daughters and son. She was buried in Springvale cemetery.

D. Fraser, *Dawn* (2001); *Australian Women's Weekly*, 4 Mar 1950, p 26; *Argus* (Melbourne), 16 Feb 1954, p 6; *Herald* (Melbourne), 13 Apr 1954, p 21, 10 Feb 1968, p 27; private information.

JOHN RICKARD

HOBBS, HOWARD FREDERICK (1902-1982), inventor, was born on 21 September 1902 at East Marden, Adelaide, fifth of six surviving children of South Australian-born parents James Harris Hobbs, fruit-grower, and his wife Mary Eliza, née Pitt. Educated at Prince Alfred College, as a boy Howard showed an aptitude for things mechanical. At 14 he built a full-size aeroplane (without wings) that was taxied around the family's garden, powered by a motorcycle engine. On leaving school he worked at his father's orchard and market garden at Paradise. He married Phyllis Dorothy Reid, a schoolteacher, at Payneham Methodist Church on 12 May 1925. Next year he applied for his first patent, an improved appliance for the grading of fruit.

Driving motorcars and lorries from an early age, Hobbs cherished an ambition to eliminate the need for gear changing. After many experiments he had a light car fitted with the 'Hobbs gearless drive' ready for testing; Professors (Sir) Robert Chapman and (Sir) Kerr Grant [qq.v.7,9] of the University of Adelaide found it satisfactory and simple to operate. Hobbs Gearless Drive Ltd was formed in 1931 to market the device and to administer the patent rights. In June 1931 Hobbs, with his wife and daughter, sailed for Britain, where he also took out patents. For the next thirty-five years the family were to live at Leamington Spa, Warwickshire; two sons were born. Hobbs was unable to persuade car manufacturers to use the 'gearless drive': based on rotating weights, it incorporated a free-wheel clutch, or ratchet, which was probably the weakness in the device. Other inventors with similar ideas also failed to attract interest in their mechanisms.

After engaging in war work, in 1946 Hobbs was helped by a wealthy industrialist to form Hobbs Transmission Ltd. He discarded the gearless drive and developed the 'Mechamatic' transmission. The new automatic gearbox was more complicated, with epicyclic gears and hydraulically operated friction clutches. Mechamatic, with four forward gears, unusual at that time, was lightweight and suitable for small cars. Many well-known makers built prototypes but the only one to reach production was the Lanchester Sprite, produced in

1955 by the Birmingham Small Arms Co. Ltd. For financial reasons BSA soon abandoned the project.

Westinghouse Brake & Signal Co. Ltd bought BSA's shares in Hobbs Transmission and, anticipating its use in the Ford Cortina, built a factory at Manchester to manufacture the Mechamatic. When Ford decided not to proceed, Hobbs Transmission went into liquidation. In the 1960s Hobbs's son David successfully drove a Lotus Elite fitted with the Mechamatic gearbox in international motor races. The family moved to Napton, near Rugby, about 1965 and Hobbs and his son John set up a workshop. They went back to the original concept of the infinitely variable drive, but this time hydraulic, not mechanical. Hobbs took out an Australian patent in the name of Variable Kinetic Drives Ltd, but like its predecessors this also failed commercially. In 1977 Hobbs was invited to participate in the British Genius Exhibition at Battersea.

Hobbs was a keen golfer, playing to a handicap close to scratch. His son David remembered him as friendly and likeable, with a sense of humour, but not forceful enough in business. Although regarded as a genius where automatic transmissions were concerned, he was not accepted into engineering societies because of his lack of qualifications. Survived by his wife, sons and daughter, he died on 15 December 1982 at Bulcote, Nottinghamshire, and was buried in England.

R. M. Gibbs, *Bulls, Bears and Wildcats* (1988); *Advertiser* (Adelaide), 10 June 1931, p 9; *Modern Motor*, May 1983, p 17; *Classic and Sportscar*, May 1983, p 9.   G. H. BROOKS

HODGKIN, MARY CONSTANCE (1909-1985), anthropologist, lecturer and student adviser, was born on 5 April 1909 at Mobberley, Cheshire, England, daughter of Arnold McKerrow, manager of a lithographics works, and his wife Gwendolen Mary, née Jones. Mary was educated at Altrincham County High School for Girls and Victoria University of Manchester (B.Sc., 1930), where she majored in botany. On 13 February 1931 at the register office, St Pancras, London, she married Ernest Pease Hodgkin, a fellow student, who had been appointed government medical entomologist in the Federated States of Malaya. Four months later, after gaining her teaching diploma, she joined Ernest in Kuala Lumpur. A daughter and three sons were born there. She taught at several schools and was involved in the Girl Guides movement.

Following the Japanese invasion of Malaya Mary Hodgkin and her four children were evacuated in January 1942 to Perth and her husband was interned in Singapore. Helped by local Quakers to find temporary accommodation, she soon bought a house at Cottesloe, using a legacy from an uncle. She taught part time (1942-55) at various schools, including Presbyterian Ladies College (1942-54), and continued her association with the Girl Guides, becoming a district commissioner. In October 1945 Ernest joined his family and next year was appointed a lecturer in biology at the University of Western Australia.

In 1956 Mary Hodgkin returned to study as one of the first students in the new department of anthropology and comparative sociology established by R. M. Berndt [q.v.] at UWA (BA Hons, 1959; MA, 1962). In her honours thesis —published as *The Asian Student in the University of Western Australia* (1958)—she made useful suggestions (later implemented by the university) for assisting overseas students. Research for her master's thesis covered a wider sample of students including those attending schools and technical colleges.

Appointed by the government of Malaya (Malaysia from 1963), Mrs Hodgkin served (1959-72) as a liaison officer for the country's students at UWA, providing generous hospitality, practical help and emotional support to hundreds of them. From 1965 she also cared for students from Singapore. A Freda Bage [q.v.7] fellowship of the Australian Federation of University Women enabled her to spend eight months in 1961 in Malaya to gauge the adjustment of returned graduates. Assisted by a grant from the Myer [qq.v.10,15] Foundation, she travelled to Britain and the United States of America in 1967 to learn how these countries aided Malaysian students. In 1972-80 she was UWA's honorary adviser to overseas students.

Mary Hodgkin tutored and lectured (1965-77) in the department of anthropology; her students remembered her as a lively, interesting and caring teacher. Her publications included *Australian Training and Asian Living* (1966) and *The Innovators: The Role of Foreign Trained Persons in South-East Asia* (1972). Active in the Anthropological Society of Western Australia, she was made an honorary life member in 1982. She served on the council of the Girl Guides Association of Western Australia until 1974. In 1972 she was awarded an honorary Ahli Mangku Negara by the Malaysian government, and in 1976 the British Empire medal. She enjoyed painting in watercolours. Survived by her husband and their four children, she died on 1 March 1985 at her Mosman Park home and was cremated.

A. Wood (ed), *If This Should Be Farewell* (2003); *Anthropology News*, vol 22, no 3, 1985, p 2; *Weekend News* (Perth), 12 Jan 1963, p 29; *West Australian*, 7 Mar 1981, p 45; family information.
                                            DOROTHY PARKER

HOGBIN, HERBERT IAN PRIESTLEY (1904-1989), anthropologist, was born on 17 December 1904 at Serlby, Harworth, Nottinghamshire, England, and named Herbert William, son of Herbert Hogbin, landscape gardener, and his wife Edith Fanny, née Smart. After migrating to Australia with his parents, he attended a school at Penrith, New South Wales, and then Fort Street Boys' High School, Sydney. He graduated with honours in English and geography at the University of Sydney (BA, 1926; Dip.Ed., 1927; MA, 1929). In 1929 he changed his name by deed poll to Herbert Ian Priestley Hogbin. His graduation had coincided with the arrival of A. R. Radcliffe-Brown [q.v.11] to take up Australia's first chair of anthropology. Having Rockefeller Foundation funds for research in Melanesia, in 1927 Radcliffe-Brown persuaded—as Hogbin remarked later—a scarcely prepared 22-year-old to join an expedition to Rennell Island and Ontong Java.

Two years later Hogbin went on a Rockefeller Foundation fellowship to the London School of Economics and Political Science, University of London (Ph.D., 1931), where under Professor Bronislaw Malinowski he wrote his doctoral dissertation. It was published as *Law and Order in Polynesia* (1934). He returned to Sydney in 1931 to make this city his academic base for the rest of his career. Regular visits to London on sabbatical leave enabled him to develop his love for Italian Renaissance painting in the galleries of Europe. In 1933 and 1934 Hogbin conducted a series of field studies in Melanesia, first in Guadalcanal and Malaita in the British Solomon Islands Protectorate, and then in Wogeo in the Mandated Territory of New Guinea. He was appointed to a permanent position in the anthropology department at the University of Sydney in 1936. His Malaita study was published as *Experiments in Civilization* (1939).

In 1942 Hogbin was appointed a member of the Australian government's Committee on National Morale. Next year he travelled to the British Solomon Islands Protectorate to advise the administration on the rehabilitation of the people after the war. Commissioned in the Australian Military Forces on 3 January 1944, he served in the Directorate of Research (and Civil Affairs) as a temporary lieutenant colonel. Much of his service was in Papua and New Guinea, where his duties included studying the impact on village life of the army's employment of local men as labourers, and making contact with villages on their liberation from the Japanese. He also lectured at the army's School of Civil Affairs (later the Australian School of Pacific Administration), first in Canberra and then in Sydney. After his demobilisation in March 1946, he continued to advise the Australian government on policy towards the Territory of Papua-New Guinea.

Hogbin was awarded the Wellcome (1944) and Rivers (1946) medals of the Royal Anthropological Institute of Great Britain and Ireland. He returned to the University of Sydney in 1946 and was promoted to reader in 1948. In the mid-1940s he had begun his final field study, in the village of Busama, resulting in *Transformation Scene* (1951), which described the effects of World War II, and *Kinship and Marriage in a New Guinea Village* (1963). He again visited Wogeo, later writing *The Island of Menstruating Men* (1970), an exploration of religion and gender, and *The Leaders and the Led* (1978), on social control. At the University of Birmingham in 1953 he gave the Josiah Mason lectures, published as *Social Change* (1958).

Following his retirement from the University of Sydney in 1969, Hogbin lectured at Macquarie University for ten years and also served as an external examiner for the University of Papua New Guinea. He published nine books, several reports for governments and a steady flow of scholarly articles, mostly in the journal *Oceania*. Malinowski, Radcliffe-Brown and Raymond Firth were the dominant influences on his work. His interests were ethnographic rather than theoretical, but he was among the first to write on the changes resulting from colonial government, missions and labour recruitment. While providing advice to colonial governments, he regarded these topics, particularly the development of native Christianity, as worthy of anthropological study.

Described as a memorable, somewhat flamboyant lecturer, Hogbin was generous with his time in reading the work of graduate students and younger colleagues. For their part, they had to accept his increasingly severe demands for simple style and clarity. His retirement was marked by a festschrift, *Anthropology in Oceania* (1971). An honorary fellow (1968) of the Royal Anthropological Institute of Great Britain and Ireland, he was awarded an honorary D.Litt. by the University of Sydney in 1983. Never married, he died on 2 August 1989 at Potts Point and his body was given to the University of Sydney.

J. Beckett, *Conversations with Ian Hogbin* (1989) and 'Ian Hogbin', *American Ethnologist*, vol 13, no 4, 1986, p 799; R. M. MacLeod (ed), *Science and the Pacific War* (2000); *Oceania*, vol 60, no 2, 1989, p 158; G. Gray, ' "The Next Focus of Power to Fall Under the Spell of This Little Gang" ', *War & Society*, vol 14, no 2, 1996, p 101; *SMH*, 18 Mar 1972, p 7; B883, item NX202820 (NAA); A. McGrath, interview with I. Hogbin (ts, 1983, NLA); Hogbin papers (Univ of Sydney Archives).
JEREMY BECKETT
GEOFFREY GRAY

HOGG, MARGARET STELLA; *see* LEE, M.

HOLMES, AUSTIN STEWART (1924-1986), economist, was born on 16 June 1924 at Narrogin, Western Australia, first of three surviving children of Australian-born parents Peter Holmes, farmer, and his wife May Sylvia, née Stewart. Austin grew up on his parents' wheat and sheep farm near Dumbleyung. After taking correspondence lessons, he attended a ten-pupil bush school and Albany High School. He did a year of science at the University of Western Australia before enlisting in the Royal Australian Air Force on 22 May 1943. Qualifying as a navigator-wireless operator, he flew in Dakotas with No.35 Squadron and in Vultee Vengeance dive-bombers with No.25 Squadron in Australia in 1944-45, and in Liberator bombers with No.12 Squadron in the Netherlands East Indies in 1945. He rose to temporary warrant officer in October 1945 and was discharged on 1 February 1946.

Returning to UWA (BA, 1949), Holmes switched to economics and graduated with first-class honours and a Hackett [q.v.9] scholarship, which took him to Clare College, Cambridge (BA, 1952; MA, 1957). On 24 September 1951 at the register office, Cambridge, he married Edith Hansen, a Western Australian secondary science teacher. Next year they returned to Australia, where he took up a lectureship at the University of Queensland. His research on savings prompted the Commonwealth Bank of Australia to offer him a two-year contract in 1957 to compile flow-of-funds estimates. He moved to Sydney, where he also held for two years a senior lectureship at the University of New South Wales.

In 1960 Holmes joined the permanent staff of the newly formed Reserve Bank of Australia. From 1966 until 1973, when he was appointed an adviser, and again from 1978 to 1981 he headed the research department. Between these two periods he worked in Canberra, first as director of the priorities review staff in the Department of the Special Minister of State and, when the PRS was disbanded, as consultant economist in the Department of the Prime Minister and Cabinet. He was appointed OBE in 1977.

At the Reserve Bank Holmes was in the forefront of argument for market-determined interest rates and a floating exchange rate. In Canberra he argued for tariff cuts, the reduction of subsidies, and other structural reforms. Pursuing policy objectives through market measures was in his view not a matter of political philosophy but of economic and social efficiency; regulation often confounded the achievement of its goals.

In 1980 Holmes delivered the (L. F.) Giblin [q.v.8] memorial lecture, which he called 'The Good Fight'. He said: 'the good fight to which I refer is the struggle to get good sense (economic rationality if you like) into our economic affairs and, more specifically, into the econ-

omic policies which influence those affairs'. A prodigious worker, he carried on the good fight for thirty years. With rigorous analysis and persistence he gradually persuaded others—including academics, politicians, bureaucrats and journalists—of the merits of his cause.

Beneath a bluntness and earthiness of speech there was a kind and compassionate man, self-effacing and encouraging. Aussie Holmes loved good company, food and drink. He was an avid reader, with a special love for Australian history. His favourite relaxation was travelling from his home at St Ives, Sydney, to the remotest corners of the outback. He retired from the Reserve Bank in March 1986. A few months later he was in the Northern Territory to supervise postgraduate theses. He died of myocardial infarction on 15 July at Alice Springs and was cremated with Uniting Church forms. His wife and their two daughters and son survived him.

C. Ulyatt (ed), *The Good Fight* (1989); C. B. Schedvin, *In Reserve* (1992); *Economic Record*, vol 62, no 179, 1986, p 506, and for publications; *SMH*, 29 Aug 1973, p 6; *Age* (Melbourne), 18 July 1986, p 19; *Financial Review*, 24 July 1986, p 34; private information.   M. R. HILL

HOLMES, MARGARET (1886-1981), lay religious leader and welfare worker, was born on 8 March 1886 at Prahran, Melbourne, fourth surviving child and only daughter of English-born parents Charles Morell Holmes, accountant, and his wife Margaret, née Byers. The family belonged to the Congregational Church; its tolerant theology and commitment to women's education were fundamental to Holmes's career. After matriculating from Tintern Ladies' College, she enrolled in 1905 at the University of Melbourne (BA, 1909; MA, 1911; Dip.Ed., 1911). There she was an active member of the Australasian Student Christian Union, becoming president of the women's branch in 1907. After graduating in classics she taught briefly at Tintern then continued her university studies.

Faced with staff shortages during World War I, the ASCU (from 1930 the Australian Student Christian Movement) invited Holmes to become part-time general secretary. Based at the Melbourne office, she helped guide the movement through the turmoil of war and postwar adjustment until 1922. After a brief period on the staff of the Associated Teachers' Training Institute (later Mercer Hall) Holmes returned to the ASCU. From 1924 to 1945 she served as the efficient and effective headquarters secretary (executive officer) for this vast non-denominational organisation with branches in Australian universities, colleges and schools. Committed to the ASCM's liberal, social and ecumenical theology, she participated in the preparation of study books for its large annual national conferences, and co-edited the ASCM journal, *Australian Intercollegian*, a forum for intellectual theological discussion. Although family responsibilities restricted her ability to travel, she was a consummate and assiduous letter writer, binding the ASCM together and strengthening its extensive and influential networks.

In the challenging decade of the 1930s Holmes, with others in the ASCM, was involved in the League of Nations' Union in Melbourne; she assisted in the organisation of the 1937 Australian Peace Conference. On the executive, from 1928, of the World Student Christian Federation, with which the ASCM was affiliated, and vice-chairman in 1933-41, she strove to bring international issues before Australian students through conferences, articles and overseas visitors.

During World War II, Holmes began a new career in refugee work. She had helped Constance Duncan [q.v.14] to establish the Victorian International Refugee Emergency Committee in 1938-39, and in 1940, because of her contacts with the WSCF, she was asked to look after the interests of internees (mostly Jewish refugees from Nazi Germany) transported from Britain in the *Dunera*. The ASCM made arrangements for the '*Dunera* boys' to take university courses and, as they were released from detention camps, assisted with resettlement. Holmes's unstinting support and advocacy resulted in enduring friendships. In 1945-49 she was Australian secretary for World Student Relief.

After retiring from the ASCM, Holmes travelled abroad to attend conferences in Britain, Europe and North America. In 1951 she was appointed executive officer of a new resettlement department (later the Ecumenical Refugee Agency) of the Australian Council of Churches. Initially operating from her Kew home, it assisted thousands of migrants to Australia, mostly 'displaced persons' who did not qualify for the mass migration program. Holmes worked closely with immigration ministers, especially Arthur Calwell [q.v.13], in pioneering Australia's postwar migration. Her work was a major contribution to human rights and a great achievement in the xenophobic Australia of the period. She was appointed MBE in 1958.

Margaret Holmes never married. She was a modest woman but firm, focused and a meticulous organiser. Her significant contribution was shaped by the ASCM's liberal theology, international vision and enlightened attitudes to women. At the heart of her life of public service were intense inner strength, belief in and care for the individual, and a broad non-sectarian view of Christianity. Retiring to Deepdene in 1962 she coached migrants in

English, maintained her wide correspondence, gardened, read, enjoyed symphony concerts and attended the Collins Street Independent Church. She died on 13 April 1981 at Brighton and was cremated.

S. Willis, *Women, Faith & Fetes* (1977); P. R. Bartrop and G. Eisen (eds), *The Dunera Affair* (1990); F. Engel, *Christians in Australia* (1993); *Austn Intercollegian*, 1 Mar 1949, p 6; *SMH*, 15 Feb 1951, p 4, 1 Jan 1958, p 4; Holmes papers (NLA).

RENATE HOWE

HOLMES À COURT, MICHAEL ROBERT HAMILTON (1937-1990), businessman, was born on 27 July 1937 at Johannesburg, South Africa, elder son of English-born Peter Worsley Holmes à Court, a former British naval officer, and his wife Ethnee Celia, née Cumming, born in South Africa. Robert was brought up mainly in Southern Rhodesia (Zimbabwe) but from the age of 9 boarded at Cordwalles Preparatory School and then at Michaelhouse School, Natal (KwaZulu-Natal), South Africa. In 1957-58 he was in New Zealand studying at the University of Auckland and Massey Agricultural College, Palmerston North. He returned to South Africa, and in 1962 moved to Perth to study law at the University of Western Australia (LL B, 1966). A skilled debater, he represented the university in inter-varsity competitions. He was also founding president of the University Flying Club. On 18 May 1966 at St Lawrence's Church of England, Dalkeith, Perth, he married Janet Lee, née Ranford, a schoolteacher. Admitted to practise on 17 April 1968, he established his own legal firm, M. R. H. Holmes à Court & Co., in Perth; at weekends he and Janet would drive 435 miles (700 km) to Esperance to operate a branch office. For a time Nicholas Hasluck was his partner.

In 1970 Holmes à Court acquired Western Australian Worsted & Woollen Mills Ltd, Albany, which was in danger of closure. He 'turned it around' financially, ceased practising law, and in 1974 bought a controlling interest in Bell Bros Holdings Ltd, an earthmoving and transport group. In 1976 he incorporated these and other companies into the Bell Group Ltd. He had a gift for seeing an opportunity and soon developed a legendary reputation for his daring company raids. He bid in 1979 for Ansett [q.v.] Transport Industries Ltd and, before he could take control, sold his interest to News Ltd for an $11 million profit. In 1981 he pulled out of a proposed takeover of Elder Smith Goldsbrough Mort [qq.v.4,6,5] Ltd, making a $16 million profit.

Interested in the media industry, in 1980-87 Holmes à Court published a weekly newspaper in Perth, the *Western Mail*. Late in 1981 he failed in an attempt to win control of the Herald

& Weekly Times Ltd but, through a merger with TVW Enterprises Ltd in 1982, gained television channels in Perth and Adelaide and four radio stations. Identifying business prospects offshore, in 1980 he unsuccessfully pursued control of *The Times*, London. In 1982 he acquired Lord Grade's Associated Communications Corporation, a major British entertainment group, which included the Stoll Moss group of thirteen theatres in London's West End. He was particularly proud of a 1987 deal in which Bell Publishing Group Pty Ltd bought West Australian Newspapers Ltd from News Corporation Ltd.

Holmes à Court's most significant assault in Australia was on the Broken Hill Proprietary Co. Ltd in 1983-86. His company Bell Resources Ltd's shareholding eventually reached 29.93 per cent; he had a seat on the board. After the stock market crash in October 1987 he sold his interest for $2.3 billion. Withdrawing from the world of listed companies, in less than three months he disposed of $5 billion in assets. The price of Bell Group's shares fell at one point from nearly $10 to $1.30; Holmes à Court received twice the latter amount when the control of his group passed to another mercurial Western Australian businessman, Alan Bond.

Retaining the London theatres, a number of Australian pastoral properties, vineyards, a winery, a transport company and several thoroughbred studs, Holmes à Court quietly worked at rebuilding the family companies. The flagship was Heytesbury Holdings Ltd, which he described as the 'family castle'; none of its assets was for sale. Carisbrook Pty Ltd was his trading company, of which he once said everything was 'for sale at the right price'. Most of his revenue in that period came from trading in shares, and he spent more time at his Georgian mansion in Regents Park, London, bought in 1988. By this time he had his own Boeing 727 aircraft, in which he commuted to and from Australia. He formed associations with European companies such as Elf Aquitaine, and made a highly profitable investment in Christie's auction house. In 1988 he established the Holmes à Court Foundation, with a brief to encourage people with 'talent and imagination'. Next year Heytesbury acquired the Sherwin Pastoral Co. Ltd's cattle properties, including Victoria River Downs in the Northern Territory.

Working eighteen-hour days, Holmes à Court did not usually move quickly in making decisions about his acquisitions. Many followed months of planning, and some were then abandoned at the last minute. He laughed at suggestions that he was a swashbuckling corporate pirate plunging impulsively into deals worth hundreds of millions of dollars. While his staff found his work regimen exhausting, they respected his abilities to go to the core of a problem and to display a cool nerve. A tall, unassuming man with a quiet voice and manner, he was courteous but capable of ruthlessness. In his understated style, a raised eyebrow could be a stern rebuke. He used words with precision, and enjoyed debate, particularly elegantly phrased arguments with journalists.

Although Holmes à Court stayed aloof from the local Establishment, he enjoyed gossip and could be acerbic when discussing his corporate enemies. He also appreciated jokes against himself. Describing his entrance to a party at Beverly Hills, California, at a time when he owned a film company, he recalled standing alone in his conservative grey suit, among the flamboyant creatures of the industry, one of whom told him that he looked 'like ET'. His main hobby was breeding thoroughbred horses—in 1984 his horse Black Knight won the Melbourne Cup—and he relaxed at weekends at his Heytesbury stud at Keysbrook. He collected vintage cars and European, Australian and Aboriginal art. In 1986-90 he chaired the board of the Art Gallery of Western Australia.

Survived by his wife and their three sons and a daughter, Holmes à Court died of myocardial infarction on 2 September 1990 at Kelmscott, Perth, and was cremated. He died intestate, with assets estimated to be worth over $800 million. The Holmes à Court collection of Australian and Indigenous art is located in Perth.

Business Review Weekly, 5 Sept 1986, p 47, 12 Sept 1986, p 55, 19 Sept 1986, p 17, 26 Sept 1986, p 51, 3 Oct 1986, p 47; *Austn Financial Review*, 3 Sept 1990, p 1; *Australian*, 3 Sept 1990, p 1; *West Australian*, 3 Sept 1990, p 1; *Bulletin*, 11 Sept 1990, p 166; J. McIlwraith, 'Holmes à Court: The End of an Era', *Australian Business*, 12 Sept 1990, p 32; *Australian*, 6-7 Apr 1991, 'Review', p 1.   JOHN McILWRAITH

HOLT, BEATRICE (1900-1988), medical practitioner and mother- and baby-care advocate, was born on 4 January 1900 at North Carlton, Melbourne, elder child of Victorian-born parents William Henry Sharwood [q.v.11], clerk, and his wife Emily, née Brown. Beatrice attended Princes Hill State School, South Melbourne College, and Methodist Ladies' College, Kew (dux 1917), before proceeding to the University of Melbourne (MB, BS, 1923). In 1927, when her father was appointed crown solicitor, she left infant-welfare work in Melbourne and moved to Canberra with her parents, opening a practice in Northbourne Avenue.

Hospitalised with an infection after an accidental needle prick, she met Dr John Ackland Holt (d.1972), who helped to save her arm from possible amputation. They were married on 1 December 1931 at the Presbyterian Church, Braddon. After living in Brisbane for a year, they returned to Canberra in 1934 and settled at Kingston (formerly Eastlake) where John, who was particularly skilled in orthopaedics and obstetrics, practised for the next thirty-five years. Beatrice acted as medical superintendent at Canberra Community Hospital during World War II and occasionally as pathologist, but never re-entered general practice.

Of their five children, the first was the victim of a cot-death and the last was stillborn. Although Bea Holt rarely spoke of these sad experiences, they may have intensified her concern for mother and child care, especially in Canberra, where many recently transferred people lived in temporary accommodation without the support of extended families. She did not believe that a maternal instinct was all that was necessary for the welfare of mothers and babies.

Holt became involved in the Canberra Mothercraft Society, which had been formally established in February 1927. A baby health clinic, the first of many, opened at Eastlake in July. Soon every newborn baby was being checked by an infant-welfare sister and mothers were receiving advice on important subjects such as the benefits of breast-feeding. Other ideas led to Canberra's first preschool system, an emergency housekeeping service, occasional child-care centres and the separation of the hospital's maternity wing from wards treating illnesses. Appointed a life member of the society in 1937, Holt served as president in 1935-37, 1940-44 and 1948-51—years of considerable pressure. From 1946 to 1951 the Australian Capital Territory had by far the highest birth rate in Australia. The society also suffered divisions, exacerbated by bureaucratic measures and by the community's high expectations of social planning.

Reticent in private, Bea Holt could be forceful in public but always maintained a natural dignity and composure. In 1949-50 she was president of the Canberra High School Parents and Citizens Association. From 1962 to 1964 she was president of the Canberra Association of University Women and in 1964 acting president of the Australian Federation of University Women. She spoke on subjects as varied as 'Immunisation against Infectious Diseases in Childhood' (1941) and 'The Changing Place of Women' (1965), gently advocating in the latter the removal of barriers to the advancement of women in Australia. Professionally qualified in dressmaking, millinery and bookbinding, she also maintained an interest in engineering, perhaps best expressed in her taste for sporty cars, including a powder-blue Karmann Ghia. Survived by two of her three daughters and her elder son, she died on 1 June 1988 at Bruce and was cremated.

H. Crisp and L. Rudduck, *The Mothering Years* (1979); J. Newman and J. Warren, *Royal Canberra Hospital* (1993); A. J. Proust (ed), *History of Medicine in Canberra and Queanbeyan* (1994); Canberra and District Hist Soc, *Newsletter*, Aug 1988, p 8; funeral address by R. Sharwood (Canberra and District Hist Soc); Canberra Mothercraft Soc records (ACT Heritage Lib); private information.

JILL WATERHOUSE

HOLT, EDGAR GEORGE (1904-1988), poet, journalist and public relations officer, was born on 27 December 1904 at Burnley, Lancashire, son of George Andrew Holt, commercial traveller, and his wife Mary Ann, née Smith. When Edgar was 9 the family migrated to Australia, eventually settling in Queensland; he attended Brisbane State High School. He served a cadetship at the *Daily Mail* and in 1924 transferred to the Brisbane *Telegraph*. Holt, an 'eccentric and casual' student in the diploma of journalism course at the University of Queensland in 1926, edited and contributed poetry and cultural commentaries to the student newspaper *Galmahra*. In 1929 he published a volume of poetry, *The Merlin Papers*, with his friend Colin Bingham [q.v.]. On 11 October 1930 he married with Presbyterian forms Dorothy Lester Vaughan at her home at New Farm, Brisbane.

Advised by the expatriate composer Arthur Benjamin [q.v.7] to 'go south' as Brisbane was only 'all right from the neck down', Holt had joined the venerable Melbourne *Argus* in 1929. He caused a sensation when he became a leader-writer at the age of 26; he editorialised against fascism. He contributed verse to the short-lived modernist magazine *Stream* (1931) and in 1932 published *Lilacs Out of the Dead Land*, which was influenced by T. S. Eliot and the later Romantic poets.

A special and leader-writer on the Melbourne *Herald* from 1935, Holt contributed book reviews and articles about Australian literature and culture. Two years later, his play *Anzac Reunion* was published. In 1939 he was elected federal president of the Australian Journalists' Association (and was awarded its gold honour badge), but resigned later that year when he moved to Sydney to join the dynamic *Daily* and *Sunday Telegraph*s. He was a political columnist and chief leader-writer, but he gained little satisfaction pontificating 'on affairs great and small' at the behest of proprietors and editors. In October 1944 he took an active role in the production of a union newspaper during a Sydney newspaper strike, relishing the opportunity 'to be off the chain'. After falling out with Brian Penton [q.v.15], editor of the *Daily Telegraph*, he joined *Smith's Weekly* in 1945. A passionate cook, he wrote about food using the pseudonym 'Toby Belch'. He compiled the waspish 'Political Form

Guide', and edited the paper from 1947 to 1950, when it ceased publication.

An admirer of John Curtin and J. B. Chifley [qq.v.13], until the bank nationalisation scheme, Holt was appointed federal public relations officer of the Liberal Party of Australia in November 1950. He had ambitious plans: a closer liaison between the federal secretariat, the State divisions and the parliamentary and extra-parliamentary wings of the party, and measurement of public opinion on major issues. Although he never received the resources he required, he wrote summaries of parliamentary and policy initiatives, pamphlets such as *The First Ten Years* (1959), and other publicity material for Federal and State elections, including Harold Holt's [q.v.14] policy speech. In 1959 he visited Britain and the United States of America to investigate the use of television in political campaigning. He also appeared on the panel of the Australian Broadcasting Commission's 'Any Questions?' and published poetry in *Southerly* and *Meanjin*.

Public relations, he commented, 'is largely salesmanship, but one must know precisely what is to be sold'. For Holt, being a member of the Liberal Party entailed rejecting totalitarianism—the 'crude forms of power-organisation with which this century is familiar'—and advancing the dignity and freedom of the individual. As early as 1943 he had identified (Sir) Robert Menzies [q.v.15] as having the most lucid and disciplined intellect in parliament, and being the best debater, but lacking some political gifts. With the federal secretariat, Holt made the prime minister and his family the focus of party publicity, fostering the image of the fatherly 'Bob Menzies' and then the statesmanlike 'Sir Robert Menzies'. He wrote *Politics Is People: The Men of the Menzies Era* (1969) at a time when the party leadership was fracturing.

Short and rotund, Holt had an unruly mop of grey hair, a ruddy complexion and a boisterous laugh. He joined his confrères Kenneth Slessor [q.v.16] and Cyril Pearl [q.v.] in establishing the Condiments Club, which met at restaurants in Sydney. Becoming increasingly vocal in his condemnation of the media, Holt blamed it for creating 'instant politics' and for manufacturing political crises. In September 1972 the party replaced him as senior public relations officer and gave him the title of senior political adviser to the secretariat. Following the election defeat in December, some officials grumbled about the generation of 'forty-niners'. Critical of the parliamentary wing's increasing dominance over the federal secretariat and as an admirer of E. G. Whitlam, Holt was eased out of the organisation in 1974. Roman history occupied the last years of the self-described 'nonconformist' and 'civilised amateur'. Survived by his wife and their son

and daughter, he died on 11 October 1988 at Potts Point and was cremated.

G. Blaikie, *Remember Smith's Weekly?* (1966); C. Turnbull (ed), *Hammond Innes Introduces Australia* (1971); I. Hancock, *National and Permanent?* (2000); B. Griffen-Foley, 'A "Civilised Amateur"', *Austn Jnl of Politics and Hist*, vol 49, no 1, 2003, p 31; *Austn Liberal*, Sept 1960, 'supp', p 3, Aug 1971, p 7, Nov 1971, p 7; *Nation*, 7 Oct 1961, p 7; M. Pratt, interview with E. G. Holt (ts, 1978, NLA); C. Bingham papers (NLA); Liberal Party of Aust, federal secretariat papers (NLA).

BRIDGET GRIFFEN-FOLEY

HOLT, SIR JAMES ARTHUR (1899-1982), engineer and public servant, was born on 30 April 1899 at Lithgow, New South Wales, eldest of three children of James Holt, hotel-keeper, and his wife Delia, née Trill, both born in New South Wales. James was educated at Lithgow Public and Sydney Boys' High schools and the University of Sydney (BE, 1921), where he graduated with first-class honours in civil engineering. First an engineering draftsman with the New South Wales Department of Public Works, employed under J. J. C. Bradfield [q.v.7] on the design and construction of the Sydney Harbour Bridge, Holt was promoted in 1927 to supervising engineer. On 30 November 1932 at St Philip's Church of England, Sydney, he married Audrey May Benson. After the bridge opened to traffic that year he spent two years as officer-in-charge of the Narooma office of the Department of Main Roads.

When Bradfield was appointed consulting engineer in 1933 for Brisbane's new cross-river bridge (named Story [q.v.12] Bridge in 1937), he invited Holt to join him. In 1934-40 Holt was supervising engineer for the project under the direction of the Bureau of Industry's Bridge Board, chaired by (Sir) John Kemp [q.v.15]. Early in World War II he taught mathematics and navigation to trainee pilots at the Central Technical College. Effectively becoming Kemp's 'right-hand man' after the latter was appointed director of the Allied Works Council in Queensland in February 1942, he was engineer-in-charge in 1943-44 of all AWC works in the Cairns region. From 1944 Holt was chief engineer with the Bridge Board.

In 1946, when the co-ordinator-general of public works took over the functions of the Bureau of Industry's boards, Holt was delegated to supervise construction of the University of Queensland's new campus at St Lucia. In 1949 he was appointed chief engineer, Co-ordinator-General's Department, with oversight of both the bridge and hydraulics branches. He superintended the completion of the Somerset dam, and the design and construction of bridges over the Fitzroy, Burdekin and North Johnstone rivers and of water conservation and hydro-electricity schemes for the Tully, Barron and Burdekin rivers. In 1953 he took responsibility for compiling Queensland's annual co-ordinated plan of works and in June 1954 succeeded Kemp as co-ordinator-general.

With government policy increasingly oriented towards resources development, Holt and his department took a dominant role in the planning, design and implementation of the State's major infrastructure projects. As chairman of the Burdekin River Authority, he advanced its proposed huge irrigation and hydro-electricity scheme. Through the Bureau of Investigation of land and water resources, he maintained a program of surveying and reporting on the conservation and future development of regional resources, out of which came the first river and beach protection models. He represented Queensland at Australian Loan Council meetings, seeking funding for public works. Chairman of the Queensland Traffic Commission (1958-63) and of the Standards Association of Australia's Queensland committee (1950-76), he participated in numerous interdepartmental and advisory committees.

Holt was active in the Institution of Engineers, Australia, serving as a committee member of the Queensland division (1939-48), division chairman (1943, 1947) and member of council (1948-54); in 1971 he was elected an honorary fellow. He was awarded the (W. H.) Warren memorial prize (1939), the R. W. Chapman medal (1953) and the (Sir) Peter Nicol Russell [qq.v.6,7] medal (1961). An external member of the University of Queensland's engineering faculty (1948-56) and member of senate (1955-68), he received an honorary doctorate of engineering in 1965.

A sound administrator, Holt did not seek the limelight and was determinedly apolitical. His recommendations for projects were always decided on technical merit, supported by meticulous attention to detail, specialist knowledge and an overall sense of the benefits accruing to Queensland. Respected for his integrity, he had an open and enthusiastic yet serious manner. In place of the traditional, formal meeting with local government representatives held annually in Brisbane, he preferred to visit them informally on their own ground.

Whenever possible Holt spent time at his Caloundra beach house, away from the telephone, playing lawn bowls, fishing and surfing. He was a founding member of the St Lucia Bowls Club, and a member of the Johnsonian Club. Knighted in 1960, he retired as co-ordinator-general in 1968 and took up several directorships: Evans [q.v.8] Deakin Ltd (1970-75), Crusader Oil NL (1970-79) and the Metropolitan Permanent Building Society (1972-79).

Sir James died on 1 May 1982 at Auchenflower and was cremated. He was survived by his wife and their three sons and a daughter.

C. Lack (ed), *Three Decades of Queensland Political History* (1962); G. Cossens (ed), *Eminent Queensland Engineers Volume II* (1999); Co-ordinator-General of Public Works, Qld, *Annual Report*, 1947, 1953, 1954, 1982; J. Minnery, Coordination and the Queensland Co-ordinator General (MPubAd thesis, Univ of Qld, 1988); K. Cohen, J. R. Kemp, 'The Grand Pooh-Bah' (PhD thesis, Univ of Qld, 2002); private information.   KAY COHEN

HOLT, ROBERT WILFRED (1913-1985), politician and solicitor, was born on 9 June 1913 at Launceston, Tasmania, third child of Wilfred John Holt, Presbyterian clergyman, and his wife Lilian Ann Janet, née Parkhill, both New South Wales born. Educated at Scotch College, Melbourne, and the University of Melbourne (LL B, 1940), he represented Australia in Rugby Union football.

Mobilised in the Militia as a lieutenant on 3 January 1941, Holt transferred to the Australian Imperial Force on 21 February and was allotted to the 8th Armoured Regiment. At Holy Trinity Church, East Melbourne, on 4 March 1942 he married with Anglican rites Norma Rose Edwards, a nurse; they were to have four children before being divorced. Promoted to temporary captain in April (substantive in September), he was posted to headquarters, 1st Armoured Division. He performed staff duties at headquarters, New Guinea Force, and at Land Headquarters, Melbourne, and was promoted to temporary major in October 1944. On 17 May 1945 he transferred to the Reserve of Officers. He was admitted as a barrister and solicitor on 1 April 1946. He practised at Portland, and later at Preston and Ringwood.

Having joined the Australian Labor Party in 1942, Holt was elected to the Victorian Legislative Assembly for Portland in 1945. He lost the seat in 1947, but won it back in 1950. Regarded as a protégé of the State ALP secretary P. J. Kennelly [q.v.], he was embroiled from the start in the developing factionalism. In December 1952 he became commissioner of crown lands and survey, minister of soldier settlement and for conservation, and president of the Board of Land and Works in John Cain's [q.v.13] Labor government, but in December next year on the floor of the assembly he tore up a land settlement amendment bill that he was handling, walked out and resigned from cabinet. He later claimed that B. A. Santamaria, the leader of the Catholic Social Studies Movement and the National Catholic Rural Movement, had used unreasonable pressure to have the government accept as part of the bill a proposal for the rural movement to use crown land in Gippsland for an Italian farming settlement; Santamaria denied this accusation.

Holt's seat was abolished in 1955 following a redistribution. Promoted as a man of principle and courage by the new left-wing controllers of the Victorian ALP branch after the split, he was endorsed for the safe Labor Federal seat of Darebin, which he held from 1955 to 1958, when he resigned due to ill health. He was elected State president of the party in 1962. Critics perceived him as a moderate, respectable face for an authoritarian, electorally ineffectual left-wing union machine in which the Communist Party of Australia had significant influence. His behaviour gave him a reputation, rightly or wrongly, for being anti-Catholic.

Influenced by criticism of the Victorian branch and its poor electoral performance, Holt attacked the State executive and lost the presidency in 1965. He resigned from the ALP in 1973, citing inappropriate union control, and told the press that he would vote Liberal and might join the Australia Party. Active in the Victorian National Parks Association, he was also president (1973-74) of the Victorian Animal Aid Trust. In a civil ceremony on 16 December 1976 at Olinda he married Barbara Ann Rothque, née Quittenton, a widow. An ambitious, energetic, well-intentioned professional man attracted to public life, Bob Holt lacked the guile and emotional balance required for the exceptional complexities of the politics of his time. Survived by his wife, and by the two sons and two daughters of his first marriage, he died on 26 April 1985 at Montrose and was cremated.

R. Murray, *The Split* (1970); K. White, *John Cain & Victorian Labor 1917-1957* (1982); *Canberra Times*, 29 July 1965, p 3; *Herald* (Melbourne), 8 May 1973, p 13; *Age* (Melbourne), 8 May 1973, p 1, 1 May 1985, p 18; B884, item V62288, B883, item VX39826 (NAA).   ROBERT MURRAY

HOLT, DAME ZARA KATE (1909-1989), fashion designer and businesswoman, was born on 10 March 1909 at Kew, Melbourne, younger daughter and second of four children of Victorian-born Sydney Herbert Dickins, merchant, and his wife Violet, née MacDonald, from Scotland. She was educated at home before attending Ruyton Girls' School, Kew (1919-24), and Toorak College (1925). When she was 16 she met Harold Holt [q.v.14], then a law student at the University of Melbourne.

In 1930, in the depths of the Depression, Zara Dickins borrowed £150 from her father and established a dress shop in Little Collins Street, Melbourne, with her friend Betty (Bettine) James. Two years later, Betty having

left to marry (Sir) Roy Grounds [q.v.], Zara sold the business. Unable to persuade the ambitious but impecunious Holt to marry before he had sufficient funds, she departed on a round-the-world cruise to England. On the return voyage she met James Heywood Fell, a British army officer serving with the 15th Lancers. She married him with Congregational forms on 4 May 1935 at Kew. For the next four years they lived at Jubbulpore (Jabalpur) and Meerut in India, Zara returning to Melbourne for visits and for the births of her three sons. After the birth in 1939 of the second and third, twin boys and probably Holt's sons, she remained in Melbourne. The Fells were amicably divorced in 1946.

During World War II Zara Fell worked with her father's food packaging business, Trading & Agency Co., designing display boxes and plastic wraps. On 8 October 1946 at Toorak she married Holt, now a solicitor and member of the House of Representatives. Her husband frequently away in Canberra and her sons at school, she opened a boutique, Magg, in Toorak Village with Betty Grounds. By her own admission she could neither cut nor sew, but she was creative and could manage people. After postwar austerities, the extravagant handmade evening dresses at which Magg excelled were very popular. Another Magg shop was opened at Double Bay, Sydney, and a Magg boutique in the Myer [q.v.10] Emporium Ltd, Melbourne. In 1961 a Magg evening dress was voted 'Gown of the Year', and in 1962 Miss Australia, Tania Verstak, wore a Magg gown in the Miss International contest, which she won. Zara Holt also advised on Australian uniforms for events such as Expo '67 in Montreal and the Mexico Olympic Games in 1968.

On her return from overseas trips with her husband (deputy-leader in the Menzies [q.v.15] government from 1956 and treasurer from 1958), Mrs Holt was in demand as a speaker on overseas fashion trends. She rarely spoke on political matters or visited Canberra, dividing her time between her home in St George's Road, Toorak, their house at Portsea and 'the shack' at Bingil Bay, North Queensland.

In January 1966 Harold Holt became Australia's seventeenth prime minister. As chatelaine of the Lodge, Canberra, Zara was noted for her dramatic refurbishments and her energetic role as hostess. She was at the Lodge when her husband disappeared at Cheviot Beach, Victoria, on 17 December 1967. Following his memorial service in Melbourne she left in January 1968 for a two-month trip, during which she attended another memorial service, at Westminster Abbey, London, lunched with Queen Elizabeth II at Sandringham, and stayed with President Lyndon Johnson and his wife at the White House, Washington. She was appointed DBE in 1968. Her autobiography, *My Life and Harry* (1968), was launched by Sir Henry Bolte [q.v.].

On 19 February 1969 at Toorak Zara married the flamboyant federal politician Henry Jefferson Percival Bate (d.1984). She continued to live in Melbourne and regularly visited Bate's houses at Tilba Tilba, New South Wales. Although she sold Magg in 1976 she retained an interest in designing. In 1979 she was appointed chairman of the Yves St Laurent Board in Melbourne. Next year she retired to Surfers Paradise, Queensland. She re-emerged into public view briefly in January 1985 to comment on a television program that had raised the question of Harold Holt's infidelities—which she acknowledged but had chosen to ignore.

Short (5 ft 2 ins or 158 cm) and plump, Zara Bate claimed that her 'impossible figure' had inspired her interest in fashion. Portrayed as 'zany' or 'daffy', she was a gift to the press, but her ebullient exterior hid an astute and successful business brain. Dame Zara died on 14 June 1989 at Surfers Paradise and was buried in Sorrento cemetery, Victoria. She was survived by her three sons, who had taken the name Holt in 1957. Her estate was sworn for probate at $5 173 165.

D. Langmore, *Prime Ministers' Wives* (1992); P. Pemberton, *Harold Holt: Guide to Archives of Australia's Prime Ministers* (2003); *Bulletin*, 2 Sept 1967, p 30; *Age*, 15 June 1989, p 4; Holt papers (NAA and NLA).   P. A. PEMBERTON

HOOK, EDWIN JOHN (1910-1990), lawyer and public servant, was born on 3 April 1910 at Forest Lodge, Sydney, eldest of three sons of Edwin John Hook, printer, and his wife Emily Jane, née Brown, both English born. Young Edwin was educated at Summer Hill Public School and (on a bursary) at Fort Street Boys' High School (dux 1926). A reference from a master commended him as 'a lad of exceptional all round ability ... exceedingly well behaved, industrious in habits and of high moral character'.

In February 1927 Hook was appointed to the New South Wales Department of the Attorney-General and of Justice as a junior clerk in the Prothonotary's Office. Attending evening classes at the University of Sydney (BA, 1930; LL B, 1933), he gained first-class honours and the university medal in law, and shared the John George Dalley prize. He was admitted to the Bar on 26 May 1933 and as a solicitor on 27 May 1938. While working as a law clerk with Minter, Simpson [q.v.11] & Co., he had married Valerie Norma Fowler Macmillan, a clerk, on 31 July 1937 at St Andrew's Church of England, Summer Hill; they were to remain childless.

On 29 January 1942 Hook enlisted in the Citizen Military Forces. He was 5 ft 9½ ins (177 cm) tall, dark complexioned, with dark brown hair and brown eyes. Posted to the 130th General Transport Company, he transferred to the Australian Imperial Force in September and was promoted to sergeant in October. From December he was attached to Alf Conlon's [q.v.13] research section at Land Headquarters, Melbourne. Discharged on 7 April 1943, he was appointed to the Commonwealth Office of Education, Sydney. He was secretary of the Universities Commission in 1946-50, then worked as assistant-director, Commonwealth Office of Education, until 1951 when he was appointed to the Attorney-General's Department, Canberra. A photograph of the older Hook shows a steady, reticent gaze behind heavy glasses, thinning hair, a no-nonsense mouth and resolute chin.

Hook advanced steadily and on 3 February 1964 was promoted to secretary of the department, succeeding Sir Kenneth Bailey [q.v.13]. He served four attorneys-general, Sir Garfield Barwick, (Sir) Billy Snedden, (Sir) Nigel Bowen and Tom Hughes, and had been associated with major legislation including important amendments in 1960 to the Crimes Act (1914-59), and the Marriage Act (1961). In 1967 he was appointed CBE. A former colleague recalled his 'level-headedness, tolerance, politeness, common sense' and his 'fairness' and 'modesty'. When not working, he enjoyed a round of golf at the Royal Canberra Golf Club; gardening, too, afforded a change from the demands of office. Excessive conscientiousness resulted in a stress-related illness that forced his retirement on 2 February 1970. Always considerate of others, he requested that, instead of a retirement present, the E. J. Hook Trust Fund be established to provide prizes for able young lawyers.

Ted Hook and his wife moved to the Gold Coast, Queensland; they relaxed with lawn bowls and took several overseas trips. Survived by his wife, he died on 2 April 1990 at Benowa and was cremated. Barwick paid tribute to a 'very sound lawyer' and a 'good and reliable friend'. Others remembered him as 'hard-working and intelligent', an 'essentially decent person, highly principled and fair to his staff and respected by everyone'.

Austn Law Jnl, vol 64, no 7, 1990, p 446; *Canberra Times*, 5 Apr 1990, p 7; B883, item NX141374 (NAA); private information.   ROSEMARY JENNINGS

HOOPER, KEVIN JOSEPH (1928-1984), politician, was born on 9 July 1928 in Brisbane, eldest child of Queensland-born parents George Cyril Hooper, labourer, and his wife Catherine, née Moriarty. The family lived at

Torwood; Kevin attended Rosalie convent, Rainworth and Milton State schools, and Marist Brothers' College, Rosalie, to grade eight level. He worked as a shop assistant at Bayards Pty Ltd and McDonnell & East [qq.v.10,8] Ltd. On 19 December 1953 at St Michael's Catholic Church, Dorrington, he married Beryl Therese Kelly, a clerk-typist. In 1956 they moved into a Queensland Housing Commission house at Inala, a poorly serviced satellite suburb between Brisbane and Ipswich with the largest accumulation of QHC housing in the State.

While employed at a dental hospital Hooper joined the Federated Miscellaneous Workers' Union of Australia; in the early 1960s he became a State organiser. Having joined the Rosalie branch of the Australian Labor Party in 1953, he transferred to Inala, where he later became secretary. On 27 May 1972 he was elected the member for the new seat of Archerfield in the Legislative Assembly. That year he was also elected president of the Oxley federal divisional executive; several times he was campaign director for the Federal member W. G. (Bill) Hayden.

Archerfield was an electorate with a heavy workload and Hooper soon entrenched himself as an effective member. In 1974-77 he was secretary of the parliamentary Labor Party. Opposition spokesman for works and housing, he spoke frequently in the House, always with a colourful turn of phrase and a waspish sense of humour. Never afraid to test under parliamentary privilege allegations of maladministration, incompetence or corruption, he became known as 'Buckets'. In 1975 he raised issues such as the accounting practices and performance of building societies (forcing the government to update the legislation), malpractice in the building industry, sales of flood-prone land on Russell Island, and the use of the National Party minister Russell Hinze's office phone to promote land sales. He had a flair for publicity and he cultivated journalists.

In February 1980 Hooper was named Opposition spokesman for police and prisons. He commented on drug trafficking, prostitution and gambling, claiming that 'crime of this magnitude could not operate without political and police permission at the highest level'. Responding in 1981 to a denial by Hinze, then minister for police, that there were illegal casinos at Fortitude Valley, he identified three premises and named Geraldo Bellino and Vittorio Conte as 'Mafia' figures who ran them. In 1982 he named the police commissioner Terence Lewis and the assistant-commissioner Tony Murphy as 'protected criminals'. However, when he advocated reform of the ALP State branch he lost party support and Wayne Goss replaced him as police spokesman in October 1982. Hooper's last campaign was for justice for detective senior constable Lorrelle Saunders, who spent ten months in prison as a result of a fabricated tape recording used in evidence. She was eventually declared 'completely innocent' by the minister for justice N. J. Harper on 21 January 1984.

A dedicated family man, Hooper loved books and classical music, especially opera. He died of Hodgkin's disease on 9 March 1984 at Prince Charles Hospital, Chermside, after surgery, and was buried in Mount Gravatt cemetery. His wife, and their five sons and one daughter, survived him. He is remembered at Inala by Kev Hooper Park.

G. E. (Tony) Fitzgerald's commission of inquiry into possible illegal activities and associated police misconduct was established in May 1987. It paved the way for the major reforms in Queensland to the police, public service and parliament that Hooper had championed.

M. B. Cribb and P. J. Boyce (eds), *Politics in Queensland* (1980); P. Dickie, *The Road to Fitzgerald* (1988); *PD* (Qld), 19 Sept 1972, p 608, 27 Mar 1984, p 2005; *Telegraph* (Brisbane), 23 Mar 1979, p 12; *National Times*, 22-28 Apr 1983, p 14; *Sunday Mail* (Brisbane), 22 Jan 1984, p 1, 11 Mar 1984, pp 2, 19; *Courier-Mail* (Brisbane), 10 Mar 1984, p 3, 5 Sept 1988, p 4; private information.

MANFRED CROSS

HOPKINS, RONALD NICHOLAS LAMOND (1897-1990), army officer, was born on 24 May 1897 at Stawell, Victoria, son of William Fleming Hopkins, surgeon, and his wife Rose Margaret Burton, née Lamond, both Victorian born. His father died in 1900 while serving in the South African War. Educated at Melbourne Church of England Grammar School, Ronald entered the Royal Military College, Duntroon, Federal Capital Territory, in February 1915. He graduated in December 1917 and was commissioned lieutenant, Australian Imperial Force, on 1 January 1918. Arriving in the Middle East in April, he served in Palestine with the 6th Light Horse Regiment, on the staffs of the 2nd and 3rd Light Horse brigades and the Anzac Mounted Division, and at AIF Headquarters, Cairo, where he helped to supervise the repatriation of Australians from Egypt.

Returning, himself, in August 1919, Hopkins held the usual succession of regimental and staff postings characteristic of the period, including a stint as orderly officer to the inspector-general Sir Harry Chauvel [q.v.7] in 1921-22. Known as 'Hoppy' to his friends, he was promoted to captain in January 1926. On 15 December that year at St Michael's Church of England, Mitcham, Adelaide, he married Nora Frances Reissmann (known as Riceman), before sailing for India, where he attended the Staff College, Quetta, in 1927-28. Further staff jobs in Australia followed, with the 1st and 3rd Cavalry brigades and at Army Headquarters, Melbourne. He rose to major in September 1936.

Hopkins's professional focus since commissioning had been on the mounted arm, and the 1930s were characterised by intense and growing debate on mechanisation, motorisation and the future of the horse in war. At the beginning of 1937 he was sent to Britain to undertake training with armoured vehicles and to report on moves to mechanise the British Army. Attached to the 1st Light Battalion, Royal Tank Corps, he became an ardent exponent of armoured forces and after his return to Australia in April 1939 was posted as general staff officer, grade 2 (mechanisation and armoured fighting vehicles), at Army Headquarters. While in Britain he had sent back reports advocating the wholesale conversion of the Australian army from horses to horsepower which, while prescient, were also premature in that they largely ignored the severe financial constraints under which the interwar army operated.

Promoted to temporary lieutenant colonel in November 1939, Hopkins was given command of the 7th Divisional Cavalry Regiment, AIF, in April 1940. In November, however, he was seconded to Army Headquarters, where he played an important part in planning the organisation of what became the 1st Armoured Division. Having been promoted to colonel in May 1941, he reached the Middle East in June and served with the 7th Division for only a month before returning to Australia and the position of GSO1 on the headquarters of the 1st Armoured Division. There his knowledge of armour and armoured operations was put to good use as the division formed and trained for possible deployment to the Middle East.

The remainder of Hopkins's war service involved increasingly more senior staff positions. Made temporary brigadier in August 1942, he was brigadier, general staff, at headquarters, New Guinea Force, from September to February 1943, and liaison officer with the United States of America's VII Amphibious Force in 1943-44 during the landings at Lae and Finschhafen. He was appointed CBE (1943) for his 'marked energy and drive' while with New Guinea Force, and to the United States' Legion of Merit (1944) in recognition of his 'judgment, industry, and high professional military skill'. From September 1944 he headed the Staff School (Australia), which was renamed the Australian Staff College in February 1946.

Opportunity for extended leadership in the field came only with the occupation of Japan and the command (from April 1946) of the 34th Infantry Brigade, formed especially for that purpose. The early period of the occupation posed numerous challenges, although most were not of a purely military nature. The manpower needs of the Australian Regular Army, established in 1947, saw the gradual run-down of the Australian component of the British Commonwealth Occupation Force, and Hopkins returned to Australia at the end of 1948. While in Japan he had worked closely and amicably with the commander-in-chief of BCOF, Lieutenant General (Sir) Horace Robertson [q.v.16].

Back in Australia, Hopkins assumed command of the 4th Military District (from January 1949) and of Central Command (from January 1950), before becoming deputy-chief of the General Staff in May 1950 as a temporary major general (substantive 21 September). In February 1951 he received his final appointment in uniform, that of commandant of RMC, Duntroon. He retired from the army on 25 May 1954. His retirement was highly active. He cultivated business interests, and for twelve years worked in public relations with the *Advertiser* newspaper in Adelaide. Appointed chief executive officer of the first Adelaide Festival of Arts, in 1960, he provoked public controversy when he threatened to resign if the festival staged Alan Seymour's play *The One Day of the Year*, a critique of Anzac Day and returned servicemen. The festival board backed him, and the play was withdrawn. He was also a keen golfer.

Hopkins wrote the history of the Royal Australian Armoured Corps, published as *Australian Armour* (1978). Far more than a parochial regimental history, the book engaged seriously with the development and use of armour by the Australian army from World War II to Vietnam, and was informed by his close personal knowledge of its genesis. Survived by his wife and their son, he died on 24 November 1990 at Walkerville and was cremated. His career exemplified the increasing professionalism of the Australian army, particularly during World War II, while his intellect, energy and sense of curiosity helped to guide and shape the armoured corps and the adoption of armour more generally.

D. M. Horner, *Crisis of Command* (1978); S. Cockburn, *The Patriarchs* (1983); P. Dennis et al, *The Oxford Companion to Australian Military History* (1995); *Advertiser* (Adelaide), 26 Nov 1990, p 15; B2455, item Hopkins R N L Lieutenant (NAA).

JEFFREY GREY

HOPMAN, HENRICK CHRISTIAN (HARRY) (1906-1985), sportsman and tennis coach, was born on 12 August 1906 at Glebe, Sydney, third child of New South Wales-born parents John Henry Hopman, schoolteacher, and his wife Jennie Siberteen, née Glad. At 13 Harry turned to tennis from a first enthusiasm for soccer, and—playing barefoot—won an open singles tournament on a court levelled into the playground of Rosehill Public School, where his father was headmaster. His successes continued during secondary schooling at Parramatta and Fort Street Boys' high schools; at 17 he represented New South Wales in the Linton [q.v.10] Cup national junior teams' competition.

After leaving school, Hopman worked as a salesman for a Sydney sports goods retailer, who allowed him generous time to play and practise. In 1925 he teamed up with Jack Crawford, and they won—for three years in a row—the Australian junior doubles championship, and then the Australian senior doubles championships (1929, 1930). Crawford, a tall and stylish baseline stroke-player, was always the better player; Hopman, nimble and energetic with a busy volleying game, lost to him in twenty-seven finals and was runner-up to him in the Australian singles titles of 1931 and 1932. Their contrasting styles meshed ideally in doubles.

In 1933 Hopman joined the staff of the Melbourne *Herald* as a sportswriter. The arrangement suited both parties: his hours were flexible, so long as his copy met deadlines, and he was allowed leave when selected to play Davis Cup tennis overseas; the paper gained exclusive use of his comments, which were then sometimes syndicated. On 19 March 1934 at St Philip's Church of England, Sydney, he married Eleanor Mary (Nell) Hall [q.v.14 Hopman], whom he had met during a junior tennis competition and with whom he formed a successful mixed doubles combination. They won four Australian titles and in 1935 became the first husband-and-wife team to reach the final at Wimbledon.

The Hopmans settled in a modest, rented house at Hawthorn: Harry—a fitness fanatic who often ran to the *Herald* office in the city—won the Australian amateur squash title in 1933, 1934 and 1936. He was a playing member of the unsuccessful Australian Davis Cup tennis teams of 1928, 1930 and 1932, and in 1938 captained the team. For the first time in fourteen years, Australia reached the Challenge Round final, going down 3-2 to the United States of America. In September 1939, again under his captaincy, Australia won the Cup 3-2 after Adrian Quist and John Bromwich both won their final singles matches.

When the Davis Cup competition tournaments resumed in 1946 after World War II, Hopman—who had also revived his private coaching sessions—was overlooked as captain; he watched as Australia was crushed by the American players Jack Kramer and Ted Schroeder, both exponents of the serve-volley power game. After four such losses, Hopman was recalled; his second stint, as non-playing captain-coach (1950-69), became known as the Hopman era.

Hopman was respected as the architect of Australia's postwar tennis supremacy. From 1950 to 1967 Australia won the Davis Cup fifteen times, and, as successive waves of young champions disqualified themselves from the competition by succumbing to the lure of professionalism, he cultivated replacements. He first developed the outstanding juniors Frank Sedgman and Ken McGregor into two of the finest players in the world. When Sedgman was left out of the 1948 squad, Hopman persuaded the *Herald* to raise funds to send the youngster abroad and to support his own coverage of both the Olympic Games and Wimbledon—enabling him to manage Sedgman's tour. When his 1950-51-52 winners, Sedgman and McGregor, turned professional, he held the Cup with the teenage newcomers Lew Hoad and Ken Rosewall. When they in turn became professionals, he brought on Ashley Cooper, Neale Fraser, Rod Laver, Roy Emerson and Mal Anderson, following them in the late 1960s with John Newcombe, Fred Stolle and Tony Roche. This process was seen by some in Britain and the USA as an assembly line; its results, however, were undeniable. Among the players who came to prominence under Hopman's care, the following won at Wimbledon: Sedgman, Hoad (twice), Cooper, Fraser, Emerson (twice), Laver (four times) and Newcombe (three times).

Primarily a strategist, conditioner and motivator, Hopman once remarked: 'I don't teach people, I stretch them'. Alrick Man, the non-playing captain of the 1947 American Davis Cup team, quipped that Hopman's presence on the sidelines was worth fifteen points a game to Australia. Tony Trabert, who with Vic Seixas went down to Hoad and Rosewall in the 1953 Challenge Round, said that they were 'beaten by two babies and a fox'—alluding to one of the gentler of Hopman's many nicknames, 'the Old Fox', which he liked. Once, after hearing a weather report that Sydney was to have a rainy day, he flew his entire squad to Brisbane to gain the advantage of an extra day's practice. On the eve of a Wimbledon final he arranged for Mal Anderson to win at poker, to give him confidence for the match ahead. When Hoad fell on wet turf during his 1953 five-setter against Trabert, and sprawled there, apparently drained emotionally and physically, Hopman walked across and threw a towel in his face. The mood broken, Hoad got up, went back and won the match.

Hopman was appointed OBE (1951) and CBE (1956). In 1955 he was presented with nearly £6000 contributed to a testimonial fund that relieved for a time the strains of living on a modest journalistic wage. For all his success, however, he was not universally admired. Childless, he was often accused of treating his young international players as children. On tours he used a much-ridiculed fining system to discipline his 'boys' for misdemeanours including poor table manners and breaches of curfew. He was not beyond using his newspaper column to highlight (for the benefit of umpires) an opposing player's tendency to foot-fault. Among his many public disputes was a war of words with Jaroslav Drobny, who beat Rosewall at Wimbledon in 1954, and, in 1962, criticism of Margaret Smith, who disliked travelling under the management of his wife.

Vigorously campaigning against the professional game that plundered his talent, in 1961 Hopman won £20 000 damages after Mirror Newspapers were found to have defamed him in 1958 by claiming he had been paid for coaching in South Africa. The case was settled after appeal on undisclosed terms. In defending the amateur system he was effectively propping up the 'shamateur' practices that saw players rewarded with under-the-table payments. As president of the Lawn Tennis Association of Victoria (1964-69) and an aspiring leader of the Lawn Tennis Association of Australia (selector 1962-69), he was often caught up in the bitter internal politics of tennis. His book *Aces and Places* (1957) gave an anecdotal account of his experiences in that world.

A wiry, nut-brown man of middle height whose weight of 10 stone (63.5 kg) rarely varied, Hopman suffered from deafness for much of his career, and wore a hearing aid installed in horn-rimmed glasses. He had left daily journalism in 1956, first undertaking public relations work and then becoming an investment adviser. In 1962 he purchased a seat on the Melbourne Stock Exchange for £10 000, but neglected to disclose that he had borrowed the money. Legal action commenced when, in 1965, he failed to repay the full debt; he soon resigned the seat. An inveterate punter, he would sometimes ask Ian Occleshaw, whose task it was to telephone his hand-written copy to the *Herald* news desk, to drive him to Caulfield racecourse—'You get better odds at the course'—between matches at Kooyong. It was not uncommon for him to bet £500 on a favourite. Ever since a string of wins at the Monte Carlo casino in 1928 convinced him that five was his lucky number, Hopman arose each day at 5.55 precisely, took comfort in the knowledge that he had five sisters, and that Davis Cup tennis was played over five matches.

In 1970 Hopman left for the USA to conduct a series of tennis camps: some said he sensed the end of the game's golden age in Australia. Nell had died in 1968; on 2 February 1971 he married Lucy Pope Fox, a divorcee, at Port Washington, Long Island, where he was running a tennis academy. His early American protégés included John McEnroe and Vitas Gerulaitis. By the mid-1970s Harry Hopman's

International Tennis camp was run from a vast complex of fifty-five courts at Largo, Florida. Innately generous, he had never been financially secure in Australia—even while seeing his young players grow wealthy; in the USA he prospered, embracing professionalism and investing in real estate, oil and gas. On 27 December 1985 Harry Hopman died at Seminole, Florida, survived by his wife; he was cremated. The annual Hopman Cup, a men's and women's team competition founded in 1989, commemorates his contribution to Australian tennis.

J. Hetherington, *Australians* (1960); H. Gordon, *Young Men in a Hurry* (1961); N. Fraser, *Power Tennis* (1962); R. Yallop, *A Serve to Authority* (1992); A. Trengove, *Australia and the Davis Cup* (2000); *Bulletin*, 5 Dec 1964, p 26; *Sun News-Pictorial* (Melbourne), 30 Dec 1985, p 25; private information.

HARRY GORDON

HORTON, MERVYN EMRYS ROSSER (1917-1983), art patron, editor and company director, was born on 27 July 1917 at Glebe, Sydney, only child of Harry Horton, an English chartered accountant, and his Welsh wife Ethel Mabel, née Harris. Harry was involved in developing the local builders' hardware firm Traversi Jones Pty Ltd, in which he soon became a major shareholder. Mervyn was often seriously ill as a child. He grew up as a Baptist and attended the Methodist Newington College, where for five or six years he edited the school magazine. The family spent 1936 in Europe and attended the Berlin Olympic Games. On his return Horton sent articles to the *Sydney Morning Herald*; they were rejected but he was offered a job there. His strict father insisted on his studying medicine instead but, after Horton spent an unhappy year at the University of Sydney, allowed a shift to law. Horton was articled to a city firm of solicitors; he abandoned the law with relief after his father died in 1940. Traversi Jones became his major source of income. Following repeated rejections for war service on physical grounds, and a nervous breakdown, work with the photographer Olga Sharpe provided convalescent therapy. In 1945-48 Horton was an assistant to the modernist commercial photographer Max Dupain.

After eighteen months in Britain, in 1951 he was appointed by Sam Ure Smith to replace Gwen Morton Spencer [q.v.16] as publisher's editor at Ure Smith Pty Ltd; he was also made a director. Ure Smith handed over to him the small jobs of secretary to the Society of Artists and gallery manager of its annual exhibitions and Horton was thereby launched into the Sydney art world. Contemporary art began to keep company with the antique furniture and silver he had enjoyed since childhood. The artist and art critic Wallace Thornton was a forceful mentor. 'Outraged' by Horton's conservative and closeted lifestyle, he began to convert him into a bon viveur.

In 1956, inspired by a visit to Italy, Horton opened one of Sydney's earliest modern Milanese-design coffee bars, Galleria Espresso, in Rowe Street, and ran it until 1962. Contemporary paintings were displayed, and art students worked there. He met a dancer with Katherine Dunham's black American company, Lenwood Morris, who became his first male lover. Horton hosted big parties, first at St Ives, then in a weekend house at Palm Beach, and from 1959 at Potts Point, where Christopher Davis lived with him for over a decade. Horton studied cooking with Sue du Val, who became his closest friend. Bustling, immensely good-natured and generous, 5 ft 8 ins (173 cm) tall and well-fed, and with a then unusual grey goatee beard (to disguise a scar on his chin) and brown eyes, Horton was described as 'a rubicund Mr Pickwick'.

The first issue of the quarterly *Art and Australia* (its title designed to closely resemble that of the earlier Sydney Ure Smith [q.v.11] publication *Art in Australia*) appeared in May 1963; Sam Ure Smith was the proprietor and Horton the editor. Production and design standards, with lavish colour illustration, were extremely high. Its chief concern was to make known the best of Australian art, both past and present, but it also brought foreign, especially Pacific, art to the attention of Australian readers. Horton edited several picture books of contemporary Australian art. He visited most Venice Biennales, and his overseas contacts made him an excellent commissioner for Australia at the 1975 Bienal de São Paulo in Brazil. For twenty years the magazine occupied him for three days a week.

Horton had a range of investments and properties to look after, among them, from 1964, Christopher Davis Antiques, and in 1978-82 he served on the board of Traversi Jones Ltd. He was a councillor (1955-72) and secretary (1962-72) of the Art Gallery Society of New South Wales, a trustee (1973-76) of the Art Gallery of New South Wales, a committee-member of the National Trust of Australia (New South Wales) and the New South Wales division of the Arts Council of Australia, and a patron of the Creative Leisure Movement. In 1982 he was appointed AM.

Horton died of cancer on 22 February 1983 at Potts Point and was cremated. He had planned his High Anglican funeral service, held at Christ Church St Laurence, and a party with a reading of his will to the many recipients of legacies of paintings, antiques, money or property. One-fifth of the residue of the estate went to two daughters of Christopher Davis, another fifth to two cousins, and the remaining three-fifths to the Art Gallery of New South Wales to fund the purchase of works of art *not* executed by 'Australian Nationals and/or residents'. Mistrustful of local Gallery trustees, he stipulated that the works were to be selected by the Tate Gallery, London, or the Museum of Modern Art, New York (which soon delegated the responsibility to the gallery in Sydney). Bryan Westwood's portrait (1968) of Horton is held by the Art Gallery of New South Wales.

Art and Aust, vol 20, no 4, 1983, p 454; D. Thomas, 'The Mervyn Horton Collection', *Art and Aust*, vol 21, no 1, 1983, p 72, see p 35 for other tributes; *SMH*, 4 Dec 1975, p 17, 23 Feb 1983, p 8, 20 Sept 1983, p 12; *Bulletin*, 12 Apr 1983, p 51; H. de Berg, interview with M. Horton (ts, 1972, NLA); *Art and Aust* records (NLA); private information and personal knowledge.   DANIEL THOMAS

HOWARD, FREDERICK JAMES (1904-1984), journalist and author, was born on 17 October 1904 at Wandsworth, London, son of George Octavius Howard, commercial clerk, and his wife Josephine, née Mitchell. Fred was educated at Alleyn's School, Dulwich, until he migrated with his parents to Australia in 1920. He worked in a bank and, with ambitions to become a writer, contributed to publications including the *Saturday Evening Post*. When his novel *The Emigrant* (1928) was accepted, he took up writing full time. Praised by the *Bulletin* for recounting 'with rare insight and sympathy' the story of a young man's progression from militant communism to a new life as 'an individualist' in Australia, the novel ran to a second edition. It was followed by *Return Ticket* (1929), also on Anglo-Australian themes, the publication of which coincided with his travelling in South and North America. Back in Australia he edited (1929-31) *Stead's Review*.

On 6 June 1930 at St John's Church of England, Toorak, Howard married Stella Victoria Gertrude Miller. In 1931 he joined the Melbourne *Herald*. Presentable looks and good manners, a positive international outlook and experiences, and a well-demonstrated commitment to his craft, brought him into favour with the newspaper magnate (Sir) Keith Murdoch [q.v.10]. Encouraged by Murdoch, Howard visited Russia in 1935 and spent nine months roaming Europe and North America, finishing another Anglo-Australian family saga, *Leave Us the Glory* (1936), in London. A photograph from this time in the Herald and Weekly Times Ltd's *House News* captured him with the Hollywood film stars Barbara Stanwyck and Herbert Mundin, typically at ease and charming.

On his return to Melbourne, Howard edited (1937-40) the *Austral-Asiatic Bulletin* for the Victorian division of the Australian Institute of International Affairs, wrote *The Negroes Begin at Calais* (1938), a satirical investigation of Europe's myriad problems, and, succeeding C. J. Dennis [q.v.8], brought a new freshness and diversity as the *Herald*'s columnist 'The Rouseabout'.

Commissioned in the Militia on 11 December 1939, Howard was appointed a captain in the Australian Imperial Force in June 1940 and posted to Corps headquarters as historical records officer. In 1940-42 he served in the Middle East, where he edited *Active Service* (1941) and was mentioned in despatches. He returned to Australia and in 1942-44, a public relations liaison officer with General Douglas MacArthur's [q.v.15] General Headquarters, South-West Pacific Area, he spent most of the time in Papua and New Guinea, and observed GHQ's practice of issuing distorted news reports of operations. Having divorced his first wife, he married Margaret Laura De Visme Gipps, a poet, on 9 February 1943 at the Albert Street Methodist Church, Brisbane. On 28 September 1944 he transferred to the Reserve of Officers.

Howard returned to the *Herald* and remained with the paper for the rest of his working life. He served as president of the Melbourne PEN Club (1946-48, 1955) and of the Victorian AIIA (1957-59). Another novel, *No Music for Generals*, was published in 1951. In 1953-57 he reported on East Asia and afterwards became chief leader-writer, producing elegant if bland daily copy, conforming to the newspaper's predictable stance on public issues and its anti-Labor bias. From 1963 he chaired Channel 7's Sunday evening television program 'Meet the Press'. In contrast to his predecessor Reg Leonard's controversial 'red-baiting', Howard was unfailingly courteous to his celebrity guests. According to his fellow panellist John Fitzgerald, the presence of 'assault troops' on the panel enabled Howard to 'sit back and, almost apologetically, close out the interview on a conciliatory note with a disarming smile and softly-spoken charm'.

Although friendly, Howard was not gregarious and did not frequent journalists' watering holes. Well groomed and urbane, he could have been a diplomat, judged his colleague Harry Gordon; to his sub-editor Neil Newnham, he was 'a gentleman journalist, experienced, knowledgeable, unflappable, and confident in his craft'. In 1969, following diagnosis of a tumour of the pelvis, he had a leg amputated. Remarkably resilient, he survived and returned to the *Herald* and to television, but lasted only a year. He retired in 1970 but continued writing, completing a biography of Sir Wilfrid Kent Hughes [q.v.15] in 1972 and, in 1978, the history of a family of New South Wales pioneers, *The Moleskin Gentry*. Childless and survived by his wife, Frederick Howard died on 20 August 1984 at Heidelberg West; he was cremated.

D. Zwar, *In Search of Keith Murdoch* (1980); R. M. Younger, *Keith Murdoch* (2003); *Bulletin*, 24 Sept 1930, p 5, 17 Oct 1951, p 23; private information.   DAVID DUNSTAN

HOWARD, WILLIAM STEWART McPHEE (1903-1983), journalist, author and public relations consultant, was born on 13 October 1903 at Balmain, Sydney, only child of Sydney-born parents William John Howard, bank clerk, and his wife Florence Irene, née Falconer. At Fort Street Boys' High School, Stewart contributed to the school magazine and became a prefect. He won an exhibition to the University of Sydney but did not continue past first-year economics.

In the 1920s Howard held executive positions with various manufacturing, agricultural and marketing firms. On 11 February 1928 at St Philip's Church of England, Sydney, he married Dorothy Annie Elizabeth Young, a stenographer. He worked as a freelance journalist and published short stories in the *Bulletin* and *Triad*. Associate editor of the *Sydney Opinion* during its brief existence (1929-30), he contributed short stories and theatre and film reviews.

Howard was part of Sydney's bohemian literary circles in the 1930s. His first novel, the slapstick *You're Telling Me!* (1934), centred on a party involving a group of thinly disguised *Smith's Weekly* journalists. Other humorous novels followed, including *Uncle Aethelred* (1944), dedicated to Adam McCay [q.v.10]. In 1934 Howard joined (Sir) Frank Packer's [q.v.15] Sydney Newspapers Ltd, where he reviewed books for the *Daily Telegraph* and the *Australian Women's Weekly* and edited the latter's film supplement. Frustrated by having to observe 'certain rigid taboos' at a women's magazine, Howard joined *Smith's Weekly* in 1938 and the *Sydney Morning Herald* in 1940.

Between 1939 and 1941 Howard had two spells as publicity officer for (Sir) William McKell [q.v.]. He moved increasingly into public administration, serving as secretary of the State War Effort Co-ordination Committee before becoming, in 1942, Packer's deputy-director of personnel for the Allied Works Council. Trade union and newspaper suggestions that Howard had implemented a 'dictatorship' and employed 'Gestapo methods' helped to precipitate an inquiry into the AWC; Sir Harry Brown's [q.v.7] report in 1943 concluded that Howard's behaviour generally showed him to be 'a human, sympathetic type'.

Divorced in 1945, Howard married Marie Winifred McKinney, née Ducker, a divorcee, on 28 July at Fullerton Memorial Presbyterian Church, Sydney. Something of a dandy who wore a monocle, he enjoyed sailing, swimming, cooking and 'loafing' at his weekend retreat at Church Point. In 1947 Brian Penton [q.v.15], who regarded Howard as 'the best critic in Australia', despatched Dymphna Cusack [q.v.] there to discuss her unwieldy manuscript of *Come in Spinner*; Cusack found him sensitive and helpful but later had cause to suspect that he was two-faced. Miles Franklin [q.v.8] thought him 'poisonous' and Frank Browne [q.v.] wrote in *Things I Hear* that he had an 'uncanny felicity' for looking after himself.

Howard had returned in 1945 to the *Sydney Morning Herald*, where he was reputedly Rupert Henderson's [q.v.] 'white-haired boy'. He specialised in writing on industrial matters. Worried about totalitarianism and the prospect of people becoming the servants of the state, Howard began working privately as a public relations adviser in 1946 and established a 'Research Service' in 1947. His statistical reports 'proving' communist instrumentality in strikes found ready outlets in the *Sydney Morning Herald* and the *Daily Telegraph*.

In February 1949 R. G. (Lord) Casey [q.v.13] persuaded the federal executive of the Liberal Party of Australia to choose Howard—one of Australia's 'most capable, resourceful and experienced public relations' men—as (Sir) Robert Menzies' [q.v.15] public relations adviser. Several State divisions were uneasy about his appointment. Howard supported conscription and advocated legislation amending the Constitution to make bank nationalisation impossible without a referendum. Despite the success of Menzies' nationwide tour, Howard was asked in September to accept a two-thirds cut in his remuneration, and the Hansen-Rubensohn [q.v.16] advertising agency declined to employ him as the December election neared.

From his dingy office in George Street, Sydney, Howard represented the interests of, among others, the Australian Council of Employers' Federations, the Graziers' Association of New South Wales and some Sydney bookmakers, and produced periodicals for his clients. Adamant that public relations work must 'build up, in the public mind, a feeling of informed friendliness towards … industry and an appreciation of the role it plays in the nation's economic and social life', in 1952 through his Research Service Howard started to publish a monthly industrial index and economic analysis. Next year he began hosting a weekly 'Book Parade' on the Macquarie network for Angus & Robertson [qq.v.7,11] Ltd.

Stewart Howard & Associates Pty Ltd, his public relations consultancy, continued until 1977. He moved to New Zealand in 1982. Survived by his wife and the daughter of his first marriage, he died on 30 September 1983 at Palmerston North, New Zealand. The death of that enigmatic and often controversial pioneer of the Australian public relations industry went largely unnoticed.

P. Buckridge, *The Scandalous Penton* (1994); B. Griffen-Foley, *The House of Packer* (1999); M. North (ed), *Yarn Spinners* (2001); *Meanjin*, vol 10, no 1, 1951, p 56; *Things I Hear*, 3 Mar 1947, p 1, 21 Feb 1949, p 3, 14 Mar 1949, p 2, 6 Nov 1952, p 3, 8 Jan 1953, p 2; *Daily Telegraph* (Sydney), 16 Feb 1949, p 11; *Record* (Melbourne Chamber of Commerce), Oct 1950, p 18; A1608, AK27/1/2 (NAA); AWM93, item 50/2/23/219 (AWM); Casey family papers and D. Cusack papers and Liberal Party of Australia records (NLA).

BRIDGET GRIFFEN-FOLEY

HOWELL, EDWARD WELSFORD ROWSELL (1902-1986), actor, writer and producer, was born on 15 July 1902 at Bromley, Kent, England, younger son of Edwin Gilburt Howell, bank clerk and actor, and his wife Madeline Anne, née Rowsell. Edward travelled to Australia in 1912, aged 10, to perform with his father in a J. C. Williamson [q.v.6] Ltd touring production of Maurice Maeterlinck's *The Blue Bird*. His parents decided to settle in Australia and he completed his education at Sydney Grammar School. In 1919 his father moved to Suva; he followed and studied law while he worked for the government legal department and then the Colonial Sugar Refining Co. Ltd. Together they founded the Suva Dramatic Guild.

On his return to Sydney in 1924, Howell joined the Playbox Theatre, where he met Mary Cecilia Long, an English actress known as Molly and professionally as Therese Desmond. On 11 May 1927 they married at St Mary's Catholic Cathedral, Sydney. They ran the (Royal) Academy of Dramatic Art for a few years. After some early film and stage work, including the film *For the Term of His Natural Life* (1927), Howell moved into radio in 1929, when he was asked by the Australian Broadcasting Co. (Commission from 1932) to present a radio play. Author of one of the first variety shows for the ABC in 1930, he later worked as a radio actor, writer, producer and director. He is perhaps best known as the creator and producer of, and an actor in, the popular radio serial 'Fred and Maggie Everybody'. This program, which ran under a number of titles from 1932 to 1953, co-starred his wife and depicted the everyday lives of a middle-class couple in a gently comic style. The show was sold to many countries, including New Zealand. At its peak, it was heard on fifty-six stations in Australia.

Howell was the chief drama producer for Amalgamated Wireless (Australasia) Ltd from 1936 to 1947, then a freelance producer and actor in commercial radio until he travelled to England in April 1949. He worked on British

Broadcasting Corporation radio productions and stage plays before returning in June 1950 to Sydney, where he and his wife continued to work for radio and the stage. In 1955 Molly had a stroke that ended her acting career; she died in 1961. Involved in television drama from the 1950s, Howell finished his career in the 1980s in the role of Bert Griffiths in 'A Country Practice'. He also appeared in the film *Careful, He Might Hear You* (1983).

On his retirement from acting in 1985 Howell advised aspiring actors to 'learn to speak properly'. An astute spotter of emerging talent, he gave a number of actors their first roles in radio. Known as 'Teddy' to his friends, he was a dapper, well-dressed man who, according to the radio historian Richard Lane, never looked or sounded like a romantic leading man. He was, however, ideally suited to the 'everybody' roles for which he was well known, and his adaptable stage presence allowed him to play a broad range of characters. Survived by his daughter, he died on 20 August 1986 at Chatswood, Sydney, and was cremated.

R. Lane, *The Golden Age of Australian Radio Drama 1923-1960* (1994); *SMH*, 7 July 1962, p 11, 14 July 1962, p 10; H. de Berg, interview with E. Howell (ts, 1978, NLA); Howell papers (SLNSW).
MICHELLE ARROW

HOWELL, LUCY (LUCIE) (1888-1985), soprano and singing teacher, was born on 6 July 1888 in Perth, fourth of nine children of Western Australian-born parents Thomas John Howell, law clerk and later a nurseryman and gardener, and his wife Clara Ellen, née Birch. Educated at White Gum Valley State School and Princess May Girls' High School, Fremantle, Lucy worked as a dental nurse for several years at Fremantle. She studied singing with several teachers including Eva Randell and Gertrude Hutton. Appearing in many local operatic and oratorio productions and recitals, she earned a reputation as 'Westralia's first soprano'. On 12 November 1919 at Johnston Memorial Church, Fremantle, she married with Congregational forms a Welsh-born returned soldier, William Henry Date, who was then resident in an army hospital at Cottesloe Beach. They had no children. Date suffered from ongoing ill health and died of cancer on 7 October 1928. Lucy (professionally known as Lucie) then lived with her parents and younger sister Hilda in their Cottesloe Beach (Mosman Park) home. She and Hilda stayed on there after the deaths of their parents in 1947 and 1948.

In the 1920s Howell had sung on radio; she continued to sing in public until the late 1930s. She began teaching singing at 'Studio 6' in the Musgrove's Ltd building, Murray Street, Perth, in 1926. Her professionalism was such that she always employed a trained accompanist. By 1930 her students were appearing in public recitals and were heard in radio broadcasts. In 1939 16-year-old Gwen Cordingley won the Deanna Durbin contest at the Piccadilly Theatre. In 1944-69 thirty-eight of her pupils were State vocal winners of the Australian Broadcasting Commission's concerto and vocal competitions; four won national finals: Elise Longwill (1950), Patricia Connop (1957), Lynette Howieson (1958) and Glenys Fowles (1967). Fowles later won a scholarship to study at the New York Metropolitan Opera; Megan Sutton was a finalist in the 1967 'Sun Aria' contest. Another of her pupils and sometime studio accompanist was the soprano Molly McGurk, who won a Churchill fellowship in 1967.

Howell had first joined the Western Australian Music Teachers' Association as an associate-member in 1918; she became a full member in 1929. From 1932 she served almost continuously on the executive: she was president in 1964, vice-president for seven terms, social president or vice-president (1968-82) and patron (1978-84). The association conferred a life membership on her in 1973. She was also active on the Western Australia Orchestral Subscribers Committee and was made patron of the Guild of Young Artists in 1961. For more than forty years Howell was the doyen of classical singing teachers in Perth. Although she became increasingly set in her ways, her capacity to find and develop talent and to select appropriate repertoire remained second to none. In 1969 she was appointed MBE; she retired in 1973. She died on 27 October 1985 at Nedlands and was cremated.

D. Popham (ed), *Reflections* (1978); R. Jamieson, *What Harmony Is This?* (1986); *West Australian*, 29 Oct 1985, p 24; *Music Teachers' Bulletin*, Nov-Dec 1985, p 12.
DAVID BLACK

HUDSON, RAY TREVOR (1919-1986), air force officer and pilot, was born on 26 July 1919 at Waverley, Sydney, son of New South Wales-born parents John Joseph Hudson, motor driver, and his wife Lillie Hunter, née Halyday. Educated to Intermediate certificate level, Ray worked as a motor salesman before enlisting in the Royal Australian Air Force on 19 August 1940. He was 5 ft 8½ ins (174 cm) tall, with a fair complexion, grey-blue eyes and fair hair.

Following pilot training in Southern Rhodesia (Zimbabwe), Hudson was commissioned on 21 May 1941 and sent to the Middle East to fly Hurricanes and later also Spitfires with No.451 Squadron, an army co-operation squadron supporting operations in the Western Desert. He was mentioned in despatches in 1942 and promoted to temporary flight lieutenant in May 1943. That month he skilfully and quickly ditched a burning Hurricane, escaping with only minor burns. This capacity for cool and decisive action in the face of danger served him well throughout the war.

From October 1943 Hudson flew Kittyhawk fighter-bombers with No.450 Squadron in Italy. He rapidly gained respect as a flight commander. In January 1944 he led a formation in attacking a large armed merchant vessel near Sibenik Harbour, Yugoslavia, 'in the face of a heavy barrage from the harbour defences and the ship's guns'. For his 'courage', and his 'skilful leadership and determined efforts' which 'contributed materially to the success achieved', and for displaying 'skill and courage' on 'a large number of sorties', he was awarded the Distinguished Flying Cross.

Made acting squadron leader in April 1944 (temporary in July), Hudson commanded the squadron until June. He won a Bar to his DFC for leading many successful missions against ground targets and shipping with 'courage and the greatest determination, often in the face of intense anti-aircraft fire'. His bombing accuracy was 'of a high order' and did 'much damage to enemy installations'. The citation concluded by stating that his 'ability in supporting troop movements has been striking' and in some areas 'has greatly facilitated the advance of our army'. His superior officer, Colonel L. A. Wilmot, described him as 'an outstanding squadron commander, very capable operationally and administratively'.

His skill and self-confidence now well appreciated, Hudson was sent to the United States of America in October 1944 for helicopter training before returning to Australia next month. Demobilised on 7 September 1945—there were no military helicopters in Australia at the time—he joined Trans-Australia Airlines in November 1946 and flew as a first officer in DC-3s and as a captain in Viscounts. On 20 November 1947 at St Peter's Church of England, Brighton Beach, Melbourne, he married Valerie Henley Wilkinson, an air hostess.

TAA sent Hudson to the USA for helicopter training in 1956. In 1960 he flew a helicopter from the ship *Magga Dan* in Antarctica, helping it to navigate through pack ice to the shore base. He then joined the Bell Helicopter Co. as a sales representative and pilot, flying to check power grids, drop geologists in remote locations and muster cattle. Survived by his wife and their two daughters, Ray Hudson died of cancer on 12 August 1986 at Currumbin, Queensland, and was cremated.

J. Herington, *Air Power over Europe 1944-1945* (1963); N. Parnell and T. Boughton, *Flypast* (1988);

L. L. Barton, *The Desert Harassers* (1991), and (comp), *Bankstown to Berlin with 451 (R.A.A.F.) Squadron, 1941-1946* (1996); G. Morley-Mower, *Messerschmitt Roulette* (1993); *Wings*, Mar 1989, p 12; AWM65, item 2749, AWM76, item B255 (AWM); A9300, item Hudson R T (NAA); private information.

DOUG HURST

HUDSON, WILFRED FRANK FLEXMORE (1913-1988), poet, short-story writer and schoolteacher, was born on 22 September 1913 at Charters Towers, Queensland, eldest of four sons of Wilfred Flexmore Hudson, a Tasmanian-born Baptist minister, and his wife Irene Maud, née Rathbone, from Rockhampton. The family moved often before settling in Adelaide in 1924; Flexmore attended thirteen primary schools in Australia and New Zealand. Completing his secondary education at Adelaide High School, he was a keen rower, sculler, swimmer and boxer. A student at Adelaide Teachers' College, he also enrolled in the arts faculty at the University of Adelaide, but did not finish his degree. He taught at small country schools including Narrowie (1936), Caliph (1937), Hammond (1939-41) and Lucindale (1942-45).

On 17 January 1938 at the office of the principal registrar, Adelaide, Hudson married Myrle Desmond (d.1979). In 1941 he launched *Poetry*, an influential periodical that he edited for six years and which was initially very successful. Although a friend of 'Rex' Ingamells [q.v.14], he was a lukewarm Jindyworobak supporter, not sharing the enthusiasm for Aboriginal culture that partly characterised the movement. Invited to edit the 1943 *Jindyworobak Anthology*, he chose an initial selection of poems deemed by Ingamells to be insufficiently 'Jindyworobak'. Hudson made a few changes and the anthology was published, more or less with Ingamells's blessing.

In 1946 Hudson resigned from the Education Department and freelanced. He wrote for the Australian Broadcasting Commission and produced a children's history that was serialised in an educational 'comic' and later published as a book, *The Story of the Polynesians* (1948). Living on the proceeds of a Commonwealth Literary Fund fellowship awarded in 1946, he began a novel but abandoned it. Forced to discontinue *Poetry* in 1947 and left with a crippling debt of £400, he escaped to sea in a schooner for about a year. In 1950-63 he was senior English master at Scotch College. Also the school's rowing coach, he was proud of the success achieved by his teams. He later taught at King's College, Henley High and, finally, at Adelaide Boys High schools, retiring in 1978.

As a writer, Hudson had a minor but distinct talent. He published six books of poetry between 1937 and 1959, displaying in them a lyrical skill in depicting the Australian landscape and a tendency to polemicise. Probably the collections *As Iron Hills: Poems* (1944) and *Pools of the Cinnabar Range* (1959) contain the best examples of his poetry. 'Song of Australia' and 'Drought' have been frequently anthologised while his reflective, philosophical 'To a Cuttlefish' was thought by the poet himself to be probably his best work. In 1985 a collection of his short stories, *Tales from Corytella* (compiled and edited by Adam Dutkiewicz), was published.

A humanist, Hudson leaned towards Buddhism. He had been active in the peace movement and the Fellowship of Australian Writers in the 1950s. Despite a succession of life-threatening illnesses, he was fit and physically compact, with handsome features and brown hair. He usually sported a small moustache. In later years he developed diabetes and Alzheimer's disease, and suffered a stroke. Survived by his son, he died on 14 May 1988 at Kings Park, Adelaide, and was cremated.

J. Tregenza, *Australian Little Magazines 1923-1954* (1964); B. Elliott (comp), *The Jindyworobaks* (1979); P. Depasquale, *Flexmore Hudson* (1981); K. Preiss and P. Oborn, *The Torrens Park Estate* (1991); H. de Berg, interview with F. Hudson (ts, 1969, NLA); J. Dally, The Jindyworobak Movement, 1935-1945 (PhD thesis, Flinders Univ, 1978); Hudson papers (NLA and SLSA); personal knowledge.

JOHN DALLY

HUGHAN, HAROLD RANDOLPH (1893-1987), potter, was born on 11 July 1893 at Mildura, Victoria, second of ten children of Victorian-born Randolph Hughan, gardener, and his English-born wife Emily, née Clayton. Much of Harold's childhood was spent at Hamilton, Victoria, where—after leaving school in 1906—he completed an apprenticeship as a mechanical engineer. In 1910 he moved to Geelong and retrained, by correspondence, as an electrical engineer. Having served in the Militia for some years, on 27 October 1915 Hughan enlisted in the Australian Imperial Force. He saw action on the Western Front in 1916-18 with the 3rd Divisional Signal Company and the 44th Battalion. In November 1917 he was commissioned and in March 1918 promoted to lieutenant. At the parish church of St James, Toxteth Park, Liverpool, England, on 2 September 1919 he married Lily Booth. They arrived in Melbourne in February 1920 and his AIF appointment terminated on 14 April. He continued to serve in the Militia, rising to major in the Volunteer Defence Corps during World War II.

After several jobs, Hughan moved to Melbourne and joined the firm of Oliver J. Nilsen, for whom he worked as an electrical engineer until his retirement in 1963. Long interested in crafts—including woodwork and weaving— he was introduced to pottery in the early 1940s by his wife and their son, Robert, who had taken it up as a hobby. Bernard Leach's *A Potter's Book* (1940) attracted him to studio pottery in the Anglo-Japanese tradition; C. F. Binns's *The Potter's Craft* (1910) taught him to throw pots on a wheel he devised from the crankshaft of a motorcar engine. He soon built his own kiln and made stoneware in a workshop behind his Glen Iris home.

Hughan drew inspiration from the Kent [q.v.15] collection of Chinese ceramics at the National Gallery of Victoria: his great love was the pots of the Song and T'ang Dynasties, but his interests encompassed many aspects of historic and contemporary practice. Seeking an 'Australian idiom', he also experimented with new forms. It was important to him that his pots were domestic, functional and affordable; yet they were also distinguished by subtle shapes and beautiful glazes, particularly the Orient-inspired celadons and tenmokus. He gained a devoted following, especially for his large platters, decorated with oriental motifs, native iris or sprays of bamboo. While prolific, he worked at his own pace well into his nineties. 'I do not make pottery for a living', he said in 1984, 'it [is] purely for pleasure, and always has been'.

An exhibition of Hughan's work at Georges Gallery, Melbourne, in 1950, led to his becoming one of the first contemporary studio potters to be represented in the National Gallery of Victoria. Later exhibitions included major retrospectives at the NGV (1969, 1983). His work has also been collected by the National Gallery of Australia, most Australian State and regional galleries, and by the Victoria and Albert Museum, London. A member of the Arts and Crafts Society of Victoria since 1949, he was invited in 1970 to be the patron of the Victorian Ceramic Group, which established an award in his name. In 1978 he was appointed MBE.

Of slight build, and known to close friends simply as 'Buzz', Hughan was described by Kenneth Hood, who had championed his work, as being, like his pots, 'reserved and unassuming'. Predeceased by his wife (1966), and survived by his son, he died at Prahran, Melbourne, on 23 October 1987, and was buried in Springvale cemetery.

H. R. Hughan Retrospective Exhibition (1969); K. Fahy et al (eds), *Australian Art Pottery 1900-1950* (2004); *Craft Australia*, winter 1983, p 68; H. de Berg, interview with H. R. Hughan (ts, 1965, NLA).

TERENCE LANE

HUGHES, RICHARD JOSEPH (1906-1984), journalist, was born on 5 March 1906 at

Prahran, Melbourne, eldest child of Victorian-born parents Richard Hughes, salesman, and his wife Katie, née McGlade. Educated at Christian Brothers' College, St Kilda, Richard worked briefly as a poster artist before joining the Victorian Railways as an apprentice shunter. The articles he contributed to the *Railways Magazine* and his skills as a debater were noticed by (Sir) Harold Clapp [q.v.8], chairman of the Victorian Railway Commissioners, who appointed him to his personal staff as a public relations officer. On 29 September 1930 Hughes married May Lillian Bennett at the Collins Street register office. Their marriage ended tragically when May committed suicide in July 1933.

In 1934 Hughes joined a short-lived evening paper, the Melbourne *Star*, and in 1936—leaving his son in the care of his parents—he moved to Sydney, joining (Sir) Frank Packer's [q.v.15] *Daily Telegraph* and later becoming chief of staff (1939) of the *Sunday Telegraph*. Remembering a promise he had made to Clapp to concentrate on Asia rather than the more traditional focus on Europe, in 1940 he took leave and travelled to Japan, from where he filed reports warning that it was likely to enter World War II against the Allies. A trip to the United States of America followed before Hughes returned to regular reporting in Australia.

While covering Federal parliament in Canberra in 1942 Hughes wrote an article, satirising a Senate debate, that was deemed a breach of privilege: he and other *Telegraph* representatives were banned from the parliament for four months. In 1943 he went to North Africa as an accredited war correspondent but returned prematurely after developing rheumatic fever in Cairo. An interest in Asia remained, and when the war ended he seized the opportunity to cover the Allied occupation of Japan.

Thus began Hughes's long and happy but often financially insecure career as a foreign correspondent. Having always endured poor relations with Brian Penton [q.v.15], his editor at the *Telegraph*, and to some degree with Packer himself, Hughes resigned from the paper after reluctantly accepting recall to Sydney. Returning to Japan, he was appointed manager of the Foreign Correspondents' Club in Tokyo—a poorly paid and difficult job from which he was soon sacked. In 1948, with the help of Ian Fleming, then foreign manager of the London *Sunday Times*, he was employed by the *Sunday Times* and the *Economist*. Over the following years these newspapers provided his main income, although in 1953 he rejoined the Packer organisation on a regular retainer, an arrangement lasting over a decade until he transferred to Rupert Murdoch's News Ltd. His contacts were extensive and included (it was later suggested) British and Russian intel-ligence agencies. He wrote with a sharply analytical, open mind and keen sense of anec-dote and was seen as the doyen of Asia's foreign press corps. In February 1956 he achieved an international scoop when he obtained an exclusive interview in Moscow with the British diplomats Donald Maclean and Guy Burgess, who had defected to the Soviet Union in 1951.

Tall, solidly built, and imposing, Hughes was described by the journalist Pat Burgess [q.v.] as 'fleshy and pale with a big head and a noble dome with thinning silver hair'. His second wife, Adele, née Redapple, whom he had married on 17 November 1945, died in Tokyo in 1950. Hughes moved to Hong Kong, where, from 1971, he also wrote for the *Far Eastern Economic Review*. Generous and toler-ant, he became a fixture in the city's Foreign Correspondents' Club and Hilton Grill, dining and conversing with friends. His trademark was the ecclesiastical language he affected. Titles such as 'Your Grace' and 'Monsignor' and other episcopal terms of expression pep-pered his conversation and correspondence. His third wife, whom he married in a Hong Kong registry office on 7 October 1973, was Oi-ying (Ann) Lee, the daughter of a Chinese general who had served in Chiang Kai-shek's Nationalist army.

Appointed CBE in 1980, Hughes inspired characters in novels by Ian Fleming and John le Carré: 'Dikko' Henderson in *You Only Live Twice* (1964); and 'Old Craw' in *The Honour-able Schoolboy* (1977). He wrote several books, including *The Chinese Communes* (1960), *Hong Kong: Borrowed Place, Borrowed Time* (1968), and his autobiographical *Foreign Devil* (1972). On 4 January 1984 Richard Hughes died in Hong Kong. He was survived by his third wife and a son from his first marriage, Richard (Dick), who had become a renowned jazz pianist and author.

N. Macswan, *The Man Who Read the East Wind* (1982); P. Burgess, *Warco* (1986); D. Hughes, *Don't You Sing!* (1994); *NY Times*, 5 Jan 1984, 'section II', p 14; R. Hughes papers and D. Warner papers (NLA).

PRUDENCE TORNEY-PARLICKI*

HULME, SIR ALAN SHALLCROSS (1907-1989), politician, accountant and cattle breeder, was born on 14 February 1907 at Mosman, Sydney, second child of Thomas Shallcross Hulme, an English-born civil ser-vant, and his wife Emily Clara, née Hynes, born in New South Wales. Alan left North Sydney Boys' High School at the age of 15 ambitious to go on the land. This was beyond the family's resources, and his first job was as a messenger-boy for Burns, Philp [qq.v.7,11] & Co. Ltd. He later trained as an accountant and joined the firm of Cullen-Ward (& Co.). In 1934 he moved to Queensland to open its Brisbane office. He was made a fellow of the Institute of Chartered Accountants in Australia in 1938. On 3 May that year he married Jean Frances Archibald at the Methodist Church, West End. She shared his interest in both politics and the land.

In 1943 Hulme was a founding member of the Queensland People's Party. He became its president (from 1946) and campaign manager, but backed its merger with the Liberal Party of Australia which, as a national party, he regarded as better suited to dismantling wartime controls and advancing liberalism. A believer in free enterprise, low taxation and small government, he stood for the Liberal Party in the Federal election in 1949 and was elected to the Brisbane seat of Petrie. Although a committed 'Menzies [q.v.15] man', he was at first sometimes seen as a 'burr in the saddle-bag' of the coalition government, which he believed made too many concessions to government regulation. He served on the House Committee (1950-58) and the Joint Committee of Public Accounts (1952-58), and chaired the Commonwealth Committee on Rates of Depreciation (1954-55) and the Commonwealth Immigration Planning Council (1956-58). On 10 December 1958 he was appointed minister for supply.

Hulme lost his seat in the swing against the Menzies government in 1961. Becoming a business consultant, he was a director of Chandlers (Australia) Ltd and the J. B. Chandler [q.v.13] Investment Co. Ltd. In 1963 he won Petrie back and on 18 December he was appointed postmaster-general. He was responsible for the Australian Broadcasting Commission in an increasingly turbulent period. Believing there to be bias, not balance, in ABC news and commentary, he was frequently in confrontation with some reporters (whom he saw as leftist propagandists) and commissioners (whom he considered ineffectual). Commenting on the ABC's budget estimates for 1970-71, he proposed in a letter to the chairman of the commission that cuts be made to television current affairs programs (such as 'Four Corners' and 'This Day Tonight'). ABC staff leaked the letter to the newspapers and, in the subsequent furore over the independence of the ABC, Hulme withdrew his suggestion but remained unrepentant.

As postmaster-general, Hulme announced the introduction of FM radio, colour television, international telephone calls using satellites, and the inclusion of health warnings on broadcast tobacco advertisements. The controversial communications tower on Black Mountain, Canberra, remains a monument to his record term as postmaster-general. He was also vice-president of the Executive Council from 1966 to 1972.

A courteous, conscientious, meticulous man, Hulme was respected as a political peace-maker. He loyally supported the five prime ministers under whom he served—(Sir) Robert Menzies, Harold Holt, (Sir) John McEwen [q.v.14,15], (Sir) John Gorton and (Sir) William McMahon [q.v.]. On Holt's death, he had worked to make (Sir) Paul Hasluck the next prime minister but, when Gorton resigned as prime minister after failing to win a party-room vote of confidence, Hulme moved a vote of thanks by acclamation. Both in parliament and as president of the Queensland division of the Liberal Party (1946-49 and 1962-63), he was a federalist (with a respect for the rights of both the States and the Commonwealth) and a strong coalitionist (often called on to mediate in the inter-party disputes so frequent in Queensland). But he was also a tough negotiator: 'Nothing is agreed', he once declared, 'until everything is agreed'.

Appointed KBE in 1971, Sir Alan did not contest the 1972 election, having won the seat of Petrie in eight elections. Some years earlier he had purchased land at Eudlo, near Nambour, Queensland, where he and his wife established a successful Droughtmaster stud. After leaving politics he was able to satisfy his youthful ambition to go on the land. His wife died in June 1983. Survived by his two sons and daughter, he died on 9 October 1989 at Nambour; he was accorded a state funeral and was cremated.

K. S. Inglis, *This Is the ABC* (1983); *PD* (Senate), 16 Oct 1989, p 1865; *PD* (HR), 24 Oct 1989, p 1659; *Business Review*, Feb 1971, p 2; private information.

PETER COLEMAN

HUMMERSTON, FLORENCE ELLEN (1889-1983), community leader and city councillor, was born on 6 March 1889 at Fremantle, Western Australia, fourth of eight surviving children of George Hayman, labourer and later accountant, and his wife Emily, née Mason. A robust child, Florence attended St Joseph's convent school, Fremantle, and Underwood Business College and then worked as a typist for her father. She married Victor William Hummerston (d.1973), an engineer, on 22 September 1909 at St Patrick's Catholic Church, Fremantle.

Flo Hummerston's charity work began when her only child, 7-year-old Emily, was concerned about a poor family whose father was ill. Her philanthropic involvement increased after her daughter's death, from kidney failure, in 1928. Living in Perth, Mrs Hummerston became involved in the Women's Service Guilds of Western Australia (vice-president 1937-40). In World War II she helped to establish the Women's Australian National Service and, as its State commander, was involved in the foundation of the Australian Women's Land Army in Western Australia. She set up an emergency housekeeping service in 1943. That year under the WANS banner she also established a home which became Wanslea Hostel (for Children of Sick Mothers). She was an honorary director of the home for twenty-five years. In 1946 the Women's Service Guild established a women's parliament to train them for high office; Mrs Hummerston was its first minister for housing and immigration. She launched the League of Home Help for Sick & Aged in 1953 and Meals on Wheels in 1954 and was president of the latter for twenty years.

The first woman councillor (1951-69) of the City of Perth, Hummerston needed to be confident. Lord Mayor Totterdell had hoped no woman would be elected because they 'were inclined to prolong discussions and so waste time'. Others worried that her success would 'ruin the old club permanently'. Health issues, such as improved methods of handling foodstuffs and the inclusion of electric hand dryers and incinerators in women's rest rooms, were among her interests. She objected to 'double dealing' by sitting councillors and inconsistent re-zoning that favoured developers. Despite the slogan 'Don't say no to Flo', she was unsuccessful in the 1953 State election and in her bid for the position of lord mayor in 1964. She believed that women's 'stepping stone is through Local Government, co-operating with men in the framing of social measures so closely associated with the home and family life'.

A tall, gaunt and visionary woman with high standards and singled-minded determination, although noted for her sense of humour, Mrs Hummerston was called 'Battleaxe Hummerston' by her detractors. She was president of the Tuberculosis (and Chest) Association of Western Australia and the women's auxiliary of the Perth Chest (Sir Charles Gairdner) Hospital and an executive member of the Children's Protection Society of Western Australia and the National Fitness Council of Western Australia. A justice of the peace from 1952, she was appointed OBE in 1960 and a freeman of Perth in 1979. Mrs Hummerston was an ardent monarchist. She died on 31 December 1983 at Como and was buried in the Catholic section of Karrakatta cemetery. A child-minding centre, a small park and a residential lodge for the elderly bear her name.

D. Popham (ed), *Reflections* (1978); P. Wellstead, *The WANS* (2005); *West Austn*, 28 Nov 1951, p 2, 16 May 1964, p 11, 23 May 1974, 'Fremantle section', p 6, 23 July 1979, p 63, 2 Jan 1984, p 12; *Sunday Times* (Perth), 1 Sept 1957, p 14; R. Jamieson, interview with F. Hummerston (ts, 1981-82, SLWA); Hummerston papers (SLWA).   JENNY GREGORY

HUMPHRIES, JOHN THOMAS (1903-1987), sailor, was born on 26 October 1903 at Sebastopol, Victoria, first surviving child of John Thomas Humphries, a miner who later served in the Australian Imperial Force, and his wife Susannah, née Thomas, both Victorian born. Educated at Redan State and Ballarat Technical schools, he entered the Royal Australian Navy on 18 July 1918 as a boy, 2nd class, listing his trade as messenger. He spent fourteen months in the training ship HMAS *Tingira* before moving into the seagoing fleet, signing on for a seven-year engagement at the end of his training.

Promoted to petty officer in 1928, Humphries left the navy on 25 October that year and settled in Brisbane. He served briefly with the Commonwealth Lighthouse Service, then trained as a diver on the Grey Street Bridge foundations, later performing similar work on the Story [q.v.12] Bridge and receiving high praise for his skills and courage. In 1938 he enrolled in the Royal Australian Fleet Reserve. Mobilised on 4 September 1939, he joined the armed merchant cruiser HMS *Kanimbla*. In August 1941 *Kanimbla* was sent to Bandar Shapur, Iran, as part of a combined Allied force. Eight enemy merchant vessels were sheltering in the port, and to avoid capture their crews attempted to scuttle them. One vessel, the 15 000-ton *Hohenfels*, sank in 48 ft (15 m) of water. On board was a vital cargo of 7000 tons of ilmenite sand, used for case-hardening steel.

Although Humphries was not trained as a naval diver, his expertise was called upon. For five weeks he dived for up to three hours at a time and, despite working in total darkness, he completed the repairs that allowed *Hohenfels* to be refloated and towed to a British port. On twelve occasions he descended into the flooded engine-room to shut bilge suction valves. This required him to go down three long ladders, thence forward along the entire length of the engine-room and then down two short ladders to the tunnels under the bunker. At least 120 ft (37 m) of air pipe and rope were required, with the constant risk of the lines becoming fouled. Because there was no telephone communication, as soon as Humphries descended the first ladder he was out of contact with his attendants, with no hope of assistance should something go wrong.

Humphries was quoted as saying, 'It was a job to be done, and I did it', and claimed that the greatest incentive to complete the task was the thought of seeing again his (then de facto) wife and daughters. For his 'skill and undaunted devotion to duty in hazardous diving operations' he was awarded the George Medal, the only such award made to an Australian rating during the war. He was also granted the non-substantive rank of diver, 1st class. On 2 February 1942 at the Albert Street Methodist

Church, Brisbane, he married Vera Staines, née Shead, a divorcee. In December he was posted to the Brisbane shore establishment HMAS *Moreton*. Demobilised on 29 May 1946, he later worked as a watchman. He died on 23 August 1987 at the Repatriation General Hospital, Greenslopes, and was cremated; his wife and their two daughters survived him.

G. H. Gill, *Royal Australian Navy 1942-1945* (1968); A6770, item Humphries J T (NAA); PR88/194 (AWM); Humphries biog file (Naval Hist Section, Dept of Defence, Canberra).

DAVID STEVENS

HUNKIN, LESLIE CLAUDE (1884-1984), politician and public servant, was born on 10 January 1884 at George Town, Tasmania, eldest of ten children of Joseph Hunkin, gold-miner, and his wife Elma Blanche, née Edwards. Educated at home and at local schools, Leslie began studying law but at 19 required treatment in a sanatorium for tuberculosis. He was to suffer several bouts of poor health during his life. Taking a job at Dempsters Ltd, drapers, he was soon in charge of the Launceston workroom. Advised for health reasons to move to the mainland, he joined the staff of Foy & Gibson [qq.v.4,8] Ltd in Perth, and in 1908 transferred to the firm's Adelaide store. He then worked for Goode [q.v.4], Durrant & Co. Ltd at their Grenfell Street warehouse. On 6 August 1910 at the office of the registrar-general, Victoria Square, he married Myrtle Florence Evans (d.1977). They had two sons and a daughter.

Attracted to the labour movement, in 1912 Hunkin became secretary of the Distributing Trades Union (from 1917 the South Australian branch of the Shop Assistants and Warehouse Employees' Federation of Australia) and helped to found the local branch of the Federated Storemen and Packers' Union of Australia in 1915. He gained a reputation as an outstanding industrial advocate in State and Federal industrial courts; the deputy-president of the former remarked during one case that the nation owed him a debt of gratitude 'for the manner in which he had dealt with a [particularly] difficult situation'. In 1920 Hunkin travelled to Narbethong, Victoria, to help friends revive a flagging timber-milling company. On his return to Adelaide he established with Ralph Hains the retail furnishing company Hains Hunkin Ltd. Still engaged in labour issues, he played a major part in preparing South Australia's Industrial Code, enacted in 1920. In January 1921, under the new legislation, he was appointed one of two employee members of the Board of Industry.

In 1921-27 Hunkin, representing the Australian Labor Party, was a member for East Torrens in the House of Assembly. He was also general secretary (1922-29) of the Public Service Association of South Australia and editor of the *Public Service Review*. A clear and logical debater in the House, he decisively shaped significant amendments to the Public Service (1925) and Superannuation (1926) Acts. He was defeated at the April 1927 election but, recognising his abilities, the conservative government of (Sir) Richard Layton Butler [q.v.7] named him public service commissioner (his appointment to take effect from 1 January 1930) and chairman of the Public Service Classification and Efficiency Board. He was to hold several other administrative posts, among them the chairmanship (1933-69) of the Forestry Board.

During the Depression Hunkin sat on various economic committees, including the South Australian Advisory Committee on State Finance, and represented South Australia at national finance meetings. Aware of the Australian Loan Council's pressure on the States to reduce government expenditure, he formed an advisory budget committee to deflect its demands. Showing a fierce sense of justice, he addressed the Public Service Association one night in 'Black October' (1930) and persuaded its members to make voluntary salary sacrifices (on top of general reductions already in place) so that the government could retain officers otherwise threatened with retrenchment.

In February 1942 Hunkin became deputy-director of manpower, responsible for implementing the Commonwealth government's labour distribution scheme in South Australia. This post demanded all his diplomacy in labour matters and his ability to concentrate on the matter at hand and to interpret complex and shifting legislation. His phenomenal memory and commercial acumen were also important. Justifiably proud of his performance, he was appointed CMG in 1945. He resumed his State government role in 1946 and retired in January 1949. Intending to return to politics, he gained endorsement as the ALP candidate for the Federal seat of Angas in April that year, but an eye injury forced his withdrawal in August.

His father's Cornish background was apparent in Hunkin's rather short frame, dark hair and clipped speech. Interested in sport, he was delighted when the South Australian Jockey Club made him a life member. He was a crack shot—the duck-hunting season saw him donning waders and pack until well into his eighties—and he enjoyed fishing. At his Toorak Gardens home he played the piano, read voraciously, especially ancient history and politics, and tended the garden. He was a member of Tattersalls Club.

Hunkin's family relationships did not mirror his success in public life. Work and a sense of community responsibility absorbed him. His family remembered him as 'always right' and very organised; he expected others to 'mind their Ps and Qs'. Towards the end of his life he moved into the Masonic Memorial Village, Somerton Park. On 8 September 1984, aged 100, he died in Adelaide and was cremated. His daughter and one son survived him.

Advertiser (Adelaide), 14 Feb 1922, p 6, 16 Apr 1949, p 1, 12 Nov 1981, p 3, 17 Nov 1981, p 5, 10 Jan 1984, p 2; *Public Service Review*, 30 Jan 1924, 31 Oct 1925; *South Australiana*, Sept 1981, p 64; C. S. Fort, Developing a National Employment Policy (PhD thesis, Univ of Adelaide, 2000); Hunkin papers (SLSA).
                                                              CAROL FORT

HUNT, EDWARD ALAN (1896-1982), solicitor and Presbyterian layman, was born on 26 November 1896 at Kirkton, near Branxton, New South Wales, third of six children of Henry Edward Fripp Hunt, schoolteacher, and his wife Barbara, née Brown. Educated first in his father's rural schools then at Maitland Boys' High School, Edward completed the Solicitors' Admission Board examinations while an articled clerk in Sydney. He was admitted as a solicitor on 29 August 1919. Employed by Harold T. Morgan & Morgan, he showed great aptitude in insurance work.

Through the Presbyterian Fellowship Association, Hunt met Edna Bell; they married on 3 April 1924 at St Stephen's Presbyterian Church, Sydney. In 1929 he lost his job but he and his brother Hector Robert, also a solicitor, established the firm of Hunt & Hunt. Specialising in litigation, Edward found his insurance work was a lifeline during the Depression. He conducted all the accident investigations—interviews, statements and client reports—himself. His legal work included workers' compensation and conveyancing. When they qualified, his two sons entered the firm.

After moving to Eastwood in 1939, the Hunt family joined the local Presbyterian Church. Hunt's church roles included those of trustee, elder and convenor of the war memorial committee. He became law agent (honorary solicitor) for the Presbyterian Church of Australia in the State of New South Wales in 1947, and served until 1973.

In 1947 Hunt was elected to the Dundas Shire Council. After it merged with the Parramatta City Council, he served from 1948 to 1959 (mayor 1956-57). Following his wife's death in 1956, Hunt reduced his law practice, devoting his time to church and community involvements. He married Gladys May Stewart, a widow, on 14 December 1957 at Willoughby Presbyterian Church.

The complex will of the benefactor C. B. Alexander (d.1947) of Tocal, in the Hunter district, where he had played and fished as a child, interested Hunt. He suggested that the development of Tocal as an agricultural college (as well as support of St Andrew's Home for Boys, Leppington), would comply with Alexander's wish to provide training for destitute and orphaned children. The Alexander trustees, the Presbyterian Church and the Supreme Court of New South Wales (in 1963) agreed. A college council, with 'E.A.' as chairman, was formed, work began in 1964 and next year the C. B. Alexander Presbyterian Agricultural College opened. Its scholarship program gave priority to disadvantaged students. In 1970 the State government took it over. Hunt's account of these events, *The Tocal Story*, was published in 1972. He also served as director of Burnside Presbyterian Homes for Children, Parramatta, from 1973 until his death. These projects became a consuming passion.

Hunt was appointed MBE in 1974. His wife died in 1980. On the centenary of Kirkton Public School, where his father had been the teacher, Ted Hunt was guest speaker on 1 May 1982. He talked about his schooldays, eighty years before, and presented an illuminated scroll. Amid the applause, he sat down and died. Survived by the two sons and two daughters of his first marriage, he was cremated.

J. White, *Tocal* (1986); F. R. Ramsay, *Three Score Years and Ten: The Story of St Andrew's Presbyterian Church, Eastwood (1907-1977)* (1989); S. O'Flahertie, *The History of Hunt & Hunt* (2000); *Austn Law Jnl*, vol 56, no 7, 1982, p 380; private information and personal knowledge.
                                                              THEODORA HOBBS

HUPPATZ, ROSA ZELMA (1906-1982), nurse, was born on 20 July 1906 at Peters Hill, near Riverton, South Australia, fourth of eight children of Frederick Carl Huppatz, farmer, and his wife Annie, née Smith. Zelma's Lutheran family valued compassion, duty and education. With a quiet but happy disposition, she tried to respect the feelings of others and to 'discuss' but not 'argue', believing it 'a mark of a superior mind to disagree and yet be friendly'. At Riverton High School she was awarded a prize for the student who had the best influence on others. From 1929 to 1932 Zelma trained as a nurse at the (Royal) Adelaide Hospital. She then studied (1932-33) at the Metropolitan Infectious Diseases Hospital, Northfield. After her return to the Adelaide Hospital she became a senior nurse in charge of a ward in 1934. She undertook a midwifery course (1938-39) at the Queen Alexandra Hospital for Women, Hobart.

Having joined the Australian Army Nursing Service Reserve, Huppatz began full-time duty in the Australian Imperial Force on 9 February

1940. She sailed for the Middle East in April and disembarked in Egypt next month. At first she worked in a British military hospital at Alexandria, nursing soldiers, sailors, airmen and merchant seamen of many nationalities. From August she was with the 2/2nd Australian General Hospital at El Kantara. She was given responsibility for assisting junior staff to adjust to their hazardous work and living conditions. Her spare time and money were spent visiting Palestine. Back in Australia in March 1942, Huppatz was matron of the 101st AGH at Katherine, Northern Territory, before her promotion to temporary lieutenant colonel and appointment as matron of the 105th (Adelaide) Military Hospital in July 1945. Her loyalty and devotion to duty impressed her superiors. She was transferred to the Reserve of Officers on 2 August 1946.

Huppatz was then appointed assistant-matron at the Royal Adelaide Hospital; she obtained her infant welfare certificate in 1947 at Torrens House. In order to promote better nursing education she helped to establish (1949) in Melbourne the College of Nursing, Australia, of which she became a fellow and later president (1959-60). In 1950 she studied nursing administration there. Concerned that schools of nursing sometimes operated as service units rather than places of education, she advocated the 'block system' in which students would have several weeks out of the hospital to attend lectures and study. She was appointed matron of RAH in 1955, a post that she held until her retirement in 1966.

A member (1957-65) of the Nurses Board of South Australia, Huppatz was also State councillor (1948-65) and State president (1962-65) of the (Royal) Australian Nursing Federation. She was an active member of the Returned Sisters sub-branch of the Returned Sailors', Soldiers' and Airmen's Imperial League of Australia. In retirement she served (1967-79) on the board of the Home for Incurables and pursued her interests in theatre and music. She was awarded the Florence Nightingale medal by the International Committee of the Red Cross in 1963 and was appointed MBE in 1966. Never married, she died on 13 December 1982 at the hospital where she had nursed so many others, and was cremated.

J. Durdin, *They Became Nurses* (1991), and *Eleven Thousand Nurses* (1999); *Advertiser* (Adelaide), 4 May 1955, p 5, 11 Aug 1959, p 14, 30 May 1963, p 29, 15 Dec 1982, p 9; *A'asian Nurses Jnl*, Jan-Feb 1983, p 8; B883, item SX1490, A463, item 1965/5831 (NAA).   SALLY-ANNE NICHOLSON

HURREN, FRANK EMERY (1899-1982), structural engineer, was born on 18 December 1899 at Birkenhead, South Australia, youngest of four children of Charles Hurren, clerk, and his wife Amy Catherine, née Emery. Educated at the South Australian School of Mines and Industries, Frank left home at 16 to take employment with Stone & Siddeley Ltd, Sydney-based consulting engineers and pioneers in the use of reinforced concrete. He returned to Adelaide in 1916 with Edward Stone who was supervising construction of the Glenelg breakwater, destroyed in a storm before completion. In 1922 he joined M. S. Stanley, a Sydney consulting engineer, as a draughtsman. On 10 May 1926 at St Paul's Church of England, Port Adelaide, he married Selina Muriel Wallace, a typist. Next year he travelled to the United States of America and Europe to investigate developments in the use of gypsum and, on his return to Adelaide, established a partnership in Gawler Place with W. W. Langman early in 1928.

Responsible for the structural frameworks of many large buildings in Adelaide, including the offices of the Shell Co. of Australia Ltd, the Australian Mutual Provident Society, the Bank of New South Wales and the Savings Bank of South Australia, the partners developed strong bonds of trust. The early years of practice involved hard work, with frequent interstate travel. As the number of commissions increased in the mid-1930s they concentrated on local projects and took in another partner, W. H. James. Hurren, Langman & James became the pre-eminent consulting structural engineering firm in Adelaide, recognised for the high quality of its work and for innovations such as the development of the pier-and-beam foundation system to reduce cracking in houses built on Adelaide's reactive clay soils. Hurren served on advisory committees, including the parliamentary by-laws and standards committee, and lectured at the School of Mines.

Hurren established the first modern sustained structural engineering consultancy in Adelaide and was influential in the acceptance of reinforced concrete as a structural material in South Australia. In 1936 his health broke down because of pressure of work, and next year he took his family to the USA. After his return difficulties gradually emerged between the partners and on 30 June 1956 their partnership was dissolved. Hurren retired and never again practised engineering, devoting his time instead to other interests and to charitable work.

Remarkably self-motivated, driven and obsessional, Hurren was also generous, trusting and loyal. Although socially awkward he made many close friends. He was an excellent host, a good correspondent and a man of diverse interests including art, theatre, shipping, travel and conservation. In March 1951 he helped to organise the meeting that led to the formation that year of the National Trust for South Australia. He was a devout Anglican.

Survived by his wife and their son and daughter, he died on 8 August 1982 at Stirling and was buried in the local cemetery.

D. A. Cumming and G. C. Moxham, *They Built South Australia* (1986); B. Stacy, '"A Mad Scramble"', *Jnl of the Hist Soc of SA*, no 33, 2005, p 87; *Advertiser* (Adelaide), 10 Aug 1982, p 6; Hurren, Langman & James records (Louis Laybourne Smith School of Architecture Archive, Univ of SA Lib); private information.   BILL STACY

HURSEY, FRANCIS JOHN BERTRAM (1912-1990), wharf labourer, commercial fisherman and timber-cutter, was born on 30 August 1912 in South Hobart, second of three children of Tasmanian-born parents James Alexander Hursey, fireman, and his wife Ellen Catherine, née Smith. Educated by the Christian Brothers at St Virgil's College, Frank began work as a labourer and house-builder. On 6 January 1933 in Hobart he married with Catholic rites Ella Olive Webberley (d.1969). They lived on a small farm at Saltwater River on the Tasman Peninsula until 1935, when Hursey became a wharf labourer at Hobart. Injured at work in 1947, he used his compensation to purchase a ketch and entered the fishing industry. He bought land at Raminea, near Dover. A tall, thin, garrulous man with a glass eye, he was noted for his extravagant language and his habit of making pronouncements. He was a member of the Australian Labor Party from about 1936. In 1954 he failed to gain endorsement as a candidate for the State election.

In 1955 Hursey moved to Warrane and applied to work again on the Hobart wharves. Initially the shipowners' association and the Australian Stevedoring Industry Board opposed his re-registration but, assisted by the local branch committee of the Waterside Workers' Federation, he won the right to return. His son Dennis also became a wharf labourer and union-member. In 1956 Hursey joined the newly formed Australian Labor Party (Anti-Communist) (Democratic Labor Party from 1957), and was endorsed for the district of Franklin in the State election. Both he and Dennis refused to pay a levy struck by the Hobart branch of the WWF to help the ALP finance its election campaign. A long-running dispute ensued: the Hurseys were expelled from the union and protracted industrial action followed, aimed at preventing them from reporting for work.

The Hurseys won a Supreme Court of Tasmania injunction in June 1958 against the WWF. Represented by Senator (Sir) Reginald Wright [q.v.] in a case beginning in July, they claimed in two writs that the branch had no authority to impose special levies for political purposes, or to stop them from working. A counter writ by the union argued that the Hurseys should not have been rostered for work when they were not union members. The Hurseys won the case and were awarded £3200 each for lost wages and suffering. Supported by the Australian Council of Trade Unions, the WWF appealed to the High Court of Australia, which, in September 1959, found in favour of the union and reduced the damages awarded to the Hurseys. Despite the decision, the ACTU reached a national agreement that saw unions abandon compulsory political levies. Amanda Lohrey based her novel *The Morality of Gentlemen* (1984) on the case.

Leaving the waterfront in 1959, Hursey and his son returned to fishing and also won a timber-cutting contract. As secretary of the new Tasmanian Fishermen's Union, in 1970 Hursey lodged a challenge in the Supreme Court to the Tasmanian government's control of waters below the low-water mark. On 17 May 1987 at St Mary Our Hope Catholic Church, Dover, he married Adelina Arbues, née Abubo, a divorcee. He died on 30 March 1990 at Dover and was buried in the local cemetery. His wife and the two daughters and four sons of his first marriage survived him.

T. Bull, *Politics in a Union* (1977) and *Life on the Waterfront* (1998); M. Beasley, *Wharfies* (1996); *SMH*, 8 Nov 1958, p 1, 17 Sept 1959, p 7; *Sunday Examiner Express* (Launceston), 14 Mar 1970, p 2; *Bulletin*, 21 Mar 1970, p 23; *Saturday Evening Mercury* (Hobart), 7 Oct 1972, p 26; *Mercury* (Hobart), 17 Apr 1973, p 3, 7 Dec 1977, p 3; *Examiner* (Launceston), 3 Apr 1990, p 35; A1533, item 1953/793, pt 1, and files on F. J. Hursey in series A10145 (NAA).   ROD HUNT

HUTCHISON, IAN (1913-1982), soldier, was born on 2 August 1913 at Paddington, Sydney, son of James Alexander Charles Hutchison, a bank accountant from Scotland, and his wife Annie Maud, née Thorburn, born in New South Wales. Educated at Middle Harbour Public School, Ian embarked on a clerical career with the shipping firm James Patrick & Co. Ltd and completed accountancy studies. A keen soldier in the Militia, he was commissioned as a lieutenant in the 17th Battalion (North Sydney Regiment) in September 1934. Next year he transferred to the 30th Battalion (New South Wales Scottish Regiment). On 6 November 1937 at the Presbyterian Church, Mosman, he married Moyra Aileen Lane.

Promoted to captain in October 1939, Hutchison was seconded to the Australian Imperial Force on the 13th and posted to the 2/3rd Battalion. In January 1940 the unit embarked for the Middle East, where it underwent extensive training. Commanding 'A' Company during the attack on Bardia, Libya, on

3 January 1941, Hutchison led his men, while under heavy fire, in capturing a large enemy fort and taking over five hundred prisoners. He had personally seized one machine-gun and turned it on the enemy. When six Italian tanks attempted a counter-attack, he organised a successful defence of the post, despite his rifle being knocked from his hands by a shell. He was awarded the Military Cross.

On 21 January Hutchison was badly wounded in the left arm near the starting line for the attack on Tobruk. He rejoined his battalion in May and during the Syrian campaign (June-July) took a leading part in the actions at Mezze, near Damascus, in the heavy fighting for Jebel Mazar on the road to Beirut, and in the battle of Damour. In March 1942 the battalion sailed to Ceylon (Sri Lanka). Hutchison was made a temporary major in July (substantive in September) and the unit returned to Australia in August.

Sent to Papua in September, the 2/3rd was soon fighting the Japanese in engagements along the Owen Stanley Range. When the commanding officer Lieutenant Colonel J. R. Stevenson [q.v.16] was wounded at Eora Creek late in October, Hutchison took temporary command. Although still young, he was, according to K. Clift, 'an experienced tactician, a daring leader and a man of great determination, possessing the confidence of all ranks'. The battalion was subsequently in action at Oivi and on the Sanananda Track. He was mentioned in despatches.

From January 1943 the battalion re-formed and trained on the Atherton Tableland, Queensland. In April Hutchison was promoted to lieutenant colonel and appointed commanding officer. He brought his men up to a high standard and instilled an *esprit de corps*. In December 1944 the 2/3rd embarked for the north coast of New Guinea, where it fought in the Aitape-Wewak area. The battalion harried and pursued the enemy, with Hutchison determined to hold the initiative, before the war ended in August 1945. For showing 'exceptional ability as a commanding officer' he was awarded the Distinguished Service Order. He transferred to the Reserve of Officers on 26 March 1946.

Back in Sydney, Hutchison became a partner in a manufacturing company, but soldiering was in his blood, and in April 1948 he was appointed to re-establish and command the 30th Battalion, Citizen Military Forces. In August 1949 he transferred to the Interim Army. He attended the Staff College, Queenscliff, Victoria, in 1950 and was appointed to command the 13th National Service Training Battalion in December that year. In November 1951 he took command of the 1st Battalion, Royal Australian Regiment.

Hutchison guided his battalion through its build-up and preparation stages and then took it to the Republic of (South) Korea in April 1952. His good training, experience and administration were evident in its early contacts with the enemy. Its first action, Operation Blaze, commenced on 2 July. The battalion remained at the 'sharp end' until the end of September, actively engaged in fighting patrols, ambush patrols and minefield protection. He was appointed OBE (1953) for his 'wise leadership' and 'untiring personal efforts'.

Relinquishing command of 1RAR in October 1952, Hutchison returned to Australia in November and performed staff duties. He was senior officer, cadets, and commander, 3rd Cadet Brigade, from March 1955 and commander, 2nd Cadet Brigade, from November 1959. On 3 August 1963 he transferred to the Retired List with the rank of colonel. Short, compact and dapper with a neat moustache, he was a friendly and active man. He had a deep interest in the army's history and traditions. Known fondly to a few as 'the little king', he was more universally called 'Hutch'. He was 'a boots and gaiters soldier' who preferred working with troops—with whom he had a genuine empathy—to sitting in the office.

Hutchison became a director of several companies and remained active in ex-service organisations, including the Royal Australian Regiment Association, Legacy and the Army Museum of New South Wales. He also worked for the establishment of the Royal Australian Regiment Memorial in Sydney. Survived by his wife, and his son and two daughters, he died of myocardial infarction on 13 December 1982 at Wahroonga and was cremated. His son, named after him, became a regular army officer.

G. Long, *To Benghazi* (1952), *Greece, Crete and Syria* (1953) and *The Final Campaigns* (1963); D. McCarthy, *South-West Pacific Area—First Year* (1959); K. Clift, *War Dance* (1980); T. F. Wade-Ferrell (comp), *In All Things Faithful* (1985); M. J. Buckley, *Scarlet and Tartan* (1986); D. Horner (ed), *Duty First* (1990); G. L. Maitland, *The Battle History of the Royal New South Wales Regiment*, vol 2 (2002); *SMH*, 16 Dec 1982, p 10; B883, item NX57963 (NAA); private information.   PETER BURNESS

HUTLEY, FRANCIS CHARLES (1914-1985), judge, was born on 22 October 1914 at Lithgow, New South Wales, elder child of Arthur Hutley, an English-born medical practitioner, and his Sydney-born wife Ethel Mary, née Plomley (d.1916). After the family moved to Sydney early in the 1920s, Frank was educated at Chatswood Boys' Intermediate High and North Sydney Boys' High schools. Having won an exhibition to the University of Sydney (BA, 1935; LL B, 1939), he graduated with first-class honours in English, philosophy and law and was awarded university medals in philosophy and law. The uncompromising intellectual integrity and rigorous academic discipline for which he became renowned were cultivated by his contact with Professor John Anderson [q.v.7], who held Hutley in the highest esteem. He became a lecturer in jurisprudence and private international law at the Sydney University Law School and in 1940 edited *Blackacre*, the law students' publication. While still a student he had been articled to G. L. Baldick and on 21 February 1941 he was admitted as a solicitor.

On 22 December that year Hutley enlisted in the Australian Imperial Force. Commissioned in July 1942, he joined Alfred Conlon's [q.v.13] research section before transferring to the Australian Army Legal Department (later Corps), with which he served in Papua (May-November 1944). He then returned to Conlon's Directorate of Research and Civil Affairs. Having attended (July-October 1945) the United States Army's School of Military Government, Charlottesville, Virginia, he carried out military liaison duties as a temporary major with the British Commonwealth Occupation Force, Japan, from April to December 1946. He transferred to the Reserve of Officers on 3 January 1947.

Hutley briefly resumed his academic career at the Sydney University Law School, before commencing practice at the Bar in 1948. He had been admitted as a barrister on 18 February 1944, while serving in the legal corps. An acknowledged expert in probate law and all matters concerning estates, he was also retained by several trade unions in important industrial litigation. His undoubted forensic abilities and his professional competence were recognised by his appointment as QC in 1967. He had an unusual mannerism of speech that he seemed to have deliberately cultivated, by which he underlined a statement, an oratorical hit or the punch-line in a story, with a growling sound that continued for many seconds after the words concluded.

A part-time lecturer in probate, succession and admiralty law at the Sydney University Law School, Hutley acquired, and almost certainly delighted in, a fearsome reputation for imposing high standards. No academic leniency or compromise was ever allowed by him, although doubtless many solicitors, and perhaps even judges, relished the subsequent opportunities for revenge. He wrote two standard works, *Cases and Materials on Succession* (1967) and *Australian Wills Precedents* (1970), and contributed articles to the *Australian Law Journal* and other learned publications in law and philosophy. The last editor (1970-71) of the *New South Wales State Reports*, he was the first editor (1971-72) of its successor, the *New South Wales Law Reports*; he also edited (1970-71) the *New South Wales Weekly Notes*. He was

a director (1958-72) of the mining company Coffs Harbour Rutile NL.

Hutley was appointed a judge of the Supreme Court of New South Wales and an additional judge of appeal on 9 October 1972. His appointment to the Court of Appeal became permanent on 9 February 1973. As a judge he was relentless in his pursuit and exposure of error, whether from a lower court or in the legal submissions being presented to him. He was fearless, as a practitioner and as a judge, in expressing his conclusions as to what was right and just. The story that he once advised a client to sue his instructing solicitor (albeit very much in character) was rebutted by Hutley upon his retirement. Despite his daunting image, he was a most generous and helpful colleague at the Bar and his advice was leavened with the most denunciatory and defamatory anecdotes and comments. On the Court of Appeal, although he could be equally as devastating to counsel as the colleagues with whom he sat, his manner was dictated not by any personal animus but by an overwhelming desire for right to be done.

Within the Supreme Court administration Hutley was a member, and later chairman, of the New South Wales and of the Commonwealth-State joint law courts library committees. He was also a member (1973-74) and president (1975) of the Joint Examinations Board of the Supreme Court. Following a three-month visit to the United States of America in 1979 on a Fulbright scholarship, he lectured on his experiences.

Opposed to cronyism, whether by solicitors in briefing counsel or by governments in making judicial appointments, at his 1984 retirement ceremony Hutley said: 'A solicitor who briefs counsel on the basis of cronyism, social or political, is as much a menace to his client as one who raids the trust account'. He denounced the tendency for the executive government to interfere in proceedings between citizens and to pressurise the courts, stating that the judgment of which he was most proud was in *Corporate Affairs Commission* v. *Bradley; Commonwealth of Australia (Intervener)* (1974).

Hutley had married Margaret Walkom, a broadcasting executive, on 6 March 1946 at St Stephen's Presbyterian Church, Sydney; they divorced in May 1949. On 2 July at St Andrew's Presbyterian Church, Chatswood, he married Lelia (Lee) Frances Walshe, a solicitor. She served as an alderman (1962-71) on the Mosman Municipal Council. Their country property, Robin Hill at Mount Wilson in the Blue Mountains, acquired in the mid-1950s, was a much-loved family retreat. Hutley was able to indulge his delight in gardening, and to participate in acrimonious disputes among the local residents (including Dr C. H. Currey [q.v.13]) at meetings of the Mount Wilson

Progress Association. Survived by his wife and their two sons and two daughters (all of whom were lawyers), he died of myocardial infarction on 2 September 1985 at St Leonards, Sydney. An agnostic, he was cremated without religious rites.

J. Kerr, *Matters for Judgment* (1978); NSW Bar Assn, *Annual Report*, 1984, p 17; *Austn Law Jnl*, vol 46, no 10, 1972, p 540, vol 59, no 1, 1985, p 59, vol 59, no 11, 1985, p 689; *Austn Bar Review*, vol 1, no 3, 1985, p 185; Mt Wilson & Mt Irvine Hist Soc, *Hist Papers*, Sept 2001, p 5; B883, item NX79702 (NAA); A. McGrath, interview with F. Hutley (ts, 1983, NLA); private information.

JOHN KENNEDY MCLAUGHLIN

HUTTON, BEATRICE MAY (1893-1990), architect and craftswoman, was born on 16 July 1893 at The Folly, Lakes Creek, Queensland, second of seven children of Falconer West Hutton, a surveyor born in New South Wales, and his Queensland-born wife Clara Susannah, née Holt. Bea spent much of her childhood at Comet Downs, Comet, Central Queensland, until the effects of the great drought at the turn of the century forced the Hutton family off the land. They moved to Rockhampton, where Falconer practised as a surveyor and Bea attended Rockhampton Girls' Grammar School. Resolving on an independent career, she entered her father's office for a year to learn the rudiments of drafting.

In June 1912 Hutton began her architectural career as an articled pupil of the leading Rockhampton architect Edwin Morton Hockings, principal of the firm E. M. Hockings & L. T. Palmer. With the departure of Hockings on active service during World War I, she became the firm's chief draftsman. In March 1916, on completion of her articles, she applied to become an associate of the Queensland Institute of Architects. Her application was accepted at the institute's meeting of 30 October without debate or controversy, making her the first woman admitted to an architectural institute in Australia. An earlier application, to the Institute of Architects of New South Wales, by Florence Taylor [q.v.12], had been rejected in 1907 because she was a woman.

Late in 1916 Hutton moved to Sydney for wider experience. She worked briefly for the architects Wardell & Denning and in April 1917 joined the office of the Queensland expatriate architect and consulting engineer Claude William Chambers. She assisted Chambers with major works in Sydney: the New South Wales Masonic Club in Castlereagh Street and Sirius House in Macquarie Place. In 1923 Hutton was registered as an architect in New South Wales and in 1931

became the junior partner of Chambers, in the restyled firm of Chambers & Hutton. That year she joined the Society of Arts and Crafts of New South Wales to pursue an interest in handicrafts nurtured by her mother.

Hutton believed that the greatest contribution of women to architecture was in the domestic sphere, in the design of homes suited to climate and equipped for modern living. Houses are among the best-known works attributed to her: the J. W. Dalzell residence, in Spencer Street, Rockhampton (c.1916); the Frank Rudd residence for a friend, in Agnes Street, Rockhampton (c.1923); Ngarita for an uncle, Sir William Vicars [q.v.12], in Cranbrook Road, Rose Bay (Bellevue Hill), Sydney (c.1926); and a retirement cottage for her parents, in Brecknell Street, Rockhampton (c.1926).

In 1933 Beatrice cut short her architectural career to return to Rockhampton to care for her ageing parents. Following her father's death in November that year, she and her mother moved to Brisbane, settling at Toowong and becoming actively involved in handiwork. Beatrice joined the Arts and Crafts Society of Queensland and took lessons in wood carving from L. J. Harvey [q.v.9]. In 1936 she opened a craft studio, The Glory Box, in Brisbane's Colonial Mutual Life Building, where she sold her work and that of her mother, including embroideries, knitted dresses, rugs, ceramics, wood carving and rolled paper and bead curtains. She also undertook commissions for carved portraits. In 1940-42, following her mother's death, she returned briefly to architecture, working for the retailers Penneys Ltd.

In her later years Hutton was surrounded by her creative handiwork. She never married. A reserved and gracious woman, she was tall and slim, with large, observant eyes and a ready smile. She retained the poise that had made her, in her youth, a champion horsewoman. She died on 7 October 1990 at Indooroopilly, Brisbane, and was cremated. Her work is represented in the collection of the Queensland Museum, South Bank, Brisbane, and in a name-plate that she carved for Miegunyah, Bowen Hills, the home of the Queensland Women's Historical Association, of which she was a member. She is honoured by the Beatrice Hutton award for commercial architecture, made annually by the Royal Australian Institute of Architects Queensland chapter, by the Beatrice Hutton room of the Rockhampton Art Gallery, and by Beatrice Hutton House of Capricornia College, Central Queensland University, Rockhampton.

D. Watson and J. McKay, *A Directory of Queensland Architects to 1940* (1984); G. R. Cooke, *Lady Woodcarvers of Rockhampton* (2000); *Daily Mail* (Brisbane), 21 Oct 1916, p 12; *Morning Bulletin*

(Rockhampton), 23 Nov 1933, p 6; J. Mackay [McKay], 'Beatrice Hutton', *Lip*, no 8, 1984, p 100; private information and personal knowledge.

JUDITH M. McKAY

HUTTON, GEOFFREY WILLIAM (1909-1985), journalist, was born on 18 October 1909 at Southampton, Hampshire, England, son of Thomas John Hutton, commercial traveller, and his wife Lavina Annette, née Shilling. Geoff's education began there at King Edward VI School, was interrupted by his family's migration to Australia in 1924, and resumed at Scotch College, Melbourne, where he edited the *Collegian* (1927) and won a scholarship to the University of Melbourne (BA Hons, 1931). His flair as editor (1930) of *Melbourne University Magazine* (for which he also wrote many articles under numerous *noms de plume*) secured a cadetship (1931) at the *Argus*, where he was to cover Australian politics and international affairs, and review books, theatre and ballet. On 12 June 1933 at All Saints' Church of England, East St Kilda, he married Necia Noel Bednall, a secretary.

In 1935 Hutton travelled to Europe for twelve months as an *Argus* correspondent. Following the entry of Japan into World War II, he was assigned to General Headquarters in Melbourne, and then as a field correspondent at Townsville, Queensland. He relieved George Johnston [q.v.14] in Port Moresby in August 1942 and, as an *Argus* correspondent, reported the fighting in Papua before covering the Allied offensives in New Guinea. In December 1943 he was transferred to Washington and then to the Supreme Headquarters, Allied Expeditionary Force, London. Landing in France shortly after D-Day, he followed the Allied advance from Normandy to the fall of Berlin. In March 1945 he was mentioned in despatches for his reporting of the Papuan and New Guinea campaigns. With the coming of the Cold War, his attention turned to eastern Europe, China, the Korean peninsula and Indo-China.

Necia died in September 1950 and, after a period as London correspondent, Hutton returned to Melbourne. On 17 March 1952 at South Yarra Presbyterian Church, he married NANCY ESTELLE Charlholmes (1917-1984), a divorcee and fellow journalist. He joined the *Age* in 1954 as a feature writer and, although suspected by the Australian Security Intelligence Organization of having once been a member of the Communist Party of Australia, and of retaining 'communistic views', he returned to London as the *Age* correspondent (1957-59). Back in Melbourne as chief leader-writer, he complemented his international

reportage with theatre and literary reviews, and in 1968 became chief drama critic. Retiring in 1974, he was widely respected as—his editor, Graham Perkin [q.v.15], noted—'a writer of grace, style and temperate judgement'.

Hutton continued reviewing for the *Age* and served as the *Australian*'s Melbourne theatre critic. A handsome, urbane man, and a literary and artistic nationalist, he wrote a biography of Dame Nellie Melba [q.v.10] (1962), a history of the Melbourne Theatre Company (1974) and studies of C. J. Dennis (1976) and Adam Lindsay Gordon [qq.v.8,4] (1978). He edited a historical anthology of the *Age* (1979) with the cartoonist Les Tanner, and *Australia's Natural Heritage* (1981) for the Australian Conservation Foundation, and collaborated with Geoffrey Blainey in a revised edition of Blainey's *Gold and Paper 1858-1982* (1983). His wife's career in journalism encompassed writing for leading magazines, including *Woman's Day* (1952-58) and, from 1967 to 1980, a column in the *Age*; in 1971 she was a founding member of the Melbourne Press Club. Nan died of cancer on 2 May 1984. Predeceased by a son of his first marriage, and survived by the daughter of his second, Geoffrey Hutton died on 1 December 1985 at Prahran and was cremated.

Argus (Melbourne), 9 Mar 1945, p 12; *Age* (Melbourne), 19 Oct 1974, p 17, 2 Dec 1985, p 5; private information.

TOM HEENAN

HUXLEY, SIR LEONARD GEORGE HOLDEN (1902-1988), physicist and vice-chancellor, was born on 29 May 1902 at Dulwich, London, eldest son of George Hambrough (or Hamborough) Huxley, and his wife Lilian Sarah, née Smith, both school-teachers. George's grandfather was the uncle of T. H. Huxley [q.v.1]. Although he carried with him throughout his life many attributes of his English heritage, Leonard considered himself very much an Australian; he spent more than three-quarters of his life in this country, including his formative years. His parents migrated to Australia in 1905. Following a brief sojourn in Western Australia, the family moved to Tasmania, where they were to remain.

From a small country school at Mathinna, Huxley won a State scholarship to The Hutchins School (1915-20), Hobart, where he excelled not only academically but also as a sportsman; in his final year he was dux, and captain of the athletics team. He continued to support his education through a series of bursaries and, finally, a scholarship to the University of Tasmania. There he won the Sir Philip Fysh [q.v.8] prize for physics in 1922.

Awarded the Rhodes scholarship for Tasmania in 1923, he left for Oxford with his first degree incomplete.

At New College, Oxford (BA, 1925; D.Phil., 1928; MA, 1929), Huxley relished the cultural as well as the academic experiences his new environment afforded him. There he met his distant cousin (Sir) Julian Huxley, then a fellow of the college and a reader in biology, with whom he formed a firm and lasting friendship. There, too, he first met (Sir) John Townsend, who was to have a profound influence on him. In 1925 Huxley commenced work for his doctorate under Townsend, who had pioneered the subject of his research, electrical breakdown in gases. Another of Townsend's interests, electron transport in gases, was to become one of Huxley's longer-term interests and the field to which he made many distinguished contributions.

After completing his doctorate, Huxley undertook post-doctoral research at Oxford. He married Ella Mary Child ('Molly') Copeland on 5 October 1929 at the parish church, Esher, Surrey. Intellectually they were well matched. Molly took a first in history at Somerville College and was to become the first (part-time) lecturer in British history at the new Canberra University College.

From January 1930 to September 1931 Huxley was in Canberra as a member of staff of the Radio Research Board, an adjunct to the Council for Scientific and Industrial Research, where he worked on ionospheric disturbances. He returned to England to take up academic appointments, first as lecturer in physics at University College, Nottingham, then (from 1932) as head of the physics department at University College, Leicester.

World War II transformed Huxley's professional career as it did those of many physicists in Britain. Immediately war was declared, he found himself recruited to the distinguished group at the Bawdsey Research Station (later the Telecommunications Research Establishment), which was to develop radar and introduce it to the services with amazing speed. Following an initial posting to Fighter Command, he was given the task of establishing and heading a radar training school for both civilian and service personnel. By the end of the war an estimated seven thousand had attended it. The war years at TRE provided Huxley with the material for his influential book *A Survey of the Principles & Practice of Wave Guides* (1947).

Though Huxley was first and foremost a physicist, his wartime experience qualified him well for his appointment in 1946 as reader in electromagnetism in the department of electrical engineering at the University of Birmingham. However, his stay was to be short-lived. In 1948 (Sir) Mark Oliphant, him-

self about to become foundation director of the Research School of Physical Sciences at the Australian National University, Canberra, drew his attention to an advertisement for the (Sir Thomas) Elder [q.v.4] chair of physics at the University of Adelaide. Huxley successfully applied for the position, taking up his appointment in February 1949. The university conferred on him a Ph.D., *ad eundem gradum*, in 1950.

Huxley's appointment coincided with the introduction of Ph.D. courses throughout Australia, and the more generous allocation of Commonwealth money to the universities in the late 1950s following the report of Sir Keith Murray's committee on Australian universities. Encouraged by an enthusiastic vice-chancellor, A. P. Rowe [q.v.16], Huxley took full advantage of these innovations. He recruited staff—some home-grown and some from overseas—and established Ph.D. training programs around new research groups. Drawing on his wartime experiences, he started a large and active group to track meteor trails and upper-atmosphere winds using radar. He formed another team to conduct laboratory studies of electron drift and diffusion in gases to complement his interest in electromagnetic wave propagation in the ionosphere. His staff began equally active programs in biophysics, solid-state physics and seismology.

Although Huxley now had a greatly enlarged and flourishing department to his credit, his later days in Adelaide were marked by increasing friction with the vice-chancellor. Huxley did not accept Rowe's view that a university should be managed like a government department or research institution, or even a business enterprise. In 1960 he was appointed to the executive of the Commonwealth Scientific and Industrial Research Organization, but he had scarcely become settled in his new position when he was invited to succeed Sir Leslie Melville as vice chancellor of the ANU. Accepting the invitation, he entered on the most influential period of his career, both within academia and outside it.

On 30 September 1960 Huxley assumed office. Next day an amendment to the Australian National University Act (1946) came into effect, amalgamating the ANU and Canberra University College. The college was incorporated in the enlarged ANU as the School of General Studies, while the old university became the Institute of Advanced Studies. Huxley's initial task was to bring about a harmonious university community from these two components, neither of which fully welcomed the association. It was a challenge he was well equipped to meet. On the one hand, he had a deep and continuing commitment to research; on the other hand, he maintained a keen interest in teaching, to which he had devoted a considerable portion of his professional life.

When Huxley joined the ANU, the old Canberra University College had no permanent buildings, apart from one housing the arts departments, while only two of the research schools of the old ANU were permanently housed, or partly so. The four existing research schools—the John Curtin School of Medical Research, and the research schools of Physical Sciences, Social Sciences and Pacific Studies—together had about one hundred postgraduate students. The college had about eight hundred undergraduates. In 1961 the university's budget was approximately £2.25 million. When Huxley retired in 1967, there were some five hundred postgraduate students and over three thousand undergraduates, and the budget was over $17.5 million.

Huxley had presided over a period of great change and growth. The research schools of Chemistry and Biological Sciences were established, the Australian Forestry School was subsumed and its role expanded as it became the department of forestry, and a second observational site was established at Siding Spring, New South Wales, for the department of astronomy. Meanwhile, many permanent buildings were erected for departments within the School of General Studies and for research schools in the institute. Huxley was appointed KBE in 1964.

Although Huxley had been actively involved in physics since his postgraduate years at Oxford, his heavy teaching loads at both Leicester and Birmingham, and his full-time service at TRE during the war, had left him relatively little time to devote to his research interests until he took up his professorial appointment in Adelaide. At Birmingham he had laid the foundations for the two research fields he was to pursue for many years. With J. A. Ratcliffe he explored the 'Luxembourg effect', a phenomenon whereby the transmission from one radio broadcasting station is superimposed on the other. This investigation brought home to Huxley the importance of laboratory studies of electron motion in gases, in this instance the constituents of air. He therefore initiated such studies at Birmingham, and a continuation of that work formed the basis of research at the University of Adelaide and later still at the ANU. To this program he brought a continuing flow of ideas and much of the theoretical backing.

The years in Adelaide were Huxley's most scientifically productive and influential. In addition to his work on electron motion in gases and the Luxembourg effect, he produced papers reporting the first results from his highly successful project to detect the trails of ionised gases left by meteors, and hence to determine wind patterns in the upper atmosphere. Being mainly interested in theoretical work, he was content to leave the development of the laboratory and field-work to his group of graduate students, some of whom continued as members of staff. As at Leicester he found himself responsible for training the first batch of Ph.D. students to graduate from the university.

With his appointment to the ANU, Huxley's interests in the areas he had promoted in Adelaide had necessarily narrowed. Encouraged by Oliphant, he established the Electron and Ion Diffusion Unit to pursue the laboratory studies that had gathered considerable momentum in Adelaide. Though his time was limited, he retained a keen interest in the unit's progress throughout his term as vice-chancellor and wrote several papers, stimulated by particular developments either within the unit or brought to his attention through its work.

On his retirement, Huxley returned to physics. Many advances had been made and a major revision of his theoretical work on electron motion in gases was required. The publication in 1974 of a major monograph, *The Diffusion and Drift of Electrons in Gases*, written with R. W. Crompton, and the three papers that resulted from its preparation, brought to a close his many contributions to the field that he had pioneered.

Huxley was a member of the council of the University of Adelaide (1953-60), the ANU (1956-59) and the newly established Canberra College of Advanced Education (1968-74). The University of Tasmania (1962) and the ANU (1980) both awarded him honorary doctorates of science. A foundation fellow (1954) of the Australian Academy of Science, he served on its council in 1956-62 and as vice-president in 1957-58. He chaired the National Standards Commission (1953-65) and the Radio Research Board (1958-64). In 1962-65 he was the foundation president of the Australian Institute of Physics. Invited to the board of the United States Educational Foundation in Australia in 1960, he became the first chairman (1965-69) of the Australian American Educational Foundation which succeeded it. He also chaired (1964-73) the general council of the Britannica Australia Awards and served (1961-72) on the council of the National Library of Australia. His own large library revealed his catholic tastes in history, natural history, literature, music and the arts.

Sir Leonard Huxley was a man of integrity who belonged to the generation of scholars whose depth of learning was matched by its width, and who had a clear vision of the age-old function of universities. He had a warm personality, although that was sometimes masked by his somewhat formal manner. Blessed with an incredible memory right up to his death, he had an enviable capacity for recalling what he had read and where he had read it. He combined his gift for words and the breadth of his interests in the preparation of scholarly speeches, which often also revealed his puckish sense of humour.

Huxley's physical resilience was as remarkable as his mental vigour. At 86 his bearing was still that of a man twenty years younger, and he looked little different from the excellent portrait of him painted by June Mendoza in 1972 and held by the ANU. It shows a man of medium height with an undiminished head of hair, now grey but still with a tinge of its earlier pale ginger hue. His wife died in 1981. Survived by their son and daughter, he died on 4 September 1988 at Camden, London, during a short visit overseas, and was cremated. A building at the ANU was named after him.

S. G. Foster and M. M. Varghese, *The Making of the Australian National University 1946-1996* (1996); *ODNB*, vol 29 (2004), p 97; R. W. Crompton, 'Leonard George Holden Huxley 1902-1988', *Hist Records of Austn Science*, vol 8, no 4, 1991, p 249; *ANU Reporter*, 23 Sept 1988, p 5; *CoResearch*, Sept 1988, p 8; M. Pratt, interview with L. G. H. Huxley (ts, 1971, NLA); Huxley papers (Basser Lib); personal knowledge.　　　ROBERT W. CROMPTON

HUXLEY, VICTOR NELSON (1906-1982), speedway motorcycle rider, was born on 23 September 1906 at Wooloowin, Brisbane, third of four children of Sydney-born parents William Henry Huxley, shirt cutter, and his wife Eva Amanda, née Lippiatt. Vic attended Fortitude Valley and Kelvin Grove state schools. Employed as a battery mechanic, he had been riding motorcycles for three years when a major motorcycle speedway competition was introduced at the Brisbane Exhibition Ground in October 1926. Winning the first event on the program, the One-Mile Handicap, he became one of the 'broadsiding' stars of the inaugural night races. He also won speedway events at the Toowoomba Showground and Brisbane's Davies Park. It was probably at this stage that he acquired the nickname 'Broadside'. After success in Australia, including a stint at Adelaide's Wayville Showground, he left for England in 1928 with a group of other leading speedway riders, including Frank Arthur [q.v.13], to introduce the new Australian sport of 'dirt-track racing'.

Speedway was a huge success in England and at one stage it was the second most popular sport (after horse-racing) in the country. For many years London was its heart, and Australians—especially Huxley—were nearly always winners. To celebrate his victories, the Ogden's branch of the Imperial Tobacco Co. (of Great Britain & Ireland) Ltd issued a 'Vic Huxley' cigarette card in their 1929 set of 'Famous Dirt-Track Riders'. On the card, he was portrayed in his characteristic 'broad-siding' manoeuvre on the track. That year he was the subject of one of a series of articles on 'Daredevils of the Speedway' published in the magazine *Modern Boy*.

In June 1930 Huxley led an Australian team to victory in the first official speedway Test match against England. Unbeaten at this meeting, he was to become the most successful rider in Tests in the early 1930s. Captain of the Harringay and then the Wimbledon speedway teams, he won the Star championship (forerunner of the world championship) in 1930 and next year became the British open champion. He was almost unbeatable: he broke speedway records all over England; won eight major championships; and also set and broke lap records at speedway tracks in Australia and New Zealand. His earnings were over £5000 per year, making him then one of the highest-paid sportsmen in the world. Members of the royal family and T. E. Lawrence were among those who congregated around Huxley's team at the speedway.

On 23 October 1931 at the register office, St Marylebone, London, Huxley married Sheila Alice Katherine King. He featured in numerous speedway magazine articles and books on speedway riding in England and Australia. When the British Broadcasting Corporation interviewed him in 1934 for its 'In Town Tonight' program, he became the first speedway rider to broadcast on radio. In the same year he won the Australian solo championship after being placed first in every event he entered.

In his eleven years as a speedway rider on a range of different manufacturers' machines, Huxley had only one serious accident. He left speedway racing in 1937 and opened the British Motorcycle Co. in Brisbane. Mobilised in the Militia as a lieutenant on 5 August 1941 he trained motorcycle dispatch riders. His appointment terminated on 5 February 1945 and he returned to his motorcycle business, retiring in 1957. He kept few trophies and never sought any publicity. Despite being 'bigger than Bradman' in his day, Vic Huxley remained throughout his life a modest and simple man. Three months after the death of his wife, he died on 24 June 1982 at Kangaroo Point, and was cremated. His son survived him.

T. Stenner, *Thrilling the Million* (1934); J. Shepherd, *Encyclopedia of Australian Sport* (1980) and *A History of Australian Speedway* (2003); *Brisbane Courier*, 18 Oct 1926, p 16; *SMH*, 19 Nov 1930, p 18; private information.

JONATHAN RICHARDS

HYLAND, CHARLES KEITH (1914-1989), businessman, was born on 15 November 1914 at Randwick, Sydney, second child of

Victorian-born parents Charles David Hyland, exporter, and his wife Jessie Emma, née Jobbins. Educated at The Armidale School, Keith moved to Melbourne, where he attended business college and began working for the family company, David Hyland & Sons Pty Ltd. The firm had a subsidiary, Australian Feather Mills Pty Ltd, in Sydney.

Two months after World War II started in September 1939, Hyland was appointed a lieutenant in the Army Service Corps, Militia. He transferred to the Australian Imperial Force on 19 June 1942 and served at a succession of supply depots as a captain. In May 1945 he embarked for Morotai and on arrival joined the 2/27th Transport Platoon. By the time the war ended in September 1945, Australian Feather Mills was experiencing difficulties due to the unavailability of down from China. Hyland decided to travel to Hong Kong with a view to placing new orders. In February 1946 he left Morotai aboard a military aircraft, without first obtaining proper authority. His quest took him to several Asian countries. Returning in April, he was court martialled for being absent without leave and dismissed from the army on 24 May.

Hyland moved to Bangkok and, with little capital, established a factory to process feathers and manufacture items such as quilts and sleeping-bags. In the mid-1950s he set up a feather-processing plant at Cholon, Saigon (Ho Chi Minh City). His father died in 1953 and he took over the family company in Sydney, but Bangkok and Saigon remained his bases. Diversifying his operations, he added timber and agricultural products to the range of goods he shipped to Europe, Australia and the United States of America. He became an advocate of increased trade between Australia and South-East Asia and developed an affection for the peoples of the region. In Saigon he lived with Ann Chi Quang; their son, Charles Hap, was born in 1964. On 17 March 1967 in Bangkok he married Lisa Ludlow, an American model whom he had met on a skiing holiday in Austria; they had a daughter and a son before separating.

During the Vietnam War, Hyland continued to spend part of the year in Saigon. On 6 February 1968 he was driving from the city to Cholon, when he was captured by the People's Liberation Armed Forces (Viet Cong). Bound and blindfolded, marched through the jungle, periodically confined in a cage or covered pit, incessantly interrogated, chained more securely after an attempted escape, and suffering from dysentery, he was eventually released on 25 November. In his account of his ordeal (Sydney *Sun*, 19-20, 23-24 December 1968), he expressed no animosity towards his former captors who, overall, had treated him as well as their circumstances and limited supplies of food and medicine permitted.

Hyland's fair and honourable business dealings in South-East Asia had gained him the trust of the locals and helped to make him rich. He tried to convince the Australian and American governments that, to reduce the influence of the Viet Cong, they needed to subsidise production by South Vietnamese farmers, who were unable to export because of their country's overvalued currency.

Five ft 11 ins (180 cm) tall, Hyland was physically 'tough as teak'. From 1976 he divided his time between Thailand and Australia. The flamboyant 'duck-feather king' built a beach house at Pattaya, Thailand, and a ski-lodge in the shape of a Thai temple at Falls Creek, Victoria, and drove a silver and maroon Bentley formerly owned by Ingrid Bergman. He died on 16 April 1989 at Darlinghurst, Sydney, and was cremated. His children survived him, as did Ann who, with Charles Hap, carried on the business.

Australian, 5 Apr 1969, p 8, 16 July 1976, p 5; *Herald* (Melbourne), 22 May 1969, p 5; *SMH*, 22 Oct 1971, p 14, 10 Nov 1972, p 6; *Sun-Herald* (Sydney), 20 Aug 1989, p 28; A471, item 78167, A1838, item 2034/14/55, B883, item VX104217 (NAA); private information.   DARRYL BENNET

I

IFOULD, EDWARD LISTER (1909-1981), air force officer, industrial chemist and company director, was born on 6 April 1909 at St Peters, Adelaide, eldest of three sons of South Australian-born parents William Herbert Ifould [q.v.9], librarian, and his wife Carrie Eugenie, née Foale. After the family moved to Sydney, Lister was educated at Turramurra College and North Sydney Boys' High School. In 1926 he joined the Colonial Sugar Refining Co. Ltd; he worked as a production chemist in the company's factories in North Queensland and New South Wales. A keen sportsman, he joined Palm Beach Surf Life-Saving Club and Northern Districts Hockey Club, Sydney, and in 1931 was a member of the New South Wales Andrews Pennant hockey team. He played Rugby League football at Innisfail, Queensland, and belonged to Tweed Heads Golf Club, New South Wales.

Five ft 8 ins (173 cm) tall, with brown eyes and hair, strong features, and a dark complexion, Ifould enlisted in the Royal Australian Air Force on 22 July 1940 under the Empire Air Training Scheme. Commissioned on 14 March 1941 as an air observer, he arrived in England in July and undertook operational training before being posted in December to No.97 Squadron of the Royal Air Force's Bomber Command. The squadron was equipped with Manchesters, but in January 1942 new four-engined Lancasters began to arrive. Ifould quickly gained a reputation as a skilled navigator and bomb-aimer.

On 17 April 1942 he participated in a highly dangerous daylight, low-level attack by twelve Lancasters on the diesel-engine factory at Augsburg in southern Germany. Due to enemy flak and fighters, just eight Lancasters succeeded in bombing the target and only five returned to England. Ifould was awarded the Distinguished Flying Cross. He was afterwards appointed squadron navigation officer and in July promoted to acting flight lieutenant. In all, he completed one mission in a Manchester and seventeen in Lancasters before being posted to No.109 Squadron in October.

Flying Mosquito light bombers, No.109 Squadron was one of the first squadrons in Pathfinder Force (No.8 Group). Ifould was again appointed squadron navigation officer. His first sortie was a special mission on the night of 20 December 1942. Leading six Mosquitoes to bomb a power station at Lutterade, the Netherlands, he and his pilot, Squadron Leader H. E. Bufton, were the first to use a blind-bombing technique known as Oboe. On 31 December at Düsseldorf, Germany, they employed Oboe for the first time to mark targets, dropping flares to guide in the main bomber force of Lancasters. Target-marking trials using Oboe continued into the new year and on 4-13 January 1943 Ifould and Bufton guided bombers over the Ruhr. Having been mentioned in despatches, Ifould was awarded a Bar to his DFC.

Made acting squadron leader in March 1943 (temporary July 1944), Ifould served with No.109 Squadron until September, logging up forty-five missions in Mosquitoes. For his skill and outstanding devotion to duty in flying a large number of sorties to targets in the Ruhr and Rhineland, he was awarded the Distinguished Service Order. The citation referred to him as 'a navigator of high merit' whose energy in training others had produced good results. In September-November he was a member of an RAF delegation visiting Washington, and its representative during United States Army trials of special radar equipment.

Back in Britain, Ifould was posted to headquarters, Pathfinder Force, then in January 1944 to headquarters, No.100 (Special Duties) Group, where he became group navigation officer. The most decorated navigator in the RAAF, he returned to Sydney in June and was transferred to the RAAF Reserve on 25 November. That year both his brothers were killed, Elton Murray while serving with the RAAF and Frank Henry while serving with the Royal Australian Navy. On 3 February 1945 at St James's Church of England, King Street, Sydney, Ifould married Mary Frankcomb, née Blackwood, a pilot's widow with a young daughter.

Ifould returned to CSR and rose to managing director of CSR Chemicals Pty Ltd before his retirement in 1971. He was later a director of Marbon Chemical (Australia) Pty Ltd, William Adams & Co. Ltd, QUF Industries Ltd and New Guinea Goldfields Ltd. Two of his passions were surfing and golf. He was president (1972-79) of the Elanora Country Club and a member of the board of the Australia Club. Sailing was another love; he had been a crew member aboard the sloop *Struen Marie* when it won the Sydney to Hobart race in 1951. Survived by his wife and their two daughters and son, and by his stepdaughter, he died on 29 January 1981 at Wahroonga, Sydney, and was cremated. His portrait (1946) by Harold Freedman is held by the Australian War Memorial, Canberra.

J. Herington, *Air War against Germany & Italy 1939-1943* (1954); M. Middlebrook and C. Everitt, *The Bomber Command War Diaries* (1985); K. Delve and P. Jacobs, *The Six-Year Offensive* (1992); A9300, item Ifould E L (NAA); AWM65, item 2788 (AWM); private information.   DENNIS NEWTON

INGAMELLS, LORIS (1892-1981), pharmacist and theosophist, was born on 24 May 1892 at Hawthorn, Melbourne, elder child of Ernest Ingamells, warehouseman, and his wife Otelia, née Lee, both English born. When the family moved to Sydney Loris attended Fort Street Superior Public School. Aged 15, he was apprenticed to a city chemist, J. C. Hallam. In 1911, having completed the prescribed course of study at the University of Sydney, he passed the final examination of the Pharmacy Board of New South Wales but, being under age, was obliged to wait until 1913 for registration as a pharmacist. Of slight build and sharp-featured, he had an activist's temperament: as a student he had complained about the scheduling of botany classes; in 1915 he questioned the election procedures for the Pharmacy Board.

On 10 August 1915 Ingamells enlisted in the Australian Imperial Force and was allocated to the Australian Army Medical Corps. He worked as a dispenser in ships of the Sea Transport Service, and in April 1916 was promoted to staff sergeant. In 1918-19 he served with the 2nd Light Horse Field Ambulance in Palestine and Egypt. Granted leave, he was briefly attached to a firm of manufacturing chemists, Allen & Hanburys Ltd, London, before being discharged from the AIF in Sydney on 31 March 1920.

That year he was appointed chief dispenser at Sydney Hospital. In 1924 he went into private practice; his first shop was at Petersham. He married Madge Renetta Noble, also a chemist, on 28 April 1930 at St Mark's Church of England, Darling Point; they had no children. They moved to Waverley in the Eastern Suburbs, where he later had land interests.

After serving as vice-president of the Pharmaceutical Society of New South Wales, in 1924 Ingamells was elected for a three-year term as president. He addressed the vexed issue of dangerous drugs legislation, with the strong support of the profession. Anxious for professional harmony, and an early champion of a national pharmacy guild, he became the first president (1928-32) of the New South Wales branch of the Federated Pharmaceutical Service Guild of Australia. This organisation soon superseded the New South Wales Association of Master Pharmacists, to which he had also belonged. Ingamells was a member (from 1926) of the Pharmacy Board of New South Wales and its president in 1933 when the University of Sydney decided to introduce a graduate diploma course in the field, but he did not survive the 1935 board elections. In the late 1940s he campaigned against 'free

medicine' and in 1954 evinced concern about reductions in pensioner benefit provisions.

Like his father before him, Ingamells had joined (1909) the Sydney lodge of the Theosophical Society. In January 1921 he served as acting-editor of the Sydney journal of the Order of The Star in the East. He urged world reconstruction 'on saner lines' and opposition to detrimental postwar behaviour such as strikes. By late 1921 he was the honorary organiser of the Theosophical Society Loyalty League. Following the Sydney lodge's agitation for an inquiry into Charles Leadbeater's [q.v.10] conduct, Ingamells, with others, was expelled from the Theosophical Society in 1923. He became a lecturer and the manager of the book depot for a new group, the Independent Theosophical Society.

A member of the Isis Lodge, Sydney, Ingamells published *An Outline of Freemasonry* (1933?). He was captain (1927-32) of the Moore Park Golf Club, Sydney's first public course. Survived by his wife, he died on 23 September 1981 at Turramurra and was cremated.

G. Haines, *'The Grains and Threepenn'orths of Pharmacy'* (1976) and *A History of the Pharmacy Board of New South Wales* (1997); J. Roe, *Beyond Belief* (1986); E. Huber, *For the Common Good: Moore Park Golf Club 1920-2000* (2001); *SMH*, 2 Dec 1924, p 8, 19 Dec 1928, p 13, 13 Apr 1933, p 10, 14 June 1933, p 12, 27 Apr 1948, p 2, 8 June 1954, p 2; B2455, item Ingamells Loris (NAA).   JILL ROE

IRVINE, KENNETH JOHN (1940-1990), Rugby League footballer, was born on 5 March 1940 at Cremorne, Sydney, only son of Sydney-born parents John Bernard Irvine, butcher, and his wife Doris May, née McCabe. Ken grew up at Cammeray, was educated at Marist Brothers' Boys' School, Mosman, and worked briefly as a beer plumber. Initially attracted to baseball, he was talent-spotted at a local Rugby League schools' carnival by a North Sydney official. He played his maiden first-grade game for the club in 1958. The following season 'Mongo', nicknamed apparently because of his slightly Asiatic appearance, scored twenty-three tries. He was a member of the 1959 Kangaroo tour to England and France, quickly overcoming the negative connotation attached to the sobriquet 'Better Brakes' that he had attracted (implying a proclivity to slow down before tackles).

Of nuggety build (5 ft 8 ins or 173 cm; 11 st. 8 lb. or 73.5 kg) Irvine was blessed with scorching speed, flawless positional sense and safe hands. Together with Brian Bevan, the expatriate Australian who played for Warrington in the British competition, Irvine was the code's most outstanding winger after World War II, of comparable status to Harold Horder [q.v.9] in an earlier era. In fifteen years in the game, twelve with North Sydney, Irvine scored some 300 tries in about 340 games, including 33 in 31 Test matches. He retired from football after winning the premiership with the Manly-Warringah club in 1972 and 1973. At Dubbo in 1963 he had run 100 yards (91 m) in 9.3 seconds, setting a world professional sprint record. A celebrated attempt to outrun a racehorse was predictably unsuccessful —though popular memory of the contest against Gili over 60 yards (55 m) at Kembla Grange racecourse in August 1963 often suggests otherwise. He also enjoyed all forms of watersports.

Irvine had married Mavis Marguirite (Valerie) Simmonds, a typist, on 25 November 1961 at St Mary's Catholic Church, North Sydney. Outside professional sprinting and football, he worked as a sales representative for sporting goods companies and as a sports journalist. His rugged good looks led to some modelling and made him a 'natural' for the game's increasing commercialism. Despite his contractual battles with the club, North Sydney fans likened him, as the journalist Mike Gibson quipped, to 'Captain Marvel, Superman, Brick Bradford and Batman and Robin all rolled into one'. An unassuming, likeable and knockabout Australian, Irvine was an enthusiastic punter and part-time larrikin.

In 1982 Irvine moved to the Gold Coast, where he worked as a sales representative with a poker-machine manufacturer and as a journalist. Part of a robust community of retired Sydney footballers, he played touch football with a local hotel team, briefly acted as sprint trainer for a Gold Coast league team and led Kangaroo supporters' tours to England. In 1983 he was diagnosed with chronic myeloid leukaemia. Survived by his wife and their daughter and son, he died on 22 December 1990 at Brisbane and was cremated. The scoreboard at North Sydney Oval, named in his honour in 1991, is a fitting testimonial to his try-scoring prowess.

M. Andrews, *ABC of Rugby League* (1992); I. Heads, *True Blue* (1992); A. Moore, *The Mighty Bears!* (1996); private information.

ANDREW MOORE

IRVING, FREDA MARY HOWY (1903-1984), journalist, was born on 16 September 1903 at Victoria Barracks, Melbourne, third and youngest child of Godfrey George Howy Irving [q.v.9], military officer, and his wife Ada Minnie Margueritha, daughter of Frederick Thomas Derham [q.v.4]. Freda was educated at Lauriston Girls' School, Malvern. The family was utterly military: her brother, Ronald Godfrey Howy Irving (1898-1965), became a brigadier; her sister, Sybil Howy Irving [q.v.14], was the first controller of the Australian Women's Army Service. Barely five feet (152 cm) tall, Freda was perhaps destined for a different profession.

A meeting with the women's editor of the *Evening Sun* in 1925 led to her employment as a journalist and a social writer for that paper. In 1932, after it was taken over by the Herald & Weekly Times Ltd and renamed the *Sun News-Pictorial*, she was appointed social editor. Her first big break came in 1936, when she went to London for the *Herald* to cover the abdication of King Edward VIII and the coronation of King George VI. In 1940 she became publicity officer for the Victorian Red Cross Society and in 1943—almost inevitably—joined the AWAS. Commissioned next month, she served on Sybil's staff as amenities officer for the three women's army services and later in the Directorate of Public Relations. She left the army in December 1945 as a captain.

Feisty and direct, Irving could handle those in authority, whether editors or senior officers, with ease. In 1946 she returned to the *Sun* and, after freelance work in 1948, joined the *Argus*, working for Gladys Hain [q.v.9] on its women's magazine. In 1952, in poor health, she left, briefly tried farming, then rejoined and covered the Royal Tour in 1954. Women's editor when the paper closed in 1957, she made sure that every member of her staff got a job. It was not so easy finding one for herself: she termed this condition being 'on the beach', and she was there a number of times during her career. She worked in public relations (1958-63) and, after a period (1963-65) as Melbourne editor of the *Women's Weekly*, she had a merry if unsuccessful attempt at running a licensed grocery at Croydon.

With diverse connections and respected for her generosity, integrity and versatility, Irving returned to journalism on the *Sunday Observer* in 1967, and over the following years worked on the *Camberwell Free Press*, the *Age*, and as Melbourne editor for *Woman's Day*, and wrote the gossip page for the Sydney *Sun-Herald* and articles for *Pol* magazine. The first female president (1972) of the Melbourne Press Club, she was appointed MBE in 1981 and honoured by colleagues from around Australia at a dinner at Melbourne's Hilton Hotel in September. Apart from journalism, her greatest passion was horse-racing: she was a member of a small syndicate that owned a mare, Freda's Joy. Gravel-voiced, hard-drinking, hard-smoking and, on occasions, hard-swearing, Freda Irving was still writing when she died, unmarried, on 26 September 1984 at Kilmore. She was buried in Fawkner cemetery.

L. Ollif, *Women in Khaki* (1981); K. Dunstan, *Informed Sources* (2001); *Age* (Melbourne), 30 Oct 1981, p 26; *Australian*, 28 Sept 1984, p 9.

KEITH DUNSTAN

IRWIN, Sir JAMES CAMPBELL (1906-1990), architect and lord mayor, was born on 23 June 1906 in North Adelaide, eldest of four sons of Australian-born parents Francis James Irwin, sharebroker, and his wife Annabella Margaret Campbell, née Mann. James was educated first at private North Adelaide schools and then at the Collegiate School of St Peter (1918-23). Articled to the architect G. K. Soward [q.v.12] in 1924, he entered the South Australian School of Mines and Industries. He joined the firm of Woods, Bagot [q.v.7], Jory & Laybourne Smith [q.v.11] as a draughtsman in 1927 and next year was admitted as an associate of the South Australian Institute of Architects. In 1930 he was made a partner and the firm became Woods, Bagot, Laybourne Smith & Irwin. After co-winning the competition to design a new wing of Adelaide Children's Hospital, he married Kathleen Agnes Orr on 23 November 1933 at St Stephen's Presbyterian Church, Sydney.

With an open face and erect stance, Irwin was regarded as 'a gentle gentleman'; later, to building contractors his insistence on standards made him a 'tough nut'. His first independent designs included Callendale, near Lucindale (1933), the Elder, Smith [qq.v.4,6] & Co. Ltd sheep-sales building (1933) and the merchandise pavilion (1937) at Wayville Showgrounds, Adelaide, and city and suburban houses.

Having been commissioned as a lieutenant in the Militia in 1933, Irwin was promoted to captain in 1939. On 6 May 1940 he transferred to the Australian Imperial Force as a major and was posted to the 2/7th Field Regiment. He arrived in the Middle East in December and was appointed brigade major, Royal Australian Artillery, 9th Division, in June 1941. Five months later he became general staff officer, 2nd grade (operations), at 9th Division headquarters. He returned to Australia in February 1943. Made GSO1 of the 11th Division and promoted to lieutenant colonel in July, he flew to Papua, where the division trained before operating in the Ramu Valley, New Guinea. He was appointed OBE in 1945. From May 1944 he instructed at the Staff School (Australia). In March 1945 he was appointed GSO1 (combined operations), Advanced Land Headquarters, Morotai, Netherlands East Indies. He served in Manila in May-September. His AIF appointment terminated in Adelaide on 7 January 1946.

Irwin succeeded Walter Bagot as the architect for St Peter's Cathedral (1945-74) and filled the same role for St Peter's College. In 1957 his firm became co-ordinating architects to the University of Adelaide, with Irwin in charge. The second architect for the Cottage Homes Inc., he served on its committee from 1935 to 1975. He was his firm's main architect and supervisor for the Anglican St Laurence's Home for the Aged (1951-63). A member of the board of management of the Home for Incurables from 1935, he was chairman of its building and grounds committee and the home's president in 1967-81. He designed the Advertiser Newspapers Ltd building (1959) and was the architect for General Motors-Holden's [q.v.9] Pty Ltd at Woodville and at Elizabeth.

From 1965 until his retirement in 1974, Irwin was senior partner of his firm. The 'biggest influence' on his architectural thinking was his cousin Leighton Irwin [q.v.9], but Bagot, Le Corbusier, Charles A. Platt, Walter Gropius, Sir Edwin Lutyens and John Nash contributed to his neo-Georgianism and his practical and stylistic reticence. He also practised Dutch modernism, touched neo-Bauhaus principles obliquely, and embraced steel-frame functionalism, although he believed that in Adelaide to enclose buildings with glass was 'the ultimate in stupidity'.

President (1956-58) of the South Australian Institute of Architects, Irwin was a fellow (1940), federal president (1962-63) and life fellow (1970) of the Royal Australian Institute of Architects. He became a fellow of the Royal Institute of British Architects (1956), the (Royal) Australian Planning Institute (1957), the Royal Society of Arts, London (1960), and the Institute of Directors in Australia (1965). In 1964-70 he served on the National Capital Planning Committee. After his retirement he was made an honorary member of the Master Builders' Association of South Australia.

Irwin was an Adelaide city councillor (1935-40, 1949-53), alderman (1953-63, 1966-72) and lord mayor (1963-66). He formed (1963) the Lord Mayor's Cultural Committee, from which the Festival Theatre evolved, and served the Adelaide Festival of Arts as president (1964-66), chairman of the board of governors (1969-73) and board member (1967-68, 1974-78). He was president of the South Australian branch of Toc H (1952-55, 1985-88), the council of the South Australian School of Art (1966-72), the Adelaide International Film Festival (1968-71) and the Pioneers' Association of South Australia (1968-73), and founding chairman (1981-86) of the Co-op Foundation. His precision and integrity brought commendation in both his architectural and civic activities. He was knighted in 1971.

Sir James died on 22 June 1990 in Adelaide and was cremated with Anglican rites. Predeceased by his wife (1989) and daughter (1990), he was survived by his son, Jamie (1937-2005), who became president (1997-2002) of the Legislative Council. Sir Ivor Hele's portrait of Irwin is held by the family.

M. Page, *Sculptors in Space* (1986); *Advertiser* (Adelaide), 5 Nov 1984, p 2, 23 June 1990, p 19; B883, item SX3200 (NAA); series S177, S202 and S255

(Architecture Museum, Univ of SA); taped reminiscences by J. C. Irwin (ts, 1978, Adelaide City Council Archives); J. Gasper, interview with J. C. Irwin (ts, 1980, SLSA); Irwin papers (SLSA); Royal Austn Inst of Architects (SA) records (SLSA); private information.   BRIDGET JOLLY

IWANOFF, IWAN (1919-1986), architect, was born on 2 July 1919 at Küsstendil (Kyustendil), Bulgaria, elder son of Nickolai Iwanow, journalist and poet, and his wife Maria, née Schopowa. Raised in an artistic family, Iwan studied fine arts before undergoing military training. On his father's advice, in 1941 he enrolled in architecture in Germany at the Technische Hochschule, Munich (Dip.Eng. and Arch., 1946). He graduated with high praise for an exceptional final project, a design for a chapel. Known as Iwan Nickolow Iwanow as a child, he changed his name to Iwan Nickoloff Iwanoff during his student years, and soon further simplified it to Iwan Iwanoff. In the difficult postwar years, he lived at Laufen, Bavaria, and supplemented his income by selling caricatures. On 25 October 1947 at the registrar office, Laufen, he married Dietlinde Hildegunde Zenns. In 1948-49 he worked with the modernist architect Emil Freymuth at Munich.

Migrating to Australia as part of the International Refugee Organization resettlement scheme, Iwanoff and his wife arrived at Fremantle, Western Australia, on 2 March 1950. He was offered employment as a draughtsman with Krantz & Sheldon, Perth, a large architectural firm specialising in the design of flats, and in time became senior draughtsman in charge of staff. He also took on private architectural projects. In 1956 he was naturalised. He worked with the Melbourne architectural firm of Yuncken, Freeman Bros, Griffiths & Simpson in 1960. After a visit to West Germany, where he was accepted as a member of the Bund Deutscher Architekten (Federation of German Architects), he returned in December 1961 to Krantz & Sheldon. In 1963 he obtained registration as an architect in Western Aus-

tralia and Victoria, and immediately established the Studio of Iwanoff in Perth. He became an associate of the Royal Australian Institute of Architects in 1964 and a fellow in 1972.

A gifted architect, Iwanoff had exceptional drawing abilities, an innovative 'expressionistic' approach to design and detailing and, above all, a conviction that architecture was an art. In 1963-86 his small office produced work of high quality, including numerous houses. His creative use of concrete blocks drew richness out of every aspect of the utilitarian. The Iwanoff house, Lifford Road, Floreat Park (1965-67), a combination of architectural office and living accommodation, is a fine example. He also designed shop fronts and interiors in central Perth, and one larger project, the civic administration centre and public library at Northam (1969-74).

Although dapper and charming, Iwanoff displayed many contradictions. He could be cautious with strangers but was outgoing with friends and clients. Architectural students regarded him as a friend and mentor. Despite his commitment to Australia Iwanoff remained a European in spirit, valuing the artistic traditions and standards of excellence that Europe represented and hopeful that Australians would aspire to these values. Survived by his wife and their two sons, he died of pneumonia on 7 October 1986 in Perth and was buried in Karrakatta cemetery. In 1991 the Library and Information Service of Western Australia held an exhibition of his architectural drawings, most of which are held by the State Archives of Western Australia.

J. Nichols and D. Richards, *The Art of Architecture* (1991); S. Anderson and M. Nordeck (eds), *Krantz & Sheldon* (1996); *Architect, W.A.*, vol 25, no 4, 1985, p 22, vol 26, no 4, 1986, p 20; D. Richards, 'A Temple for Suburban Living', *Transition*, no 44/45, 1994, p 48; *Monument*, Aug/Sept 2001, p 104; A446, items 1955/26451 and 1960/35627, A12014, item 252-253, K1331, item Iwanoff (NAA); Iwanoff papers, and Krantz & Sheldon papers (SLWA); private information.   DUNCAN RICHARDS

J

JACKA, BERYL ELAINE (1913-1989), administrator, was born on 9 June 1913 at Hawthorn, Melbourne, fifth of seven children of Victorian-born parents William John Jacka, butcher, and his wife Edith Selina, née Oscar. Educated at Auburn State and Milverton schools, Beryl won a gold medal for shorthand at Stotts Business College and in 1936 joined the Australasian Institute of Mining and Metallurgy as a typist (the only woman in its office); she became acting secretary in 1945. Appointed secretary in 1948, over the next twenty-eight years she saw the institute grow from a membership of 1200 in fourteen branches to 6500 in thirty-five branches. Imparting 'a vital air of efficiency' (according to the *Age*), she was closely involved with all aspects of this expansion.

As secretary Jacka reported to the AusIMM council, in particular to the annually elected president, who came to rely on her judgment. She travelled regularly to the institute's branches across Australia and attended several overseas congresses, while also publishing many volumes of technical papers and proceedings and developing a wide, often first-hand knowledge of Australian mining science and industry. Planning and managing thirty-one highly successful annual conferences for the institute, she was also organising secretary for two large international meetings in Australia and New Zealand: the Empire Mining and Metallurgical Congress (1953) for some five hundred delegates, and the Eighth Commonwealth Mining and Metallurgical Congress (1965), with 2300 registrations. In 1959 the Australian Minerals Industry Research Association Ltd was established under her expert administration, with (Sir) Maurice Mawby [q.v.15] as inaugural president.

Tough but fair, authoritative and demanding, Jacka drew on her experience in Baptist Church youth groups and the Girl Guides movement. She set exacting standards of work, behaviour and dress to her younger, female staff, and rewarded good results. At her retirement in 1976, she was made an honorary member of the institute—a remarkable tribute in a then essentially male-dominated profession. The president, C. H. Martin, praised 'the concentration, the search for perfection, and the originality of ideas which characterize Miss Jacka's services'. She was then appointed executive officer of the new Australian Academy of Technological Sciences (Engineering was added in 1987), and similarly assisted in its development, organising thirteen symposia and two international convocations before illness forced her resignation in 1989.

Miss Jacka's prodigious memory extended to details of the lives of those with whom she worked: she never forgot birthdays and was charming and hospitable to staff in social gatherings. She had little time for hobbies but as often as possible she watched her favourite Australian Rules football team, Melbourne, play on Saturday afternoons. Conservative in her dress, she could seem reserved behind the strong, dark-rimmed spectacles she wore from middle age. She was appointed MBE (1965) and AM (1979). Beryl Jacka died on 27 December 1989 at Glen Iris and was cremated. An annual award in her name was established to recognise service to the AusIMM.

Austn Academy of Technological Sciences and Engineering, *Annual Report*, 1989-90, p 51; *Age* (Melbourne), 30 Aug 1949, p 5; private information and personal knowledge.

D. F. FAIRWEATHER

JACKLIN, PAUL SEYMOUR (1914-1982), radio producer and compère, and advertising executive, was born on 25 January 1914 in Pretoria, South Africa, one of three sons of Seymour Jacklin, public servant, and his wife Annette Hope, née Palfrey. Aged 12 he moved to Geneva, where his father worked at the League of Nations. Educated in South Africa and England, Paul excelled at Cranleigh School, Surrey, and briefly studied English literature at St Catharine's College, Cambridge. He turned to the theatre, learning stage-managing at the Croydon Repertory Theatre and acting in John Van Druten's *Young Woodley*. On his return to South Africa in 1935, Jacklin joined the African Broadcasting Co., which became the South African Broadcasting Corporation. In Cape Town he changed the style of children's programs, modelling them on those for adults. On 11 June 1938 at the Rondebosch Congregational Church, Cape Town, he married Olwen Porzig; four days later they sailed for Australia.

From February 1939 Jacklin worked for the Australian Broadcasting Commission as a producer in Sydney. His first production of note was the serial 'Singapore Spy'. In April he was assigned by the ABC to cover in Sydney the embarkation of Prime Minister Joseph Lyons's [q.v.10] body for carriage by sea to Tasmania. The *Wireless Weekly* admired 'his beautiful and sympathetic commentary'. Equally accomplished as an on-air voice and as a director and creator of programs, Jacklin devised, compèred and produced the variety show 'Merry-Go-Round', among others, for the ABC in

Melbourne; a one-hour weekly presentation, performed before a studio audience, it ran for nearly two years. A government restriction order, issued in March 1941 because of his alleged anti-British views, prevented him from broadcasting. (On arrival in Australia he had attempted to 'build up a more theatrical personality' by claiming to be a Boer.) He enlisted in the Australian Imperial Force on 13 June 1941 but was discharged as medically unfit in April next year without serving overseas. The restriction order was amended in April 1943 to allow him to write material and was revoked in June 1945.

Jacklin joined the commercial broadcasting station 2UE, where he remained for twelve years. He produced 'Crackerjack', another variety show, but soon turned predominantly to drama. As 2UE's head of production he was responsible for all broadcasts, including Max Afford's [q.v.13] serials 'Danger Unlimited' and 'Hagen's Circus'. After approving the purchase of a series, he directed the early episodes himself to establish its character. He was the national program director for the Major Broadcasting Network, of which 2UE was the key station.

When the 'Lux Radio Theatre' returned on 2UE in 1955, Jacklin became its producer-director. After its demise a year later he left the station to join J. Walter Thompson Australia Pty Ltd, the advertising agency behind Lux. Jacklin's energy, self-confidence and talent led to his becoming a director of the Australian company in 1963, director of creative services and deputy-chairman in 1971, vice-president of the parent company in the United States of America and chairman and chief executive of the Australian agency in 1973. He retired in 1980. Survived by his wife and their son, he died of cancer on 24 December 1982 at Bowral and was cremated.

R. Lane, *The Golden Age of Australian Radio Drama 1923 1960* (1994); *SMH*, 11 July 1938, p 5, 2 Aug 1938, 'Women's Supp', p 2, 15 May 1954, p 4, 19 Oct 1961, p 1, 16 Oct 1963, p 20; *Wireless Weekly*, 19 Apr 1939, p 3; *Austn Financial Review*, 18 Dec 1973, p 9; B883, item VX57644, A367, item C65511, MP529/2, item Jacklin/PS (NAA); private information.   RICHARD LANE

JACKSON, DENYS GABRIEL MAURICE (1899-1986), writer, commentator and Catholic apologist, was born on 8 August 1899 at Toxteth Park, Liverpool, England, sixth of eight children of Fred Jackson, commercial clerk, and his wife Charlotte Amy Fuller, née Lester. At first educated at home by his mother, Denys was briefly at the Worcester Cathedral and Westminster Abbey choir schools before attending Liverpool Institute High School for Boys. Fascinated from an early age by history,

he had read Gibbon's *Decline and Fall of the Roman Empire* by the age of 14. By 17 he had converted from High Anglicanism via an enthusiasm for the Orthodox Church to Catholicism, mainly under the influence of John Henry Newman's writings and example. Like his mother he favoured a militant Christianity.

Commissioned in the Gloustershire Regiment on 23 June 1918, Jackson served in England during World War I. He then studied at the University of Liverpool (BA, 1921; MA, 1925), specialising in Jacobean and medieval history. After instructing in a dancing academy, he taught history at St Edmund's College, Ware—one of his fellow teachers was the renowned Catholic priest and writer Ronald Knox—and from 1924 at St Bede's College, Manchester. Having responded successfully to a government advertisement for teachers in Victoria, he sailed for Australia in 1926. From Durban he sent a cable to Charlotte Augusta ('Rose') Heckford, asking her to follow him; they were married at St Francis's Church, Melbourne, on 6 May 1927. His first posting was to Warracknabeal. In 1928-34 he taught at Melbourne High School.

In 1931 Jackson joined a group of young Catholic intellectuals eager to study their faith in depth and to apply it actively. Forming the Campion Society, they discussed the writings of Hilaire Belloc, G. K. Chesterton, Christopher Dawson, Jacques Maritain and others, as well as the papal encyclicals on social issues. Jackson himself found a kindred spirit in Charles Maurras, founder of the right-wing Action Française movement, of which the Vatican disapproved. Older than most members of the Campion Society, some of whom were later to achieve distinction in academic, legal and diplomatic fields, he exerted a strong influence on them.

Soon Jackson's deep knowledge of history and his gifts as a writer and speaker attracted wider notice: in 1933 he was engaged as an editorial writer for the weekly *Advocate*, of which he became a full-time staff member in 1934. That year he commenced regular Sunday night broadcasts on radio-station 3AW's 'Catholic Hour'. It was the beginning of a half-century-long career as one of the most influential Catholic lay figures in Australia. His prolific writing also appeared regularly in Melbourne's other Catholic weekly, the *Tribune*, which he edited from 1935, and, from the early 1940s, in *News Weekly*. He once estimated that he wrote ten thousand words for publication every week.

Confidently offering usually well informed comment on a wide range of global, national and religious affairs, Jackson used several pseudonyms, including 'Sulla' (in the *Advocate*), 'John C. Calhoun' (in *News Weekly*) and 'The Onlooker' on the 'Catholic Hour'. His forthright views came to be regarded by many of his Catholic readers and listeners in Victoria as the settled Church position on major issues, some of them contentious. In the 1930s he defended Mussolini's invasion of Abyssinia, although he was not uncritical of Italian fascism, much preferring the style and policies of Salazar in Portugal. While he showed no sympathy for Nazism, he believed for some time that conventional diplomatic and peacemaking means could be effective in dealing with Hitler. He deplored all attacks on the Jewish people, once intervening to prevent the Advocate Press printing the outpourings of a notoriously anti-Semitic Carmelite priest. His support for Franco during the Spanish Civil War derived from his unqualified opposition to communism, a position he maintained during and after World War II.

Jackson's anti-communism was also central to his approach to national politics, and particularly to the split in the Australian Labor Party after 1955. He consistently backed the policies advocated by one of his closest friends from the Campion Society, B. A. Santamaria. In his pamphlet *Australian Dream* (1947) Jackson propagated a utopian vision of a less urbanised and largely Catholic Australia, where idealised feudal and medieval ways would be revived. He applauded the work of the National Civic Council and the Democratic Labor Party, and fully endorsed American and Australian involvement in the Vietnam War.

In spite of his English origin and monarchist sympathies, Jackson became an ardent Australian nationalist, insisting that his adopted land be seen as 'no mere satellite of a distant country'. He denounced the White Australia policy, calling for an increased intake of migrants. On most matters, he shared the views of another of his close friends, Archbishop Daniel Mannix [q.v.10]. Jackson remained cautiously conservative on theological questions. He developed serious misgivings about tendencies in Catholic observance and ecumenism associated with the Second Vatican Council (1962-65). Equally, towards the end of his life, he admitted that his anti-communism had adversely affected his judgment on some matters including the true nature of fascism in Europe.

Larger than life and mildly eccentric, Jackson was described by some as an Australian Chesterton. His high tenor voice, with its occasionally vehement and sarcastic tone, might have given the impression of a prickly and formidable character. To those who knew him, however, he was a simple, humble, kindly man, unattached to money or material goods and deeply devoted to his family. He gave his last broadcast in 1980 and his writing slowed at that time as he suffered several strokes and fading eyesight—an especially heavy blow for such a prodigious reader. Predeceased by his wife (1979), and survived by two sons and a daughter, Denys Jackson died on 7 November 1986 at Wantirna South and was buried in Brighton cemetery. A portrait by Bernard Lawson was once entered for the Archibald prize.

N. Brennan, *The Politics of Catholics* (1972); G. Henderson, *Mr Santamaria and the Bishops* (1982); C. H. Jory, *The Campion Society* (1986); P. Ormonde (ed), *Santamaria* (2000); B. Duncan, *Crusade or Conspiracy* (2001); *Advocate* (Melbourne), 29 May 1980, p 3, 28 Apr 1983, p 10, 13 Nov 1986, p 5; *News Weekly* (Melbourne), 19 Nov 1986, p 11; private information.   MICHAEL COSTIGAN

JACKSON, DONALD ROBERT (1915-1986), soldier, was born on 12 October 1915 at Sunningdale, Surrey, England, elder son of ROBERT EDWARD JACKSON (1886-1948), army officer, and his wife Edith Marguerite, née Vautin. Robert had been born on 1 January 1886 at Crows Nest, Queensland. In 1907 he was commissioned in the Commonwealth Cadet Corps and in 1911 in the Permanent Military Forces, with which he served in Western Australia. Joining the Australian Imperial Force in November 1914, he embarked as adjutant of the 10th Light Horse Regiment. On 29 May 1915 he was wounded in action on Gallipoli. He convalesced in England then held staff appointments with the 3rd Division on the Western Front. For this work, he was appointed to the Légion d'honneur (1917), awarded the Distinguished Service Order (1918) and appointed CMG (1919).

Back in Australia in 1920, Jackson resumed his career in the permanent forces. He was appointed to lead Northern Command in May 1940 and promoted to substantive major general in July. Twelve months later he was removed to Western Command, and effectively from the chance of a fighting command. He believed that he was sidelined for having opposed the 'Brisbane Line' strategy while in Queensland. Early in 1942 he retired. His disappointment is recorded in Donald Jackson's unpublished memoir held by the Australian War Memorial, Canberra. Robert Jackson died of pneumonia on 24 November 1948 at Heidelberg, Melbourne, and was cremated. His wife, and their daughter and two sons, survived him.

Donald was educated at Sydney Boys' High School and entered the Royal Military College, Duntroon, Federal Capital Territory, in the small class of 1934, becoming head cadet in his final year. After graduation he was allocated to the infantry and posted to the Sydney University Regiment so that he could study at the university (BA, 1949). He was with Darwin Mobile Force when World War II broke out in 1939. Transferring to the AIF, he sailed for the Middle East as adjutant of the 2/1st Battalion with the rank of captain. In 1940-41 he performed well in the fighting in Libya. He participated in the Greek campaign (April 1941) as a staff officer on the headquarters of I Corps. When the evacuation began, he supervised the embarkation of the nursing staff. Following a rearguard action near Argos, he was captured but escaped the same afternoon. He collected a force of about two hundred Allied troops and, after a hazardous journey, arrived on Crete, from which he was evacuated to Palestine. His actions won him the DSO.

Appointed brigade major of the 24th Brigade in Syria, Jackson moved to Egypt in June 1942 for the operations that culminated in the battle of El Alamein in October-November. Next year he sailed for Australia, arriving in February. He was an assistant to the director of military intelligence at Advanced Land Headquarters, Brisbane, before becoming second-in-command of the 2/28th Battalion in July 1944. From June 1945 he fought in British North Borneo. In 1946-47 he commanded the 67th Battalion in Japan. His postwar appointments included director of infantry at Army Headquarters, Melbourne, and commandant of the Officer Cadet School, Portsea. He retired from the army in 1968 as a brigadier.

Jackson was a man of solid build and character. His fellow officers found him dour and taciturn, though he was a shrewd judge of the temperament of Australian soldiers. From 1968 he held management positions with Hammersley Iron Pty Ltd at Dampier, Western Australia. He was the first member and chairman (1975) of the Defence Forces Credit Union, Australian Capital Territory. In retirement he lived for a time in Fiji. On 25 January 1944 at St Andrew's Presbyterian Church, Southport, Queensland, he had married Peggie Elaine Taylor, a Women's Auxiliary Australian Air Force security officer; the marriage was dissolved in 1947. He married Anita Mary Edith Urquhart on 6 December 1949 at St John's Church of England, Toorak, Melbourne. Survived by his wife and their daughter and two sons, he died of myocardial infarction on 12 January 1986 in Canberra and was cremated with Anglican rites.

G. Long, *To Benghazi* (1952), *Greece, Crete and Syria* (1953), and *The Final Campaigns* (1963); B. Maughan, *Tobruk and El Alamein* (1966); D. M. Horner, *Crisis of Command* (1978); Donald Robert Jackson memoir (AWM); private information.

MICHAEL O'BRIEN

JACOBS, HENRY OSBORNE (1888-1988), musician, was born on 13 July 1888 at Edgbaston, Birmingham, England, son of Welsh-born Solomon Jacobs, musician, and his wife Louisa Jane, née Stockham. Educated at Catholic schools at Blackpool, Harry showed an early musical talent. In 1908, already an experienced performer—singing, playing the piano and leading a small band—he was engaged by the music hall star Ada Reeve as her accompanist. Skilled at orchestration, he became her musical director and conductor on tours to South Africa and North America, and of Australia, where he gave patriotic concerts in 1914, 1917 and 1918. On 7 February 1921 at St Paul's Church of England, Marton, near Blackpool, Lancaster, he married Violet Lucie Maud Bishop, a solo dancer with Reeve's company. After a long season of *Spangles*, a variety show, at Melbourne's Palace theatre in 1922, Jacobs, his wife and his mother-in-law settled in Australia.

For the next six years Jacobs was based in Sydney as conductor and arranger for J. C. Williamson's [q.v.6] Ltd, touring Australia and New Zealand with musicals such as *No No Nanette* and Gilbert and Sullivan operas. For a time involved with the Tivoli vaudeville circuit, in 1927 he was appointed conductor at the new Palais Theatre at St Kilda, Melbourne, where, until 1949, immaculately dressed in bow-tie and tails, he led an orchestra that supported variety acts and played light classics before film screenings. Amid manpower shortages in the 1940s he also formed and conducted the highly regarded Palais ladies' orchestra. As Madame Saronova, his wife became a noted ballet teacher of the Cecchetti method.

During the 1930s Jacobs conducted and orchestrated scores for Eftee Films, composed music for Charles Chauvel's [q.v.7] film *Heritage* (1935) and was musical arranger for Frank Thring's [q.v.12] première production of Varney Monk's [q.v.10] musical *Collits' Inn*, with Gladys Moncrieff and George Wallace [qq.v.10,12] at the Princess Theatre, Melbourne, in 1933. From 1941 his ensemble played for the popular 3UZ radio programs 'Fifty and Over', a nostalgic show for 'old-timers', and 'Are You an Artist?', an amateur talent quest. Encouraging stars such as the mouth organist Horrie Dargie in their early careers, Jacobs also directed variety at the Plaza, Northcote, and appeared in Tivoli shows featuring Tommy Trinder and Winifred Atwell. In later years he worked as music librarian for the Tivoli and for Crawford Television Productions, and directed, arranged and conducted Melbourne's Carols by Candlelight concerts. At eighty years of age he still accompanied his wife's Australian National Theatre ballet school classes.

In the chancy world of show business, Jacobs was never unemployed. He won respect from orchestra members for his sound musicianship. Theatre and radio managers could rely on him. He was always sober, cheerful and polite; he led a quiet life in suburban Brighton, where he served as a vestryman at

St Andrew's Church of England. Survived by his wife and daughter, Harry Jacobs died on 17 January 1988 at East Brighton and was cremated.

K. Dreyfus, *Sweethearts of Rhythm* (1989); *Herald* (Melbourne), 15 July 1968, p 9, 13 July 1987, p 16; private information. MIMI COLLIGAN

JACOBS, SIR ROLAND ELLIS (1891-1981), businessman, was born on 28 February 1891 in Adelaide, youngest of six children of Samuel Joshua Jacobs [q.v.9], a South Australian-born merchant, and his wife Caroline, née Ellis, from Victoria. Roland was educated at Geelong College, Victoria, and the Adelaide Shorthand and Business Training Academy. Rejected on medical grounds for active service in World War I, he served as a training and administrative officer in army camps in South Australia. On 29 August 1917 at New Farm, Brisbane, he married with Jewish rites Olga Hertzberg (d.1969). After working in several clerical positions he became South Australian agent for the Perth firm F. A. Henriques Ltd, acquired in 1930 by the Sydney-based company Mauri Bros & Thomson Ltd, suppliers to the brewing industry. Appointed assistant-manager and then manager, in 1942-43 he was president of the Adelaide Chamber of Commerce.

In 1948 Jacobs joined the board of his father's old firm, the South Australian Brewing Co. Ltd. Two months later he was named managing director and in 1951 chairman. His strong leadership in this dual role was a crucial factor in the development of the company after the difficult times of the Depression and World War II. In 1950 he selected a competent general manager in C. R. Aitken, allowing him to devote more time to the promotion of the company and the brewing industry. In June 1961 Jacobs stepped down as managing director but he continued as chairman until March 1965 and finally retired as a director two years later. He was chairman (1965-74) of the Executor Trustee & Agency Co. of South Australia Ltd.

Committed to community service, through his corporate associations Jacobs raised funds for the more than thirty organisations that he represented. He was president of the Crippled Children's Association of South Australia (1947-51); the Australian Advisory Council for the Physically Handicapped (from 1951); the South Australian branch of the Royal Society for the Prevention of Cruelty to Animals (1949-65); and Meals on Wheels (1964-69). Vice-president of the South Australian division of the National Heart Foundation from 1960, with Sir Ivan Jose [q.v.14] he supported the establishment in 1963 of the Medical Foundation, University of Adelaide. He served on the board of management of the Royal Adelaide and Queen Elizabeth hospitals (1954-57).

In the 1940s Jacobs had sat on the State advisory committee of the Australian Broadcasting Commission and in 1948-65 on the committee of the South Australian Orchestral Association. He was a founding member (1960-64) of the board of governors of the Adelaide Festival of Arts. President of the Rotary Club of Adelaide (1938-39) and of Adelaide's Commonwealth Club (1952), he was also a member of the Adelaide Club. He was knighted in 1963.

Sir Norman Young, Jacobs's successor as chairman of the SA Brewing Co., said: 'He had great charm, modesty, simplicity and impeccable manners. He never pretended. He commanded both respect and affection'. Although born into the Jewish faith, Jacobs was not a strict follower of its rituals. On 30 November 1970 he married Esther Cook MBE, formerly Lipman, a widow and daughter of V. L. Solomon [q.v.12], in a civil ceremony at her Leabrook home. Survived by his wife and the two daughters and son of his first marriage, Sir Roland died on 28 June 1981 at Leabrook and was buried in Centennial Park cemetery. His portrait by Sir William Dargie is held by his daughter Doreen Bridges AM.

M. Cudmore (comp), *History of the South Australian Brewing Company Limited* (1988); N. S. Young, *Figuratively Speaking* (1991); J. Healey (ed), *S.A.'s Greats* (2001); *News* (Adelaide), 13 Sept 1961, p 20; *Advertiser* (Adelaide), 30 June 1981, p 3; private information. ALISON PAINTER

JAMES, RICHARD HAUGHTON ('JIMMY') (1906-1985), designer, advertising executive and painter, was born on 22 August 1906 at West Grinstead, Sussex, England, son of Montague Gifford James, a major in the Indian Army soon to become an Anglican clergyman, and his wife Violet, née Royston-Pigott. Educated at Denstone College, Staffordshire, James intentionally failed a university entrance examination and went to London to become a cartoonist with the *Daily Graphic* and later a commercial artist at Grafton Art. By 21 he was studio manager of a design company and had launched his own advertising school. On 26 July 1930 at the parish church, Kensington, he married Dorothy ('Terry') Charlotte Stephens; they had one son.

In the 1930s James held senior positions with the small agency Erwin Wasey and the international McCann-Erikson. When unemployed because of mergers or company failures, he turned his hand to designing book jackets, sports clothes and even perfume bottles for Schiaparelli. He wrote and drew 'Our Nellie', a comic strip for the *Sunday Express*, and became interested in easel painting. In an attempt to save their marriage, the Jameses decided in 1938 to migrate to Australia. They arrived in Sydney in February 1939 after nearly six months in Tahiti, a period to which he would ever more refer.

Appointed senior creative director with J. Walter Thompson Australia Pty Ltd—the nation's biggest advertising agency—James soon established himself in the artistic life of the city. A fellow of the Royal Society of Artists, he founded the Design Centre with Geoff and Dahl Collings, wrote for Sydney Ure Smith's [q.v.11] *Australia: National Journal* and gave weekly radio broadcasts and frequent lunch-time lectures. He vigorously defended the work of the Contemporary Art Society and joined Ure Smith in launching the Design and Indus-tries Association of Australia in 1940. In 1944 he appeared as a witness for (Sir) William Dobell [q.v.14] in the Supreme Court case initiated to overturn his winning of the Archibald [q.v.3] prize.

Having enlisted in the Militia on 28 October 1942, James transferred to the Australian Imperial Force in January 1943 and was com-missioned as a lieutenant in May. He served as a camouflage officer (1943-44) and as an education officer (1944-45), writing booklets such as *Art Every Day* (1945). His duties took him to northern Australia and Horn Island. He retired from the army in May 1945.

Divorced in 1943, on 5 August that year at St John's Church of England, Darlinghurst, James had married Wilga (Wylga) Sheppard, a clerk. They moved to Melbourne, where he established Haughton James Services, a de-sign consultancy. His landmark Red Cross Modern Homes Exhibition (1949) featured the work of Robin Boyd [q.v.13] and Grant Feather-ston. Joining the Victorian Artists Society in 1946, James founded and edited the *Australian Artist* (1947-49). He was the first president (1948-55) of the Society of Designers for Industry, and also president (1965-67) of the National Gallery Society.

In 1952 James established with John Briggs an advertising agency which, by 1961, had become the highly successful and respected Briggs Canny James & Paramor Pty Ltd. After BCJP was acquired by the major international firm Foote Cone & Belding in 1964, he de-voted himself to painting. Working in a studio next to the house Boyd had designed for him in Kew, within a few years he won acceptance as a serious painter. His work is represented in the art galleries of New South Wales and Victoria.

Of medium height, balding, ebullient and urbane, James retired to Positano, Italy, in 1967. Widowed in 1972, he immersed himself in philosophy and experimented with LSD. Disconsolate and lonely, he composed an advertisement setting out his ideas on life and marriage, reputedly published in the *New*

Statesman, with instant results. On 18 January 1974 at the office of the government statist, Melbourne, he married Jean Rosemary Edwards, a translator and widow. They led a sybaritic life in Australia, Europe and places that each had dreamed of visiting until Rose-mary's death in 1981, after which he returned to Melbourne and lived with the daughter of his second marriage. 'Jimmy' James died on 12 July 1985 at South Caulfield and was cremated. His daughter and son survived him. In 2004 he was inducted into the Paperpoint/ Australian Graphic Design Centre Hall of Fame.

M. Bogle, *Design in Australia* (1988); R. Haese, *Rebels and Precursors* (1988); *Bulletin*, 3 Dec 1985, p 86; R. Marginson papers (Powerhouse Museum, Sydney); private information and personal knowl-edge.
                                            NEIL CLEREHAN

JAMIESON, COLIN JOHN (1923-1990), carpenter and politician, was born on 26 May 1923 in Perth, son of Western Australian-born George Archibald Jamieson, clerk, and his wife Mona, née Colvin, from Victoria. Colin's mother died when he was 5; he was reared by his father's sister and, after she died, by his maternal grandfather. Educated at Leederville State and Perth Junior Technical schools until 1937, he worked first in a vehicle body-building workshop and in 1938-42 for a fruit and veg-etable business. In World War II he served in Australia in the Australian Army Service Corps, Australian Imperial Force (1942-44), and as a wireless assistant and radar mechanic in the Royal Australian Air Force (1944-46). He was a labourer and storeman with the Midland Railway Co. of Western Australia before training as a carpenter and joiner in 1949-53. A member of the Australian Labor Party from 1946, he was active in local branches of the Amalgamated Society of Carpenters and Joiners' Union and the Building Workers Industrial Union of Australia.

On 14 February 1953 Jamieson won the seat of Canning in the State's Legislative Assembly. Subsequently he was returned for the seats of Beeloo (1956-68), Belmont (1968-74) and Welshpool (1974-86). From 1959 to 1976 he was State president of the ALP. In John Tonkin's government (1971-74) he held the portfolio of works and water supplies, and at times was also responsible for electricity and traffic safety. Elected deputy-leader in 1974, he succeeded Tonkin as leader in 1976. Next year the party suffered a decisive electoral defeat and in February 1978 replaced him as leader with Ronald Davies. Jamieson held sev-eral shadow portfolios before retiring from parliament at the 1986 election. From 1977 he was known as 'Father of the House'.

A staunch supporter of the parliamentary system, Jamieson had a reputation for his careful scrutiny of every piece of legislation and for his command of standing orders. He was an original member (1984-89) of the Parliamentary History Advisory Committee. In his last speech to the assembly, on 17 October 1985, he asserted that he entered parliament as 'a socialist with commitments. In my travels and experiences I have seen nothing which has convinced me that my commitment at that time was not a correct one. Indeed, the more I think about it, the more I think that left is right'. He was described by the Liberal premier Sir Charles Court as 'honest and straightforward', a man who 'took his duty seriously and always kept his word'. His former press secretary observed that he was regarded as a 'walking encyclopaedia'.

Jamieson supported numerous community organisations. He was president (1971-83) of the executive committee of the Western Australian Amateur Football League and a keen tennis player. A member of several horticultural societies, he successfully exhibited roses, dahlias and chrysanthemums. He was appointed AO in 1988. Jamieson had married Emily Margaret Male, a schoolteacher, on 14 May 1960 at the Holy Family Catholic Church, Como; they lived in the Perth suburb of Cloverdale. Survived by his wife and their son and daughter, he died of pulmonary embolism on 27 March 1990 at Subiaco and was cremated.

D. Black (ed), *The House on the Hill* (1991); *PD* (WA), 17 Oct 1985, p 2529; *West Australian*, 12 Apr 1974, p 1, 26 Mar 1976, p 1, 14 Feb 1978, p 9, 22 Feb 1978, p 1, 28 Mar 1990, p 9; *Sunday Times* (Perth), 23 June 1985, 'Sunday Magazine', p 1; S. Reid, interview with C. Jamieson (ts, 1989, SLWA).

HARRY C. J. PHILLIPS

JANGARI, BEETALOO BILL; *see* BILL

JARRETT, PATRICIA IRENE HERSCHELL (1911-1990), journalist, was born on 9 March 1911 at Albert Park, Melbourne, elder daughter of Victorian-born parents Cyril Chalmers Jarrett, station manager, and his wife Jessie Mabel, née Herschell. Although her Christian names were registered as Irene Herschell, she was always known as Patricia. Her family lived with Cyril's parents on their property near Kyneton, where the fair-haired, blue-eyed Pat had an idyllic early childhood. In 1917 she moved with her mother and sister to Melbourne. Educated at Middle Park State and Elwood Central schools, she excelled at sport. The Olympic champion (Sir) Frank Beaurepaire [q.v.7] encouraged her as a swimmer. In 1927 she began work in Herschell's Film Lab-

oratories, owned by an uncle, while also freelancing for the *Sporting Globe*, in which she soon had her own column. At the same time she successfully competed in championship swimming and athletics.

Ambitious and confident, in 1933 Pat joined Sir Keith Murdoch's [q.v.10] *Herald* as a woman sportswriter. She covered the first English women's cricket tour of Australia in 1934-35, and in 1937 accompanied the Australian team's return tour of England. In 1939 Murdoch approved her request to visit North America. En route she renewed acquaintance with Maie (Lady) Casey [q.v.], travelling to join her husband, Richard (Lord) Casey [q.v.13], who was setting up Australia's first legation in Washington. Thus began a lifelong friendship with the Caseys, especially Maie, whose secretary she became. Forthright and honest, Jarrett found the 'social racket' accompanying diplomatic life tedious, but an American woman journalist dubbed her the 'dynamic blond lady from down under' who brought 'a refreshing touch to the diplomatic scene'. She was then the only foreigner to be admitted to the National Women's Press Club, Washington. In May 1941 she was named press liaison officer for the legation. Returning to Australia in February 1942 Jarrett became a war correspondent, although, as a woman, she was confined to Australia. Early in 1943 she joined the Caseys in Calcutta when Richard Casey, newly appointed governor of Bengal, invited her to be Maie's assistant. Pat accompanied her on all official duties, and helped her to run the household and entertain dignitaries such as Mahatma Gandhi and Louis (Lord) Mountbatten.

After the Caseys left Calcutta in February 1946, Jarrett worked briefly in New York as a publicity officer. She returned to Melbourne and journalism in March 1947. Next year Murdoch offered her the position of women's editor of the *Sun News-Pictorial*. Initially reluctant to be relegated to the 'butterfly department', Pat accepted and became known to her colleagues as 'P. J.'. She transformed the women's pages into a respected vehicle for contemporary women's issues, while her column, 'Fair Comment', became a household word. She was equally popular on her 1967 radio 3DB program, 'Talk It Over', and her weekly television appearance on HSV-7's 'Meet the Press'.

Short, sturdily built, with a ready smile and great sense of humour, Miss Jarrett served as women's editor until 1973 and then continued as editorial consultant until 1985; altogether she spent fifty-two years with the Herald and Weekly Times Ltd. In 1972 she was appointed MBE and awarded the Queen's Jubilee medal. Having lived at Berwick, near the Caseys, for more than two decades, she moved to Mt Eliza in 1981. She died on 28 August 1990 at Frankston and was cremated.

W. J. Hudson, *Casey* (1986); A. Tate, *Fair Comment* (1996); *Sun News-Pictorial* (Melbourne), 29 Aug 1990, p 15; M. Cranfield, interview with P. Jarrett (ts, 1984, NLA); L. Mills, From the 'Butterfly Department' to Beirut: Australian Women Reporting in Wartime 1939-1979 (BA Hons thesis, Univ of Melbourne, 1989); Herald and Weekly Times Ltd Archives (Melbourne); Jarrett papers (SLV); private information.   AUDREY TATE

JARRETT, THELMA EILEEN (1905-1987), soroptimist, was born on 25 February 1905 at Gladesville, Sydney, second child of New South Wales-born parents Robert Loxton Jarrett, accountant, and his wife Elizabeth, née Hill. Educated at Fintona Girls' School, Camberwell, Melbourne, Thelma trained as a teacher and in 1927-36 and 1938-39 was senior geography mistress at Tintern Ladies' College, Hawthorn. She completed a diploma in geography (1937) at the London School of Economics and Political Science, and, after leaving Tintern, accepted a post in public relations for the Murray Valley Passenger Service. In 1940-47 she was assistant administrative superintendent at the Munitions Supply Laboratories, Maribyrnong.

Pursuing an interest in personnel management, Jarrett investigated it in North America and Britain before becoming general secretary (1952-70) of the Good Neighbour Council of Victoria. She travelled extensively around the State, co-ordinating resettlement and assimilation services; she was appointed MBE (1957) in recognition of this work. Based in London in 1960-62, she lectured for the Commonwealth Department of Immigration, addressing audiences throughout the United Kingdom to raise awareness of the opportunities for migrants in Australia.

Jarrett had joined the Soroptimist Club of Melbourne in 1952, and while in London she was the Victorian representative on the board of governors of the Federation of Soroptimist Clubs of Great Britain and Ireland. For much of the 1960s she served as Victorian representative on the Australia and New Zealand co-ordinating committee; in 1964-66 she was president of the State's divisional union. The first person from outside Britain to be vice-president (1969-71) of the federation, Jarrett was elected president at its 1972 conference, held at Killarney, Ireland. She faced a huge task in making the presidency work from such a distance, but with large postal, telephone and airline bills, she effectively fulfilled the office. In Sydney in August 1973, shortly before the end of her term, Jarrett chaired the first conference of the federation to be held in the Southern hemisphere.

Arguing for the increasing relevance of soroptimism at a time of substantial change in 'the pattern of women's lives', Jarrett sought to advance their access to health and family planning, education, employment and economic security. Her particular interest in conditions in underdeveloped countries was reflected in her work as representative of the Victorian branch of the National Council of Women (1971-83) on the State division of the United Nations Association of Australia (secretary 1973-74; executive director 1974-75) and as the honorary secretary of the UNAA's Status of Women Committee (1976-84).

With an upright carriage and insistence on the deference due to the many offices she held, Jarrett was a formidable if respected figure for younger soroptimists. Yet she had a delightful sense of humour and a warm manner, and was a generous mentor. An active member of the Business and Professional Women's Club, Melbourne (president, 1955-57), she also served (1963-68) on Fintona's board of directors. Thelma Jarrett died on 13 August 1987 at Hawthorn, Melbourne, and was cremated.

Soroptimist International of Victoria, Australia (1982); *Herald* (Melbourne), 28 Dec 1970, p 23, 21 Oct 1972, p 41; *Sun* (Sydney), 24 Oct 1972, p 23; National Council of Women (Vic), *Quarterly Bulletin*, Mar/Apr 1973, p 3; private information.
                                        JOAN M. BANKS

JENKINS, FREDERICK JOHN (1892-1983), soldier and farmer, was born on 17 June 1892 at Kangaroo Flat, Bendigo, Victoria, seventh child of Morgan Jenkins, a miner from Wales, and his locally born wife Fanny, née Oldfield. Educated at the Bendigo Continuation School, he began teaching in the Victorian Education Department in 1909. He gained his trained teacher's certificate in 1913 and was at Chute State School, near Beaufort, when he enlisted in the Australian Imperial Force on 23 February 1915. He was posted to the 23rd Battalion.

In May Jenkins sailed for Egypt. His troopship, the *Southland*, was torpedoed en route to Gallipoli on 2 September and he was admitted to hospital at Mudros suffering from deafness. Joining his unit on the peninsula early in October, he served there until December. In March 1916 he went with his battalion to France as a substantive sergeant. He was awarded a Military Medal for his actions on 28 July at Pozières, where, with two other soldiers, he destroyed an enemy machine-gun while under heavy fire; he was wounded in the right hand.

Jenkins was commissioned in August 1917. For his conduct during the third battle of Ypres, Belgium, in September-October, in which he 'set a splendid example to his men', he was awarded the Military Cross. He had been mentioned in despatches. In November he was promoted to lieutenant. On 23 April 1918 he was again wounded, in his right arm and face. After recovering, he returned to his unit in July and was awarded a Bar to his MC for his actions as company commander in the capture of Mont St Quentin, France, on 1 September. The citation read: 'by his splendid leadership, courage and initiative he was able to advance 600 yards [549 m] in the face of fierce machine-gun fire, capturing eighty prisoners and causing heavy enemy casualties. Later he made a daring reconnaissance over very exposed ground'.

After his AIF appointment terminated in Melbourne on 15 July 1919, Jenkins went back to schoolteaching for a short time, but resigned to take up a soldier-settlement block at Red Cliffs on the Murray River. On 15 September 1926 he married Doris Holliwell Lewis, a dressmaker, at the Church of England, Red Cliffs. In 1936 the family moved to a 3000-acre (1214 ha) property at Condamine, Queensland, and began a cattle-fattening business, then switched to dairy farming and, later, growing wheat and other grain crops.

Mobilised in the Militia on 23 October 1942, Jenkins was posted to the 31st Employment (Works) Company in Brisbane. He transferred to the AIF in February 1943, was made temporary captain in October and appointed second-in-command of his company in July 1944. His AIF appointment terminated on 7 September and he returned to his property. Tall and slim, he had the medium complexion of his father's Welsh forebears. He had a strong character and was a natural leader, whether on active service or duck-hunting or fishing with friends. Jenkins took a close interest in the Condamine Rodeo, the Condamine State School and the Miles Soldiers' Club. He died on 27 June 1983 at Miles and was cremated; his three sons and daughter survived him. His eldest son, Glyn, was a member of the Victorian Legislative Council in 1970-82 and a minister in 1981-82.

Victoria: The Education Department's Record of War Service, 1914-1919 (1921); C. E. W. Bean, *The A.I.F. in France 1918* (1942); K. M. Wright, *A Land Fit for Heroes* (1995); R. J. Austin, *Forward Undeterred* (1998); B2455, item Jenkins Frederick John, B883, item QX50131 (NAA); private information.

A. ARGENT

JENNER, DOROTHY HETTY FOSBURY ('ANDREA') (1891-1985), actress, journalist and radio broadcaster, was born on 1 March 1891 in Sydney, eldest of four children of William Alexander Gordon, a station manager born in India, and his Melbourne-born wife Dora Ellen, née Fosbury. Dorothy grew up on Edgeroi, a property near Narrabri, and was educated by governesses before the family moved to Darlinghurst, Sydney, in 1903. She then attended a private school at Goulburn, Ascham School, Edgecliff, and the Sydney Church of England Girls' Grammar School, Darlinghurst, displaying more interest in singing, dancing and ice-skating than in academic pursuits. After further private tuition she sailed to England, stayed with relatives and had a lively social life. Recalled to Australia by her parents around 1913, she established a dressmaking business in George Street, Sydney, and helped J. C. Williamson [q.v.6] Ltd stage a fund-raising revue for the war effort.

In 1915 Dorothy departed for San Francisco, United States of America. She moved to Hollywood and worked as an extra and sometimes a stuntwoman on film sets. On 5 March 1917 at Stockton, California, she married Murray Eugene McEwen, whom she later labelled an alcoholic and a gigolo; the marriage broke down in 1921. Dorothy became a stock actress with Paramount Pictures Inc. and obtained generally small parts in several films, including *The Chorus Girl's Romance* (1920) and *Clarence* (1922). Unable to earn enough money as an actress, she worked as a production assistant on *The Ten Commandments* (1923) and resumed dressmaking. A 'fool for handsome men', she married George Onesiphorus Jenner, an advertising writer and a divorcee, on 25 March 1923 at Hollywood. In 1925 she fled to Sydney and the marriage, as disastrous as her first, was subsequently dissolved.

Dorothy Jenner played the lead in Raymond Longford's [q.v.10] *Hills of Hate* (1926) and was an art director on *For the Term of His Natural Life* (1927). She accepted in 1927 a gentleman friend's offer of a ticket to England, where she fell ill. Convalescence in Switzerland was followed by a tour of Europe. Her impressions of a Spanish bullfight were cabled back to the Sydney *Sun*. This led to a weekly column under the byline 'Andrea', chosen from a numerology list. She thought of herself as 'the playgirl of the western world'. In 1934 she agreed to chaperone a wealthy young Indian in the USA, and continued her column —a mixture of gossip, character sketches, royal news, fashion reportage and theatre criticism—from New York.

In May 1939 Jenner flew back on a visit to Sydney, where she was stranded by World War II. She came third in the Australian Red Cross Society (New South Wales division) fund-raising 'queen' competition in 1941. Accredited as a war correspondent for the *Sun* in September, she went to Singapore. She despatched several stories from Asia and had a brief liaison with a wing commander, her one true love. In January 1942 she was interned in the Stanley prisoner-of-war camp, Hong Kong. Through a diary kept on toilet paper she recorded military developments and drily profiled her fellow internees. She helped to allocate supplies and participated in lectures and plays. The sight of her irrigating her colon dissuaded a Japanese officer from raping her, and she invoked dysentery as an excuse not to make propaganda broadcasts to Allied forces in the Pacific.

Thin and unwell, Jenner returned to Australia in October 1945. She joined the speaking circuit, persuaded Associated Newspapers Ltd, owners of the *Sun*, to pay her half her salary for the past four years, and invested the proceeds with her nephew in a business venture that failed. Associated Newspapers sent her overseas in 1947. Recalled to Sydney in 1950, Jenner resigned from the *Sun* and joined (Sir) Frank Packer's [q.v.15] *Daily Telegraph*, where she wrote the 'Postscripts' column. Although uneasy with her volatile boss, Jenner, never a fan of trade unions, joined him in his battles against the authority of the Australian Journalists' Association and its code of ethics.

In 1953 Jenner left for Ezra Norton's [q.v.15] *Truth* and *Daily Mirror*, where she covered society events. She served (1954-60) on the board of the Phillip Street Theatre, which staged revues. She went along good-naturedly with Gordon Chater's impersonation of her there as Andrea in 'Little Lady Make Believe', but maintained, nevertheless, that she knew most of the people whose names she dropped.

With small, elegant hands and shapely legs, Jenner was always immaculately groomed and expensively dressed. She put on a beauty spot each morning, had a face-lift and remained circumspect about her age. She appeared on an Australian Broadcasting Commission television panel game show and moved into radio just as the *Daily Mirror* proposed that she retire. In the late 1950s she joined radio station 2UE to host a morning show with Tom Jacobs, dispensing a mixture of worldly wisdom and 'horse sense'. 'Hello, Mums and Dads', uttered in a deep resonant voice—a result of rupturing a vocal cord while a prisoner of war and of years of smoking—became her trademark.

Early in the 1960s Jenner was lured to 2GB, where she secured a secretary, a salary of £5000, and a promise of £10 a week in retirement. She studied newspapers and magazines before recording the next day's show. Her pungent patter resulted in numerous complaints from listeners. In 1967 Jenner became the host of an early talkback program but in 1969 her session was dropped by 2GB. In 1970 she presented a national morning program on the ABC before being replaced by a music format, and a similar fate befell her at 2CH in 1972.

Jenner worked for the Black and White committee of the Royal Blind Society of New South Wales, the State Meals on Wheels Association and the Wayside Chapel, and was named a life governor of Sydney Hospital. She

was appointed OBE in 1968. A supporter of the Liberal Party of Australia, she was accused in parliament of smearing Australian Labor Party supporters as communists, and attracted libel writs from Gough and Margaret Whitlam and Jim Cairns. Several co-authors dropped by the wayside before her memoir *Darlings, I've Had a Ball!* (1975), written with Trish Sheppard, was published and widely serialised. Jenner appeared on various television shows including 'This Is Your Life'. Surviving a serious car crash in 1976, she died on 24 March 1985 at her Potts Point flat and was cremated. Her friend Judy Cassab twice painted her portrait.

Newspaper News, 1 June 1935, p 1; *Sun* (Sydney), 13 Sept 1945, p 4, 25 July 1967, p 4, 26 July 1967, p 13, 27 July 1967, p 13, 28 July 1967, p 13, 31 July 1967, p 13; *Daily Telegraph* (Sydney), 8 Apr 1950, p 21; *Bulletin*, 12 Jan 1963, p 15, 11 Sept 1965, p 26; *Age* (Melbourne), 31 May 1968, p 5; *Woman's Day*, 18 Jan 1971, p 14; *SMH*, 25 Mar 1985, p 5; Jenner papers (SLNSW); boxes 200.27/1-2, 4, 26 (John Fairfax Holdings Ltd archives, Sydney).

BRIDGET GRIFFEN-FOLEY

JENNINGS, DOUGLAS BERNARD (1929-1987), businessman and politician, was born on 30 October 1929 at Glenhuntly, Melbourne, second surviving son of (Sir) Albert Victor Jennings (d.1993), auctioneer, and his wife Ethel Sarah, née Johnson. Educated at Murrumbeena State, Ivanhoe Grammar and Melbourne Church of England Grammar schools, Doug was a keen and able sportsman, winning championships in swimming and boxing and representing Victoria in water polo and swimming. In 1947 he joined the speculative building company his father had founded in 1932, A. V. Jennings Industries Ltd, which had expanded to encompass the development of housing estates. On 11 November 1953 he married Patricia Downey.

Early in his work Jennings exhibited the characteristics that would shape his life: extroverted and popular, he was too outspoken and idiosyncratic to be a team leader. His enthusiasm first found a niche in sales and marketing, but his elder brother, Vic, and several senior executives, grew concerned at some of his innovations, including the establishment of furnishing and real-estate subsidiaries, especially given the company's exposure to the Federal government's 1960-61 credit squeeze.

Leaving the firm, Jennings moved to North Queensland in 1961 and took up the Mount Surprise Brahman cattle station. Building a highly successful business, again adopting several innovative practices, he also became active in community affairs, serving on the Etheridge Shire Council (1964-67) and joining the Queensland Country Party. He gave particular attention to the interests of his Aboriginal stockmen, introducing a superannuation scheme for them and paying award wages. Selling the property in 1968, he returned to Victoria and established the Mornington Park Brahman stud at Flinders. He was State founding chairman (1968-72) of the Australian Brahman Breeders' Association.

Still a substantial shareholder in the family company, and with support from his father, Jennings began urging it to diversify into areas such as cattle breeding and mining. Family and company unrest led to A.V.'s resignation as chairman in 1972 and to Doug Jennings's relinquishing his interests. Frustrated by planning controls on land development at Flinders, he entered politics and in 1976 won the Legislative Assembly seat of Westernport for the governing Liberal Party. He gained a reputation as a quixotic, outspoken advocate for public probity and, with his fellow Liberal Charles Francis, criticised his government for covering up corrupt land deals by the Housing Commission of Victoria. In 1977 he abstained from voting in support of (Sir) Rupert Hamer's government in an Opposition no confidence motion, and in 1979 was expelled from the party. Later that year he stood unsuccessfully as an Independent.

In 1980, at the invitation of Premier (Sir) Joh Bjelke-Petersen, Jennings contested and won the Queensland State seat of Southport for the National Party. With views oscillating from far right to slightly left, at times he was a thorn in the side of his government but held his seat with increasing majorities. Already a trustee of the Victorian Aboriginal Advancement League, he now sought to improve policies relating to Queensland Aboriginal communities. He also saved from development a spit of land on the Gold Coast, part of which was later named the Doug Jennings Park.

Divorced in 1980, Jennings married Susan Frances Leister, a secretary, at Mornington on 28 February 1981. They were divorced in 1984. He remained obsessed with physical fitness, ignoring the signs of over-exertion. On 9 April 1987 Doug Jennings died of coronary heart disease in the sauna of the gymnasium at Parliament House, Brisbane. Survived by a son and daughter of his first marriage, he was buried in Flinders cemetery, Victoria. His estate was valued for probate at $3 820 000.

D. Garden, *Builders to the Nation* (1992); *PD* (Vic), 14 Apr 1987, p 1195; *Courier-Mail* (Brisbane), 10 Apr 1987, p 5; *Age* (Melbourne), 15 Apr 1987, p 16; *Gold Coast Bulletin*, 16 Dec 1987, p 4; private information.   DONALD S. GARDEN

JENNINGS, JOSEPH NEWELL (1916-1984), geomorphologist, was born on 29 June 1916 at Wortley, Leeds, Yorkshire, England, only child of Joseph Newell Jennings, commercial traveller, and his wife Alice, née Rhodes. Educated at the Oldershaw School for Boys, Wallasey, Cheshire, young Joe studied geography at St Catharine's College, Cambridge (BA, 1938; MA, 1945). He conducted research in Iceland in 1937 and on Jan Mayen island in 1938. At the outbreak of World War II he interrupted his doctoral studies in the department of botany to enlist in the British Army. Commissioned in the Royal Regiment of Artillery in June 1941, he was promoted to lieutenant in October 1942 and to temporary captain in April 1946. He served mainly in Iceland. On 14 March 1941 at the register office, Otley, Yorkshire, he had married Betty Mary Priest, a doctor's receptionist.

Demobilised in 1946, Jennings accepted a lectureship in physical geography at the University of Leicester. Regulations inhibited him from resuming his doctoral studies, but a grant from the Royal Geographical Society allowed him to continue his work on the origin of the Norfolk Broads. Although the analysis was meticulous and the conclusions valid from the data obtained, his further work with Dr Joyce Lambert demonstrated that his findings were incorrect. With Lambert's assistance, he published an able self-refutation. Turning to Australia 'in search of wider horizons', in 1952 he was appointed reader in geomorphology in the department of geography, Research School of Pacific Studies, at the Australian National University, Canberra. He arrived, with his family, in January 1953 and was naturalised in 1963. Made a professorial fellow in 1966, he was a foundation member of the department of biogeography and geomorphology in 1968.

Jennings's academic career blossomed and covered a wide range of Australian landscapes —from changing sea levels to the highest peaks and from deserts to coral reefs. He began caving as a recreational activity but soon became immersed in the science of caves and karst, eventually becoming a world authority on karst geomorphology. In 1968-77 he edited the seven-volume series *An Introduction to Systematic Geomorphology*, of which his own contribution, *Karst* (1971), is a standard authority. He also edited the long-running series 'Australian Landform Examples' in the *Australian Geographer* and was an associate-editor for the *Zeitschrift für Geomorphologie*. Ultimately his publications numbered over two hundred.

His research was not confined to Australia but extended to the Territory of Papua and New Guinea, Malaysia, China, New Zealand, Canada and the United States of America. As well as geomorphological studies, he also published in the fields of zoology, climatology, and European exploration and land use in Australia. He enthusiastically accepted new ideas, methodologies and technologies. In 1972 the University of Cambridge awarded him a Ph.D. by letters. At his insistence, the doctorate was in botany rather than geography, marking the culmination of his pre-war research. It was recognised that his achievements warranted a D.Sc., but again he insisted that he be given the lesser degree appropriate to his original enrolment. President of the Institute of Australian Geographers, in 1975 he was awarded the (W. B.) Clarke [q.v.3] medal of the Royal Society of New South Wales and the Victoria medal of the Royal Geographical Society, London. Retiring in 1977 'to make way for a younger man', he continued to work as a visiting fellow until his death.

A remarkable mentor for his students, coworkers and the caving community, Jennings offered his unflagging friendship and advice to landscape scientists around the world. He had an enormous influence on Australian cave science and exploration, with particular emphasis on the Eastern Highlands, the Nullarbor and the Kimberleys, as well as the sandstone karstlands across northern Australia. Jennings was perhaps the first to publish on the unusual young karst landscapes of southern coastal Australia: the so-called 'syngenetic' karsts. He was a founder (1956) and president (1958-60) of the Australian Speleological Federation. In 1983 the United States' National Speleological Society bestowed honorary life membership on him.

Jennings was fascinated by, and revelled in, the Australian bush. He was an active camper, bushwalker and skier, as well as an enthusiastic lover of Australian red wines. Genial, extrovert and forthright, he had an abundantly vital personality, a fine brain and goodness of heart. He died of myocardial infarction on 24 August 1984 at Eucumbene, New South Wales, while skiing in the Snowy Mountains, where he had conducted much of his research. Survived by his wife, and their son and two daughters, he was cremated.

Geographical Jnl, vol 151, no 1, 1985, p 151; *Austn Geographer*, vol 16, no 3, 1985, p 169; O. H. K. and A. P. Spate, 'Obituary: Joseph Newell Jennings 1916-1984', *Austn Geographical Studies*, vol 23, no 2, 1985, p 325, and for publications; *Canberra Times*, 29 Aug 1984, p 16; *ANU Reporter*, 14 Sept 1984, p 7; private information.   ANDY SPATE

JEROMIN, HEINZ (1925-1987), carpenter and works foreman, was born on 11 May 1925 at Lyck, East Prussia, Germany (Ełk, Poland), son of Franz Jeromin and his wife Maria. From 1942 Heinz served as a private in the German Army. Captured in Normandy in 1944, he was interned as a prisoner of war in Britain and in the United States of America, where he picked cotton. After he was repatriated in 1949,

he worked as a carpenter at Hamburg. He had lost contact with most of his family in World War II and his homeland had been taken over by Soviet forces.

In 1951 Jeromin was one of about 650 German tradesmen recruited by an Australian engineer, Roy Robinson, to work for the Snowy Mountains Hydro-electric Authority. Eager to leave the chaos of postwar Germany, he signed up for an initial two-year contract, his fare (approximately £160) to be repaid from his wages of about £10 a week. Understanding the word 'snowy', he took his old German Army greatcoat with him—a boon in the subzero temperatures around Cooma, New South Wales. He was 5 ft 8½ ins (174 cm) tall, sturdily built, blond and blue-eyed.

Germans were the third largest ethnic group on the 'Snowy scheme', after Italians and those then known as Yugoslavs. In the early years particularly, German workers attracted hostility from their former foes, especially Poles. Jeromin was among a group of Germans locked up for the night at Cabramurra township for a rowdy celebration of Hitler's birthday. But gradually the workforce of forty nationalities evolved into a harmonious and cohesive community, the Snowy proving a social as well as a physical engineering feat.

Appointed to the salaried staff of the SMHEA in 1961, Jeromin was made a temporary works foreman in the field construction division. By 1963 he had decided to quit his job and move to Sydney, hoping to find a wife. He had married Ursula Marie Inge, possibly on a visit to Germany in 1956, but the marriage had ended in divorce and he had lost touch with his son. As he was preparing to leave for Sydney, however, he was transferred in January 1964 to the construction of the new town of Jindabyne. He was overcome to be offered such an important task: 'Me, a little squarehead, got an order to build Jindabyne! So that's what I had to do'.

In 1987 Jeromin reflected on his life in Australia. He knew he had become institutionalised, dependent on his unvarying routine of work and hostel accommodation: 'I need someone to tell me what to do'. Although he never remarried, he had found a place for himself on the Snowy, and was proud of the contribution he had made through his work. 'We just wanted to show you, we can make something for peace too', he said. Survived by his son, he died of myocardial infarction and alcoholic cardiomyopathy on 5 June 1987 in the SMHEA staff hostel at Jindabyne and was cremated.

M. Unger, *Voices from the Snowy* (1989); S. McHugh, *The Snowy* (1995); F. Robinson, *A Study of Occupational Health and Safety Practice in the Construction of the Snowy Mountains Hydro-Electric Scheme* (2000); A11394, item Jeromin H, A11395, item Jeromin H, SP908/1, item German/Jeromin Heinz (NAA); S. McHugh, taped interview with H. Jeromin (1987, SLNSW).

SIOBHÁN MCHUGH

JOHNSON, RAYNOR CAREY (1901-1987), physicist, college master and mystic, was born on 5 April 1901 at Leeds, Yorkshire, England, eldest son of John William Johnson, bank clerk, and his wife Jane, née Wade. Educated at Bradford Grammar School, Raynor won an open scholarship in natural science to Balliol College, Oxford (BA, 1922; MA, 1926). He was invited to become a research student in spectroscopy, working with Professor (Sir) Thomas Merton. In 1923-26 he lectured in physics at Queen's University, Belfast. On 7 October 1925 in Belfast he married Mary Rubina Buchanan with Methodist forms.

While at Balliol Johnson had also completed a B.Sc. (1922) at the University of London, gaining first-class honours in physics. He later graduated Ph.D. (1924) and D.Sc. (1927) from the University of London and was appointed a lecturer there in 1927. Between 1923 and 1933 he wrote or co-authored twenty-one papers, published a book, *Spectra* (1928), and laid the foundations for later texts *Atomic Spectra* (1946) and *Introduction to Molecular Spectra* (1949). His publications placed him among the leading research scientists in spectroscopy.

Johnson's Methodist background and early friendship with the prominent nonconformist preacher and author Leslie Weatherhead shaped his commitment to use his vocation in the service of others. He believed that blood serum could be analysed by spectroscopy, leading perhaps to the discovery of the causes of diseases such as cancer. Accordingly, he began a medical course while continuing full-time research. With Weatherhead he pursued an interest in psychotherapy. He also became associated with the Society for Psychical Research.

Keen for a new challenge, in 1934 Johnson accepted the position of master at Queen's College, University of Melbourne. His personal integrity and devotion to the interests of students soon overcame initial reservations that he was neither ordained nor Australian. Known affectionately as 'Sam', he contributed much to Queen's academic, intellectual and social life, although until the 1950s he was frustrated in his plans for the renovation and extension of facilities. Having hoped to establish a wing for women students, he took the initiative in founding St Hilda's College in 1964. He was disappointed by the council's refusal to allow him to complete his medical course.

Unorthodox in some of his public views as master, Johnson also turned to a study of the paranormal in his personal research—an interest stimulated by his friendship with Ambrose Pratt [q.v.11]. In little more than a decade he published four major books on the intersections of natural science, psychical research and mystical experience, applying to this work the same care and integrity as he had given to his scientific experiments. *The Imprisoned Splendour* (1953), *Nurslings of Immortality* (1957), *Watcher on the Hills* (1959) and *The Light and the Gate* (1964) were widely read and reviewed throughout the English-speaking world, establishing Johnson as a leading authority in the field. Abandoning his belief in the divinity of Christ and in redemptive theology, Johnson accepted Jesus only as a great spiritual leader. Such views troubled members of the Methodist Conference, yet he retained the confidence of his college council and community and his tenure continued until his retirement in 1964.

In the summer of 1962-63 Johnson visited India, where he had an audience with the president and philosopher Dr Sarvepalli Radhakrishnan, who had invited him to address both houses of parliament on science and spirituality. The main purpose of his travels, however, was to meet two noted Indian mystics, Vinoba Bhave at Santiniketan, an ashram founded by Rabindranath Tagore, and Swami Pratyagatmananda at Calcutta. The visit strengthened his conviction that he would never understand the meaning of life by intellectual endeavour alone. Returning to Melbourne he affirmed the certainty of God's existence and the possibility of knowing Him through the discipline of contemplation. On retirement he and his wife committed themselves to this quest at their cottage in the Dandenong Ranges.

Small, of slight build with domed forehead and slightly receding chin, Johnson had a warm, friendly, expressive face, twinkling eyes and a genial sense of humour. His outstanding qualities were sincerity, humility and simplicity. He had a mind that spanned the whole of human experience, but he never displayed his learning for its own sake. His goal was to understand the meaning of life and he was always ready to help others in their quest. His later books included *The Spiritual Path* (1971) and *Pool of Reflections* (1975). Shunning publicity for himself, he was distressed when a cult with which he was associated, known as The Family, received adverse media attention in the 1970s.

Survived by his wife, and their two daughters and two sons, Raynor Johnson died at Upper Ferntree Gully on 16 May 1987 and was buried in Macclesfield cemetery. A portrait by Louis Kahan is held at Queen's, and a wing of the college is named in his honour.

O. Parnaby, *Queen's College, University of Melbourne* (1990); J. Arriens, *The Writings and Beliefs of Raynor Johnson* (1998); *Age* (Melbourne), 18 May 1987, p 10; Johnson papers (Queen's College Archives, University of Melbourne); private information and personal knowledge.

OWEN PARNABY

JOHNSTON, EDGAR CHARLES (1896-1988), aviator and public servant, was born on 30 April 1896 in East Perth, tenth of eleven children of Western Australian-born Harry Frederick Johnston [q.v.9 E. Bertram Johnston], surveyor, and his wife Maria Louisa, née Butcher, from Tasmania. Bertram was his brother; M. W. Clifton [q.v.3] was his great-grandfather. Educated at Guildford Grammar School, in 1914 Edgar took up an engineering apprenticeship with the surveys branch of the State's Department of Lands and enrolled in the engineering degree course at the University of Western Australia.

Enlisting in the Australian Imperial Force on 29 April 1915, Johnston served on Gallipoli with the 28th Battalion and on the Western Front with the 24th Field Artillery Brigade. On 16 March 1916 he was discharged to take a commission in the Royal Flying Corps. He flew first with No.24 Squadron then with No.88 Squadron, in which he became a flight commander with the rank of captain. A 'brilliant and most dashing leader', he won the Distinguished Flying Cross for his conduct in two engagements on 4 September 1918 in which the four Bristol Fighters under his command accounted for seven enemy aircraft. In aerial combat overall, he and his observers claimed twenty victories. He was demobilised from the Royal Air Force and repatriated in 1919.

Back in Perth, Johnston resumed his post with the Department of Lands and qualified as a surveyor. On 23 February 1921 at St Mary's Church of England, South Perth, he married Margaret Allison, daughter of Andrew Gibb Maitland [q.v.10]. He had been appointed superintendent of aerodromes in the new civil aviation branch, Commonwealth Department of Defence, in January. Based in Melbourne, and with little assistance, he chose sites for and laid out aerodromes—including Mascot (Sydney), Essendon (Melbourne), Archerfield (Brisbane) and Parafield (Adelaide)—and other landing fields and emergency strips. He was also responsible for navigation beacons.

Captain Johnston became deputy-controller of civil aviation in 1929 and acting-controller in 1931, succeeding H. C. Brinsmead [q.v.7] as controller in 1933. He was chairman of an interdepartmental committee on air communications and a member of the Air Accidents Investigation Committee. In 1936 he was appointed controller-general and foundation chairman of the Civil Aviation Board. He sup-ported the adoption by Australian airlines of the American Douglas DC-2 and DC-3 aircraft, thus antagonising people 'in high places' who wished to restrict imports to British machines. Responsible for international aviation negotiations, he helped Qantas Empire Airways Ltd to obtain a share of the England-Australia route. The report on the crash in October 1938 of the DC-2 airliner *Kyeema* at Mount Dandenong, Victoria, censured him for having delayed installation of new ultra-high-frequency navigational beacons and for other administrative failures. The leader of the Opposition, John Curtin [q.v.13], claimed that Johnston was 'a possible scapegoat'. In 1939 when the board was superseded by the Commonwealth Department of Aviation, he was passed over for the post of head, becoming assistant director-general under A. B. Corbett [q.v.13].

A founding member (1940) of the Tasman Air Commission, Johnston later sat on the Tasman Empire Airlines Ltd policy committee. During World War II he was heavily engaged in the department's activities in support of the war effort; his bargaining skills and technical expertise often proved crucial. He was an inaugural member (1946-52) of the Australian National Airlines Commission, which operated as Trans-Australia Airlines. After the war he again became extensively involved in setting up international airline agreements and played a leading role at the first assembly meeting (1947) of the International Civil Aviation Organization. He was a board-member of British Commonwealth Pacific Airlines Ltd, formed in 1946, and of TEAL (1954-55).

Johnston retired from the Department of Civil Aviation in 1955. International adviser (1955-67) to Qantas, he took part in negotiations when the company was developing its 'Kangaroo Route' to London and also seeking to extend its service across the Pacific Ocean. He supported the Department of Aviation Historical Society (later Civil Aviation Historical Society) from its formation in 1982. Patron of the Victorian/Tasmanian division, he was elected first national life member in 1984. The society inaugurated a series of memorial lectures in his honour in 1988. A keen fisherman and bushwalker, Johnston promoted both forms of recreation in Victoria. He died on 24 May 1988 at Malvern, Melbourne, and was cremated. His wife and their daughter and son survived him.

C. A. Butler, *Flying Start* (1971); I. Sabey, *Challenge in the Skies* (1979); *Aviation Retrospect* (1985); J. Gunn, *The Defeat of Distance* (1985), *Challenging Horizons* (1987), *High Corridors* (1988), and *Contested Skies* (1999); C. Shores et al, *Above the Trenches* (1990); *SMH*, 9 Dec 1938, p 13; B2455, item Johnston E C (NAA); Johnston papers (Civil Aviation Hist Soc, Vic/Tas division, Melbourne).   J. D. WALKER

JOHNSTON, FREDERICK AUSTIN (1909-1990), smallgoods manufacturer, meat exporter and political party organiser, was born on 9 October 1909 at Blaydon, Durham, England, son of William Oliver Johnston, master butcher, and his wife Elizabeth Florence, née Johnston. Educated at Wallsend-on-Tyne secondary school, Fred migrated in 1926 with his family to Perth. He joined his father and two brothers in opening a butcher's shop in Barrack Street; in 1929 they moved to larger premises in Beaufort Street. On 23 March 1935 at St Mary's Church of England, West Perth, he married Nance Jessie Dethridge.

From about 1932 the family business traded as W. O. Johnston & Sons; Fred Johnston became managing director in 1942. The company developed into one of Western Australia's biggest meat-processing firms and was a member of the State division of the Meat and Allied Trades Federation of Australia. Representing that organisation, Johnston was president of the Western Australian Employers' Federation (1948-53) and of the Australian Council of Employers' Federations (1953-55). He was a council-member (1949-57) of the West Australia Chamber of Manufactures. During the 1950s the firm rapidly expanded its export trade and in 1960 Johnston helped to form the Western Australian Meat Exporters' Association.

A founding member (1945) of the State division of the Liberal Party of Australia, Johnston took a leading role in mobilising business support in the campaign leading up to the State election in March 1947. The Liberal Party and Country and Democratic League coalition unexpectedly won and the Liberal leader (Sir) Ross McLarty [q.v.15] became premier. Labor regained power in 1953; next year Johnston, elected State president of the Liberal Party, undertook a thorough reorganisation of the party's structure. Vivian Ockerby was engaged as general secretary of the Liberal and Country League.

Business commitments obliged Johnston to stand down in 1955 but he returned to the presidency in 1957-61. During his term he pressed the views of the Liberal organisation and the business community on the parliamentary party. Blaming A. R. G. Hawke's [q.v.] Labor government for the relative economic stagnation of Western Australia, Johnston rallied business support in the 1959 election campaign. Electoral success saw (Sir) David Brand, who had replaced McLarty in 1957, commence a record twelve years as premier with (Sir) Charles Court as minister for industrial development. After Brand retired in 1972, Johnston's influence behind the scenes ensured Court's succession to the leadership. Before the 1974 election he vigorously supported an advertising campaign by business interests that helped to defeat John Tonkin's Labor government. Maintaining an active interest in party affairs until the end of his life, he never failed to attend crucial meetings of the Liberal Party State council. He was appointed CBE in 1956 and CMG in 1963.

In 1964 W. O. Johnston & Sons Pty Ltd was declared insolvent and in 1967 it was taken over by Talloman Holdings Pty Ltd. Johnston retained directorships of several companies. Active in community groups, he had been charter president (1949-50) of the Rotary Club of Mount Lawley and in 1955-56 district governor. In 1950-52 he was president of the Western Australian Golf Club, Mount Yokine. A former champion badminton player and president of the Badminton Association of Western Australia, he was chairman of the finance committee for the British Empire and Commonwealth Games held in Perth in 1962. He was a Perth city councillor in 1963-65. A councillor (1971-82) of the Tuberculosis and Chest Association of Western Australia, he was chairman (1974-82) of the Sir Charles Gairdner [q.v.] Hospital Board and president (1978-84) of the Cancer Council of Western Australia (from 1983 the Cancer Foundation of Western Australia). Survived by his wife and their daughter and son, he died on 19 May 1990 at Subiaco and was cremated.

Leading Personalities of Western Australia (1950); C. Riedel, *Rotary in Western Australia* (1983); *Austn Exporter*, Nov 1963, p 23, Sept 1964, p 31; *West Australian*, 21 May 1990, p 20; private information.

JEREMY BUXTON

JOHNSTON, HENRY ALOYSIUS (1888-1986), Jesuit priest and seminary rector, was born on 17 October 1888 at Downpatrick, Northern Ireland, son of Henry Johnston, clerk, and his wife Kate, née Woods. A younger brother also became a Jesuit. Henry was educated at Mungret College, Limerick, and entered the novitiate of the Society of Jesus at Tullabeg College in 1906. He studied at the Royal (National after 1909) University of Ireland (BA, 1910; MA, 1912), gaining first-class honours in ancient classics in his masterate while also teaching at St Stanislaus College, Tullamore (1910-11). In 1912-14 he taught at Clongowes Wood College, Kildare. After reading philosophy at St Mary's Hall, Stonyhurst, England (1914-16), he returned to Ireland to teach at Tullabeg (1916-18) and then studied theology at Milltown Park, where he was ordained priest on 24 October 1920. Back at Tullabeg, in 1922 he completed a doctorate in theology for the Gregorian University, Rome, although the degree was not conferred until 1963.

Responding to a call from Corpus Christi College, the recently established seminary at Werribee, in 1923 Johnston travelled to

Victoria, and, after teaching at Xavier College, Melbourne, took up his appointment in 1925. Essentially a professor of philosophy, he also taught liturgy and music, and on occasion scripture and moral theology. In 1930 he became rector of the college, remaining so until 1947. Almost four hundred student priests came under his influence. Noted for his professional poise, practical equanimity and unshakeable self-confidence, he was a rigid, seemingly aloof disciplinarian: he treated all students alike and set an example of impeccable priestly behaviour. Industrious and orderly, without being pettifogging, he had a passion for detailed knowledge and accuracy.

The years at Werribee were the highlight of Johnston's life in Australia, but his work extended beyond them. He taught (1949-53) at Canisius College, Pymble, Sydney, and then served as parish priest and superior (1954-56) at St Mary's, North Sydney. In 1957 and again in 1961 he was tertian instructor at Sevenhill College, Clare, South Australia, and between those appointments taught Greek, Latin and history at Loyola College, Watsonia, Melbourne. From 1962 to 1966 he served as parish priest and superior at Immaculate Conception Church, Hawthorn. After further stints of teaching at Werribee (1967-70) and Watsonia (1970-73), he worked (1974) with the Marist Brothers at Campion College, Kew. He spent 1975-77 at the provincial's residence, Hawthorn, before returning to St Mary's (1978-82) as chaplain to the nearby Josephite Sisters.

Incisive of mind and tenacious of purpose, Johnston was a formidable Irish gentleman, scholar and cleric. A passion for knowledge and accuracy also informed his work as a polemicist, a writer of apologetic tracts, and a radio personality. His somewhat steely smile and halo of tightly curled white hair gave him a special aura. He maintained an iceberg calm and relentless logic at all times. Yet, although he appeared reserved, even cold, he could be counted on for sympathetic advice. He had a respect for individuality, if within strictly defined boundaries. His popular publications included *Plain Talks on the Catholic Religion* (1936), *A Critic Looks at the Catholic Church* (1944) and *A Seed That Grew* (1956), a history of North Sydney parish. Father Henry Johnston died on 4 September 1986 at Kew and was buried in Boroondara cemetery.

Corpus Christi, no 1, 1962, p 46, no 2, 1967, p 163, no 3, 1974, p 25; *Jesuit Life*, no 22, 1986, p 27; private information and personal knowledge.   J. EDDY

JOHNSTONE, BRIAN WILLIAM WAL-LACE (1920-1988), army officer and art gallery owner, was born on 21 November 1920 at Mussoorie, India, only child of Noel William Wallace Johnstone, army officer, and his wife Kathleen Violet, née Hart. The family migrated to Australia and Brian was educated (1933-38) at the Collegiate School of St Peter, Adelaide. He entered the Royal Military College, Duntroon, Australian Capital Territory, in 1939. After graduating in 1941, he transferred to the Australian Imperial Force and performed training and staff duties in the South-West Pacific Area. In 1945-48 he served in the United States of America and Europe. Captain Johnstone transferred to the Reserve of Officers on 29 June 1949, in order to take the post of aide-de-camp to the governor of Queensland, Sir John Lavarack [q.v.15]. On 8 September 1950 at St Mary's Church of England, Kangaroo Point, Brisbane, he married Marjorie Rose Mant, a 38-year-old actress. Next year they became founding members of the Queensland (National) Art Gallery Society.

In partnership with Hugh Hale, a Brisbane-based interior designer, on 8 December 1950 Johnstone opened the Marodian Gallery, at the back of Hale's shop in Upper Edward Street. Probably intended as a trial, the venture had a fairly safe beginning, but in 1951 Hale's intolerance of more challenging art by Donald Friend [q.v.] and Arthur Boyd led to the dissolution of the partnership.

After Johnstone left his post with the governor on 14 July 1951, he and his wife opened the Johnstone Gallery, on 5 February next year, in the Brisbane Arcade, Queen Street. The small basement space—a former bomb shelter—was decorated in a modern and inexpensive fashion. In a letter to clients Johnstone outlined his intention to exhibit 'the most creative work in Australia today', particularly that of 'brilliant' younger artists. Drawing on new schools of painting that were emerging in Melbourne and Sydney, in the first year he arranged solo exhibitions for Friend, Laurence Hope, (Sir) Sidney Nolan and Carl Plate [q.v.15 Lewers]. Michael Kmit showed his work for the first time in Brisbane. In 1954 at their home, 6 Cintra Road, Bowen Hills, the Johnstones opened the 'Home Salon' to complement the city gallery. Their confidence was high and the market-place responsive; however, they closed the Johnstone Gallery on 19 December 1957. Johnstone then spent ten months in hospital with tuberculosis before reopening it at 6 Cintra Road.

This gallery combined a semi-domestic setting, modern designer wares and good contemporary art with a dramatic décor: walls were painted dark or white and theatrically placed curtains, furniture, ceramics and arrangements of dried flowers, sticks or plants created a distinctive aura. The nature of the space with its twists, turns and vistas, placement of works around every corner and up small flights of stairs, and sophisticated lighting, all helped to show the art to its greatest advantage. Boyd, Friend and Nolan, as well as other artists including Charles Blackman, Margaret Olley, Ray Crooke, Lawrence Daws, Keith Looby, Lloyd Rees and (Sir) Russell Drysdale [qq.v.] and the local sculptors Leonard and Kathleen Shillam, were among the exhibitors.

The Johnstones had a unique style. Marjorie's theatrical personality was evident not only in the gallery's presentation but also at frequent opening events, often in a tropical garden setting. The couple developed methods of marketing and of promoting the artists whose work they exhibited: they travelled interstate and sold from slides, used catalogues with additional information and forewords, issued invitations to events, and established links with the press. The gallery gained national significance and pervasive influence. Its location in Brisbane, often derided before the 1980s as a place of little culture, makes the Johnstones' achievement all the greater.

In the 1960s the Johnstones made available a block of land adjacent to their home, and helped to raise funds, for a new Twelfth Night Theatre, which opened in 1971. Fatigued, and in ill health, they retired and closed the gallery in December 1972. Survived by his wife (d.1993), Johnstone died of a ruptured aortic aneurysm on 22 June 1988 in Brisbane and was cremated. There were no children. 'The Jabirus', a sculpture by Leonard and Kathleen Shillam, was presented in 1992 to the City of Brisbane Collection (now held by the Museum of Brisbane) as a memorial to the Johnstone Gallery. In 1994 the Johnstones' extensive private art collection was auctioned. The Johnstone Gallery archive and portraits of Brian and Marjorie Johnstone, painted and donated by Ray Crooke in 2003, are held by the State Library of Queensland.

Art and Australia, June 1978, p 395; A. Archer, Back Room—Bomb Shelter—Bowen Hills (BA Hons thesis, Univ of Qld, 1990); L. Martin-Chew, "Like Topsy": The Johnstone Gallery 1950-1972 (MCA thesis, JCU, 2001); B2458, item 3319 (NAA).

LOUISE MARTIN-CHEW

JONES, PHYLLIS MANDER (1896-1984), librarian and archivist, was born on 2 January 1896 at Homebush, Sydney, eldest of five children of Queensland-born George Mander Jones, physician, and his wife Margaret Fleming, née Arnott, born in New South Wales. George was a grandson of the merchant David Jones [q.v.2]; Margaret was a daughter of the biscuit manufacturer William Arnott [q.v.3]. Phyllis was educated at Abbotsleigh and at the University of Sydney (BA, 1917), where she resided at Women's College and graduated with first-class honours in German and second-class honours in French. Following a brief stint of teaching at Abbotsleigh, she tutored privately.

In May 1925 Miss Jones joined the staff of the Public Library of New South Wales as a library assistant. By 1933 she was a fully qualified librarian. She became particularly well informed about the history of the book, its manufacture and decoration and in 1941 was appointed to the position of bibliographer. During World War II her knowledge of languages proved useful to the Department of the Army, which employed her on its censorship staff; she also assisted in the bibliographic work carried out by the Mitchell Library, under the direction of Ida Leeson [q.v.10], for the Allied Geographical Section.

In November 1946 Jones was appointed Mitchell librarian. She had responsibility for a library (which also functioned as the State archives) that had experienced difficulties during the war years, the practices of which needed modernisation, and the staff of which was generally not equipped to deal with the problems confronting them. She trained the staff and established new standards in the care and recording of the collections, giving particular attention to the conservation and processing of manuscripts, maps and pictorial material and to the creation of finding aids to help researchers. She acquired important original documents, including the second collection of Macarthur [q.v.2 Elizabeth, James, John, q.v.5 Sir William] papers and the records of the early Supreme Court of New South Wales. She addressed groups and conferences in Australia and overseas and prepared publications promoting the library's valuable resources. In 1956 George Mackaness [q.v.10] wrote to her: 'The Mitchell owes to you far more than the Trustees will ever be able to repay'.

Miss Mander Jones (as she was commonly known) also helped to establish the archival profession in Australia. During 1948 she investigated archival practices and conservation techniques and explored holdings of records relating to Australia in Britain, the United States of America and South America, and attended the inaugural conference of the International Council on Archives. In 1949 she prepared a report about archives in New South Wales for a conference of Commonwealth and State authorities. For many years she was an examiner in bibliography and archives for registration examinations of the Library Association of Australia. She helped to establish its archives section (which in 1975 became the Australian Society of Archivists) and was co-editor of the first issue of the journal *Archives and Manuscripts*, in 1955.

In 1956 Mander Jones went to London to work on the records of the London Missionary

Society and other papers. Next year she resigned as Mitchell librarian and became the State Public Library's liaison officer in London. In 1960 she took over the work of the Australian Joint Copying Project, a program initiated in 1945 for the copying of records of Australian, and later Pacific, interest in the United Kingdom. In 1964 she was appointed to direct the project, jointly administered by the Australian National University and the National Library of Australia, which led to the publication *Manuscripts in the British Isles Relating to Australia, New Zealand, and the Pacific* (1972), popularly known as the 'Mander-Jones guide'. After returning to Australia, she contributed to the bibliography of J. C. Beaglehole's *The Life of Captain James Cook* (1974) and researched the history of the Arnott family. Moving to Medindie, Adelaide, she published (1981) a guide to the manuscript holdings of the South Australian branch of the Royal Geographical Society of Australasia.

Phyllis Mander-Jones (she hyphenated her surname in later life) was appointed MBE in 1971. She was made a fellow of the Library Association of Australia in 1963 and received its 1981 H. C. L. Anderson [q.v.7] award. The Australian Society of Archivists made her an honorary member (1976) and in 1996 inaugurated the Mander Jones awards. She was a skilled artist and photographer, an adventurous traveller and a meticulous scholar. According to Professor G. G. Nicholson [q.v.11], she had 'a grace of character and rare distinction of manner'. Never married, she died on 19 February 1984 at Prospect, Adelaide, and was cremated.

Archives and Manuscripts, vol 14, no 1, 1986, pp 7-45; B. Berzins, interview with P. Mander-Jones (ts, 1983, SLNSW); Mander-Jones papers (SLNSW).

BAIBA BERZINS

JONES, RICHARD (1936-1986), conservationist, was born on 19 September 1936 at Sarina, Queensland, eldest of three sons of George Jones, an English-born tobacco-farmer, and his wife Isabella Mary, née Arbuthnot, from North Queensland. Dux of Mackay State High School in 1954, next year Richard trained as a primary school teacher at Queensland Teachers' Training College, Kelvin Grove, Brisbane, and in 1956-57 taught in the Mackay district.

In 1958 Jones enrolled at the University of Queensland (B.Sc., 1961; M.Sc., 1963), and subsequently majored in botany. For his master's thesis he investigated the mountain mallee heath of the McPherson Ranges. He was president of the metropolitan section of the Australian Country Party, Queensland branch. On 25 May 1963 at Scots Memorial Church, Clayfield, Brisbane, he married with Presbyterian forms Patricia Campbell Cribb, a schoolteacher. In 1963 he lectured at the University College of Townsville; next year he commenced doctoral studies at the University of Melbourne (Ph.D., 1967). His thesis, supervised by Raymond Specht, was on 'Productivity and Water Use Efficiency of a Victorian Heathland'. He joined the Commonwealth Scientific and Industrial Research Organization's Division of Plant Industry in 1967. Based at its Riverina Laboratory, Deniliquin, New South Wales, as a dry-land ecologist, he researched saltbush as a food source for sheep.

A senior lecturer in botany at the University of Tasmania from 1970, 'Dick' Jones became the dominant early figure in the environment movement that soon emerged in Tasmania. He was founding chairman of the Lake Pedder Action Committee (1971), which fought unsuccessfully to save the lake from inundation, and of the United Tasmania Group (1972-79), the world's first 'green' political party. As co-manager of the group's campaign for the Tasmanian House of Assembly 1972 elections, he produced a pamphlet, *A New Ethic*. Inaugural director (1974-86) of the university's Centre for Environmental Studies, he edited publications on a range of contentious Tasmanian conservation issues, including logging of rainforests, wood-chip production, endangered wildlife, and the activities of the Hydro-Electric Commission. He helped to establish the Tasmanian Environment Centre, opened in Hobart in 1973, and served on its board, and was a councillor (1973-82), vice-president (1973-81) and life member (1982) of the Australian Conservation Foundation. In 1974 and 1975 he contested Senate elections as a UTG candidate.

Although (Senator) Robert (Bob) Brown became the public face of Tasmanian environmental politics after the Lake Pedder campaign, Jones continued to be a dauntless and formidable activist. He supported the Tasmanian Wilderness Society's crusade against both options for future dam sites presented to voters in a State referendum in 1981; as a result 33 per cent wrote 'no dams' on their ballot papers. In 1985 he was appointed to the Tasmanian World Heritage Area Council's consultative committee. Survived by his wife and their daughter and son, he died on 19 March 1986 in Hobart, after a fall from a ladder at his Sandy Bay home, and was cremated with Anglican rites. He left behind him Australia's most tactically adept and politically prominent regional environment movement.

D. Johnson, *Lake Pedder* (1972); P. Hay et al (eds), *Environmental Politics in Australia and New Zealand* (1989); M. Mulligan and S. Hill, *Ecological Pioneers* (2001); *Public Administration* (Sydney), vol 31, no 1,

1972, p 21; *Togatus*, Apr 1986, p 8; P. Walker, The United Tasmania Group (BA Hons thesis, Univ of Tas, 1987); private information.   PETER HAY

JORDAN, DENIS OSWALD (1914-1982), physical and inorganic chemist, was born on 23 September 1914 at Southgate, London, second son of Walter William Jordan, accountant's clerk, and his wife Rosa, née Waters. Denis attended Minchenden Grammar School, Southgate. Leaving school in 1933, he was fortunate to obtain, in a time of economic depression, the position of laboratory assistant at the British Launderers' Research Association, which was supported by the Department of Scientific and Industrial Research. He attended night classes at the Sir John Cass Technical Institute (College), University of London (B.Sc. (Special) Chemistry, 1936; M.Sc., 1938; Ph.D., 1945; D.Sc., 1953). For his master's degree he researched the hydrolysis of soaps, using the novel glass electrode to determine the acidity or alkalinity (pH) of aqueous solutions. In 1939 'Doj' was appointed assistant lecturer in applied chemistry at University College, Nottingham (University of Nottingham). He married Margery Gauge on 30 December 1939 at Fox Lane Congregational Church, Palmers Green, Southgate.

For his doctoral thesis Jordan worked on the surface chemistry of soap solutions. With the organic chemist J. Masson Gulland he attempted the physico-chemical characterisation of the little understood nucleic acids. In 1947 Gulland, Jordan and C. J. Threlfall perfected a method for preparing highly polymeric deoxyribonucleic acids from calf thymus glands. By carrying out pH titrations Gulland, Jordan and H. F. W. Taylor confirmed that DNA was a linear polymer of phosphate-linked sugar groups and that there was specific hydrogen bonding between the purine and pyrimidine bases. These results contributed to the postulation of a molecular structure for DNA in 1953 by J. D. Watson and F. H. C. Crick. In 1948 Jordan was awarded a Commonwealth Fund fellowship to study at Princeton University, United States of America, with the physical chemist (Sir) Hugh Taylor. Back in England he continued work on nucleic acids and surface chemistry and commenced studies of synthetic polymers, completing his time at Nottingham as a reader.

In 1953 Jordan was appointed to the chair of physical and inorganic chemistry at the University of Adelaide. Arriving in Australia early in 1954, he found a discipline and a department needing renewal. He applied himself to this task with characteristic energy and enthusiasm and by 1966 the department, with nineteen academic staff members, was acknowledged as the foremost polymer chemistry school in Australia. A busy supervisor and an excellent lecturer, Jordan also published ninety-seven research articles and a book, *The Chemistry of Nucleic Acids* (1960). He was dean of the faculty of science (1958-59), a member of the finance committee (1969-77) and the university council (1971-80), and pro vice-chancellor (1974-75). In 1979 he retired as professor emeritus from the university.

Jordan was a member (1958-75) and president (1958-59, 1961-62) of the council of the Australian Institute of Nuclear Science and Engineering. In 1970 the South Australian government appointed him chairman of a committee to investigate all aspects of pollution in the State. The report, which resulted in the setting up of a Department of Environment and Conservation and an advisory, extra-governmental Environmental Protection Council, was seminal for subsequent environmental planning in South Australia. He was a fellow (1970) of the Australian Academy of Science and a member (1976-79) of its council. President (1978-79) of the Royal Australian Chemical Institute, he was awarded its Batteard-Jordan Australian Polymer (1974) and Leighton memorial (1981) medals. In 1980 he was appointed AO. Next year the University of Adelaide named its physical and inorganic chemistry building after him.

A keen patron of Scotch College, Adelaide, he served on the council of governors from 1956 (chairman 1961-81), and claimed that in the interest of the college he had consumed more haggis than most native-born Scots. His hobbies were camping, gardening and listening to music. Survived by his wife and their two daughters, he died of carcinoid syndrome on 12 February 1982 at St Georges, Adelaide, and was cremated.

R. J. Best, *Discoveries by Chemists* (1987); J. H. Coates, 'Denis Oswald Jordan 1914-1982', *Hist Records of Austn Science*, vol 6, no 2, 1985, p 237; *Cluaran*, 1982, p 112.   JOHN COATES

JORDAN, ELLEN VIOLET (1913-1982), politician, was born on 29 June 1913 at Ipswich, Queensland, eldest of three children of English-born James Bertie Norman Perrett, a railway fitter, and his Queensland-born wife Ann Jane, née Brown. Educated at Brassall State and Ipswich Girls' Grammar schools, Vi won, but did not take up, a scholarship to attend the Teachers' Training College in Brisbane. An accomplished musician, she had become an associate of the London College of Music and of the Trinity College of Music, London. Headstrong and determined, at 18 she married David Jordan, a railway porter, on 14 May 1932 at St Thomas's Church of

England, North Ipswich. A member of one of Ipswich's brass bands, David shared her love of music.

At the beginning of World War II Vi Jordan was fiercely opposed to conscription and Australian support for the British at war. Nevertheless she became secretary of the first aid and air raid precautions committee and president of the Ipswich civilian welfare committee for service women at the Royal Australian Air Force base at Amberley. She also devoted time to a servicewomen's hostel at Ipswich.

When the Soviet Union became a wartime ally, Jordan joined the Australian Friends of the Soviet Union; as a result her knowledge of Marxist philosophy developed. From a family steeped in the trade union movement, Jordan believed that the militant attitude of some communist unions was detrimental to the workers but she remained sympathetic to the philosophy of the Communist Party of Australia. Affected by the communist takeover of Czechoslovakia and Prime Minister (Sir) Robert Menzies' [q.v.15] attempt in 1950-51 to have the Communist Party declared illegal, Jordan burnt all her relevant books and papers and severed her connections with the Friends of the Soviet Union.

A member of the Australian Labor Party from the late 1940s, at the time of the split in Queensland Labor in 1957 Jordan remained staunchly loyal to the ALP: she was president (1956-67) of the Labor women's central organising committee, secretary (1958-65) of the Somerset executive committee and secretary of both the Somerset and Ipswich West ladies' branches. At the Labor-in-Politics Convention in Brisbane in 1960, she moved a successful resolution that women be allowed direct representation on the Queensland central executive. She was chosen as that representative and thus became the first woman other than a union delegate on the executive. In 1961 she was the first woman elected to the Ipswich City Council; she held this position until 1967. She was a delegate to conferences of the Local Government Association of Queensland.

The ALP chose Jordan as their candidate for the State seat of Ipswich West for the 1966 election. Under the campaign leadership of Bill Hayden, she defeated Jim Finimore, who had been the mayor of Ipswich for seventeen years. Serving for three terms, during which the ALP was in opposition, Jordan engaged in the struggle for the rights of the working class and for political, economic and social equality for women. In 1966 she spoke in parliament in a grievance session advocating equal pay for women. She was re-elected in 1969 and 1972 but defeated in 1974. In the lead-up to the 1977 election Jordan won the ALP plebiscite for Ipswich West but a redistribution changed the boundaries of her electorate and the QCE,

deciding to appoint candidates centrally, did not choose her.

Jordan was president (1974-76) of the federal women's executive of the ALP. In 1975 she was made a member of the Council of Queensland Women, set up to advise the State government on the status of women. She was appointed AM in 1976 and next year awarded the Queen's jubilee medal. A keen lawn-bowler, she served on the committee of the North Ipswich Bowling Club. Predeceased (1967) by her husband and survived by her son, she died of myocardial infarction on 7 May 1982 at Ipswich and was buried in the city's general cemetery. She was praised for her 'ability to always keep Ipswich on the Map' and will be remembered as the first woman from the ALP, and only the second of any political persuasion, to become a member of the Queensland parliament.

M. Reynolds, *The Last Bastion* (1995); *PD* (Qld), 4 Aug 1982, p 11; *Refractory Girl*, no 4, 1973, p 13; *Qld Review*, vol 12, no 2, 2005, p 63; *Courier-Mail* (Brisbane), 9 Aug 1977, p 1, 10 May 1982, p 25; *Qld Times*, 30 June 1980, p 7, 8 May 1982, p 2, 7 Nov 1991, p 18; private information.

PATRICIA FALLON

JOSKE, SIR PERCY ERNEST (1895-1981), politician and judge, was born on 5 October 1895 at Albert Park, Melbourne, youngest of three children of Ernest Joske, a German-born solicitor, and his Victorian-born wife Evalyne, née Richards. Evalyne died giving birth to him and Ernest remarried in 1898. Percy was educated at Wesley College, where he formed a lifelong friendship with (Sir) Robert Menzies [q.v.15], and at the University of Melbourne (LL B, 1915; LL M, 1918; BA, 1921; MA, 1923), winning the (Sir) John Madden [q.v.10] exhibition and graduating with first-class honours. He signed the Bar roll on 25 June 1917.

Specialising in matrimonial law, Joske acquired an extensive and varied practice. He was a prolific author of legal textbooks, publishing *The Remuneration of Commission Agents* (with Alan S. Lloyd, 1924), *The Law of Marriage and Divorce* (1925), *The Law and Procedure at Meetings of Councils* (1925), *The Law and Principles of Insurance in Australasia* (1933), *The Law and Procedure at Meetings in Australia and New Zealand* (1938) and *Sale of Goods in Australia* (1949). On 12 January 1928 at the Methodist Church, Highbury Grove, Kew, he married Hilda Mavis Connell, a teacher of music. From 1936 to 1956 he edited the *Victorian Law Reports*. Succeeding his father as registrar of the Dental Board of Victoria in 1940, he was to hold the position until 1957. On 16 October 1944 he took silk. He lectured part time in dental jurisprudence at the Australian College of Dentistry and in the law of domestic relations at the University of Melbourne.

Having stood unsuccessfully as an Independent Liberal and Country Party candidate for the Legislative Council seat of Monash in June 1949, Joske succeeded (Sir) Thomas White [q.v.16] to the safe Liberal seat of Balaclava in the House of Representatives at a by-election on 28 July 1951. The *Sun-Herald* described him as a 'fluent debater', although his 'thin voice' was 'sometimes lost in House debates'. He was a member of various parliamentary committees, an Australian delegate (1955) to the tenth session of the General Assembly of the United Nations in New York, a councillor (1956-60) of the Australian National University and chairman (1959-60) of the Commonwealth Immigration Planning Council.

A keen advocate of uniform divorce law in Australia, Joske pressed the government to introduce a Federal divorce bill. He drafted a private member's bill, passed as the Matrimonial Causes Act (1955), which enabled married women to institute divorce proceedings in the State or Territory of their residence. In 1957 he introduced, again as a private member, a comprehensive measure that dealt with the grounds of divorce as well as with questions of jurisdiction. The bill was vigorously debated; (Sir) Howard Beale [q.v.] led the campaign against it on the grounds that it was too narrow and conservative. Eventually it was replaced by a government bill that became law as the Matrimonial Causes Act (1959). The attorney-general, Sir Garfield Barwick, acknowledged a 'great debt' to Joske's efforts, which made the uniform divorce legislation possible.

On 3 June 1960 Joske was appointed a judge of the Commonwealth (Australian) Industrial Court. He also served as a judge of the Supreme Court of the Australian Capital Territory (from 1960), of the Northern Territory (from 1961) and of Norfolk Island (from 1966). He worked regularly in the Supreme Court in Canberra, but in the early 1970s became involved in a series of 'often-spectacular exchanges' with counsel who 'disliked his interventionist technique' on the bench. Continuing to write on a wide range of legal subjects, he published *The Law of Partnership in Australia and New Zealand* (1957), *Australian Federal Government* (1967) and *Family Law* (1976), as well as numerous new editions of his previous works. In 1977 the *Australian Law Journal* declared that, apart from H. V. Evatt [q.v.14], 'no other Australian judge has been the author of so many standard books on legal subjects'.

Mavis had died in 1968. On 4 October 1969 at the chapel of the Pacific Theological College, Suva, Fiji, Joske married her cousin Hilda Dorothy Larcombe, née Thomas, a widow. He moved from Brighton, Melbourne, to her Georgian-revival house, Somerset, designed by B. J. Waterhouse [q.v.12], at Strathfield, Sydney. Appointed CMG in 1967, he was knighted in 1977. Later that year he retired. Usually affable and mild mannered, he listed his recreations as gardening and writing. In 1978 he published *Sir Robert Menzies 1894-1978: A New, Informal Memoir*. He was Australian president of the Royal Life Saving Society from 1951 to 1979. Sir Percy died on 25 April 1981 at his Strathfield home and was cremated with Anglican rites. His wife survived him, as did the son of his first marriage, Thomas Roderick, a judge (1976-2005) of the Family Court of Australia.

H. Beale, *This Inch of Time* (1977); D. Marr, *Barwick* (1980); *The Dental Board of Victoria* (1993); *PD* (HR), 14 May 1959, p 2222; *Austn Law Jnl*, vol 34, no 2, 1960, p 59, vol 51, no 10, 1977, p 735, vol 55, no 8, 1981, p 607; *Sun-Herald* (Sydney), 14 Apr 1957, p 30; *SMH*, 14 Sept 1977, p 3, 27 Apr 1981, p 8; *Canberra Times*, 17 Dec 1977, p 7, 27 Apr 1981, p 3; Joske papers (NLA); private information.

JOLYON HORNER

JOYCE, ERROL BLAIR DE NORMANVILLE ('BARNEY') (1908-1983), grazier and cattle-breeder, was born on 28 June 1908 at Bundaberg, Queensland, second of six children of Fitzpierce de Normanville Joyce, grazier, from Galway, Ireland, and his Queensland-born wife Rose Eileen, daughter of De Burgh Persse [q.v.5]. Educated at home by governesses and at The Armidale School, New South Wales (1921-25), Barney worked on the family's cattle property, Eidsvold station, in the Burnett district of Queensland. In the 1930s he travelled extensively in Australia and overseas, and investigated cattle-raising in Brazil and Argentina. After his father's death in 1936 Barney, his brother Raoul and his mother formed the partnership of Joyce & Joyce. They acquired Gyranda, near Cracow, in Dawson River country; Barney managed Eidsvold and Raoul Gyranda. Their mother, who had a 'good business head', was reputedly a guiding force in the venture until her death in 1959.

On 1 December 1938 at St Mark's Church of England, Darling Point, Sydney, Joyce married Joan Willoughby Dowling, granddaughter of V. J. Dowling [q.v.4]. In 1942-45 he served as a private in the Volunteer Defence Corps. He was a member (1949-67) of Eidsvold Shire Council. In 1946-82 he was a board-member of Mactaggarts Primary Producers' Co-operative Association Ltd (from 1977, Primac Holdings Ltd).

The Joyce properties initially ran and bred Hereford cattle, but after King Ranch (Australia) Pty Ltd introduced American-bred Santa

Gertrudis cattle into Australia in 1952, Joyce & Joyce acquired four imported bulls in 1953-54, and ten heifers in 1955. These were crossed with Herefords to produce, over time, some ninety progeny, and the first cross-bred Eidsvold bulls were sold in January 1958. Thereafter Joyce actively promoted the breed. He clashed with breeders of 'British' cattle, most notably during and following a lecture on 'breeding for the environment' that he gave in 1959 at Armidale. A frequent speaker on the rural programs of the Australian Broadcasting Commission, Radio Australia and the British Broadcasting Corporation's Asia Pacific service, he was an early advocate of dehorning cattle and of flexible fencing. He worked with the Queensland Department of Agriculture and Stock in experiments comparing Hereford and Santa Gertrudis cross-steers and provided field-work opportunities for agricultural students on Eidsvold station.

Helping to form the Santa Gertrudis Breeders' (Australia) Association in 1955, Joyce served as a permanent councillor (1955-72), vice-president and deputy-president (1955-62), president (1964-66) and patron (1978-82); he was elected an honorary life member in 1973. While president he established a publicity fund; produced a booklet, *Santa Gertrudis in Australia*; instituted a formal stud-book; and extended membership to breeders from Western Australia and the Northern Territory. A cattle judge at shows throughout Australia, he lectured on the Santa Gertrudis breed in Britain, the United States of America, the Pacific islands and Africa. He also promoted Eidsvold station, number two in the stud register, inviting such notables as Joyce Grenfell, Dame Annabelle Rankin [q.v.], (Sir) Zelman Cowen and Prince Richard of Gloucester to open its well-publicised annual cattle sales. The Joyces twice entertained Prince Charles at Eidsvold and attended his wedding in 1981.

A patron of the arts, Joyce owned a highly regarded collection of Australian art by both established and emerging artists; he often displayed paintings at his cattle sales. He was a benefactor of the University of Queensland, donating money and paintings for a new music shell (1971), finance for Dutch stained-glass windows in Mayne [q.v.10] Hall (1972), and funding for pathology laboratories in the department of veterinary medicine (1978). In 1971 he was appointed OBE.

Sometimes dubbed the 'squire of Eidsvold', Joyce was colourful in both dress and manner. He sported a distinctive thin white moustache and frequently wore a calfskin vest with a varied choice of hats. Often accompanied on tours by his wife, he was a consummate showman: charismatic, witty and charming, and equally at home with stockmen and royalty. He was neither a 'shrinking violet' nor a 'quiet achiever', believing it 'better to be deplored than to be ignored'. He unabashedly promoted Eidsvold, Santa Gertrudis, and Australia—in that order. Survived by his wife, he died on 21 January 1983 at Nambour and was cremated. There were no children.

K. Nutting, *The Joyces of the Overflow and Eidsvold* (1972); J. Hanley, *Santa Gertrudis* (1995); *Qld Country Life*, 1 Oct 1959, p 9; *Santa Gertrudis Review*, Dec 1982, p 27, July 1983, p 9; *Sunday Mail* (Brisbane), 23 Jan 1983, p 3; *Times* (London), 7 Feb 1983, p 12; The History of Eidsvold Station (booklet, 1969?, copy held at Univ of Qld Lib); J. Francis, Mr Errol Blair de Normanville (Barney) Joyce, O.B.E. (ts, 1983, Univ of Qld Lib).
                                                                M. FRENCH

JOYNT, WILLIAM DONOVAN (1889-1986), soldier, printer and publisher, was born on 19 March 1889 at Elsternwick, Melbourne, third son of Edward Kelly Joynt, a commercial traveller from Ireland, and his Victorian-born wife Alice, née Woolcott. He attended the Grange Preparatory School, South Yarra, and Melbourne Church of England Grammar School (1904) before taking office jobs, including one with an accountancy firm in 1906-07. In 1909 he sailed for Rockhampton, Queensland, walked to Mackay, joined a coastal steamer bound for Cairns, and did bush and farm jobs in North Queensland. He then worked in the Victorian Mallee and in Western Australia, and was dairying and digging potatoes on Flinders Island, off Tasmania, when World War I began.

Having served as a corporal in the Victorian Rifles, Militia, Joynt enlisted in the Australian Imperial Force on 21 May 1915. Commissioned on 24 December, he arrived in France in May 1916 and joined the 8th Battalion in July. On 30 September he was shot in the shoulder during a raid on the German trenches at The Bluff in the Ypres sector, Belgium. He was evacuated to England, commended in divisional orders and in December promoted to lieutenant. In January 1917 he rejoined his battalion and, except for three months at an army school and on leave during the 1917-18 winter, served with the unit on the Western Front until August 1918, fighting in the second battle of Bullecourt and at Menin Road and Broodseinde. C. E. W. Bean's [q.v.7] official history published his vivid diary account of the fighting near Merris on the Somme on 12-14 April 1918.

On 23 August 1918, when an attack near Herleville was pinned down, with heavy losses, by intense fire from Plateau Wood, Joynt rallied the attackers and led an advance which cleared the wood's approaches, then in a bayonet charge captured it and over eighty prisoners. For his 'most conspicuous bravery' he won the Victoria Cross. He was seriously wounded in the buttock on 26 August and evacuated to England. Promoted to captain in October, he was posted to AIF Headquarters, London, in March 1919. In February 1920 he returned to Melbourne, where his AIF appointment terminated on 11 June. His elder brother Gerald, a lieutenant in the 57th Battalion, had been killed at Polygon Wood, Belgium, on 25 September 1917.

Joynt had studied agriculture and sheep-breeding in England in 1919, and in 1920 he became a soldier settler, dairy farming near Berwick. By 1926 he had a manager on his block, and when it was resumed in 1929 was pursuing interests in Melbourne. He was a pioneer of colour printing in Australia. About 1920 he had formed Queen City Printers Pty Ltd and with W. E. Dexter [q.v.8] arranged an exhibition of war photographs in colour, and printed its catalogue. He then formed Colarts Studios Pty Ltd and bought the rights to a German colour-printing process. The business failed during the Depression, but under various business names Joynt remained a printer and publisher for over sixty years. He called himself a 'master printer' when he married Edith Amy Garrett, a trained nurse, in a civil ceremony at Hawthorn on 19 March 1932, his forty-third birthday.

An inaugural member of Melbourne Legacy in 1923, Joynt helped to lead the club's successful campaign to have Melbourne's Shrine of Remembrance built in its present form on its present site. He was active in the Militia in 1926-33, being promoted to major in February 1930. Mobilised on 26 September 1939, he commanded the 3rd Garrison Battalion at Queenscliff and then, from March 1941, Puckapunyal camp. From June 1942 he was camp staff officer then quartermaster at Seymour camp. He was placed on the Retired List as an honorary lieutenant colonel on 10 October 1944. He and his wife rented then bought Tom Roberts's [q.v.11] old home, Talisman, at Kallista and lived there until they built their own home nearby. Joynt wrote three autobiographical books: *To Russia and Back through Communist Countries* (1971), *Saving the Channel Ports, 1918* (1975) and *Breaking the Road for the Rest* (1979).

Short and dark, with twinkling grey eyes, Donovan Joynt was a chirpy cock sparrow of a man, self-reliant, dogmatic, conservative, a nominal Anglican, a Freemason from 1924, a dedicated advocate of returned-soldier causes, a special constable during the 1923 Melbourne police strike, a keen club-man and a life member of the Naval and Military Club. In 1979 he described himself as a 'Royalist' with a 'love of all things British', while an old Legacy comrade called him 'a dedicated "King's Man", a true-blue adherent of all the best traditions and heritages of his British ancestry'. His wife

died in 1978. The last surviving of Australia's World War I VC winners, he died on 5 May 1986 at Windsor and was buried with full military honours in Brighton cemetery. He had no children.

C. Blatchford, *Legacy* (1932); C. E. W. Bean, *The A.I.F. in France 1917* (1933), *The A.I.F. in France 1918*, 2 vols (1937, 1942); L. Wigmore (ed), *They Dared Mightily* (1963); R. J. Austin, *Cobbers in Khaki* (1997); *Mufti*, 1 Dec 1937, p 17; *Age* (Melbourne), 7 May 1986, p 5; 2DRL/0765 (AWM); B884, item V80044 (NAA); private information.

BILL GAMMAGE

JUNGWIRTH, Sir WILLIAM JOHN (1897-1981), public servant, was born on 10 August 1897 at Richmond, Melbourne, third child of Victorian-born parents Vincent John Jungwirth, labourer, and his wife Jane, née Thomson. Educated at Abbotsford State School, Jack—as he was known—worked as a junior clerk with Dalgety [q.v.4] & Co. before joining the Department of Lands in 1915. He studied shorthand at Zercho's Business College, qualified as a licentiate (1920) of the Commonwealth Institute of Accountants, and in 1920 transferred to the premier's office, in the Chief Secretary's Department, where he became private secretary (1922) to the premier, (Sir) Harry Lawson [q.v.10]. His high regard for the Presbyterian and teetotal premier reflected his similar outlook. On 22 December 1923 at North Richmond Methodist church he married Alice Ruth Powell.

Chief clerk from 1931, Jungwirth was appointed secretary of the newly established Department of Premier in 1936, the youngest first division officer in the Victorian public service. An outstanding administrator and organiser, he was calm in approach, unruffled in crises and firm in his advice to the thirteen premiers and twenty-three ministries he was to serve as private or official secretary. For these premiers he was a trusted constant through frequent periods of political change. He defined his role as 'supplying political masters with information and advice on which to base policy, accepting the policy when made and working loyally to implement it'.

Between 1927 and 1959 Jungwirth played official roles in eight royal visits, including those of State director of Queen Elizabeth II's 1954 national tour and organiser of the Duke of Edinburgh's official opening of the 1956 Olympic Games. Appointed CMG (1948) and knighted in 1957, by his retirement in 1962 he was Victoria's senior and pre-eminent public servant, his department having replaced the Treasury and Chief Secretary's Department as the originator of new activities. A shrewd observer, he reflected in his unpublished memoirs that, over forty years, close association with politics had convinced him that the efficient functioning of democratic government required that members of the Executive should be 'responsible to parliament and not to their respective parties'.

Jungwirth was a man of strong faith and an active member of the Methodist Church; his personal qualities, coupled with his knowledge of government and legislation, drew him into extensive community service. He had joined the Independent Order of Rechabites in 1913 and was secretary of the Richmond Tent (1923-37), district chief ruler (1931) and a trustee (1940-81). A board-member (1940-76) and president (1966-73) of Prince Henry's Hospital, he was also president (1954-56, 1964-65) of the Young Men's Christian Association of Melbourne, and a committee-member of Orana Children's Home and Overton Homes for the Aged. He joined the Rotary Club of Melbourne in 1954 (director, 1962-64; president 1964-65) and remained an active member until 1978. Colleagues recalled his keen sense of humour coupled to firm convictions, resolutely defended.

In retirement Jungwirth served on the Victorian Tourist Development Authority (1962-64); chaired the board of inquiry (1963-64) into the State Library of Victoria that recommended major reforms in library services in Victoria, including the replacement of the Board of Trustees and the Free Library Service Board with a single body, the Library Council of Victoria; and was a member (1973-79) of the executive of the Patriotic Funds Committee of Victoria. In 1949-79 he served on the board of management for the Sir Colin MacKenzie [q.v.10] Sanctuary, Healesville, which he chaired for fifteen years.

Of trim build and average height, with short-cropped black hair and neatly trimmed moustache, Jungwirth favoured a black bowler or homberg hat. He rose early, often collecting newspapers from the shop opposite his home in pyjamas and gown so as to brief himself before leaving for the office. A keen sportsman, he played football in his youth, cricket into his fifties (with a slow left-hand delivery), and then bowls, becoming president of the North Balwyn Bowling Club. Recalled as 'a mad, one eyed Richmond supporter', he was a frequent visitor to the team's rooms after games. His first wife had died in 1938, and on 28 March 1942 at the Methodist Church, South Camberwell, he had married Annie Edna Tamblyn. A devoted family man, he stimulated discussion across all topics with his children and was an inveterate practical joker. Sir John died on 25 January 1981 at Kew, and was cremated. His wife survived him, together with a son and daughter of his first marriage and the two sons of his second.

Herald (Melbourne), 24 Nov 1956, p 27; *Sun News-Pictorial* (Melbourne), 19 Sept 1959, p 9; *Rechabite*, May 1981, p 98; Jungwirth papers (SLV); private information and personal knowledge.

F. J. KENDALL

K

KANE, JOHN THOMAS (1908-1988), politician, was born on 23 July 1908 at Burraga, New South Wales, eldest of three children of Australian-born parents Cornelius Kane, engine driver, and his wife Kate, née Williams. In 1911 the family moved to Lithgow, where Jack attended St Patrick's convent school and in 1921 found work as a shop assistant. With the death of his father three years later, he became a miner to earn enough to support the family. On 24 March 1928 at St Patrick's Catholic Church, Lithgow, he married Rose Emily Martin. Forced onto the dole during the Depression, he began selling produce door-to-door and eventually ran a greengrocer's shop. After the venture failed, he was a self-employed truck driver from 1937 to 1952. He left Lithgow in 1942 to pursue work for his trucking business and in 1947 settled at Haberfield, Sydney.

Having grown up in a family steeped in unionism and Labor politics, Kane joined the Miners' Federation and in 1929 the Australian Labor Party. A fellow miner tried to recruit him to the Communist Party of Australia but, although something of a militant, he refused the offer. He was a strong supporter of J. T. Lang [q.v.9]. Kane became increasingly active in the labour movement and in the 1946 Federal election was deputy campaign director in J. B. Chifley's [q.v.13] electorate of Macquarie. He was also active in the Transport Workers' Union, becoming vice-president of the New South Wales branch.

The growing influence of the Communist Party in the unions and the constant industrial disruption of the late 1940s led Kane to join the ALP industrial groups. His considerable organising ability meant that he rose rapidly, becoming New South Wales secretary of the groups in 1950. A strong Catholic, he was approached to join B. A. Santamaria's Catholic Social Studies Movement. His involvement with 'the Movement' grew, particularly after meeting Santamaria in 1947. Kane, a good platform orator, toured the coalfields during the 1949 miners' strike, arguing the government's case at mass meetings. A 'blunt reforming zealot', he was part of a rebel group which in the early 1950s challenged the existing leadership of the TWU, alleging that it was corrupt. In 1952 the industrial groups and their allies took control of the New South Wales branch of the ALP, and Kane joined the executive. A year later he was assistant State secretary.

When the 1955 federal conference in Hobart withdrew recognition of the industrial groups, their supporters in New South Wales split into two factions. One, which included the State Labor government and the Sydney Catholic hierarchy, took the approach that a compromise could be negotiated with the federal authorities and that it was better to 'stay in and fight' than split the party. Kane strongly supported the opposing view that federal intervention should be resisted at all costs. His inflexibility and single-mindedness reinforced his intransigence. In any event, his skills as a political operator and central role in the groups made him a marked man. A compromise, hammered out in June 1956, left the executive in the control of a group of moderates around the party officers. Part of the deal was the removal of Kane, accomplished at an executive meeting on 29 June. Premier J. J. Cahill [q.v.13] had earlier offered him a job as chairman of the Board of Fire Commissioners. He rejected it, stating characteristically: 'I am better at lighting fires than putting the bastards out'.

After the banning of the groups a similar body, the Industrial Labor Organisation, was set up, with Kane as full-time secretary from July 1956. The federal executive responded by proscribing the new organisation, putting Kane out of a job again. On 29 September the Democratic Labor Party was formed in New South Wales with Kane as its secretary. The Catholic hierarchy's injunction to 'stay in and fight' meant that the DLP attracted relatively little support in New South Wales. Its base was further diminished when Kane broke with the first president, Alan Manning, who resigned in 1958. The DLP in New South Wales became a Catholic, strongly anti-communist splinter group controlled by Kane and his supporters and dedicated to keeping Labor out of office until it accepted the new party's hard right policies.

Kane was also federal secretary of the DLP from 1957. When both positions became honorary, in 1966 he was appointed secretary to the Queensland DLP senator Vince Gair [q.v.14] to provide him with a salary while he carried out his party duties. In November 1970 Kane himself was elected to the Senate for the DLP—assisted by a flow of ALP preferences. As a senator, he spoke against political strikes and mergers between left-wing unions. He pushed a hard anti-communist line on defence and foreign policy, arguing that Australia should develop a nuclear capability. Kane also campaigned against the foreign takeover of Australian firms and for the abolition of death duties. He took a strong stand against 'permissive' attitudes to social questions, attacking moves to liberalise censorship by the minister for customs and excise Don Chipp. Like all other DLP senators, he was defeated at the election after the May 1974 double dissolution.

Continuing his party activities, he served as a member of the executive of Santamaria's National Civic Council and worked as an industrial relations consultant. He returned briefly to the headlines late in 1974 when a defamation action was brought against him by the left-wing journalist Wilfred Burchett [q.v.] over allegations in the DLP's journal *Focus* that Burchett had been a spy and collaborator with the Chinese and Soviet governments. Kane won the case and a subsequent appeal.

In 1970 a newspaper article described Kane as 'a surprisingly shy and diffident man behind his gruff exterior and the look and manner of the seasoned political pro'. Six feet (183 cm) tall, he moved ponderously. 'The hair above his thick-set face is streaked with grey and his big miner's fingers are lightly browned with nicotine. His voice is unexpectedly soft and deep'. He expressed a 'cheerful contempt' for the notion that he had time for any recreation other than politics. Survived by his wife, their daughter and younger son, he died on 27 October 1988 at Darlinghurst and was buried in Botany cemetery. His political memoirs, *Exploding the Myths*, were published in 1989.

R. Murray, *The Split* (1970); B. Duncan, *Crusade or Conspiracy?* (2001); *Canberra Times*, 24 Nov 1970, p 4; *SMH*, 12 Dec 1970, p 2, 2 Nov 1974, p 1, 1 Feb 1975, p 9, 3 Dec 1975, p 7; *Bulletin*, 19 Dec 1970, p 25; V. Keraitis, interview with J. T. Kane (ts, 1980, NLA); R. Hurst and R. Raxworthy, interviews with J. T. Kane (tss, 1985, NLA).   DAVID CLUNE

KARAVA, GABRIEL EHAVA (c.1921-1985), soldier, village leader and politician, was born possibly in September 1921 at Heavala village, Moveave, Papua, only son of Karava Poevare and his wife Taise Auapo. Gabriel inherited high traditional status through both his mother's and father's lineages. He attended Catholic schools at the nearby village of Terapo and at Bomana, near Port Moresby; he later claimed to have had five years of schooling, the most then available, and to be literate in Police Motu, Pidgin and 'some English'.

After working at a native hospital, he enlisted in the Papuan Infantry Battalion as Gabriel Ehava on 1 January 1942 and was given the rank of lance corporal. He was then 5 ft 4 ins (163 cm) tall, athletic, and commanding in appearance. In July-August the PIB engaged the invading Japanese as they advanced from Buna to Kokoda. Serving with Sergeant John Ehava Sefe, who also came from Heavala and who was to win the Distinguished Conduct Medal, Gabriel Ehava was by late 1942 in frequent combat with Japanese forces retreating along the north coast. He was awarded the Military Medal for going to the aid of a patrol under attack near the Opi River on 21 February 1943: 'Armed with an automatic weapon he surprised and attacked the enemy from the flank, killing four and putting the remainder to flight'.

Rested and retrained at Bisiatabu, inland from Port Moresby, Karava flew to Wau, New Guinea, with 'B' Company in June and served in the Markham and Ramu valleys. He was discharged on 16 May 1944, probably one of several 'time finish' men who were then allowed to go home. Re-enlisting in the PIB on 26 March 1945, he was promoted to sergeant and given further training at Bisiatabu. In May the PIB landed at Torokina, Bougainville, and Karava went north to the Bonis Peninsula with 'A' Company. He was in several 'fire-fights' before the Japanese surrender. The PIB moved to Torokina then to Fauro Island and finally in March 1946 to Rabaul to guard Japanese prisoners. Karava was discharged on 17 June.

Back at Moveave, Karava and others who had served in the war were determined to bring change; they had some cash and their army experience made them ready to unite across clan and village lines, but they had little education and almost no supporting economic or political infrastructure. In 1948 Karava became the first chairman of the Heavala Co-operative Society, set up to buy copra and sell goods through village stores. From 1958 he was director of the Toaripi Association of Native Societies. When local government was introduced in the late 1950s, he was elected chairman of the Toaripi and then the East Kerema councils. He served on the Gulf District Advisory Council and in 1962 was selected to travel to Australia with a group observing Australian political institutions.

At the first election for the Territory of Papua and New Guinea's House of Assembly in 1964, Karava won the Lakekamu open electorate. He had promised the people roads, bridges, schools, hospitals and more chances to grow cash crops; and in short speeches (sometimes given in Police Motu) in the House of Assembly he supported the Australian administration, was cautious about moves towards self-government, and asked for social and economic development in his electorate. In 1968 he was defeated by the younger and better educated Tore Lokoloko. After leaving national politics, he owned trade stores, a cattle farm and coconut, cocoa and rubber plantations, and supplemented his income by shooting crocodiles. He had married Josephine Sariman (with whom he had one daughter), Feareka Luvu (one son), Lauhari Kake (seven sons and four daughters) and More Kake (two sons and four daughters). Gabriel Ehava Karava died of asthma on 28 August 1985 in the Kerema General Hospital.

Territory of PNG, *The Members of the House of Assembly* (1964); G. M. Byrnes, *Green Shadows* (1989); J. Sinclair, *To Find a Path*, vol 1 (1990); A. E. Hooper, *Love, War & Letters* (1994); *New Guinea Research Bulletin*, no 25, 1968; AWM52, item 8/4/4, AWM54, item 419/5/10 (AWM); B884, item PN4040 (NAA); private information.   H. N. NELSON

KASTNER, WINIFRED (1903-1987), community leader and welfare worker, was born on 29 June 1903 at Chesterfield, Derby, England, eldest of five children of Ernest Stubbs, engineers' pattern-maker, and his wife Florence, née Blank. At 16 Winifred moved to Sheffield, where she studied at the local school of art and became a certificated arts and crafts teacher. In 1930 she migrated to Western Australia in search of better prospects. First she presented talks on handicrafts for a 6WF radio session popular with countrywomen. A foundation member in 1932 of the Country Women's Association's handicraft and home industries committee, that year she toured the outback demonstrating and promoting various arts and crafts on behalf of the CWA and 6WF. She also became involved with the Young Women's Christian Association. On 3 December 1932 at St George's Cathedral, Perth, she married with Anglican rites Eric Oscar Kastner (d.1975), a German-born taxi driver. They had one daughter.

In the 1940s Winifred Kastner was superintendent of the Metropolitan Emergency Service Corps of the Australian Red Cross Society. She enjoyed working with children and in 1945 set up handicrafts and library services at the Children's Hospital (Princess Margaret Hospital for Children), Subiaco; she was later director of handicraft services. In 1950 she helped to establish and became a director of a kindergarten for emotionally disturbed, abused and underprivileged children run by the Child Welfare Department at the Government Receiving Home, Mount Lawley. Later recalling that this was her most important and satisfying work, she and her husband made special equipment and toys to provide the children with a sense of security and love. For some ten years from 1952 she was 'camp mother' at annual holiday camps for children with disabilities. On the committee of the Slow Learning Children's Group of Western Australia from 1956, she was part-time (1958-61) and full-time (1961-66) welfare officer at the Irrabeena Diagnostic and Referral Centre—a challenging post that involved being on call for twenty-four hours and home-visiting. In 1956-59 she was president of the Kindergarten Union of Western Australia.

Mrs Kastner had joined (1940) the Women's Service Guilds of Western Australia, a prominent feminist organisation; she served as State president in 1953-55 and 1969 and represented the guilds on the committees of many organisations. A founding member of the Swan River Pollution (Conservation) Committee (1948-54), she later remembered 'countless Saturdays spent, covered with mud, clearing slush from the river around industrial buildings'. In 1952 she participated in a campaign for citizenship rights for Aborigines and in 1953 chaired a public meeting called by the guilds to establish the Association of Civilian Widows. She was a council-member of the League of Home Help for the Sick and Aged, Meals on Wheels and the Good Neighbour Council of Western Australia, a member (1948-78) of the Marriage Guidance Council of Western Australia (chairman 1958) and deputy-chairman (1974-77) of the Citizens Advice Bureau of Western Australia.

A justice of the peace from 1952, Kastner sat on the bench of the Married Persons' (Summary) Relief Court for twenty-four years. She was president (1960-62) of the Women Justices' Association of Western Australia. In the 1950s she was on the State council of the Girl Guides Association of Western Australia. Later she was president of the YWCA's Retired Ladies Club. Over the years she attended several international conferences at her own expense, including the jubilee congress (1955) of the International Alliance of Women in Ceylon (Sri Lanka).

Winifred Kastner was a quiet and unassuming woman who worked energetically for her causes. She was awarded Queen Elizabeth II's coronation medal in 1953 and appointed MBE in 1976. In later life she moved from her Mount Hawthorn home into Gracewood Lodge, Manning. She died on 10 February 1987 at Nedlands and was cremated. Her daughter survived her.

D. Popham (ed), *Reflections* (1978); J. Clarke, *Just Us* (1988); D. Davidson, *Women on the Warpath* (1997); P. D. Ingham, *Setting the Pace in the Aged Care Industry* (2005); J. Teasdale, interview with W. Kastner (ts, 1975, SLWA).

DIANNE DAVIDSON

KATTER, ROBERT CUMMIN (1918-1990), businessman and politician, was born Cummin Katter on 5 September 1918 in South Brisbane, fourth child of Carl Robert Katter, a Lebanese draper, and his locally born wife Vivian Bridget, née Warby. He became known as Robert Cummin Katter. The family later moved to Cloncurry to run a general store. Bob was educated at Mount Carmel College, Charters Towers, where he excelled at athletics, Rugby League football and debating. On matriculation, he returned to Brisbane to enrol in law at the University of Queensland but his studies were interrupted by war. Having enlisted in the Militia in October 1936, he was appointed as a lieutenant in April 1940. He was called up for full-time duty in September 1941 and promoted to temporary captain but his appointment was terminated on medical grounds in July 1942. Returning to Cloncurry, he leased a clothing store and, later, a picture theatre. On 22 April 1944 at the Church of the Holy Spirit, New Farm, Brisbane, he married with Catholic rites Mabel Joan Horn.

Politics soon beckoned. Belonging to a family that boasted an engagement with Labor politics from the 1891 shearers' strike, Bob joined the Australian Labor Party and later became its Cloncurry branch secretary. In 1946 he was elected to the Cloncurry Shire Council; he served as chairman in 1949-52 and again in 1964-67. As Australia's youngest local government head, Katter oversaw numerous advances, including the provision of housing for pensioners. His advocacy of Aboriginal rights also marked him as ahead of his time; for example, he raised eyebrows when he removed from his theatre the steel partitions dividing Aborigines from other patrons. In the late 1950s he hosted his own community radio program, 'Katter's Candid Comments'.

Following a short stint as a union delegate on the Brisbane wharves, Katter moved towards Labor's anti-communist wing. He split from the ALP in 1957 and stood, unsuccessfully, as a candidate for the breakaway Queensland Labor Party (later the Democratic Labor Party) for the State seat of Flinders (1957-58) and for the Federal electorate of Kennedy (1958). Vehemently opposed to the principle of one vote, one value, in 1964 Katter joined the Country Party, for which he won in 1966 the Federal seat of Kennedy. Re-elected, with increasing margins, a further nine times, he was a powerful advocate of northern interests.

A man of rugged appearance with at all times polished shoes, Katter soon earned a reputation as a no-nonsense member, a 'blue heeler' who 'dug his teeth in', and a 'battler' with a 'gloves off' approach. Regarded as an 'old style bush politician', he became an early hawk on the Vietnam War. Katter later served, from February to December 1972, as minister for the army and, from June 1974 to November 1975, as shadow minister for northern development and the Northern Territory. He was chairman of the parliamentary committee on road safety, and an adviser to the United Nations General Assembly in 1970 and 1984 and during the Zimbabwean elections in 1980. Later he was an inaugural director of the Australian Stockman's Hall of Fame at Longreach.

Katter did not recontest Kennedy at the 1990 poll. After the death of his first wife in 1971, he had married Joycelyn Marjorie Steel, a secretary, on 22 May 1976 at his old school chapel. Katter was deeply committed to his family, his faith and his constituents. He died on 18 March 1990 at Mount Isa and was buried in Sunset lawn cemetery; his wife and their two sons and daughter survived him, as did the two sons and daughter of his first marriage. His eldest son, Robert, followed him into the House of Representatives in 1993.

PD (HR), 8 May 1990, p 32; *Courier-Mail* (Brisbane), 8 Dec 1966, p 10, 19 Mar 1990, p 1; *Review* (Melbourne), 29 Jan-4 Feb 1972, p 404; *Australian*, 19 Mar 1990, p 3; *Canberra Times*, 19 Mar 1990, p 2; Katter biog information (Parliamentary Lib, Canberra); private information.

PAUL D. WILLIAMS

KAYE, GEOFFREY ALFRED (1903-1986), anaesthetist, was born on 9 April 1903 at St Kilda, Melbourne, fourth child of Prussian-born Alfred Kornblum, merchant, and his Victorian-born wife Rosetta, née Levinson. Geoffrey was educated in England at Gresham's School, Holt, Norfolk, and—adopting the surname Kaye—studied at the University of Melbourne (MB, 1926; BS, 1927; MD, 1929). By 1927, as a resident medical officer at the Alfred Hospital, he had decided to specialise in the then relatively undeveloped field of anaesthetics. While presenting a paper at the Australasian Medical Congress in Sydney in 1929, he met Dr Francis McMeckan, one of the pioneers of anaesthetics in the United States of America, who encouraged him to pursue further studies overseas. Appointed an honorary anaesthetist at the Alfred Hospital in 1930, Kaye then travelled to the United Kingdom, Germany and North America, expanding his knowledge of new research, apparatus and techniques and developing enduring personal networks.

On his return in 1931, Kaye strove to raise the standing and standards of anaesthetics in Australia. He edited *Practical Anaesthesia* (1932), the first Australian textbook on the subject, written with colleagues at the Alfred Hospital and published by its Baker [q.v.7] Medical Research Institute. Through travel, lectures and demonstrations he assisted in the professional co-ordination of his speciality. In 1934 the Australian Society of Anaesthetics was established, largely as a result of his lobbying; one of its seven founders, he edited its newsletter and served as its first secretary (1934-46). A part-time lecturer (1938-57) in anaesthetics at the University of Melbourne, in 1939 he completed a diploma in the subject, jointly awarded by the Royal colleges of Surgeons, England, and of Physicians, London.

From 1937 Kaye worked on the design and manufacture of anaesthetic equipment for the Australian Military Forces. Giving his religion as Jewish, on 13 October 1939 he was appointed a captain in the Australian Army Medical

Corps, Australian Imperial Force. While serving (1940-42) in the Middle East with the 2/2nd Australian General Hospital he was appointed adviser in anaesthetics to the AIF, in which role he ensured the availability of workshops and trained personnel to maintain and repair the equipment. He returned to Australia and on 24 October 1943 transferred to the Reserve of Officers.

From his English education and natural inclination Kaye was formal in style. Tall, lean and idealistic, he was a man of incisive mind and complex personality: reserved, demanding, sometimes intemperate and unforgiving but capable on closer acquaintance of generosity and warmth. He was elected an honorary life member of the ASA in 1944. From 1945 he added to his duties lecturing at the College of Dentistry and serving as honorary anaesthetist to the Dental Hospital. He collaborated with Robert Orton and Douglas Renton in *Anaesthetic Methods* (1946) and in 1949 was elected a fellow of the faculty of anaesthetics, Royal College of Surgeons. Still seeking the full national, professional representation of anaesthetics, he vigorously opposed moves to amalgamate the ASA within the Royal Australasian College of Surgeons, but acquiesced in election as a foundation fellow of the RACS's faculty of anaesthetics in 1952.

Kaye's particular interest in the design and production of anaesthetic equipment was increasingly evident in the development, under his curatorship (1939-55), of a museum for the ASA. He envisaged the collection not merely as having historical value but as an integral dimension of the society's teaching role. In 1958 the museum was named in his honour, becoming a lasting monument to his work. He welcomed new technology, later even selling a treasured eighteenth-century coffee pot to purchase a computer.

Withdrawing from practice and teaching, in 1957 Kaye became a consulting anaesthetist at the Alfred. He continued research in his own laboratory and published papers on a wide range of topics. Among the most unusual works was 'Anaesthesia for Snakes' (1952), which summarised his observations while engaged by the Melbourne zoo to assist in making plaster replicas of their more dangerous reptiles. With interests extending well beyond his profession, he wrote cogently and with considerable expertise on topics as diverse as religion in Ancient Egypt and Chinese monochromes. Aesthetically attracted to the Georgian period, he acquired an extensive collection of furniture, decorative art and glassware, much of which he donated to the University of Melbourne in 1980 and 1986.

Rarely separated from his typewriter, Kaye maintained a voluminous correspondence with colleagues at home and abroad. He was hard to know but worth the effort. In 1974 he received the Orton medal from the faculty of anaesthetics, which elected him an honorary fellow in 1978. On the fiftieth anniversary in 1984 of the founding of the ASA, he addressed an international meeting of anaesthetists at the Sydney Opera House. Geoffrey Kaye never married. He died on 28 October 1986 at East Melbourne and was cremated.

G. Wilson, *Fifty Years* (1987) and *One Grand Chain* (1996); *Alfred Hospital: Faces and Places* (1996); B. Baker, *Australia's First Anaesthetic Department* (2005); *Anaesthesia and Intensive Care*, vol 15, no 1, 1987, p 107, vol 17, no 2, 1989, p 213.

RAY MARGINSON

KAYE, LOUIS; *see* NORMAN, N.

KEEFFE, JAMES BERNARD (1919-1988), trade union official and politician, was born on 20 August 1919 at Atherton, Queensland, son of James Keeffe, a New South Wales-born farmer, and his Queensland-born wife Augusta, née Holzappel. Educated at Mothar Mountain State School, near Gympie, Jim left at 13 to work as a farmhand but continued his studies by correspondence. He joined the Australian Labor Party in 1936. On 25 January 1941 at St Patrick's Catholic Church, Gympie, he married Elizabeth Merle Garrett (d.1965), a domestic worker; they had a daughter and a son. He had enlisted in the Citizen Military Forces on 18 April 1939. Called up for full-time duty in December 1941 as an acting sergeant with the 9th Battalion, he transferred to the Australian Imperial Force on 10 July 1942. He served at Milne Bay, Papua, later that year and on Bougainville from November 1944. While in action in January 1945 he suffered a gunshot wound to the right forearm, which left it permanently disfigured. Invalided home, he was discharged from the army on 27 October.

After a rehabilitation course in cooping, he was court advocate for, and for two years part-time secretary of, the coopers' union. In 1951-56 he was employed as a clerk with the Plumbers & Gasfitters Employees' Union, Queensland branch. He was an ardent champion of the working classes and in the 1940s had helped to establish the Young Labor Association. A member of the ALP's 'Left' faction and a Queensland central executive organiser (1956-60), in 1960 he was elected State secretary following J. M. Schmella's [q.v.16] death. It was a particularly turbulent period for the Queensland branch, in the aftermath of its 1957 split. Keeffe was federal president of the ALP in 1962-70. Winning a seat in the half-Senate election in December 1964, he entered Federal parliament on 1 July 1965. On 6 August 1966 at St Margaret Mary's Catholic

Church, Hyde Park, Townsville, he married Sheila Denise Nichols, a secretary. They lived at Townsville and had two daughters and a son before divorcing in 1981.

In parliament Keeffe soon earned the nickname the 'knocker from the north' for his record as a 'formidable' debater who, at times, fell into 'fierce' and 'abrasive' argument. Even his maiden speech saw a fiery break from convention when he lambasted the stark disparity in living standards between the city and the bush. After 1967 he clashed repeatedly with the new Opposition leader, Gough Whitlam, who was determined to reform the ALP into a modern and moderate party. Keeffe's parliamentary performances, while always vigorous, proved especially effective during adjournment debates where he pursued issues close to his heart, including the development of northern Australia, Aboriginal land rights, and the establishment of an essential aircraft industry. Known as a 'hard' campaigner, he was suspended from the chamber several times.

Keeffe was parliamentary representative (1967-76) on the council of the Australian Institute of Aboriginal Studies. In 1971-80 he sat on various Senate committees. Deputy Opposition leader in the Senate and shadow minister for Northern Australia and Aboriginal affairs in 1976-77, he was as comfortable sitting cross-legged on the ground with Aborigines as he was in his Parliament House office. Outside the parliament he was known as a kind man committed to assisting the less fortunate. Indeed, his Townsville electorate office often resembled a de facto branch of the Department of Social Security. He also campaigned on peace and environmental issues, with a particular emphasis on conserving the Great Barrier Reef. Such interests saw him straddle the ideological divide between 'old' and 'new' Labor, a trait that became manifest in his support for federal intervention in 1980 into the moribund Queensland ALP. He had rejoined the national executive in 1976.

Retiring from politics in February 1983, later that year Keeffe was made a life member of the ALP. He enjoyed gardening and fishing, and even turned his hand to writing children's fairy tales on environmentally based themes. He died of myocardial infarction on 15 May 1988, while returning to Townsville by train after attending the opening of the new Parliament House in Canberra, and was buried in Woongarra cemetery. His five children survived him.

Parliamentary Handbook of the Commonwealth of Australia (1982); R. Fitzgerald and H. Thornton, *Labor in Queensland* (1989); *PD* (Senate), 17 May 1988, p 2287; *Austn Aboriginal Studies*, no 2, 1988, p 117; *Australian*, 16 May 1988, p 2; *Courier-Mail* (Brisbane), 16 May 1988, p 4.

PAUL D. WILLIAMS

KELLAWAY, HAROLD LIONEL (LEON) (1897?-1990), ballet dancer and teacher, was born possibly in 1897 in London. He was always secretive about his birth but his parents may have been Edwin John Kellaway, caretaker at Parliament House, Cape Town, and his wife Rebecca Annie, née Brebner. He spent his childhood in South Africa, gaining billing as 'Baby Kellaway' in a professional theatrical troupe that included his three elder brothers, two of whom—Cecil [q.v.9] and Alec (d.1973) —became actors in Australia. His interest in dance developed in his teenage years. After studying in London with Serafina Astafieva and Nicolai Legat, he toured the variety circuit in England, Australia and the United States of America with Ivy Schilling, and then partnered Lydia Kyasht. He danced with Anna Pavlova's company in 1929-31. Returning to Australia in 1934, he performed with Olga Spessivtzeva in the Dandré-Levitoff Russian Ballet under the stage name of Jan Kowsky (or Kowski). At the end of that tour he decided to settle in Sydney.

After appearing in musical productions and operettas with J. C. Williamson [q.v.6] Ltd, in 1937 Kellaway opened a ballet school. He was a popular and inspiring teacher, attentive to fine details of movement and expression, and often spicing his instruction with blunt and memorable advice. As Christine Perry recalls, he 'taught ballet scientifically long before it became fashionable to do so'. Welcoming the sheer enthusiasm of Australian dancers, he was an inventive choreographer to his own small, skilled and dedicated company, Ballet Nationale. He became a mentor to many students who would gain significant reputations, notably Kathleen Gorham [q.v.] and Elaine Fifield. During World War II he worked with Ernest C. Rolls in the production of musicals, and after the war he danced with the Borovansky [q.v.13] Ballet Company as a character artist.

Appointed maître de danse of the National Theatre Ballet, Melbourne, in 1949, Kellaway contributed significantly to building the company and encouraging dancers including Lynne Golding, Margaret Scott and Alison Lee. Returning to the Borovansky Ballet in 1954, he was assistant to the ballet master, Harcourt Algeranoff [q.v.13] in 1959. On the foundation of the Australian Ballet, in 1962, he was invited by the director, (Dame) Peggy van Praagh [q.v.], to become associate ballet master. A skilled mime, he continued to take character parts in the company's productions until 1968, appearing as 'the Wowser' in *Melbourne Cup* in 1962—a memorable role repeated at the Royal Opera House, Covent Garden, London, in 1965—and as 'the Duke' in *Giselle* (1964) with Dame Margot Fonteyn and Rudolf Nureyev. He was loved and respected by such artists, who sought his advice on matters of technique. When the Australian

Ballet School opened in 1964, he joined the staff. He retired as emeritus professor of dance in 1980 and was awarded the OAM in 1986.

Kellaway was humorous, even tempered, unfailingly direct and keenly interested in the lives of his students. He was a gifted raconteur. Severe arthritis afflicted him in his last years of teaching; in retirement he took up drawing until that too became impossible. Leon Kellaway died at Murrumbeena on 30 April 1990 and was cremated. He was unmarried. As both a teacher and a character dancer, he had made an immense contribution to Australian ballet.

F. Salter, *Borovansky* (1980); E. Pask, *Ballet in Australia* (1982); F. van Straten, *National Treasure* (1994); *Dance Australia*, Aug-Sept 1990, p 25; personal knowledge.   NOËL PELLY*

KELLY, EMILY CAROLINE (1899-1989), theatre producer and anthropologist, was born on 24 April 1899 at West Didsbury, Manchester, England, one of four children of Robert Francis Watson, warehouse manager, and his wife Caroline, née Tennant. Young Caroline acted in little theatre at Manchester and Birmingham. After moving to Australia in the early 1920s, Carrie Tennant, as she was known, performed for charity in Sydney. In 1925-26 she had elocution lessons with Barbara Sisley [q.v.Supp.] in Brisbane. There Carrie was fired from her first professional appearance—at the Cremorne Theatre, Brisbane, in 'The Snapshots of 1926'—for 'rotten' acting. Back in Sydney she started a playreading circle for radio 2KY, and produced two series of one-act plays at Burdekin House, taking the leading role in her own *Outback*. This work and her other one-act plays *Reprieve* and *Secrecy* were published in *Three Plays for Little Theatre* (1930). On 23 January 1929 at St James's Church of England, Sydney, she married Francis Angelo Timothy Kelly, a copywriter with Ferguson Advertising Co. Ltd, shortly to become editor of *Health and Physical Culture*, and later an advertising agent.

In 1929 Carrie Kelly opened the Community Playhouse in St Peter's Church hall, Darlinghurst. On 7 December her troupe of experienced actors performed *Echoes* (1918) by Adrian Consett Stephen. Intending to foster an Australian theatre tradition, she ran competitions for the best Australian one-act play, promising that all entries would be performed. It proved a recipe for disaster. The many entries for her second competition over-taxed her players; performances were underrehearsed; judges disagreed. In 1931 Tennant transferred to the Aeolian Hall, incorporating her players into the Australian Play Society.

On the final night of her third one-act competition, Lady Game, wife of the governor Sir Philip Game [q.v.8], left at interval denouncing the 'distasteful moral tone' of the plays she had seen, one being Tom Moore's [q.v.15] 'No Robbery'. 'Does Lady Game object to "Carmen", to "Madam Butterfly?"' Tennant retorted. Disheartened, she abandoned Australian theatre. Producer of more than seventy one-act and five full-length plays, she had created opportunities for coming authors—Leslie Haylen's [q.v.14] *Two Minutes' Silence* (1933) was the basis for a film by the McDonagh [q.v.10] sisters—and more generally for promoting theatre. She included Shaw and Ibsen in the Community Playhouse's repertoire.

In 1931 Kelly enrolled in anthropology at the University of Sydney (Dip.Anth., 1945). Margaret Mead had persuaded her that it was a great field for women 'interested in the betterment of humanity'. This was a sustaining belief. Forty years later Kelly wrote that anthropology taught tolerance and was 'far more important than throwing ironmongery at the moon'. Under A. P. Elkin's [q.v.14] supervision she undertook fieldwork among Aboriginal communities in New South Wales and, for four months in 1934, at Cherbourg Aboriginal Settlement, Queensland, where she discovered the tenacious nature of Aboriginal memory. The elders guarded their religious secrets 'very jealously', she wrote in a paper delivered in January 1935 to the Australian and New Zealand Association for the Advancement of Science.

With Elkin as mentor Kelly proposed to the Aborigines Protection Board in 1936 a scheme for social re-organisation of its reserves, intended to combat apathy. Promoted as the application of anthropological knowledge to problems of administration, it was a modest proposal for a social club with acknowledgment of the traditional authority of elders and for occupancy rights for cultivators within reserves. Before she reached Burnt Bridge Settlement, near Kempsey, in August 1937, to implement her scheme, the board's policy of concentration had brought about confrontation with the Moseleys [q.v.Supp.] and distress for recent arrivals. Kelly's critical 1937 report supplied ammunition for others—Elkin, the Association for the Protection of Native Races and feminist organisations—to demand changes. Contrasting the situation at Burnt Bridge with that at Wreck Bay, Kelly stressed the importance of the availability of paid employment and criticised the exclusion of Aborigines from work relief.

When the parliamentary select committee on the administration of the Aborigines Protection Board (appointed in November 1937) lapsed without reporting, Kelly continued to badger the premier, (Sir) Bertram Stevens [q.v.12]. He admitted to 'infrequent contacts' with Aborigines and commissioned advice from the Public Service Board, which consulted Kelly and Elkin and adopted their recommendations for a reconstructed board to include an anthropologist and for the appointment of a full-time protector of Aborigines.

Kelly's writing subtly shifted direction. An early emphasis on education and training implicitly directed towards assimilation was replaced by respect for Aboriginal culture. She warned missionaries in 1944 that the Aborigine accepted from Christianity only that which fitted his 'old way'. Later she was outspoken against forcing Aborigines into factories and cities, 'trying to ... turn them into greedy grasping people in our own image'.

Between 1942 and 1948 Kelly wrote several reports for the Commonwealth government on the assimilation of immigrants—Jewish refugees, 'orphaned' children and non-British migrants. Noting prejudice, anti-Semitism and tensions between Australian Jews and new arrivals, she was emphatic about the need to 'condition' public opinion before any large-scale immigration.

Kelly gave lectures on the social aspects of town planning at the universities of Sydney and Melbourne. She is remembered as an intellectually stimulating teacher at Sydney Kindergarten Teachers' College but her academic career petered out. Her interests shifted to urban planning and she ended her working life in the employment of the State Planning Authority of New South Wales, advising on housing projects south of Sydney. Always a lively controversialist she advocated the restoration of the verandah as the 'children's place', corner shops for people to meet, and grants to young couples to build granny flats.

Reputed to have been living as a semi-recluse in a caravan, Caroline Kelly died on 1 September 1989 at Kyogle. Following a requiem Mass at St Mary's Catholic Church, North Sydney, she was buried in the Catholic section of Northern Suburbs cemetery. Predeceased by her husband, she was survived by her adopted son.

T. Wise, *The Self-made Anthropologist* (1985); Assn for the Protection of Native Races, *Annual Report*, 1937-38, p 9; *Hecate*, vol 24, no 2, 1998, p 8; *SMH*, 30 Sept 1931, p 15, 28 Apr 1932, p 13, 27 July 1937, p 22, 19 Aug 1958, p 26, 21 June 1960, p 7, 21 Oct 1971, p 8, 12 July 1972, p 7; *B.P. Mag*, 1 Mar 1932, p 26; *Daily Mirror* (Sydney), 18 Aug 1970, p 16; A434, item 1950/3/44230, A436, item 1948/5/330, A441, item 1952/13/2687, A441, item 1952/13/2684, A1336, item 39459, A2998, item 1952/105 (NAA); NSW Aborigines Board Protection, Minutes, 1936-37, reel 2792, frames 226-305, and Premier's Dept Special Bundles, Treatment of Aborigines in NSW, reel 1862, frames 424-494 (SRNSW); Carrie Tennant papers (Univ of Qld Lib); A. P. Elkin papers (Univ of Sydney Archives).   HEATHER RADI

KELLY, JOHN HENRY (1895-1983), farmer, public servant and rural-industries consultant, was born on 17 May 1895 at Hornsby, Sydney, eleventh of fourteen children of Irish-born parents Henry Edward Kelly, railway ganger and later funeral director, and his wife Mary, née Monaghan. Jack received his early education at the Good Samaritan convent school, Campbelltown, and at the Christian Brothers' school, Lewisham, where he found the discipline hard. He was intelligent but 'wild and unmanageable' and after his authoritarian father enrolled him at St Joseph's College, Hunters Hill, as a first step towards the priesthood, he ran away from home at the age of 12. (Six of his eight sisters became nuns.) Posing as an orphan, he was taken in by a family at Jesmond, near Newcastle, with whom he stayed for about six months while working at a coalmine. A year later, after labouring in a variety of rural jobs mainly on the Liverpool Plains, he was apprehended by the police and returned home.

Leaving school at 15, Kelly found employment as a conveyor-belt operator at the Darling Harbour wheat terminal, as a general hand for a well-boring contractor, and at an abattoir. In 1912 he was gaoled briefly for refusing to carry out his compulsory military training, but on the outbreak of World War I he tried to enlist, only for his father to refuse permission. He went to Brisbane and worked at Thomas Borthwick's freezing works before joining the Australian Imperial Force on 1 July 1915. Sailing for the Middle East in September, two months later he was posted as a temporary corporal to a composite light horse regiment that fought in Egypt as part of Western Frontier Force; he was wounded in the foot on 13 December. After recovering, he saw action in the Sinai and Palestine campaigns, serving as a sapper in the 1st Field Squadron and then as a driver in the Anzac Mounted Divisional Train. He was discharged from the AIF on 27 September 1919 in Sydney.

Impressed by the Rothschild settlements of small farmers in Palestine, Kelly was granted a 134-acre (54 ha) farm in the Murrumbidgee Irrigation Area in August 1921. On 26 November at St Matthew's Church of England, Manly, Sydney, he married Gwenllian Mary Morris Jenkins. He soon became involved in local politics and journalism. The first president (1928-29) of the Wade Shire Council, he opposed the 'home maintenance area' and 'living maintenance' concepts of land settlement as they presupposed a 'peasant standard'. In 1930 he unsuccessfully contested the State seat of Murrumbidgee for the Country Party. He farmed throughout the difficult 1930s and averred that the rural crisis was the result of 'too many farmers on too many farms which are not economic units'. In January 1939 he organised a convention at Griffith to examine the possibility of diverting westward the waters of the Snowy River and suggested that a national survey of Australia's water resources be undertaken.

On 15 July 1940 Kelly enlisted in the Royal Australian Air Force. He stood again as a United Country Party candidate for Murrumbidgee in 1941 but came last in a field of five. Serving as a clerk in the RAAF, he rose to temporary sergeant before being discharged on 31 March 1942. Next day he enlisted for full-time duty in the Volunteer Defence Corps as an acting staff sergeant. Stationed in the Wollongong area, he was promoted to warrant officer, class two, in June, commissioned as a lieutenant in October 1943 and made temporary captain in November. In March 1944 he was posted to headquarters, Newcastle Fortress, as a staff officer. He resigned his commission on 31 October and, at the invitation of J. B. Chifley [q.v.13], joined the Department of Post-War Reconstruction, Canberra, in January 1945, soon becoming a foundation member of (Sir) John Crawford's [q.v.] Bureau of Agricultural Economics. Using his previous experience as a soldier settler, he helped to plan the War Service Land Settlement Scheme and played an important part in preventing the establishment of farms that were too small.

In 1948 Kelly undertook the first survey of the beef cattle industry in northern Australia. He travelled extensively and met much hostility in his investigations, especially when he commented on the plight of Aboriginal stockmen and the deficient land management of absentee landlords, but his BAE report of 1952 was generally well received. It recommended greater government involvement in the north, the abandonment of the inefficient and wasteful open-range system of cattle-raising in favour of smaller properties, the use of the brigalow country of Queensland for beef cattle and fodder crops, and a better deal for Aboriginal workers. He next completed surveys of the region of the Ord and Victoria rivers in the North-West and the Leichhardt-Gilbert area of Queensland in 1954, and with Dr Rex Patterson conducted a study on the road transport of cattle that led to a Commonwealth program of developing beef roads. In 1959 he underwent an operation to save his sight. He retired in 1960, but continued his research as a consultant.

An indefatigable worker and enthusiast for northern development, Kelly gave interviews, lectures and broadcasts, and published his views in newspapers, journals and BAE reports. His ideas and vision were articulated in *Struggle for the North* (1966), which showed how the ownership of the northern cattle lands and their mineral resources had been acquired by international monopolies and large financial consortiums. His provocative *Beef in Northern Australia* (1971), in which he

maintained that the north could support three times its cattle population if the government imposed more stringent controls on lease-holders, was the outcome of a research fellowship (1967-70), held in the Research School of Social Sciences at the Australian National University, and funded by the Reserve Bank of Australia.

Spade-bearded, spare and fit, with precise diction and a twinkle in his eye, 'Kelly of the North' had an immense gusto for life, work, friends and fun. An expert bushman, he loved the outback, enjoyed a drink and was a renowned talker and storyteller. A highly practical economist and agrarian reformer, radical in most things, he identified with the battler and the underdog. He died on 9 April 1983 in Canberra and was cremated; his wife, three of their four sons and their daughter survived him.

People (Sydney), 21 Nov 1951, p 24; *Canberra Times*, 13 Mar 1968, p 23, 30 May 1974, p 3, 27 Aug 1981, p 3, 11 Apr 1983, p 7; *Courier* (Canberra), 15 Jan 1970, p 2; *Austn Financial Review*, 22 Apr 1983, p 28; B2455, item Kelly J H, A9301, item 32328, B884, item N391298 (NAA); M. Pratt, interview with J. H. Kelly (ts, 1971 and 1974, NLA); Kelly papers (NLA).

G. P. WALSH

KELLY, JOHN PATRICK (1907-1984), solicitor, Catholic lay leader and hospital administrator, was born on 15 February 1907 at Bulimba, Brisbane, second of three surviving children of Michael Kelly, an Irish-born police constable, and his wife Beatrice Annie, née Baldwin, from Queensland. John was educated at Our Lady of the Sacred Heart School, Thursday Island, when his father was stationed there, and in Brisbane by the Christian Brothers at St James's and St Joseph's (Gregory Terrace) colleges. At Terrace he was captain of the first XIII and first XI and also represented the school in swimming and athletics. Later he played first-grade Rugby League and Rugby Union. He graduated from the University of Queensland (BA, 1930).

Admitted to the Bar on 6 September 1932, Kelly formed his own firm of solicitors (known from 1939 as John P. Kelly & Co.) and practised until the 1970s. (Sir) James Duhig was a client; in 1950 Kelly briefed A. D. McGill, a Protestant and a Freemason, when Duhig was sued for professional fees by Hennessy [qq.v.8,10,9], Hennessy & Co., the architectural firm that had drawn up plans for Holy Name Cathedral.

President of the Christian Brothers Old Boys' Association in the 1930s, Kelly supported its objectives, including the influencing of national affairs, assertion of a Christian concept of society and resistance to the spread of anti-Christian principles and propaganda.

He founded (1933) the Aquinas Library, which was to become a Brisbane cultural institution: among other activities it established study groups based on those run by the Campion Society of Melbourne and published Kelly's 1944 inaugural Aquinas lecture *Aquinas and Modern Practices of Interest Taking*, with an introduction by Colin Clark [q.v.]. In the 1940s Kelly was lay director of Catholic Action's Brisbane secretariat. He was chairman (1938-80) of the Mater Misericordiae hospitals advisory boards; stressing that they were 'advisory', he would say wryly: 'the nuns on Mater Hill run that hospital'. The Sisters of Mercy, grateful for his contribution, established the John P. Kelly Mater Research Foundation in 1982. He had been appointed OBE in 1966.

A friend said that Kelly had 'a somewhat formidable personality' but that he was 'generous and compassionate under his somewhat severe and authoritarian exterior'. Outside the Church, his interests were gardening and reading. He was deputy-chairman (1954-57) and chairman (1957-77) of the State's Literature Board of Review. On 23 January 1937 at St Patrick's Catholic Church, Fortitude Valley, Brisbane, he had married Margaret Maud Hishon (d.1968), a public servant. Survived by his four daughters and son, he died on 12 June 1984 in the Canossa Hospital, Oxley, and was buried in Hemmant cemetery. At his funeral Mass Archbishop Francis Rush referred to his warmth and wit and 'quiet enjoyment of the absurd'. Kelly's portrait by Sir William Dargie, commissioned by the Sisters of Mercy, is held at the Mater.

H. Gregory, *Expressions of Mercy* (2006); F. Hills, 'The Rise and Fall of the Aquinas Library 1933-1991', *Proceedings* (Brisbane Catholic Hist Soc), vol 4, 1994, p 47, and 'John P. Kelly (1907-1984)', *Proceedings* (Brisbane Catholic Hist Soc), vol 5, 1996, p 76; *Madonna*, Mar 1994, p 39; *Courier-Mail* (Brisbane), 3 Feb 1983, p 5, 13 June 1984, p 16; private information and personal knowledge.   FRANK HILLS

KELLY, MARGARET ELIZABETH (MARGOT) (1894-1983), restaurateur, was born on 15 March 1894 at Enoggera, Brisbane, third of five children of English-born Walter Pamley Emerson, drayman, and his wife Catherine, née McNair, from Scotland. Apprenticed to a dressmaker at W. J. Overell & Sons, Fortitude Valley, Margot was responsible for picking up pins from the floor with a magnet. She also studied cooking, millinery and fashion at a technical college. In her early twenties, assisted financially by her father, she opened a small clothing boutique. On 7 April 1928 at St Mary's Catholic Church, Charleville, she married Edward Charles Patrick Kelly, a licensed victualler. Helping him to run the Hotel Charleville, she reputedly always referred to him as 'Mr Kelly'.

The Kellys moved to Brisbane and during World War II ran the National Hotel. Margot Kelly's dining room became well known for its hospitality and the quality of its food. According to Alexander McRobbie, General Douglas MacArthur [q.v.15], when in Brisbane, preferred to eat his meals at her establishment rather than at Lennons Hotel, which had been requisitioned by the United States Army. Lieutenant Philip Mountbatten, RN (later Prince Philip, Duke of Edinburgh), was also a guest when in port. The Kellys invested in a mineral resources company and bought a house at Surfers Paradise named Maison de Rêve.

After her husband died in 1949 Mrs Kelly moved to the Gold Coast. She bought several properties, including the site in Hanlan Street, Surfers Paradise, where in 1954 she opened a restaurant named the Hibiscus Room. It became the most elegant place on the coast to dine. Frequented by well-to-do holiday-makers and visiting celebrities, it set the tone for Surfers Paradise's increasingly sophisticated self-image. Kelly ruled her domain with a rod of iron. The musician Ron Roman, who came from Sydney to perform at the Hibiscus Room, described her as 'a very tough boss—but also a very lovely lady'.

Determined to create an impression of the 'good life' on the Gold Coast, Kelly made an 'appearance' every night in the restaurant, dressed in a formal and elaborate gown, a hibiscus in her carefully coiffed hair. She was famous for her taste and style, in a place not generally known for either attribute. Her standards never slipped: she regularly checked the silver cutlery for cleanliness and shine and the food for quality and presentation. By 1980, however, both Kelly's age and the restaurant's dated décor were beginning to tell. A review on 3 January in the *Courier-Mail* attacked the standard of food, service and furnishings, and complained: 'If the Hibiscus Room is part of Surfers' past, its prices are firmly in the present'.

Kelly sold the business later that year; the building was soon demolished to make way for a high-rise development. Always secretive about her age, she lived the last years of her life quietly in her Isle of Capri home. In her eighties she was still chic, with impeccable hair and make-up. Childless, she died on 25 September 1983 at Kangaroo Point, Brisbane, and was buried in Nudgee cemetery. Her obituarist in the *Gold Coast Bulletin* described her as the 'legendary lady of Surfers Paradise'.

The Gold Coast Story (1966); A. McRobbie, *The Surfers Paradise Story* (1982), and *The Real Surfers Paradise* (1988), and *20th Century Gold Coast People*

(2000); J. Marston (ed), *150 Years in Paradise* (1993); *Gold Coast Bulletin*, 14 Aug 1983, p 28, 28 Sept 1983, p 13, 7 Oct 1983, p 4.   PAMELA MURRAY

KELSALL, DENIS FLETCHER (1918-1982), chemical engineer, was born on 10 February 1918 at Broadbottom, Cheshire, England, son of William Fletcher Kelsall, police constable, and his wife Annie Elizabeth, née Mason. He attended (1930-36) Altrincham Grammar School for Boys, where he became a prefect and played football in the first XI. Awarded state and county scholarships to Queens' College, Cambridge (BA, 1939; MA, 1943; Ph.D., 1969), he gained first-class honours in both parts of the natural sciences tripos. He worked for Imperial Chemical Industries Ltd for a short period before joining the Royal Air Force in 1941 and serving as a pilot. Commissioned in June 1943, he was promoted to flying officer in December. On 1 January 1944 he married Bessie Dutton at the parish church of St Ambrose, Widnes, Lancashire.

Demobilised from the RAF in 1945, Kelsall studied at Cambridge University Training College for Schoolmasters and in 1946-47 taught at his old school. He then took up an appointment as principal scientific officer in the chemical engineering division of the Atomic Energy Research Establishment, Harwell. Part of his time was spent on secondment in Canada, where he commenced his work on mineral separation techniques. In 1952 he was awarded the Moulton medal of the Institution of Chemical Engineers for his research at Harwell on hydraulic cyclones. His study of cyclones was to lead to his becoming the first non-American recipient of the Robert H. Richards award of the American Institute of Mining, Metallurgical, and Petroleum Engineers, in 1977.

Appointed chief concentration metallurgist for Rhoanglo Mine Services Ltd in 1953, Kelsall worked for the company at Kitwe, Northern Rhodesia (Zambia), before joining the chemical engineering section, division of industrial chemistry, of the Commonwealth Scientific and Industrial Research Organization in Melbourne in 1959. At first his work spanned diverse fields but he soon came to concentrate on size separation and then on grinding and eventually on flotation processes for separating minerals.

Kelsall became chief of the CSIRO's division of chemical engineering in 1974, by which time he had written or co-authored some forty-two scientific papers. For a time (1979-81) he was also chief of the division of applied geomechanics. Active in the affairs of his profession, he was the leading author of a workshop course, 'Exploiting the Modern Approach to Crushing, Grinding, Classification and Flotation', held by the Australian Mineral Foundation in 1975. In 1976 he was elected a fellow of the Australian Academy of Technological Sciences, for whom he convened a symposium on Australia's mineral resources in 1979. He was a member of the Institution of Chemical Engineers, the Institution of Mining and Metallurgy, and the Australasian Institute of Mining and Metallurgy.

Although Kelsall had become an Australian citizen in 1970 and expressed strong loyalties to the Australian way of life, he always regarded himself as a 'scientific missionary'. 'Kelly', as he was known in Australia, lived an organised, disciplined life and expected no less of his professional colleagues. For many years he took part in amateur theatricals as a member of the Beaumaris Players. Until his final year he played golf and jogged, combining the latter with exercising his dog. Survived by his wife and their three daughters, he died of cancer on 15 April 1982 at East Bentleigh and was cremated.

Austn Financial Review, 27 Mar 1974, p 47; Univ of Melbourne Archives; Cambridge Univ Archives; CSIRO Archives, Canberra; private information.
                                          IAN D. RAE

KEMP, FRANCIS RODERICK (ROGER) (1908-1987), artist, was born on 3 July 1908 at Long Gully, Bendigo, Victoria, second of three children of locally born parents Francis Herbert Henry Kemp, mining-engine driver, and his wife Rebecca Jane, née Harvey. Roger's infancy was spent in a close-knit Cornish community at St Just Point, Eaglehawk, which provided the elements of Methodist faith and Penwith superstition that shaped his visionary outlook. His family moved to South Yarra, Melbourne, on the eve of World War I, following Frank's injury in a mine accident. Roger received basic schooling and entered the workforce at 14. He had musical ambitions, having joined a youth choir and received formal training as a singer. In 1929 he enrolled in night classes in drawing at the National Gallery of Victoria Art School. After briefly studying commercial art at the Working Men's College in 1932, he returned to the gallery school, where, financially supported by his sister Adelaide he undertook full-time studies in painting (1933-35).

While initially following the academic program, in his final year Kemp veered towards the flattened, angular forms of early cubism and was singled out for rebuke. He was torn between his loves for singing and painting in the mid-1930s; however, the arrival of Colonel de Basil's *Ballets Russes* in Melbourne in 1936 led Kemp to believe it might be possible to create a dynamic fusion of visual art and music.

Entranced by the stirring music, colourful costumes and whirling figures in the company's *Spectre de la Rose* and the symphonic ballet, *Les Présages*, designed by the surrealist André Masson, Kemp experimented with vividly coloured semi-abstract and geometricised figures. Notes in an early sketchbook suggest that, influenced by Christian Science and theosophy, he sought to convey mystical ideas about the spiritual progress of humanity in his compositions.

At first Kemp made no effort to exhibit: his work was seen only by friends from the theatre scene, including Harry Tatlock Miller and Loudon Sainthill [q.v.16]. This self-imposed isolation ended after he met Edna Merle McCrohan, an art teacher, whom he married with Anglican rites on 10 September 1943 at Christ Church, South Yarra. With her encouragement, he held his first solo exhibition at the Velasquez Gallery in June 1945. While he sold nothing, apart from an abstract bought by the designer Frances Burke, the show drew favourable reviews from the *Sun*, *Argus* and *Herald*. They were not appealing paintings. Wartime shortages had forced him to work in enamel on masonite; green and white were removed from his palette, and black, which he had rarely used before, predominated. Focused on stark schematic figures, these works were dark, troubled and brooding, and suggested that his faith in human destiny was being tested. Nevertheless, critics such as Alan McCulloch and Laurie Thomas [q.v.16] praised their apocalyptic overtones, later claiming that they encapsulated the mood of a world traumatised by war.

Further solo exhibitions in 1947 and 1950 attracted positive notices and the interest of artists who saw Kemp as a leader in the push towards abstraction. He was employed in the printing industry but his paintings increasingly featured in most of Melbourne's contemporary art shows and in nationally touring exhibitions of the Blake prize for religious art. Evolving through the 1950s, Kemp's mature style was expressed in paintings set prevailingly in deep blues and reds, balancing rectangular bodies, soaring bird-forms and mandala motifs within a loose geometric scaffold of broad black lines. His works were charged with symbolism and a distinctly Gothic visual richness, often likened to stained-glass windows.

Strong exhibition sales and a series of awards, including the John McCaughey memorial prize (1961), the Georges Invitation art prize (1965), the Transfield prize (1965) and the Blake prize for religious art (1968, 1970), enabled Kemp by 1966 to devote himself fully to painting. An unstoppable, sometimes baffling talker on the subject of art and metaphysics, he was increasingly revered as a 'modern master'. He became a charismatic figure who found many disciples among younger artists,

Leonard French, Jan Senbergs and George Baldessin [q.v.13] being the most prominent. Still, there was a homespun humility to the man, for he never put on airs, greeting acquaintances with a warm hug. Dark and of average build, he dressed simply in a tweedy jacket, corduroy trousers, desert boots and his signature woven tie.

In the early 1970s Kemp worked in London after touring Europe, and on return featured in the inaugural Sydney Biennale (1973), in *Ten Australians*—a landmark contemporary art exhibition sent overseas by the Federal government (1974-75)—and in a major touring retrospective in 1978-80. Appointed OBE (1978) and AO (1987), and awarded the Society of Painters and Sculptors medal (1986), he kept painting steadily through the 1980s despite declining health. Survived by his wife and four daughters, Roger Kemp died at Sandringham on 14 September 1987 and was cremated.

Roger Kemp: Cycles and Directions 1935-1975 (1978); H. Kolenberg, *Roger Kemp* (1991); C. Heathcote, *A Quiet Revolution* (1995); *Art and Australia*, vol 8, no 2, 1970, p 143; *Age* (Melbourne), 25 May 1985, p 16, 8 Nov 1986, p 9.

CHRISTOPHER HEATHCOTE

KEMSLEY, SIR ALFRED NEWCOMBE (1896-1987), businessman, was born on 29 March 1896 at Prospect, South Australia, son of English-born parents Alfred Kemsley, boiler-maker, and his wife Clara Kate, née Newcombe. 'Kem' was educated at Nailsworth Public School, Adelaide, then at Howard's Commercial and Correspondence College and the Adelaide Shorthand and Business Training Academy. He passed the South Australian civil service and railway clerical examinations. From 1911 he was employed as a clerk in the State Lands Department before enlisting in the Australian Imperial Force on 5 March 1915. Recognising his gifts as a manager and administrator, the army employed him on supply duties in Egypt (1916) and on the Western Front (1916-19). In October 1916 he was awarded the Meritorious Service Medal and commissioned. He was demobilised as an honorary captain on 6 December 1919.

Returning to Adelaide, Kemsley entered a brief real-estate partnership before moving to Melbourne and joining the head office of Broken Hill Proprietary Ltd in 1920. On 6 September 1921 at the Pirie Street Methodist Church, Adelaide, he married Glydus Annie May Logg. In 1923-29 he was secretary of Melbourne's Metropolitan Town Planning Commission. He was active in the Militia (1921-28) and in the right-wing White Army (League of National Security); in 1923 he became the secretary of the Special Constabulary Force deployed during the police strike in October. Widowed in 1922 he married Janet Oldfield on 22 December 1925 at St Paul's Church of England, Bendigo.

Appointed secretary (1930-34) to the Liquor Trade Defence Union, Kemsley organised the resoundingly successful referendum campaign against the proposed abolition of licences to sell liquor—although he was uncomfortable with some aspects of the organisation and always denied responsibility for a poster featuring an image of an injured pedestrian and the caption 'A Drop of Brandy Might Have Saved Him'. In 1934 he became general manager of radio-station 3UZ and in 1935-36 also served as vice-president of the Australian Federation of Broadcasting Stations. At 3UZ he engaged Sir Thomas Blamey [q.v.13], with whom he had served during World War I, to give a series of regular Sunday night commentaries in 1938, 'The Perils of War'. These broadcasts, delivered under the pseudonym 'The Sentinel', provided a valued opportunity for the unemployed Blamey: such a gesture was typical of Kemsley's support for colleagues and friends.

A foundation member (1923) of the Melbourne Legacy Club, Kemsley had exercised forceful leadership on many of its committees, and as recording secretary (1926-27), chairman of committees (1927-28), vice-president (1928-30) and president (1932-33). He sought to expand the club's welfare activities. Together with his friend Donovan Joynt, VC [q.v.], he became one of the most committed advocates for the creation of a Shrine of Remembrance on St Kilda Road as a 'worthy' memorial to Victoria's 'unparalleled efforts during the Great War'. He played an active role in the defeat of a counter-proposal for an Anzac Square in Spring Street. In 1938 he was appointed to the trust established to administer the Shrine, later serving as its deputy-chairman (1952) and chairman (1978-84).

In June 1941 Kemsley began full-time service in the Militia (AIF from July) as director of organisation and recruiting at Army Headquarters, Melbourne, with the rank of temporary colonel (substantive in March 1943). He was seconded to the civilian post of business adviser to the Department of the Army in 1943-46, and was concurrently army representative on the Board of Business Administration. In March-April 1946 he was also business member of the Military Board. On 12 June 1946 he was transferred to the Reserve of Officers.

Back in civilian life, Kemsley established a successful advertising agency, United Service Publicity Pty Ltd (U. S. P. Benson Pty Ltd after 1962). He was a director from 1946 and chairman in 1960-64. Questions of urban development again claimed his attention following his appointment to the Victorian Town and Coun-

try Planning Board (1946-68), for which he conducted a traffic census of Melbourne and its suburbs (1948) and served on the government finance committee relating to the proposed city underground railway scheme. He was an early supporter of the movement to create a national trust in Victoria, and sought to secure the board's support for its activities. A member of the National Trust of Australia (Victoria) from 1958, he resigned in 1974 troubled that it had expanded beyond its initial functions. Already an honorary member (1941) of the Town and Country Planning Association, in 1964 he was awarded its Sir James Barrett [q.v.7] memorial medal.

Kemsley had joined the Melbourne Chamber of Commerce in 1947 and was elected to its council every year until 1976. He became a constructive influence during years of transformation in the Chamber's interests in social and economic policy, serving on many of its committees including those dealing with public relations (chairman 1952-53), civic affairs and environmental protection—a cause he particularly supported. In 1956-68 he represented the Associated Chambers of Commerce of Australia on the Australian National Travel Association (deputy-chairman 1967).

The evolution of Legacy also continued to concern him in the postwar years. As secretary (1948) of the club's finance committee, he was closely involved in the establishment and maintenance of the Melbourne Army Transit House (Blamey House) and in obtaining a gift of £20 000 to purchase a house at Beaumaris for the orphan boys of deceased ex-servicemen. Aware of increasing demands and expectations, in 1960 he presented a paper reminding 'legatees' that there would still be children of World War II veterans to care for in the 1990s. On that basis he opposed any further extension of eligibility to Legacy benefits and of welfare programs. As Mark Lyons noted, for younger colleagues, keen to embrace new forms of assistance in areas such as education, his concerns seemed overly negative. While his paper expressed an older man's exasperation with such enthusiasms, it also raised issues that in time would demand increasing attention.

Of medium height, balding, tending to a gruff appearance and capable of amazing bursts of energy, Kemsley sought to temper his views with balanced argument, sensitivity and humanity. His occasional bluntness was at odds with the geniality and approachability that encouraged many young people to seek his advice. Often taken into the confidence of political and business leaders, he declared his political independence but was open in his opposition to socialism, communism and religious bigotry.

Kemsley's business interests included a directorship (1964-69) of Ponsford Newman

& Benson Ltd. He maintained support for many charities and causes, joining the Victorian branch of the Proportional Representation Society in his youth and remaining a member for the rest of his life; serving as trustee (1948-68) of the Henry George Foundation; and being actively involved with the Free Enterprise Foundation and the Land Values Research Group. He served on the council of the (War) Nurses Memorial Centre (1948-83), the Blamey Memorial Committee from 1954 (chairman 1978) and the Discharged Servicemen's Employment Board (1969-74). A member of Melbourne's Naval and Military Club from 1936 (honorary life member 1983), in his eighties he would scoff at colleagues who took the lift to the dining room, climbing the stairs to arrive red-faced but victorious.

Appointed CBE (1960) and CMG (1973), and knighted in 1979, Sir Alfred could still gain headlines in 1985 by deploring the congestion that would affect Melbourne's streets if buildings were allowed to exceed height restrictions. His second wife had died in 1972. On 16 November of that year at East Malvern he married Annie Elizabeth Copsey. Remembered by the *Age* as one of Melbourne's 'great characters', he died on 24 February 1987 at Brighton, survived by his wife and the son and daughter of his second marriage (the son of his first marriage had died in 1941); he was cremated. An annual prize in his name was established for the best student in marketing communications at the University of Melbourne.

J. S. Gawler, *A Roof over My Head* (1963); W. D. Joynt, *Breaking the Road for the Rest* (1979); M. Lyons, *Legacy* (1978); *Herald* (Melbourne), 24 Jan 1985, p 1; *Melbourne Legacy Bulletin*, Mar 1987, p 3; *Age* (Melbourne), 25 Feb 1987, p 10; private information.   MICHAEL INGAMELLS

KENNA, PETER JOSEPH (1930-1987), playwright, was born on 18 March 1930 at Balmain, Sydney, eleventh of thirteen children of James O'Connor Kenna, carpenter, and his wife Agnes Charlotte, née Horne, both born in rural New South Wales. Peter was educated at the Christian Brothers' School, Lewisham; during his schooldays he performed as a boy soprano and in a concert party to entertain the troops. After leaving school at the age of 14, he worked in a pickle factory, as an apprentice window-dresser at Mark Foy's [qq.v.4,8] Ltd and as a 'juvenile' in radio serials. While selling art materials in a shop, he acted and made props for the Genesian and Independent theatres; in 1954 he auditioned successfully for the Australian Eizabethan Theatre Trust. He also wrote eleven plays, none of which was performed.

In 1958 Kenna's entry in an Australian play competition sponsored by the trust and General Motors-Holden [q.v.9] Ltd won the first prize of £300. *The Slaughter of St. Teresa's Day* (revised version published 1972) constituted, in a later assessment by the critic H. G. Kippax, a 'vivid and idiomatic depiction of a slice of the Irishry of old Sydney life'. One of the judges, Kylie Tennant [q.v.], praised Kenna for his practical working knowledge of the theatre, appreciation of character and ability to make his creations walk and live. The play opened at the trust's Newtown theatre in March 1959. Critics commended Neva Carr-Glyn's [q.v.13] performance as Oola Maguire, an Irish-Australian underworld leader, but were more equivocal about the play—although later it would be widely performed and studied.

As a result of the British Broadcasting Corporation's interest in this play Kenna travelled in 1960 to London, where he worked in an art showroom. The Hampstead Theatre Club performed his new work *Talk to the Moon* (published 1977) in 1963. He wrote plays for radio and television including *Goodbye, Gloria, Goodbye* for the BBC. Back in Australia, in 1966 he directed the Independent Theatre's production of his play *Muriel's Virtues?*, a farce set in a suburban lounge room. Although the *Sun-Herald* described him as 'one of Australia's leading dramatists', a reviewer condemned the play as a 'catastrophe'. He worked as a stage director and performed in pantomime. In search of better treatment for his kidneys, damaged by the large doses of Bex powders that he had taken for tension headaches, he went back to England and began dialysis.

Kenna returned to Australia in 1971. *Listen Closely* (published 1977), a play about the generation gap between a university-educated young man and his bush-town-dwelling father, was performed at Sydney's Independent Theatre in 1972. Next year he received a three-year grant from the Literature Board of the Australian Council for the Arts, and the Nimrod Street Theatre staged *A Hard God* (published 1974), directed by John Bell. The play dealt with the Cassidys, driven off the land and into Sydney by drought. In Aggie Cassidy, movingly performed by Gloria Dawn [q.v.13], Kenna created perhaps the finest tragic role for a female actor in the Australian canon. The play attracted large audiences in Melbourne, Brisbane and Sydney, was televised by the Australian Broadcasting Commission and became a school text. After he received a kidney transplant from his sister Agnes in 1974, Kenna's health improved temporarily.

In 1975 the Nimrod Street Theatre staged Kenna's one-act play *Mates* (published 1977), the story of a confrontation between a shearer and a drag queen. *Trespassers Will Be Prosecuted* (published 1977) opened at the Jane

Street Theatre in 1976; its theme was the cruelty of conventional society in its treatment of outcasts. In 1978 'The Cassidy Album', his trilogy consisting of *A Hard God*, *Furtive Love* (published 1980) and *An Eager Hope*, opened at the Adelaide Festival of Arts, before moving to Sydney's Seymour Centre. Heavily auto-biographical, the second play, in particular, extended the theme of *A Hard God* to focus on Joe Cassidy's struggle to reconcile his Catholic faith with his homosexuality. Kenna's health deteriorated in the 1980s. He wrote articles for the *Sydney Morning Herald* and created the screenplay for the film *The Umbrella Woman* (1987).

The Irish, Catholic, working-class and rural values that his parents embodied influenced Kenna. John Bell described him as acerbic, passionate, sincere and generous. In a series of contrasts Kenna wrote about the ordinary but revealed it to hold beauty and inspiration; he found comfort in Catholicism, but agonised over its compatibility with his homosexuality; and although he lived most of his life in inner Sydney, he was haunted by the 'bush' legend that perhaps inspired his spirited nationalism. He died of hepatitis and liver failure on 29 November 1987 at St Leonards and was buried in the Catholic section of Rookwood cemetery.

J. Bell, *John Bell: The Time of My Life* (2002); *SMH*, 16 Dec 1958, p 5, 19 Dec 1958, p 2, 23 Feb 1959, p 2, 12 Mar 1959, p 5, 30 June 1965, p 2, 15 Apr 1966, p 12, 9 May 1972, p 8, 26 Aug 1972, p 20, 20 Aug 1973, p 9, 11 Jan 1975, p 8, 31 July 1975, p 10, 24 Nov 1976, p 11, 25 Mar 1978, p 16, 3 Apr 1978, p 8, 30 Nov 1987, p 3; *Sun-Herald* (Sydney), 11 Dec 1966, p 112; *National Times*, 23 Dec 1978, p 44; *New Theatre Aust*, Feb 1988, p 5; H. de Berg, interview with P. Kenna (ts, 1972, NLA).

RICHARD WATERHOUSE

KENNEDY, BYRON ERIC (1949-1983), film producer, was born on 18 August 1949 in Melbourne, elder child of Victorian-born parents Eric James Kennedy, engineer, and his wife Lorna, née Flynn. Byron was educated at Footscray High School and began making films with an 8-mm camera. He met George Miller, a medical student, at a film workshop in Melbourne.

In 1971 Kennedy and Miller made *Violence in the Cinema, Part I*; Kennedy was the lighting cameraman, co-writer and co-editor. Made with an extremely small crew and running for fourteen minutes, it was shown at the Sydney Film Festival. In the film, a dry lecture on violence in the cinema is interrupted by a shotgun-wielding thug. The lecturer, despite having part of his head blown away, continues with the lecture and is finally incinerated. The film won a silver award in the fiction section of the 1972 Australian Film Institute awards.

A recipient of a travel grant from the (Australian) Film and Television School, Kennedy travelled through thirty countries; this trip further sharpened his sense of the international language of film. His passion for cinema and his curiosity about the film-making process was immense. In 1972 he gave an impressive and largely improvised performance in *The Office Picnic*. On another low-budget film, *Come Out Fighting* (1973), he worked as the lighting cameraman.

Kennedy, as producer, and Miller, as director, spent more than a year preparing the film *Mad Max*, and two years raising the money. Thirty non-government investors put up $380 000 and shooting began in spring 1977. The focus on road rage and carnage sprang from Miller's work as a doctor treating motor-car crash victims. Critics praised the film's technical brilliance but Phillip Adams described it as having 'all the moral uplift of *Mein Kampf*'. It launched the career of Mel Gibson. At the 1979 AFI awards *Mad Max* won the jury prize and those for editing, music and sound. Overseas it received the special jury prize at the Avoriaz International Festival of Fantastic Film. In the late 1990s the *Guinness Book of Records* listed *Mad Max* as the most profitable film on a cost-to-revenue basis.

Mad Max 2, also known as *The Road Warrior*, was filmed in 1981 on a considerably bigger budget. It was a striking, often electrifying film that displayed more technical polish than its predecessor. In *Mad Max* some dialogue was drowned out by the roar of machines whereas *Mad Max 2* was the first Australian feature film mixed in stereo: Kennedy was one of the sound mixers. The film was a critical and commercial success: it won AFI awards for direction, editing, production design, costume design and sound. In 1982 it won the grand prize at the Avoriaz Fantasy Film Festival and the Los Angeles Film Critics Association's award for best foreign film. Kennedy Miller Entertainment Pty Ltd changed direction dramatically in its next venture. With Kennedy as executive producer, the company embarked on *The Dismissal* (1983), a six-hour television mini-series dealing with the political events of 1974-75.

A shy and intense man with a dark beard, Kennedy had a laconic expression and a dry sense of humour. He had not married. An experienced pilot, on 17 July 1983 he flew his helicopter over Lake Burragorang, near Sydney, and crashed when the engine cut out. Kennedy died next day from his injuries and was cremated. The Byron Kennedy award for a film-maker who has displayed outstanding creative enterprise has been given at the AFI awards since 1984.

Bulletin, 24 Apr 1979, p 66, 1 May 1979, p 38, 12 Jan 1982, p 56, 15 Feb 1983, p 70; *National Times*,

12-18 July 1981, p 30, 22-28 July 1983, p 7; *Variety* (NY), 26 May 1982, p 5, 20 July 1983, p 41; *Daily Telegraph* (Sydney), 19 July 1983, p 13; *Equity*, Sept 1983, p 26; personal knowledge.

RICHARD BRENNAN

KENNEDY, DAISY FOWLER (1893-1981), violinist, was born on 16 January 1893 at Kooringa (Burra), South Australia, fifth of six children of Joseph Arthur Kennedy, a schoolteacher born in Northern Ireland, and his wife Elizabeth Isabella, née Lorimer, born in South Australia. At the age of 7 Daisy began violin lessons in Adelaide with Mrs R. G. Alderman and in 1906 won a scholarship to the Elder [q.v.4] Conservatorium of Music as a student of Hermann Heinicke [q.v.9]. In 1908 she played for the visiting virtuoso Jan Kubelik, who recommended that she study in Europe.

After tuition with Otakar Ševčík in Prague and at the Vienna Meisterschule, she made her début in Vienna in October 1911 and in London two months later. She settled in England in 1912. Equally adept as a recital artist and a concerto soloist, she played regularly with leading orchestras under such conductors as Sir Henry Wood and (Sir) Landon Ronald. Her tours took her to Poland, Bohemia, Austria, France, Hungary, North America and Egypt.

On her tour of Australia and New Zealand in 1919-20 Kennedy was greeted with acclaim. On 17 April 1914 at the register office, Marylebone, London, she had married the Russian pianist Benno Moiseiwitsch, with whom she often performed. The marriage ended in divorce in 1924. On 16 December that year she married the poet and dramatist John Drinkwater, also a divorcee, at the register office, Kensington, London.

Kennedy possessed a brilliant technique and striking stage presence, and was much admired for her innovative repertoire. *The New York Times* praised her 'breadth of style', 'powerful tone', and 'certainty of intonation'. In 1927 she caused a stir when she publicly complained of insufficient rehearsal time for a Promenade Concert engagement in London. The music critic Ernest Newman observed: 'I am delighted to find, for once, an artist with the will and the pluck to fight her own battle'. In the late 1920s Kennedy concentrated on her role as wife and mother. She performed less often, although in 1932 she formed the Kennedy Trio with her cousin, the cellist Lauri Kennedy [q.v.], and his pianist wife Dorothy McBride. She was seriously injured in a motorcar accident in 1937, and her husband died shortly after. Left impecunious, she became the conductor and leader of a light orchestra at the Regent Palace Hotel in London, remaining there until 1950.

Survived by two daughters from her first marriage and one from her second, Daisy Kennedy died on 30 July 1981 at Hammersmith, London, and was cremated. Her ashes were scattered in the Adelaide hills. A woman of independence and determination, she moved in the highest social circles and was famed for her beauty and glamour. Kennedy's Columbia recordings, now rare, are a testimony to her considerable artistry as a musician. Her eldest daughter, Tanya Moiseiwitsch (1914-2003) was an influential designer for the theatre.

A. G. Stephens, *Interviews* (1921); I. Moresby, *Australia Makes Music* (1948); J. Creighton, *Discopaedia of the Violin 1889-1971* (1974); *New Age: A Weekly Review of Politics, Literature and Art*, 7 Mar 1918, p 377; *New York Times*, 5 Mar 1921, p 18; *Sunday Times* (London), 28 Aug 1927, p 5; *Advertiser* (Adelaide), 26 Nov 1948, p 7, 21 Sept 1964, p 8, 14 Feb 1978, p 26; W. Hancock, Daisy Kennedy and her Adelaide Concerts (ts, 1995, copy on ADB file); Kennedy papers (Performing Arts Collection, Adelaide Festival Centre).　WAYNE HANCOCK

KENNEDY, IRVINE ROBERT LAURI(E) (1896-1985), cellist, was born on 5 July 1896 at Randwick, Sydney, third son of English-born Samuel Robert Kennedy, commission agent, and his New South Wales-born wife Bertha Frederickson, née Chapman. Daisy Kennedy [q.v.] was his cousin. Laurie had no formal education. He began performing in 1906 as the comic turn with the family troupe, the Kennedy Concert Company, as they toured Australia, New Zealand, South Africa and India. Starting with the piano and progressing to the cello, he showed striking musical promise. After studying with Herbert Walenn at the Royal College of Music, London, and Paul Brummer in Vienna, he toured with his brothers before settling in Melbourne. In 1916 he was appointed professor of violoncello at the Albert Street Conservatorium, East Melbourne. There he was noticed by (Dame) Nellie Melba [q.v.10], who encouraged him to pursue further study in New York. On 12 August 1918 at St Mary's Cathedral, Sydney, he married with Catholic rites Dorothy Evelyn McBride, a pianist. After touring Australia on the Fullers [q.v.8] theatre circuit, they had saved enough to follow Melba's advice.

Leaving Australia in 1919, the Kennedys were offered positions as assisting artists on the 1920 tour of the United States of America by the Irish tenor John McCormack. Lauri (having dropped the 'e') maintained an association with McCormack for over six years, on stage and in recordings. In 1921 the Kennedys moved to London, where Lauri accompanied the Russian bass Feodor Chaliapin, appeared in numerous Royal Albert Hall recitals, and toured with artists including Melba, McCormack and Luisa Tetrazzini. Already a celebrated soloist, in 1930 for the British Broadcasting Corporation he became principal cellist in (Sir) Adrian Boult's BBC Symphony Orchestra. In 1935 he joined the London Philharmonic and Covent Garden orchestras. He also performed with several chamber ensembles, notably the Kreisler and London string quartets and the Chamber Music Players, and became a professor at the RCM.

Early in 1938 the Kennedys toured Australia for the Australian Broadcasting Commission, Lauri being celebrated for his 'great artistry'. Returning to the USA in June, he joined Arturo Toscanini's National Broadcasting Company orchestra and then settled in Hollywood, where he recorded many film scores, including that of Disney's *Fantasia*. Back in Australia in 1944, the Kennedys decided to rest from the rigours of performance. They purchased Fotheringham's Hotel, Taree, New South Wales, and later the Phillip Hotel, Sydney. From 1947 Lauri was again a soloist in ABC subscription series. He tutored at youth music camps until 1966, when Ernest Llewellyn [q.v.] appointed him lecturer in cello at the new Canberra School of Music; he resigned at the end of the year due to poor health.

Jovial and energetic, 'with a touch of Rudolf Valentino' in his appearance, Kennedy was admired both on and off the platform. He did not possess the most powerful tone, especially later in his career, but his playing—aided by his 1713 Grancino cello—was as beautiful and sensuous as any of his day. Predeceased (1972) by Dorothy, Lauri Kennedy died on 26 April 1985 at Sacramento, California, where he had lived with their eldest son, David; he was cremated.

Lauri's second son, JOHN KENNEDY (1923-1980), was born on 30 December 1923 in London. His parents' touring commitments seem to have produced an enduring estrangement from them. Educated at Brighton College, he entered Balliol College, Oxford, but abandoned law after winning a scholarship to study cello at the Royal Academy of Music, London, in 1943. Next year he married Priscilla Stoner, a pianist. He joined the Royal Philharmonic Orchestra (1946) and became principal cellist (1947) with the Liverpool Symphony Orchestra. In 1949 he was reunited with his parents when he was appointed to the Sydney Symphony Orchestra as principal cellist under (Sir) Eugene Goossens [q.v.14].

Like his father, Kennedy was an entertaining, sometimes flamboyant, character who played with 'gentle refinement and silky tone'. In Sydney he also appeared with the ABC String Quartet. Resigning from the SSO in 1951, he returned to England and became principal cellist (1952) in Sir Thomas Beecham's Royal Philharmonic Orchestra. Divorced from his first wife, in 1957 he married Joan Dargavel, a singer, with whom he travelled to Australia in 1959 to become senior lecturer in cello at the University of Melbourne; they were later divorced. In 1965 he was made a fellow of the Royal Academy of Music, London. He played with the Ormond and Melbourne trios and appeared frequently in concerts and broadcasts until ill health forced his retirement in 1975. John Kennedy died of chronic liver disease on 9 February 1980 at Box Hill and was cremated. He was survived by the son of his first marriage, Nigel, an internationally renowned violinist, and two daughters of his second, one of whom, Laurien, a cellist, won the ABC Instrumental and Vocal Competition in 1978.

I. Moresby, *Australia Makes Music* (1948); P. Sametz, *Play On!* (1992); *Austn Musical News*, Apr 1916, p 299, Dec 1937, p 2, Apr 1938, p 6, May 1938, p 28; *Canon*, July 1949, p 572; *Daily Telegraph* (Sydney), 7 June 1952, p 11; *Herald* (Melbourne), 11 Feb 1980, p 12; *Age* (Melbourne), 13 Oct 1991, 'Sunday Agenda', p 4.   PETER CAMPBELL

KENNEDY, MARGARET ('MARNIE') (1919-1985), domestic servant and writer, was born in 1919 on the bank of Coppermine Creek, near Cloncurry, Queensland, daughter of Rosie Baker, a Kalkadoon woman, and an unknown white man. Marnie was sent as a young child, with her mother, to Palm Island Aboriginal reserve. She witnessed the traumatic events in 1930 when officials shot dead the settlement's superintendent, Robert Curry [q.v.Supp.], who had run amok, killing his two children, wounding other white staff and setting fire to buildings. At 13 she was sent to work as a domestic servant at Blue Range station, north-west of Charters Towers.

On 28 July 1936 at St George's Church of England, Palm Island, Marnie married Alwyn Kennedy, an Aboriginal stockman on Blue Range. Rev. Ernest Gribble [q.v.14] officiated. A son, Alwyn Patrick, was born later that year. The couple was granted exemption from the Aboriginals Protection and Restriction of the Sale of Opium Act (1897) that controlled Aboriginal life. Separating from her husband, Marnie Kennedy moved to Ingham, where she stayed with the Illins, a Russian-Aboriginal family, and worked on cane-farms. She returned to Blue Range and another son was born in 1945. From 1948, now living with a man she called 'Sam', she worked on Oban, Oxton Downs, Walgra and Carandotta stations in western Queensland; a daughter was born in 1949. She made sure that her children received a good education.

About 1970 Mrs Kennedy moved to Charters Towers, and later to Townsville. In 1982 she published a short story, 'God's Gift to the Aborigines', in *Identity*. It was brief but powerful, depicting the knowledge and wisdom of Aboriginal culture in simple and effective language. In her view, the land and its resources should be shared between the original inhabitants and any 'invaders'. In a poem, 'Our History', featured in the same issue, she described Aboriginal people as 'wild and free' until Captain Cook [q.v.1] 'came for a look', with his 'goats, chooks and crooks', and asserted that 'now there are chains on our necks to our knees'.

'Our History' was reprinted in the *Asian Bureau Australia Newsletter* in 1984, with her article 'The Human Cost …', which argued that the Aboriginal experience of European law and culture had been confusing and destructive. On Palm Island some officials were obsessed with personal hygiene and sexual morality, while others were intent on systematically and ruthlessly destroying Aboriginal culture, dividing Aboriginal families and repressing any sign of resistance. Unable to understand what Indigenous people had done to deserve this cruel punishment, she hoped that white Australians would eventually realise that terrible injustices had been inflicted on them. She wanted future generations of Aborigines to know 'this part of our history', but looked forward to the day when 'young white Australians will help to heal the damage the government did over a hundred years'.

In 1985 Marnie Kennedy published her autobiography, *Born a Half-caste*. She and Alwyn were divorced in 1959. Later known as Mrs James Chester, she died of cancer on 30 September 1985 at Townsville and was buried with Catholic rites in Belgian Gardens cemetery. Her three children survived her.

E. Govor, *My Dark Brother* (2000).

JONATHAN RICHARDS

KENNELLY, PATRICK JOHN (1900-1981), Australian Labor Party official and politician, was born on 3 June 1900 at Northcote, Melbourne, fifth child of Irish-born parents John Kennelly, warder, and his wife Mary, née O'Dea. Educated at St Joseph's School, Northcote, and St Patrick's College, East Melbourne, Pat set his life's course from an early age: at 15 he joined the Australian Labor Party. When he commenced work he joined the Federated Clerks' Union of Australia and by 19 he was secretary of the Northcote branch of the ALP, where he began a lifelong association with John Cain [q.v.13]. While working at the Yallourn open-cut mine in 1925 he coached the local football team, foreshadowing an enduring association with Australian Rules football, which included the Port Melbourne and Richmond clubs.

In 1926 Kennelly began full-time political work as a clerk in the ALP office, becoming organising secretary in 1930. On 1 November that year at St Patrick's Cathedral he married Jessie Milne, a finisher; they were to have four children. His skills as a 'machine' man were honed in the office as Labor squabbled and split during the Depression. He was elected to the State executive in 1932 and held the position until 1950. In May 1938 he began a long parliamentary career by winning a by-election for the Legislative Council province of Melbourne West, but he retained his party position, rising to assistant-secretary in 1940. He was a minister without portfolio in the five-day Cain ministry of September 1943.

A 'stocky, hook-nosed Irishman with a bull neck', Kennelly was, by the end of World War II, well entrenched in the Victorian party machine. In the second Cain ministry (November 1945-November 1947) he was commissioner of public works, minister-in-charge of electrical undertakings and vice-president of the Board of Land and Works. He was elected federal secretary (1946-54) of the ALP and general secretary (1947-49) of the Victorian branch. In 1947 the Richmond Football Club, of which he had been vice-president and chairman of selectors, made him a life member. At this stage his legendary role as a 'numbers man' and political 'fixer'—resting on an interconnected network of Labor, Catholic and football associates—was clearly established. He was an influential strategist in the Cain government; an informal adviser to J. B. Chifley [q.v.13] on tactical matters; an adept fundraiser who some critics said was too close to John Wren [q.v.12]; and a highly numerate factional operator in party and preselection ballots where his preferred 'horses for courses' usually won, although the process was sometimes questioned. Known as the 'kingmaker', he was reported to have said, with his characteristic stutter, 'I d-d-don't care who's got the n-n-numbers brother, so long as I get to c-c-count the v-v-votes'.

Recognising his role in the party, in 1949 the State caucus elected Kennelly leader of the ALP in the Legislative Council. However, in 1952, as the Catholic Social Studies Movement became more assertive, a bitter faction fight saw Kennelly, Cain and several others challenged in preselection ballots. While he was in the midst of defending his Melbourne West position, his 13-year-old son, Neil, was killed in a motor accident. Grief sharpened his bitterness towards the Industrial Groups when he was defeated.

In 1953 Kennelly won Federal preselection and was elected to the Senate. Despite his new role, he concentrated much of his energy on defeating the 'groupers' within the ALP. He blocked their moves at meetings of the federal executive and federal conference in 1953, openly denounced them at the June 1954 State conference and worked behind the scenes to establish the 1954 ALP inquiry into the Victorian branch, to which he gave critical evidence. He played a decisive role in excluding the 'grouper' delegation from the 1955 Hobart federal conference that formalised the Labor split, and was given the task of re-establishing the Victorian ALP office afterwards.

Although in Opposition during his Senate career, Kennelly was an active committee and party member. He was deputy-leader of the Opposition in the Senate (1956-67), a member of the Joint Committee on Constitutional Review (1956-59), a trustee of the Parliamentary Retiring Allowances Trust (1967-71) and, perhaps ironically, a member of the Committee of Disputed Returns and Qualifications (1953-66). He was an adept parliamentary tactician and an effective speaker, despite his speech impediment, which he occasionally used to vulgar comic effect, especially when referring to the Country Party.

After retiring from the Senate in 1971, Kennelly continued a very active life, serving as chairman (from 1964) of the Industrial Printing & Publicity Co. (owner of radio 3KZ), as a trustee of the Melbourne Cricket Ground, and as the resolute and active chairman (1947-81) of the Albert Park Committee of Management. Under his leadership, Albert Park was transformed from a tip to one of Melbourne's best-equipped sporting reserves. He also maintained his association with the Richmond Football Club. As a party 'fixer', he helped to reform the Victorian branch of the ALP in the early 1970s to clear the way for the election of the Whitlam government. In 1978 he was appointed AO. Survived by his wife, one of their three sons and their daughter, he died on 12 October 1981 at Richmond. A practising Catholic whose devotion to the Church was sorely tested in the 1950s, he was accorded a state funeral and a requiem Mass at the Church of St Peter and St Paul, South Melbourne, and was buried in Melbourne general cemetery.

R. Murray, *The Split* (1970); K. White, *John Cain & Victorian Labor 1917-1957* (1982); R. McMullin, *The Light on the Hill* (1991); *PD* (HR), 13 Oct 1981, p 1842; *PD* (Senate), 13 Oct 1981, p 1079; *PD* (Vic), 13 Oct 1981, pp 1280, 1317; *Bulletin*, 10 Mar 1962, p 11; *Fact* (Carlton), 2 Nov 1964, p 5; *Age* (Melbourne), 22 May 1971, 'Sat Review', p 8, 13 Oct 1981, p 11, 16 Oct 1981, p 3.   PETER LOVE

KENTWELL, WILBUR DAVIES (1914-1981), musician, was born on 20 January 1914 at Castle Hill, Sydney, sixth surviving child of John Amos Kentwell, carpenter, and his wife Lucretia, née Davies, both born in New South Wales. Wilbur attended Parramatta High School to Intermediate level. Possessing innate musical ability, he had begun some limited formal musical tuition at the age of 8. After later instruction in organ playing, in his early teens he played for services at his local church. He was introduced to the theatre organ and public entertainment through the large Christie instrument at the Roxy Theatre, Parramatta, where he later performed professionally. From 1939 he was resident organist at the Savoy Theatre, New Lambton, Newcastle, for some five years, using a Hammond electronic organ. He also worked as a salesman.

On 29 June 1940 at Christ Church Cathedral, Newcastle, he married with Anglican rites Euphemia Cowan, a theatre usherette. Called up for full-time duty in the Militia on 4 August 1942, Kentwell served in the artillery in the Newcastle area before being discharged as medically unfit on 27 March 1945. He had continued to play the organ at the Savoy Theatre, and at the Century Theatre, Broadmeadow, whenever he could obtain a leave pass.

In the later 1940s Kentwell became resident organist at the Vogue Theatre, Double Bay, while playing regularly at several other theatres and at the Trocadero ballroom, Sydney—sometimes dashing between two engagements in the one evening. He was also staff organist at radio-station 2CH until appointed director of music to Macquarie Broadcasting Services Pty Ltd. There he attained national fame, particularly through his association with Jack Davey [q.v.13], who enjoyed an enormous following. Kentwell undertook freelance work for 2KY and 2UE, and for Australian Broadcasting Commission radio, on which he performed both as a soloist and in a trio. He also composed songs, writing words and music. His musicianship brought him engagements on radio as an associate artist with many celebrities, including Bob Hope, Nat King Cole, Anne Ziegler and Webster Booth, Peter Dawson, Gladys Moncrieff [qq.v.8,10] and George Formby.

After local television transmission started, Kentwell moved to Brisbane as director of music at Channel 9; he later worked for Channel 0. He also began teaching his techniques of theatre organ entertainment, and continued until his death. As well as making many recordings on traditional theatre organs, he used electronic instruments, particularly the Hammond organs (produced in the United States of America from the 1930s), which became popular with radio stations, theatres and nightclubs.

Reputed to be able to play more than one thousand melodies from memory, Kentwell was one of the last of a group of versatile musicians who provided 'live' incidental, accompaniment and effect music, which was a characteristic feature of radio broadcasts up to the end of the 1950s. Predeceased by his wife, he died of head injuries and barbiturate intoxication on 9 February 1981 at Toowong and was cremated. His daughter survived him.

Sun (Sydney), 28 Feb 1957, p 30; *Courier-Mail* (Brisbane), 11 Feb 1981, p 25; *T.O.S.A. News*, Mar 1981, p 9, Apr 1981, p 8, May 1981, p 5; B884, item N284116 (NAA).   G. D. RUSHWORTH

KEON, STANDISH MICHAEL (1913-1987), trade union official and politician, was born on 3 July 1913 at Carlton, Melbourne, third surviving son of Australian-born parents Philip Tobyn Keon, lorry driver, and his wife Jane, née Scott. His Christian names were registered as Horace Stanley, Horace being the name of a brother who had died the previous year as a result of a domestic accident. Educated at Catholic schools in East Melbourne and Richmond, Stan won a scholarship to Xavier College but was unable to take it up. Reduced family circumstances compelled him to start work at the age of 12. He held various jobs, including those of office-boy at a city music store, wireless salesman, and employee of the Hospitals and Charities Board.

Sponsored by Arthur Calwell [q.v.13], in 1927 Keon joined the East Melbourne branch of the Australian Labor Party. In 1933 he had a short stint editing, for Calwell, the *Irish Review*. He was also a committed member of the Catholic Young Men's Society of Victoria, which provided a form of higher education and a social network that he would later draw on in his political career. A member of the CYMS board of management (1937-39 and 1941-42), he was also a prominent debater and secretary of the society's amateur athletic club. His principal duty as a member of the editorial committee of the *Catholic Young Man* (1937-38) was to 'secure the development of Catholic Action' within the society. Catholic Action, in the wake of the Depression, was understood by many socially aware Catholics to mean militant opposition to both capitalism and communism.

In 1939-49 Keon was general secretary of the Victorian Public Service Association. He initiated an aggressive campaign against the parsimony of (Sir) Albert Dunstan's [q.v.8] Country Party ministry, which retained office by virtue of Labor Party support. Under Keon's leadership, the VPSA secured its first general salary increase for fifteen years, long-service leave, the five-day week and the principle of permanency for women. A central issue for him was the fulfilment of a twenty-year battle by the VPSA for the establishment of an independent Public Service Board, one of the three members of which was an elected representative of the VPSA. Continued dissatisfaction over interference by Dunstan with the board's independence was one of the immediate causes of the defeat of the Dunstan-Hollway [q.v.14] government in September 1945. In 1946 the Cain [q.v.13] Labor ministry introduced a bill guaranteeing the full independence of the PSB. Keon strove behind the scenes to ensure its passage through the Legislative Council.

Through a brilliantly organised campaign, mobilising his connections in the VPSA and CYMS, Keon had won Labor preselection for the blue-ribbon Legislative Assembly seat of Richmond in 1945. He and his 'crusaders' were to dominate Richmond politics for the next decade. After he entered parliament at the general election in November, his contributions to debate were often belligerent and provocative. Suspended in November 1948, he marked his departure from the chamber by giving a Nazi salute, an action that brought about a further suspension. Earlier that year he had created a sensation by a savage attack on John Wren [q.v.12], accusing him of switching his support from the ALP to the Country Party in return for legislation favouring his horse-racing and trotting interests.

Imbued with a powerful sense of social justice, Keon despised what he saw as attempts by business and rural sectional interests to preserve or gain privileges at the expense of working-class members of the community. He was an extremely effective local member: Janet McCalman described him as 'the first parliamentarian in Richmond's history who had the nerve, the commitment and the skill to fight for Richmond people's immediate and daily needs'.

Keon's public life was marked by fierce anti-communism. In July 1946 he had debated with a communist union leader in front of a polarised audience of five thousand people at the Richmond Town Hall. His position was more considered than might have appeared from his relish for invective and confrontation. In his parliamentary speeches he recognised the attractions of communism to the young, and admitted that 'mere suppression' was no remedy. The only answer was a reaffirmation of 'Christian values', reinforced by education. To Keon, Christian values meant that: 'Every human being is precious in his own right … His protection and full development are the purpose and measure of social institutions'. Having contested the deputy-leadership of the State branch of the ALP in 1947, he secured preselection for the Federal seat of Yarra next year, winning comfortably at the general election in December 1949.

His maiden speech in the House of Representatives considered ways of dealing with the internal and external threat of communism. Although remaining ambivalent about repressive legislation, he appeared to suggest that suppression should not be aimed just at trade unions, and he attacked journalists and academics, describing them as 'parlour pinks' and 'pink professors'. In 1952 he claimed that the Commonwealth Literary Fund was being used to support communist sympathisers. Intemperate personal attacks were balanced by careful and original analysis. The latter was evident in a speech in August 1954, in which he pointed out the inevitability of British withdrawal from Asia, questioned the popular left-wing argument that 'wars of liberation' were necessarily the legacy of colonialism, doubted the value of the South-East Asia Treaty Organization, and argued that Australia should seek its own regional alliances.

At this time Keon was a dark-haired, trim, sharp-nosed figure. Intense, ambitious, pugnacious, widely read, formidably intelligent and articulate, he left a strong impression. His voice was described as having 'an electric character'. Frank Hardy, in *Power without Glory* (1950), caricatured the unmarried Keon in his malign portrait of the devious, sexually repressed Michael Kiely. Writing in 2004, Philip Jones, who knew Keon, characterised him as 'a very closeted gay'. There were other sides to Keon's character: he appreciated good food and wine, and enjoyed a wide circle of friends.

In October 1954 Dr H. V. Evatt [q.v.14], the leader of the federal Labor Party, publicly accused 'a small minority' of members, mostly from Victoria, of disloyalty to the labour movement and of being under the control of B. A. Santamaria. Evatt's statement brought to a head the deep sectarian and personal antagonisms between left and right. In April 1955 seven Federal parliamentarians, including Keon, were expelled from the party. Keon became deputy-leader of the Australian Labor Party (Anti-Communist) (later Democratic Labor Party). At the general election in December he was narrowly defeated by the ALP's Dr Jim Cairns after a vicious campaign by both sides.

Keon's parliamentary career was over, although he stood for Yarra at the next four general elections. He decried the influence of Santamaria on the DLP and lamented the public perception of it as a 'church party'. By 1960 he held no office in the DLP. Elected secretary of a revived Victorian branch of the party in 1977, he unsuccessfully contested the Legislative Council seat of Ballarat at a by-election in 1978 and the Legislative Assembly seat of Kew at the general election in 1979.

Stan Keon became a successful wine merchant, and built up a significant collection of Australian art. He died on 22 January 1987 at Richmond and was buried in Boroondara cemetery, Kew. His estate was sworn for probate at $720 560. He was often described as a potential prime minister but, despite his great talents, it was never likely that he would attain that position. Throughout his political career he remained an irascible, volatile individualist.

R. Murray, *The Split* (1970); A. Curthoys and J. Merritt (eds), *Australia's First Cold War 1945-1953*, vol 1 (1984); J. McCalman, *Struggletown* (1984); *Copping It Sweet: Shared Memories of Richmond* (1988); R. McMullin, *The Light on the Hill* (1991); M. Keon, *Glad Morning Again* (1996); P. Love and P. Strangio (eds), *Arguing the Cold War* (2001); B. Duncan, *Crusade or Conspiracy?* (2001); P. Jones, *Art & Life* (2004); *PD* (LA, Vic), 27 July 1948, p 1867, 23 Nov 1948, p 3645, 11 May 1949, p 952; *PD* (HR), 14 Mar 1950, p 687, 11 Aug 1954, p 186; *PD* (Senate), 17 Feb 1987, p 57; *Labour History*, no 87, 2004, p 167; *Age* (Melbourne), 24 Jan 1987, p 16; *Sun News-Pictorial* (Melbourne), 27 Jan 1987, p 21; *Advocate* (Melbourne), 5 Feb 1987, p 5; private information.
GEOFF BROWNE

KERNOT, EDITH BETTY (1910-1984), golfer, was born on 26 July 1910 at Geelong, Victoria, third child of Walter Charles Kernot, chemist, and his wife Edith Latham, née Hobday [q.v.15 Kernot]. Both parents were locally born; Walter came from a well-established Geelong family, his uncle, Charles [q.v.5], having founded a successful chemist's and stationery business. Betty was educated at the Hermitage, Geelong. Showing an early talent for golf, she joined the Geelong Golf Club in 1923 and was attracted to the increasingly competitive side of a sport still largely regarded as a pastime for women of wealth and leisure. By her mid-twenties she was playing her best golf, securing her standing as an elite competitor and displaying a rare grace of swing and great accuracy.

Triumphant in the Victorian Champion of Champions title in 1935 and 1936, Kernot then won the Australian Ladies' Amateur Championship (1937, 1938) and, with E. M. Hutton, the Australian Ladies' Foursomes Championship (1937). Described that year by the *Sun News-Pictorial* as 'a brilliant little machine, hitting her shots with plenty of devil, and scoring par golf', she matched visiting British (1935) and American (1936) players in her long game, if not always near the green. She was selected for Tasman Cup teams in 1937 and 1938. By 1939 she was on a handicap of four and played in an exhibition match against the flamboyant Texan 'Babe' Didrickson. Known for her immaculate appearance, Kernot found the advice given to her by the big hitter disquieting: 'Betty, you've got to take off your girdle and let her rip'.

When the ALAC resumed in 1946 after World War II, Kernot was still playing good golf and in 1947 was runner-up in the championship. Ranked number one for Royal Melbourne Golf Club and later for the South Western

District Golf Association in pennant tournaments, she won championships at several clubs: Geelong (thirteen times), Royal Melbourne (four times), Metropolitan and Barwon Heads (both six times). In 1955 she set a course record at Geelong. She represented Victoria eleven times.

Increasingly recognised for leadership qualities, Kernot was Victorian delegate to the Australian Ladies' Golf Union (1939, 1948, 1950, 1953, 1956, 1957), and manager (1949) and captain (1950-52) of the Tasman Cup teams. A committee member (1934-67), life member (1939), and president (1952-56) of the Geelong Golf Club, she also served as president (1962) and patron (1963) of the SWDGA, which, in 1971, named a scratch foursome event for district players in her honour. In 1966 she was involved, through the Victorian Ladies Golf Association, in launching a camp for juniors at the Anglesea club.

While devoted to her sport, Betty Kernot was also an active member of the Victorian Ladies' Benevolent Association and the Victorian Red Cross Society. A revered and popular figure, she continued to play until her death on 19 October 1984 at Geelong; she was cremated. The Betty Kernot memorial trophy was established by the Geelong Golf Club in her honour.

P. Perry, *From Green to Gold* (1976); G. Long, *The History of the Geelong Golf Club* (1992); *SMH*, 26 Aug 1937, p 25; *Sun News-Pictorial* (Melbourne), 27 Aug 1937, p 20; private information.   J. E. SENYARD

KEWLEY, THOMAS HENRY (1911-1989), public servant and university lecturer in public administration, was born on 21 May 1911 at Waterloo, Victoria, fourth surviving child of Thomas Arthur Kewley, wood-carter, and his wife Helen Eugenie, née Ansaldi, both locally born. After completing his secondary education at the Ballarat School of Mines, he worked (1929-31) for the Young Men's Christian Association of Sydney. He proceeded to the University of Sydney (BA, 1935; Dip.Pub. Admin., 1938; Cert.Soc.Stud., 1939; MA, 1947), where he studied with John Anderson and F. A. Bland [qq.v.7,13] and lived at St Andrew's College.

In 1936 Kewley joined the Commonwealth Public Service. He worked in the Postmaster-General's Department, the national insurance branch of the Department of the Treasury, the Department of Trade and Customs and the Prime Minister's Department, undertaking research and administrative work. On 26 December 1940 at St James's Church of England, Sydney, he married Ethel Doreen Gardner, a schoolteacher.

When, in 1940, the University of Sydney absorbed the Board of Social Study and Training to establish a university qualification in social work, Kewley was recruited to teach social legislation and administration. In 1944 he transferred to Professor Bland's department of public administration; he was promoted to senior lecturer in 1947. His unfailing helpfulness, courtesy and encouragement to his students were widely admired. He served on the university's board of social studies (1951-64).

By 1941 Kewley had begun to publish articles on the history of social services. His MA thesis was titled 'Social Services: New South Wales and the Commonwealth of Australia'. *Social Security in Australia* (1965), his first major publication, was marked by a wealth of detail and an understanding of administrative process. He brought this study up to date in *Social Security in Australia 1900-72* (1973) and *Australian Social Security Today: Major Developments from 1900 to 1978* (1980). A reviewer commented that the first book laid a solid historical foundation on which other people would build but that more work needed to be done on the social and political milieu in which the events occurred. This comment foreshadowed later criticism of Kewley's work. During the 1970s his brand of empirical study was overtaken by more comparative, theoretical and critical approaches. Nevertheless, his books continued to be cited in scholarly, administrative and legislative documents as the standard reference for the history of social security.

In addition to his major interest in social security, Kewley studied the administration of public enterprises. In 1954 he attended, as a guest of the United Nations, a conference in Rangoon on public enterprises. This subject was central to his sabbatical leaves at the London School of Economics and Political Science (on a Rockefeller Foundation fellowship in 1950), and, in the United States of America, at Colgate University, New York State (Fulbright scholarship in 1959) and the University of Hawaii (1965). He retired from the University of Sydney in 1974.

A council member of the State regional group of the (Royal) Institute of Public Administration, Kewley had been assistant-editor (1951-52) and editor (1953, 1970, 1974) of the journal *Public Administration*. In 1968 he was seconded to the Commonwealth Department of Social Services as adviser to the public servants reporting to the cabinet committee on social welfare.

In the late 1970s Kewley served on the management committee, and as director, of the centre for social welfare studies at the Kuring-gai College of Advanced Education, where he helped to establish graduate courses in social and public administration; he was appointed the college's first fellow. From 1977 to 1981 he was a member of the Commonwealth government's Social Security Appeals Tribunal. He was awarded the OAM in 1982 and became a fellow of the Royal Australian Institute of Public Administration in 1983. During his retirement he cared for his wife, who was in failing health. She had compiled the indexes of his books. Survived by his wife and their two sons, Kewley died on 2 April 1989 at St Leonards and was cremated.

L. Foster, *High Hopes* (1986); *Policy: A Jnl of Public Policy and Ideas*, vol 5, no 2, 1989, p 64; Kewley file (Univ of Sydney Archives); eulogies at funeral (copy on ADB file); private information.

MICHAEL HORSBURGH

KEYS, GEORGE ERIC MAXWELL (1904-1986), headmaster, was born on 30 January 1904 at Christchurch, New Zealand, son of James Herbert Keys, clerk, and his wife Annie Paton, née Maxwell, both born in New Zealand. James died in 1918, leaving the family, then living at Palmerston North, in straitened circumstances. That year Maxwell completed his schooling at the local high school and in 1919 became a pupil-teacher at Christchurch West District High School. Gaining a teaching diploma at Christchurch Training College in 1922, he studied part time from 1921 at Canterbury University College, University of New Zealand (BA, 1925; Dip.Ed., 1926; Dip.Soc.Sc., 1931; MA, 1936) while teaching at high schools and Cathedral Grammar School. In 1926 he transferred to the Christchurch Technical College and also established a vocational guidance department of the local Young Men's Christian Association.

Five feet 9 ins (175 cm) and of rugged build, Keys was handsome, with dark hair and blue eyes. In 1927-28 he travelled in North America and Britain; he experienced tough periods of unemployment in Canada and a three-month stint with the Royal Canadian Mounted Police. In the United States of America he made contacts in the vocational guidance field. A love of outdoor life, respect for disciplined male teamwork and skill as a poker player were legacies of this time.

Back at Christchurch, Keys married Eileen Constance Mitchell on 24 January 1929 at St Andrew's Presbyterian Church. Having studied in London, she was to become an accomplished potter. Keys rejoined the staff at the technical college as vocational guidance master. During the Depression he helped to set up counselling and placement services and later to introduce vocational guidance into New Zealand schools. In 1939, having gained a Carnegie Foundation of New York fellowship, he began studies at the Institute of Education, University of London, that were cut short by World War II. In 1941-46 he continued his teaching and youth work at Christchurch and served as a flight lieutenant in the Air Training Corps.

In January 1947 Keys succeeded P. C. Anderson [q.v.7] as headmaster of Scotch College, Perth. The school was in poor shape after years of penury during the Depression and World War II; Keys appointed new staff and encouraged the development of music, drama and art. He formed a pipe band and expanded cadet training through the introduction of Air Training and Sea Cadets corps. A new post-matriculation class assisted in the transition between school and work, and in 1958 he engaged the State's first school counsellor. He instigated a major building program: a war memorial hall (1957), new junior school (1961), science block (1961), more boarding accommodation (1962-68) and a chapel (1968). Enrolments increased from 325 to 700.

In 1959 Keys gained a doctorate in education from the University of Toronto, Canada; travelling in North America he was appalled by the 'blackboard jungle' mentality that characterised many schools. He returned to Perth with a more conservative philosophy of education. Impressed by Geelong Church of England Grammar School's Timbertop in Victoria, he made an ill-fated attempt to establish a similar program. He was more successful in implementing the Duke of Edinburgh's award scheme at the school and introduced a service club modelled on Rotary.

Keys was not universally loved. A combination of rigidity and freedom marked his years at Scotch; young innovative masters taught alongside men whose teaching methods had stultified years earlier. His study was nicknamed 'the lubritorium'; there he oiled the wheels and smoothed over difficult situations. He was active in professional organisations: in 1959 he hosted the eleventh triennial Headmasters' Conference of the Independent Schools of Australia at Scotch. A founding member (1959) and a fellow (1967) of the Australian College of Education, he was chairman of the Western Australia chapter. In 1966 he served as president of the Association of Independent Schools of Western Australia.

Appointed OBE in 1968, Keys retired in December that year and moved to Roleystone. In 1969-73 he chaired the Youth Council of Western Australia. He was a keen sailor and a committed Rotarian. Survived by his wife and their son and two daughters, he died on 10 March 1986 at Roleystone and was cremated.

J. Gregory, *Building a Tradition* (1996) and for bib; *Reporter* (Claremont), vol 79, 1986, p 2; Scotch College, *Clan*, Apr 1986, p 1.   JENNY GREGORY

KILPATRICK, SIR WILLIAM JOHN (1906-1985), businessman and charity-worker, was born on 27 December 1906 at Surry Hills, Sydney, third child of Scottish-born James Parke Scott Kilpatrick, hotel waiter, and his wife Georgina, née Banks, a native of Sydney. Raised in the Wollongong area, Bill left school when his family returned to Sydney in 1920 and began work at Pincombe Ltd, an office equipment supplier. He obtained qualifications in accounting, auditing and commercial law and began a rapid rise in the firm: appointed company secretary and assistant-manager in 1927, he moved to Melbourne in 1933 as director and manager of its Victorian and Tasmanian branch. On 29 October 1932 at St David's Presbyterian Church, Haberfield, Sydney, he married Alice Margaret Strachan, a typist.

Enlisting in the Royal Australian Air Force on 23 February 1942, Kilpatrick was commissioned next month. He was employed as an identification officer in a number of fighter sectors in the South-West Pacific Area and as a personnel officer at headquarters, Southern Area, Melbourne. In January 1945 he was promoted to acting squadron leader. His appointment was terminated on 15 June that year.

In 1946 Kilpatrick established his own import company, Business Equipment Holdings Pty Ltd, an enterprise which, when acquired by Litton Industries Inc. of the United States of America in 1965, employed a thousand people in thirty offices across Australia. His other business interests included investments in urban land, beef and dairy properties in Victoria and New South Wales, and the plastics industry. Deciding to work part time in 1955, he devoted his extraordinary drive to community service and charity work. That year he organised Operation Gratitude to raise funds for war veterans' and war nurses' homes. He served as treasurer of the Victoria Promotion Committee and as a Melbourne city councillor (1958-64).

Kilpatrick made his greatest and most enduring contributions, however, as a health campaigner and fund-raiser for medical research. A member of the Anti-Cancer Council of Victoria (1957-76) and chairman of several of its committees, he was founding president of the Australian Cancer Society (1961-64, 1974-77). As world chairman (1962-74) of the International Union Against Cancer's finance council, he travelled widely. In 1960-64 he was the first vice-president of the National Heart Foundation of Australia and in 1970-72 chairman of the National Drug Education Committee.

To support these causes, Kilpatrick introduced the door-knock concept from the United States of America and directed the three largest charity appeals attempted in Australia: the 1958 Anti-Cancer Campaign, which raised £1 350 000; the 1961 National Heart Appeal (£2 562 745); and the Winston Churchill Memorial Appeal of 1965, which nearly doubled its target of £1 million to support the trust of which Kilpatrick was founding national president (1965-80) and patron (1980-85). Praised in the *Age* in 1964 as a man of 'great humanity, tireless energy, constructive thinking, inspired leadership and outstanding organising ability', he was appointed CBE (1958), KBE (1965) and AO (1981). In 1977 he was awarded an honorary doctorate of laws by the University of Melbourne.

Modest, gracious, persistent and persuasive, Sir William lived at Toorak and enjoyed golf and swimming. He suddenly became ill while attending an NHF meeting in Canberra, where he died on 25 May 1985. Survived by his wife, a partner in his philanthropic work, and by their three daughters and son, he was cremated. A portrait by Sir William Dargie is privately held.

Anti-Cancer Council of Vic, *Annual Report*, 1985, p 36; *Herald* (Melbourne), 7 Sept 1961, p 12; *Age* (Melbourne), 22 May 1964, p 2, 27 May 1985, p 6; *Canberra Times*, 27 May 1985, p 7.

DAMIAN VELTRI

KING, DONALD (1926-1989), geologist, was born on 3 June 1926 at Rose Park, Adelaide, third child of English-born parents Charles William King, cabinet-maker, and his wife Daisy Maud Evelyn, née Canhan. Don was educated at Adelaide High School and the University of Adelaide (B.Sc., 1948; M.Sc., 1950), where Professor Sir Douglas Mawson [q.v.10] steered him towards a career in geology. On 2 September 1950 at St Peter's Cathedral, Adelaide, he married with Anglican rites Joyce Hamp Walker, daughter of Hurtle Walker [q.v.12]. Joining the Geological Survey of South Australia, King developed his geological mapping and mineral exploration skills under the tutelage of some of the country's most able geologists. Seconded to the Commonwealth Bureau of Mineral Resources, Geology and Geophysics in 1951, he took part in a geological survey of northern Pakistan conducted under the auspices of the Colombo Plan. After returning he made a wide-ranging contribution to the survey's activities, especially the search for uranium in the Olary province. He also discovered a phosphate mineral known as 'Kingite'. When the government geologist (Sir) Samuel Benson Dickinson resigned in 1956 to become director of exploration with Rio Tinto Mining Co. of Australia Ltd, he took King with him and appointed him manager of Rio's Tasmanian exploration activities.

In 1961 King joined Utah Development Co. and moved to Queensland with a brief to explore the Bowen Basin for deposits of coking coal amenable to low-cost open-cut mining. The coal potential of the Bowen Basin had hitherto attracted little attention. He noted the orderly progression in rank of the coal northwards along the Dawson Valley to a geologically complex structural belt, and set about examining the wider possibilities of this relationship. Assembling evidence that suggested seams present in the largely concealed Permian sediments along the central-western edge of the Bowen Basin were likely to contain medium- and low-volatile coking coals, he convinced Utah that it should explore the area, despite their reluctance to consider mining so far from the coast.

Drilling in the Blackwater district south of the Mackenzie River in 1962 resulted in the discovery of huge deposits of medium- and low-volatile coking coal. A year later much more extensive deposits of similar high quality coking coal were discovered north of the river. They later supported several very large open-cut mines, as well as towns, railways, ports and other export-related infrastructure. By 2000 they were producing fifty million tonnes of coking coal annually. The discovery of this rich coking coal province is regarded as one of the great achievements of modern mineral exploration.

Promoted in 1964 to the position of UDC's chief geologist in Australia, King was transferred to its head office in Melbourne. The move south did not suit him and led to his resignation in 1965 to become an associate-director of Brisbane-based Mines Administration Pty Ltd, which managed a group of Australian oil companies keen to extend their exploration activities to minerals and coal. At a time when others believed there were no new fields to be found in the Bowen Basin, Minad made several noteworthy discoveries that led to its takeover by CSR Ltd in 1977. King chose this time to establish his own geological consultancy, Energy Minerals Pty Ltd, which he operated successfully in Brisbane until his death.

King was the author of forty-seven papers on a wide range of geological subjects. He was a foundation member (1952) of the Geological Society of Australia and chairman of its Queensland division in 1964, and a member of the Australasian Institute of Mining and Metallurgy, for which he co-edited a highly acclaimed monograph on coal (1975), the second in its *Economic Geology of Australia and Papua New Guinea* series. In 1987 he was appointed AO. An outstanding exploration geologist and recognised authority on coal in Queensland, King had a robust constitution, and boundless energy and enthusiasm for field investigations. His magnetic personality enabled him to exert an influence for good on young geologists and colleagues. He died on 3 August 1989 at his home at The Gap and was cremated. His wife and their three sons survived him.

A. Trengove, *Discovery* (1979); B. Galligan, *Utah and Queensland Coal* (1989); P. Goscombe, 'Donald King AO, MSc', *AusIMM Bulletin and Procs*, Oct 1989, p 34, and 'Donald King A.O., M.Sc.', *Bowen Basin Symposium 1990* (1990), p 3; private information and personal knowledge.

PETER W. GOSCOMBE

KING, HADDON RYMER FORRESTER (1905-1990), geologist, was born on 4 February 1905 in Georgetown, British Guiana, son of George Forrester King and his wife Jessie Ann, née Kingsland. He began his career as a surveyor's assistant on the Geological Survey of British Guiana in 1926 under the supervision of H. J. C. (Terence) Conolly, and obtained his surveyor's licence in 1929. Moving to Canada, he studied mining engineering at the University of Toronto (B.A.Sc., 1934) and gained experience in mineral exploration in the Timmins and Sudbury regions, working with Conolly.

In 1934 King was invited to join the newly formed Western Mining Corporation Ltd in Western Australia 'to apply the latest ideas in geology, geophysics, geochemistry and aerial photography to the scientific search for new mineral deposits', collaborating with American consultants. He became senior geologist in 1936. Research at Norseman revealed a repetition of the original gold ore body, increasing the life of the mine by more than fifty years. He married Noreen Sheahan (d.1965), an accountant, on 19 January 1937 at St Mary's Catholic Cathedral, Perth.

On 8 April 1942 King was called up for full-time duty in the Militia. Serving with the Australian Army Ordnance Corps (later the Corps of Australian Electrical and Mechanical Engineers) in Western Australia, he was commissioned as a lieutenant in May. He transferred to the Australian Imperial Force in October and was promoted to captain in January 1943. Posted to the 12th Advanced Workshop, he served on Bougainville from October 1944 to December 1945. His AIF appointment terminated on 18 January 1946.

That year King was appointed chief geologist of the Zinc Corporation Ltd at Broken Hill, New South Wales. He moved to Melbourne in 1953 as chief geologist at Consolidated Zinc Pty Ltd. In 1962, when the company became part of Conzinc Riotinto of Australia Ltd, he was made director of exploration. He oversaw the discovery and development of the vast iron deposits in the Hamersley Range, Western Australia, and the Panguna copper deposit on Bougainville. From 1965 he also chaired the Baas Becking Geobiological Laboratory. Retiring in 1970, he continued to work as a consultant. On 16 August 1969 at the Collins Street Independent Church, Melbourne, he had married with Congregational forms Eleonore Umbach, a secretary.

King's major contribution to mining geology came from his recognition that the Broken Hill ore body, and other similar deposits worldwide, originated as sedimentary layers of metals, rather than later replacements from metallic solutions. Although King was supported in his work by some colleagues, the concept initially 'raised fierce opposition' in both Australia and North America. Over the following twenty years it gained wide acceptance, based on Lourens Baas Becking's evidence of deposition of ore sulphides by bacteria in sea water. King's ideas are encapsulated in a book of essays, *The Rocks Speak* (1989).

A shy man, Haddon King was renowned for his quiet, thoughtful, positive response to people's ideas, although he was not afraid to criticise academic conservatism. He received many awards: the Penrose medal of the Society of Economic Geologists (1970), the (W. B.) Clarke [q.v.3] medal of the Royal Society of New South Wales (1972), the Australasian Institute of Mining and Metallurgy medal (1973), an honorary D.Sc. from the University of New England (1975), an honorary fellowship of the Institution of Mining and Metallurgy, London (1975), and the W. R. Browne [q.v.13] medal of the Geological Society of Australia (1984). Survived by his wife and the two daughters and son of his first marriage, he died on 11 March 1990 at Kippa-Ring, Brisbane, and was cremated with Catholic rites.

AusIMM Bulletin, no 3, 1990, p 43; *Economic Geology*, vol 86, no 2, 1991, p 460; *Jnl and Procs of the Royal Soc of NSW*, vol 124, 1991, p 85; King papers (Univ of Melbourne Archives).

D. F. BRANAGAN

KING, NORMAN JOSEPH (1905-1981), sugar technologist and administrator, was born on 27 December 1905 at Toowoomba, Queensland, fifth child of Queensland-born parents Philip King, engine driver, and his wife Margaret, formerly Bourke, née McMahon. Raised at Ipswich and Brisbane, Norman completed his secondary education at St Laurence's College, Brisbane, and in 1922 joined the Queensland Public Service as a clerk in the Registrar-General's Department. In 1925 he took up a post as records clerk at the Bureau of Central Sugar Mills. Gaining a diploma of industrial chemistry from Central Technical College in 1927, he transferred to the agricultural chemical laboratory, Department of Agriculture and Stock. In 1932 he was seconded to the Queensland Bureau of Sugar Experiment Stations, Bundaberg, to conduct a soil survey in the district. On 10 June 1933 at the bride's home Mayfield House, Montville, he married with Catholic rites Myrtle Mary Dart (d.1979). A permanent employee of BSES from 1933, he was appointed chemist-in-charge at Bundaberg (1937), senior adviser (1945) and assistant-director (1947).

Back in Brisbane from 1947, King was named director in 1948. He welded men returning from wartime service or secondment and well-chosen new staff into an effective organisation. In 1950-51 he served on the royal commission appointed to prepare a plan for the orderly development of the sugar industry. The BSES was removed from public service control in 1951 and a board established to oversee its operations. Under King's direction BSES staff, including R. W. Mungomery [q.v.15], monitored the various diseases and pests affecting cane and assessed the efficacy of insecticides and other control measures. By 1956 two important industry problems were contained: cane grubs and ratoon stunting disease. King recruited sufficient staff to provide for the first time an adequate extension service to the State's scattered sugar areas, and strengthened the breeding programs developing cane varieties suitable for the Queensland environment. A new head office was opened in Brisbane in 1958, additional stations in the Burdekin and Tully districts established, and existing facilities expanded or rebuilt.

An able administrator, King delegated day-to-day operations to his deputy and concentrated on major industry issues, including funding of research and future directions. He compiled *The Australian Sugar Industry: Some Facts and Figures* (1953), one of several publications showing his good grasp of detail. Visiting country areas regularly, he was noted for giving staff a fair hearing. He raised the profile of regional officers-in-charge and enhanced their status as the bureau's representatives.

King was active in the Queensland and International societies of sugar cane technologists. In 1950 he hosted the international group's conference in Brisbane. President (1953) of the local society and a general vice-president of the international body (1953-56), he was made a life member of both in 1971. He advised on methods to improve the productivity of cane in the Philippines (1956) and Puerto Rico (1970). In 1963 he served on a committee of inquiry into matters concerning the expansion of the Australian sugar industry. Appointed OBE in 1968, he retired in 1972. He enjoyed fishing, and the industry's traditional drink, rum. Survived by his son and daughter, he died on 25 May 1981 at his Greenslopes home and was cremated.

Bureau of Sugar Experiment Stations 1900-1975 (1975); Bureau of Sugar Experiment Stations, *Annual Report*, 1948-72; *Courier-Mail* (Brisbane),

28 May 1981, p 16; *Bundaberg News-Mail*, 28 May 1981, p 16; Public Service Board staff file (QSA).

JOHN D. KERR*

KINGHORN, JAMES ROY (1891-1983), zoologist, museum curator and broadcaster, was born on 12 October 1891 at Richmond, New South Wales, second of three children of a Scottish-born Presbyterian minister James Kinghorn and his wife (Bertha) Ethel, née Campbell, born in Sydney. Roy attended All Saints' College, Bathurst, and Sydney Church of England Grammar School. In 1907 he joined the Australian Museum in Sydney as a cadet, working mainly on crustaceans. He attended zoology lectures at the University of Sydney and studied part time at the Sydney Technical College, but after he failed a college examination, his position as cadet was reviewed and he was appointed a zoologist's clerk. In 1914 he resigned in anticipation of becoming a zoological clerk for the Commonwealth Fisheries' investigation ship *Endeavour* but it was lost at sea.

Enlisting in the Australian Imperial Force on 21 June 1915, Kinghorn served with the Dental Corps in Egypt and on Lemnos (1915-16) and for a few weeks (November-December 1917) on the Western Front as a driver with the artillery before an accidental injury to his knee caused him to be repatriated and discharged on 23 July 1918. He married Winifred Mance on 12 November 1921 at St Stephen's Presbyterian Church, Sydney.

On his return to the Australian Museum in 1918 Kinghorn had been appointed zoologist in charge of reptiles and amphibians; in 1921 birds were added. Despite later admitting that he had never liked the species, he published *Snakes of Australia* (1929). He also wrote herpetological and ornithological papers focusing on Australia, New Guinea and the Solomon Islands for scientific publications and natural history articles for magazines and newspapers. Handsome, versatile and personable, he educated the public, including children, about science by giving lectures for the museum and throughout the State. He was a corresponding member (1923) of the Zoological Society of London and was awarded (1935) the diploma of the Museums' Association of Great Britain. A member of the Wildlife Preservation Society of Australia and a fellow of the California Academy of Sciences, he served as president (1927-28, 1950-56) of the Royal Zoological Society of New South Wales.

Under a Carnegie Corporation of New York grant, Kinghorn visited (1937-38) museums in the United States of America, Britain and Europe. On appointment as assistant to the director of the Australian Museum in 1941, he declared: 'Museums are not morgues and should expand along modern lines'. In World War II he assisted with army recruiting and while serving in the Volunteer Defence Corps, lectured soldiers on camouflage techniques. He was commissioned as a lieutenant. With C. H. Kellaway [q.v.9] he wrote *The Dangerous Snakes of the South-West Pacific Area* (1943).

In 1956, almost fifty years after he first joined the museum, Kinghorn retired. For four years he appeared in a children's program on Channel 7 television. He then worked (1961-71) with the Australian Broadcasting Commission, for which he had given school programs from the 1930s; one of his roles was Linnaeus on the 'Argonauts'. Predeceased (1977) by his wife, and childless, he died on 4 March 1983 at Concord and was cremated.

R. Strahan, *Rare and Curious Specimens* (1979); *Austn Museum Mag*, vol 12, no 4, 1956, p 125; *SMH*, 4 Apr 1935, p 15, 13 Oct 1956, p 4; *Austn Women's Weekly*, 15 Feb 1941, p 2; B2455, Kinghorn James Roy, B884, N447506, ST3624/1, J R Kinghorn (NAA); H. de Berg, interview with J. R. Kinghorn (ts, 1977, NLA); Austn Museum archives, Sydney; private information.   ROSE DOCKER

KIRWAN WARD, EDWARD BERNARD (1909-1983), newspaper columnist, was born on 2 April 1909 at Shotover, near Oxford, England, one of eight children of Norman Francis Kirwan Ward, electrical engineer, and his wife Bertha Marie Thomas, née Van der Heyden. He was educated locally. After migrating to Western Australia with his family at age 18, he worked in agricultural jobs, and as a shoe salesman and insurance clerk, and struggled with Australian slang as part of a rampant literary ambition. He wrote under the name Kirwan Ward (which he sometimes hyphenated in everyday life), but was known to friends as Bernie Ward. At Perth College chapel on 12 November 1938 he married with Anglican rites Helen Curtis Inkpen.

Mobilised in the Royal Australian Naval Volunteer Reserve as a paymaster sub-lieutenant on 30 November 1942, Kirwan Ward was promoted to provisional lieutenant (special branch) in March 1943. In Darwin Jim Macartney [q.v.15], the editor of the Perth *Daily News*, asked him, over a bottle of gin, what he would do after the war. Kirwan Ward was unenthusiastic about his prospects in insurance. When his RANVR appointment terminated on 2 May 1946, Macartney offered him a job as writer and illustrator of 'Peepshow', a daily column with a 9.30 a.m. deadline. His first stylish sentence read: 'If you're looking for a simple recipe for success, here it is: Find out what people want and then give it to them'. He was writing about the proprietor of a roadside café, but it could have been his own motto. He tapped, with increasingly wry humour and polish, the attitudes and interests of the people of small-town Perth.

Travellers on public transport turned automatically to the back page of the afternoon tabloid for the exploits of Kirwan Ward's politically incorrect character Clueless Chloe or the letter sorters, the Postal Pixies. Readers saw him as one of them, but this was not altogether true. He was a serious reader, with a touch of David Niven, the English gentleman, and of the 'oddball'; he was an impeccable dresser who would wear a silk cravat to the local football. But he was a sports fanatic: a welterweight boxer noted for a 'terrible right hand', a golfer, and a fan of the Claremont Football Club and of soccer in Britain.

Macartney employed the illustrator Paul Rigby as a cartoonist in 1952. Kirwan Ward and Rigby were a perfect match, although the older Kirwan Ward and the often outrageous Rigby were opposites in personality. Macartney sent them on assignment throughout Australia and overseas, including a visit to China in 1958 during the Great Leap Forward. With their favourite city pubs in Perth being demolished, and to avoid being 'buttonholed', Kirwan Ward, with Rigby, moved over the railway line to the Victoria Hotel in James Street. In the front bar—where he mixed easily with detectives, criminals, reporters, magistrates and magnates—was born many a story for his column as well as the Lager Lovers' League.

Kirwan Ward wrote six columns a week for twenty-eight years until he retired in 1974, and another two a week for the next nine years. His columns remained non-judgmental of individuals but critical of institutional interventions such as censorship and 'archaic liquor laws'. He could be critical of the media: his last column pondered whether the sexiness of R. J. L. (Bob) Hawke was really the election issue. His skill as a raconteur made him a 'natural' for Australian Broadcasting Commission talks, and he wrote ten books on history, travel and old buildings. In 1978 he was appointed MBE. He died on 5 March 1983 at Fremantle and was cremated. His wife and their daughter and son survived him.

Tom's Weekly (Perth), 9 June 1973, p 6; *Western Mail* (Perth), 1 May 1982, p 18; *West Australian*, 7 Mar 1983, p 4; *Daily News* (Perth), 7 Mar 1983, p 3; A6769, item Ward B E K (NAA); private information.

RON DAVIDSON

KLEINIG, CYRIL NATHANIEL (1912-1982), pilot and airline manager, was born on 19 November 1912 at Roseworthy, South Australia, third child of South Australian-born parents Friedrich Nathaniel Kleinig, chaff merchant, and his wife Louisa Bertha, née Linke. He was educated at Scotch College, Adelaide (1919-29), where he played in the first XVIII and rowed in the first VIII, and later at the South Australian School of Mines and Industries and at Perth Technical College.

One of many young men who became interested in aviation during this period, in 1930 Kleinig began voluntary weekend work at 'Horrie' Miller's [q.v.10] hangar at Adelaide Airport to gain experience. He also took flying lessons and studied for an engineer's licence. He then started flying for MacRobertson [q.v.11 Robertson]-Miller Aviation Co. Ltd on regular routes and charter flights in South Australia. During the worst of the Depression he took part in a flying circus that toured country towns to keep the company in business. When MMA transferred its main operations to Western Australia in 1934, he remained to manage its operations in South Australia, serving as chief pilot and engineer. On 2 December 1939 at St Stephen's Lutheran Church, Adelaide, he married Rona Elsa Thiele, a clerk.

In 1939 MMA's services were centralised in Western Australia and Kleinig transferred to Perth as a pilot-engineer. He was appointed assistant managing director in 1947. That year he was the first pilot of the Air Beef scheme, which transported beef by air from abattoirs in the North-West. In 1955 MMA amalgamated with Airlines (WA) Ltd to form MacRobertson Miller Airlines Ltd; Kleinig was appointed to the board as managing director. When the airline became a wholly owned subsidiary of Ansett [q.v.] Transport Industries Ltd in 1969, he became general manager of MacRobertson Miller Airline Services. He retired in 1977, having overseen the introduction of the turboprop and jet airliners that revolutionised transport in Western Australia, particularly in remote areas.

Kleinig was a perfectionist who liked to experiment with new methods. A leader in the travel industry, he was widely recognised for his role in developing tourism in Western Australia. He was a fellow (1959) and councillor of the (Chartered) Institute of Transport; president (1964-66) and a life member of the Perth division of the Australian Institute of Management; an honorary fellow (1966) of the Institute of Sales and Marketing Executives; a member (from 1967) of the Western Australian Transport Advisory Council; president (1971-73) of the Federated Chambers of Commerce of Western Australia; and chairman (1973-75) of the Western Australian branch of the Australian National Travel Association. In 1979 he was appointed AO.

Serving the community with enthusiasm and dedication, Kleinig was president (1966-67) of the Rotary Club of Perth and governor (1979-80) of Rotary District 945, as well as vice-president of the Royal West Australian Institute for the Blind. He listed his recreations as gardening, fishing and boating. Survived by his wife, and their son and daughter, he died of coronary artery disease on 17 February 1982 at Nedlands and was cremated with Uniting Church forms. In July the first Fokker F-28-4000 to enter the fleet of Airlines of Western Australia was named after him.

H. C. Miller, *Early Birds* (1968); F. Dunn, *Speck in the Sky* (1984); N. Parnell and T. Boughton, *Flypast* (1988); R. C. Adkins, *I Flew for MMA* (1996); *Weekend News* (Perth), 22 Sept 1962, p 13; MacRobertson Miller Airlines Ltd, *Jetstream*, Apr 1966, p 1, Dec 1977, p 1; *West Australian*, 28 Oct 1977, p 11, 23 May, 'Western Australia Week', p 11, 18 Feb 1982, p 5; private information.   LEIGH EDMONDS

KNIGHT, ALFRED VICTOR (1897-1983), naval officer and master mariner, was born on 20 February 1897 at Dover, Kent, England, son of William Knight, grocer's manager, and his wife Annetta Louisa, née Howgego. Educated at St Mary's School, Dover, Victor was active in the local Scout troop as well as the church choir. He joined the Roberts Steamship Co. as a cadet in 1912 and served his apprenticeship in the tramp steamer *Batiscan*. On 21 April 1915 he was appointed midshipman in the Royal Naval Reserve.

After serving in the armed merchant cruiser HMS *Victorian* on blockade duty in the North Sea, Knight was posted to destroyers, first HMS *Owl* on escort duty to France and then HMS *Crusader* on the Dover Patrol. He was promoted to temporary acting sub-lieutenant in February 1917 and to temporary sub-lieutenant in February 1918. On 23 April that year he was in HMS *Sirius* during the attack on Ostend (Oostende) harbour, Belgium. The raid, designed to block the port to prevent its use by the Germans as a destroyer and U-boat base, failed in its objective but was a substantial propaganda success. Knight was awarded the Distinguished Service Cross for his 'great coolness under heavy fire'. He was mentioned in despatches for his actions during a second assault on 10 May. In February 1919 he was promoted to temporary acting lieutenant and appointed to HMS *Northolt*, which was employed on postwar minesweeping duties.

Leaving the navy in January 1920, Knight obtained his master's certificate next month and resumed his career in the merchant navy, sailing on voyages to the Americas and the Far East. He worked for the Booth and Blue Funnel lines, and also for a time with Malayan Customs in their campaign against rubber smuggling. Following a visit to Australia, he was appointed as a lieutenant, Royal Australian Naval Reserve (Seagoing), on 1 January 1923. In 1925 he joined the Union Steam Ship Co. of New Zealand Ltd. On 12 April 1930 at St Nicolas's Church of England, Coogee, Sydney, he married Irene Ethel Pain (d.1967), an artist.

He was promoted to lieutenant commander, RANR, in 1931 and to commander in 1937.

Mobilised for full-time duty on 16 March 1940, Knight served at Navy Office, Melbourne, in the trade division. In February 1941 he was appointed commanding officer of the Bathurst-class corvette HMAS *Lithgow*, which was commissioned in June. *Lithgow* swept for mines in Bass Strait, assisted in the destruction of the Japanese submarine *I 124* off Darwin in January 1942, escorted troop convoys to Papua and took part in the campaign to recapture Buna in December. He was appointed OBE (1943).

In February 1943 Knight took command of HMAS *Westralia*, then being converted as a landing ship, infantry. Under his command *Westralia* trained more than 21 000 men in amphibious warfare, transported more than 19 000 men and 30 000 tons of military equipment to forward areas, and took part in the Allied landings at Arawe, New Britain (December 1943), Humboldt Bay, Netherlands New Guinea (April 1944), and Leyte Gulf, the Philippines (October 1944). He was appointed to the United States of America's Legion of Merit (1946). The citation described him as a 'forceful leader' who, by his 'splendid cooperation in the conduct of a vital training programme, aggressive determination and untiring energies ... contributed materially to combined large-scale operations'.

Appointed sea transport officer, Sydney, in November 1944, Knight was promoted to captain in December 1946. He was demobilised on 1 July 1947. Transferring to the Australian Shipping Board (Australian National Line from 1956), he commanded various merchant ships. He was made ANL's first commodore soon after his retirement in 1962 and honorary commodore of the fleet in 1972. On 17 October 1968 at the registrar-general's office, Sydney, he had married Hilda Marian Menlove, née Stevens (d.1975), the divorced wife of D. A. Menlove [q.v.]. He was chairman of the Glebe Island Committee, a director of Altikar Pty Ltd (later associate-director of Multicon & Altikar Engineering Pty Ltd), and an active member of many naval and merchant-navy associations. His recreations included golf and fishing. Survived by the daughter of his first marriage, he died on 22 January 1983 in his home at Double Bay and was cremated following a funeral at the naval chapel, HMAS *Watson*.

F. M. McGuire, *The Royal Australian Navy* (1948); W. N. Swan, *Spearheads of Invasion* (1953); G. H. Gill, *Royal Australian Navy 1939-1942* (1957) and *1942-1945* (1968); *Naval Hist Review*, June 1975, p 3; *SMH*, 27 Jan 1983, p 11; A6769, item Knight A V (NAA); ADM 240/40 (National Archives, London).
                                          GREG SWINDEN
                                          DAVID STEVENS

KNIGHT, JOHN LANGFORD (1912-1988), chemist and public servant, was born on 25 August 1912 at Cressy, Victoria, son of Gabriel Knight, schoolteacher, and his wife Laura Mabel, née Langford, both Victorian born. Jack was educated at University High School, Melbourne, and the University of Melbourne (B.Sc., 1932; M.Sc., 1933), where he shared the Dixson and Wyselaskie [q.v.6] scholarships in chemistry and was a member of intervarsity swimming and water-polo teams. In August 1933, after working in the university's chemistry department, he became a chemist with Nobel (Australasia) Pty Ltd at Deer Park, analysing raw materials and carrying out developmental work on acids and explosives, including the manufacture of tetrazene for the Ammunition Factory, Footscray. On 12 September 1936 at the Methodist Church, Canterbury, he married Lillian Fo'Velle Moulton, a saleswoman. Next month he joined the Department of Defence as a chemist at the Explosives Factory, Maribyrnong, and was placed in charge of propellants.

In October 1941 Knight was transferred to the directorate of explosives supply, Department of Munitions. Part of an explosives mission to North America from November to May 1942, he studied the manufacture of smokeless powder and became involved in the planning of a new explosives factory for Australia at Mulwala, New South Wales. In 1942-45 he was its assistant-manager, with responsibility for the design, layout and construction of the buildings and plant to make synthetic ammonia and methanol and produce nitric acid and nitrocellulose.

After World War II Knight returned to central administration as assistant to the consultant on explosives, A. E. Leighton [q.v.10], and oversaw more than twenty armament chemical annexes. From 1947 he also served as secretary and executive officer of the Explosives Committee. In 1949-51 he was explosives and chemical engineering representative for the Department of Supply and Development in Britain, responsible for liaison with research establishments and factories.

Back in Melbourne in the Department of Defence Production, Knight was an assistant-manager of the Maribyrnong factory in 1952-54; manager of the Explosives Factory, Albion, which he reopened as a government concern, in 1954-56; and chief chemical engineer in the explosives branch in 1957-58. Joining the Department of Supply in 1958 he was controller, explosives supply (later explosives and ammunition supply) until 1967, and deputy-controller of munitions supply, in Canberra, in 1967-76. He was chairman of the Operational Safety Committee in 1958-76. Knight travelled abroad regularly on government business, and between 1969 and 1973 attended the second, third and fourth Quadripartite Ammunition Conferences, in the United States of America, Britain and Canada respectively. While visiting Paris in 1965, he noticed the poor condition of the Australian exhibit at the Musée de l'Armée; he lobbied the Australian government to upgrade it.

Tall and spare with an oval face, Knight was a dedicated and respected public servant. He was a fellow of the (Royal) Australian Chemical Institute (1946) and the Australian Institute of Management (1961), and a member of the Royal Society of Victoria (1961). Reading, gardening and bowls were his recreations; he was a member of the Canberra Bowling Club, and also of the Melbourne Cricket Club and the Royal Automobile Club of Victoria. He retired due to ill health in 1976 and next year was appointed ISO. His unpublished 'Explosives in Australia', written in retirement, argued that D. P. Mellor's [q.v.15] *The Role of Science and Industry* contains 'substantial errors' in its treatment of chemicals and explosives. In 1983 he returned to live in Melbourne. Survived by his wife, and their two sons and daughter, he died on 22 January 1988 at Blackburn and was cremated with Presbyterian forms.

Knight papers (Noel Butlin Archives Centre, ANU, Canberra).   G. P. WALSH

KNIGHT, JOHN WILLIAM (1943-1981), politician and diplomat, was born on 20 November 1943 at Armidale, New South Wales, son of Jack Albert Knight, grocer, and his wife Myrene Ruth, née Porter, both New South Wales born. Educated at Armidale Demonstration and High schools, John was captain of both. He proceeded on a teacher's scholarship to the University of New England (BA Hons, 1965), where he majored in modern history and shared the Shell prize for arts. On 9 May 1964 at All Saints Church of England, Kempsey, he married his childhood sweetheart, Jennifer Major, a schoolteacher; they were to separate in 1968 and to be divorced in October 1971. In 1965 he was one of fifteen selected from more than four hundred applicants to join the Department of External Affairs. After training he spent two years in New Delhi as third secretary at the Australian High Commission.

In 1968 Knight won a Fulbright scholarship to the East-West Center at the University of Hawaii (MA, 1969), where he studied modern Asian history. Returning to External Affairs in 1969, he was posted to Suva. There on 8 November 1971 he married with Anglican rites Karla Havholm, an American-born hairdresser. Back in Australia in 1973, he was appointed senior private secretary to the leader of the Opposition (Sir) Billy Snedden [q.v.], who stirred his interest in politics. After six months as a visiting fellow in the department of international relations at the Australian National University, he rejoined the Department of Foreign Affairs in May 1975 and in August was posted as counsellor to the Australian Embassy in Saudi Arabia. He returned to Canberra in November and next month stood for the Senate, becoming the first Liberal senator for the Australian Capital Territory.

Re-elected in 1977 and again in 1980, Knight was appointed the Senate's government deputy-whip in 1978 and government whip in 1980. He was chairman (from 1976) of the joint parliamentary committee on the Australian Capital Territory, and a member of the Senate standing committees on foreign affairs and defence (from 1976), library (from 1978) and standing orders (from 1980), and the Senate select committee on parliamentary appropriations and staffing (from 1980). He also served on government committees on health and welfare, foreign affairs and defence, the arts and government tactics.

Knight was heavily involved in the International Year of Disabled Persons and had just finished the manuscript for a book on the role of a back-bencher in foreign policy when he suffered a heart attack on 28 February 1981 after water-skiing on Lake Jindabyne, New South Wales. Survived by his wife and their two sons, he died on 4 March in Canberra and was cremated. Politicians from both sides mourned the death of the 'small-l' Liberal, who was respected for his sincerity, dedication, sense of fair play, love of home and family, and his devotion to his adopted city. His Liberal colleague John Haslem recalled him as an 'interesting and thoughtful person' with 'a fresh, confident, energetic air', who 'mixed easily' and was 'thoroughly good company'. Knight was posthumously named Canberran of the Year in 1981.

PD (Senate), 4 Mar 1981, p 303; *PD* (HR), 4 Mar 1981, p 403; *Canberra Times*, 15 Nov 1975, p 6, 7 Dec 1977, p 21, 1 Mar 1981, p 1, 5 Mar 1981, pp 1, 2, 14, 7 Mar 1981, pp 1, 13, 27 Nov 1982, p 12; *Australian*, 5 Mar 1981, p 11; private information.

JOHN FARQUHARSON

KNIGHT, JULIUS FREDERICK VALENTINE (1909-1986), surveyor, was born on 16 June 1909 at Drouin, Victoria, son of Frederick John Gregory Knight, engineer's fitter, and his wife Mabel, née Dobson, both Victorian born. He attended primary schools at Swan Hill, South Melbourne and South Yarra, Melbourne Junior Technical School (1921-23) and, on a scholarship, the Working Men's College (1924). In February 1925 he started work with Kodak (Australasia) Pty Ltd.

Developing an interest in surveying, 'Jule' was indentured to Frank Doolan and licensed on 16 June 1930, becoming one of the youngest qualified surveyors; the previous November he had been elected a member of the Victorian Institute of Surveyors. When planning of the Ray of Light for Melbourne's Shrine of Remembrance was deputed to the government astronomer Dr J. M. Baldwin [q.v.7] and the surveying firm of Doolan & Goodchild, Knight's calculations in 1931 positioned the floor plate and roof slit to ensure that the sun would shine on the Stone of Remembrance at 11 a.m. on 11 November each year. He worked in and around Melbourne, as well as at Warrnambool, where on 22 December 1934 at Christ Church he married with Anglican rites Martha Mary ('Mollie') Moore.

After a brief stint in 1937 as a mining surveyor at Norseman, Western Australia, Knight was appointed chief surveyor of Lake George Mines Ltd at Captains Flat, New South Wales. In 1939 he joined the Department of the Interior, Canberra. He defined various wartime defence facilities in the States and the Northern Territory, including a 100-mile (161 km) section of the Stuart Highway. Postwar surveys included the rocket range at Woomera, South Australia. In Canberra he surveyed residential subdivisions, and worked on topographical and engineering projects. As chief development officer from 1952, he helped to effect the transfer of Melbourne-based departments. The establishment in 1957 of the National Capital Development Commission altered his duty statement, but he retained control of leases of land for business, industries and embassies. He brought to this responsibility a reputation for meticulous detail. His quiet and modest but resolute and ethical character, combined with a sharp memory, won respect, as did his generosity in sharing knowledge with subordinates.

Following his retirement in 1969, Knight worked part time for both the Australian Capital Territory Electricity Authority and the Australian National University. Joining the staff of the registrar, property and plans, at the ANU, he drew on his vast knowledge of planning and regulatory requirements. He was retained as a consultant until his death.

A foundation member of the Canberra division of the Institution of Surveyors, Australia, Knight was elected president (1963) and a fellow (1964). He was a member of the Royal Australian Planning Institute. His knowledge of the development of the national capital enriched the Canberra and District Historical Society. Belonging for almost forty years to the Royal Canberra Golf Club, he relished his win in 1985 of the Scrivener [q.v.11] Cup. He was also a keen gardener. Julius Knight died on 12 November 1986 in Canberra and was cremated; his wife and their two daughters and son survived him.

W. B. Russell, *We Will Remember Them* (1991); *Canberra Times*, 1 Dec 1986, p 11; *ANU Reporter*, 12 Dec 1986, p 7; *Austn Surveyor*, Mar 1987, p 457; private information.   JOHN ATCHISON

KNOKE, GARY JAMES (1942-1984), athlete, teacher and coach, was born on 5 February 1942 at Punchbowl, Sydney, eldest son of James Leslie Knoke, clerk, and his wife Freda Adelaide, née Rees, both Sydney born. Gary attended Eastwood Public and Enmore High schools. A very popular student, he excelled in sport, particularly tennis, but he was to make his name in track and field athletics. In 1959 he joined the Randwick-Botany Amateur Athletic Club, where he was coached by Ernie Watson. With a 'sinewy torso and lean legs', Knoke became an outstanding hurdler. He won his first senior State title, the 120-yards hurdles, in 1962 and his last, the 400-metres hurdles, in 1973. In all, he claimed nine New South Wales and ten Australian hurdles titles, as well as six State sprint titles.

After completing (1962) a diploma in physical education at Teachers' College, Sydney, Knoke taught briefly at Kingsgrove High School. From 1967 he studied at the University of Oregon (B.Sc.(PE), 1969), United States of America, having been awarded an athletics scholarship. He ran for his university while in the USA and was never defeated in the 400-metres hurdles. On 25 January 1969 at Eugene, Oregon, he married Ann Michelle Reinmuth, a student. He returned to Australia later that year and taught at Drummoyne Boys' High School, Sydney.

Knoke represented Australia in the 1962, 1966, 1970 and 1974 Commonwealth Games and in the 1964, 1968 and 1972 Olympic Games. He was placed fourth in the final of the 400-metres hurdles in the Tokyo Olympics in 1964 and fifth in his semi-final in Mexico City in 1968. In his semi-final in Munich, West Germany, in 1972 he mistook an echo of the starter's gun for a recall and slowed to a walk before realising his error. He finished sixth and out of the final. Thereafter, any Australian athlete doing likewise or missing the start was said to have 'done a Knoke'.

In 1981 Knoke was appointed to the Australian Institute of Sport, Canberra, where he successfully coached the Olympic sprinter Paul Narracott, the Olympic hurdler Don Wright and the Commonwealth Games hurdler and gold medallist Garry Brown. He held the national 400-metres hurdles record (on Australian soil) of 49.4 seconds for over ten years before it was finally broken by Brown. Knoke

was a quiet and popular man of great inner strength and religious conviction. He died of cancer on 9 July 1984 at Calvary Hospital, Bruce, and was cremated with Anglican rites. His wife and their two sons survived him. He is commemorated at the AIS by the Gary Knoke memorial scholarship for athletics.

P. Jenes (comp), *Australian Athletics at 'the Games'* (1982); R. P. B. White and M. Harrison, *100 Years of the NSW AAA* (1987); *SMH*, 23 Sept 1969, p 17, 11 July 1984, p 44; *Age* (Melbourne), 11 July 1984, p 37; private information.   JOHN A. DALY

KNOX, ALISTAIR SAMUEL (1912-1986), architect and builder, was born on 8 April 1912 at South Melbourne, second child of locally born parents Arthur Jean François Knox, clerk, and his wife Margaret Longmore, née Brown. Educated at Scotch College, at 15 Alistair began work as a clerk in the State Savings Bank of Victoria. On 20 March 1937 he married Mernda Mabel Clayton, a domestic arts teacher, at the college chapel. He began a part-time pottery course at Melbourne Technical College in 1941 but his studies were interrupted from June 1942 when his spare time was taken up by the Volunteer Defence Corps. Transferring to the Naval Auxiliary Patrol in 1943 and, next year, to the Royal Australian Naval Volunteer Reserve, he served in Papuan and New Guinean waters in the *Martindale* and was discharged in Melbourne as a leading seaman on 3 September 1945.

Resuming work at the bank, Knox also began studying architecture and building construction at Melbourne Technical College. While he did not complete the diploma, the course influenced him: in 1948 he resigned from the bank to explore the possibilities of building his own style of house. With the post-war shortage of building materials, and encouraged by an enthusiastic client in Frank English, he created his first earth building, a simple rectangle, at Montmorency. His next project was a study for W. Macmahon Ball [q.v.] in the same materials at his Eltham home. For Knox, mud-brick was becoming his means of both survival and creative expression.

Drawn to the Montsalvat artists' colony centred on Justus Jorgensen [q.v.14], Knox moved with his family to Eltham in 1949. His developing architectural style was showing the influence of Frank Lloyd Wright, the inspiration of Francis Greenway and Walter Burley Griffin [qq.v.1,9] (including the latter's preference for planting indigenous flora) and his admiration for the modernist work of Robin Boyd [q.v.13] and (Sir) Roy Grounds [q.v.]. Buildings, landscape and environment began to merge in his work; as Bruce Mackenzie noted, a Knox house 'grew in the landscape in the way that trees adapted ... to inevitable forces'. In landscape design he was particularly impressed by the work of Ellis Stones [q.v.16] and Gordon Ford, whose espousal of 'bush gardens' he helped to promote.

Knox's career evolved over three distinct phases. In the first, from the 1940s to the 1960s, he followed Wright in embracing simple building structures. Notable houses from this period include the Ball, Busst and Le Gallienne-Downing [qq.v.15,14] houses. The more sophisticated designs of the second phase, until the late 1970s, incorporated the use of mud, stone and timber, as evident in the Coller (1974) and Huggett (1975) homes. A final phase came in the 1980s, when a Knox house was widely sought.

Even with this increasing popularity, Knox remained closely identified with the Eltham community. Mernda died in 1954, and on 15 September that year at the office of the government statist he married Margot, née Edwards, who had changed her name to Knox. Their home provided shelter, nurture and support for two generations of painters, potters, sculptors, poets and thinkers. In 1972-75 Knox was a councillor (president, 1975) on the Eltham Shire Council. He was drawn to the environmental movement, publishing three books on housing and the environment, writing for newspapers, speaking on radio, and hosting 'open houses' to demonstrate his building and landscaping theories. Although academically unqualified, he was a founding member (1967) and fellow (1983) of the Australian Institute of Landscape Architects, and a frequent lecturer on environmental design, architecture, building and landscape. He received an honorary doctorate of architecture from the University of Melbourne in 1984.

Short, with intense eyes and a wiry physique, Knox evoked unequivocal responses. Remembered by his son Hamish—also a mud-brick builder—as 'interested in everyone he met, enthusiastic, easy going, a raconteur, a lover of people', he possessed, in Geoff Sanderson's words, a 'powerful memorable personality'. Above all, he presented a vision of integrating the earth's elements into landscapes and living environments. He demonstrated how Australians could live in harmony with the landscape and established the mud-brick home as an attractive option for a wide cross-section of the Australian community. Christian beliefs informed his practice and wider social commitments.

Alistair Knox died on 30 July 1986 while visiting clients at Sunnycliffs, near Mildura, and was buried in Eltham cemetery. He was survived by a son and two daughters from his first marriage, and by his wife and their four sons and daughter. A park in Eltham is named in his honour.

T. Howard, *Mud and Man* (1992); *Landscape Aust*, vol 8, no 4, 1986, p 320, vol 9, no 1, 1987, p 34; B. Blackman, interview with Alistair Knox (ts, 1986, NLA); private information.   FAY WOODHOUSE

KNOX, DOROTHY ISABEL (1902-1983), headmistress, was born on 27 August 1902 at Benalla, Victoria, youngest of three children of Victorian-born parents Edward Knox, factory manager, and his wife Robina Dewar, née Brodie. A gifted student, Dorothy was educated at Benalla, Grassmere, Warrnambool and Warragul, before matriculating from Melbourne High School. At the University of Melbourne (BA, 1923; MA, 1925) she lived at Janet Clarke [q.v.3] Hall.

Appointed to teach English, history and French at Presbyterian Ladies' College, Goulburn, New South Wales, in 1923, Knox became senior mistress in December 1925. From 1927 to 1929 she undertook a working holiday in England and Europe, before returning to Goulburn as senior mistress and, later, acting principal. One referee claimed that 'her ability to impart is of the highest class, her scholarship is excellent, and her discipline more than usually good'.

In 1932 Knox was named principal of the new Presbyterian Ladies' College, Orange, where her organising and administrative abilities were fully tested. In July 1936 she became headmistress of PLC, Pymble, Sydney, which under her guidance greatly expanded in the 1950s and 1960s. She retired in 1967, as the first cohort of students under the Wyndham [q.v.] scheme (which she praised) completed the Higher School certificate. She resumed work as acting headmistress (1969-71) of PLC Armidale.

A woman of high Christian ideals and exceptional strength of character, 'Knocky' was a diminutive figure, with penetrating blue eyes, a kindly smile and a peaches-and-cream complexion. She was secretary (1939-47) and president (1948-50, 1955-56, 1963-64) of the Teachers' Guild of New South Wales and president (1950-52) of the Headmistresses' Association of Australia. A foundation member (1959) and fellow (1969) of the New South Wales chapter of the Australian College of Education, she served (1962-67) on the State Secondary Schools Board.

Miss Knox's enduring encouragement of women students, especially those from country districts, motivated her determination to see another women's college established at the University of Sydney, under the auspices of the Presbyterian Church of New South Wales. In 1948 she convened a planning committee, with Isabel McKinney (Harrison) as honorary secretary. When no suitable and affordable site had been found, the Presbyterian Assembly agreed in 1967 to establish a college, named for John Dunmore Lang [q.v.2], at Macquarie University. Knox chaired (1970-78) the foundation council of the college, which opened in March 1972 and became co-educational. She rejoiced in the number of international and women students that the college attracted. The Dorothy Knox fellowship enabled the periodic appointment there of a distinguished scholar or artist.

An inveterate traveller, Miss Knox undertook overseas trips in 1958 and 1973, described in her memoirs, *Time Flies* (1982). On her retirement she lived in a unit at Waverton until blindness forced her to enter a hostel at Roseville. She was appointed OBE in 1958 and AM in 1980. Never married, she died on 7 November 1983 at Terrey Hills and was cremated. Memorial services were held at the renamed Pymble Ladies' College and at Orange; the Dorothy Knox Centre at PLC, Armidale, was opened in 1989.

M. Coleman, *This Is Pymble College 1916-1991* (1991); B. Mansfield and M. Hutchinson, *Liberality of Opportunity* (1992); C. Pound and A. Atkinson, *The Common Task* (1995); *SMH*, 9 Nov 1983, p 15; H. de Berg, interview with D. Knox (ts, 1981, NLA); private information.   RUTH TEALE

KNOX, JAMES ROBERT (1914-1983), Catholic cardinal, was born on 2 March 1914 at Bayswater, Perth, second of three sons of Irish-born parents John Knox, storekeeper, and his wife Alice Emily, née Walsh. James attended Catholic schools at Gooseberry Hill and Midland before becoming a tailor's assistant. In 1933 he applied to the Perth archdiocese to study for the priesthood. Rejected because it was cheaper to recruit and educate priests in Ireland, he then successfully applied to become a diocesan priest in the territorial abbacy of New Norcia, and in 1934 went to St Ildephonsus' College, New Norcia, to complete his secondary education. He entered New Norcia Seminary in March 1936 and appeared such a promising student that he was transferred to the Pontifical Urban College of Propaganda Fide, Rome, in September. Ordained priest on 22 December 1941, he pursued postgraduate studies, obtaining doctorates in theology (1944) and canon law (1949), and published *De necessitudine deiparum inter et Eucharistiam* (1949). Unable to return to Australia during World War II, he had been assigned to Propaganda College staff, becoming a vice-rector in 1945.

From 1948 Knox assisted Monsignor Montini (later Pope Paul VI) in the Vatican Secretariat of State, until sent in 1950 as secretary to the apostolic delegate in Japan. Appointed apostolic delegate in British East and West Africa and the Territories of the Persian Gulf and named titular archbishop of Melitene on 20 July 1953, he received episcopal ordination on 8 November in Rome. After successful work in Africa, implementing the policy of indigenising the colonial Church structures, he was promoted in February 1957 to be apostolic internuncio to India and apostolic delegate to Burma and Ceylon (Sri Lanka). He was involved in much innovation and expansion, which encompassed Mother Teresa's Missionaries of Charity.

On 13 April 1967 Knox was appointed archbishop of Melbourne. Crowds enthusiastically welcomed him on his installation in St Patrick's Cathedral on 30 July. They sought decisive leadership, as Archbishop Mannix [q.v.10] had retired from public life by 1950—although governing the archdiocese until his death in 1963—and the episcopate of his successor, Archbishop Simonds [q.v.16], had been largely ineffectual due to his ill health. Moreover, the decrees of the Second Vatican Council (1962-65) were waiting to be implemented.

Although Knox had not lived in Australia for thirty years and had never served as a parish priest, he quickly settled into the application of the council's directives, the driving force of his time in Melbourne. He unquestioningly accepted the council's decisions as the will of God, and established the physical and organisational frameworks necessary to put them into practice. In-service training was arranged for priests and the reformed liturgical rites were introduced. The archdiocesan governance structure, in place since the episcopate of Archbishop Goold [q.v.4], was completely reorganised by the division of the archdiocese into four regions headed by auxiliary bishops, the creation of twelve archdiocesan departments headed by episcopal vicars, and the establishment of a Senate of Priests and other advisory bodies.

Seeing education as pivotal, Knox proposed one central theological college rather than separate seminaries for diocesan priests and those of religious institutes. Although not all the religious institutes joined the dioceses in Victoria and Tasmania to form the Catholic Theological College, the final result was successful and the granting of degrees through the Melbourne College of Divinity brought a new standard to theological education for clergy and laity. He recognised the need for an Institute of Catholic Education to unite the separate small Catholic teacher-training colleges in Victoria. The ICE later became a core part of the Australian Catholic University.

Knox's initiatives required major building works, with which he proceeded despite much opposition. His construction program included the replacement of the existing seminaries with a new one at Clayton, more suited to the modern training of priests; the bold reordering of the interior of St Patrick's Cathedral;

and the razing of the nineteenth-century St Patrick's College and cathedral presbytery to enable the construction of imaginative and work-efficient diocesan offices and a cathedral residence. At one stage trade unions declared the cathedral precinct black. Knox was not intimidated and the project was completed.

His vision brought involvement in ecumenism. He established a Commission for Ecumenical Affairs and encouraged participation in the Victorian Council of Churches. In 1968 he founded the Melbourne Overseas Missions to provide assistance by way of personnel, equipment and finance to struggling dioceses in developing countries. When asked whether Melbourne could afford to lend priests to other places, he replied that we could not expect God to be generous to us unless we were generous.

One great achievement was the celebration of the Fortieth International Eucharistic Congress in Melbourne in 1973. The original proposal in 1968 was generally opposed by the clergy who feared a repetition of congresses based on theology predating Vatican II. Knox showed extraordinary tenacity in making 'The People's Congress' happen. Radically innovative, it was the model for succeeding ones. Knox had the ability to identify priests and laypersons gifted with abilities in certain fields, to give them responsibilities, then to trust and support them.

On 5 March 1973 Pope Paul VI named Knox cardinal with the title of Santa Maria in Vallicella. It was widely believed that the Pope had sent him to Melbourne to have the pastoral experience of governing a diocese before being recalled to a senior Vatican position. Most were not surprised when he was appointed in January 1974 prefect of two congregations, Discipline of the Sacraments and Divine Worship. He left Melbourne for the Vatican in March and on 1 July his resignation as archbishop was accepted. The Church in Melbourne bore little resemblance to the one he had inherited seven years earlier.

In Rome Knox worked in the same methodical way. By mid-1975 the two congregations he headed were united into one, a task requiring sensitivity, tact and firm management. In 1981, to his disappointment, he was made president of the newly established Pontifical Council for the Family. He approached this assignment with his usual commitment and drive. From 1973 he was also president of the Permanent Committee for International Eucharistic Congresses. In 1982 his health declined and in May 1983 he became seriously ill with a circulatory problem. He died on 26 June that year at Gemelli Hospital, Rome, and was buried in the crypt of St Patrick's Cathedral, Melbourne.

Knox had been a hard-working enthusiast rather than a brilliant intellectual. He would research a matter thoroughly, then doggedly defend his position once he had made a decision. He was astute, never devious, decisive, approachable, and willing to take counsel. He abhorred racism. Invariably he was pleasant, patient, courteous and kind; he was a genuinely simple and uncomplicated person. Physically wiry, he was proficient in many sports, and a competent tennis player all his life. He was a man of deep faith and prayer, devoted to the Eucharist and the Virgin Mary, and noted for his fidelity to the Pope; his spirituality was based on trying to discern God's will and to follow it. Perceived as saintly, he lived simply and had no interest in possessions besides books. Paul Fitzgerald's portrait (1974) of Knox is held by St Patrick's Cathedral.

Advocate (Melbourne), 22 June 1967, p 5, 29 June 1967, p 5, 3 Aug 1967, p 1, 7 Mar 1974, p 1, 14 Mar 1974, p 1, 30 June 1983, p 1, 7 July 1983, p 1, 14 July 1983, p 1; *Herald* (Melbourne), 25 Sept 1972, p 2, 8 Mar 1974, p 4, 27 June 1983, p 3; *National Times*, 22-28 Mar 1974, p 723, 4-9 Aug 1975, p 44; *L'Osservatore Romano* (weekly English edn), 4 July 1983, p 12, 11 July 1983, p 2; Knox correspondence (Benedictine Community of New Norcia, WA, Archives); Knox papers (Melbourne Diocesan Hist Commission); private information.

IAN B. WATERS

KOGAN, MISCHA (1904-1982), violist, was born in 1904 at Kertch, the Ukraine, Russia, into a prosperous Jewish family. Putting aside an early interest in medicine, he studied violin and viola at the Moscow Conservatorium until unrest following the Bolshevik revolution in October 1917 prompted him to leave Russia for Constantinople. At 16 he moved to Vienna, where he continued his musical studies with Arnold Rosé (Gustav Mahler's brother-in-law) and further nurtured his love of chamber music. After studying in Berlin with Professor Alexander Fiedelmann, he settled in Jerusalem, becoming a Palestinian national; he joined two brothers on service with British military forces there. In 1928 he migrated to Melbourne (as 'Michael'), living first at Carlton and later at Toorak.

Playing with the Victorian, Melbourne and Sisserman string quartets, Kogan became a prominent concert performer, expanding local repertoires with works from his extensive library and gaining recognition for the viola as a solo instrument. In 1931 he joined the staff of the New Conservatorium, Spring Street, and founded his first exclusive chamber music club. An active member of the Association of Music Teachers of Victoria, he also taught at the St Kilda Conservatory and took private students. In 1938 he was appointed a permanent member of the Melbourne Symphony Orchestra and during World War II—having been rejected for military service on medical grounds—organised and performed in chamber music groups for the forces. After returning from overseas, having played in 1948-49 with the London Symphony and London Philharmonic orchestras, in 1950 Kogan became a practical instructor (senior lecturer 1960-63) in viola at the University of Melbourne conservatorium.

In 1950 Kogan also established the Soirées Musicales Chamber Music Society, through which—as Verdon Williams recalled—he 'carved himself an important and unique niche' in Melbourne's musical life. The society's earliest annual concert seasons were held in private homes on Sunday afternoons, but their popularity soon required public venues, including Coppin Hall, South Yarra, the Caulfield Arts Centre, the Methodist Ladies' College and Melba [q.v.10] Hall at the university. Kogan persuaded the Australian Broadcasting Commission to allow visiting international musicians to perform in the society's recitals: over time its programs featured Sir John Barbirolli (cello), Evelyn Rothwell (oboe), Ruggiero Ricci and Fritz Kreisler (violin), Daniel Barenboim and Alfred Brendel (piano), and Jean Pierre Rampal (flute). Often introducing new works, some by Australian composers, the group also hosted local artists, Hephzibah Menuhin [q.v.], Raymond Lambert (piano), John Amadio [qq.v.15,7] (flute), Paul McDermott (violinist) and John Kennedy [q.v.] (cello) among them.

A fine violist and an intense and committed musician, Kogan continued to direct and perform in a variety of ensembles. With thick-lensed glasses and wild, wiry but receding hair, he became one of the Melbourne (in 1949-65 Victorian) Symphony Orchestra's most recognised members until his retirement in 1975. He was awarded the British Empire Medal (1977) for his services to music. On 27 August 1982 Mischa Kogan died, unmarried, at St Kilda; he was buried in the Chevra Kadisha cemetery, Springvale.

Austn Musical News, May 1931, p 18, Apr 1935, p 25, June 1957, p 34, Jan 1960, p 12; *Sun News-Pictorial* (Melbourne), 17 July 1945, p 4; *Herald* (Melbourne), 27 Oct 1977, p 34; private information.

JILLIAN GRAHAM

KOMON, RUDOLPH JOHN (1908-1982), art dealer, wine judge and *bon vivant*, was born on 21 June 1908 in Vienna, one of four children of Czech parents Rudolf Komon, tailor, and his wife Anna, née Soucek. His parents later lived in Berlin, where his mother was to be killed by Allied bombing during World War II. After he left high school Rudy worked for a Czech newspaper as a sports and political journalist.

Based in Vienna he travelled through Austria and Germany, observing the rise of Hitler. In 1938 Komon moved to Czechoslovakia and joined the underground movement. He also began dealing in art. Many of the Prague painters who worked as newspaper cartoonists were his friends and he sold their paintings on the black market. At the end of the war he became a correspondent for Associated Press; after the 1948 communist assumption of power he crossed borders again—into Switzerland. He rarely spoke about his European life.

When Komon migrated to Australia in 1950 his suitcase contained a number of European etchings; he sold one by Edvard Munch to the Public Library, Museum and Art Gallery of Western Australia. Speaking a colourful brand of English—he never lost his thick Czech accent—he began selling rugs and Meissen porcelain from a small antique shop in the Sydney suburb of Waverley. At weekends he hawked (Sir) William Dobell's [q.v.14] paintings from the back of a truck. He was 42 years old when he arrived in a culturally unsophisticated, beer-drinking Australia and he never ceased to rail amiably against the 'bloody barbarians' he found everywhere in his new country. As cellarmaster (1956-76) of the Wine and Food Society of New South Wales he befriended many of the people who would later become his clients. Credited with one of the best palates in Australia, Komon judged wine at shows in Sydney, Brisbane, Perth and Canberra from 1959 to 1979. Art and wine were his two great interests—a risky combination as his cellar was occasionally raided by his artists.

In 1959 Komon bought a wineshop at Woollahra that he converted into the Rudy Komon Art Gallery. While the consumption of wine dropped, the quality improved. The rubicund, ebullient, beetle-browed Komon nurtured a stable of artists including the Melburnians Fred Williams, Clifton Pugh [qq.v.], George Baldessin [q.v.13], John Brack, Leonard French and Jan Senbergs, as well as Jon Molvig [q.v.15], John Olsen and Robert Dickerson. He liked the company of men and rarely showed women painters—his fellow European migrant Judy Cassab was one exception. Those who gathered for Saturday brawn and sausage lunches in the upstairs backroom of his gallery included prime ministers, business leaders, restaurateurs, journalists and winegrowers.

Komon was the first art dealer in Sydney to introduce the European practice of paying artists a wage in return for the right to sell their work. He had a close relationship with his artists—he found them studios, lent them money, organised their travel and wined and dined them. On trips overseas he often chose them as travelling companions. He pitched their prices high. When Olsen joined the

Komon stable—a rocky relationship that did not last—he sold one of his paintings for a then unheard-of 1000 guineas. To stimulate sales Komon would often sprinkle an exhibition with red stickers 'as an encouragement'; often he was the buyer. He brought a new professionalism to art dealing and, exercising considerable roguish charm, made it fashionable to buy and collect paintings. Known for playing games with his buyers, he would, for example, refuse to sell a Fred Williams because the 'barbarian' would-be purchaser did not have enough appreciation of the artist's work. Clients were sometimes expected to buy works by lesser artists before being allowed to graduate to the big names.

Naturalised in 1955 Komon married an English-born high-school teacher, Ruth Spenser Stevens, on 9 January 1959 at the registrar general's office, Sydney; they had no children. A keen swimmer, he also enjoyed cooking. In 1973 he was appointed MBE. He died on 27 October 1982 at Camperdown, Sydney, and was cremated. Two years later Ray Hughes bought the contents of the Komon gallery. The same year the Rudy Komon memorial fund was established to buy works by younger artists for the Art Gallery of New South Wales; the gallery was a major beneficiary when Ruth Komon died in 2001. It holds Eric Smith's portrait of Komon, which had won the 1981 Archibald [q.v.3] prize.

R. Raymond (ed), *52 Views of Rudy Komon* (1999); A446, item 1955/21868 (NAA); Rudy Komon Art Gallery records (NLA).   LENORE NICKLIN

KORMAN, STANLEY (1904-1988), industrialist, property developer and entrepreneur, was born on 27 August 1904 at Radom, Poland, a manufacturing town 60 miles (97 km) south of Warsaw, second of seven children of Abraham Korman and his wife Malka, née Tschaikovsky. Named Shaja, he was educated at a Jewish school and was fluent in several languages besides Polish, including Russian and Hebrew. Poor living conditions and anti-Jewish attitudes in Poland persuaded the family to move in 1925 to Palestine, where they established a candle-making business. Within two years Korman migrated to Australia, in search of better prospects. Arriving in Melbourne on 6 June 1927, he adopted the name Stanley. First he obtained a labouring job at Australian Glass Manufacturers Co. Ltd, Spotswood, and later he became a presser in a Brunswick hosiery mill. On 10 September 1930 at the Jewish Synagogue, East Melbourne, he married English-born Sylvia Lazarus.

Naturalised on 28 October 1932, Korman set up a small hosiery business at North Carlton, soon renamed Centenary Woollen Mills Pty Ltd. In 1935-39 he brought his father and other family members to Australia. His firm moved to a larger mill at Bentleigh in 1939 and in World War II enjoyed profitable defence contracts. In 1945 he formed a family company, Stanhill Pty Ltd, its name deriving from a combination of his own name and that of his brother Hilel; the headquarters were at 34 Queens Road. He sold Centenary in 1948.

Korman has been described by Trevor Sykes as 'short and dapper in a pinstripe suit and meticulously trimmed pencil moustache', and as having 'boundless vision and energy'. When visiting Miami, Florida, United States of America, in 1952, he was impressed with the artificial island developments and the international-standard hotels. Next year Stanhill acquired the Chevron Hotel, near Queens Road, and in 1955 Scott's Hotel in the city. The Korman family bought up several thousand acres at Broadmeadows in 1954-58 and 750 acres (304 ha) at Heidelberg in 1958 for housing developments. At Surfers Paradise, Queensland, Korman developed Chevron Island and the Paradise Island canal estate and built the first stage of the Chevron Hotel (opened in 1958). By 1959 construction of the Chevron Hotel, Sydney, and further stages of the Surfers Paradise hotel were under way.

Not content with these projects, in late 1957 Stanhill Holdings Ltd had acquired Automobile Finance Co. of Australia Ltd, renamed next year Factors Ltd. Factors soon had controlling interests in the clothing chain stores Rockman's Showrooms Ltd and Roger David Pty Ltd, and in Queensland Mines Ltd. Returning to his pre-war textile interests, in 1960 Korman arranged for Factors to take over Holeproof Industries Ltd, Holeproof Industries Ltd (New Zealand) and Australian Knitting Mills Ltd. By 1960 he presided over a group of 150 companies with interlocking share holdings and board memberships. In 1956-61 corporate assets grew from £2.3 million to £54.3 million.

Portrayed in the press in the 1950s as an imaginative and successful entrepreneur, Korman took risks that ultimately collided with the duties inherent in running public companies. The Federal government's credit squeeze in 1960 dealt Stanhill and Factors a severe blow: valuations of their properties fell; a too rapid expansion of Rockman's into junior department stores incurred heavy trading losses; and the Sydney Chevron had been over-capitalised. Shares in Stanhill Consolidated Ltd fell from a high of 23 shillings to five pence by 1963 and that year Factors went into receivership. In 1964 he was charged with authorising the issue of a false prospectus. The Victorian government commissioned three reports by Peter Murphy, QC, into Stanhill and Factors, all with adverse findings and all particularly critical of Korman, whom Murphy found 'unprincipled and untrustworthy'. Shareholders had lost about £24 million. Korman was convicted on 26 October 1966, and sentenced to six months' gaol. Losing a court appeal and harbouring considerable bitterness at being singled out, he served four and a half months.

On his release Korman's family persuaded him to start afresh in the USA. Aged 63, he began again at Phoenix, Arizona, and Las Vegas, Nevada, building a hotel, several supermarkets, mobile-home parks and office developments. Back in Queensland in 1985, he was warmly welcomed as the man who had put Surfers Paradise on the map. He planned new ventures there but, after adverse reportage by southern newspapers, returned to America in 1986. Survived by his wife and sons, he died on 26 July 1988 at Las Vegas and was buried in a Chevra Kadisha cemetery, Melbourne. The cardiovascular diagnostic centre at the Alfred Hospital, Melbourne, which he funded in 1959, and the Korman wing of the Mount Scopus (War Memorial) College, Burwood, were named after him.

A. Lemon, *Broadmeadows* (1982); T. Sykes, *Two Centuries of Panic* (1988); A. McRobbie, *The Real Surfers Paradise!* (1988) and *20th Century Gold Coast People* (2000); Investigation … into the Affairs of Stanhill Development Finance Ltd and Other Companies, Interim Reports, *V&P* (Vic), 1964-65, vol 1, p 813, and 1965-66, vol 1, p 830; *Third and Final Report* [of the investigation] (1967); *Herald* (Melbourne), 5 Oct 1957, p 21, 17 Sept 1964, p 1, 24 Aug 1967, p 1, 30 Nov 1967, p 1; *Australian Business*, 14 Sept 1988, p 32; A1/15, item 1932/5834 (NAA); personal knowledge.   PETER SPEARRITT
                                       JOHN YOUNG

KRASKER, ROBERT (1913-1981), cinematographer, was born on 21 August 1913 at Alexandria, Egypt, youngest of five children of Leon Krasker, a merchant from Romania, and his Austrian-born wife Matilde, née Rubel. Robert arrived in Perth with his family on 15 November and his birth was registered in Western Australia. In 1930 he sailed for Europe to study art in Paris and optics and photography at Dresden, Germany. He worked with the cinematographer Philip Tannura at Paramount's Joinville studios in France before moving permanently to London in 1932. Joining (Sir) Alexander Korda's London Film Productions as a camera operator, he assisted the studio's chief cameraman Georges Périnal, whose influence on Krasker's subsequent development was crucial. He absorbed lessons in lighting, composition and camera placement, putting them to use in his best work in the 1940s and beyond.

Sometimes credited as Bob Krasker, he worked on such major productions as *Rem-*brandt and *Things to Come* (both 1936) and *The Thief of Bagdad* (1940). He contracted malaria in the Sudan while a camera operator on *The Four Feathers* (1939) and subsequently became diabetic. Promoted to associate-photographer, he worked on *One of Our Aircraft is Missing* (1942). He was the cinematographer for the wartime propaganda piece *The Gentle Sex* (1943), co-directed by Leslie Howard and Maurice Elvey. That work prompted (Sir) Laurence (Lord) Olivier to hire him, with Jack Hildyard, to film, in colour, *Henry V* (1944). By this time considered to be among the front rank of cinematographers, he shot the celebrated *Brief Encounter* (1945), scripted by (Sir) Noël Coward and directed by (Sir) David Lean. This film was as sensitive and small scale in black-and-white as *Henry V* had been epic and celebratory in colour: Krasker was equally accomplished in both genres. The association with Lean ended mortifyingly when the director fired him from *Great Expectations* (1946), claiming that his work was 'too polite' and that he wanted something 'harder'. Krasker's memorable rendering of the film's opening graveyard scenes remains, however, an indication of what might have been.

With *Odd Man Out* (1947), the first of four films made with (Sir) Carol Reed, Krasker began probably the most artistically rewarding partnership of his career. It reached its apogee with *The Third Man* (1949), scripted by Graham Greene, in which Krasker's atmospheric use of unusual perspectives, wide angle lenses and a tilted camera helped to win him in 1950 the American Academy of Motion Picture Arts and Sciences' award for black-and-white cinematography. His style, eschewing glamour in favour of realism and employing high-contrast images and unconventional compositions, remains undated. It is particularly evident in the series of epic spectacle-films with which the final phase of his career is mostly identified. Robert Rossen's magisterial *Alexander the Great* (1956), and a succession of large-scale films for the director Anthony Mann such as *El Cid* (1961) and *The Fall of the Roman Empire* (1964), demonstrated Krasker's art at its most confident and mature.

Unhappy with cinematic trends of the late 1960s and struggling with health problems, Krasker virtually retired after shooting *The Trap* (1966). He had worked with some of the great directors of his time, including John Ford, Joseph Losey, William Wyler, Anthony Asquith, Joseph L. Mankiewicz, Michael Powell, Emeric Pressburger, Luchino Visconti and (Sir) Peter Ustinov. Colleagues remember an unassuming, modest man, about 5 ft 8 ins (173 cm) tall, gregarious despite superficial shyness, and easy to work with. If unsure of a technicality, he was never too proud to consult his junior assistants. He attached so little importance to worldly fame that his Oscar statuette served as a doorstop in his Ealing house. A gifted linguist, he was fluent in French and had a good working knowledge of Spanish and Italian. There appears to be no record of his marrying. He died of aortic stenosis on 16 August 1981 in London.

D. Petrie, *The British Cinematographer* (1996); *ODNB*, vol 32 (2004); *Bulletin*, 1 Dec 1981, p 128; *Cinema Papers*, Apr 1997, p 18; private information.

JOEL GREENBERG

KRATZMANN, NOEL AUSTIN (1917-1989), builder and property developer, was born on 12 December 1917 at Murgon, Queensland, second child of Queensland-born parents Herman William August Kratzmann, builder, and his wife Emma May, née Fick. When Noel was 7 the family moved to Toowong, Brisbane, where he attended the local state school. He was to live at Toowong for the greater part of his life. Starting work in his father's construction firm, he studied trade and design subjects at Central Technical College and in 1938 won the Master Builders' Federation of Australia's federal building construction prize. On 23 December 1939 at Albert Street Methodist Church, Brisbane, he married Olive Eileen Mulligan, a shop assistant. They were to have three sons.

In the 1940s Kratzmann bought the business from his father. He operated as a sole trader until 1954, when he formed N. A. Kratzmann Pty Ltd. As business grew he established new companies, based in Brisbane and Townsville, and won contracts for a number of large projects: hospitals, power stations, hotels (including Stanley Korman's [q.v.] Chevron Hotel, Surfers Paradise), banks, buildings at the University of Queensland, and housing developments, both public and private. Among the high-rise apartment buildings erected late in the 1950s by Kratzmann, using new construction techniques such as lift slab, were Torbreck at Highgate Hill and Paradise Towers at Surfers Paradise. He pioneered the establishment of suburban business centres, including Toowong.

In 1960 Kratzmann sold out to Reid Murray Holdings Ltd. Retained to run the construction enterprises, he continued to trade under the Kratzmann name. The collapse of Reid Murray in 1963 and N. A. Kratzmann Pty Ltd's subsequent bankruptcy was the subject of a special investigation into their affairs by Peter Connolly, QC. In his report, presented to the Queensland parliament in 1964, Connolly criticised Kratzmann's for 'the chaotic state of the company's books' and an inflated estimate of its profitability at the time of the take-over. A resilient businessman, Kratzmann expanded and diversified his interests. In 1973 he bought and restored Cintra House, a grand colonial house at Bowen Hills that became the home of Cintra House Galleries. He developed the Toowong Private Hospital, an acute-care psychiatric facility that opened in May 1976, and chaired the hospital board until his death.

Patrons of the Twelfth Night Theatre, in the 1960s Kratzmann and his wife helped to finance the company's new theatre at Bowen Hills. They were a stylish couple; always fashionably dressed, Kratzmann had a fondness for fine tailoring and for colourful shirts and ties. Often photographed at the races, they were usually at Flemington for the Melbourne Cup. Kratzmann was a founding member (1979) of the Queensland Art Gallery Foundation, a justice of the peace, and a fellow of the Australian Institute of Building. He was a member of the Queensland Turf and Tattersall's clubs. Interested in sport, he played tennis and golf.

Kratzmann's last major building project was a 120-square (1115 sq.m) mansion on what had been the site of Sir John Chandler's [q.v.13] estate at St Lucia. At the time he and his wife were living in semi-retirement at the Gold Coast. He died on 23 February 1989 in Brisbane, just before the family's planned move to the new property, and was buried in Toowong cemetery. His wife and two sons survived him. The family has since endowed (1997) the Kratzmann chair of psychiatry at the University of Queensland, and assisted the university to restore the Customs House, its city campus. Sir William Dargie's portrait of Kratzmann is held by the family.

P. Connolly, *Report of a Special Investigation into Reid Murray Developments ...* (1964); *Sunday Mail* (Brisbane), 5 Mar 1989, p 23; *Sunday Sun* (Brisbane), 5 Mar 1989, p 30; private information.

GREGORY KRATZMANN

KRIPS, HENRY JOSEPH (1912-1987), conductor, composer and pianist, was born on 10 February 1912 in Vienna, youngest of five sons of Josef Jakob Krips, medical doctor, and his wife Aloisia, née Seitz. Named Heinrich Josef, he grew up in a musical household; the conductor Josef Krips was his brother. Heinrich was educated at the Vienna Conservatory of Music and Vienna University; he made his conducting début at the city's Burgtheater in 1932. Further appointments followed at Innsbruck and Salzburg, at the Vienna Volksoper and at open-air festivals. He also composed an opera, *Fiordaliso* (1936). Although Krips's parents were both Catholic, he had Jewish ancestry. On 3 September 1938 in Vienna he married Luise Pauline Deutsch;

they migrated to Australia, arriving in Sydney in November.

Now calling himself Henry, Krips soon found work in the music industry. He composed and directed the scores for several Australian films, including *Gone to the Dogs* (1939), *Come up Smiling* (1939), *Dad Rudd, M.P.* (1940) and *The Power and the Glory* (1941). For the Kirsova [q.v.15] Ballet he wrote the music for *Faust* (1941) and *The Revolution of the Umbrellas* (1943) and provided piano accompaniment for performances. In 1942-43 he was employed as musical director with George Patterson [q.v.15] Pty Ltd's radio unit. He was naturalised on 10 July 1944. That year he conducted the Australian Broadcasting Commission's Sydney Symphony Orchestra during the opera season presented by the newly formed Krips-de Vries Grand Opera Company. With his wife he developed a passion for collecting Australian art, Aboriginal artefacts and carved Chinese jade.

In 1946-48 Krips conducted the SSO, and the Sydney Light Symphony Orchestra at its *Music for Millions* concerts. He was appointed conductor of the Perth Symphony Orchestra in 1948. Described by a critic, Raymond Bowers, as a 'powerhouse of enthusiasm', he promised to perform 'Mahler, Britten, Bax, Bruckner, a pageant of composers known only to Perth from recordings and hearsay'. He wrote the music for the films *Smithy* (1946) and Charles Chauvel's [q.v.7] epic *Sons of Matthew* (1949).

In 1949 Krips became resident conductor of the newly constituted South Australian Symphony Orchestra. Over the following years, with his customary energy and enthusiasm, he raised it to a very high standard. He also performed as guest-conductor in other States. Six ft (183 cm) tall, with fair hair and blue eyes, he was a charming personality, both on and off the concert platform. He wrote music, winning prizes for several compositions: *Land of Mine*, a national song (1951); *Southern Intermezzo*, a piece for the saxophone (1956); and *Kirribilli*, a light orchestral composition (1959). In 1953 he took leave for nine months to study trends in music in Britain and Europe, and to conduct orchestras in Vienna and London. Further leave was granted in 1955 and 1957; eventually Krips spent a part of each year overseas, where he conducted many leading British and European orchestras at concerts, operas and recording sessions. He developed his skills and reputation as a conductor and took back to Australia orchestral works that had never been performed there before. Credited with introducing Australian audiences to Mahler, in 1963 he was awarded honorary membership of the International Gustav Mahler Society, Vienna. In 1967 the president of Austria conferred on him the title of professor 'in recognition of his outstanding work for Austrian music in Australia'. He was appointed MBE in 1970.

After retiring from his post with the SASO in March 1972, Krips continued to work as a guest-conductor in Australia and overseas, making appearances in Korea (1978) and Canada (1979). He enjoyed playing tennis and squash. Survived by his wife (d.2001) and their two sons, he died on 25 January 1987 in North Adelaide and was cremated. Next month Harold Tidemann wrote in the Adelaide *Advertiser*:

His debonair charm, not forgetting the Austrian accent which never left him, endeared him to a wide circle. No other conductor could quite as effectively reproduce that Viennese lilt and few will forget that irrepressible movement of his which so aptly expressed the German walzen, 'to revolve'.

C. Buttrose, *Playing for Australia* (1982); *Advertiser* (Adelaide), 9 Sept 1949, p 2, 15 June 1951, p 1, 20 Apr 1954, p 2, 27 Oct 1970, p 9, 17 May 1980, p 14, 26 Jan 1987, p 3, 26 Feb 1987, p 20; *24 Hours*, Apr 1987, p 10; A446, item 1953/23591 (NAA).

                                    ZAIGA SUDRABS

KRUGER, EDWARD NORMAN (1897-1987) and **PERCY JOHN** (1905-1989), sawmillers and racehorse-breeders, were born on 10 October 1897 and 28 March 1905 at Mutdapilly, Queensland, sixth and tenth of the thirteen children of German-born parents Carl August Kruger, blacksmith and farmer, and his wife Elizabeth, née Hertrich. In 1912 the family moved to Bundamba, Ipswich, and Carl worked as a 'colliery carpenter'. Ted completed his education at Mount Forbes State School and was briefly a miner; Percy attended both Mount Forbes and Bundamba state schools.

Ted, and later Perc, joined their father in a handle-manufacturing business, registered in 1924 as C. A. Kruger & Son Pty Ltd. Ted had designed the prototype of an axe-handle. The firm eventually became the biggest producer of wooden handles for tools in Australia, with Slash as the brand name and 'we'll handle you right' as its slogan. It also developed as a sawmilling enterprise with its own leases in timber reserves. From 1927 Ted was manager; several brothers and other relations were involved in the business, which struggled for capital until Carl won £6000 in a Golden Casket art union shortly before his death in 1933. On 20 April 1929 at St Mary's Catholic Church, Ipswich, Ted had married Catherine Ellen Tobin (d.1985), a typist, and on 3 February 1934 at St Stephen's Presbyterian Church,

Ipswich, Percy married Olive Sloan, a weaver. They and other family members were to live in the Bundamba-Booval area of Ipswich for most of their lives. By 1947-48 the Kruger firm was one of the main hardwood processors in Queensland. Percy later became joint-manager.

The two brothers took up horse-breeding as their main recreation. Although horses were often registered in the name 'E. N. and P. J. Kruger', Percy mostly led the racing initiatives. Founding the City View stud at Bundamba about 1944, the Krugers were long-standing committeemen of the Ipswich Amateur Turf Club. They bought Lyndhurst, near Warwick, from the McDougall [q.v.10] family, and moved their stock there in March 1956. The Krugers intensively redeveloped the property, installing a large irrigation system and constructing new buildings and other appointments. Percy's enthusiasm for Stardust blood led them to buy the imported stallion Smokey Eyes (a paternal half-brother of Star Kingdom) in 1958 from T. J. Macknamara of Victoria, just before his progeny began to prove their worth. According to *Australian Bloodhorse Review*, Smokey Eyes (d.1973) was reputedly 'the most prolific sire of winners in world bloodstock history', his stock winning about three thousand races. He was champion stallion of Australia in terms of races won by his offspring for twelve consecutive seasons (1961/62-1972/73). His best Queensland progeny included Eye Liner (winner of the 1965 Australian Jockey Club's Champagne Stakes), Charlton Boy (winner of the 1974 Doomben Ten Thousand) and Intrepid Clipper, who, when owned by Alfred Grant [q.v.], won the Queensland Derby in 1969.

The Krugers increasingly kept their best fillies, including Eye Liner, for breeding after racing. Percy raced two of the four Queensland Oaks winners sired by Smokey Eyes, and an Oaks-winning granddaughter. Smokey Eyes' daughters foaled many winners to later Lyndhurst sires such as Lysander II, Hail to Success, Grand Chaudiere, Head over Heels, and Celestial Dancer. Both brothers were often committee-men of the Bloodhorse Breeders' Association of Australia, Queensland division; Percy was president in 1968-70.

On 31 October 1975 the brothers sold the mill site to accommodate a relocated Ipswich technical college. They began a substantial separation of their interests: broadly, Ted took the timber and manufacturing interests, Percy and his son Merrell the Lyndhurst stud. Percy continued to live at Ipswich. Reluctant to close a business with about 140 employees, Ted doggedly negotiated its progressive transfer to a 12-ha site at Dinmore, Ipswich. In November 1981 Besser (Qld) Ltd acquired the firm, then called Kruger Enterprises, and Ted retired from the managing directorship.

In group photographs the Krugers stand suited and wearing 'pork-pie' hats, Percy smiling and a little more nuggety, Ted rather more serious. Ted was keen on tennis, bowls and football, and active in local community organisations; he was named Ipswich Citizen of the Year in 1979. Survived by a daughter, he died on 14 July 1987 at Ipswich and was buried in Warrill Park lawn cemetery. Percy died on 14 September 1989 at Warwick and was cremated. His wife and their son survived him; a daughter had predeceased him.

City of Ipswich Queensland Australia (1959); P. Pring, *The Thoroughbred Encyclopaedia of Australia & New Zealand* (1981); R. du Bourg, *The Australian and New Zealand Thoroughbred*, 3rd edn (1991); *Ipswich Adviser*, 19 Apr 1962, p 1; *Austn Bloodhorse Review*, 'Austn Sire Liftout', Sept 1989, p 40, Nov 1989, p 15; *Qld Times*, 15 Sept 1979, p 1, 18 Dec 1980, p 7, 18 Nov 1981, p 7, 15 July 1987, p 2, 21 Sept 1989, p 24; Qld Timber Industry Inquiry Commission (1949-50), RSI236/1/123, SRS1043/1/2326/box 757, RSI236/1/128 (QSA); private information.

S. J. ROUTH

KRYGIER, HENRY RICHARD (1917-1986), publisher, journalist and businessman, was born on 9 September 1917 in Warsaw, elder son of Jewish parents Benedykt Krygier, timber merchant, and his wife Flora, née Schoenman, and was named Henryk Ryszard. He studied law at the Jozef Pilsudski (Warsaw) University, where he was elected chairman of the protest committee of Jewish students that in 1938 successfully campaigned against the exclusion from examinations of Jewish students who refused to sit in the officially segregated 'ghetto benches'. He graduated in 1939.

On 8 January 1939 Krygier married Romualda (Roma) Halpern in Warsaw. In September the Polish Command ordered all able-bodied young men to leave the city and walk east to the nearest army recruiting centre. Instead, unable to find the army, Krygier walked and hitch-hiked to Lithuania. Roma joined him and they settled at Kaunas. Roma had been a member of, and Richard was sympathetic to, the Polish Communist Party. Their political faith, already shaken by the Moscow trials of the 'Old Bolsheviks' (1936-38), was shattered by the Hitler-Stalin pact of August 1939, the division of Poland between Germany and the Soviet Union and their experience of Sovietisation in Lithuania from June 1940. The Krygiers obtained Japanese transit visas, which enabled them to travel by train to Vladivostok and thence by ship to Japan. They lived in a hostel at Kobe for some weeks until they were both appointed to the Polish relief committee in Tokyo.

About nine months later the Krygiers left for Australia via Shanghai, arriving in Sydney on 21 November 1941. After eighteen months as a waiter in Romano's [q.v.11] restaurant, Krygier was appointed correspondent of the Polish Telegraphic Agency, London (effectively press officer in the Polish Consulate, Sydney), responsible for writing and distributing news releases in support of the Polish government (in exile) in London. He also served as a war correspondent for the Polish press in the Netherlands East Indies and the Philippines. In these capacities he became familiar with Sydney newspapers and journalists and Australian politics. He supported the Australian Labor Party. In 1947 he was naturalised.

When the postwar communist government in Warsaw closed down the consulate in July 1945, Krygier and his Polish boss from Japan had begun a business, K. Zyngol & Co. Pty Ltd, which exported food and clothing parcels to Europe. He set up another business, Vistula (Aust.) Pty Ltd, importer of European books and magazines, which amalgamated with Overseas Periodicals (Aust.) Pty Ltd; at different times Krygier was chairman of directors and managing director.

The events of Krygier's youth, especially his loss of his native land and his survival of the Holocaust and the Gulag, produced in him a democratic, anti-totalitarian perspective that the years would deepen. It attracted him in particular to the liberal internationalist Congress for Cultural Freedom, which one hundred intellectuals, mainly refugees from Hitler and Stalin, had formed in Berlin in June 1950. He became its honorary 'Australian representative', that is, distributor (and sometimes translator) of its publications.

In 1954 Krygier formed and became secretary of the Australian Committee (Association from 1957) for Cultural Freedom. Under the chairmanship (1954-61) of Sir John Latham [q.v.10], the committee's principal activities were judicious statements on such matters as the reform of laws on immigration, censorship, defamation and Aborigines, and occasionally on wider issues ranging from South African apartheid to Soviet oppression. It also published a bulletin, *Free Spirit*, which debated these issues in a livelier, journalistic style.

The Australian Committee's—and Krygier's —greatest achievement was the creation of the literary-political magazine *Quadrant* under the editorship of the poet and critic James McAuley [q.v.15]. At first a quarterly and later a monthly, it published poetry, fiction and cultural criticism of a high standard and political essays of literary quality. Although never editor of *Quadrant*, Krygier was publisher, business manager and fund-raiser as well as contributor and 'ideas man'.

Krygier arranged lecture tours (by Stephen Spender, Malcolm Muggeridge, Leszek Kolakowski and Zbigniew Brzezinski) and overseas exhibitions by Australian artists (John Olsen in Paris, Peter Laverty in Tokyo). He organised several international conferences (in Canberra 1960; Port Moresby 1964-65; and Kuala Lumpur 1966) on the problems of establishing constitutional or democratic institutions in 'developing states'. Another major conference, in Sydney in 1962 on the role of 'little magazines', brought together editors of these publications from the United States of America, Africa, Asia and Australia.

On Latham's retirement as president in 1961, some members of the Australian association saw an opportunity to appoint not only a new president but also a new secretary—one less preoccupied with the dissolution of the Soviet Union or the liberation of Central Europe and more responsive to the new ideas of the 1960s. In the presidential election they supported (Sir) John Kerr, QC, while Krygier's supporters backed Dr Lloyd Ross [q.v.] of the Australian Railways Union. Ross narrowly won.

It was revealed in the 1960s that the US Central Intelligence Agency had funded the Congress for Cultural Freedom and that some of this money had trickled down to the Australian association and *Quadrant*. There was no evidence that any member of the Australian group was aware of the source of the congress's funds or that any subvention from the congress had ever influenced a decision by the committee or *Quadrant*, but the fact of any secret subsidy was deplorable. In subsequent years Krygier ensured that all funding was open, transparent and Australian. He was appointed OBE in 1981.

Survived by his wife and their daughter and son, Krygier died of cancer on 27 September 1986 at Darlinghurst and was cremated. Tributes to him in the November 1986 edition of *Quadrant* emphasised not only his civic courage and contribution to Australian intellectual life but also the warmth of his personality. H. W. Arndt found him 'invariably cheerful, imperturbably optimistic and completely secure in his convictions'. Sir Zelman Cowen and Owen Harries described his capacity for warm friendship. Zbigniew Brzezinski (US national security adviser) noted that his commitment to democracy was 'a life-long epic'.

P. Coleman, *The Liberal Conspiracy* (1989); *Quadrant*, Nov 1986, pp 8-43, Oct 1996, p 12; A12508, item 50/1311, A435, item 1946/4/6884 (NAA); J. D. B. Miller, interview with R. Krygier (ts, 1984, NLA).   PETER COLEMAN

KYLE, SIR WALLACE HART (1910-1988), air force officer and governor, was born on 22 January 1910 at Kalgoorlie, Western Australia, sixth surviving child of Victorian-born parents Alfred Kyle, builder, and his wife Christina Ellen, formerly Winning, née Beck. After attending Kalgoorlie State School in 1920-22, he went to Guildford Grammar School, Perth, as a boarder. He excelled at sport, representing the school in swimming, Australian Rules football, cricket and athletics, and becoming school champion in tennis and badminton; he was also a prefect and house captain.

In 1928 Kyle followed the example of a former Guildford pupil, (Sir) Edmund Hudleston, in entering on a scholarship the Royal Air Force College, Cranwell, Lincolnshire, England. There he was called 'Digger' and the name stuck throughout his air force career. When he graduated in December 1929 he was first sent to a fighter squadron equipped with Bulldog biplanes, but in September 1930 began training on naval reconnaissance aircraft and from 1931 served with the Fleet Air Arm. A flying instructor from 1934, Flight Lieutenant Kyle served on exchange with the Royal Australian Air Force in 1936-38. In addition to teaching at Point Cook, Victoria, and at Richmond and Mascot, New South Wales, he was one of the first pilots to instruct on the prototype of the RAAF's Wirraway basic combat trainer. As second-in-command of No.23 (City of Perth) Squadron, he led the transfer of the unit's Hawker Demon aircraft from Laverton, Victoria, to their new base outside Perth in March 1938. He returned to England two months later and was promoted to squadron leader in July.

After a further year of instructional duty, Kyle was posted to the staff of Training Command. As a temporary wing commander he headed No.139 (Jamaica) Squadron from December 1940, leading this unit of Blenheim light bombers on dangerous daylight formation raids against targets in Europe. During one daring attack in April 1941 on steel works at Ijmuiden, the Netherlands, he released his bombs from only 50 ft (15 m), then skilfully evaded pursuing enemy fighters by flying close to sea level; for his leadership in this successful action, he was awarded the Distinguished Flying Cross. In July he was made acting group captain (substantive July 1947) and given command of an operational training unit. On 4 September 1941 at the parish church, Yattendon, Berkshire, he married Mary (Molly) Rimington Wilkinson, a Women's Auxiliary Air Force cipher officer.

Kyle commanded the RAF station at Horsham St Faith, Norfolk, in July 1942. Working with another ex-Western Australian officer, (Sir) Hughie Edwards [q.v.], he devised the tactics and techniques that enabled his two bomber squadrons to best employ their new Mosquito aircraft. In September he was trans-ferred to command at Marham, where Mosquitoes were used by the Pathfinder Force, and in March 1944 he took over the station at Downham Market. At Bomber Command headquarters from October, he was involved in planning and organising raids until the end of the war. Mentioned in despatches four times, he was awarded the Distinguished Service Order (1945) and appointed CBE (1946).

Sent to the Staff College, Bracknell, Berkshire, in August 1945, Kyle joined the directing staff in February 1946. In October 1948 he was posted to headquarters, Mediterranean and Middle East, at Ismailia, Egypt. He became deputy-commandant of the RAF College, Cranwell, in 1951, and next year was appointed director of operational requirements at the Air Ministry as an air commodore. At the end of 1954 he departed for Malaya (Malaysia), where, the following January, he assumed duty as air officer commanding, with the acting rank of air vice-marshal (substantive in July). His command included the Lincoln bombers of No.1 Squadron, RAAF.

Returning to England in 1957, Kyle became assistant-chief of the Air Staff. In September 1959 he was promoted to acting air marshal (substantive January 1961) and made commander-in-chief of Technical Training Command. Succeeding Hudleston as vice-chief of the Air Staff (1962-64), he rose to air chief marshal on 1 January 1964. From February 1965 he led Bomber Command, until it merged with Fighter Command in April 1968, whereupon he headed the new Strike Command for four months. To mark his final command he flew in a Lightning jet fighter at 1000 miles (1609 km) per hour, thereby qualifying as a member of the 'Ten Ton Club'. On 9 November he was placed on the Retired List. He had been appointed CB (1953), KCB (1960) and GCB (1966). Several times he had returned to Australia, representing the RAF at defence talks in Canberra in 1967 and at the golden jubilee of the RAAF in 1971.

Sir Wallace retired to Tiptoe, Hampshire. An avowed monarchist—he had been an aide-de-camp to King George VI (1949-52) and Queen Elizabeth II (1952-56 and 1966-68)—he accepted an approach in 1975 by the premier of Western Australia, Sir Charles Court, to become the State's governor after Edwards retired in April. Arriving in November, he threw himself into his new position with enthusiasm, undeterred by strong republican sentiment in large segments of the Australian community. With his craggy features and unpretentious outgoing personality he appeared quintessentially Australian, although in reality he was totally Anglicised and out of sympathy with many local values. His public remarks in favour of developing a uranium processing plant at Kalgoorlie caused a brief uproar in 1978. He fought with the staff at

Government House, but otherwise enjoyed a successful period in office. Appointed a knight of grace of the Order of St John (1976) and KCVO (1977), he was awarded honorary doctorates by the Western Australian Institute of Technology (1979) and the University of Western Australia (1980).

Accepting an extension of his original three-year term to enable him to participate in the celebrations marking the State's 150th anniversary in 1979, Sir Wallace left Perth with Lady Kyle in May 1980 in anticipation of his term officially ending on 30 September. They resumed retirement in England but returned on later occasions to visit family, and he was president of the Fairbridge [q.v.8] Society in Britain and Western Australia from 1980. He died on 31 January 1988 at his home at Lymington, Hampshire, and was cremated; his wife and their three sons and daughter survived him. His eldest son, Richard, became an air vice-marshal in the RAF, while his youngest, Timothy, served as a pilot in the Fleet Air Arm. The Rotary Club of Perth, in conjunction with the University of Western Australia, inaugurated the Sir Wallace Kyle oration in 1980.

C. D. Coulthard-Clark, *The Third Brother* (1991); T. A. G. Hungerford (ed), *Tall Stories* (1996); *ODNB*, vol 32 (2004), p 131; *Canberra Times*, 7 Dec 1967, p 3, 15 Sept 1975, p 1; *West Australian*, 20 Apr 1968, p 7, 15 Sept 1975, p 1, 25 Nov 1975, p 1, 1 June 1978, p 3, 18 Dec 1979, p 1, 17 Dec 1980, p 1, 13 Jan 1983, p 26, 2 Feb 1988, pp 1, 32; *Australian*, 17 Aug 1976, p 11; *Times* (London), 2 Feb 1988, p 16, 19 Mar 1988, p 10; AWM65, item 3074 (AWM); W. H. Kyle RAF record (RAF Personnel Management Agency, Innsworth, Gloucester, Eng); private information.

CHRIS CLARK